A Casebook on Labour L

A Casebook on Labour Law

EWAN McGAUGHEY

LLB, Dip German Law, LLM, PhD, Senior Lecturer in Private Law,
King's College, London and Research Associate, Centre for Business Research,
University of Cambridge

·HART·

OXFORD · LONDON · NEW YORK · NEW DELHI · SYDNEY

HART PUBLISHING

Bloomsbury Publishing Plc

Kemp House, Chawley Park, Cumnor Hill, Oxford, OX2 9PH, UK

HART PUBLISHING, the Hart/Stag logo, BLOOMSBURY and the Diana logo are
trademarks of Bloomsbury Publishing Plc

First published in Great Britain 2019

A catalogue record for this book is available from the British Library.

Library of Congress Cataloging-in-Publication data

Names: McGaughey, Ewan, author.

Title: A casebook on labour law / Ewan McGaughey.

Other titles: Casebook on labor law

Description: Oxford [UK] ; Portland, Oregon : Hart Publishing, 2019.

Identifiers: LCCN 2018044042 (print) I LCCN 2018044157 (ebook) I
ISBN 9781849469302 (Epub) I ISBN 9781849465298 (paperback)

Subjects: LCSH: Labor laws and legislation—Great Britain. I
Labor laws and legislation—European Union countries. I Labor laws and legislation.

Classification: LCC KD3009 (ebook) I LCC KD3009 .M259 2018 (print) I DDC 344.01—dc23

LC record available at https://lccn.loc.gov/2018044042

ISBN: PB: 978-1-84946-529-8
       ePDF: 978-1-84946-931-9
       ePub: 978-1-84946-930-2

Typeset by Compuscript Ltd, Shannon
Printed and bound in Great Britain by CPI Group (UK) Ltd, Croydon CR0 4YY

To find out more about our authors and books visit www.hartpublishing.co.uk.
Here you will find extracts, author information, details of forthcoming events
and the option to sign up for our newsletters.

Preface

The *Bathers at Asnières*, on this book's front cover, happened to find its home in the National Gallery in London. From 1884, it is one of two masterpieces by the French painter, Georges Seurat. The second, on the back cover, is *A Sunday Afternoon on the Island of La Grande Jatte*. It found a home at the Art Institute of Chicago. Although one is in London, the other Chicago, they were probably intended to be viewed side by side. Like the opposite banks of the river, they represent opposite visions of the future. When you look at the bathers, the scene is bright, full of optimism. The figures bask in the sun. They swim and relax, probably on a break from work at factories like those in the distance. They are the Parisian working class. The boy in the red hat calls out across la Seine. He would be heard on the island of la Grande Jatte, where almost every figure is cast in shadows: shadows of trees, shadows of umbrellas, shadows of each other. One woman is fishing. Another trails a monkey. Why are they doing that? We see from their clothes they are from the bourgeoisie, and Seurat is making suggestions. Those women are 'fishing' for clients. These people are 'monkeying' around, lives leashed into hypocrisy and vice. Everyone, it seems, is staring at the river drifting by them like time, except for a little girl dressed in white. She is looking at you, right from the centre. Is the boy with the red hat trying to call her? I think he is, and he's saying: 'Leave them and join us, and the future will be on our side.'

Back then, in Seurat's time, labour law barely existed. Laws about labour were always there, but not taught except through snippets of contract, property or statutory enactment. Labour law only won its own place on a legal curriculum at the London School of Economics in 1895. But even now, a dozen decades on, there are still some people who say that labour law is not quite a proper subject, like the classical legal subjects. Labour law, it is said, is merely a 'contextual' topic that discusses an area of life. 'There is nothing wrong', this argument goes, 'with categories of that kind.' But labour law has no 'unity of concept or event' like the mighty foundations of public and private law.[1] The state on the one hand, and then on the other persons, property, obligations: contracts, torts and unjust enrichment. These are the great pillars of law built in the minds of its classical proponents. In this scheme, labour law ranks on the plane of 'the laws about cyberspace' or 'the law of the horse'. There is nothing wrong with it but, supposedly, it will not enlighten us about the whole of the law as classical subjects do. As a 'contextual' topic, it is said to be more an appendage, not the substance, of a proper legal education.[2]

There is an element of truth in this view. It is certainly true that through the twentieth century labour law's foundations were slowly, and painstakingly, pieced together from the neglected chapters of 'traditional' subjects, like panning through silt for gold. 'The technique of bourgeois society and its law', wrote Otto Kahn-Freund, had been,

> to cover social facts and factors of social existence with abstractions: property, contract, legal person. All these abstractions contain within them socially opposed and contradictory

---

[1] P Birks, *Introduction to the Law of Restitution* (1984) 73.
[2] FH Easterbrook, 'Cyberspace and the Law of the Horse' [1996] *University of Chicago Legal Forum* 207.

phenomena: property used for production and property used for consumption, agreements between equal parties and agreements between unequal parties, capitalist and worker. Through abstraction it is possible to extend legal rules, which are appropriate to the social phenomenon for which they were originally developed, to other social phenomena, thereby concealing the exercise of social power behind a veil of law.[3]

'Bourgeois society and its law', as Kahn-Freund put it, had of course been progress. Across the tattered seams of legal history, as slavery and serfdom had broken down, everyone was recognised as having full personhood. Labour relations were said to have shifted from 'status to contract'.[4] When people first spoke about 'freedom of contract', in the trade union debates of the 1870s, this language initially took the side of human liberation: workers stopped being punished for demanding better contracts at work. Around the turn of the twentieth century, rights to own property and the right to vote were slowly becoming universal. Labour law was certainly a contextual topic, but its coming together coincided with a reformation in classical law.

The problem is, classical law's own categories were also contextual. The original context developed in Ancient Rome. The first pillar of 'private law', the law of persons, originally distinguished those with 'full' personhood from slaves and women. Slaves were 'things', the property of real 'persons'. Second, in the law of property, rights *in rem* were (and for many remain) a relation between a person and a 'thing', and the most important 'things' the wealthy could own were other human beings. Third, the law of obligations, or rights *in personam*, were meant to involve relations between 'proper' persons. Slaves could not own property, they could only be property. As someone else's property, they could only create 'personal rights' such as contracts at their masters' behest. Fourth, this 'private' law of individuals was divided from a 'public' law that concerned the 'state'.[5] As well as this very division being contextual (necessarily making all subdivisions the same), individual rights did not truly need to extend to the state, because the Emperor monopolised its power. Reformed though it is now, the original context of public–private categories, of classical law, was enslavement, patriarchy and dictatorship.

Roman law's categories fitted intimately with the dominant conception of justice in the ancient world. As Plato wrote, stepping out of the job you were born for was 'the worst of evils' that 'spells destruction to our state'. When 'each of our three classes ... does its own job and minds its own business, that, by contrast, is justice and makes our state just'.[6] Aristotle expanded on this. Ideals of justice were said to be objectively identifiable, like an arithmetical or geometric equation.[7] 'Corrective justice', to remedy wrongs, mapped onto private law. 'Distributive justice', to share things fairly, mapped onto public law. Each would exist in a separate field, private and public. And if justice were objective, it could be administered by experts, the philosopher kings, the aristocracy. The power of this conception of law lay not just in its elegant simplicity, but in the fact that it did not require deliberative democracy. Labour law stood in direct opposition, the partner of rapid social development, as people demanded the vote.

---

[3] O Kahn-Freund, 'Hugo Sinzheimer 1875–1945' in *Labour Law and Politics in the Weimar Republic* (1981) 102.
[4] HJS Maine, *Ancient Law* (1861) ch 6.
[5] Ulpian, *Institutes* 1.1.4; *Digests* 1.1.2.
[6] Plato, *The Republic*, Book IV, Part V, 139, translated by D Lee.
[7] Aristotle, *Nicomachean Ethics*, Book V.

Did it matter if labour law would not fit the classical unities of 'concept and event'? For many it seemed that it did. Ideally, labour law should be forced back into the old rules: contract, tort and property. The pioneers of this view happened to work at the University of Chicago, founded by the oil tycoon, JD Rockefeller. Rockefeller described the university in 1896 as the 'best investment I ever made in my life'.[8] He owned the Standard Oil cartel (now mainly ExxonMobil[9]) and it was on his watch that striking mineworkers in Ludlow, Colorado were massacred in 1914. Labour lawyers had urged that in contracts for work, bargaining power between employees and employers was unequal. 'Freedom of contract' was all on the employer's side, especially when employers were large corporations. This justified labour rights, over rights of property and contract. The Chicago School replied that unequal bargaining power had 'no economic basis'.[10] Any unequal distribution of rights was irrelevant for an efficient economy. Problems of fairness might be an issue for tax policy set by government, but not for markets. Markets almost always allocate resources to their most productive use. The only real economic problem was transaction costs,[11] not unequal bargaining power. There should be no special labour rights. Instead, regulatory barriers to mobility and flexibility should be removed.

So, on the Chicago view, rights such as the minimum wage, paid holidays or childcare were harming the very people they were intended to help. By increasing costs on employers, labour rights caused unemployment, and social exclusion of society's most vulnerable.[12] Labour lawyers argued that law should promote collective action by trade unions, to counteract the unequal bargaining power of collectivised capital, usually organised in a corporate form. But the Chicago School said unionised workers were just the same as a price-fixing cartel. They should be shut down by tort or competition law.[13] Labour lawyers argued for the right to equality, so employers could not unjustifiably discriminate against different people, to break human solidarity. But the Chicago School said equality rights would simply raise costs and cause unemployment again. If racism or sexism were genuinely bad for production, the market would sanction it as irrational behaviour. There was no need for new law.[14] Labour lawyers argued for people to have job security, to ensure basic continuity and stability of income and livelihood. But again, said the Chicago School, this would lead to unemployment.[15] Labour law's 'noble' intentions would do no more than repave the road to serfdom.[16]

More than this, Chicago's theorists argued they now had the very reason for all law. 'Social justice', which labour lawyers and democrats talked about, was just a 'mirage'.[17] The 'meaning of justice', it was said, 'perhaps the most common, is – efficiency' because

---

[8] In an 1896 address to the university convocation, according to D Yergin, *The Prize: The Epic Quest for Oil, Money & Power* (2008) 33.

[9] *Standard Oil Co of New Jersey v United States*, 221 US 1 (1911) broke up the monopoly under the Sherman Act of 1890. See particularly the judgment of Harlan J. Standard Oil was divided into 34 companies: parts are owned by Shell, BP, Chevron, Sonoco, etc, but mainly ExxonMobil. The former CEO of ExxonMobil, Rex Tillerson, was made Secretary of State by Donald Trump.

[10] R Posner, 'Reflections on Consumerism' (1973) 20 *University of Chicago Law School Records* 19, 24–25.

[11] RA Coase, 'The Problem of Social Cost' (1960) 3 *Journal of Law and Economics* 1.

[12] M Friedman, 'The Methodology of Positive Economics' in *Essays in Positive Economics* (1953) ch 1.

[13] RA Posner, *Economic Analysis of Law* (1973) ch 11.

[14] G Becker, *The Economics of Discrimination* (1957).

[15] R Epstein, 'In Defense of the Contract at Will' (1984) 51(4) *University of Chicago Law Review* 947.

[16] FA Hayek, *The Road to Serfdom* (1943).

[17] FA Hayek, *Law, Legislation and Liberty* (1970).

'in a world of scarce resources waste should be regarded as immoral'.[18] With this new theory of justice, the context of the classical categories of public and private law, person-hood, property and obligation, had transformed. Now, unlike in Ancient Rome, every human being was a full 'person'. Corporations, incidentally, were as well. Now, property in natural persons no longer existed. Now, all people were formally free to make con-tracts and have other personal rights. The law's classical context had been imperial power. Now, the law's context was remade for a market society, and a market ideally controlled through unrestricted corporate power.

This book, written as it is not from Chicago, but London takes a different approach. It is not with Seurat's shadowy figures on *La grande Jatte*, but on the side of the *Bathers*. It is not based on divisions of public and private, but sees the law as a uni-fied social whole. All law pursues common goals. 'Democracy and social justice' as an American labour advocate once told an older Chicago audience, are the values we should pursue.[19] Democracy means power in the hands of people, whether power emanates from government or corporations in the marketplace. Social justice means everyone being able to fulfil their potential, expand their capacity and be able to improve the content of their character.[20] In a just society this is what we are due. As we receive the benefits of an improving society, we owe a duty to each other to lend a helping hand.[21] All law, including labour law, and every social institution, should promote 'the utmost possible development of faculty in the individual human being',[22] and ensure 'the opportunity to develop individuality becomes fully actualised'.[23]

In this tradition of thought, social justice has turned Plato's justice on its head. It appeals to something older, a promise of justice that follows the voice of the people, and sees that rigid laws must sometimes 'bend in season'.[24] Instead of the individual being subordinated to the 'public' good, every social institution exists to serve human freedom and human development. It goes hand in hand with democracy, where power and its 'administration is in the hands of the many and not of the few'.[25] The objective ideal-ism of old Athenians, the belief that justice may be deduced like arithmetic or geometric truth, is the mirage. So is the binary divide, mapping justice as correction and distribu-tion onto private and public law. The concept of justice exists only within the societies that shape their own morals. Different legal systems must innovate, as laboratories of democracy, to test how alternative visions of justice are best to be realised.[26]

Social justice requires social law. Unlike a 'public and private law' scheme, it sees that every legal subject concerns *associations* among people: from exchanges, to partnerships, to polities. Some laws create rights in associations (such as contracts, or assurances that people rely on). Others laws protect rights (such as breach of contract, torts, insolvency). In all fields of law, people owe duties to one another that mirror rights to enter into and exit from the association, rights of voice, and minimum rights of fair

---

[18] R Posner, *Economic Analysis of Law* (2011) 37.
[19] L Brandeis, 'The Living Law' (1916) 10(7) *Illinois Law Review* 461.
[20] T Paine, *The Rights of Man* (1792) Part II, ch 3.
[21] B Spinoza, *On the Improvement of the Understanding* (1677) §§13–14.
[22] S Webb and B Webb, *Industrial Democracy* (9th edn 1926) Part IV, ch 4, 849.
[23] AA Berle, 'Property, Production and Revolution' (1965) 65(1) *Columbia Law Review* 1, 17.
[24] Sophocles, *Antigone* (441 BC) translated by RC Jebb (1917) in words of Haemon to King Creon.
[25] Thucydides, *History of the Peloponnesian War* (c 411 BC) Book 2, para 37.
[26] See *New State Ice Co v Liebmann*, 285 US 262 (1932).

dealing. Labour law is simply the part of the law of enterprise (literally 'doing things') about human work. Law makes people in power accountable, so the rule of law means an ever more democratic rule of, by and for the people.[27] It was once said, by an old enemy of democracy, that if we recognised '[t]his principle of equality' in Parliament, if we got a democratic basis for that institution, we would have imposed upon ourselves 'the task of re-modelling the whole of [our] institutions, in reference to the principles that [we] have set up'.[28] I agree, and think that this probably remains one of labour law's most important and unfinished goals.

* * *

As a legal resource, this book aligns with a liberal tradition of education: the goal is not to tell students or practitioners what to think, but to offer a way to go about thinking, be honest about where we stand, and let people make up their own minds. Conflicting arguments should be faithfully recounted, not silenced, because even views that seem flawed may contain an element of truth, or they may ensure our own views are not held in prejudice.[29] This is the method followed through the book's five parts. It is based on cases and statutory materials that attempt to encapsulate all central principles.[30] Because precedent binds, the book chooses higher courts over lower courts in the main extracts. Cases bring statute to life, while the organisation of the book holds the conceptual structure. The text, notes and questions typically probe the principles behind the existing case law, rather than neutrally leave it to speak for itself. Readers deserve a clash of opinions to make up their minds, and we only live once. We do not yet have a Labour Code, and until we do, textbooks function as a rough replacement. Yet, even if we had a code, the words of statutes, and of judges themselves, are golden. Real lawyers read the law, and not just another author's summary of it.

Why call it 'labour law' and not, say, 'employment law'? Or what about, as in many civil systems, the 'law of work' (*droit du travail* or *Arbeitsrecht*)? In the UK labour law is preferred to 'law of work' mostly out of tradition. Perhaps this tradition makes some sense, because one of the labour movement's central goals, like the bathers at Asnières, has been to be free from work. 'Employment' might not capture it all, first, because labour law goes beyond the employment relationship to involvement by the state, to international trade, and to union and corporate governance. Second, 'employment' carries an unfortunate connotation of subordination, where the 'employer' uses the 'employee' for its own ends. Should people not be able to use an employing entity for *their* ends? Other languages are similar: in German the employee is the *Arbeitnehmer* ('work taker') and the employer is the *Arbeitgeber* ('work giver', or worse yet, 'job creator'). But is it not the employee who really 'gives' labour, and the employer who 'takes'? Language often reflects cultural change: more and more, in real life, we talk not about employees, but colleagues, members, co-workers (or *Mitarbeiter*).[31] Language is not neutral. It makes politically meaningful choices. In this book the word 'labour' in 'labour law' refers not

---

[27] A Lincoln, *Gettysburg Address* (1863) and cf Aristotle, *Politics*, Book 3, ch 16.
[28] Mr Robert Lowe MP, Hansard HC Debs (15 July 1867) col 1543. See ch 1(2).
[29] JS Mill, *On Liberty* (1859) ch 1.
[30] CC Langdell, *Selection of Cases on the Law of Contracts* (1871).
[31] See books.google.com/ngrams. Enter words (especially *Mitarbeiter*) for their usage in books over time.

just to the action of labouring, but to the goals of the labour movement as a whole: to free people from work by subordination to others, for the utmost development of humankind.

Beyond the name, what defines the scope of labour law and its internal logic? Necessarily, a scope must depend on a purpose. An academic subject (including 'law') does not have boundaries that we may draw neat lines around, any more than there is a 'right' point for the focus in the zoom on a camera. There is no objective 'concept' out there to be revealed by an author,[32] but an argument to be made. Depending on the panorama or the detail we seek, depending on the purpose of the picture, the focus will change. This book attempts to encompass everything that matters for people to pursue fulfilling lives, so far as laws relating to work can do it. Looking back at the some of the leading texts in UK literature,[33] it is natural that the focus of each will change. Topics that have been in and out of labour law textbooks, such as tax, pensions and policies for full employment, are included here. Fields integral to modern labour law internationally are also included, such as corporate governance, fiscal and monetary policy.

The book's thematic structure is as follows. Part 1 elaborates labour law history and theory. Part 2 concerns the tension between contract and rights at work. Part 3 explores the all-important right to participate in enterprise governance through unions and votes at work. Part 4 discusses the principle of equality. Part 5 is about job security, starting with policies to achieve full employment. This book does not distinguish 'individual' from 'collective' labour law, any more than it is possible, or desirable, to conceptually (rather than contextually) distinguish 'private' from 'public' law. All private rights depend on public or, better said, social assistance for their existence and enforcement.[34] Similarly, individual rights rest ultimately on the quality of collective regulation through the courts, government regulators, trade unions and non-governmental organisations. Like the individual–collective distinction, the private–public distinction may still be kicking, but it has long been philosophically dead for any kind of principled analysis.[35] The book's themes centre on mechanisms of good governance in what is probably among the most important of human institutions: work.

The end of each chapter summarises important academic writings for further reading. The problem questions also try to draw us back to the living world. Sometimes we forget, with our heads buried in commentaries and statutes, we learn most from talking to people in the world around us. When you have read, talk. I am incredibly grateful to all my labour law teachers and colleagues, particularly Keith Ewing, Aileen McColgan, Hugh Collins, Paul Davies, David Kershaw, Eva Micheler, Wanjiru Njoya, Brian Langille, Nicola Countouris, Simon Deakin and Peer Zumbansen for their inspiration. I also want to say a special thank you to Franck Lecomte, Valerio de Stefano, Vincenzo Pietrogiovanni,

---

[32] This was the preoccupation of much legal philosophy after HLA Hart, *The Concept of Law* (1961). Contrast L Wittgenstein, *Philosophical Investigations* (1953) §§23, 43 and 199–203, and perhaps more accessibly, Q Skinner, *Visions of Politics* (2002) vol 1, ch 2.

[33] eg S Deakin and G Morris, *Labour Law* (6th edn 2012). H Collins, KD Ewing and A McColgan, *Labour Law* (2012). M Freedland and P Davies, *Labour Law: Text and Materials* (1984). Lord Wedderburn, *The Worker and the Law* (3rd edn 1986). S Webb and B Webb, *Industrial Democracy* (1920).

[34] R Hale, 'Coercion and Distribution in a Supposedly Non-Coercive State' (1923) 38 *Political Science Quarterly* 472 and R Hale, 'Bargaining, Duress and Economic Liberty' (1943) 43 *Columbia Law Review* 625.

[35] See *Civil Rights Cases*, 109 US 3 (1883) per Harlan J (dissenting) and *Lochner v New York*, 198 US 45 (1905) per Harlan J and Holmes J (dissenting).

Zoe Adams, Patrick Kessler, Danny Fairfax, Jacob Eisler, Tim Parker and Liv Jores. Finally, I thank all my students: together with teachers, and all members of staff: they make universities one of the best places to work. I am constantly filled with hope for the future, by the energy, intelligence, organisation and passion of our next generation of labour lawyers.

King's College, London, May Day 2018

Publisher's Note

The author and publisher gratefully acknowledge the authors and publishers of extracted material which appears in this book, and in particular the following for permission to reprint from the sources indicated.

Alfred A Knopf: MS Eccles, Beckoning Frontiers: Public and Personal Recollections, edited by Sidney Hyman, 1961.

Deakin, S, Malmberg, J and Sarkar, P: 'Do Labour Laws Increase Equality at the Expense of Higher Unemployment? The Experience of Six OECD Countries, 1970–2010' (2014) University of Cambridge Faculty of Law Research Paper No. 11/2014 7–9 and 26.

Liverpool University Press: KD Ewing, 'The State and Industrial Relations' (1998) 5 *Historical Studies in Industrial Relations* 1, 16–25.

Oxford University Press: O Kahn-Freund: 'Industrial Democracy' *Industrial Law Journal*, Volume 6, Issue 1, 1 January 1977 65–84.

Penguin Classics: Sir Thomas More, *Utopia* (1516) Book 1 translated by Paul Turner, 46–49.

Simon and Schuster: OE Williamson, The Economic Institutions of Capitalism (1985); imprint: The Free Press (Macmillan) chs 10 and 12 241–262 and 298–306 (parts).

University of California Press: Martin Luther King Jr, *Speech to the Fourth Constitutional Convention AFL-CIO*, Miami, Florida (11 December 1961), The Papers of Martin Luther King, Jr., Volume VII: To Save the Soul of America, January 1961 August 1962, 333–341.

University of Chicago Law School: RA Epstein, 'In Defense of the Contract at Will' *University of Chicago Law Review* (1984) 51(4) 973–976.

University of Chicago Press: M Friedman, 'The Methodology of Positive Economics', *Essays in Positive Economics* (1953) ch 1 4–7.

Wiley: J Stiglitz, 'Employment, social justice and societal well-being' (2002) 141 *International Labour Review* 9 9–18 and 21 (parts).

While every care has been taken to establish and acknowledge copyright, and to contact the copyright holders, the publishers apologise for any accidental infringement and would be pleased to come to a suitable agreement with the rightful copyright owners in each case.

Contents

Preface	*v*
Publisher's Note	*xiii*
Table of Cases	*xxix*
Table of Legislation	*lv*
List of Abbreviations	*xcvii*

PART ONE: HISTORY AND THEORY

1. HISTORY — 3

(1) Slavery, Serfdom and the Commons — 3
    J Froissart, The Chronicles of Froissart — 4
    T More, Utopia — 6
    Somerset v Stewart — 9

(2) Freedom of Contract — 11
    R v Lovelass — 11
    S Webb and B Webb, The History of Trade Unionism — 12
    F Engels, The Condition of the Working Class in England — 15
    Eleventh and Final Report of the Royal Commissioners appointed
        to Inquire into the Organization and Rules of Trades Unions
        and Other Associations — 18

(3) Modern Labour Law — 21
    (a) Democracy — 21
        KD Ewing, 'The State and Industrial Relations' — 21
        O Kahn-Freund, 'Industrial Democracy' — 28
    (b) Equality — 32
        Martin Luther King Jr, Speech to the Fourth Constitutional
            Convention AFL-CIO, Miami, Florida — 32
        Equal Pay (No 2) Bill, Hansard HC Debs — 35
    (c) Internationalism — 38
        Treaty on the Functioning of the European Union, Article 153 — 38
        ILO, Declaration on Fundamental Principles and Rights at Work — 39
Additional Reading — 41

2. THEORY — 45

(1) Equality and Freedom — 46
    A Smith, The Theory of Moral Sentiments — 46
    A Smith, An Inquiry into the Nature and Causes of the Wealth of
        Nations — 48
    JS Mill, Principles of Political Economy — 51
    K Marx, Capital: A Critique of Political Economy — 53
    S Webb and B Webb, Industrial Democracy — 62

(2) Economic Efficiency 67
   M Friedman, 'The Methodology of Positive Economics' in Essays in Positive Economics 67
   RA Epstein, 'In Defense of the Contract at Will' 70
   OE Williamson, The Economic Institutions of Capitalism 72
   E McGaughey, 'Can Behavioural Psychology Inform Labour Law?' in A Ludlow and A Blackham, New Frontiers in Empirical Labour Law Research 75
(3) Human Development 82
   J Stiglitz, 'Employment, social justice and societal well-being' 82
   S Deakin, J Malmberg and P Sarkar, 'Do Labour Laws Increase Equality at the Expense of Higher Unemployment? The Experience of Six OECD Countries, 1970–2010' 87
Additional Reading 90

PART TWO: CONTRACT AND RIGHTS

3. SCOPE AND ENFORCEMENT 95
(1) Principles of Construction 96
   Johnson v Unisys Ltd 96
   Gisda Cyf v Barratt 98
   Autoclenz Ltd v Belcher 101
(2) Who is an Employee or Worker? 105
   (a) Statutory Tests 105
     Employment Rights Act 1996 s 230 105
   (b) Employee: Multiple Factors 106
     City of Montreal v Montreal Locomotive Works Ltd 107
     Ready Mixed Concrete (South East) Ltd v Minister for Pensions and National Insurance 108
   (c) Employee: Mutuality of Obligation? 112
     O'Kelly v Trusthouse Forte plc 113
     Nethermere (St Neots) Ltd v Gardiner 116
     Carmichael v National Power plc 119
     Stringfellow Restaurants Ltd v Quashie 121
   (d) Workers, and Not Employees 124
     Clyde & Co LLP v Bates van Winkelhof 124
   (e) Employed, Without Rights? 128
     Edmonds v Lawson QC 128
     X v Mid Sussex Citizens Advice Bureau 130
(3) Who are the 'Employers'? 133
   (a) Subcontracting 133
     Catholic Child Welfare Society v Institute of the Brothers of the Christian Schools 133
   (b) Agency Work 136
     Dacas v Brook Street Bureau (UK) Ltd 136
     Cable & Wireless plc v Muscat 141

(c) Corporate Groups   145
    Chandler v Cape plc   145
(4) Enforcement Bodies   148
    R (UNISON) v Lord Chancellor   149
Problem Question   157
Additional Reading   158

4. **CONTRACT OF EMPLOYMENT**   163
(1) Formation   164
  (a) Enforceable Agreements   164
    CSC Computer Sciences Ltd v McAlinden   164
    Ford v Warwickshire CC   168
  (b) Unjust or Vitiating Factors   169
    Hounga v Allen   170
  (c) Statutory Control for Unfair Terms?   177
    Unfair Contract Terms Act 1977 s 2(1)   177
    Johnstone v Bloomsbury Health Authority   178
    Commerzbank AG v Keen   180
(2) Incorporation of Terms   181
  (a) Incorporation: Workplace Rule Book   182
    French v Barclays Bank plc   182
  (b) Incorporation: Collective Agreements   184
    The Trade Union and Labour Relations (Consolidation)
      Act 1992 s 179   184
    Kaur v MG Rover Group Ltd   185
    Malone v British Airways plc   186
  (c) Right to Notice of Terms   188
    Employment Rights Act 1996 ss 1–2   188
    Scally v Southern Health and Social Services Board   190
(3) Choice and Conflicts of Law   191
  (a) Contract   192
    Rome I Regulation (EC) 593/2008, Arts 3 and 8   192
    Lawson v Serco Ltd; Botham v Ministry of Defence; Crofts v Veta Ltd   194
    Ravat v Halliburton Manufacturing and Services Ltd   198
  (b) Tort   201
    Rome II Regulation (EC) No 864/2007   201
Additional Reading   203

5. **IMPLIED TERMS AND VARIATION**   207
(1) Implied Rights of Employing Entities   208
  (a) Right to Direct and Limits   208
    Lister v Romford Ice & Cold Storage Co Ltd   208
    Wilson v Racher   211
  (b) Right to Appropriate and Limits   214
    Stevenson, Jordan & Harrison Ltd v MacDonald & Evans   214

(c) Right to Employee Loyalty and Limits   216
    Attorney General v Blake   216
(2) Implied Employee Rights   221
(a) Good Faith or Mutual Trust and Confidence   221
    Malik and Mahmud v Bank of Credit and Commerce International SA   221
    Transco plc v O'Brien   224
    Mallone v BPB Industries plc   226
(b) Work for Pay in Normal Hours   228
    Devonald v Rosser & Sons   228
(c) A Safe System of Work   230
    Johnstone v Bloomsbury Health Authority   230
(d) Notice and Fair Process for Dismissal   233
    West London Mental Health NHS Trust v Chhabra   233
(3) Variation   236
(a) No Variation Without Consent   236
    Rigby v Ferodo Ltd   236
(b) Unilateral Variation or 'Flexibility' Clauses   239
    Wandsworth LBC v D'Silva   239
(c) Dismissal After Variation Refused Could Be Fair   241
    Hollister v National Farmers' Union   241

Problem Question   242
Additional Reading   243

6. WAGES, TAXES, PENSIONS   245

(1) A Living Wage for Work   246
(a) Just Enrichment and *Quantum Meruit*   246
    Patel v Mirza   246
(b) The Minimum Living Wage   249
    France v James Coombes & Co   249
(c) Pay Period   253
    British Nursing Association v Inland Revenue   253
    Walton v Independent Living Organisation   255
(d) Deduction Limits   256
    Employment Rights Act 1996 s 13   257
    Miles v Wakefield Metropolitan District Council   259
    Nerva v United Kingdom   263
(2) Unjustified Pay   265
    Companies (Model Articles) Regulations 2008 Sch 3, paras 3 and 23 266
    Companies Act 2006 s 439A   269
(3) Tax and National Insurance   270
(a) Taxation of Employment Income   270
    Finance Act 2017 s 2   271
    Income Tax Act 2007 ss 10–12, 35 and 57A   271
(b) National Insurance Contributions   274
    Social Security Contributions and Benefits Act 1992 ss 1, 8–15   274

(4) Occupational Pensions   276
    (a) Right to an Occupational Pension   277
       Pensions Act 2008 ss 1–20   278
    (b) Governance   281
Additional Reading   282

7. WORKING TIME AND CHILD CARE   285

(1) Days   286
    (a) What Are Holidays?   286
       Russell v Transocean International Resources Ltd   286
       Stringer v Her Majesty's Revenue and Customs   289
    (b) Level of Pay   292
       Robinson-Steele v RD Retail Services Ltd   292
       Williams v British Airways plc   294

(2) Hours   296
    (a) Right to Regular Hours   296
       Borrer v Cardinal Security Ltd   297
    (b) Maximum Hours   299
       Pfeiffer v Deutsches Rotes Kreuz   300
       Sindicato de Medicos de Asistencia Publica v Conselleria de Sanidad
          y Consumo de la Generalidad Valenciana   303
       Landeshauptstadt Kiel v Jaegar   304
    (c) Breaks and Night Work   308
       Hughes v Corps of Commissionaires Management Ltd (No 2)   308
    (d) Enforcement   310
       Barber v RJB Mining (UK) Ltd   310

(3) Child Care   311
(4) Right to Request Flexible Working Time   315
       Commotion Ltd v Rutty   316
Problem Question   318
Additional Reading   318

PART THREE: PARTICIPATION

8. TRADE UNIONS   323

(1) Freedom of Association   324
       European Convention on Human Rights 1950 Art 11   324
(2) Voting Rights   327
    (a) Elections   327
       Trade Union and Labour Relations (Consolidation)
          Act 1992 ss 46 and 50   327
       Breen v Amalgamated Engineering Union   330
    (b) Political Funds   335
       Trade Union and Labour Relations (Consolidation)
          Act 1992 ss 71–72 and 82   335

(3) Other Rights in Court 337
   (a) Right to Enforce the Constitution 337
      Edwards v Halliwell 338
   (b) Money and Transparent Accounts 341
      Trade Union and Labour Relations (Consolidation) Act 1992 s 28 ... 341
   (c) Fairness in Disciplinary or Expulsion 344
      Bonsor v Musicians' Union 344
      Cheall v APEX 349
      ASLEF v United Kingdom 351
(4) Anti-Discrimination 354
      Wilson and Palmer v United Kingdom 355
      Council of Civil Service Unions v Minister for the Civil Service ... 360
      Bass Taverns Ltd v Burgess 364
      Employment Relations Act 1999 (Blacklists) Regulations 2010
        (SI 2010/493) 366
Additional Reading 369

9. COLLECTIVE BARGAINING 371
(1) Recognition for Bargaining 372
      Trade Union and Labour Relations (Consolidation)
        Act 1992 Sch A1, paras 3–7, 11, 12, 18, 22–26 and 35–36 ... 372
      Pharmacists' Defence Association Union v Secretary of State
        for Business, Innovation and Skills 378
      R (National Union of Journalists) v CAC 381
      R (Kwik-Fit (GB) Ltd) v Central Arbitration Committee 384
      Lidl Ltd v Central Arbitration Committee 386
(2) Collective Agreement Terms 389
   (a) Enforceability 389
      Trade Union and Labour Relations (Consolidation) Act 1992 s 179 ... 389
   (b) Standard Collective Agreement Terms 391
      Joint Negotiating Committee for Higher Education Staff 391
(3) Rights Essential for Bargaining 393
   (a) Automatic Enrolment and Closed Shop 393
      Trade Union and Labour Relations (Consolidation) Act 1992 s 146 ... 394
      Young, James and Webster v United Kingdom 396
   (b) Information for Collective Bargaining 403
   (c) Rights to Time Off and Representation 404
Additional Reading 405

10. COLLECTIVE ACTION 407
(1) The Right to Collective Action 408
   (a) Common Law and Equity 408
      British Airways Plc v Unite the Union 409
      Certification of the Constitution of the Republic of South Africa ... 415

(b) Statutory Codified Rights   419
     Trade Union and Labour Relations (Consolidation)
          Act 1992 ss 219 and 244   419
     BBC v Hearn   424
(c) International Law   429
     RMT v United Kingdom   430
(d) European Union   439
     The Rosella or ITF v Viking Line ABP   439
     Laval Un Partneri Ltd v Svenska Byggnadsarbetareförbundet   445
     FNV Kunsten Informatie en Media v Staat der Nederlanden   450

(2) Solidarity Action and Picketing   453
(a) Solidarity Action and the Corporate Veil   453
     Trade Union and Labour Relations (Consolidation) Act 1992 s 224   453
     Dimbleby and Sons Ltd v NUJ   455
(b) Picketing   458
     Trade Union and Labour Relations (Consolidation)
          Act 1992 ss 220–21 and 241   459

(3) Balloting   462
     Trade Union and Labour Relations (Consolidation)
          Act 1992 ss 226–34A   463
     P v NASUWT   466

(4) Dispute Resolution, Dismissal, Detriment   471
     Trade Union and Labour Relations (Consolidation) Act 1992
          ss 20–22 and 212–18   472
     The Nawala or NWL Ltd v Woods   474
     Trade Union and Labour Relations (Consolidation) Act 1992 s 238A 477

Additional Reading   479

11. VOTES AT WORK   481

(1) Rights Over Enterprise Executives   482
(a) Votes for Corporate Boards   482
     Statutes and Ordinances of the University of Cambridge 2017,
          Statutes A and C   482
     Companies Act 2006 ss 21, 112–13, 154, 168–69 and 282–84   486
     Companies (Model Articles) Regulations 2008 Sch 3, paras 3–5, 20,
          23, 34   488
     Financial Reporting Council, UK Corporate Governance Code
          (July 2018)   490
     Board Representation (Private Sector Employees) Act 1987
          (SFS 1987:1245)   493
     Employee Involvement Directive 2001/86/EC   496
(b) Enforcing Directors' Duties?   500
     Companies Act 2006 ss 170–75   500
     Companies Act 2006 ss 260–63   504

(2) Work Councils   506
   (a) Principles   507
       Control Council Law No 22 (10 April 1946) Works Councils   507
       Work Constitution Act 1972 (BGBl I S 2518)   509
   (b) Economic Changes for 50+ Employees   511
       Information and Consultation Directive 2002/14/EC Arts 1–7   511
       Information and Consultation of Employees Regulations 2004
         (SI 3426/2004) regs 2–32   512
   (c) Economic Changes for 1000+ EU Employees   516
       Transnational Works Council Directive 2009/38/EC arts 6–13   516
       Transnational Information and Consultation of Employees
         Regulations 1999   518
(3) Rights in Workers' Capital   521
       Pensions Act 2004 ss 241–43   521
       Pensions Act 2008 ss 67–69 and Sch 1   523
       Association of Member Nominated Trustees, The Red Lines: Voting
         Instructions (2016)   526
Additional Reading   529

PART FOUR: EQUALITY

12. DISCRIMINATION   533

(1) Principles and Protected Characteristics   534
   (a) General Principle of Equality?   534
       Kruse v Johnson   534
       Kücükdeveci v Swedex GmbH & Co KG   539
   (b) Protected Characteristics   544
       Mandla v Dowell Lee   544
       Redfearn v United Kingdom   547
       Coleman v Attridge Law   552
       English v Sanderson Blinds Ltd   556
(2) Direct Discrimination   559
   (a) Comparison   559
       Equality Act 2010 ss 13, 18, 23 and 29   559
       Shamoon v Chief Constable of the Royal Ulster Constabulary   561
   (b) Proof and Remedies   565
       Equality Act 2010 s 136   565
       Rookes v Barnard   567
   (c) Justifications   570
       Equality Act 2010 Sch 9, paras 1–4   570
       Seldon v Clarkson Wright & Jakes   572
(3) Harassment   575
       Equality Act 2010 ss 26 and 40   575
       Majrowski v Guy's and St Thomas's NHS Trust   576

(4) Victimisation   579
            Equality Act 2010 s 27   579
            St Helen's MBC v Derbyshire   580
Problem Question   582
Additional Reading   582

13. DISADVANTAGE   585

(1) Indirect Discrimination   586
      (a) Particular Disadvantage of Neutral Practices   586
            Equality Act 2010 s 19   586
            R (Seymour-Smith) v SS for Employment   587
            Homer v Chief Constable of West Yorkshire Police   590
      (b) Objective Justification   594
            Griggs v Duke Power Co   595
            Eweida v United Kingdom   598
            Kutz-Bauer v Freie und Hansestadt Hamburg   603
(2) Reduced Protection on Gender Pay Equality   605
      (a) Comparators   606
            Equal Treatment Directive 2006   606
            Allonby v Accrington and Rossendale College   607
            Equality Act 2010 ss 64–66 and 79   609
      (b) Genuine Material Factor Defence   611
            Equality Act 2010 s 69   611
            Clay Cross (Quarry Services) Ltd v Fletcher   612
Additional Reading   613

14. INCLUSION   615

(1) Positive Action   616
            Equality Act 2010 ss 158–59   616
            Re Badeck's application   618
(2) Pregnancy   621
            Parviainen v Finnair Oyj   621
(3) Disability   623
      (a) Meaning   624
            Equality Act 2010 s 6 and Sch 1   624
      (b) Reasonable Adjustments   626
            Equality Act 2010 ss 13(3), 15, 20–21, 60 and Sch 8   626
            Archibald v Fife Council   629
Additional Reading   633

15. ATYPICAL WORK   635

(1) Part-Time Workers   636
      (a) Equality or Justification?   636
            Part-time Work Directive 1997 clauses 3–4   636

Part-time Workers (Prevention of Less Favourable Treatment) Regulations 2000	638
Matthews v Kent & Medway Towns Fire Authority	639
Wippel v Peek & Cloppenburg GmbH & Co KG	641
O'Brien v Ministry of Justice	644
(b) Right to Full-Time Work?	647
Part-time Work Directive 1997 clauses 5–6	647
Employment Rights Act 1996 s 80F–G	649
(2) Fixed-Term Employees	650
(a) Equality or Justification?	650
Fixed-Term Work Directive 1999 clauses 3–4	650
Fixed-Term Employees (Prevention of Less Favourable Treatment) Regulations 2002 regs 2–5	651
Del Cerro Alonso v Osakidetza-Servicio Vasco de Salud	653
(b) Right to Permanent Work?	655
Fixed Term Work Directive 1999 clauses 5 and 6	655
Mangold v Helm	657
Fixed-Term Employees (Prevention of Less Favourable Treatment) Regulations 2002 regs 3(6)–(7) and 8	660
Duncombe v Secretary of State for Children, Schools and Families	661
(3) Agency Work	663
(a) Equality or Justification?	664
Temporary Agency Work Directive 2008 Arts 2–3	664
Agency Workers Regulations 2010 reg 5	666
(b) Right to Direct Work?	668
Temporary Agency Work Directive 2008 Arts 4 and 6	669
Agency Workers Regulations 2010 reg 13	670
Problem Question	670
Additional Reading	671

PART FIVE: JOB SECURITY

16. FULL EMPLOYMENT

16. FULL EMPLOYMENT	**675**
(1) Fiscal Policy	676
(a) Investment	678
White Paper, Employment Policy (May 1944) Cmd 6527	678
MS Eccles, Beckoning Frontiers: Public and Personal Recollections (1951) 75–77	686
Economic Policies Recommendation (EU) 2015/1184	691
Employment Decision 2015/1848	692
Greece: Memorandum of Understanding on Specific Economic Policy Conditionality (3 May 2010) 60–71	695
Employment Promotion and Protection against Unemployment Recommendation 1988 (no 176)	700

(b) Procurement   702
    Rüffert v Land Niedersachsen   702
(c) Education and Retraining   707
(2) Monetary Policy   708
    Bank of England Act 1998 ss 1–2, 10–13 and 19   708
    Treaty on European Union, Art 3   712
    Treaty on the Functioning of the European Union, Arts 9,
       127 and 282   712
(3) Income Insurance and Employment Agencies   716
(a) Unemployment Insurance   716
    Jobseekers Act 1995 ss 1–6J   717
    Welfare Reform Act 2012 ss 1–17   720
    R (Reilly) v Secretary of State for Work and Pensions   723
(b) Employment Agencies   729
    Höfner and Elser v Macrotron GmbH   730
    Employment Agencies Act 1973   732
    Gangmasters Licensing Act 2004 ss 4–13   734
(4) Trade Policy   735
    EU–South Korea Free Trade Agreement (14 May 2011) [2011]
       OJ L127, Art 13   736
Additional Reading   739

17. DISMISSAL CONCEPT AND PROCESS   741

(1) Concept of Dismissal   742
    Western Excavating (ECC) Ltd v Sharp   743
    Buckland v Bournemouth University   745
    Adamas Ltd v Cheung   749
(2) Notice   752
    Employment Rights Act 1996 ss 86 and 89   752
    Société Générale, London Branch v Geys   754
(3) Fair Hearing   763
    ACAS Code of Practice 1: Disciplinary and Grievance
       Procedures (2015)   764
    Trade Union and Labour Relations (Consolidation) Act 1992 s 207A 767
    Salford Royal NHS Foundation Trust v Roldan   769
    R (G) v Governors of X School   771
(4) Injunctions to Follow Procedure   775
    Edwards v Chesterfield Royal Hospital NHS Foundation Trust   775
Problem Question   777
Additional Reading   778

18. FAIR REASONS FOR DISMISSAL   779

(1) Right Against Unjust Dismissal   780
    Dean v Bennett   780
    Johnson v Unisys Ltd   783

(2) Fairness of Dismissal 787
  (a) Qualifications for the Statutory Right 787
      Employment Rights Act 1996 ss 97, 108, 111 and 212 787
  (b) Reasonableness 791
      Employment Rights Act 1996 s 98 791
      HSBC Bank plc v Madden 793
      Turner v East Midlands Trains Ltd 797
  (c) Reasons: Conduct and Capability 802
      Bowater v Northwest London Hospitals NHS Trust 802
      McAdie v Royal Bank of Scotland plc 805
(3) Remedies After Dismissal 806
  (a) Damages, Statutory Cap and Exceptions 806
      Employment Rights Act 1996 ss 119, 123–24 and 227 807
      Johnson v Unisys Ltd 810
  (b) Injunctions After Dismissal 815
      Employment Rights Act 1996 ss 114–15 816
      Port of London Authority v Payne 817
  (c) Compromise Agreements 819
      Employment Rights Act 1996 s 203 819
Additional Reading 820

19. REDUNDANCY AND TRANSFERS 823
(1) Conceptions of Redundancy 824
  (a) Redundancies 824
      Trade Union and Labour Relations (Consolidation) Act 1992 s 195 824
      Employment Rights Act 1996 s 139 825
      University and College Union v University of Stirling 826
      Murray v Foyle Meats Ltd 830
  (b) Some Other Substantial Reason 833
      Employment Rights Act 1996 s 98(1)(b) 833
      Hollister v National Farmers' Union 834
      Reilly v Sandwell Metropolitan Borough Council 837
  (c) Transfer of Undertakings 839
      Transfer of Undertakings Directive 2001/23/EC Arts 1, 3–4 and 6 840
      Oy Liikenne Ab v Liskjärvi and Juntunen 844
      Parkwood Leisure Ltd v Alemo-Herron 848
(2) Consultation, Selection, Notification 853
  (a) General Duty to Consult 854
      Williams v Compair Maxam Ltd 854
  (b) Over 20 Redundancies 857
      Collective Redundancies Directive 98/59/EC 857
      Trade Union and Labour Relations (Consolidation) Act 1992 s 188 858
      Lyttle v Bluebird UK Bidco 2 Ltd 862
      AEK ry v Fujitsu Siemens Computers Oy 864
      Transfer of Undertakings Directive 2001/23/EC Art 7 869

(c) Limits of EU Competence   870
                AGET Iraklis v Ypourgos Ergasias, Koinonikis Asfalisis kai Koinonikis
                    Allilengyis   870
(3) Right to Pay or Redeployment   875
     Employment Rights Act 1996 ss 135, 141, 162   875
Problem Question   878
Additional Reading   878

Index   881

Table of Cases

UNITED KINGDOM

A v B [2003] IRLR 405 . . . . 770, 798
AB v CD [2001] IRLR 808. 335
Abbey National plc v Fairbrother [2007] IRLR 320. 747
Abbott v Sullivan [1952] 1 KB 189 346
Abdulla v Birmingham CC [2012] UKSC 47. 611
Abercrombie v Aga Rangemaster Ltd [2013] EWCA Civ 1148 259
Abernethy v Mott, Hay and Anderson [1974] ICR 323 791
Abu Dhabi National Tanker Co v Product Star Shipping Ltd (The Product Star)
    (No 2) [1993] 1 Lloyd's Rep 397 227
Achilleas, The. *See* Transfield Shipping Inc v Mercator Shipping Inc
Adamas Ltd v Cheung [2011] UKPC 32 . . . . **749**
Addis v Gramophone Co Ltd [1909] AC 488. . . . . .198, 333,
                                                                        780, 783–86, 811
Advocate General v MacDonald, 2001 SC 1 563
Agnew v Commissioners of Inland Revenue [2001] UKPC 28 104
Agricultural Sector (Wales) Bill, Re [2014] UKSC 43. 251
Airfix Footwear Ltd v Cope [1978] ICR 1210 . . . . 116, 117
Allen v Flood [1898] AC 1 . . . . 20, 359, 413
Allonby v Accrington and Rossingdale College [2004] ICR 1328. 668
Alstom Transport v Tilson [2010] EWCA Civ 1308 144
Amalgamated Engineering Union v Minister of Pensions and National Insurance
    [1963] 1 WLR 441, [1963] 1 All ER 864. 109
Amalgamated Society of Carpenters and Joiners v Braithwaite [1922] 2 AC 440. 347
Amalgamated Society of Railway Servants v Osborne [1910] AC 87 337
American Cyanamid Co v Ethicon Ltd [1975] AC 396 . . . . 457, 474, 475
Amicus v Macmillan Publishers Ltd [2007] IRLR 378 (EAT). 515
Annamunthodo v Oilfield Workers' Trade Union [1961] AC 945 . . . . 347, 349
Aramis, The [1989] 1 Lloyd's Rep 213. 142–44
Archibald v Fife Council [2004] UKHL 32 . . . . **629**
Ashby v White (1703) 92 ER 126. . . . . 538, 775, 810
Aslam and Farrar v Uber BV (2016) 2202550/2015 128
ASLEF v London & Birmingham Railway [2011] EWCA Civ 226 471
Associated Provincial Picture Houses Ltd v Wednesbury Corp
    [1948] 1 KB 223. . . . . 227, 334, 506, 766
Atkin v Acton (1830) 172 ER 67 753
Attorney General v Blake [2000] UKHL 45 . . . . **216**, 220

Attorney General of Belize v Belize Telecom Ltd [2009] UKPC 10,
    [2009] 1 WLR 1988 . . . . 302, 334, 380, 757, 801
Autoclenz Ltd v Belcher [2011] UKSC 41 . . . .**101**, 105, 106,
    108, 112, 113, 118, 120, 121, 123,
    124, 127, 132, 133, 136, 140, 144,
    159, 161, 163, 167, 177, 207, 221,
    223, 230, 241, 297, 298, 359, 413, 452,
    470, 471, 525, 652, 664, 668, 672, 777, 832
Azmi v Kirklees MBC [2007] IRLR 434 (EAT) 601
Bahl v Law Society [2004] EWCA Civ 1070. 594
Bailey Case (1854) 3 E & B 607 117
Bailey v Williamson (1873) LR 8 QB 118 535
Baird v Wells (1890) 44 Ch D 661 346
Bank voor Handel en Scheepvaart NV v Slatford [1953] 1 QB 248,
    [1951] 2 TLR 755, [1951] 2 All ER 779 110
Barber v RJB Mining (UK) Ltd [1999] 2 CMLR 833 . . . .**311**
Barber v Somerset CC [2004] UKHL 13 815
Barings (No 5), Re [2000] 1 BCLC 523 502
Bass Taverns Ltd v Burgess [1995] EWCA Civ 40 . . . .**364**, 365
Bateman v ASDA Stores Ltd [2010] IRLR 370 240
BBC v Hearn [1977] 1 WLR 1004, [1977] ICR 686. . . . . 421, **424**, 426, 467
BCE Inc v 1976 Debenture Holders, 2008 SCC 69 505
Bell v Midland Railway Co, 10 CBNS 287 568
Benedetti v Sawiris [2013] UKSC 50. . . . . 248, 249
Benham v Gambling [1941] AC 157 568
Bennett v National Amalgamated Society of Operative House
    and Ship Painters and Decorators (1916) 85 LJ Ch 298 337
Bhasin v Hrynew [2014] 3 SCR 494 224
Bhullar v Bhullar [2003] EWCA Civ 424 219
Blackpool and the Fylde College v National Association of Teachers
    in Further and Higher Education [1994] ICR 648 469
Blackpool Corp v Locker [1948] 1 KB 349 724
Boardman v Phipps [1967] 2 AC 46. 248
Bolam v Friern Hospital Management Committee [1957] 1 WLR 582 793
Bonsor v Musicians' Union [1956] AC 104 . . . .**344**, 346, 349
Borrer v Cardinal Security Ltd [2013] UKEAT 0416_12_1607 . . . .**297**, 298
Boulting v Association of Cinematograph, Television and Allied
    Technicians [1963] 2 QB 606. . . . . 127, 620
Bouzir v Country Style Foods Ltd [2011] EWCA Civ 1519 565
Bowater v Northwest London Hospitals NHS Trust [2011] EWCA Civ 63 . . . .**802**
Boyo v Lambeth LBC [1994] ICR 727. . . . . 756, 759, 763
Bradford City Metropolitan Council v Arora [1991] 2 QB 507 569
Braganza v BP Shipping Ltd [2015] UKSC 17 228
Breen v Amalgamated Engineering Union [1971] 2 QB 175 . . . .**330**, 335, 506
Brigden v American Express Bank Ltd [2000] IRLR 94 181
Brimnes, The [1975] QB 929 98
Briscoe v Lubrizol [2002] EWCA Civ 508 184

Bristow v City Petroleum [1987] 1 WLR 529 258
British Aerospace plc v Green [1995] EWCA Civ 26 856
British Airways plc v Noble [2006] EWCA Civ 537 296
British Airways plc v Unite the Union (No 1) [2009] EWHC 3541 (QB) 470
British Airways plc v Unite the Union [2010] EWCA Civ 669 .... **409**, 412, 471
British Coal Corp v Smith [1996] IRLR 404 610
British Fuels Ltd v Baxendale [1999] 2 AC 52 853
British Homes Stores Ltd v Burchell (Note) [1978] ICR 303 839
British Leyland UK Ltd v Swift [1981] IRLR 91 .... 792, 797
British Nursing Association v Inland Revenue [2002] EWCA Civ 494 .... **253**
British Telecommunications plc v Ticehurst [1992] ICR 383 .... 220, 263
Broome v DPP [1974] AC 587 461
Browning v Morris (1778) 2 Cowp 790 247
Bryant v Foreign and Commonwealth Office [2003] UKEAT 174 196
Buckland v Bournemouth University [2010] EWCA Civ 121 .... **745**, 748
Burchell v British Home Stores [1980] ICR 303 .... 770, 794, 839
Burns v Santander plc [2011] IRLR 639 258
Burton and Rheule v De Vere Hotels [1997] ICR 151 579
Butt v Kelson [1952] Ch 197 528
Byrne Bros (Formwork) Ltd v Baird [2002] ICR 667 125
Cable & Wireless plc v Muscat [2006] EWCA Civ 220 .... **141**, 387, 663
Camden Exhibition & Display Ltd v Lynott [1966] 1 QB 555 184
Camilla M, The [1979] 1 Lloyd's Rep 26 475
Caparo Industries plc v Dickman [1989] QB 653 146
Carl v University of Sheffield [2009] ICR 1286 644
Carlen v Drury (1812) 35 ER 61 779
Carmichael v National Power plc [1999] UKHL 47 .... **119**, 120, 121, 832
Carter v Boehm (1766) 3 Burr 1905 224
Cartwright v King's College London [2010] EWCA Civ 1146 769
Catamaran Cruisers Ltd v Williams [1994] IRLR 384 837
Catholic Child Welfare Society v Institute of the Brothers
  of the Christian Schools [2012] UKSC 56, [2013] 2 AC 1 .... **133**, 136, 664, 668
Caulfield v Marshall Clay Products [2004] EWCA Civ 422 294
Chadwick v Pioneer Private Telephone Co Ltd [1941] 1 All ER 522 117
Chagger v Abbey National plc [2010] ICR 397 566
Chandler v Cape plc [2011] EWCA Civ 525 .... **145**, 203, 457, 861
Chartbrook Ltd v Persimmon Homes Ltd [2009] UKHL 38,
  [2009] 1 AC 1101 .... 102, 103
Cheall v APEX [1983] 2 AC 180 .... **349**, 401
Chhabra v West London Mental Health NHS Trust [2013] UKSC 80 .... 214, 478
Chief Constable of the Royal Ulster Constabulary v A [2000] NI 261 563
Chief Constable of West Yorkshire Police v Khan [2001] UKHL 48 .... 580, 581
Choithram Int SA v Pagarani [2000] UKPC 46 499
City of Montreal v Montreal Locomotive Works Ltd
  [1946] UKPC 44 .... 106, **107**, 108
Claridge v Daler Rowney Ltd [2008] ICR 1267 747
Clark v Nomura International plc [2000] IRLR 766 227

Clark v Oxfordshire Health Authority [1998] IRLR 125 . . . . 119, 120
Clark's of Hove v Bakers Union [1978] ICR 1076 868
Clarkson International Tools Ltd v Short [1973] ICR 191 809
Clay v AJ Crump Ltd [1964] 1 QB 533 146
Clay Cross (Quarry Services) Ltd v Fletcher [1978] IRLR 361 . . . . **612**
Clouston & Co Ltd v Corry [1906] AC 122 . . . . 782, 783
Clyde & Co LLP v Bates van Winkelhof [2014] UKSC 32 . . . .**124**, 359,
620, 652, 664
CMS v Dolphin Ltd v Simonet [2001] 2 BCLC 704 177
Cobbe v Yeoman's Row Management Ltd [2008] UKHL 55 167
Cockburn v Alexander (1848) 6 CB 791, 136 ER 1459 759
Coles v Ministry of Defence [2016] ICR 55. 670
Collier v Sunday Referee Publishing Co Ltd [1940] 2 KB 647 117
Collins v National Theatre [2004] EWCA Civ 144 . . . . 631, 632
Combe v Combe [1951] 2 KB 215 167
Commerzbank AG v Keen [2006] EWCA Civ 1536 . . . . **180**
Commotion Ltd v Rutty [2006] IRLR 171. . . . . **316**, 649
Connelly v Rio Tino Zinc Corp [1997] UKHL 30 146
Consistent Group v Kalwak [2008] EWCA Civ 430, [2007] IRLR 560 . . . . 144, 297
Constantine v Imperial Hotels Ltd [1944] KB 693. . . . . 32, 538, 539, 546
Conway v Wade [1908] 2 KB 844 425
Cook v Deeks [1916] UKPC 10, [1916] 1 AC 554. . . . . 219, 503
Cormie v Robert Rodger (UKEATS/0036/11) 122
Cornwall CC v Prater [2006] IRLR 362. 121
Cory Lighterage Ltd v Transport and General Workers' Union
    [1973] 1 WLR 792 425
Cotter v National Union of Seamen [1929] 2 Ch 58 339
Council of Civil Service Unions v Minister for the Civil Service
    [1984] UKHL 9 . . . . **361**
Courtaulds Northern Textiles Ltd v Andrew [1979] IRLR 84 223
Cowan v Scargill [1985] Ch 270. 701
Cowen v Haden Carrier Ltd [1982] IRLR 225 831
Crabb v Arun DC [1975] EWCA Civ 7 167
Credit Suisse First Boston (Europe) Ltd v Lister [1999] ICR 794 853
Creen v Wright (1875–76) LR 1 CPD 591 754
Cresswell v Board of Inland Revenue [1984] ICR 508 210
Crofter Hand Woven Harris Tweed Co Ltd v Veitch [1941] UKHL 2,
    [1942] AC 435 . . . . .325, 408, 412,
414, 419, 421, 422
Crossley v Faithful & Gould Holdings Ltd [2004] EWCA Civ 293. . . . . 191, 757
Crouch v Great Northern Railway Co (1856) 11 Ex 742 568
CSC Computer Sciences Ltd v McAlinden [2013] EWCA Civ 1435 . . . . **164**, 167
Customs and Excise Commissioners v Barclays Bank [2007] 1 AC 181 146
Cutter v Powell (1795) 101 ER 573 262
Dacas v Brook Street Bureau (UK) Ltd [2004] EWCA Civ 217 . . . . **136**, 143, 663
Daimler Co Ltd v Continental Tyre and Rubber Co (Great Britain) Ltd
    [1916] 2 AC 307. 861

Darlington School Case, 12 LJ (QB) 124, 14 LJ (QB) 67 781
Davidson v Comparisons [1980] IRLR 360 833
DC Thomson & Co Ltd v Deakin [1952] Ch 646. 423
Dean v Bennett (1870) LR 6 Ch 489. . . . . 359, **780**, 782, 783
Delaney v Staples [1992] 1 AC 687 258
Derry v Peek (1889) 14 AC 337 488
Devonald v Rosser & Sons [1906] 2 KB 728 . . . . 117, **228**, 230, 259, 296
Dhunna v Creditsights Ltd [2014] EWCA Civ 1238 201
Dimbleby & Sons Ltd v NUJ [1983] 1 WLR 427 . . . . 148, **455**, 458
Diocese of Hallam Trustees v Connaughton [1996] ICR 860 (EAT) 607
Dorset Yacht Co Ltd v Home Office [1970] AC 1004 146
DPP v Jones [1999] 2 AC 240 461
Drane v Evangelou [1978] 1 WLR 455 . . . . 570, 809
Dresdner Kleinwort Ltd v Attrill [2013] EWCA Civ 394. 167
Dryden v Greater Glasgow Health Board [1992] IRLR 469 210
Dubai Aluminium Co Ltd v Salaam [2002] UKHL 48, [2003] 2 AC 366 . . . . 135, 577
Dumfries and Galloway Council v North [2013] UKSC 45 149
Duncombe v Secretary of State for Children, Schools and Families
    [2011] UKSC 36 . . . . 198, 200, **661**
Dunk v George Waller & Sons Ltd [1970] 2 QB 163. 129
Dunn v AAH Ltd [2010] IRLR 709 234
Dunnachie v Kingston-upon-Hull CC [2004] UKHL 36 809
Duport Steel Ltd v Sirs [1980] ICR 161 455
E Green & Son (Castings) Ltd v Association of Scientific, Technical
    and Managerial Staffs [1984] ICR 352 (EAT) 861, 862
Eagle Place Services Ltd v Rudd [2010] IRLR 486 632
Eastwood v Magnox Electric plc [2004] UKHL 35 . . . . 224, 814
Ecclestone v National Union of Journalists [1999] IRLR 166 334
Edmonds v Lawson QC [2000] EWCA Civ 69 . . . . **128**, 253, 282
Edwards v Bairstow [1956] AC 14 113
Edwards v Chesterfield Royal Hospital NHS Foundation Trust
    [2011] UKSC 58, [2012] 2 AC 22 . . . . .129, 130, 235, 311,
                                          775, 778, 805, 815, 852, 853
Edwards v Halliwell [1950] 2 All ER 1064. . . . . **338**
Edwards v Levy (1860) 2 F&F 94 211
Edwards v Society of Graphical and Allied Trades [1971] Ch 354 . . . . 348, 350
Eley v Positive Government Security Life Assurance Co Ltd (1876) 1 Ex D 88 505
Ellis v Brighton Co-operative Society Ltd [1976] IRLR 419. . . . . 241, 835
Enfield Technical Services Ltd v Payne [2008] EWCA Civ 393,
    [2008] ICR 1423 171
English v Sanderson Blinds Ltd [2008] EWCA Civ 1421 . . . . **556**, 558
Equitable Life Assurance Society v Hyman [2000] UKHL 39,
    [2002] 1 AC 408. . . . . .98, 144, 191, 207,
                                          227, 232, 241, 299, 334
Essop v Home Office and Naeem v Secretary of State for Justice
    [2017] UKSC 27 597
Esterman v NALGO [1974] ICR 625 . . . . 348, 349

Etam plc v Rowan [1989] IRLR 150 571
Express & Echo Publications Ltd v Tanton ("Tanton") [1999] ICR 693 102
Express Newspapers Ltd Respondents v McShane [1980] AC 672 . . . . 426, 455
Faccenda Chicken Ltd v Fowler [1986] ICR 297 220
Falcke v Scottish Imperial Insurance Co (1886) 34 Ch 234 248
Farley v Skinner [2001] UKHL 49 808
Fecitt v NHS Manchester [2011] EWCA Civ 1190 582
Fender v St John-Mildmay [1938] AC 1 233
Ferguson v John Dawson & Partners (Contractors) Ltd [1976] 1 WLR 1213 112
Financial Times Ltd v Bishop [2003] UKEAT 0147 196
Firthglow Ltd v Szilagyi [2009] IRLR 365 297
Fitzpatrick v British Railways Board [1992] ICR 221 363
Foley v Post Office [2000] ICR 1283 . . . . 797, 838, 839
Ford v Warwickshire CC [1983] 2 AC 71, [1983] ICR 273 . . . . 115, 119,
123, 140, **168**, 656, 790
Ford Motor Co Ltd v Amalgamated Union of Engineering and Foundry
    Workers [1969] 2 QB 303 390
Fort Gilkicker, Re [2013] EWHC 348 505
Foss v Harbottle (1843) 67 ER 189 338–41
France v James Coombes & Co [1929] AC 496 . . . . 65, **249**
French v Barclays Bank plc [1998] EWCA Civ 1092, [1998] IRLR 646 . . . . . . **182**, 228
Frewin v Consignia plc, unreported 18 July 2003 (EAT) 805
Fullarton Computer Industries Ltd v CAC [2001] Scot CS 168 386
G4S Cash Solutions (UK) Ltd v Powell [2016] IRLR 820 632
GAB Robins (UK) Ltd v Triggs [2008] EWCA Civ 17 809
Gallagher v Alpha Catering [2004] EWCA Civ 1559 309
Gallagher v Post Office [1970] 3 All ER 712 390
Gamlestaden Fastigheter AB v Baltic Partners Ltd [2007] UKPC 26 505
Gan Insurance Co Ltd v Tai Ping Insurance Co Ltd (No 2)
    [2001] 2 All ER (Comm) 299 227
Garratt v Mirror Group Newspapers Ltd [2011] EWCA Civ 425,
    [2011] ICR 880 . . . . 165, 187
Gate Gourmet London Ltd v TGWU [2005] EWHC 1889 473
General Billposting Ltd v Atkinson [1909] AC 118 177
George v Luton BC, 16 September (EAT) 99
George Mitchell (Chesterhall) Ltd v Finney Lock Seeds Ltd
    [1982] EWCA Civ 5 . . . . 177, 233, 427
Geys v Société Générale [2013] 1 AC 523 235
Gillian's case 346
Gisda Cyf v Barratt [2010] UKSC 41 . . . . **98**, 100, 105, 144,
145, 163, 184, 221, 263,
359, 422, 454, 471, 751, 790
Glasgow City Council v McNab [2007] IRLR 476 571
Goodwin v Patent Office [1999] ICR 302 625
Governing Body of Clifton Middle School v Askew [1999] EWCA Civ 1892 132
Govia GTR Ltd v Associated Society of Locomotive Engineers and Firemen
    [2016] EWCA Civ 1309 476

Grainger plc v Nicholson [2010] IRLR 4 (EAT) 551
Gray v Fire Alarm Fabrication Services Ltd [2007] ICR 247. 146
Guinness plc v Saunders [1990] 2 AC 663 . . . . 270, 502
Gunton v Richmond-upon-Thames LBC [1980] ICR 755 . . . . .237, 755,
760, 761, 763, 778
Haddon v Van Den Bergh Foods Ltd [1999] ICR 1150 (EAT). 793, 839
Hadmor Productions Ltd v Hamilton [1983] 1 AC 191 426
Hainsworth v Ministry of Defence [2014] EWCA Civ 763 556
Halfpenny v IGE Medical Systems Ltd [1997] ICR 1007 311
Hall v Woolston Hall Leisure Ltd [2000] EWCA Civ 170. . . . . 171, 176
Hanley v Pease & Partners Ltd [1915] 1 KB 698 261
Harman v Flexible Lamps Ltd [1980] IRLR 418 751
Harries v Church Commissioners of England and Wales [1992] 1 WLR 1241 701
Harrison v Kent CC [1995] ICR 434 (EAT). 363
Harrods v Remmick [1998] ICR 156 144
Harron v Chief Constable of Dorset Police [2016] IRLR 481 (EAT). 552
Hart v AR Marshall & Sons (Bulwell) Ltd [1978] 2 All ER 413 751
Hartley v King Edward VI College [2017] UKSC 39 . . . . 263, 478
Hartog v Colin & Shields [1939] 3 All ER 566 191
Harvela Investments Ltd v Royal Trust of Canada (CI) Ltd [1986] AC 207 165
Hellyer Bros v McLeod [1987] ICR 526 119
Henderson v Merrett Syndicates Ltd [1994] UKHL 5 201
Henry v London General Transport Services Ltd [2002] EWCA Civ 488. 186
Herbert Morris Ltd v Saxelby [1916] 1 AC 688 176
Hewage v Grampian Health Board [2012] UKSC 37. 565
High Table Ltd v Horst [1997] EWCA Civ 2000 833
Hill v CA Parsons & Co Ltd [1972] Ch 305. 777
HK (An Infant), Re [1967] 2 QB 617. 331
Hodgson v National and Local Government Officials Association
[1972] 1 WLR 130 341
Hoenig v Isaacs [1952] EWCA Civ 6. 262
Hollister v National Farmers' Union [1979] ICR 542. . . . . **241**, 834, 836
Holman v Johnson (1775) 1 Cowp 341, 98 Eng Rep 1120. 172
Home Office v Evans [2007] EWCA Civ 1089 239
Homer v Chief Constable of West Yorkshire Police [2012] UKSC 15 . . . . **590**, 594
Horkulak v Cantor Fitzgerald International [2004] EWCA Civ 1287 815
Hornby v Close (1867) LR 2 QB 153. 18
Hospital Medical Group Ltd v Westwood [2012] EWCA Civ 1005. . . . . 125, 127
Hounga v Allen [2014] UKSC 47 . . . .**170**, 176,
246, 247, 412
Howard v Pickford Truck Co Ltd [1951] 1 KB 417 238
HSBC Bank plc v Madden [2000] EWCA Civ 3030 . . . . **793**, 797
Hudson v Department for Work and Pensions [2012] EWCA Civ 1416 653
Hughes v Corps of Commissionaires Management Ltd (No 2)
[2011] EWCA Civ 1061 . . . . **308**
HV McKay, Ex parte (1907) 2 CAR 1 246
Iceland Frozen Foods Ltd v Jones [1983] ICR 17 (EAT) 792, 794

Igbo v Johnson, Matthey Chemicals Ltd [1986] ICR 505 820
Igen Ltd v Wong [2005] EWCA Civ 142 565
Imperial Group Pension Trust Ltd v Imperial Tobacco Ltd [1991] 1 WLR 589. 224
Inco Europe Ltd v First Choice Distribution [2000] 1 WLR 586. 793
Inderwick v Snell (1850) 42 ER 83 782
Interfoto Picture Library Ltd v Stiletto Visual Programmes Ltd
    [1987] EWCA Civ 6. 183
Irani v Southampton AHA [1985] ICR 590 777
Isle of Wight Tourist Board v Coombes [1976] IRLR 413. 223
J Lyons & Sons v Wilkins [1896] 1 Ch 811, [1899] 1 Ch 255 460
J Spurling Ltd v Bradshaw [1956] EWCA Civ 3 183
Jackson v Ghost Ltd [2003] IRLR 824. 196
James v Eastleigh BC [1990] 2 AC 751 564
James v Greenwich LBC [2008] EWCA Civ 35 . . . . 144, 664, 668
James v Redcats (Brands) Ltd [2007] IRLR 296 124
Jarvis v Swans Tours Ltd [1972] EWCA Civ 8 808
Jivraj v Hashwani [2011] UKSC 40 . . . . 125, 132, 575
Johnson v Unisys Ltd [2001] UKHL 13, [2003] 1 AC 518 . . . .**96**, 100, 105,
                                                            184, 235, 539, 546, 780,
                                                            783, 786, 809, **811**, 814
Johnstone v Bloomsbury Health Authority [1992] QB 333 . . . .**178, 230**, 303
Joint English Stock Board, Re (1867) LR Eq 350 661
Jones v Gwent CC [1992] IRLR 521 777
Jones v Post Office [2001] EWCA Civ 558 632
Jones v University of Manchester [1993] ICR 474. 590
JT Stratford & Son v Lindley [1965] AC 269. . . . . 421, 423
Kaur v MG Rover Group Ltd [2004] EWCA 1507. . . . . **185**
Keech v Sandford [1726] EWHC Ch J76. . . . . 528, 768
Kelly v National Society of Operative Printers'
    Assistants (1915) 84 LJKB 2236 . . . . 344, 346
Kerr v Sweater Shop (Scotland) Ltd [1996] IRLR 425 258
King v Great Britain-China Centre [1992] ICR 516. 565
Kingston v Preston (1773) 2 Doug KB 689 . . . . 413, 415
Kiriri Cotton Co Ltd v Dewani [1960] AC 192 247
Kirklees MBC v Radecki [2009] EWCA Civ 298 99
Kruse v Johnson [1898] 2 QB 91 . . . . **534**, 536, 543, 546
Kuddus v Chief Constable of Leicestershire [2002] 2 AC 122. 569
Kulkarni v Milton Keynes Hospital NHS Foundation Trust [2010] ICR 101. 235
Kwik-Fit (GB) Ltd v Lineham [1992] ICR 183 749
L'Estrange v F Graucob Ltd [1934] 2 KB 394 102
Ladele v Islington LBC [2009] EWCA Civ 1357. 601
Lambeth LBC v Commission for Racial Equality [1990] ICR 768 572
Lawlor v Union of Post Office Workers [1965] Ch 712 333
Laws v London Chronicle (Indicator Newspapers) Ltd [1959] 1 WLR 698 754
Lawson v Serco Ltd; Botham v Ministry of Defence;
    Crofts v Veta Ltd [2006] UKHL 3 . . . . **194**, 197, 201, 205
Lee v Lee's Air Farming Ltd [1960] UKPC 33. . . . . 126, 620

Lee v Showmen's Guild of Great Britain [1952] 2 QB 329 347
Lee Ting Sang v Chung Chi Keung [1990] UKPC 9 112
Leisure Employment Services Ltd v HM Revenue & Customs
    [2007] EWCA Civ 92. 265
Leonard v Southern Derbyshire Chamber of Commerce [2001] IRLR 19. 625
Lesney Products & Co v Nolan [1976] EWCA Civ 8 829
Lewisham LBC v Malcolm and EHRC [2008] UKHL 43 628
Lidl Ltd v Central Arbitration Committee [2017] EWCA Civ 328. . . . . **386**
Lister v Hesley Hall Ltd [2002] 1 AC 215 577
Lister v Romford Ice & Cold Storage Co Ltd [1956] UKHL 6,
    [1957] AC 555 . . . . **208**, 209, 757
Litster v Forth Dry Dock & Engineering Co Ltd [1988] UKHL 10. 852
Liverpool CC v Irwin [1976] AC 239. . . . . 207, 757
Logan Salton v Durham CC [1989] IRLR 99. 820
London Ambulance Service v Charlton [1992] ICR 773 404
London Fire and Civil Defence Authority v Betty [1994] IRLR 384. 805
London Transport Executive v Clarke [1981] ICR 355 . . . . 99, 237, 756, 760
London Underground Ltd v Edwards (No 2) [1999] ICR 494 . . . . 592, 604
London Underground Ltd v National Union of Railwaymen, Maritime
    and Transport Staff [1996] ICR 170. . . . . 408, 411, 412, 418
Lord Bruce's case (1728) 93 ER 870 782
Lubbe v Cape plc [2000] 1 WLR 1545. 145
Luce v Bexley LBC [1990] ICR 591 404
Luke v Stoke on Trent City Council [2007] EWCA Civ 761 210
Lumley v Gye (1853) 2 E&B 216. . . . . 421, 422
Lungowe v Vedanta Resources plc and Konkola Copper Mines plc
    [2017] EWCA Civ 1528. 203
Lyddon v Englefield Brickwork Ltd [2008] IRLR 198. 293
Macarthys Ltd v Smith (No 2) [1981] QB 180. 607
Madarassy v Nomura International plc [2007] EWCA Civ 33. 565
Majrowski v Guy's and St Thomas's NHS Trust [2006] UKHL 34 . . . . **576**
Malik and Mahmud v Bank of Credit and Commerce International SA
    [1997] UKHL 23, [1998] AC 20 . . . . .214, **221**, 223,
                                                                        747, 780, 783–85, 812
Malloch v Aberdeen Corp [1971] 1 WLR 1578 . . . . 784, 813
Mallone v BPB Industries plc [2002] EWCA Civ 126 . . . . **226**
Malone v British Airways plc [2010] EWCA Civ 1225. . . . . **186**
Mandla v Dowell Lee [1983] QB 1, [1983] 2 AC 548 . . . . **544**, 559
Market Investigations Ltd v Minister for Social Security [1969] 2 QB 173 . . . . . 111, 112
Marks and Spencer plc v BNP Paribas Securities Services
    Trust Co (Jersey) Ltd [2015] UKSC 72. 302
Massey v Crown Life Insurance Co [1978] ICR 590 . . . . 112, 123
Matadeen v Pointu [1998] UKPC 9 . . . . 226, 533, 543
Mathewson v RB Wilson Dental Laboratory Ltd [1988] IRLR 512. 804
Matthews v Kent & Medway Towns Fire Authority [2006] UKHL 8 . . . . **639**
Maxim Nordenfelt Guns and Ammunition Co v Nordenfelt [1893] 1 Ch 630. 172
McAdie v Royal Bank of Scotland plc [2007] EWCA Civ 806. . . . . **805**

McBride v Scottish Police Authority [2016] UKSC 27 818
McCartney v Oversley House Management [2006] IRLR 514 254
McClelland v Northern Ireland General Health Services [1957] 1 WLR 594 100
McGahie v Union of Shop, Distributive and Allied Workers (1965) 1966 SLT 74 340
McMaster v Manchester Airport plc [1998] IRLR 112 (EAT). 99
McMeechan v Secretary of State for Employment [1996] EWCA Civ 1166,
    [1997] IRLR 353 . . . . 121, 140
McMenemy v Capita Business Ltd [2007] CSIH 25 643
Mercury Communications Ltd v Scott-Garner [1984] ICR 74. 428
Merkur Island Shipping Corp v Laughton [1983] 2 AC 570 423
Mersey Docks and Harbour Board v Coggins & Griffith (Liverpool) Ltd
    [1947] AC 1 134
Metrobus Ltd v Unite the Union [2009] EWCA Civ 829. . . . . 408, 470, 861
Mezey v South West London & St George's Mental Health NHS Trust
    [2010] IRLR 512 777
Miles v Wakefield MDC [1987] UKHL 15, [1987] AC 539 . . . . **259**, 478
Milford Haven Port Authority v Unite the Union [2010] EWCA Civ 400. 471
Mingeley v Pennock [2004] EWCA Civ 328 132
Ministry of Defence v DeBique [2010] IRLR 471 (EAT) 594
Ministry of Defence v Fletcher [2010] IRLR 25 569
Ministry of Defence v Jeremiah [1980] ICR 13 581
Ministry of Justice v Prison Officers' Association [2008] EWHC 239 429
Mogul Steamship Co Ltd v McGregor, Gow & Co
    [1892] AC 25 . . . . 358, 408,
                                                                                               413, 414, 423
Mohamed v Alaga & Co [2000] 1 WLR 1815 247
Montgomery v Johnson Underwood [2001] EWCA Civ 318,
    [2001] IRLR 264 . . . . 137, 140
Montgomery v Lanarkshire Health Board [2015] UKSC 11 793
Moorcock, The (1889) 14 PD 64 . . . . 207, 229
Moray Council v Stewart [2006] ICR 1253 (EAT). 515
Morgan v Fry [1968] 2 QB 710 . . . . 408, 412, 414, 419
Morgan v Simpson [1975] QB 151. 470
Morris v Ford Motor Co Ltd [1973] 1 QB 792. 209
Moss v McLachlan [1985] IRLR 76. 462
Murray v Foyle Meats Ltd [1999] UKHL 30. . . . . 829, **830**, 832
Muschett v HM Prison Service [2010] EWCA Civ 25. 144, 668
Nambalat v Taher [2012] EWCA Civ 1249 252
Nash v Paragon Finance [2001] EWCA 1466 . . . . 226, 227
National Sailors' and Firemen's Union v Reed [1926] Ch 536. 428
National Union of Gold, Silver, and Allied Trades v Albury
    Brothers Ltd [1979] ICR 84. 404
National Union of Mineworkers (Kent Area) v Gormley, 20 October 1977,
    The Times. 340
National Westminster Bank plc v Morgan [1985] UKHL 2 170
Nawala, The. *See* **NWL Ltd v Woods**
Nelson v British Broadcasting Corporation [1977] IRLR 148. . . . . 830, 831

Nelson v British Broadcasting Corporation (No 2) [1979] IRLR 346,
    [1980] ICR 110 . . . . 810, 813, 830, 831
Nethermere (St Neots) Ltd v Gardiner [1984] ICR 612 . . . . .101, 112, 113,
    116, 119–21, 665, 666
Netjets Management Ltd v CAC [2013] EWCA Civ 127;
    [2012] EWHC 2685 . . . . 384, 386
Network Rail Infrastructure Ltd v National Union of Rail,
    Maritime and Transport Workers [2010] EWHC 1084 (QB) 409, 471
Newnham Farms Ltd v Powell (2003) EAT/0711/01/MAA 166, 167
News Group Newspapers Ltd v Society of Graphical
    and Allied Trades [1987] ICR 181 478
Ngcobo v Thor Chemicals Holdings Ltd, January 1996 146
NHS Leeds v Larner [2012] EWCA Civ 1034 292
Nokes v Doncaster Amalgamated Collieries Ltd [1940] AC 1014 843
Norman v Yellow Pages Sales Ltd [2010] EWCA Civ 1395 820
North v Dumfries and Galloway Council [2013] UKSC 45 611
North Riding Garages v Butterwick [1967] 2 QB 56 828
Northgate HR Ltd v Mercy [2007] EWCA Civ 1304 860
Norton Tool Co Ltd v Tewson [1972] EW Misc 1 . . . . 808, 809, 813
Norwest Holst Group Administration Ltd v Harrison [1985] ICR 668 237
Notcutt v Universal Equipment Co (London) Ltd [1986] EWCA Civ 3 . . . . 751, 821
Nottingham University v Fishel [2000] IRLR 471 219
NWL Ltd v Woods [1979] 1 WLR 1294 . . . . **474**
O'Brien v Ministry of Justice [2013] UKSC 6 . . . . 605, 613, **644**
O'Kelly v Trusthouse Forte plc [1983] ICR 728, [1984] QB 90 . . . .**113**, 115,
    116, 118–20, 122,
    123, 126, 359, 652
O'Laire v Jackal Ltd [1990] IRLR 70 817
O'Reilly v Mackman [1983] 2 AC 237 361
OBG Ltd v Allan [2007] UKHL 21 . . . . 412, 423, 471
Okpabi v Royal Dutch Shell plc [2018] EWCA Civ 191 203
Optical Express Ltd v Williams [2007] IRLR 936 877
Orr v Milton Keynes Council [2011] EWCA Civ 62 . . . . 801, 838
P v NASUWT [2003] UKHL 8 . . . . 427, **466**
P&O European Ferries (Dover) Ltd v Byrne [1989] ICR 779 478
Padfield v Minister of Agriculture, Fisheries and Food [1968] AC 997 . . . . 331, 332
Paris v Stepney BC [1951] AC 367 231
Parish of St Pancras Middlesex v Parish of Clapham,
    Surrey (1860) 2 El & El 742 106
Park Cakes Ltd v Shumba [2013] EWCA Civ 974 164
Parr v Whitbread and Co plc [1990] ICR 427 . . . . 795, 797
Patel v Mirza [2016] UKSC 42 . . . . 176, **246**, 248
Paul and Fraser v NALGO [1987] IRLR 413 337
Pawson v Watson (1778) 2 Cowp 786 224
Pearce v Foster (1886) 17 QBD 536 . . . . .219 782
Pearce v Governing Body of Mayfield School [2003] UKHL34;
    [2001] EWCA Civ 1347, [2002] ICR 198 . . . . 563, 579

Pepper v Hart [1992] UKHL 3 . . . . 37, 833
Pharmacists' Defence Association Union v Secretary of State
   for Business, Innovation and Skills [2017] EWCA Civ 66 . . . . **378**, 383
Phillips Products Ltd v Hyland [1987] 1 WLR 659 179
Pickstone v Freemans plc [1989] AC 66 610
Piddington v Bates [1961] 1 WLR 162 461
Pimlico Plumbers Ltd v Smith [2017] EWCA Civ 51 127
Pink v White [1985] IRLR 489 831
Polkey v AE Dayton Services Ltd [1987] UKHL 8 . . . . 767, 805
Port of London Authority v Payne [1993] EWCA Civ 26 . . . . **818**
Porter v Magill [2001] UKHL 67 235
Post Office v Roberts [1980] IRLR 347 223
Post Office v Union of Post Office Workers [1974] 1 WLR 89 365
Potter v Hunt Contracts Ltd [1992] IRLR 108 258
Potter v RJ Temple plc, 18 December 2003, The Times (EAT) 99
President of the Methodist Conference v Preston [2013] UKSC 29 . . . . 132, 782
Printing and Numerical Registering Co v Sampson (1875) 19 Eq 462 233
Product Star, The. *See* Abu Dhabi National Tanker Co v Product
   Star Shipping Ltd
Prohibitions del Roy (1607) 12 Co Rep 63 395
Protectacoat Firthglow Ltd v Szilagyi [2009] EWCA Civ 98 102
Pulse Healthcare Ltd v Carewatch Care Services Ltd, UKEAT/0123/12 297
Qua v John Ford Morrison Solicitors [2003] ICR 482 315
Quinn v Leathem [1901] UKHL 2 . . . . 20, 422
R v Gaming Board for Great Britain, Ex parte Benaim and Khaida
   [1970] 2 QB 417 331
R v Ghosh [1982] EWCA Crim 2 264
R v Journeymen-Taylors of Cambridge (1721) 88 ER 9 42
R v Lovelass (1834) 172 ER 1380 . . . . **11**
R v Lyons [2002] UKHL 44, [2003] 1 AC 976 174
R v Richardson (1758) 97 ER 426 . . . . 782, 783
R v Secretary of State for Employment, Ex p Seymour-Smith (No 2)
   [2000] 1 WLR 435 645
R v Secretary of State for the Home Department, Ex p Leech
   [1994] QB 198 . . . . 151, 152
R v Welch (1853) 2 E&B 357 117
R (Age UK) v Secretary of State for Business, Innovation and Skills
   [2009] EWHC 2336 (Admin) 574
R (Amicus) v Secretary of State for Trade and Industry
   [2004] EWHC 860 (Admin) 571
R (BTP Tioxide) v Central Arbitration Committee [1981] ICR 843 403
R (Carson and Reynolds) v Secretary of State for Work and Pensions
   [2005] UKHL 37 572
R (Daly) v Secretary of State for the Home Department [2001] UKHL 26 . . . . . . 151, 152
R (Equal Opportunities Commission) v Secretary of State for Employment
   [1994] UKHL 2, [1995] 1 AC 1 637
R (G) v Governors of X School [2011] UKSC 30 . . . . **771**

R (Kwik-Fit (GB) Ltd) v Central Arbitration Committee
[2002] EWCA Civ 512. . . . . **384**
R (Laporte) v Chief Constable of Gloucestershire [2006] UKHL 55. 461
R (National Union of Journalists) v CAC [2005] EWCA Civ 1309 . . . . **381**
R (Reilly) v Secretary of State for Work and Pensions
[2013] UKSC 68 . . . . 720, **723**, 728
R (Seymour-Smith) v Secretary of State for Employment
[2000] UKHL 12 . . . . **587**, 594, 603, 789
R (Shoesmith) v Ofsted [2011] EWCA Civ 642. 786
R (UNISON) v Lord Chancellor [2017] UKSC 51 . . . . **149**, 728, 806, 810
R (Williamson) v Secretary of State for Education and Employment
[2005] UKHL 15 . . . . 551, 552
R (Wright) v Secretary of State for Health [2009] 1 AC 739 798
Rainey v Greater Glasgow Health Board [1987] IRLR 26. 613
Ravat v Halliburton Manufacturing and Services Ltd
[2012] UKSC 1 . . . . **198**, 201, 205
RCO Support Services Ltd v Unison [2002] EWCA Civ 464 847
Reading v Attorney-General [1951] UKHL 1, [1951] AC 507. . . . . 198, 217
Ready Mixed Concrete (South East) Ltd v Minister of Pensions
and National Insurance [1968] 2 QB 497 . . . . .101, 104, **108**,
117, 122, 137
Reda v Flag Ltd [2002] UKPC 38 . . . . 235, 786
Redcar and Cleveland BC v Bainbridge [2007] EWCA Civ 929 612
Reilly v Sandwell MBC [2018] UKSC 16. . . . . 834, **837**, 839
Reilly v Secretary of State for Work and Pensions [2016] EWCA Civ 413 728
Revenue and Customs Commissioners v Annabel's (Berkeley Square) Ltd
[2009] EWCA Civ 361. . . . . 79, 264
Revenue and Customs Commissioners v PA Holdings
[2011] EWCA Civ 1414. 273
Richardson v Koefod [1969] 1 WLR 1812. 754
Richmond Precision Engineering Ltd v Pearce [1985] IRLR 179 837
Ridge v Baldwin [1964] AC 40. . . . . 780, 784
Rigby v Ferodo Ltd [1988] ICR 29 . . . . **236**, 745, 837
RMT v Serco Ltd [2011] EWCA Civ 226 . . . . 408, 471
Robb v Green [1895] 2 Q.B. 315 209
Roberts v Hopwood [1925] AC 578 . . . . 34, 702
Robertson v British Gas Corp [1983] ICR 351 239
Robinson v Harman (1848) 1 Ex 850. . . . . 217, 296
Roebuck v National Union of Mineworkers (Yorkshire Area) No 2
[1978] ICR 676 348
Roger Bullivant Ltd v Ellis [1987] ICR 464. 220
Rolls Royce plc v Unite the Union [2009] EWCA Civ 387 857
Rooke's Case (1598) 77 ER 209 782
Rookes v Barnard [1964] UKHL 1, [1964] AC 1129. . . . . .333, 421–23,
567, 569, 647, 809
Rose & Frank Co v JR Crompton & Bros Ltd [1924] UKHL 2 . . . . 132, 167, 390
Royal Mail Group Ltd v CWU [2009] EWCA Civ 1045 870

Russell v Transocean International Resources Ltd [2011] UKSC 57 . . . . **286**
Rutherford v Secretary of State for Trade and Industry [2006] UKHL 19 590
Saad v Secretary of State for the Home Department [2001] EWCA Civ 2008 427
Safeway Stores plc v Burrell [1997] ICR 523 829–31
Sagar v Ridehalgh & Sons Ltd [1931] 1 Ch 310 258
Sainsbury's Supermarkets v Hitt [2003] IRLR 23 CA 797
Salford Royal NHS Foundation Trust v Roldan
    [2010] EWCA Civ 522. . . . . **769**, 797, 798
Salomon v Salomon and Co Ltd [1897] AC 22 . . . . 456, 457
Samuels v London Bus Services Ltd (2008) ET Case No 3202466/2008 402
Sanders v Ernest A Neale Ltd [1974] ICR 565. . . . . 755, 756
Sandle v Adecco UK Ltd [2016] IRLR 941 745
Sayers v Cambridgeshire CC [2007] IRLR 29 303
Scala Ballroom (Wolverhampton) Ltd v Ratcliffe [1958] 1 WLR 72. 538
Scally v Southern Health and Social Services Board [1992] 1 AC 294. . . . . . . **190**, 222
Schmidt v Secretary of State for Home Affairs [1969] 2 Ch 149. 332
Scottbridge Construction Ltd v Wright [2002] ScotCS 285. 254
Seaford Court Estates Ltd v Asher [1949] 2 KB 481 384
Secretary of State for Employment v ASLEF (No 2) [1972] ICR 19. 220
Secretary of State for Employment v Chapman [1989] ICR 771 877
Secretary of State for Justice v Windle [2016] EWCA Civ 459. 127
Secretary of State for Trade and Industry v Bottrill [1999] EWCA Civ 781 127
Seldon v Clarkson Wright & Jakes [2012] UKSC 16. 572
Shamoon v Chief Constable of the Royal Ulster Constabulary
    [2003] UKHL 11, [2003] IRLR 285 . . . . **561**, 581
Sharma v Manchester City Council [2008] IRLR 336. 641
Shepherd v Williamson [2010] EWHC 237 503
Shields v E Coomes (Holdings) Ltd [1978] 1 WLR 1408 612
Simmons v Heath Laundry Co [1910] 1 KB 543 114
Smith v Carillion (JM) Ltd [2015] EWCA Civ 209 . . . . 123, 144, 668
Smith v Glasgow City DC [1987] ICR 796 . . . . 792, 804
Smith v Hughes (1871) LR 6 QB 597 164
Smith v Littlewoods Ltd [1987] AC 241. . . . . 146, 147
Smith v Safeway plc [1996] ICR 868 564
Smith and Fawcett Ltd, Re [1942] Ch 304 506
Société Générale, London Branch v Geys [2012] UKSC 63 . . . . **754**, 763, 778
Somerset v Stewart (1772) 98 ER 499 . . . . **9**, 401
South Wales Miners' Federation v Glamorgan Coal Co
    [1905] AC 239 . . . . 20, 412, 422
Southern Cross Healthcare Co Ltd v Perkins [2010] EWCA Civ 1442 189
Southern Foundries (1926) Ltd v Shirlaw [1940] AC 701 127
Spackman v London Metropolitan University [2007] IRLR 741 263
Spectrum Plus Ltd, Re [2005] UKHL 41 525
St Helen's MBC v Derbyshire [2007] UKHL 16 . . . . 358, **580**
Stack v Dowden [2007] UKHL 17 249
Standard Life Health Care Ltd v Gorman [2009] EWCA Civ 1292. 177
Stephenson v Delphi Diesel Systems [2003] ICR 471 122

Sterling Engineering Co Ltd v Patchett [1955] AC 534 216
Stevens v Northolt High School, Teach 24 Ltd, unreported, 15 July 2014 668
Stevenson v United Road Transport Union [1977] ICR 893 . . . . 348, 349
Stevenson, Jordan & Harrison Ltd v MacDonald & Evans
   [1952] 1 TLR 101 . . . . **214**
Stilk v Myrick [1809] EWHC KB J58 . . . . 167, 429
Stockton on Tees BC v Aylott [2010] EWCA Civ 910 628
Stratford (JT) & Son Ltd v Lindley [1964] 2 WLR 1002 . . . . 415, 423
Stringfellow Restaurants Ltd v Quashie [2012] EWCA Civ 1735 . . . . **121**, 126
Sumsion v BBC (Scotland) [2007] IRLR 678 . . . . 287, 288
Susie Radin Ltd v GMB [2004] EWCA Civ 180 861
System Floors (UK) Ltd v Daniel [1982] ICR 54 . . . . 189, 204
Taff Vale Railway Co v Amalgamated Society of Railway Servants
   [1901] UKHL 1 . . . . 20, 21, 69, 358,
                                                419, 422, 460, 461
Tailors of Ipswich Case (1614) 11 Co Rep 53a 395
Tarleton v M'Gawley (1790) 1 Peake NPC 270 422
Taylor v Caldwell (1863) 122 ER 309 751
Taylor v Kent CC [1969] 2 QB 560 877
Taylor v National Union of Seamen [1967] 1 WLR 532 333
Taylor v Secretary of State for Scotland [2000] UKHL 28 100
Thaine v London School of Economics [2010] ICR 1422 (EAT) 576
Thomas v Times Book Co Ltd [1966] 2 All ER 241 264
Thomas Marshall (Exports) Ltd v Guinle [1979] Ch 227 . . . . 755, 760
Thomas Wragg & Sons Ltd v Wood [1976] ICR 313 877
Thompson v Renwick Group Ltd [2014] EWCA Civ 635 148
Timeload Ltd v British Telecommunications plc [1995] EMLR 459 180
Tinsley v Milligan [1994] 1 AC 340 171
Todd v British Midland Airways Ltd [1978] ICR 959 195
Torquay Hotel Co Ltd v Cousins [1969] 2 Ch 106 423
Transco plc v O'Brien [2002] EWCA Civ 379 . . . . 77, **224**, 539, 664
Transfield Shipping Inc v Mercator Shipping Inc, The Achilleas
   [2008] UKHL 48 216
True v Amalgamated Collieries of Western Australia Ltd [1941] AC 537 203
Turberville v Stampe (1697) 91 ER 1072 133
Turner v East Midlands Trains Ltd [2012] EWCA Civ 1470 . . . . **797**, 801, 821
Turner v Sawdon & Co [1901] 2 KB 653 117
Twinsectra Ltd v Yardley [2002] UKHL 12 525
United States v Nolan [2015] UKSC 63 868
Universe Sentinel, The. *See* Universe Tankships Inc of Monrovia
   v International Transport Workers Federation 427
Universe Tankships Inc of Monrovia v International Transport
   Workers Federation, The Universe Sentinel [1983] 1 AC 366 . . . . 426, 427
University and College Union v University of Stirling
   [2015] UKSC 26 . . . . **826**, 829, 832
University College London Hospitals NHS Trust v Unison
   [1998] EWCA Civ 1528 458

University of Oxford v Humphreys [1999] EWCA Civ 3050 . . . . 413, 853
University of Technology, Jamaica v Industrial Disputes Tribunal
    [2017] UKPC 22 795
Vakante v Addey & Stanhope School [2004] EWCA Civ 1065 176
Vandervell's Trusts (No 2), Re [1974] Ch 269 829
Various Claimants v McAlpine [2016] EWHC 45 (QB) 368
Vento v Chief Constable of West Yorkshire Police [2002] EWCA Civ 1871 566
Viasystems (Tyneside) Ltd v Thermal Transfer (Northern) Ltd
    [2005] EWCA Civ 1151. . . . . 133, 134, 136
Vicary v BT plc [1999] IRLR 680 625
Vining v Wandsworth LBC [2017] EWCA Civ 1092. 384, 775
WA Goold (Pearmak) Ltd v McConnell [1995] IRLR 516 97
Walton v Independent Living Organisation [2003] EWCA Civ 199 . . . . **255**
Wandsworth LBC v D'Silva [1998] IRLR 193 . . . . **239**
Watson v University of Strathclyde [2011] IRLR 458 235
Watt (or Thomas) v Thomas [1947] AC 484. 333
Welton v Deluxe Retail Ltd (t/a Madhouse) [2013] ICR 428. 790
West London Mental Health NHS Trust v Chhabra [2013] UKSC 80 . . . . **233**, 742,
                                                                        748, 763, 777, 780
West Midlands Cooperative Society v Tipton [1986] AC 536 766
Western Excavating (ECC) Ltd v Sharp [1977] EWCA Civ 2,
    [1978] ICR 221 . . . . **743**, 747, 749
Whelpdale v Cookson (1747) 27 ER 856. 768
Whitbread plc v Hall [2001] IRLR 275 CA 797
Whitney v Monster Worldwide Ltd [2010] EWCA Civ 1312 239
Whittle v Frankland (1862) 2 B & S 49 117
Wilkes case, Lofft 1 568
William Hill Organisation Ltd v Tucker [1999] ICR 291 176
Williams v Compair Maxam Ltd [1982] ICR 156 (EAT) **854**, 856, 875
Williams v Natural Life Health Foods Ltd [1998] UKHL 17. 209
Wilson v Racher [1974] ICR 428 . . . . .210, **211**, 214,
                                                                    223, 234, 478, 546,
                                                                742, 748, 780, 786, 787
Wilson v St Helens BC [1998] UKHL 37. 852
Wilsons & Clyde Coal Co Ltd v English [1938] AC 57 . . . . 230, 232
Wiluszynski v Tower Hamlets LBC [1989] ICR 493 262
Woods v WM Car Services (Peterborough) Ltd [1981] ICR 666 . . . . 224, 744
Wragg Ltd, Re [1897] 1 Ch 796 . . . . 60, 246
Wrotham Park Estate Co Ltd v Parkside Homes Ltd [1974] 1 WLR 798 217
X v Mid Sussex Citizens Advice Bureau [2012] UKSC 59 . . . . **130**
Yeboah v Crofton [2002] IRLR 634 770
Young v Canadian National Railway [1930] UKPC 94 390
Young v Ladies' Imperial Club [1920] 2 KB 523. 346
Young & Woods Ltd v West [1980] EWCA Civ 6, [1980] IRLR 201 . . . . . . 114, 118, 276
Zockoll Group Ltd v Mercury Communications Ltd [1998] ITCLR 104 180
Zucker v Astrid Jewels Ltd [1978] ICR 1088 365
Zuijs v Wirth Bros Proprietary Ltd (1955) 93 CLR 561 109

CANADA

Bazley v Curry [1999] 2 SCR 534 135
Bhasin v Hrynew, 2014 SCC 71 360
Smart v Board of Governors of South Saskatchewan Hospital Centre
    (1989) 60 DLR (4th) 8 759
Wallace v United Grain Growers Ltd (1997) 152 DLR (4th) 1 . . . . 783, 785, 812

FRANCE

Seco Desquenne et Giral Construction SA v Sobeca SA [2003] ECC1 448

GERMANY

BVerfGE 3, 383, 399 (1954) 594
Bank Guarantee Case or Bürgschaft (19 October 1993) BVerfGE 89, 214 224
Federal Labour Court, BAG (7 December 2005) 5 AZR 535/04 299

SOUTH AFRICA

Certification of the Constitution of the Republic of South Africa
    [1996] ZACC 24, [1996] ZACC 26 415
Minister of Posts and Telegraphs v Rasool, 1934 AD 167 536

UNITED STATES

14 Penn Plaza LLC v Pyett, 556 US 247 (2009). 167
Adams v Tanner, 244 US 590 (1917) 663, 730
AT&T Mobility v Concepcion, 563 US 333 (2011). 167
Brennan v Plaza Shoe Store, Inc, 522 F2d 843 (8th Cir 1975). 135
Busser v Snyder, 282 Pa 440 (1925). 688
Castaneda v Partida, 430 US 482 (1977) 590
CGTF v Collector of Internal Revenue, 275 US 87 (1927) 245
Civil Rights case. *See* United States v Stanley
Commonwealth v Hunt, 45 Mass 111 (1842). 14, 412
Coppage v Kansas, 236 US 1 (1915) 479
Davis v Alexander, 269 US 114 (1925) 148
Debs, Re, 158 US 564 (1895). 414
Dunlop v Ashy, 555 F2d 1228 (5th Cir 1977). 135
FedEx Home Delivery v NLRB, 563 F3d 492 (DC 2009) 115
Garner v Teamsters Local 776, 346 US 485 (1953) 445

Gaston County v United States, 395 US 285 (1969) 595
Griggs v Duke Power Co, 401 US 424 (1971) **595**, 597
Hazelwood School District v United States, 433 US 299 (1977) 590
Hoffman Plastic Compounds v NLRB, 535 US 137 (2002). 176
Howard Johnson Co v Detroit Local Joint Executive Board, 417 US 249 (1974) 843
Johnson v Transportation Agency, Santa Clara County, 480 US 616 (1987) 618
Lochner v New York, 198 US 45 (1905). 285, 852
Loewe v Lawlor, 208 US 274 (1908) 414
Nationwide Mutual Insurers Co v Darden, 503 US 318 (1992). 106
New Process Steel LP v NLRB, 560 US 674 (2010) 389
New State Ice Co v Liebmann, 285 US 262 (1932) 45
New York State Department of Social Services v Dublino, 413 US 405 (1973) 739
Nizamuddowlah v Bengal Cabaret Inc, 399 NYS 2d 854 (1977). 176, 247, 248
NLRB v Gissel Packing Co, 395 US 575 (1969) 388
Railroad Retirement Board v Alton Railroad Co, 295 US 330 (1935). 688
Ricci v DeStefano, 557 US 557 (2009) 597
San Diego Building Trades Council v Garmon, 359 US 236 (1959) 445
Shelley v Kraemer, 334 US 1 (1948) 207
State Board of Control v Buckstegge, 158 Pac 837 (1916) 688
United States v Silk, 331 US 704 (1946) 109
United States v Stanley, Civil Rights Case, 109 US 3 (1883). 537, 786
United States v Workingmen's Amalgamated Council of New Orleans,
    57 F 85 (5th Cir 1893) 414
United Steelworkers of America v Weber, 443 US 193 (1979) 618

EUROPEAN COURT OF HUMAN RIGHTS

Abdulaziz, Cabales and Balkandali v United Kingdom
    (A/94) (1985) 7 EHRR 471 550
Ahmed v United Kingdom (22954/93) [1999] IRLR 188 548
ASLEF v United Kingdom (11002/05) [2007] IRLR 361 . . . . **351**
Bah v United Kingdom (56328/07) (2012) 54 EHRR 21 550
Barbulescu v Romania (61496/08) [2017] IRLR 1032, [2016] ECHR 61 804
Campbell v United Kingdom (7511/76) (1982) 4 EHRR 293 551
Cheall v United Kingdom (10550/83) (1986) 8 EHRR CD74 . . . . 351, 352, 353
CN v United Kingdom (4239/08) (2013) 56 EHRR 24 174
Demir and Baykara v Turkey (34503/97) [2009] IRLR 766,
    [2008] ECHR 1345 . . . . 384, 434, 435, 438
DH v Czech Republic (57325/10) (2008) 47 EHRR 3 550
Enerji Yapı-Yol Sen v Turkey (28602/95) (2008) 46 EHRR 19,
    [2009] ECHR 2251 . . . . 433, 438
Evans v United Kingdom (6339/05) (2008) 46 EHRR 34 600
Eweida v United Kingdom (48420/10) [2013] IRLR 231, [2013] ECHR 37. . . . **598**, 602
Féret v Belgium (15615/07) 16 July 2009 548
Gaskin v United Kingdom (A/160) (1990) 12 EHRR 36 353

Gustafsson v Sweden (1996) 22 EHRR 409. . . . . 356, 402
Handyside v United Kingdom (A/24) (1979-80) 1 EHRR 737 . . . . 353, 399, 549
Hatton v United Kingdom (36022/97) (2003) 37 EHRR 28. 353
Heinisch v Germany (28274/08) [2011] IRLR 922, [2011] ECHR 1175. . . . . 126, 548
Hizb Ut-Tahrir v Germany (31098/08) (2012) 55 EHRR SE12. 548
Hoffmann v Austria (A/94) (1994) 17 EHRR 293 550
Hrvatski Lijecnicki Sindikat v Croatia [2014] ECHR 1337. 438
James v United Kingdom (A/98) (1986) 8 EHRR 123. 353
Jersild v Denmark (A/298) (1995) 19 EHRR 1 549
Karaçay v Turkey (6615/03) 27 March 2007 433
Karner v Austria (40016/98) (2004) 38 EHRR 24 600
Kart v Turkey (8917/05) (2010) 51 EHRR 40 435
National Union of Belgian Police v Belgium (A/9) (1979–80) 1 EHRR 578 356
Nerva v United Kingdom (42295/98) (2003) 36 EHRR 4 . . . . 79, **263**
Palomo Sanchez v Spain (28955/06) [2011] IRLR 934, [2011] ECHR 1319 360
Pay v United Kingdom (32792/05) [2009] IRLR 139, [2008] ECHR 1007. 804
Petrenco v Moldova (20928/05) [2011] EMLR 5. 798
Pfeifer v Austria (12556/03) (2009) 48 EHRR 8 798
Rantsev v Cyprus and Russia (25965/04) (2010) 51 EHRR 1 174
Redfearn v United Kingdom (47335/06) [2013] IRLR 51,
    [2012] ECHR 1878 . . . . 354, **547**, 552
RMT v United Kingdom [2014] ECHR 366 . . . . **430**, 438, 453, 454, 471
Sanchez v Spain (28955/06) (2012) 54 EHRR 24 . . . . 798, 799
Schalk and Kopf v Austria (30141/04) (2011) 53 EHRR 20,
    [2010] ECHR 1996 600
Schmidt and Dahlstrom v Sweden (A/21) (1979-80) 1 EHRR 632,
    [1976] ECHR 1 438
Schuitemaker v Netherlands (15906/08) 4 May 2010 725
Sigurjonnson v Iceland (1993) 16 EHRR 462 402
Siliadin v France (73316/01) (2006) 43 EHRR 16. 174
Sindicatul "Păstorul cel Bun" v Romania (2330/09) 9 July 2013 434
Smith v United Kingdom (54357/15) [2017] IRLR 771, [2016] ECHR 805. 368
Sørenson v Denmark [2006] ECHR 24 . . . . 402, 548
Stedman v United Kingdom (29107/95) (1997) 23 EHRR CD168,
    [1997] ECHR 178 . . . . 548, 551
Stummer v Austria (37452/02) (2012) 54 EHRR 11 435
Svenska Transportarbetareförbundet and Seko v Sweden (29999/16)
    1 December 2016. 450
Swedish Engine Drivers' Union v Sweden (5614/72) [1976] ECHR 2 356
Syndicat national de la police belge v Belgium (A/19) 27 October 1975 443
Talmon v Netherlands [1997] ECHR 207. 725
Timishev v Russia (55762/00 and 55974/00) (2007) 44 EHRR 37 550
Unison v United Kingdom (53574/99) [2002] IRLR 497 458
United Communist Party of Turkey v Turkey (19392/92) (1998) 26 EHRR 121 549
Van Der Mussele v Belgium (8919/80) (1984) 6 EHRR 163. . . . . 725, 726
Von Hannover v Germany (No 2) (40660/08 and 60641/08) (2012) 55 EHRR 15 435

Wilson and Palmer v United Kingdom (30668/96, 30671/96
and 30678/96) (2002) 35 EHRR 20 . . . . .115, 352, **355**,
359, 382–84, 443
Young, James and Webster v United Kingdom (7601/76 and 7806/77)
[1981] ECHR 4 . . . . .352, 353,
383, **396**, 548
Zielinski v France (24846/94) (2001) 31 EHRR 19 728

EUROPEAN UNION

3F v Commission (C-319/07 P) EU:C:2009:435 451
Abrahamsson and Anderson v Fogelqvist (C-407/98) EU:C:2000:367 618
Achbita v G4S Secure Solutions NV (C-157/15) EU:C:2017:203 602
Adeneler v Ellinikos Organismos Galaktos (C-212/04) EU:C:2006:443,
[2006] IRLR 716 . . . . .308, 309,
654, 656, 662
AEK ry v Fujitsu Siemens Computers Oy (C-44/08) EU:C:2009:533 . . . . **864**, 868
AGET Iraklis v Ypourgos Ergasias, Koinonikis Asfalisis kai Koinonikis
Allilengyis (C-201/15) EU:C:2016:972 . . . . 870, 874
AKT ry v Shell Aviation Finland Oy (C-533/13) EU:C:2015:173 669
Alabaster v Woolwich plc (C-147/02) EU:C:2004:192 621
Albany International BV v Stichting Bedrijfspensioenfonds
Textielindustrie (C-67/96) EU:C:1999:430 . . . . 441, 451
Alemo-Herron v Parkwood Leisure Ltd (C-426/11) EU:C:2013:521 . . . . .848, 852,
872, 874
Allen (C-234/98) [1999] ECR I-8643 845
Allonby v Accrington and Rossendale College (C-256/01)
EU:C:2004:18 . . . . .124, 125, 140,
451, 452, **607**, 610
Amministrazione delle Finanze dello Stato v Simmenthal SpA (106/77)
[1978] ECR 629 659
Angé Serrano v European Parliament (C-496/08P) [2010] ECR I-1793 645
Angelidaki v Organismos Nomarchiakis Autodioikisis Rethymnis (C-378/07)
EU:C:2009:250 663
Arblade, Criminal Proceedings against (C-369/96) EU:C:1999:575 . . . . 442, 448, 449
Arjona Camacho v Securitas Seguridad Espana SA (C-407/14) EU:C:2015:831 569
Asklepios Kliniken Langen-Seligenstadt GmbH v Felja (C-680/150)
EU:C:2017:317 852
Asscher v Staatssecretaris van Financiën (C-107/94) EU:C:1996:251 127
Association de médiation sociale v Union locale des syndicats CGT (C-176/12)
EU:C:2014:2 516
Athinaïki Chartopoiïa AE v Panagiotidis (C-270/05) EU:C:2007:101 . . . . . . 862, 863, 865
Auto-ja Kuljetusalan Työntekijäliitto AKT ry v Öljytuote ry (C-533/13)
EU:C:2015:173 735
Badeck's Application, Re (C-158/97) EU:C:2000:163 . . . . **619**, 620

Barber v Guardian Royal Exchange Assurance Group (C-262/88)
    EU:C:1990:209 . . . . 280, 313, 314
Bartsch v Bosch und Siemens Hausgerate (BSH) Altersfursorge
  . GmbH (C-427/06) [2008] ECR I-7245 540
Becu, Criminal Proceedings against (C-22/98) EU:C:1999:419 452
Betriebsrat der Ruhrlandklinik gGmbH v Ruhrlandklinik gGmbH (C-216/15)
    EU:C:2016:883 665
Bilka-Kaufhaus GmbH v Weber von Hartz (170/84) EU:C:1986:204 602
Boyle v Equal Opportunities Commission (C-411/96) EU:C:1998:506 314
Bundesdruckerei GmbH v Stadt Dortmund (C-549/13)
    EU:C:2014:2235 . . . . 449, 705, 706
Caballero v Fondo de Garantia Salarial (FOGASA) (C-442/00)
    [2002] ECR I-11915. 659
Centros Ltd v Erhvervs- og Selskabsstyrelsen (C-212/97) EU:C:1999:126. 498
Centrum voor Gelijkheid van Kansen en voor Racismebestrijding
    v Firma Feryn NV (C-54/07) EU:C:2008:397. 564
Chacón Navas v Eurest Colectividades SA (C-13/05) EU:C:2006:456 624–26
CILFIT Srl v Ministry of Health (283/81) EU:C:1982:335 288
Cimade v Ministre de l'Interieur, de l'Outre-mer, des Collectivites
    territoriales et de l'Immigration (C-179/11) EU:C:2012:594 850
Claes v Landsbanki Luxembourg SA (C-235/10) EU:C:2011:119 . . . . 868, 869
CLECE SA v Valor (C-463/09) EU:C:2011:24 846
Coleman v Attridge Law (C-303/06) EU:C:2008:415 . . . . **552**, 556, 559, 626
Commission v France (C-483/99) EU:C:2002:327 873
Commission v France (C-334/02) [2004] ECR I-2229. 440
Commission v Germany (C-271/08) EU:C:2010:426 . . . . 444, 449, 705
Commission v Greece (C-244/11) EU:C:2012:694 873
Commission v Italy (C-518/06) EU:C:2009:270 . . . . 871, 872
Commission v Italy (C-326/07) EU:C:2009:193 . . . . 872, 873
Commission v Luxembourg (C-519/03) [2005] ECR I-3067. 290
Commission v Netherlands (2012) C-542/09. 646
Commission v Spain (C-463/00) EU:C:2003:272 871
Commission v United Kingdom (C-383/92) EU:C:1994:234 . . . . 825, 863, 864, 872
Commission v United Kingdom (C-484/04) EU:C:2006:526 311
Confederación Española de Empresarios de Estaciones de Servicio (C-217/05)
    EU:C:2006:784 . . . . 451, 452
Confédération générale du travail (C-385/05) EU:C:2007:37 863
Courage Ltd v Crehan (C-453/99) EU:C:2001:465 108
Dansk Metalarbejderforbund and Specialarbejderforbundet i Danmark (284/83)
    EU:C:1985:61 872
De Weerd v Bestuur van de Bedrijfsvereniging voor de Gezondheid,
    Geestelijke en Maatschappelijke Belangen (C-343/92) [1994] ECR I-571. 604
Decker v Caisse de Maladie des Employes Prives (C-120/95)
    [1998] ECR I-1831. 440
Defrenne v Belgium (80/70) EU:C:1971:55. 313
Defrenne v Sabena (No 2) (43/75) EU:C:1976:56 . . . . 37, 441, 540, 608

Del Cerro Alonso v Osakidetza-Servicio Vasco de Salud (C-307/05)
  EU:C:2007:509 . . . . **653**
Della Rocca v Poste Italiane SpA (C-290/12) EU:C:2013:235 651
Deutsches Weintor (C-544/10) EU:C:2012:526 851
Dominguez v CICOA (C-282/10) EU:C:2012:33. 289
Enderby v Frenchay Health Authority (C-127/92) EU:C:1993:859 613
Erzberger v TUI AG (C-566/15) EU:C:2017:562. 498
Faccini Dori v Recreb Srl (C-91/92) [1994] ECR I-3325. . . . . 301, 541
FNV Kunsten Informatie en Media v Staat der Nederlanden (C-413/13)
  EU:C:2014:2411 . . . . 104, **450**
France v Stoeckel (C-345/89) EU:C:1991:324. 310
Francovich v Italy (C-6/90) EU:C:1991:428 . . . . .286, 288,
                                                                              301, 652, 868
Fuß v Stadt Halle (C-243/09) EU:C:2010:609 307
Gauweiler v Deutsche Bundestag (C-62/14) EU:C:2015:400 715
GB-INNO-BM NV v Vereniging van de Kleinhandelaars
  in Tabak (13/77) [1977] ECR 2115 731
Gebhard v Consiglio dell'Ordine degli Avvocati e Procuratori
  di Milano (C-55/94) [1995] ECR I-4165. 442
Gillespie v Northern Health and Social Services Board (C-342/93)
  [1996] ECR I-475. 621
Guisado v Bankia SA (C-103/16) EU:C:2018:99. 874
Handels- og Kontorfunktionaerernes Forbund i Danmark v Dansk
  Arbejdsgiverforening, Ex p Danfoss (109/88) EU:C:1989:383. 655
Hennigs v Eisenbahn-Bundesamt; Land Berlin v Mai (C-297/10
  and C-298/10) [2012] 1 CMLR 18. 592
Hill and Stapleton (C-243/95) [1998] ECR I-3739. 604
Höfner and Elser v Macrotron GmbH (C-41/90) EU:C:1991:161 . . . . 730, 731, 841
Høj Pedersen (C-66/96) EU:C:1998:549 621
Huet v Université de Bretagne Occidentale (C-251/11) EU:C:2012:133. 663
Impact v Minister for Agriculture and Food (C-268/06) [2008] ECR I-2483 153
International Transport Workers' Federation and Finnish Seamen's Union
  v Viking Line ABP (C-438/05) [2008] IRLR 143 .39, **439**, 445,
                                                                           448, 449, 451, 477,
                                                                           655, 705, 852, 873
Italy v Sacchi (155/73) [1974] ECR 409 731
Jørgensen v Foreningen af Speciallaeger (C-226/98) EU:C:2000:191. 604
Junk v Kühnel (C-188/03) [2005] ECR I-885, [2005] 1 CMLR 42 . . . . .515, 836,
                                                                           856, 865, 870
Kalanke v Freie und Hansestadt Bremen (C-450/93) EU:C:1995:322. 617
Kaltoft v Municipality of Bilund (C-354/13) EU:C:2014:2463 626
Kamer van Koophandel v Inspire Art Ltd (C-167/01) EU:C:2003:512 . . . . 194, 498
Kampelmann v Landschaftsverband Westfalen-Lippe (C-253/96)
  EU:C:1997:585 . . . . 189, 204
KHS AG v Schulte (C-214/10) EU:C:2011:761. 292
Kiiski v Tampereen Kaupunki (C-116/06) [2007] ECR I-7643 290
Köbler v Austria (C-224/01) EU:C:2003:513. 294

Kohll v Union des Caisses de Maladie (C-158/96) [1998] ECR I-1931 440
Kreil v Germany (C-285/98) EU:C:2000:2 571
Kücük v Land Nordrhein-Westfalen (C-586/10) EU:C:2012:39 663
Kücükdeveci v Swedex GmbH & Co KG (C-555/07)
    EU:C:2010:21 . . . . **539**, 543, 592
Kutz-Bauer v Freie und Hansestadt Hamburg (C-187/00)
    EU:C:2003:168 . . . . 602, **603**, 613
Landeshauptstadt Kiel v Jaegar (C-151/02) EU:C:2003:437 . . . . 300, **304**, 307
Laval Un Partneri Ltd v Svenska Byggnadsarbetareförbundet
    (C-341/05) EU:C:2007:809 . . . .**445**, 449, 477,
                                                                                                            702, 703, 705, 852
Lawrence v Regent Office Care Ltd (C-320/00) EU:C:2002:498 . . . . 607, 608, 610
Lawrie-Blum v Land Baden-Wurttemberg (66/85) EU:C:1986:284 . . . . 104, 125, 211
Lindqvist, Criminal Proceedings against (C-101/01) EU:C:2003:596,
    [2004] QB 1014 849
Lock v British Gas Trading Ltd (C-539/12) EU:C:2014:351 296
Lyttle v Bluebird UK Bidco 2 Ltd (C-182/13) EU:C:2015:317 . . . . **862**
Mangold v Helm (C-144/04) EU:C:2005:709 . . . . 539–43, 553, **657**
Marks & Spencer (C-62/00) [2002] ECR I-6325 301
Marks & Spencer (C-446/03) [2005] ECR I-10837 . . . . 440, 871
Marleasing SA v La Comercial Internacional de Alimentacion
    SA (C-106/89) EU:C:1990:395 . . . . 286, 289, 302, 541
Marschall v Land Nordrhein Westfalen (C-409/95) EU:C:1997:533 617
Marshall v Southampton and South West Hampshire AHA (152/84)
    EU:C:1986:84 . . . . 289, 301
Marshall v Southampton and South West Hampshire AHA (No 2)
    (C-271/91) EU:C:1993:335 289
Mascolo v Ministero dell'Istruzione, dell'Università e della Ricerca
    (C-22/13) EU:C:2014:2103 656
Merino Gómez (C-342/01) [2004] ECR I-2605, [2005] ICR 1040 . . . . 288, 290, 293
Michaeler v Amt für sozialen Arbeitsschutz and Autonome Provinz
    Bozen (C-55/07) [2008] ECR I-3135 648
Milkova v Izpalnitelen director na Agentsiata za privatizatsia i sledprivatizatsionen
    control (C-406/15) [2017] IRLR 566 543
Omega Spielhallen- und Automatenaufstellungs GmbH v Bundesstadt
    Bonn (C-36/02) [2004] ECR I-9609 . . . . 440, 441, 444
Ordem dos Técnicos Oficiais de Contas (C-1/12) EU:C:2013:127 . . . . 451, 452
Oy Liikenne AB v Liskojärvi and Juntunen (C-172/99) EU:C:2001:59 844
P v S and Cornwall CC (C-13/94) EU:C:1996:170 544
Palacios de la Villa v Cortefiel Servicios SA (C-411/05) EU:C:2007:604 . . . . 540, 574
Parviainen v Finnair Oyj (C-471/08) EU:C:2010:391 . . . . **621**
Pereda v Madrid Movilidad SA (C-277/08) EU:C:2009:542 291
Pfeiffer v Deutsches Rotes Kreuz (C-397/01) [2004] ECR 8835 . . . . 98, 296, **300**, 541
R v HM Treasury, Ex p Daily Mail and General Trust (81/87)
    [1988] ECR 5483 442
R v Ministry of Agriculture, Fisheries and Food, Ex p Agegate (C-3/87)
    EU:C:1989:650 452

R (BECTU) v Department of Trade and Industry (C-173/99)
   [2001] ECR I-4881. . . . . 288, 293
R (Omega Air Ltd) v Secretary of State for the Environment, Transport and
   the Regions (C-27/00 and C-122/00) [2002] ECR I-2569, [2002] 2 CMLR 9 553
R (Seymour-Smith and Perez) v Secretary of State for Employment
   (C-167/97) EU:C:1999:60 . . . . 39, 603, 637
R (Wells) v Secretary of State for Transport, Local Government
   and the Regions (C-201/02) EU:C:2004:12. 301
Regiopost GmbH & Co KG v Stadt Landau in der Pfalz (C-115/14)
   EU:C:2015:760 . . . . 449, 706
Rinner-Kühn v FWW Spezial-Gebaudereinigung GmbH & Co KG (171/88)
   EU:C:1989:328 602
Robinson-Steele v RD Retail Services Ltd (C-131/04)
   EU:C:2006:177 . . . . **292**, 295, 296
Rockfon A/S v Specialarbejderforbundet i Danmark (C-449/93)
   [1995] ECR I-4291. . . . . 861, 862, 866
Rosella, The. *See* International Transport Workers' Federation
   and Finnish Seamen's Union v Viking Line ABP
Rosenbladt v Oellerking Gebäudereinigungsges (C-45/09) EU:C:2010:601 575
Rüffert v Land Niedersachsen (C-346/06) EU:C:2008:189 . . . . 449, **702**, 704
Rush Portuguesa Lda v Office National d'Immigration (C113/89)
   EU:C:1990:142 448
Schmidberger v Austria (2003) C-112/00. 440–42, 444, 462
Schönheit v Stadt Frankfurt am Main (C-4/02 and C-5/02) EU:C:2003:583 644
Schultz-Hoff and Stringer Revenue and Customs Commissioners
   (C-350/06 and C-520/06) [2009] ECR I-179. . . . . 295, 296
Segers v Bestuur van de Bedrijfsvereniging voor Bank- en Verzekeringswezen,
   Groothandel en Vrije Beroepen (79/85) EU:C:1986:308. 871
Sindicato de Medicos de Asistencia Publica (SIMAP) v Conselleria
   de Sanidad y Consumo de la Generalidad Valenciana (C-303/98)
   EU:C:2000:528 . . . . 300, **303**, 305, 306
Sirdar v Secretary of State for Defence (C-273/97) EU:C:1999:523 571
Sky Österreich GmbH v Osterreichischer Rundfunk (C-283/11)
   EU:C:2013:28 . . . . 851, 872
Solred SA v Administración General del Estado (C-347/96)
   [1998] ECR I-937. 659
Spijkers v Gebroeders Benedik Abattoir CV (24/85) EU:C:1986:127. . . . . . 844, 846, 847
Steymann v Staatssecretaris van Justitie (196/87) EU:C:1988:475 131
Stringer v Her Majesty's Revenue and Customs; Schultz-Hoff
   v Deutsche Rentenversicherung Bund (C-520/06) EU:C:2009:18 . . . . **289**
Süzen v Zehnacker Gebaeudereingung GmbH Krankenhausservice
   (C-13/95) EU:C:1997:141 844–46
Syndesmos ton en Elladi Touristikon kai Taxidiotikon Grafeion
   (SETTG) v Ergasias (C-398/95) EU:C:1997:282 873
Überseering BV v Nordic Construction Company Baumanagement
   GmbH (C-208/00) EU:C:2002:632 498
United Kingdom v Council (C-84/94) EU:C:1996:431 305

Vassallo v Azienda Ospedaliera Ospedale San Martino di Genova
(2006) (C-180/04) 663
Von Colson and Kamann v Land Nordrhein-Westfalen (C-14/83)
EU:C:1984:153 .... 301, 541
Werhof v Freeway Traffic Systems GmbH & Co KG (C-499/04)
EU:C:2006:168 .... 847, 849, 850, 852
Williams v British Airways plc (C-155/10) EU:C:2011:588 .... **294**
Wippel v Peek & Cloppenburg GmbH & Co KG (C-313/02)
EU:C:2004:607 .... **641**, 643, 651, 672
Wolf v Stadt Frankfurt am Main (C-229/08) EU:C:2010:3 574
Wouters v Algemene Raad van de Nederlandse Orde van Advocaten (C-309/99)
EU:C:2002:98 396
Zentralbetriebsrat der Landeskrankenhäuser Tirols v Land Tirol (C-486/08)
EU:C:2010:215 .... 644, 648

Table of Legislation

UNITED KINGDOM

Statutes

Act for the Relief of the Poor 1601 729
Agricultural Wages Act 1948 251
  s 3 167
Apportionment Act 1870
  s 2 478
Armed Forces Act 2006
  s 374 790
Army Act 1955
  s 31 429
Bank of England Act 1694 711
Bank of England Act 1946 712
  s 4(3) 711
Bank of England Act 1998 710
  s 1 709
  ss 1–2 708
  s 2 709
  ss 10–13 708
  s 11 710
  s 13 709
  s 19 . . . . 708, 710
Bill of Rights 1689 156
  Art 4 273
Bills of Exchange Act 208
Brick Making Act 1725 (12 Geo 1, c 35) 48
BT Act 1981 428
Bubble Act 1720 50
Bubble Companies, etc Act 1825 712
Cambridge University Act 1856
  ss 5–6 486
Charities Act 2011 499
Charter of the Forest 1217 . . . . 4, 6
Children and Families Act 2014
  s 117 314
  s 131 316

Civil Evidence Act 1972
  s 3 368
Civil Partnership Act 2004 598
Combination Act 1799 42
Combination Act 1800 42
Combinations of Workmen Act 1825 19
Communications Act 2003
  s 87 428
Companies Act 1862 346
Companies Act 1947 752
Companies Act 2006 . . . . .65, 268, 327,
                                                                            393, 486, 488, 500
  ss 3–6 499
  ss 7–9 482
  s 20 189
  s 21 . . . . 329, **486**, 488
  s 31 700
  s 33 340
  ss 112–13 . . . . **486**, 488
  s 154 . . . . 482, **486**
  s 168 . . . . 235, 268, 269, 489
  ss 168–69 . . . . .127, 328,
                                                                       486, 620, 752, 786
  s 169 488
  s 170 502
  ss 170–75 . . . . **500**
  s 171 . . . . .338, 502,
                                                                                         539, 700
  ss 171–77 340
  s 172 . . . . 490, 503, 505
  s 174 502
  s 175 503
  s 177 503
  ss 188–89 270
  ss 215–22 270
  s 232 338
  s 251 502
  s 260 505
  ss 260–63 . . . . 340, **504**, 505
  s 263 505
  ss 265–69 505
  s 282 488
  ss 282–83 268
  ss 282–84 . . . . **486**
  s 283 488
  s 284 488
  s 301 329

s 314 329
s 366 488
ss 366–68 . . . . 20, 336
s 378 336
s 414A 403
ss 414A–C 503
s 414C 503
s 415 403
s 420 403
s 422A 269
s 423 403
s 430 403
s 437 488
s 439A **269**
s 489 488
ss 495–97 342
s 549 493
s 566 493
ss 580–86 493
s 1166 493
Company Directors Disqualification Act 1986
    s 6 502
Competition Act 1998
    s 2 414
Conspiracy and Protection of Property Act 1875 . . . . 20, 421
    s 3 . . . . 20, 414, 419
    s 7 . . . . 20, 460
Constitutional Reform Act 2005 832
    s 3 119
Consumer Credit Act 1974 30
Consumer Rights Act 2015 65
Contracts of Employment Act 1963 . . . . 37, 188,
                                                                                        204, 752–54
Contracts of Employment and Redundancy Payments Act
    (Northern Ireland) 1965
    s 11(2)(b) 831
Contracts (Rights of Third Parties) Act 1999
    s 1 264
Co-operative and Community Benefit Societies Act 2014 499
Copyright Act 1911
    s 5(1) 214
Copyright Act 1956 567
Coroners and Justice Act 2009
    s 71 174
Corporation Tax Act 2010 273
Criminal Justice Act 1991
    s 17(1) 368

Criminal Justice Act 1993
   s 52 246
Criminal Justice and Public Order Act 1994
   s 127 429
   s 127A 429
   s 128 429
Data Protection Act 1998
   ss 17–21 366
Deregulation and Contracting Out Act 1994 732
Disability Discrimination Act 1995 . . . . .130, 552,
                                                                      623, 629, 631, 633
   s 3B 558
   s 4 552
       (2)(b) 630
   s 5(2)(b) 631
   s 6 629
       (1) 630, 631
       (3)(c) 630
       (4) 631
   s 53 629
   s 54 629
Disabled Men (Facilities for Employment) Act 1919 623
Disabled Persons (Employment) Act 1944 . . . . 623, 631
Education Act 2002
   s 175(2) 837
Education Reform Act 1988 485
   ss 124–28 482
   s 124A 485
   s 128 485
   Sch 7 . . . . 482, 485
       para 3 485
   Sch 7A 485
       para 3 485
Employment Act 1980 . . . . .323, 394,
                                                                      399, 435, 789
   s 17 456
       (1)(b) 457
       (3) 456, 457
       (4) 456, 457
       (7) 456
Employment Act 1982
   s 18 455
Employment Act 1990
   s 4 458
Employment Act 2002 . . . . 769, 776
   ss 29–33 768
   Sch 2 769

Employment Act 2008 . . . . 769, 776
  s 3 768
  s 19 354
Employment Act 2010
  s 120 768
  s 127 768
Employment Agencies Act 1973 . . . . **732**
  ss 1–3 732
  s 3A 733
  s 6 733
  s 9 733
  s 13 733
Employment Protection Act 1975 . . . . 259, 311, 475
  s 4 581
  s 6 581
    (2)(b) 581
  Sch 1, para 6(1)(b) 241
Employment Protection (Consolidation) Act 1978 37
  s 57(3) 794
  s 58 113
  s 153 113
  Sch 13, para 9 168
Employment Relations Act 1999 . . . . 371, 469
  s 3 366
  ss 10–15 404
Employment Relations Act 2004 368
Employment Rights Act 1996 . . . . 97, 126, 188,
189, 294, 393,
549, 663, 751, 789
  Pt X 812, 813, 827
  s 1 . . . . 119, 182, 655
  ss 1–2 . . . . **188**
  s 3 97
    (1) 814
  s 12 189
  s 13 . . . . 164, 170, 239,
241, 256, **257**, 258,
259, 289, 479, 605
  s 14 257
    (5) 259
  s 17 257
  s 23 . . . . 257, 289, 768
  s 24(2) 257
  s 27 258
  ss 27A–B 299
  s 28 258
  s 29 259

ss 29–32 358
s 31(1). 259
s 41 288
ss 43A–43L 124
s 43C. 126
s 43E. 126
s 43F. 126
s 43G 126
s 43H 126
s 45A 299, 311
s 47B. 582
ss 55–80E 313
s 57A 315
s 63D 492
s 64(2). 790
s 80F. 317, 318, 492
ss 80F–G. **649**
ss 80F–H. 647
ss 80F–I 316
s 80G 316
s 80H(1)(b)316
s 86 . . . . 539, **752**, 756
    (1) 753
    (3) 754, 756, 762
    (6) 757
ss 86–89 752
s 89 . . . . **752**, 753
s 94 . . . . .128, 136, 170,
                                                                             194, 196, 198, 492,
                                                                             546, 743, 746, 787
    (1) 195–97, 199, 200
s 95 746
    (1) 743
        (a) 820
        (b) 656, 820, 827
        (c) 743, 744
ss 95–110 787
s 97 . . . . 99, **787**, 788
    (1) 98
    (3)–(5) 788
s 98 . . . . .127, 241, 533,
                                                                                  656, 661, 744,
                                                                             791, 794, 802, 826
    (1) 791
        (b) 825, **833**, 838
        (b)–(3). 791
    (1)–(3) 838

(2) 825, 833
  (b) 838
(4) 779, 792,
                                                                    794, 835, 838
s 98A 769
  (2) 770
s 99 . . . . 623, 789
s 100 789
ss 100–03 808
s 101 288
s 101A 299, 789
ss 101–ZA 789
s 102 789
s 103 789
s 103A 789
s 104 789
s 104A 789
s 104B 790
s 104C 790
s 104D 790
s 104E 790
s 104F 790
s 104G 790
s 105 790
s 108 . . . . **787**, 789
  (1) 547
  (2)–(5) 787, 789
s 111 . . . . **787**, 789, 790
  (2) 811
ss 113–17 817
s 114 818
ss 114–15 . . . . **816**
s 116 . . . . **816**
s 117 . . . . **817**
s 119 . . . . **807**, 808
s 120 808
s 121 808
s 122 808
s 123 . . . . 808, 809
ss 123–24 . . . . **807**
s 124 96
  (1ZA)(a) 810
  (b) 810
  (6) 810
s 126 808
s 128 817
s 135 . . . . 492, **875**, 877

s 138 877
s 139 . . . . 824, **825**, 826
  (1) 825, 830
    (b) 830
s 141 . . . . **875**, 877
  (3)(b) 875
  (4)(d) 877
s 146 877
s 162 . . . . **875**, 877
s 196 . . . . 194, 195
s 203 . . . . **819**, 820
s 205A 132, 492
  (2)(b) 492
s 209 789
s 212 . . . . 115, 121, 123,
                                                                168, 656, **787**, 790
  (3)(b) 168
s 224 . . . . 458, 753
s 227 . . . . **807**, 808
s 230 . . . . **106**, 782
  (2) 106
  (3) 101, 124
    (a) 106
    (b) 124, 249
s 231 . . . . 133, 457, 458, 877
s 244 458
Employment Tribunals Act 1996 771
  s 3 189
Enterprise and Regulatory Reform Act 2013 579
  ss 7–24 771
  s 72 251
  s 79 269
Equal Pay Act 1970 . . . . 37, 605, 612, 640
  s 1(3) 612
    (6) 611
      (c) 608
  s 2(3) 611
Equality Act 2006
  s 1 566
  s 20 566
  s 30 566
Equality Act 2010 . . . . 34, 154, 534,
                                                                544, 561, 575, 583,
                                                                585, 591, 605,
                                                                614, 623, 631, 633
  s 4 . . . . 585, 623
  s 5 . . . . 572, 590, 857

ss 5–12 544
s 6 . . . . **624**, 625
  (1) 624
  (5) 625
s 9 544
s 10 546
s 12 556
s 13 . . . . **559**, 561, 572
  (1) 553, 564
  (2) 572
  (3) 561, **626**
  (6) 623
s 14 594
s 15 . . . . **626**, 628
s 16 561
s 18 . . . . **559**, 623
s 19 . . . . 154, **586**, 590, 857
  (2)(d) 154
s 20 . . . . 556, 629
  (3) 628
ss 20–21 . . . . **626**
s 21 628
s 22 629
s 23 . . . . **559**, 561
s 26 . . . . **575**, 576
  (1)(ii) 579
s 27 . . . . 358, **579**, 580
  (1) 580
s 29 . . . . **559**
s 39 . . . . .132, 561,
                                                              572, 590, 857
  (2)(c) 170
  (3)–(4) 580
  (5) 556
s 40 . . . . 556, **575**, 576, 579
s 60 . . . . **626**
ss 64–66 . . . . **609**
s 65 . . . . 37, 610
s 66 610
ss 67–68 610
s 69 . . . . **611**
  (1)(b) 611
  (3) 611
s 71 605
s 78 620
s 79 . . . . **609**, 611
  (9) 610

s 83 . . . . 130, 620
  (2) 106, 125
    (a) 127
s 85(1). 585
s 108 566
ss 109–10 566
s 111 566
s 112 566
s 119 566
  (2)(a) 171
s 123 . . . . 566, 605
s 124 569
  (6) 171
s 129 . . . . 566, 605
s 136 . . . . **565**
s 158(2). 617
ss 158–59 . . . . **616**, 620
s 159 617
s 192 571
Sch 1. . . . . **624**
  para 1 625
  para 2(1) 625
Sch 8. . . . . **626**
  para 2(1) 628
  para 5(1) 628
Sch 9, para 1(1) 575
  paras 1–4 . . . . **570**
  para 4(2) 571
  paras 10–13 574
Sch 11. 585
Sch 22, para 2. 571
Sch 23, para 2. 571
European Communities Act 1972. . . . . 38, 868
Factory Act 1833. 286
Factory Act 1844. 17
Fair Trading Act 1973 30
Finance Act 2015 273
Finance Act 2017 272
  s 2. . . . . **271**
Financial Services and Markets Act 2000. . . . . 65, 687
  s 1B(6)(a) 491
Fixed-term Parliaments Act 2011 . . . . 328, 329
Frauds by Workmen Act (22 Geo 2, c 27). 48
Friendly Societies Act 1992 499
Gangmasters Licensing Act 2004
  ss 4—13 . . . . **734**, 735

s 12 735
s 13 735
Great Reform Act 1832 14
Growth and Infrastructure Act 2013
s 31 132
Higher Education Governance (Scotland) Act 2016 486
Highway Act 1980
s 137 461
Human Rights Act 1998 . . . . 408, 412, 728
s 3 . . . . .115, 126, 325,
354, 359, 378, 381, 800
s 4 . . . . 325, 379, 470, 728
s 6(3)(a) 325
s 8 325
Immigration Act 1971
s 24(1)(b)(ii) 170, 171
Immigration and Asylum Act 1999
s 153A 252
Inclosure Act 1773 14
Inclosure Acts 6, 8, 14, 42
Income Tax Act 2007 . . . . 270, 272
s 3 272
ss 10–12 . . . . **271**
s 35 . . . . **271**
s 57A **271**, 273
(7) 274
Income Tax (Earnings and Pensions) Act 2003 274
ss 14–41L 274
ss 48–61 273
ss 63–226E 274
ss 227–326B 274
ss 327–85 274
ss 386–681 274
Income Tax (Trading and Other Income) Act 2005 274
s 5 274
Indian Slavery Act 1843 10
Industrial Relations Act 1971 . . . . 37, 743, 787, 796, 812, 814, 833
s 22 811
ss 22–33 789
s 106(4) 811
(5) 811
s 116 811
s 118(1) 811
Sch 6, para 5 811
Industry Act 1975 27
Iron and Steel Act 1967 27

Iron and Steel Act 1975. 455
Jobseekers Act 1995 . . . . 717, 719, 724
    ss 1–6J **717**, 720
    s 17A 720, 723, 724
        (1) 724
    s 18 728
    s 35 723
Jobseekers (Back to Work Schemes) Act 2013. 728
    s 1 728
Joint Stock Companies Act 1856 50
King's College London Act 1997
    s 15 . . . . 106, 485
Labour Exchange Act 1909. . . . . 729, 730
Land Registration Act 2002
    Sch 3, para 2. 843
Landlord and Tenant Act 1985 65
Law Reform (Miscellaneous Provisions) Act 1934 569
    s 1(2)(a) 567
Legal Services Act 2007
    s 12 395
    s 18 395
    Sch 10 395
Limitation Act 1980
    s 5 605
Limited Liability Partnerships Act 2000. 499
    ss 3–4 482
    s 4(4). 124, 126
Limited Partnerships Act 1908 499
Local Government Act 1888
    s 16 535
    s 17 . . . . 706, 707
        (1) 706
        (5) 706
Local Government Act 1999
    s 3 707
Lord Cairn's Act 217
Magna Carta 1215. 4
    cl 40 151
    cl 12 . . . . 4, 273
    cl 29 . . . . 156, 763
    cl 47 4
    cl 48 4
Magna Carta 1297
    Ch 29 150
Masters and Servants Act 1823 (4 Geo 4, c 34) 117
Merchant Shipping Act 1995
    s 59 429

Mines and Collieries Act 1842 17
Misuse of Drugs Act 1971 804
Modern Slavery Act 2015
  s 54 503
National Health Service Act 2006
  ss 30–39 482
  Sch 7 . . . . 482, 500
National Health Service (Private Finance) Act 1997 458
National Insurance Act 1911 20,
                                                                                    274, 716, 720
National Insurance Act 1946 720
  s 1(2) 107
National Insurance Act 1965
  s 1(2) 108
National Labor Relations Act 1935
  s 1 65
National Minimum Wage Act 1998 . . . . .101, 128,
                                                                                    129, 251, 252, 263
  s 1 . . . . 249, 251
    (3) 252
  s 2(1) 252
  s 3(1A) 252
  s 4(2) 251
  s 10 256
  s 13 256
  s 14 256
  ss 17–18 256
  s 19 256
  s 19A 256
  ss 23–25 256
  s 24 768
  s 28 251
  s 34 251
  s 35 251
  s 37 252
  s 41 251
  s 43 252
  s 45 252
  s 45B 252
  s 54 . . . . 106, 128, 251
Official Secrets Act 1911 216
Official Secrets Act 1989 218
  s 1 218
    (3) 218
Official Secrets Acts 218
Old Age Pensions Act 1908 . . . . 20, 276
Ordinance of Labourers 1349 4

Oxford University Act 1854 32
   s 16 486
   s 21 486
Partnership Act 1890 . . . . .482, 499
   s 10 135
Pensions Act 1995
   ss 16–21 522
Pensions Act 2004 . . . . .521, 522, 525
   s 241 522
   ss 241–42 522
   ss 241–43 . . . .**521**
   s 242 . . . . .522, 523
   s 243 522
      (2) 522
   ss 259–61 516
Pensions Act 2008 . . . . .112, 277,
                                     278, 279, 394, 523
   s 1 . . . . .106, 395
   ss 1–3 278
   ss 1–20 . . . .**278**
   s 8 . . . .**278**
   s 13 278
   s 20 278
   ss 67–69 . . . . .278, **523**
   s 69 524
   Sch 1 . . . . .278, **523**, 524
      para 1 524
      (6) 524
Police Act 1919 428
Police Act 1996
   s 89(2) 461
Poor Act 1575 8
Poor Acts 42
Poor Law Amendment Act 1834 729
Poor Relief Act 1662 729
Port of London Act 1908 . . . . .27, 491, 530
Post Office Act 1969 390
Post Office Act 1977 . . . . .27, 491
Preferential Payments in Bankruptcy Act 1897 249
Prices and Incomes Act 1966
    Sch 2, para 14 690
Prisoners' Earnings Act 1996
   s 2(1)(b) 252
Protection from Harassment Act 1997 . . . . .576, 578, 579
   s 1 576
      (1) 576
   s 3 577

Public Order Act 1986
  s 14A 461
Public Schools Act 1868 585
Public Service Pensions Act 2013
  ss 4–5 523
Race Relations Act 1965 . . . . 34, 539
Race Relations Act 1968 34
Race Relations Act 1975 34
Race Relations Act 1976 . . . . 170, 545, 546, 578, 629
  s 3 544
    (1) 544
  s 16(2)(a) 563
  s 56(1)(b) 171
  s 57(1) 171
  s 78 132
Race Relations Acts 37
Railways Act 1920 27
Railways Act 1993
  s 25 476
Redundancy Payments Act 1965 . . . . 37, 828
Reform Act 1867 . . . . 17, 90
Representation of the People Act 1883 27
Representation of the People Act 1918 27
Representation of the People Act 1928 27
Representation of the People Act 1969 27
Reserve and Auxiliary Forces (Protection of Civil Interests) Act 1951
  s 13(2) 567
Royal Exchange and London Assurance Corporation Act 1719 712
Safeguarding Vulnerable Groups Act 2006
  Sch 3, para 3(3) 773
    paras 3–4 771
Sex Discrimination Act 1975 37
Sale of Goods Act 1979 208
Sex Discrimination Act 1975 . . . . 605, 629
Shops Act 1950 288
Slave Trade Act 1807 10
Slavery Abolition Act 1833 10
Small Business, Enterprise and Employment Act 2015
  s 153 299
Social Security Act 1935 . . . . 109, 110, 878
Social Security Administration Act 1992
  s 71A 728
Social Security Contributions and Benefits Act 1992
  s 1 . . . . **274**
  ss 8–15 . . . . **274**
  s 9 274
  s 15 274

ss 43–55C 276
s 157 314
ss 164–71 314
Sch 3, para 5 276
South Sea Company Act 1711 711
South Sea Company Act 1720 (7 Geo 1, stat 1, c 13) 48
Statute of Artificers 1562 8
Statute of Cambridge 1388 729
Statute of Labourers 1351 . . . . 4–6, 11, 41
Sunday Trading Act 1994 288
Supreme Court of Judicature Act 1873
 s 25(11) 782
Tax Credits Act 2002 790
Taxation of Chargeable Gains Act 1992 273
Teaching and Higher Education Act 1998 585
Theft Act 1968
 s 1 264
 s 7 265
Trade Boards Act 1909 . . . . 20, 25, 65, 250
Trade Boards Act 1918 . . . . 23, 25, 65
 s 1(2) 25
 s 8 249
 s 78 24
Trade Disputes Act 1906 . . . . 20, 69,
                                                      325, 421, 422, 428
 ss 1–4 419
 s 2 461
Trade Disputes Act 1965 . . . . 423, 569
Trade Disputes and Trade Unions Act 1927 . . . . 26, 337
Trade Disputes and Trade Unions Act 1946 337
Trade Union Act 1871 . . . . 19, 42, 69,
                                                      184, 325, 329, 346, 389
 s 2 19
 s 3 19
 s 4 . . . . 20, 346, 389
Trade Union Act 1913 337
Trade Union Act 1984 . . . . 329, 337, 369, 462
Trade Union Act 2016 470
Trade Union and Labour Relations Act 1974 . . . . 390, 456, 812, 835
 s 13 474
 s 17(2) 475
 s 30(5) 456, 457
 Sch 1 744
  para 4 743
  para 5 743
  para 6(8) 835
  para 10 789

Trade Union and Labour Relations (Consolidation)
   Act (TULRCA) 1992 .... 106, 358, 393, 467, 468, 789
   Pt V.. 410, 411
   s 1.. 327
   ss 2–4 327
   s 5.. 327
   ss 6–9 327
   s 10... 346, 347
   ss 10–23 327
   s 13.. 356
   s 18(4)... 419
   s 20... 424, 473
   ss 20–22 .... **472**
   s 21... 424, 473
      (3) 473
   s 22... 424, 473
   s 24.. 469
   ss 27–45D... 342
   s 28... **341**
   s 46... **327**, 328
   s 47... 330, 334, 335
   s 48... 329, 768
   s 49.. 330
   s 50... **327**, 328
      (2)(c) 328
   s 51.. 330
   ss 51A–56A 330
   s 63.. 338
   ss 64–67 344
   s 65(6)... 344
   ss 71–72 .... **335**, 336
   s 72(1)(f).. 337
   s 72A 336
   s 73.. 336
   s 77.. 336
   s 82... **335**, 336
   s 111... 768
   s 137... 544
   ss 137–39 363
   ss 145A–B 358
   ss 145A–46.. 768
   s 146..115, 123, 145,
                                      355, 358, 359, 368, **394**, 569
      (1)(c) 395
      (2) 365
      (3) 402
   ss 146–48 357

s 148(3). 355, 358
  (a). 355
s 152. . . . . 115, 359
  (2) 365
s 163. 768
s 168. 404
s 170. 404
s 174. . . . . 347, 351–53
  (2) 344
s 179. . . . . **184, 389**, 390
  (3) 184
  (4) 185
s 180. . . . . .412, 413,
                                                                  419, 421, 422, 470
s 181. . . . . 366, 403
s 182. 366
s 188. . . . . .825, 836,
                                                      858, 860, 862, 868, 875
  (1) 827
  (2) 826, 856, 860
  (2)–(4) 856
  (4) 827, 860, 861
  (7) 868
ss 188–92 384
s 189(1). 827, 860
  (b) 860
  (2) 827
  (3) 827
  (4) 827, 860, 861
  (5) 860
ss 189–90 860
s 190(1). 860
  (2) 860
s 191. 860
s 192. 860
s 193. 827
ss 193–94 870
s 194. 827
s 195. . . . . **824**, 825, 826
  (1) 827
  (2) 826
s 199. 765
s 207. 776
s 207A 742, 765, **767**, 768, 832
ss 212–18 . . . . **472**
s 219. . . . . **419**, 421, 474
  (1)(a) 422

(2) 422
(3) 460
s 220 460
ss 220–21 . . . . **459**
s 220A 460
s 221 . . . . 473, 474
s 223 432
s 224 . . . . 148, 432, **453**
(1) 460
(3) 460
s 224A 418
s 226 . . . . 466, 470
(2) 466
ss 226–32 411
ss 226–34A **463**
ss 226–35 . . . . 418, 431, 470
s 226A 411, 430, 466, 469
(1) 470
(2A) 470
(2H) 470
(3A) 469
s 226B 470
s 227 470
(1) 466, 468
(2) 468
s 228 470
s 228A 470
s 229 470
(4) 470
s 230 . . . . 466, 470
(2) 467–69
(2A) 466, 467
(2B) 466
s 231 . . . . 409–11, 471
(a)–(d) 410
s 231A 470
s 231B 470
s 232A 466–68
s 232B 466, 467, 469
(2) 467
s 233 470
s 234 470
s 234A 418, 470
s 237 478
s 238 478
s 238A **477**, 478
(5) 477

s 238B. 477
s 239(1). 477
s 241 . . . . **459**, 461
s 244 . . . . **419**, 421, 466
s 275 360
s 296 106
s 297 . . . . 133, 877
s 298 827
Sch A1 . . . . .377, 380,
381, 383, 386, 405
Pt I 379, 380
Pt VI. 379, 380, 382
Pt VIII 379
paras 3–7 . . . . **372**, 378
paras 4–7 377
para 7 378
para 11 . . . . **372**
(2) 384
paras 11–18 . . . . 377, 384
para 12 . . . . **372**
para 18 . . . . **372**
para 19B 384, 387, 388
(3)(c) 386, 387
para 22 386
paras 22–26 . . . . **372**, 377
paras 22–27 388
para 24 388
para 27A 388
paras 31–32 377
para 35 377–83
paras 35–36 . . . . **372**
para 36 377
para 39 388
para 134(1) 379
para 137 379
para 146 768
Sch A2 768
Trading with the Enemy Act 1914 861
Transportation Act 1717 11
Tribunals, Courts and Enforcement Act 2007. 149
s 42 152
(1) 151
Truck Act 1831
s III 258
Truck Act 1887 258
Truck Act 1896 258

Trustee Act 2000
  s 3 281
    (1) 701
  s 4(3)(b) 834
Unemployment Insurance (No 2) Act 1924
  s 4(1). 24
Unfair Contract Terms Act 1977 . . . . 179, 181, 232
  s 1. 180
    (1) 179
    (3) 178, 179
  s 2. . . . . 179, 181
    (1) **177**, 178–80, 232
    (2) 179, 180
        . . . .
  ss 2–7 180
  s 3. . . . . 180, 181, 528
  s 6. 178
  s 7. 178
  s 11(4). 178
  s 13. 179
    (1) 179
  s 20. 178
  s 21. 178
  Sch 1, para 4. 179–81
  Sch 2. 178
Universities (Scotland) Act 1966 486
Unlawful Oaths Act 1797 . . . . 11, 12
Unlawful Societies Act 1799. . . . . 11, 12
Vagabond Acts 42
Vagabonds Act 1597 11
Vagrancy Act 1547 8
Wages Act 1986 . . . . 251, 258
Wages Council Act 1945. 251
Wages Council Act 1959. 251
Wages Council Act 1979. 251
Welfare Reform Act 2009 720
Welfare Reform Act 2012 . . . . 717, 720
  ss 1–17 . . . . **720**
  s 4. 722
  s 5. 722
  ss 13–19 723
  s 16(3). 723
      (e) 723
  ss 26–29 728
  s 33. 722
  s 96. 723

Welfare Reform and Work Act 2016
  s 1 676
  ss 8–14 676
  s 11 723
  ss 13–19 723
Woollen Manufacturers Act 1725 (12 Geo 1, c 34) 48

Statutory Instruments

Additional Paternity Leave Regulations 2010 (SI 2010/1055) 314
Agency Worker Regulations 2010 (SI 2010/93) 226, 667
  reg 3 667
  reg 5 . . . . **666**, 668
    (1)–(2) 667
  reg 6(3) 667
  reg 7 667
  reg 10 668
  reg 13 . . . . 669, **670**
  reg 17 790
Certification Officer (Amendment of Fees) Regulations 2005 (SI 2005/713) 327
Collective Redundancies and Transfer of Undertakings (Protection
  of Employment) (Amendment) Regulations 1995 (SI 1995/2587) 868
Companies (Cross-Border Mergers) Regulations 2007 (SI 2007/2974)
  regs 46–47 790
Companies (Miscellaneous Reporting) Regulations 2018 (SI 2018/860) 490
Companies (Model Articles) Regulations 2008 (SI 2008/3229) **190**, 393, 489
  Sch 3, para 2 328
  Sch 3, para 3 . . . . **266**, 268, 489
    paras 3–5 . . . . **488**
    para 4 . . . . 268, 489
    para 5 489
    para 20 . . . . **488**, 489
    para 23 . . . . **266**, 267, **488**, 489
    para 34 . . . . **488**
Conduct of Employment Agencies and Employment Businesses
  Regulations 2003 (SI 2003/3319) 734
  reg 6 734
  reg 7 734
  reg 27 734
Consumer Protection from Unfair Trading Regulations 2008 (SI 2008/1277)
  reg 5 265
  reg 8 265
  reg 13 265
Cross-border Railway Services (Working Time) Regulations 2008
  (SI 2008/1660)
  reg 17 768

Employment Equality (Age) Regulations 2006 (SI 2006/1031)
  reg 3(1)(b) 591
    (2) 591
  reg 17 572
  reg 30 592
Employment Equality (Sexual Orientation) Regulations 2003 (SI 2003/1661)
  reg 5 . . . . 556, 557
    (1) 558
Employment Relations Act 1999 (Blacklists) Regulations 2010
  (SI 2010/493) **366**, 368
  reg 9 768
Employment Rights (Increase of Limits) Order 2016 (SI 2016/288) 259
Employment Rights (Increase of Limits) Order 2018 (SI 2018/194) 810
Employment Tribunal Extension of Jurisdiction (England and Wales)
  Order 1994 (SI 1994/1623) 768
  Art 4(d) 189
Employment Tribunals and the Employment Appeal Tribunal Fees
  Order 2013 (SI 2013/1893) 149, 152, 153, 154
Equality Act 2010 (Disability) Regulations 2010 (SI 2010/2128) 629
  reg 3 626
  regs 3–8 625
  reg 4 626
  reg 5 626
  reg 6 626
  reg 7 626
  reg 8 629
European Cooperative Society (Involvement of Employees)
  Regulations 2006 (SI 2006/2059)
  reg 31 790
  reg 34 768
European Public Limited-Liability Company Regulations 2004
  (SI 2004/2326)
  reg 42 790
  reg 45 768
European Public Limited-Liability Company (Employee Involvement)
  (Great Britain) Regulations 2009 (SI 2009/2401) 790
Fixed-term Employees (Prevention of Less Favourable Treatment)
  Regulations 2002 (SI 2002/2034) 485, 656, 662, 671
  regs 2–3 652
  regs 2–5 . . . . **651**
  reg 3(3)(b) 652
    (6)–(7) **660**
  reg 5 652
  reg 8 . . . . 653, **660**, 661, 663
    (2) 655, 656, 660
    (5) 661
  reg 12(2) 652

reg 18 653
   (1) 653
Flexible Working Regulations 2014 (SI 2014/1398)
   reg 4 318
Industrial Relations (Northern Ireland) Order 1976 (SI 1976/1043)
   art 2(7) 830
Information and Consultation of Employees Regulations 2004
   (SI 3426/2004)
   reg 2 515
   regs 2–32 . . . . **512**
   reg 4(3) 516
   reg 8 515
   reg 19 515
   reg 20 515
      (4)(d) 515
   regs 22–23 515
   reg 30 790
   reg 33 768
   Sch 2 515
International Development Association (Seventh Replenishment)
   Order 1985 (SI 1985/80) 267
   Art 82 267
Jobseeker's Allowance (Employment, Skills and Enterprise Scheme)
   Regulations 2011 (SI 2011/917) 724, 726, 728
   reg 2 . . . . 723, 724
   reg 4(1) 724
      (2) 724
         (c) 723, 724
         (e) 724
Jobseeker's Allowance (Schemes for Assisting Persons to Obtain Employment)
   Regulations 2013 (SI 2013/276) 728
Local Government Pension Scheme Regulations 2013 (SI 2013/2356)
   reg 53(4) 523
Maternity and Parental Leave, etc Regulations 1999 (SI 1999/3312) 314
Modern Slavery Act 2015 (Transparency in Supply Chains)
   Regulations 2015 (SI 2015/1833)
   reg 2 503
National Employment Savings Trust (Consequential Provisions)
   Order 2010 (SI 2010/9)
   reg 3 524
National Minimum Wage Regulations 1999 (SI 1999/584)
   reg 2(2) 252
   reg 3 256
   reg 4(1) 254
   reg 15 256
      (1) 253
      (1A) 254

reg 28 255
reg 31(e) 263, 264
National Minimum Wage Regulations 1999 (Amendment)
    Regulations 2009 (SI 2009/1902)
    reg 5 . . . . 79, 264
National Minimum Wage Regulations 2015 (SI 2015/621) 251
    reg 4 249
    regs 4–4A 252
    reg 6 253
    reg 7 253
    regs 11–16 265
    reg 17 253
    reg 21 . . . . 253, 254
    regs 21–29 254
    reg 22 254
    reg 23 254
    reg 30 253
    regs 30–35 254
    reg 32 254
        (1) 253, 254
    regs 33–34 254
    reg 35 254
    reg 36 253
    regs 36–43 254
    regs 41–43 254
    reg 44 253
    regs 44–50 254
    reg 45 254
    reg 49 254
    reg 50 254
    reg 59 256
Occupational and Personal Pension Schemes (Automatic Enrolment)
    Regulations 2010 (SI 2010/772) 279
Occupational and Personal Pension Schemes (Automatic Enrolment)
    (Amendment) Regulations 2012 (SI 2012/1257) 279
Occupational and Personal Pension Schemes (Consultation by Employers
    and Miscellaneous Amendment) Regulations 2006 (SI 2006/349)
    reg 8 516
    regs 11–13 516
    Sch, para 5 790
        para 8 768
Part-time Work (Prevention of Less Favourable Treatment)
    Regulations 2000 (SI 2000/1551) 140, 485, 637, **638**, 647, 652, 671
    reg 2(1)–(2) 639
        (3) 639
        (4) 638, 641
            (a)(ii) 639

reg 3 639
reg 4 639
reg 5 . . . . 638, 639, 641, 644
   (2) 644
   (3) 644
reg 6 638
Paternity and Adoption Leave Regulations 2002 (SI 2002/2788) 314
Prisoners' Earnings Act 1996 (Commencement) (England and Wales)
   Order 2011 (SI 2011/1658) 252
Public Contracts Regulations 2015 (SI 2015/102) 702
   reg 56 702
Sex Discrimination (Northern Ireland) Order 1976 (SI 1976/1042) 561
   Art 3(1). 563
      (a) 563
Statutory Maternity Pay (General) Regulations 1986 (SI 1986/1960) 314
Statutory Paternity Pay and Statutory Adoption Pay (General)
   Regulations 2002 (SI 2002/2822) 314
Statutory Paternity Pay and Statutory Adoption Pay (Weekly Rates)
   Regulations 2002 (SI 2002/2818) 314
Trade Boards (Boot and Shoe Repairing) Order 1919 249
Trade Union and Labour Relations (Consolidation) Act 1992
   (Amendment) Order 2013 (SI 2013/763)
   Art 3 860
Transfer of Undertakings (Protection of Employment) Regulations 1981
   (SI 1981/1794). 141, 164
Transfer of Undertakings (Protection of Employment)
   Regulations 2006 (SI 2006/246) 430, 840, 842,
                                              848, 849, 853
   reg 3 841
   reg 4 852
   regs 4–5 841
   regs 4–7 847
   reg 5 849
   reg 6 841
   reg 7 841
   regs 13–15 870
Transnational Information and Consultation of Employees
Regulations 1999 (SI 1999/3323). **518**, 520, 790
   reg 32 768
Unfair Dismissal and Statement of Reasons for Dismissal (Variation of
   Qualifying Period) Order 1999 (SI 1999/1436)
   Art 3 789
Unfair Dismissal and Statement of Reasons for Dismissal (Variation
   of Qualifying Period) Order 2012 (SI 2012/989). 789
Unfair Dismissal (Variation of Qualifying Period) Order 1979 (SI 1979/959) 789
Unfair Dismissal (Variation of Qualifying Period) Order 1985
   (SI 1985/782). 587, 589

Unfair Dismissal (Variation of the Limit of Compensatory Award)
  Order 2013 (SI 2013/1949) 806
Welfare Benefits Up-rating Order 2015 (SI 2015/30). 314
Working Time Regulations 1998 (SI 1998/1833) 101, 233, 311, 789
    reg 2(1) 106
    reg 4 310
        (3)(b) 303
    regs 4–5 299
    reg 5 299
    regs 6–7 310
    reg 10 308
        (1) 255
    reg 11 308
    reg 12 308
        (1) 255
        (3) 308
    reg 13 286
    regs 14–16 289
    reg 15 287
        (2) 287
    regs 18–24A 303
    reg 20 303
    regs 20–21 520
    reg 21 309
    reg 24 308
    reg 30 768

AUSTRALIA

Excise Tariff Act 1906. 246
Immigration Restriction Act 1901 34

AUSTRIA

Working Time Act (Arbeitzeitgesetz) 641

BERMUDA

Companies Act 1981
    s 93 235

CANADA

British North America Act
  s 125 107

DENMARK

Companies Acts 1973 28

FRANCE

Code du travail
  Art L 213-1 310
  Art L 223-2 289
  Art L 223-4 289
  Art L 1111-3 516

GERMANY

Civil Code (Bürgerliches Gesetzbuch) (BGB)
  § 134 730
  § 242 77
  § 566 843
  § 613 843
  § 613a 852
  § 622 . . . . .539, 540,
                                                                      542, 754
    (2) 540, 541
  § 631 847
  § 950 216
Co-determination Act 1976 (Mitbestimmungsgesetz) 28, 494
  § 1 . . . . 494, 499
  § 7 494
  § 9 494
  § 18 494
  §§ 27–29 494
  § 33 . . . . 28, 157, 494
Control Council Law No 22 (10 April 1946) Works Councils **507**, 764
  Art V 508
    (b) 763
Employment Promotion Act 1996 (Beschäftigungsförderungsgesetz) (AFG) 657
  Art 3 731
First Law for the Provision of Modern Services on the Labour Market 2002 658

Minimum Wage Law 2014 (Mindestlohngesetz) 251
One Third Participation Act 2003
 § 1 494
Part-time and Fixed-term Work Act 2001 (Teilzeit- und Befristungsgesetz)
 § 12 299
 § 14 657
  (3) 539, 657, 659
Posted Worker Act 1996 (AEntG) 703, 704
Social Code (Sozialgesetzbuch)
 §§ 35–39 603
 § 41 575
State Procurement Act (Lower Saxony) (Landesvergabegesetz) 702, 704
 § 3 702
 § 8 702
Weimar Constitution 1919 . . . . 65, 363
Work Constitution Act 1972 (Betriebsverfassungsgesetz) **509**, 510, 525
 § 1 510
 § 87 510
 § 99 665
 § 102 766
 § 111 766
 §§ 111–13 510
Work Councils Act 1920
 §§ 84–87 796
Work Promotion Act (Arbeitsförderungsgesetz)
 § 13 730
Working Time Act 1994 (Arbeitszeitgesetz)
 § 3 300
 § 5 III 304
 § 7 300

INDIA

Caste Acts 34

NEW ZEALAND

Workers' Compensation Act 1922 126

SOUTH AFRICA

Constitution
 Ch 2, § 23 418
  (4)(c) 418

Immorality Act 1927. 424
Industrial Conciliation Act 1956. 424
Interim Constitution 1994. 415–17
    CP XXVIII. 416, 417
    NT 23 415–17
Labour Relations Act 28 of 1956 416
Labour Relations Act 66 of 1995 417
Prohibition of Political Interference Act 1968 424
Reservation of Separate Amenities Act 1953 424
South Africa Act 1909. 34

SPAIN

Basque Decree 231/2000 653
Law 55/2003 of 16 December 2003 653
Royal Decree No 1561/95. 303

SWEDEN

Board Representation (Private Sector Employees) Act 1987 . . . . **493**, 494
    s 6. 494
Law (1915: 218) on Agreements and other Legal Acts in the Field
    of Property Law
    § 36. 246

UNITED STATES

Age Discrimination in Employment Act of 1967
    §§ 621–34. 572
Civil Rights Act of 1875. 537
Civil Rights Act of 1964 . . . . .32, 34, 533,
                                                                         538, 594, 595, 605
    Title VII 594, 595
    § 2000e-2 594
Clayton Antitrust Act of 1914. . . . . 40, 69
    § 6. . . . . 414, 453
Constitution
    14th Amendment 285, 537
Davis–Bacon Act of 1931
    §3141-8 706
Delaware General Corporation Law of 1969
    § 141(h) 267
Emergency Relief Appropriation Act of 1935 684

Employee Retirement Income Security Act of 1974
  § 407(d)(6) 79
Employment Act of 1946 688
  § 1021 714
Equal Pay Act of 1963 . . . . 34, 605
Fair Labor Standards Act of 1938 . . . . 68, 79, 445, 605
  § 3(r) 135
  §§ 203(m) 265
Federal Emergency Relief Act of 1933 684
Federal Reserve Act of 1913
  § 225a 714
Foreign Assistance Act of 1948 715
Humphrey–Hawkins Full Employment Act of 1978 688
Internal Revenue Code
  § 4975(e)(7) 79
McNamara–O'Hara Service Contract Act of 1965
  §6701-7 706
National Industrial Recovery Act of 1933 92
National Labor Relations Act of 1935 (or the Wagner Act) 27, 33, 405, 445
  § 2(11) 127
  § 8(a)(2) 326, 327
Pension Protection Act of 2006
  § 902 279
Reciprocal Trade Agreements Act of 1934 684
Recovery and Reinvestment Act of 2009 699
Securities Act of 1933 687
Securities and Exchange Act of 1934 687
Sherman Antitrust Act of 1890 . . . . 414, 453
  § 1 453
Small Business Job Protection Act of 1996 . . . . 79, 265
Smoot–Hawley Tariff Act of 1930 684
Social Security Act of 1935 . . . . 687, 775
Taft–Hartley Act of 1947 . . . . 402, 714
  §158(b)(4) 454
    (c) 388
  § 185 843
Walsh–Healey Public Contracts Act of 1936
  §6501-11 706

EUROPE

Charter of Fundamental Rights of the European Union 2000 . . . . 154, 326,
                                                                      439, 850, 852
  Art 2(1) 540
  Art 12 . . . . 326, 705

Art 16 . . . . 705, 851, 852, 872, 874
Arts 20–21 544
Art 27 516
Arts 27–28 700
Art 28 . . . . 326, 439, 440
Art 30 . . . . .774, 786,
810, 873, 874
Arts 30–31 700
Art 31(2) 295
Art 33 874
Art 34 700
Art 47 . . . . 153, 810, 868
Art 52(1) 873
(7) 851
Community Charter of the Fundamental Social Rights of Workers 1989 305
pt 8 305
pt 19(1) 305
Comprehensive Economic and Trade Agreement between Canada and the EU 738
Council of Europe Convention on Action against Trafficking
in Human Beings 2005 174
Art 1 174
Art 4 174
(a) 174
Art 15 174
EU–South Korea Trade Agreement (14 May 2011) [2011] OJ L127 738
Art 13 . . . . **736**
(2) 738
European Convention on Human Rights 264, 324–26,
412, 429, 430, 438, 450,
470, 536, 566, 593, 600, 774
Art 4 . . . . 174, 175, 723, 725–27
(2) 726
(3) 725
(d) 725, 726, 727
Art 6 . . . . 153, 728, 771–74
(1) 772
Art 8 . . . . .368, 775,
798, 799, 801, 804
(2) 799
Art 9 . . . . .368, 401, 544,
547, 551, 598–600
(1) 398
(2) 398
Art 10 . . . . .125, 365,
401, 547, 552, 799
(1) 398
(2) 398, 551

Art 11 . . . . .115, **324**, 325, 326,
334, 350–56, 359, 365,
368, 378–84, 386, 393,
394, 396–402, 404, 430,
433–39, 458, 460, 470,
547–49, 552, 700, 849
 (1) 352, 356, 398
 (2) 352, 354,
398, 399, 433, 437, 551
 Art 13 . . . . 153, 810
 Art 14 . . . . .381, 383,
544, 572,
598, 600, 775
 Art 34 450
 Art 35 450
 Protocol 1, Art 1 . . . . 263, 264
European Social Charter 1961 . . . . 400, 435, 436
 Art 1 676
 Art 2 . . . . 286, 296
 (1) 738
 Art 4 69
 Art 5 355
 Art 6(2) 356
 (4) 430
 Art 25 355
Single European Act (Treaty of Maastricht) 1986 . . . . 38, 678
Statute of the Court of Justice of the EC
 Art 20 306
Statute of the ECB 714
 Arts 10–11 714
Transatlantic Trade and Investment Partnership (USA – EU) 738
Treaty Establishing the European Community
 Art 10 301
 Art 13 . . . . 552, 553, 555
 Art 43 439–41
 Art 49 . . . . 445, 447, 448, 704
 Art 81(1) 441
 Art 82 730
 Art 85(1) 441
 Arts 85–94 731
 Art 86 731
 Art 90 730
 (1) 731
 (2) 731
 Art 119 . . . . 587, 588
 Art 137 . . . . 440, 655
 (4) 445

Art 141 . . . . 37, 607

   (1) 608

Treaty on European Union

Art 2 439

Art 3 . . . . 676, 713

   (3) 694, 874

Art 4 499

Art 6(1). 295, 540, 851

Art 9 . . . . **712**

Art 118a 300

Art 127 . . . . **712**

Art 282 . . . . **712**

Treaty on the Functioning of the European Union (TFEU)

Art 49 . . . . .439–41, 444,

                                           452, 477, 655, 705, 871

Art 54 . . . . 442, 871

Art 56 . . . . 444, 445, 450, 702, 704, 705

Art 57 444

Art 63 . . . . 871, 872

Art 101 . . . . 414, 450, 452

   (1) 450, 451, 452

Art 102 730

Art 106 . . . . 441, 730

Art 123 . . . . 714, 715

Art 153 . . . . **38**, 439

   (1) 655

      (a) 286

      (i) 655

   (4) 439, 445

   (5) 439, 444, 655

Arts 154–55 636

Art 156 442

Art 157 . . . . .37, 280, 313,

                                         587, 605–07, 637, 655

   (5) 440

Art 158(a). 300

Art 267 542

Art 283(2). 714

Art 288 541

EU SECONDARY LEGISLATION

Regulations

Brussels I Regulation (EC) No 44/2001

Art 19 196

Brussels I Regulation (Recast) (EU) No 1215/2012. 193
   Art 20(2). 193
   Art 21(1)(a) 193
      (b) 194
Capital Requirements Regulation (EU) No 575/2013
   Art 450 270
Company Regulation (EC) No 2157/2001 495
Generalised Tarriff Preferences Regulation (EC) No 732/2008
   Arts 7–8 41
   Art 15 41
   Art 27 41
Rome I Regulation (EC) 593/2008 . . . . 200, 205
   Recital 23 . . . . 193, 201
   Recital 34 449
   Art 3 . . . . **192**, 193
      (2) 193
   Art 8 . . . . **192**
      (1) 193
      (2) 193
      (3) 193
      (4) 193, 197
Rome II Regulation (EC) No 864/2007 . . . . **201**
   Art 1 202
      (2)(d) 203
   Art 2 202
   Art 4 202
   Art 7 203
   Art 9 202

Directives

Access Directive 2002/19/ EC
   Arts 3–4 429
Acquired Rights Directive 77/187/EC 843, 845, 850
   Art 3(1). 850
Capital Requirements Directive 2013/36/EU
   Art 94 270
Collective Redundancies Directive 75/129/EEC 866
Collective Redundancies Directive 98/59/EC 825, **857**, 862,
                                           863, 865–68, 870, 871
   Recital 2 865
   Art 1 858
      (1)(a) 862, 864
         (i) 861, 863
         (ii) 862, 863
      (2)(b) 868

Art 2 . . . . 856, 858, 865
   (1) 864–67
   (2) 865, 866
   (3) 866
      (b) 866
   (4) 864–66
Arts 2–4 863
Art 3(1). 865, 866
   (2) 866
Arts 3–4 870
Art 5 . . . . 863, 864
Art 6 860
Credit Institutions Directive 2013/36/EU
  Art 95(2). 499
Cross Border Merger Directive 2005/56/EC
  Art 16(2)–(4) 498
Employee Involvement Directive 2001/86 . . . . 405, 495, **496**
  Recital 18 497
  Arts 3–4 497
  Arts 3–13 498
  Art 7 497
  Annex, Pt 3. 497
     (b) 497
Employment Information Directive 91/533/EEC 188
Equal Treatment Directive 76/207/EEC 310, 557, 606, 619
  Art 2 617
   (1) 604, 619, 642
   (4) 619
  Art 5(1). 604, 642
Equal Treatment Directive 2006/54/EC. 544, 605, **606**, 619
  Art 2(1)(b) 586
  Art 7 607
Equality Framework Directive 2000/78/EC 130, 539–42, 544,
                                                          555–57, 605, 606, 630, 659
  Recital 17 630
  Recital 37 555
  Art 1 . . . . 552, 555, 557, 630
  Art 2(1). 552, 555
    (2)(a). 539, 555
      (b) 586
  Art 3 . . . . 130, 131
   (1)(a) 130
    (b) 131
    (c) 555
   (4) 571
  Art 4(1). 571, 573, 574
   (2) 571

Art 5 556
Art 6 . . . . 539, 572, 574
   (1) 540, 574, 658, 659
Art 8(2). 630
Art 10 565
European Works Council Directive 2009/38/EC 405, 518, 868
Fixed Term Work Directive 1999/70/EC 308, 644, 650,
651, 654, 655, 658, 659
Art 2 651
   (1) 650
   (2) 651
Arts 3–4 . . . . **650**
Art 4 654
   (1) 653
Art 5 . . . . 651, 653, 654, **655**, 656, 657, 659
   (1)(a) 653
Art 6 . . . . **655**, 656
   (1) 660
Art 8 659
Annex 657, 658
Information and Consultation Directive 2002/14/EC 512, 868
Arts 1–7 . . . . **511**
Art 2 515
Art 4(2). 512
   (4)(e) 515
Art 6 512
Art 7 512
Art 8 . . . . 512, 515
Art 9 512
Parental Leave Directive 2010/18/EU. 313
Art 2(2). 314
Art 7 315
Part-time Work Directive 97/81/EC. 140, 637, 644–46, 650
Art 2(1). 644
Art 3 637
Arts 3–4 . . . . **636**
Art 4 637
Art 5(1). 648
   (3) 315, 492
      (a) 647
      (b) 649
Arts 5–6 . . . . **647**
Annex 642, 644
Posted Workers Directive 96/71/EC 194, 445,
447–49, 702–04, 706
Recital 17 445
Arts 1–3 702

Art 3(1). 445, 446, 703
    (a)–(g). 446, 447, 703
    (c) 703
  (7) 447, 703
  (8) 446, 447, 702–04
  (10) 447
Pregnant Workers Directive 92/85/EEC 313, 622, 874
  Art 5(1). 621
    (2) 621–23
  Art 10(2). 874
  Art 11 621
    (1) 622, 623
    (2)(b) 314, 621
    (3) 621
    (4) 622
  Annex I. 621
Public Procurement Directive 92/50/EEC 705, 844
Public Procurement Directive 2004/18/EC. 705, 706
Public Procurement Directive 2014/24/EU
  Art 18 706
    (2) 702
Public Procurement Directive 2014/25/EU
  Art 18 450
Race Equality Directive 2000/43/EC 34, 37, 544
  Art 2(2)(b) 586
  Art 3 132
Temporary and Agency Work Directive 2008/104/EC 144, 666, 672
  Art 1 666
  Art 2 . . . . 136, 663, 665
  Arts 2–3 . . . . **664**
  Art 3(f) 665
  Art 4 . . . . **669**, 735
  Art 5 . . . . **665**
    (1) 665
    (2) 665
  Art 6 . . . . 665, **669**, 670
  Art 7 665
  Art 8 665
Trafficking Directive 2011/36. 175
  Art 17 175
Transfer of Undertakings Directive 2001/23/EC 840, 842, 848–50
  Art 1 . . . . **840**, 841, 847
    (1)(b) 844
      (c) 842
  Art 2(2). 870
  Art 3 . . . . 847, 850–52
    (1) 840, 841, 848, 849

Arts 3–4 . . . . **840**, 847
Art 4 841
    (1) 840
Art 6 . . . . **840**, 841
Art 7 . . . . 849, **869**
    (1) 870
    (2) 870
Art 8 . . . . 850, 851
Transnational Works Council Directive 2009/38/EC
Arts 6–13 . . . . **516**
Working Time Directive 93/104/EC 233, 290, 299–307
Preamble 306
Recital 4 305
Art 1(1) 300
    (3) 300
Art 6 . . . . 301, 304
    (2) 301, 302
Art 7(1) 290
Art 18(1)(b) 319
        (i) 300
Working Time Directive 2003/88/EC 233, 287–90, 303
Recital 5 287
Recital 6 290
Art 2 . . . . 287, 310
Art 3 308
Art 4 308
Art 5 308
Art 6 . . . . 299, 300
Art 7 . . . . 286, 288, 292–95
    (1) 290–93, 295
    (2) 293
Arts 8–13 310
Art 15 293
Art 17 . . . . 303, 309
    (2) 309
Art 18(3) 293
Art 22 299
    (1) 299
Working Time in Civil Aviation Directive 2000/79/EC
Art 3 294

Decisions

Employment Decision (EU) 2015/1848 . . . . **692**

Recommendations

Economic Policies Recommendation (EU) 2015/1184 . . . . **691**

INTERNATIONAL

General Agreement on Tariffs and Trade 1947 . . . . 41, 736
ILO Abolition of Forced Labour Convention 1957 (c 105) 40
ILO Collective Bargaining Convention 1949 (c 98) 40, 365
   Art 1 355
   Art 2 355
ILO Declaration on Fundamental Principles and Rights at Work 1998 . . . . **39**
ILO Discrimination (Employment and Occupation)
   Convention 1958 (c 111) 34, 40, 100, 547
ILO Employment Policy Convention 1964 (c 122) 675
   Art 1(2) 707
ILO Employment Promotion and Protection against Unemployment
   Recommendation 1988 (No 176) **700**
ILO Employment Relationship Recommendation 2006 (No 198) **160**
ILO Equal Remuneration Convention 1951 (c 100) 40
ILO Forced Labour Convention 1930 (c 29) 40, 725
ILO Freedom of Association and Protection of the Right to Organise
   Convention 1948 (c 87) 40, 127,
                                             176, 429, 430, 436
   Art 2 355
   Art 3 . . . . 325, 352, 431
     (1) 429
   Art 5 352
   Art 10 431
ILO Holidays with Pay Convention 1970 (c 132) 290, 291
   Art 9(1) 292
ILO Hours of Work (Industry) Convention 1919 (c 1)
   Art 2 285
ILO Labour Clauses (Public Contracts) Convention 1949 (c 94) 702
   Art 2 702
ILO Maternity Protection Convention 2000 (c 183) 315
ILO Minimum Age Convention 1973 (c 138) 40
ILO Night Work (Women) Convention 1948 (c 89) 310
ILO Part-Time Work Convention 1994 (c 175) 637
ILO Private Employment Agencies Convention 1997 (c 181) 663, 730
   Art 7(1) 730
ILO Promotion and Protection against Unemployment Convention 1988 (c 168)
   Art 2 729
   Art 7 708
ILO Protection of Wages Convention 1949 (c 95) 258

ILO Resolution Concerning Statistics of the Economically Active Population,
  Employment, Unemployment and Underemployment 1982 677
ILO Termination of Employment Convention 1982 (c 158). 786
  Art 3(3). 656
  Art 11 754
ILO Termination of Employment Recommendation 1963 (No 119) 780
ILO Unemployment Convention 1919 (c 2) 663, 730
ILO Unemployment Recommendation 1919 (No 1) 663, 730
ILO Workers' Representatives Convention 1971 (c 135)
  Art 1 355
ILO Worst Forms of Child Labour Convention 1999 (c 182). 40
International Covenant on Civil and Political Rights (ICCPR) 1966
  Art 22 326
International Covenant on Economic, Social and Cultural Rights
  (ICESCR) 1966 . . . . 326, 412
  Art 8 452
    (1)(d) 429
  Art 9 . . . . 729, 775
Trans-Pacific Partnership (between the USA, Canada, Mexico
  and nine Pacific countries) 738
Treaty of Utrecht. 711
United Nations General Assembly Resolution 1598, On Race Conflict
  in South Africa 1961 424
United Nations Protocol to Prevent, Suppress and Punish Trafficking
  in Persons (Palermo Protocol) 2000. 174
  Art 3 173
    (a). 174
  Art 6(6). 175
Universal Declaration of Human Rights 1948 . . . . 326, 359, 429, 740, 775
  Art 7 100
  Art 16 100
  Art 20 326
    (2) 394, 396, 397
  Art 22 774
  Arts 22–23 700
  Art 23 . . . . 100, 452
    (1) 402, 675, 729
    (2) 360
    (3) 69, 245, 371, 677
    (4) 355, 359, 430
  Art 24 286
Versailles Treaty
  Pt XIII. 21
  Art 427 414
Vienna Convention 1969. 695
  Arts 6–7 700

List of Abbreviations

TEXTBOOK READING IN EACH CHAPTER

Collins	H Collins, *Employment Law* (2nd edn 2010)
CEM	H Collins, KD Ewing, A McColgan, *Labour Law: Law in Context* (Cambridge University Press 2012)
D&M	S Deakin and G Morris, *Labour Law* (6th edn Hart 2012)

UNITED KINGDOM STATUTES

UCTA 1977	Unfair Contract Terms Act 1977
IA 1986	Insolvency Act 1986
TULRCA 1992	Trade Union and Labour Relations (Consolidation) Act 1992
ERA 1996	Employment Rights Act 1996
NMWA 1998	National Minimum Wage Act 1998
PA 2004	Pensions Act 2004
CA 2006	Companies Act 2006
PA 2008	Pensions Act 2008
EA 2010	Equality Act 2010

UNITED KINGDOM REGULATIONS

WTR 1998	Working Time Regulations 1998
PTWR 1999	Part-time Worker Regulations 1999
NMWR 1999	National Minimum Wage Regulations 1999
FTER 2002	Fixed-term Employee Regulations 2002
ICER 2004	Information and Consultation of Employees Regulations 2004
TUPER 2006	Transfer of Undertakings (Protection of Employment) Regulations 2006

TICER 1999	Transnational Information and Consultation of Employees Regulations 1999
AWR 2010	Agency Worker Regulations 2010
NMWR 2015	National Minimum Wage Regulations 2010

INTERNATIONAL INSTRUMENTS AND BODIES

EU	European Union
EWCD 2009	European Works Councils Directive 2009
ICED 2002	Information and Consultation of Employees Directive 2002
ILO	International Labour Organization
ICESCR	International Covenant on Economic, Social and Cultural Rights
TFEU	Treaty on the Functioning of the European Union
TEU	Treay on European Union
UDHR	Universal Declaration of Human Rights
WTO	World Trade Organization
WTD 2003	Working Time Directive 2003

Part One

History and Theory

History

Why has UK labour law developed in the way we see it today? Why does the UK have a minimal floor of rights at work, but with very incomplete enforcement? Why are there limited rights to equal treatment? Why are there rights to join a trade union to get fair terms over the minimum, and basic rights against unjust dismissal? Legal history helps answer questions such as these, and improves us as practising lawyers. To understand what the law 'is' now (or to argue for an interpretation before a tribunal or a court), we must know why laws emerged. This is a fairly standard view of the value of legal history. If history were airbrushed from textbooks, it would diminish our capacity for reasoned argument. When we see things as they are, and ask 'why?', we are empowered to compare the reasons with our experience today. If the original justifications cease to match outcomes, the law should be better interpreted or change (OW Holmes, *The Common Law* (1890) 5).

A second, similar view is that legal history has value because, just as we see the law changed before, we see it can change again. We cannot only see things as they are and ask 'why?' but imagine things that never were and ask 'why not?' (cf GB Shaw, *Back to Methuselah* (1921) Act I, §i) A serious academic argument was made in 1990 that there was an 'end of history' after the fall of the Berlin Wall. Liberal democracy, based on a market economy, had triumphed. Soon, labour law was implicated as it was said shareholder dominance of corporate governance was superior to systems where labour has a meaningful voice at work (H Hansmann and R Kraakman, 'The End of History for Corporate Law' (2000) 89 Georgetown Law Journal 439). These arguments appeal to the superiority of a fixed social or economic model. To test whether they are right or wrong, we can use theoretical and empirical research, and history provides a wealth of data. This chapter sketches the turning points, from feudalism, to industrial revolution, to today.

(1) SLAVERY, SERFDOM AND THE COMMONS

Legal subordination of some people to others was an integral part of ancient economies. When the Domesday Book was compiled by William the Conqueror for levying taxes in 1086, at least 12 per cent of people were recorded as free, 30 per cent as serfs, 35 per cent as subservient bordars and cottars, and 9 per cent as slaves (DD McGarry, *Medieval History and Civilization* (1976) 242). The King monopolised all power through force, without any distinction between political and economic control. The aristocracy were originally military commanders, delegated rights of land ownership by the Crown. With land came people. Discontent about taxation among the barons during the Third Crusade led to the Magna Carta 1215 being signed by King John. One of the promises included rights for barons to representation in what became Parliament, so as not to be taxed without their consent (clause 12).

In contrast, 'commoners' were given rights under clauses 47 and 48 to land that had been increasingly been taken over by the Crown ('afforested') in the last century. This formed the basis of the Charter of the Forest 1217, the foundation for the right of free people to use and work on common property. Yet for the majority, still legally tied to their landlords, the character of labour relations did not alter until the Black Death in 1348, when England probably had around 3.3 million inhabitants. Plague probably halved Europe's population, and killed 60 per cent of London. Among survivors, many serfs and slaves suddenly found they had no lords, and lords found there was a labour shortage, pressing wages to rise. In response, Edward III's Ordinance of Labourers 1349 required that all unfree *and* 'free' people had to work if they were needed, for wages no higher than the local custom. Leaving the employer or failing to work was criminal. Building on this, the Statute of Labourers 1351, blaming the 'malice of servants, who were idle and refused to serve after the pestilence', specified the wage rates for different work. It was enforced by Justices of the Peace. Along with their officials they were generally despised (LR Poos, 'The Social Context of the Statute of Labourers Enforcement' (1983) 1(1) *Law and History Review* 27, 31–33). But enforcement did not work. Falling profits for landlords meant falling revenue for the Crown. It introduced a poll tax in 1377, and triggered the Peasants' Revolt in 1381, chronicled by the French observer Jean Froissart.

J Froissart, *The Chronicles of Froissart* (1385) Translated by GC Macaulay (1895) 250–52

It was a marvellous thing and of poor foundation that this mischief began in England, and to give ensample to all manner of people I will speak thereof as it was done, as I was informed, and of the incidents thereof. There was an usage in England, and yet is in divers countries, that the noblemen hath great franchise over the commons and keepeth them in servage, that is to say, their tenants ought by custom to labour the lords' lands, to gather and bring home their corns, and some to thresh and to fan, and by servage to make their hay and to hew their wood and bring it home. All these things they ought to do by servage, and there be more of these people in England than in any other realm.

Thus the noblemen and prelates are served by them, and specially in the county of Kent, Essex, Sussex and Bedford. These unhappy people of these said countries began to stir, because they said they were kept in great servage, and in the beginning of the world, they said, there were no bondmen, wherefore they maintained that none ought to be bond, without he did treason to his lord, as Lucifer did to God; but they said they could have no such battle, for they were neither angels nor spirits, but men formed to the similitude of their lords, saying why should they then be kept so under like beasts; the which they said they would no longer suffer, for they would be all one, and if they laboured or did anything for their lords, they would have wages therefor as well as other. And of this imagination was a foolish priest in the country of Kent called John Ball, for the which foolish words he had been three times in the bishop of Canterbury's prison: for this priest used oftentimes on the Sundays after mass, when the people were going out of the minster, to go into the cloister and preach, and made the people to assemble about him, and would say thus:

'Ah, ye good people, the matters goeth not well to pass in England, nor shall not do till everything be common, and that there be no villains nor gentlemen, but that we may be all unied together, and that the lords be no greater masters than we be.

What have we deserved, or why should we be kept thus in servage? We be all come from one father and one mother, Adam and Eve: whereby can they say or shew that they be greater lords than we be, saving by that they cause us to win and labour for that they dispend?

They are clothed in velvet and camlet furred with grise, and we be vestured with poor cloth: they have their wines, spices and good bread, and we have the drawing out of the chaff and drink water: they dwell in fair houses, and we have the pain and travail, rain and wind in the fields; and by that that cometh of our labours they keep and maintain their estates: we be called their bondmen, and without we do readily them service, we be beaten; and we have no sovereign to whom we may complain, nor that will hear us nor do us right.

Let us go to the king, he is young, and shew him what servage we be in, and shew him how we will have it otherwise, or else we will provide us of some remedy; and if we go together, all manner of people that be now in any bondage will follow us to the intent to be made free; and when the king seeth us, we shall have some remedy, either by fairness or otherwise.'

Thus John Ball said on Sundays, when the people issued out of the churches in the villages; wherefore many of the mean people loved him, and such as intended to no goodness said how he said truth; and so they would murmur one with another in the fields and in the ways as they went together, affirming how John Ball said truth.

NOTES AND QUESTIONS

1. John Ball's sermons, as reconstructed by Froissart, highlight an old fact of employment: that employers appropriate, or take property over, the benefits that his workers' labour produces: 'by that that cometh of our labours they keep and maintain their estates'. Ball's solution is that 'everything be common' so that the 'lords be no greater masters than we be'. Ball was imprisoned and tortured, before being released, but then joined Wat Tyler and marched on London. They met with the King's delegation, which was purporting to offer peace and compromise. The King was lying, and he had all the rebels killed.
2. Lord Sumption, elevated to the UK Supreme Court in 2012, describes Ball as 'an ideologue, a prophet and a seer' who embraced 'an intense, messianic utopianism which ultimately rejected all political authority, lay and ecclesiastical' (J Sumption, *Divided Houses: Hundred Years' War* (2012) vol 3, 422–23). There are few sources, but from Froissart, do you find this to be an accurate representation of Ball's preaching?
3. Geoffrey Chaucer's famous compendium of pilgrim stories, *The Canterbury Tales* (1380–1400) gives us a stylised cross-section of well-to-do professions in this period: a knight, miller, pardoner, nun, reeve, and so on. The wages of those characters were not fixed by the Statute of Labourers 1351, that is except for the 'Plowman', who actually represented the vast majority of the population. But Chaucer never got to write a 'Ploughman's Tale'. *The General Prologue* describes him as treating his neighbours well 'at alle times, thogh him gamed or smerte'

(ie people ripped him off) but 'God loved he the beste'. Otherwise, Chaucer gave him no voice during the journey. The Ploughman's wages would have been suppressed to a pre-plague rate that was paid in 1347, and his hire had to extend to a whole year, or according to custom, but not day to day. See M Bailey, 'The Ploughman' in SH Rigby, *Historians on Chaucer* (2014) ch 20, who refers to cases prosecuting ploughmen in R Sillem, *Records of Some Sessions of the Peace in Lincolnshire 1360–1375* (1936). What practical difficulties do you think arise if the state fixes wage scales – maximum, minimum, both – for people at work? What are the possible benefits to partially or completely replacing employer–employee wage bargaining with government wage orders?

4. After the plague, serfdom and slavery among English people was in terminal decline (EP Cheyney, 'The Disappearance of English Serfdom' (1900) 15(57) *English Historical Review* 20). By 1523, a judge of the Common Pleas, Anthony Fitzherbert, wrote that servitude had become 'the greatest inconvenience that nowe is suffred by the lawe. That is to have any christen man bounden to an other, and to have the rule of his body, landes, and goodes, that his wyfe, children, and servantes have laboured for, all their life tyme, to be so taken, lyke as it were extorcion or bribery' (A Fitzherbert, *Surueyenge* (1546) 31).

5. While servitude dwindled, people who were 'free', if not literally compelled to work by the Statute of Labourers 1351, remained practically compelled unless they could forge a living on common land or waters. The Charter of the Forest 1217, which governed public access rights to common land persisted, and generated a large volume of case law for centuries (still largely unresearched). However, the Inclosure Acts gradually brought this to an end, privatising previously common land. A large incentive to do this came from the greater profits that could be earned by landowners from livestock. Sir Thomas More, Lord Chancellor from 1529 to 1532, described the process in the early sixteenth century, through the voice of his fictional character Raphael Hythloday, in conversation with a Cardinal, a lawyer and More himself listening.

T More, *Utopia* (1516) Book I
Translated by P Turner (Penguin edn 2004)*

'But that's not the only thing that compels people to steal. There are other factors at work which must, I think, be peculiar to your country.'

'And what are they?' asked the Cardinal.

'Sheep,' I told him. 'These placid creatures, which used to require so little food, have now apparently developed a raging appetite, and turned into man-eaters. Fields, houses, forests, towns, everything goes down their throats. To put it more plainly, in those parts of the kingdom where the finest, and so the most expensive wool is produced, the nobles and gentlemen, not to mention several saintly abbots, have grown dissatisfied with the income that their predecessors got out of their estates. They're no longer content to lead lazy, comfortable lives, which do no good to society – they must actively do it harm, by enclosing all the land they can for pasture, and leaving none for cultivation. They're even tearing down houses and demolishing whole towns – except, of course, for the churches, which they preserve for use as sheepfolds. As though they didn't waste enough of your soil already on their coverts and game-preserves,

* Reproduced by permission of Penguin Books Ltd.

these kind souls have started destroying all traces of human habitation, and turning every scrap of farmland into a wilderness.

So what happens? Each greedy individual preys on his native land like a malignant growth, absorbing field after field, and enclosing thousands of acres with a single fence. Result – hundreds of farmers are evicted. They're either cheated or bullied into giving up their property, or systematically ill-treated until they're finally forced to sell. Whichever way it's done, out the poor creatures have to go, men and women, husbands and wives, widows and orphans, mothers and tiny children, together with all their employees, whose great numbers are not a sign of wealth, but simply of the fact that you can't run a farm without plenty of manpower. Out they have to go from the homes they know so well, and they can't find anywhere else to live. Their whole stock of furniture wouldn't fetch much of a price, even if they could afford to wait for a suitable offer. But they can't, so they get very little indeed for it. By the time they've been wandering around for a bit, this little is all used up, and then what can they do but steal – and be very properly hanged? Of course, they can always become tramps and beggars, but even then they're liable to be arrested as vagrants, and put in prison for being idle – when nobody will give them a job, however much they want one. After all, it only takes one shepherd or cowherd to graze animals over an area that would need any amount of labour to make it fit for corn production.

'For the same reason, corn is much dearer in many districts. The price of wool has also risen so steeply that your poorer weavers simply can't afford to buy it, which means a lot more people thrown out of work. This is partly due to an epidemic of the rot, which destroyed vast numbers of sheep just after the conversion of arable to pasture land began. It almost looked like a judgement on the landowners for their greed – except that *they* ought to have caught it instead of the sheep.'

'Not that prices would fall, however many sheep there were, for the sheep market has become, if not strictly a monopoly – for that implies only one seller – then at least an oligopoly. I mean it's almost entirely under the control of a few rich men, who don't need to sell unless they feel like it, and never do feel like it until they can get the price they want. This also accounts for the equally high prices of other types of livestock, especially in view of the shortage of breeders caused by the demolition of farms, and the general decline of agriculture. For the rich men I'm talking about never bother to breed either sheep or cattle themselves. They merely buy scraggy specimens cheap from someone else, fatten them up on their own pastures, and resell them at a large profit. I imagine that's why the full effects of the situation have not yet been felt. So far they've only inflated prices in the areas where they sell, but, if they keep transferring animals from other districts faster than they can be replaced, stocks in the buying areas too will gradually be depleted, until eventually there'll be an acute shortage everywhere.

'Thus a few greedy people have converted one of England's greatest natural advantages into a national disaster. For it's the high price of food that makes employers turn off so many of their servants – which inevitably means turning them into beggars or thieves. And theft comes easier to a man of spirit.

'To make matters worse, this wretched poverty is most incongruously linked with expensive tastes. Servants, tradesmen, even farm-labourers, in fact all classes of society are recklessly extravagant about clothes and food. Then think how many brothels there are, including those that go under the names of wine-taverns or ale-houses. Think of the demoralizing games people play – dice, cards, backgammon, tennis, bowls, quoits – what are they but quick methods of wasting a man's money, and sending him straight off to become a thief? Get rid of these pernicious practices. Make a law that anyone responsible for demolishing a farm or a country town must either rebuild it himself or else hand over the land to someone who's willing to do so. Stop the rich from cornering markets and establishing virtual monopolies. Reduce the number of people who are kept doing nothing. Revive agriculture and the wool industry, so that there is plenty of honest, useful work for the great army of unemployed – by which I mean not only existing thieves, but tramps and idle servants who are bound to become thieves eventually.

1. Book I of More's *Utopia* is a dialogue in Latin between a quiet and observant More, an unnamed obnoxious lawyer, a Cardinal and a traveller called Raphael Hythloday (who is in the first person here) on the state of English society, compared with other fictional lands that Hythloday has visited. In Book II, Hythloday describes *Utopia*, a supposedly 'ideal' society from which England might learn. *Utopia* is properly interpreted as an ironic reply to Plato's *Republic*. More did not think that a 'perfect' society could be created without unacceptable controls on personal freedom. The giveaways are in the names 'Utopia' (Greek for 'no place') and 'Hythloday' (which means 'Nonsenso'), as well as the descriptions of life in Utopia itself. Much 'utopian' literature missed this basic point as it attempted to construct theories of ideal worlds (perhaps the most unwittingly comical and recent example is R Nozick, *Anarchy, State and Utopia* (1977)). *Utopia*'s true value is a covert critique of English society: open criticism was impossible at the time. Indeed, as Lord Chancellor, More refused to give his blessing to Henry VIII's reformation and split from the Catholic Church, and was executed in 1535.
2. More's passage highlights human dispossession through structural economic change (crops to sheep), legal change (the Inclosure Acts), the resulting 'great army of unemployed' and the criminalisation of the poor. 'Placid' sheep become instruments of social destruction under the 'control of a few rich men'. The possession by these men of property, and their refusal to supply, allows them to raise prices because they 'don't need to sell unless they feel like it, and never do feel like it until they can get the price they want.' Thus More argues unemployment results from unequal distribution of resources. Is this convincing? What factors do you think contribute to unemployment?
3. To deal with the unemployed, a Vagrancy Act 1547 stated that the homeless would be placed in servitude or slavery for a second offence. It was repealed after Kett's Rebellion in 1549, but enclosure and vagrancy continued. The first Poor Act 1575 empowered parishes to put paupers into workhouses. This also had little success.
4. Further on, More wrote: 'As for the theory that peace is best preserved by keeping the people poor, it's completely contradicted by the facts. Beggars are far the most quarrelsome section of the community. Who is more likely to start a revolution than a man who's discontented with his present living conditions? Who could have a stronger impulse to turn everything upside down in the hope of personal profit than a man who'd got nothing to lose? No, if a king is so hated or despised by his subjects that he can't keep them in order unless he reduces them to beggary by violence, extortion, and confiscation, he'd far better abdicate. Such methods of staying in power may preserve the title, but they destroy the majesty of a king. There's nothing majestic about ruling a nation of beggars – true majesty consists in governing the rich and prosperous.' Do you agree?
5. The Statute of Artificers 1562 continued to regulate wages, free movement and training for specified classes of worker. Section 15 allowed justices of the peace to fix yearly wage schedules for the locality. This system, though enforcement was very defective, remained in place until the late eighteenth century. See further, S Deakin and F Wilkinson, 'The Origins of the Contract of Employment' in *The Law of the Labour Market* (2005) ch 2.

6. From this time, English labour law (of sorts) began to reach abroad, first with the East India Company (established 1600). The Royal Africa Company was created in 1660, which enslaved people in Western Africa, and brought them to work in British American colonies. Shortly after the United Kingdom formed in 1707, the South Sea Company was incorporated to trade slaves in South America. Sale of its stocks, and the fact that it actually failed to produce anything, precipitated the world's first stock market crash, further tarnishing the reputation of an already mistrusted institution: the corporation (A Smith, *The Wealth of Nations* (1776) Book V, ch I, §107). Although slavery was an integral part of the growing British Empire's economy, it was equally reviled, and was finally declared unlawful at common law by one phenomenal judgment in 1772.

Somerset v Stewart (1772) 98 ER 499

James Somerset claimed that he was free, and that Charles Stewart could not enforce his title to Somerset as a slave owner, despite having purchased Somerset while in Boston, Massachusetts (then a British colony). Stewart had brought Somerset to England in 1769. In 1771, Somerset escaped. He was baptised, with three new 'godparents' (who were abolitionist campaigners). In November he was recaptured and imprisoned on a ship that would travel to Jamaica where Somerset would be forced to labour on the plantations. The godparents applied on Somerset's behalf for a writ of habeas corpus, supported by other abolitionist campaigners and donors. Somerset's counsel contended that, although colonial laws might permit slavery, neither English common law nor Parliament recognised it. Slavery was, therefore, unlawful. A contract for slavery was unlawful in English common law. Stewart's counsel contended that the right of property was inviolable, and the consequences of any decision otherwise would be dangerous, as around 15,000 slaves were in England at that time.

Lord Mansfield: Mr. Stewart advances no claim on contract; he rests his whole demand on a right to the negro as slave, and mentions the purpose of detainure to be the sending of him over to be sold in Jamaica. If the parties will have judgment, *fiat justitia, ruat cœlum*, let justice be done whatever be the consequence. 50*l.* a head may not be a high price; then a loss follows to the proprietors of above 700,000*l.* sterling. How would the law stand with respect to their settlement; their wages? How many actions for any slight coercion by the master? We cannot in any of these points direct the law; the law must rule us. In these particulars, it may be matter of weighty consideration, what provisions are made or set by law. Mr. Stewart may end the question, by discharging or giving freedom to the negro.

[Despite Lord Mansfield's encouragement, no settlement was reached, and he gave judgment.]

We pay due attention to the opinion of Sir Philip York and Mr. Talbot in the year 1729, by which they pledged themselves to the British planters for the legal consequences of bringing slaves into this kingdom, or their being baptized; which opinion was repeated and recognized by Lord Hardwicke, sitting as Chancellor on the 19th of October, 1749. ...

...

The cause returned is, the slave absented himself, and departed from his master's service, and refused to return and serve him during his stay in England; whereupon, by his master's orders, he was put on board the ship by force, and there detained in secure custody, to be carried out of the kingdom and sold. So high an act of dominion must derive its authority, if any such it has, from the law of the kingdom where executed. A foreigner cannot be imprisoned here on the authority of any law existing in his own country: the power of a master over his servant is different in all countries, more or less limited or extensive; the exercise of it therefore must always be regulated by the laws of the place where exercised.

The state of slavery is of such a nature, that it is incapable of now being introduced by Courts of Justice upon mere reasoning or inferences from any principles, natural or political; it must take its rise from positive law; the origin of it can in no country or age be traced back to any other source: immemorial usage preserves the memory of positive law long after all traces of the occasion; reason, authority, and time of its introduction are lost; and in a case so odious as the condition of slaves must be taken strictly, the power claimed by this return was never in use here; no master ever was allowed here to take a slave by force to be sold abroad because he had deserted from his service, or for any other reason whatever; we cannot say the cause set forth by this return is allowed or approved of by the laws of this kingdom, therefore the black must be discharged.

NOTES AND QUESTIONS

1. Lord Mansfield's judgment is one of the most important in the history of international law. First, he identifies that (in conflict-of-laws principles) the applicable law must be the jurisdiction where the purported slave physically is at the date of trial. Second, Lord Mansfield effectively identifies a *jus cogens* norm (in public international law) that slavery is unlawful in *every* jurisdiction, unless legitimised by positive law.

2. Before giving final judgment, Lord Mansfield says: *'fiat justitia, ruat cœlum*, let justice be done whatever be the consequence.' This is a philosophical rejection of empiricism: that the value of a law can be measured by its effects. It follows the view that some principles are so basic, there should be no empirical enquiry into their validity. Do you agree? Can you think of 'principle'-based arguments that people would have made for slavery? Are there strong consequentialist arguments against slavery?

3. Four years later, in 1776, thirteen American colonies declared independence. There were multiple causes of the Revolution: in the North, people demanded no taxation without representation. But in the South, with an agricultural economy dependent on slaves, Lord Mansfield's judgment was a major grievance: quite a 'consequence'. See AW Blumrosen, 'The Profound Influence in America of Lord Mansfield's Decision in *Somerset v Stuart*' (2007) 13 *Texas Wesleyan Law Review* 645.

4. The transatlantic slave trade counts among the most tremendous crimes against humanity in world history. There were numerous rebellions, inevitably and brutally suppressed, as indeed there have been throughout history (one of the best known was led by Spartacus, in Ancient Rome). Although the slave trade enriched the British Empire's elites, traders and plantation owners, this was a pittance compared to its total economic and humanitarian cost.

5. William Wilberforce was a pioneer of the campaign that eventually produced the Slave Trade Act 1807, which abolished the *trade* within the Empire, and the Slavery Abolition Act 1833, which abolished slavery everywhere in the Empire, except areas finally dealt with by Indian Slavery Act 1843. The 1833 Act provided market rate compensation for all slave owners, but kept former slaves bonded to their 'employers' for a further six years. Details of the compensation paid, which

amounted to history's largest 'bailout' until the banking crisis of 2007–08, are now online: ucl.ac.uk/lbs

6.   A famous indictment of slavery, but still justifying colonisation of the 'new world' and genocide of native inhabitants, is J Locke, *Second Treatise on Civil Government* (1689) chs IV and V, §§36–37. From the Vagabonds Act 1597 (39 Eliz c 4) penal transportation was introduced to ship people to America, and later Australia, extended by the Transportation Act 1717. Many also chose to emigrate from the desperate poverty generated by the industrial revolution.

(2) FREEDOM OF CONTRACT

By the start of the industrial revolution, mass enslavement was gradually being brought to an end in the Commonwealth, serfdom no longer existed, but 'freedom' of people to work on terms they chose was constrained. Economically, people who had no property were still practically compelled to work for others, or starve. Legally, the Master and Servant Acts criminalised leaving an employer in breach of contract: according to W Blackstone, *Commentaries* (1765) Book I, ch 14 the standard duration, under the Statute of Labourers 1351, was still one year. Employers could organise trusts and partnerships, or ask Parliament to grant a corporation's charter, to amalgamate their proprietary power. But organisations of workers to collectively bargain were prohibited. In other words, although there was freedom to contract, the rich were far more free than the poor.

Historians typically date the industrial revolution to the 1780s, when manufacturing production took off, beyond anything previously known.[1] But the wealth generated was not shared equitably. The poverty of work in early industrial Britain inspired the poet William Blake to write about 'dark Satanic Mills' and call to build a new 'Jerusalem' in 'England's green & pleasant Land' (1808). Politically, this was difficult because there was no representation in the UK for the vast majority of people to shape the laws that governed their lives. The response of Parliament to domestic unrest inspired by the revolutions in America (1776) and France (1781) involved suppression of almost any labour or democratic association. But over the course of the nineteenth century, laissez-faire theory became common currency, centred around the notion of 'freedom of contract'. Initially, this ideal represented liberation from the perspective of workers, but eventually it was used to justify suppression of labour organisations. A classic episode in the story of liberation was the 'Tolpuddle Martyrs'.

R v Lovelass (1834) 172 ER 1380

James Lovelass and five others were prosecuted under the Unlawful Oaths 1797 and Unlawful Societies Act 1799 for a organising a union to improve their wages. Specifically, the account of Edward Legg, a witness, was as follows:

> I went with the last witness; they told us something about striking, or that they meant to strike, and that we might do the same if we liked. There was nothing said about the time when we should

---

[1]   See E Hobsbawm, *The Age of Revolution* (1962) ch 2.

strike. There was something said about our masters having notice of it, but I don't remember any-thing about it. We kissed a book when we were blinded. When we were on our knees, we repeated something that was said by somebody, but who said it I don't know. I believe it was like the voice of James Lovelass. I think the words which we repeated were something about being plunged into eternity, and about keeping secret what was done by the society. I don't know what book it was that I kissed. When I was unblinded I saw a book on the table that resembled a Testament. They shewed us the picture of death, and one of them said, 'Remember your end!'

The Court read the following directions to the jury.

Williams B: If you are satisfied that an oath, or obligation tantamount to an oath, was admin-istered to either of the witnesses Legg or Lock by means of the prisoners, you ought to find them guilty. The prisoners are indicted under the [Unlawful Oaths Act 1797], the preamble of which refers to seditious and mutinous societies; but I am of opinion that the enacting part of the statute extends to all societies of an illegal nature: and the second section of the [Unlawful Societies Act 1799], enacts that all societies shall be illegal, the members whereof shall, accord-ing to the rules thereof, be required to take an oath or engagement not required by law. If you are satisfied from the evidence respecting the blinding, the kneeling, and the other facts proved, that an oath or obligation was imposed on the witnesses, or either of them, you ought to find the prisoners guilty; and if you come to that conclusion, I wish you to state whether you are of opinion that the prisoners were united in a society.

NOTE

1.   This case report extract exemplifies the way in which legal abstraction, in splendid technical solitude, can obscure social reality. It discusses the concept of 'oaths', and various requisite components to prove that an unlawful oath was taken. What was really happening was explained later by the Webbs.

S Webb and B Webb, *The History of Trade Unionism* (1894) ch 3, 144–48

The story of the trial and transportation of the Dorchester labourers is the best-known episode of early Trade Union history. The agricultural labourers of the southern counties, oppressed by the tacit combinations of the farmers and by the operation of the Corn Laws, as well as exceptionally demoralised by the Old Poor Law, had long been in a state of sullen despair. The specially hard times of 1829 had resulted in outbursts of machine-breaking, rick-burning, and hunger riots, which had been put down in 1830 by the movement of troops through the disturbed districts, and the appointment of a Special Commission of Assize to try over 1000 prisoners, several of whom were hung and hundreds transported. The whole wage-earning population of these rural dis-tricts was effectually cowed. With the improvement of trade a general movement for high wages seems to have been set on foot. In 1832 we find the Duke of Wellington, as Lord-Lieutenant of Hampshire, reporting to Lord Melbourne that more than half the labourers in his county were contributing a penny per week to a network of local societies affiliated, as he thought, to some National Union. "The labourers said that they had received directions from the Union not to take less than ten shillings, and that the Union would stand by them."

These societies, whatever may have been their constitution, had apparently the effect of raising wages not only in Hampshire, but also in the neighbouring counties. In the village of Tolpuddle, in Dorsetshire, as George Loveless tells us, an agreement was made between the farmers and the men, in the presence of the village parson, that the wages should be those paid in other districts. This involved a rise to ten shillings a week. In the following year the farmers repented of their decision, and successively reduced wages shilling by shilling until they were paying only seven shillings a week. In this strait the men made inquiries about "the Trades Union," and two delegates from the Grand National visited the village. Upon their information the Lovelesses established "the Friendly Society of Agricultural Labourers," having its "Grand Lodge" at Tolpuddle. For this village club the elaborate ritual and code of rules of one of the national orders of the Grand National Consolidated Trades Union were adopted. No secrecy seems to have been observed, for John Loveless openly ordered of the village painter a figure of "Death painted six feet high for a society of his own," with which to perform the initiation rites. The farmers took alarm, and induced the local magistrates, on February 21, 1834, to issue placards warning the labourers that any one joining the Union would be sentenced to seven years' transportation. This was no idle threat. Within three days of the publication of the notice the Lovelesses and four other members were arrested and lodged in gaol.

The trial of these unfortunate labourers was a scandalous perversion of the law. The Lovelesses and their friends seem to have been simple-minded Methodists, two of them being itinerant preachers. No accusation was made, and no evidence preferred against them, of anything worse than the playing with oaths, which, as we have seen, formed a part of the initiation ceremony of the Grand National and other Unions of the time, with evidently no consciousness of their statutory illegality. Not only were they guiltless of any intimidation or outrage, but they had not even struck or presented any application for higher wages. Yet the judge (John Williams), who had only recently been raised to the bench, charged the grand jury on the case at portentous length, as if the prisoners had committed murder or treason, and inflicted on them, after the briefest of trials, the monstrous sentence of seven years' transportation.

The action of the Government shows how eagerly the Home Secretary accepted the blunder of an inexperienced judge as part of his policy of repression. Lord Melbourne expressed his opinion that "the law has in this case been most properly applied"; and the sentence, far from exciting criticism in the Whig Cabinet, was carried out with special celerity. The case was tried on March 1834; before the 30th the prisoners were in the hulks and by the 15th of the next month Lord Howick was able to say in the House of Commons that their ship had already sailed for Botany Bay.

The Grand National Consolidated Trades Union prove to have a wider influence than the Government expect

The whole machinery of the organisation was turned to the preparation of petitions and the holding of public meetings, and a wave of sympathy rallied, for a few weeks, the drooping energies of the members. Cordial relations were established with the five great Unions which remained outside the ranks, for the northern counties were mainly organised by the Builders' Union, the Leeds, Huddersfield and Bradford District Union, the Clothiers' Union, the Cotton-spinners' Union, and the Potters' Union, which on this occasion sent delegates to London to assist the executive of the Grand National. The agitation culminated in a monster procession of Trade Unionists to the Home Office to present a petition to Lord Melbourne the first of the great "demonstrations" which have since become a regular part of the machinery of London politics. The proposal to hold this procession had excited the utmost alarm, both in friends and to foes. The Times, with the Parisian events of 1830 still in its memory, wrote leader after leader condemning the project, and Lord Melbourne let it be known that he would refuse to receive any deputation or petition from a procession. Special constables were sworn in, and troops brought into London to prevent a rising. ...

... The demonstration, in point of numbers, was undoubtedly a success. We learn, for instance, that the tailors alone paraded from 5000 to 7000 strong, and the master builders subsequently complained that their works had been entirely suspended through their men's participation. Over a quarter of a million signatures had been obtained to the petition, and, even on the admission of the Times, 30,000 persons took part in the procession, representing a proportion of the London of that time equivalent to 100,000 to-day.

Meanwhile Radicals of all shades hastened to the rescue. A public meeting was held at the Crown and Anchor Tavern at which Roebuck, Colonel Perronet Thompson, and Daniel O'Connell spoke; and a debate took place in the House of Commons in which the ferocious sentence was strongly attacked by Joseph Hume. But the Government, far from remitting the punishment, refused even to recognise that it was excessive; and the unfortunate labourers were allowed to proceed to their penal exile.

...

[Footnote] The agitation for their release was kept up, both in and out Parliament, by the "London Dorchester Committee"; and in 1836 remainder of the sentence was remitted. Through official blundering it was two years later (April 1838) before five out of the six prisoners turned home. The sixth, as we learn from a circular of the Committee dated August 20, 1838, had even then not arrived. "Great and lasting honour," writes a well-informed contemporary, "is due to this body of workmen (the London Dorchester Committee), about sixteen in number by whose indefatigable exertions, extending over a period of five year and the valuable assistance of Thomas Wakley, MP for Finsbury, the same Government who banished the men were compelled to pardon them and bring them home free of expense."

NOTES AND QUESTIONS

1. A striking feature of the Webbs' account is the depths of (what are now) human rights violations carried out by the UK government: a criminal sentence for exercising a right of free speech, and then transportation to a colony where the government backed genocide of the indigenous population, and torture of the inhabitants was routine. Popular mobilisation was ineffective at making the government blink during the protest, but the pressure resulted in the commutation of the sentences, and a lasting desire among the trade union movement to change the law.

2. *Commonwealth v Hunt*, 45 Mass 111 (1842) is an example of the international ramifications of *R v Lovelass*. A few years later, the Massachusetts Supreme Court held that English common law was not applicable in its jurisdiction, and organising and taking action to improve wages pursued a legitimate purpose unless proven otherwise.

3. The years preceding the Tolpuddle Martyrs tale had involved significant social upheaval. In the relative calm that followed the defeat of Napoleon in 1815, industrial unrest grew, until in 1830 displaced agricultural workers rioted and destroyed threshing machines in the south of England. The primary cause was common land continuing to be forcibly taken by private landowners under the Inclosure Act 1773 and its successors. See E Hobsbawm and G Rudé, *Captain Swing* (1969).

4. Working people were powerless to prevent the robbery of the commons because to vote for Parliament, people needed 'real' property – ie is a proprietary interest in land. Propelled by the unrest, the so-called Great Reform Act 1832 harmonised the various qualifications for voting: in boroughs an elector needed to have a £10 yearly value of a freehold, and in counties £2 freehold value, £10 copyhold or £50 rental value. This enfranchised roughly 10 per cent of the adult population.

What arguments can you think of against a property qualification for participation in political power? To what extent (if at all) should participation in economic power be different?

5.   Agricultural work could be backbreaking, but might have been a blessing compared with the unspeakable conditions and child labour common in industry.

F Engels, *The Condition of the Working Class in England* (1844) ch 9, The Mining Proletariat

The production of raw materials and fuel for a manufacture so colossal as that of England requires a considerable number of workers. But of all the materials needed for its industries (except wool, which belongs to the agricultural districts), England produces only the minerals: the metals and the coal. While Cornwall possesses rich copper, tin, zinc, and lead mines, Staffordshire, Wales, and other districts yield great quantities of iron, and almost the whole North and West of England, central Scotland, and certain districts of Ireland, produce a superabundance of coal.

In the Cornish mines about 19,000 men, and 11,000 women and children are employed, in part above and in part below ground. Within the mines below ground, men and boys above twelve years old are employed almost exclusively. The condition of these workers seems, according to the Children's Employment Commission's Report, to be comparatively endurable, materially, and the English often enough boast of their strong, bold miners, who follow the veins of mineral below the bottom of the very sea. But in the matter of the health of these workers, this same Children's Employment Commission's Report judges differently. It shows in Dr. Barham's intelligent report how the inhalation of an atmosphere containing little oxygen, and mixed with dust amid the smoke of blasting powder, such as prevails in the mines, seriously affects the lungs, disturbs the action of the heart, and diminishes the activity of the digestive organs; that wearing toil, and especially the climbing up and down of ladders, upon which even vigorous young men have to spend in some mines more than an hour a day, and which precedes and follows daily work, contributes greatly to the development of these evils, so that men who begin this work in early youth are far from reaching the stature of women who work above ground; that many die young of galloping consumption, and most miners at middle age of slow consumption; that they age prematurely and become unfit for work between the thirty-fifth and forty-fifth years; that many are attacked by acute inflammations of the respiratory organs when exposed to the sudden change from the warm air of the shaft (after climbing the ladder in profuse perspiration) to the cold wind above ground; and that these acute inflammations are very frequently fatal. Work above ground, breaking and sorting the ore, is done by girls and children, and is described as very wholesome, being done in the open air. ...

... we find again the lodging-houses and sleeping-places with which we have already become acquainted in the towns, and in quite as filthy, disgusting, and overcrowded a state as there. Commissioner Mitchell visited one such sleeping barrack, 18 feet long, 15 feet wide, and arranged for the reception of 42 men and 14 boys, or 56 persons altogether, one-half of whom slept above the other in berths as on shipboard. There was no opening for the escape of the foul air; and, although no one had slept in this pen for three nights preceding the visit, the smell and the atmosphere were such that Commissioner Mitchell could not endure it a moment. What must it be through a hot summer night, with fifty-six occupants? And this is not the steerage of an American slave ship, it is the dwelling of free-born Britons!

In the coal and iron mines which are worked in pretty much the same way, children of four, five, and seven years are employed. They are set to transporting the ore or coal loosened by the miner from its place to the horse-path or the main shaft, and to opening and shutting the doors (which separate the divisions of the mine and regulate its ventilation) for the passage of workers and material. For watching the doors the smallest children are usually employed, who thus pass twelve hours daily, in the dark, alone, sitting usually in damp passages without even having work enough to save them from the stupefying, brutalising tedium of doing nothing. The transport of coal and iron-stone, on the other hand, is very hard labour, the stuff being shoved in large tubs, without wheels, over the uneven floor of the mine; often over moist clay, or through water, and frequently up steep inclines and through paths so low-roofed that the workers are forced to creep on hands and knees. For this more wearing labour, therefore, older children and half-grown girls are employed. One man or two boys per tub are employed, according to circumstances; and, if two boys, one pushes and the other pulls. The loosening of the ore or coal, which is done by men or strong youths of sixteen years or more, is also very weary work. The usual working-day is eleven to twelve hours, often longer; in Scotland it reaches fourteen hours, and double time is frequent, when all the employees are at work below ground twenty-four, and even thirty-six hours at a stretch. Set times for meals are almost unknown, so that these people eat when hunger and time permit.

The standard of living of the miners is in general described as fairly good and their wages high in comparison with those of the agricultural labourers surrounding them (who, however, live at starvation rates), except in certain parts of Scotland and in the Irish mines, where great misery prevails. ...

The children and young people who are employed in transporting coal and iron-stone all complain of being overtired. Even in the most recklessly conducted industrial establishments there is no such universal and exaggerated overwork. The whole report proves this, with a number of examples on every page. It is constantly happening that children throw themselves down on the stone hearth or the floor as soon as they reach home, fall asleep at once without being able to take a bite of food, and have to be washed and put to bed while asleep; it even happens that they lie down on the way home, and are found by their parents late at night asleep on the road. It seems to be a universal practice among these children to spend Sunday in bed to recover in some degree from the overexertion of the week. Church and school are visited by but few, and even of these the teachers complain of their great sleepiness and the want of all eagerness to learn. The same thing is true of the elder girls and women. They are overworked in the most brutal manner. This weariness, which is almost always carried to a most painful pitch, cannot fail to affect the constitution. The first result of such overexertion is the diversion of vitality to the one-sided development of the muscles, so that those especially of the arms, legs, and back, of the shoulders and chest, which are chiefly called into activity in pushing and pulling, attain an uncommonly vigorous development, while all the rest of the body suffers and is atrophied from want of nourishment.

...

When the Children's Employment Commission's Report was laid before Parliament, Lord Ashley hastened to bring in a bill wholly forbidding the work of women in the mines, and greatly limiting that of children. The bill was adopted, but has remained a dead letter in most districts, because no mine inspectors were appointed to watch over its being carried into effect. The evasion of the law is very easy in the country districts in which the mines are situated; and no one need be surprised that the Miners' Union laid before the Home Secretary an official notice, last year, that in the Duke of Hamilton's coal-mines in Scotland, more than sixty women were at work; or that the Manchester Guardian reported that a girl perished in an explosion in a mine near Wigan, and no one troubled himself further about the fact that an infringement of the law was thus revealed. In single cases the employment of women may have been discontinued, but in general the old state of things remains as before.

NOTES AND QUESTIONS

1. The bill from Lord Ashley, the Tory peer also known as the Earl of Shaftesbury, that this passage refers to was the Mines and Collieries Act 1842. It resulted from the Children's Employment Commission, *First Report of the Commissioners. Mines* (1842) documenting the effects of working in mines on the health of children, county by county across the UK, over thousands of pages. To take just one (ordinary, not bad) case of child labour at random, see Appendix, Part II, 293, Derbyshire, No 110: Richard Clarke 'Is 12 years old. Has worked in a pit five years; drives the ass and wears the belt. … Goes down at five to eight, for a whole day … never receives any rewards and is punished by sticks or anything the loader or corporal lays his hands on … his mother last week got a summons for the loader, who had beaten him with a piece of wood like a trap-bat until his back and head were all over with bruises.'

2. Despite International Labour Organization Conventions 138 and 182 requiring abolition of child labour, the ILO, *Global Trends in Child Labour 2008 to 2012* (2013) estimated 120 million 5 to 14 year olds are in child labour, and 37 million in hazardous work in 2012. This represents an overall 2.7 per cent and 1.2 per cent reduction since 2008. Sub-Saharan Africa had a 21.7 per cent rate of child labour, Asia and the Pacific 8.3 per cent, Latin America and the Caribbean 7.2 per cent, and other regions 4.8 per cent. Should there be criminal penalties for company directors whose subsidiaries or supply chains use child labour?

3. The very long, slow history of factory or health and safety regulation proceeded inch by inch through the nineteenth century to limit child labour, and limit women's labour, in industries such as textiles, mines or manufacturing, limit the working day, require rest breaks, limit night work, and have inspections. See, in particular, the Factory Act 1844. Meanwhile, in the field of tort law, there was a total absence of effective remedies if people were injured or killed at work. The unholy trinity of defence that employers could run were *volenti non fit injuria* (workers 'voluntarily' ran the risk of death or injury at work), contributory negligence (if an accident was partly a worker's 'fault', they were completely barred from compensation), and common employment (people 'accepted' being injured or killed by their co-workers).

4. Democratic reform was slow. In the view of the Prime Minister Lord Palmerston, in a letter to Lord Russell of October 1862, 'Power in the Hands of the Masses throws the Scum of the Community to the Surface. … Truth and Justice are soon banished from the Land.' Others took a different view, and after various aborted attempts by the Liberal Party, the Conservative Prime Minister Disraeli managed to pass the Reform Act 1867. The right to vote came with a £10 pa rental value of any lodger's home in boroughs, and £12 pa value in counties. It enfranchised roughly 20 per cent of the adult population.

5. Within the Liberal Party, a leading opponent of the 1867 Act was also the author of the first modern company laws, Robert Lowe MP, who subsequently became Chancellor of the Exchequer. In opposing the Act, he said this: 'This principle of equality which you have taken to worship, is a very jealous power; she cannot be worshipped by halves. … When you get a democratic basis for your institutions,

> you must remember that you cannot look at that alone, but you must look at it in reference to all your other institutions. When you have once taught the people to entertain the notion of the individual rights of every citizen to share in the Government, and the doctrine of popular supremacy, you impose on yourselves the task of re-modelling the whole of your institutions, in reference to the principles that you have set up ... the elite of the working classes you are so fond of, are members of trades unions ... founded on principles of the most grinding tyranny not so much against masters as against each other. ... It was only necessary that you should give them the franchise, to make those trades unions the most dangerous political agencies that could be conceived; because they were in the hands, not of individual members, but of designing men, able to launch them in solid mass against the institutions of the country' (HC Hansard Debs (15 July 1867) vol 188, cols 1543–46).
>
> 6.   As the Act passed, the Queen's Bench in *Hornby v Close* (1867) LR 2 QB 153 decided that maybe all trade unions were illegal as a general principle, as its objects were in 'restraint of trade'. This propelled Disraeli to appoint a Commission on union laws.

Eleventh and Final Report of the Royal Commissioners appointed to Inquire into the Organization and Rules of Trades Unions and Other Associations (1868–69)

(60.) With regard to the general question of the right of workmen to combine together for determining and stipulating with their employer the terms on which only the will consent to work for him, we think that, provided the combination be perfectly voluntary, and that full liberty be left to all other workmen to undertake the work which the parties combining have refused, and that no obstruction be placed in the way of the employer resorting elsewhere in search of a supply of labour, there is no ground of justice or of policy for withholding such a right from the workmen. It cannot be doubted that a demand backed by the resolution of a large body of workmen to decline work if the demand be not acceded to, comes with more force than that of an isolated workman; and we think that the workmen may reasonably claim to be allowed any advantage which they can derive from such concerted action, in bargaining with their employer from time to time as to the terms on which they will dispose of their labour.

(61.) In every bargain there is, more or less, a struggle between the buyer and the seller, the seller desiring to get as much as he can, and the buyer to pay as little as possible; but, as between the employer and the workmen, there is in general this advantage on the side of the employer, that he can more easily wait – i.e., can hold out longer than the workman. Moreover, the holding out singly of any one workman out of a large number does not much affect the employer; his works go on, though perhaps not in complete efficiency, until a further supply of labour is obtained; but the workman is generally in such a position that he must starve unless he either accept the terms offered, or is able speedily to find work elsewhere. He in general cannot wait. It is to redress this inequality that the power of combining is justified by the promoters of trades unions.

    ...

(81.) The distinction we propose to draw is to allow registration in the one case, so that a trades union whose rules and byelaws were found by the Registering Officer to be unobjectionable, would be entitled to be registered, and acquire the benefits intended to be conferred by such registration; while in the other case a trades union whose rules and byelaws were found by him to be framed for the promotion of certain objects deemed objectionable, which we shall presently specify, would not be entitled to registration so long as the objectionable rules and byelaws should remain.

...

(83.) These [objectionable] objects are:
1. To prevent the employment or to limit the number of apprentices in any trade.
2. To prevent the introduction or to limit the use of machinery in any trade or manufacture.
3. To prevent any workman from taking a sub-contract, or working by the piece, or working in common with men not members of the union.
4. To authorize interference, in the way of support from the funds of the union, by the council or governing body of the union, with the workmen of any other union when out on strike, or when otherwise engaged in any dispute with their employer, in any case in which such other union is an unconnected union.

...

DISSENT (III.)

We, the undersigned, Commissioners appointed by Your Majesty, find ourselves reluctantly compelled to dissent from the foregoing Report, in which we are unable to concur for the following reasons:—

It is in our opinion essential to any serious amendment of the law relating to trades unions that the doctrine of the Common Law whereby it is presumed that all combinations, whether of workmen or employers, are unlawful, and according to some authorities are punishable as conspiracies – a doctrine, we must observe, which has long had none but indirect effects – should be broadly and unequivocally rescinded.

...

We are of the opinion that no adequate ground has been shown for the continuance of special laws relating exclusively to the employment of labour.

NOTES AND QUESTIONS

1. The particular 'special law' referred to was the Combinations of Workmen Act 1825, which made organisation illegal, and picketing criminal. The split between the Conservative majority and the Liberal minority comes down to two essential rules, which remain an intense source of controversy today. These are what are called the 'closed shop' and 'secondary action'. Unions have always sought to agree with employers that new employees be enrolled in the union, and have always aimed to take collective action against anyone who could influence their pay and conditions (not just the employer identified by a contract). The Minority report simply favoured total repeal of all special laws. See HW McCready, 'British Labour and the Royal Commission on Trade Unions 1867–1869' (1955) 24(4) *University of Toronto Quarterly* 390.
2. In the event, the Liberal government won the 1868 election, and the Trade Union Act 1871 was passed on the model suggested by the Minority Report. See Hansard HC Deb 14 (February 1871) vol 204, cols 257–73. Sections 2 and 3 stated trade union rules and agreements were not to be criminal or void, even if (in the courts'

view) they were in restraint of trade. With the intention of keeping courts away from union affairs, section 4 provided that no proceedings should enforce agreements between members, or use of funds, but nothing would make those agreements unlawful.

3.   The Conspiracy and Protection of Property Act 1875, passed by Disraeli's next Conservative government, dealt with a lingering question of picketing and strikes. Section 7 provided that peaceful picketing, 'merely to obtain or communicate information', was lawful, while section 3 introduced the 'golden formula'. Any 'act in contemplation or furtherance of a trade dispute' would not be a conspiracy or crime if it was lawful when done by one person.

4.   In *Allen v Flood* [1898] AC 1, the House of Lords held that a union could not be sued for refusing to work with non-union workers: a strike against the employer, even if it was 'malicious', if no unlawful means were used, and no pre-existing right was infringed, was unlawful. As the workers were hired day to day, they technically did not need to threaten breach of contract. It was thought by many that the Lords had effectively held trade disputes to be out of the scope of litigation. Presumably, it was also open for the courts to say that there is an implied contractual right to cease work in contemplation or furtherance of a trade dispute. This could be contracted out of, for instance by a 'no strike' clause in a collective agreement, but an individual agreement could hardly exclude this right because it would not reflect the true agreement of the parties.

5.   A differently constituted House of Lords then changed its mind over an infamous trilogy of cases. *Taff Vale Railway Co v Amalgamated Society of Railway Servants* [1901] UKHL 1 held that trade unions could be liable in tort for economic loss to employers resulting from an employee (purportedly) breaching a contract of employment: this was the 'unlawful means'. *Quinn v Leathem* [1901] UKHL 2 held that a combination of people intending to cause economic harm would be unlawful, even though, for a single person, it would be regarded as legitimate competition. *South Wales Miners' Federation v Glamorgan Coal Co* [1905] AC 239 held that it was no defence to have an honest desire to improve wages if the result was harm to an employer. *Quinn* inspired one of the most important articles in legal theory's history, condemning its reasoning, in WN Hohfeld, 'Some Fundamental Legal Conceptions as Applied in Judicial Reasoning' (1913) 23 *Yale Law Journal* 16, 42 ff. The *Taff Vale* case caused the meeting of a Labour Representation Committee at Farringdon Hall, which led to the creation of a Labour Party that would campaign for Parliament.

6.   The 1905 election returned a Liberal government, more radical than ever before, pushed by the return of 29 Labour MPs. One of the first Acts was the Trade Disputes Act 1906, which stated that a trade union could not be liable in tort for any act in 'contemplation or furtherance of a trade dispute'. Led by the two charismatic figures of David Lloyd George as President of the Board of Trade and Chancellor, and Winston Churchill as a successor, the government passed the Old Age Pensions Act 1908, creating the first state pension, the Trade Boards Act 1909, establishing minimum wages in 'sweated industries', and the National Insurance Act 1911, introducing unemployment, sickness and health insurance. It also brought about World War One.

(3) MODERN LABOUR LAW

The involvement of the labour movement in politics after *Taff Vale*, and the reforms after the 1905 election, heralded the modern era of labour law. This is what we are concerned with today, though it is fair to say that most of today's law comes from the era that began in 1979. Three main features can be identified. First, the essential model of labour regulation was to create a minimum floor of rights, and to rely on collective regulation to get fair standards above the minimum. For fair wages above the minimum, law sought to extend democracy to the economy. Workplace participation also inspired the nature of minimum rights, and this is why a 'voice at work' has remained the most politically contentious issue in labour law. It is probably the central division in modern politics. Second, as the British Empire disintegrated, and the civil rights movement spread from the United States, there was a new development of anti-discrimination law to achieve equality. Third, following the creation of the International Labour Organization (ILO) in 1919, labour regulation was increasingly coordinated with and inspired by countries abroad. The ILO's central principle was that 'peace can be established only if it is based upon social justice' (Versailles Treaty, Part XIII). This expresses the view that labour regulation is not just a social issue, or an economic one, but ultimately an issue of geopolitical importance.

(a) Democracy

KD Ewing, 'The State and Industrial Relations' (1998) 5 *Historical Studies in Industrial Relations* 1, 16–25

In his well-known essay published in 1959, Kahn-Freund argued that a dominant characteristic of labour law in the first half of the twentieth century was the 'principle' of 'collective laissez-faire'. This he defined to mean 'allowing free play to the collective forces of society, and to limit the intervention of the law to those marginal areas in which the disparity of these forces, that is … the forces of organised labour and of organised management, is so great as to prevent the successful operation of what is so very characteristically called "negotiating machinery"'. 'Seen from the lawyer's point of view', he continued, the 'main characteristic' of the British trade-union movement was 'its aversion to legislative intervention, its disinclination to rely on legal sanctions, its almost passionate belief in the autonomy of industrial forces'.[2] Although not denying a role for law in the process, Kahn-Freund was later to remark on 'the astonishing fact that in a country in which collective bargaining is so highly developed and of such comparatively ancient origin, the bulk of collective bargaining and collective agreements continues to exist outside the law and without any development of a "collective labour law" of any major proportion'.[3]

But despite the enduring influence of 'collective laissez-faire' as an aid to our understanding of the development of the British system, it nevertheless provides an incomplete picture

---

[2] O. Kahn-Freund, 'Labour Law', in M. Ginsberg (ed.), *Law and Opinion in England in the 20th Century* (Stevens: 1959), p. 224.

[3] O. Kahn-Freund, 'Report on the Legal Status of Collective Bargaining and Collective Agreements in Great Britain', in O. Kahn-Freund (ed.), *Labour Relations and the Law* (Stevens: 1965), pp. 30–4. To the extent that law had a part to play, it was 'to promote the willingness to bargain and the observance of agreements', by the creation of 'legal substitutes for non-functioning collective bargaining machinery which at the same time operate as inducements to negotiate and observe agreements'.

of the relationship between the state and industrial relations. The evidence suggests that the state has been a much more active player in the building of collective bargaining and other institutions than a concentration on legal regulation would tend to indicate, thereby reflecting the fact that legal regulation is only one method of intervention, but that there are others – sometimes less formal yet not necessarily less effective. ...

The Nature and Form of State Intervention

... what we have in the British system is (i) a process of socialization in the sense of state intervention in industrial relations, which (ii) took the form of 'administrative regulation' rather than statutory intervention, and (iii) was undertaken with the support of trade unions. The most systematic forms of intervention were to take place during and immediately after the First World War,[4] when active steps were taken to encourage what Kahn-Freund has referred to as the 'regulatory function of collective forces in society'.[5]

  ...

The Whitley Committee

Post-First World War reconstruction saw important intervention by the state to implement the report of the Whitley Committee which had been established by the Prime Minister in 1916 to 'make and consider suggestions for securing a permanent improvement in the relations between employers and workmen'.[6] The committee produced five reports on industrial relations issues, with the first recommending that the government should 'propose without delay to the various associations of employers and employed the formation of Joint Standing Industrial Councils [JICs] in each industry' where they did not already exist, and the second recommending 'an adaptation and expansion of the system of Trade Boards working under an amended Trade Boards Act' for 'trades where organisation is at present very weak or non-existent'.[7] The sheer ambition of the project was revealed in the final report of the committee where it was said that: 'Taking our first and second reports together they constitute a scheme designed to cover all the chief industries of the country and to equip each of them with a representative joint body capable of dealing with matters affecting the welfare of the industry in which employers and employed are concerned.' It was not suggested that there should be legal intervention to set up the JICs, and none was introduced, though again the role of the law was not ruled out, it being suggested in the first report of the committee that 'it may be desirable at some later stage for the State to give the sanction of the law to agreements made by the Councils', while accepting also that the initiative should come from the councils themselves.[8]

According to Clegg, the government of the day accepted the proposals of the committee, so that 'during 1918 and 1919 the new Ministry of Labour called meetings of the two sides of almost every industry which lacked an industry-wide procedure agreement in order to promote the establishment of joint industrial councils'.[9] This led to the creation of 73 JICs,

---

[4] For a full account of which see D. Brodie, 'The Evolution of British Labour Law', *Juridical Review* (1997), p. 287, which makes much more sceptical judgements than those made here.

[5] Kahn-Freund, 'Labour Law', p. 223.

[6] Ministry of Reconstruction, Committee on Relations between Employers and Employed (Whitley), *Final Report* (1 July 1918), Cd 9153(1918), para. 1.

[7] Whitley Committee, Final Report, para. 3. For details of the second report, see note ... .

[8] Whitley Committee, Interim Report, para. 21.

[9] H. A. Clegg, *The System of Industrial Relations in Great Britain* (Blackwell, Oxford: 1972), pp. 202–5. The government also produced a model constitution for JICs on which most councils were 'largely based': see Ministry of Labour, *Industrial Relations Handbook* (HMSO: 1961), p. 24. See further, I. G. Sharpe, *Industrial Conciliation and Arbitration in Great Britain* (Allen and Unwin: 1950), p. 328, and more recently Brodie, 'Evolution of British Labour Law', pp. 291–2.

with 47 surviving the early inter-war depression to remain in existence by 1926, and although it is said that only 20 survived by 1939 these were nevertheless 'by far the largest and most important'.[10] Also, according to Clegg, the process was rejuvenated during and after the Second World War when the 'return of full employment and government control was ... used to extend the system to industries which had not yet achieved it or had slipped back between the wars', leading to another 56 JICs being set up or revived between 1939 and 1946.[11] Although this intervention was undertaken without legislation (though not without the law to the extent that the government acted in accordance with its discretionary legal powers), the process was underpinned by legislation in the form of the Trade Boards Act 1918, which allowed for the creation of trade boards in the unorganized sectors, a power which was used by ministers to persuade employers to enter into voluntary arrangements for the creation of JICs. Together these devices of state intervention were said to have been responsible for the extension to some five million workers of procedures for the joint regulation of working conditions,[12] a considerable achievement when it is recalled that only one half of that number were believed to have been covered by collective agreements in 1910.[13]

Trade Boards Act 1918

The second limb of the Whitley proposals was for the creation of trade boards, for those industries 'in which organisation on the part of employers and employed is less completely established than in the industries covered in the [first] report' of the committee.[14] In developing these proposals the committee acknowledged that trade boards had been established initially in 1909 'to secure the establishment of a minimum standard of wages in certain unorganised industries', but argued that the functions of trade boards should change so that they might be regarded also as a means of supplying a regular machinery for negotiation and decision on certain groups of questions dealt with in other circumstances by collective bargaining between employers' organizations and trade unions. The committee also recommended that the powers of the trade boards should be expanded to deal not only with wages but also with hours of labour 'and questions cognate to wages and hours', it being further proposed that they should be empowered 'to initiate and conduct enquiries on all matters affecting the industry or the section of the industry concerned'.[15] The effect of the Whitley blueprint was that there would thus be 'broadly two classes of industries in the country – industries with Industrial Councils and industries with Trade Boards'.[16] In fact some industries would have both, for although trade boards were designed for those industries where collective machinery was weak or non-existent, there were also well-organized industries with 'sections or areas in which the degree of organisation ... falls much below what is normal in the rest of the industry', where 'the general body of employers and employed ... should have some means whereby they may bring the whole of the trade up to the standard of minimum conditions which have been

---

[10] A. Fox, *History and Heritage: The Social Origins of the British Industrial Relations System* (Allen and Unwin: 1985), p. 297.

[11] Clegg, *System of Industrial Relations*, p. 206. See also Ministry of Labour, *Industrial Relations Handbook*, p. 24.

[12] According to the Committee Appointed to Enquire into the Working and Effects of the Trade Boards Acts (Cave), Report, Cmd 1645 (1922), some three million workers were covered by the trade boards, while it has been estimated that the new JICs in operation in 1923 employed on average (between 1919 and 1939) some 2.05 million workers: R. Charles, *The Development of Industrial Relations in Britain 1911–1939* (Hutchinson: 1973), pp. 124–5.

[13] *Report on Collective Agreements* (1910).

[14] Whitley Committee, *Second Report on Joint Standing Industrial Councils* (18 October 1917), Cd 9002 (1918).

[15] Ibid., para. 11.

[16] Ibid., para. 17.

agreed upon by a substantial majority of the industry'.[17] A trade board for the area or section in question was the way in which this was to be done.

...

Two Steps Forward, One Step Back: the Retreat of the Ministry

The Ministry of Labour intervention of 1918–21 proved to be enduring and set a pattern for the conduct of industrial relations for at least forty years, in addition to its immediate impact in extending the scope of collective bargaining coverage.[18] But state support was by no means unbroken, with the policy changing radically following the trade depression towards the end of 1920 when 'higher wages began to press severely upon manufacturers'.[19] There was no longer any interest in promoting collective bargaining on the one hand, while the trade boards strategy came to an abrupt end on the other. By the end of the 1920s, policy had thus swung radically from one in which the state had actively intervened to support and sustain trade-unionism, collective bargaining and joint wage regulation, to one in which that support was withdrawn. But by withdrawal it is not meant that the state removed the institutions which it helped to create, though some did perish, no doubt for want of nourishment by public offi-cials. Rather, by withdrawal is meant the retreat of continuing support for the policy of insti-tution building and for those institutions already in place. Even here the retreat was far from complete, the Ministry of Labour continuing to acknowledge responsibility for the implementa-tion of the Whitley strategy, with departmental officials still attending meetings of JICs. There were also contradictions, as in the case of the modest gain won during the short-lived Labour government in 1924 when the trade dispute disqualification from unemployment benefit was removed where the dispute was caused by the employer's breach of a collective agreement.[20] The repeal of this amendment in 1927, however, only serves to reinforce the trend in public policy in the 1920 s.78.

The Pendulum Swings

It has been suggested that the 'keen proselytisation campaign'[21] pursued by Ministry of Labour officials came to an end in 1922, when the number of staff charged with responsibility for JICs was cut from 115 to 20.[22] It is also the case that a number of JICs collapsed during this period (not to be superseded by a trade board). The change of policy on the part of the administration coincided with the first annual reports of the Ministry of Labour. A marked difference in tone is to be found in the content of these reports between the years 1923–33 and 1934–48. So far as the former are concerned, it is true, as already suggested, that they acknowledge that one of the 'principal' responsibilities of the Ministry was to provide 'assistance in the settlement of industrial disputes, and in the formation of Conciliation Boards and Joint Industrial Councils'.[23] In practice, however, the early reports are fairly anodyne at least so far as they relate to the JICs,

[17] Ibid., para. 15.

[18] It is in this context that we must assess the impact of these measures, though others have been more sceptical. See G. R. Askwith, *Industrial Problems and Disputes* (Murray: 1920), p. 457, noting that the Whitley scheme had not been adopted by coalmining, cotton, engineering, shipbuilding, iron and steel, and the railways, all of which preferred to 'follow their own lines of agreement or arrangements'. See also Ministry of Labour, *Industrial Relations Handbook*, p. 24, and Lowe, *Adjusting to Democracy*.

[19] Cave Committee, Report, para. 12.

[20] Unemployment Insurance (No 2) Act 1924, s. 4(1). See K. Ewing, 'Collective Agreements, Trade Dis-putes and Unemployment Benefit: The Employers' Breach Exemption', *Northern Ireland Legal Quarterly* 32 (1981), p. 305.

[21] Fox, *History and Heritage*, p. 297.

[22] Charles, *Development of Industrial Relations*, pp. 204, 210–11. See also Brodie, 'Evolution of British Labour Law', pp. 298–9.

[23] MoL Report 1923 and 1924, p. 8. See also MoL Report 1925, Cmd 2736 (1926), p. 7.

merely commenting on the powers of the ministry and the activities of the councils in the years in question, being noticeably silent on any initiatives on the part of the ministry,[24] despite a formal recognition of the good work which the councils performed during the General Strike of 1926.[25] In 1927, for example, it was reported simply that the position in regard to JICs 'showed very little change', and that some councils displayed 'little activity or limit their work mainly to questions of wages and working conditions', while acknowledging that 'the Councils as a whole have provided an effective and valuable means for providing satisfactory relations in their various industries'.[26] Two years later it was reported that although no councils had been dissolved' a few found but little to occupy their attention', though again some councils did accomplish 'much valuable work to the advantage of the industries concerned'.[27]

The change of strategy on the trade boards is associated with the report of the Cave Committee, which had been appointed in 1921 to examine the operation of the legislation. ... The view of the committee was that the 'coercive powers of the State should be used [only] to prevent the oppression of the worker by forcing him to work at wages below the level of subsistence and under conditions injurious to his health', but not 'as an instrument for the public regulation of wages throughout the industries concerned'.[28] It therefore recommended that the minister should have power to establish a trade board only where wages were exceptionally low and where there was no adequate collective bargaining machinery, replacing the existing legislation which allowed for a trade board to be established where only the latter condition was met.[29] This recommendation was duly accepted by the government, but it was reluctant to devote 'the expenditure of considerable time and labour' to a bill in order to implement this and other recommendations for change which Cave had made. Consequently it proposed to proceed 'within the limits of the existing statutes', and announced that no new trade board would be established unless both conditions were met, surely an example of the misuse of government power."

State Intervention and Voluntarism

The period from 1922 to 1934 is perhaps the nearest the UK came to the 'voluntarist paradigm'.[30] The state retreated in terms of its role as institution builder, with the result that the parties were left largely to their own devices, albeit in some cases within a framework which had been created with the help of the state. The retreat is captured by the spirit of the report of the Balfour Committee on Industry and Trade which had been set up by the Labour government in 1924 to inquire into the conditions and prospects of British industry and commerce, with special reference to the export trade.[31] As part of its inquiry this committee

---

[24] See especially MoL Report 1925.

[25] MoL Report 1926, Cmd 2856 (1927), pp. 7–8. The effect of the General Strike was said 'definitely to strengthen the position of the Industrial Councils and their power for good'. It was also reported that there was 'every ground for satisfaction at the way in which the Whitley Council system has stood the severe test to which the General Strike exposed it'.

[26] MoL Report 1927, p. 8.

[27] MoL Report 1929, Cmd 3579 (1930), p. 80.

[28] Cave Committee, Report, para. 53.

[29] Though under the Trade Boards Act 1918, the minister was directed to have regard to the rates of wages prevailing in the trade: s. 1(2). Under the Trade Boards Act 1909, which was amended by the 1918 Act, on this point a board could be established where rates were exceptionally low without reference to bargaining machinery.

[30] Subject to such qualifications as the Trade Disputes and Trade Unions Act 1927, passed in the wake of the General Strike, though not directly aimed at collective bargaining machinery.

[31] Balfour Committee, Final Report. The terms of reference included specifically 'the relations between those engaged in production. This will involve inquiry into methods of industrial remuneration, the main causes of unrest and disputes, and the methods of avoidance or settlement of disputes, as, for example, co-partnership, co-operation, wages Boards and voluntary arbitration, State regulation of wages and compulsory arbitration and compulsory enforcement and extension of agreements'.

surveyed the industrial relations scene, acknowledging that it was 'highly desirable in the general interest of trade and employment that voluntary arrangements for the collective settlement of wages should ... be extended to cover as large an area of industry as possible'.[32] But it saw no occasion to make any specific recommendation to the development of collective bargaining machinery. So far as JICs were concerned, 'the greater part of the field' was 'already covered',[33] while it 'cordially commended' the policy of the Ministry of Labour's practice 'to keep a continuous watch on the means available for the peaceful adjustment of disputes, and to take every reasonable opportunity to secure that adequate joint machinery shall exist, whether in the shape of a Joint Industrial Council or of some other suitable and acceptable means for joint consultation and negotiation'.[34] In fact the Ministry of Labour annual reports from 1923 to 1929 reveal only one newly created JIC in that time, for which the Ministry claimed no responsibility.[35]

NOTES AND QUESTIONS

1. Ewing's central argument is that before World War Two UK labour policy was not, contrary to the influential theory of Otto Kahn-Freund, one of collective laissez faire. Unions depended on government promotion by the Ministry of Labour for more members, bargaining power and better working conditions. Figure 1.1, discussed in E McGaughey, 'Do Corporations Increase Inequality?' (2015), suggests a strong causal relation in the UK's system between union membership and income inequality.

Figure 1.1 UK union membership and income inequality 1900–2010

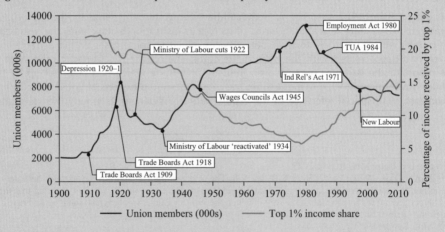

— Union members (000s)   — Top 1% income share

Sources: N Brownlie, Trade Union Membership 2011 (DBIS 2012) 22–23. T Piketty, Capital in the Twenty-First Century (2014) Technical Appendices, Table S9.2.

[32] Ibid., p. 89.
[33] Despite the fact that collective bargaining covered only 42% of the workforce, with total coverage of collective agreements and wages orders being 51%: Milner, 'The Coverage of Collective Pay-Setting Institutions', *BJIR*, p. 76.
[34] Balfour Committee, Final Report, p. 113.
[35] The Printing Ink and Roller Trades JIC: MoL Report 1929, p. 80.

2. The conception of 'industrial democracy' implemented after the Whiteley Reports was mirrored in the United States through the short-lived National War Labor Board: RB Gregg, 'The National War Labor Board' (1919) 33(1) *Harvard Law Review* 39 and see generally JR Commons, *Principles of Labor Legislation* (2nd edn 1920). In Germany, unions sought enforceable legal rights in the Weimar constitution, as opposed to discretionary administrative action that depended on changes in government; see H Sinzheimer, 'The Development of Labor Legislation in Germany' (1920) 92 *Annals of the American Academy of Political and Social Science* 35. What do you think are the potential strengths and weaknesses of administrative regulation compared to legal rights?

3. The UK had some of the world's first laws on direct legal participation rights, for instance, in the Port of London Act 1908, and was on the verge of legislating in the Railways Act 1920 for one-third of company directors to be elected by workers, under a Conservative–Liberal coalition. But opposition from management, and focus of unions at the time on nationalisation of industry, meant the proposals were never implemented. See E McGaughey, 'Votes at Work in Britain: Shareholder Monopolisation and the "Single Channel"' (2017) 46(4) *Industrial Law Journal* 444. In the United States, after the Wall Street Crash of 1929 triggered the Great Depression, President Franklin D Roosevelt's central labour plank of the New Deal was the National Labor Relations Act 1935, piloted by German-born New York Senator, Robert Wagner. This creates a duty on employers to bargain in good faith with a union, if the union wins a majority in a ballot of workers in a 'bargaining unit'.

4. Over the period Ewing covers, political as well as economic democracy emerged. The Representation of the People Act (RPA) 1883 enfranchised around one-third of men, according to the value of property they held. The RPA 1918 gave every man aged 21 the vote, and every woman aged 30. The RPA 1928 equalised voting ages between men and women. RPA 1948 ended double voting for graduates of London, Cambridge and Oxford. After that the RPA 1969 reduced the voting age to 18. Do you think that economic change drives political change, or political change drives economic change, or both?

5. After the controversial report, *In Place of Strife* (1969) Cmnd 3888, the centre of discussion moved. Many Labour Party politicians criticised reliance on ongoing strikes as the 'single channel' for social progress. They said British industry was inflexible in adopting the latest technological and administrative practices. To simplify somewhat, three basic positions were (1) union power needed to be restrained; (2) union bargaining should be restructured and decentralised, to combine fairness and flexibility; (3) a second channel for a voice at work should be opened. After a few experiments in the Iron and Steel Act 1967, the Industry Act 1975, and the Post Office Act 1977, the government commissioned the *Report of the Committee of Inquiry on Industrial Democracy* (1977) Cmnd 6706. It proposed that workers elect half the boards of private companies. It remained controversial even among labour law's finest minds.

O Kahn-Freund, 'Industrial Democracy' (1977) 6 *Industrial Law Journal* 65

The Proposals

The implementation of the report would make it necessary to reconstitute the boards of the companies to which the new law would apply, and indeed to embark on a far reaching reform of company law. The scope of this reform would however be limited: the proposals made by the committee would, for the time being, apply only (i) to companies employing 2,000 or more employees in the United Kingdom, (ii) to the holding companies, or. in the case of foreign based multi-national groups, the top United Kingdom subsidiaries, of enterprises, i.e. groups of companies, employing that number though each of the companies of the group employs a smaller number (Chap. 11, para. 4, 59). The committee envisages that, in the fullness of time, the key number may be reduced to 1,000 (Chap. 11. para. 5), but for the time being the new system would apply to some 738 enterprises and to 1.800 companies employing six or seven million people in the United Kingdom (out of a total of about 24 or 25 million employees, 18 in the private and six or seven in the public sector (Chap. 2, para. 5)). We would have two different systems of company law. Since the coming into force of the Co-Determination Law of 1976[36] this has also been true of the law of the Federal Republic of Germany, where different rules as to participation apply to enterprises (including groups of companies) employing more than 2,000 employees and those employing 2,000 or less.

The second big decision made by the committee was to reject what is often called the "two-tier" and sometimes (including the shareholders' meeting) the "three-tier" structure of companies, i.e. the co-existence of a supervisory board and of a board of management which is obligatory, e.g. in Germany, and optional, e.g. in France[37] (Chap. 8, para. 14). No "supervisory board" is to be introduced, and employee representation is to be effectuated through a reconstitution of the unitary board of directors. The minority arrived at the opposite conclusion (para. 35 of its report).

This however, and the need for preventing a distribution of functions depriving the employee directors of effective influence, led to a third decision, concerning the powers of the various corporate organs. The board would have a number of "attributed" functions. It would have the exclusive non-delegatable power of submitting to the shareholders' meeting resolutions for the winding up of (he company, for changes in the memorandum or articles, for the payment of dividends, for changes in the capital structure or the relation between board, meeting, and senior management, for the disposal of a substantial part of the undertaking. It would also have the ultimate but delegatable responsibility for the "allocation or disposition of resources" not constituting a substantial part of the undertaking, and non-delegatable power to appoint, remove and control managerial employees and to determine their remuneration (Chap. 8, para. 19).

...

The committee has, fourthly, accepted the principle of parity of share-holder and employee representation on the board, but rejected the "half and half" principle. The board is to consist of equal numbers of shareholder and employee representatives (at least four on either side)

[36] Mitbestimmungsgesstz of May 4, 1976. I am using the leading Commentary by Fitting, Wlotzke and Wissmann (Munich, 1976). The new law provides not only for a complete reorganisation of the supervisory council, but also (s. 33) for a labour director as a member of the board of management. This institution of the "labour director," hitherto known only in the coal, iron and steel industries under the Law of 1951, raises special problems, not directly germane to those raised by the Bullock Report.

[37] For the Danish system (Companies Acts of June 13, 1973) which is a half-way home see P. L. Davits in Bastone and Davies, Industrial Democracy, European Experience. Two Reports prepared for the Industrial Democracy Committee. H.M.S.O., 1976, p. 55, and the "Green Paper" of the EEC Commission (see below note ...), pp. 56 et seq.

and a third group of (at least three) co-opted members, not necessarily "independent" or "neutral," but chosen for their expertise and experience (Chap. 9, paras. 13. 14, 19). If a majority of the shareholder and a majority of the employee representatives cannot agree on who is to be co-opted, an independent Industrial Democracy Commission (see Chap. 12) would try to conciliate, and, failing conciliation, make binding nominations (Chap. 9. para. 43). ...

This is the so-called "2 X plus Y" formula (X being the members representing the two sides, Y the co-opted group) with which not only the Minority Report, but also the (on this point) dissenting member of the majority, Mr. N. S. Wilson, disagreed. Reading the report one has to make a determined mental effort not to see in this structure a replica of the traditional pattern of committees, boards, tribunals, operating in the sphere of labour relations (which it is not intended to be). The committee cannot be accused of confusing corporate decision making with collective bargaining – whether such confusion may be the unintended consequence of its proposals is a different question. ...

But who are the employee representatives? What is to be the "channel of representation"? Here is a fifth major decision: the employee representatives are not to be elected by a ballot of the workforce as a whole nor nominated or appointed by a works council representing them (which in this country does not, of course, exist), but the system of representation is to be "based on trade union machinery" (Chap. 10, para. 8). In general the choice of the representatives would lie with a Joint Representation Committee formed by the shop stewards or other representatives at plant or enterprise level of the various unions who have members there (Chap. 10, para. 29). Overall something of the order of 70 per cent of all (blue and white collar) employees in the enterprises within the proposals are union members. One must not however jump to the conclusion that the 30 per cent who are not organised are to be entirely disenfranchised. Though they would not be represented on the boards, they would have a say in deciding whether the system is to be introduced at ail and whether it is (after a certain lapse of time) to continue.

This is because the new system is not to be imposed by law from on high – quite different from, e.g. the German system. For each company it must be introduced separately, at the request of a union or unions recognised by the employer and representing at least 20 per cent of the workforce of the enterprise. ...

Pluralistic or Unitary Patterns?

If the present vogue for representation of employees in corporate organs can partly be understood as the outcome of the need for filling the gap between territorial and plant (establishment, workshop, shop-floor) bargaining and for a system of organised channels of union influence on entrepreneurial and managerial decisions, the first question to be asked and answered is whether it is preferable to satisfy these needs through a reform of the collective bargaining system or through a reform of company law. The Bullock Committee discussed at some length the problem how far its proposed scheme was compatible with the existing system of collective bargaining (Chap. 10, paras. 7, 52 et seq.), but its terms of reference precluded it from asking and answering the question whether the purposes of its own proposals could not equally well or better be attained by an expansion of collective negotiations … . In the result, it produced a proposal for a board structure, looking, as said above, very much like that of a negotiating or bargaining body, whilst the minority sought to dilute the right of representation into a right to make representations.

...

Underlying the report there is an assumption that there exists a self-perpetuating entity, the company or the enterprise, whose "interests" transcend those of any of its component elements. This is to be represented by the new board of directors. "The new concept of a partnership between capital and labour in the control of companies will supersede the idea that a company and its shareholders (i.e. the 'owners' or 'members') are the one and the same thing" (Chap. 8, para. 26). This presupposes that the interest of the company may be as different from that of a given individual shareholder or group of shareholders as it may be from that of a given individual employee or group of employees, and that it is the function of a board of directors to reconcile these (potentially antithetic) interests through the synthesis of the "company's interest."

...

The so-called "interest of the company" is always identical with an interest of its shareholders, not the interest, but an interest. But the employees concerned with the dispute about the introduction of labour-saving machinery may have nothing to gain from this measure: the company's interest may be irreconcilably opposed to that of each member of that employee group. He will lose his job – this may be very indirectly to his benefit because the improved performance of the company resulting from rationalisation may lead to increased exports or lower prices or better quality of production, all of which may benefit the worker as" a citizen or as a consumer, but not as an employee of that company. In other words: the company's interests may be opposed to those of the workers in a sense in which they cannot be opposed to the shareholders, nor, for that matter, those of the creditors. Not as if a conflict of interests between the company and the workers could not be mitigated and settled by conciliation and bargaining, e.g. about redundancy pay or the staggering of dismissals etc. But from the company's point of view such a settlement is a compact with an outside force: it is different from the settlement of a conflict between groups of shareholders inside the company.

...

What is good for big business is not necessarily good for the nation, nor is that which is good for the trade unions. It cannot be supposed that in the committee's view, that which is good for big business and the trade unions combined is necessarily in the national interest It would be insulting to demonstrate that it is not – the matter is too obvious. Clearly, in the committee's view, consumer interests may be in need of protection, partly through "the constraints of competition in the marketplace, however imperfect" (Chap. 6, para. 44), partly through legislation such as the Fair Trading Act 1973 and the Consumer Credit Act 1974, partly through the existing consumer organisations. These organisations, however, could, in the committee's view, not be considered as a "consumer constituency equivalent to that of employees and shareholders." Moreover, "the involvement of employees and shareholders in a company is different in kind from that of the consumers" (Chap. 6, paras. 46, 47). The committee rejected the idea of a representation of consumer interests on the reconstituted boards. In doing so – rightly or wrongly – it implicitly rejected the idea that these boards would represent anything that could be characterised as a "public interest" Consumer interests are to be accommodated *extra muros*, employee interests and shareholder interests *intra muros*. The public interest included all of them and much else besides (e.g. the protection of the people against the destruction of their health or of their environment). Of all these different interests "industrial democracy" covers only those of the workers (represented by the unions) and of the shareholders. These are the only interests (of many others) to be accommodated and reconciled within the company structure.

...

There may well be a strong case against any legal regulation of employee representation at plant level in this country, or, alternatively, shop stewards with enhanced and statutory guaranteed powers (something like the French sections syndicates and *diliguis syndicaux*) may be preferable to the German model of works councils. This does not dispose of the argument that an edifice of statutory participation must be built from the bottom upwards, and not (as at one point the report seems to suggest) (Chap. 6, para. 11) from the top downwards.

...

It is not suggested here that the measure recommended by the Bullock Committee would be a disaster remotely comparable to the 1971 Act. It is too peripheral to day-to-day relations to be anything of that kind. Yet two things must be said about it: it would introduce at a sensitive point of these relations a measure of legalism which may be excessive. And, secondly, it can only work if management and organised labour both want to work it. Whether and what measure of understanding between the unions and between the union movement as a whole and management can be achieved is a political question the answer to which is unpredictable.

Though it may be a little unusual, I should like to have the privilege of ending this paper with a personal observation. My scepticism towards employee representation in the corporate organs of business enterprise goes back to the time of the experiment made in this direction more than half a century ago under the Weimar Republic I recognise that much water has flown under the bridges of the Thames and also of the Rhine since those days, and that both the proposals of the Bullock Report and the present law of the Federal Republic and of other European countries are very different from the feeble and half-hearted German scheme between the Wars. Nor can I forget how difficult it is, at an advanced age to abandon firm views formed in the past, and perhaps under conditions which are no more. For all these and other reasons I was determined to read the Bullock Report with an open mind – I was doing my best to find the road to Damascus and to turn from a sceptic into a believer. It is my painful duty to confess that I did not succeed.

NOTES AND QUESTIONS

1. Kahn-Freund explains that his (highly influential) scepticism of direct participation came from the tragic experience in the collapse of the Weimar Republic into fascism. As a young man, having been a Berlin Labour Court judge, he argued the Reich Labour Court pursued a fascist doctrine in the late 1920s that converted employee-elected work councils into tools for the employer, fuelling the economic authoritarianism that played the prelude to the Nazi catastrophe. See O Kahn-Freund, 'The Social Ideal of the Reich Labour Court – A Critical Examination of the Practice of the Reich Labour Court' (1931) in O Kahn-Freund, R Lewis and J Clark (eds), *Labour Law and Politics in the Weimar Republic* (1981) ch 3. Judge Kahn-Freund awarded maximum damages in 1934 to radio employees, who were dismissed by the Nazi regime, on concocted accusations of being communists. His house was then ransacked, he was dismissed for 'political unreliability', and he and his wife were forced to leave Berlin for London. With a rare candour and honesty, he says his emotional aversion to codetermination (which he thought vulnerable to state takeover) may apply 'no more', but he could not abandon it.

2. At page 72 of the article, Kahn-Freund's historical analysis appears to be footed on a mistaken premise that in Germany itself, codetermination was 'resumed … in the law', separately from collective bargaining. In fact, codetermination (the right of employees to participate in enterprise governance) was initially a product of collective bargaining in the so-called Stinnes-Legien Abkommen 1918, and then again from 1945 to 1951 through collective bargains throughout the economy, but particularly in the coal and steel industries. See E McGaughey, 'The Codetermination Bargains: The History of German Corporate and Labour Law' (2017) 23(1) *Columbia Journal of European Law* 135. Also mistaken was the view that US unions 'reject[ed]' workplace participation at the time: like in the UK, the US labour movement was divided. But a number of large unions were using collective agreements at that very moment to win seats on boards, notably in the car company Chrysler. Why do you think trade unions would have an interest in collectively bargaining for employee representation in a company's management?

3. As chapter 11 will elaborate, when he was writing, Kahn-Freund himself happened to work in a corporation where, as an employee he had legal rights to vote for his workplace's management, namely under the Oxford University Act 1854. This is common to almost all UK universities. Most also have student representation. But the UK now sits alongside a minority of EU countries (mostly poorer and more unequal) without any general workplace participation laws. See E McGaughey, 'Votes at Work in Britain: Shareholder Monopolisation and the "Single Channel"' (2017) 46(4) *Industrial Law Journal* 444. In light of Kahn-Freund's critique of consumer and public interests, what similarities or differences do you think there are between universities and other corporations? Can there be a unified theory of stakeholder representation for all sectors of enterprise?

4. In the end, after the Bullock Report, a government White Paper (1978) Cmnd 7231 proposed companies adopt a two-tier board, with a minority of representatives on the lower 'supervisory board' appointed solely by unions (as opposed to a direct vote for employees). Because of bickering on details, 'unremitting hostility' from the City to union control of voting, an outbreak of strikes in the 'Winter of Discontent', and the election of 1979, no law was passed. After 1979, existing rights of direct participation in the Post Office and other enterprises were removed.

(b) Equality

Economic discrimination between rich and poor often compounds social inequality, particularly based on gender and race. The common law was gradually developing around World War Two to combat discrimination, in employment and more generally, to ensure people are judged according to the 'content of their character', not other unjust factors. In *Constantine v Imperial Hotels Ltd* [1944] KB 693, a black cricket player, and star of the West Indies team, was told by a hotel manager that he would have to be moved after white US soldiers, from segregated southern states, objected to being in the same accommodation. Constantine won damages in the High Court in tort. Birkett J (who went on to judge the Nuremberg trials) found that a common law duty of an innkeeper to house people was breached. Discrimination became effectively unlawful at common law. Plainly, however, tackling discrimination required more than ad hoc ingenuity of the rare judge. Within the United States, the figurehead of the movement to end institutional racism was Martin Luther King Jr. Because the UK's first modern legislation was modelled on the US Civil Rights Act 1964, a comparative perspective is particularly important.

Martin Luther King Jr, Speech to the Fourth Constitutional Convention AFL-CIO, Miami, Florida (11 December 1961)*

This revolution within industry was fought mercilessly by those who blindly believed their right to uncontrolled profits was a law of the universe, and that without the maintenance of the old order catastrophe faced the nation.

---

* Reprinted by arrangement with The Heirs to the Estate of Martin Luther King Jr., c/o Writers House as agent for the proprietor New York, NY.

History is a great teacher. Now, every one knows that the labor movement did not diminish the strength of the nation but enlarged it. By raising the living standards of millions, labor miraculously created a market for industry and lifted the whole nation to undreamed levels of production. Those who today attack labor forget these simple truths, but history remembers them.

Labor's next monumental struggle emerged in the thirties when it wrote into federal law the right freely to organize and bargain collectively. It was now apparently emancipated. The days when workers were jailed for organizing, and when in the English Parliament Lord Macauley had to debate against a bill decreeing the death penalty for anyone engaging in a strike, were grim but almost forgotten memories.

Yet, the Wagner Act, like any other legislation, tended merely to declare rights but did not deliver them. Labor had to bring the law to life by exercising its rights in practice over stubborn, tenacious opposition. It was warned to go slow, to be moderate, not to stir up strife. But labor knew it was always the right time to do right, and it spread its organization over the nation and achieved equality organizationally with capital. The day of economic democracy was born.

Negroes in the United States read this history of labor and find it mirrors their own experience. We are confronted by powerful forces telling us to rely on the good will and understanding of those who profit by exploiting us. They deplore our discontent, they resent our will to organize, so that we may guarantee that humanity will prevail and equality will be exacted. They are shocked that action organizations, sit-ins, civil disobedience, and protests are becoming our everyday tools, just as strikes, demonstrations and union organization became yours to insure that bargaining power genuinely existed on both sides of the table. ...

This unity of purpose is not an historical coincidence. Negroes are almost entirely a working people. There are pitifully few Negro millionaires and few Negro employers. Our needs are identical with labor's needs: decent wages, fair working conditions, livable housing, old age security, health and welfare measures, conditions in which families can grow, have education for their children and respect in the community. That is why Negroes support labor's demands and fight laws which curb labor. That is why the labor-hater and labor-baiter is virtually always a twin-headed creature spewing anti-Negro epithets from one mouth and anti-labor propaganda from the other mouth. ...

Discrimination does exist in the labor movement. It is true that organized labor has taken significant steps to remove the yoke of discrimination from its own body. But in spite of this, some unions, governed by the racist ethos, have contributed to the degraded economic status of the Negro. Negroes have been barred from membership in certain unions, and denied apprenticeship training and vocational education. In every section of the country one can find local unions existing as a serious and vicious obstacle when the Negro seeks jobs or upgrading in employment. Labor must honestly admit these shameful conditions, and design the battle plan which will defeat and eliminate them. In this way, labor would be unearthing the big truth and utilizing its strength against the bleakness of injustice in the spirit of its finest traditions. ...

The two most dynamic and cohesive liberal forces in the country are the labor movement and the Negro freedom movement. Together we can be architects of democracy in a South now rapidly industrializing. Together we can retool the political structure of the South, sending to Congress steadfast liberals who, joining with those from northern industrial states, will extend the frontiers of democracy for the whole nation. Together we can bring about the day when there will be no separate identification of Negroes and labor.

There is no intrinsic difference, as I have tried to demonstrate. Differences have been contrived by outsiders who seek to impose disunity by dividing brothers because the color of their skin has a different shade. I look forward confidently to the day when all who work for a living will be one with no thought to their separateness as Negroes, Jews, Italians or any other distinctions.

This will be the day when we shall bring into full realization the American dream – a dream yet unfilled. A dream of equality of opportunity, of privilege and property widely distributed;

a dream of a land where men will not take necessities from the many to give luxuries to the few; a dream of a land where men will not argue that the color of a man's skin determines the content of his character; a dream of a nation where all our gifts and resources are held not for ourselves alone but as instruments of service for the rest of humanity; the dream of a country where every man will respect the dignity and worth of human personality – that is the dream.

And as we struggle to make racial and economic justice a reality, let us maintain faith in the future. We will confront difficulties and frustrating moments in the struggle to make justice a reality, but we must believe somehow that these problems can be solved.

NOTES AND QUESTIONS

1. Martin Luther King Jr's famous 'I Have a Dream' speech to the 'March on Washington' on 28 August 1963 was practised in various forms on many occasions, including here before the American Federation of Labour and Congress of Industrial Organizations. King's essential argument is that people should be judged by the 'content of their character', and not irrelevant factors such as race, because this is necessary to reach the goal of human freedom and justice.

2. The US Civil Rights Act 1964, in contrast to King's frame, identified categories of protected characteristic on which people may *not* be judged. UK and EU discrimination law was modelled on this approach – the opposite premise of King – starting with the Race Relations Act 1965 (for public places), the RRA 1968 (for employment), the RRA 1975, the Race Equality Directive 2000/43/EC, now all recodified in the Equality Act 2010. See chapter 12.

3. Within the British Empire, to give just a few examples, the principal South African apartheid laws date from the South Africa Act 1909. The 'White Australia Policy' was effected by the first Prime Minister, Edmund Barton, by the Immigration Restriction Act 1901. In India, Caste Acts entrenched systems of ethnic divisions, at the top of which sat the imperial 'Britishers'. In Kenya, there was a system of segregation and violence so entrenched it was decided during decolonisation that every white family should be compensated to relocate to the UK. This partly explains why the UK objected to the International Labour Organization Discrimination (Employment and Occupation) Convention 1958 (No 111) until finally adopting it in 1999.

4. The movement for gender equality succeeded in legal enactment at the same time. As far back as 1888, the TUC had passed a resolution that 'it is desirable in the interest both of men and women that in trades where women do the same work as men they shall receive the same payment'. This sentiment was not shared in the UK judiciary. When a local council attempted to pay equal wages to its staff in 1924, the House of Lords said the action was *ultra vires*, Lord Atkinson blustering that the policy was motivated by 'some eccentric principles of socialistic philanthropy, or by a feminist ambition to secure the equality of the sexes in the matter of wages in the world of labour' (*Roberts v Hopwood* [1925] AC 578, 594). The US Equal Pay Act 1963 was the model for the UK. A Labour government finally legislated in 1970. The Second Reading went as follows.

Equal Pay (No 2) Bill, Hansard HC Debs
(9 February 1970) vol 795, cols 913–17 and 966–67, 1019–24

The First Secretary of State and Secretary of State for Employment and Productivity (Mrs. Barbara Castle)

I beg to move, That the Bill be now read a Second time.

...

There can be no doubt that this afternoon we are witnessing another historic advance in the struggle against discrimination in our society, this time against discrimination on grounds of sex. In introducing the Bill, I hope that there will be no difference between the two sides of the House about the principle. The only difference is that the present Government have had the will to act.

While other people have talked – lots of people have talked – we intend to make equal pay for equal work a reality, and, in doing so, to take women workers progressively out of the sweated labour class. We intend to do it, if the House will back us, in ways which will give a lead to other countries whose governments have left us behind in adopting the principle but who are still striving for effective ways of implementing it. ...

Since then the struggle against discrimination against women in rates of pay has had a chequered course. There was that great moment during the war when Mrs. Thelma Cazalet Keir, with strong Labour support, led a successful revolt against the Government on the issue of sex discrimination in teachers' pay, and the great man himself, Winston Churchill, had to come down to the House the next day to make the reimposition of sex discrimination a vote of confidence.

Since then, the cause of equal pay has had its partial victories: the non-industrial Civil Service, non-manual local authority workers and teachers all got the first of seven instalments towards equal pay in 1955, and full equality in 1961. But its extension to that far greater number of women in industry for whom the T.U.C. fought so long ago has so far eluded us. The trade union movement has realised that this can be done only by legislation, and previous Governments have refused to legislate. Up to now, the extension of equal pay in industry has always foundered on three arguments: how should we define equal pay for equal work? How can we enforce it?

The C.B.I. was all in favour of the definition embodied in the Treaty of Rome: "Equal pay for the same work" but the T.U.C. emphatically rejected this as inadequate. The T.U.C. wanted the I.L. Convention definition: "Equal pay for work of equal value" which the C.B.I., in turn, rejected as being far too open ended and indefinite. I think that they were both right: "Equal pay for the same work" is so restrictive that it would merely impinge on those women, very much in the minority, who work side by side with men on identical work, while, equally, the I.L. definition is far from satisfactory.

...

It is for this reason that the Government decided that they must look at the old definitions afresh and try to work out methods of enforcement which would have an effective practical impact on inequality. I think that in the Bill we have succeeded. Its aim is to eradicate discrimination in pay in specific identifiable situations by prescribing equally specific remedies.

The Bill deals with three different situations. The first situation is where men and many women are doing the same or "broadly similar" work, not only in the same establishment but in different establishments of the same employer where these are covered by common terms and conditions. The second is where they are doing jobs which are different but which have been found to be equivalent under a scheme of job evaluation. The third is where their terms and conditions of employment are laid down in collective agreements, statutory wages orders or employers' pay structures.

This three-pronged approach does all that can be done in legislation, and goes beyond anything in the law of other major countries. It gets away from abstractions like "equal pay for work of equal value", and brings equal pay out of the debating room and into recognisable situations in factories, offices and shops, and into the black and white of pay agreements.

...

Mr. Ronald Bell (Buckinghamshire, South)

The Bill forbids a man being paid more even when his work is worth more, and does so in the cause of social engineering; yet men carry, and must always carry, the main economic burden of the community.

The result of the Bill will, in all probability, be depression of the common rate of pay, and that is the real nature of the threat to the family. Such folly can only lead to the French position of massive allowances according to the size of family. But in France this was an instrument of Government population policy, and our population problem is the exact opposite. This is the industrial millstone which the French Government have hung round the necks of their Common Market colleagues in Article 119 of the Treaty of Rome. Therefore, we should not underestimate the trigger which we are pulling by this Bill. It must lead, as is conceded by both sides, to a sex discrimination Act, and it must lead, I say, whether it is conceded or not, to massive family allowances. ...

Legislation is absolutely wrong in this field. Attempts to rig the market always fail. For that reason my colleagues and I voted against the Prices and Incomes Bill and its renewal. This Bill is exactly that thing again. It is unjust and economically dangerous; and it is folly to think that inflation and over-employment will float anything. As the Royal Commission presciently said in its report, actions like this would in days of a strict gold standard and floating rates have met swift retribution. Therefore, I invite the House to believe that this Bill and its proposals are economically superficial and naïve. They introduce into yet another field of human affairs the influence of Statute law. I ask the House whether it is thought really necessary that we must have laws about everything and actions in the courts about everything with injunctions and damages and prescription spreading even wider through the community, until eventually freedom is wholly destroyed.

...

Mrs. Margaret Thatcher (Finchley)

When I was a pupil at the Bar, my first master at law gave me a very sound piece of advice which I tried to follow. He said, "Always express your conclusion first, so that people do not have to wait for it". I therefore gladly express my conclusion first on the Bill. I welcome it ...

...

My hon. and learned Friend the Member for Buckinghamshire, South (Mr. Ronald Bell) made what I am sure we all found was an interesting speech and a carefully argued one. My hon. and learned Friend referred to the Report of the Royal Commission. ...

In reply to my hon. and learned Friend, I take one or two quotations from the minority report ... in paragraph 14: "The majority do not base their case mainly upon the evidence. They appear to rely chiefly upon an a priori argument ...". The conclusion in paragraph 19 of the minority report was: "To sum up: the theoretical argument advanced by the majority to account for the lower wages of women in terms of lower efficiency, used in its widest sense, seems to us unconvincing and on the evidence their case is not proven." My hon. and learned Friend used a phrase from the report, "The market mirrors the truth". Perhaps the best argument which I can put about the market in relation to certain jobs is this. Let us suppose that the question of application to be a candidate for Member of Parliament were judged entirely on market forces. I think that there would probably still be candidates to be Members of Parliament even though there were no pay at all, for Members would be sponsored or would have enough money to do it, or some would come who had other means of support. But, in that case, I think that we should probably find ourselves without a number of very valuable Members. ...

1. Statements by the Minister introducing the Second Reading of an Act of Parliament are influential in construing the intention of Parliament, when interpreting legislation, since *Pepper v Hart* [1992] UKHL 3. Here Barbara Castle MP had advocated that 'specific' wording would be most effective against inequality. In fact the Act was subsequently amended many times, and both the EU Directive and the Equality Act 2010 s 65 adds the ILO definition.

2. Mr Ronald Bell QC also opposed the Race Relations Acts. At one point, another MP shouted at him, 'Whom do you dislike most – coloureds or women?' While this bitter individual's views may now seem absurd, John Stuart Mill, the great liberal philosopher, who campaigned for gender equality in his later life, reminds us that understanding arguments that seem completely wrong is still important: '[S]ince the general or prevailing opinion on any object is rarely or never the whole truth, it is only by the collision of adverse opinions that the remainder of the truth has any chance of being supplied.' *On Liberty* (1859) ch 2. Remarkably, during the debates Margaret Thatcher MP provides what was possibly the most courteously damning reply to Bell's contention that markets made anti-discrimination law unnecessary. She argues by analogy that market actors consider things other than money, and seems to suggest that markets do not always act 'rationally'.

3. The immediate background to US reform was the *Presidential Commission on the Status of Women* (1961) chaired by Eleanor Roosevelt until she passed away in 1962. The Report recommended an equal pay law, but also public childcare and paid maternity leave. In this way, equality has always been tied to the pursuit of substantive justice. On the other hand, if the only childcare leave available is for women, is that not state-sponsored sex discrimination?

4. In the UK, the immediate cause of the Equal Pay Act 1970 was the 1968 strike in the Dagenham plant of Ford Motor Company. Women sewing machinists, making car seat covers, demanded pay equal to the men doing comparable work. The government intervened, and subsequently promised legislation. The Act did not take effect until 1975, when the Sex Discrimination Act 1975 was also passed, and after the UK joined the European Economic Community (now the EU). The Treaty, Art 141 (now TFEU Art 157) required equal pay between men and women. The European Court of Justice stated memorably in *Defrenne v Sabena (No 2)* (1976) C-43/75, [10] that: '[T]his provision forms part of the social objectives of the community, which is not merely an economic union, but is at the same time intended, by common action, to ensure social progress and seek the constant improvement of the living and working conditions of their peoples.'

5. The final major area of labour law to develop post-war, covered comprehensively in Part Five, is job security. The Contracts of Employment Act 1963 codified people's right to a written statement of their contracts, and statutory notice before dismissal. The Redundancy Payments Act 1965 introduced severance pay for economic dismissals. The Industrial Relations Act 1971 introduced the first unfair dismissal protection. Because it also attempted to suppress collective action, the unions boycotted the Act, and forced a change of government. Unfair dismissal law, however, was kept in the subsequent Employment Protection (Consolidation) Act 1978. At all times, legislation drew inspiration from collective agreements, and knowledge of what worked abroad.

(c) Internationalism

After 1979, much of the UK's labour law framework was transformed: the majority of this book is concerned with the paradigm established since Margaret Thatcher became Prime Minister. However, significant development occurred through the UK's membership of the European Union, since the European Communities Act 1972. In the Treaty of Maastricht, the UK opted out of the 'social chapter', which contained some labour regulation. In 1997, the UK opted back in (and may not opt out again without the consent of all Member States, or by leaving the EU altogether). At the time of writing, and despite the so called 'Brexit' poll, it remains unclear whether the UK will in fact remain or leave the EU, or if some other treaty will result which requires UK adherence to common market rules. In any event, it matters what the EU does. Its power to legislate in the field of labour law is now in TFEU Article 153.

Treaty on the Functioning of the European Union, Article 153

1. With a view to achieving the objectives of Article 151, the Union shall support and complement the activities of the Member States in the following fields:
    (a) improvement in particular of the working environment to protect workers' health safety;
    (b) working conditions;
    (c) social security and social protection of workers;
    (d) protection of workers where their employment contract is terminated;
    (e) the information and consultation of workers;
    (f) representation and collective defence of the interests of workers and employers, including co-determination, subject to paragraph 5;
    (g) conditions of employment for third-country nationals legally residing in Union territory;
    (h) the integration of persons excluded from the labour market, without prejudice to Article 166;
    (i) equality between men and women with regard to labour market opportunities and treatment at work;
    (j) the combating of social exclusion;
    (k) the modernisation of social protection systems without prejudice to point (c).
    ...
4. The provisions adopted pursuant to this Article:
    — shall not affect the right of Member States to define the fundamental principles of their social security systems and must not significantly affect the financial equilibrium thereof,
    — shall not prevent any Member State from maintaining or introducing more stringent protective measures compatible with the Treaties.
5. The provisions of this Article shall not apply to pay, the right of association, the right to strike or the right to impose lock-outs.'

NOTES AND QUESTIONS

1. Although the EU may not legislate on pay (eg, an EU-wide minimum wage), trade unions, and collective action, the ECJ has decided many cases where those labour policies conflict with other EU law norms. It also appears to be silent on the question of job security rights, such as unfair dismissal. For example, a long qualifying

period for unfair dismissal rights may mean fewer young people or women get protection of the right, and could therefore raise questions of discrimination, or the courts' protection of the EU right for companies to establish a business in any member state could conflict with an international trade union's right to strike. See *R (Seymour-Smith) v Secretary of State for Employment* (1999) C-167/97, [2000] UKHL 12; and *The Rosella* (2008) C-438/05, [2008] IRLR 143.

2.   The four major themes of legal development in this chapter have been liberation from forced labour, the ending of child labour, the development of the right to participate in setting the terms of work, and the development of equality. In its 1998 Declaration, the ILO determined that these four policies were mandatory for all member nations.

ILO, *Declaration on Fundamental Principles and Rights at Work* (1998)

Whereas the ILO was founded in the conviction that social justice is essential to universal and lasting peace;

Whereas economic growth is essential but not sufficient to ensure equity, social progress and the eradication of poverty, confirming the need for the ILO to promote strong social policies, justice and democratic institutions;

Whereas the ILO should, now more than ever, draw upon all its standard-setting, technical cooperation and research resources in all its areas of competence, in particular employment, vocational training and working conditions, to ensure that, in the context of a global strategy for economic and social development, economic and social policies are mutually reinforcing components in order to create broad-based sustainable development;

Whereas the ILO should give special attention to the problems of persons with special social needs, particularly the unemployed and migrant workers, and mobilize and encourage international, regional and national efforts aimed at resolving their problems, and promote effective policies aimed at job creation;

Whereas, in seeking to maintain the link between social progress and economic growth, the guarantee of fundamental principles and rights at work is of particular significance in that it enables the persons concerned, to claim freely and on the basis of equality of opportunity, their fair share of the wealth which they have helped to generate, and to achieve fully their human potential;

Whereas the ILO is the constitutionally mandated international organization and the competent body to set and deal with international labour standards, and enjoys universal support and acknowledgement in promoting Fundamental Rights at Work as the expression of its constitutional principles;

Whereas it is urgent, in a situation of growing economic interdependence, to reaffirm the immutable nature of the fundamental principles and rights embodied in the Constitution of the Organization and to promote their universal application;

THE INTERNATIONAL LABOUR CONFERENCE
   1. Recalls:
   (a)   that in freely joining the ILO, all Members have endorsed the principles and rights set out in its Constitution and in the Declaration of Philadelphia, and have undertaken to work towards attaining the overall objectives of the Organization to the best of their resources and fully in line with their specific circumstances;
   (b)   that these principles and rights have been expressed and developed in the form of specific rights and obligations in Conventions recognized as fundamental both inside and outside the Organization.

2. Declares that all Members, even if they have not ratified the Conventions in question, have an obligation arising from the very fact of membership in the Organization to respect, to promote and to realize, in good faith and in accordance with the Constitution, the principles concerning the fundamental rights which are the subject of those Conventions, namely:

    (a)   freedom of association and the effective recognition of the right to collective bargaining;

    (b)   the elimination of all forms of forced or compulsory labour;

    (c)   the effective abolition of child labour; and

    (d)   the elimination of discrimination in respect of employment and occupation.

3. Recognizes the obligation on the Organization to assist its Members, in response to their established and expressed needs, in order to attain these objectives by making full use of its constitutional, operational and budgetary resources, including, by the mobilization of external resources and support, as well as by encouraging other international organizations with which the ILO has established relations, pursuant to article 12 of its Constitution, to support these efforts:

    (a)   by offering technical cooperation and advisory services to promote the ratification and implementation of the fundamental Conventions;

    (b)   by assisting those Members not yet in a position to ratify some or all of these Conventions in their efforts to respect, to promote and to realize the principles concerning fundamental rights which are the subject of these Conventions; and

    (c)   by helping the Members in their efforts to create a climate for economic and social development.

NOTES AND QUESTIONS

1. The four pairs of Conventions (eight in total) are binding on every member, even those states that have not ratified Conventions. In effect, these become *jus cogens* norms: the abolition of forced labour (1930, No 29 and 1957, No 105), the abolition of child labour (1973, No 138 and 1999, No 182), freedom of association including the right to strike (1948, No 87 and 1949, No 98), and the principle of equal treatment (1951, No 100 and 1958, No 111).

2. The ILO's motto, 'Labour is not a commodity' is intended as a reference, in part, to the argument by Karl Marx in *Capital* (1867) ch 1, that under a capitalist economic system all things, including human beings, are turned into commodities by the production process. Marx argued people, like any other commodity, are exploited for their labour power, and they are alienated from the product of their labour. The phrase was first seen in law in the US Clayton Antitrust Act 1914. On the history of the phrase, see P O'Higgins, 'Labour Is Not a Commodity – An Irish Contribution to International Labour Law' (1997) 26(3) *Industrial Law Journal* 225.

3. There are many more Conventions as well as Recommendations, which form the major sources of international labour law. Does the isolation of 'core' Conventions represent a backward step in the ILO's evolution – a narrowing of horizons – or an admission of failure to raise standards? Out of all Conventions, which would you choose as 'core'?

4. In 2000, the United Nations released the eight Millennium Development Goals (concerning poverty, education, gender equality, health, and environment) and the ten principles of the Global Compact. The Global Compact is addressed to corporations to help states realise the development goals. In turn, it refers to the core ILO Conventions.

5. The third article requires Members to realise core labour standards, not merely in their own territory, but also to help other members to do the same. Which avenues of government policy, trade policy or corporate regulation do you think could achieve that?

6. The World Trade Organization has a potentially huge indirect impact on labour law policy, even though the Singapore Ministerial Declaration (13 December 1996) said labour policy should not be part of an amended General Agreement on Tariffs and Trade. Trade treaties formerly sought to reduce tariffs and customs taxes on goods, services and capital, while more modern treaties seek to pass substantive regulation of enterprise. One effect of the failure to amend the GATT or treaties forming the WTO is that more bilateral trade deals have made (cursory) reference to labour standards, as part of conditions to liberalise, eg Council Regulation (EC) No 732/2008 Arts 7–8, 15 and 27. See BA Hepple, *Labour Laws and Global Trade* (2005) and MJ Trebilcock and R Howse, *The Regulation of International Trade* (2012) ch 18, 716–55.

Additional Reading for Chapter 1

BH Putnam, *Enforcement of the Statute of Labourers* **(1908)**
Putnam examines the 1351 Act, as the subtitle says, 'During the First Decade after the Black Death 1349–1359' through primary sources including reports from Justices of the Peace, proceedings before the Court of King's Bench and the Common Pleas.

EM Dodd, 'From Maximum to Minimum Wages: Six Centuries of Regulation of Employment Contracts' (1943) 43(5) *Columbia Law Review* **643**
Dodd explores the regulation of wages since the Statute of Labourers 1351, up to what was, in effect, the New Deal's 'maximum wage' regulation in the United States by the Wage Stabilization Unit.

P Blumberg, *Industrial Democracy: The Sociology of Participation* **(1968) chs 1–3**
Blumberg recounts the Hawthorne experiments of Elton Mayo. He concludes that although the workers were unaffected by lighting variation, it was significant that their productivity greatly improved when they were in the test laboratory, as opposed to the factory. Blumberg argues that, from Mayo's own documents, it was clear that the workers performed better because the workers did not have draconian supervisors and were consulted on how their work would be done, and when they would get breaks. Blumberg suggests that greater participation in the workplace, for example through legal rights in works councils and elections to the board of directors, would improve productivity and have social benefits.

K Marx, *Capital: A Critique of Political Economy* **(1887) vol I, chs 10, 15 and 27–28**
In chapters 10 and 15, the German refugee, writing from the British Library, traces the evolution of child and factory labour in respect of changes to the working day, and the introduction of machinery through the countless reports of Royal Commissions, newspaper and contemporary sources. Marx argues that ultimately the 'chronic misery' inflicted by people on workers lays the foundations for revolution. Chapters 27 and 28 recount the development of English land law through 'expropriation' of people from land they used to inhabit in a feudal system. Marx traces the Inclosure Acts, followed by Poor Acts and Vagabond Acts to prohibit begging and eventually to put people into workhouses. He finishes by suggesting that although criminalisation of trade unions had gradually been lifted by the Trade Union Act 1871, the process was incomplete. *Capital* was first published in German in 1867, and translated into English in 1887.

JV Orth, *Combination and Conspiracy* **(1991)**
With the subtitle 'A Legal History of Trade Unionism, 1721–1906', Orth explores the gradual liberalisation of worker combinations from common law suppression, particularly through statutes and torts relating to unlawful 'conspiracy' from the emergent years of the United Kingdom. Starting with *R v Journeymen-Taylors of Cambridge* (1721) 88 ER 9, Orth contends that the Combination Acts of 1799 and 1800, which codified suppression of worker combinations, actually marked liberalisation because they coincided with the abandonment of wage fixing. Gradual development over the nineteenth century brought the modern right to take collective action.

S Deakin and F Wilkinson, *The Law of the Labour Market* **(2005) ch 2**
In chapter 2, on 'The Origins of the Contract of Employment', Deakin and Wilkinson contend that the contract of employment was created historically by the change in economic system from feudal to capitalist production. The authors document how the dividing line between employed and self-employed was evident in early Poor Law cases, and suggest that state welfare policy has always been instrumental in shaping the scope of employment.

R Lewis and J Clark (eds), *Labour Law and Politics in the Weimar Republic* **(1981)**
This book summarises modern German labour law history, and collects various essays from Otto Kahn-Freund. It includes a translation from German of his astonishing critique of the 'Social Ideal of the Reich Labour Court' in its 1920s and early 1930s case law. Kahn-Freund concluded from an examination of the Court's decisions that it pursued a fascist agenda, which systematically dismantled the post-World War One system of workplace democracy, in elected works councils, allowed open discrimination of trade union representatives, but imposed social obligations on employers to care for their subordinated workforce.

KW Wedderburn, *The Worker and the Law* **(2nd edn 1986)**
'Most workers want nothing more of the law than that it should leave them alone.' So begins Lord Wedderburn's classic treatise on labour relations. Wedderburn analyses by topic the state of labour law, focusing on its evolution through the early to mid-twentieth century, and the particular tension between the judiciary and statutory

rights. He concludes with a recommendation that positive rights for trade unions should be codified in statute.

P Davies and M Freedland, Labour Legislation and Public Policy (2nd edn 1993)
Davies and Freedland cover the evolution of labour law primarily from 1945 to 1992, a project they say was motivated partly by wishing to grapple with 'the colossal rate of legislative change from the mid-1960s onwards, and the lack of continuity in recent years'. Starting with a critique of Otto Kahn-Freund's theory of British collective laissez faire, they trace the shift from a public policy of using collective agreements as the primary instruments to improve labour rights, to reliance on minimum labour standards in legislation, coinciding with the juridification and dismantling of trade union organisation in the majority of British workplaces. If collective bargaining was to be reconstructed in a viable way, it would need to be accompanied by the legal guarantee of rights for employees within workplaces and as union members.

Theory

What should labour law aim for, and what are the means to get there? The word 'theory' usually mixes two things. First, there are descriptive or 'positive' theories about how the world works. What happens to the unemployment rate if we raise or decrease the minimum wage? How will people's living standards change with greater or fewer union rights, and more or less employee voice? When politicians or economists predict what will happen with some legal change, we must look for evidence. This can include quantitative data (on what happened before when countries changed their laws), qualitative research in interviews and surveys (what people say about legal changes), or behavioural and psychological experiments (which suggest how humans might react to legal changes).

Second, there are political or 'normative' theories about the goals that labour law (or all law) should pursue. (For this author's views, see the Preface.) What values does the law aim to uphold? Big concepts such as democracy, freedom, equality, liberty, solidarity, efficiency, development, prosperity or dignity shape our vocabulary on what 'the good life' should mean. Human societies seldom arrive at rounded conceptions of justice through abstract reasoning (cf J Rawls, *A Theory of Justice* (1971) 65, on a 'reflective equilibrium' between conflicting views). Once people agree upon (or impose) a model of justice, we usually put principles into practice, and then revise those principles in light of experience, before starting again. In this way, it might be hoped that a reflexive equilibrium is reached, not by pure reason, but by reason and experience. Societies become 'laboratories of democracy', so long as law does not shut down experiment (see *New State Ice Co v Liebmann*, 285 US 262 (1932) per Brandeis J).

Since the industrial revolution, labour theory has become increasingly sophisticated. Philosophers and political economists used to reason in terms of values (equality, freedom, etc) by appeal to allegory and anecdote. In the twentieth century, as more statistical data were collected and available, a clash developed around the 'social science' of advancing welfare or economic efficiency. Nevertheless, many dominant theories remained unconnected to evidence. In the twenty-first century, as discussion has advanced, and computing power allows unprecedented access to information, the global debate has shifted towards the language of human development. Basic clashes of values remain, however, and colour people's understanding, or willingness, to accept evidence. This chapter outlines (1) early theory, centred on equality and freedom, (2) economic efficiency theories, and (3) contemporary theories and evidence on human development.

(1) EQUALITY AND FREEDOM

Since the industrial revolution, labour was central to all theories of politics and economics. Of course it was: almost everyone worked for a living, and for the first time in human history people's work could increase their material well-being beyond subsistence. For the first time, laws and social institutions were seen as instruments for a progressively better existence. Could expanding production by labour and capital bring more equality and freedom, or would it lead to the immiseration of a subjugated working class? In the first extracts the great Glaswegian lawyer, moral philosopher, and father of economics, Adam Smith, grapples with the way that tensions in human behaviour play out in labour markets.

A Smith, *The Theory of Moral Sentiments* (1759) Part I, ch I and Part IV, ch I

Part I Of the Propriety of Action

Chapter I Of Sympathy

How selfish soever man may be supposed, there are evidently some principles in his nature, which interest him in the fortune of others, and render their happiness necessary to him, though he derives nothing from it except the pleasure of seeing it. Of this kind is pity or compassion, the emotion which we feel for the misery of others, when we either see it, or are made to conceive it in a very lively manner. That we often derive sorrow from the sorrow of others, is a matter of fact too obvious to require any instances to prove it; for this sentiment, like all the other original passions of human nature, is by no means confined to the virtuous and humane, though they perhaps may feel it with the most exquisite sensibility. The greatest ruffian, the most hardened violator of the laws of society, is not altogether without it.

...

Part IV Of the Effect of Utility upon the Sentiment of Approbation

Chapter I Of the beauty which the appearance of Utility bestows upon all the productions of art, and of the extensive influence of this species of Beauty

...

The earth by these labours of mankind has been obliged to redouble her natural fertility, and to maintain a greater multitude of inhabitants. It is to no purpose, that the proud and unfeeling landlord views his extensive fields, and without a thought for the wants of his brethren, in imagination consumes himself the whole harvest that grows upon them. The homely and vulgar proverb, that the eye is larger than the belly, never was more fully verified than with regard to him. The capacity of his stomach bears no proportion to the immensity of his desires, and will receive no more than that of the meanest peasant. The rest he is obliged to distribute among those, who prepare, in the nicest manner, that little which he himself makes use of, among those who fit up the palace in which this little is to be consumed, among those who provide and keep in order all the different baubles and trinkets, which are employed in the oeconomy of greatness; all of whom thus derive from his luxury and caprice, that share of the necessaries of life, which they would in vain have expected from his humanity or his justice. The produce of the soil maintains at all times nearly that number of inhabitants which it is capable of maintaining. The rich only select from the heap what is most precious and agreeable. They consume little more than the poor, and in spite of their natural selfishness and rapacity, though they mean only their own conveniency, though the sole end which they propose from the labours of all the thousands whom they employ, be the gratification of their own vain and insatiable desires, they divide with the poor the produce of all their improvements. They are led by an invisible hand to make nearly the same distribution of the necessaries of life, which would have been made, had the earth been divided into equal portions among all its inhabitants, and thus without intending it, without knowing it, advance the interest of the society, and afford means to the multiplication of the species. When Providence divided the earth among a few lordly masters, it neither forgot nor abandoned those who seemed to have been left out in the partition. These last too enjoy their share of all that it produces. In what constitutes the real happiness of human life, they are in no respect inferior to those who would seem so much above them. In ease of body and peace of mind, all the different ranks of life are nearly upon a level, and the beggar, who suns himself by the side of the highway, possesses that security which kings are fighting for.

NOTES AND QUESTIONS

1. Smith argues that almost all people gain pleasure from helping others. But even if an individual is particularly selfish and greedy, Smith contends that the incapacity of that person to consume all their wealth forces them to expend their wealth in a way that helps. An 'invisible hand' in labour markets, he thought originally, would 'make nearly the same distribution' of wealth as if the earth had 'been divided into equal portions'. Do you share Smith's normative view that markets should follow a goal of equality?

2. In modern terminology, Smith is basing his positive argument that markets make equality on an unlimited 'propensity to consume' by employers, an early version of the view that wealth would 'trickle down'. As we shall see, Smith evidently thought employers would all remain in small partnerships rather than large corporations. But if that had remained true (and it did not), would you find this theory persuasive on its own terms?

3. Smith's *Lectures On Justice, Police, Revenue and Arms* (1763) though often forgotten, probably had an impact even more enduring than William Blackstone's *Commentaries* (1769). Most significantly, Smith states contracts are founded upon 'reasonable expectations', a view adopted by the House of Lords and the Supreme Court: see chapter 5.

4. In the year of the American revolution, Smith published *The Wealth of Nations*, which in today's eyes has made him the father of economics. By then he had subtly developed his view of labour markets.

A Smith, *An Inquiry into the Nature and Causes of the Wealth of Nations* (1776) Book I, ch 8 and Book V, ch 1

Book I, ch 8, Of the Wages of Labour

The produce of labour constitutes the natural recompence or wages of labour.

In that original state of things, which precedes both the appropriation of land and the accumulation of stock, the whole produce of labour belongs to the labourer. He has neither landlord nor master to share with him.

Had this state continued, the wages of labour would have augmented with all those improvements in its productive powers, to which the division of labour gives occasion. All things would gradually have become cheaper. They would have been produced by a smaller quantity of labour; and as the commodities produced by equal quantities of labour would naturally in this state of things be exchanged for one another, they would have been purchased likewise with the produce of a smaller quantity.

But though all things would have become cheaper in reality, in appearance many things might have become dearer than before, or have been exchanged for a greater quantity of other goods. ...

As soon as land becomes private property, the landlord demands a share of almost all the produce which the labourer can either raise, or collect from it. His rent makes the first deduction from the produce of the labour which is employed upon land.

It seldom happens that the person who tills the ground has wherewithal to maintain himself till he reaps the harvest. His maintenance is generally advanced to him from the stock of a master, the farmer who employs him, and who would have no interest to employ him, unless he was to share in the produce of his labour, or unless his stock was to be replaced to him with a profit. This profit makes a second deduction from the produce of the labour which is employed upon land. ...

What are the common wages of labour, depends every where upon the contract usually made between those two parties, whose interests are by no means the same. The workmen desire to get as much, the masters to give as little as possible. The former are disposed to combine in order to raise, the latter in order to lower the wages of labour.

It is not, however, difficult to foresee which of the two parties must, upon all ordinary occasions, have the advantage in the dispute, and force the other into a compliance with their terms. The masters, being fewer in number, can combine much more easily; and the law, besides, authorizes, or at least does not prohibit their combinations, while it prohibits those of the workmen.[1] We have no acts of parliament against combining to lower the price of work; but many against combining to raise it. In all such disputes the masters can hold out much longer. A landlord, a farmer, a master manufacturer, a merchant, though they did not employ a single workman, could generally live a year or two upon the stocks which they have already acquired. Many workmen could not subsist a week, few could subsist a month, and scarce any a year without employment. In the long run the workman may be as necessary to his master as his master is to him; but the necessity is not so immediate.

We rarely hear, it has been said, of the combinations of masters, though frequently of those of workmen. But whoever imagines, upon this account, that masters rarely combine, is as ignorant of the world as of the subject. Masters are always and every where in a sort of tacit, but constant and uniform combination, not to raise the wages of labour above their actual rate.

---

[1] E.g., 7 Geo. I., stat. 1, c. 13, as to London tailors; 12 Geo. I., c. 34, as to woolcombers and weavers; 12 Geo. I., c. 35, as to brick and tile makers within fifteen miles of London; 22 Geo. II., c. 27, §12, as to persons employed in the woollen manufacture and many others.

To violate this combination is every where a most unpopular action, and a sort of reproach to a master among his neighbours and equals. We seldom, indeed, hear of this combination, because it is the usual, and one may say, the natural state of things which nobody ever hears of. Masters too sometimes enter into particular combinations to sink the wages of labour even below this rate. These are always conducted with the utmost silence and secrecy, till the moment of execution, and when the workmen yield, as they sometimes do, without resistance, though severely felt by them, they are never heard of by other people. Such combinations, however, are frequently resisted by a contrary defensive combination of the workmen; who sometimes too, without any provocation of this kind, combine of their own accord to raise the price of their labour. ...

But though in disputes with their workmen, masters must generally have the advantage, there is however a certain rate below which it seems impossible to reduce, for any considerable time, the ordinary wages even of the lowest species of labour.

A man must always live by his work, and his wages must at least be sufficient to maintain him. They must even upon most occasions be somewhat more; otherwise it would be impossible for him to bring up a family, and the race of such workmen could not last beyond the first generation. ...

Book V, ch 1, Of the Expences of the Sovereign or Commonwealth

Of the Public Works and Institutions which are necessary for facilitating particular Branches of Commerce

The object of the public works and institutions above mentioned is to facilitate commerce in general. But in order to facilitate some particular branches of it, particular institutions are necessary, which again require a particular and extraordinary expence.

...

In a private copartnery, each partner is bound for the debts contracted by the company to the whole extent of his fortune. In a joint stock company, on the contrary, each partner is bound only to the extent of his share.

The trade of a joint stock company is always managed by a court of directors. This court, indeed, is frequently subject, in many respects, to the control of a general court of proprietors. But the greater part of those proprietors seldom pretend to understand anything of the business of the company, and when the spirit of faction happens not to prevail among them, give themselves no trouble about it, but receive contentedly such half-yearly or yearly dividend as the directors think proper to make to them. This total exemption from trouble and from risk, beyond a limited sum, encourages many people to become adventurers in joint stock companies, who would, upon no account, hazard their fortunes in any private copartnery. Such companies, therefore, commonly draw to themselves much greater stocks than any private copartnery can boast of. The trading stock of the South Sea Company, at one time, amounted to upwards of thirty-three millions eight hundred thousand pounds. The divided capital of the Bank of England amounts, at present, to ten millions seven hundred and eighty thousand pounds. The directors of such companies, however, being the managers rather of other people's money than of their own, it cannot well be expected that they should watch over it with the same anxious vigilance with which the partners in a private copartnery frequently watch over their own. Like the stewards of a rich man, they are apt to consider attention to small matters as not for their master's honour, and very easily give themselves a dispensation from having it. Negligence and profusion, therefore, must always prevail, more or less, in the management of the affairs of such a company. It is upon this account that joint stock companies for foreign trade have seldom been able to maintain the competition against private adventurers. They have, accordingly, very seldom succeeded without an exclusive privilege, and frequently have not succeeded with one. Without an exclusive privilege they have commonly mismanaged the trade. With an exclusive privilege they have both mismanaged and confined it.

NOTES AND QUESTIONS

1. Smith's suggests workers lack bargaining power compared with employers because they have fewer resources to 'hold out' in negotiations. This flows from unequal distribution of property in land and capital goods. To what extent do you think the same holds true today? What do you think influences the distribution of wealth the most?

2. The idea that unequal distribution of property is the basis for inequality of bargaining power has probably been the most important idea in the history of labour law theory. While the law enforces private property rights, and property rights are very unequally distributed, people are not truly free. See also, from Germany, and co-author of the social democratic Weimar Constitution of 1919, H Sinzheimer, *Grundzüge des Arbeitsrechts* (1926) ch 2, 22.

3. Smith also contends that law unfairly repressed worker combinations, but did not do this equally for employer combinations. Since the Bubble Act 1720, corporations had been unlawful without an Act of Parliament. Smith obviously approved. 'Negligence and profusion' was the result, he wrote, in most cases where directors of joint-stock companies managed 'other people's money'. His ideal world, where the 'invisible hand' led to equality, was one of small partnerships of the 'butcher, baker and brewer'. He seemed to think this worked only so long as corporations were unlawful, and he heavily criticised those Parliament did create, unless they were for banking, accident insurance, canal-making and water supply (Book V, ch 1, Part III, §§104–21). Smith was, however, wrong that corporations were not as competitive as partnerships, at least with the very considerable regulation since their general legalisation, first consolidated in the Joint Stock Companies Act 1856. Corporations, at least in UK law today, are effectively a combination of capital investors, and are the most common form of employer today. However, most ultimate investors are themselves employees saving for retirement (see chapters 6 and 11).

4. Following on from Smith's remarks about sufficient wages, T Malthus, *An Essay on the Principle of Population* (1798) developed a theory that wages could *never* go beyond subsistence because the working classes would procreate to eliminate any surplus. The normative conclusion was that policies to provide food and relief, such as the poor law, were wasteful. Why do you think these sorts of theories become popular?

5. The next most prominent political economist of his time, D Ricardo, *On the Principles of Political Economy and Taxation* (1817) ch 5, was more sceptical than Smith that anything but supply and demand, and the costs of maintaining workers' existence, affected wages. Ricardo also argued that the development of machinery inevitably harms the interests of workers. More enduring was his theory of comparative advantage: if countries producing different commodities open to free trade, no matter how comparatively inefficient any one is, they will all gain a comparative advantage in price. Ricardo's theories therefore had no conception of bargaining power in labour relations, or in international relations.

6.   By far the most influential thinker of the late nineteenth century was John
     Stuart Mill, an intensively educated child, civil servant, philosopher, and
     economist, who also became the Member of Parliament for Westminster. In this
     extract Mill gives his rationalisation for labour legislation, as he saw it at the time.

JS Mill, *Principles of Political Economy*
(1848) Book VI, ch VI and Book V, ch XI

Book IV, ch VI, Of the Stationary State

§1. The preceding chapters comprise the general theory of the economical progress of society,
in the sense in which those terms are commonly understood; the progress of capital, of population, and of the productive arts. But in contemplating any progressive movement, not in its
nature unlimited, the mind is not satisfied with merely tracing the laws of the movement; it
cannot but ask the further question, to what goal? Towards what ultimate point is society tend-
ing by its industrial progress? When the progress ceases, in what condition are we to expect
that it will leave mankind?
    ...

§2. ... I confess I am not charmed with the ideal of life held out by those who think that the
normal state of human beings is that of struggling to get on; that the trampling, crushing,
elbowing, and treading on each other's heels, which form the existing type of social life, are
the most desirable lot of human kind, or anything but the disagreeable symptoms of one of
the phases of industrial progress. It may be a necessary stage in the progress of civilization,
and those European nations which have hitherto been so fortunate as to be preserved from it,
may have it yet to undergo. It is an incident of growth, not a mark of decline. ... But it is not a
kind of social perfection which philanthropists to come will feel any very eager desire to assist
in realizing. Most fitting, indeed, is it, that while riches are power, and to grow as rich as possible the universal object of ambition, the path to its attainment should be open to all, without
favour or partiality. But the best state for human nature is that in which, while no one is poor,
no one desires to be richer, nor has any reason to fear being thrust back by the efforts of others
to push themselves forward. ...

Book V, ch XI, Of the Grounds and Limits of the Laisser-faire or Non-Interference Principle

§7. ... *Laisser-faire*, in short, should be the general practice: every departure from it, unless
required by some great good, is a certain evil. ... The maxim is unquestionably sound as a general rule; but there is no difficulty in perceiving some very large and conspicuous exceptions to
it. These may be classed under several heads.
    First:—The individual who is presumed to be the best judge of his own interests may be
incapable of judging or acting for himself; may be a lunatic, an idiot, an infant: or though not
wholly incapable, may be of immature years and judgment. In this case the foundation of the
laisser-faire principle breaks down entirely. ...

§10. A second exception to the doctrine that individuals are the best judges of their own interest, is when an individual attempts to decide irrevocably now, what will be best for his interest
at some future and distant time. ...

§11. The third exception which I shall notice, to the doctrine that government cannot manage
the affairs of individuals as well as the individuals themselves, has reference to the great class

of cases in which the individuals can only manage the concern by delegated agency, and in which the so-called private management is, in point of fact, hardly better entitled to be called management by the persons interested, than administration by a public officer. Whatever, if left to spontaneous agency, can only be done by joint-stock associations, will often be as well, and sometimes better done, as far as the actual work is concerned, by the state. Government management is, indeed, proverbially jobbing, careless, and ineffective, but so likewise has generally been joint-stock management. The directors of a joint-stock company, it is true, are always shareholders; but also the members of a government are invariably taxpayers; and in the case of directors, no more than in that of governments, is their proportional share of the benefits of good management equal to the interest they may possibly have in mismanagement, even without reckoning the interest of their case. It may be objected, that the shareholders, in their collective character, exercise a certain control over the directors, and have almost always full power to remove them from office. Practically, however, the difficulty of exercising this power is found to be so great, that it is hardly ever exercised except in cases of such flagrantly unskilful, or, at least, unsuccessful management, as would generally produce the ejection from office of managers appointed by the government. …

§12. To a fourth case of exception I must request particular attention, it being one to which as it appears to me, the attention of political economists has not yet been sufficiently drawn. There are matters in which the interference of law is required, not to overrule the judgment of individuals respecting their own interest, but to give effect to that judgment: they being unable to give effect to it except by concert, which concert again cannot be effectual unless it receives validity and sanction from the law. For illustration, and without prejudging the particular point, I may advert to the question of diminishing the hours of labour. Let us suppose, what is at least supposable, whether it be the fact or not – that a general reduction of the hours of factory labour, say from ten to nine, would be for the advantage of the workpeople: that they would receive as high wages, or nearly as high, for nine hours' labour as they receive for ten. If this would be the result, and if the operatives generally are convinced that it would, the limitation, some may say, will be adopted spontaneously. I answer, that it will not be adopted unless the body of operatives bind themselves to one another to abide by it. A workman who refused to work more than nine hours while there were others who worked ten, would either not be employed at all, or if employed, must submit to lose one-tenth of his wages. However convinced, therefore, he may be that it is the interest of the class to work short time, it is contrary to his own interest to set the example, unless he is well assured that all or most others will follow it. But suppose a general agreement of the whole class: might not this be effectual without the sanction of law? Not unless enforced by opinion with a rigour practically equal to that of law. For however beneficial the observance of the regulation might be to the class collectively, the immediate interest of every individual would lie in violating it: and the more numerous those were who adhered to the rule, the more would individuals gain by departing from it.

NOTES AND QUESTIONS

1.   In another of his books, *Utilitarianism* (1863) ch 5, Mill expounded his position that the ultimate goal was pursuit of utility, by which he meant as many people's happiness as possible. This underpinned the maxim 'to do to each according to his deserts', which in turn was the 'highest abstract standard of social and distributive justice towards which all institutions, and the efforts of all virtuous citizens, should be made in the utmost possible degree to converge'. Above, Mill argues that a 'stationary state', where competitive society of struggling, trampling and elbowing has been superseded, should be the end-point. Laissez faire (freedom of contract) would be the method to get there, although Mill's range of exceptions where laissez faire does not work (particularly in labour markets and

corporations) is striking. Mill did not elaborate whether a stationary state would still have markets and institutions in the form he advocated for the present.

2. In Book I, 'Production', Mill advances the view that there are fixed economic 'laws' of labour, capital and competition, based on human nature, according to which actual laws can be configured to realise the greatest production of economic wealth. In Book II, 'Distribution', he sums up, saying we 'cannot alter the ultimate properties either of matter or mind, but can only employ those properties more or less successfully'. Then, Mill says it 'is not so with the Distribution of wealth. That is a matter of human institution solely. The things once there, mankind, individually or collectively, can do with them as they like.' Do you think the distribution of wealth itself affects the frontier of possible production?

3. Mill's fourth exception to laissez faire was the first economic explanation of 'collective action problems' (contrast the anti-labour but oft-quoted M Olson, *The Logic of Collective Action* (1957)). Law is necessary to give effect to 'the judgment of individuals respecting their own interest' which collective action problems prevent. While Smith had observed legal obstacles for workers to combine relative to employers, Mill concludes that the costs of taking collective action will be higher among people who are in greater need. Mill uses the example of reducing working time. Can you think of any labour regulation that could not be justified under this exception?

4. Mill's third exception to laissez faire was whenever an enterprise is necessarily run for administrative efficiency through 'delegated agency', generating what is now usually known in economic literature as the 'agency problem'. Mill says corporations are the chief example, and then says that government will usually do such tasks that corporations perform better, because they are more accountable to the public. Can you think of any enterprise that could not be justifiably nationalised under this exception?

5. Mill believed, like most political economists of his age, that prices for all goods and services reflected supply and demand, and should, if markets were not imperfect, reflect the value of the labour contained within them. See J Locke, *Second Treatise on Government* (1689) ch 5. For Mill, of course, labour markets were inherently imperfect, and so wages and prices did not reflect the true value of labour in them. The labour theory of value was also the starting point for the critique of Karl Marx.

K Marx, *Capital: A Critique of Political Economy* **(1867)**
vol I, chs 13, 32 and 33

Chapter 13, Co-operation

... We saw in a former chapter, that a certain minimum amount of capital was necessary, in order that the number of labourers simultaneously employed, and, consequently, the amount of surplus-value produced, might suffice to liberate the employer himself from manual labour, to convert him from a small master into a capitalist, and thus formally to establish capitalist production. We now see that a certain minimum amount is a necessary condition for the conversion of numerous isolated and independent processes into one combined social process.

We also saw that at first, the subjection of labour to capital was only a formal result of the fact, that the labourer, instead of working for himself, works for and consequently under the capitalist. By the co-operation of numerous wage-labourers, the sway of capital develops into a requisite for carrying on the labour-process itself, into a real requisite of production. That a capitalist should command on the field of production, is now as indispensable as that a general should command on the field of battle.

All combined labour on a large scale requires, more or less, a directing authority, in order to secure the harmonious working of the individual activities, and to perform the general functions that have their origin in the action of the combined organism, as distinguished from the action of its separate organs. A single violin player is his own conductor; an orchestra requires a separate one. The work of directing, superintending, and adjusting, becomes one of the functions of capital, from the moment that the labour under the control of capital, becomes co-operative. Once a function of capital, it acquires special characteristics.

The directing motive, the end and aim of capitalist production, is to extract the greatest possible amount of surplus-value,[2] and consequently to exploit labour-power to the greatest possible extent. As the number of the co-operating labourers increases, so too does their resistance to the domination of capital, and with it, the necessity for capital to overcome this resistance by counterpressure. The control exercised by the capitalist is not only a special function, due to the nature of the social labour-process, and peculiar to that process, but it is, at the same time, a function of the exploitation of a social labour-process, and is consequently rooted in the unavoidable antagonism between the exploiter and the living and labouring raw material he exploits.

Again, in proportion to the increasing mass of the means of production, now no longer the property of the labourer, but of the capitalist, the necessity increases for some effective control over the proper application of those means.[3] Moreover, the co-operation of wage labourers is entirely brought about by the capital that employs them. Their union into one single productive body and the establishment of a connexion between their individual functions, are matters foreign and external to them, are not their own act, but the act of the capital that brings and keeps them together. Hence the connexion existing between their various labours appears to them, ideally, in the shape of a preconceived plan of the capitalist, and practically in the shape of the authority of the same capitalist, in the shape of the powerful will of another, who subjects their activity to his aims. If, then, the control of the capitalist is in substance two-fold by reason of the two-fold nature of the process of production itself, which, on the one hand, is a social process for producing use-values, on the other, a process for creating surplus-value in form that control is despotic. As co-operation extends its scale, this despotism takes forms peculiar to itself. Just as at first the capitalist is relieved from actual labour so soon as his capital has reached that minimum amount with which capitalist production, as such, begins, so now, he hands over the work of direct and constant supervision of the individual workmen, and groups of workmen, to a special kind of wage-labourer. An industrial army of workmen, under the command of a capitalist, requires, like a real army, officers (managers), and sergeants (foremen, overlookers), who, while the work is being done, command in the name of the capitalist. The work of supervision becomes their established and exclusive function. When comparing the mode of production of isolated peasants and artisans with production by slave-labour,

---

[2] "Profits ... is the sole end of trade." (J. Vanderlint, l.c., p. 11.)

[3] That Philistine paper, the Spectator, states that after the introduction of a sort of partnership between capitalist and workmen in the "Wirework Company of Manchester," "the first result was a sudden decrease in waste, the men not seeing why they should waste their own property any more than any other master's, and waste is, perhaps, next to bad debts, the greatest source of manufacturing loss." The same paper finds that the main defect in the Rochdale co-operative experiments is this: "They showed that associations of workmen could manage shops, mills, and almost all forms of industry with success, and they immediately improved the condition of the men; but then they did not leave a clear place for masters." Quelle horreur!

the political economist counts this labour of superintendence among the *faux frais* of production.[4] But, when considering the capitalist mode of production, he, on the contrary, treats the work of control made necessary by the co-operative character of the labour-process as identical with the different work of control, necessitated by the capitalist character of that process and the antagonism of interests between capitalist and labourer.[5] It is not because he is a leader of industry that a man is a capitalist; on the contrary, he is a leader of industry because he is a capitalist. The leadership of industry is an attribute of capital, just as in feudal times the functions of general and judge, were attributes of landed property.[6]

The labourer is the owner of his labour-power until he has done bargaining for its sale with the capitalist; and he can sell no more than what he has i.e., his individual, isolated labour-power. This state of things is in no way altered by the fact that the capitalist, instead of buying the labour-power of one man, buys that of 100, and enters into separate contracts with 100 unconnected men instead of with one. He is at liberty to set the 100 men to work, without letting them co-operate. He pays them the value of 100 independent labour-powers, but he does not pay for the combined labour-power of the hundred. Being independent of each other, the labourers are isolated persons, who enter into relations with the capitalist, but not with one another. This co-operation begins only with the labour-process, but they have then ceased to belong to themselves. On entering that process, they become incorporated with capital. As co-operators, as members of a working organism, they are but special modes of existence of capital.

...

This power of Asiatic and Egyptian kings, Etruscan theocrats, &c., has in modern society been transferred to the capitalist, whether he be an isolated, or as in joint-stock companies, a collective capitalist.

Co-operation, such as we find it at the dawn of human development, among races who live by the chase,[7] or, say, in the agriculture of Indian communities, is based, on the one hand, on ownership in common of the means of production, and on the other hand, on the fact, that in those cases, each individual has no more torn himself off from the navel-string of his tribe or community, than each bee has freed itself from connexion with the hive. Such co-operation is distinguished from capitalistic co-operation by both of the above characteristics. The sporadic application of co-operation on a large scale in ancient times, in the middle ages, and in modern colonies, reposes on relations of dominion and servitude, principally on slavery. The capitalistic form, on the contrary, pre-supposes from first to last, the free wage-labourer, who sells his labour-power to capital. Historically, however, this form is developed in opposition to peasant agriculture and to the carrying on of independent handicrafts whether in guilds or not.[8] From the standpoint of these, capitalistic co-operation does not manifest itself as a particular

---

[4] Professor Cairnes, after stating that the superintendence of labour is a leading feature of production by slaves in the Southern States of North America, continues: "The peasant proprietor (of the North), appropriating the whole produce of his toil, needs no other stimulus to exertion. Superintendence is here completely dispensed with." (Cairnes, l.c., pp. 48, 49.)

[5] Sir James Steuart, a writer altogether remarkable for his quick eye for the characteristic social distinctions between different modes of production, says: "Why do large undertakings in the manufacturing way ruin private industry, but by coming nearer to the simplicity of slaves?" ("Prin. of Pol. Econ.," London, 1767, v. I., pp. 167, 168.)

[6] Auguste Comte and his school might therefore have shown that feudal lords are an eternal necessity in the same way that they have done in the case of the lords of capital.

[7] Linguet is improbably right, when in his "Théorie des Lois Civiles," he declares hunting to be the first form of co-operation, and man-hunting (war) one of the earliest forms of hunting.

[8] Peasant agriculture on a small scale, and the carrying on of independent handicrafts, which together form the basis of the feudal mode of production, and after the dissolution of that system, continue side by side with the capitalist mode, also form the economic foundation of the classical communities at their best, after the primitive form of ownership of land in common had disappeared, and before slavery had seized on production in earnest.

historical form of co-operation, but co-operation itself appears to be a historical form peculiar to, and specifically distinguishing, the capitalist process of production.

Just as the social productive power of labour that is developed by co-operation, appears to be the productive power of capital, so co-operation itself, contrasted with the process of production carried on by isolated independent labourers, or even by small employers, appears to be a specific form of the capitalist process of production. It is the first change experienced by the actual labour-process, when subjected to capital. This change takes place spontaneously. The simultaneous employment of a large number of wage-labourers, in one and the same process, which is a necessary condition of this change, also forms the starting-point of capitalist production. This point coincides with the birth of capital itself. If then, on the one hand, the capitalist mode of production presents itself to us historically, as a necessary condition to the transformation of the labour-process into a social process, so, on the other hand, this social form of the labour-process presents itself, as a method employed by capital for the more profitable exploitation of labour, by increasing that labour's productiveness. ...

Chapter 32, Historical Tendency of Capitalist Accumulation

What does the primitive accumulation of capital, i.e., its historical genesis, resolve itself into? In so far as it is not immediate transformation of slaves and serfs into wage labourers, and therefore a mere change of form, it only means the expropriation of the immediate producers, i.e., the dissolution of private property based on the labour of its owner. Private property, as the antithesis to social, collective property, exists only where the means of labour and the external conditions of labour belong to private individuals. But according as these private individuals are labourers or not labourers, private property has a different character. The numberless shades, that it at first sight presents, correspond to the intermediate stages lying between these two extremes. The private property of the labourer in his means of production is the foundation of petty industry, whether agricultural, manufacturing, or both; petty industry, again, is an essential condition for the development of social production and of the free individuality of the labourer himself. ... The expropriation of the immediate producers was accomplished with merciless Vandalism, and under the stimulus of passions the most infamous, the most sordid, the pettiest, the most meanly odious. Self-earned private property, that is based, so to say, on the fusing together of the isolated, independent labouring individual with the conditions of his labour, is supplanted by capitalistic private property, which rests on exploitation of the nominally free labour of others, i.e., on wage labour.[9]

As soon as this process of transformation has sufficiently decomposed the old society from top to bottom, as soon as the labourers are turned into proletarians, their means of labour into capital, as soon as the capitalist mode of production stands on its own feet, then the further socialisation of labour and further transformation of the land and other means of production into socially exploited and, therefore, common means of production, as well as the further expropriation of private proprietors, takes a new form. That which is now to be expropriated is no longer the labourer working for himself, but the capitalist exploiting many labourers. This expropriation is accomplished by the action of the immanent laws of capitalistic production itself, by the centralisation of capital. One capitalist always kills many. Hand in hand with this centralisation, or this expropriation of many capitalists by few, develop, on an ever-extending scale, the co-operative form of the labour process, the conscious technical application of science, the methodical cultivation of the soil, the transformation of the instruments of labour into instruments of labour only usable in common, the economising of all means of

---

[9] "Nous sommes dans une condition tout-à-fait nouvelle de la societé ... nous tendons a séparer toute espèce de propriété d'avec toute espèce de travail." [We are in a situation which is entirely new for society ... we are striving to separate every kind of property from every kind of labour.] (Sismondi: "Nouveaux Principes d'Econ. Polit." t. II, p. 434.)

production by their use as means of production of combined, socialised labour, the entanglement of all peoples in the net of the world market, and with this, the international character of the capitalistic regime. Along with the constantly diminishing number of the magnates of capital, who usurp and monopolise all advantages of this process of transformation, grows the mass of misery, oppression, slavery, degradation, exploitation; but with this too grows the revolt of the working class, a class always increasing in numbers, and disciplined, united, organised by the very mechanism of the process of capitalist production itself. The monopoly of capital becomes a fetter upon the mode of production, which has sprung up and flourished along with, and under it. Centralisation of the means of production and socialisation of labour at last reach a point where they become incompatible with their capitalist integument. This integument is burst asunder. The knell of capitalist private property sounds. The expropriators are expropriated.

The capitalist mode of appropriation, the result of the capitalist mode of production, produces capitalist private property. This is the first negation of individual private property, as founded on the labour of the proprietor. But capitalist production begets, with the inexorability of a law of Nature, its own negation. It is the negation of negation. This does not re-establish private property for the producer, but gives him individual property based on the acquisition of the capitalist era: i.e., on co-operation and the possession in common of the land and of the means of production.

The transformation of scattered private property, arising from individual labour, into capitalist private property is, naturally, a process, incomparably more protracted, violent, and difficult, than the transformation of capitalistic private property, already practically resting on socialised production, into socialised property. In the former case, we had the expropriation of the mass of the people by a few usurpers; in the latter, we have the expropriation of a few usurpers by the mass of the people.

Chapter 33, The Modern Theory of Colonisation

Political economy confuses on principle two very different kinds of private property, of which one rests on the producers' own labour, the other on the employment of the labour of others. It forgets that the latter not only is the direct antithesis of the former, but absolutely grows on its tomb only. In Western Europe, the home of Political Economy, the process of primitive accumulation is more of less accomplished. Here the capitalist regime has either directly conquered the whole domain of national production, or, where economic conditions are less developed, it, at least, indirectly controls those strata of society which, though belonging to the antiquated mode of production, continue to exist side by side with it in gradual decay. To this ready-made world of capital, the political economist applies the notions of law and of property inherited from a pre-capitalistic world with all the more anxious zeal and all the greater unction, the more loudly the facts cry out in the face of his ideology. It is otherwise in the colonies. There the capitalist regime everywhere comes into collision with the resistance of the producer, who, as owner of his own conditions of labour, employs that labour to enrich himself, instead of the capitalist. The contradiction of these two diametrically opposed economic systems, manifests itself here practically in a struggle between them. Where the capitalist has at his back the power of the mother-country, he tries to clear out of his way by force the modes of production and appropriation based on the independent labour of the producer. The same interest, which compels the sycophant of capital, the political economist, in the mother-country, to proclaim the theoretical identity of the capitalist mode of production with its contrary, that same interest compels him in the colonies to make a clean breast of it, and to proclaim aloud the antagonism of the two modes of production. To this end, he proves how the development of the social productive power of labour, co-operation, division of labour, use of machinery on a large scale, &c., are impossible without the expropriation of the labourers, and the corresponding transformation of their means of production into capital. In the interest of the so-called national wealth, he seeks for artificial means to ensure the poverty of the people. ...
    ...

We have seen that the expropriation of the mass of the people from the soil forms the basis of the capitalist mode of production. The essence of a free colony, on the contrary, consists in this – that the bulk of the soil is still public property, and every settler on it therefore can turn part of it into his private property and individual means of production, without hindering the later settlers in the same operation.[10] This is the secret both of the prosperity of the colonies and of their inveterate vice – opposition to the establishment of capital. "Where land is very cheap and all men are free, where every one who so pleases can easily obtain a piece of land for himself, not only is labour very dear, as respects the labourer's share of the produce, but the difficulty is to obtain combined labour at any price."[11]

...

How, then, to heal the anti-capitalistic cancer of the colonies? If men were willing, at a blow, to turn all the soil from public into private property, they would destroy certainly the root of the evil, but also – the colonies. The trick is how to kill two birds with one stone. Let the Government put upon the virgin soil an artificial price, independent of the law of supply and demand, a price that compels the immigrant to work a long time for wages before he can earn enough money to buy land, and turn himself into an independent peasant. The fund resulting from the sale of land at a price relatively prohibitory for the wage-workers, this fund of money extorted from the wages of labour by violation of the sacred law of supply and demand, the Government is to employ, on the other hand, in proportion as it grows; to import have-nothings from Europe into the colonies, and thus keep the wage labour market full for the capitalists. Under these circumstances, *tout sera pour le mieux dans le meilleur des mondes possibles*. This is the great secret of "systematic colonization."

NOTES AND QUESTIONS

1. Marx's central argument was that capitalism was inherently exploitative, expansionist but unstable. It needed to be overthrown to let human freedom flourish. Workers produce society's wealth, but they are left only with a bare subsistence after the surplus value is taken by the employer. Marx equated capitalism with private ownership of the means of production: an absence of public ownership, with property and contract law that recognises no social obligation. Private property led to workers' position of subordination, and exploitation. Do you agree that working for another is inherently 'exploitation'?

2. Although Marx recognised the concept of unequal bargaining power (see *Wage Labour and Capital* (1847)), Marx's concept of 'surplus value' was not the difference between actual market prices and the idea of a 'just price' in a procedurally fair exchange. Marx asserts that everything exchanges at its 'value', which for him is the amount of labour embodied in it. But in labour contracts 'surplus value' was the difference between the average wages necessary to keep workers alive (ie the average worker does get paid according to the 'value' of their labour time) and the profit that would be gained when workers' labour power was combined with capital (see *Capital*, chs 5 and 6). It seems that Marx absorbed Friedrich Carl von Savigny's 'abstraction principle' during his Berlin legal education: the idea that a *contract* exchanging labour time is distinct from the location of *property* rights

---

[10] "Land, to be an element of colonization, must not only be waste, but it must be public property, liable to be converted into private property." ([E. G. Wakefield: "England and America"], Vol. II, p. 125.)

[11] l.c., p. 17.

over the capital that is worked on. Thus (in the abstract, at least) it becomes possible to say simultaneously that a worker's wage equals the 'value' they receive (by the contract) and that it does not (in the 'property'). Do you agree that in a work–wage bargain, it is conceptually useful to abstract labour time from labour power? Do you agree that a person who makes their capital (land, equipment, computers, etc) available to work on can contribute nothing of value to the bargain?

3.   K Marx, *Economic & Philosophic Manuscripts* (1844) argued that labour exploitation also led to alienation. 'What, then, constitutes the alienation of labour? First, the fact that labour is external to the worker, ie, it does not belong to his intrinsic nature; that in his work, therefore, he does not affirm himself but denies himself, does not feel content but unhappy, does not develop freely his physical and mental energy but mortifies his body and ruins his mind. The worker therefore only feels himself outside his work, and in his work feels outside himself. He feels at home when he is not working, and when he is working he does not feel at home. His labour is therefore not voluntary, but coerced; it is forced labour. It is therefore not the satisfaction of a need; it is merely a means to satisfy needs external to it. Its alien character emerges clearly in the fact that as soon as no physical or other compulsion exists, labour is shunned like the plague. External labor, labor in which man alienates himself, is a labour of self-sacrifice, of mortification.' Do you agree?

4.   Since the end of the cold war, individuals who accuse people who engaged with Marx of being Marxist have become became rarer. This is a positive development, because twentieth-century political, economic and legal authors often wrote in reference to Marx (whether opposed, sympathetic or critical) without specifically citing him. For example, the most important theory in modern company law drew direct parallels and contrasts to *Capital*, without ever mentioning it: AA Berle and GC Means, *The Modern Corporation and Private Property* (1932) 5 and 64. Until 1989 people regularly self-censored, for fear of career damage. For a notable exception among labour lawyers, see H Collins, *Marxism and Law* (1980). Collins argued the Marxist contention (from Engels and Lenin, rather than Marx himself) that law and the state is destined to 'wither away' was misplaced. Law is inevitable, and desirable, while communist revolution is not. Can you imagine a society without law of any type? On the other hand, can you imagine a society where social norms do not require the use of force by the state against members of the population who break the law?

5.   K Marx and F Engels, *Communist Manifesto* (1848) had a ten-point plan for after the communist revolution. Communists split about the way this revolution should occur. Many saw violent revolt as necessary, though Marx remarked once in a letter that in England, if the working classes got the vote, this would be tantamount to revolution in itself. At least six points of the *Communist Manifesto* were partially put into effect as the UK Parliament democratised, namely (2) progressive income tax, (3) inheritance tax – though not abolition of inheritance, (5) centralisation of credit – though only a regulatory central bank, which licenses out its monopoly rights to private banks today, (6) centralisation of communications and transport – though today those enterprises have been partially reprivatised, with specific regulation, (7) land planning law – though not progressive nationalisation

of factories any longer, (10) free education, and abolition of child labour. These ideas are now conservative, not revolutionary. Point (1) was abolition of property in land: natural resources are state owned, before being licensed out, there is still some social housing, and we have national parks. However, complete abolition of all private land seems unlikely. The remaining points were (4) confiscating emigrant and rebel property, (8) equal liability of all to labour and (9) equal distribution of the population over the country. In many communist countries, these points were put into effect, accompanied by massive human rights abuse. Apart from points (8) and (10), and given the basics of the theory in *Capital*, why do you think the *Communist Manifesto* had so little to say about labour law itself?

6. In the former Soviet bloc, where dictators claimed they were carrying through Marxist ideology (or at least the parts that suited the dictators), workplaces were authoritarian. For example, on East Germany, see CE Shaw, 'Management–Labor Committees' (1950) 3(2) *Industrial and Labor Relations Review* 229 and VI Lenin, *Role and Functions of the Trade Unions under the New Economic Policy* (1922).

7. Marx believed the immiseration of exploited and alienated workers would be so strong that a communist revolution was inevitable. This was supposedly a scientific claim, adapted from the dialectical theory of history of the Berlin law professor GWF Hegel, *Lectures on the History of Philosophy* (1826). See G Kitching, *Marxism and Science: Analysis of an Obsession* (1994). After the Soviet Union fell, F Fukuyama, *The End of History and the Last Man* (1992) claimed that liberal democracy was the end-point of development because of this system's apparent ability to generate more wealth and prosperity for everyone in society than any other alternative. Why do you think that a quality of 'inevitability' in political theory could be psychologically so appealing?

8. Marx's theory of colonisation posits that a capitalist economic system is impelled by the pursuit of profit to open new markets in places with a different system of property rights: Marx gives an example of workers who own their own labour, by an artificial price being placed on land, being required to join a system of private property and sell their labour to others. In essence, to Marx the capitalist took over rival systems. VI Lenin, *Imperialism, the Highest Stage of Capitalism* (1917) expanded this notion to say that capitalism, in its highest stage, would result in war against economies that did not comply. To what extent do you think this theory is consistent with actual historical evolution since the British Empire began to collapse, and the International Labour Organization and United Nations were established? Can you think of invasions or wars driven by a desire to take economic resources? What proportion of the total are they?

9. Very soon after the publication of the first volume of *Capital*, a group of economists, particularly UCL's WS Jevons, *Principles of Economics* (1871), argued that the classical labour theory of value was wrong. Prices, including for people's work, in competitive markets reflected the value of the things exchanged in the sense of the 'marginal utility' added to production: what people believe the things are worth. In law, contrast *In re Wragg Ltd* [1897] 1 Ch 796, 831. The theory of marginal utility has remained the most influential among some economists to explain market prices. However, there is substantial disagreement about the extent to which competitive markets fail.

10. F Jenkin, *The Graphic Representation of the Laws of Supply and Demand and other Essays on Political Economy* (1887) devised the first supply-and-demand graphs. These show the familiar view that equilibrium prices are where the quantity of a good or service supplied matches the quantity demanded. Theoretically, this reflects the marginal utility of the good or service. Jenkin thought the same principles wholly inapplicable to labour markets, because he did not view markets for corn as equivalent to markets for labour, where matters can change depending on whether the workforce contracts individually or might collectively bargain. Jenkin believed, because of unequal bargaining power, the chart shown in Figure 2.1 simply cannot be graphically represented in the same way, and he declined to produce charts in relation to labour and trade unions.

Figure 2.1 First Law of Supply and Demand

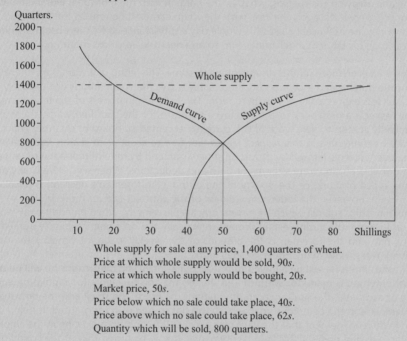

Whole supply for sale at any price, 1,400 quarters of wheat.
Price at which whole supply would be sold, 90s.
Price at which whole supply would be bought, 20s.
Market price, 50s.
Price below which no sale could take place, 40s.
Price above which no sale could take place, 62s.
Quantity which will be sold, 800 quarters.

11. The graph became known as the 'Marshallian cross', after the author who adopted Jenkin's work, and is now found in all introductory microeconomics texts. Alfred Marshall, professor of economics in Cambridge, also did not believe the same principles applied to commercial sales markets as to labour. *Principles of Economics* (3rd edn 1895) Book VI, ch 4, 649, '[T]he effects of the laborer's disadvantage in bargaining are therefore cumulative in two ways. It lowers his wages; and, as we have seen, this lowers his efficiency as a worker, and thereby lowers the normal value of his labor. And in addition it diminishes his efficiency as a bargainer, and thus increases the chance that he will sell his labor for less than its normal value.' The same point was expanded considerably by two founders of the London School of Economics.

S Webb and B Webb, *Industrial Democracy*
(1897) Part III, ch 2 (655–62, 671–72, 692) and ch 4 (847–48)

Part III, ch 2, The Higgling of the Market

… When the workman applies for the post to the employer's foreman, the two parties to the bargain differ considerably in strategic strength. There is first the difference of alternative. If the foreman, and the capitalist employer for whom he acts, fail to come to terms with the workman, they may be put to some inconvenience in arranging the work of the establishment. They may have to persuade the other workmen to work harder or to work overtime; they may even be compelled to leave a machine vacant, and thus run the risk of some delay in the completion of an order. Even if the workman remains obdurate, the worst that the capitalist suffers is a fractional decrease of the year's profit.[12] Meanwhile he and his foreman, with their wives and families, find their housekeeping quite unaffected; they go on eating and drinking, working and enjoying themselves, whether the bargain with the individual workman has been made or not. Very different is the case with the wage-earner. If he refuses the foreman's terms even for a day, he irrevocably loses his whole day's subsistence. If he has absolutely no other resources than his labor, hunger brings him to his knees the very next morning. …

…

There is an even more serious disadvantage to come. The hiring of a workman, unlike a contract for the purchase of a commodity, necessarily leaves many conditions not precisely determined, still less expressed in any definite form. This indeterminateness of the labor contract is in some respects a drawback to the employer. In return for the specified wage, the workman has impliedly agreed to give work of the currently accepted standard of quantity and quality. The lack of definiteness in this respect leaves him free to skulk or to scamp. But against this the employer protects himself by providing supervision and by requiring obedience to his foreman, if not also by elaborate systems of fines and deductions. Whenever there is any dispute as to the speed of work, or the quality of the output, the foreman's decision is absolute. To the workman, however, the indeterminateness of the contract is a far more fruitful source of personal hardship, against which he has no practicable remedy. When an additional "hand" is taken on in a manufacturing establishment, practically the only point explicitly agreed upon between him and the foreman is the amount of the weekly wage, or possibly the scale of piece-work rates. How many hours he shall work, how quickly or how intensely he is to exert himself, what intervals will be allowed for meals, what fines and deductions he will be subject to, what provision is made for warmth and shelter, the arrangements for ventilation and prevention of accidents, the sanitary accommodation, the noise, the smell and the dirt, the foreman's temper and the comrades' manners all this has to be taken for granted, it being always implied in the engagement that the workman accepts the conditions existing in the employer's establishment, and obeys all his lawful commands. It may be urged that, if the conditions are worse than is customary, the workman will not accept the situation, unless he is offered higher wages. But until he has made his contract and actually begun work, he cannot know what the conditions are, even if he could estimate their disadvantage in terms of money, and stand out for the higher price. …

… When the unemployed are crowding round the factory gates every morning, it is plain to each man that, unless he can induce the foreman to select him rather than another, his chance of subsistence for weeks to come may be irretrievably lost. …

---

[12] The latest critic of the theory of Trade Unionism denies this inequality, on the ground that whilst the wage-earners must starve if the employers stand out, the employers may be driven into bankruptcy if the workmen revolt (*A Criticism of the Theory of Traded Unions*, by T. S. Cree, Glasgow, 1891, p. 20). But this very argument assumes "a stoppage of work through a strike" – that is to say, deliberately concerted action among the wage-earners – the very Trade Unionism which the writer declares to be unnecessary.

... the typical capitalist manufacturer of the present generation, with his increasing education and refinement, his growing political interests and public spirit, will, so long as his own customary income is not interfered with, take a positive pleasure in augmenting the wages and promoting the comfort of his workpeople. Unfortunately, the intelligent, far-sighted, and public-spirited employer is not master of the situation. Unless he is protected by one or other of the dykes or bulwarks presently to be described, he is constantly finding himself as powerless as the workman to withstand the pressure of competitive industry. How this competitive pressure pushes him, in sheer self-defence, to take as much advantage of his work-people as the most grasping and short-sighted of his rivals, we shall understand by examining the next link in the chain.

Paradoxical as it may appear, in the highly-developed commercial system of the England of to-day the capitalist manufacturer, stands at as great a relative disadvantage to the wholesale trader as the isolated, workman does to the capitalist manufacturer. In the higgling of the market with the wholesale trader who takes his product, the capitalist manufacturer exhibits the same inferiority of strategic position with regard to the alternative, with regard to knowledge of the circumstances, and with regard to bargaining capacity.

...

We thus arrive at the consumer as the ultimate sources of that persistent pressure on sellers, which, transmitted through the long chain of bargaining, finally crushes the isolated workman at the base of the pyramid. Yet, paradoxical as it may seem, the consumer is, of all the parties to the transaction, the least personally responsible for the result. For he takes no active part in the process. In the great market of the world, he but accepts what is spontaneously offered to him. He does not, as a rule, even suggest to the shopkeeper that he would like prices lowered. All he does – and it is enough to keep the whole machine in motion – is to demur to paying half a crown for an article, when some one else is offering him the same thing for two shillings. It may be urged that he ought to be ready to pay a higher price for a better quality. ... With regard to the vast majority of the purchases of daily life, no one but an expert can, with any assurance, discriminate between shades of quality, and the ordinary customer is reduced to decide by price alone. Nor could he, even on grounds of the highest philanthropy, reasonably take any other course. As a practical man, he knows it to be quite impossible for him to trace the article through its various stages of production and distribution, and to discover whether the extra sixpence charged by the dearer shop represents better wages to any workman, or goes as mere extra profit to one or other of the capitalists concerned. ... In the same way the great fall in prices, which is so marked a feature of our time, is undoubtedly due, in the main (if not, as some say, to currency changes), to the natural and legitimate reduction of the real cost of production; to the improvement of technical processes, the cheapening of transport, the exclusion of unnecessary middlemen, and the general increase in intelligence and in the efficiency of social organisation. It follows that the consumers, as consumers, are helpless in the matter. The systematic pressure upon the isolated workman which we have described has reference to them alone, and serves their immediate interests, but it cannot be said to be caused by anything within their volition, or to be alterable by anything which they, in their capacity of consumers, could possibly accomplish.

...

... the shareholders' meeting, the board of directors, and the salaried general manager inevitably bring in "business principles," and pay no more for labor than they are compelled. ... It is not too much to say that, so far as concerns the personal life of the 50,0000 employees of the London and North-Western Railway Company, the 55,000 ordinary shareholders, who own that vast enterprise, are even more ignorant, more inaccessible, and more irresponsible than the millions of passengers whom they serve. ... Thus it is only in exceptional instances, and then only temporarily, that the wage-earners as a class get any share of the extra profits, secured, to the capitalists, by their dykes and bulwarks. These exceptional profits are quickly capitalised by their owners, and transferred to new shareholders who come in at a premium. The more complete and legally secured is the monopoly, the more certain it is to be disposed of at a price which yields only a low rate of interest – in extreme cases, such as urban waterworks, approximating actually to the return on government securities themselves. On the other hand, the position of the wage-earner is positively worsened, in the colossal capitalist corporations, by the absence of effective competition for his services by rival employers. The difference in strategic position becomes so overwhelming that the wage-contract ceases to be, in any genuine sense, a bargain at all. …

Ch 4, Trade Unionism and Democracy

If, then, we are asked whether democracy, as shown by an analysis of Trade Unionism, is consistent with Individual Liberty, we are compelled to answer by asking, What is Liberty? If Liberty means every man being his own master, and following his own impulses, then it is clearly inconsistent, not so much with democracy or any other particular form of government, as with the crowding together of population in dense masses, division of labor, and, as we think, civilisation itself. What particular individuals, sections, or classes usually mean by "freedom of contract," "freedom of association," or "freedom of enterprise" is freedom of opportunity to use the power that they happen to possess; that is to say, to compel other less powerful people to accept their terms. This sort of personal freedom in a community composed of unequal units is not distinguishable from compulsion. It is, therefore, necessary to define Liberty before talking about it, a definition which every man will frame according to his own view of what is socially desirable. We ourselves understand by the words "Liberty" or "Freedom," not any quantum of natural or Inalienable rights, but such conditions of existence in the community as do, in practice, result in the utmost possible development of faculty in the individual human being. Now, in this sense democracy is not only consistent with Liberty, but is, as it seems to us, the only way of securing the largest amount of it. It is open to argument whether other forms of government may not achieve a fuller development of the faculties of particular individuals or classes. To an autocrat, untrammelled rule over a whole kingdom may mean an exercise of his individual faculties, and a development of his individual personality, such as no other situation in life would afford. An aristocracy, or government by one class in the interests of one class, may conceivably enable that class to develop a perfection in physical grace or intellectual charm attainable by no other system of society. Similarly, it might be argued that, where the ownership of the means of production and the administration of industry are unreservedly left to the capitalist class, this "freedom of enterprise" would result in a development of faculty among the captains of industry which could not otherwise be reached. We dissent from all these propositions, if only on the ground that the fullest development of personal character requires the pressure of discipline as well as the stimulus of opportunity. But, however untrammelled power may affect the character of those who possess it, autocracy, aristocracy, and plutocracy have all, from the point of view of the lover of liberty, one fatal defect. They necessarily involve a restriction in the opportunity for development of faculty among the great mass of the population. It is only when the resources of the nation are deliberately organised and dealt with for the benefit, not of particular individuals or classes, but of the entire community; when the administration of industry, as of every other branch of human affairs, becomes the function of specialised experts, working through deliberately adjusted Common Rules; and when the ultimate decision on policy rests in no other hands than those of the citizens themselves, that the maximum aggregate development of individual intellect and individual character in the community as a whole can be attained.

NOTES AND QUESTIONS

1. The Webbs analyse the economy as a whole as a 'chain of bargaining', where unless businesses are capable of erecting 'dykes and bulwarks' against

unrestricted competition, they will not be able to maintain stable business. They saw unequal bargaining power (or how the 'two parties to the bargain differ considerably in strategic strength') as synonymous with a relative lack of 'alternative'. Their understanding of the causes of unequal bargaining power appears consistent with the evolution of theory from Smith, Mill and Jevons, respectively: the building blocks of unequal bargaining power are (i) unequal distribution of wealth and resources, (ii) disparity in collective organisation, and (iii) asymmetry of information. Do you agree that these factors, particularly the first, represent a significant concern?

2. In the UK, the theory was partly put into practice in labour law through the Trade Boards Act 1909 and 1918. In *France v James Coombes & Co* [1929] AC 496, 505–06, Lord Atkin, reading for Lord Blanesburgh, remarked that minimum wages were seen as necessary to stop low pay 'either as a result of competition in the labour market or deficient bargaining power'. In the United States, the clearest consequence of the theory was the National Labor Relations Act 1935 §1, which states its purpose to remedy the 'inequality of bargaining power between employees who do not possess full freedom of association or actual liberty of contract and employers who are organized in the corporate or other forms of ownership association'.

3. O Kahn-Freund, *Labour and the Law* (Hamlyn Lectures, 1972) 7: '[T]he relation between an employer and an isolated employee or worker is typically a relation between a bearer of power and one who is not a bearer of power. In its inception it is an act of submission, in its operation it is a condition of subordination, however much the submission and the subordination may be concealed by the indispensable figment of the legal mind known as the 'contract of employment. The main object of labour law has been, and … will always be a countervailing force to counteract the inequality of bargaining power which is inherent and must be inherent in the employment relationship. … [Labour law] is an attempt to infuse law into a relation of command and subordination.' Do you agree that counteracting unequal bargaining power is labour law's 'main' object?

4. The vast majority of contractual transactions day to day are regulated to counteract unequal bargaining power, such as for consumers under the Consumer Rights Act 2015, for tenants under the Landlord and Tenant Act 1985, or investors under the Companies Act 2006 and Financial Services and Markets Act 2000. To what extent are workers, consumers, tenants or small investors in stocks and shares in a similar position? See H Arthurs, 'Labor Law as the Law of Economic Subordination and Resistance: A Thought Experiment' (2013) 34 *Comparative Labor Law and Policy* Journal 585.

5. M Weber, *The Theory of Social and Economic Organization* (1915) 152, the great sociologist, classically defined power as 'the probability that one actor within a social relationship will be in a position to carry out his own will, despite resistance, regardless of the basis on which this probability rests'. Again, this appears to rest on similar causes to those the Webbs identified. Also in Germany, see H Sinzheimer, *Grundzüge des Arbeitsrechts* (1926) ch 2, 22, who says of the dependence of labour: 'The foundation is the relationship between work and property.' Sinzheimer coauthored the Weimar Constitution in 1919 in Germany.

6. Sidney Webb wrote the UK Labour Party's original Clause IV, believing that socialism would not merely come through labour policy, but by progressively extending 'the common ownership of the means of production, distribution and exchange'. 'Common' ownership was typically equated with 'state' ownership. Clause IV was rewritten in 1995 to aim for a 'community in which power, wealth and opportunity are in the hands of the many, not the few'. This is the definition of democracy from Pericles' Funeral Oration, see Thucydides, *History of the Peloponnesian War* (c 411 BC) Book 2, para 37.

7. In *Industrial Democracy* (1897) Part III, ch 4, 818–22, the Webbs initially argued that economic organisation should be based on a kind of separation of powers: consumers deciding what should be produced, employers deciding the manner of production, and workers deciding the conditions of production. This approach (i) assumed that employers and employees were distinct classes of people and (ii) cut employees out of the right to determine who their employers were. As the Webbs envisaged that industry would be nationalised, they presumably thought this would be a question for Parliament. However, in *The History of Trade Unionism* (1920) Appendix VIII, they said: 'In 1920, after nearly a quarter of a century of further experience and consideration, we should, in some respects, put this differently. The growth, among all classes, and especially among the manual workers and the technicians, of what we may call corporate self-consciousness and public spirit, and the diffusion of education coupled with further discoveries in the technique of democratic institutions would lead us today to include, and even to put in the forefront, certain additional suggestions. ... We ourselves look for the admission of nominees of the manual workers, as well as of the technicians, upon the executive boards and committees, on terms of complete equality with the other members, in all publicly owned industries and services.'

8. The Wall Street Crash and the ensuing Great Depression shook economic theory. In the United States, the primary intellectuals included Berle and Means (1932) mentioned above, calling for careful legal reform to corporate law and financial regulation. Moreover, Berle was the intellectual architect of the New Deal, and the development of a programme for economic and social rights, see FD Roosevelt, *Campaign Address on Progressive Government at the Commonwealth Club in San Francisco, California* (1932) written by Berle, and later 'Property, Production and Revolution' (1965) 65 *Columbia Law Review* 1. In the UK, the primary response within economics came from JM Keynes, *The General Theory of Employment, Interest and Money* (1936), which developed 'macroeconomics' as a field focused on aggregate shifts in wages, prices, inflation and employment. This has come to be seen as distinct from 'microeconomics', which maps more neatly onto problems of contract, property, tort company or labour law. Keynes argued that active government policy was needed to counteract economic downturns, for example through greater spending on public works. Some combination of these two approaches (social and economic rights, plus active government) formed a basic basic post-war policy consensus until the revival of another school of thought.

(2) ECONOMIC EFFICIENCY

After 1945, as politics democratised, it was generally accepted that labour policy should aim to increase welfare and growth. Few remained who would seriously argue that improvements in basic living standards were not desirable or needed. Opponents of labour rights and active government therefore shifted their criticism to the methods used to achieve the common aim. Economic theory had always appealed to empirical evidence to support its claims (eg S Webb, 'The Economic Theory of a Legal Minimum Wage' (1912) 20 *Journal of Political Economy* 973). But whereas before, theoretical debate was heavily abstract, new masses of data, produced by government departments, enabled ever more sophisticated arguments to be made about the economic effects of law.

M Friedman, 'The Methodology of Positive Economics'
in *Essays in Positive Economics* (1953) ch 1, 4–7

Positive economics is in principle independent of any particular ethical position or normative judgments. ... Its task is to provide a system of generalizations that can be used to make correct predictions about the consequences of any change in circumstances. Its performance is to be judged by the precision, scope, and conformity with experience of the predictions it yields. In short, positive economics is, or can be, an "objective" science, in precisely the same sense as any of the physical sciences. Of course, the fact that economics deals with the interrelations of human beings, and that the investigator is himself part of the subject matter being investigated in a more intimate sense than in the physical sciences, raises special difficulties in achieving objectivity at the same time that it provides the social scientist with a class of data not available to the physical scientist. But neither the one nor the other is, in my view, a fundamental distinction between the two groups of sciences.[13]

Normative economics and the art of economics, on the other hand, cannot be independent of positive economics. Any policy conclusion necessarily rests on a prediction about the consequences of doing one thing rather than another, a prediction that must be based – implicitly or explicitly – on positive economics. There is not, of course, a one-to-one relation between policy conclusions and the conclusions of positive economics; if there were, there would be no separate normative science. Two individuals may agree on the consequences of a particular piece of legislation. One may regard them as desirable on balance and so favor the legislation; the other, as undesirable and so oppose the legislation.

I venture the judgment, however, that currently in the Western world, and especially in the United States, differences about economic policy among disinterested citizens derive predominantly from different predictions about the economic consequences of taking action – differences that in principle can be eliminated by the progress of positive economics – rather than from fundamental differences in basic values, differences about which men can ultimately only fight. An obvious and not unimportant example is minimum-wage legislation. Underneath the

[13] The interaction between the observer and the process observed that is so prominent a feature of the social sciences, besides its more obvious parallel in the physical sciences, has a more subtle counterpart in the indeterminacy principle arising out of the interaction between the process of measurement and the phenomena being measured. And both have a counterpart in pure logic in Godel's theorem, asserting the impossibility of a comprehensive self-contained logic. It is an open question whether all three can be regarded as different formulations of an even more general principle.

welter of arguments offered for and against such legislation there is an underlying consensus on the objective of achieving a "living wage" for all, to use the ambiguous phrase so common in such discussions. The difference of opinion is largely grounded on an implicit or explicit difference in predictions about the efficacy of this particular means in furthering the agreed-on end. Proponents believe (predict) that legal minimum wages diminish poverty by raising the wages of those receiving less than the minimum wage as well as of some receiving more than the minimum wage without any counterbalancing increase in the number of people entirely unemployed or employed less advantageously than they otherwise would be. Opponents believe (predict) that legal minimum wages increase poverty by increasing the number of people who are unemployed or employed less advantageously and that this more than offsets any favorable effect on the wages of those who remain employed. Agreement about the economic consequences of the legislation might not produce complete agreement about its desirability, for differences might still remain about its political or social consequences; but, given agreement on objectives, it would certainly go a long way toward producing consensus.

Closely related differences in positive analysis underlie divergent views about the appropriate role and place of trade-unions and the desirability of direct price and wage controls and of tariffs. Different predictions about the importance of so-called "economies of scale" account very largely for divergent views about the desirability or necessity of detailed government regulation of industry and even of socialism rather than private enterprise. And this list could be extended indefinitely.[14] Of course, my judgment that the major differences about economic policy in the Western world are of this kind is itself a "positive" statement to be accepted or rejected on the basis of empirical evidence.

If this judgment is valid, it means that a consensus on "correct" economic policy depends much less on the progress of normative economics proper than, on the progress of a positive economics yielding conclusions that are, and deserve to be, widely accepted. It means also that a major reason for distinguishing positive economics sharply from normative economics is precisely the contribution that can thereby be made to agreement about policy.

NOTES AND QUESTIONS

1. Friedman's method of argument is to concede we all want a living wage, but to suggest that enacting a minimum wage law (in the United States, this was the Fair Labor Standards Act of 1938) will have an unintended consequence of raising unemployment. The 'micro' policy of a minimum wage has a 'macro' effect that harms the people it was meant to help: those who would have low-paid jobs, but now have no job at all because fewer employers can afford to pay the wage. Friedman believed this would be confirmed by empirical evidence, or at any rate not falsified by evidence to the contrary. He did not himself provide evidence for his theory.

2. In fact, most empirical evidence on the minimum wage suggests that a reasonable minimum wage increases employment, as well as improving wages for lower

---

[14] One rather more complex example is stabilization policy. Superficially, divergent views on this question seem to reflect differences in objectives; but I believe that this impression is misleading and that at bottom the different views reflect primarily different judgments about the source of fluctuations in economic activity and the effect of alternative countercyclical action. For one major positive consideration that accounts for much of the divergence see "The Effects of a Full-Employment Policy on Economic Stability: A Formal Analysis," infra, pp. 117–32. For a summary of the present state of professional views on this question see "The Problem of Economic Instability," a report of a subcommittee of the Committee on Public Issues of the American Economic Association, American Economic Review, XL (September, 1950), 501–38.

earners. The theory consistent with this suggests fairer pay raises productivity, encourages more people to enter the labour market, and stimulates 'effective aggregate demand' (ie with higher wages, people buy more stuff, so businesses hire more), which more than compensates for any employers that actually reduce or cease business. Thus, the absence of a minimum wage increases unemployment in a state where workers lack bargaining power. See DE Card and AB Krueger, *Myth and Measurement: The New Economics of the Minimum Wage* (1995) and S Machin and A Manning, 'Minimum Wages and Economic Outcomes in Europe' (1997) 41 *European Economic Review* 733. Do you think evidence always persuades people for 'producing consensus' as Friedman suggests?

3. The language of economic efficiency contrasts starkly with the language of rights, in a way that many would find unacceptable. On a strict rights-based view, a decent wage should be assured regardless of the consequences. See the Universal Declaration of Human Rights 1948 Art 23(3) and the European Social Charter 1961 Art 4. One way to view rights instruments is as an attempt to draw a line under a debate about consequences that has already been played out and won. Consequentialist argument often aims to prise open those debates once more, although the two angles are not always irreconcilable. See ACL Davies, *Perspectives on Labour Law* (2nd edn 2009). Do you think consequentialist or principles-based arguments are more important? Depending on who you aim to persuade, could both be equally important?

4. In a short article, L Summers, 'Some Simple Economics of Mandated Benefits' (1989) 79(2) *American Economic Review* 177, 181, posited that any labour right that costs an employer money (eg paid holidays, paid parental leave, an occupational pension) would result in employers reducing wages by the same amount, or if they could not (like Friedman argued on the minimum wage), they would fire staff. Summers appeared to view this, in his theory, as more efficient in some cases than government provision. Like Friedman's theory, Summers's theory leaves empirical evidence for another time. Although he mentions information problems, he does not address the argument that absence of labour rights might reflect a labour market failure, rather than a market in competitive equilibrium. Why do you think 'simple economics' might often turn out to be not so simple at all?

5. RA Posner, 'Some Economics of Labor Law' (1984) 51(4) *University of Chicago Law Review* 988, argued the purpose of US collective labour law is to make the labour market anti-competitive. Promoting trade unions is supporting 'cartelisation', and ideally unions should be broken up by competition law and sued for economic loss to employers for strike action in breach of contract. That position existed in the United States before the Clayton Act 1914 and in the UK either before the Trade Union Act 1871, or between *Taff Vale* and the Trade Disputes Act 1906. If a union is a 'cartel' of labour, is a corporation a 'cartel' of capital? Is the economic loss caused by a strike different to the loss caused by a dismissal?

6. From the same symposium that produced Posner's paper above, Epstein set out his views on why there should be no law requiring fairness in dismissals.

RA Epstein, 'In Defense of the Contract at Will'
(1984) 51(4) *University of Chicago Law Review* 947, 973–76

The persistent tension between private ordering and government regulation exists in virtually every area known to the law, and in none has that tension been more pronounced than in the law of employer and employee relations. During the last fifty years, the balance of power has shifted heavily in favor of direct public regulation, which has been thought strictly necessary to redress the perceived imbalance between the individual and the firm. …

…

The first way to argue for the contract at will is to insist upon the importance of freedom of contract as an end in itself. Freedom of contract is an aspect of individual liberty, every bit as much as freedom of speech, or freedom in the selection of marriage partners or in the adoption of religious beliefs or affiliations. Just as it is regarded as prima facie unjust to abridge these liberties, so too is it presumptively unjust to abridge the economic liberties of individuals.

…

In the employment-contracting situation, the employer is the sole residual claimant upon the earnings of the firm, while the employee receives a fixed wage.[15] But this important difference does not mean that the advantages of the at-will arrangement are of no importance to the employment relationship. On the contract it is possible to identify a number of reasons why the at-will contract usually works for the benefit of both sides in employment as well as partnership contexts. …

[Epstein sets out four theoretical benefits to firms and employees that derive from both employers and employees being able to terminate at will and continues]

The account thus far given of the contract at will in no way depends upon any notion of an inherent inequality of bargaining power that pervades all employment contracts. Indeed if such an inequality did govern the employment relationship, we should expect to see conditions that exist in no labor market. Wages should be driven to zero, for no matter what their previous level, the employer could use his (inexhaustible) bargaining power to reduce them further, until the zero level was reached. Similarly inequality of bargaining power implies that the employee will be bound for a term while the employer (who can pay the peppercorn consideration) retains the power to terminate at will. Yet in practice we observe both positive wages and employees with the right to quit at will.

…

… the description of the employment relationship does suggest one way in which inequality can arise, even within the framework of generally competitive markets. In the course of an ongoing relationship between employee and employer, each side gains from the contract more than it could obtain by returning to the open market. The surplus that is created must be divided between the parties. In principle, either the worker or the employer could receive the entire surplus without inducing the other party, who still receives a competitive return, to sever the relationship. A fortiori any solution that divides the surplus between the parties should be stable as well. The contract at will thus creates a bilateral monopoly, but only to the extent of the surplus.

The question of inequality of bargaining power can now be helpfully restated: which side will appropriate most of the surplus in any negotiations between them? Unlike the typical

---

[15] Sometimes the employee's wage will be fixed, not in dollar terms, but as a function of his own productivity (for example, a sales personnel who works on commission). But even if the employee's claim is a function of the firm's profit from particular transactions, he is in a different position than is an owner. An individual salesman can make a fortune while the firm loses money; a pure equity partner cannot.

formulations of the problem, this leaves the set of possible solutions strictly bounded because the employee cannot be driven below the competitive wage and the employer cannot be driven to a wage above the sum of the competitive wage plus the full amount of the surplus. An employer can therefore be said to possess an inequality of bargaining power when he is able to appropriate more than half the surplus, while the employee can be said to possess inequality of bargaining power if he can appropriate more than half the surplus. To take an example, assume the employer is prepared to pay 20, while the worker is willing to work for 10. The agreed wage therefore could fall anywhere between those two numbers. If the employer is systematically able to appropriate more than 5 of this surplus, by keeping the wage level below 15, then he has unequal bargaining power, though still within the framework of overall competitive markets.

...

It still remains to be determined which side is likely to appropriate most of this contract-specific surplus. One might guess that the employer will be able to achieve this objective, perhaps because his experience in repeat transactions with many workers fosters greater skills in negotiation. In addition, the employer may know in general the market wages available to beginning workers, as these typically will be public knowledge. Yet a number of considerations suggest the opposite conclusion. First, the employer often bargains through subordinate managers and thus faces an agency-cost problem avoided by the worker who bargains on his own account. Second, the worker's opportunity cost for his time will often be lower than the employer's, so that the increased time he can spend on the transaction may offset the employer's greater skill, if any, per unit of time. Third, the worker may be able to learn something about the employer's reservation price (i.e., the maximum wage he would be willing to pay) because the employer must reveal some information about his willingness to pay in negotiations with other long-term workers. Finally, it is not clear that the employer gains any real advantage because of his greater relative wealth, if any. To be sure, the wealthy employer can hold out for a larger share of the surplus because he has less, proportionally, to lose. Yet by the same token the employer's resolve may be weaker because he has less to gain by holding out.

This modest catalogue of considerations shows how difficult is to determine the exact division of the surplus, although my suspicion is that in the broad run of cases it will tend to be evenly divided. But even if this guess is wrong, there is no reason for the law to interfere in the bargaining process. The whole question of inequality of bargaining power arises in the bounded context of how much of a supra competitive wage the worker will obtain. At the very worst, the worker will get the amount that is offered in some alternate employment where he has built up no specific capital. To try to formulate and administer a set of legal rules that will allow some trier of fact to measure the size of the surplus embedded in the ongoing transaction, and to allocate half (or more) of it to the worker, cannot be done at any social cost that is less than the expected size of the surplus itself, if it can be done at all. ...

...

The size of the surplus and thus the scope of any inequality problem can be reduced more effectively by adopting legal rules that remove or minimize legal impediments to labor mobility.

NOTES AND QUESTIONS

1. Epstein contends that, even if workers are poorer than their employers, this is irrelevant because rational employers have less to gain from workers by holding out in an industrial dispute. He says if inequality of bargaining power exists (and this means an ability to take more of the joint surplus in production), there should be evidence of this, but he says he suspects this does not happen in reality. But even if the empirical evidence went against him, Epstein would deny the public concern in private ordering because intervention is usually damaging.

2.   Given what Epstein says about freedom of contract, is this a rights-based theory, an empiricist theory, or both?
3.   It is not clear who Epstein had in mind when he posits that if proponents of unequal bargaining power were right, workers' wages should be pressed to zero. Presumably the actual argument (eg from the Webbs) was that unequal bargaining power pushes wages close to subsistence as even exploitative employers would not want their workforce to starve. More poignant is Epstein's claim that bargaining power does not allow employers to take a larger share of the joint surplus. Do you think labour's share of income in the economy an appropriate proxy for the manner in which the joint surplus is shared? If so, then it would appear that unequal bargaining power is pervasive: see F Rodriguez and A Jayadev, 'The Declining Labor Share of Income' (2010) 3(2) *Journal of Globalization and Development* 1.
4.   A less radically deregulatory theory comes from Oliver Williamson.

OE Williamson, *The Economic Institutions of Capitalism* (1985) chs 10 and 12

Chapter 10, The Organization of Labor

...

A central thesis of this book is that a common theory of contract applies to transactions of all types – labor market transactions included. The organization of labor organization is nevertheless a very complicated matter. No single approach to the study of labor organization is at present adequate – which is to say that the study of these matters is usefully informed from several points of view. Transaction cost economics focuses on efficiency aspects. Among the areas in which potential benefits might be realized through collective organization are wage and benefit determination; the enhancement of productivity through human asset development; dispute settlement; efficacious adaptation; and regard for dignity.

...

Recall that the principal dimensions for describing transactions are frequency, uncertainty and asset specificity. The transactions of interest here are ones of a recurring kind. Accordingly, frequency will be set aside and emphasis placed on uncertainty and asset specificity.

For the reasons given previously, the labor market transactions for which continuity between firm and worker are valued are those for which a firm-specific human asset condition develops. Note in this connection that skill acquisition is a necessary but not a sufficient condition for asset specificity features to appear. The nature of the skills also matters. Thus physicians, engineers, lawyers and the like possess valued skills for which they expect to be compensated, but such skills do not by themselves pose a governance issue. Unless those skills are deepened and specialized to a particular employer, neither employer nor employee has a productive interest in maintaining a continuing employment relation. The employer can easily hire a substitute and the employee can move to alternative employment without loss of productive value.

Mere deepening of skills through job experience does not by itself pose a problem either. Thus typing skills may be enhanced by practice, but if they are equally valued by current and potential employers there is no need to devise special protection for an ongoing employment relation. Knowledge of a particular firm's filing system, by contrast, may be highly specific (non-transferable). Continuity of the employment relation in the latter case is a source of added value.

Thus whereas neoclassical reasoning links skills to productivity and compensation, transaction cost reasoning introduces organizational consideration. Specifically, skills that are acquired in a learning-by-doing fashion and that are imperfectly transferable across employers have to be embedded in a protective governance structure lest productive values be sacrificed if the employment relation is unwittingly severed. ...

... As with intermediate product market transactions, an increase in parametric uncertainty is troublesome mainly for transactions in which human asset specificity is great. Possible transaction costs aside,[16] neither party has a continuity interest in transactions in which asset specificity is negligible. ...

...

The claim or suggestion that power rather than efficiency is responsible for decisions to organize exchange relations one way rather than another runs through much of the social science commentary on labor organization. Rarely is power defined, however. Partly this is because it is widely believed that while power "may be tricky to define ... it is not that difficult to recognize" (Pfeffer, 1981, p. 3). I submit, however, that much of what is "recognized" as power is the result of looking at individual contracts in an *ex post* state rather than, as comparative institutional analysis requires, considering the *set* of relevant contracts in their entirety.

Sometimes what is referred to as power reduces to a preference for an alternative distribution of income. Those who have fewer resources would have greater purchasing "power" if this were accomplished. But the organization of labor need not be affected on that account. To be sure, the mix of goods and services would probably change. But the way in which work is organized need not. Indeed, if efficiency is driving organizational outcomes, modes that are efficient under one distribution of income will normally remain efficient under another. Since mutual gains are potentially available whenever a move from a less to a more efficient configuration is accomplished, the incentive to choose more efficient modes is transparent.

... A common misconception that runs through much of the power literature is that aggregate power can be inferred by ascertaining which of two contestants will win in an *isolated* confrontation.

...

The suggestion that employers rather than employees or society at large is the gainer whenever more efficient work practices are implemented assumes that workers lack bargaining power and neglects the competitive process. Work rule changes made during a contract are normally subject to arbitration, however. And those made during contract renewal negotiations are part of a much larger package in which tradeoffs are worked out.

Thus assume a more efficient practice can be identified and suppose that the employer initially appropriates the whole of the efficiency gain. Even though workers are no better off (indeed, depending on the particulars, some may be released and need to find new employment), society stands to gain in two respects. First, the resources saved by the reorganization of work can be productively reemployed in alternative uses. Second, the immediate profits that accrue to the firm will rarely be durable ... significant reforms will be detected and imitated by others, and prices will fall as margins are restored to earlier levels. ...

Chapter 12, Corporate Governance

...

Supporters of codetermination regard participation for informational purposes as inadequate. They maintain that codetermination should extend the influence of workers. ...

That argument is clearly mistaken as applied to workers with general purpose skills and knowledge. ... Such workers can quit and be replaced without productive losses to either

---

[16] These transaction costs are asymmetrically concentrated on the employee side of the transaction. They mainly arise in conjunction with the disruptive effects on family and social life that job termination and reemployment sometimes produces. Protection against arbitrary dismissals is thus warranted even for nonspecific jobs. Provided, however, that short notice requirements are respected, the firm cannot be said to have a symmetrical interest in preventing unexplained quits.

worker or firm.[17] ... Consider, therefore, workers who make firm-specific investments. ... Ordinarily, it can be presumed that workers and firms will recognize the benefits of creating specialized structure of governance to safeguard firm-specific assets. Failure to provide such safeguards will cause demands for higher wages. ...

... Labor membership on the board of directors for informational purposes is one means of achieving that result. ... Labor membership on boards of directors can be especially important during periods of actual or alleged adversity, especially when firms are asking workers for give-backs. Labor's board membership might mitigate worker's skepticism by promoting the exchange of credible information. Douglas Fraser's inclusion on the Chrysler board during the company's recovery is an illustration.

The practice does not, however, enjoy widespread support. Some opponents fear that it will be difficult to resist the transformation of information into decision-making participation. It is also possible, however, that the informational benefits of labor membership are not adequately appreciated. ...

...

... suppliers of finance bear a unique relation to the firm: The whole of their investment in the firm is potentially placed at hazard. By contrast, the productive assets (plant and equipment; human capital) of suppliers of raw material, labor, intermediate product, electric power, and the like normally remains in the suppliers' possession. ... therefore, these suppliers can costlessly redeploy their assets to productive advantage. Suppliers of finance must secure repayment or otherwise repossess their investments to effect redeployment. ...

Stockholders are also unique in that their investments are not associated with particular assets. The diffuse character of their investments puts shareholders at an enormous disadvantage in crafting the kind of bilateral safeguards. ...

... What to do? ... invent a governance structure that holders of equity recognize as a safeguard against expropriation and egregious mismanagement. Suppose that a board of directors is created that (1) is elected by the pro-rata votes of those who hold tradable shares, (2) has the power to replace management. ... Thus regarded, the board of directors should be seen as a governance instrument of the stockholders. Whether other constituencies also qualify depends on their contracting relation to the firm.

NOTES AND QUESTIONS

1. Williamson argues that inequality of bargaining power is not a real concern because he thought it lacked definition. The real risk in any labour relation, to which law should respond, is that people make 'asset-specific investments' in their workplace, by learning some special, non-transferable skill. In his scheme, this might justify minimal protections against unfair dismissals, but in most cases shareholder monopoly of corporate governance is justified: there should not be labour representation on company boards, except potentially for information purposes.
2. Do you agree with Williamson that 'power' is 'rarely defined'? Alternatively, his contention that power 'reduces to a preference for an alternative distribution of income' could be accurate to the extent that many of the authors (Adam Smith, John Stuart Mill, Sidney and Beatrice Webb) who explored unequal bargaining

---

[17] This is an oversimplification. It assumes easy reemployment and ignores transitional costs, including the impact on the family. As Knight observes, "Laborers are attached to their homes and even to their work by sentimental ties to which market facts are ruthless" (1965, p. 346). I will assume that those effects are constant across (or vary directly with) human asset specificity. Accordingly, the cutting edge is the degree of human asset specificity.

power did believe that unequal wealth distribution was economically problematic. However, it was also a factual observation: unequal distribution of property weakens bargaining power, and perpetuates inequality into every transactional term.

3.   Williamson asserts that distribution does not matter economically because, following the view championed by one of his tutors, RA Coase, 'The Problem of Social Cost' (1960) 3 *Journal of Law and Economics* 1, distribution of income does not affect efficiency of production. Can efficiency and distribution be segregated?

4.   Williamson's 'central thesis', that there is a 'common theory of contract that applies to all transactions', was probably being abandoned 40–50 years earlier in legal theory. See F Kessler, 'Contracts of Adhesion – Some Thoughts About Freedom of Contract' (1943) 43(5) *Columbia Law Review* 629, 636, where he asked: '[C]an the unity of the law of contracts be maintained in the face of the increasing use of contracts of adhesion?' This is reflected today in the multitude of rights in specific contracts, such as those for consumers, tenants, shareholders and employees.

5.   Williamson treats 'suppliers of finance', who he suggests should get voting rights for company boards to protect their interests, as being synonymous with 'shareholders'. Most shareholders today, which hold voting rights, are institutions – asset managers and banks – who handle other people's money that is saved in pensions, life insurance or mutual funds. However, the true suppliers of finance (mostly employees saving for retirement) are separated from those voting rights. Thus Williamson's defence of shareholder monopolisation of corporate governance is, in fact, a misguided defence of asset managers and bankers – who on Williamson's own grounds have legitimacy in voting. See E McGaughey, 'Does Corporate Governance Exclude the Ultimate Investor?' (2016) 16(1) *Journal of Corporate Law Studies* 221.

6.   Williamson shared the 'Bank of Sweden Prize in Economic Science in Memorial of Alfred Nobel' in 2008, as did Milton Friedman in 1976. This is often referred to as the 'Nobel Prize in Economics' although unlike the prizes in peace, physics or literature, it has no connection to Alfred Nobel or his will. Nobel's name was added to the prize, issued from 1969, but it is funded by the Bank of Sweden. Does this present a problem of misrepresentation?

7.   The next extract examines modern behavioural research and what it suggests about rational choice economic theories on labour law.

**E McGaughey, 'Can Behavioural Psychology Inform Labour Law?'
in A Ludlow and A Blackham, *New Frontiers in Empirical Labour
Law Research* (2015) ch 6**

... in 1984 Richard Posner memorably wrote in 'Some Economics of Labor Law' that:

because labor law is ... founded on a policy that is the opposite of the policies of competition and economic efficiency that most economists support, the field is unlikely to attract as a subject for teaching and scholarship, the lawyer who is deeply committed to economic analysis; it is likely to repel him.[18]

Thus, a standard view in law and economics came to be that inequality of bargaining power had 'no economic basis',[19] that anything other 'at-will' employment was economically inefficient,[20] and collective action to any end by a union was virtually indistinguishable from a price-fixing cartel.[21]

But was this all true? Does labour law undermine a competitive economy? In 1998 Posner wrote that behavioural psychology could not present 'an alternative theory' to rational choice because 'it is profoundly unclear what "behavioral man" will do in any given situation'.[22] However this view, even if it was accurate then, is wrong now because a growing number of specific experiments are creating a superior positive understanding of how people act in economic affairs. Case-by-case experimentation can always be repeated, which means that unlike rational choice theory,[23] the theories it generates are built on falsifiable evidence.[24]

...

1. Fairness and Productivity

One of the most important contributions that behavioural economics has made to social science relates to our understanding of the human motivation at work. The motivation to work matters because it naturally affects the productive efficiency of people and the organisations they work in. The normative relevance this has is that if a first institutional arrangement tends to demotivate people, and leads to less productive outcomes compared to a second, the first may be classified as a market failure.

Probably the most important experiment in this respect was conducted by Alain Cohn, Ernst Fehr, Benedikt Hermann and Frédéric Schneider. ... The test participants were temporary workers who got jobs for two weekends in two German towns.[25] These workers did not know they were part of an experiment, and worked in pairs, handing out cards to pedestrians on the High Street for entry into nightclubs and bars. They had to either sell the cards for €5 or would give out the cards for free in return for the customer's information. There were a total of 96 workers in 48 pairs, and they were subjected to three different treatments. A first group worked at a wage of €12 an hour. A second group were hired at €12 an hour, but then were told shortly into their first shift that both workers in the pair would be receiving a wage cut to €9 per hour. The third group, most importantly, were also hired at €12 an hour but were then told the following: 'Worker 1 continues to earn €12 per hour while worker 2 receives €9 instead

---

[18]   RA Posner, 'Some Economics of Labor Law' (1984) 51 *University of Chicago Law Review* 988, 990.

[19]   RA Posner, 'Reflections on Consumerism' (1973) 20 *University of Chicago Law School Records* 19, 24–25. See also OE Williamson, *The Economic Institutions of Capitalism* (New York, The Free Press, 1985) 237–58.

[20]   RA Epstein, 'In Defense of the Contract at Will' (1984) 51 *University of Chicago Law Review* 947.

[21]   RA Posner, *Economic Analysis of Law* (New York, Little Brown and Co, 1973) ch 11, effectively restating the view of the US Supreme Court in *Loewe v Lawlor*, 208 US 274 (1908).

[22]   RA Posner, 'Rational Choice, Behavioral Economics and the Law' (1998) 50 *Stanford Law Review* 1551, 1559–60. Note the examples of elaborate reasoning to deduce what 'rational man' would do hypothetically: RA Coase, 'The Problem of Social Cost' (1961) 3 *Journal of Law and Economics* 1, and OE Williamson, *The Economic Institutions of Capitalism* (New York, The Free Press, 1985).

[23]   Cf A Smith, *Theory of Moral Sentiments* (1758) 1.

[24]   The evidence also indicates that some conclusions of behavioural law and economics previously, notably of Cass Sunstein and Christine Jolls, cannot realistically be supported. See further, E McGaughey, 'Behavioural Economics and Labour Law' (LSE Working Paper Series 20/2014, 2014): papers.ssrn.com/sol3/papers.cfm?abstract_id=2460685.

[25]   A Cohn, E Fehr, B Herrmann and F Schneider, 'Social Comparison in the Workplace: Evidence from a Field Experiment' (2014) 12 *Journal of the European Economic Association* 877.

of €12 per hour. This was the manager's decision'. Obviously, worker two could do very little, except leave at this point. It was that or unemployment, and so they had very little bargaining power against 'the manager's decision'. The terms of the employment contract allowed for variation.[26] The productivity of the workers was measured both in terms of the number of cards distributed, and in the accuracy of the customer information that was recorded.

Among the second group, where wages were cut to €9 an hour, there was a 15 per cent drop in productivity for both workers in the pair, compared to workers in the first group who stayed on €12 an hour. In the third group, where only one participant's wage was cut, there was an overall drop of 34 per cent in productivity between the participants in the team. This was entirely due to the one team member whose wage was cut to €9. The average worker who remained with pay of €12 continued to work as normal. So, the effect of cutting one worker's wage was a greater productivity loss than if both workers' wages were cut. The conclusion of the German nightclub card study authors is that, not only absolute levels of pay matter for performance, but also relative pay matters. In short, people's motivation to work is affected by their perception of fairness of their pay relative to other people in their group.

This study has important implications for one of the central issues in labour law, because it shows the connection between motivation to work and fairness in pay: a direct consequence of the capacity that employees have to bargain with employers.

...

Is it true that labour law, when it mitigates inequality of bargaining power, is concerned merely with distribution and not with economic efficiency? There are, of course, multiple reasons why specific labour rights can have positive efficiency consequences, and these have been extensively discussed before.[27] These discussions have concerned labour law's reduction of collective action problems, information asymmetries, transaction costs, improving aggregate demand, and mitigating monopsony.[28] Yet it also seems the German nightclub card study indicates why counteracting inequality of bargaining power has important and positive consequences for productive efficiency in itself. If workers as a group perceive themselves to be paid unfairly compared to their co-workers then the likely outcome is a drop in their productivity. Unfair wages in this context represent a market failure. Whenever inequality of bargaining power produces unfair distribution of rights in the workplace this represents a market failure, because it undermines the motivation to work. None of this should come as a dramatic surprise for economic thought, because it is experimental confirmation of much of what Alfred Marshall in 1890,[29] or Adam Smith in 1776,[30] had already realised.

...

There is one more main question raised by this experiment. Unfair wages diminish the productivity of the person who feels relatively undervalued, but could there be any effect on people who are substantially overvalued? ... Originally ... the matter was indeed posed as a

---

[26] Although the express terms of the contract allowed for the variation, the change in the experiment probably amounted to a breach of an implied term in employment contracts. In Germany, this is called 'Treu and Glauben' (see Civil Code (BGB) §242) and is referred to as either 'good faith' or 'mutual trust and confidence' in the Commonwealth and the United States. In the UK, see *Transco plc v O'Brien* [2002] EWCA Civ 379.

[27] See, eg S Deakin and F Wilkinson, 'Labour Law and Economic Theory: A Reappraisal' in H Collins, P Davies and RW Rideout (eds), *Legal Regulation of the Employment Relation* (Kluwer Law International, 2000).

[28] On this, see A Manning, *Monopsony in Motion: Imperfect Competition in Labor Markets* (Princeton, Princeton University Press, 2003). Manning's theory models how a monopsonistic labour market produces sub-optimal results, and contends that labour markets are always monopsonistic. Unpacking why labour markets fit into this model of monopsony, however, is a tricky issue that must be left for another time. It would seem that, as Manning suggests in ch 1, it is a specific example of the general phenomenon of inequality of bargaining power.

[29] A Marshall, *Principles of Economics* (3rd edn 1895) Book VI, ch 4, 649.

[30] A Smith, *An Inquiry into the Nature and Causes of the Wealth of Nations* (1776) Book 1, ch 8, §§43 and 47.

question of the damaging efficiency consequences, namely by AA Berle and Gardiner Means in *The Modern Corporation and Private Property*. Berle and Means pointed out that if they were unaccountable, company directors could 'serve their own pockets better by profiting at the expense of the company than by making profits for it'.[31] So overvaluation, unjust enrichment at the expense of others, was an economic efficiency issue, not simply a distributive issue, because it would lead to less productive effort by the person who was unjustly enriched.

2. Security and Productivity

A second issue, for which behavioural psychology has interesting implications, concerns not just the distribution of rights at work, but the security of rights: particularly security of pay, and potentially job security. In the Madurai game studies designed by Dan Ariely, Uri Gneezy, George Loewenstein and Nina Mazar, a group of people were asked to play six different games and depending on their performance, they would get different rewards.[32] The experiment was conducted by a group of Masters students at Narayanan College, in Madurai, which is in Tamil Nadu, India. In total, 87 residents of the town took part. Each person played the six games, and at the start of each a dice was rolled to determine at random whether person would receive a 'low', 'medium' or 'high' reward for their performance. The high reward was set at 400 rupees per game, and so 2,400 rupees was the maximum possible winnings, equivalent to around five months of the average per capita consumer expenditure of the locality.[33] The games required creative thinking, memory and motor skills of one kind or another, for instance, guiding a metal ball through a tiltable labyrinth which has holes in it that the ball should avoid.[34] They found that for all of the games, the participants who were told they could receive the high reward performed the worst.[35]

In a variation of the experiment, the same games were set up where participants were first given the maximum amount of money they could win, and were told it would be taken away again in proportion to how far their score fell below the highest possible. The idea here was to see if people performed differently if they felt they already had something which they could then lose. 'Loss aversion' is a well-established phenomenon which means that changes which appear to make things worse loom larger in people's minds than changes which appear to be gains.[36] On average people prefer avoiding losses to making gains of the same magnitude by a factor of two to one.[37] Unfortunately, as Dan Ariely later reported, the experiment could not be completed. The first test participant was given the money, performed poorly and then left the test room politely. The second participant, however, 'was so nervous that he shook the whole time and couldn't concentrate'. He then ran away with all of the money.[38] It was thus felt to be inappropriate to continue.

Why did the prospect of a large money payment negatively affect people's performance in the tests? 'Increased motivation', wrote the authors,

> tends to narrow individuals' focus of attention on a variety of dimensions ... including the breadth of the solution set people consider. This can be detrimental for tasks that involve

[31] AA Berle and GC Means, *The Modern Corporation and Private Property* (1932) 114.
[32] D Ariely, U Gneezy, G Loewenstein and N Mazar, 'Large Stakes and Big Mistakes' (2009) 76 *Review of Economic Studies* 451.
[33] Ibid, 454.
[34] The six games were called 'Packing Quarters', 'Simon', 'Recall Last Three Digits', 'Labyrinth', 'Dart Ball', and 'Roll-Up'.
[35] Ariely et al, n 53, 458 and the graphs therein.
[36] D Kahneman, JL Knetsch and RH Thaler, 'Anomalies: The Endowment Effect, Loss Aversion, and Status Quo Bias' (1991) 5 *Journal of Economic Perspectives* 193, 199.
[37] A Tversky and D Kahneman, 'Loss Aversion and Riskless Choice: A Reference Dependent Model' (1991) 106 *Quarterly Journal of Economics* 1039.
[38] D Ariely, *The Upside of Irrationality* (New York, Harper Collins, 2011) 33.

insight or creativity, since both require a kind of open-minded thinking that enables one to draw unusual connections between elements.

In fact, the authors had expected that on the games which required only memory skills, the higher payment would induce better performance, but even this prediction was proven to be unsound.[39] In a subsequent experiment with 24 MIT students, they found there was a statistically significant difference in performance between participants who did a task where they hit either the 'N' or the 'V' key on a keyboard, and those who did a task having to find numbers in a matrix that added up to 10.[40] This led to the conclusion that if work involves absolutely no thought, no creativity, no 'cognitive resources and effort', but instead 'requires only physical effort', then higher stakes can motivate better performance.

There are several important and immediate implications from this line of work, and several very interesting questions raised by it. First, the test was designed with the problem of bonus pay in mind. It had previously been thought, and prominently advocated in a large amount of law and economics literature, that it would be desirable to give company directors, senior managers, and perhaps all employees, significant variable components in their pay.

…

The theory that bonuses and performance related pay could be economically beneficial has not just been restricted to corporate boards and financial services. A tipping culture has become an increasingly important part of food catering work, many service industries have introduced discretionary or performance related elements to their work, and there has been a concerted attempt to promote employee share schemes. This is not to say that things like tipping, or employees buying stocks are necessarily bad, but laws which subsidise overindulgence in these practices are. That has happened with tipping, whenever pay from tips can be used to subsidise the employer's payment of the minimum wage,[41] and it has happened through tax advantages for employee share schemes.[42] All these measures make people's income less secure, particularly share schemes which fail the first rule that any prudent investor must follow: diversify. In doing so they lead to consequences opposed to what is desired. Going by the Madurai game studies, unless someone is doing a job which requires no cognitive effort, the impact of such practices (if any) will probably be negative. Even if someone's job does involve purely mechanical actions a human is not a resource, and treating people like they are no better than cogs in need of oil damages the moral character of the employer.

The outcomes of the Madurai game studies when loss aversion was brought into the equation points toward an interesting question about job security. Would there be similar results if future tests looked at not simply high stakes in pay, but high stakes in keeping one's job? There should be little doubt that, when the decision is made by one's peers or an impartial judge, dismissal is a necessary final sanction for poor job performance and is necessary to respond to changes in economic demand. But if people work under a constant threat of dismissal, how does this affect their performance and productivity? One of the beliefs that supports labour market 'flexicurity' in Europe, or at-will employment in the United States, seems to be that if a trumped up authority figure can bark 'you're fired' when they like, staff will be encouraged

---

[39] D Ariely, U Gneezy, G Loewenstein and N Mazar, 'Large Stakes and Big Mistakes' (2009) 76 *Review of Economic Studies* 451, 458–59.

[40] Ibid, 460–61.

[41] In the UK this was true until an amendment in the National Minimum Wage Regulations 1999 (Amendment) Regulations 2009 (SI 2009/1902) reg 5. Before this see *Revenue and Customs Commissioners v Annabel's (Berkeley Square) Ltd* [2009] EWCA Civ 361. A challenge to the European Court of Human Rights, on the basis that employers' taking tips to pay the minimum wage, was found to be within a Member State's margin of appreciation in *Nerva v United Kingdom* (2003) 36 EHRR 4. In the US, tips still form a large part of people's pay in most service industries because the Fair Labor Standards Act 1938 allowed for deviations, particularly since the Small Business Job Protection Act 1996.

[42] See, eg in the US, the Employee Retirement Income Security Act 1974, §407(d)(6) and Internal Revenue Code, §4975(e)(7).

to work properly. The reality may well be that the irrational threat of losing one's job has the same impact that any high stake has for productive output. In addition to important issues of justice and fairness,[43] it may damage rather than improve productivity.

3. Participation, Satisfaction and Productivity

A third major finding of behavioural studies sheds light on the importance of participation in workplace management and productivity. Shedding light on participation was not, however, the intended consequence of the original Hawthorne experiments, which were probably the first of their kind in the workplace. In 1924, an Australian researcher at Harvard Business School called Elton Mayo formulated an experiment with the employees at the Hawthorne Works of the Western Electric Company. ...

...

Mayo wished to substantiate a hypothesis that lighting intensity would affect workers' productivity. He borrowed five factory workers from Western Electric and brought them to an observation laboratory. They would work as normal putting together telephone relays as Mayo's two research colleagues varied the lighting. Unfortunately, as the switches were changed there were no effects. It was then determined to examine the effects of varying rest breaks, lunches, and daily or weekly working times. The observers were instructed to observe, but not to interfere with the work, and simply make the workers feel comfortable so they could get on with the job. Presumably, Mayo wanted to try and avoid 'contaminating' the test environment. So the observers asked the workers when breaks would suit them, and things like what meals they would prefer. Otherwise they stayed out of the way. Again, productivity went up when breaks were introduced, when meals were given, and also when an hour was taken off the day. But even more curious, productivity continued to improve when these benefits were removed. Mayo generated a large amount of data and findings, which he later wrote up,[44] but he did not exactly get what he wanted.

The proper interpretation of the Hawthorne experiments became an important point of debate, and it has remained one of the most important experiments in psychology and the workplace. What came to be known as the 'Hawthorne effect' is still widely discussed today. This term appears to have first been coined by Herbert Simon, to mean at a great level of generality that 'the very act of observing people in organizations and making them the subject of study and experimentation may well change their attitudes and behavior'.[45] Quite what changes might result was left open, but the more important view was to follow. 'We now have', said Simon,

> a considerable body of evidence to support the participation hypothesis – the hypothesis that significant changes in human behavior can be brought about rapidly only if the persons who are expected to change participate in deciding what the change shall be and how it shall be made.[46]

On this theme, in 1968, sociologist Paul Blumberg looked back at the archives Mayo left, and highlighted the one absolutely solid finding.[47] Workers in the test lab consistently outperformed

---

[43] For a discussion of competing values, see H Collins, *Justice in Dismissal* (Oxford, Oxford University Press, 1992) 13–23.

[44] E Mayo, *The Human Problems of an Industrial Civilization* (New York, Macmillan Company, 1933).

[45] HA Simon, 'Recent Advances in Organization Theory' in SK Bailey, *Research Frontiers in Politics and Government* (The Brookings Institution, 1955) 28.

[46] Ibid, 29.

[47] P Blumberg, *Industrial Democracy: The Sociology of Participation* (New York, Schocken Books, 1968) chs 2–3.

those who stayed in the factory in productivity. Even stranger, the workers seemed happier at work, and began to socialise with each other more after their shifts. Among the interviews were several statements about how they were glad to escape the authoritarian managers back at the factory.[48] But Mayo's main objective was to show how workers can be made productive, so the employer can appropriate the gains.[49] Blumberg concluded this is why Mayo missed the same conclusion that Simon was drawing: that what was making the Hawthorne workers more productive was their new ability to participate in workplace decisions. Even when benefits were taken away, the act of joining people in the process of decision (because it was genuine) meant that the staff had a reason to want to work more effectively. Productivity only dropped as the experiments continued toward 1932, and involvement in workplace decisions dropped away.[50] Participation in the workplace improved productivity.

Law and economics literature has since sought to ignore or side-line the view that meaningful workplace participation (and not simply information and consultation) could lead to productive gains. For instance, Oliver Williamson sought to address Blumberg's claims, albeit indirectly,[51] by pointing to alternative papers. These papers showed, said Williamson, that there was 'serious doubt that efforts to effect participation can be justified on profitability grounds'. Moreover 'evidence relating job satisfaction to productivity', said Williamson, 'discloses little or no association between the two'.[52] The difficulty is that the literature Williamson cited included Herbert Simon, who as we have just seen, did think there was evidence that participation improved productivity. If Williamson had attempted to address the findings of Blumberg, he might have reached a different conclusion. If he had looked to chapter five of Blumberg's book, he would have seen a large catalogue of experiments up to 1968. If he had aimed to refute the findings, it would have been necessary to conduct a study demonstrating participation in the workplace has no positive effect on productivity. But he did not. ...

NOTES AND QUESTIONS

1. The main contention in this extract is that, when confronted with hard evidence, many claims from law and economics theorists that justify labour deregulation fail scrutiny. This particularly includes the claims that unequal bargaining power has no detrimental economic impact (it affects pay, which affects productivity), that 'flexible' pay and job conditions improve productivity (it can frighten people, and reduce the quality of their work), and that workplace participation is irrelevant (it makes people happier and more productive). Is this persuasive?

2. It would be mistaken to think behavioural experiments produce conclusions on everybody's behaviour: they show average tendencies in people's behaviour, while minorities can (and often do) act differently. Do you think it is possible to develop a social science of human behaviour that can be used for labour policy decisions? What problems (if any) can you envisage?

[48] Ibid, 25.

[49] See also, E Mayo, *Teamwork and Labor Turnover in the Aircraft Industry of Southern California* (Harvard, Harvard University Press, 1944).

[50] Blumberg, [above], 37–39.

[51] OE Williamson, *The Economic Institutions of Capitalism* (New York, The Free Press, 1985) 269–70, cites S Bowles and H Gintis, *Schooling in Capitalist America: Educational Reform and the Contradictions of Economic Life* (New York, Basic Books, 1976) 79–80, for a quote from Blumberg.

[52] Williamson, ibid, 270. Job satisfaction obviously differs from participation itself. However, the evidence shows a clear positive correlation between job satisfaction and productivity. See D Ariely, E Kamenica and D Prelec, 'Man's Search for Meaning: The Case of Legos' (2008) 67 *Journal of Economic Behavior & Organization* 671.

3.   RA Posner, 'Rational Choice, Behavioral Economics, and the Law' (1998) 50(5)
     Stanford Law Review 1551 argued that behavioural economics could not replace
     rational choice theory because it is 'antitheoretical' and offered no positive basis
     for predicting behaviour and outcomes. What do you think?

(3) HUMAN DEVELOPMENT

Since the late 1970s, a gradual shift took place within the economics profession. First, economic efficiency and growth was reconceptualised: from being an overriding objective, that would be sacrificed to achieve distributive justice (a view popularised by AM Okun, *Equality and Efficiency: The Big Tradeoff* (1971)), to a subcategory of the greater goal of human development. The United Nations Inequality-adjusted Human Development Index, since 2010, compiles a figure for social progress across countries, based on (1)(a) gross domestic product, (1)(b) reduced according to unequally income is distributed, (2) years of education, (3) life expectancy. This measure leaves much to be desired, but is itself developing. It symbolises the efforts both to reintegrate economics into mainstream social science, humanities and legal policy, and also to emphasise in non-economic subjects the importance of engaging with economic theory (of which there are many kinds). Second, in contrast to the strand of economics favoured by the authors above, more people focused on producing macro-empirical evidence for policy predictions. As well as 'micro' empirical data from surveying, interviews, or behavioural experiments, researchers would seek to identify close correlations of data on economic outcomes (growth, unemployment, inequality, etc) with legal or regulatory change, to deduce a possible effect.

J Stiglitz, 'Employment, social justice and societal well-being'
(2002) 141 *International Labour Review* 9

The purpose of economic activity is to increase the well-being of individuals, and economic structures that are able to do so are more desirable than those that do not. This proposition might seem anodyne, but on closer inspection it is far more complex. To be sure, all politicians – left, right and centre – pay homage to it. Yet, the policies that are pursued often turn out to be antithetical to it. Much of traditional economics has indeed provided considerable comfort to those politicians who have a different agenda, and created considerable confusion for those who are sympathetic.

A second proposition, also deceptively anodyne, is that for a large fraction of the world's population, work – employment – is important. For individuals who lose their jobs, it is not just the loss of income that matters, it is also the individual's sense of self. Unemployment is associated with a variety of problems and pathologies, from higher divorce rates, higher suicide rates to higher incidences of alcoholism. And the relationship is not just a correlation: there is a causal connection. Some individuals can keep themselves happy and gainfully "employed" without a job. But for many, employment – the fact that someone else recognizes their "contribution" by paying them – is important. ...

Labour and Neoclassical Economics

One of the great "tricks" (some might say "insights") of neoclassical economics is to treat labour like any other factor of production. Output is written as a function of inputs – steel, machines, and labour. The *mathematics* treats labour like a commodity, lulling one into thinking of labour like an ordinary commodity, such as steel or plastic. But labour is unlike any other commodity. The work environment is of no concern for steel; we do not care about steel's well-being (though to be sure, we may take care that the environment does not lead to its rusting or otherwise adversely affect its performance characteristics). Steel does not have to be *motivated* to work as an input. Steel does whatever it is "told" to do. But management is generally highly concerned with *motivating* labour.

The distinction arises from labour's human aspect. Individuals decide how hard they work, and with what care. The environment affects their behaviour, including the incentives with which they are confronted. In standard theory, individuals contract to perform a certain job, and are paid if and only if they complete that job. It is assumed that contract enforcement is costless – partly because of the assumption that information exists about whether the task (which is specified in infinite minutia) has been completed. Yet, information imperfections abound in the economy, and these information imperfections have profound impacts on the way an economy behaves, a fact recognized by the 2001 Nobel Prize (which focused in particular on information asymmetries). While this is not the occasion to review all of the implications of information imperfections, I want to highlight three that are particularly germane to the theses of this article.

First, imperfect information leads to imperfect competition; but the striking result of our research was that even a little bit of information imperfection – even a small cost of searching for a new job, for instance – can have a large effect. Economists always knew that information was imperfect, but they hoped that a little bit of imperfection would only change the equilibrium in a small way, and that the imperfections were indeed small. These hopes were not based on analytical work, but rather on the realization that if these assumptions were not true, the models that economists have used for decades, and the conclusions derived from these models, would be of little relevance. To put it perhaps over-grandly, it would have made much of economic analysis obsolete overnight. The new information economics showed, however, that even a small search cost could enable the equilibrium real wage to fall from the competitive level to the monopsony level.[53]

Observers of labour markets had long been concerned with bargaining power asymmetries. Workers' mobility is limited; employees who are fired – e.g. because they demand higher wages or better working conditions – may have a stigma, making it difficult for them to obtain another job, even if employers do not act collusively (and there may be tacit collusion); credit market imperfections (credit rationing, which itself can be explained by information imperfections) can make it difficult for a worker who is unemployed to live well for long, putting the worker in a far more precarious position than the employer who has lost whatever rents were gained from the worker's labour. What our analysis showed is that, despite other market imperfections that may exist, these alone put workers in a decidedly disadvantageous position.

Second, imperfect information leads to unemployment: even when wages are so high that the demand for labour is less than the supply, wages will not fall; for if a firm lowers its wages, workers' effort or the quality of workers hired may decrease (or their turnover costs increase). To most of the world, this is hardly news. But to standard economic theory it is: neoclassical theory said that markets always clear; what seemed to be unemployment was nothing more than a sudden change in the demand for leisure. Information economics also emphasized that the decentralized adjustment process often worked imperfectly, leading to temporary

---

[53] See P Diamond, 'A model of price adjustment' (1971) 3 *Journal of Economic Theory* 156, J Stiglitz, 'Equilibrium wage distributions' (1985) 95 *Economic Journal* 595, and J Stiglitz, 'The causes and consequences of the dependence of quality on prices' (1987) 25(1) *Journal of Economic Literature* 1.

unemployment rates which even exceeded the equilibrium unemployment rates associated with efficiency wages. Yet traditional theory paid no attention to this – after all, with perfect information it is easy to move to the new equilibrium whenever the economy is disturbed.

Third, information economics has challenged the traditional economic theory which argues that markets are self-adjusting and efficient, and that the nature of the equilibrium (and its efficiency) depends neither on distribution nor on institutions. To traditional economists, the law of demand and supply determines the allocation of resources (including incomes), not institutions like sharecropping. Issues of efficiency could thus conveniently be separated from issues of distribution. Information economics has challenged each of these propositions: Bruce Greenwald and I showed that when information is imperfect or markets incomplete – that is, always – markets are not even constrained Pareto efficient, i.e. that in principle, there existed interventions in the market which took account of the costs of information and of creating a market, and which made everyone better off.[54] Our analysis found that there were pervasive market failures that might, in principle, be addressed by government intervention. The retort that we ignored information imperfections in the public sector was simply wrong. We took them into account. We had, in fact, gone further, and identified reasons which made government's information set, powers and constraints different from those of a decentralized private sector, and which provided an explanation for why, at least in principle, government might undertake welfare-improving actions.[55]

We also showed that the nature of the equilibrium, including its efficiency, could well depend on the distribution of wealth. This can be seen most clearly in the case of simple agricultural economies, but in fact it holds true more generally. The agency problems associated with sharecropping arise because of the disparity between the ownership of land and capital. Problems of information asymmetry do not arise when workers work their own land. ...

In standard competitive models, any interference with the free workings of the economy had an adverse effect on efficiency, whether it was minimum wage laws or trade unions – which introduced imperfect competition in labour markets – or requirements on working conditions. ...

It was, of course, inconvenient that many of the central propositions had little empirical support. Card and Krueger's (1995) work strongly demonstrated that minimum wage legislation does not have the serious adverse effect on employment predicted by the standard theory – and that it may even have a positive effect.[56] But economic theory did not lend credence to many of the propositions either, even without recourse to modern information theories. Even if benefits did not depend on contributions, payroll taxes should largely be shifted backwards (except for minimum wage workers), and hence have no effect on employment; and to the extent that benefits depend on contributions, there may be little or no effect on labour supply (not even a positive one). But information economics explained clearly why market equilibrium was generally inefficient, e.g. why firms "undersupplied" contract provisions enhancing job security.[57]

In short, the mantra of increased labour market flexibility was only a thinly disguised attempt to roll back – under the guise of "economic efficiency" – gains that workers had achieved over years and years of bargaining and political activity. To be sure, sometimes unions may have more than corrected the imbalance of bargaining power that previously existed, and used their power to push for excessive protection for their members, at the expense of other workers in the economy. If that happens, however, the answer is not to pretend that in the absence of

---

[54] See B Greenwald and J Stiglitz, 'Externalities in economies with imperfect information and incomplete markets' (1986) 101(2) *Quarterly Journal of Economics* 229.

[55] See for example J Stiglitz, 'The economic role of the State: Efficiency and effectiveness' (1989) in Arnold Heertje (ed), *The economic role of the State* (1989) 9.

[56] D Card and AB Krueger, *Myth and measurement: The new economics of the minimum wage* (1995)

[57] See, in particular, C Shapiro and JE Stiglitz, 'Equilibrium unemployment as a worker discipline device' (1984) 74(3) *American Economic Review* 433.

such protections, the competitive market place would lead to efficient or equitable outcomes; but rather to try to redress the imbalances.

While freedom of association and trade union rights are important in correcting the power imbalances that exist in labour markets, even workers enjoying such rights are typically in a disadvantageous position. It is far easier for an employer to replace recalcitrant workers than for employees to "replace" a recalcitrant employer, especially when the unemployment rate is high. Thus, there is an important role for government, e.g. in ensuring occupational health and safety.

...

"Labour market flexibility" and "capital market liberalization" may thus appear as symmetric policies, freeing up the labour and capital markets, respectively; but they have very asymmetric consequences – and both serve to enhance the welfare of capital at the expense of workers. So ingrained have these prescriptions become in the mantra of good policy that their distributional consequences have been almost totally ignored; and of course, if efficiency and distribution could be separated, as traditional theory argued they could be, the lapse might not have been so important.

It is not, of course, just that the advocates of these policies overlook the imperfections of competition and information. There are other market imperfections (some derived from imperfections of information) to which they turn a blind eye too. With imperfect insurance markets, individuals worry about the volatility of their income. They can smooth only imperfectly and often at great cost. Risk matters more than it would if markets were perfect. Indeed, surveys of poor workers suggest that insecurity is among their main concerns, and that instability is among the most important causes and manifestations of poverty (see World Bank, 2000).[58] Yet, the so-called Washington Consensus has not only pushed policies which enhanced instability, but it has also pushed for the elimination of job security protections (which markets by themselves will often not provide).

Another important set of market imperfections concerns corporate governance. Managers of firms may not act in the interests of shareholders, majority shareholders may not act in the interests of minority shareholders and, more broadly, the concerns of other stakeholders may not be adequately reflected in the firm's decision-making process.[59]

...

Another manifestation of "capital market friendly policies" is the recent push for privatization of social security [ie the basic state pension in the US], with the replacement of defined-benefit programmes by defined-contribution programmes. While this is not the occasion for a full debate on the issues,[60] it should be clear that privatization would be of immense benefit to those firms that managed the pension funds and provided the annuities, but it would at the same time impose greater risks on workers, since the market in most countries does not provide securities that are fully indexed for inflation. Moreover, there is evidence suggesting that even in highly efficient capital markets, like the United Kingdom's, transaction costs are so high that benefits under privatization are reduced by 40 per cent.[61]

...

In development, transition and crises – or even in ordinary economic downturns – markets do not automatically quickly lead to full employment, and it is now almost universally recognized

---

[58] World Bank, *World Development Report, 2000/2001: Attacking poverty* (2000).

[59] See J Stiglitz, 'Credit markets and the control of capital' (1985) 17(2) *Journal of Money, Credit and Banking* 133.

[60] For a discussion of some of the fallacies underlying the standard arguments for privatization, see PR Orszag and JE Stiglitz, 'Rethinking pension reform: Ten myths about social security systems' in R Holzmann and JE Stiglitz (eds), *New ideas about old age security: Toward sustainable pension systems in the 21st century* (2001) 17.

[61] M Murthi, MJ Orszag and PR Orszag, 'The charge ratio on individual accounts: Lessons from the U.K. experience' (1999) Birbeck College Working Paper 99-2.

that government has an important role in facilitating employment creation and the maintenance of the economy at full employment. We now know a great deal about how to design
effective stimulus programmes. We know that monetary policy is more effective in constraining
an economy in a boom than in stimulating an economy in recession, and that we therefore
need to rely on fiscal measures. We also know a great deal about how to design effective fiscal
measures, i.e. measures which operate quickly, which have high multiplier effects, and which
do not exacerbate social divisions in countries where such divisions are strong.[62] An example
might be policies which change intertemporal prices to encourage consumption and investment during a period of expected unemployment (in which the shadow prices of resources
are low) and which reduce liquidity constraints that limit expenditures either on investment
or on consumption.[63] Such policies are indeed more effective than, say, tax cuts for the rich or
permanent investment tax credits.

No matter how well we manage the economy, there will be downturns and, with downturns, unemployment. Yet while we know more about macroeconomic management,[64] economic crises have become more frequent and deeper around the world: close to a hundred
countries experienced crises in the last quarter of the twentieth century. I believe there are
some reasons for this: changes in the global economic architecture, including capital market
liberalization, have heightened risks beyond the coping ability of many developing countries.
Thus, while countries need to be urged to construct adequate safety nets,[65] anyone who is
concerned with employment and decent work must be concerned about those features of the
global economic architecture which contribute to volatility. ...

...

If, however, development is to be broader based, then we must pay at least as much attention to workers and their security. We must persuade them that change can benefit them. But
if they are exposed to increased insecurity and higher unemployment it will not; and many of
the "reform" policies have done exactly that. On a more positive note, successful democratic
development entails questioning authority and participation in decision-making: democratic
workplaces[66] as well as democratic political processes. These entail more democratic governance structures at all levels.[67]

NOTES AND QUESTIONS

1.   Joseph Stiglitz, who was Chief Economic Adviser to the World Bank, and also a
recipient of the Bank of Sweden Prize in Economics (or 'Nobel' Prize) in 2001,
identifies systemic market failures in producing 'well-being', particularly through
employment, in 'information asymmetries'. This refers to the simple idea that
when people in a market for labour cannot adequately evaluate the worth of something, markets fail to adequately match supply and demand. Stiglitz then relates

[62] These are, of course, not the only desiderata that stimulus packages should meet: they should also
strengthen the economy's long-run position, or at least not do undue harm.

[63] The constraints themselves are explained by asymmetries of information (see, for example, Stiglitz and
Weiss, 1981).

[64] Indeed, in the United States, while there are still economic fluctuations, there is little evidence of a regular business cycle; expansions have become longer, and contractions shorter.

[65] Though, at the same time, one should recognize the inadequacy of such safety nets – even in advanced
industrialized countries – in the agricultural and self-employment sectors, sectors which predominate in less
developed countries.

[66] There is some evidence that more democratic workplaces enhance economic efficiency, see AS Blinder
(ed), *Paying for productivity: A look at the evidence* (1990) and DI Levine, *Reinventing the workplace: how
business and employees can both win* (1995).

[67] By contrast, IMF conditionality often serves to undermine democratic processes, especially when (as in
Korea) the conditionality extends beyond issues directly related to the crisis, and into core political issues, see
M Feldstein, 'Refocusing the IMF' (1998) 77(2) *Foreign Affairs* 20.

this to unequal bargaining power, which he connects to distribution of wealth. What, precisely, do you think the relationship is between the two?

2.	T Piketty, *Capital in the Twenty-First Century* (2014) ch 9, 331–34 contends that because the true nature of marginal productivity (of labour or other inputs to production) is hard to know in practice, 'hierarchical relationships' determine the outcome. Would you agree, in economic terms, that unequal bargaining power is best regarded as a market failure, because unfairly paid people are less motivated to work, and this damages productive efficiency?

3.	Stiglitz uses the language of 'government intervention' in markets, although from a legal perspective 'intervention' in markets is a logical impossibility. Markets (based in the law of property, contract, etc) are themselves products of law, and so labour legislation internally redefines the character of markets. If a market is law, how can law interfere? It may be that the view law interferes with markets is particularly prevalent in common law systems where the rules of property and contract derive from judge-made case law, and labour legislation alters the employer prerogatives that the common law had set up, whereas in a codified civil law system, most law is legislation already.

4.	The next extract covers some of the most recent macro-empirical work on the effect of labour rights.

S Deakin, J Malmberg and P Sarkar, 'Do Labour Laws Increase Equality at the Expense of Higher Unemployment? The Experience of Six OECD Countries, 1970–2010' (2014) University of Cambridge Faculty of Law Research Paper No 11/2014

3. Empirical Evidence on Time Trends in Labour Laws: Data from the CBR Labour Regulation Index

Although the literature examining the economic impact of labour laws is large, very little of it uses time series data, even though this is the kind of evidence 'that most empiricists would regard as providing a stronger and more valid test of any claim' than time-invariant data of the kind commonly used in cross-sectional regressions (Freeman, 2005: 14). Part of the reasons is the lack, until recently, of reliable time series on legal and related institutional changes. The dataset most heavily relied on in empirical studies of labour legislation, the OECD's Employment Protection Index ('EPI'), has only a limited longitudinal dimension. Data have been collected at various points since the EPI's inception in the 1990s (see Grubb and Wells, 1993) but there are gaps in the time series. In any event the EPI only covers employment protection laws, mostly relating to unfair dismissal legislation. Laws on working time and industrial action are not contained in the EPI, and those governing codetermination, employee involvement and collective worker representation are only covered in so far as they relate to collective dismissals and related aspects of employment terminations. The right to strike is not covered at all in the EPI. The index prepared by Botero et al. (2004) does cover these areas of labour law (as well as some aspects of social security laws) but is not longitudinal. The various Doing Business Report indices relating to labour law, building on Botero et al. (2004), provide limited longitudinal data, but going back only to the early 2000s.

The Labour Regulation Index (LRI) is one of a number of databases developed at the Centre for Business Research in Cambridge since the mid-2000s which provide longitudinal data on changes in labour and company law. The LRI is based on a 'fine-grained' approach to the coding of primary legal sources which makes it possible to indicate not just the presence or absence of a worker-protective law in a given country, but to estimate magnitudes concerning the degree of protection conferred on workers by a given legal rule. These are represented using graduated scores between 0 (indicating little or no protection of workers) and 1 (indicating high protection of workers). Coding algorithms or protocols are used in an attempt to ensure consistency in the scoring of legal rules, and primary sources are reported in full alongside the scores for particular variables.[68]

The LRI contains forty indicators in all, spread across 5 sub-indices, covering, respectively, the regulation of alternative employment contracts (self-employment, part-time work, fixed-term employment and temporary agency work), working time (daily and weekly working time limits and rules governing overtime and nightwork), dismissal (procedural and substantive rules on termination of employment), employee representation (rules on collective bargaining, the closed shop and codetermination) and the industrial action (the extent of legal support for the right to strike, including rules on secondary and political strikes).[69]

In this paper we report findings from data coding exercises covering six countries (France, Germany, Sweden, Japan, the UK and USA) for the period from the early 1970s to more or less the present day. France, Germany, the US and USA are among the five countries initially coded up to 2006 (see Deakin et al., 2007). Japan and Sweden have been added to the dataset and their coding covers the period 1970–2010.

Figures 1–6 present data on labour laws in these six countries over the four decades from 1970. Scores are represented as five-year averages in order to illustrate general trends over time. Figure 1 represents the trend in labour laws as a whole (that is, covering each of the five sub-indices). The time trend is represented in terms of five- year moving averages. As Figure 1 makes clear, the individual country experiences vary greatly. Labour law is much more worker-protective in France and Sweden than in the United States, for example. There is also considerable variation over time, particularly in the UK and Sweden. In the USA and Japan, on the other hand, labour law has changed very little over the period covered by the dataset.

Figure 1 Labour laws (all) in six OECD countries, 1970–2010

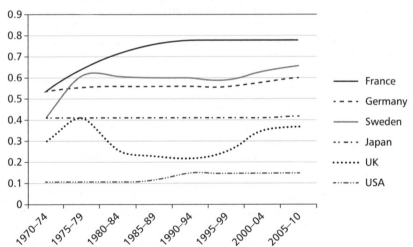

Source: CBR Labour Regulation Index (LRI): http://www.cbr.cam.ac.uk/research/projects/project2-20output.htm.

---

[68] For further details, see Deakin, Lele and Siems, 2007. For more general discussion of the 'leximetric' methods used to create these datasets, see Deakin and Sarkar, 2008; Siems and Deakin, 2010), and for helpful discussion of coding such 'synthetic' indices more generally, see OECD, 2013: ch. 2. The LRI dataset is publicly available (at http://www.cbr.cam.ac.uk/research/projects/project2-20output.htm).

[69] As such, the index does not cover all aspects of employment law. There may be a case for extending the LRI to cover other areas of labour law, such as discrimination law, in future. The analysis presented in the text

[Five further charts depict changes in the protectiveness of employment contracts, working time, dismissal protection, employee representation, and industrial action. Then, two charts show changes in countries' unemployment rates and labour's share of income.]

5. Assessment

Our panel data analysis suggests that there is no consistent relationship, either negative or positive, between labour laws in general and unemployment in developed countries. Some specific types of labour regulation may have the effect of reducing unemployment. In the case of working time regulation, this effect could be the combined result of work-sharing arrangements and improved labour productivity. In the case of worker representation laws, the impact could be derived from the positive effects of these laws on employee motivation and morale.

There is some evidence, then, that labour laws are compatible with improved efficiency at the level of the firm and with enhanced economic performance at national level. This is consistent with some aspects of the literature on labour regulation. ... Our other finding is that labour laws in general, and working time laws and employee representation laws in particular, have positive distributional effects. In this respect our findings tally with the consensus from other empirical studies. ...

The absence of clear findings on two of our sub-indices, those relating to employment protection and strike law, suggests that further research is needed to disentangle their possible effects. ...

NOTES AND QUESTIONS

1.   This article by Simon Deakin, Jonas Malmberg and Prabirjit Sarkar is part of a larger project at the Centre for Business Research to 'encode' and assess economic impacts of the laws of enterprise. See J Armour, S Deakin, P Lele and M Siems, 'How Do Legal Rules Evolve? Evidence from a Cross-Country Comparison of Shareholder, Creditor, and Worker Protection' (2009) 57(3) *American Journal of Comparative Law* 579. It was motivated to correct the defective attempts at the same thing by financial economists at the World Bank and the OECD, from the 1990s, who had no legal understanding, and generally concluded that US corporate and insolvency law was good, and labour law everywhere was bad.

2.   The obvious difficulty of this method is the subjectivity of 'coding' laws with points on a scale of 0 to 1. For example, points might be given to countries with a requirement to give notice before dismissal, more for employers to provide reasons, and more to pay compensation for redundancy. But how can quality of laws be compared on a numerical scale when laws entail no quantities? The authors' reply is to frankly admit the shortcomings of the method, but point out that because all data and evaluations are transparent, readers can assess for themselves whether the results are trustworthy. Moreover, once one research group (at the World Bank, etc) has begun the game, it cannot be stopped, and the only response it to undertake the same research, and try to do it better.

3.   S Deakin, C Fenwick and P Sarkar, 'Labour Law and Inclusive Development: The Economic Effects of Industrial Relations Laws in Middle-Income Countries'

---

represents work in progress (see Deakin, Lele and Siems, 2007). For some other areas of regulation, such as minimum wage laws, there is less need for a 'synthetic' index such as the LRI, as the effects of legal regulation can be studied using widely-available country-level earnings data. See, for a recent example, Grimshaw (2013).

(2014) University of Cambridge Faculty of Law Research Paper No 13/2014, studied Brazil, Russia, India, China and South Africa (the 'BRICS') and found positive effects for worker representation laws, but negative effects for laws favouring freer strike action, which are said to be specific for development. Only a larger sample – or indeed further historical analysis for developed countries – will reveal if these findings are anomalous.

4. If empirical evidence does favour more protective labour law, to what extent do you think this will change political discourse?

Additional Reading for Chapter 2

JS Mill, *Chapters on Socialism* (1879) Fortnightly Review

Mill critiqued the socialist writers of the mid-nineteenth century who sought to abolish private property, to establish 'the economic constitution of society on an entirely new basis', arguing it instead needed reform. As the working classes had gained male suffrage in America and France, said Mill, and with the Reform Act 1867 moving closer to suffrage in the UK, it was important to scrutinise the changes in legislation people would inevitably require. Mill suggests that total state ownership would require, if it were to function, a strident improvement in people's moral character. This could not be achieved by an Act of Parliament alone. But because the idea of property is variable, not fixed, any right of property can be altered that stood in the way of the public good.

L Brandeis, *The Fundamental Cause of Industrial Unrest* (1916)

Brandeis, who made his name as the 'People's Advocate' before being appointed to the US Supreme Court, argued before the US Commission on Industrial Relations that collective bargaining was the best mechanism to resolve labour disputes. It would be wrong to replace the 'tyranny of capital' with a tyranny of labour, because the 'social justice for which we are striving is an incident of our democracy, not its main end'. Brandeis favoured a system of labour freedom and voice, to remove legal restrictions on collective bargaining and strikes. As he said, 'the end for which we must strive is the attainment of rule by the people, and that involves industrial democracy as well as political democracy'.

JR Commons and JB Andrews, *Principles of Labor Legislation* (1916)

The foundational US textbook by Commons and Andrews is also an early masterpiece of concision and comparative law. The thematic structure of the book reflects the early struggles of labour lawyers to refute the dogma of 'freedom of contract' and property put forward by the US Supreme Court. It emphasises unequal bargaining power, and analyses individual and collective bargaining, before exploring wage and hours regulation. The latter chapters engage the labour law roots of the emerging welfare state: on unemployment, health, social insurance and public administration.

R Dukes, *The Labour Constitution: The Enduring Idea of Labour Law* (2014)
Dukes explores the theory of labour regulation, which first emerged in early-twentieth-century Germany, that labour rights should be embedded in a country's constitutional framework, in order to democratise the economy as much as politics. Dukes presents this rights-centred view of labour regulation, developed by Hugo Sinzheimer, as a contrast to Otto Kahn-Freund's opinion that labour law did not need the state, or the later view, represented by Paul Davies and Mark Freedland, that labour law should be regarded as an integral element of a market's functioning. However, Dukes suggests that regarding labour law as a critical extension of a democratic state could inform a coherent narrative to correct the 'dearth of democratic institutions at the global level'.

AA Berle, 'Property, Production and Revolution' (1965) 65 *Columbia Law Review* 1
Berle, a leading architect of US President Roosevelt's New Deal, suggests that the economic changes in modern enterprise had warranted the extension of a scheme of economic and social rights, embedded in legislation. Modern corporations had changed the nature of private property, so that more obligations should attach to property used for 'productive' purposes, than 'passive' property used for consumption. In a reflection of the 'Great Society' programme passed at the time, Berle identified the growing regulation of consumer affairs, labour relations and public services by specialised laws and government administrators as writing what was in substance a 'Second Bill of Rights'.

H Collins, 'The Productive Disintegration of Labour Law' (1997) 26 *Industrial Law Journal* 295
Collins recounts a thematic development of UK labour law theory over the late twentieth century. He contends that the paradigm of analysis, which drew on sociological and industrial relations accounts of the workplace, exhibited a 'deafness' to other theoretical traditions. While collective laissez faire or 'legal abstentionism', represented by Kahn-Freund and Wedderburn, contained powerful critiques of legal formalism, they were closed to economic analysis, the language of individual rights, and institutions for social dialogue and partnership. The pages of the *Industrial Law Journal* showed an increasing openness to multiple discourses. The new 'disintegration' of labour law theory was 'productive'.

ACL Davies, *Perspectives on Labour Law* (2nd edn 2009)
Davies systematically explores UK labour law based on two primary competing perspectives: human rights instruments, and economic theory, focusing on the last 70 years. While stating that the book does not argue 'that either perspective is 'correct' or preferable to the other', it aims to show how the internal dialogues of each perspective have reached very different conclusions. Part II analyses eight major topics in UK labour law, against particular theories as they apply to that policy field.

H Arthurs, 'Labor Law as the Law of Economic Subordination and Resistance: A Thought Experiment' (2013) 34 *Comparative Labor Law and Policy Journal* 585
Reflecting on the general decline in the power of labour organisations, Arthurs contends that our understanding of the dependence of labour should be integrated with understanding of the dependence of other social groups: consumers, tenants, pensioners, investors, etc.

He proposes a counterfactual: what if labour law had never developed as an autonomous field? Presumably it would still exist, but integrated with other forms of law. With the Great Depression in the United States particularly in mind, and the (aborted) National Industrial Recovery Act 1933, Arthurs argues that in times of economic and social crisis people have recognised their identities as something broader that just a 'worker'. When successful, they have sought legal reform to resolve subordinate positions in whatever field they arise. He posits that the next generation of legal reform may be successful in turning the reality of subordination itself into a counterfactual.

SL Willborn, 'Individual Employment Rights and the Standard Economic Objection: Theory and Empiricism' (1988) 67 *Nebraska Law Review* 101
Willborn explains, complete with supply and demand schedules, the standard objections among American law and economics theorists to labour rights that create minimum standards (such as the minimum wage, or anything in chs 3–7). This view suggests that all rights are inefficient because they do not merely set default rules and lower transaction costs, but mandate non-waivable rights. Willborn offers what might be seen as an immanent critique, suggesting that if one follows economic logic, minimum terms can be viewed as underproduced goods, respond to externalities, information asymmetries, and so on. (None of these, however, draw attention to the economic significance of unequal bargaining power.) Willborn says that whether a right is efficient is ultimately a question of empirical evidence (on which the literature is notably silent).

G Davidov and B Langille (ed), *The Idea of Labour Law* (2011) Parts I and II
This collection gathers contributions from various authors seeking to uncover the essential 'idea' of labour law and its normative foundations. To give examples of chapters, Hepple suggests labour law results from a contest of ideologies, still very alive. Weiss explains how labour law transcends the public–private divide and should be integrated with social security, although even texts and courses in Germany have not succeeded in this. Hyde outlines 22 'ideas' of labour law and, writing from a US perspective, suggests each has lost touch with the practical reality of labour's crisis on the ground. Langille contends that focus on bargaining power is out of date, and a positive conception of promoting people's capacity is needed. Fudge argues that, if one views labour law as a way to expand people's capabilities, one should include unpaid workers in its scope. Deakin argues that labour law does not merely correct market failures, but constitutes what markets do.

A Ludlow and A Blackham (eds), *New Frontiers in Empirical Labour Law Research* (2015)
This edited collection focuses on ways in which empirical research into the consequences of labour regulation has been developing. It discusses empirical methods and their application to work, including qualitative, quantitative and behavioural research.

Part Two

Contract and Rights

3

Scope and Enforcement

The 'scope and enforcement' of labour rights refers to who gets rights, who has to rely on contract alone, and how effectively the law is upheld. Labour rights, according to the majority view, are for people who perform work for others, but might lack the bargaining power to get decent terms in a contract (O Kahn-Freund, *Labour and the Law* (1972) 7). They replace terms that individuals might reach by contract with employing corporations or other entities, with decisions reached by democratic deliberation. They build part of a charter for economic and social rights. The minimum rights that exist through the employment relationship are explored through part 2, while parts 3, 4 and 5 are devoted to the rights of a different nature: to workplace participation, equality, and job security. Implicitly the law says to employing entities, 'you must provide these minimum standards, and if you are not efficient enough to do so, you are not good enough to be an employer at all'. In this way, the law usually aims to protect 'dependent' labourers, but equally it aims to prevent unjust enrichment of employing entities at the expense of employees and basic social development. The law does not always achieve this aim – making social rights effective – unless its purpose is recognised.

Labour 'rights' always imply a correlative duty. Usually the duty is fulfilled by employing entities, but also governments. However, the law also allows people to be 'self-employed', and so in effect to be responsible for the minimum standards that labour rights seek. Should we allow the risk that self-employed have less income than a minimum wage? Should we allow people to have fewer holidays, or less job security, where state welfare (on less income than in employment) and insolvency law are the only guarantees? If the answer is 'yes', the task is to separate people who 'voluntarily' accept the risks of self-employment from those who had no real option. The alleged employers (and maybe employees who could pay less tax) have strong incentives to deny an employment relation. Big corporations or public bodies who deny they have employees seldom attract judicial sympathy. But the UK is also nation of small and medium sized enterprises, and many highly skilled workers: blurring the division between the self-employed and employed. Lack of bargaining power may create a factual presumption in a judge's mind that someone is an employee, before looking at the contract. While universal rules for who gets labour rights elude the law (and the best minds in legal theory for most of modern history) the law must begin with principles.

Introductory reading: Collins ch 2 (38–42). CEM ch 6 (185–225). D&M ch 3 (131–234).

(1) PRINCIPLES OF CONSTRUCTION

To decide if someone is entitled to labour rights, courts have increasingly 'fused' their thinking on three levels: first, the construction of contracts has been fused with equitable principle; second, judge-made law is fused with statutory policy; third national law is being fused with international instruments. At the same time as these 'three fusions', the unity of contract law has 'diffused'. Equity, statute and international law recognised people's real social positions, unlike contract law's notional equality between each party. 'Construction' means a combined process of identifying which terms are incorporated, interpreting them, resolving conflicts (if any) in textual sources (chapter 4), and deciding what to 'read' into the gaps, or to read down, so the contract matches the parties' reasonable expectations (chapter 5). EU law prevails over UK law, legislation prevails over contracts, and because the law's purpose is to ensure basic social and economic rights, the employee's expectations usually hold greater weight than an employing entity's. The next three cases elaborate on this basic point. The disputes concerned (1) the measure of damages for unfair dismissal in *Johnson*, (2) time limits for unfair dismissal claims in *Barratt*, and (3) principles to determine who is an employee in *Autoclenz*. The interest lies in how the thinking of the UK's highest court has evolved in the early twenty-first century.

Johnson v Unisys Ltd [2001] UKHL 13

Mr Johnson had worked for Unisys Ltd for 20 years, in Milton Keynes, before suffering a mental breakdown, involving depression, heavy drinking and suicidal thoughts. He claimed damages after he was dismissed by Unisys Ltd for not having a fair hearing, in breach of the company's own contractual disciplinary procedure. The Employment Rights Act 1996 section 124, at the time, limited damages for dismissal for an unfair *reason* to £11,000, regardless of an employment contract's terms. Mr Johnson received a maximum award, which came to £11,691.88 including interest. However, he claimed that the economic consequences of his loss were over £400,000, in line with general principles on damages in tort for psychiatric injury. He argued that, because his claim was based in breach of contract for the implied term of mutual trust and confidence in the *procedure* of dismissal, the limits on statutory compensation for the *reason* for dismissal were irrelevant. The House of Lords held that this would, in effect, undermine the purpose of the legislation. Mr Johnson's claim was limited: common law rights should be interpreted consistently with a statutory scheme.

Lord Hoffmann:

35. My Lords, the first question is whether the implied term of trust and confidence upon which Mr Johnson relies, and about which in a general way there is no real dispute, or any of the other implied terms, applies to a dismissal. At common law the contract of employment was regarded by the courts as a contract like any other. The parties were free to negotiate whatever terms they liked and no terms would be implied unless they satisfied the strict test of necessity

applied to a commercial contract. Freedom of contract meant that the stronger party, usually the employer, was free to impose his terms upon the weaker. But over the last 30 years or so, the nature of the contract of employment has been transformed. It has been recognised that a person's employment is usually one of the most important things in his or her life. It gives not only a livelihood but an occupation, an identity and a sense of self-esteem. The law has changed to recognise this social reality. Most of the changes have been made by Parliament. The Employment Rights Act 1996 consolidates numerous statutes which have conferred rights upon employees. European law has made a substantial contribution. And the common law has adapted itself to the new attitudes, proceeding sometimes by analogy with statutory rights.

36. The contribution of the common law to the employment revolution has been by the evolution of implied terms in the contract of employment. The most far reaching is the implied term of trust and confidence. But there have been others. For example, in *W A Goold (Pearmak) Ltd v McConnell* [1995] IRLR 516, Morison J (sitting in the Employment Appeal Tribunal) said that it was an implied term of the contract of employment that an employer would reasonably and promptly afford employees an opportunity to obtain redress of grievances. He inferred such a term from what is now section 3 of the Employment Rights Act 1996, which requires that an employee be provided with a written statement of the particulars of his employment, including a note of how he may apply if he has any grievances. So statute and common law have proceeded hand in hand.

37. The problem lies in extending or adapting any of these implied terms to dismissal. There are two reasons why dismissal presents special problems. The first is that any terms which the courts imply into a contract must be consistent with the express terms. Implied terms may supplement the express terms of the contract but cannot contradict them. Only Parliament may actually override what the parties have agreed. The second reason is that judges, in developing the law, must have regard to the policies expressed by Parliament in legislation. Employment law requires a balancing of the interests of employers and employees, with proper regard not only to the individual dignity and worth of the employees but also to the general economic interest. Subject to observance of fundamental human rights, the point at which this balance should be struck is a matter for democratic decision. The development of the common law by the judges plays a subsidiary role. Their traditional function is to adapt and modernise the common law. But such developments must be consistent with legislative policy as expressed in statutes. The courts may proceed in harmony with Parliament but there should be no discord.

Lord Bingham agreed with **Lord Hoffmann** and **Lord Millett**. **Lord Nicholls** concurred. **Lord Steyn** dissented on the reasoning. **Lord Millett** agreed with **Lord Hoffmann**.

NOTES AND QUESTIONS

1. *Johnson*, which is a leading authority on job security, has come to stand for the proposition that the relationship of 'mutual trust and confidence' that must subsist throughout employment may not provide remedies beyond what is already found in statute (the *Johnson*-exclusion zone). See chapter 18(3)(a). For now, the essential point made by Lord Hoffmann is that statute and common law should be construed as a unified whole, and not contradict one another. Do you agree that Mr Johnson's claim, which their Lordships rejected, necessarily contradicted the statutory scheme?

2. 'Freedom of contract', says Lord Hoffmann, 'meant that the stronger party, usually the employer, was free to impose his terms upon the weaker.' The same position

was adopted by the European Court of Justice in *Pfeiffer v Deutsches Rotes Kreuz* (2005) C-397/01, [2004] ECR 8835, [82] that employment rights are 'necessary to prevent the employer being in a position to disregard the intentions of the other party to the contract or to impose on that party a restriction of his rights without him having expressly given his consent in that regard'.

3.   Lord Hoffmann also highlights that the 'strict test of necessity' for 'implied terms' in commercial contracts differs from the employment context. This was a reference to the notion that implied terms should be necessary for business efficacy. In fact, the test for implied terms had already changed by then to terms that are 'essential to give effect to the reasonable expectations of the parties', per Lord Steyn, *Equitable Life Assurance Society v Hyman* [2000] UKHL 39. See chapter 5.

4.   The limits on unfair dismissal awards now update each year with inflation. In 2018, the maximum basic and compensatory awards were £15,240 and £83,682. See chapter 18.

5.   Lord Steyn, dissenting on the reasoning, stated at [20]: 'It is no longer right to equate a contract of employment with commercial contracts. One possible way of describing a contract of employment in modern terms is as a relational contract.' See IR Macneil, 'Contracts: Adjustment of Longterm Economic Relations under Classical, Neoclassical and Relational Contract Law' (1978) 72 *Northwestern University Law Review* 854. Given that a self-employed person can have a 'relational contract' with another self-employed person, how (if at all) is this notion specifically relevant to employment law? What more makes employment different?

Gisda Cyf v Barratt [2010] UKSC 41

Ms Barratt claimed damages for unfair dismissal and sex discrimination against her employer, which alleged she 'behaved inappropriately' (whatever that allegation meant) at a private party. She had not been at home when, on 30 November 2006, a letter arrived from the employing entity informing her that her job was terminated. She returned on 3 December and opened it. She brought a claim for unfair dismissal on 2 March 2007. The employing entity contended she was outside the three-month time limit to bring claims to an Employment Tribunal, under the Employment Rights Act (ERA) 1996 s 97(1). It relied on the commercial contract case, *The Brimnes* [1975] QB 929, which holds a notification binds a commercial party when it is reasonable to have seen it during working hours. Ms Barratt contended that time should only begin running when she had actually been informed of the dismissal, by opening the letter. The Supreme Court held that Ms Barratt was correct, because employment law is meant to favour the employee, and cannot be regarded the same as commercial context. Lord Kerr, delivering judgment for a unanimous court, referred to two Employment Appeal Tribunal decisions, and continued.

Lord Kerr:

34. Underlying both decisions (although not expressly articulated in either) is the notion that it would be unfair for time to begin to run against an employee in relation to his or her unfair dismissal complaint until the employee knows – or, at least, has a reasonable chance to

find out – that he or she has been dismissed. This is as it should be. Dismissal from employ-ment is a major event in anyone's life. Decisions that may have a profound effect on one's future require to be made. It is entirely reasonable that the time (already short) within which one should have the chance to make those decisions should not be further abbreviated by complications surrounding the receipt of the information that one has in fact been dismissed.

35. These considerations provide the essential rationale for not following the conventional contract law route in the approach to an interpretation of section 97. As Mummery LJ said, it is a statutory construct. It is designed to hold the balance between employer and employee but it does not require – nor should it – that both sides be placed on an equal footing. Employees as a class are in a more vulnerable position than employers. Protection of employees' rights has been the theme of legislation in this field for many years. The need for the protection and safeguarding of employees' rights provides the overarching backdrop to the proper construc-tion of section 97.

36. An essential part of the protection of employees is the requirement that they be informed of any possible breach of their rights. For that reason we emphatically agree with the EAT's view in *McMaster* that the doctrine of constructive knowledge has no place in the debate as to whether a dismissal has been communicated. For the short time of three months to begin to run against an employee, he or she must be informed of the event that triggers the start of that period, namely, their dismissal or, at least, he or she must have the chance to find out that that short period has begun. Again, this case exemplifies the need for this. During the three months after Ms Barratt's dismissal, she pursued an internal appeal; she learned that she was unsuccessful in that appeal; she sought advice in relation to the lodging of a complaint of unfair dismissal; and she presumably required some time to absorb and act upon that advice. Viewed in the abstract, three months might appear to be a substantial period. In reality, however, when momentous decisions have to be taken, it is not an unduly generous time.

37. We do not consider, therefore, that what has been described as the "general law of contract" should provide a preliminary guide to the proper interpretation of section 97 of the 1996 Act, much less that it should be determinative of that issue. With the proposition that one should be aware of what conventional contractual principles would dictate we have no quarrel but we tend to doubt that the "contractual analysis" should be regarded as a starting point in the debate, certainly if by that it is meant that this analysis should hold sway unless displaced by other factors. Section 97 should be interpreted in its setting. It is part of a charter protecting employees' rights. An interpretation that promotes those rights, as opposed to one which is consonant with traditional contract law principles, is to be preferred.

38. For these reasons we reject the thesis that cases such as *London Transport Executive v Clarke, Kirklees Metropolitan Council v Radecki, Potter v RJ Temple plc* and *George v Luton Borough Council* represent a general acceptance that statutory rights given to employees should be interpreted in a way that is compatible with common law contractual principles, if indeed they are as they have been represented to be. (On this latter point, we have not received contrary argument on the common law position and we wish to make clear that this judgment should not be taken as an endorsement of the appellant's argument as to the effect of those principles). Of course, where the protection of employees' statutory rights exactly coincides with common law principles, the latter may well provide an insight into how the former may be interpreted and applied but that is a far cry from saying that principles of contract law should dictate the scope of employees' statutory rights. These cases do no more, in our opinion, than recognise that where common law principles precisely reflect the statutorily protected rights of employees they may be prayed in aid to reinforce the protection of those rights.

39. The need to segregate intellectually common law principles relating to contract law, even in the field of employment, from statutorily conferred rights is fundamental. The common law recognised certain employment rights, but the right at common law not to be wrongfully dismissed is significantly narrower than the statutory protection against unfair dismissal. The deliberate expansion by Parliament of the protection of employment rights for employees considered to be vulnerable and the significance of the creation of a separate system of rights was recognised by the House of Lords in *Johnson v Unisys Ltd* [2001] UKHL 13, [2003] 1 AC 518.

Lord Hope, **Lord Saville**, **Lord Walker** and **Lady Hale** agreed.

NOTES AND QUESTIONS

1. The Supreme Court judgment was the most powerful statement of change in the common law of employment. The 'general law of contract' was not even 'a preliminary guide'. The 'need to segregate intellectually common law principles, even in the field of employment, from statutorily conferred rights is fundamental'.
2. Some contractual documents conflict with themselves, and courts will have a choice between results favouring the employer or an employee. Inevitably unwritten norms of social policy are applied. In *McClelland v Northern Ireland General Health Services* [1957] 1 WLR 594, Mrs McClelland's contract stated that a 'Female officer will on marriage be required to tender their resignations to the board'. But condition 12 said the only grounds on which she could be dismissed were for 'gross misconduct' or if 'inefficient and unfit' for the job. The House of Lords could have construed the contract so that the more specific rule (resign on marriage) took precedence over the more general (dismissal only for gross misconduct, etc). But Lord Oaksey, Lord Goddard and Lord Evershed held condition 12 was exhaustive, and so dismissal for marriage was wrongful. Lord Tucker and Lord Keith dissented. Lord Keith said he could find 'no reason' for abrogating 'the ordinary common law rules governing the relations between master and servant'. But why not? Obviously the question of social policy was whether Lord Tucker and Lord Keith wanted to uphold the right to equality, embedded in the Universal Declaration of Human Rights 1948 Arts 7, 16 and 23, and the ILO Discrimination Convention 1958 (c 111) which was being finalised at the time. The contract's assumption, that women should quit and have babies once they are married, was sexist. If their Lordships did not feel able to say the term was void for that reason alone, why were they not at least prepared to use principles of construction to achieve the result that the society around them plainly viewed as just?
3. Contrast *Taylor v Secretary of State for Scotland* [2000] UKHL 28 where the House of Lords held that a contractual requirement for a prison officer to retire at 55 years old was not ousted by another clause requiring no discrimination on grounds of age. The House, reflecting a widespread view that direct age discrimination can be justified, held the more specific norm prevailed over the general. See chapter 12(2)(c).
4. The landmark case on the scope of employment rights followed the year after *Gisda*.

Autoclenz Ltd v Belcher [2011] UKSC 41

Mr Belcher and 19 other car valets cleaned cars for British Car Auctions in Measham, through Autoclenz Ltd. They claimed compensation for their rights to paid holidays, and minimum wage, under the Working Time Regulations 1998 and the National Minimum Wage Act 1998. Their contract with Autoclenz Ltd, signed in 2007, stated that each was a 'self-employed independent contractor'. They were to provide their own materials, they had no obligation to provide their services, and Autoclenz Ltd had no obligation to offer them work. They could provide a suitably qualified substitute to do their work. Autoclenz Ltd contended they were not entitled to a minimum wage or holiday pay because they were neither 'employees' nor 'workers'.

At the Employment Tribunal, Foxwell J held that the car valets were employees, and even if they could not be regarded as employees, they were definitely workers. In the Employment Appeal Tribunal, Peter Clark J held the car valets were workers, but not employees. In the Court of Appeal, Smith LJ, Aikens LJ, and Sedley LJ held that the car valets were employees and workers even though the contract described the car valets as 'self-employed', that and the other provisions were merely a sham that did not reflect the reality of the relationship. The Supreme Court unanimously held that the car valets were employees and workers, and entitled to paid holidays and the minimum wage.

Lord Clarke:

17. It is common ground that the issues are (1) whether the ET was correct to find that the claimants were at all material times working under contracts of employment and were therefore workers within limb (a) of the definition [of a 'worker' in the ERA 1996 section 230(3), namely as having a 'contract of employment'] and (2) whether in any event the ET was correct to find that they were at all material times within limb (b). This involves consideration of whether and in what circumstances the ET may disregard terms which were included in a written agreement between the parties and instead base its decision on a finding that the documents did not reflect what was actually agreed between the parties or the true intentions or expectations of the parties.

18. As Smith LJ explained in the Court of Appeal at para 11, the classic description of a contract of employment (or a contract of service as it used to be called) is found in the judgment of MacKenna J in *Ready Mixed Concrete (South East) Ltd v Minister of Pensions and National Insurance* [1968] 2 QB 497, 515C:

> "A contract of service exists if these three conditions are fulfilled. (i) The servant agrees that, in consideration of a wage or other remuneration, he will provide his own work and skill in the performance of some service for his master. (ii) He agrees, expressly or impliedly, that in the performance of that service he will be subject to the other's control in a sufficient degree to make that other master. (iii) The other provisions of the contract are consistent with its being a contract of service. ... Freedom to do a job either by one's own hands or by another's is inconsistent with a contract of service, though a limited or occasional power of delegation may not be."

19. Three further propositions are not I think contentious:

i)   As Stephenson LJ put it in *Nethermere (St Neots) Ltd v Gardiner* [1984] ICR 612, 623, "There must ... be an irreducible minimum of obligation on each side to create a contract of service".

ii)   If a genuine right of substitution exists, this negates an obligation to perform work per-
       sonally and is inconsistent with employee status: *Express & Echo Publications Ltd v Tanton*
       (*"Tanton"*) [1999] ICR 693, per Peter Gibson LJ at p 699G.
iii)   If a contractual right, as for example a right to substitute, exists, it does not matter that it
       is not used. It does not follow from the fact that a term is not enforced that such a term
       is not part of the agreement: see eg *Tanton* at p 697G.

20. The essential question in each case is what were the terms of the agreement. The position
under the ordinary law of contract is clear. It was correctly summarised thus by Aikens LJ in the
Court of Appeal:

> "87. ... Express contracts (as opposed to those implied from conduct) can be oral, in writing
> or a mixture of both. Where the terms are put in writing by the parties and it is not alleged
> that there are any additional oral terms to it, then those written terms will, at least prima
> facie represent the whole of the parties' agreement. Ordinarily the parties are bound by
> those terms where a party has signed the contract: see eg *L'Estrange v F Graucob Ltd* [1934]
> 2 KB 394. If a party has not signed a contract, then there are the usual issues as to whether
> he was made sufficiently aware of the clauses for a court to be able to conclude that he
> agreed to the terms in them. That is not an issue in this case.
>
> 88. Once it is established that the written terms of the contract were agreed, it is not pos-
> sible to imply terms into a contract that are inconsistent with its express terms. The only
> way it can be argued that a contract contains a term which is inconsistent with one of its
> express terms is to allege that the written terms do not accurately reflect the true agreement
> of the parties.
>
> 89. Generally, if a party to a contract claims that a written term does not accurately reflect
> what was agreed between the parties, the allegation is that there was a continuing common
> intention to agree another term, which intention was outwardly manifested but, because of
> a mistake (usually a common mistake of the parties, but it can be a unilateral one) the con-
> tract inaccurately recorded what was agreed. If such a case is made out, a court may grant
> rectification of a contract. See, generally, the discussion in the speech of Lord Hoffmann,
> [48] to [66], in *Chartbrook Ltd v Persimmon Homes Ltd* [2009] UKHL 38, [2009] 1 AC 1101
> with whom all the other law lords agreed. ..."

21. Nothing in this judgment is intended in any way to alter those principles, which apply to
ordinary contracts and, in particular, to commercial contracts. There is, however, a body of case
law in the context of employment contracts in which a different approach has been taken.
Again, Aikens LJ put it correctly in the remainder of para 89 as follows:

> "But in cases of contracts concerning work and services, where one party alleges that the
> written contract terms do not accurately reflect the true agreement of the parties, rec-
> tification principles are not in point, because it is not generally alleged that there was a
> mistake in setting out the contract terms as they were. There may be several reasons why
> the written terms do not accurately reflect what the parties actually agreed. But in each
> case the question the court has to answer is: what contractual terms did the parties actu-
> ally agree?"

...

32. Aikens LJ stressed at paras 90 to 92 the importance of identifying what were the actual
legal obligations of the parties. He expressly agreed with Smith LJ's analysis of the legal position in *Szilagyi* and in paras 47 to 53 in this case. In addition, he correctly warned against

focusing on the "true intentions" or "true expectations" of the parties because of the risk of concentrating too much on what were the private intentions of the parties. He added:

> "What the parties privately intended or expected (either before or after the contract was agreed) may be evidence of what, objectively discerned, was actually agreed between the parties: see Lord Hoffmann's speech in the *Chartbrook* case at [64] to [65]. But ultimately what matters is only what was agreed, either as set out in the written terms or, if it is alleged those terms are not accurate, what is proved to be their actual agreement at the time the contract was concluded. I accept, of course, that the agreement may not be express; it may be implied. But the court or tribunal's task is still to ascertain what was agreed."

I agree.

33. At para 103 Sedley LJ said that he was entirely content to adopt the reasoning of Aikens LJ:

> "recognising as it does that while employment is a matter of contract, the factual matrix in which the contract is cast is not ordinarily the same as that of an arm's length commercial contract."

I agree.

34. The critical difference between this type of case and the ordinary commercial dispute is identified by Aikens LJ in para 92 as follows:

> "92. I respectfully agree with the view, emphasised by both Smith and Sedley LJJ, that the circumstances in which contracts relating to work or services are concluded are often very different from those in which commercial contracts between parties of equal bargaining power are agreed. I accept that, frequently, organisations which are offering work or requiring services to be provided by individuals are in a position to dictate the written terms which the other party has to accept. In practice, in this area of the law, it may be more common for a court or tribunal to have to investigate allegations that the written contract does not represent the actual terms agreed and the court or tribunal must be realistic and worldly wise when it does so. ..."

35. So the relative bargaining power of the parties must be taken into account in deciding whether the terms of any written agreement in truth represent what was agreed and the true agreement will often have to be gleaned from all the circumstances of the case, of which the written agreement is only a part. This may be described as a purposive approach to the problem. If so, I am content with that description.

Lord Hope, **Lord Walker**, **Lord Collins** and **Sir Nicholas Wilson** concurred.

NOTES AND QUESTIONS

1. The Supreme Court affirms that 'relative bargaining power of the parties must be taken into account in deciding whether the terms of any written agreement in truth represent what was agreed'. This is a 'purposive approach'. Lord Clarke's language here is imperative. It is not optional for tribunals and courts: they 'must' take relative bargaining power into account. Moreover, this rule is not confined to terms affecting employment status, but generally applies to 'the terms of any written agreement'. Can you think of reasons why some courts, academics or practitioners, might be slow to shift their standard practice?

2. The multiple factors set out by Lord Clarke appear to be exhaustive. But no factor in the multiple-factor test is decisive in itself or has greater weight. A persuasive lawyer can manipulate arguments about the factual matrix (as we will see below). Hence, the only way to make sense of those factors is the purpose of the exercise. This is not a problem unique to law. On the general indeterminacy, and context dependence of language, see L Wittgenstein, *Philosophical Investigations* (1953).

3. Lord Clarke makes 'bargaining power' key to interpreting the parties' 'true agreement'. In effect this suggests that the quality of a contracting party's autonomy, and equally the state's legitimacy in enforcing contracts, decreases as the employee's bargaining power decreases. Do you think this is an appropriate way to reconcile the tension between intention and factual freedom?

4. In *Agnew v Commissioners of Inland Revenue* [2001] UKPC 28, to identify a floating charge (which matters for how much employees can get from an insolvent company, see chapter 20), Lord Millett said there should be a 'two-stage process'. First, one must look at a contract 'to gather the intentions of the parties from the language they have used'. The object is not to decide which legal category the parties wanted (fixed or floating charge, or by analogy, employed or self-employed) but 'to ascertain the nature of the rights and obligations which the parties intended to grant each other'. 'Once these have been ascertained, the Court can then embark on the second stage of the process, which is one of categorisation. This is a matter of law. It does not depend on the intention of the parties.' Do you agree that Lord Clarke sees the same two-step process for deciding who is an employee?

5. In addition to the general principle of remedying unequal bargaining power, Lord Clarke endorses *Ready Mix Concrete*, namely that employment contracts involve work for a wage under another's direction, and multiple factors should determine the details of who is an employee. This is reflected in EU law, in *Lawrie-Blum v Land Baden-Wurttemberg* (1986) C-66/85.

6. In *FNV Kunsten Informatie en Media v Staat der Nederlanden* (2014) C-413/13 the First Chamber of the CJEU advised a Dutch court that orchestra workers, who were described as self-employed by contract, could well have been 'in fact "false self-employed", that is to say, service providers in a situation comparable to that of employees'. The CJEU further took the view that as such there could be no question of competition law applying to such employees, who were therefore free to organise a trade union. The CJEU might also have noted that core international labour rights to organise are rights for everyone who works, including self-employed people, such as criminal law barristers or London Hackney taxi drivers (as opposed to taxi corporation employees), both of which have gone on strike in the last few years.

7. This case involved a three-party employment relationship, with the employees providing work to British Car Auctions (BCA) through an outsourcing agency, Autoclenz Ltd. Had Autoclenz Ltd become insolvent before the employees claimed, presumably the Supreme Court would not have allowed BCA to retain the benefits of the employees' work without giving an account. This meets problems in the law

of subrogation. Do you think it would make a difference if BCA had paid Auto-clenz in advance for the employees' labour, or if BCA's payment would follow at the end of the month?

8. Together *Johnson*, *Gisda Cyf* and *Autoclenz* stand for three essential principles:
   (i) Courts must construe statute and common law in a consistent manner, to give the purpose of the legislative policy genuine effectiveness.
   (ii) For the construction of statutory rights, the general law of contract as it applies in a commercial context must be intellectually segregated from employment.
   (iii) The relative bargaining power of the parties must be taken into account when interpreting every term of a contract relating to employment.

(2) WHO IS AN EMPLOYEE OR WORKER?

(a) Statutory Tests

To apply the basic principles just outlined, there are further legal tests to determine 'employee' or 'worker' or other protected statuses. The case law, however, has historically been contradictory, frequently unprincipled, and unjust. In essence, a core of people have 'employee' rights, and a larger number of people have 'worker' rights. The self-employed do not have 'employee' rights, and self-employed people who personally perform work, but not for a 'client' or 'customer', do not have 'worker' rights. In each case, this begs the question of where the dividing line should be, and statute does not help.

Employment Rights Act 1996 s 230

230 **Employees, workers etc.**

(1) In this Act "employee" means an individual who has entered into or works under (or, where the employment has ceased, worked under) a contract of employment.

(2) In this Act "contract of employment" means a contract of service or apprenticeship, whether express or implied, and (if it is express) whether oral or in writing.

(3) In this Act "worker" (except in the phrases "shop worker" and "betting worker") means an individual who has entered into or works under (or, where the employment has ceased, worked under)—

(a) a contract of employment, or
(b) any other contract, whether express or implied and (if it is express) whether oral or in writing, whereby the individual undertakes to do or perform personally any work or services for another party to the contract whose status is not by virtue of the contract that of a client or customer of any profession or business undertaking carried on by the individual;

and any reference to a worker's contract shall be construed accordingly.

1. Because statute defines 'employee' as someone with a 'contract of service', but does not define this, like in other common law jurisdictions it 'explains nothing', *Nationwide Mutual Insurers Co v Darden*, 503 US 318 (1992) per Souter J.

2. Some statutes, such as the King's College London Act 1997 section 15, distinguish between different employees or 'staff' for the purpose of granting direct participation rights in governance. Many partnership or company constitutions achieve the same. Thus subgroups of 'employees' often have rights beyond statute. See chapter 10.

3. The most important 'employee' rights involve dismissals (chapters 17–20), childcare (chapter 7(3)), rights relating to the contract of employment (chapters 4 and 5), information and consultation (chapter 10(2)) and equal treatment as a fixed-term staff member (chapter 13).

4. An 'apprentice', which counts as an employee under section 230(2), is someone who 'gives his services in order to be taught'. *The Parish of St Pancras Middlesex v The Parish of Clapham, Surrey* (1860) 2 El & El 742, 754, per Blackburn J.

5. Section 230(3)(a) means all employees are workers, but some workers are not employees. This larger group of 'workers' have rights in the National Minimum Wage Act 1998 s 54 (chapter 6), the Working Time Regulations 1998 regulation 2(1) (chapter 7), and in the Trade Union and Labour Relations (Consolidation) Act (TULRCA) 1992 (chapters 9–12).

6. The 'worker' definition effectively makes any contracting party an employer when they are not 'a client or customer of any profession or business undertaking'. Implicitly the burden of proof is shifted to the employer to show the person is not a worker. But what, exactly, is a client or customer?

7. The TULRCA 1992 predominantly uses the concept of 'worker' (s 296). By contrast, the International Labour Organization's position is that self-employed people who personally perform work have the right to collective bargaining and the right to take collective action. This could logically include people who are self-employed. The definition of 'client' or 'customer' should be interpreted in compliance with all core international labour rights.

8. The Equality Act 2010 s 83(2) covers workers, and anyone providing a service personally to clients or customers. Why do you think that anti-discrimination protection would have a wider scope than other employment rights?

9. The Pensions Act 2008 s 1 states that a 'jobholder' (a concept that draws a linguistic analogy to a shareholder in a corporation) is a worker, but only those ordinarily working in Great Britain, aged between 16 and under 75, and with qualifying earnings. Jobholders have a right to be automatically enrolled in a defined contribution occupational pension plan by the employer. See chapter 6(3).

(b) Employee: Multiple Factors

As Lord Clarke reaffirmed in *Autoclenz Ltd v Belcher*, within the overall duty of courts to construe who is an employee in light of the relative bargaining power of the parties, multiple factors are taken into account. *Montreal Locomotive* first took this approach.

City of Montreal v Montreal Locomotive Works Ltd [1946] UKPC 44

In the course of a tax dispute, under the British North America Act section 125, between the City of Montreal and Montreal Locomotive Works Ltd, the Privy Council gave general remarks on the nature of an agency relationship, including employment.

Lord Wright: The great difference of opinion on this question in the Courts below illustrates the difficulty which is inherent in deciding questions like this. In earlier cases a single test, such as the presence or absence of control, was often relied on to determine whether the case was one of master and servant, mostly in order to decide issues of tortious liability on the part of the master or superior. In the more complex conditions of modern industry, more complicated tests have often to be applied. It has been suggested that a fourfold test would in some cases be more appropriate, a complex involving (1) control; (2) ownership of the tools; (3) chance of profit; (4) risk of loss. Control in itself is not always conclusive. Thus the master of a chartered vessel is generally the employee of the shipowner though the charter can direct the employment of the vessel. Again the law often limits the employer's right to interfere with the employee's conduct, as also do trade union regulations. In many cases the question can only be settled by examining the whole of the various elements which constitute the relationship between the parties. In this way it is in some cases possible to decide the issue by raising as the crucial question whose business is it, or in other words by asking whether the party is carrying on the business, in the sense of carrying it on for himself or on his own behalf and not merely for a superior. In the present case the business or undertaking is in the manufacture of the war-like vehicles. The respondent might have been making them with a view to selling them to the Government for its own profit. … The respondent supplied no funds and took no financial risk and no liability, with the significant exception of bad faith or wanton neglect: every other risk was taken by the Government.

NOTES AND QUESTIONS

1. Lord Wright suggests the increased complexity of tests for who is an employee reflects increased complexity of work: the image of a worker on a factory-assembly line was replaced by the increasingly educated worker, expected to exercise independent discretion. People were no longer merely 'controlled' as before. Does having multiple factors increase the discretion of the judiciary over employment status? If so, what determines, and what should determine, how that discretion will be used?

2. Lord Wright's opinion coincides with the establishment of the universal welfare state in the UK, a development shared across Commonwealth and European countries. The National Insurance Act 1946 s 1(2) adopted the distinction between employed and self-employed for mass administration of who would make contributions to the state pension, unemployment insurance, etc. S Deakin and F Wilkinson, *The Law of the Labour Market: Employment, Industrialisation and Legal Evolution* (2005) ch 2 suggest that the employment relationship has always been shaped by welfare policy dating back to the poor laws. Do you agree that state policy (rather than litigation by employees, unions and employers) is likely to have an important impact on the scope of labour rights? Why might that be?

3. M Freedland, 'Contract of Employment to Personal Work Nexus' (2006) 35 ILJ 1, 13, criticises the 'binary divide' between the employed and self-employed, and favours making labour rights depend on a 'family of personal work contracts'

approach. As Freedland writes, there 'is no bright-line binary divide or partly or wholly rejected out-group within this family of contracts. It becomes easier in this construct to recognise specific typologies within the contract of employment, but, even more important, also to accept typologies which transcend the boundaries of the contract of employment.' Deakin has replied that in substance, this does not abandon the binary divide but merely draws 'that line in a different place' (2007) 26 ILJ 68. If there are some people who get labour rights, and some who do not, is a binary divide inevitable? If so, how could universal protection in labour rights be guaranteed for everyone?

4. A curiosity of *Montreal Locomotive* is the way Lord Wright explains employment tests in a business agency context, suggesting chains of bargains in long-term business relations involve unequal bargaining power, and may be functionally equivalent to contracts for personal performance of work. In competition law, on vertical restraints, see *Courage Ltd v Crehan* (2001) C-453/99, [32]–[33].

5. As we saw, *Autoclenz* expressly approved the *Ready Mixed Concrete* case. Although a High Court decision, the multiple factors it identified are widely adopted.

Ready Mixed Concrete (South East) Ltd v Minister for Pensions and National Insurance [1968] 2 QB 497

The Minister claimed that Ready Mixed Concrete Ltd had to pay National Insurance contributions for Mr Latimer, a lorry driver in Kent, contending he was an 'employed person' under the National Insurance Act 1965 section 1(2). Mr Latimer's contract described him as an 'independent contractor'. He was in the process of acquiring his lorry on hire-purchase from Ready Mixed Finance Ltd, in the same company group. Mr Latimer was required to decorate his lorry in company colours and logos, wear a company uniform, to use its mixing units, only to use it for the company, carry out orders, and pay running costs. Mr Latimer was paid according to the loads he carried and the miles covered. He was allowed to employ substitute drivers. The Minister had determined that Mr Latimer was an employee. The High Court reversed this, finding Mr Latimer was an independent contractor, so that Ready Mixed Concrete Ltd did not need to make national insurance contributions on his behalf.

MacKenna J: I must now consider what is meant by a contract of service.

A contract of service exists if these three conditions are fulfilled. (i) The servant agrees that, in consideration of a wage or other remuneration, he will provide his own work and skill in the performance of some service for his master. (ii) He agrees, expressly or impliedly, that in the performance of that service he will be subject to the other's control in a sufficient degree to make that other master. (iii) The other provisions of the contract are consistent with its being a contract of service.

I need say little about (i) and (ii).

As to (i). There must be a wage or other remuneration. Otherwise there will be no consideration, and without consideration no contract of any kind. The servant must be obliged to provide his own work and skill. Freedom to do a job either by one's own hands or by another's is inconsistent with a contract of service, though a limited or occasional power of delegation may not be: see Atiyah's Vicarious Liability in the Law of Torts (1967) pp. 59 to 61 and the cases cited by him.

As to (ii). Control includes the power of deciding the thing to be done, the way in which it shall be done, the means to be employed in doing it, the time when and the place where it shall be done. All these aspects of control must be considered in deciding whether the right exists in a sufficient degree to make one party the master and the other his servant. The right need not be unrestricted.

> "What matters is lawful authority to command so far as there is scope for it. and there must always be some room for it, if only in incidental or collateral matters." – *Zuijs v. Wirth Brothers Proprietary, Ltd.* (1955) 93 C.L.R. 561, 571.

To find where the right resides one must look first to the express terms of the contract, and if they deal fully with the matter one may look no further. If the contract does not expressly provide which party shall have the right, the question must be answered in the ordinary way by implication.

The third and negative condition is for my purpose the important one, and I shall try with the help of five examples to explain what I mean by provisions inconsistent with the nature of a contract of service.

> (i) A contract obliges one party to build for the other, providing at his own expense the necessary plant and materials. This is not a contract of service, even though the builder may be obliged to use his own labour only and to accept a high degree of control: it is a building contract. It is not a contract to serve another for a wage, but a contract to produce a thing (or a result) for a price.
> (ii) A contract obliges one party to carry another's goods, providing at his own expense everything needed for performance. This is not a contract of service, even though the carrier may be obliged to drive the vehicle himself and to accept the other's control over his performance: it is a contract of carriage.
> (iii) A contract obliges a labourer to work for a builder, providing some simple tools, and to accept the builder's control. Notwithstanding the obligation to provide the tools, the contract is one of service. That obligation is not inconsistent with the nature of a contract of service. It is not a sufficiently important matter to affect the substance of the contract.
> (iv) A contract obliges one party to work for the other, accepting his control, and to provide his own transport. This is still a contract of service. The obligation to provide his own transport does not affect the substance. Transport in this example is incidental to the main purpose of the contract. Transport in the second example was the essential part of the performance.
> (v) The same instrument provides that one party shall work for the other subject to the other's control, and also that he shall sell him his land. The first part of the instrument is no less a contract of service because the second part imposes obligations of a different kind: Amalgamated Engineering Union v. Minister of Pensions and National Insurance.[1]

[MacKenna J cited Commonwealth authority, including Montreal Locomotive and continued]

U.S. v. Silk[2] was the most important of the American cases cited to me. The case disposed of two suits raising the question whether men working for the plaintiffs, Silk and Greyvan, were "employees" within the meaning of that word in the Social Security Act, 1935. The judges of the Supreme Court agreed upon the test to be applied, though not in every instance upon its application to the facts. It was not to be what they described as "the common law test," viz., "power of control, whether exercised or not, over the manner of performing service to the

---

[1] [1963] 1 W.L.R. 441, 451, 452; [1963] 1 All E.R. 864.
[2] (1946) 331 U.S. 704.

undertaking." The test was whether the men were employees "as a matter of economic real-ity." Important factors were said to be "the degrees of control, opportunities of profit or loss, investment in facilities, permanency of relation and skill required in the claimed independent operation."

Silk sold coal by retail, using the services of two classes of workers, unloaders and truck drivers. The unloaders moved the coal from railway vans into bins. They came to the yard when they wished and were given a wagon to unload and a place to put the coal. They provided their own tools and were paid so much per ton for the coal they shifted. All the nine judges held that these men were employees[3]:

> "Giving full consideration to the concurrence of the two lower courts in a contrary result, we cannot agree that the unloaders in the Silk case were independent contractors. They provided only picks and shovels. They had no opportunity to gain or lose except from the work of their hands and these simple tools. That the unloaders did not work regularly is not significant. They did work in the course of the employer's trade or business. This brings them under the coverage of the Act. They are of the group that the Social Security Act was intended to aid. Silk was in a position to exercise all necessary supervision over their simple tasks. Unloaders have often been held to be employees in tort cases."

Silk's drivers owned the trucks in which they delivered coal to Silk's customers. They paid all the expenses of operating their trucks including the wages of any extra help they needed or chose to employ. They came to the yard when they pleased and were free to haul goods for other people. They were paid for their deliveries at a rate per ton. Greyvan carried on a road haulier's business. Their drivers too owned their trucks and were required to pay all the costs of opera-tion. They were not allowed to work for anyone else but Greyvan, and had to drive the trucks themselves or, if they employed a relief driver, to be present when he drove. They had to follow all the rules, regulations and instructions of Greyvan. They were paid a percentage of the tariff which Greyvan charged the customers.

By a majority of the court both sets of drivers were held to be independent contractors[4]:

> "… where the arrangements leave the driver-owners so much responsibility for investment and management as here, they must be held to be independent contractors. These driver-owners are small business men. They own their own trucks. They hire their own helpers. In one instance they haul for a single business, in the other for any customer. The distinction, though important, is not controlling. It is the total situation, including the risk undertaken, the control exercised, the opportunity for profit from sound management, that marks these driver-owners as independent contractors."

This reasoning apparently requires that there should be some power of control vested in the driver if he is to qualify as an independent contractor. That the power need not be very exten-sive appears from the facts in Greyvan's case. The driver's investment, and the risk undertaken by him, seem to be the important things.

...

There is, as well, the dictum of Denning L.J. in *Bank voor Handel en Scheepvaart N.V. v. Slatford*,[5] repeated in his Hamlyn Lectures:

> "In this connection I would observe that the test of being a servant does not rest nowa-days on submission to orders. It depends on whether the person is part and parcel of the organisation."

---

[3] Ibid. 716.
[4] (1946) 331 U.S. 719.
[5] [1953] 1 QB 248, 295; [1951] 2 TLR 755; [1951] 2 All ER 779.

This raises more questions than I know how to answer. What is meant by being "part and parcel of an organisation"? Are all persons who answer this description servants? If only some are servants, what distinguishes them from the others if it is not their submission to orders? Though I cannot answer these questions I can at least invoke the dictum to support my opinion that control is not everything.

...

If (as I assume) it must be shown that he has freedom enough in the performance of these obligations to qualify as an independent contractor, I would say that he has enough. He is free to decide whether he will maintain the vehicle by his own labour or that of another, and, if he decides to use another's, he is free to choose whom he will employ and on what terms. He is free to use another's services to drive the vehicle when he is away because of sickness or holidays, or indeed at any other time when he has not been directed to drive himself. He is free again in his choice of a competent driver to take his place at these times, and whoever he appoints will be his servant and not the company's. He is free to choose where he will buy his fuel or any other of his requirements, subject to the company's control in the case of major repairs. This is enough. It is true that the company are given special powers to ensure that he runs his business efficiently, keeps proper accounts and pays his bills. I find nothing in these or any other provisions of the contract inconsistent with the company's contention that he is running a business of his own. A man does not cease to run a business on his own account because he agrees to run it efficiently or bo accept another's superintendence.

A comparison of Latimer's profits with the wages earned by men who are admittedly the company's servants confirms my conclusion that his status is different, that he is, in the words of the judgment in Silk's case, a "small business man," and not a servant.

NOTES AND QUESTIONS

1. The clarity of MacKenna J's reasoning should not obscure the difficult, border-line nature of the case. MacKenna J squarely bases his findings on being 'free to choose' – a concept coterminous with bargaining power. But presumably the Minister deemed Mr Latimer's notional ownership of the lorry (from which the company profited through the hire-purchase agreement) as hardly decisive given the exclusive nature of Mr Latimer's service. Should greater deference have been given to the Minister, in his legitimate role of applying the government's policy behind the law?

2. If we assume (and this is highly debatable) that a court would not find Mr Latimer is an employee today, do you agree he would at least be a worker? If so, the curi-ous result would be that the Pensions Act 2008 requires the employing entity administers his basic occupational pension, but Mr Latimer would need to admin-ister contributions for his basic state pension. Would that make sense?

3. Another High Court case around the same time, *Market Investigations Ltd v Minister for Social Security* [1969] 2 QB 173, found that Ms Irving, who carried out questionnaires for the company, was an employee. Cooke J posed the question: '[I]s the person who has engaged himself to perform these services performing them as a person in business on his own account? ... factors, which may be of importance, are such matters as whether the man performing the services pro-vides his own equipment, whether he hires his own helpers, what degree of finan-cial risk he takes, what degree of responsibility for investment and management he has, and whether and how far he has an opportunity for profiting from sound management in the performance of his task.' Does this approach resemble the *dictum* of Denning LJ that MacKenna J doubts?

4. Did the reasoning of MacKenna J actually place any weight on the declaration in the contract that Mr Latimer was an independent contractor? After *Autoclenz*, the position is that express declarations of employment status can simply be disregarded in light of the parties' bargaining power. In *Ferguson v John Dawson & Partners (Contractors) Ltd* [1976] 1 WLR 1213, 1223, Megaw LJ colourfully emphasised that the parties cannot 'by their own whim, by the use of a verbal formula, unrelated to the reality of the relationship, ... influence the decision on whom the responsibility for the safety of workmen, as imposed by statutory regulations, should rest'. By contrast in *Massey v Crown Life Insurance Co* [1978] ICR 590, 595, Lord Denning MR said: '[W]hen it is a situation which is in doubt or which is ambiguous, so that it can be brought under one relationship or the other, it is open to the parties by agreement to stipulate what the legal situation shall be.' Presumably, this refers to 'doubt' which only arises from the fact that the parties' bargaining power is relatively equal.

5. In *Lee Ting Sang v Chung Chi Keung* [1990] UKPC 9 Lord Griffiths, delivering the Privy Council's advice, found that a mason, Mr Sang, who provided his own tools, was an employee under the Hong Kong Employees' Compensation Ordinance. Lord Griffiths applied the multiple factors listed by *Market Investigations*, and disapproved Denning LJ's 'part and parcel' test to say Mr Sang was 'clearly' an employee. This meant Mr Keung and the co-defendant Shun Sing Construction & Engineering Co Ltd were jointly liable to compensate Mr Sang for injuries. At one point Lord Griffiths doubted the utility of a 'purposive construction' of the Ordinance, however presumably this approach would have yielded the same outcome. In any case, a purposive is compulsory for all courts since *Autoclenz*.

(c) Employee: Mutuality of Obligation?

As we have seen, *Autoclenz* set out an exhaustive test for who is an employee. It approved the view that there must be 'an irreducible minimum of obligation on each side to create a contract of service' (at [19], quoting Stephenson LJ in *Nethermere*, below). He went on to approve the view that this means 'there were mutual obligations, namely the provision of work in return for money' (at [37], quoting Foxwell J in the Employment Tribunal). It follows, in the context of employment, 'mutuality of obligation' means the consideration of the contract: work for a quid pro quo, usually money. Consideration is the irreducible minimum for a contract in common law, and (though often misunderstood) in most civil law systems, in absence of a deed. The purpose of employment rights would be frustrated if it were harder to make an employment contract than any other contract.

But since 1983 there has been a competing definition of 'mutuality of obligation', as voluntary undertakings by the alleged employee and employer to offer and accept work on an ongoing basis (see S Deakin and GS Morris, *Labour Law* (6th edn 2012) 164). The logical effect was that if the employer asserted they had never accepted any ongoing duty to employ someone, claiming no more than a relationship 'at will' (which could be ended at a moment's notice, for any reason), the employer could argue it was unbound from employment duties (eg the duty to give reasonable notice before dismissal for a fair reason). The clarification in *Autoclenz* that the 'consideration' view of mutuality is correct is welcome, because the 'ongoing' view of mutuality amounts to no more than a logical circularity that evades employment rights for precarious workers: the very people who lack bargaining power that labour law aims to protect. However, the 'ongoing' view of mutuality has not yet been eliminated from judicial discourse. This makes it necessary to have a twelve-page section recounting the confused history of case law on this point.

O'Kelly v Trusthouse Forte plc [1983] ICR 728, [1984] QB 90

Mr O'Kelly and two others claimed they were unfairly dismissed from their wine butler and bar jobs with Trusthouse plc at the Grosvenor House Hotel, under the former Employment Protection (Consolidation) Act 1978 sections 58 and 153. They organised a trade union. To have the right not to be unfairly dismissed, the Act required them to be 'employees'. Irvine QC, representing Trusthouse, contended they were not. Their contract was silent, although Trusthouse deducted tax and social security contributions as if they were employees. They were on a list of around 100 'casuals' who were called up from time to time. Their hours fluctuated, but two worked an average of 31 hours, and one 42 hours, over the last year. The Tribunal found that they were not employees because there was 'no obligation for the worker to offer his services and there is no obligation for the employer to provide work'. It reasoned that, following a High Court decision in *Airfix* and an Appeal Tribunal decision in *Nethermere* (discussed below), that this was decisive. Browne-Wilkinson J in the Appeal Tribunal reversed this finding, and held they were employees. A majority of the Court of Appeal reinstated the Tribunal's decision, while Ackner LJ would have remitted the question to the Tribunal to consider whether there was a 'single or successive contract'.

Sir John Donaldson MR: Whilst it may be convenient for some purposes to refer to questions of "pure" law as contrasted with "mixed" questions of fact and law, the fact is that the appeal tribunal has no jurisdiction to consider any question of mixed fact and law until it has purified or distilled the mixture and extracted a question of pure law.

The purification methods are well known. In the last analysis all courts have to direct themselves as to the law and then apply those directions in finding the facts (in relation to admissibility and relevance) and to the facts as so found. When reviewing such a decision, the only problem is to divine the direction on law which the lower court gave to itself. Sometimes it will have been expressed in its reasons, but more often it has to be inferred. This is the point of temptation for the appellate court. It may well have a shrewd suspicion, or gut reaction, that it would have reached a different decision, but it must never forget that this may be because it thinks that it would have found or weighed the facts differently. Unpalatable though it may be on occasion, it must loyally accept the conclusions of fact with which it is presented and, accepting those conclusions, it must be satisfied that there must have been a misdirection on a question of law before it can intervene. Unless the direction on law has been expressed it can only be so satisfied if, in its opinion, no reasonable tribunal, properly directing itself on the relevant questions of law, could have reached the conclusion under appeal. This is a heavy burden on an appellant. I would have thought that all this was trite law, but if it is not, it is set out with the greatest possible clarity in *Edwards v Bairstow* [1956] AC 14.

Why, then, is there a problem in relation to an issue as to whether an applicant to an industrial tribunal is or is not employed under a contract of employment? The answer lies in the interpretation which the appeal tribunal has placed upon a passage in a judgment of Stephenson LJ in *Young & Woods Ltd v West* [1980] IRLR 201, 205, which Browne-Wilkinson J has interpreted as authority for the proposition:

> "the question was one of pure law, so that the appellate court can, and indeed must, reach its own view on whether or not, on the findings of fact made by the lower court, the true analysis is that there was a contract of employment."

If this is the true interpretation of Stephenson LJ's judgment, it represents a sudden and unexplained departure from what has been understood to be the law for over 70 years, for it was as long ago as that that this court went so far, in *Simmons v Heath Laundry Co.* [1910] 1 KB 543, as to describe the issue as one of fact with which an appellate court could not interfere in the absence of reason to believe that the arbitrator had misdirected himself. For my part I do not think that Stephenson LJ can be taken as having intended to make such a departure.

...

In the instant appeal the industrial tribunal directed itself to

> "consider all aspects of the relationship, no single factor being in itself decisive and each of which may vary in weight and direction, and having given such balance to the factors as seems appropriate, to determine whether the person was carrying on business on his own account."

This is wholly correct as a matter of law and it is not for this court or for the appeal tribunal to re-weigh the facts.

The industrial tribunal then concluded that there was no contract of employment extending over a series of engagements. This conclusion was based upon an evaluation of the large number of factors set out in their reasons, but it is clear that the majority attached great importance to the fact that, as they saw it, there was no mutuality of obligation and that in the industry casual workers were not regarded as working under any overall contract of employment.

The appeal tribunal refused to interfere with this conclusion and in my judgment they were right to do so. So far as mutuality is concerned, the "arrangement," to use a neutral term, could have been that be company promised to offer work to the regular casuals and, in exchange, the regular casuals undertook to accept and perform such work as was offered. This would have constituted a contract. But what happened in fact could equally well be attributed to market forces. Which represented the true view could only be determined by the tribunal which heard the witnesses and evaluated the facts. Again, although how the industry and its casual workers regarded their status is not directly material, any generally accepted view would be part of the contractual matrix and so indirectly material, although in no way decisive. This again was a matter for the industrial tribunal.

Although I, like the appeal tribunal, am content to accept the industrial tribunal's conclusion that there was no overall or umbrella contract, I think that there is a shorter answer. It is that giving the applicants' evidence its fullest possible weight, all that could emerge was an umbrella or master contract for, not of, employment. It would be a contract to offer and accept individual contracts of employment and, as such, outside the scope of the unfair dismissal provisions.

This leaves the question of whether the applicants entered into individual contracts of employment on each occasion when they worked for the company ...

[The industrial tribunal ...] had weighed the relevant factors governing the relationship between the parties with great care in the course of determining whether any umbrella contract was one of employment or for the provision of services. It had rejected the umbrella contract on the grounds that there was no contract at all, but it had also concluded:

> "the applicants were in business on their own account as independent contractors supplying services and are not qualified for interim relief because they were not employees who worked under a contract of employment."

This, unless erroneous in law, was wholly sufficient reason for holding that the individual contracts, which clearly existed, were contracts for the provision of services. If and in so far as the appeal tribunal was criticising the industrial tribunal for failing to say so, it should be pointed out that there was only one question which it had to decide, namely, whether the applicants were employees who worked under a contract of employment.

...

The appeal tribunal justified its own conclusion by saying:

"Standing back and looking at the matter in the round, what we have to ask is whether these applicants can be said to have been carrying on business on their own account. We can well understand that casuals who have their services to sell, and sell them in the market to whoever needs them for the time being, can be said to be in business on their own account in the marketing or selling of their services; but we find it difficult to reach that conclusion in a situation where the services are, in fact, being offered to one person only against a background arrangement (albeit not contractual) which requires the services to be offered to one person only and which involves a repetition of those contracts (albeit under no obligation to do so) as is shown by the weekly pay packet, the holiday pay and other matters of that kind. In our judgment, each of these individual contracts is a contract of employment, not a contract for services."

This must involve a misdirection on a question of law or every independent contractor who is content or able only to attract one client would be held to work under a contract of employment. ...

Fox LJ gave a judgment concurring with Sir John Donaldson MR.

NOTES AND QUESTIONS

1. Almost immediately, the House of Lords appeared to reverse the effect of *O'Kelly* in *Ford v Warwickshire CC* [1983] 2 AC 71, holding that short breaks in employment did not matter: an employment relation continues. See ERA 1996 s 212.
2. As the majority of *O'Kelly* allowed employers to sack casual staff for organising a union, it is now plainly wrong. The idea that workers can be subjected to any 'detriment' for union organising was rejected in *Wilson v United Kingdom* [2002] ECHR 552, under the European Convention on Human Rights Art 11. The relevant legislation, TULRCA 1992 s 146, was amended to embody this principle in relation to 'workers', but section 152 on dismissals (which presumably is a graver form of detriment) was not also unamended: its scope still relates only to 'employees'. The Human Rights Act 1998 section 3 requires interpretation of primary legislation in a way that is compatible with Convention case law, so the concept of 'employee' must be interpreted to cover people such as those in *O'Kelly*'s case. Fortunately, as stated above, *Autoclenz* has reversed the idea that mutual obligations means anything more than the consideration given in the typical work–wage bargain, and so *O'Kelly* has been consigned to the dustbin of shoddy precedent.
3. There is no shortage of examples internationally for courts and judges attempting to unravel employment rights through dishonest manipulation of the law. In the United States most recently, see *FedEx Home Delivery v NLRB*, 563 F3d 492 (DC 2009), where a majority of the DC Circuit of the Federal Court of Appeals

adopted the submission of the FedEx lawyer, Ted Cruz, that truck drivers had no rights to organise a union because they voluntarily assumed 'entrepreneurial opportunity'. Garland J, who was nominated by Barack Obama to fill the US Supreme Court vacancy in 2016, dissented.

4. The alternative view of 'mutuality of obligation' propounded in Irvine QC's submissions, and adopted by Sir John Donaldson MR, was in substance introduced by Slynn J in *Airfix Footwear Ltd v Cope* [1978] ICR 1210, based on a fudging of the opposite idea articulated by M Freedland, *The Contract of Employment* (1976) 21–22. Freedland said an employment contract embodies 'exchange of work for remuneration' and then 'exchange of mutual promises for future performance' which 'provides the arrangement with its stability and with its continuity as a contract. The promises to employ and to be employed may be of short duration or may be terminable at short notice; but they still form an integral and most important part of the contract. They are the mutual undertakings to maintain the employment relationship in being which are inherent in any contract of employment so called.' Similarly, many classical labour lawyers argued long-term contractual relations acquired a character akin to proprietary rights (eg O Gierke, *The Social Role of Private Law* (1889)). At no point was this meant to be more than an academic and factual analysis about *every* act performing work, to justify more employment rights. It was never advanced as a precondition for employment to exist.

5. Sir John Donaldson MR invents the language of an 'umbrella contract' in this case, adopted in many cases since, while Ackner LJ and Fox LJ speak of a 'successive' contract. This is only relevant if it is accepted that the employer accepting an 'ongoing' relationship is a precondition to an employment relationship (which it is not). But in any case, what does this mean? If you are paid by the hour, and you stop work at the weekend (or indeed, at 6pm) is there a need to find an 'umbrella contract' before you are an employee? If not, why would it make a difference for a person who is given different hours day to day?

6. The next Court of Appeal decision contradicted *O'Kelly*'s reasoning on 'mutuality'.

Nethermere (St Neots) Ltd v Gardiner [1984] ICR 612

Mrs Taverna and Mrs Gardiner claimed holiday pay from Nethermere Ltd, for their jobs as homeworkers, sewing pockets onto trousers for 5–7 hours a day, 40–44 weeks a year. They used Nethermere's sewing machines. The Industrial Tribunal held the claimants were not in business 'on their own account' and therefore were employees. The Appeal Tribunal upheld this finding, although stated that the question of employment status was a pure question of law. The Court of Appeal found the claimants were employees, although clarified that the question was a mixed question of fact and law.

Stephenson LJ: Was there then any misdirection in law on the part of the industrial tribunal? I do not see how it could be submitted that the tribunal erred in directing itself by the "business on her own account" test in the light of the approval given to the similar direction in *O'Kelly v Trusthouse Forte Plc*. The appeal tribunal thought that the industrial tribunal had mistaken the *ratio decidendi* of *Airfix Footwear Ltd v Cope* [1978] ICR 1210, but in my judgment it was the appeal tribunal who misunderstood it and erred in correcting the industrial tribunal on the point. Tudor Evans J said [1983] ICR 319, 326:

> "It was argued for the employers in the *Airfix* case that they were not obliged to provide work for the applicant nor was she obliged to perform it and that, in such circumstances, no reasonable tribunal acting judicially could find that there was a contract of service. The appeal tribunal acknowledged that the absence of mutual obligations, where work is offered and performed sporadically, might lead to the conclusion that there was a series of contracts of service or a contract for services but that the answer would depend on the facts of each individual case. The court then reviewed the evidence as found by the tribunal, including the fact that the work had been done for seven years and for five days a week and concluded that, on the material before it, the tribunal was well entitled to come to the conclusion that there was, by reason of the duration of the relationship, a continuing contract of employment. We do not read the judgment as establishing the proposition that before a contract of service can exist there must be the mutual obligations for which Mr. Blair contends."

Mr. Blair had contended for the company that there must indeed be mutual obligations before a contract of service can exist; that is, a continuing obligation on the employer to provide work and pay and a continuing obligation on the employee to do the work provided. But he also submitted, at p. 323F, that a true analysis of *Airfix Footwear Ltd v Cope* [1978] ICR 1210 showed that "where the same quantity of work is accepted and performed over a long period, the proper inference is that there may be a mutual obligation to provide and perform it"; that crucial prerequisite was not, however present in this case.

Does the law require any and what mutual obligations before there can be a contract of service? If the law as to contracts of service is that there must be mutual obligations which were not found by the industrial tribunal or cannot be inferred from the evidence, then the industrial tribunal misdirected itself in law and its determination can and should be set aside. That was Mr. Tabachnik's main contention for the company before this court. I at first thought that Mr. Tabachnik's task had been made easier by a concession, but that concession has been withdrawn, and I have come to the conclusion that his interesting and forceful argument must fail and that no misdirection on the point can fairly be attributed to the industrial tribunal.

For the obligation required of an employer we were referred to old cases where the courts had held that justices had jurisdiction to convict and punish workmen for breaches of contracts to serve masters under the statute 4 Geo. 4, c. 34. For that purpose the court had to decide that there was mutuality of obligation, an obligation on the master to provide work as well as wages, complementing an obligation on the servant to perform the work: *Reg v Welch* (1853) 2 E&B 357; *Bailey Case* (1854) 3 E. & B. 607 and *Whittle v Frankland* (1862) 2 B. & S. 49. But later cases have shown that the normal rule is that a contract of employment does not oblige the master to provide the servant with work in addition to wages: *Collier v Sunday Referee Publishing Co. Ltd.* [1940] 2 KB 647, 650, per Asquith J. An obligation to provide work was not implied by this court in a salesman's contract: *Turner v Sawdon & Co* [1901] 2 K.B. 653; it was in a pieceworker's contract: *Devonald v Rosser & Sons* [1906] 2 KB 728.

The obligation required of an employee was concisely stated by Stable J in a sentence in *Chadwick v Pioneer Private Telephone Co. Ltd.* [1941] 1 All E.R. 522, 523D: "A contract of service implies an obligation to serve, and it comprises some degree of control by the master." That was expanded by Mackenna J in *Ready Mixed Concrete (South East) Ltd v Minister of Pensions and National Insurance* [1968] 2 QB 497, 515:

> "A contract of service exists if these three conditions are fulfilled. (i) The servant agrees that, in consideration of a wage or other remuneration, he will provide his own work and skill in

the performance of some service for his master. (ii) He agrees, expressly or impliedly, that in the performance of that service he will be subject to the other's control in a sufficient degree to make that other master. (iii) The other provisions of the contract are consistent with its being a contract of service."

Of (iii) MacKenna J. proceeded to give some valuable examples, none on all fours with this case. I do not quote what he says of (i) and (ii) except as to mutual obligations:

"There must be a wage or other remuneration. Otherwise there will be no consideration, and without consideration no contract of any kind. The servant must be obliged to provide his own work and skill."

There must, in my judgment, be an irreducible minimum of obligation on each side to create a contract of service. I doubt if it can be reduced any lower than in the sentences I have just quoted and I have doubted whether even that minimum can be discerned to be present in the facts as found by the industrial tribunal, particularly in paragraph 8 of its decision, and what the appeal tribunal said about it and counsel's interpretation of it. Tudor Evans J said [1983] I.C.R. 319, 325:

"At the end of the argument, we asked counsel for further submission as to whether, in paragraph 8, the tribunal clearly refer to the lack of mutual obligation or whether the find-ings were that there was no obligation as to the number of hours the applicants should work or how many garments they should complete with the implication that the applicants were obliged to do some work. Both counsel agreed that there was a reference to a lack of mutual obligations in the sense for which Mr. Blair contends."

Mr. Blair's contention had been, as I have indicated, that on the evidence the company were not obliged to supply the applicants with work and that the applicants were not obliged to do it. If the decision of the industrial tribunal is to be understood in the sense apparently given it by the appeal tribunal, there was a misdirection in law, for there could have been no contract of service, and perhaps no contract at all. The position of the applicants would have been that of the casual "regulars" as found by the industrial tribunal in *O'Kelly v. Trusthouse Forte Plc.* [1983] I.C.R. 728, 743, namely that they had the right to decide whether or not to accept work, and the company had no obligation to provide any work.

Kerr LJ gave a dissenting judgment. **Dillon LJ** gave a concurring judgment.

NOTES AND QUESTIONS

1.   Stephenson LJ, giving the majority judgment, accepts a criticism in *O'Kelly* of his previous decision in *Young & Woods Ltd v West* [1980] IRLR 201 (in which Ackner LJ and Sir David Cairns had concurred) that employment status is solely a question of law. However, it clearly rejects the view of 'mutuality of obligation' as a requirement for ongoing offer and acceptance of work. Quoting Mackenna J, he agrees it means in return for work there 'must be a wage or other remunera-tion. Otherwise there will be no consideration'. This passage, at [1984] ICR 612, 623, was expressly endorsed in *Autoclenz* at [19]. When two Court of Appeals are at odds, a third Court of Appeal decision is in a position to choose, in lieu of a decision by the House of Lords or Supreme Court. Once again, *Autoclenz* has favoured the 'consideration' view.

2. In *Hellyer Bros v McLeod* [1987] ICR 526, the Court of Appeal decided that a group of fisherman claiming redundancy pay would have to prove they had ongoing mutuality of obligation between separate voyages out to sea, when they were (ostensibly) 'free' to take other jobs. The court made reference to *Ford v Warwickshire CC* [1983] 2 AC 71 (noted above), but did not appear to think that the absence of any reference to this additional requirement in the House of Lords judgment was an issue.

3. Who was the 'Mr Blair', mentioned as counsel for the employer in the Employment Appeal Tribunal, and why did he not appear in the Court of Appeal? During the case's progress, he was elected to Parliament. His pupil master at 11 King's Bench Walk had been Irvine QC from *O'Kelly*. Ten years later Blair had become the leader of the Labour Party, and in 1997 the UK Prime Minister. Blair appointed Irvine QC as the Lord Chancellor. Although appointed politically, rather than through the ordinary process required for judges, the Lord Chancellor could sit on court cases in the House of Lords until the Constitutional Reform Act 2005 section 3.

Carmichael v National Power plc [1999] UKHL 47

Mrs Carmichael and Mrs Leese claimed a written statement of a contract of employment from National Power plc, under ERA 1996 section 1. To do this they needed to be 'employees'. They worked as tour guides for the Blyth Power Stations in Northumberland, formerly operated by the Central Electricity Generating Board (CEGB). Their contracts stated: 'I am pleased to note that you are agreeable to be employed by the CEGB at Blyth "A" and "B" power stations on a casual as required basis as a station guide.' They worked an average of 3.75 hours a week in 1990, 6 hours a week in 1991, and around 25 hours by 1995. National Power plc contended they were not employees because there was no 'mutuality of obligation', in the sense of the employer accepting an ongoing duty to provide work. The Court of Appeal reversed the Tribunal and Appeal Tribunal, finding by a majority that they were employees. The House of Lords held they were not employees.

Lord Irvine LC: If this appeal turned exclusively – and in my judgment it does not – on the true meaning and effect of the documentation of March 1989, then I would hold as a matter of construction that no obligation on the C.E.G.B. to provide casual work, nor on Mrs. Leese and Mrs. Carmichael to undertake it, was imposed. There would therefore be an absence of that irreducible minimum of mutual obligation necessary to create a contract of service (*Nethermere (St. Neots) Ltd v Gardiner* [1984] ICR 612, 623C-G per Stephenson L.J., and *Clark v Oxfordshire Health Authority* [1998] IRLR 125, 128 per Sir Christopher Slade, at paragraph 22).

In my judgment it would only be appropriate to determine the issue in these cases solely by reference to the documents in March 1989, if it appeared from their own terms and/or from what the parties said or did then, or subsequently, that they intended them to constitute an exclusive memorial of their relationship. The industrial tribunal must be taken to have decided that they were not so intended but constituted one, albeit important, relevant source of material from which they were entitled to infer the parties' true intention, along with the other objective inferences which could reasonably be drawn from what the parties said and did in March 1989, and subsequently.

The documents contained no provisions governing when, how, or with what frequency guide work would be offered; there were no provisions for notice of termination on either side; the sickness, holiday and pension arrangements for regular staff did not apply; nor did the grievance and disciplinary procedures. Significantly, as Kennedy LJ in his dissenting judgment with which I agree emphasised, in 1994, for example, Mrs. Carmichael was not available for work on 17 occasions nor Mrs. Leese on 8. (p. 1174D). No suggestion of disciplining them arose. The objective inference is that when work was available they were free to undertake it or not as they chose. This flexibility of approach was well suited to their family needs. Just as the need for tours was unpredictable so also were their domestic commitments. Flexibility suited both sides. As Mrs. Carmichael said in her application form, "the part-time casual arrangement would suit my personal circumstances ideally!" The arrangement turned on mutual convenience and goodwill and worked well in practice over the years. The tribunal observed that Mrs. Leese and Mrs. Carmichael had a sense of moral obligation to the C.E.G.B., but would infer no legal obligation. Mr. Lovatt also gave evidence for the C.E.G.B. that "neither ladies are required to work if they do not wish to do so." In my judgment, therefore, the industrial tribunal was well entitled to infer from the March 1989, documents, the surrounding circumstances and how the parties conducted themselves subsequently that their intention neither in 1989 nor subsequently was to have their relationship regulated by contract whilst Mrs. Leese and Mrs. Carmichael were not working as guides. The industrial tribunal correctly concluded that their case "founders on the rock of absence of mutuality." I repeat that no issue arises as to their status when actually working as guides.

Thus, even if the words, "employment will be on a casual as required basis" in the March 1989 documentation were, as Mr. Langstaff Q.C. contends, capable of imposing an obligation to undertake guide work when required – and in my judgment they are not – that interpretation is negated by the findings of the industrial tribunal. So also, even if the March 1989 documentation were capable of bearing the primary constructions which found favour with Ward L.J. and Chadwick L.J. – and in my judgment they are not – the terms which each implied, by invoking business efficacy may not be implied because there may be no implication on that ground unless into a relationship itself contractual.

For all these reasons I would allow this appeal and reinstate the industrial tribunal's reserved decision of 11 September 1995.

Lord Goff, **Lord Jauncey**, **Lord Browne-Wilkinson** and **Lord Hoffmann** concurred.

NOTES AND QUESTIONS

1.   The opinion of Lord Irvine LC is not well expressed. The other Law Lords (possibly aware of the personal angle of this line of cases) concur without saying much. In fact, the effect is to approve the *Nethermere* view at [1984] ICR 612, 623 (which *Clark v Oxfordshire HA* simply referred back to) of the meaning of mutuality of obligation: that is consideration. As Stephenson LJ said, there 'must be a wage or other remuneration. Otherwise there will be no consideration'. This therefore contradicts *O'Kelly*. Thus, whether or not Lord Irvine LC meant to refer to the 'ongoing' view of mutuality, he did the opposite. This is what the other Law Lords concurred with. Thus, Lord Irvine LC overrules the submissions he made as counsel in *O'Kelly*, and Blair made in *Nethermere*. On this reading of *Carmichael* there is no precondition for the employer to accept that the employee will do ongoing work. There is only a requirement of consideration: such as work for a wage.

2.   *Carmichael* is not referred to in *Autoclenz* and therefore has ceased to be relevant.

3.   In light of the clarification in *Autoclenz*, would the tour guides be found to be employees? Taking into account the relative bargaining power of the parties,

presumably they would. They were part-time employees, and it is irrelevant that employees have variable hours, as indeed the car valets did.

4.   Lord Hoffmann gives the only other reasoned opinion, although he focuses on the history of the 'mixed fact and law' nature of employment status. Presumably the 'fact' element is the economic reality of the parties' positions, and the 'law' element is the policy of labour rights to protect workers who could not bargain for labour rights themselves, and prevent unjust enrichment of employers.

5.   Since *Autoclenz*, there have still been Court of Appeal decisions applying old law, strangely failing to apply the precedents that bind them.

Stringfellow Restaurants Ltd v Quashie [2012] EWCA Civ 1735

Ms Quashie claimed she was an employee of Stringfellow Restaurants Ltd and had been unfairly dismissed in her job as a lap dancer in their nightclubs. She had worked for 18 months on a rota basis, earning around £200,000 per annum. She had received a booklet of 'house rules' appended to the agreement. Stringfellow customers bought vouchers, which included a tip out fee, house fee fines and a commission, that Quashie then cashed in. She was not required to work any set number of nights per week. The Employment Tribunal found that Quashie was not an employee. The Employment Appeal Tribunal held there was a contract of employment, as she was integrated in the business. Stringfellow Ltd argued that the Tribunal's conclusions were misread, and there was nothing continuing that might establish an umbrella contract. The Court of Appeal agreed that Quashie was not an employee.

Elias LJ:

10. An issue that arises in this case is the significance of mutuality of obligation in the employment contract. Every bilateral contract requires mutual obligations; they constitute the consideration from each party necessary to create the contract. Typically an employment contract will be for a fixed or indefinite duration, and one of the obligations will be to keep the relationship in place until it is lawfully severed, usually by termination on notice. But there are some circumstances where a worker works intermittently for the employer, perhaps as and when work is available. There is in principle no reason why the worker should not be employed under a contract of employment for each separate engagement, even if of short duration, as a number of authorities have confirmed: see the decisions of the Court of Appeal in *Meechan* [sic] *v Secretary of State for Employment* [1997] IRLR 353 and *Cornwall County Council v Prater* [2006] IRLR 362.

11. Where the employee working on discrete separate engagements needs to establish a particular period of continuous employment in order to be entitled to certain rights, it will usually be necessary to show that the contract of employment continues between engagements. (Exceptionally the employee can establish continuity even during periods when no contract of employment is in place by relying on certain statutory rules found in section 212 of the Employment Rights Act.)

12. In order for the contract to remain in force, it is necessary to show that there is at least what has been termed "an irreducible minimum of obligation", either express or implied, which continue during the breaks in work engagements: see the judgment of Stephenson LJ in *Nethermere (St Neots) v Gardiner* [1984] ICR 612, 623, approved by Lord Irvine of Lairg in *Carmichael v National Power plc* [1999] ICR 1226, 1230. Where this occurs, these contracts are

often referred to as "global" or "umbrella" contracts because they are overarching contracts punctuated by periods of work. However, whilst the fact that there is no umbrella contract does not preclude the worker being employed under a contract of employment when actually carrying out an engagement, the fact that a worker only works casually and intermittently for an employer may, depending on the facts, justify an inference that when he or she does work it is to provide services as an independent contractor rather than as an employee. This was the way in which the employment tribunal analysed the employment status of casual wine wait-ers in *O'Kelly v Trusthouse Forte plc* [1983] ICR 728, and the Court of Appeal held that it was a cogent analysis, consistent with the evidence, which the Employment Appeal Tribunal had been wrong to reverse.

13. In *Stephenson v Delphi Diesel Systems* [2003] ICR 471 I sought to bring some of these strands concerning mutuality together in the following way (paras 11–14):
[His Lordship repeated three similar points to the above, and continued …]

"14. The issue whether the employed person is required to accept work if offered, or whether the employer is obliged to offer work if available is irrelevant to the question whether a contract exists at all during the period when the work is actually performed. The only question then is whether there is sufficient control to give rise to a conclusion that the contractual relationship which does exist is one of a contract of service or not."

14. On reflection, it is clear that the last sentence of paragraph 14 is too sweeping. Control is not the only issue. Even where the work-wage relationship is established and there is substan-tial control, there may be other features of the relationship which will entitle a tribunal to con-clude that there is no contract of employment in place even during an individual engagement. *O'Kelly* and *Ready Mixed* provide examples.
…

45. The critical question was as to whether the nature of those contractual obligations. Were they such as to render it a contract of employment? To use the language of McKenna J, were the provisions of the contract consistent with it being a contract of service? In my view, the most important finding in that regard was the Tribunal's inference from the evidence that the employer was under no obligation to pay the dancer anything at all. The principal evidence for that was that she negotiated her own fees with the clients, took the risk that on any particular night she would be out of pocket and received back from the employer only monies received from clients (whether by way of cash or Heavenly Money) after deductions.

46. In my judgment, this was an inference which the Tribunal properly made on that evidence. It could not be said to be perverse and the EAT was not, with respect, entitled to conclude that the arrangement for payment was no more than the mechanism whereby the club discharged its obligation to pay the dancer. Even if the EAT was correct to find that the Tribunal had wrongly concluded that there was no contract at all in existence, that would not in my view have justified it in opening up all the Tribunal's findings and substituting its own analysis of the evidence.
…

51. The fact that the dancer took the economic risk is also a very powerful pointer against the contract being a contract of employment. Indeed, it is the basis of the economic reality test, described above. It is not necessary to go so far as to accept the submission of Mr Linden that absent an obligation on the employer to pay a wage (or to secure or arrange for its payment by a third party, as in *Cormie v Robert Rodger* (UKEATS/0036/11), the relationship can never as a matter of law constitute a contract of employment. But it would, I think, be an unusual case where a contract of service is found to exist when the worker takes the economic risk and is

paid exclusively by third parties. On any view, the Tribunal was entitled to find that the lack of any obligation to pay did preclude the establishment of such a contract here. Indeed, in the *Trusthouse Forte* case the waiter was found to be engaged as an independent contractor even though in that case he was paid remuneration by the employer.

52. The Employment Tribunal's conclusion was strongly reinforced by the fact that the terms of the contract involved the dancer accepting that she was self employed, and she conducted her affairs on that basis, paying her own tax. In addition, and again consistently with that classification, she did not receive sick pay or holiday pay. It is trite law that the parties cannot by agreement fix the status of their relationship: that is an objective matter to be determined by an assessment of all the relevant facts. But it is legitimate for a court to have regard to the way in which the parties have chosen to categorise the relationship, and in a case where the position is uncertain, it can be decisive, as Lord Denning recognised in *Massey v Crown Life Insurance* [1978] 2 All ER 576, 578.

Pitchford LJ and **Ward LJ** agreed.

NOTES AND QUESTIONS

1. Why did Elias LJ not make reference to the Supreme Court in *Autoclenz*, which said he 'must take into account the relative bargaining power of the parties'? Mr Linden QC, who represented Stringfellow Restaurants Ltd, had also represented the car valets in *Autoclenz*. Given Ms Quashie's high income and capacity to find alternative work, do you think Elias LJ implicitly took bargaining power into account?
2. Elias LJ's obiter references to *O'Kelly* as examples of people outside the scope of employment are regrettable. It is not a reasonable position to suggest that fundamental human rights violations have remained a part of UK labour law.
3. Elias LJ devotes some time to discussing 'umbrella' contracts, but presumably this is an unnecessary gloss on the law, for the reason he gives at paragraph [10]. If people are hired intermittently, but the breaks in employment are merely temporary cessations of work, there is a continuing employment contract (see ERA 1996 s 212 and *Ford v Warwickshire CC* [1983] 2 AC 71). The sole relevance of this lies in fulfilment of the qualifying period for an employment right. It has no relevance to being an employee, because otherwise it would frustrate the purpose of employment rights by withdrawing protection from people who are least able about to bargain for rights in their contracts.
4. In *Smith v Carillion (JM) Ltd* [2015] EWCA Civ 209, Elias LJ, this time making reference to *Autoclenz* at [30], felt able to hold that Mr Smith, who worked through an employment agency for a construction company, was not an employee and had no rights to protection from dismissal from the company under TULRCA 1992 s 146. Apparently Elias LJ thought *Autoclenz* required no 'departure from the established jurisprudence with respect to agency workers' (see below at chapter 3(3)(b)) even though *Autoclenz* was itself an intermediated job case, and contained no limitations in respect of agency work for its principles. For this reason, *Smith* should be regarded as entirely inadequate, and a failure to recognise that some of the 'established jurisprudence' from past judgments is now wrong. The common law is not a dead establishment, but lives.

5. After an additional twelve pages of discussion, it is respectfully submitted that the language of 'mutuality of obligation' is unnecessary. As the CJEU found for the purpose of defining a 'worker' in EU law, it is 'of no consequence' (see *Allonby v Accrington and Rossendale College* (2004) C-256/01, [72]). As *Autoclenz* made clear, it means consideration and no more. A clarification of this point by the Supreme Court or Court of Appeal would fulfil Parliament's intention, comply with international law, reduce litigation, and reduce the pages in this book's second edition.

(d) Workers, and Not Employees

Who is a worker, but not an employee, under ERA 1996 s 230(3)? Before *Autoclenz*, it appeared that many people who lacked bargaining power benefited from protection, while the 'ongoing' version of the 'mutuality of obligation' test persisted. For example, in *James v Redcats (Brands) Ltd* [2007] IRLR 296, Elias J found that a postal courier, who was not being paid the minimum wage, was a worker as there was no requirement for 'mutuality of obligation'. Arguably that claimant would today also be regarded as an employee. This suggests people who are workers, but not employees, will be a group that have very significant autonomy in their work, or a special position of authority if they are in an organisation.

Clyde & Co LLP v Bates van Winkelhof [2014] UKSC 32

Ms Bates van Winkelhof claimed that she was a 'worker' under ERA 1996 s 230(3)(b) for the purpose of protection from detriment for whistleblowing under ss 43A–43L, against her law firm, Clyde & Co LLP. She was an equity partner in the firm. She reported to management that a Tanzanian client had been involved in money laundering and bribery in November 2010. She was suspended and expelled in January 2011. In the Court of Appeal, Elias LJ held that because the Limited Liability Partnerships Act 2000 s 4(4) states a member of an LLP would not be regarded as 'employed', the claimant could not be an employee or a worker. The Supreme Court unanimously reversed this decision.

Lady Hale:

30. Having reached the conclusion that section 4(4) of the 2000 Act does not operate so as to exclude the appellant from being a "worker" within the meaning of section 230(3)(b) of the 1996 Act, it is necessary to consider the "more subtle" analysis addressed in the Court of Appeal, that "underlying the statutory definition of worker is the notion that one party has to be in a subordinate relationship to the other" (para 71). Elias LJ would have been "minded to hold that the member of an LLP would not by virtue of that status alone constitute either an employee or a worker" (para 73). If by that he meant only that there are some members of an LLP who are purely investors and do not undertake personally to work for the LLP, then of course I would agree. But if by that he meant that those members who do so undertake (whether by virtue of the membership agreement or otherwise) cannot be workers, then I respectfully disagree.

31. As already seen, employment law distinguishes between three types of people: those employed under a contract of employment; those self-employed people who are in business

on their own account and undertake work for their clients or customers; and an intermediate class of workers who are self-employed but do not fall within the second class. Discrimination law, on the other hand, while it includes a contract "personally to do work" within its definition of employment (see, now, Equality Act 2010, s 83(2)) does not include an express exception for those in business on their account who work for their clients or customers. But a similar qualification has been introduced by a different route.

32. In *Allonby v Accrington and Rossendale College* (Case C-256/01) [2004] ICR 1328, the European Court of Justice was concerned with whether a college lecturer who was ostensibly self-employed could nevertheless be a "worker" for the purpose of an equal pay claim. The Court held, following *Lawrie-Blum v Land Baden-Wurttemberg* (Case C-66/85) [1987] ICR 483 that "there must be considered as a worker a person who, for a certain period of time, performs services for and under the direction of another person in return for which he receives remuneration" (para 67). However, such people were to be distinguished from "independent providers of services who are not in a relationship of subordination with the person who receives the services" (para 68). The concept of subordination was there introduced in order to distinguish the intermediate category from people who were dealing with clients or customers on their own account. It was used for the same purpose in the discrimination case of *Jivraj v Hashwani*.

33. We are dealing with the more precise wording of section 230(3)(b). English cases in the EAT have attempted to capture the essential distinction in a variety of ways. Thus in *Byrne Bros (Formwork) Ltd v Baird* [2002] ICR 667, Mr Recorder Underhill QC suggested, at para 17(4), that

> "[t]he reason why employees are thought to need such protection is that they are in a subordinate and dependent position vis-a-vis their employers: the purpose of the Regulations is to extend protection to workers who are, substantively and economically, in the same position. Thus the essence of the intended distinction must be between, on the one hand, workers whose degree of dependence is essentially the same as that of employees and, on the other, contractors who have a sufficiently arm's-length and independent position to be treated as being able to look after themselves in the relevant respects."

...

39. There can be no substitute for applying the words of the statute to the facts of the individual case. There will be cases where that is not easy to do. But in my view they are not solved by adding some mystery ingredient of "subordination" to the concept of employee and worker. The experienced employment judges who have considered this problem have all recognised that there is no magic test other than the words of the statute themselves. As Elias J recognised in *Redcats*, a small business may be genuinely an independent business but be completely dependent upon and subordinate to the demands of a key customer (the position of those small factories making goods exclusively for the "St Michael" brand in the past comes to mind). Equally, as Maurice Kay LJ recognised in *Westwood*, one may be a professional person with a high degree of autonomy as to how the work is performed and more than one string to one's bow, and still be so closely integrated into the other party's operation as to fall within the definition. As the case of the controlling shareholder in a company who is also employed as chief executive shows, one can effectively be one's own boss and still be a "worker". While subordination may sometimes be an aid to distinguishing workers from other self-employed people, it is not a freestanding and universal characteristic of being a worker. ...

41. I have reached that conclusion without the help of the European Convention on Human Rights. But it may be worth noting that that conclusion is entirely consistent with the appellant's rights under article 10, whereas a different conclusion would pose more problems. Article 10 provides for a qualified right to freedom of expression.

[Lady Hale referred to Heinisch v Germany [2011] ECHR 1175 and others and continued]

43. Hence it is argued that, if the appellant's claims as to the reasons for her dismissal are made good, it would be incompatible with her convention rights for the law to deny her a remedy. If the whistle-blowing provisions of the 1996 Act apply to her, she would have such a remedy. Those provisions are consistent with the proportionality calculation carried out in *Heinisch*. The expectation is that disclosure will first be made to the employer or the person responsible for the wrong doing or to a prescribed regulator (see sections 43C, 43E, 43F). Disclosure may only be made to other persons in more limited circumstances (see sections 43G, 43H), for example where the worker reasonably believes that she will be subject to a detriment if she discloses to her employer, and it must be reasonable in all the circumstances of the case. If those provisions do not apply to the appellant, then it is difficult to see what other protection she would have, given that she is not entitled to protection from unfair dismissal. Hence it is our duty under section 3 of the Human Rights Act 1998 to interpret the 1996 Act so as to give her that protection. …

45. Fortunately, however, as the appellant already has that protection under the 1996 Act as interpreted in a completely conventional way, it is not necessary for us to decide whether her convention rights would require and permit us to interpret it compatibly.

Lord Neuberger and **Lord Wilson** agreed with **Lady Hale**. **Lord Clarke** and **Lord Carnwath** gave short concurring judgments.

NOTES AND QUESTIONS

1.   Lady Hale's decision is threefold: that the true construction of the Limited Liability Partnerships Act 2000 s 4(4) did not preclude solicitor partners being workers, that there is no need for a worker to be regarded as 'subordinate', and that a human rights compatible interpretation of the ERA 1996 would likely require the claimant to have protection. The latter point appears to be the most significant. Above it was remarked how *O'Kelly*, despite Elias LJ's unfortunate references to it in *Quashie*, is bad law now, as it purported to evade labour rights through cutting bar staff out of the scope of employment. What other rights could this strong human rights focused approach to construction affect?

2.   The judgment appears to presume that Ms Bates van Winkelhof, as a partner, was a worker but not an employee because partners participate equally in the governance of the partnership: unfair dismissal rights are replaced with the standard terms of a partnership deed requiring a majority vote of partners; childcare rights are presumably seen as less necessary since (in theory) partners will want to ensure a family-friendly environment for their colleagues so that they may enjoy it themselves. Would it matter if governance participation was weighted or very unequal among partners?

3.   Should company directors, who have similar managerial power, be classed as workers but not employees? The position in UK law is that company directors will be employees. In *Lee v Lee's Air Farming Ltd* [1960] UKPC 33 the Privy Council advised that Mr Lee, who owned 2,999 of 3,000 shares and was the sole director of the aeroplane fertiliser company, was a 'worker' by virtue of his contract to be its chief pilot. This meant, under the New Zealand Workers' Compensation Act 1922, that his widow was entitled to claim statutory compensation after

Mr Lee was killed in an aircraft crash. Subsequently, it has been consistently held that company directors are employees (and 'workers'). See *Secretary of State for Trade and Industry v Bottrill* [1999] EWCA Civ 781, but contrast *Asscher v Staatssecretaris van Financiën* (1996) C-107/94, the CJEU holding a director and sole shareholder of a company was not regarded as a 'worker' with 'a relationship of subordination' in EU law.

4. In *Boulting v Association of Cinematograph, Television and Allied Technicians* [1963] 2 QB 606, Lord Denning MR dissenting suggested that managerial staff including company directors should not be seen as employees. This mirrors a stance taken under the US National Labor Relations Act of 1935 §2(11), where it was originally thought that if managers were members of unions, it could dilute solidarity. Other jurisdictions also say directors or senior managers are not employees, but unlike the unique position of the United States, say they are protected through having 'employee-like' status with full rights to organise. This is the position under the ILO Right to Organise Convention 1948 (c 87). In the UK, every worker is protected in the right to organise. Paid childcare leave and dismissal rights are the key 'employee' rights that would be questioned for directors. Do you agree that everyone working in an organisation should have these rights?

5. The Companies Act 2006 ss 168–69 regulates director removal from office: a simple majority vote of members in the company general meeting removes any director, if they have 28 days notice and an opportunity to circulate their case to remain. Removal from office could breach the employment contract for which damages must be paid, but an injunction cannot be available (see *Southern Foundries (1926) Ltd v Shirlaw* [1940] AC 701). Do you agree that the proper deliberation by the general meeting should always be regarded as justifying dismissal under ERA 1996 s 98?

6. In *Hospital Medical Group Ltd v Westwood* [2012] EWCA Civ 1005, the Court of Appeal approved a statement by Aikens LJ in *Autoclenz* that worker status was determined by a threefold test of (i) entering a contract for work, (ii) performing work personally and (iii) that the other party is not a client or customer. This meant that a surgeon who did hair transplants was rightly held to be a non-employee worker.

7. However, in *Secretary of State for Justice v Windle* [2016] EWCA Civ 459, Underhill LJ decided to make 'mutuality of obligation' a condition for worker status as well (below). He held that court interpreters working for Her Majesty's Courts and Tribunals Service were not doing a contract 'personally to do work' within the meaning of the Equality Act 2010 s 83(2)(a). Windle claimed race discrimination, but Underhill LJ took the view that because HMCTS was 'under no obligation to offer them work; nor were they under any obligation to accept it when offered', they could not be said to be personally performing work. He said: 'The factors relevant in assessing whether a claimant is employed under a contract of service are not essentially different from those relevant in assessing whether he or she is an employee in the extended sense.' On what rational or legal basis can this decision be defended?

8. In *Pimlico Plumbers Ltd v Smith* [2017] EWCA Civ 51, the Court of Appeal held that a plumber, Mr Smith, was a worker but not an employee. His contract from

2009 stated that he was an independent contractor, although a previous contract from 2004 stated he was a 'sub contracted employee'. After having a heart attack and no longer being engaged, he claimed unfair dismissal under ERA 1996 s 94, or wrongful dismissal at common law. As a non-employee worker, however, he could only claim outstanding holiday pay, sick pay, unlawful wage deductions and discrimination. Sir Terence Etherton MR held that the Tribunal had reached a correct decision on the facts. Do you agree?

9. *Aslam and Farrar v Uber BV* (2016) 2202550/2015 held that drivers of cars using the popular software application from Uber BV were, at least, workers. Uber's contracts asserted that their drivers were independent contractors. The drivers claimed rights to the minimum wage and paid holidays (although not any rights that required 'employee' status). The Tribunal found at [48]–[53] that Uber gives drivers detailed instructions, requires standards of presentation, has sophisticated surveillance through its app, and penalty mechanisms for failing to work to meet Uber's demand. It also held that Uber's contracts were an 'excellent illustration ... of "armies of lawyers" contriving documents in their clients' interests which simply misrepresent the true rights and obligations on both sides' [96]. Do you agree that Uber drivers (as they have been held in Germany, South Africa, California, etc) are employees, as well as workers? Do you agree that 'contriving' to 'misrepresent' something is fraud, and justifies punitive damages in claims for breaches of labour rights?

(e) Employed, Without Rights?

Two anomalous cases, involving pupil barristers and volunteers for the Citizens Advice Bureau, held people who appeared vulnerable to be outside the scope of the minimum wage and discrimination protection. It is very unclear whether either still stands as good precedent, and appears particularly unfortunate as both involved the legal profession.

Edmonds v Lawson QC [2000] EWCA Civ 69

Rebecca Jane Edmonds, a criminal law pupil with Michael Lawson QC's chambers, 23 Essex Street, claimed the minimum wage. Her pupillage had been 'unfunded'. The Code of Conduct stated duties of pupils were to be 'conscientious in receiving the instruction given and to apply yourself full-time to your pupillage'. The chambers argued there was no intention to create legal relations, or consideration, but even if there were, Edmonds was not an apprentice, or employee, or a worker for the purpose of the National Minimum Wage Act 1998 s 54. Sullivan J held that Miss Edmonds was a worker. The chambers appealed. The Court of Appeal found that there was an intention to create legal relations, and consideration, but held that a pupil barrister is neither an apprentice nor a worker because, in its view, there is an absence of commitment to serve and the general practice was that pupils receive no payment.

Lord Bingham CJ

8. The object of the National Minimum Wage Act 1998 was not, as we understand, to enlarge the categories of those entitled to be paid wages but to ensure that those entitled to be paid

wages are not paid at anything less than a specified minimum level. ... It makes no difference that, if the pupil defaulted, the chambers would be most unlikely to sue; the same is true if an employer engages a junior employee under an employment contract which is undoubtedly binding, and the employee fails to turn up on the appointed day.

...

34. Since the issue in this case is whether pupil barristers aged over 26 are entitled to be paid the national minimum wage, it cannot be conclusive that pupils are not now generally paid. This is true even of funded pupils since, as we understand, chambers grants are treated as professional earnings for tax purposes only in part. But the fact that the generality of barrister pupils have been unpaid, not just in the distant past but also in modern times, is in our view of significance in determining whether a relationship of or equivalent to apprenticeship exists. For although trade apprentices have always received reduced wages, reflecting both the value of the practical training they receive and their reduced productivity, they have always in modern times received some wages and in earlier times received board and lodging. In *Dunk v George Waller & Sons Ltd* [1970] 2 QB 163 at 169 Widgery LJ said:

"A contract of apprenticeship secures three things for the apprentice: it secures him, first, a money payment during the period of apprenticeship; ..."

While solicitors' articled clerks may once have been in very much the same position as pupil barristers, they have in more recent times been entitled to payment. The fact that pupil barristers have up to the present been unpaid in our view reflects the lack of expectation that they will render services of value; hence the requirement in the Code of Conduct that, if they do produce work of value, they shall be paid.

Pill LJ and **Hale LJ** concurred.

NOTES AND QUESTIONS

1. Immediately following this case, the Bar Council resolved that its member chambers should pay to pupils a bursary of £10,000, which reflected the minimum wage at the time. In 2015, the minimum wage for a pupillage set by the Bar Council is £1000 per month. Although most chambers pay much more, this would mean that if a pupil does not work more than 34.3 hours per week, they will be earning the minimum wage. Given that paragraph 34 relies on the 'generality' of pupils being unpaid, does the change in practice mean that all barristers are employees?

2. Was it accurate for Lord Bingham CJ to suggest that the National Minimum Wage Act 1998 was not intended to enlarge the categories of covered workers? In the Second Reading, Margaret Becket MP suggests that it was meant to reverse, among other things how 'young people were removed from coverage by the wages council system' from 1986. See Hansard HC Debs (16 December 1997) vol 303, col 164.

3. It might be tempting (even more if you are going to the bar) to view this decision as motivated by unconscious judicial bias against interference in the Inns' traditions. It could be argued to reveal a romantic but inappropriate attachment to the aura of 'self-employment', even for pupils, that damages equal opportunity by deterring entry for people who are not from privileged backgrounds. Interestingly, Lady Hale, who concurred in the judgment, suggested in *Edwards v Chesterfield*

Royal Hospital NHS Foundation Trust [2011] UKSC 58, [110] that because she was the only one who had 'spent a substantial proportion of her working life as an employee rather than as a self-employed barrister or tenured office holder' she intuitively took a different approach to employment rights. On the other hand, it could be viewed as a technical decision (based on the practice of paying wages at the time) whose basis has now changed.

4. Substantial media attention, but less case law, has arisen on unpaid interns. The legal position is that – at the least – anyone performing work for someone that is not a client or a customer is a worker, and anyone who is dependent is an employee. Interns are therefore to be regarded as employees, and some are apprentices.

X v Mid Sussex Citizens Advice Bureau [2012] UKSC 59

X, a volunteer adviser at the Mid Sussex Citizens Advice Bureau, claimed that she was unlawfully dismissed on grounds of her disability. Her volunteer agreement said it was 'binding in honour only' and 'not a contract of employment'. The Tribunal, Appeal Tribunal held that as a volunteer, she was not protected by the Disability Discrimination Act 1995 (now the Equality Act 2010 section 83) interpreted in light of the Equality Framework Directive 2000/78/EC. In the Court of Appeal, Elias LJ held that this was correct as X was not an 'employee' or a 'worker' under UK or EU law or had an 'occupation'. The Supreme Court held this was correct.

Lord Mance:

39. … the European Parliament did during the consultation process which preceded the making of the Framework Directive propose amendments to article 3(1)(a), to make it refer to:

> "(a) conditions for access to employment, *unpaid and voluntary work, official duties*, self-employment and occupation, including selection criteria and recruitment conditions, *finding of employment by public and private employment agencies and authorities*, whatever the sector or branch of activity and at all levels of the professional hierarchy, including promotion;" (added words italicised)

It gave as the justification that:

> "Official duties, unpaid and voluntary work should likewise fall within the scope of this directive. It would not be right for official (i.e. public) duties to become a separate field of application: they should be covered by the definition of the term 'employment'." (A5-0264/2000 final, p 20)

40. The Commission decided to amend its proposal to take up the Parliament's suggestion (COM/2000/652 final), though with slight differences, in a form according to which article 3 would have read:

> "This Directive shall apply to *all persons in both the public and private sectors, including public authorities, with regard to*:
> (a) conditions for access to employment, self-employment and occupation, *unpaid or voluntary work* including selection criteria and recruitment conditions, whatever the sector or branch of activity and at all levels of the professional hierarchy, including promotion;

(b) access to all types and to all levels, of vocational guidance, vocational training, advanced vocational training and retraining, *including practical work experience*;" (added words italicised)

In an Explanatory Memorandum, the Commission described such amendments as involving:

"Clarification of the material scope of the proposal, indicating that it covers both the public and private sectors, including public authorities. It is also stated that the proposal also applies to unpaid or voluntary work and practical training ….".

41. In the event, however, the Council, while substantially accepting (with a qualification and some verbal reformulation) the amendment to the opening words and while accepting the addition to article 3(1)(b), notably did not accept the addition to cover "unpaid or voluntary work". The Equality and Human Rights Commission suggests that was because that addition was a mere unnecessary "clarification". That is a misreading of the Commission's Explanatory Memorandum, where "clarification" is a word used only in relation to the proposed amendment of the opening words of article 3. Further, it is not credible to suggest that the reason for the Council's failure to adopt the one proposed alteration in this area which it did not adopt is that it regarded the addition of the words "unpaid or voluntary work" as unnecessary and intended that, without them, the Directive would cover voluntary activity. The appellant's and the Equality and Human Rights Commission's current case thus runs contrary to a deliberate choice made by the relevant European legislator.

Lord Neuberger, **Lord Walker**, **Lady Hale** and **Lord Wilson** agreed.

NOTES AND QUESTIONS

1. The Supreme Court did not have the benefit of submissions from counsel on the case of *Steymann v Staatssecretaris van Justitie* (1988) Case 196/87. Here, Mr Steymann was classed as a 'worker' for the purpose of the right to free movement in the European Union (and therefore not to be discriminated against on grounds of nationality) after he volunteered for work in the Bhagwan community, doing plumbing and household duties. He did not receive a wage, but the community provided 'for the material needs of its members in any event, irrespective of the nature and the extent of their activities'. The Supreme Court had no other chance to find this out, however, because it stated the law was *acte clair*, and declined to make a reference to the CJEU. This suggests that *X v Mid Sussex* proceeded on an erroneous footing and should not be followed.
2. Lord Mance's account of the legislative history could be construed in the opposite way, as the Council of the EU made no statement of why it did not include the Parliament's amendment. Could they have thought an amendment unnecessary, because to them *Steymann* suggested that unpaid volunteers were workers?
3. The peculiar effect of *X* is that the claimant, while giving advice to citizens, could be discriminated against for disability, or maybe even racial and sexual harassment. However, if while working the same claimant refused to give advice to someone who entered a Citizens Advice Bureau office on grounds of their disability, race, gender, etc, then the Citizens Advice Bureau would be liable for discrimination. Does this make sense?
4. Suppose a volunteer is told by their employer 'You're fired you ******* dirty ******, I hate ******s like you.' Whatever the position in EU law (including the

general principle of equality: see chapter 14), do you think this does (or should) constitute a violation of a right at common law, and in equity? Do you agree that such prejudiced conduct is so odious that it could only be legitimised by positive law, if at all?

5. Do you think the statement that an agreement is 'binding in honour only' is relevant in an employment, as opposed to a commercial, context? Contrast *Rose & Frank Co v JR Crompton & Bros Ltd* [1924] UKHL 2. Given that such documents are take-it-or-leave-it deals, why should an employing entity be able to contract away other people's social rights?

6. In *Jivraj v Hashwani* [2011] UKSC 40 a commercial arbitrator was held by the Supreme Court not to have the requisite 'subordination' needed to be in 'employment' to make a discrimination claim based on religion or belief. The decision may have been motivated in part by a concern for independence of the judiciary, and the notion of 'subordination' appeared antithetical to that.

7. In *President of the Methodist Conference v Preston* [2013] UKSC 29 the Supreme Court held that a Methodist Church minister was not an employee, and could not claim unfair dismissal. In Lord Sumption's view, the minister did not even have a contract with the church, and was solely engaged by unilateral actions under the church constitution. Lady Hale dissented, arguing that everything in the relationship appeared contractual, and would have followed the findings of the Employment Appeal Tribunal and the Court of Appeal below that the minister was entitled to bring a claim. Do you think the Supreme Court views judges and church ministers to be in equivalent official positions, where public policy should preclude a finding of employment?

8. In *Mingeley v Pennock* [2004] EWCA Civ 328 Maurice Kay LJ held that a minicab driver had no claim for race discrimination under what was the Race Relations Act 1976 s 78 (now Equality Act 2010 s 39) because he had no duty to personally perform the driving work. He found the idea 'unsustainable' that UK law had to be interpreted in light of the scope required by the Race Equality Directive 2000/43/EC Art 3 because he believed it was relevant that the UK law 'has been in existence for more than a quarter of a century and which has been given authoritative interpretation by the Court of Appeal and the House of Lords'. It is submitted that Maurice Kay LJ incorrectly interpreted UK law (particularly since the comments on substitution in *Autoclenz*), and failed to appreciate the duty to interpret UK law to meet EU law's minimum standards.

9. *Governing Body of Clifton Middle School v Askew* [1999] EWCA Civ 1892 held an 'employment relationship' did not exist between a teacher and his school's governing body, which would mean Mr Askew's employment contract was protected from variation without justification under the Transfer of Undertakings (Protection of Employment) Regulations 1993.

10. ERA 1996 s 205A, inserted by Growth and Infrastructure Act 2013 s 31, created a new 'employee shareholder status' which enabled employees to 'sell' non-EU-based dismissal or childcare rights in return for shares in the employing company. Despite high hopes from the then Chancellor of the Exchequer, George Osborne, virtually nobody took up this option. See J Prassl, 'Dismantling the Contract of Employment? The New Employee Shareholder Status in the UK' (2013) 42 *ILJ* 307.

(3) WHO ARE THE 'EMPLOYERS'?

Because labour rights mean someone has correlative duties, the case law could equally have developed a test to establish who are the 'employers'. For instance, a multifactor test based on the functions that typical employers perform could clarify who is responsible for employment rights. Outside small business it is rare for the employer to be a natural person, rather than a corporation, partnership, public body or some other legal entity. These entities exist because of voluntary actions: an agreement among people to incorporate, set up a charitable trust, government department, and so forth. Other entities can also be associated through voluntary obligations, in groups of companies, or a looser 'network', where potentially one entity has influence or substantially benefits from another. To ensure the efficacy of labour rights, the law may recognise that multiple entities form one de facto enterprise. For example, ERA 1996 s 231 and TULRCA 1992 s 297 treat employers as 'associated' if one is a company controlled by the other, or they in a company group, that another controls. A key element, identified by the common law as far back as *Turberville v Stampe* (1697) 91 ER 1072 is that an employer is a party that factually benefits from someone's labour, regardless of transactional form: if there are multiple parties, they become joint-bearers of labour duties. This will be particularly important if there are several potential employers, but one or more is insolvent, or if one party should be responsible for an act that warrants targeted liability, such as malicious sex discrimination. The persistent difficulty is that in the chains of bargaining that make up any modern economy, *everyone* ultimately benefits from a worker's labour: direct employers, to trading partners, to consumers, to the consumer's employer, and so on. The task of drawing conceptual differences becomes frustrated, as there are only degrees of benefit, not differences of kind. This means the essential purpose of the exercise matters, as it does when defining 'employee': to guarantee basic social and economic rights despite unequal bargaining power, and to prevent unjust enrichment.

(a) Subcontracting

As we saw, *Autoclenz* involved an intermediary subcontractor, which was responsible for labour rights (the minimum wage and holiday pay) of car-valet employees, while working for another business. Since *Viasystems (Tyneside) Ltd v Thermal Transfer (Northern) Ltd* [2005] EWCA Civ 1151, it was acknowledged that an employee can have two or more employers. This meant two employers were jointly liable for damage to a third party caused by their subcontracted employee. In the following case, the Supreme Court addressed the concept of an 'enterprise', which may be formed through subcontracting.

Catholic Child Welfare Society v Institute of the Brothers of the Christian Schools [2012] UKSC 56, [2013] 2 AC 1

A group action of 170 claimants had successfully claimed that between 1958 and 1992 they were raped or sexually abused by Brother James Carragher, and various others, at the St William's school. The Catholic Child Welfare Society (CCWS, a charitable company, referred to as the 'Middlesbrough defendants') supplied the teachers and managed the school directly. The Institute of the Brothers of the Christian Schools (IBCS), an unincorporated association, also controlled which schools its 'Brothers' taught at. The Court of Appeal found that the CCWS was liable, but the IBCS was not jointly liable. CCWS appealed, contending that IBCS should also be vicariously liable. The Supreme Court found the IBCS was jointly liable because it formed part of the whole.

Lord Phillips:

41. At para 16 [of the *Viasystems* case, noted below] May LJ … held that the enquiry should concentrate on the relevant negligent act and then ask whose responsibility it was to prevent it. Who was entitled, and perhaps theoretically obliged, to give orders as to how the work should or should not be done? The answer on the facts of the case was both the second and the third defendants. There was dual control and thus there should be dual vicarious liability.

42. Rix LJ reached the same conclusion, but his reasoning was not the same. At para 55 he commented that the basis of vicarious liability was, generally speaking, that those who set in motion and profit from the activities of their employees should compensate those who are injured by such activities, even when performed negligently. Liability was extended to the employer on the practical assumption that because he could spread the risk through pricing and insurance, he was better organised and able to bear the risk and was, at the same time, encouraged to control the risk.

43. Dealing with the test of control, Rix LJ observed at paras 59 and 64 that the right to control the method of doing work had long been an important and sometimes critical test of the master/servant relationship. The courts had, however, imperceptibly moved from using the test of control as determinative of the relationship of employer and employee to using it as the test of vicarious liability of a defendant. At para 79 he questioned whether the doctrine of vicarious liability was to be equated with control. Vicarious liability was a doctrine designed for the sake of the claimant, imposing a liability incurred without fault because the employer was treated at law as picking up the burden of an organisational or business relationship which he had undertaken for his own benefit. Accordingly, what one was looking for was:

> "a situation where the employee in question, at any rate for relevant purposes, is so much a part of the work, business or organisation of both employers that it is just to make both employers answer for his negligence."

44. The brothers who taught at the school were not contractually employed by the Institute; they were contractually employed by or on behalf of the Middlesbrough Defendants. By this appeal the Middlesbrough Defendants seek to establish dual vicarious liability. The question arises of whether the approach of May LJ or that of Rix LJ should be applied in determining whether the Institute is also vicariously liable for the brothers' torts.

45. The test that May LJ applied was that applied in *Mersey Docks*. I do not consider that there is any justification for applying this stringent test when considering whether there is dual vicarious liability. Where two defendants are potentially vicariously liable for the act of a tortfeasor it is necessary to give independent consideration to the relationship of the tortfeasor with each defendant in order to decide whether that defendant is vicariously liable. In considering that question in relation to each defendant the approach of Rix LJ is to be preferred to that of May LJ.

 …

67. … it is of interest to note that 11 days after the English Court of Appeal held in *Viasystems* that it was possible in law to have dual vicarious liability for a single tortious act, McLachlin CJ,

giving the judgment of the Supreme Court, reached the same conclusion in *Blackwater v Plint* (2005) 258 DLR (4th) 275.
   [...]

75. In *Dubai Aluminium Co Ltd v Salaam* [2002] UKHL 48; [2003] 2 AC 366 the relevant issue was whether dishonest conduct by a solicitor could involve the firm in liability under section 10 of the Partnership Act 1890 as having been carried on "in the ordinary course of the business of the firm". Giving the leading speech Lord Nicholls held that it was necessary to apply the legal policy underlying vicarious liability, which he stated at para 21:

> "is based on the recognition that carrying on a business enterprise necessarily involves risks to others. It involves the risk that others will be harmed by wrongful acts committed by the agents through whom the business is carried on. When those risks ripen into loss, it is just that the business should be responsible for compensating the person who has been wronged."

This has strong echoes of the "enterprise risk" approach of the Canadian Supreme Court and, indeed, Lord Nicholls went on at para 23 to cite with approval from the judgment of McLachlin CJ in *Bazley*.

76. When considering the stage 2 test of "the ordinary course of employment" he suggested at para 23 that the wrongful conduct must be so closely connected with the acts the employee was authorised to do that the wrongful conduct might "fairly and properly be regarded" as done in the ordinary course of employment.
   ...

93. There was a very close connection between the brother teachers' employment in the school and the sexual abuse that they committed, or must for present purposes be assumed to have committed. There was no Criminal Records Bureau at the time, but the risk of sexual abuse was recognised, as demonstrated by the prohibition on touching the children in the chapter in the Rule dealing with chastity. No doubt the status of a brother was treated by the managers as an assurance that children could safely be entrusted to his care. The placement of brother teachers in St William's, a residential school in the precincts of which they also resided, greatly enhanced the risk of abuse by them if they had a propensity for such misconduct.

94. This is not a borderline case. It is one where it is fair, just and reasonable, by reason of the satisfaction of the relevant criteria, for the Institute to share with the Middlesbrough Defendants vicarious liability for the abuse committed by the brothers. I would allow this appeal.

Lady Hale, Lord Kerr, Lord Wilson and **Lord Carnwath** agreed.

NOTES AND QUESTIONS

1.   What should be the limits of what counts as 'the enterprise'? Should the Vatican City ultimately be liable for the actions of a Catholic school? See AA Berle, 'The Theory of Enterprise Entity' (1947) 47(3) *Columbia Law Review* 343.
2.   The US Fair Labor Standards Act 1938 §3(r) states the 'enterprise', which is jointly liable for federal the minimum wage, is any group of companies or entities that perform (i) 'related activities', (i) under 'unified operation or common control' and (iii) for a 'common business purpose'. See further *Dunlop v Ashy*, 555 F2d 1228 (5th Cir 1977) and *Brennan v Plaza Shoe Store, Inc*, 522 F2d 843 (8th Cir 1975).

3.   *Viasystems (Tyneside) Ltd v Thermal Transfer (Northern) Ltd* [2005] EWCA Civ 1151 held that two employers could be jointly liable for an accident caused by a subcontracted worker. Rejecting arguments against a person having two employers in principle, May LJ decided that control of employers, and therefore responsibility, could be equally shared. If control was unequal, joint liability would probably not be necessary.

4.   A finding of vicarious liability often protects a third party to an employment relationship who is injured by an employee, and who logically is not in a position to bargain for compensation. It often also protects the person who is injured, but if they are in a weak bargaining position, they are equally incapable of protecting themselves as a third-party tort victim. What do you think justifies vicarious liability for employees?

(b) Agency Work

What happens if an employer employs someone using the services of an employment agency? Following the principles set out by the Supreme Court in *Autoclenz* and *CCWS*, the logical answer is that the agency is the primary employer, because it is the closest party. The user will be jointly liable, unless it breaches an employment right (eg sexual harassment) in a way that suggests it should be primarily liable. The Court of Appeal cases on this point were inconsistent and unsatisfactory, although the Temporary and Agency Work Directive 2008, Article 2 had required courts to recognise 'temporary-work agencies as employers'. This seems to be confirmed by *Autoclenz* (in the EU jargon, a case of 'incidental vertical direct effect'). The remaining question is the circumstances under which a user would be regarded as the joint-employer.

Dacas v Brook Street Bureau (UK) Ltd [2004] EWCA Civ 217

Mrs Dacas claimed that she was unfairly dismissed from her job as a cleaner in a mental health hostel, held for four years, with Wandsworth London Borough Council (LBC) through an employment agency named Brook Street Ltd, under the Employment Rights Act 1996 section 94. Wandsworth LBC paid Brook Street Ltd, and Brook Street Ltd paid Mrs Dacas. Brook Street Ltd stated it was 'dissatisfied' with the way Mrs Dacas had queried her holiday pay. Subsequently, Wandsworth LBC informed Brook Street Ltd she was no longer wanted, for allegedly being rude to a visitor, and Brook Street declined to find her further work. Mrs Dacas brought a claim to Tribunal against both the agency and council, which both denied that she was an 'employee'. The Tribunal found she was not an employee of anyone. Mrs Dacas appealed, but dropped a claim against Wandsworth LBC, and pursued the claim solely against Brook Street Ltd. The Employment Appeal Tribunal held that Mrs Dacas was employed by Brook Street Ltd. Brook Street Ltd appealed. The majority of the Court of Appeal held that Mrs Dacas was not an employee of Brook Street Ltd because she was an employee of Wandsworth LBC.

Mummery LJ:

19. If the applicant has a contract of service in a triangular situation of this kind, it may be with (a) the end-user, the contract usually being an implied one, or (b) the employment agency,

depending on the construction of the express contract between the applicant and the agency and on other admissible evidence or, though this is more problematical, (c) more than one entity exercising the functions of an employer, namely the employment agency and the end-user jointly (see Freedland at pp. 42–43).

...

43. ... Mrs Dacas did not join the Council as a respondent to her appeal and it took no part in it. This was unfortunate. The result was that the focus of argument in the Employment Appeal Tribunal was understandably on the particular situation of Brook Street rather than on the whole of the complex triangular situation involving the Council, Mrs Dacas and Brook Street.

45. In those circumstances it was important that the Council should be given the opportunity to make submissions on the appeal. ... Regardless of the outcome of the appeal by Brook Street, it was not open to Mrs Dacas to contend on this appeal that the Council was liable to her in relation to any claim arising from the termination of the arrangements pursuant to which she worked as a cleaner. ...

...

58. The judgments of this court in *Montgomery v Johnson Underwood* [2001] IRLR 264 support Brook Street on this appeal. The court held that the applicant was not employed by the employment agency, which exercised no control over the work to be done by the applicant as a part time receptionist/ telephonist for the end-user. Applying the criteria laid down in *Ready Mixed Concrete* the court held that, in the absence of a framework of control, direction or supervision by the agency, there was no contract of service with it. As for the client of the employment agency, it was joined as a party to unfair dismissal proceedings in the Employment Tribunal, which held that the applicant was an employee of the agency and not of the end-user. In the Employment Appeal Tribunal, the end-user, as well as the agency, took part and the appeal was dismissed. The end-user took no part in the appeal to the Court of Appeal, which was only concerned with the issue whether the applicant was employed by the agency. The appeal by the agency was allowed. It was held that the applicant had no contract of service with the agency, as there was no mutuality of obligation between her and the agency and there was no control of her by the agency. The question of an implied contract of service between the applicant and the end-user did not arise for consideration in the Court of Appeal.

...

64. On Brook Street's appeal I would hold that the Employment Tribunal correctly concluded that the express contract between the employment agency and Mrs Dacas was not a contract of service. Brook Street was under no obligation to provide Mrs Dacas with work. She was under no obligation to accept any work offered by Brook Street to her. It did not exercise any relevant day to day control over her or her work at West Drive. That control was exercised by the Council, which supplied her clothing and materials and for whom she did the work. The fact that Brook Street agreed to do some things that an employer would normally do (payment) does not make it the employer. ... I would allow the appeal by Brook Street.

Sedley LJ:

71. The conclusion of the Employment Tribunal that Mrs Dacas was employed by nobody is simply not credible. There has to be something wrong with it. The EAT clearly thought so. Their conclusion that she was employed by the agency, Brook Street, is intelligible but still odd. In some degree it may reflect the fact that, for some reason which has not been explained to us, Wandsworth was not made a respondent to the appeal against the Employment Tribunal's decision. ...

72. It is important to bear in mind that a great deal more hangs on the legal status of a worker than the worker's own rights, though they are important enough. An employer is vicariously liable for injury to others caused by an employee's carelessness, and is required by statute to insure against it; but an enterprise will have no such liability for harm done by somebody working for it who is not an employee. Suppose for a moment that Mrs Dacas had injured a resident or a visitor in the course of her work by carelessly leaving cleaning materials in a dangerous place. She would have been in breach of her obligation to Brook Street under clause 4(d) of the temporary worker agreement, but that would have been of no value to the victim. Any competent solicitor to whom the victim went would have issued proceedings against Wandsworth on the footing that Wandsworth was vicariously liable as Mrs Dacas' employer; and if it were so held, the borough's compulsory insurance would cover the damages. If Wandsworth denied that Mrs Dacas was their employee it would be obliged to say whether it contended that she was employed by somebody else or by nobody. For the reasons explained by Lord Justice Mummery it is highly unlikely that it could succeed in either such contention. If the facts established at trial were those I have postulated, it is a near-certainty that the county court or the High Court would find Wandsworth vicariously liable for Mrs Dacas' negligence. ...

...

75. The argument for Wandsworth proceeds from the fact that it had no written agreement of any kind with Mrs Dacas to the submission that there was accordingly nothing into which any terms could be implied. This, however, misses the critical point that there are more means of expressing mutual intentions than putting them in writing. In the field of employment it is not uncommon to find that a contract of employment has come into being through the conduct of the parties without a word being put in writing or even, on occasion, spoken. In particular, conduct which might not have manifested such a mutual intention had it lasted only a brief time may become unequivocal if it is maintained over weeks or months. Once the intention to enter into an employment relationship is so expressed, the common law will imply a variety of terms into it and simultaneously will spell vicarious liability out of it; and statute will add a series of other rights and obligations.

76. It is correct that the written terms of the temporary worker agreement allowed Brook Street to move Mrs Dacas daily from job to job, or from a job to no job, and to send a different cleaner each day or week to the West Drive hostel. Had this or something like it happened, I accept readily that it would have been difficult, though not necessarily impossible to spell out of it any contract of employment between Wandsworth and Mrs Dacas. But it is not what happened; it was very possibly something that Wandsworth would not have wanted to happen; and the Employment Tribunal's task was to make a legally proper appraisal of what did happen. This they failed to do. As Lord Justice Mummery has demonstrated, their single paragraph of findings about Mrs Dacas' relationship with Wandsworth fails to identify, much less address, the determinative questions.

77. For my part, I would doubt whether, at least on the facts found by the tribunal, those questions were susceptible of more than one answer – namely that by the date of her dismissal she was an employee of the borough with a statutory right not to be unfairly dismissed. In saying this, I should make it clear that there is nothing special about the length of time for which, as it happens, Mrs Dacas had been working for Wandsworth. Until a year had gone by she had no protection in any case against unfair dismissal; but once arrangements like these had been in place for a year or more, I would have thought that the same inexorable inference would have arisen.

78. As Lord Justice Mummery has made clear, nothing we decide at this level can now fix Wandsworth with liability. But my principal reason for agreeing that Brook Street was not Mrs Dacas' employer is that, in my judgment, the evidence before the Employment Tribunal

pointed to the conclusion that Wandsworth was. Had Wandsworth remained a party it would have been necessary to remit the claim against it for a correctly approached decision on its liability, not least because the possibility that she had no employer defies common sense. The possibility mentioned by Lord Justice Mummery (paragraph 19) of a trilateral contract of service, meaning simply a contract in which one side's obligations are divided or shared between two of the three parties, would also remain for consideration.

Munby J (dissenting):

81. The case raises a point of fundamental importance not merely to large numbers of workers but also to the whole of an industry in which Brook Street is merely one, albeit a very prominent, player. Lord Justice Mummery's judgment (and even more so Lord Justice Sedley's judgment) seem to me to put in question the most basic assumptions upon which the whole of that industry has hitherto conducted its business. Therefore, whilst recognising that this is an area of law in relation to which my Lords have vastly greater knowledge and experience than I could ever possibly claim, I feel that I must explain why I have very serious misgivings about the course on which they would have us embark.

82. The approach of the industry is founded on assumptions that, reduced to their simplest form, can be summarised as follows:

i)   There can be no contract of employment – no contract of service – unless there is (a) mutuality of obligation as between the employer and the employee and (b) "control" of the employee by the employer.
ii)   There can be no mutuality of obligation in the absence of an obligation on the part of the employer to pay a wage or other remuneration.
iii) Therefore there can be no contract of service unless there is (a) an obligation on the part of the employer to remunerate the employee and (b) "control" of the employee by the employer.
iv)   It follows that if the obligation to remunerate the worker is imposed on one person whilst control of the worker is vested in another, there cannot be a contract of employment with either.

Hence the triangular arrangements that one finds in the present and many other similar cases. The obligation to remunerate the worker is imposed on the agency whilst control of the worker is vested in the end-user.
    …

101. Where, with all respect, I part company with my Lords is in relation to three matters. The first is the suggestion that the objective fact and degree of control over the work done by Mrs Dacas over the years is crucial. That, as it seems to me, somewhat overstates the position. …

102. The second is the suggestion that there is mutuality of obligation because the Council was under an obligation to pay for the work that Mrs Dacas did for it and she received payment in respect of such work from Brook Street. In this connection my Lord asks rhetorically, What was the Council paying for, if not for the work done by Mrs Dacas under its direction and for its benefit? The difficulty with this approach, as Mr Swift correctly pointed out, is that the Council had no obligation to pay Mrs Dacas, that Brook Street's obligation to pay her arose independently of whether or not Brook Street was paid by the Council, and that the Council did not set the rate of her pay. …

104. The final matter is the assumption that any very useful purpose is likely to be served by remitting a case such as this for rehearing by the Employment Tribunal. I rather doubt that it

will, for I find it very difficult to imagine that any Tribunal correctly directing itself in law could find that there is in these circumstances any contract, let alone a contract of service, between Mrs Dacas and the Council. I agree with the submission made on this point by Mr Foy QC. Such a finding is likely to be extremely rare, because there can only be an employment relationship if the end-user is responsible for the payment of remuneration to the worker, and in most cases – of deliberate purpose – it is the agency and not the end-user who undertakes to pay the worker.

NOTES AND QUESTIONS

1. The learned judges give three different reasons for the result: Mummery LJ says there was no 'mutuality of obligation' between Mrs Dacas and Brook Street Ltd, on the 'ongoing' definition, which is now discredited by *Autoclenz*. Sedley LJ appears to suggest Mrs Dacas is not an employee for the same reasons, but then says that there could be joint liability with the end-user, as Mummery LJ mooted at [19]. Munby J, dissenting on reasoning, posits the view that Mrs Dacas could indeed be an employee of nobody. On the reasoning in *Autoclenz*, do you agree that Mrs Dacas would have succeeded?

2. Note that unlike in paragraph 77, the qualifying period for unfair dismissal was raised to two years in 2012. See chapter 17.

3. Munby J suggests, presumably on the strength on submissions by counsel for Brook Street Ltd, that employment agencies were relying for their business model on the opinion that their staff did not get employment rights. If that were true (and it is doubtful) that users of agency workers could evade employment rights, do you agree that this creates an anti-competitive, and unjustified subsidy for the employment agency industry? See E McGaughey, 'Should Agency Workers Be Treated Differently?' (2010) LSE Legal Studies Working Paper No 7/2010.

4. *McMeechan v Secretary of State for Employment* [1996] EWCA Civ 1166 held that Mr McMeechan was an 'employee' of an agency, for the purpose of a claim to the National Insurance Fund for unpaid wages when the agency went insolvent. Giving judgment, Waite LJ left open whether Sutcliffe Catering, where Mr McMeechan worked, was also an employer. Waite LJ rejected that 'mutuality of obligation' (or any term excluding it) is relevant to whether someone is employed for a particular engagement or 'single stint' of work. Presumably the only further question (noted above at chapter 3(2)(c) and extracted in chapter 4) is whether between engagements, there is only a 'temporary cessation of work' or not: *Ford v Warwickshire CC* [1983] 2 AC 71. However this only affects the period of time for which someone is employed for the purpose of qualifying for rights (eg time off for childcare, job security), not their employment status. (But contrast *Montgomery v Johnson Underwood Ltd* [2001] EWCA Civ 318.)

5. In *Allonby v Accrington and Rossendale College* (2004) C-256/01 a part-time teacher claimed equal pay compared to a full-time employee of the College under the Part-time Work Directive, as implemented by the Part-time Work (Prevention of Less Favourable Treatment) Regulations 2000. The College argued that because Ms Allonby had been employed through an agency, Education Learning Services, she was not entitled to claim she was unequally paid: the employers were different. The CJEU held that the minimum requirements of the Directive

only mandated that Member State law grant a claim when discrimination was attributable to a 'single source'. It ascribed the agency as the employer, stating at [72]: 'The fact that no obligation is imposed on them to accept an assignment is of no consequence in that context.'

6.   Why would a contract have to be 'implied' between an employee and the employer that he or she works for through an agency? If I give you a pen and you give me a pound without saying anything, is our contract not still 'expressed' by our conduct?

Cable & Wireless plc v Muscat **[2006] EWCA Civ 220**

Mr Muscat claim he was unfairly dismissed from his job as a telecommunication specialist from before March 2001 to December 2002, under the Transfer of Undertakings (Protection of Employment) Regulations 1981. He was originally employed by Exodus Ltd. To make the company more attractive for a takeover bid, in October 2001 Mr Muscat and other staff were rehired under an arrangement where E-Nuff Ltd paid his wages, but otherwise his work remained identical. In April 2002, C&W plc took over Exodus Ltd. In August 2002, Mr Muscat was told his contract would be shifted again to an employment agency called Abraxas plc. The contract stated the contract would be 'one of independent Suppliers and nothing contained in this agreement shall be construed as constituting or establishing any partnership or joint venture or relationship of employee and employer between the parties'. Internal documents of C&W plc continued, however, to refer to Mr Muscat as an 'employee'. In December 2002, C&W plc dismissed him, but alleged that Abraxas plc rather than itself was the employer. The Tribunal held that Mr Muscat had an implied contract with C&W plc. In the Appeal Tribunal, Serota QC dismissed C&W plc's appeal. The Court of Appeal upheld that Mr Muscat was the employee of C&W plc.

Smith LJ (joined by **Sir Anthony Clarke MR** and **Maurice Kay LJ**):

41. ... In our view, it is right that, when considering the possible existence of an implied contract of employment, all the evidence should be considered. However, we cannot see why Mr Muscat's contract for services with Abraxas should preclude the existence of a contract of employment with C&W. C&W was not a party to the contract for services. Nor was it a signatory to the Works Schedule. There does not appear to be any essential inconsistency between Mr Muscat's position in promising Abraxas that he would undertake an assignment at the premises of C&W and an implied contract of employment with C&W when that assignment began. ...

42. Mr Reynold also contended that, when it came to considering whether there was any mutuality of obligation between C&W and Mr Muscat, one had to look at the terms of the written contract between Abraxas and Mr Muscat. Mummery LJ had said that the obligations spelled out in the contract between Mrs Dacas and Brook Street could be 'read across' so as to establish what Mrs Dacas's obligations were towards Wandsworth. If the written agreement between the agency and the worker was taken into account, it would negative the existence of a contract of employment between the worker and the end-user. We do not accept that. It may be possible to infer the existence of a contract of employment between the worker and the end-user from their conduct, although its precise terms might not be clear. If there is a contract between the worker and the agency, that must be examined to see whether it excludes

the possibility of there being a contract of employment between the worker and the end-user. That contract might also be useful as a means of determining what the precise terms are of the implied contract of employment between the worker and end-user. In the present case, it is possible to infer a contract of employment by examining the conduct of C&W and Mr Muscat. This is a particularly clear case because of the existence of a contract of employment between Mr Muscat and EIL and the transfer of that contract upon the transfer of undertakings. ...

43. Finally, Mr Reynold submitted that the ET had given no proper consideration to the question of whether it was necessary to imply a contract of employment between Mr Muscat and C&W in order to give business reality to what was happening. We were referred to the well-known passages in the judgment of Bingham LJ in *The Aramis* [1989] 1 Lloyd's Rep 213. The facts of that case are not germane but Bingham LJ made some general observations about the circumstances in which a contract might be implied. At page 224 column 1, he said:

> "As the question whether or not any such contract is to be implied is one of fact, its answer must depend upon the circumstances of each particular case – and the different sets of facts which arise for consideration in these cases are legion. However, I also agree that no such contract should be implied on the facts of any given case unless it is necessary to do so; necessary that is to say, in order to give business reality to a transaction and to create enforceable obligations between parties who are dealing with one another in circumstances in which one would expect that business reality and those enforceable obligations to exist."

Later, on the same page in column 2, he said that, in a case where there was no express agreement, the court considering whether a contract was to be implied must answer the question whether it would be reasonably understood from the conduct of the parties that there was an agreement between them. He continued:

> "I do not think it is enough for the party seeking the implication of a contract to obtain 'It might' as the answer to these questions for it would, in my view, be contrary to principle to countenance the implication of a contract from conduct if the conduct relied on is no more than consistent with an intention to contract than with an intention not to contract. It must surely be necessary to identify conduct referable to the contract contended for or at the very least, conduct inconsistent with there being no contract made between the parties to the effect contended for. Put another way, I think it must be fatal to the implication of a contract if the parties would or might have acted exactly as they did in the absence of a contract."

44. Mr Reynold submitted that, in giving guidance in *Dacas*, Mummery LJ had not mentioned the need for the ET to consider whether the implication of a contract of employment between worker and end-user was necessary to give business reality to what was happening between the parties. The ET had not expressly referred to this requirement in their decision and the EAT had accepted that they could not say whether or not the ET had given consideration to this issue. However, they observed that it may be that the Court of Appeal in Dacas had considered that in the particular circumstances of the case, it was necessary to imply a contract of employment because, to adopt the expression Mummery LJ had used at paragraph 53 of his judgment, that 'would accord with practical reality and common sense'.

45. We do not accept these submissions. In paragraph 16 of his judgment, Mummery LJ said:

> "Depending on the evidence in the case, a contract of service may be implied – that is, deduced – as a necessary inference from the conduct of the parties and from the circumstances surrounding the parties and the work done."

We take that to be an express appreciation of the principles referred to in *The Aramis*. Moreover, in the decision of the ET in the present case, there is a reference to "the most relevant and helpful passages" in the decision of the Court of Appeal in *Dacas*. The first paragraph there listed is paragraph 16 in the judgment of Mummery LJ which includes the passage just cited. Thus, quite apart from the inherent unlikelihood of Mummery LJ not having considered the basic contractual principles, we are satisfied that he actually referred to the criterion of necessity and, by express incorporation, so did the ET in the present case.

...

48. We accept that the question whether it is necessary to infer the existence of an employment contract between two parties may sometimes be difficult. In this particular case, we do not think it is. It is common ground that, from April until 13th August 2002, Mr Muscat was employed by C&W. True it is that C&W did not think he was their employee but what the parties may think or say about their relationship is not conclusive. The issue must be determined objectively. The ET held that, for that period, the relationship was that of employer and employee. The employment had been transferred from EIL and, until the terms were varied, they would remain as they were with EIL. That meant that C&W were under an obligation to provide Mr Muscat with work. Mr Muscat was under an obligation to attend their premises and do the work of a telecommunications specialist, subject to the direction and control of C&W management. There were other indicia which tended to confirm that the relationship was indeed that of employer/employee. Mr Muscat arranged his annual leave with his C&W managers. C&W provided equipment and paid Mr Muscat's mobile telephone bill. They gave him an employee number. There can be no doubt that, before Mr Muscat signed the agreement with Abraxas, C&W were under an obligation to pay Mr Muscat. They defaulted on that obligation for about three months. Then they made arrangements with Abraxas that Abraxas would pay Mr Muscat's invoices and, on 13th August, Mr Muscat signed a contract with Abraxas.

...

51. Applying the words of the test established in *The Aramis*, it was necessary to infer the continuing existence of the employment contract in order to give business reality to the relationship and arrangements between Mr Muscat and C&W. There was no other possible explanation for what they were doing. Also, it was necessary to infer the existence of an employment contract in order to establish the enforceable obligations that one would expect to see in these circumstances. Before 13th August, there were enforceable obligations between Mr Muscat and C&W. After that, it cannot be said that those obligations had disappeared. Abraxas had not affected them. If Abraxas had for some reason ceased to function, that would not have brought the relationship between C&W and Mr Muscat to an end. Their mutual obligations to each other would have continued and C&W would either have had to pay Mr Muscat itself or make some other arrangement for payment. We reject Mr Reynold's final submission.

...

53. We add this. In the course of argument there was a suggestion that, if the court were to uphold the ET's decision, it would be doing so from a desire to change the established law by 'judicial creativity'. That should not be done; if the law needed to changed, as a matter of policy, it should be done by Parliament. We wish to make it plain that this decision is not driven by policy considerations. The decision of the ET was correct, according to the established law.

1. The Court of Appeal held that Mr Muscat was an employee of C&W plc, because it was 'necessary to give business reality to the relationship'. Do you agree that the reality is that agency staff are always employees of the end-users where they work, and an employment agency is, in a natural and legal sense, the employer's 'agent'?

2. The Court of Appeal and Mr Reynold QC, counsel for C&W plc, referred to *The Aramis*, for the test of finding an 'implied contract'. But in fact, in *Equitable Life Assurance Society v Hyman* [2000] UKHL 39 the test for implied terms (and therefore 'implied' contracts) was changed to ask what is necessary to reflect the 'reasonable expectations of the parties'. This draws attention to the non-contractual expectations people have at work, and the social expectation that everyone, unless genuinely self-employed, has to labour rights. Arguably, the Court of Appeal interpreted the (outdated) test in line with the actual law. But now, *Gisda Cyf v Barratt* [2010] UKSC 41 supersedes both, by clarifying that construction of contracts, when it relates to statutory rights, is to be 'segregated intellectually' from the commercial context: the purpose is to protect the weaker party.

3. In *James v Greenwich LBC* [2008] EWCA Civ 35, Mummery LJ, giving judgment in the Court of Appeal came to the conclusion that Mrs James, who had worked through Brook Street Ltd for Greenwich LBC for a number of years had no employer and so could not bring an unfair dismissal claim. He took the view there was no 'mutuality of obligation' with the agency, and no contract could be 'implied' with the end-user. He remarked that if it seemed unfortunate that this (according to him) was the law, Parliament should act.

4. In the event, Parliament did act by bringing an Act to regulate agency work to a Second Reading. The Prime Minister's office, however, then persuaded backbenchers supporting the Bill to allow the stalled draft of the Temporary and Agency Work Directive to proceed. This places primary responsibility for employment rights on an agency, although leaves open the extent of liability of an end-user.

5. It is submitted that the agency is always primarily liable for all employment rights and for vicarious liability, but that an action may be brought against the end-user jointly. The end-user will be able to seek contribution from the agency, as established in *Harrods v Remmick* [1998] ICR 156.

6. Before *Autoclenz* there was a series of decisions holding precarious workers to be outside the scope of employment protection of all kinds based on very flimsy reasoning, and usually connected to mutuality of obligation. These include *Consistent Group v Kalwak* [2008] EWCA Civ 430 (expressly rejected in *Autoclenz*), *Alstom Transport v Tilson* [2010] EWCA Civ 1308 (finding an agency employee to have no rights), *Muschett v H M Prison Service* [2010] EWCA Civ 25 (denying an agency worker for a prison a discrimination claim). These were plainly wrong at the time, and should have been eliminated by the principles laid down in *Autoclenz*.

7. There continued, however, to be a disturbing lack of clarity in the case law on agency workers. In *Smith v Carillion (JM) Ltd* [2015] EWCA Civ 209, Elias LJ again applied the outdated 'necessity' test, without reference to the authorities that were binding upon him regarding 'reasonable expectations' from either *Hyman* or

Gisda Cyf v Barratt. He found that a construction worker was not employed by an end-user, and so not protected against blacklisting, as detriment, under TULRCA 1992 s 146. Elias LJ declined to interpret the law so as to be compatible with international labour rights. This appears to be less to do with careful legal acknowledgement of binding precedent, and more to do with a natural human bias that people, including judges, have for the status quo (in this case, a judge's decisions on an issue for many years). See D Kahneman, JL Knetsch and RH Thaler, 'Anomalies: The Endowment Effect, Loss Aversion, and Status Quo Bias' (1991) 5(1) *Journal of Economic Perspectives* 193, 199.

(c) Corporate Groups

Chandler v Cape plc [2011] EWCA Civ 525

David Chandler claimed damages against Cape plc for personal injury, due to asbestosis, contracted between 1959 and 1962 as he worked for a subsidiary, Cape Building Products Ltd. Cape Building Products Ltd had gone insolvent, and had had no insurance policy. Asbestosis is a disease caused by small asbestos fibres lodging in the lungs, but potentially with an 'incubation' period of decades. After discovering his condition in 2007, Mr Chandler claimed that Cape plc should be jointly and severally liable with the subsidiary. The High Court found that Cape plc was liable on the ground that it exercised control over the subsidiary. The Court of Appeal upheld the decision, based on the finding that the parent had interfered in the subsidiary's affairs.

Arden LJ:

8. Cape acquired at least a majority of the share capital of Cape Products in 1945, and the outstanding shares in about 1953. Cape installed the necessary plant into the empty factory. A manager was appointed "to manage this plant as a branch of Cape" (see The Cape Asbestos Story produced by Cape Asbestos, 1953, page 71). Production of Asbestolux, a new form of non-combustible asbestos board, started. "In a short time, [Cape Products] was an invaluable feature in Cape's economy" (op. cit. page 72). However, it is noteworthy that at no relevant point in time did Cape cease to be an operating company itself or merely hold the shares in its subsidiaries as if it were an investment holding company.

...

40. Although it appears that there is no reported case of a direct duty of care on the part of a parent company, Mr Weir cites the passage from the speech of Lord Bingham in *Lubbe v Cape Plc* [2000] 1 WLR 1545. That case concerned the question whether proceedings, which had been brought by former employees of a former South African subsidiary of Cape in England and Wales, should be stayed on the grounds that the proper forum was South Africa. The House did not therefore have to consider the basis of which such an action might succeed. However, at page 1555 Lord Bingham expressly contemplated that it might involve as in this case a detailed examination of the relationship between the parties based on the surviving documentary material. ...

...

62. The basis on which the judge found there was a duty of care on the part of Cape is on the basis of an assumption of responsibility. This falls within the second and third parts of

the three-part Caparo test for determining whether there is a duty of care, namely proximity and the further requirement that it be fair, just and reasonable to impose liability. These two requirements are directed to the essentially same question. As Lord Oliver pointed out in *Caparo*:

> "'Proximity' is, no doubt a convenient expression so long as it is realised that it is no more than a label which embraces not a definable concept but merely a description of circumstances in which, pragmatically, the courts conclude that a duty of care exists." (page 633)

63. The development of the law of negligence has to be incremental and the judge was in my judgment correct to hold that the analogous line of cases in negligence to the instant case is the line of authority on the duty of a person to intervene to prevent damage to another. As Lord Goff pointed out in *Smith v Littlewoods Ltd* [1987] AC 241 at 270, there is in general no duty to prevent third parties causing damage to another. But Lord Goff recognised that there were exceptions to this principle, for example where there was "a relationship between the parties which gives rise to an imposition or assumption of responsibility" on the part of the defendant (page 272D).

64. Lord Goff speaks of the imposition or assumption of responsibility. Whether a party has assumed responsibility is a question of law. The court does not have to find that the relevant party has voluntarily assumed responsibility (see also on this point *Customs and Excise Commissioners v Barclays Bank* [2007] 1 AC 181, cited by Mr Weir). The word "assumption" is therefore something of a misnomer. The phrase "attachment" of responsibility might be more accurate.

65. Responsibility was imposed in *Dorset Yacht Co Ltd v Home Office* [1970] AC 1004, where the Home Office was held liable for damage done by escaping Borstal boys over whom the Home Office had had control. Its control over them gave rise to a special relationship in law between the plaintiffs and the Home Office. An assumption of a duty of care has also been found to exist as between an independent contractor and employees of the employer: see, for example, *Gray v Fire Alarm Fabrication Services Ltd* [2007] ICR 247; *Clay v AJ Crump Ltd* [1964] 1 QB 533.

66. Likewise, it has been held on two occasions that it is arguable that a parent company may owe a duty of care to employees of subsidiaries: see *Connelly v Rio Tino Zinc Corporation* and *Ngcobo v Thor Chemicals Holdings Ltd*, January 1996, per Maurice Kay J, unreported. There is nothing in either judgment or the general law to support the submission advanced by Mr Stuart-Smith that the duty of care can only exist in these cases if the parent company has absolute control of the subsidiary. Moreover, if a parent company has responsibility towards the employees of a subsidiary there may not be an exact correlation between the responsibilities of the two companies. The parent company is not likely to accept responsibility towards its subsidiary's employees in all respects but only for example in relation to what might be called high level advice or strategy.

   ...

69. I would emphatically reject any suggestion that this court is in any way concerned with what is usually referred to as piercing the corporate veil. A subsidiary and its company are separate entities. There is no imposition or assumption of responsibility by reason only that a company is the parent company of another company.

70. The question is simply whether what the parent company did amounted to taking on a direct duty to the subsidiary's employees.

   ...

78. Given Cape's state of knowledge about the Cowley Works, and its superior knowledge about the nature and management of asbestos risks, I have no doubt that in this case it is appropriate to find that Cape assumed a duty of care either to advise Cape Products on what steps it had to take in the light of knowledge then available to provide those employees with a safe system of work or to ensure that those steps were taken. The scope of the duty can be defined in either way. Whichever way it is formulated, the injury to Mr Chandler was the result. As the judge held, working on past performance and viewing the matter realistically, Cape could, and did on other matters, give Cape Products instructions as to how it was to operate with which, so far as we know, it duly complied.

79. In these circumstances, there was, in my judgment, a direct duty of care owed by Cape to the employees of Cape Products. There was an omission to advise on precautionary measures even though it was doing research and that research had not established (nor could it establish) that the asbestosis and related diseases were not caused by asbestos dust. Moreover, while I have reached my conclusion in my own words and following my own route, it turns out that, in all essential respects, my reasoning follows the analysis of the judge in paragraphs 61 and 72 to 75 of his judgment.

80. In summary, this case demonstrates that in appropriate circumstances the law may impose on a parent company responsibility for the health and safety of its subsidiary's employees. Those circumstances include a situation where, as in the present case, (1) the businesses of the parent and subsidiary are in a relevant respect the same; (2) the parent has, or ought to have, superior knowledge on some relevant aspect of health and safety in the particular industry; (3) the subsidiary's system of work is unsafe as the parent company knew, or ought to have known; and (4) the parent knew or ought to have foreseen that the subsidiary or its employees would rely on its using that superior knowledge for the employees' protection. For the purposes of (4) it is not necessary to show that the parent is in the practice of intervening in the health and safety policies of the subsidiary. The court will look at the relationship between the companies more widely. The court may find that element (4) is established where the evidence shows that the parent has a practice of intervening in the trading operations of the subsidiary, for example production and funding issues.

Moses LJ and **McFarlane LJ** agreed.

NOTES AND QUESTIONS

1. In the High Court, Wynn-William J had applied Lord Goff's dictum in *Smith v Littlewoods Organisation Ltd* [1987] UKHL 18 to say that a parent company which exercised control over a subsidiary would be liable for its actions. By contrast, Arden LJ favoured a test that could be interpreted even more radically: a parent that interferes in its subsidiary's affairs in any way will be 'attached' with responsibility for all its affairs. According to the leading company law treatise, PL Davies and S Worthington, *Gower and Davies Principles of Modern Company Law* (2012) 218, the Court of Appeal decision is still best interpreted as resting upon the ability to control.

2. Under either approach, is control or interference just as achievable through contract, as it is through share ownership? Suppose a corporation outsources production through a supply chain, whose tasks they dominate, and that outsourced entity further outsources to another entity, either within the UK or EU or globally. Should the end-user be liable for what those down the supply chain do?

This meets problems raised in the topic of conflicts of laws. See chapter 4(3) and E McGaughey, '*Donoghue v Salmon* in the High Court' [2011] *Journal of Personal Injury Law* 249.

3. In the US, *Davis v Alexander*, 269 US 114 (1925) Brandeis J held that, among railways companies, if one 'company actually controls another and operates both as a single system, the dominant company will be liable for injuries due to the negligence of the subsidiary company'. Thus ability to control, and its actual exercise, are not alternatives but complementary tests.

4. A differently constituted Court of Appeal in *Thompson v Renwick Group Ltd* [2014] EWCA Civ 635 found that a parent company was not liable for injuries caused by a subsidiary. Tomlinson LJ held that the parent was no more than a 'holding company', which had shares but did not operate together, and that it had 'superior knowledge or expertise' to 'protect its employees from risk of injury'. Why is this relevant?

5. What if an employee is injured in another country, but works for an employing entity whose parent company is headquartered in the UK? See chapter 4(3)(b).

6. Could a private equity firm be liable for the employment rights of a company that goes insolvent? This increasingly interesting question is answered affirmatively by J Prassl, *The Concept of the Employer* (2015) chs 2 and 3. Prassl contends that private-equity firms exercise all the functions of a typical employer. In the long run, do you think private-equity consortia would be more or less profitable if they could not avoid employment rights in the firms where they invested?

7. TULRCA 1992 s 224 makes it unlawful for a trade union to take collective action against a party that is not an 'employer'. In *Dimbleby & Sons Ltd v NUJ* [1983] 1 WLR 427 the House of Lords held that there could be situations where another company is treated as having the same identity. Presumably, construing a parent company as an employer of a subsidiary's employee would be necessary so that the right to strike is effective against the ultimate decision-makers in a 'trade dispute'.

(4) ENFORCEMENT BODIES

Although the scope of labour law is important in theory, it matters little that someone is arguably an 'employee' or a 'worker' in law, and has a claim against multiple entities, if those rights are not enforced. There are three main alternatives: individual claims in court, enforcement by government bodies, and trade unions. Each type of body has strengths and weaknesses. The efficacy of modern labour law rests on all of them.

First, individual claims in court are fundamental to the rule of law. Individual access to justice avoids problems of organising collective action. No individual may need to wait for official permission before instigating a claim, and should be guaranteed a fair and impartial hearing. Practically, however, litigation is time consuming and daunting. Most people have not been educated in court procedures, or how the law works, and even if they invest the time, the expense and time involved to become informed, the process may still be frightening. Many may choose not to pursue claims because they fear reputational damage or wasted time, and believe they should move on. In addition, from 2013 to 2017, the government imposed around £1200 in Employment Tribunal fees for bringing each claim. This barrier was removed by the Supreme Court.

R (UNISON) v Lord Chancellor [2017] UKSC 51

UNISON, the union, claimed that fees for Employment Tribunals were ultra vires. The UK government introduced £1200 fees to bring a typical case to an Employment Tribunal through the Employment Tribunals and the Employment Appeal Tribunal Fees Order 2013 (SI 2013/1893). The Lord Chancellor purported to exercise this power, to 'prescribe fees', under section 42(1) of the Tribunals, Courts and Enforcement Act 2007. That power does not come with express limitations, but UNISON claimed that the Order was ultra vires. The effect of the 2013 Order as it stood was to undermine access to justice and the rule of law. The Supreme Court agreed, and struck down the Order.

Lord Reed (with whom **Lord Neuberger**, **Lord Mance**, **Lord Kerr**, **Lord Wilson** and **Lord Hughes** agree):

The constitutional right of access to the courts

66. The constitutional right of access to the courts is inherent in the rule of law. The importance of the rule of law is not always understood. Indications of a lack of understanding include the assumption that the administration of justice is merely a public service like any other, that courts and tribunals are providers of services to the "users" who appear before them, and that the provision of those services is of value only to the users themselves and to those who are remunerated for their participation in the proceedings. The extent to which that viewpoint has gained currency in recent times is apparent from the consultation papers and reports discussed earlier. It is epitomised in the assumption that the consumption of ET and EAT services without full cost recovery results in a loss to society, since "ET and EAT use does not lead to gains to society that exceed the sum of the gains to consumers and producers of these services".

67. It may be helpful to begin by explaining briefly the importance of the rule of law, and the role of access to the courts in maintaining the rule of law. It may also be helpful to explain why the idea that bringing a claim before a court or a tribunal is a purely private activity, and the related idea that such claims provide no broader social benefit, are demonstrably untenable.

68. At the heart of the concept of the rule of law is the idea that society is governed by law. Parliament exists primarily in order to make laws for society in this country. Democratic procedures exist primarily in order to ensure that the Parliament which makes those laws includes Members of Parliament who are chosen by the people of this country and are accountable to them. Courts exist in order to ensure that the laws made by Parliament, and the common law created by the courts themselves, are applied and enforced. That role includes ensuring that the executive branch of government carries out its functions in accordance with the law. In order for the courts to perform that role, people must in principle have unimpeded access to them. Without such access, laws are liable to become a dead letter, the work done by Parliament may be rendered nugatory, and the democratic election of Members of Parliament may become a meaningless charade. That is why the courts do not merely provide a public service like any other.

69. Access to the courts is not, therefore, of value only to the particular individuals involved. That is most obviously true of cases which establish principles of general importance. ... For example, the case of *Dumfries and Galloway Council v North* [2013] UKSC 45 ... concerned

with the comparability for equal pay purposes of classroom assistants and nursery nurses with male manual workers such as road workers and refuse collectors, had implications well beyond the particular claimants and the respondent local authority. The case also illustrates the fact that it is not always desirable that claims should be settled: it resolved a point of genuine uncertainty as to the interpretation of the legislation governing equal pay, which was of general importance, and on which an authoritative ruling was required.

   ...

71. But the value to society of the right of access to the courts is not confined to cases in which the courts decide questions of general importance. People and businesses need to know, on the one hand, that they will be able to enforce their rights if they have to do so, and, on the other hand, that if they fail to meet their obligations, there is likely to be a remedy against them. It is that knowledge which underpins everyday economic and social relations. That is so, notwithstanding that judicial enforcement of the law is not usually necessary, and notwithstanding that the resolution of disputes by other methods is often desirable.

72. When Parliament passes laws creating employment rights, for example, it does so not merely in order to confer benefits on individual employees, but because it has decided that it is in the public interest that those rights should be given effect. It does not envisage that every case of a breach of those rights will result in a claim before an ET. But the possibility of claims being brought by employees whose rights are infringed must exist, if employment relationships are to be based on respect for those rights. Equally, although it is often desirable that claims arising out of alleged breaches of employment rights should be resolved by negotiation or mediation, those procedures can only work fairly and properly if they are backed up by the knowledge on both sides that a fair and just system of adjudication will be available if they fail. Otherwise, the party in the stronger bargaining position will always prevail. It is thus the claims which are brought before an ET which enable legislation to have the deterrent and other effects which Parliament intended, provide authoritative guidance as to its meaning and application, and underpin alternative methods of dispute resolution.

73. A Lord Chancellor of a previous generation put the point in a nutshell, in a letter to the Treasury:

   "(i)   Justice in this country is something in which all the Queen's subjects have an interest, whether it be criminal or civil.
   (ii)   The courts are for the benefit of all, whether the individual resorts to them or not.
   (iii) In the case of the civil courts the citizen benefits from the interpretation of the law by the Judges and from the resolution of disputes, whether between the state and the individual or between individuals."

(Genn, *Judging Civil Justice* (2010), p 46, quoting a letter written by Lord Gardiner in 1965)

74. In English law, the right of access to the courts has long been recognised. The central idea is expressed in chapter 40 of the Magna Carta of 1215 ("Nulli vendemus, nulli negabimus aut differemus rectum aut justiciam"), which remains on the statute book in the closing words of chapter 29 of the version issued by Edward I in 1297:

   "We will sell to no man, we will not deny or defer to any man either Justice or Right."

Those words are not a prohibition on the charging of court fees, but they are a guarantee of access to courts which administer justice promptly and fairly.

   ...

80. Even where a statutory power authorises an intrusion upon the right of access to the courts, it is interpreted as authorising only such a degree of intrusion as is reasonably necessary to fulfil the objective of the provision in question. This principle was developed in a series of cases concerned with prisoners. The first was *R v Secretary of State for the Home Department, Ex p Leech* [1994] QB 198, which concerned a prison rule under which letters between a prisoner and a solicitor could be read, and stopped if they were of inordinate length or otherwise objectionable. The rule did not apply where the letter related to proceedings already commenced, but the Court of Appeal accepted that it nevertheless created an impediment to the exercise of the right of access to justice in so far as it applied to prisoners who were seeking legal advice in connection with possible future proceedings. The question was whether the rule was authorised by a statutory power to make rules for the regulation of prisons. That depended on whether an objective need for such a rule, in the interests of the regulation of prisons, could be demonstrated. As Steyn LJ, giving the judgment of the court, stated at p 212:

"The question is whether there is a self-evident and pressing need for an unrestricted power to read letters between a prisoner and a solicitor and a power to stop such letters on the ground of prolixity and objectionability."

The evidence established merely a need to check that the correspondence was *bona fide* legal correspondence. Steyn LJ concluded:

"By way of summary, we accept that [the statutory provision] by necessary implication authorises some screening of correspondence passing between a prisoner and a solicitor. The authorised intrusion must, however, be the minimum necessary to ensure that the correspondence is in truth bona fide legal correspondence." (p 217)

...

82. A similar approach was adopted in *R (Daly) v Secretary of State for the Home Department* [2001] UKHL 26 ... which concerned a policy that prisoners must be absent from their cells when legal correspondence kept there was examined. Lord Bingham of Cornhill, with whose speech the other members of the House agreed, summarised the effect of the earlier authorities concerning prisoners, including ... *Ex p Leech*:

"Among the rights which, in part at least, survive [imprisonment] are three important rights, closely related but free standing, each of them calling for appropriate legal protection: the right of access to a court; the right of access to legal advice; and the right to communicate confidentially with a legal adviser under the seal of legal professional privilege. Such rights may be curtailed only by clear and express words, and then only to the extent reasonably necessary to meet the ends which justify the curtailment." (pp 537–538)

After an examination of the evidence, Lord Bingham concluded that "the policy provides for a degree of intrusion into the privileged legal correspondence of prisoners which is greater than is justified by the objectives the policy is intended to serve, and so violates the common law rights of prisoners" (para 21). Since that degree of intrusion was not expressly authorised by the relevant statutory provision, it followed that the Secretary of State had no power to lay down the policy.

...

The right of access to justice in the present case

86. The 2007 Act does not state the purposes for which the power conferred by section 42(1) to prescribe fees may be exercised. There is however no dispute that the purposes which underlay

the making of the Fees Order are legitimate. Fees paid by litigants can, in principle, reasonably be considered to be a justifiable way of making resources available for the justice system and so securing access to justice. Measures that deter the bringing of frivolous and vexatious cases can also increase the efficiency of the justice system and overall access to justice.

87. The Lord Chancellor cannot, however, lawfully impose whatever fees he chooses in order to achieve those purposes. It follows from the authorities cited that the Fees Order will be ultra vires if there is a real risk that persons will effectively be prevented from having access to justice. That will be so because section 42 of the 2007 Act contains no words authorising the prevention of access to the relevant tribunals. That is indeed accepted by the Lord Chancellor.

88. But a situation in which some persons are effectively prevented from having access to justice is not the only situation in which the Fees Order might be regarded as ultra vires. As appears from such cases as *Leech* and *Daly*, even where primary legislation authorises the imposition of an intrusion on the right of access to justice, it is presumed to be subject to an implied limitation. As it was put by Lord Bingham in *Daly*, the degree of intrusion must not be greater than is justified by the objectives which the measure is intended to serve.

   ...

91. In order for the fees to be lawful, they have to be set at a level that everyone can afford, taking into account the availability of full or partial remission. The evidence now before the court, considered realistically and as a whole, leads to the conclusion that that requirement is not met. In the first place, as the Review Report concludes, "it is clear that there has been a sharp, substantial and sustained fall in the volume of case receipts as a result of the introduction of fees". While the Review Report fairly states that there is no conclusive evidence that the fees have prevented people from bringing claims, the court does not require conclusive evidence: as the Hillingdon case indicates, it is sufficient in this context if a real risk is demonstrated. The fall in the number of claims has in any event been so sharp, so substantial, and so sustained as to warrant the conclusion that a significant number of people who would otherwise have brought claims have found the fees to be unaffordable.

   ...

96. Furthermore, it is not only where fees are unaffordable that they can prevent access to justice. They can equally have that effect if they render it futile or irrational to bring a claim. As explained earlier, many claims which can be brought in ETs do not seek any financial award: for example, claims to enforce the right to regular work breaks or to written particulars of employment. Many claims which do seek a financial award are for modest amounts, as explained earlier. If, for example, fees of £390 have to be paid in order to pursue a claim worth £500 (such as the median award in claims for unlawful deductions from wages), no sensible person will pursue the claim unless he can be virtually certain that he will succeed in his claim, that the award will include the reimbursement of the fees, and that the award will be satisfied in full. If those conditions are not met, the fee will in reality prevent the claim from being pursued, whether or not it can be afforded. In practice, however, success can rarely be guaranteed. In addition, on the evidence before the court, only half of the claimants who succeed in obtaining an award receive payment in full, and around a third of them receive nothing at all.

   ...

Can the Fees Order be justified as a necessary intrusion on the right of access to justice?

99. The primary aim of the Fees Order was to transfer some of the cost burden of the ET and EAT system from general taxpayers to users of the system. That objective has been achieved to some extent, but it does not follow that fees which intruded to a lesser extent upon the

right of access to justice would have been any less effective. In that regard, it is necessary to point out an error in the Review Report, repeated in the Lord Chancellor's submissions. The Review Report states that the Ministry of Justice have considered whether it would be more proportionate to charge lower fees, but that "the result of reducing fees would reduce the income generated by fees, and thereby reduce the proportion of cost transferred to users from the taxpayer" (para 307). That statement is unsupported by any evidence, and appears to be regarded as axiomatic. Similarly, in his written case, the Lord Chancellor states that, in pursuing the aim of transferring the costs of the tribunals from taxpayers to users, "the higher the fees are, patently the more effective they are in doing so". This idea is repeated: in recovering the cost from users, it is said, "the higher the fee, the more effective it is".

100. However, it is elementary economics, and plain common sense, that the revenue derived from the supply of services is not maximised by maximising the price. In order to obtain the maximum revenue, it is necessary to identify the optimal price, which depends on the price elasticity of demand. In the present case, it is clear that the fees were not set at the optimal price: the price elasticity of demand was greatly underestimated. It has not been shown that less onerous fees, or a more generous system of remission, would have been any less effective in meeting the objective of transferring the cost burden to users.

101. Nor, on the evidence before the court, have fees at the level set in the Fees Order been shown to be necessary in order to achieve its secondary aims: namely, to incentivise earlier settlements and to disincentivise the pursuit of weak or vexatious claims.

   …

105. The Court of Appeal identified 24 of the rights enforceable in ETs as having their source in EU law. They include, for example, the right to equal pay, the rights to equal treatment and maternity leave, and the various rights granted under the Working Time Directive. Subject to the exceptions discussed earlier, the ET is the only forum in which those rights can be enforced. It follows that, so far as applicable to these rights, restrictions on the right of access to ETs and the EAT fall within the scope of EU law.

106. EU law has long recognised the principle of effectiveness: that is to say, that the procedural requirements for domestic actions must not be "liable to render practically impossible or excessively difficult" the exercise of rights conferred by EU law: see, for example, *Impact v Minister for Agriculture and Food* (Case C-268/06) [2008] ECR I-2483, para 46. It has also recognised the principle of effective judicial protection as a general principle of EU law, stemming from the constitutional traditions common to the member states, which has been enshrined in articles 6 and 13 of the European Convention on Human Rights and which has also been reaffirmed by article 47 of the Charter of Fundamental Rights of the European Union.

   …

117. Given the conclusion that the fees imposed by the Fees Order are in practice unaffordable by some people, and that they are so high as in practice to prevent even people who can afford them from pursuing claims for small amounts and non-monetary claims, it follows that the Fees Order imposes limitations on the exercise of EU rights which are disproportionate, and that it is therefore unlawful under EU law.

Lady Hale:

121. … as the existing Fees Order is unlawful, the Lord Chancellor will no doubt wish to avoid any potentially unlawful discrimination in any replacement Order.

   …

124. It is not suggested that the Fees Order is directly discriminatory on any of the grounds prohibited either under the Charter or the 2010 Act. Rather, it is suggested that the Order is indirectly discriminatory within the meaning of section 19 of the 2010 Act, which is itself based on the concept of indirect discrimination in EU law. ...

125. ... it is suggested that the higher fees payable, either for Type B claims in general or for discrimination claims in particular, are indirectly discriminatory against women (and others with protected characteristics too). In relation to Type B claims in general, this is because a higher proportion of women bring Type B claims than bring Type A claims. Before the Court of Appeal, UNISON suggested that 54% of Type B claimants were women, whereas only 37% of Type A claimants were women. However, the Lord Chancellor put in figures suggesting that 45% of Type B claimants were women. The Court of Appeal accepted that this was still a disparate impact (para 85). This meant that the higher fees for Type B claims might put women at a particular disadvantage when compared with men. Both the Court of Appeal and the Divisional Court therefore proceeded on the basis that "the situation" had to be justified and this has not been challenged by the Lord Chancellor.

126. Under section 19(2)(d), a PCP which puts or would put people with a protected characteristic at a particular disadvantage when compared with people who do not share that characteristic is not discriminatory if the person who applies it can show that the PCP is a proportionate means of achieving a legitimate aim. In other words, unlike the case of direct discrimination, it is the PCP itself which requires to be justified, rather than its discriminatory effect. So can the higher fees for Type B claims be justified?

127. Given that we have already held that the whole Fees Order cannot be justified, this is a somewhat artificial exercise. ...

   ...

134. ... If the fee charged for unfair dismissal claims had been lower than the fee charged for discrimination claims, then it might well have been necessary (and very difficult) to demonstrate that the higher fee for discrimination claims was a proportionate means of achieving a legitimate aim. But that is not this case. And in any event, it is accepted that the higher fees generally have a disparate impact and in my view it has not been shown that they are justified.

NOTES AND QUESTIONS

1. The Supreme Court held that the rule of law was compromised by the 2013 Order, and was therefore ultra vires. It rejects that access to courts is like any other public service, where people seeking justice are mere 'users' of the service. Lord Reed says without the rule of law, which includes the enforcement, 'democratic election of Members of Parliament may become a meaningless charade' [68]. Lady Hale spells out that fees can have a disproportionate impact on some groups, and therefore may also be unlawful because they indirectly discriminate against people of certain protected characteristics (see chapter 13).

2. Many people bringing employment cases do not have legal representation. One possibility is to ask a workplace trade union to provide representation. Another option is to go to Citizens Advice, or another agency, and request to be referred for representation to another organisation, such as the Free Representation Unit (FRU). Volunteers at the FRU (http://www.thefru.org.uk/) can be anyone from law students who have not yet qualified, to established barristers or solicitors (some times even professors) who take cases on a pro-bono basis. To join the

FRU, a volunteer must complete a short training day and a test, attend an office induction, and then simply pick up a case file. When a volunteer finds a case file that they feel competent to take, they will have discuss the arguments with the FRU manager, and then phone the client to offer their services. A hearing date will already have been set, and so the volunteer must simply prepare their case and appear at Tribunal. Since Tribunal fees have been abolished, the number of claims and demand for volunteer representation is likely to rise.

3.   To file an Employment Tribunal claim, a claimant must notify the Advisory, Conciliation and Arbitration Service (ACAS) about the claim. This is to attempt to reach 'early conciliation' and a settlement. If the employer refuses to cooperate, or offer compensation to which a claimant is legally entitled, the claimant should and fill out an 'ET1' form within 3 months of the event giving rise to the claim. This is usually the effective date of a dismissal. The ET1 form has fields for personal details, the ACAS certificate, and a short description of the claims being made. This is submitted online at www.employmenttribunals.service.gov.uk or can be done by post. A date for a case management hearing may be set, and then a date for Tribunal hearing. The claimant and his or her representative will be able to call witnesses, and cross-examine the witnesses on the other side. The claimant should put their full case to the Tribunal through these witnesses, before closing submissions. Hearings can last less than a day, or go on for four or more days in a longer, complex case.

4.   The time and effort involved in bringing and completing a claim can be daunting, and there is no guarantee that a Tribunal's judge, and its two lay members, will resolve the case in a satisfactory manner, or with an accurate understanding of the law. For this reason, an appeal to the Employment Appeal Tribunal is possible within 42 days of a Tribunal judgment on the substance of a claim. Remedies hearings in longer cases are often done separately. For a full guide to claims, see N Cunningham and M Reed, *Employment Tribunal Claims: Tactics and Precedents* (2013).

5.   A second type of body to enforce labour rights can be a government agency. Currently there is no overarching government regulator for all labour rights, rather than a series of agencies who are meant to oversee enforcement of particular areas. These include:

Government body	*Functions*
Agricultural Wages Boards (Scotland and Wales)	Minimum wages, farms, chapter 6(1)(b)
Her Majesty's Revenue and Customs	Minimum wage and tax, chapter 6(3)
Central Arbitration Committee	Union recognition, chapter 9(1)
Equality and Human Rights Commission	Anti-discrimination, chapter 12
Employment Agency Standards Inspectorate	Agency inspections, chapter 16(3)(c)
Gangmasters Licensing Authority	Farm agency licensing, chapter 16(3)(c)
Advisory, Conciliation and Arbitration Service	Unions, Codes of Practice, chapter 17(3)

6. In addition, actual government departments directly accountable to the Minister may play a role in labour rights enforcement. From 1916 to 1968, the Ministry of Labour existed, and under Labour governments, and some Conservative governments, used its powers to promote trade union membership. It was renamed the Department of Employment and Productivity, then just the Department of Employment in 1970, the Department for Education and Employment in 1995, and the Department for Work and Pensions in 2001. The Department for Work and Pensions no longer has any active policy around encouraging union membership, or workplace self-regulation. Rather, its remit has become confined to (theoretically) improving the employment rate and managing welfare policy: chapter 16.

7. A potential weakness of government agencies is that, unlike courts and unions, they are vulnerable to political parties which are hostile to the enforcement of law in power, even if they cannot command the political credibility to pass legislation. In this context, Lord Reed's judgment appears as one of the most profound restatements of the rule of law in modern times. He quotes Magna Carta, cl XXIX, that: 'We will sell to no man, we will not deny or defer to any man either Justice or Right.' He might have added that the first clause of the Bill of Rights 1689 reads: 'That the pretended power of suspending the laws or the execution of laws by regal authority without consent of Parliament is illegal.' This has precisely been the strategy of a growing hyperconservative political sect, in the USA and UK, intent on 'government shut down'. Formerly independent regulators are defunded, or have officials appointed that cease to allow the authority to work, without legislative change. In the United States, a prime example is the National Labor Relations Board, which oversees collective bargaining like the UK's Central Arbitration Committee. In the UK, though less extreme, an example was the fate of the Gangmasters Licensing Authority, when Home Secretary, Theresa May in 2014 halted virtually all investigations. See further, on arbitration clauses in contracts, chapter 4(1)(c).

8. A third type of enforcement body is a trade union. As well as providing services such as collective bargaining, one of a trade union's core functions is to oversee compliance with basic rights and workplace agreements on the ground. Unions assist and represent people in dismissal cases in any dispute. Perhaps most basically, they can pressure management to acknowledging people are indeed employees with rights, rather than outsourced independent contractors. In practice, the weakened memebership of trade unions has meant less enforcement. See KD Ewing, 'The function of trade unions' (2005) 31(1) *ILJ* 1.

9. As an extension of a trade union, many workplaces across Europe have democratically elected works councils. These must be distinguished from sham 'company unions' or sham 'consultative committees' controlled by management. Works councils can perform an important function of supervising and enforcing workplace rights and rules. In elections, union candidates often win by virtue of their organisation, although independent candidates may also contest and win. This is probably good for unions, to keep them on their toes. The practice has been growing very slowly in the UK, but is much more developed in countries such as Norway or Germany.

10. Without unions, workplace rights may be left entirely in the hands of the employing entity's 'human resource management' staff. There is a danger that poor education and training in 'HR' can lead to an anti-social, anti-union ethic, where any
questioning of management is met with reprisals, and 'troublemakers' who 'raise
their voice' are vilified. While HR departments will often present themselves as
there to help or provide a service, from a labour rights perspective they are a tool
of managerial control: chapter 8(4). In Germany, the company executive responsible for staffing issues must hold the confidence of the workforce, or be elected.
See the Codetermination Act 1976 §33 (Mitbestimmungsgesetz 1976). Should
HR managers be selected with the participation of the workplace union, or elected
by all employees?

Problem Question

G Orwell, *Nineteen Eighty-Four* (1949)

Since 1984, Winston has worked at the offices of the Ministry of Truth, a government
department devoted to adjusting historical records to comply with official policy on the
use of language. He has received a written statement entitled 'Contract Terms' stating
the following:

> 'You are accepted to work under a contract for services. You agree this is not an employment
> contract. You are a self-employed independent contractor. If you cannot work, you may pro-
> vide a suitably qualified substitute. We have no obligation to offer you ongoing work, and you
> have no obligation to accept work from us.'

In 1997, Winston was informed that he would continue in his job through an employment
agency named Big Brother Ltd. He is given a new contract to sign which is the same as
before, but expressly adds that he has 'no employment relationship and no contract of
any kind' with the Ministry of Truth. He continued to work in his office.

Last month Winston was dismissed, without any notice or investigation. Big Brother
Ltd is now insolvent. Winston comes to seek your advice, and tells you that his pay has
not been raised since 1997, and he was still earning £3 per hour. He also says that he
attempted to volunteer for a housing charity, called Room 101, but was told that they did
not recruit homosexuals.

Advise Winston on whether, as a preliminary matter, he has standing to make claims
for (1) unfair dismissal (2) the minimum wage or (3) discrimination. Who could you tell
him to also ask for help?

NOTE

1. With this, as with all problem questions, start by identifying the list of claims
the claimant will want to make. Then, for each claim, structure your answer in
four parts. First, identify the issue: what the claimants want to claim, and from

who. Second, state the relevant legal rules: so set out any relevant statutory provisions or cases, and summarise them in a concise and accurate way. Third, apply the law: say how the general rule fits on the specific circumstance at hand. Fourth, conclude by stating the likelihood of who will succeed. If the conclusion could be ambiguous or go both ways, give the interpretation of the law that you think most plausible and/or the outcome that is fair and just. This scheme is easy to remember as the 'IRAC' method: Issue, Rule, Apply, Conclude. You should be able to answer this well in about 1000–1200 words.

Additional Reading for Chapter 3

O Kahn-Freund, 'A Note on Status and Contract in British Labour Law' (1967) 30 *Modern Law Review* **685**
Kahn-Freund takes issue with the misused argument of Henry Summer Maine that after having moved from 'status to contract' in the nineteenth century, labour rights were moving people from 'contract to status' again. Kahn-Freund points out that in a modern employment contract 'its existence and its termination depended on the volition of the parties, but its substance was determined by legal norms withdrawn from the parties' contractual freedom'. People who attempted to link labour rights with pre-industrial revolution servitude were exhibiting a 'somewhat desperate but also occasionally somewhat tendentious inclination'.

B Hepple, 'Restructuring Employment Rights' (1986) 15 *ILJ* **69**
Hepple suggests that the scope of employment rights should be enlarged to cover any 'employment relationship' (which combines elements of contract and status) that covers intermittent exchanges of work for pay and a single continuous contract.

H Collins, 'Independent Contractors and the Challenge of Vertical Disintegration to Employment Protection Law' (1990) 10 *Oxford Journal of Legal Studies* **353**
Collins argues the various tests used by courts to separate employees are 'dysfunctional' because their application leads to results that 'defeat the clear purposes of labour law regulation'. Yet 'economic reality' and 'bargaining power' cannot function alone, as they still risk judicial misconception of regulation's purpose. Collins proposes a test that places a presumption that someone is an employee when they personally perform work, and the employer cannot show it is merely a 'performance contract' and that (in a metaphorical sense) no 'badges of organisation' are present.

M Freedland, *Personal Employment Contract* **(2003)**
Continuing the themes from his 1976 book, Freedland argues that a 'personal scope of work' test ought to become the primary determinant of labour rights.

S Deakin, "Enterprise Risk': The Juridical Nature of the Firm Revisited' (2003) 32 *Industrial Law Journal* **97**
Criticising decisions by the House of Lords that a 'close connection' test between an actor and tortious damage define vicarious liability, Deakin contends these and other historical tests offer little more than 'vague verbal formulae' to what is an essentially economic problem. It would be preferable to substitute a test based on the 'scope of risk creation', because 'risk' is not a verbal rather than an economic formula. The goal of vicarious liability should be to ensure that risk are 'internalised' by firms, in order for them not to have an anti-competitive advantage in their enterprise by 'externalising' costs onto others.

G Davidov, 'Who Is a worker?' (2005) 34 *ILJ* **57**
Observing that a new word 'worker' was replacing 'employee' in a number of statutes, not just in the UK, Davidov argues it should include anyone who has 'significant dependency'. Creating an intermediate category of 'worker' between employed and self-employed might even make the delineation of those concepts easier. Davidov stresses that the purpose of the regulation should drive the definition.

E McGaughey, 'Should Agency Workers Be Treated Differently?' (2010) LSE Legal Studies Working Paper No 7/2010
Cases that held agency workers were nobody's employee created an unjustified regulatory subsidy for the agency industry. An 'employee' should be acknowledged according to the purpose of labour legislation to remedy unequal bargaining power (as was, in the event, achieved the following year by *Autoclenz Ltd v Belcher* [2011] UKSC 41, [35]). Mutuality of obligation is a circular concept if it means anything more than consideration, and requires ongoing future exchanges. Because employment agencies and clients carry out all the same functions as conventional employers, under the orthodox tests for implication of terms, a joint employment should be found between the staff member on the one hand and both the agency and the end-user on the other. For some claims, such as harassment, primary liability would fall on the wrongdoer, but secondary liability would follow the second employer in the event of the first's insolvency. Agency workers should not be treated differently simply because an agency stands in the middle.

J Prassl, *The Concept of the Employer* **(2015)**
Prassl sets out a set of empirically grounded arguments for who should be regarded as within the concept of an employer. Looking at the way that agency work and private equity functions in practice, Prassl suggests that the functions of an employer can be broken into several parts, and shared between different entities. For instance, an agency might provide a staff member with pay and general directions, while the end-user gives day-to-day instructions, and both benefit from the fruits of the employee's work. In private equity, the shareholders behind a company, often organised by a partnership, set goals, and procure redundancies, through several legal forms, but clearly exercise employer functions. If they do so, they should be responsible for employment rights.

ILO, Employment Relationship Recommendation 2006 (No 198)
Preamble

...

Considering that laws and regulations, and their interpretation, should be compatible with the objectives of decent work, and

Considering that employment or labour law seeks, among other things, to address what can be an unequal bargaining position between parties to an employment relationship, and

Considering that the protection of workers is at the heart of the mandate of the International Labour Organization, and in accordance with principles set out in the ILO Declaration on Fundamental Principles and Rights at Work, 1998, and the Decent Work Agenda ...

1. Members should formulate and apply a national policy for reviewing at appropriate intervals and, if necessary, clarifying and adapting the scope of relevant laws and regulations, in order to guarantee effective protection for workers who perform work in the context of an employment relationship.

...

4. National policy should at least include measures to:

(a) provide guidance for the parties concerned, in particular employers and workers, on effectively establishing the existence of an employment relationship and on the distinction between employed and self-employed workers;

(b) combat disguised employment relationships in the context of, for example, other relationships that may include the use of other forms of contractual arrangements that hide the true legal status, noting that a disguised employment relationship occurs when the employer treats an individual as other than an employee in a manner that hides his or her true legal status as an employee, and that situations can arise where contractual arrangements have the effect of depriving workers of the protection they are due;

(c) ensure standards applicable to all forms of contractual arrangements, including those involving multiple parties, so that employed workers have the protection they are due;

(d) ensure that standards applicable to all forms of contractual arrangements establish who is responsible for the protection contained therein;

(e) provide effective access of those concerned, in particular employers and workers, to appropriate, speedy, inexpensive, fair and efficient procedures and mechanisms for settling disputes regarding the existence and terms of an employment relationship;

(f) ensure compliance with, and effective application of, laws and regulations concerning the employment relationship; and

(g) provide for appropriate and adequate training in relevant international labour standards, comparative and case law for the judiciary, arbitrators, mediators, labour inspectors, and other persons responsible for dealing with the resolution of disputes and enforcement of national employment laws and standards.

5. Members should take particular account in national policy to ensure effective protection to workers especially affected by the uncertainty as to the existence of an employment relationship, including women workers, as well as the most vulnerable workers, young workers, older workers, workers in the informal economy, migrant workers and workers with disabilities.

...

9. For the purposes of the national policy of protection for workers in an employment relationship, the determination of the existence of such a relationship should be guided primarily by the facts relating to the performance of work and the remuneration of the worker, notwithstanding how the relationship is characterized in any contrary arrangement, contractual or otherwise, that may have been agreed between the parties.

10. Members should promote clear methods for guiding workers and employers as to the determination of the existence of an employment relationship.

11. For the purpose of facilitating the determination of the existence of an employment relationship, Members should, within the framework of the national policy referred to in this Recommendation, consider the possibility of the following:

(a) allowing a broad range of means for determining the existence of an employment relationship;
(b) providing for a legal presumption that an employment relationship exists where one or more relevant indicators is present; and
(c) determining, following prior consultations with the most representative organizations of employers and workers, that workers with certain characteristics, in general or in a particular sector, must be deemed to be either employed or self-employed.

12. For the purposes of the national policy referred to in this Recommendation, Members may consider clearly defining the conditions applied for determining the existence of an employment relationship, for example, subordination or dependence.

13. Members should consider the possibility of defining in their laws and regulations, or by other means, specific indicators of the existence of an employment relationship. Those indicators might include:

(a) the fact that the work: is carried out according to the instructions and under the control of another party; involves the integration of the worker in the organization of the; is performed solely or mainly for the benefit of another person; must be carried out personally by the worker; is carried out within specific working hours or at a workplace specified or agreed by the party requesting the work; is of a particular duration and has a certain continuity; requires the worker's availability; or involves the provision of tools, materials and machinery by the party requesting the work;
(b) periodic payment of remuneration to the worker; the fact that such remuneration constitutes the worker's sole or principal source of income; provision of payment in kind, such as food, lodging or transport; recognition of entitlements such as weekly rest and annual holidays; payment by the party requesting the work for travel undertaken by the worker in order to carry out the work; or absence of financial risk for the worker.

[The UK is not in compliance with this Recommendation by setting out definitions in legislation. The *Autoclenz* judgment complies fully with the Recommendation, yet conflicting Court of Appeal cases, particularly on 'mutuality of obligation' and agency workers, still fall short of the requirements under the Preamble, sections 5 and 12.]

4

Contract of Employment

As chapter 3 discussed, the employment relation is a mix of contract and rights. In principle, rights exist for people who lack or possibly could lack bargaining power to get them in contract. But also, whatever type the contract is, '[n]ot everything is contractual in a contract'. The relation is 'set against the background of usage, familiar to all who engage in similar negotiations and which may be supposed to govern the language of a particular agreement' (E Durkheim, *The Division of Labour in Society* (1893) book I, ch VII). In *Gisda Cyf v Barratt* [2010] UKSC 41, [39] the Supreme Court emphasised that the 'need to segregate intellectually common law principles relating to contract law, even in the field of employment, from statutorily conferred rights is fundamental'. *Autoclenz Ltd v Belcher*, [2011] UKSC 41, [35] stated that courts must scrutinise 'the terms of any written agreement' – not just terms on employee status – to see if they 'in truth represent what was agreed'. This matters because if the rules on a contract's formation, validity and content are not subordinated to labour rights, the efficacy of those rights could be compromised. An objective manifestation of consent between two or more parties usually unlocks the employment relation: conduct, as Adam Smith put it in his *Lectures on Jurisprudence* (1763), that generates 'reasonable expectations'. But because the employee usually has fewer alternatives than the employing entity, the minimum terms of the relation are set in law. It is a reasonable social expectation that courts will ensure all rules of contract guarantee social and economic rights. This chapter analyses (1) contractual formation and 'unjust factors' that cancel the contract or its terms, (2) how terms are incorporated by reference and the extent of the right to be informed about them, and (3) the choice of which legal system, internationally, can apply.

Introductory reading: Collins ch 2 (27–34). CEM ch 3 (93–130). D&M ch 4 (259–95).

(1) FORMATION

(a) Enforceable Agreements

The basic rule about conduct to form a contract in English law, since *Smith v Hughes* (1871) LR 6 QB 597, is that if 'whatever a man's real intention may be, he so conducts himself that a reasonable man would believe that he was assenting to the terms proposed', and the other party enters into the contract on that belief, both 'would be equally bound'. Because the contract of employment guarantees labour rights, the courts' standards for the 'agreement' element of contractual formation matter. An offer of money mirrored by acceptance to work, written or oral, is plainly enough. More interesting are the standards for creation of obligations through assurances and conduct. The next case focuses on the creation of a new term in a contract, but not by agreement in the normal fashion.

CSC Computer Sciences Ltd v McAlinden [2013] EWCA Civ 1435

Mr McAlinden claimed that, because CSC Computer Sciences Ltd had assured his wages would rise in line with the Retail Price Index (RPI) but did not pay up, it made an unlawful wage deduction under the Employment Rights Act (ERA) 1996 s 13. CSCCS Ltd had taken over IT Services Ltd in 2000, and had believed that the employees were legally entitled to RPI wage increases (as opposed to no annual increase, or increases under the Consumer Price Index, which does not take account of house price inflation) under the Transfer of Undertakings (Protection of Employment) Regulations 1981. CSCCS Ltd communicated its understanding in emails and at a pay review meeting, but it was mistaken about this. The Judge found the communication of a right to pay increases created a right for employees to have the pay increases. CSCCS Ltd argued that conduct based on its mistaken belief could not give rise to contractual obligations. The Court of Appeal rejected this.

Underhill LJ:

11. The correct approach in cases where employees seek to rely on terms to be implied on the basis of "custom and practice and/or the conduct of the parties" was very recently reviewed by this Court in *Park Cakes Ltd v Shumba* [2013] EWCA Civ 974 ... and although the term asserted in that case concerned enhanced redundancy benefits the same principles would apply in the present case. Since that decision was handed down after the argument before us we gave the parties the opportunity to submit further written submissions by reference to it. I see no point in reproducing in extenso here what was said in Park Cakes. But I would draw attention to the fact that the Court, following the lead given by Leveson LJ in *Garratt v Mirror Group Newspapers Ltd* [2011] EWCA Civ 425, [2011] ICR 880, focused less on the language of "custom and practice" and more on the essential question of what the employees will reasonably have understood from the employer's conduct and words, applying ordinary contractual principles.
    ...

16. ... It is important to appreciate that this is not a case of the kind (in my experience more usual) where the employer confers the benefit in question in the belief that he is doing so without obligation but the employees assert that he has nevertheless conveyed the contrary

impression. In such a case a finding that the employer had communicated a "policy" of confer-ring the benefit would indeed probably mean that what was communicated fell short of an acknowledgment of legal obligation. But here CSC's case has to be that, while itself believing that it was under a legal obligation to pay the increases, it said or did nothing that should have conveyed that impression to the employees. That is rather more of a tall order for an employer; and the Judge may be forgiven for not being wholly precise in his wording. I believe that what he meant in para. 103 was that CSC had communicated not only a policy of paying RPI increases but its belief, as found in the previous paragraph, that it was obliged to do so. That is in my view confirmed by the documents to which he refers in para. 103 – being those summarised at para. 5 above. The significance of all three is that they acknowledge a legal obligation; one is addressed to an employee, and another prescribes what should be said to employees if they ask.

17. ... this is a case where CSC itself believed that it was under a legal obligation in this regard; and ex-ITS employees were differently treated from their colleagues for that reason. It would hardly be very surprising if it had conveyed that impression to the employees. But the Judge had more to go on than that general consideration. ... the documents to which he referred clearly showed CSC both telling an individual employee that he had a contractual right to RPI increases and authorising managers to give that message more generally. The grievance state-ments to which he referred in para. 103 also clearly conveyed (though without much speci-ficity) that the ex-ITS employees had been given the impression that they were contractually entitled to RPI increases. Taking it as a whole, there was in my view ample evidential basis for the Judge's finding; and it is clear on what basis he reached that finding.

18. I turn to Mr Gorton's second point. He fastened on the passage in the Judge's Reasons where he considers whether CSC was in fact correct in its belief that the ITS employees enjoyed a contractual right, as at the moment of transfer, to an RPI increase: see para. 99 of the Rea-sons, quoted at 11 (7) above. He submitted that that passage constitutes a finding that they did not in fact enjoy such a right and thus that CSC's belief that they did was mistaken; and he submitted that conduct based on a mistaken belief could not give rise to contractual obliga-tions. In this connection he relied on the decision of the House of Lords in *Harvela Investments Ltd v Royal Trust of Canada (C.I.) Ltd* [1986] AC 207.

19. I should start by noting that the point does not appear to have been put this way in the ET. Accordingly the Judge was not required to, and did not, make an explicit finding as to whether CSC's belief that the ex-ITS employees had enjoyed, pre-transfer, a right to RPI increases was mistaken. His conclusion that the Claimants had not proved that they enjoyed such a right is not, on a strict analysis, sufficient: while the burden of proving the existence of the right pre-transfer was on the Claimants, the burden of proving any mistake – that is, the non-existence of the right – would be on CSC. The Judge had acknowledged in para. 99 the existence of evidence pointing to at least an accepted "practice" of paying RPI increases pre-transfer; and the openings of both paras. 99 and 100 are carefully worded. Nevertheless I am prepared to accept for the purposes of argument that in the circumstances of this case what the Judge says in those paragraphs can be treated as an implicit finding that CSC's belief was indeed mistaken.

20. Even on that basis, I cannot accept Mr Gorton's submission. We are concerned here with the effect of communications by an employer to (a class of) his employees, partly in words and partly by conduct. As a matter of principle, what matters is the effect of those communica-tions, viewed objectively: the employer's subjective understanding is irrelevant. If, as the Judge found, CSC's communications conveyed the impression to the Claimants that RPI increases were a contractual right, the fact that it may have been acting on a mistaken belief is thus

irrelevant. It is of course trite law that, other things being equal, unilateral mistake cannot invalidate a contract.

21. The decision in Harvela on which Mr Gorton relied is concerned with a wholly different situation. The facts can be sufficiently summarised as follows. The vendors of a parcel of shares invited offers from two potential purchasers and bound themselves to accept the higher bid. One party ("A") submitted a bid in a "referential" form which was eventually held not to comply with the terms of the offer. The vendors believed that they were bound to accept that offer and sent a telex saying so. A contended that even if its original bid was invalid as an acceptance of the original invitation it could and should be treated as a fresh offer, which the vendor had accepted by its telex. The House of Lords rejected that argument. A's bid was not a fresh contractual offer, nor was the vendors' telex an acceptance of such an offer. In the context of the prior dealings the bid could only be understood as a purported acceptance of the offer to sell constituted by the prior invitation, and the telex as an acknowledgment (as it turned out, a mistaken acknowledgment) of a legal obligation created by that prior offer and acceptance. Both Lord Diplock and Lord Templeman, who delivered the only two substantial speeches, did indeed refer to the fact that both A and the vendors mistakenly believed that A's bid had created a binding contract (see at pp. 226 D–E and 235 F–G), but it was no part of their reasoning that that mistake invalidated what would otherwise have been a binding contract: their reasoning was, rather, as I have said, that in the context created by the parties' (mistaken) belief A's bid was not intended – nor, critically, could it have been understood to be intended – as a fresh contractual offer.

CONCLUSION
22. I therefore cannot accept either of Mr Gorton's challenges to the reasoning of the Employment Judge and I would dismiss the appeal. The Claimants in their Respondents' Notice sought to argue that the Judge should in any event have found that ITS's policy had crystallised into a contractual term prior to the transfer to CSC; but that is now academic and I need not consider it.

Lord Thomson CJ and **Tomlinson LJ** agreed.

NOTES AND QUESTIONS

1. Underhill LJ reasons that because the employer 'conveyed the impression' that their wages would increase in line with the RPI as a contractual right, this became an enforceable obligation. He rejects that it was a vague statement of policy, and suggests the employer would have to argue that it 'said or did nothing that should have conveyed that impression to the employees'.

2. In *Newnham Farms Ltd v Powell* (2003) EAT/0711/01/MAA, the Employment Appeal Tribunal upheld the finding that a contract was formed by conduct, in 'absence of any specific meetings or conversations which were alleged expressly to constitute a contract', but as it was put, 'a very good example of an implied contract of employment'. Mrs Powell had done administrative and light agricultural work on the farm for her husband's company until their marriage broke down. Recorder Burke QC noted there were no 'specific meetings or conversations' discussing any contract, but held that there was one, and that Mrs Powell was therefore entitled to be paid a minimum wage under an order pursuant to the

former Agricultural Wages Act 1948 section 3. Both courts in *Powell* and *McAlinden* stated that the contract or the terms were 'implied'. Is the better view that that conduct 'expresses' a contract and its terms? See also chapter 3(1)(b) note 7.

3.   While a contractual relationship already existed in *McAlinden*, do you agree that in substance the employer gave a clear assurance, on which employees could reasonably rely, and from which it became inequitable for the employer to resile? Obviously the employees went on performing their contractual duties as normal without giving any 'fresh' consideration. This seems to have directly overturned the old case of *Stilk v Myrick* [1809] EWHC KB J58, where sailors in a trade dispute were denied the wages they were promised. Also, the claimants succeeded in using estoppel as a 'sword', winning expectation damages. This contradicts *Combe v Combe* [1951] 2 KB 215.

4.   In Australia, the United States and virtually all civil law systems, estoppel has long founded a cause of action, as it has in English law when it concerns a claim over property. See *Crabb v Arun DC* [1975] EWCA Civ 7. Is it backward for English law to make it easier to claim estoppel for proprietary rights than for personal rights? Lord Scott may have agreed in *Cobbe v Yeoman's Row Management Ltd* [2008] UKHL 55, [14] where he described proprietary estoppel as a 'sub-species' of promissory estoppel. Logically, this means promissory estoppel cannot be more restrictive than proprietary estoppel.

5.   For an agreement to be enforceable, it must be made in a context where courts presume legal relations are created. In commerce, rather than domestic or social spheres, this is always presumed, unless a term states, for example, that the deal 'shall not be subject to legal jurisdiction in the law courts' (*Rose & Frank Co v JR Crompton & Bros Ltd* [1924] UKHL 2). But presumably such a clause would not represent the truth of the bargain in an individual employment relation: *Autoclenz*, [35] but see chapter 3(2)(e) note 5.

6.   *Dresdner Kleinwort Ltd v Attrill* [2013] EWCA Civ 394 held that when a CEO of the bank declared there was a guaranteed minimum bonus pool in 2008 this was binding: there was no need for acceptance. The declaration could not be later revoked.

7.   Do the foregoing cases suggest that, whatever the position for commercial contracts, obligations in employment form based on the average employee's understanding?

8.   Can employees contract away their rights to be decided solely by private arbitration panels, 'adjudicated' by appointees of large corporations? In *14 Penn Plaza LLC v Pyett*, 556 US 247 (2009) the Republican appointees to the US Supreme Court held, 5 to 4, that all arbitration clauses in individual employment contracts must be enforced according to their terms. Souter J for the dissent said it was a 'bald assertion' by the majority that '[n]othing in the law suggests a distinction between the status of arbitration agreements signed by an individual employee and those agreed to by a union representative'. This view was extended to negate consumer and employment right class actions by 5 to 4 in *AT&T Mobility v Concepcion*, 563 US 333 (2011). In the UK, *Autoclenz* suggests that any such arbitration clauses are entirely void. *14 Penn Plaza* is foreign to democratic values and human rights.

9.   In addition to 'agreement', some quid pro quo is required from either side at the outset of a bargain, in absence of a deed, for the court to find a deal was 'enforceable'. 'A consideration' in English law used to refer to a reason of justice (and 'just exchange' under the English analogue to the medieval *laesio enormis* doctrine) for a court to enforce the deal. Gradually 'consideration' came to mean anything of value in the eyes of the law. In employment, work and an assurance of some payment suffices. Statutory rights long replaced courts' ad hoc attempts to ensure just exchange.

10. If consideration is necessary for a contract, what happens when there are breaks for periods of time during the course of employment? Plainly a break over night, or over a weekend, does not stop the continuation of a contractual relationship. Under ERA 1996 s 212(3)(b), nor does a 'temporary cessation of work'. The next case exemplifies how this works.

Ford v Warwickshire CC [1983] 2 AC 71

Mrs Ford claimed damages for unfair dismissal from Warwickshire County Council. She worked from September to July on successive fixed-term contracts for eight academic years as a part-time lecturer at the Warwickshire College of Further Education until September 1979. Then she was told her contracts would not be renewed. The question was whether her summer holiday breaks counted as merely a 'temporary cessation of work' under the Employment Protection (Consolidation) Act 1978 Sch 13, para 9 (now ERA 1996 s 212). She sought to claim her dismissal was unfair, but was told that her year-long fixed-term contract was not enough to meet the necessary qualifying period. The House of Lords held that her summer breaks were indeed only temporary, and she had the right to claim unfair dismissal.

Lord Diplock:

My Lords, I am quite unable to be persuaded that paragraph 9 (1) is not applicable to cases where a contract of employment for a fixed term has expired and upon expiry has not been renewed by the employer, in exactly the same way as it is applicable to contracts of employment of indefinite duration which are terminated by the employer by notice. One looks to see what was the reason for the employer's failure to renew the contract on the expiry of its fixed term and asks oneself the question: was that reason "a temporary cessation of work," within the meaning of that phrase in paragraph 9(1)?

There are many employments, of which teaching is one of the largest and most obvious, in which it is perfectly possible to predict with accuracy the periods in which the educational institution at which a teacher who is employed to conduct courses in particular subjects will have no work available for that teacher to do, i.e. during the three annual school holidays or during vacations at universities and other institutions of further education. As the evidence in the instant case discloses, it is a common practice to employ part-time teachers of courses at institutions of further education under successive fixed term contracts the length of which is fixed according to the duration of the particular course and expires at the end of it. In the interval between successive courses which may coincide with the end of p one academic year at an institution of further education and the beginning of the next but may be considerably longer, there is no work available at the institution for the teacher to do, and he remains without any contract of employment until the course is resumed, when he again becomes employed under a fresh fixed term contract.

Lord Keith, Lord Roskill and **Lord Brandon** concurred.

Lord Brightman:

Suppose that in August 1977 the appellant was engaged under a contract of employment of indefinite duration, starting in September 1977, subject to one week's notice on either side. Suppose that on July 1, 1978, the council gave the appellant one week's notice because her pottery class would not extend beyond July 8, 1978. Suppose that in August 1978 she was engaged under a similar but new contract of employment for an indefinite term starting in September 1978. It could not, I apprehend, be doubted that she would have been absent from work within the meaning of the Act during the 1978 summer vacation on account of a temporary cessation of her work.

Suppose that her contract was determinable by one month's notice on either side, and that such notice was therefore given on June 8, 1978. Again, I apprehend that there is no doubt that the vacation period would "count" on the true construction of the Act.

...

I therefore reach the conclusion that the appellant can properly be described as "absent from work" during each of the vacation periods which spanned her successive contracts of employment and that such absence can properly be described as "on account of a temporary cessation of work" notwithstanding that the contract was brought to an end by the expiry of its fixed term, instead of by the expiry of the term of the dismissal notice; and that an expected cessation of work which governs the length of the fixed term satisfies the words "on account of a temporary cessation of work," just as an expected cessation of work which leads to a dismissal notice would have satisfied those words.

NOTES AND QUESTIONS

1.   The House of Lords holds that a summer break, even of a few months, was a temporary cessation. Therefore, there is a continuous contract of employment, despite the apparent break in obligations for the employee to provide work, and the employer to provide a wage.
2.   How long do you think the longest possible 'temporary cessation' would be? Presumably the question should be approached by regarding the context in which the question is asked: whether Parliament intended to confer employment rights in that situation.

(b) Unjust or Vitiating Factors

Ideally the creation of a binding contract, to which society lends the machinery of state enforcement, should be founded on fully informed and true consent of all parties, and not contravene the law. For this reason, any contract can be deemed 'unjust', and may be vitiated at the election of a wronged party, if there was misrepresentation, duress or undue influence. In the vast majority of everyday contracts, non-disclosure of material terms and inequality of bargaining power are also unjust factors. Many think that these are exceptions, because the rules are scattered through statutory enactments on consumer products and finance, shareholder or investor contracts, tenancy laws and labour law. But although there is no general doctrine of disclosure and unequal bargaining power (*National Westminster Bank plc v Morgan* [1985] UKHL 2), these unjust factors are fundamental to most everyday contracts. Another unjust factor is illegality. It has been a problematic, historically, because some have argued it should render a contract unenforceable, regardless of the effects.

Hounga v Allen [2014] UKSC 47

Mary Hounga, an undocumented migrant, sued Adenike Allen for unpaid wages and unfair dismissal under ERA 1996 ss 13 and 94, and direct discrimination under the Race Relations Act 1976 (now the Equality Act 2010 s 39(2)(c)). Hounga, probably then aged 14, was brought to the UK from Lagos, Nigeria on a fraudulent passport as the 'granddaughter' of Mrs Allen. She worked as a domestic servant from January 2007 in Allen's home in Hanworth, Middlesex. Hounga cared for Mrs Allen's three smaller children. The Immigration Act 1971 s 24(1)(b)(ii) made her contract of employment a criminal offence. The tribunal found Hounga, though a child, knew coming to the UK was unlawful, and she understood the difference between right and wrong. She was never paid, as promised, and was beaten and abused. In July 2008 Hounga was kicked out of the house, had water poured on her, and slept in her wet clothes in the front garden. When she tried to get back in at 7am, nobody answered. She went to a supermarket carpark. Social services found her. The UK Human Trafficking Centre took care of her, and assisted with the legal action against Allen. The Employment Tribunal found Hounga could claim racial discrimination, but rejected a claim in contract for unpaid wages, and unfair dismissal, as it required asserting the existence of an illegal contract. On appeal, Silber J upheld the decision. On appeal of the discrimination issue (but not unfair dismissal or wage deductions) the Court of Appeal, Rimer LJ, held the claim was 'inextricably linked' with the illegal conduct, and it would be condoning illegality to allow the claimant to rely on her own illegal actions. Hounga, appealed, with Anti-Slavery International intervening in her support. The Supreme Court unanimously reversed the Court of Appeal and allowed Hounga's racial discrimination claim.

Lord Wilson (with whom **Lady Hale** and **Lord Kerr** agree):

THE DEFENCE OF ILLEGALITY

23. ... of the various claims and complaints made by Miss Hounga against Mrs Allen in the tribunal, the only one to reach this court is the complaint of discrimination in relation to her dismissal. This particular complaint may well be said not to capture the gravamen of Miss Hounga's case against Mrs Allen. Irrespective of whether all of it can form the subject of a civil claim, the case which, on the tribunal's exiguous findings, Miss Hounga makes against Mrs Allen relates centrally to her participation in the plan to secure her entry into the UK on a false basis; to Mrs Allen's failure to pay her the promised wages and, in particular, to secure for her the promised education (although the tribunal made no finding that Mrs Allen had never intended to secure it for her); and to her acts of serious violence towards Miss Hounga over 18 months, coupled with threats of imprisonment which were entirely convincing to Miss Hounga and which in effect disabled her from taking any steps to rescue herself from her situation in Mrs Allen's

home. In the event it was Mrs Allen's eviction of her which precipitated her rescue. Cruel though the manner of its execution was, the dismissal was, in a real sense, a blessing for Miss Hounga. But, while the facts upon which the present appeal is founded may not represent Miss Hounga's essential case against Mrs Allen, the clean legal issue remains: was the Court of Appeal correct to hold that the illegality defence defeated the complaint of discrimination?

24. The application of the defence of illegality to a claim founded on contract often has its own complexities. But, in that it was unlawful (and indeed a criminal offence under section 24(1)(b)(ii) of the Immigration Act 1971) for Miss Hounga to enter into the contract of employment with Mrs Allen, the defence of illegality in principle precluded her from enforcing it. In this regard a claim for unfair dismissal might arguably require analysis different from a claim for wrongful dismissal. But a claimant for unfair dismissal is nevertheless seeking to enforce her contract, including often to secure her reinstatement under it. In *Enfield Technical Services Ltd v Payne* [2008] EWCA Civ 393, [2008] ICR 1423, the Court of Appeal, while rejecting its applicability to the two cases before it, clearly proceeded on the basis that a defence of illegality could defeat a claim for unfair dismissal. This present appeal proceeds without challenge to the conclusion of the tribunal, upheld by the appeal tribunal, that the defence indeed precluded Miss Hounga's claim for unfair dismissal. Equally there is no challenge to the dismissal on that same basis of her claim for unpaid wages although the considerations of public policy to which I will refer from para 46 onwards might conceivably have yielded a different conclusion.

25. Unlawful discrimination is, however, a statutory tort: in relation to discrimination in the field of employment, see sections 56(1)(b) and 57(1) of the 1976 Act, now sections 124(6) and 119(2)(a) of the 2010 Act. The application of the defence of illegality to claims in tort is highly problematic.

[His Lordship summarised case law up to *Tinsley v Milligan* [1994] 1 AC 340, which introduced a 'reliance' test, and a subsequent 'inextricable link' test used, for example, in *Hall v Woolston Hall Leisure Ltd* [2000] EWCA Civ 170, and continued:]

37. Every formulation of a requirement to identify the active or effective cause of an event – or an act to which it is inextricably linked – has a potential for inconsistent application driven by subjective considerations. In his article entitled "Ex Turpi Causa – when Latin avoids liability" in the Edinburgh Law Review, 18 (2014) 175, Lord Mance made a related point at p 184:

"Your painter negligently leaves your front door open, and a thief enters. Of course, in your action for negligence against the painter, the painter is responsible for causing the loss of your goods. Equally, however, in your action for theft of the goods against the thief, if he is caught, he is the cause. Causation, like much else in the law, depends on context."

38. The subjectivity inherent in the requisite value judgement is well demonstrated by the facts of the present case. Three judges in the Court of Appeal were of the view, articulated in the judgment of Rimer LJ, that Miss Hounga's complaint was inextricably linked to her own unlawful conduct – "obviously" so. They considered that the only difference between the complaints of Miss Hounga and of Mr Vakante was that, whereas his employers were unaware of the illegality, Mrs Allen and Miss Hounga were "equal participants" in entry into the illegal contract of employment. "Whichever party bore the greater responsibility for making of the illegal contract", said Rimer LJ, "[Miss Hounga] was a willing participant in it." He made a further point:

"Ms Hounga's dismissal discrimination case was dependent upon the special vulnerability to which she was subject by reason of her illegal employment contract: she was relying on the facts that she was an illegal immigrant, had no right to be employed here, effectively had no rights here at all and so could be treated less well because of her inferior situation."

39. But were Mrs Allen and Miss Hounga equal participants in entry into the illegal contract? Was there any doubt about the identity of the party who bore greater responsibility for it? And, despite the superficial attraction in logic of Rimer LJ's further point, should Mrs Allen's cruel misuse of Miss Hounga's perceived vulnerability arising out of the illegality, by making threats about the consequences of her exposure to the authorities, be a further justification for the defeat of her complaint? As I will explain in para 49, such threats are an indicator that Miss Hounga was the victim of forced labour but in the hands of the Court of Appeal they become a ground for denial of her complaint.

40. If, indeed, the test applicable to Mrs Allen's defence of illegality is that of the inextricable link, I, for one, albeit conscious of the inherent subjectivity in my so saying, would hold the link to be absent. Entry into the illegal contract on 28 January 2007 and its continued operation until 17 July 2008 provided, so I consider, no more than the context in which Mrs Allen then perpetrated the acts of physical, verbal and emotional abuse by which, among other things, she dismissed Miss Hounga from her employment.

41. But the bigger question is whether the inextricable link test is applicable to Mrs Allen's defence.

PUBLIC POLICY

42. The defence of illegality rests upon the foundation of public policy. "The principle of public policy is this..." said Lord Mansfield by way of preface to his classic exposition of the defence in *Holman v Johnson* (1775) 1 Cowp 341, p 343, 98 Eng Rep 1120, p 1121. "Rules which rest upon the foundation of public policy, not being rules which belong to the fixed or customary law, are capable, on proper occasion, of expansion or modification": *Maxim Nordenfelt Guns and Ammunition Co v Nordenfelt* [1893] 1 Ch 630, 661 (Bowen LJ). So it is necessary, first, to ask "What is the aspect of public policy which founds the defence?" and, second, to ask "But is there another aspect of public policy to which application of the defence would run counter?"

...

44. Concern to preserve the integrity of the legal system is a helpful rationale of the aspect of policy which founds the defence even if the instance given by McLachlin J of where that concern is in issue may best be taken as an example of it rather than as the only conceivable instance of it. I therefore pose and answer the following questions:

(a) Did the tribunal's award of compensation to Miss Hounga allow her to profit from her wrongful conduct in entering into the contract? No, it was an award of compensation for injury to feelings consequent upon her dismissal, in particular the abusive nature of it.
(b) Did the award permit evasion of a penalty prescribed by the criminal law? No, Miss Hounga has not been prosecuted for her entry into the contract and, even had a penalty been thus imposed upon her, it would not represent evasion of it.
(c) Did the award compromise the integrity of the legal system by appearing to encourage those in the situation of Miss Hounga to enter into illegal contracts of employment? No, the idea is fanciful.
(d) Conversely, would application of the defence of illegality so as to defeat the award compromise the integrity of the legal system by appearing to encourage those in the situation of Mrs Allen to enter into illegal contracts of employment? Yes, possibly: it might engender a belief that they could even discriminate against such employees with impunity.

45. So the considerations of public policy which militate in favour of applying the defence so as to defeat Miss Hounga's complaint scarcely exist.

46. But what about the second question posed in para 42? It requires the court to consider whether Mrs Allen was guilty of "trafficking" in bringing Miss Hounga from Nigeria to the UK and into the home in Hanworth.

47. The accepted international definition of trafficking is contained in the UN Protocol to Prevent, Suppress and Punish Trafficking in Persons ("the Palermo Protocol") signed in 2000 and ratified by the UK on 9 February 2006. Article 3 provides:

> "(a) 'Trafficking in persons' shall mean the recruitment, transportation, transfer, harbouring or receipt of persons, by means of the threat or use of force or other forms of coercion, of abduction, of fraud, of deception, of the abuse of power or of a position of vulnerability … for the purpose of exploitation. Exploitation shall include, at a minimum, … sexual exploitation, forced labour or services, slavery or practices similar to slavery, servitude or the removal of organs;
> (b) The consent of a victim of trafficking in persons to the intended exploitation set forth in subparagraph (a) of this article shall be irrelevant where any of the means set forth in subparagraph (a) have been used;
> (c) The recruitment, transportation, transfer, harbouring or receipt of a child for the purpose of exploitation shall be considered 'trafficking in persons' even if this does not involve any of the means set forth in subparagraph (a) of this article."

So did Mrs Allen, together with other members of her family, recruit and/or transport and/or receive Miss Hounga, being then a child, for the purpose of exploitation, namely forced labour or servitude?

48. In her claim form Miss Hounga alleged that the UK Human Trafficking Centre had accepted her as a victim of human trafficking. Before the tribunal she filed a report on herself made by Ms Skrivankova, Trafficking Programme Coordinator, Anti-Slavery International, which intervenes in this appeal. The report must be handled with care because Ms Skrivankova did not interview Miss Hounga and relied on written material, in particular her witness statement, which included disputed allegations in relation to which the tribunal made no findings. At all events Ms Skrivankova reported that all the elements in the definition of trafficking in the Palermo Protocol were present in Miss Hounga's case. She suggested that it was a classic case of the trafficking of a vulnerable child, lacking family support, by people known to her, who abused her natural trust in them with promises which were not kept and who subjected her to forced labour. In this latter regard Ms Skrivankova referred to a list of six indicators of forced labour published by the International Labour Organisation ("the ILO"), which takes the view that, if at least two of the indicators are present, forced labour exists.

49. The tribunal made no finding whether Miss Hounga was the victim of trafficking. No doubt it considered that it had no need to do so. It is only at this third level of appeal that the issue crops up again; and this court's duty to be fair to Mrs Allen demands that it should approach the issue with the utmost caution. Nevertheless, although the court should remember, for example, that Miss Hounga was not actually locked into the home, it is hard to resist the conclusion that Mrs Allen was guilty of trafficking within the meaning of the definition in the Palermo Protocol. Thus, of the ILO's six indicators of forced labour, there might be argument about the existence of the second (restriction of movement) but, on the tribunal's findings, there certainly existed the first (physical harm or threats of it), the fourth (withholding of wages) and the sixth (threat of denunciation to the authorities where the worker has an irregular immigration status). Judicious hesitation leads me to conclude that, if Miss Hounga's case

was not one of trafficking on the part of Mrs Allen and her family, it was so close to it that the distinction will not matter for the purpose of what follows.

50. The Council of Europe Convention on Action against Trafficking in Human Beings CETS No 197 ("the Convention") was done in Warsaw on 16 May 2005 and, following ratification, the UK became obliged to adhere to it, as a matter of international law, on 1 April 2009. Among the purposes of the Convention, set out in article 1, are the prevention of trafficking, the protection of the human rights of victims and the design of a comprehensive framework for their protection and assistance. By article 4, the Convention imports the definition of trafficking set out in the Palermo Protocol. Article 15 provides:

> "3. Each party shall provide, in its internal law, for the right of victims to compensation from the perpetrators."

It is too technical an approach to an international instrument to contend that paragraph 3 relates to compensation only for the trafficking and not for related acts of discrimination. In my view it would be a breach of the UK's international obligations under the Convention for its law to cause Miss Hounga's complaint to be defeated by the defence of illegality. As Lord Hoffmann said in *R v Lyons* [2002] UKHL 44, [2003] 1 AC 976, at para 27,

> "Of course there is a strong presumption in favour of interpreting English law (whether common law or statute) in a way which does not place the United Kingdom in breach of an international obligation."

51. Article 4 of the European Convention on Human Rights provides:

> "1. No one shall be held in slavery or servitude.
> 2. No one shall be required to perform forced or compulsory labour."

In *Rantsev v Cyprus and Russia* (2010) 51 EHRR 1 a Russian woman, aged 20, had gone to work as an artiste in a cabaret in Cyprus. Three weeks later she was found dead in a street. The European Court of Human Rights ("the ECtHR") upheld her father's complaint that Cyprus was in breach of article 4 in that its regime for the issue of visas for cabaret artistes had failed to afford effective protection to her against trafficking and that its police had failed properly to investigate events during those weeks which suggested that she was the victim of it. For present purposes the importance of the court's judgment lies in the following:

> "282. There can be no doubt that trafficking threatens the human dignity and funda-mental freedoms of its victims and cannot be considered compatible with a democratic society and the values expounded in the Convention. In view of its obligation to interpret the Convention in light of present-day conditions, the Court considers it unnecessary to identify whether the treatment about which the applicant complains constitutes 'slavery', 'servitude' or 'forced and compulsory labour'. Instead, the Court concludes that trafficking itself, within the meaning of article 3(a) of the Palermo Protocol and article 4(a) of the Anti-Trafficking Convention, falls within the scope of article 4 of the Convention."

52. In *Siliadin v France* (2006) 43 EHRR 16 the ECtHR ruled that a 15-year-old girl, brought from Togo to France and made to work for a family without pay for 15 hours a day, had been held in servitude and required to perform forced labour and that France had violated article 4 by having failed to introduce criminal legislation which would afford effective protection to her. In *CN v United Kingdom* (2013) 56 EHRR 24 the court made an analogous ruling against the UK. After the events in that case, Parliament had provided, by section 71 of the Coroners and Justice Act 2009 which extends to England, Wales and Northern Ireland, that it is a specific

criminal offence to hold a person in slavery or servitude or to require her (or him) to perform forced labour. No doubt mindful of their obligations under article 4, the UK authorities are striving in various ways to combat trafficking and to protect its victims. I refer, for example, to the Draft Modern Slavery Bill, Cm 8770, presented to Parliament in December 2013 and in particular to the amendments to it proposed by the government in its paper, Cm 8889, presented in June 2014 by way of response to the report of a parliamentary committee on the draft Bill. I note, for example, that one such amendment would provide a statutory defence to a victim of trafficking who, as a result, has been compelled to commit a crime. Although Miss Hounga is not in that category, the decision of the Court of Appeal to uphold Mrs Allen's defence of illegality to her complaint runs strikingly counter to the prominent strain of current public policy against trafficking and in favour of the protection of its victims. The public policy in support of the application of that defence, to the extent that it exists at all, should give way to the public policy to which its application is an affront; and Miss Hounga's appeal should be allowed.

Lord Hughes (with whom **Lord Carnwath** dissented on reasoning):

65. … It is not possible to interpret [the Palermo Protocol] as requiring English law to permit Miss Hounga to recover damages for the statutory tort of discrimination. That statutory tort is not in any sense co-extensive with trafficking or for that matter with exploitation. For the same reasons, it would not be possible to interpret this article as requiring English law to depart from its general principles of illegality so as to enable a person such as Miss Hounga to recover wages under an unlawful contract of employment. Moreover, the EU Directive [2011/36/EU], now in force, is more specific and explains what article 6(6) appears to have in mind:

> "Article 17 Compensation to victims
> Member States shall ensure that victims of trafficking in human beings have access to existing schemes of compensation to victims of violent crimes of intent."

> […]

67. For these reasons my conclusion is that Miss Hounga succeeds in her appeal, on the particular facts of this case, on the ground that there is insufficiently close connection between her immigration offences and her claims for the statutory tort of discrimination, for the former merely provided the setting or context in which that tort was committed, and to allow her to recover for that tort would not amount to the court condoning what it otherwise condemns. But it is not possible to read across from the law of human trafficking to provide a separate or additional reason for this outcome. Even if one assumes in Miss Hounga's favour that her treatment by Mrs Allen in England amounted to slavery or forced labour, and even if one assumes, without any findings of fact, that Mrs Allen brought her to England with the purpose of so treating her, she does not appear to have been compelled to commit the immigration offences which she certainly did commit.

NOTES AND QUESTIONS

1. The majority of the Supreme Court favour fusion of the common law doctrine of illegality with international instruments against forced labour and trafficking. As Lord Wilson indicates, the Palermo Protocol Art 6(6) requires that compensation is paid to the trafficked victim, not the employer. Lord Hughes contends that 'compensation' means public criminal compensation schemes, as the EU Trafficking Directive 2011 refers to, not damages from the employer. He favours a 'close connection' test for illegality, instead of the majority's purposive approach.

The majority suggests at [24] and [50]–[52] that the wage and unfair dismissal claims could succeed, while the minority at [65] doubts it. Why should an employer ever be unjustly enriched from a worker's labour, whether the contract is illegal or not?

2. In effect, counsel for Allen was arguing illegality was simultaneously an unjust factor (rendering a contract unenforceable) and a defence, both against recovery of a factual enrichment to the employer in the provision of valuable labour, and against the legal enrichment through failure to fulfil a right. What is the best way to prevent an employer's unjust enrichment at the expense of an employee's illegal work? Does the minority have any answer for this?

3. The reasoning of the majority in *Hounga v Allen* was subsequently approved by a majority in *Patel v Mirza* [2016] UKSC 42, and the possibility of a wage claim via *quantum meruit* endorsed by Lord Toulson at [74] and Lord Sumption at [243] referring also to New York authority, *Nizamuddowlah v Bengal Cabaret Inc*, 399 NYS 2d 854 (1977).

4. Sadly, the Republican appointees to the US Supreme Court in *Hoffman Plastic Compounds v NLRB*, 535 US 137 (2002) held 5 to 4 that an undocumented migrant who organised a union could be dismissed with impunity (a violation of ILO Conventions 87). In the dissent by the Democratic judges, Breyer J reasoned that awarding 'back pay' in compensation did not interfere with immigration policy, it could not seriously increase the incentives for people to migrate illegally, but not doing so would increase the incentives of employers to hire illegal immigrants.

5. At [33] Lord Wilson discussed *Hall v Woolston Hall Leisure Ltd* [2000] EWCA Civ 170, where an employee who 'turned a blind eye' to the employer's tax evasion through her payslip could still bring a sex discrimination claim. For discussion of the argument that rights are enforceable regardless of illegality, see C Mogridge, 'Illegal Contracts of Employment: Loss of Statutory Protection' (1981) 20 *ILJ* 23.

6. At [35] Lord Wilson noted *Vakante v Addey & Stanhope School* [2004] EWCA Civ 1065, where the Court of Appeal held a Croatian asylum seeker could not claim racial discrimination because he did not have a work permit. Why should an employing entity have immunity for its racism because it was lucky, unwitting or even criminal enough to have employed someone illegally?

7. Another important category of illegal contracts are those in 'restraint of trade'. This concept is inherently difficult, because there is a lack of consensus about what should count as legitimate restraints on people's freedom to trade, or ability to inflict economic loss on others through competition. In *Herbert Morris Ltd v Saxelby* [1916] 1 AC 688, the House of Lords found that any clause that purports to restrict an employee's freedom to work after their job terminates will be unenforceable. This does not extend to employees who take confidential information, or directors who divert maturing business opportunities: see *CMS Dolphin Ltd v Simonet* [2001] 2 BCLC 704.

8. In *William Hill Organisation Ltd v Tucker* [1999] ICR 291 the Court of Appeal refused an employer's claim for an injunction to prevent Mr Tucker working in a 6 month notice clause in his employment contract. As Mr Tucker was a spread better, he needed to continue to work to maintain his skills, and refusal to let him

do this was a repudiation of the contract. In addition, the contract could not be construed to prevent work if this would be in 'restraint of trade'.

9. In *Standard Life Health Care Ltd v Gorman* [2009] EWCA Civ 1292 the Court of Appeal granted an injunction for a 3-month notice period against employees, without pay, who wished to resign immediately and work for a competitor. The resignation was said to be a breach good faith and a duty of loyalty. Was this restraint of trade? Is it desirable for private contracts to force people onto unemployment benefits?

10. In *General Billposting Ltd v Atkinson* [1909] AC 118 the House of Lords refused to enforce a non-compete clause against an employee, because the employer had wrongfully dismissed the employee.

(c) Statutory Control for Unfair Terms?

Statutory control of unfair terms was originally deemed necessary by Parliament because of the courts' historical failure to develop a principled approach to unfair terms (see *George Mitchell (Chesterhall) Ltd v Finney Lock Seeds Ltd* [1982] EWCA Civ 5, per Lord Denning MR). The theory of 'freedom of contract' professed the idea that the state should not interfere in people's lives, whilst simultaneously lending state enforcement for contracts (an intimate interference in people's lives, funded by society through taxation). With *Autoclenz Ltd v Belcher*, the principle is established that terms must be enforced with regard to the bargaining power of the parties. This allows the courts to achieve in substance what statutory regulation of unfair terms has done. The difference is that statute structures judicial discretion. But it has been doubted that it all applies to employment.

Unfair Contract Terms Act 1977 s 2(1)

2.—Negligence liability.

(1) A person cannot by reference to any contract term or to a notice given to persons generally or to particular persons exclude or restrict his liability for death or personal injury resulting from negligence.

(2) In the case of other loss or damage, a person cannot so exclude or restrict his liability for negligence except in so far as the term or notice satisfies the requirement of reasonableness.

(3) Where a contract term or notice purports to exclude or restrict liability for negligence a person's agreement to or awareness of it is not of itself to be taken as indicating his voluntary acceptance of any risk.

[...]

3.—Liability arising in contract.

(1) This section applies as between contracting parties where one of them deals on the other's written standard terms of business.

(2) As against that party, the other cannot by reference to any contract term—

(a) when himself in breach of contract, exclude or restrict any liability of his in respect of the breach; or

(b) claim to be entitled—

(i) to render a contractual performance substantially different from that which was reasonably expected of him, or

>   (ii)   in respect of the whole or any part of his contractual obligation, to render no
>   performance at all,
> except in so far as (in any of the cases mentioned above in this subsection) the contract term
> satisfies the requirement of reasonableness.
>   …

11.—The "reasonableness" test.
    (1) In relation to a contract term, the requirement of reasonableness for the purposes of
this Part of this Act… is that the term shall have been a fair and reasonable one to be included
having regard to the circumstances which were, or ought reasonably to have been, known to
or in the contemplation of the parties when the contract was made.
    …

Schedule 2 "Guidelines" for Application of Reasonableness Test
    The matters to which regard is to be had in particular sections 6(1A), 7(1A) and (4), 20 and
21 are any of the following which appear to be relevant—
    (a)   the strength of the bargaining positions of the parties relative to each other, taking
           into account (among other things) alternative means by which the customer's
           requirements could have been met.…

NOTES AND QUESTIONS

1.   The Unfair Contract Terms Act (UCTA) 1977 s 1(3) states the Act covers things
      done 'in the course of a business'. Section 11(4) adds that to determine what is
      reasonable, a party's 'resources' to meet a liability, and ability to 'cover himself by
      insurance', should also be considered. Although Schedule 2 itself refers to ss 6, 7,
      20 and 21 and the 'customer', it has been consistently held that its guidelines are
      also relevant for applying the reasonableness test in all other sections. Bargaining
      power is probably the most important element of regulating unfair terms among
      consumer contracts, tenancies, or small to big businesses.

Johnstone v Bloomsbury Health Authority **[1992] QB 333**

Dr Chris Johnstone claimed that Bloomsbury Health Authority had breached his contract
by demanding he follow a term to work 'on average' 48 hours beyond a standard 40-hour
week. He was a junior doctor in the Obstetric Department at University College Hospital.
Paragraph 4(b) of his contract said he should be on call 48 hours a week 'on average', on
top of his 40 hour contract. His working time had been 'in some weeks exceeding 100,
with inadequate periods of sleep; over one weekend he worked a 32-hour shift with only
30 minutes' sleep'. That is, in some weeks he was working over 14 hours a day, every
day; there are 168 hours in a week. Dr Johnstone claimed damages for personal injury, as
he had 'stress and depression; is lethargic and his appetite and ability to sleep are diminished. He has been physically sick on occasions from exhaustion and has felt desperate
and suicidal.' Dr Johnstone claimed being required to work over 72 hours a week was
contrary to public policy at common law, a breach of an implied term to provide a 'safe
system of working' (on this point, see chapter 5(2)(c)) and that it was a further breach of
UCTA 1977 s 2(1). The hospital claimed that Dr Johnstone's claim was 'frivolous and
vexatious' and he was bound to the express contract terms. The Court of Appeal held the
claims should not be struck out.

Stuart-Smith LJ:

There is no dispute that the defendants' liability, if any, is for personal injury resulting from negligence: see section 1(1) and (3) and the section operates in favour of the plaintiff, if it is applicable. By paragraph 4 of Schedule 1 it is provided that section 2(1) and (2) "do not extend to a contract of employment, except in favour of the employee." I take this to mean that if there is in a contract of employment a term excluding or restricting the liability of the employer to the employee, the latter can rely on the provisions of section 2(1) and (2).

Section 13(1) is also relevant:

"To the extent that this Part of this Act prevents the exclusion or restriction of any liability it also prevents – (a) making the liability or its enforcement subject to restrictive or onerous conditions; (b) excluding or restricting any right or remedy in respect of the liability, or subjecting a person to any prejudice in consequence of his pursuing any such right or remedy ... and (to that extent) sections 2 and 5 to 7 also prevent excluding or restricting liability by reference to terms and notices which exclude or restrict the relevant obligation or duty."

When considering the operation of section 2 of the Act the court is concerned with the substance and not the form of the contractual provision. In *Phillips Products Ltd v Hyland* [1987] 1 WLR 659, 666, Slade L.J. said:

"In applying section 2(2), it is not relevant to consider whether the form of a condition is such that it can aptly be given the label of an 'exclusion' or 'restriction' clause. There is no mystique about 'exclusion' or 'restriction' clauses. To decide whether a person 'excludes' liability by reference to a contract term, you look at the effect of the term. You look at its substance."

If, contrary to my opinion, the defendants are entitled to succeed on the submissions they advanced in support of the appeal in relation to the statement of claim, it is arguable that they can only do so because the effect of paragraph 4(b) of the contract must be construed as an express assumption of risk by the plaintiff (a plea of *volenti non fit injuria*) or because it operates to restrict or limit the ambit and scope of the duty of care owed by the defendants. If that is the correct analysis, then the substance and effect, though not the form, of the term is such that it can properly be argued to fall within section 1(1) of the Act. For this reason, in my judgment, paragraph 4(i) of the reply should not be struck out.

Leggatt LJ and **Browne-Wilkinson VC** concurred.

NOTES AND QUESTIONS

1. The reasoning of Stuart-Smith LJ suggests that any contract term that could lead to personal injury, directly or indirectly, is unlawful. Section 13 makes clear that it is irrelevant what form the unfair clause takes: what matters is its effect or 'substance'. To what extent can this type of regulation tackle the problem of a 'long hours culture'?

2. Apart from the UCTA 1977 question, Dr Johnstone's claim that there to be a common law right to health and safety, with some complication, was approved (see chapter 5).

Commerzbank AG v Keen [2006] EWCA Civ 1536

Mr Keen claimed that Commerzbank AG acted in breach of contract, or its employment contract violated UCTA 1977 s 3, by not awarding him a 'discretionary' bonus in 2005. Mr Keen had a basic salary of £120,000 on the bank's proprietary trading desk, and had received bonuses of €2.8m in 2003 and €2.95m in 2004. In May 2005, the desk was closed, and he was made redundant in June. His contract said: 'No bonus will be paid to you if on the date of payment of the bonus you are not employed.' In March 2006, the bank refused to pay a bonus for the time Mr Keen worked in 2005. He claimed that the bank's exercise of discretion breached an implied contract term because it was irrational or perverse, or alternatively, that the requirement to be 'employed' at the time was an unreasonable standard form provision under UCTA 1977 s 3. The Court of Appeal held that section 3 was not meant to apply to employment contracts.

Mummery LJ:

77. Mr Robin Knowles QC submitted that the Bank is not entitled to rely on the provision requiring Mr Keen to be in the employment of the Bank in order to participate in the discretionary bonus scheme. He submits that if it has the meaning contended for by the Bank, it is an unfair contract term within section 3 of the 1977 Act and is subject to the statutory requirement of reasonableness. The Bank, he contended, is claiming to be entitled to render a contractual performance substantially different from that which was reasonably expected of it: see *Timeload Ltd v. British Telecommunications plc* [1995] EMLR 459 at 468 and *Zockoll Group Ltd v. Mercury Communications Ltd & Anor* [1998] ITCLR 104 at 118E–119D.

78. The first question is whether the 1977 Act applies at all to a contract term for the remuneration of an employee. Section 1 of the 1977 Act provides that sections 2 to 7 of the Act apply only to business liability, that is liability for breach of obligations or duties arising from things done or to be done by a person in the course of a business and references to liability are to be read accordingly.
[His Lordship read UCTA 1977 section 3 and continued:]

82. No express mention is made to contracts of employment in respect of section 3, but there is a provision that section 2(1) and (2) do not extend to a contract of employment, except in favour of an employee: Schedule 1 paragraph 4....

...

87. In this case the question of construction falls into two parts: the first is whether Mr Keen was dealing with the Bank "as a consumer" in contracting with it (the consumer point). The second is whether Mr Keen was dealing with the Bank on its "written standard terms of business" (the standard terms point).

...

101. I do not see how it can be argued with any real prospect of success that under such a term for remuneration Mr Keen "deals as consumer" with the Bank. As a matter of principle and of construction of section 3 I have been assisted in reaching this conclusion by the analysis of Professor Mark Freedland in the 2nd edition of his work "The Personal Contract of Employment" at pp 190–191. I agree with his general conclusion that

"This body of regulation is of marginal application to personal work or employment contracts, both as to its scope and its substance."

102. As he says, the regulation of fairness of contract terms by section 3 of the 1977 Act is not primarily directed at personal work or employment contracts and is not particularly appropriate to them. After citing *Brigden* and referring to the article of Loraine Watson, he rightly comments that such contracts do not really fit naturally into the categories of consumer contracts or standard form contracts, as it involves treating workers as users or recipients of goods or services when in truth they are providers of their services. It is artificial and unconvincing to read section 3 as extending to payment provisions in respect of personal services rendered by the employee to the employer. I do not think that there is a real prospect of a trial judge coming to a contrary conclusion after hearing all the arguments.

103. For similar reasons I have reached the same conclusion on the issue whether Mr Keen contracted on the Bank's "written standard terms of business" in relation to the provision in the discretionary bonus scheme requiring him to be in the employment of the Bank at the date of payment of the bonus.

104. As Morland J pointed out in Brigden the relevant business in that case, as in this case, is the business of banking. The terms as to the payment of discretionary bonuses were not the standard terms of the business of banking. They were the terms of the remuneration of certain employees of the Bank, such as Mr Keen, who were employed in part of the Bank's business.

Jacob LJ and **Moses LJ** concurred.

NOTES AND QUESTIONS

1. Mummery LJ reasons that section 3 does not apply to an employee on the basis that Mark Freedland said this 'body of regulation is of marginal application'. Arguably the better view is that UCTA 1977 is in general terms because it aimed to regulate all 'Unfair Contract Terms'. Because UCTA 1977 Sch 1, para 4 clarifies its application regarding s 2, this suggests it applies in its entirety to employment unless it targets other groups such as consumers. This was an unnecessary gloss on the statute.

2. It is respectfully suggested that Professor Freedland's argument in *The Personal Employment Contract* (2003) ch 3, was taken out of context. He did not say UCTA 1977 s 3 (aside from provisions on consumers) was inapplicable to employment. He was merely made the point that the primary regulation of the employment relationship is found in specialised statutory rights. Although employees, consumers, tenants or small investors all lack bargaining power, it does not follow that one-size-fits-all regulation is sufficient for them. Moreover, Professor Freedland at no point stated that most employment contracts were not in 'standard form'. Usually they are.

(2) INCORPORATION OF TERMS

Generally speaking, when an employee signs a contract everything in the document will form part of the agreement unless this contradicts a statutory right, the application of UCTA 1977, or if it does not 'in truth represent what was agreed' (as in *Autoclenz*). Beyond the written agreement, more terms may be 'incorporated'. While the 'implied terms' discussed in chapter 5 exist because of the parties' inaction, incorporated terms exist because of the actions of one or both of the parties: terms can be incorporated by reference to other documents, particularly a workplace rule book or a collective agreement. If there is no written document, or it is silent, these sources of terms can still be incorporated through verbal agreements, assurances or conduct. This section considers those two main sources and (though it is a right) the employer's duties to notify the employee of his or her contractual rights under ERA 1996 s 1.

(a) Incorporation: Workplace Rule Book

French v Barclays Bank plc **[1998] EWCA Civ 1092**

Mr French claimed that his employer, Barclays Bank plc, was in breach of contract by refusing to give him an interest-free bridging loan to move house, which was referred to in the staff manual. Under a contractual mobility clause, Mr French was required to relocate from Oxfordshire to Essex. He needed to sell his family home in Radley and buy another in Billericay, and he thought he could rely on the bridging loan to complete the purchase of the new house before selling the old one. However, the housing market collapsed, meaning by October 1989 the Radley house was valued at £150,000, when he had been trying to sell it for £195,000. At this point, the bank refused to provide the loan. The Court of Appeal held that this constituted a breach of contract.

Waller LJ:

The starting point must be Mr French's contract of employment. That is the relevant contract looking at the matter chronologically. What is more, it is under the contract of employment that Mr French is obliged to relocate at the request of the Bank, and it is in the context of that request, together with the contract of employment, in which the terms of the loan must be construed.

When Mr French joined the staff of the Bank he did so by virtue of a letter of appointment dated 28 June 1967 and his acknowledgement of that letter dated 2 July 1967. It was an express term of his engagement that it was subject to "the other regulations and conditions of service contained in a staff handbook enclosed herewith". In acknowledging receipt of the letter Mr French accepted the engagement on the basis of the "staff handbook and pension fund regulations." Not surprisingly, the staff handbook and rules altered from time to time and Mr French ultimately, in 1981, acknowledged receipt of the booklet dated October 1980 setting out the rules for, and giving information relating to, the managerial and clerical staff of the Bank. There is no dispute that the relevant handbook and rules applicable to Mr French, as at the material time, are those dated January 1985. The first rule of conduct was that "every member of the staff must be willing to serve at any office of the Bank, or at any of its subsidiary companies in the United Kingdom, as may be required and will serve the Bank faithfully diligently to the best of his or her ability." The rules provided that "applications by any member of staff who requires an advance from the Bank, whether or not supported by approved security, must be submitted to his/her manager. No advance, either by way of loan or by way of overdraft may be made to a member of the staff, ... until sanction has been obtained from the appropriate authority."

...

The rules referred to included some general rules of some materiality. Under the heading "Removal Expenses and Removal Grants" "Members of the staff who are householders and who are transferred from one office to another to suit the convenience of the Bank may claim reasonable expenses incurred in the move if this of necessity involves a change of residence. They may also be entitled to receive a removal grant and a disturbance allowance" Under the heading "Staff Housing Loans" "Special schemes are available to assist members of the pensionable staff in the necessary purchase of houses for their own occupation.

Interest is charged at specially reduced rates and in certain circumstances, the Bank will give some assistance should the subsequent sale of the house involve the applicant in financial loss. Full details may be obtained from the staff manual."

It is common ground that the relevant version of the staff manual is that dated September 1988. The section relating to staff loans includes in the general conditions the following: – "The present facilities available to staff and the guidelines relating to the sanctioning of loans are detailed in this section but the decision to grant a loan is entirely at the discretion of the Bank. Staff loans can in no sense and for no purpose be regarded as a term or condition of service."

...

Once the Bank in the exercise of its discretion had granted a bridging loan interest-free on the terms of the staff manual, there was an obligation on the Bank to maintain that position, unless of course Mr French failed in some way to carry out his obligation to market the house at the agreed price. The Bank was of course able to make the loan as short term as they liked by buying the house at the agreed price i.e. by adopting the Hambro or Mann & Company policy but offering a price by reference to the original valuations rather than by reference to a value six months on.

Thus, under ordinary contractual principles, it seems to me that the 10 October 1989 letter was a breach of the loan contract. What it made clear was that if Mr French did not accept a different scheme from that under which his interest-free bridging loan had been agreed, that bridging loan would not be interest-free after twelve months. That is the clearest notice that the Bank did not intend to fulfil their contractual obligations under the loan terms.

...

I accept that in considering whether there was a breach of the terms of the loan, it adds nothing to say that in breaching the terms the Bank was involved in a change of policy. However, in considering whether there was a breach of the implied term not to breach trust and confidence, the quality of the conduct of the Bank is clearly relevant. To seek to invoke a change of a policy or a change in the terms on which loans were made to employees requested to relocate which (a) has been applied to other employees over many years and (b) appeared in terms in the manual at the time when the loan was made, is conduct which would be likely to destroy the confidence and trust between the Bank and its employees.

In my view Mr French had an entitlement to damages flowing first from a breach of the terms on which he received the bridging loan originally, and second from a breach of the implied terms of his contract of employment that trust and confidence would not be undermined. On this aspect thus I would dismiss the Bank's appeal.

Walker LJ and **Hobhouse LJ** agreed.

NOTES AND QUESTIONS

1.   Waller LJ based his decision on 'ordinary contractual principles' to say that the bank's withdrawal of the bridging loan constituted a breach. Those principles were set out in cases such as *J Spurling Ltd v Bradshaw* [1956] EWCA Civ 3 (concerning liability for orange juice barrels breaking) and *Interfoto Picture Library Ltd v Stiletto Visual Programmes Ltd* [1987] EWCA Civ 6 (a term requiring high payments for retaining photo transparencies was not incorporated through a slip inside the unopened bag). Terms are incorporated by reasonable notice, but 'the more unreasonable a clause is, the greater the notice ... must be given of it.'

2. On a post-*Johnson* and *Gisda Cyf* approach, instead of 'ordinary' contractual principles, should specialised principles for the employment relation be developed? Presumably it would follow that terms onerous for the employee (if not contrary to law) would require explicit notice, while terms benefiting the employee would be incorporated on any assurance that an employing entity objectively manifests to staff.

3. In *Briscoe v Lubrizol* [2002] EWCA Civ 508, Potter LJ stated obiter that details of the employment relation are often found in a handbook, which are incorporated and binding even without express reference in written statements that are handed to the employee. Do you think this should hold regardless of the nature of the terms?

(b) Incorporation: Collective Agreements

The Trade Union and Labour Relations (Consolidation) Act 1992 s 179

179 Whether agreement intended to be a legally enforceable contract.
(1) A collective agreement shall be conclusively presumed not to have been intended by the parties to be a legally enforceable contract unless the agreement—
    (a) is in writing, and
    (b) contains a provision which (however expressed) states that the parties intend that the agreement shall be a legally enforceable contract.
(2) A collective agreement which does satisfy those conditions shall be conclusively presumed to have been intended by the parties to be a legally enforceable contract...

NOTES AND QUESTIONS

1. Section 179(3) goes on to say that parts of a collective agreement could be identified as binding, or not. This codifies a labour law theory, dating from the Trade Union Act 1871, that collective agreements were to be outside of the purview of the courts' enforcement, since the working people (not without justification in the nineteenth century) did not trust judges. To what extent is this still a good approach?

2. O Kahn-Freund, 'Collective Agreements' (1941) 4 *MLR* 225, suggested that although collective agreements were presumed not to intend to create legal relations, the rights they created for employees could not be derogated from to the detriment of the employee. Adopting this view, there would in effect be a four-tier system of labour regulation: (1) a minimum floor of rights created by law, (2) a first floor of rights by collective agreement, (3) a second floor of rights created by individual contracts, and (4) a third level of rights subject to the employing entity's discretion. See chapter 5(1).

3. In *Camden Exhibition & Display Ltd v Lynott* [1966] 1 QB 555 the Court of Appeal first held by a majority that a collective agreement provision was incorporated into individual employment contracts. However, this was done to enforce a clause that overtime for 'due and proper performance of contracts shall not be subject to restriction'. The effect was that employees could not refuse to work

overtime during industrial action: seemingly the opposite of what Kahn-Freund had advocated.

4. TULRCA 1992 s 179(4) says that parts of a collective agreement that are not binding can still be referred to 'for the purpose of interpreting a part of the agreement which is such a contract'. The same is true for construing an individual contract of employment, which can be held to incorporate the collective agreement's terms.

Kaur v MG Rover Group Ltd **[2004] EWCA 1507**

Mrs Kaur claimed an injunction against being made compulsorily redundant from MG Rover Ltd on the basis of her workplace collective agreement. Her employment contract said it was 'in accordance with and, where appropriate, subject to … collective agreements'. The collective agreement, named 'The Way Ahead Partnership Agreement', said in para 2.1: 'As with the successful introduction of "Rover Tomorrow – The New Deal', THERE WILL BE NO COMPULSORY REDUNDANCY.' Paragraph 2.3 read that any 'reductions in manpower' would be achieved 'with the co-operation of all employees … after consultation with trade unions'. In 2003, Mrs Kaur was threatened with redundancy. The Court of Appeal held that para 2.1 was not 'apt' to be incorporated because this was not 'intended'.

Keene LJ:

31. I can accept that The Way Ahead does generally have the character of a bargain, struck between the appellant and the unions, and that what is said in it about compulsory redundancy reflected the statements about more flexible working by the workforce. But that does not get the respondent very far at all. It is what one would expect of a collective agreement, which as both sides accept is an agreement but not something which is in itself normally enforceable at law. At a collective level, various assurances and statements as to the future were undoubtedly made by both the employer and the trade unions. But the fact that paragraph 2.1 was not unilateral but part of such a package tells one nothing about its aptness for incorporation as a term of individual contracts of employment.

32. That issue is one to be resolved by looking at the words relied on in their context. That context contains a number of features, which seem to me to indicate that those words are expressing an aspiration rather than a binding contractual term. First, the preceding sentence in the same paragraph is important. It describes enabling employees who want to work for Rover to stay with Rover as "an objective," something therefore which it is hoped to achieve. But that objective is the very same thing as saying that there will be no compulsory redundancy. It is only if the objective is achieved that there would be no compulsory redundancy. It follows that the character of the crucial second sentence is to be viewed in the light of the first sentence, indicating that this is an objective, rather than a binding promise.

33. Secondly, that is reinforced by the opening words of the second sentence, "as with the successful introduction of 'Rover Tomorrow – The New Deal'," which suggest that the statement about no compulsory redundancy is to be seen as a repeat of the earlier position in The New Deal. Yet, as I have already concluded, the position under The New Deal was one where the statements about employees being able to stay with Rover were not contractual commitments. Thirdly, paragraph 2.3 of The Way Ahead is relevant, as it is the positive counterpart of

the statement about no compulsory redundancy. Paragraph 2.3 spells out how future reductions in manpower will be achieved and so, implicitly, how compulsory redundancies can be avoided. It is the other side of the coin to paragraph 2.1. But it states that such reductions "will be achieved in future, with the co-operation of all employees, through natural wastage ... (etc)." As Mr Goudie submits, this indicates that avoiding compulsory redundancies is contingent on the co-operation of the workforce as a whole, whatever that may mean. That makes it very difficult to see the reference to "no compulsory redundancy" as an enforceable term in each employee's contract of employment, both because of the vagueness of the language of paragraph 2.3 and because any entitlement would depend on the activities of others in the workforce. I regard paragraph 2.3 as highly relevant when one comes to consider the significance of paragraph 2.1. Seen together, the aspirational nature of the company's statement is plain, as indeed is its collective rather than individual character.

34. I conclude, therefore, that the words relied on by the respondent in paragraph 2.1 of The Way Ahead were not intended to be incorporated into the contracts of employment of individual employees and were not apt for such incorporation. In so far as they formed part of a bargain with the unions, the commitment was solely on a collective basis. For these reasons and, in respect of the cross-appeal, for the reasons given earlier in this judgment, I would allow the appeal and dismiss the cross-appeal.

Jonathan Parker LJ and **Brooke LJ** agreed.

NOTES AND QUESTIONS

1. Keene LJ's reasons for saying para 2.1 was not apt or intended to be incorporated are that avoiding redundancies was an 'objective' that might not be achieved and was 'contingent' on the cooperation of the workforce. The 'vagueness' of para 2.3 infected para 2.1. If collective agreements were presumed to create legal relations, would the result have differed?
2. In *Henry v London General Transport Services Ltd* [2002] EWCA Civ 488, the Court of Appeal described a collective agreement as 'implied', rather than incorporated, following a series of cases suggesting that collective agreements become the 'custom' of a workplace. What is to be gained (if anything) by saying collective agreement terms are implied rather than incorporated?

Malone v British Airways plc [2010] EWCA Civ 1225

Miss Malone and other crew claimed that British Airways breached their employment contracts by reducing the number of cabin crew on their planes. Section 7.1 of the workplace collective agreement specified minimum crew on board. The reduced number of cabin crew was still above the level required by law. British Airways contended that section 7.1 of the collective agreement was not 'apt' for incorporation. Miss Malone contended that it was, because having fewer colleagues affected her individual working conditions. The Court of Appeal held that, though it affected working conditions, the undertakings were not directed in favour of individual employees and not incorporated.

Smith LJ:

60. … It is not clear from the language whether section 7.1 is intended to be enforceable by an individual employee. In that it is unlike several other subsections which clearly impose duties on an individual employee or obligations on the employer towards individual employees. In my view, examining the context of the agreement as a whole does not help with the construction of section 7.1.

61. I am satisfied that crew complements do impact to some extent upon the working conditions of individual employees and that that is a pointer towards section 7.1 being intended as an individually enforceable term. I also accept that the fact that crew complements have, in the past, been negotiated as part of a productivity deal is another pointer towards enforceability. I accept also that an undertaking as to the size of the team of workers who will undertake a task may, in some circumstances, be enforceable by individuals.

62. Set against that are the disastrous consequences for BA which could ensue if this term were to be individually enforceable. It seems to me that they are so serious as to be unthinkable. By that I mean that if the parties had thought about the issue at the time of negotiation, they would have immediately have said it was not intended that section 7.1 could have the effect of enabling an individual or a small group of cabin crew members to bring a flight to a halt by refusing to work under complement. So, if I apply the rule by which a term of uncertain meaning is to be construed, that of asking what, objectively considered in the light of the factual matrix against which the agreement was made, the parties must be taken to have intended the provision to mean, I am driven to the conclusion that they did not mean this term to be individually enforceable. I accept that there are pointers towards individual enforceability but these are not conclusive. In the end, I think that the true construction of this term is that it was intended as an undertaking by the employer towards its cabin crew employees collectively and was intended partly to protect jobs and partly to protect the crews, collectively, against excessive demands in terms of work and effort. I think that it was intended to be binding only in honour, although it created a danger that, if breached, industrial action would follow.

Ward LJ and **Jackson LJ** agreed.

NOTES AND QUESTIONS

1. Was it helpful to suggest that it would be 'disastrous' and 'unthinkable' if an individual crew member could refuse to fly in breach of their employment contract?
2. In *Garratt v Mirror Group Newspapers* [2011] EWCA 425 the Court of Appeal held that a workplace 'custom' of signing a compromise agreement, which would waive legal claims, was effective to limit a right to enhanced redundancy pay that derived from collective agreements. Which principles, if any, justify such a stance?
3. What do you think are the potential drawbacks and benefits of collective agreements becoming legally enforceable in their entirety?

(c) Right to Notice of Terms

Does it matter whether the employee knows or understands the content of the contract of employment? The Contracts of Employment Act 1963 originally introduced the right to receive a statement of the contract from the employer, 'to have the terms of his contract which affect him most closely set down in black and white' (Hansard HC Debs (14 February 1963) vol 671, col 1511). The Employment Information Directive 91/533/EEC harmonised various basic standards throughout the EU, which the ERA 1996 now reflects.

Employment Rights Act 1996 ss 1–2

1.—Statement of initial employment particulars.
    (1) Where an employee begins employment with an employer, the employer shall give to the employee a written statement of particulars of employment.
    (2) The statement may (subject to section 2(4)) be given in instalments and (whether or not given in instalments) shall be given not later than two months after the beginning of the employment.
    (3) The statement shall contain particulars of—
        (a) the names of the employer and employee,
        (b) the date when the employment began, and
        (c) the date on which the employee's period of continuous employment began (taking into account any employment with a previous employer which counts towards that period).
    (4) The statement shall also contain particulars, as at a specified date not more than seven days before the statement (or the instalment containing them) is given, of—
        (a) the scale or rate of remuneration or the method of calculating remuneration,
        (b) the intervals at which remuneration is paid (that is, weekly, monthly or other specified intervals),
        (c) any terms and conditions relating to hours of work (including any terms and conditions relating to normal working hours),
        (d) any terms and conditions relating to any of the following—
            (i)   entitlement to holidays, including public holidays, and holiday pay (the particulars given being sufficient to enable the employee's entitlement, including any entitlement to accrued holiday pay on the termination of employment, to be precisely calculated),
            (ii) incapacity for work due to sickness or injury, including any provision for sick pay, and
            (iii) pensions and pension schemes,
    (e) the length of notice which the employee is obliged to give and entitled to receive to terminate his contract of employment,
    (f) the title of the job which the employee is employed to do or a brief description of the work for which he is employed,
    (g) where the employment is not intended to be permanent, the period for which it is expected to continue or, if it is for a fixed term, the date when it is to end,
    (h) either the place of work or, where the employee is required or permitted to work at various places, an indication of that and of the address of the employer,
    (i) any collective agreements which directly affect the terms and conditions of the employment including, where the employer is not a party, the persons by whom they were made, and

(j) where the employee is required to work outside the United Kingdom for a period of more than one month—
  (i)   the period for which he is to work outside the United Kingdom,
  (ii) the currency in which remuneration is to be paid while he is working outside the United Kingdom,
  (iii) any additional remuneration payable to him, and any benefits to be provided to or in respect of him, by reason of his being required to work outside the United Kingdom, and
  (iv) any terms and conditions relating to his return to the United Kingdom.
(5) Subsection (4)(d)(iii) does not apply to an employee of a body or authority if—
  (a) the employee's pension rights depend on the terms of a pension scheme established under any provision contained in or having effect under any Act, and
  (b) any such provision requires the body or authority to give to a new employee information concerning the employee's pension rights or the determination of questions affecting those rights.

NOTES AND QUESTIONS

1. Given this provision's complexity, would it be preferable to append a 'model employment contract' to the ERA 1996, where the details relevant to the parties could be filled in? This could reduce contract length. The terms of the model would be deemed to apply by default of amendment. This is done for company constitutions: Companies Act 2006 section 20 and Companies (Model Articles) Regulations 2008.
2. J Kenner, 'Statement or Contract – Some Reflections on the EC Employer Information (Contract or Employment Relationship) Directive after *Kampelmann*' (1999) 28 *ILJ* 205, suggests that, while the right to a statement of a contract marked the birth of individual employment rights in 1963, its spread through EU law coincided with a dismantling of more significant labour law protection, such as wage councils or collective bargaining.
3. *Southern Cross Healthcare Co Ltd v Perkins* [2010] EWCA Civ 1442 held that a Tribunal has no power to interpret or construe the written statement, if it is ambiguous, and to enforce it. Instead an employee must go to a civil court for contractual construction issues, because under the Employment Tribunals Act 1996 section 3, and the Employment Tribunals Extension of Jurisdiction (England and Wales) Order 1994 Art 4(d) does cover breach of contract claims for dismissals but generally not other breach of contract claims. This is so even though ERA 1996 s 12 allows the tribunal to declare what particulars in the statement should have been given. Is the *Perkins* result intellectually coherent?
4. The written statement of the contract is not to be confused with the contract itself: oral agreement and the conduct of the parties often supplement or override the written document. However, the ECJ in *Kampelmann v Landschaftsverband Westfalen-Lippe* (1997) C-253/96, essentially following *System Floors (UK) Ltd v Daniel* [1982] ICR 54, held that the statement will be 'very strong prima facie evidence' of the contract, but not binding. Here, the employer mistakenly stated an employee's contract began a week earlier. Browne-Wilkinson J disregarded this, so as to deny the employee was within the statutory qualifying period to claim unfair dismissal. When it confers a benefit on the employee, should the written statement bind the employer conclusively?

Scally v Southern Health and Social Services Board [1992] 1 AC 294

Dr Scally and three other doctors claimed damages against the Board for an alleged breach of duty to inform them that, to get full superannuation benefits, they needed to make extra contributions to their occupational pension scheme. This formed part of their contract, but they were unaware of this until after a 12-month time limit had already expired. They contended that, although there was no explicit duty on the employer, one should be implied as part of their contract of employment, because this was necessary to know the express, but complex, contractual rights. The House of Lords held that there was an implied right to be informed on the facts.

Lord Bridge:

... in the modern world it is increasingly common for individuals to enter into contracts, particularly contracts of employment, on complex terms which have been settled in the course of negotiations between representative bodies or organisations and many details of which the individual employee cannot be expected to know unless they are drawn to his attention.

...

There are three possible views of the legal consequences arising from this situation. The first is that it could be properly be left to individual employees, knowing that they were compulsory contributors to a superannuation scheme, to make enquiries and ascertain the details of the scheme for themselves. In the light of the judge's findings, I think this view can be confidently rejected. There was no reason whatever why young doctors embarking on a career in the health services should appreciate the necessity to enquire into the details of the superannuation scheme to which they were contributors in order to be in a position to enjoy its benefits. The second view is that the law provided no means of ensuring that the intended beneficiaries of the opportunity to buy added years became aware of it, so that it would be a matter of chance whether or not, in relation to any individual employee, the relevant provision of the Regulations of 1974 achieved its intended purpose. I find this view so unattractive that I would accept it only if driven to the conclusion that there was no other legally tenable alternative. The third view is that there was an obligation on either the employing board or the department to take reasonable steps to bring the relevant provision to the notice of employees in time to avail themselves of the opportunity to buy added years if they so decided.

...

Will the law then imply a term in the contract of employment imposing such an obligation on the employer? ... I fully appreciate that the criterion to justify an implication of this kind is necessity, not reasonableness. But I take the view that it is not merely reasonable, but necessary, in the circumstances postulated, to imply an obligation on the employer to take reasonable steps to bring the term of the contract in question to the employee's attention, so that he may be in a position to enjoy its benefit. Accordingly I would hold that there was an implied term in each of the plaintiffs' contracts of employment of which the boards were in each case in breach.

Lord Roskill, Lord Goff, Lord Jauncey and **Lord Lowry** concurred.

NOTES AND QUESTIONS

1. *Scally* decided that employees had a common law right (on the basis of an implied term, discussed in chapter 5) to have the pension right brought 'to the employee's attention' because only then would the employee 'be in a position to enjoy its benefit'. Two months after the decision the proprietor of *The Mirror* newspaper,

Robert Maxwell, died after falling off his yacht, and it was revealed he had been stealing his employees' pension savings. This led to significant change after the Goode Report, *Pension Law Reform* (1993) Cm 2342, particularly recommending employee representatives to participate in pension governance. See chapters 6(3) and 12.

2. To reach the result, Lord Bridge states the implied right fulfilled the required test of 'necessity'. He did not articulate a general principle by which the right might be necessary, other than 'to enjoy' full pension rights. The House of Lords has since made clear that terms are to be implied as 'necessary to reflect the reasonable expectations of the parties': *Equitable Life Assurance Society v Hyman* [2002] 1 AC 408.

3. In *Crossley v Faithful & Gould Holdings Ltd* [2004] EWCA Civ 293 the Court of Appeal held that a director, who suffered a nervous breakdown, took leave, and then resigned after consulting the employer's staffing department, had no right to be informed that would end his workplace incapacity benefits. Dyson LJ said the test of 'necessity' was an 'elusive concept'. He did not have the benefit of submissions on the recent developments which had made the necessity test less elusive: the importance of 'reasonable expectations' (see chapter 5). He went on to say courts should 'recognise that, to some extent at least, the existence and scope of standardised implied terms raise questions of reasonableness, fairness and the balancing of competing policy considerations'. This led to the conclusion that the director, who was in a state of nervous breakdown, was not entitled to be informed of his incapacity benefits as that would be 'an unfair and unreasonable burden on employers'.

4. With the greatest respect, the Court of Appeal's reasoning in *Crossley* could have been improved. To assess relative burdens it is necessary to quantify the financial detriment to the company compared to the financial impact on the employee and his family: it was simply assumed to be a zero-sum game. Then, whatever the financial results show, the relative positions of the employee and the corporation should be weighed, and the employee's interests should be given greater weight than the corporation's. Further, it should be questioned how the parties conducted themselves. Especially since this was an employment case, it appears worse than a situation where in bad faith a defendant 'snaps up' an offer which is known to be mistaken: *Hartog v Colin & Shields* [1939] 3 All ER 566. After all, Mr Crossley merely sought the contractual benefit for which he had given good consideration by his labour. The employing entity cheated him.

(3) CHOICE AND CONFLICTS OF LAW

In a globalising economy, with more work that goes across borders between legal systems, contracting parties may seek to choose the legal system that applies to their relationship. There would be a 'race to the bottom' in labour rights if employing entities could use a 'choice of law' clause to select systems with worse protection than in the UK (or indeed, if an employer abroad chose the UK to avoid a system with better labour rights). It follows that the justifications for regulating choice and conflicts of law are essentially the same as the justifications for having labour rights at all: standards should apply to ensure employing entities compete on efficiency and quality of product or services, not on cutting people's living standards. This means the contractual element of employment is different to commercial or other contracts. This section overlaps with the next chapter, as it covers what happens when the parties are silent on the choice of law.

Introductory reading: CEM ch 2 (57–60). D&M ch 1 (118–30).

(a) Contract

This section considers the position in the European Union. UK courts have decided that, at common law, an essentially identical result transpires by interpreting statutory rights.

Rome I Regulation (EC) 593/2008, Arts 3 and 8

Whereas:

...

(23) As regards contracts concluded with parties regarded as being weaker, those parties should be protected by conflict-of-law rules that are more favourable to their interests than the general rules.

...

(34) The rule on individual employment contracts should not prejudice the application of the overriding mandatory provisions of the country to which a worker is posted in accordance with Directive 96/71/EC of the European Parliament and of the Council of 16 December 1996 concerning the posting of workers in the framework of the provision of services.

(35) Employees should not be deprived of the protection afforded to them by provisions which cannot be derogated from by agreement or which can only be derogated from to their benefit.

(36) As regards individual employment contracts, work carried out in another country should be regarded as temporary if the employee is expected to resume working in the country of origin after carrying out his tasks abroad. The conclusion of a new contract of employment with the original employer or an employer belonging to the same group of companies as the original employer should not preclude the employee from being regarded as carrying out his work in another country temporarily.

...

Article 3 Freedom of choice
    1. A contract shall be governed by the law chosen by the parties. The choice shall be made expressly or clearly demonstrated by the terms of the contract or the circumstances of the case. By their choice the parties can select the law applicable to the whole or to part only of the contract.

2. The parties may at any time agree to subject the contract to a law other than that which previously governed it, whether as a result of an earlier choice made under this Article or of other provisions of this Regulation. ...

3. Where all other elements relevant to the situation at the time of the choice are located in a country other than the country whose law has been chosen, the choice of the parties shall not prejudice the application of provisions of the law of that other country which cannot be derogated from by agreement.

4. Where all other elements relevant to the situation at the time of the choice are located in one or more Member States, the parties' choice of applicable law other than that of a Member State shall not prejudice the application of provisions of Community law, where appropriate as implemented in the Member State of the forum, which cannot be derogated from by agreement.

...

Article 8 Individual employment contracts

1. An individual employment contract shall be governed by the law chosen by the parties in accordance with Article 3. Such a choice of law may not, however, have the result of depriving the employee of the protection afforded to him by provisions that cannot be derogated from by agreement under the law that, in the absence of choice, would have been applicable pursuant to paragraphs 2, 3 and 4 of this Article.

2. To the extent that the law applicable to the individual employment contract has not been chosen by the parties, the contract shall be governed by the law of the country in which or, failing that, from which the employee habitually carries out his work in performance of the contract. The country where the work is habitually carried out shall not be deemed to have changed if he is temporarily employed in another country.

3. Where the law applicable cannot be determined pursuant to paragraph 2, the contract shall be governed by the law of the country where the place of business through which the employee was engaged is situated.

4. Where it appears from the circumstances as a whole that the contract is more closely connected with a country other than that indicated in paragraphs 2 or 3, the law of that other country shall apply.

NOTES AND QUESTIONS

1. The Regulation makes clear that the employee, as the 'weaker' party (recital 23), may not lose labour rights that 'cannot be derogated from by agreement' (Arts 8(1) and 3(2)), but that otherwise (for terms of a contract that go beyond the minimum) the parties have 'freedom of choice' (Art 3). If a contract term does not identify a choice of law, it is governed by the law in 'which the employee habitually carries out' work, disregarding temporary moves (Art 8(2)), or where the 'employee was engaged' (Art 8(3)), or wherever the 'contract is more closely connected' (Art 8(4)). If there are two possible answers under Article 8(4), in whose favour should the court err?

2. In addition to the parties' 'choice of law', conflicts of laws asks whether Member State courts have 'jurisdiction'. The Brussels I Regulation (EU) No 1215/2012 concerns whether a court in EU trade has jurisdiction to hear a claim. Employers can be sued in Member States in which they are domiciled (Art 21(1)(a)) or at least have a branch (Art 20(2)), or wherever the employee habitually works

or was engaged (Art 21(1)(b)). But employees can be sued only where they are domiciled. Thus there are two steps for a UK court: (1) is there jurisdiction to hear a claim, and (2) which laws did the parties choose?

3. 'Jurisdiction' is thought to be an issue separate from choice of law because it is assumed that courts should have jurisdiction to reject claims from people who are unrelated to their territory, and should not be allowed to contract in (eg should contractors in Tipperary be free to choose the law of Timbuktu?). This is not inevitable: in the United States, people may register a corporation in any of the 50 states' legal systems, even if all business, profits, employees and shareholders are entirely in another state, and have done no more than post a letter with the registration documents. The US Supreme Court requires that state courts acknowledge those corporations are established. The EU position on the 'right of establishment' is not dissimilar, but enables Member States to impose rules as public policy requires. See *Kamer van Koophandel v Inspire Art Ltd* (2003) C-167/01.

4. In the next case, although the EU Regulations were already in force, the House of Lords considered the issues under UK law. It reached a curiously similar result.

Lawson v Serco Ltd; Botham v Ministry of Defence; Crofts v Veta Ltd **[2006] UKHL 3**

In three joined cases, employees claimed the right to a fair dismissal under ERA 1996 s 94, but the employers contended that they were not subject to UK law as they worked wholly or partly abroad. ERA 1996 s 196 had previously identified the Act's territorial scope, but was repealed in 1999 and left to judicial interpretation. This coincided with the Posted Workers Directive 96/71/EC, which required people working abroad to enjoy protection of the host state. Mr Lawson worked on Ascension Island in the south Atlantic Ocean as a security guard. He claimed constructive dismissal for his poor treatment. Mr Botham was a youth worker in Germany for the Ministry of Defence, dismissed allegedly for gross misconduct. Mr Crofts, and other pilots, worked for a Hong Kong company named Veta Ltd, a wholly owned subsidiary for the airline company Cathay Pacific plc in Hong Kong. They were 'peripatetic' workers, flying between the UK and Hong Kong. Different Court of Appeals had held that Mr Lawson and Mr Botham were not covered by UK law, because they were all abroad, while Mr Crofts and his colleagues were held by a majority to be covered (Lord Phillips MR dissenting). The House of Lords held that all claimants were entitled to bring unfair dismissal claims in the UK.

Lord Hoffmann:

5. ... Thus in *Lawson* and *Botham*, employer and employee both had close connections with Great Britain but all the services were performed abroad. In *Crofts* the employer was foreign but the employee was resident in Great Britain and although his services were peripatetic, they were based in Great Britain. ...

9. ... it was submitted that Parliament must have intended to widen the territorial scope of the various provisions to which section 196 had applied. Counsel said that support for

this argument could be found in the brief statement of the Minister of State, Department of Trade and Industry (Mr Ian McCartney) when recommending the repeal of section 196 to the House of Commons: see Hansard (HC Debates) 26 July 1999, cols 31–32. It is no criticism of Mr McCartney's moment at the despatch box to say that I have not found his remarks particularly helpful in dealing with problems which he is unlikely to have had in mind ... Parliament was content to accept the application of established principles of construction to the substantive rights conferred by the Act, whatever the consequences might be.

...

23. ... Of course this question should be decided according to established principles of construction, giving effect to what Parliament may reasonably be supposed to have intended and attributing to Parliament a rational scheme. But this involves the application of principles, not the invention of supplementary rules ...

...

29. As I said earlier, I think that we are today more concerned with how the contract was in fact being operated at the time of the dismissal than with the terms of the original contract. But the common sense of treating the base of a peripatetic employee as, for the purposes of the statute, his place of employment, remains valid. It was applied by the Court of Appeal to an airline pilot in *Todd v British Midland Airways Ltd* [1978] ICR 959, where Lord Denning MR said, at p 964:

> 'A man's base is the place where he should be regarded as ordinarily working, even though he may spend days, weeks or months working overseas. I would only make this suggestion. I do not think that the terms of the contract help much in these cases. As a rule, there is no term in the contract about exactly where he is to work. You have to go by the conduct of the parties and the way they have been operating the contract. You have to find at the material time where the man is based.'

30. ... now that section 196 has been repealed, I think that Lord Denning provides the most helpful guidance.

31. Like the majority in the Court of Appeal, I think that Lord Denning's approach in *Todd v British Midland Airways Ltd* points the way to the answer in *Crofts v Veta Ltd*. ... Unless, like Lord Phillips of Worth Matravers MR, one regards airline pilots as the flying Dutchmen of labour law, condemned to fly without any jurisdiction in which they can seek redress, I think there is no sensible alternative to asking where they are based. And the same is true of other peripatetic employees. ...

...

35. The problem of what I might call the expatriate employees is rather more difficult. The concept of a base, which is useful to locate the workplace of a peripatetic employee, provides no help in the case of an expatriate employee. The Ministry of Defence accepts that Mr Botham fell within the scope of section 94(1), but his base was the base and the base was in Germany.

36. The circumstances would have to be unusual for an employee who works and is based abroad to come within the scope of British labour legislation. But I think that there are some who do. I hesitate to describe such cases as coming within an exception or exceptions to the general rule because that suggests a definition more precise than can be imposed upon the many possible combinations of factors, some of which may be unforeseen. Mr Crow submitted that in principle the test was whether, despite the workplace being abroad, there are other relevant factors so powerful that the employment relationship has a closer connection with

Great Britain than with the foreign country where the employee works. This may well be a correct description of the cases in which section 94(1) can exceptionally apply to an employee who works outside Great Britain, but like many accurate statements, it is framed in terms too general to be of practical help. I would also not wish to burden tribunals with inquiry into the systems of labour law of other countries. In my view one should go further and try, without drafting a definition, to identify the characteristics which such exceptional cases will ordinarily have.

37. First, I think that it would be very unlikely that someone working abroad would be within the scope of section 94(1) unless he was working for an employer based in Great Britain. But that would not be enough. Many companies based in Great Britain also carry on business in other countries and employment in those businesses will not attract British law merely on account of British ownership. The fact that the employee also happens to be British or even that he was recruited in Britain, so that the relationship was "rooted and forged" in this country, should not in itself be sufficient to take the case out of the general rule that the place of employment is decisive. Something more is necessary.

38. Something more may be provided by the fact that the employee is posted abroad by a British employer for the purposes of a business carried on in Great Britain. He is not working for a business conducted in a foreign country which belongs to British owners or is a branch of a British business, but as representative of a business conducted at home. I have in mind, for example, a foreign correspondent on the staff of a British newspaper, who is posted to Rome or Peking and may remain for years living in Italy or China but remains nevertheless a permanent employee of the newspaper who could be posted to some other country. He would in my opinion fall within the scope of section 94(1). The distinction is illustrated by *Financial Times Ltd v Bishop* [2003] UKEAT 0147, a decision of the Employment Appeal Tribunal delivered by Judge Burke QC. Mr Bishop was originally a sales executive working for the Financial Times in London. At the time of his dismissal in 2002 he had been working for three years in San Francisco selling advertising space. The Employment Tribunal accepted jurisdiction on the ground that under European rules it had personal jurisdiction over the Financial Times: see article 19 of Regulation EC 44/2001. But that was not a sufficient ground: the Regulation assumes that the employee has a claim to enforce, whereas the question was whether section 94(1) gave Mr Bishop a substantive claim. Having set aside this decision, the EAT was in my opinion right in saying that the findings of fact were inadequate to enable it to give its own decision. The question was whether Mr Bishop was selling advertising space in San Francisco as a part of the business which the Financial Times conducted in London or whether he was working for a business which the Financial Times or an associated company was conducting in the United States: for example, by selling advertising in the Financial Times American edition. In the latter case, section 94 would not in my view apply. (Compare *Jackson v Ghost Ltd* [2003] IRLR 824, which was a clear case of employment in a foreign business).

39. Another example is an expatriate employee of a British employer who is operating within what amounts for practical purposes to an extra-territorial British enclave in a foreign country. This was the position of Mr Botham working in a military base in Germany. And I think, although the case is not quite so strong, that the same is true of Mr Lawson at the RAF base on Ascension Island. While it is true that Mr Lawson was there in a support role, employed by a private firm to provide security on the base, I think it would be unrealistic to regard him as having taken up employment in a foreign community in the same way as if Serco Ltd were providing security services for a hospital in Berlin. I have no doubt that *Bryant v Foreign and Commonwealth Office* [2003] UKEAT 174, in which it was held that section 94(1) did not apply to a British national locally engaged to work in the British Embassy in Rome, was rightly decided. But on Ascension there was no local community. In practice, as opposed to

constitutional theory, the base was a British outpost in the South Atlantic. Although there was a local system of law, the connection between the employment relationship and the United Kingdom were overwhelmingly stronger.

40. I have given two examples of cases in which section 94(1) may apply to an expatriate employee: the employee posted abroad to work for a business conducted in Britain and the employee working in a political or social British enclave abroad. I do not say that there may not be others, but I have not been able to think of any and they would have to have equally strong connections with Great Britain and British employment law. For the purposes of these two appeals, the second of these examples is sufficient. It leads to the conclusion that the appeals of both Mr Lawson and Mr Botham should be allowed.

Double claiming

41. Finally I should note that in the case of expatriate employees, it is quite possible that they will be entitled to make claims under both the local law and section 94(1). For example, the foreign correspondent living in Rome would be entitled to rights in Italian law under the Posted Workers Directive and although the Directive does not extend to claims for unfair dismissal, Italian domestic law may nevertheless provide for them. Obviously there cannot be double recovery and any compensation paid under the foreign system would have to be taken into account by an Employment Tribunal.

Lord Woolf, Lord Rodger, Lord Walker and **Baroness Hale** concurred.

NOTES AND QUESTIONS

1. Lord Hoffmann reasoned that peripatetic workers would be able to claim from the place where they are based, which means where someone is 'ordinarily working', which may ignore periods of work overseas. If part of the reason for the law is to ensure employers cannot make contracts to undercut labour rights, why not allow the employee to select the most advantageous law to which their work connects?

2. This author's first experience on a mini-pupillage happened to be shadowing counsel for Veta Ltd in the Court of Appeal. A memorable episode in those submissions was when the Master of the Rolls asked counsel how it might be possible to decide the case so that British Airways pilots could always be covered by UK law, but so that pilots of Veta Ltd might not be. Counsel had a ready point-by-point response that was duly written down. This advice is reflected in the dissenting judgment. Which pressures do you think might be operating on judges to turn employees, as Lord Hoffmann joked, into 'the flying Dutchmen of labour law'?

3. For 'expatriate workers', Lord Hoffmann mentions the 'close connections' of *Lawson* and *Botham* at paragraph 5 (which is the test in Rome I Regulation Article 8(4)) and then lists various examples (the foreign correspondent of a UK newspaper, the person working for the foreign embassy but recruited locally). Which principles run through the results that Lord Hoffmann favours in these cases?

4.   As an historical matter, in cases such as *Addis v Gramophone Co Ltd* [1909] AC 488, where a man was posted by a UK company to work in Kolkata, courts readily accepted the British claimants were covered by UK law. It seemed irrelevant that they worked in a jurisdiction where colonial law applied, for a wrongful dismissal claim.

5.   In *Reading v Attorney-General* [1951] UKHL 1, Mr Reading, working in Egypt as a sergeant in the Royal Army Medical Corps, was assumed to be covered by UK law. That case concerned whether bribes he took were held on constructive trust for the Crown, his employer. Supposing those bribes had been used to buy an asset from another who knew about the bribes, and the asset had fallen in value, the Crown would have been entitled to cherrypick the best remedy to ensure the efficacy of its rights. Why should employees not simply be able to cherrypick the best system of rights?

6.   In *Duncombe v Secretary of State for Children, Schools and Families* [2011] UKSC 36 the Supreme Court held that a British employee working for the European School in Karlsruhe, Germany, who was employed by the UK government, could bring a claim for unfair dismissal under the Employments Rights Act 1996 section 94. Lady Hale noted that it was 'fair to say that had this issue stood alone it is unlikely that permission would have been given to bring an appeal to this Court'. On the other issue in the appeal, whether giving Duncombe a fixed-term contract was objectively justified, see chapter 11.

Ravat v Halliburton Manufacturing and Services Ltd [2012] UKSC 1

Mr Ravat claimed he was unfairly dismissed by Halliburton Ltd (a subsidiary of the US oil group, Halliburton Inc), after he was made redundant from his job as an accounts manager in Algeria and Libya, from 1990 to 2006. He would fly to Libya for 28 days work, and then go back to Preston for 28 days at home. His supervisor, Mr Strachan, was in Cairo. The company was incorporated in the UK. Mr Ravat was hired in the UK. He was told the UK grievance procedure for redundancy would apply to him. Mr Strachan originally chose to hold a grievance hearing in Aberdeen. But in court the company argued he was outside the scope of the right against unfair dismissal in ERA 1996 s 94. In the Aberdeen Employment Tribunal, Mr Christie held it did have jurisdiction to consider Mr Ravat's claim. In the Employment Appeal Tribunal Lady Smith reversed this finding. The Court of Session held by a majority that Mr Ravat's case could be heard. Lord Osborne reasoned Mr Ravat was a peripatetic worker, while Lord Carloway held he was an expatriate worker, with a close connection with the UK. Lord Brodie, dissenting, held he was an expatriate worker, but did not have a close connection with the UK. The Supreme Court held that Mr Ravat had a close connection with the UK because of the assurance that UK law would apply.

Lord Hope:

4. ... As Louise Merrett, The Extra-Territorial Reach of Employment Legislation (2010) 39 Industrial Law Journal 355, has pointed out, increasing labour mobility together with the

proliferation of multinational companies and groups of companies has made the international aspects of employment law important in an ever-growing number of cases. ...

...

28. ... The expatriate cases that Lord Hoffmann identified as falling within its scope were referred to by him as exceptional cases: para 36. This was because, as he said in para 36, the circumstances would have to be unusual for an employee who works and is based abroad to come within the scope of British labour legislation. It will always be a question of fact and degree as to whether the connection is sufficiently strong to overcome the general rule that the place of employment is decisive. The case of those who are truly expatriate because they not only work but also live outside Great Britain requires an especially strong connection with Great Britain and British employment law before an exception can be made for them.

30. It is true that at the time of his dismissal the respondent was working in Libya and that the operations that were being conducted there and in which he worked were those of a different Halliburton associated company which was incorporated and based in Germany. It is true also that the decision to dismiss him was taken by Mr Strachan who was based in Cairo. But I would not attach as much importance to these details as I would have done if the company for which the respondent was working in Libya was not another associated Halliburton company. The vehicles which a multinational corporation uses to conduct its business across international boundaries depend on a variety of factors which may deflect attention from the reality of the situation in which the employee finds himself. As Mr Christie said in the employment tribunal, it is notorious that the employees of one company within the group may waft to another without alteration to their essential function in pursuit of the common corporate purpose: para 53. All the other factors point towards Great Britain as the place with which, in comparison with any other, the respondent's employment had the closer connection.

31. The appellant's business was based in Great Britain. It was to provide tools, services and personnel to the oil industry. That was why it sent the respondent to Libya, even though the actual work itself was in the furtherance of the business of another Halliburton subsidiary or associate company: see the employment tribunal's judgment, para 53. It chose to treat him as a commuter for this purpose, with a rotational working pattern familiar to workers elsewhere in the oil industry which enables them to spend an equivalent amount of time at home in Great Britain as that spent offshore or overseas. In the respondent's case this meant that all the benefits for which he would have been eligible had he been working in Great Britain were preserved for him.

32. Lady Smith said in the EAT that the employment tribunal was wrong to take account of the proper law of the parties' contract and the reassurance given to the respondent by the appellant about the availability to him of UK employment law, as neither of them were relevant. The better view, I think, is that, while neither of these things can be regarded as determinative, they are nevertheless relevant. Of course, it was not open to the parties to contract into the jurisdiction of the employment tribunal. As Mr Cavanagh put it, the parties cannot alter the statutory reach of section 94(1) by an estoppel based on what they agreed to. The question whether the tribunal has jurisdiction will always depend on whether it can be held that Parliament can reasonably be taken to have intended that an employee in the claimant's position should have the right to take his claim to an employment tribunal. But, as this is a question of fact and degree, factors such as any assurance that the employer may have given to the employee and the way the employment relationship is then handled in practice must play a part in the assessment.

33. The assurances that were given in the respondent's case were made in response to his understandable concern that his position under British employment law might be compromised

by his assignment to Libya. The documentation he was given indicated that it was the appellant's intention that the relationship should be governed by British employment law. This was borne out in practice, as matters relating to the termination of his employment were handled by the appellant's human resources department in Aberdeen. This all fits into a pattern, which points quite strongly to British employment law as the system with which his employment had the closest connection.

34. Mr Cavanagh submitted that the fact that the respondent's home was in Great Britain was of no relevance. Why, he said, should the place where you are living when you are not working be relevant at all? All that mattered was the place where he was working. His place of residence did not matter, and it should be left out of account. It is true that his place of work was in Libya and not in Preston. But the fact that his home was in Great Britain cannot be dismissed as irrelevant. It was the reason why he was given the status of a commuter, with all the benefits that were attached to it which, as he made clear, he did not want to be prejudiced by his assignment. Here too the fact that his home was in Preston fits into a pattern which had a very real bearing on the parties' employment relationship.

35. As the question is ultimately one of degree, considerable respect must be given to the decision of the employment tribunal as the primary fact-finder. Mr Christie said in para 54 of his judgment that his conclusion that the balance was in favour of the respondent fell within the band of reasonable responses available to a reasonable chairman of employment tribunals. This remark was seen by both Lady Smith in para 36 of her judgment in the EAT and by Lord Osborne in the Extra Division, 2011 SLT 44, para 19 as an indication that he considered the task that he was undertaking as the exercise of a discretion. His remark was perhaps not very well chosen, but I do not think that his judgment when read as a whole is open to this criticism. The test which he applied was whether there was a substantial connection with Great Britain: see paras 39 and 47. It would have been better if he had asked himself whether the connection was sufficiently strong to enable it to be said that Parliament would have regarded it as appropriate for the tribunal to deal with the claim: see para 29, above. But I think that it is plain from his reasoning that he would have reached the same conclusion if he had applied that test. Lord Osborne said in para 20 of his opinion that the tribunal reached a conclusion that it was entitled to reach and that it was a correct conclusion. I agree with that assessment. So I too would hold that section 94(1) must be interpreted as applying to the respondent's employment, and that the employment tribunal has jurisdiction to hear his claim.

Lady Hale, Lord Brown, Lord Mance and **Lord Kerr** agreed.

NOTES AND QUESTIONS

1. Lord Hope holds that Mr Ravat has a claim in the UK, because although not decisive, the assurances he was given established a close connection to the UK. He gives emphasis at [4] and [30] to the need to ensure the efficacy of labour rights with 'the proliferation of multinational companies' and the 'notorious' practices of businesses to have people move while they still perform an 'essential function in pursuit of the common corporate purpose'.
2. In most EU jurisdictions, there would be no distinction between a contract and 'statutory' rights, because contract and rights alike are founded in statutory codes. It appears that this case and *Duncombe*, noted above, were thought to involve statutory rights, rather than contract, and so the Rome I Regulation did not apply. In any case, it appears that the common law, as Lord Hope expressed, is the same.

3.   In *Dhunna v Creditsights Ltd* [2014] EWCA Civ 1238 Rimer LJ found that
     Mr Dhunna did not have a sufficiently 'close connection' to the UK to bring a
     claim against his alleged unfair dismissal. He moved from London to Dubai while
     working for a UK subsidiary of an American group, Creditsights Inc. He earned
     over £100,000, plus a bonus, but was paid in US dollars. Rimer LJ held the 'object
     of the exercise is not to decide which system of law is more or less favourable
     to the employee' and where the contract was written and company was based
     was not a 'compelling factor' ([40] and [43]). Is this reasoning compatible with
     Lord Hope's view in *Ravat* at [30] on the 'reality' of the situation, or indeed with
     Recital (23) to the Rome I Regulation? Does the approach of Rimer LJ undermine
     commercial certainty?
4.   In *Crofts v Veta Ltd*, counsel for the employers were contending that the applicable
     law should be where the employer is based (in that case, Hong Kong), while in
     Ravat and *Dhunna* employers sought to argue that where employers were was not
     as relevant as other factors. It is submitted that unless the purpose of labour rights
     is followed, to favour the employee and prevent unjust enrichment of (mostly cor-
     porate) employers, the 'close connection' test will always result in excessive and
     contradictory litigation on inherently indecisive factors.

(b) Tort

Although it may seem odd to include tort issues in a chapter titled the 'contract' of
employment, tort law functions like any other implied term in a contract. As Lord Goff
put it 'the law of tort is the general law, out of which the parties can, if they wish, contract' (*Henderson v Merrett Syndicates Ltd* [1994] UKHL 5). This comment plainly does
not apply where statute or common law creates a right, or an employee lacks the bargaining power to truly agree to a departure from the default rules of tort.

Practically, the most important tort law rules for labour law concern the employer's
duty of care, to provide a healthy environment and a safe system of work. There may also
be questions of liability for unfair practices during lockouts or strikes. Unlike the Rome I
Regulation on contract, conflicts of tort law (and other non-contractual obligations,
particularly unjust enrichment) are regulated by the Rome II Regulation.

Rome II Regulation (EC) No 864/2007

Article 1 Scope

1. This Regulation shall apply, in situations involving a conflict of laws, to non-contractual
obligations in civil and commercial matters. It shall not apply, in particular, to revenue, customs
or administrative matters or to the liability of the State for acts and omissions in the exercise of
State authority (*acta iure imperii*).

2. The following shall be excluded from the scope of this Regulation:

…

(d) non-contractual obligations arising out of the law of companies and other bodies corporate or unincorporated regarding matters such as the creation, by registration or otherwise,
legal capacity, internal organisation or winding-up of companies and other bodies corporate
or unincorporated, the personal liability of officers and members as such for the obligations of

the company or body and the personal liability of auditors to a company or to its members in the statutory audits of accounting documents. ...

Article 2 Non-contractual obligations
1. For the purposes of this Regulation, damage shall cover any consequence arising out of tort/delict, unjust enrichment, *negotiorum gestio* or *culpa in contrahendo*.
...

Article 4 General rule
1. Unless otherwise provided for in this Regulation, the law applicable to a non-contractual obligation arising out of a tort/delict shall be the law of the country in which the damage occurs irrespective of the country in which the event giving rise to the damage occurred and irrespective of the country or countries in which the indirect consequences of that event occur.
2. However, where the person claimed to be liable and the person sustaining damage both have their habitual residence in the same country at the time when the damage occurs, the law of that country shall apply.
3. Where it is clear from all the circumstances of the case that the tort/delict is manifestly more closely connected with a country other than that indicated in paragraphs 1 or 2, the law of that other country shall apply. A manifestly closer connection with another country might be based in particular on a pre-existing relationship between the parties, such as a contract, that is closely connected with the tort/delict in question.
...

Article 7 Environmental damage
The law applicable to a non-contractual obligation arising out of environmental damage or damage sustained by persons or property as a result of such damage shall be the law determined pursuant to Article 4(1), unless the person seeking compensation for damage chooses to base his or her claim on the law of the country in which the event giving rise to the damage occurred.
...

Article 9 Industrial action
Without prejudice to Article 4(2), the law applicable to a non-contractual obligation in respect of the liability of a person in the capacity of a worker or an employer or the organisations representing their professional interests for damages caused by an industrial action, pending or carried out, shall be the law of the country where the action is to be, or has been, taken.

NOTES AND QUESTIONS

1. The Rome II Regulation Arts 1 and 2 say it concerns 'non-contractual obligations' including tort, unjust enrichment, *negotiorum gestio* (a liability to pay for the costs of work one benefits from) or *culpa in contrahendo* (liability in precontractual bargaining), but makes a special exclusion (among others) for 'non-contractual obligations' arising out of the law of companies'. Article 4 says the general rule is that the law applies from the country where 'the damage occurred', and Art 9 says that for strikes, the applicable law is 'country where the action is'. Of course, most countries do not recognise that unions are liable for 'damage' from strikes, for which employers may be equally or more responsible (see chapter 10), and so this article primarily refers to the liability of the employer. However, crucially,

Art 7 says that for 'environmental damage or damage sustained by persons or property as a result' the claimant can choose to bring a claim under the law of the tortfeasor.

2. Article 7 means that if there is environmental damage, as well as a labour rights violation by a UK multinational, claims can be brought in the UK under UK law by foreign claimants. Why not allow claims under UK law for labour rights violations by themselves?

3. What does the exclusion for 'the law of companies' mean? In chapter 3(3)(c) the case of *Chandler v Cape plc* was explored, where the employee of an insolvent subsidiary was able to sue Cape plc in tort because the solvent parent had interfered in the health and safety affairs of the subsidiary. The Court of Appeal said the case did not engage the company law doctrine of 'piercing the veil of incorporation', where one company's rights and duties can be treated as another's, and shared, even though they are formally created as separate legal entities. Arguably, if a company in a country where damage takes place puts up an argument about the 'corporate veil' under that country's law, this means that the matter would then fall within the Art 1(2)(d) exception, so that the issue should be handled purely in tort law under UK principles.

4. In *Lungowe v Vedanta Resources Plc and Konkola Copper Mines Plc* [2017] EWCA Civ 1528 the Court of Appeal held that a parent company in London could be sued in tort by claimant farmers and workers in Zambia, who had suffered injury and environmental damage by a subsidiary's copper mining. Simon LJ gave the leading judgment, holding that if a parent and subsidiary company exercised similar knowledge and expertise over operations, then the parent could owe a duty of care.

5. However, in *Okpabi v Royal Dutch Shell Plc* [2018] EWCA Civ 191 the majority of the Court of Appeal held that no claim was likely to succeed for breach of the duty of care, after Royal Dutch Shell plc's subsidiary in Nigeria created a toxic oil spill, harming the environment and its citizens. Again, Simon LJ gave the leading judgment, but said it was (ostensibly) different to *Lungowe* and adding that 'the importance of multi-national parent companies conducting themselves consistently with international standards' was 'unobjectionable as an abstract principle, but is a doubtful foundation for the imposition of a duty of care' [130]–[131]. Sir Geoffrey Vos concurred in the result, while Sales LJ gave a concise, powerful, logical and compelling dissent. There was enough evidence, and liability should follow in the same way as it did in *Chandler*. This issue seems likely to see the Supreme Court soon.

Additional Reading for Chapter 4

O Kahn-Freund, 'Collective Agreements' (1941) 4(3) *Modern Law Review* 225
Examining a Privy Council case from Australia, *True v Amalgamated Collieries of Western Australia Ltd* [1941] AC 537, Kahn-Freund contends that while British law had

said little, more could be said to 'elucidate the normative effect of collective rules'. In principle, 'the individual contract of employment should not be allowed to derogate from the terms of the collective bargain to the detriment of the employee'. An individual contract must 'be deemed to have been concluded upon the terms of the collective bargain'. It is like 'other legal rules protecting the socially weaker against the socially stronger party to a contract (housing legislation, etc)'. Because of unequal bargaining power, the law 'transfers the freedom [of contract] from the individual into the collective sphere'.

F Kessler, 'Contracts of Adhesion – Some Thoughts About Freedom of Contract' (1943) 43(5) *Columbia Law Review* 629

Kessler's article, perhaps the most important in the history of contract law, argues that the growth of mass enterprise, and the need for efficient administration, led to the emergence of a qualitatively different kind of contract: the contract of adhesion. Instead of contracts where people bargain over the terms and conditions, individuals with less bargaining power typically adhere to the terms put before them by a large corporation. They are told to 'take it or leave it'. This is 'one of the many devices to build up and strengthen industrial empires'. Kessler suggests that a unified theory of contract law, based on individual freedom of contract, could no longer really be said to exist. Instead, recognising that contract is a 'social institution', the task of lawyers would be to develop multiple contract laws based on differing expectations in each context. We should realise 'that freedom of contract must mean different things for different types of contracts'.

H Collins, 'Legal Responses to the Standard Form Contract of Employment' (2007) 36(1) *ILJ* 2

Collins argues there has been a 'muffled legal response' to the paradigm-shifting rise of standard form contracts in employment. He recounts evidence how, according to the Workplace Employment Relations Survey 2004, when unions are derecognised 'it was extremely rare for any negotiation over terms and conditions'. In a casual look at one edition of Industrial Relations Law Reports, in 25 cases, 19 were clearly about employees on standard form contracts, in one there was a negotiated contract by a sport star, and in the others it was unclear or there was an oral agreement with minimum wage workers. Collins suggests 'leading authors seem to repress the significance' of this because of a 'reluctance to accept the shocking extent of the employer's unilateral rule-making power'. Collins goes on to favour greater accountability through unfair terms legislation and use of implied terms (see chapter 5).

J Kenner, 'Statement or Contract?' (1999) 28 *ILJ* 205

Kenner's article, subtitled 'Some Reflections on the EC Employee Information (Contract or Employment Relationship) Directive after *Kampelmann*', traces the background of the Directive into the Contracts of Employment Act 1963, suggesting this was one area of EU labour law, at least, where EU standards followed UK law. Kenner suggests that both UK, such as *System Floors*, and EU cases, such as *Kampelmann*, mean that (1) an employer will be bound by written statements of the contract which favour the employee, (2) an employer will have 'a heavy burden of rebuttal on the employer seeking to disprove his own statement', and (3) an employee will not necessarily be bound by the written statement: courts should 'instead construe employment contracts in the light of all the available evidence'. This reflects the policy of transparency and the law's stated 'purpose to give improved protection to employees'.

U Grušic, 'The Territorial Scope of Employment Legislation and Choice of Law' (2012) 75(5) *Modern Law Review* 722

Grušic argues that the mode of reasoning in *Lawson v Serco Ltd* (continued in *Ravat*) was incorrect to apply common law principles of statutory construction, instead of simply applying the principles of the Rome I Regulation on choice of law. Under conflicts of laws in EU law, 'contractual and statutory claims seem to have been by and large merged into a single category'. This largely reflects the fact that most countries do not have a common law/statute distinction because all law is codified. The mandatory quality of rights, and the law that an employee can choose the more favourable system reflects that 'the employer who is knowledgeable of the territorial limitations of the statutory employment rights and who employs employees to work abroad can, almost without any adverse consequences on its part, insert a choice-of-law clause' in their favour, and the law should 'eradicate such adverse consequences'.

Implied Terms and Variation

Employment, like many contracts, lasts over a period of time: it is not a simple exchange. Because few contracts spell out rules for all possible developments, implied terms come in when express terms run out. They also reflect people's expectations, which shape and amend express terms. Chapter 4 already covered two types of implied term: an employer's duty to inform employees about the contract, and rules to identify the applicable legal system (both partly codified in statute). English law used to say that terms were only to be implied if 'necessary to give ... "business efficacy" to the contract' (*The Moorcock* (1889) 14 PD 64, but contrast *Liverpool CC v Irwin* [1976] AC 239, 258). However, this test was revised in *Equitable Life Assurance Society v Hyman* [2002] 1 AC 408, 459, to what is necessary or 'essential to give effect to the reasonable expectations of the parties'. 'Reasonable expectations' were the language of contract for Adam Smith (chapter 2(1)), and they reflect the view that people's expectations differ in different contexts. Commercial, consumer, securities, housing and labour markets all differ. So does the law.

Express terms often conflict with people's reasonable expectations, and the law's standardised implied terms. Hence, there must be rules to reconcile conflicts. Since *Autoclenz Ltd v Belcher*, 'the relative bargaining power of the parties must be taken into account in deciding whether the terms of any written agreement in truth represent what was agreed' (chapter 3(1)(a)). Common law does not say 'everything is negotiable' because there are few justifications for taxpayer-funded courts upholding contract terms that society deems to be unjust (see JS Mill, *Principles of Political Economy* (1848) book V, ch 1 and *Shelley v Kraemer*, 334 US 1, 19 (1948) per Vinson CJ). This chapter divides the rules that come from implied terms, into (1) those favouring employing entities, and (2) those favouring employees. This division must not be taken too far: in a democratic enterprise, managerial power coordinates all investments of labour from workers or capital from shareholders, for the benefit of everyone. But in undemocratic workplaces, managerial power can be used to unjustly enrich directors, managers or shareholders at the expense of employees. Employment's first implied term, the right to direct, lets management (if the law does nothing more) unilaterally vary the contract's consideration without renegotiating its terms. Section (3) deals with further problems of contract variation either by consent, or by threatening or purporting to dismiss and then rehire an employee on new terms.

Introductory reading: Collins ch 2 (27–45). CEM chs 4–5 (131–84). D&M ch 4 (358–70).

(1) IMPLIED RIGHTS OF EMPLOYING ENTITIES

Theories of labour as disparate as those of Karl Marx and Richard Posner share a curious similarity: a view that one of the first incidents of an employment contract is that 'the labourer works under the control of the capitalist to whom his labour belongs' (*Capital* (1867) vol I, ch 7, 131) or that the employer has a (seemingly unfettered) right to direct or manage the worker (*Economic Analysis of Law* (2014) ch 12; also M Thatcher, *Speech to CBI Annual Dinner* (22 May 1986)). Workers have the right to leave, but while at work they are ostensibly subordinate to an unfettered employer discretion. Justinian's *Institutes*, 1.3.2 defined slavery in this way: when 'one person is subjected to the authority of another, contrary to nature'. Modern labour law has not followed these theories for a considerable period of time. First, an implied 'right to direct' does exist, but is bound by limits to use that power for a proper purpose: it should be consistent with the nature of just employment relations. Second, in order to criticise the system, Marx had contended that all benefits of work or 'the product is the property of the capitalist and not that of the labourer' (*Capital* (1867) vol I, ch 7, §1; see similarly B Cheffins, *Company Law: Theory, Structure and Operation* (1997) ch 12, 555). Labour lawyers had written less about this 'right to appropriate', but are doing more as the importance of intellectual property has increased. Here, too, modern labour law has always limited the power of employing entities to appropriate the benefits of workers' labour. The third implied right in this section is the employing entity's right to loyalty and its limits.

(a) Right to Direct and Limits

Lister v Romford Ice & Cold Storage Co Ltd **[1956] UKHL 6, [1957] AC 555**

Martin Lister Jr claimed the company should indemnify him for the cost of injuring his father at work. Lister's father, Martin Lister Sr, drove a waste disposal lorry into a slaughterhouse on Old Church Road, Romford. To get through the yard gates, Martin Sr got out to help, and Martin Jr reversed over him. Martin Sr sued the company for compensation for personal injury, claiming it was vicariously liable for his son's actions at work. McNair J awarded the Martin Sr two-thirds compensation, reduced to reflect the father's own negligence. The company's insurer paid £1600. But then, in a subrogation action (stepping into the company's rights) the insurer sued Martin Jr for its costs. The company was not consulted. Martin Jr argued that it was an implied term of the contract that he should be indemnified against the company while at work. The Court of Appeal rejected this view, Denning LJ dissenting. The House of Lords upheld the insurer's claim, and in doing so made general remarks on implied terms.

Lord Tucker:

Some contractual terms may be implied by general rules of law. These general rules, some of which are now statutory, for example, Sale of Goods Act, Bills of Exchange Act, etc., derive in the main from the common law by which they have become attached in the course of time to certain classes of contractual relationships, for example, landlord and tenant, innkeeper and guest, contracts of guarantee and contracts of personal service. Contrasted with such cases as these there are those in which from their particular circumstances it is necessary to imply a term to give efficacy to the contract and make it a workable agreement in such manner as the parties would clearly have done if they had applied their minds to the contingency which has arisen. ...

Without attempting an exhaustive enumeration of the duties imposed in this way upon a servant, I may mention: (1) the duty to give reasonable notice in the absence of custom or express agreement; (2) the duty to obey the lawful orders of the master; (3) the duty to be honest and diligent in the master's service; (4) the duty to take reasonable care of his master's property entrusted to him and generally in the performance of his duties; (5) to account to his master for any secret commission or remuneration received by him; (6) not to abuse his master's confidence in matters pertaining to his service: cf. Robb v. Green. 73

It would, I think, require very compelling evidence of some general change in circumstances affecting master and servant to justify the court in introducing some quite novel term into their contract, for example, a term absolving the servant from certain of the consequences of a breach of his recognized duty to take care, or as to the provision of insurance covering the servant's liability to third parties or his master. I find it difficult to understand what, if any, are the limitations of this theory. Is it to be confined to the relationship of master and servant with reference to motor-cars, or is it to extend to all those employed in industry or transport who, in the very nature of things, are engaged on work in which negligence on their part may result in widespread and grievous damage amounting to thousands of pounds for which they may be liable to their employers and in respect of risks which it was customary for the employer to insure against long before the advent of the motor-car?

Viscount Simonds, Lord Morton, Lord Radcliffe and **Lord Somervell** gave concurring judgments.

NOTES AND QUESTIONS

1. The contemporary importance of this judgment is Lord Tucker's point that the categories of implied term are not closed, or cannot be given 'exhaustive enumeration'. The actual outcome must now be regarded as superseded, if not expressly overturned. In *Williams v Natural Life Health Foods Ltd* [1998] UKHL 17 Lord Steyn held that a company director could not be sued by the liquidator of Natural Life Health Foods Ltd after it went insolvent for negligently misrepresenting on the company's behalf that it would perform well financially. He would only be liable if he had personally assumed liability to the company's creditors (eg by saying 'I warrant the accuracy of these predictions'). In other words, there is now an implied term that employees, including directors, are protected by a company's separate personality.

2. After the decision in *Lister*, there was an uproar by employees and unions, who argued that insurance corporations should not suddenly be entitled to sue workers for accidents at work – work from which employers profited. As described by Lord Denning MR in *Morris v Ford Motor Co Ltd* [1973] 1 QB 792, which 'distinguished' *Lister* on its facts, unions made a 'gentlemen's agreement' with insurers that they would not take advantage of the *Lister* ruling. It is likely legislation would have reversed it if the industry itself had not done so. *Williams* has probably made that unnecessary.

3. Lord Tucker's second point was that an employee should 'obey lawful orders of the master'. Generously interpreted, Lord Tucker means that in an employment contract, a director or manager will usually be entitled to direct the employee's tasks at work, within the scope of the contract's express terms, for proper purposes. While this is right, Lord Tucker's 'master' language was redolent of another age and (as *Wilson v Racher* shows below) no longer represents the law.

4. FW Taylor, *The Principles of Scientific Management* (1911) developed the notion of unbridled managerial discretion to its logical conclusion. The title's concept was popularised by Louis Brandeis (the famed labour rights attorney and later US Supreme Court judge) in his submissions to the Interstate Commerce Commission, to improve wages and reduce consumer prices through more humane and intelligent work practices. See LD Brandeis, *Scientific Management and Railroads* (1912). Taylor, however, was himself a manager, displayed utter contempt for his workers, and was interested in little more than extracting profit. To take just one example, at ch 2, 40, Taylor says of his manual labourers: 'This work is so crude and elementary in its nature that the writer firmly believes that it would be possible to train an intelligent gorilla so as to become a more efficient pig-iron handler than any man can be.' Do you think it is legitimate to work employees as hard as possible to maximise profit? Do the most profitable enterprises treat humans like mere resources?

5. An example of a unilateral variation of contractual consideration through the power to direct (by making staff work differently or harder) is *Cresswell v Board of Inland Revenue* [1984] ICR 508. The Revenue wished to introduce a computerised record system, which Cresswell and the union believed would lead to redundancies. They sought a guarantee that there would be no redundancies. When the Revenue refused, they sought a court declaration that the changes would be a breach of contract. Walton J, refuting a hypothetical argument that Cresswell might become a 'slave to the machine', held there was no breach, as it 'leaves jobs done by those who operate the new methodology precisely the same'. While it may seem obvious to a modern eye that computer training is a positive change which employing entities should be able to make, do you agree the jobs were 'precisely the same'?

6. Another example is *Dryden v Greater Glasgow Health Board* [1992] IRLR 469, where an employer led a consultation on a new ban on smoking in the Board's NHS hospitals. Ms Dryden, a nurse and long-term smoker, was told (unsurprisingly) that because there was no express contract term allowing her to smoke, the employer could change the rule. Lord Coulsfield remarked that there probably would be no implied 'right to smoke' in Ms Dryden's favour. Why do you think not?

7. *Luke v Stoke on Trent City Council* [2007] EWCA Civ 761 held that a special needs teacher could be required to move locations temporarily as part of the right to direct, without any need to imply a term. Mrs Luke alleged bullying and harassment by the headmaster, but an 'external investigator' (hired by the employing council) dismissed 32 out of 33 allegations. This meant Mrs Luke's claim for unlawful wage deductions, when she did not attend work because she refused to move, failed. While the tribunals below had implied a term that she could be

required to move, Mummery LJ said that this was 'unnecessary' on the basis of the apparent 'business efficacy' test. Laws LJ and Moses LJ agreed. Assuming these facts, the result may have been correct, but why do you think that the Court of Appeal found it unnecessary to apply the House of Lords jurisprudence binding upon them, that terms are to be implied as necessary to reflect the 'reasonable expectations' of the parties? Do you think an external investigator paid by the employing entity possibly has a conflict of interest?

8.   In EU law, *Lawrie-Blum v Land Baden-Württemberg* (1986) Case 66/85, [17], stated: 'The essential feature of an employment relationship ... is that for a certain period of time a person performs services for and under the direction of another person in return for which he receives remuneration.' In the United Staes, see the Restatement of the Law (Second) of Agency (1958) §220.

9.   The most significant limit on the right to direct was set by *Wilson v Racher*.

Wilson v Racher [1974] ICR 428

Mr Wilson claimed that his employer, Mr Racher, the owner of Tolethorpe Hall, Stamford, had wrongfully and constructively dismissed him by breaching an implied obligation of trust and confidence, before the six-month contract was up. Wilson was a 'man of considerable competence'. He worked as Racher's head gardener until, after 48 days, their 'complete conflict of personalities' yielded an argument. In defending the wrongful dismissal claim, counsel for Racher submitted that Wilson should not succeed because he had used obscene language. The Court of Appeal held that Mr Racher's behaviour caused the argument, and upheld the County Court judge's award of £421.15 in damages for wrongful dismissal.

Edmund Davies LJ:

There is no rule of thumb to determine what misconduct on the part of a servant justifies summary termination of his contract. For the purpose of the present case, the test is whether the plaintiff's conduct was insulting and insubordinate to such a degree as to be incompatible with the continuance of the relation of master and servant: per Hill J. in *Edwards v Levy* (1860) 2 F&F 94, 95. The application of such test will, of course, lead to varying results according to the nature of the employment and all the circumstances of the case. Reported decisions provide useful, but only general guides, each case turning upon its own facts. Many of the decisions which are customarily cited in these cases date from the last century and may be wholly out of accord with current social conditions. What would today be regarded as almost an attitude of Czar-serf, which is to be found in some of the older cases where a dismissed employee failed to recover damages, would, I venture to think, be decided differently today. We have by now come to realise that a contract of service imposes upon the parties a duty of mutual respect.

What happened on Sunday June 11, emerges from the judge's clear and helpful judgment, in which he reviews all the facts and sets out his findings. This court lacks the advantage of seeing and hearing the witnesses which was enjoyed by the judge. It needs to be stressed that the defendant now challenges none of the findings of fact. The story began on the preceding Friday afternoon when the plaintiff had been trimming a new yew hedge with an electric cutter. It was a damp afternoon, but the plaintiff carried on, taking shelter when the rain became heavy and then resuming his work when conditions improved. But at about 3.45 p.m. the rain was so heavy that the plaintiff could not continue because there was danger of his being electrocuted by the cutter. He then proceeded to oil and clean his tools until his day's work was over. But he did make one mistake. He left a ladder leaning against a young yew hedge, which was an unfortunate thing to do. To that extent, the plaintiff was guilty of some dereliction of duty. But on the Sunday afternoon that was by no means the only topic discussed between the parties. It was after luncheon that the defendant and his wife and three young children were in the garden when the plaintiff passed and greeted them. The defendant asked where he was going, and the plaintiff replied that he was going to the garden shed to get his boots. Thereafter the defendant showered the plaintiff with questions. He shouted at him, and he was very aggressive. He accused the plaintiff of leaving his work prematurely on the Friday afternoon. The plaintiff explained that he had stopped cutting the hedge only because it would have been dangerous to continue, whereupon the defendant said, "I am not bothered about you, Wilson, that's your lookout." Though there was some reference to the ladder, the defendant did not make clear what his complaint was. But when the defendant accused the plaintiff of shirking his work on the Friday afternoon, there is no doubt that the plaintiff used most regrettable language, and it is part of my unpleasant duty to repeat it so as to make clear what happened. The plaintiff said: "If you remember it was pissing with rain on Friday. Do you expect me to get fucking wet?" The judge, who found that Mrs. Racher and the children did not hear those words, said:

> "The plaintiff had a clear conscience, and he did reply somewhat robustly when he expressed the state of the weather. I think he felt under a certain amount of grievance at that remark."

According to the judge, "The defendant then moved to what he thought was stronger ground," thereby obviously referring to his determination to get rid of the plaintiff. The judge dealt with an allegation about a line of string having been left in the garden by the plaintiff, and commented:

> "A more trivial complaint it would be difficult to imagine … It was an extremely trivial ground of complaint, if indeed justified at all. I think it is clear from this and other evidence that [the defendant] sets very high standards and this seems tome to be an absurdly high standard of tidiness. The defendant's second barrel is very odd and illustrates that the defendant was determined to get the plaintiff on something."

There was a dispute as to whether the string belonged to the plaintiff or to the defendant, and there was a complaint about leaving other things lying about. The judge accepted that the plaintiff moved away in an attempt to avoid any further altercation. But he was called back, and was then bombarded with questions. The defendant was going on at him, and this was, indeed, confirmed to some extent by the evidence of the defendant himself. Finally, the plaintiff told the defendant, "Get stuffed," and "Go and shit yourself."

These last two expressions were used by the plaintiff immediately before he was dismissed. He later apologised to Mrs. Racher for using such language, as to which the judge said, "One cannot condone them or commend them, but he said that when subjected to a number of petty criticisms and was not being allowed to go." Despite the use of such language, the judge held that the plaintiff was entitled to say that he had been wrongly dismissed. Following upon the incident of June 11, the defendant sent to the plaintiff on June 16, a letter in the following terms:

> "In accordance with the terms of the service agreement between us I hereby give you one month's notice from the date of this letter, which confirms my oral notice given to you on Sunday, June 11, 1972. You will appreciate that no matter what your abilities as a gardener are, there can be no question of your remaining in my employment when you choose to use obscene four-letter words in the direct presence of my wife and in particular my children."

The judge held that Mrs. Racher heard the second lot of expressions, but there was no finding as to whether the children had heard them.

Mr. Connell, who appeared for the defendant below, has with admirable clarity submitted that the judge arrived at a wrong finding. He rightly stresses the domestic nature of this particular contract of service, and says that, the plaintiff being engaged in a family setting, obscene language of the kind admittedly used by him could not possibly be tolerated. At one stage he submitted that so bad was the language that the plaintiff must be regarded as having himself repudiated the contract of service. But no such plea was advanced either in the defence or, as appears from the judgment, at the hearing. The sole question that accordingly arises is whether the language most regrettably employed by the plaintiff constituted such conduct as made the continuance of the contract of service impossible.

...

... On the judge's findings, here was a competent, diligent and efficient gardener who, apart from one complaint of leaving a ladder against a yew tree, had done nothing which could be regarded as blame-worthy by any reasonable employer. Here, too, was an employer who was resolved to get rid of him; an employer who would use every barrel in the gun that he could find, or thought available; and an employer who was provocative from the outset and dealt with the plaintiff in an unseemly manner. The plaintiff lost his temper. He used obscene and deplorable language. He was therefore deserving of the severest reproof. But this was a solitary occasion. ... there was no background either of inefficiency or of insolence. The plaintiff tried to avert the situation by walking away, but he was summoned back and the defendant continued his gadfly activity of goading him into intemperate language. Such are the findings of the county court judge.

In those circumstances, would it be just to say that the plaintiff's use of this exteremely bad language on a solitary occasion made impossible the continuance of the master and servant relationship, and showed that the plaintiff was indeed resolved to follow a line of conduct which made the continuation of that relationship impossible? The judge thought the answer to that question was clear, and I cannot say that he was manifestly wrong. On the contrary, it seems to me that the parties could have made up their differences. The plaintiff apologised to Mrs. Racher. There are no grounds for thinking that if the defendant had given him a warning that such language would not be tolerated, and further, if he had manifested recognition that he himself had acted provocatively, the damage done might well have been repaired and some degree of harmony restored. Perhaps there was such instinctive antipathy between the two men that the defendant would, nevertheless, have been glad to get rid of the plaintiff when October 23, 1972, arrived.

In my judgment, in the light of the findings of fact the judge arrived at a just decision. that is not to say that language such as that employed by the plaintiff is to be tolerated. On the contrary, it requires very special circumstances to entitle a servant who expresses his feelings in such a grossly improper way to succeed in an action for wrongful dismissal. But there were special circumstances here, and they were of the defendant's own creation. The plaintiff, probably lacking the educational advantages of the defendant, and finding himself in a frustrating situation despite his efforts to escape from it, fell into the error of explosively using this language. To say that he ought to be kicked out because on this solitary occasion he fell into such grave error would, in my judgment, be wrong. I am not persuaded that the judge was in error in holding that that was unfair dismissal, that it was wrongful dismissal, and that the plaintiff was entitled to the damages awarded. I would therefore be for dismissing the appeal.

Cairns LJ and **James LJ** concurred.

1. This important judgment, approved by the Supreme Court in *Chhabra v West London Mental Health NHS Trust* [2013] UKSC 80, holds that an employer's conduct, without a good reason, repudiated an employment relationship, and justified damages. It recognises a 'duty of mutual respect'. This contains an unfettered right to direct an employee in any manner.

2. *Wilson v Racher* is a remarkable case: an employee was brave enough to claim, and a County Court judge sanctioned the menial nastiness of Mr Racher. Why do employees tolerate nasty treatment by employers, and why do a minority of managers or human resource staff feel able to treat employees nastily? Presumably, many employees are able to quit and 'go elsewhere', but many submit to abusive authority because they are in financial need: the costs of the odd 'incident' are outweighed by the social and economic gains of continuing in the job. For the abuser, abuse usually functions as a psychological replacement for poor self-esteem, low satisfaction at work or failing personal relationships (S Einarsen, 'The Nature and Causes of Bullying at Work' (1999) 20 *International Journal of Manpower* 16, 20). If they are not themselves helped, changed by the organisation or changed by law, they may perpetuate a 'czar–serf' model of workplace relations or – as this author has called it – 'the "Donald Trump" model of workplace relations'. How many people do you know who have suffered unacceptable treatment at work?

3. S Webb and B Webb, *Industrial Democracy* (1902) part III, ch 4, 842, fn 1, wrote: 'The capitalist is very fond of declaring that labour is a commodity, and the wage contract a bargain of purchase and sale like any other. But he instinctively expects his wage-earners to render him, not only obedience, but also personal deference. If the wage contract is a bargain of purchase and sale like any other, why is the workman expected to doff his hat to his employer, and to say "sir" to him without reciprocity?'

4. In addition to fault-based breaches of the 'duty of mutual respect' (such as bullying like Mr Racher's), can the right to direct be used in a way that constitutes a strict breach of the right to mutual respect? Yes: see *Malik* below. Also, statute codifies examples, such as a direction to do something dangerous, and employing entities have duties of consultation when attempting to vary workplace practices. See chapter 9.

(b) Right to Appropriate and Limits

Stevenson, Jordan & Harrison Ltd v MacDonald & Evans [1952] 1 TLR 101

Stevenson, Jordan & Harrison Ltd, an engineering firm, claimed it was entitled to the copyright of a book written by their former employee, the late Mr Evans-Hemming. The Copyright Act 1911 section 5(1) said the author of a work owns the copyright, but the employer owns it if done during the course of employment, in absence of an agreement. Some of the book came from lectures Mr Evans-Hemming wrote while not employed, and other parts came from material he acquired while working on assignment for one of the firm's clients in Manchester. The Court of Appeal held that the copyright in the 'Manchester section' belonged to the firm because it was written in the course of employment.

Denning LJ:

It is often easy to recognise a contract of service when you see it, but difficult to say where the difference lies. A ship's master, a chauffeur, and a reporter on the staff of a newspaper are all employed under a contract of service; but a ship's pilot, a taxi-man, and a newspaper contributor are employed under a contract for services. One feature which seems to me to run through the instances is that, under a contract of service, a man is employed as part of the business and his work is done as an integral part of the business; whereas under a contract for services his work, although done for the business, is not integrated into it but is only accessory to it.

...

In so far as Mr. Evans-Hemming prepared and wrote manuals for the use of a particular client of the company, he was doing it as part of his work as a servant of the company under a contract of service; but in so far as he prepared and wrote lectures for delivery to universities and to learned and professional societies, he was doing so as an accessory to the contract of service and not as part of it. The giving of lectures was no doubt very helpful to the company, in that it might serve directly as an advertisement for the company, and on that account the company paid Mr. Evans-Hemming the expenses he incurred. The lectures were, in a sense, part of the services rendered by Mr. Evans-Hemming for the benefit of the company. But they were in no sense part of his service. It follows that the copyright in the lectures was in Mr. Evans-Hemming.

Lord Evershed MR and **Morris LJ** gave concurring judgments.

NOTES AND QUESTIONS

1. This case illustrates a basic proposition that an implied term of employment is that the employer appropriates the benefits of an employee's labour. The limit set forth in this case is when work is done outside the course of employment: otherwise the copyright in the lectures would have belonged to the company. Do you think there are, or should be, further limits?

2. Intellectual property gives a salient instance of an historic common law assumption, that an employer appropriates the benefits of an employee's work (cf Froissart, ch 1(1)). The benefits from every twist of a spanner on a machine, every stroke of a key on a computer, are appropriated by an employing entity under the default assumptions of property and contract. It was irrelevant that the benefits were intangible or could be segregated from other things. What legal guarantees are there that the employee receives a just price for his or her labour, and that the employing entity is not unjustly enriched at the worker's expense?

3. JM Keynes, *The General Theory of Employment, Interest and Money* (1936) remarked that while it was difficult to reduce employees' wages, it was easier to keep them the same, despite changes in the economy or the enterprise. For example, if there is inflation, 'real' wages will reduce without any contractual change. Alternatively, if an enterprise becomes more profitable using everyone's contributions of labour and capital, the gains of growth will be disproportionately appropriated by the enterprise, without any contractual change. What can be done to remedy this? (See also chapter 9.)

4. In civil law systems, the same presumption of the common law is often embedded
    in cases, rather than being made explicit in codes. For instance, the German Civil
    Code (Bürgerliches Gesetzbuch) §950 states that the property in the work on an
    object will belong to the 'manufacturer' (*Hersteller*). In what might seem to be a
    rather backward view, courts and commentaries have said the manufacturer is not
    the worker but the property owner.

5. Aside from cases where an employee misuses confidential information,
    presumably an employer does not give consideration for any and all inventions
    or valuable creative work that an employee might come up with. In *Sterling
    Engineering Co Ltd v Patchett* [1955] AC 534, 543, Viscount Simonds remarked
    that if an employee in the course of employment 'makes an invention which it
    falls within his duty to make … he holds his interest in the invention, and in
    any resulting patent, as trustee for the employer unless he can show that he has
    a beneficial interest which the law recognises'. Presumably it is a different thing
    if there is no express contract term: that would probably not be in the contem-
    plation of the parties, or consistent with the background of social expectations,
    cf *The Achilleas* or *Transfield Shipping Inc v Mercator Shipping Inc* [2008]
    UKHL 48.

6. The United States has generated a significant body of law on intellectual property
    issues, particularly deriving from California's Silicon Valley. See O Lobel, 'Intel-
    lectual Property and Restrictive Covenants' in KG Dau-Schmidt et al, *Labor and
    Employment Law and Economics* (Elgar 2009) vol 2, ch 18, 526.

(c) Right to Employee Loyalty and Limits

Attorney General v Blake [2000] UKHL 45

The Attorney General claimed that George Blake, a Secret Intelligence Services member from 1944, breached a duty of good faith by publishing a book on his career and
should make restitution for (give back) all profits. As part of Blake's employment contract, he signed an Official Secrets Act 1911 declaration to disclose no information about
his work. This applied after Blake's employment ceased. In 1951 he became a Soviet
double agent. The British government discovered this and imprisoned him in 1961, but
he escaped to the Soviet Union. He wrote a book about his work in the secret service
called *No Other Choice* (1989). The information in the book was no longer confidential,
Blake received advanced payments from the publisher, Jonathan Cape, and was entitled
to more. The Crown sued for all the profits Blake made on the book, including those that
he had not yet received.

Lord Nicholls:

Equity reinforces the duty of fidelity owed by a trustee or fiduciary by requiring him to account
for any profits he derives from his office or position. This ensures that trustees and fiduciaries
are financially disinterested in carrying out their duties. They may not put themselves in a position where their duty and interest conflict. To this end they must not make any unauthorised

profit. If they do, they are accountable. Whether the beneficiaries or persons to whom the fiduciary duty is owed suffered any loss by the impugned transaction is altogether irrelevant. The accountability of the army sergeant in *Reading v Attorney General* [1951] AC 507 is a familiar application of this principle to a servant of the Crown.

...

Against this background I turn to consider the remedies available for breaches of contract. The basic remedy is an award of damages. In the much quoted words of Baron Parke, the rule of the common law is that where a party sustains a loss by reason of a breach of contract, he is, so far as money can do it, to be placed in the same position as if the contract had been performed: *Robinson v Harman* (1848) 1 Ex 850, 855. Leaving aside the anomalous exception of punitive damages, damages are compensatory. That is axiomatic. It is equally well established that an award of damages, assessed by reference to financial loss, is not always 'adequate' as a remedy for a breach of contract. The law recognises that a party to a contract may have an interest in performance which is not readily measurable in terms of money. On breach the innocent party suffers a loss. He fails to obtain the benefit promised by the other party to the contract. To him the loss may be as important as financially measurable loss, or more so. An award of damages, assessed by reference to financial loss, will not recompense him properly. For him a financially assessed measure of damages is inadequate.

...

An instance of this nature occurred in *Wrotham Park Estate Co Ltd v Parkside Homes Ltd* [1974] 1 W.L.R. 798. For social and economic reasons the court refused to make a mandatory order for the demolition of houses built on land burdened with a restrictive covenant. Instead, Brightman J. made an award of damages under the jurisdiction which originated with Lord Cairns' Act. The existence of the new houses did not diminish the value of the benefited land by one farthing. The judge considered that if the plaintiffs were given a nominal sum, or no sum, justice would manifestly not have been done. He assessed the damages at five per cent of the developer's anticipated profit, this being the amount of money which could reasonably have been demanded for a relaxation of the covenant.

In reaching his conclusion the judge applied by analogy the cases mentioned above concerning the assessment of damages when a defendant has invaded another's property rights but without diminishing the value of the property. I consider he was right to do so. Property rights are superior to contractual rights in that, unlike contractual rights, property rights may survive against an indefinite class of persons. However, it is not easy to see why, as between the parties to a contract, a violation of a party's contractual rights should attract a lesser degree of remedy than a violation of his property rights. As Lionel Smith has pointed out in his article 'Disgorgement of the profits of Contract: Property, Contract and 'Efficient Breach'' 24 Can. B.L.J. 121, it is not clear why it should be any more permissible to expropriate personal rights than it is permissible to expropriate property rights.

... Some years ago Professor Dawson suggested there is no inherent reason why the technique of equity courts in land contracts should not be more widely employed, not by granting remedies as the by-product of a phantom 'trust' created by the contract, but as an alternative form of money judgment remedy. That well known ailment of lawyers, a hardening of the categories, ought not to be an obstacle: see 'Restitution or Damages' (1959) 20 Ohio L.J. 175.

... there seems to be no reason, in principle, why the court must in all circumstances rule out an account of profits as a remedy for breach of contract. I prefer to avoid the unhappy expression 'restitutionary damages'. Remedies are the law's response to a wrong (or, more precisely, to a cause of action). When, exceptionally, a just response to a breach of contract so requires, the court should be able to grant the discretionary remedy of requiring a defendant to account to the plaintiff for the benefits he has received from his breach of contract. In the same way as a plaintiff's interest in performance of a contract may render it just and equitable for the court

218
8t>218

Lord Woolf, at [1998] Ch 439, 457, 458, also suggested three facts which should not be a sufficient ground for departing from the normal basis on which damages are awarded: the fact that the breach was cynical and deliberate; the fact that the breach enabled the defendant to enter into a more profitable contract elsewhere; and the fact that by entering into a new and more profitable contract the defendant put it out of his power to perform his contract with the plaintiff. I agree that none of these facts would be, by itself, a good reason for ordering an account of profits.

The present case

The present case is exceptional. The context is employment as a member of the security and intelligence services. Secret information is the lifeblood of these services. In the 1950s Blake deliberately committed repeated breaches of his undertaking not to divulge official information gained as a result of his employment. He caused untold and immeasurable damage to the public interest he had committed himself to serve. In 1990 he published his autobiography, a further breach of his express undertaking. By this time the information disclosed was no longer confidential. In the ordinary course of commercial dealings the disclosure of non-confidential information might be regarded as venial. In the present case disclosure was also a criminal offence under the Official Secrets Acts, even though the information was no longer confidential. Section 1 of the Official Secrets Act 1989 draws a distinction in this regard between members of the security and intelligence services and other Crown servants. Under section 1(3) a person who is or has been a Crown servant is guilty of an offence if without lawful authority he makes 'a damaging disclosure' of information relating to security or intelligence. The offence is drawn more widely in the case of a present or past member of the security and intelligence services. Such a person is guilty of an offence if without lawful authority he discloses 'any information' relating to security or intelligence which is or has been in his possession by virtue of his position as a member of those services. This distinction was approved in Parliament after debate when the legislation was being enacted.

Lord Hobhouse (dissenting):

… The answer given by my noble and learned friend does not reflect the essentially punitive nature of the claim and seeks to apply principles of law which are only appropriate where commercial or proprietary interests are involved. Blake has made a financial gain but he has not done so at the expense of the Crown or making use of any property of or commercial interest of the Crown either in law or equity.

1. The House of Lords held that Blake had to give up profits from the book. It was not relevant that the information was no longer confidential, nor that Blake was not classed as a fiduciary, nor that the information was not classed as 'property'. This case is sometimes seen as innovative because the normal remedy for breach of contract is compensation (to make good losses) rather than restitution (to give up gains). Many categories of employee who are bound by fiduciary duties (positions of trust, demanding loyalty and no conflicts) have long been required to make restitution: particularly company directors (eg *Bhullar v Bhullar* [2003] EWCA Civ 424 or *Cook v Deeks* [1916] UKPC 10). Lord Nicholls' best attempt to rationalise when other employees should be bound to make restitution is when an employing entity has a 'legitimate interest' in such a remedy. Do you agree that a better test would be that restitution will be available when an employee's position of responsibility (akin to directorship) requires avoiding of any possibility of conflict of interest?

2. In *Pearce v Foster* (1886) 17 QBD 536, the Court of Appeal held that a clerk, employed to give advice at a stockbroking firm, was dismissed for a good reason when he failed to disclose that he was himself speculating in buying and selling shares with other clients. Lord Esher MR and Lopes LJ said the breach lay in lack of faithful performance. By contrast, Lindley LJ said Pearce 'had so conducted himself as to make his interest conflict with his duty'. Does 'faithful' mean anything different from avoiding the possibility of conflict of interest?

3. The idea that employees should be 'loyal' to an employing entity has been fiercely disavowed throughout the history of labour law. Because employers profit from employees' work, there is an inherent tension (or even class conflict). It follows that a legal duty of 'loyalty' to a person who (potentially) profits unjustly from you is authoritarian, and antithetical to a free society. In his classic article, which earned him professional isolation by the German Academy in 1931, but made him Europe's most important labour lawyer in the mid-twentieth century, Otto Kahn-Freund wrote that the Empire Labour Court, by developing a duty of employees and unions to be faithful to the enterprise, had laid the foundations of a fascist society. See 'The Social Ideal of the Reich Labour Court – A Critical Examination of the Practice of the Reich Labour Court' (1931) in O Kahn-Freund, R Lewis and J Clark (eds), *Labour Law and Politics in the Weimar Republic* (1981) ch 3, discussed in this book at chapter 1(3)(a).

4. Against whom may restitution be available? In *Nottingham University v Fishel* [2000] IRLR 471, the university claimed restitution from Dr Simon Fishel for profits he made (1) while working privately and (2) using the services of junior embryologists, employed by the university, without gaining consent as his contract required. Dr Fishel argued that the embryologists gained experience from doing

his private work, and the university benefited: it had no loss. Elias J held that, though there was a clear breach of contract, Dr Fishel was not liable to account for his profits. He had not undertaken an obligation that would make him a fiduciary. However, he was liable to account for profits attributable to the work of junior embryologists, since he had a duty to direct their work only in the university's interests. What does this suggest about which employees will be liable for restitution?

5.   Lord Hobhouse dissents in *Blake* because he views property and confidential commercial interests as categorically different from contract. Lord Nicholls' reply, implicitly, is this exemplifies that 'well known ailment of lawyers, a hardening of the categories' which 'ought not to be an obstacle'. Do you agree that historical legal categories are irrelevant if underlying moral principles are the same?

6.   When is information classed as 'confidential'? In *Faccenda Chicken Ltd v Fowler* [1986] ICR 297, Neill LJ held that Mr Fowler had not breached his employment contract when, after resigning, he used information he learned about pricing and sales for different customers in his next business, transporting fresh chickens with refrigerated vans. While employed, Mr Fowler had to keep this information confidential. But because there was no provision in his contract classifying this information as a trade secret, after his employment ended he was free to use it.

7.   In many cases, an injunction (where a court says 'stop that!' or 'do this!') will be a preferable remedy to restitution. In *Roger Bullivant Ltd v Ellis* [1987] ICR 464, the Court of Appeal held that a company was entitled to an injunction against its former managing director using a customer index and black book of trade secrets after he had resigned. Mr Ellis had promised in his contract that, if his job terminated, he would not attempt to transact with former clients.

8.   An older line of cases suggest employees owe their employers 'good will' in performance of their contracts. The effect was that collective action by 'working to rule' (ie doing *exactly* what one's contract requires and no more) would be a breach of contract, potentially enabling damages against a trade union for partial strikes. In *Secretary of State for Employment v ASLEF (No 2)* [1972] ICR 19, train conductors' contracts required them to check each door was closed before leaving the platform. They literally opened and shut every door before departing each station, causing delays. Lord Denning MR held this literal compliance with the contract was a breach, because good will, an implicit duty, was withdrawn. Buckley LJ said there were 'breaches of an implied term to serve the employer faithfully within the requirements of the contract'. Roskill LJ preferred to formulate the duty that 'each employee will not, in obeying his lawful instructions, seek to obey them in a wholly unreasonable way which has the effect of disrupting the system'. Does this necessarily mean directors and managers have a complementary common law duty to the enterprise to bargain in good faith to avoid strikes? See chapter 11.

9.   *British Telecommunications plc v Ticehurst* [1992] ICR 383 held that where employees worked strictly to rule, this would count as 'part performance', entitling

the employing entity to withhold all pay. This applies a doctrine that is suitable for commercial contracts to employment contracts, in a way which frustrates the statutory and international right to take collective action. Can that reasoning survive the Supreme Court decision in *Gisda Cyf v Barratt*, that principles from the general law of contract must be 'segregated intellectually' from statutory rights?

(2) IMPLIED EMPLOYEE RIGHTS

Just as employing entities benefit from implied terms, employees have implied common law rights. These limit the right to direct workers and appropriate the benefits of labour, if they are purposefully construed by courts. The essential controversy is whether default common law rights may be overridden by express contract terms. In commercial contracts, there is little dispute: the principle of private autonomy requires that express terms override implied terms. Does the same logic apply to employment relationships? There is no debate about statutory rights: these cannot be contracted away. As for common law rights, a growing consensus seems to be that if employees are truly free to choose, they should be able to limit or contract out of them. An individual agreement will not usually be enough: given the 'relative bargaining power of the parties', it will not be a 'true agreement' (*Autoclenz Ltd v Belcher* [2011] UKSC 41, [35]). This suggests collective agreement is needed, but the controversy is not yet decisively resolved. The main rights discussed here are to (a) good faith or mutual trust and confidence, (b) work for pay in normal hours, (c) a safe system of work, and (d) notice and good reasons for dismissal.

(a) Good Faith or Mutual Trust and Confidence

Malik and Mahmud v Bank of Credit and Commerce International SA [1997] UKHL 23, [1998] AC 20

Mr Malik and Mr Mahmud claimed compensation from the liquidator of Bank of Credit and Commerce International SA (BCCI) for lost earnings, when they failed to find new jobs. BCCI went insolvent after public revelations that it had engaged in mass fraud, funded terrorists, laundered money and extorted politicians. Malik and Mahmud sought employment elsewhere. They found the stigma and reputational damage from BCCI hindered their prospects. This raised the question of what duty (if any) the company had owed to its employees that had been broken. Without any express contract terms, Malik and Mahmud argued there was an implied term in their employment contracts that nothing would be done that was calculated to undermine mutual trust and confidence. The House of Lords agreed.

Lord Nicholls:

There is here an important point of principle. Are financial losses of this character, which I shall call "continuing financial losses", recoverable for breach of the trust and confidence term?

This is the crucial point in the present appeals. In my view, if it was reasonably foreseeable that a particular type of loss of this character was a serious possibility, and loss of this type is sustained in consequence of a breach, then in principle damages in respect of the loss should be recoverable.

In the present case the agreed facts make no assumption, either way, about whether the appellants' handicap in the labour market was reasonably foreseeable by the bank. On this there must be scope for argument. I would not regard the absence of this necessary ingredient from the assumed facts as a sufficient reason for refusing to permit the former employees' claims to proceed further.

The contrary argument of principle is that since the purpose of the trust and confidence term is to preserve the employment relationship and to enable that relationship to prosper and continue, the losses recoverable for breach should be confined to those flowing from the premature termination of the relationship. Thus, a breach of the term should not be regarded as giving rise to recoverable losses beyond those I have described as premature termination losses. In this way, the measure of damages would be commensurate with, and not go beyond, the scope of the protection the trust and confidence term is intended to provide for the employee.

This is an unacceptably narrow evaluation of the trust and confidence term. Employers may be under no common law obligation, through the medium of an implied contractual term of general application, to take steps to improve their employees' future job prospects. But failure to improve is one thing, positively to damage is another. Employment, and job prospects, are matters of vital concern to most people. Jobs of all descriptions are less secure than formerly, people change jobs more frequently, and the job market is not always buoyant. Everyone knows this. An employment contract creates a close personal relationship, where there is often a disparity of power between the parties. Frequently the employee is vulnerable. Although the underlying purpose of the trust and confidence term is to protect the employment relationship, there can be nothing unfairly onerous or unreasonable in requiring an employer who breaches the trust and confidence term to be liable if he thereby causes continuing financial loss of a nature that was reasonably foreseeable. Employers must take care not to damage their employees' future employment prospects, by harsh and oppressive behaviour or by any other form of conduct which is unacceptable today as falling below the standards set by the implied trust and confidence term.

Lord Steyn:

The employees do not rely on a term implied in fact. They do not therefore rely on an individualised term to be implied from the particular provisions of their employment contracts considered against their specific contextual setting. Instead they rely on a standardised term implied by law, that is, on a term which is said to be an incident of all contracts of employment: *Scally v Southern Health and Social Services Board* [1992] 1 AC 294, 307B. Such implied terms operate as default rules. The parties are free to exclude or modify them. But is common ground that in the present case the particular terms of the contracts of employment of the two applicants could not affect an implied obligation of mutual trust and confidence …

… A striking illustration of this change is *Scally* to which I have already referred where the House of Lords implied a term that all employees in a certain category had to be notified by an employer of their entitlement to certain benefits. It was a change in legal culture which made possible the evolution of the implied term of trust and confidence …

…

The evolution of the implied term of trust and confidence is a fact. It has not yet been endorsed by your Lordships' House. It has proved a workable principle in practice. It has not been the subject of adverse criticism in any decided cases and it has been welcomed in academic writings. I regard the emergence of the implied obligation of mutual trust and confidence as a sound development.

…

... The motives of the employer cannot be determinative, or even relevant, in judging the employees' claims for damages for breach of the implied obligation. If conduct objectively considered is likely to cause serious damage to the relationship between employer and employee a breach of the implied obligation may arise.

Lord Goff and **Lord Mackay** agreed with both judgments. **Lord Mustill** agreed with **Lord Steyn**.

NOTES AND QUESTIONS

1. The whole House recognises the right to mutual trust and confidence. In essence it is what *Wilson v Racher* termed a 'duty of mutual respect'. Lord Steyn says such 'implied terms operate as default rules. The parties are free to exclude or modify them.' Do you agree this requires that both 'parties are free' to an equal measure? If the 'freedom' is all on the side of the employing entity, it follows there is no genuine freedom for an individual employee. Thus, the essential point of *Autoclenz* emerges again: the 'relative bargaining power of the parties must be taken into account in deciding whether the terms of any written agreement in truth represent what was agreed'.

2. In *Malik* the function of mutual trust and confidence is to require an unusual duty, to assure the claimants a remedy: not to conduct a fraudulent business, to assure compensation for future lost job opportunities. Generally, the function of open-textured standards, such as mutual trust and confidence, is to empower the judiciary to develop rules and remedies when they match principles in diverse cases. As opposed to rules, standards (such as 'negligence', 'conflict of interest' or 'proper purpose') develop categories of cases that can only be explained through category and example. Courts reason by analogy from one case to the next, in light of evolving social values about decent conduct. Rules follow from standards, just as laws follow from principles (at least most of the time). What examples in other legal fields apply the same logic?

3. A considerable body of case law had already built up between *Wilson* and *Malik*. In *Isle of Wight Tourist Board v Coombes* [1976] IRLR 413 the Employment Appeal Tribunal held that it was a breach for a director to say his personal secretary was 'an intolerable bitch on a Monday morning'. This justified the secretary resigning and claiming damages for constructive dismissal. Similarly, in *Courtaulds Northern Textiles Ltd v Andrew* [1979] IRLR 84, it was a breach for a manager to tell an employee during a heated argument, 'You can't do the bloody job anyway.' Given that in Mr Wilson swore at Mr Racher as well, does this suggest that offensive or derogatory language is worse when it comes from people in a position of authority, and is more excusable by people who are not?

4. *The Post Office v Roberts* [1980] IRLR 347 held that the Post Office breached mutual trust and confidence when its supervisor, Mr O'Keefe, wrote on Ms Roberts' personal records, without any basis, that she was irresponsible, lacked industry and comprehension skills, and this hindered her application for an office transfer. Talbot J said 'We do not think it helpful' to ask if the 'behaviour was deliberate or malicious'. It is therefore only relevant that mutual trust and confidence is breached.

5.   By contrast, in *Woods v W M Car Services (Peterborough) Ltd* [1981] ICR 666, the Court of Appeal upheld the Tribunal's finding that no breach occurred when an employer insisted on reducing Ms Woods' pay, or increasing hours, and changing her job title. According to Watkins LJ: 'The obdurate refusal of the employee to accept conditions very properly and sensibly being sought to be imposed upon her was unreasonable.' Inevitably many enterprises do need to restructure, and in some cases there will be compelling arguments for making redundancies or reducing the pay of all staff. If cuts need to be made, do you agree that it is relevant whether managers or directors are themselves sharing the burdens of restructuring proportionally? See further below, chapter 5(3)(b).

6.   In *Eastwood v Magnox Electric plc* [2004] UKHL 35 Lord Nicholls at [11] and Lord Steyn at [50] renamed the term as one of 'good faith'. This was already suggested by Sir Nicolas Browne-Wilkinson VC in *Imperial Group Pension Trust Limited v Imperial Tobacco Ltd* [1991] 1 WLR 589, 597. As well as being less of a mouthful than 'mutual trust and confidence', the language of good faith has carries considerable meaning. It was first said to be a general and probably compulsory term of all contracts by Lord Mansfield in *Carter v Boehm* (1766) 3 Burr 1905, where a colonial fort owner breached the term by failing to disclose risks of French invasion to his insurer. In addition, in *Pawson v Watson* (1778) 2 Cowp 786, 788, Lord Mansfield stated that 'by the law of merchants, all dealings must be fair and honest'. This stance was not followed in the years after. But in most countries today, 'good faith' is recognised as an organising principle for contract law and cannot be contracted away. It gives the opportunity for courts to eliminate unconscionable practices in light of contemporary social values. In Canada, see *Bhasin v Hrynew* [2014] 3 SCR 494. In Germany, see the *Bank Guarantee Case* or *Bürgschaft* (19 October 1993) BVerfGE 89, 214.

7.   The next case found that a duty of equal treatment was part of mutual trust and confidence.

Transco plc v O'Brien [2002] EWCA Civ 379

Mr Paul O'Brien claimed that Transco plc (which ran British Gas) breached his employment contract by failing to offer him enhanced contractual redundancy pay, as they did to 74 other workers. Mr O'Brien had been hired through Accountancy Personnel, an employment agency, on 1 August 1995, and before Transco plc in February 1996 invoiced the agency 'to engage Paul O'Brien's services on a permanent basis' Transco did not count Mr O'Brien as a real permanent employee. On this ground, Transco plc did not offer O'Brien the same redundancy package as other directly hired staff as it sought to sell off the property portfolio unit where he the others worked. O'Brien succeeded in establishing that he was an employee from February 1996, and claimed he should further be treated equally. The Court of Appeal upheld his claim.

Pill LJ:

5. The appellants had 75 workers who were recognised as permanent employees. They were all considered entitled to the enhanced redundancy package, with the possible exception of one employee who in the event had not chosen to accept the package. The only explanation given

for singling out the respondent was the fact that the employers had not believed him to be a permanent employee.

...

17. In this case, for good commercial reasons the appellants decided to offer their workforce (the relevant part of which was over 70 strong) a new contract on better terms. To single out an employee on capricious grounds and refuse to offer him the same terms as are offered to the rest of the workforce is in my judgment a breach of the implied term of trust and confidence. There are few things which would be more likely to damage seriously (to put it no higher) the relationship of trust between an employer and employee than a capricious refusal, in present circumstances, to offer the same terms to a single employee.

18. The matter should be looked at as one of substance. Whether the form of the change proposed by the employer is by way of variation or by way of a new contract is not in itself of great importance: the context and the substance of the matter must be considered. The substance here was an offer of fresh contractual arrangements to a workforce in order to achieve the employer's aims and objects, though the welfare of the workforce may well also have been a factor. To deprive one member of a large workforce of the same opportunity as offered to all his fellow workers is a clear breach of the implied term, in my view.

19. I have already stated in summary form the second submission made, which is that the Employment Tribunal have erred in law by their use of the expression "to treat employees in a fair and even handed manner". It is submitted that the wrong test has been applied. In my judgment, even if that is right it does not affect the outcome of this appeal. The facts are clear and are not and cannot be disputed, and it is for this court, as a matter of law (as it was for the EAT) to hold whether on those facts there was a breach of the implied term. Reference to fairness and even-handedness is surplusage. ...

20. It is not suggested on behalf of the respondent that the refusal to offer terms to him was capricious in the sense in which Mr Leiper used that term as the basis for his first submission. The reason why the terms were not offered, as the Employment Tribunal recognised, was a genuine but erroneous belief that the respondent's status was not that of a permanent employee, as contemplated in the scheme. It is submitted that such genuine and reasonable belief was a good reason for failing to make the offer to the respondent, good in the sense that it did not involve a breach of the trust and confidence term.

21. I am not able to accept that submission. Employment tribunals have found unanimously that the respondent was an employee and by a majority that he was a permanent employee. The reason given by the employers has been found to have been unsound. A reasonable belief in a state of affairs now held not to exist is not in my judgment a ground for depriving the employee of the improved terms of employment which would have been offered but for the error.

22. In the present case it was plainly a breach of contract to treat an employee as not being entitled to benefits resulting from his being a permanent employee when he was in fact a permanent employee. The good faith with which the erroneous belief was held does not alter the character of the failure. Had the employers assessed the respondent's status correctly he would have been offered the enhanced terms. The EAT were correct to conclude that the respondent must be placed in the position in which he would have been but for the breach of contract. The employers were in breach of contract in failing to offer the respondent the enhanced contractual redundancy payment, as held by the majority of the Employment Tribunal. Questions as to the loss resulting from that breach and of causation do not arise for consideration upon the present appeal.

Longmore LJ agreed. **Sir Martin Nourse** gave a short concurring opinion.

1. Pill LJ holds that an honest belief that Mr O'Brien was not a permanent employee was not enough to justify unequal treatment: Mr O'Brien had to be treated equally and it was 'capricious' to single him out. What does this suggest about cases discussed in chapter 3(3) regarding joint employment and the employee status of people hired through employment agencies?

2. While the idea that we should 'treat like cases alike' is widely accepted, and even referred to as 'a general axiom of rational behaviour' in *Matadeen v Pointu* [1998] UKPC 9, Lord Hoffmann remarked the following: 'Of course persons should be uniformly treated, unless there is some valid reason to treat them differently. But what counts as a valid reason for treating them differently?' The Court of Appeal rejects that Mr O'Brien's connection to an agency was a valid reason for differential treatment, because in substance he was a permanent employee. How do you think relevant factors can be separated from irrelevant ones? See further chapter 13.

3. Parliament has now partially codified this common law principle of equal treatment for agency workers, in respect of 'basic working conditions'. See the Agency Worker Regulations 2010, explained in chapter 12.

Mallone v BPB Industries plc [2002] EWCA Civ 126

Mr Giovanni Mallone claimed compensation for BPB plc unreasonably withdrawing his share options after being dismissed. Mallone's contract, as a managing director of BPB's Italian subsidiary, incorporated a share option, where Rule 5(b)(iii) said options be awarded to terminated employees 'as the directors in their absolute discretion shall determine'. They had passed a resolution under an express rule of the share option scheme, which allowed award of share options to terminated employees in 'appropriate proportion'. He claimed their exercise of discretion was unreasonable. The Court of Appeal agreed.

Rix LJ:

34. Mr Randall submitted that the committee's decision could not be so stigmatised. It had an "absolute discretion". The judge had accepted Mr Heard's evidence that the committee had taken into account Mr Mallone's performance, the circumstances of his dismissal (which Mr Randall pointed out included the fact that Mr Mallone had been offered alternative employment within the group, in England), and their understanding that Mr Mallone would receive Lire 1 billion in compensation. That was, he stated (albeit this was not a matter in evidence), greatly more than an executive in his position would have received by way of compensation under English law. ...

...

37. Mr Randall accepted and indeed said he adopted that reasoning, but in a case such as the present sought to argue that irrationality could best be judged by the standard of good faith, viz. not to act dishonestly, for an improper purpose, capriciously or arbitrarily, and that none of these things could be said or had been found of the committee. In this connection he cited *Nash v Paragon Finance* [2001] EWCA 1466. That was concerned with a mortgage with a variable interest rate clause. It was alleged that the mortgagee's discretion to vary the interest rate could not be exercised unreasonably. This court rejected the implication of such a term.

Having considered *Abu Dhabi National Tanker Co v Product Star Shipping Ltd (The Product Star) (No 2)* [1993] 1 Lloyd's Rep 397 and *Gan Insurance Co Ltd v Tai Ping Insurance Co Ltd (No 2)* [2001] 2 All ER (Comm) 299, this court adopted the solution of those two earlier decisions which was to apply a less restricted limitation analogous to unreasonableness in the *Wednesbury* sense: *Associated Provincial Picture Houses Ltd v Wednesbury Corporation* [1948] 1 KB 223; or what Mance LJ in the latter case called "unreasonableness in the sense of conduct or a decision to which no reasonable person having the relevant discretion could have subscribed" (at para 64). In *Nash* Dyson LJ then said (at para 41):

> "So here too, we find a somewhat reluctant extension of the implied term to include unreasonableness that is analogous to *Wednesbury* unreasonableness. I entirely accept that the scope of an implied term will depend on the circumstances of the particular contract. But I find the analogy of Gan Insurance and the cases considered in the judgment of Mance LJ helpful. It is one thing to imply that a lender will not exercise his discretion in a way that no reasonable lender, acting reasonably, would do. It is unlikely that a lender who was acting in that way would not also be acting either dishonestly, for an improper purpose, capriciously or arbitrarily. It is quite another matter to imply a term that the lender would not impose unreasonable rates."

38. Mr Randall submitted that because there was no finding of dishonesty, improper motive, capriciousness or arbitrariness against BPB in this case, therefore the judge must have been mistaken to have found that the committee's decision had been one that "no reasonable employer could have reached" (see at para 28 above).

39. I cannot accept that submission. One could debate whether an employer could act irrationally (using that term for acting as no reasonable employer would act) without it also being said that he was acting in one of the other ways described. In many cases that might be so: but I am unwilling to say that it is necessarily so. Perhaps irrationality and arbitrariness are very close to the same thing. But I think that someone may act irrationally while being honest; and as Burton J suggested in *Clark v Nomura*, capriciousness is something else (eg deciding on the basis of the colour of someone's hair or eyes). I would be reluctant to contemplate, on the facts found by the judge, that some epithet for the committee's decision other than that chosen by the judge himself should be used. I can see no ground for doing so.

40. The question remains whether the judge was justified to make the finding of irrationality that he did. In my judgment he was. The directors had what is called an absolute discretion: but their discretion still remained one to find "the appropriate proportion". The proviso indicates that, at any rate prima facie and subject to the director's discretion, the appropriate proportion is to be found by taking the length of the participant's service following the grant of an option.

Wilson J and **Waller LJ** agreed.

NOTES AND QUESTIONS

1. The Court of Appeal holds that, although the express wording of the share option scheme granted 'absolute discretion' to directors, that discretion was to be exercised in a rational way. This is repeatedly described as a requirement of 'good faith'.
2. Will the common law always control discretionary power? The House of Lords in *Equitable Life Assurance Society v Hyman* [2000] UKHL 39 suggests it must. Here, an insurance company's directors had 'absolute discretion' to change bonus

payments for people saving through life insurance schemes. Because of a history of mismanagement, Equitable Life's directors attempted to reduce the bonus payments for policyholders who had contracted for a 'guaranteed annuity rate' to subsidise those who had bought 'current annuity rate' policies, and so prop up its customer base. Despite the express contract term, their Lordships affirmed that this was a breach of contract, and control by 'implication is essential to give effect to the reasonable expectations of the parties'. The 'guaranteed' annuity rate holders had a reasonable expectation that their policies would be sheltered from 'current' market conditions, and varying bonuses undermined that. In effect one express term ('absolute discretion') is contradicted by the implications of other express terms, in light of what the court determines to be reasonable expectations. In employment, where else do employing entities have discretion that might potentially be abused?

3. In *French v Barclays Bank* [1998] IRLR 646, as described at chapter 4(2)(a), Waller LJ (Walker LJ and Hobhouse LJ agreeing) held that a bridging loan for home relocation being withdrawn was a breach of mutual trust and confidence. This was so even though it was discretionary under the contract's terms.

4. In *Braganza v BP Shipping Ltd* [2015] UKSC 17, the majority of the Supreme Court held that BP's investigation into Mr Braganza's death was not stable, and was to be reviewed on the same principles as administrative law, namely with 'honesty, good faith, and genuineness' and avoiding 'arbitrariness, capriciousness, perversity and irrationality', per Lord Neuberger (dissenting) at [104]. The company would have to pay Mrs Braganza compensation, unless Mr Braganza committed suicide. The company investigator said he committed suicide. Mrs Braganza contested this, and the courts agreed with her. Lady Hale, for the majority, said the evidence of suicide was 'straws in the wind', and could not be relied upon. She emphasised at [18]: '[T]he party who is charged with making decisions which affect the rights of both parties to the contract has a clear conflict of interest. That conflict is heightened where there is a significant imbalance of power between the contracting parties as there often will be in an employment contract.'

(b) Work for Pay in Normal Hours

Devonald v Rosser & Sons **[1906] 2 KB 728**

Mr Devonald claimed compensation for not being paid during a contractual 28-day notice period, when his employer, Rosser & Sons did not provide any work. He was bringing a test case for his fellow tinplate rollermen at a factory in Cilfrew, South Wales. Employees were paid for each completed box of 112 tin plates. In their contracts, rule 1 stated they would receive 'twenty-eight days' notice in writing, such notice to be given on the first Monday of any calendar month before 12 o'clock at noon'. In July 1903, the company announced the plant would close in two weeks, and gave notice on 3 August 1903. Thus, for a six-week period, the employer gave no work and did not pay. The Court of Appeal held that they were obliged to do so.

Lord Alverston CJ:

... the implication which is to be drawn from this contract is one which, to use the language of Bowen L.J. in *The Moorcock*,[1] is raised "from the presumed intention of the parties with the object of giving to the transaction such efficacy as both parties must have intended that at all events it should have," that "what the law desires to effect by the implication is to give such business efficacy to the transaction as must have been intended at all events by both parties who are business men." I am content to accept that test in deciding whether or not this contract involves the implication which is necessary to enable the plaintiff to recover. Now, in order to determine that question, the only facts that are material to be considered are that the plaintiff was in the defendants' regular employment, that he was paid by piece work, and that he was employed upon the terms of a rule which provides that "No person regularly employed shall quit or be discharged from these works without giving or receiving twenty-eight days' notice in writing, such notice to be given on the first Monday of any calendar month."

...

What, then, is the obligation of the employers under such a contract as the present? On the one hand we must consider the matter from the point of view of the employers who I agree will under ordinary circumstances desire to carry on their works at a profit, though not necessarily at a profit in every week, for it is matter of common knowledge that masters have frequently to run their mills for weeks and months together at a loss in order to keep their business together and in hopes of better times. On the other hand, we have to consider the position of the workman. The workman has to live; and the effect of the defendants' contention is that if the master at any time found that his works were being carried on at a loss, he might at once close down his works and cease to employ his men, who, even if they gave notice to quit the employment, would be bound to the master for a period of at least twenty-eight days during which time they would be unable to earn any wages at all. I agree with Jelf J. that that is an unreasonable contention from the workman's point of view. In my opinion the necessary implication to be drawn from this contract is at least that the master will find a reasonable amount of work up to the expiration of a notice given in accordance with the contract. I am not prepared to say that that obligation is an absolute one to find work at all events, for the evidence shewed that it was subject to certain contingencies, such as breakdown of machinery and want of water and materials. But I am clearly of opinion that it would be no excuse to the master, for non-performance of his implied obligation to provide the workman with work, that he could no longer make his plates at a profit either for orders or for stock. It is to be observed that the question how the works are to be carried on, whether they are going to work short or full time, or whether for stock or current orders, is a matter which rests entirely in the hands of the master. The men have absolutely nothing to say to it. And it seems to me that there is nothing unreasonable in the implication that the master shall look at least twenty-eight days ahead, or, to take the extreme case, as the notice has to be given on the first Monday in the month, fifty-seven days ahead, so as to place himself in a position to provide the workman with work during the period covered by the notice.

President Sir Gorell Barnes and **Farwell LJ** gave concurring opinions.

NOTES AND QUESTIONS

1. The Court of Appeal holds that, despite the workers' pay being set by 'piece' (the quantity of tinplate output), it was still a 'necessary implication' of the notice period 'that the master will find a reasonable amount of work up to the expiration of a notice given in accordance with the contract'. It follows that until an employing entity has duly dismissed an employee (in this case for redundancy) there

---

[1] 14 P. D. 64, at p. 68.

is an implied common law right to pay during the normal hours or work that an employee does. If the employing entity does not have work, this risk properly falls on the employing entity.

2.   What determines the rate of pay? The *Devonald* employees appear to have been entitled to the income they had been receiving prior to the factory closure: presumably the court can calculate an average, should hours have fluctuated.

3.   Why should employing entities bear the risk of downturns in work, rather than employees? Lord Alverstone CJ gives greater weight to the fact that the 'workman has to live'. This suggests it is morally right to protect the more vulnerable party to the employment relation: the individual human being over the organisation. But is this economically prudent if the organisation's fortunes will have consequences for other individuals? Simon Deakin and Frank Wilkinson, *The Law of the Labour Market* (2005) ch 2, 109–10 suggest that the modern economic system, of which the employment contract is a part, has been designed to fulfil both a 'coordination' and 'risk function'. On the one hand it enables enterprise to be directed according to sound economic management, and on the other it 'channels the risks of economic insecurity in such a way as to protect the individual worker against the consequences of that very same dependence on, and subordination to, the employer's superior resources'. It follows that risk is diversified in such a way (onto organisations, away from individuals) that those best placed to absorb risks do so. This reduces systemic risk. Do you agree?

4.   If an express contract term purports to give 'absolute discretion' or something similar to an employing entity to reduce hours and work to zero, will that override the common law right expressed in *Devonald*? This raises the social problem of 'zero hours contracts'. Common law authority gives a clear answer: that following *Autoclenz* such terms will not represent the parties' true agreement. However, statutory codification and business practice lags behind. See chapter 7(2)(a).

(c) A Safe System of Work

Johnstone v Bloomsbury Health Authority **[1992] QB 333**

For the facts of Dr Johnstone's claim for personal injury from overwork, see chapter 4(1)(c).

Stuart-Smith LJ:

A man who is engaged expressly to work on a particular machine or range of machinery is not thereby precluded from suing his employer if he sustains injury because the machine is dangerous. Take the case of a man whose contract requires him to work a certain number of basic hours and overtime in addition as required; if he is required to work such long hours that he is exhausted and his attention or concentration fail so that he suffers an accident, it is no defence to the employer to say that the workman expressly agreed to work such hours. So much is trite law and finds succinct expression in the speech of Lord Thankerton in *Wilsons & Clyde Coal Co Ltd v English* [1938] AC 57, 67:

> "It appears clear, then, that, when the workman contracts to do the work, he is not to be held as having agreed to hold the master immune from the latter's liability for want of due care in the provision of a reasonably safe system of working."

There is no difference between the duty to provide a safe system of working and the duty to take reasonable care for the safety of the employee. The former is merely an ingredient in the latter duty. Moreover, I cannot see, in the example I have just given, that it makes any difference that instead of the overtime being "as required" the workman is contracted to work up to 88 hours a week. If these were the hours of a contract of a heavy goods driver, and he fell asleep at the wheel through exhaustion and suffered injury I entertain no doubt that, subject to any defence of contributory negligence, the employee would have a good claim against his employer for operating an unsafe system of work. There is no obligation on the employer to require the man to drive for 88 hours in the week, and if by so doing he exposes him to foreseeable risk of injury he will be liable.

It must be remembered that the duty of care is owed to the individual employee and different employees may have different stamina. If the defendants in this case knew or ought to have known that by requiring him to work the hours they did, they exposed him to risk of injury to his health, then they should not have required him to work in excess of those hours that he safely could have done.

In my opinion paragraph 4(b) gave the defendants the power to require the plaintiff to work up to 88 hours per week on average. But that power had to be exercised in the light of the other contractual terms and in particular their duty to take care for his safety. Mr. Beloff submits that the defendants cannot be expected to treat their house officers differently according to their physical stamina. But this is not the law. In *Paris v Stepney Borough Council* [1951] AC 367 the employer owed a duty to take greater care of a one-eyed man than a normal man in respect of risk of injuries to the eyes. If employers know or ought to know that a workman has a vulnerable back they are in breach of duty in requiring him to lift and move weights which are likely to cause him injury even if a normal man can carry them without risk. Mr. Beloff's suggested solution was that if a potential house officer thought that he could not perform the hours required, he should not take he job. Although the principle that if you cannot stand the heat in the kitchen you should get out, or not go in, may often be a sound one, it would have serious implications if applied in these circumstances. Any doctor who wishes to practice has to serve at least one year as a house officer in a hospital; the National Health Service is effectively a monopoly employer. Is the aspiring doctor who has spent many years in training to this point to abandon his chosen profession because the employer may exercise its power to call upon him to work so many hours that his health is undermined? I fail to see why he should not approach the matter on the basis that the defendants will only exercise that power consistently with their duty to have proper regard to his health and safety. The fact that one doctor may have less stamina and physical strength than another does not mean that he is any less competent at his profession.

It follows that I would hold that if the pleaded facts are established, and they are of course contested, paragraph 4(b) of the contract does not preclude or limit the plaintiff's claim as contended by Mr. Beloff. I therefore have no difficulty in concluding that the prayer in the writ and statement of claim should not be struck out in the manner sought.

Leggatt LJ (dissenting):

It is suggested that during the latter period the defendants may not be entitled to call upon the plaintiff if it is foreseeable that to do so would injure his health. But I am persuaded by Mr. Beloff that there is no warrant for any distinction between the two periods: the doctor's duty to make himself available has as its correlative a right in the employer to take advantage of his availability by requiring him to work; and there can in principle be no difference in the nature or extent of the duty owed to the doctor according to whether he contracts to work or merely to be on call. It is therefore not permissible to argue that the implied duty to look out for a doctor's health may cut down the number of hours for which a doctor who is on call may be required to work, even though not the number of hours for which he is required to work in any event. The only difference between the two is that the employer has an option in the one case but not in the other: the doctor's duty is the same in both. and the implied duty cannot detract from the employer's right any more than from the doctor's duty.

Browne-Wilkinson VC:

… I agree with Leggatt L.J. and disagree with Stuart-Smith L.J. that in the present case the scope of the duty of care for the plaintiff's health owed by the defendants falls to be determined taking into account the express terms of clause 4(b) of the contract. If the contract, on its true construction, were to impose an absolute obligation to work 48 hours overtime per week on average, it would, in my judgment, preclude an argument by the employee that the employer, in requiring 48 hours per week overtime, was in breach of his implied duty of care for the employee's health.

But this case is not the same as the example I have used above. Although clause 4(b) imposes an absolute duty on the plaintiff to work for 40 hours and in addition an obligation "to be available" for a further 48 hours per week on average, the defendants have a discretion as to the number of hours they call on the plaintiff to work "overtime." There is no incompatibility between the plaintiff being under a duty to be available for 48 hours overtime and the defendants having the right, subject to their ordinary duty not to injure the plaintiff, to call on him to work up to 48 hours overtime on average. There is, in the present contract, no incompatibility between the plaintiff's duty on the one hand and the defendants' right, subject to the implied duty as to health, on the other. The implied term does not contradict the express term of the contract.

NOTES AND QUESTIONS

1. By a majority, the Court of Appeal held that an implied term controlled the express term requiring long hours. But there were three different views. Stuart-Smith LJ says that the implied right to a safe system of work overrides express terms. Leggatt LJ, dissenting, thought that express terms must always override implied terms just like in any commercial contract. Browne-Wilkinson VC chose to explain the matter as the express term's discretion being interpreted through the implied right. This reaches the same result as Stuart-Smith LJ, but by highlighting the courts' inherent jurisdiction to control private discretion, the principle later adopted by the House of Lords *Equitable Life v Hyman*. Which approach do you think is most preferable?

2. As will be recalled from chapter 4(1)(c), although Leggatt LJ dissents on the implied term point, he agrees that the Unfair Contract Terms Act 1977 (UCTA) s 2(1) limited the contract's terms. What (if anything) justifies there being one rule at common law that openly contradicts statute, accepted by Parliament for twenty-five years? Was Leggatt LJ's position that, had UCTA 1977 never been enacted, the employing entity would be immune at common law for working the junior doctor to death?

3. For the foundational House of Lords case on the non-delegable duty to provide a safe system of work, *Wilsons & Clyde Coal Co Ltd v English* [1938] AC 57, see chapter 7A.

4. Is it relevant to patterns of working time that the NHS in Stuart-Smith LJ's words is a 'monopoly employer' and that employees lack choice of employer? In countries without a publicly funded universal service, and multiple privatised health-care providers, long hours are common where labour markets are unregulated. In the United States, for example, private 'Health Maintenance Organizations' are

paid through employer health insurance contracts. They operate private hospitals where the equivalent of junior doctors, termed 'medical residents', frequently work over 100 hours a week. Consistent with classical labour law theory, the evidence suggests that 'choice' of employer is irrelevant because of the systematic inequality of labour's bargaining power. Changing employing entities will not help when all employing entities use the same standard terms of employment: they do so because their resources, organisation and informational advantages enable them to impose their will on all employees.

5. Their Lordships rejected that long hours were in themselves contrary to 'public policy' because, per Stuart-Smith LJ the 'courts should be wary of extending the scope of the doctrine beyond the well-recognised categories: see *Fender v St John-Mildmay* [1938] AC 1, 11–12, per Lord Atkin'. What does 'be wary' mean?

6. Assuming we are 'wary' about public policy preventing harmful working hours, why should we be any less wary of public policy enforcing contracts whatever their terms? In *Printing and Numerical Registering Co v Sampson* (1875) 19 Eq 462, 465, Sir George Jessel MR said: '[I]f there is one thing which more than another public policy requires it is that men of full age and competent understanding shall have the utmost liberty of contracting, and that their contracts when entered into freely and voluntarily shall be held sacred and shall be enforced by Courts of justice.' What justifies this as the dominant public policy when 'the freedom was all on the side of the big concern which had the use of the printing press'? (*George Mitchell (Chesterhall) Ltd v Finney Lock Seeds Ltd* [1982] EWCA Civ 5, per Lord Denning MR.)

7. The courts' definition of 'public policy' and the fact of public ownership of the UK health service did not change the long-hours culture for Dr Johnstone and his colleagues. Pressure from unions and human rights groups led Parliament to decide that public policy should advance, when it opted into the Social Chapter of the European Union and implemented the Working Time Directive 1993, recast in 2003/88/EC, through the Working Time Regulations 1998. See chapter 7.

(d) Notice and Fair Process for Dismissal

West London Mental Health NHS Trust v Chhabra [2013] UKSC 80

Dr Chhabra sought an injunction against her NHS employer continuing a disciplinary procedure, for being contrary to the NHS Disciplinary Procedures 2005. Dr Chhabra was investigated for breaching 'patient confidentiality' by leaving documents visible on train journeys and dictating reports. A consultant from another NHS Trust was appointed as case manager. It was agreed that a 'human resources' director of the Trust, Mr Wishart, would not take part. However, the investigator sent Wishart a draft of her report. Wishart suggested extensive amendments, against Dr Chhabra. Charges were put to a conduct panel alleging gross misconduct. There was a further allegation outside the investigator's remit. Dr Chhabra objected to this and there was a further investigation, which concluded there was no case to pursue. Dr Chhabra claimed interlocutory relief to prevent the trust investigating confidentiality concerns under its disciplinary policy.

Lord Hodge (with whom **Lady Hale**, **Lord Kerr**, **Lord Reed** and **Lord Hughes** agree):

34. ... I consider that there have been a number of irregularities in the proceedings against Dr Chhabra which cumulatively render the convening of the conduct panel unlawful as a material breach of her contract of employment. I have four concerns about the procedure which the Trust followed.

35. First, I do not think that the findings of fact and evidence, which Dr Taylor recorded, were capable when taken at their highest of supporting a charge of gross misconduct. Paragraph 13.4.1 of policy D4 speaks of conduct so serious "as to potentially make any further relationship and trust between the Trust and the employee impossible." This language describes conduct which could involve a repudiatory breach of contract: *Dunn v AAH Ltd* [2010] IRLR 709, para 6; *Wilson v Racher* [1974] ICR 428. There is no material in Dr Taylor's report to support the view that the breaches of confidentiality which she recorded, including the former secretary's allegations, were wilful in the sense that they were deliberate breaches of that duty. In my view they were qualitatively different from a deliberate breach of confidentiality such as speaking to the media about a patient.

36. Secondly, in reaching the view that Dr Chhabra's behaviour could amount to gross misconduct, Dr Broughton founded on the words added to para 13.4.1 with effect from 28 March 2011, after the incidents in this case. The list of misconduct in para 13.4.1 comprised only typical examples of what the Trust saw as amounting to gross misconduct and was not a comprehensive statement of the concept. But Dr Broughton relied on the amended provision in support of his view that the complaints might amount to gross misconduct and quoted it in his letter of 12 August 2011 relating to the disciplinary procedure (para 24 above).

37. Thirdly, I consider that the Trust breached its contract with Dr Chhabra when Mr Wishart continued to take part in the investigatory process in breach of the undertaking which the Trust's solicitors gave in their letter of 24 February 2011 (para 21 above). In particular, when Mr Wishart proposed extensive amendments to Dr Taylor's draft report and Dr Taylor accepted some of them, which strengthened her criticism of Dr Chhabra, the Trust went outside the agreed procedures which had contractual effect. Policies D4 and D4A established a procedure by which the report was to be the work of the case investigator. There would generally be no impropriety in a case investigator seeking advice from an employer's human resources department, for example on questions of procedure. I do not think that it is illegitimate for an employer, through its human resources department or a similar function, to assist a case investigator in the presentation of a report, for example to ensure that all necessary matters have been addressed and achieve clarity. But, in this case, Dr Taylor's report was altered in ways which went beyond clarifying its conclusions. The amendment of the draft report by a member of the employer's management which occurred in this case is not within the agreed procedure. The report had to be the product of the case investigator. It was not. Further, the disregard for the undertaking amounted to a breach of the obligation of good faith in the contract of employment. It was also contrary to para 3.1 of policy D4 as it was behaviour which the objective observer would not consider reasonable: Dr Chhabra had an implied contractual right to a fair process and Mr Wishart's involvement undermined the fairness of the disciplinary process.

38. Fourthly, Dr Broughton did not re-assess the decision in his letter of 12 August 2011 that the matters were considered as potential gross misconduct after he departed from the additional complaint once he had received Dr Taylor's second report. In my view he was obliged to do so under para 3.1 of policy D4: an objective observer would not consider it reasonable to fail to do so.

39. I am persuaded that the cumulative effect of those irregularities is that it would be unlawful for the Trust to proceed with the disciplinary procedure and that the court should grant relief. As a general rule it is not appropriate for the courts to intervene to remedy minor irregularities

in the course of disciplinary proceedings between employer and employee – its role is not the "micro-management" of such proceedings: *Kulkarni v Milton Keynes Hospital NHS Foundation Trust* [2010] ICR 101, para 22. Such intervention would produce unnecessary delay and expense. But in this case the irregularities, particularly the first and third, are of a more serious nature. I also bear in mind that any common law damages which Dr Chhabra might obtain if she were to succeed in a claim based on those irregularities after her employment were terminated might be very limited: *Edwards v Chesterfield Royal Hospital NHS Foundation Trust* [2012] 2 AC 22 and *Geys v Société Générale* [2013] 1 AC 523, para 73, Lord Wilson.

…

42. I would allow the appeal and substitute for Judge McMullen's orders an order restraining the Trust from (a) pursuing any of the confidentiality concerns contained in the Trust's letter of 12 August 2011 as matters of gross misconduct and (b) pursuing any confidentiality concerns without first re-starting and completing an investigation under its policy D4A.

NOTES AND QUESTIONS

1. Dr Chhabra was held at [37], to have 'had an implied contractual right to a fair process' before disciplinary or dismissal. This brief, but important, statement contains no qualification, and no qualifying period of employment before it takes effect. As *Johnson v Unisys Ltd* showed (chapter 3(1) and see chapter 15), the common law should be developed in a way that is consistent with statutory rights, and should not overtly undermine the scheme set by Parliament. How can this right to claim for an unfair dismissal procedure in a Tribunal be articulated so as not to undermine the statutory scheme?

2. In *Reda v Flag Ltd* [2002] UKPC 38, the Privy Council advised that a company director could be dismissed 'without cause' because his employment contract stated this expressly. Lord Millett accepted there was an implied term of mutual trust and confidence, but said 'it cannot sensibly be used to circumscribe an express power of dismissal without cause'. One interpretation of this case is simply that the contract bound the director whatever it said. A second interpretation is that this result is just on the basis that mandatory rules of company law typically require that a director can be removed on a vote of the general meeting, after a fair hearing (in the UK, see the Companies Act 2006 s 168) but that in the Bermuda Companies Act 1981 section 93, this result must be expressed in the by-laws: presumably the contract reflected those. Decisions reached through a democratic governance by a company's members (leaving aside, for the moment, that only shareholders are usually members) effectively function as the 'cause'. Third, it could be accepted that an express term excluding the implied right to a fair process was possible for a company director, taking into account his or her bargaining power: a director is a worker and akin to an employee, but not exactly an employee. This reasoning would not hold for other employees.

3. Would an internal grievance or disciplinary hearing be compromised if a panel has people who are friendly or connected with someone involved in a conflict with the employee? In *Watson v University of Strathclyde* [2011] IRLR 458, Lady Smith in the Employment Appeal Tribunal upheld the view that such involvement was enough to vitiate such a panel's decision, by analogy to public law standards against bias: *Porter v Magill* [2001] UKHL 67.

4. To what extent is there a structural bias in organisations if supervisors or directors are are in no way accountable through the vote to other employees?

(3) VARIATION

The implied right of employing entities to direct employees enables workplace patterns to be altered from time to time. If used, it will usually change the balance of consideration in the work–wage bargain. This may have the effect of improving productive efficiency for everyone's benefit, saving working time, or enabling higher wages. It may also be used to cynically redistribute wealth from employees to managers or shareholders. Outside the right to direct, and its limits, the basic position is that express contract terms cannot be varied without consent of all parties. However, employing entities might insert unilateral variation or 'flexibility' clauses in contracts: express terms purporting to enable employing entities to change other express terms. They might also dismiss workers who refuse to accept a proposed change. The law has not developed a clear response to either of these problems.

(a) No Variation Without Consent

Rigby v Ferodo Ltd **[1988] ICR 29**

Mr Rigby, a lathe operator, claimed damages from Ferodo Ltd for breach of contract after it purported to cut his wages. The company was experiencing 'very severe financial pressures' and proposed a total 5 per cent wage cut, while wishing to retain staff. Mr Rigby had earned £129 a week, but was told that his reduction would be around £30 per week. (It was not disclosed what pay cut the company's directors were prepared to take.) Mr Rigby's union, the Confederation of Shipbuilding and Engineering Unions, had agreed not to take strike action, but had not agreed to wage reductions. Mr Rigby did not accept his wage reductions, and claimed back a shortfall in pay around 15 months later. The House of Lords held that there had been a repudiatory breach of contract by the employer and so Mr Rigby was entitled to claim his shortfall in wages.

Lord Oliver:

Before considering the primary contention upon which the appellant bases its case, I ought to notice briefly a submission made both to the trial judge and to the Court of Appeal and rejected by both. It is common ground that the unilateral imposition by an employer of a reduction in the agreed remuneration of an employee constitutes a fundamental and repudiatory breach of the contract of employment which, if accepted by the employee, would terminate the contract forthwith. It is submitted, however, that it also constituted – at least in the circumstances of this case – the giving of the necessary 12 weeks notice required under the contract to terminate the employment. My Lords, even if this were capable of being sustained as an abstract proposition of law, which I doubt, it appears to me to be a quite impossible contention on the facts of this case. The appellant never purported to give such a notice and would, I venture to think, have been both astonished and discomfitted if anyone had contended at the time that it had. The one thing that the appellant was concerned to do was to retain its employees in its employment and, as the trial judge trenchantly observed, the deliberate implementation of a policy preferred over others in order to keep the whole workforce in work cannot sensibly be construed as evincing an intention to terminate the contract of service.

The principal argument advanced on the appellant's behalf was to the following effect. It was not contended and could not, in the light of the trial judge's findings of fact, be contended that the appellant's repudiation of its contractual obligation to pay the agreed wages in full was ever expressly accepted by Mr. Rigby. Equally it is accepted that, as a general rule, an unaccepted repudiation leaves the contractual obligations of the parties unaffected. It is, however, argued that contracts of employment form a special category of their own, constituting an exception to the general rule. The wrongful repudiation of the fundamental obligations of either party under such a contract, it is said, not only brings to an end the relationship of employer and employee (which, as a practical matter, cannot continue in the face of a refusal to perform or accept the services which the employee has agreed to perform) but also, of itself and by itself, terminates the contract of service forthwith without the necessity of any acceptance, express or implied, by the party not in default. Thus, it is argued, when the appellant's management implemented the reduction of Mr. Rigby's wages without his agreement and against his will, his contract of employment with the appellant was terminated – wrongfully terminated, no doubt, but terminated – and could no longer be claimed by him to be subsisting. His sole remedy, therefore, was to sue for damages and the only damage suffered was the amount of the shortfall from the original contractual wage over the period of 12 weeks on the expiration of which the contract could have been lawfully terminated.

Mr. Wingate-Saul Q.C., on behalf of the appellant, accepts that this argument is inconsistent with the number of reported decisions of the Court of Appeal – in particular *Gunton v Richmond-upon-Thames London Borough Council* [1980] ICR 755; *London Transport Executive v Clarke* [1981] ICR 355 and *Norwest Holst Group Administration Ltd v Harrison* [1985] ICR 668 – but submits that those cases, in so far as they rested upon the proposition that an acceptance of a wrongful repudiation of a contract of employment is necessary to bring the contract to an end, were wrongly decided and that your Lordships should prefer the dissenting views of Shaw LJ in *Gunton's case* [1980] I.C.R. 755 and of Lord Denning MR in *London Transport Executive v Clarke* [1981] ICR 355. In his dissenting judgment in *Gunton's case*, Shaw LJ expressed the view that the practical basis for according an election to the injured party has no reality in relation to a contract of service where the repudiation takes the form of an express and direct termination of the contract in contravention of its terms. The contrary (and majority) view is that, whilst from a practical point of view a wrongful dismissal puts an end to the status of the dismissed employee as an employee and confines him to a remedy in damages for breach of contract (so that there will normally be little difficulty in inferring an acceptance of the repudiation), there is no reason in principle why, if the employee clearly indicates that he does not accept the employer's breach as a termination of the contract, it should not remain on foot and enforceable so far as concerns obligations which do not of necessity depend on the existence of the relationship of master and servant. My Lords, there is much to be said for both views and the majority opinion in *Gunton's case* [1980] ICR 755 has not been without its critics. But although it seems that one reason at least why the Court of Appeal here thought it right to grant leave to appeal to your Lordships' House was to afford an opportunity for a consideration of the correctness or otherwise of that majority opinion, the instant case is not on any analysis one of wrongful dismissal but is concerned with a very different state of facts, including the actual and intended continuation of the relationship of employer and employee without interruption. Having regard to the fact that your Lordships have not found it necessary to call upon counsel for the respondent, it would not, in my view, be appropriate that your Lordships should decide a not unimportant point of law which, on the facts before your Lordships, is of academic interest only.

Whatever may be the position under a contract of service where the repudiation takes the form either of a walk-out by the employee or of a refusal by the employer any longer to regard the employee as his servant, I know of no principle of law that any breach which the innocent party is entitled to treat as repudiatory of the other party's obligations brings the contract to an end automatically. No authority has been cited for so broad a proposition and indeed Mr. Wingate-Saul has not contended for it. What he has submitted is that where there is a combination of three factors, that is to say, (a) a breach of contract going to an essential term, (b) a desire in the party in breach either not to continue the contract or to continue it in a different form and (c) no practical option in the other party but to accept the breach, then the contract is automatically brought to an end. My Lords, for my part, I have found myself unable either to accept this formulation as a matter of law or to see why it should be so. I entirely fail to see how the continuance of the primary contractual obligation can be made to depend upon the subjective desire of the contract-breaker and I do not understand what is meant by the injured party having no alternative but to accept the breach. If this means that, if the contract-breaker persists, the injured party may have to put up with the fact that he will not be able to enforce the primary obligation of performance, that is, of course, true of every contract which is not susceptible of a decree of specific performance. If it means that he has no alternative to accepting the breach as a repudiation and thus terminating the contract, it begs the question. For my part, I can see no reason in law or logic why, leaving aside for the moment the extreme case of outright dismissal or walk-out, a contract of employment should be on any different footing from any other contract as regards the principle that "an unaccepted repudiation is a thing writ in water and of no value to anybody": per Asquith LJ in *Howard v Pickford Truck Co Ltd* [1951] 1 KB 417, 421.

My Lords, the one thing that is clear in this case is that the appellant had no intention whatever of terminating the contracts of employment with its workforce except by compelling the acceptance of new contractual terms which Mr. Rigby and his fellow C.S.E.U. members were, as they made it quite clear, unwilling to accept and which they never did accept. Faced with that situation the appellant could have chosen to terminate their contracts on proper notice. It chose not to do so. It could have dismissed them out of hand and faced the consequences. It chose not to do so. It continued to employ them, week by week, under contracts which entitled them to a certain level of wages but withheld from them a part of that entitlement. I can, in those circumstances, see no answer at all to Mr. Rigby's claim and the trial judge and the Court of Appeal were, in my judgment, plainly right in the conclusions at which they arrived.

It has been submitted that there was some sort of implied acceptance on the part of Mr. Rigby of the appellant's repudiation by working on. At the trial this was put on the basis of estoppel, waiver and acquiescence. All three were rejected by the trial judge and, in my judgment, he was, on the facts which he found, quite plainly right to reject them. I can, for my part, see no other basis upon which it can be argued that the continued working by Mr. Rigby and his acceptance for the time being and under protest of the wage that the appellant, with full knowledge of his lack of agreement, chose to pay him is to be construed as an acceptance by him either of the repudiation by the appellant of the original continuing contract or of the new terms which the appellant was seeking to impose.

Finally, it has been argued that Mr. Rigby's claim is a claim for damages rather than for debt and that the ordinary rule in actions for damages for breach of contract applies, that is to say, that where a defendant has two methods of performing his contract he must be taken to have selected that which is most favourable to him. Thus the argument runs, since the appellant could have lawfully terminated Mr. Rigby's employment by 12 weeks' notice, it must be treated as if it had done so and his claim to damages must be limited to the shortfall in wages during that period. The only question, it is suggested, is whether the action is in truth one for damages rather than for debt and whether, if the latter, the same principle should apply. For my part, I derive no assistance from the distinction between debt and damages, for it seems to me entirely immaterial whether Mr. Rigby's claim be treated as one for his agreed remuneration for services rendered or as one for damages for breach of an agreement to pay it. On either view the argument advanced is, in my judgment, based on a fallacy. It assumes the very proposition which has already been rejected, namely, that the employment under the contract of service has come to an end. If it had, then no doubt there would be room for an inquiry at what date the employer could first lawfully have terminated it. But that is not the case with which this appeal is concerned. What your Lordships are concerned with here is a claim for sums due under a continuing contract which never was terminated, either lawfully or unlawfully, and there simply is no room in such a case for the application of the principle referred to. This contention likewise was rightly rejected both by the trial judge and by the Court of Appeal. My Lords, I would dismiss the appeal.

Lord Bridge, Lord Fraser, Lord Brightman and **Lord Ackner** agreed.

1. Lord Oliver emphatically affirms that a purported unilateral variation of wages by an employer constitutes a breach of – and a breach that repudiates – the contract. This gives an employee the option of quitting and claiming damages, or remaining in the job and claiming that there has been an unlawful deduction of wages: the procedure for this is codified now in the Employment Rights Act (ERA) 1996 ss 13 ff (see chapter 6). The purported wage deduction is not an implicit termination of the contract by the employer, or triggering of the notice period before dismissal. It is simply a breach of contract and in this respect, as Lord Oliver termed the argument, employment contracts are not 'a special category of their own, constituting an exception to the general rule'. While it seems fair that employees' contractual rights are not less favourable than the rights of commercial parties, does it follow that they should not be more favourable?

2. In *Robertson v British Gas Corp* [1983] ICR 351, Mr Robertson and his colleagues successfully claimed damages for a shortfall in wages based on an incorporate collective agreement. A bonus scheme for employees was fixed by collective agreement. British Gas Corp said it was terminating bonuses and withdrawing from the collective agreement. The employees' claim succeeded. 'This was another way', said Kerr LJ, 'of saying that the terms of the individual contracts are in part to be found in the agreed collective agreements as exist from time to time.'

3. In *Home Office v Evans* [2007] EWCA Civ 1089, the Court of Appeal held that the Home Office was entitled to take advantage of an express contract term to move Mr Evans' place of work from Waterloo Station to Heathrow, rather than making staff redundant. It rejected that this confounded the employee's reasonable expectations. How far do you think would be too far?

4. In *Whitney v Monster Worldwide Ltd* [2010] EWCA Civ 1312, Longmore LJ held that a 'no detriment guarantee' regarding Mr Whitney's pension was binding. The employer attempted (as a majority of employers have done) to replace the final salary pension scheme (where the employer guarantees an income from retirement until death based on an employee's income in the last year) with a money purchase scheme (which is simply a savings account that can run out before someone dies if they live longer than expected). His original pension was also linked to the Retail Price Index, albeit that increases were capped at 5 per cent per annum.

(b) Unilateral Variation or 'Flexibility' Clauses

Wandsworth LBC v D'Silva [1998] IRLR 193

Mr D'Silva and his colleagues claimed that Wandsworth LBC breached their employment contracts by attempting to unilaterally vary the Code of Practice on Staff Sickness. D'Silva's contract stated in paragraph 4: '[F]rom time to time variations in your terms and conditions of employment will occur, and these will be separately notified to you or otherwise incorporated in the documents to which you have reference.' The Code resulted from a collective agreement with Unison. The council sought to reduce the period of sick leave from 12 to 6 months before an assessment of an employee for termination or redeployment would be made. The council argued the Code was not 'apt' to be incorporated. Disagreeing with the Employment Tribunal and Employment Appeal Tribunal, the Court of Appeal held that the Code was not apt for incorporation. It also remarked on the legal position if it had been.

Lord Woolf MR (giving judgment with **Millett LJ** and **Robert Walker LJ**):

... the decision which the Industrial Tribunal came to on the first issue is not sustainable. If the language of the provisions which are to be amended are examined in the context of the scheme as a whole, they are not an appropriate foundation upon which to base contractual rights. If what was being triggered was a disciplinary or an appeal procedure, the position would probably be different. Both in the case of the short and the long term absentees the Code is doing no more than providing guidance for both the supervisors and the employees as to what is expected to happen. The Code does not set out what is contractually required to happen. The whole process in the initial stages is sensibly designed to be flexible and informal in a way which is inconsistent with contractual rights being created. At later stages of the process proposed the employees' arguments would have much more force. The appeal should therefore be allowed.

Having decided that the appeal should be allowed on the first issue, it is not strictly necessary to express any views on the second issue. However, bearing in mind this is a test case it may be useful if some general guidance is given, although the relevance of the guidance will vary much depends on the context of the particular case.

The general position is that contracts of employment can only be varied by agreement. However in the employment field an employer or for that matter an employee can reserve the ability to change a particular aspect of the contract unilaterally by notifying the other party as part of the contract that this is the situation. However, clear language is required to reserve to one party an unusual power of this sort. In addition the Court is unlikely to favour an interpretation which does more than enable a party to vary contractual provisions with which that party is required to comply. If therefore the provisions of the code which the Council were seeking to amend in this case were of a contractual nature, then they could well be capable of unilateral variation as the counsel contends. In relation to the provisions as to appeals the position would be likely to be different. To apply a power of unilateral variation to the rights which an employee is given under this part of the code could produce an unreasonable result and the courts in construing a contract of employment will seek to avoid such a result.

NOTES AND QUESTIONS

1. Lord Woolf MR holds for the Court of Appeal that the collective agreement's sickness code was not apt for incorporation because it was 'guidance for both the supervisors and the employees as to what is expected to happen' rather than what was contractually bound to happen. Is this convincing? Lord Woolf MR then suggests obiter that, had the provision been contractually binding, it could be varied unilaterally through a clause with 'clear language'. But while provisions that only state what the employing entity 'is required to comply' with could be varied, provisions that purport to allow 'variation of the rights which an employee is given ... could produce an unreasonable result' and courts 'will seek to avoid such a result'. Is this adequate?
2. In *Bateman v ASDA Stores Ltd* [2010] IRLR 370 a 'Colleague Handbook' had ostensibly 'reserved the right to review, revise, amend or replace the contents of this handbook, and introduce new policies from time to time reflecting

the changing needs of the business'. ASDA purported to reduce its 'colleagues' pay unilaterally, moving 16,000 employees to the new 'Top Rate' scheme; 6670 employees claimed this was an unlawful wage deduction under ERA 1996 s 13. Silber J at [21] recalled the judgment of 'Lord Hoffman [*sic*] that "what the parties using those words against the relevant background would reasonably have been understood to mean"', and proceeded to reject that canons of construction made any difference to enforcing the term as it stood. Nor did the dicta of Lord Woolf MR help the employees and, in his view, there could be no breach of mutual trust and confidence. Do you think this is a legally defensible result? Is it now constrained by the principles in *Autoclenz Ltd v Belcher* [2011] UKSC 41, or should it have been based on *Equitable Life Assurance Society v Hyman*?

(c) Dismissal After Variation Refused Could Be Fair

Hollister v National Farmers' Union **[1979] ICR 542**

Mr Hollister claimed unfair dismissal after he and his colleagues in Cornwall were dismissed for refusing to accept renegotiated contract terms with lower pension benefits, but slightly higher pay. Mr Hollister worked as a secretary for the National Farmers' Union, earning commission on getting insurance with Cornish Mutual Association Co for members. The head office had negotiated the new terms without consulting the Cornwall secretaries. Under the Employment Protection Act 1974 Sch 1, para 6(1)(b), now ERA 1996 s 98, the Tribunal found the dismissal was fair because it was it was for 'some other substantial reason', namely that the change had been consulted upon. The Employment Appeal Tribunal held that the dismissal was for a substantial reason, but the level of consultation was not enough to discharge the onus that their action was reasonable. The Court of Appeal held the dismissal was for a 'substantial reason of a kind such as to justify the dismissal'.

Lord Denning MR:

The question which is being discussed in this case is whether the reorganisation of the business which the National Farmers' Union left they had to undertake in 1976, coupled with Mr. Hollister's refusal to accept the new agreement, was a substantial reason of such a kind as to justify the dismissal of the employee. Upon that there have only been one or two cases. One we were particularly referred to was *Ellis v Brighton Co-operative Society Ltd* [1976] IRLR 419, where it was recognised by the court that reorganisation of business may on occasion be a sufficient reason justifying the dismissal of an employee. They went on to say, at p. 420:

> 'Where there has been a properly consulted-upon reorganisation which, if it is not done, is going to bring the whole business to a standstill, a failure to go along with the new arrangements may well – it is not bound to, but it may well – constitute "some other substantial reason".'

Certainly, I think, everyone would agree with that. But in the present case Arnold J. expanded it a little so as not to limit it to where it came absolutely to a standstill but to where there was some sound, good business reason for the reorganisation. I must say I see no reason to differ from Arnold J.'s view on that. It must depend on all the circumstances whether the reorganisation was such that the only sensible thing to do was to terminate the employee's contract unless he would agree to a new arrangement. It seems to me that that paragraph may well be satisfied, and indeed was satisfied in this case, having regard to the commercial necessity of rearrangements being made and the termination of the relationship with the Cornish Mutual, and the setting up of a new relationship via the National Farmers' Union Mutual Insurance Society Ltd. On that rearrangement being made, it was absolutely essential for new contracts to be made with the existing group secretaries: and the only way to deal with it was to terminate the agreements and offer them reasonable new ones. It seems to me that that would be, and was, a substantial reason of a kind sufficient to justify this kind of dismissal. I stress the word "kind."

Eveleigh LJ and **Sir Stanley Rees** concurred.

NOTES AND QUESTIONS

1. Do you think 'everyone would agree with that'?
2. As we will see in chapter 18, employing entities may dismiss employees after a (currently) two-year qualifying period for a closed statutory list of fair reasons: conduct, capability or qualifications, redundancy, or 'some other substantial reason'. Here, the Court of Appeal rejects that Mr Hollister and his colleagues should have a claim for breach of contract or unfair dismissal because 'some other substantial reason' is said to embrace the idea that an employing entity has consulted most staff on a unilateral variation: it was not relevant that Mr Hollister himself had not been asked. Two policies compete: the idea that enterprises should be able to restructure to adapt to the market, and the protection of employees. Should an employing entity be able to change its policies without all voices in the enterprise being able to participate in determining what is good for the whole?

Problem Question

Paddington 2 (2017)

Paddington, who had always dreamt of coming to London, has recently arrived by boat as an undocumented migrant from deepest, darkest Peru. He was fortunate enough to find a home, and began work at a local barber shop. Unfortunately, during the first week of work Paddington accidentally shaves a customer's head, and when his employer finds what has happened, Paddington is summarily dismissed. Paddington did not receive wages for two hours' work, which would have amounted to £30.

Nearby, a struggling actor called Phoenix Buchanan has been employed to work on commercials for Harley's Gourmet Dog Food. The employer handbook states that employees, such as Phoenix, 'must do everything to uphold the reputation of the brand, including the consumption of dog food according to the employer's absolute discretion'. Phoenix has signed a contract, but has not read the handbook because nobody does. As he is about to film a dog food commercial, he is handed a spoon, and told that he must take a mouthful while the camera is rolling. Because Phoenix needs the money, he puts the dog food in his mouth, and spits it out afterwards. The following morning, Phoenix is violently ill, and takes two months to recover. Because of his work in a degrading dog food commercial, he also finds it very difficult to secure new jobs.

Meanwhile, Paddington has secured as a new job in a kitchen for an employer, and head chef, called Knuckles McGinty. While on the job, Paddington perfects a recipe for marmalade, based on his prior knowledge. He writes out a short story of how he came across the recipe in Peru for Knuckles. It is a great success for the Knuckles Kitchen customers. Paddington, however, leaves the job after a few weeks. Paddington later hears that Knuckles is producing and selling large quantities of marmalade using the name with his recipe, and using Paddington's story on its label. This has become immensely profitable.

Advise the parties.

Additional Reading for Chapter 5

KV Stone, 'The New Psychological Contract: Implications of the Changing Workplace for Labor and Employment Law' (2001) 48 *UCLA Law Review* 519
Stone sets out the concept of a 'psychological contract', which operates in addition to whatever might be expressed in the legal contractual documents at work. She argues that, while old expectations of orderly promotion and long-term job security were breaking down in US (and UK) workplaces, it might also be argued there are new expectations of employability, training, human capital development and networking opportunities. These might (optimistically) reach the same results of security, fairness and justice.

D Brodie, 'Mutual Trust and Confidence: Catalysts, Constraints and Commonality' (2008) 37 *ILJ* 329
Brodie argues that mutual trust and confidence, which has become a central concept in the law of employment, should interact with 'human resource management' as it develops. He says the law on implied terms 'takes account of contemporary standards and values' and says that another source of inspiration could be the 'ethical' side of staffing practice. This literature can be, for instance, 'extremely helpful in explaining why it is important to maintain a commitment to procedural justice'. This may also have a darker side, for instance because research shows 'workers are more willing to accept negative outcomes where decision-making is transparent'. Nevertheless, the 'promotion of consistency' fits well with the requirements of mutual trust.

6

Wages, Taxes, Pensions

The Universal Declaration of Human Rights 1948 Art 23(3) says: 'Everyone who works has the right to just and favourable remuneration ensuring for himself and his family an existence worthy of human dignity, and supplemented, if necessary, by other means of social protection.' To what extent does the law achieve this? All legal systems alter wages that markets (based on reductive property and contract rules) would deliver in four main ways: (1) requiring a minimum wage, (2) procedures to limit excessive pay, (3) taxing to redistribute money for fairer incomes and public services, and (4) ensuring retirement income in pensions (see also chapter 16(3) on unemployment insurance). These rules set loose limits. Within the limits, to get fair wages, people must have a voice through trade unions and collective bargaining, and have votes at work (chapters 8–11).

Hard-line economic theory argues all these rules harm the people they are intended to help. Wages in free markets, through supply and demand, reflect the 'marginal utility' or 'product' of the worker. Rational employers pay the value that each worker adds to production (eg P Milgrom and J Roberts, *Economics, Organization and Management* (1992) and see chapter 2(1)). Regulation and tax, it is said, distort the market equilibrium wage. Minimum wages increase unemployment and exclude precarious workers. Limits to executive or banker pay move talent abroad. Tax destroys incentives to innovate. Compulsory saving is another tax. But in real life, law sets conditions by which all contracts and property rights are enforced. There is nothing pre-legal about a 'market equilibrium', no state of 'non-interference'. The only question is whether law creates a just distribution of income (see JS Mill, *Principles of Political Economy* (1848) book V, ch I, §2). Critically, the evidence shows that hard-line economic theory is wrong. Reasonable wages increase aggregate demand and boost growth. Excessively unequal pay damages productivity: it represents an unearned 'agency cost' (chapter 2(2)). Efficiently administered taxes are 'what we pay for civilized society' (*CGTF v Collector of Internal Revenue*, 275 US 87 (1927) per Holmes J). But they also correct the failure of markets (shaped by the most reductive rules of property and contract) to provide the social security needed for innovation and human development (chapter 2(3)). This said, clearly the law does not have consistent principles for wage regulation. The living wage has loopholes, pay often remains excessive, and taxation and pension policy is not yet adequately integrated with the rest of the law on the welfare state. This chapter deals with each area in turn.

Introductory text: Collins ch 4 (77–86). CEM ch 7. D&M ch 4 (304–31, 399–408).

(1) A LIVING WAGE FOR WORK

Partly because of a historical commitment to 'freedom of contract', the British Parliament developed the right to a minimum or living wage before the common law did. By contrast, courts elsewhere did develop judicial wage standards. For example, Australia passed an Excise Tariff Act 1906, which gave farmers who used harvester machines tariff protection from foreign imports, but only if they paid their workers a 'fair and reasonable' wage. This was left undefined, so in *Ex parte HV McKay* (1907) 2 CAR 1, Higgins J held 'it must be meant to secure to [workers] something which they cannot get by the ordinary system of individual bargaining with employers'. This meant the 'normal needs of an average employee, regarded as a human being in a civilised community' that would be provided by a hypothetical 'collective agreement'. It would at least give a 'condition of frugal comfort estimated by current human standards'. Other countries use contractual principles of 'unconscionability', *contra bonos mores*, or 'good faith' to require employers pay, for example, no less than two-thirds of comparable jobs. In Germany, see P Hanau, 'Entgelthöhe' in *Münchener Kommentar zum Arbeitsrecht* (2nd edn 2000) §63, 1254, on BGB §138. In Sweden, Law (1915: 218) on agreements and other legal acts in the field of property law, §36).

In the UK in the last 20 years, there has been more discussion of the principle of 'just enrichment' or *quantum meruit* for people's pay: this could be a basis for developing a common law right to a living wage for work. Whilst old common law assumed market prices were just per se, or that 'value … is measured by the price' (*In re Wragg Ltd* [1897] 1 Ch 796, 831, per Lindley LJ, on company shares), the law today acknowledges that market prices, shaped arbitrarily by bargaining power, are often unjust. This section examines (a) the developing concepts of just pay at common law, (b) the minimum or living wage as it is set by statute, (c) pay periods to calculate whether proper wages have been paid over time, and (d) any lawful categories of wage deductions.

(a) Just Enrichment and *Quantum Meruit*

Patel v Mirza [2016] UKSC 42

In the course of this securities contract case, their Lordships referred to the unresolved issue in *Hounga v Allen* (chapter 4(1)(b)): whether the illegality of a contract barred claims for unpaid wages. In this case itself, Mr Patel claimed Mr Mirza should repay him £620,000 after this money was transferred under a deal to use 'inside information' about the Royal Bank of Scotland (RBS). The information, not yet known to the public, was that the government was about to make an announcement about RBS. 'Insider dealing' is an offence under the Criminal Justice Act 1993 section 52, because it is thought that insiders should not trade on shares, and profit, when the public does not have the chance to do the same. The Supreme Court held unanimously that money could be recovered by a restitution claim, even though the contract would have been illegal. In doing so, they discussed *Hounga*.

Lord Toulson (with whom **Lady Hale**, **Lord Kerr**, **Lord Wilson** and **Lord Hodge** agreed):

74. Miss Hounga brought claims against the Allens in the employment tribunal for unfair dismissal, breach of contract and unpaid wages. They were dismissed on the ground that her contract of employment was unlawful. She appealed unsuccessfully to the appeal tribunal and she did not seek to appeal further. Neither the Court of Appeal nor the Supreme Court therefore had occasion to consider whether she was entitled to be paid for the services which she rendered on a *quantum meruit* (by analogy with cases such as *Mohamed v Alaga & Co* [[2000] 1 WLR 1815] and *Nizamuddowlah v Bengal Cabaret Inc* [399 NYS 2d 854 (1977)]).

Lord Sumption:

243. The other category comprises cases in which the application of the illegality principle would be inconsistent with the rule of law which makes the act illegal. The paradigm case is a rule of law intended to protect persons such as the plaintiff against exploitation by the likes of the defendant. Such a rule will commonly require the plaintiff to have a remedy not withstanding that he participated in its breach. The exception generally arises in the context of acts made illegal by statute. In *Browning v Morris* (1778) 2 Cowp 790, 792, Lord Mansfield expressed the point in this way:

> "Where contracts or transactions are prohibited by positive statutes for the sake of protecting one set of men from another set of men, the one, from their situation and condition being liable to be oppressed or imposed upon by the other, there the parties are not *in pari delicto*; and in furtherance of these statutes, the person injured, after the transaction is finished and completed, may bring his action and defeat the contract."

The classic modern illustration is *Kiriri Cotton Co Ltd v Dewani* [1960] AC 192, in which a tenant was held entitled to recover an illegal premium paid to the landlord, notwithstanding that his payment of it involved participating in a breach of an ordinance regulating tenancies. Lord Denning, delivering the advice of the Privy Council, observed at p 205 that: "The duty of observing the law is firmly placed by the Ordinance on the shoulders of the landlord for the protection of the tenant." *Hounga v Allen* [2014] 1 WLR 2889 on its facts illustrates the same principle. The claimant had been illegally trafficked into the United Kingdom by her employer. Her vulnerability on that account enabled her employer to exploit and ultimately to dismiss her. An attempt to bar her claim for unlawful discrimination on account of her participation in her own illegal trafficking failed. There was no claim under the employment contract itself, which was illegal, but it may well be that a claim for a *quantum meruit* for services performed would have succeeded on the same ground. There is New York authority for such a result: see *Nizamuddowlah v Bengal Cabaret Inc* (1977) 399 NYS 2d 854.

Lord Neuberger gave an opinion concurring with **Lord Toulson**. **Lord Clarke** and **Lord Mance** gave opinions preferring reasoning on illegality closer to **Lord Sumption**.

NOTES AND QUESTIONS

1. The illegality principle aside, the crucial point for this chapter is that the Supreme Court plainly accepts that regardless of contract, Miss Hounga 'may well' have succeeded in a claim for wages. Lord Toulson foots his reasoning on the purpose of the policy at play, while Lord Sumption suggests the duties fall on employers because the law is there 'for the sake of protecting' the employee. Therefore, Hounga would have had a *quantum meruit* claim to be paid for her work. How would this be quantified?

2. In *Nizamuddowlah v Bengal Cabaret Inc* 399 NYS 2d 854 (1977) the New York Supreme Court held that an undocumented migrant was entitled to claim $8,287 for the minimum wage, plus liquidated damages, court costs and interest, even though the contract for work was illegal. Deductions were made for costs the employer laid out. Calabretta J held 'the only equitable alternative' was to 'allow the employee to recover based on the theory of unjust enrichment' to stop the employer who had 'managed to run his enterprise without fairly compensating his employees'. The employee's 'violation is overshadowed by [employer's] entire course of deceptive conduct'. Would you agree the claimant's pay should be measured by the minimum wage if the amount the employing entity profits from the worker's labour is higher?

3. These cases run against an old dictum in *Falcke v Scottish Imperial Insurance Co* (1886) 34 Ch 234, per Bowen LJ that the 'general principle is, beyond all question, that work and labour done or money expended by one man to preserve or benefit the property of another do not according to English law create any lien upon the property saved or benefited, nor, even if standing alone, create any obligation to repay the expenditure. Liabilities are not to be forced upon people behind their backs any more than you can confer a benefit upon a man against his will.' By contrast, *Patel v Mirza* says that if benefits are accepted, pay must be given. It is irrelevant that an obligation is not accepted or would be illegal under an immigration statute.

4. Is the statutory minimum wage a starting point for *quantum meruit* claims in UK law? Probably not, although case law is sparse, and has dealt only with autonomous service providers rather than employees. In *Boardman v Phipps* [1967] 2 AC 46 the House of Lords upheld the Court of Appeal and High Court, that Mr Tom Boardman and Mr Tom Phipps were entitled to 'a generous remuneration' on a 'liberal scale' ([1964] 1 WLR 993, 1018; [1965] Ch 992, 1021; [1967] 2 AC 46, 104 and 112) for their services. The two Toms took the opportunity to buy shares in a company (which the trust could have done) without securing the fully informed, true consent of the trust. This breached the strict fiduciary duty to avoid any possibility of a conflict of interest with the Phipps family trust fund. But they invested time and effort in restructuring the company, which did benefit the trust's shares. While the court ordered their conflicted profits should be repaid, it recognised their honesty and valuable work, reflected by the 'generous' and 'liberal' measure in *quantum meruit*. Therefore, the general principle is people's work should merit reasonable pay. Does this differ from market price?

5. In another services case, *Benedetti v Sawiris* [2013] UKSC 50, the Supreme Court held that Benedetti, who sought to be paid like 'a partner not a shity middle man' [*sic*] for linking a buyer and seller in a telecommunications company takeover, was entitled to an award reflecting the market value for his services. Benedetti was not entitled to a share of the profits from the deal, as he hoped for. Lord Clarke at [15] said: '[T]he starting point in valuing the enrichment is the objective market value.' The Supreme Court did not consider the 'objective market value' of Sawiris' capital contribution (measured, for example, by the amount of interest on a similar loan). This aside, in contrast to a multi-million-euro takeover deal, do

you think that an objective market value provides adequate guidance in cases of employment?

6. In *Stack v Dowden* [2007] UKHL 17, with a long related line of property cases, the House of Lords recognised that people's contributions of work to the family home will be both remunerated and secured through a proprietary interest in the home. Presumably a family relationship empowers the court to treat a claim as one akin to partnership, in contrast to *Benedetti*'s case.

7. Should employees be entitled to proprietary interests to secure their pay in some circumstances? Insolvency policy has sought to achieve this very same effect in a series of ways since the Preferential Payments in Bankruptcy Act 1897. See ch 20.

8. Do you agree that, unlike commercial service contracts, a *quantum meruit* claim in employment should be assessed in accordance with (i) the profit gained by the employer, or if higher (ii) the hypothetical wage for comparable work if both parties had equal bargaining power under a collective agreement, but that this must be (iii) no less than the statutory minimum wage?

9. Relatively few cases will actually involve assessing a *quantum meruit* in employment. Nevertheless, the legal position is important because it shapes starting judicial presumptions. In the absence of a minimum wage statute, or if in doubt about a contract, what is just?

(b) The Minimum Living Wage

The National Minimum Wage Act (NMWA) 1998 s 1 requires most 'workers' receive a minimum wage: anyone with a contract to personally perform work, but not for a client or customer (Employment Rights Act (ERA) 1996 s 230(3)(b), see chapter 3(2)(d)). The government altered the label in the National Minimum Wage Regulations 2015 reg 4 to the 'national living wage'. This wage is £7.83 per hour in 2018 for people over 25. Minimum-living wages must be clearly distinguished from 'fair wages'. Fair wages come for most people with a voice at work through collective bargaining and governance rights (chapters 8–11). But laws for both are thought to exist for the same reasons. Lord Blanesburgh stated the justification for a minimum wage in *France*.

France v James Coombes & Co [1929] AC 496

Mr France, who worked for James Coombes & Co repairing boots, claimed a shortfall in the minimum wage under the Trade Boards (Boot and Shoe Repairing) Order 1919. The Minister of Labour had passed the Order under the Trade Boards Act 1909 and the Trade Boards Act 1918 s 8. It fixed minimum wage rates for managers and other classes of worker in the boot trade, confirmed on 8 August 1922. The employer contended it did pay the minimum wage for the time Mr France actually worked, which was less than half the time he was physically in the repair shop. MacKinnon J in the High Court, and Scrutton LJ, Sankey LJ and Romer J in the Court of Appeal, held that when Mr France was not actually working, there was no entitlement to be paid. The House of Lords, following the judgment of Viscount Dunedin, upheld this view by a majority. Lord Blanesburgh dissented.

Lord Blanesburgh (dissenting), read by **Lord Atkin**:

I asked Mr. Stuart Bevan whether he could under the Acts and Order justify an agreement by virtue of which, with no obligation on his part to pay a minimum wage on a time basis, an employer could, if he had need of them, retain the worker's protected services exclusively for himself, and could, if he had himself no need of these services, prevent the worker from exercising his protected skill either for his own benefit or in the service of another employer. Mr. Bevan's answer, as I understood him, was that provided the worker received the equivalent of the minimum wage in respect of repairing work actually done by him, all the other provisions of any agreement with him were matters of bargain outside the Acts altogether. The remedy of the worker if he found these provisions irksome or oppressive was to terminate the agreement.

My Lords, seeing that the presumed necessity for fixing any minimum wage rate at all in any particular trade is due to the apprehension on the part of the Minister that in its absence workmen in that trade may have imposed upon them wages which they ought not to be asked to accept, but which, either as a result of competition in the labour market or deficient bargaining power, they are not in a position to refuse, this answer of Mr. Bevan's may not, I think, be accepted as correct or adequate without very full consideration. If it be well founded it at once removes out of the way every obstacle to the wholesale evasion of these protective Acts. I proceed therefore to test its correctness by a consideration of the relevant provisions of the Acts and of the Boot and Shoe Repairing Trade Order with which your Lordships are now immediately concerned.

My Lords, in common with, I think, many similar enactments, these Acts do not require that any Order made under them shall bind the employer to find for his workers in general, if the worker is paid by the piece, work of any prescribed amount, or if he is paid on a time basis, work for any prescribed time. What is required of the employer is that the worker shall receive at least the minimum rate of remuneration for the work actually done, or for the time spent in the statutory employment. And this is in terms so provided for by s. VIII. of Part I. of Sch. I. of this Order.

Lord Warrington, **Lord Buckmaster** and **Lord Sumner** agreed with the majority.

NOTES AND QUESTIONS

1. Lord Blanesburgh states the orthodox view: workers' unequal bargaining power justifies the minimum wage. Workers' power to quit and go elsewhere does not change the inequality of bargaining power against every employer. But is unequal bargaining power in this context a justification, or more a counter-argument? Presumably the starting point is that the law, out of political or moral conviction, should ensure everyone the resources for maximum human development. When someone says 'markets do that if you leave them alone', unequal bargaining power comes up as the counter-argument. What do you think (and does it matter)?

2. The policy behind the minimum wage justifies a broad purposive interpretation for the scope of workers to be paid the minimum wage. Exceptions should be construed restrictively. Specifically, Lord Blanesburgh alludes to the absurd result if an employer demanded a worker stays in a shop without pay. The minimum wage is to be paid at all such times.

3. The Trade Boards Act 1909 was the first general statutory system to set minimum wages for specific industries through Orders. Introducing the Act, Winston Churchill MP said: 'It is a serious national evil that any class of His Majesty's

subjects should receive less than a living wage in return for their utmost exertions. It was formerly supposed that the working of the laws of supply and demand would naturally regulate or eliminate that evil. … But where you have what we call sweated trades, you have no organisation, no parity of bargaining, the good employer is undercut by the bad, and the bad employer is undercut by the worst; the worker, whose whole livelihood depends upon the industry, is undersold by the worker who only takes the trade up as a second string, his feebleness and ignorance generally renders the worker an easy prey to the tyranny; of the masters and middle-men, only a step higher up the ladder than the worker, and held in the same relentless grip of forces – where those conditions prevail you have not a condition of progress, but a condition of progressive degeneration.' Hansard HC vol 4, col 388 (28 April 1909).

4. Post-World War Two, minimum wage regulation was carried on by the Wages Councils Act 1945, 1959 and 1979. Workers in some sectors would fall through the cracks if a sectoral wage board had not yet been established. Wage boards could also be muzzled or abolished by hostile governments. The Wages Act 1986 retrenched the last wage councils, before the National Minimum Wage Act 1998. Other countries had similar problems with sectoral wage systems: one of the most recent national minimum wage laws is Germany's Mindestlohngesetz 2014. Under NMWA 1998 s 4(2) there cannot be central setting of wages for different areas or sectors. Why not? Should regional governments be able to set wages above the national minimum?

5. The Enterprise and Regulatory Reform Act 2013 s 72 abolished the last board in England, the Agricultural Wages Board, under the Agricultural Wages Act 1948. This set wages higher for farm workers, depending on skills. The Scottish Agricultural Wages Board survives, as does the Agricultural Advisory Panel for Wales, despite the UK government attempting to abolish it: see *Re Agricultural Sector (Wales) Bill* [2014] UKSC 43. Can you guess what happened to farm work wages in England since 2013?

6. NMWA 1998 ss 1 and 54 covers 'workers' of school-leaving age who ordinarily work in the UK, while ss 34 and 35 expressly include people working through job agencies and home workers. Under s 41, the Secretary of State can designate more people as being 'workers'. Under s 28, the burden of proof is on the person denying worker status.

7. The term 'living wage', now found in the National Minimum Wage Regulations (NMWR) 2015, is used by a charity (without any statutory role) called the Living Wage Foundation (www.livingwage.org.uk). This is funded by charities, think tanks and businesses (Ikea, GlaxoSmithKline, Nestle, etc). The charity's guidance for what a 'living wage' should be is higher than the statutory minimum/living wage in the UK and London. The Foundation acts as a pressure group to raise the minimum wage. It would appear that the Living Wage Foundation's corporate sponsors are more ambivalent about fair wages through collective bargaining or votes at work.

8. Why might a corporation support a higher living wage? And is there any incentive for a corporation to support fair wages in collective bargaining? Absolutely. A corporation that already pays wages higher than competitors will want to

ensure that its competitors do not compete, and become more profitable, solely by slashing their wage bill. Legal wage regulation prevents unfair competition, and helps ensure business is competing on quality, not degradation of their workforce. See S Webb, 'The Economic Theory of a Legal Minimum Wage' (1912) 20(10) *Journal of Political Economy* 973.

9.   Under NMWA 1998 ss 1(3) and 2(1) the Secretary of State sets an hourly minimum wage from time to time. As of April 2018 (NMWR 2015 regs 4–4A) it is £7.83 per hour for over 25 year olds, £7.38 per hour for 21 to 24 year olds, £5.90 per hour for 18 to 20 year olds, £4.20 per hour for under 18 year olds, and £3.70 per hour for apprentices. In April 2016, the category of over 25 year olds was introduced: before that, everyone over 21 received the top rate. In 2010, using the power in s 3(1A), a sub-minimum wage was introduced for apprentices. These relative cuts to the minimum wage respond to theories that youth unemployment is exacerbated by the minimum wage (cf chapter 2(2)). Given that businesses rely on customers who have money to buy their products, do you see any logic in the idea that cutting young workers' wages will increase employment?

10.   The NMWA 1998 contains random exclusions from the minimum wage, for instance, s 37, members of the armed forces; s 43, profit sharing fishermen; s 45, prisoners. In addition, the Prisoners' Earnings Act 1996 s 2(1)(b) says pay from prisoners who work can be taken for 'contributing towards the cost of the prisoner's upkeep', among other things. Labour, after 1997, did not put into effect. The coalition did in the Prisoners' Earnings Act 1996 (Commencement) (England and Wales) Order 2011. Will earning sub-minimum wages be likely to rehabilitate prisoners? Should corporations be enriched by prison labour, which bargains down the wages of people who are free?

11.   Under NMWA 1998 s 45B and the Immigration and Asylum Act 1999 s 153A, 'A detained person does not qualify for the national minimum wage in respect of work which he does in pursuance of removal centre rules.' Does anything justify this?

12.   Under NMWR 2015 reg 57(3)(b) there is no right to be paid if 'the worker is not a member of that family, but is treated as such, in particular as regards to the provision of living accommodation and meals and the sharing of tasks and leisure activities'. This was applied in *Nambalat v Taher* [2012] EWCA Civ 1249, where Pill LJ held that two migrant domestic workers who claimed the minimum wage were treated as members of the family, and so did not qualify under the former NMWR 1999 reg 2(2). Black LJ and Bean J concurred. The first claimant was in fact paid from £180 to £250 per week between 2000 and 2009 and had the title 'general housekeeper and child minder'. The Court of Appeal agreed with the Tribunal that: 'Time was spent with the children … which went beyond the scope of her duties, or watching television or clearing up after meals.' Pill LJ said 'particular consideration needed to be given to the sharing of tasks and leisure activities'. A serious question that, it is respectfully suggested, was not adequately reasoned is whether a non-family member, from a foreign country, who is a women, is being treated as having inherently less value than a white English person would be. It is utterly unclear that the legislation was meant to substitute the supposed joy of television viewing and games with children, with a minimum wage.

13. Recall *Edmonds v Lawson QC* [2000] EWCA Civ 69, above at chapter 3(2)(e).
14. If someone works full time, to do an easy, rough estimate of their yearly pre-tax earnings, multiply the hourly wage rate by 2000 (40 hours by 50 weeks). £3.70 per hour is about £7400 a year and £7.83 per hour is about £15,660, before tax. (In reality, 28 days paid holidays mean people should be paid 52 weeks a year, and a working week may be under or over 40 hours.) In April 2017, the pre-tax median UK salary for a full time employee was £28,600. See Office for National Statistics, *Statistical Bulletin: Annual Survey of Hours and Earnings* (26 October 2017). What do you think a 'living wage' should mean?

(c) Pay Period

Workers are entitled to the minimum wage for each hour they work. The NMWR 2015 reg 17 classifies four types of pay arrangement: by salary (regs 21 ff), for time (reg 30), output (reg 36) or unmeasured work (reg 44). If, for one lump of pay, working hours have fluctuated, the 'pay reference period' is one month or shorter (reg 6). To decide if someone has received the minimum wage, pay is simply divided by hours (reg 7). Workers being 'on call' caused early problems.

British Nursing Association v Inland Revenue [2002] EWCA Civ 494

'Bank nurses' for the British Nursing Association claimed they should be paid the minimum wage for each hour that they were required to be ready to answer telephone queries. They stayed at home overnight, and between calls could read or watch television. They were paid an amount per shift, lower than the minimum wage per hour. The employing entity argued that the NMWR 1999 reg 15(1) (now NMWR 2015 reg 32(1)) drew an implicit distinction between work at home and work at an employer's workplace: if a worker is at home, and not actually working, he or she does not need to be paid. The Court of Appeal disagreed.

Buxton LJ:

19. ... the alternative that is apparently contended for by the appellant, that the employees are only working when they are actually dealing with phone calls with all the periods spent waiting for calls excluded, would, in my view effectively make a mockery of the whole system of the minimum wage.

Peter Gibson LJ and **Neuberger J** agreed.

NOTES AND QUESTIONS

1. The Court of Appeal held that the nurses had to be paid while on call. Why do you think the health and social care sector might produce proportionally more minimum wage cases of this kind? Does this affect people who must be reachable by phone or email?

2. In *Scottbridge Construction Ltd v Wright* [2002] ScotCS 285, Mr Wright was a night watchman and was required to work seven nights a week from 5pm to 7am at his employer's office in Glasgow. He got £210 a week. He was permitted to sleep during his shifts. He had been given a mattress. He could have done so for all but four hours. If he had been paid a minimum wage for all the time on duty he would have had an extra £142.80 a week and a total of £3,427.20 by the time of his claim. The Tribunal held that the four hours when Mr Wright was required to be awake was working time, and so he should be paid for the work when he was on call. The Employment Appeal Tribunal reversed the Tribunal, but the EAT on appeal was itself reversed: Lord President Cullen said Mr Wright needed to be paid all the time, even if he was asleep.

3. After *Scottbridge*, NMWR 1999 reg 15(1A), now NMWR 2015 reg 32, was introduced to say that a worker who has 'suitable facilities for sleeping' is not doing 'work' when not awake. Should this be allowed? If you can be woken up, is it real sleep? Why should an employing corporation not have to pay for this time? Sleep deprivation can have seriously damaging consequences. On occupational health, see T Åkerstedt, 'Shift Work and Disturbed Sleep/Wakefulness' (2003) 53(2) *Occupational Medicine* 89 and S Brand et al, 'Sleep Patterns, Work, and Strain among Young Students in Hospitality and Tourism' (2008) 46(3) *Industrial Health* 199. Do the regulations violate an employer's duty to ensure a safe system of work? Could they be declared ultra vires and void in judicial review?

4. Under NMWR 2015 regs 21–29 'salaried work' is what labour relations experts often call the 'standard employment relation'. Under reg 21 a salaried worker receives an annual salary, for basic hours, usually without payments other than a bonus over weekly, monthly instalments. To tell if the hourly rate complies with the minimum wage, the instalments are divided by the basic hours (reg 22), minus absences from work or strikes (regulation 23).

5. NMWR 2015 regs 30–35 define 'time work' mainly as pay 'by reference to the time worked by the worker' or 'output in a period of time'. It expressly includes time when the worker is 'available, and required to be available, at or near a place of work … unless the worker is at home' (reg 32(1)). This was the *British Nursing* case. Training and travelling for the purpose of work (not to work) is working time (regs 33–34), and absences, strikes or non-regulated rest breaks are not time worked (reg 35).

6. Under NMWR 2015 regs 36–43, 'output work' is that paid 'by reference to a measure of output' including 'pieces made' or 'tasks performed'. Output may be 'rated' (regs 41–43). Generally, people need to be paid for the hours spent on the output.

7. Under NMWR 2015 regs 44–50, 'unmeasured work' is work that does not fall into the previous categories. If so, workers need to be paid according to hours 'which are worked' or according to 'a daily average agreement' (reg 45), made in writing that is 'a reasonable estimate' and must include 'where the worker was available to work' (regs 49 and 50).

8. In *McCartney v Oversley House Management* [2006] IRLR 514, Mrs McCartney claimed she was doing salaried work under NMWR 1999 reg 4(1) and not paid the minimum wage in her job as resident manager of Oversley House (originally

the Alcester Poor Law Union workhouse, est 1834). Her contract required her to be within three miles of the home, contactable by mobile phone, respond to emergencies 24 hours a day, 4 days a week. She got £8,750 pa, paid monthly, with rent-free accommodation. She also claimed she did not have proper rest breaks under the Working Time Regulations 1998 regs 10(1) and 12(1) (see chapter 7). Richardson J held she was properly considered as a salaried worker and on the facts not paid the minimum wage.

9.   If work is unmeasured, how should a 'daily average agreement' be made?

Walton v Independent Living Organisation [2003] EWCA Civ 199

Miss Julie Walton claimed that she should be paid more by the Independent Living Organisation to reach the minimum wage. She was a care worker for Miss E Jones, an epileptic but 'relatively easy client'. Miss Walton washed, ironed, shopped and made meals. She remained at work for 24 hours a day, three days a week and was paid £31.40 a day plus a meals allowance. She could sleep when with Miss Jones. The Inland Revenue's National Minimum Wage Team contacted the company after a complaint. The employing entity sent Miss Butler to 'assess' Miss Walton's hours of work. They concluded her tasks took 6 hours and 50 minutes a day. Miss Walton signed a form recording this. The Tribunal held that her time was 'unmeasured', and the estimation was an 'agreement' of time for the purpose of NMWR 1999 reg 28, even though her whole pay was expressed on a daily basis. She was paid £4.60 an hour, above the minimum. Miss Walton attempted to argue that her work was time work, not unmeasured work, to avoid the consequence of the form she had signed. The Court of Appeal held her work was unmeasured, and she was bound.

Aldous LJ:

34. Regulation 28 is concerned with unmeasured work. Thus the work is not paid by refer-ence to the time worked. In this case Miss Walton was paid by reference to the tasks required. Regulation 28 is concerned with that sort of employment and the necessity of ascertaining the number of hours to be used in calculating the National Minimum Wage. It does that by ascertaining from a written agreement the hours that the worker works to carry out the tasks, referred to as duties. In my view the Tribunal was entitled to conclude that there was a written agreement, that 6 hours 50 minutes was a realistic assessment of the time taken to carry out the duties and that regulation 28 applied. That being so, the Tribunal was entitled to conclude that Miss Walton's claim failed. The British Nursing Association and Scottbridge cases are not analogous. Miss Watson stayed at Miss Jones's home for 3 days. I do not believe that she "worked" a continuous period of 72 hours.

Arden LJ:

36. In making his submissions Mr Robin Allen QC recalled the well-known line from Milton: "They also serve who only stand and wait" (Milton, *When I consider how my light is spent*), thus reminding us that a person can and often does perform a service sim-ply by making himself or herself available for work. The Low Pay Commission recom-mended that the National Minimum Wage should apply to "all working time when a worker is required by the employer to be at the place of work *and available for work*" (Recommendation 4.33) and that "certain workers, such as those required to be on

call and sleep on their employer's premises ... should be entitled to the National Minimum Wage for all times when they are awake and *required to be available for work."* (Recommendation 4.34). These are undeniably important recommendations for those who serve but only stand and wait, and they were implemented, in the case of time work, by regulations 3 and 15 of the National Minimum Wage Regulations 1999.

37. As I see it, the appellants' approach in this case confuses time as a convenient unit for the quantification of a payment of remuneration with time as the yardstick by reference to which the rate of pay is determined. ...

Jacob J agreed with both judgments.

NOTES AND QUESTIONS

1. The Court of Appeals held Miss Walton's work was classified as 'unmeasured'. Therefore, the rule for time work – that time actually worked or on call had to be paid – did not apply. Instead, a rule favourable to the employing entity, that Miss Walton could 'agree' to how many hours were being 'worked', applied. Was Miss Walton implicitly threatened with being fired for enforcing her minimum wage rights? Was this duress?

2. This case highlights both the strengths and weaknesses of the minimum wage enforcement system. Under NMWA 1998 s 13, the Secretary of State has appointed compliance 'officers' to a unit in Her Majesty's Revenue and Customs to enforce the law. Under s 14, they can inspect, examine and copy records of individuals. (Under NMWR 2015 reg 59, the employer has a duty to keep records of wages.) Under s 19 they can issue an enforcement notice requiring payment of wages within 28 days, and a penalty up to £5000, or half the total arrears, can be imposed (s 19A). Compliance officers can complain and bring proceedings on worker's behalf.

3. Individuals can also bring claims, but the obvious difficulty is that the law will often be seen as difficult to understand, costly and a source of worry for most people. Under NMWA 1998 ss 17–18 individuals can claim for an unlawful wage deduction (below, ERA 1996 s 13). Somewhat fancifully, under s10, workers are entitled to inspect, examine and copy their employing entity's records if they 'believe on reasonable grounds' that they are underpaid, and failure to permit inspection enables a remedy of up to 80 times the minimum wage. Workers may suffer no detriment for exercising their rights (ss 23–25).

4. What would you advise a friend to do if they were not getting the minimum wage?

(d) Deduction Limits

Three main types of rule concern limits to deductions from pay: (i) general requirements for any deductions to be in a written agreement, (ii) specific case law on deductions in the course of strikes, and (iii) specific regulation on deductions from the minimum wage.

Employment Rights Act 1996 s 13

13. Right not to suffer unauthorised deductions.

(1) An employer shall not make a deduction from wages of a worker employed by him unless—

(a) the deduction is required or authorised to be made by virtue of a statutory provision or a relevant provision of the worker's contract, or

(b) the worker has previously signified in writing his agreement or consent to the making of the deduction.

(2) In this section "relevant provision", in relation to a worker's contract, means a provision of the contract comprised—

(a) in one or more written terms of the contract of which the employer has given the worker a copy on an occasion prior to the employer making the deduction in question, or

(b) in one or more terms of the contract (whether express or implied and, if express, whether oral or in writing) the existence and effect, or combined effect, of which in relation to the worker the employer has notified to the worker in writing on such an occasion.

(3) Where the total amount of wages paid on any occasion by an employer to a worker employed by him is less than the total amount of the wages properly payable by him to the worker on that occasion (after deductions), the amount of the deficiency shall be treated for the purposes of this Part as a deduction made by the employer from the worker's wages on that occasion.

(4) Subsection (3) does not apply in so far as the deficiency is attributable to an error of any description on the part of the employer affecting the computation by him of the gross amount of the wages properly payable by him to the worker on that occasion.

(5) For the purposes of this section a relevant provision of a worker's contract having effect by virtue of a variation of the contract does not operate to authorise the making of a deduction on account of any conduct of the worker, or any other event occurring, before the variation took effect.

(6) For the purposes of this section an agreement or consent signified by a worker does not operate to authorise the making of a deduction on account of any conduct of the worker, or any other event occurring, before the agreement or consent was signified.

(7) This section does not affect any other statutory provision by virtue of which a sum payable to a worker by his employer but not constituting "wages" within the meaning of this Part is not to be subject to a deduction at the instance of the employer.

NOTES AND QUESTIONS

1. ERA 1996 s 14, goes on to say that deductions are legitimate if the worker had been overpaid, and s 17 enables deductions for 'cash shortage' or 'stock deficiency' but only to a limit of 10 per cent of wages on any day. Most employers will not in fact utilise these provisions, because in practice people strongly object to not being fully paid for their work. If deductions relate to accidents, why should an employee be able to deduct any pay at all, rather than assume the risks of business?

2. ERA 1996 s 23 enables a worker to claim that a deduction not complying with s 13 is unlawful, and s 24(2) enables the Tribunal to declare the employer must pay 'such amount as the tribunal considers appropriate ... to compensate the worker

for any financial loss'. This could include frequently encountered problems such
as unplanned bank overdraft fees, fees for the worker's own late payment, fees for
enforcing the worker's rights, and presumably compensation for a reasonable time
spent working to understand, research and bring a claim.

3. ERA 1996 s 27 defines wages to include any pay or 'emolument referable to his
    employment' (see below, chapter 6(3)(a)). This expressly includes statutory sick,
    parental or time-off pay, 'guarantee payments', 'protective awards' and so forth.
    Delaney v Staples [1992] 1 AC 687 created a case-based exception for pay in lieu
    of notice when an employee is dismissed. Lord Browne-Wilkinson reasoned that
    pay in lieu of notice is not wages because it relates to termination, and not service
    under the contract. This enabled an employing entity to cancel a cheque, when it
    decided that Miss Delaney could be summarily dismissed, rather than dismissed
    on notice.

4. A rare exception to a s 13 claim occurred in *Burns v Santander plc* [2011] IRLR
    639. Peter Clark J held that Mr Burns, after being charged with sexual assault and
    12 other offences, did not have a claim for his wages being deducted. They could
    (unsurprisingly) stop his salary as a branch manager when he failed to show up
    for work because he was remanded in custody.

5. The origins of the law were the Truck Act 1831 s III, which required that peo-
    ple be paid 'the entire Amount of the Wages earned … in the current Coin of
    this Realm'. Partly this was to ensure people were paid with money, not food or
    non-exchangeable goods (ie 'truck'). Its updates in 1887 and 1896, which
    required that any deductions had to be 'fair and reasonable, having regard to all
    the circumstances of the case' lasted until the Wages Act 1986. This substituted
    the current rules, which set the default requirements in terms of transparency,
    rather than limits. See further *Bristow v City Petroleum* [1987] 1 WLR 529, 532
    and T Goriely, 'Arbitrary Deductions from Pay and the Proposed Repeal of the
    Truck Acts' (1983) 12 *ILJ* 236. These changes in statutory codification do not, it
    seems, affect common law limits to what counts as true agreement.

6. The UK had ratified the Protection of Wages Convention 1949 (c 95) which con-
    trolled deductions and prohibited wages being paid in kind. It was denounced,
    however, by the UK government in 1983.

7. Transparency requirements have been purposively interpreted by the Employment
    Appeal Tribunal. See *Potter v Hunt Contracts Ltd* [1992] IRLR 108 (agreement
    to repay training costs was not agreement to deductions) and *Kerr v The Sweater
    Shop (Scotland) Ltd* [1996] IRLR 425 (a workplace noticeboard was not suffi-
    cient for deductions, without personal written agreement). This suggests the old
    case of *Sagar v Ridehalgh & Sons Ltd* [1931] 1 Ch 310 is reversed. The Court of
    Appeal, overturning Farwell J, held that an employing entity could deduct wages
    for 3 yards of cloth being 'unmerchantable' because a custom of deductions was
    known well enough. No deduction was agreed in advance, and one expects a
    modern employer would invest in adequate training and skills, bearing the risk for
    otherwise undesired outcomes.

8. ERA 1996 s 28 states that if an employer provides no work, and 'an employee
    would normally be required to work in accordance with his contract of
    employment … the employee is entitled to be paid by his employer an amount in

respect of that day' so long as there is not a strike or lockout, and an employee has not refused reasonable alternative work. Under s 29, an employee must have worked for one month to qualify for this right, but under s 31(1) the limit of this 'guarantee payment' is £26 (updated last in SI 2016/288). These provisions for minimum standards, first introduced by the Employment Protection Act 1975, have not proven particularly useful against zero-hours contracts because they only relate to 'days' without work rather than 'hours' that are more often varied (see chapter 7(1)). This means a claim in contract is preferable. On the other hand, the provisions were applied in *Abercrombie v Aga Rangemaster Ltd* [2013] EWCA Civ 1148, where the Court of Appeal held it was irrelevant that workers agreeing to temporarily not work Fridays (reducing hours from 39 to 34 a week) had not thereby changed what they 'would normally be required to work'. Given the smaller than usual sums involved, it was expedient to claim under statute.

9. As explained in chapter 5(2)(b), *Devonald v Rosser & Sons* [1906] 2 KB 728 founds a claim in contract, as an implied common law right, to be paid when ready and able to work. These claims may be brought in a Tribunal or the High Court.

10. ERA 1996 s 14(5) says s 13 does not stop deductions 'where the worker has taken part in a strike or other industrial action'. What does that mean?

Miles v Wakefield Metropolitan District Council [1987] UKHL 15, [1987] AC 539

Mr Miles claimed that his wages were unlawfully deducted after he joined in collective action against the council. He worked 37 hours a week as a births, deaths and marriages registrar. In 1981, to improve wages, his union, the National and Local Government Officers' Association (now Unison) called for its members to stop work on Saturday mornings for weddings. Mr Miles did all other work. This amounted to three hours less per week. The council deducted 3/37th of his pay. Mr Miles claimed this was unlawful because he was willing to do other work. Nicholls J held the pay could be deducted. The Court of Appeal, Eveleigh LJ dissenting, held the deduction was unlawful unless Mr Miles was dismissed. The House of Lords held that 3/37th in pay could be deducted and in obiter dicta said that the employer could further refuse to accept 'part performance' of the work.

Lord Brightman:

I agree that the plaintiff's action was rightly dismissed by the trial judge. It was rightly dismissed because in an action by an employee to recover his pay it must be proved or admitted that the employee worked or was willing to work in accordance with his contract of employment, or that such service as was given by the employee, if falling short of his contractual obligations, was accepted by the employer as a sufficient performance of his contract. I leave out of account a failure to work or work efficiently as a result of illness or other unavoidable impediment, to which special considerations apply.

If an employee offers partial performance, as he does in some types of industrial conflict falling short of a strike, the employer has a choice. He may decline to accept the partial performance that is offered, in which case the employee is entitled to no remuneration for his unwanted services, even if they are performed. That is the instant case. Or the employer may accept the partial performance. If he accepts the partial performance as if it were performance which satisfied the terms of the contract, the employer must pay the full wage for the period of the partial performance because he will have precluded or estopped himself from asserting that the performance was not that which the contract required. But what is the position if the employee offers partial performance and the employer, usually of necessity, accepts such partial performance, the deficient work being understood by the employer and intended by the employee to fall short of the contractual requirements and being accepted by the employer as such? There are, as it seems to me, two possible answers. One possible answer is that the employer must pay the full wage but may recover by action or counterclaim or set-off damages for breach of contract. The other possible answer is that the employee is only entitled to so much remuneration as represents the value of the work he has done, i.e. *quantum meruit*. My noble and learned friend Lord Templeman prefers the latter solution, and so do I. My reason is this. One has to start with the assumption that the employee sues for his pay; the employer is only bound to pay the employee that which the employee can recover by action. The employee cannot recover his contractual wages because he cannot prove that he has performed or ever intended to perform his contractual obligations. If wages and work are interdependent, it is difficult to suppose that an employee who has voluntarily declined to perform his contractual work can claim his contractual wages. The employee offers partial performance with the object of inflicting the maximum damage on the employer at the minimum inconvenience to himself. If, in breach of his contract, an employee works with the object of harming his employer, he can hardly claim that he is working under his contract and is therefore entitled to his contractual wages. But nevertheless in the case supposed the employee has provided some services, albeit less than the contract required, and the employer has received those (non-contractual) services; therefore the employer must clearly pay something – not the contractual wages because the contractual work has deliberately not been performed. What can he recover? Surely the value of the services which he gave and which the employer received, i.e. *quantum meruit*.

Lord Templeman:

Mr. Sedley, who appeared for the plaintiff, submitted and the majority of the Court of Appeal accepted that significance was to be attached to the fact that the plaintiff was not a servant under a contract of employment but the holder of an office. In the olden days satirised by Dickens and Thackeray a gentleman appointed to an office, for example, in the Chancery Registry or in the Department of Circumlocution and Sealing Wax, carried out his ill-defined duties at his leisure and pleasure.

Trollope explained that a special Act of Parliament was necessary in order to control the functions and the stipend of the holder of the office of Warden of Hiram's Hospital. It is unusual for the holder of an office to take industrial action and the consequences will depend on the rights and obligations conferred and imposed on the office-holder by the terms of his appointment. But if an ambassador and the embassy porter were both on strike then I would expect both to be liable to lose or both to be entitled to claim their apportioned remuneration attributable to the period of the strike. A judge and an usher on strike should arguably be treated in the same manner. The ambassador might be required to decode a declaration of war on Sunday, and a judge might devote his Christmas holidays to the elucidation of legal problems arising from industrial action, so that it would be necessary to divide their annual salaries by 365 to define a daily rate applicable to the period of strike, whereas the weekly, daily or hourly wages of the porter and the usher provide a different basis for apportionment, but in principle it is difficult to see why there should be any difference in treatment. To decide this appeal it suffices that there is no logical distinction between a superintendent registrar who is paid a weekly salary for a 37-hour week and a municipal dustman who is paid a weekly wage for a 37-hour week if both are on strike, both are supported by their unions and both claim from the council payment in full of their salary and wages for the duration of the strike. Middle class morality must not be allowed to place Mr. Dolittle in an inferior position in this respect.

...

For the past two years teachers have been engaged in sporadic strike action, usually on one day in a week. If Mr. Sedley is right, educational authorities must pay for strike days unless after each day's strike they issue dismissal notices. To show that the educational authorities have no intention of ruining the educational system by insisting on dismissal, the dismissal notice must presumably be accompanied by a reinstatement notice. This would finally submerge the teaching profession in paper.

The consequences of Mr. Sedley's submissions demonstrate that his analysis of a contract of employment is deficient. It cannot be right that an employer should be compelled to pay something for nothing whether he dismisses or retains a worker. In a contract of employment wages and work go together. The employer pays for work and the worker works for his wages. If the employer declines to pay, the worker need not work. If the worker declines to work, the employer need not pay. In an action by a worker to recover his pay he must allege and be ready to prove that he worked or was willing to work. Different considerations apply to a failure to work by sickness or other circumstances which may be governed by express or implied terms or by custom. In the present case the plaintiff disentitled himself for his salary for Saturday morning because he declined to work on Saturday morning in accordance with his duty.

...

In those circumstances, the worker cannot claim that he is entitled to his wages under the contract because he is deliberately working in a manner designed to harm the employer. But the worker will be entitled to be paid on a *quantum meruit* basis for the amount and value of the reduced work performed and accepted.

Lord Oliver:

A plaintiff in an action for remuneration under a contract of employment must, in my judgment, assume the initial burden of averring and proving his readiness and willingness to render the services required by the contract (subject, no doubt, to any implied term exonerating him from inability to perform due, for instance, to illness). I do not, for my part, find this inconsistent with the cases to which Mr. Sedley has drawn attention and which preclude the employer from accepting the services tendered whilst at the same time seeking to penalise the employee for some other breach of his contractual obligations. For instance, *Hanley v Pease & Partners Ltd* [1915] 1 KB 698 was a case in which the employer unsuccessfully sought to withhold from his employee, as a punishment for absence on a previous day on which he had not worked, wages for a day on which the employee had worked. It is interesting to note that there does not appear to have been any dispute that that employee was not entitled to be paid for the day on which he was absent.

...

... the plaintiff cannot, for the reasons which I have given, successfully claim that he was at the material time ready and willing to perform the work which he was properly required to do on Saturdays and his action for the remuneration attributable to that work must fail. I would also prefer to reserve my opinion with regard to the question whether there may not be circumstances in which an employee engaged in industrial action might be entitled to claim remuneration on a quantum meruit basis for work actually done.

Lord Bridge concurred, doubting that *quantum meruit* would be available. **Lord Brandon** agreed with **Lord Oliver** to reserve his opinion.

NOTES AND QUESTIONS

1.   The House of Lords held the council was entitled to deduct pay for the proportion of hours not worked. Lord Brightman and Lord Templeman said that if such 'partial performance' was offered, an employer could further elect not to accept the whole, but would have to pay *quantum meruit*. Lord Brandon and Lord Oliver reserved their views. Only Lord Bridge said he found this 'difficult to understand'.

2.   Although not mentioned, the notorious case of *Cutter v Powell* (1795) 101 ER 573 used to justify the doctrine of partial performance. Mrs Cutter claimed that Powell, master of a ship sailing from Jamaica to Liverpool, should pay wages for the seven weeks work Mr Cutter performed, although he died before the ten-week voyage was complete. Lord Kenyon CJ with the other judges on the eighteenth-century King's Bench found that no money was due at all, because Mr Cutter had only partly performed an entire obligation. This principle continues for services cases today (eg *Hoenig v Isaacs* [1952] EWCA Civ 6). Should it have any application to employment today?

3.   As the Court of Appeal pointed out, the collective action by Mr Miles and NALGO 'was aimed at securing increased remuneration' [1985] 1 WLR 822, 825. Because inflation was at 18 per cent in 1980 and 11.9 per cent in 1981, Mr Miles and his colleagues were suffering a real-terms wage decrease (around a 25 per cent cut in two years, other things being equal). As we will see in chapter 11, one of the reasons that the right to take collective action is a fundamental human right is to protect people's living standards, and this is why action taken 'in contemplation or furtherance of a trade dispute' is immune by employers for economic loss. There is technical debate about whether there is an implied contractual right, or an overriding fundamental right, to take collective action. But also, could an employer be regarded as breaching the contract by doing nothing as wages are reduced (through inflation) in real terms? If not, why should an employer be entitled to make any deductions for strikes when work *is* done?

4.   Lord Templeman strangely remarked that: 'Industrial action is largely a 20th century development introduced with success by the Bermondsey matchworkers at about the turn of the century.' By contrast, see S Webb and B Webb, *The History of Trade Unionism* (rev edn 1920) ch 1, on a Hebrew brickmakers strike in ancient Egypt, c 1490 BC. They state strikes 'are as old as history itself'. See also chapter 1. Should the law require specialist judges to decide labour cases in appellate courts?

5.   In *Wiluszynski v Tower Hamlets LBC* [1989] ICR 493 Nicholls LJ applied Lord Bridge's minority opinion and refused a claim against the council for deducting all Mr Wiluszynski's wages after a partial collective action. Totalling just 3 hours over 5 weeks, he and his housing officer colleagues had refused to answer phone queries only by Liberal/SDP (now Liberal Democrat) councillors. Nicholls LJ said: 'A buyer of goods is entitled to decline to accept goods tendered to him which do not conform to a condition in the contract, without necessarily terminating the contract altogether. So with services.' If your total pay will be deducted for a partial strike, is it rational to go on total or partial strike in future? Do you think the Court of Appeal's policy was helpful at encouraging peaceful resolution of disputes?

6. In *British Telecommunications plc v Ticehurst* [1992] ICR 383 another Court of Appeal decided that simply withdrawing 'good faith' could be notified by an employer to be partial performance, and paid accordingly. In *Spackman v London Metropolitan University* [2007] IRLR 741 a County Court judge believed that no *quantum meruit* could be an 'implied term', and that an exam boycott could enable full wage deductions of the lecturers.
7. These cases must now be re-evaluated in light of the principles set up by the Supreme Court in *Hartley v King Edward VI College* [2017] UKSC 39. See chapter 10(4).
8. In *Gisda Cyf v Barratt* [2010] UKSC 41, [39] the Supreme Court said: 'The need to segregate intellectually common law principles relating to contract law, even in the field of employment, from statutorily conferred rights is fundamental.' Do you agree that principles fit for contracts providing services should no longer be applied when the fundamental right to take collective action is at stake?
9. Turning back to the NMWA 1998, the European Court of Human Rights has suggested it was not prepared to interfere with UK law on deductions regarding former provisions about restaurant tips.

Nerva v United Kingdom (2003) 36 EHRR 4

Nerva claimed that tips for work, taken by RL & G Ltd, which owned the Paradiso and Inferno restaurant on the Strand, London belonged to workers doing the waiting job, and they were not being paid the minimum wage. At the time, the NMWR 1999 reg 31(e) enabled employers to take tips to pay the minimum wage. The claimants argued that when customers gave tips, this money should be regarded as already belonging to the staff, even if received by the employer. It was, therefore, a violation of the European Convention on Human Rights, Protocol 1, Art 1, of the right to property, for an employer to be able to take tips to pay the minimum wage.

Costa J, Baka J, Bratza J, Jörundsson J, Bîrsan J, Ugrekhelidze J and **Dollé J**:

43. The applicants cannot maintain that they had a separate right to the tips and a separate right to minimum remuneration calculated without reference to those tips. In the first place, that assertion is not borne out by the legislation at issue as interpreted by the domestic courts. The fact that the domestic courts ruled in a dispute between private litigants that the tips at issue represented "remuneration" within the meaning of the applicable legislation cannot of itself be said to engage the liability of the respondent State under Article 1 of Protocol No. 1. It would observe in this connection that the interpretation and application of domestic legislation in a given dispute is essentially a matter for the domestic courts. It notes that after full argument on the competing interpretations canvassed for the notion of "remuneration", the domestic courts ruled that the employer, and not the customer, paid the tips at issue out of its own funds to the applicants and their colleagues. This conclusion cannot be considered arbitrary or manifestly unreasonable, having regard to the scope of the expression "remuneration" and indeed to the applicants' acceptance that title in the tips at issue passed to the employer. Moreover, the applicants cannot claim that they had a legitimate expectation that the tips at issue would not count towards remuneration. Such a view assumes that the customer intended that this would not be the case. However, this is too imprecise a basis on which to found

a legitimate expectation which could give rise to "possessions" within the meaning of Article 1 of Protocol No. 1 ...

Loucaides J (dissenting):

It is my opinion that the interpretation given by the domestic courts to the notion of "remuneration" constituted a disproportionate interference with the applicants' right to the peaceful enjoyment of their possessions since it allowed what was intended for and owed to the applicants to be used to satisfy the employer's debt to them under the minimum wage legislation. I agree with the view of Lord Justice Aldous in the Court of Appeal (see paragraph 23 of the judgment) that such a practice, as condoned by the domestic courts, in effect authorised the employer to enrich itself at the expense of its staff.

I do not share the view of the majority that the case simply raised a question of "interpretation and application of domestic legislation in a given dispute [which] is essentially a matter for the domestic courts". Whether the tips in this case could be regarded as "possessions of the applicants" for the purposes of Article 1 of Protocol No. 1 on the basis of the autonomous meaning of that term as established by the case-law of this Court was a matter which could and should have been determined by this Court in order to find whether there had been an interference with the relevant right of the applicants.

NOTES AND QUESTIONS

1. The European Court of Human Rights held that the UK had a margin of appreciation in determining that tips were not the property of employees. Therefore, the tips could be appropriated by the employing entity to subsidise the minimum wage. When you have given tips to workers in the past, did you give them on the basis that they would go to the workers, or the employers? Do you think most people would regard such a system as honest?

2. The majority's judgment rests solely on the UK's 'legislation at issue', namely NMWR reg 31(e) as it stood. This defined the scope of property rights, for the purpose of ECHR Protocol 1, Art 1. Otherwise, tips belong to the worker because the intention of every customer, coupled with delivery, is to leave tips for workers (either as a 'gift' or perhaps more accurately as a third-party beneficiary to a contract within the meaning of the Contracts (Rights of Third Parties) Act 1999 s 1). See *Thomas v Times Book Co Ltd* [1966] 2 All ER 241. By contrast, Loucaides J thought there should be an 'autonomous meaning' of property in ECHR Protocol 1, Art 1.

3. The UK's legislation was amended after *Revenue and Customs Commissioners v Annabel's (Berkeley Square) Ltd* [2009] EWCA Civ 361. This held, in effect, that employing entities could not fail to pay National Insurance on tips that they took from employees. As the case shone a light on the tips practice, SI 2009/1902 reg 5 removed the tips exception in NMWR 1999 reg 31(e). Now, if you pay someone a tip, it cannot lawfully go to the employer.

4. The legislative change has serious implications, which many employers wilfully ignore. It means that tips are workers' property, both in domestic case law, legislation and under the ECHR. Under the Theft Act 1968 s 1 the employer commits theft when it 'dishonestly appropriates property belonging to another with the intention of permanently depriving the other of it'. Dishonesty means knowing something is dishonest by the standards of honest people (not dishonest employers): *R v Ghosh* [1982] EWCA Crim 2. 'Property' means what UK case law and

legislation says. 'Appropriating' means takes, and 'permanently depriving' means keeping. Employers who commit wage theft are open to criminal charges. Under the Theft Act 1968 s 7, the maximum prison sentence is seven years. Workers are entitled to call the police.

5. 'Wage theft' is often a metaphorical term for wage rights violations, developed in the United States: K Bobo, *Wage Theft in America* (2011). This is distinct from the literal criminal liability issues raised above. The original idea of allowing employers to take a worker's tips seems to have been imported from the US Small Business Act of 1996, codified in the Fair Labor Standards Act of 1938, 29 USC §§203(m). In the United States, currently, the minimum wage is $7.25 an hour, but only $2.13 in a tipped job. Have you ever wondered why American customer service at restaurants is so dazzling?

6. Although employers taking tips has been prohibited, a so-called 'service charge' paid through a card machine at restaurants is often taken by the employer. What is the customer's intention here, and therefore who has 'property' for the purpose of 'theft'? If the employer takes the 'service' charge, it seems that (if not founding an action for theft), an employer could also be liable under the Consumer Protection from Unfair Trading Regulations 2008 reg 5 for causing 'the average consumer to take a transactional decision he would not have taken otherwise'. This is an offence (reg 8) leading to fines or up to two years in prison (reg 13).

7. NMWR 2015 regs 11–16 still enable an employer to make deductions from the minimum wage for services provided to employees for their 'own use and benefit' and for accommodation expenses. See *Leisure Employment Services Ltd v HM Revenue & Customs* [2007] EWCA Civ 92. But no more than £6 per day can be deducted.

8. There are no other deductions that can be made by an employer, which goes below the minimum wage, even with a worker's consent. For example, making deductions for food is unlawful. It is unlawful to pay workers in food.

(2) UNJUSTIFIED PAY

As income and wealth inequality has become increasingly extreme, the body of law on unjustified pay has been growing. The people with the greatest wealth or incomes fall into four major groups: (1) directors and senior managers of major companies, particularly in the financial sector, (2) major shareholders in companies, (3) people with inherited wealth from companies or land, and (4) sport, film and other celebrities. Has inequality increased because these people have become more talented, responsible or valuable than everyone else? If not, the law may be enabling their unjustified enrichment.

In a notorious article, two management economists argued that high pay at work for most people happened for the same reasons that sport stars (4) are highly paid. High earners are all like people with more talent who win sport tournaments, and deserve big rewards (E Lazear and S Rosen, 'Rank-Order Tournaments as Optimum Labor Contracts' (1981) 89(5) *Journal of Political Economy* 841). This theory of Lazear (a chief economic adviser to George W Bush) and Rosen did not bother to consider more obvious causes for high sportsperson rewards, including changes to sport club and broadcasting regulation, or intellectual property rights that accompanied stratospheric pay rises of sport, film and other celebrities. This aside, the argument was met with considerable derision for trying to equate talented ball-kickers, say, with corporate directors who pay themselves. See L Bebchuk and J Fried, *Pay without Performance: The Unfulfilled Promise of Executive Compensation* (2004). Collective bargaining might affect pay scales across industry and within corporations. But also, corporate governance has been intensively discussed. All company directors are employees. Their default powers and rights are in Model Articles.

Companies (Model Articles) Regulations 2008 Sch 3, paras 3 and 23

Directors' general authority
3. Subject to the articles, the directors are responsible for the management of the company's business, for which purpose they may exercise all the powers of the company.

Members' reserve power
4. (1) The members may, by special resolution, direct the directors to take, or refrain from taking, specified action.
(2) No such special resolution invalidates anything which the directors have done before the passing of the resolution.
…

Directors' remuneration
23. (1) Directors may undertake any services for the company that the directors decide.
(2) Directors are entitled to such remuneration as the directors determine—
(a) for their services to the company as directors, and
(b) for any other service which they undertake for the company.

NOTES AND QUESTIONS

1. Model Art 23 is followed by virtually every company in the UK, so that indeed directors 'are entitled to such remuneration as the directors determine'. Do you think that company directors should get to pay themselves?

Figure 6.1 UK inequality and executive pay ratios

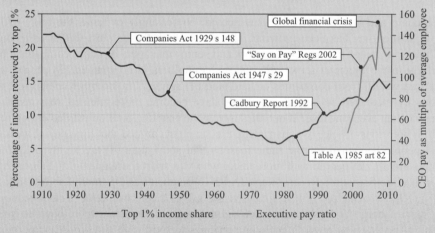

Sources: Piketty (2014) and Manifest and MM&K (2011).

2. Figure 6.1 shows data on income inequality, measured by the share of income for the top 1 per cent of earners against the pay of the average CEO as a multiple of the average employee in their firm. Sadly, there is little statistical data before 1999, but what exists suggests that an exponential rise in CEO pay began in the early 1980s. In 1985, a decisive regulatory change was that SI 1985/80, Table A, introduced a new model Art 82 (the equivalent of Art 23 today) reading 'directors shall be entitled to such remuneration as the company may by ordinary resolution determine'. The previous model rule said a company 'shall' determine director pay, or it would be fixed in a company's constitution. This reflected a long-held view that the conflicts meant directors had 'no power to vote themselves fees for salaries for their services beyond what the constitution of the company may provide' (N Lindley, *The Law of Companies* (5th edn 1889) 303). This did not mean companies never changed the model articles: in principle they could. But the default was powerful in limiting the exponential pay rises of today.

3. There is more data on pay ratios in the United States (see Figure 6.2). There, it appears executive pay ratios run alongside income inequality measured by the percentage of income received by the top 1 per cent of earners. The curve of executive pay seemed to change when the Delaware General Corporation Law 1969 §141(h) was rewritten to say 'the board of directors shall have the authority to fix the compensation of directors'. Most US companies incorporate in Delaware. S Arsht and WK Stapleton, 'Delaware General Corporation Law: 1969' (1969) 25 *Business Lawyer* 287. Other data sources are T Piketty, *Capital in the Twenty-First Century* (2014) Technical Appendices, Table S9.2. A Davis and L Mishel, 'CEO Pay Continues to Rise as Typical Workers Are Paid Less' (12 June 2014) Economic Policy Institute. WG Lewellen, *Executive Compensation in Large Industrial Corporations* (1968) ch 8, 123, Table 1, ch 9, 177, Table 13.

Figure 6.2 US inequality and executive pay ratios

Sources: Piketty (2014), Davis and Mishel (2014), Lewellen (1968).

4.   The following table shows the top 10 highest-paid executives in UK companies.

Company	Sector	CEO	£000 total pay	Change
WPP	Advertising	Martin Sorrell	70,416	+
Berkeley Group	Land	Tony Pidgeley	23,296	+
Reckitt Benckiser	Chemicals	Rakesh Kapoor	23,190	+
Sky	Media	Jeremy Darroch	16,889	+
Shire	Drugs	Flemming Ornskov	14,638	+
BP	Oil	Bob Dudley	13,296	+
Relx (Reed Elsevier)	Info	Erik Engstrom	10,869	+
Prudential	Assets	Mike Wells	10,031	+
Schroders	Assets	Michael Dobson	8,905	+
Lloyds Banking	Bank	Antonio Horta-Osorio	8,773	−

5.   According to the High Pay Centre, the average CEO is paid £5.5m a year. The median UK salary for a full-time employee in April 2017 was £28,600. Therefore, the median full-time employee must work for about 200 years to earn what an average CEO gets in one year. The average CEO earns more between New Year and April Fool's Day than the employee in a lifetime. The CEO of WPP (an advertising firm) earns more in a week than most in a lifetime. And so on.

6.   As we know, most employing entities are companies. They may also be partnerships, a local council, or a government department represented by the Secretary of State established through statute. But in all entities, governance rules exist, like in companies. The Companies Act (CA) 2006 applies to any limited corporation. The suffix 'Ltd' is used for 'private' companies, where investors generally cannot sell shares without each others' consent. 'Plc' is used for 'public' companies, which usually allow their shares to be traded on a listed exchange, such as the London Stock Exchange. As chapter 11 will discuss, 'membership' and therefore voting rights within companies are generally monopolised by shareholders: the institutions (individuals rarely) who buy shares. Under CA 2006 s 168, the 'general meeting' of shareholders (which usually takes place annually) can vote out the directors with a simple majority. But although shareholders can fire directors, there is no direct right to set directors' pay. That is considered, as in Article 3, a power of 'management'. Under Art 4, members could only instruct directors to receive a lower rate with a 75 per cent vote, known as a 'special resolution'. A 50 per cent vote is an 'ordinary resolution' (ss 282–83).

7.   What arguments justify directors paying themselves? A consistent argument has been that on boards of public companies the UK Corporate Governance Code 2017, s D requires companies to comply, or explain to the markets noncompliance, with the standard that the board will have a 'remuneration committee' with a majority of 'independent non-executive directors'. This committee is meant to set pay according to 'performance', with various 'design' principles in Schedule A. 'Non-executive' directors do not have management jobs. Their 'independence' is satisfied under the Code, B.1.1: they have not been employees

in the last five years, had a material business or service relationship, are unrelated by family, are not significant shareholders, and have not been on the board for nine years. Despite all these interesting criteria, directors will still collectively hire each other and work with each other. This seems to fail, to a considerable degree, any serious standard to avoid conflicts of interest.

8. Reform was passed in the Enterprise and Regulatory Reform Act 2013 s 79 for public companies that are 'quoted' on a stock exchange, now CA 2006 s 439A.

Companies Act 2006 s 439A

439A. Quoted companies: members' approval of directors' remuneration policy
(1) A quoted company must give notice of the intention to move, as an ordinary resolution, a resolution approving the relevant directors' remuneration policy—
  (a) at the accounts meeting held in the first financial year which begins on or after the day on which the company becomes a quoted company, and
  (b) at an accounts or other general meeting held no later than the end of the period of three financial years beginning with the first financial year after the last accounts or other general meeting in relation to which notice is given under this subsection.
...
(7) For the purposes of this section, the relevant directors' remuneration policy is—
  (a) in a case where notice is given in relation to an accounts meeting, the remuneration policy contained in the directors' remuneration report in respect of which a resolution under section 439 is required to be put to the vote at that accounts meeting;
  (b) in a case where notice is given in relation to a general meeting other than an accounts meeting—
    (i) the remuneration policy contained in the directors' remuneration report in respect of which such a resolution was required to be put to the vote at the last accounts meeting to be held before that other general meeting, or
    (ii) where that policy has been revised in accordance with section 422A, the policy as so revised.

NOTES AND QUESTIONS

1. Does CA 2006 s 439A remove the inherent conflict of interest in directors paying themselves? It requires members take a binding vote on the 'directors' remuneration policy'. This is not a binding vote on the actual figure. In the event of rejection, it is still up to the directors under s 422A to redraw the policy.
2. Why do shareholders not simply fire the directors under CA 2006 s 168 for giving themselves excessive pay rises? The answer seems to be that institutional shareholders are themselves conflicted: most registered shareholders are asset managers controlling 'other people's money', like JP Morgan, Legal & General, BlackRock, etc. Asset managers are very highly paid. They probably do not want to put a spotlight on CEO pay, because the spotlight will turn back on them. They have a social conflict of interest with the beneficiaries – mostly employees saving for retirement – whose money they manage. What do you think?
3. What would be the effect on exponentially rising pay if employees could vote in the general meeting, or for directors on the board? One indication is given in

G Charness et al, 'The Hidden Advantage of Delegation: Pareto Improvements in a Gift Exchange Game' (2012) 102(5) *American Economic Review* 2358. This behavioural economics study found that employees were more productive as a group when the choice of sharing out wages was delegated to them. By analogy, one can expect that companies as a whole become more productive and workers become more satisfied if they can determine a fair distribution of gains among themselves democratically. See chapter 11.

4. Limits on types of pay are found in CA 2006 ss 188–89 (contracts with directors over two years in length require a member vote) and ss 215–22 (payments to directors for loss of office – ie golden parachutes – cannot be made without member approval).

5. *Guinness plc v Saunders* [1990] 2 AC 663 held that procedures for pay must be followed strictly. After a successful takeover bid, Saunders, the chairman of Guinness plc, arranged for a fee of £5.2m to be paid to the American attorney, Ward, who worked on completing the deal. This was beyond the power that had been delegated to directors under the company constitution. Therefore, the money had to be paid back.

6. After the global financial crisis, the EU introduced the Capital Requirements Directive 2013/36/EU Art 94, which required the 'variable elements of remuneration' for various senior workers in financial institutions (ie banker bonuses) to be no more than 100 per cent of the salary, or 200 per cent with shareholder approval. Disclosure is required by the Capital Requirements Regulation (EU) No 575/2013 Art 450. Predictably, salaries rose, to compensate for falling bonuses. Why do you think legislators put in place a set of rules that were bound to change very little?

(3) TAX AND NATIONAL INSURANCE

Tax and National Insurance Contributions (NICs) raise a host of issues for labour lawyers. First, tax and NICs create incentives for employers to deny that their staff are employees. Improperly enforced, this can have serious effects on the formal scope of labour rights coverage. Second, it affects the transparency of real pay. When you buy a product you pay the advertised price, and this includes Value Added Tax. Why is it that when you get a job, you do not get the wages you were promised, including income tax? Does it make people overly optimistic about their real income when they spend, leading them into more debt? In every pay slip, people read deductions from their wage for income tax and NICs. Why should a corporation have to make prices transparent for consumers, but not need to make real pay transparent for workers? This section outlines (a) income tax, and (b) National Insurance.

(a) Taxation of Employment Income

Each year, the Government sets out the main rates of income tax in a Finance Act (FA). This may or may not alter the income tax rates listed in the heavily amended Income Tax Act (ITA) 2007, which lists the thresholds and limits for each rate.

Finance Act 2017 s 2

2 Main rates of income tax for tax year 2017–18
For the tax year 2017–18 the main rates of income tax are as follows—
   (a) the basic rate is 20%;
   (b) the higher rate is 40%;
   (c) the additional rate is 45%.

Income Tax Act 2007 ss 10–12, 35 and 57A

10 Income charged at the basic, higher and additional rates: individuals
(2) Income tax on an individual's income up to the basic rate limit is charged at the basic rate (except to the extent that, in accordance with section 12, it is charged at the starting rate for savings).
...
(5) The basic rate limit is £33,500.
(5A) The higher rate limit is £150,000.
(6) The basic rate limit and higher rate limit are increased in some circumstances: see–
   (a) section 414(2) (gift aid relief), and
   (b) section 192(4) of FA 2004 (relief for pension contributions).
...

12 Income charged at the starting rate for savings
(1) Income tax is charged at the starting rate for savings (rather than the basic rate) on so much of an individual's income up to the starting rate limit for savings as is savings income.
...
(3) The starting rate limit for savings is £5000. ...
...

35 Personal allowance
(1) An individual who makes a claim is entitled to a personal allowance of £11,500[1] for a tax year if the individual meets the requirements of section 56 (residence etc).
(2) For an individual whose adjusted net income exceeds £100,000, the allowance under subsection (1) is reduced by one-half of the excess.
...

57A Personal allowance linked to national minimum wage
(1) This section provides for increases in the amount specified in section 35(1) (personal allowance).
(2) It applies in relation to a tax year if—
   (a) the relevant national minimum wage at the start of the tax year is greater than it was at the start of the previous tax year, and
   (b) the amount specified in section 35(1) immediately before the start of the tax year is at least £12,500.
(3) For the tax year, the personal allowance specified in section 35(1) is to be the yearly equivalent of the relevant national minimum wage at the start of the tax year.
(4) Subsections (1) to (3) do not require a change to be made in the amounts deductible or repayable under PAYE regulations during the period beginning on 6 April and ending on 17 May in the tax year.

---

[1] This comes from the FA 2016 s 3, which amended the Finance Act 2015 s 5(1)(b), which in turn is meant to amend the ITA 2007 s 35. Sometimes even Westlaw and Lexis cannot keep up.

(5) Before the start of the tax year the Treasury must make an order replacing the amount specified in section 35(1) with the amount which, as a result of this section, is the personal allowance for the tax year.

(6) For the purposes of this section, the "relevant national minimum wage", at any time, is—

(a) the hourly rate prescribed under section 3(2)(b) of the National Minimum Wage Act 1998 in relation to persons aged 21, or

(b) if no hourly rate is so prescribed in relation to such persons, the single hourly rate prescribed under section 1(3) of that Act.

(7) For the purposes of this section, the yearly equivalent of the relevant national minimum wage at any time is the amount equal to – NMW × 30 × 52 where NMW is the relevant national minimum wage at that time.

NOTES AND QUESTIONS

1. ITA 2007 s 3 states that income tax applies to employment income, pensions, social security, and income from 'trading', property, savings and investment and other miscellaneous categories. Unlike National Insurance, its rates therefore apply to employees and the self-employed alike (but with many, many differences).

2. Together the FA 2017 and ITA 2007 require that people pay: (1) 0 per cent tax on earnings up to £11,500, (2) 20 per cent between £11,500 and £45,000, (3) 40 per cent between £45,000 and £150,000, (4) 45 per cent on earnings over £150,000.

3. Therefore, if you are an employee earning the 2017 UK median wage of £28,600, you would pay £3,420 in income tax (20 per cent on the £17,100 between £11,500 and £28,600). You also pay NICs (see below) of £2452.32 (12 per cent between £8,164 and £28,600). If you have no student loan deductions, this would mean your final yearly salary is £22,727.68. Why should an employer be allowed to advertise you get £28,600, when (ignoring other income) you really get £22,727.68?

4. Despite considerable limits, income tax remains 'progressive'. Value Added Tax, for example, is 'regressive': the greater burden of VAT falls on people who spend a higher proportion of their income on ordinary goods and services (as opposed to capital or financial products). But under ITA 2007, higher earners pay more, because it is generally thought that money for government, welfare, public infrastructure and services should come from people with the greatest ability to pay. Progressive income tax may also correct an unjust distribution of income produced by markets shaped through arbitrary bargaining power. Matters of justice are, of course, fiercely contested. Contrast JS Mill, *The Income and Property Tax* (1861) calling it 'graduated robbery', K Marx, *Critique of the Gotha Programme* (1875) 'from each according to their means, to each according to their needs', and J Rawls, *A Theory of Justice* (1971) chs 2 and 5: tax should ensure basic liberty and equal opportunity.

5. Although income tax is progressive, the top rate is a mere 45 per cent. From 1938 to 1984, with sur-tax it was never lower than 75 per cent. Similar to trade union membership, there is an obvious and logical mirror image with inequality. (See Figure 6.3.)

Figure 6.3 UK top rate of income tax and inequality 1900–2017

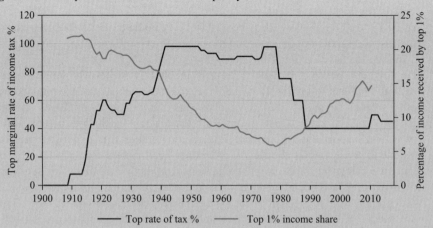

Source: T Piketty, Captial in the Twenty-First Century (2014) Technical Appendice, Table S9.2 and S14.1.

6. Very high earners cannot spend all of their income (they have a 'lower marginal propensity to consume' their income: see chaper 16(1)(a)). Hence, they save and invest money in capital assets such as houses, company shares or in managed funds. These assets generate more money in income, and also in rising asset values. Those 'capital gains' are subject to different, lower, rates in the Taxation of Chargeable Gains Act 1992, between 18 and 28 per cent. Why should wealthy asset owners pay less tax than working people?

7. Corporate income is also subject to different, lower rates of tax in the Corporation Tax Act 2010. The rates are either 19 per cent, or 30 per cent for companies with profits (not income, but profits after all wages and capital are paid) over £300,000. Why should multimillion- or multibillion-pound corporations pay less tax than working people?

8. The difference between income and corporate tax encouraged employees to incorporate a company through which they worked, solely to evade tax. The UK tax authorities issued a leaflet numbered 'IR35' (for Inland Revenue) in 2000 on how they would determine whether such a company was merely a sham. Now the Income Tax (Earnings and Pensions) Act 2003 ss 48–61 deem that there is employment, disregarding that someone's work is performed through an intermediary. See *HMRC v PA Holdings* [2011] EWCA Civ 1414.

9. Why are the tax rates set each year by a new Finance Act? Since the Magna Carta 1215 clause 12 and the Bill of Rights 1688 Art 4, there can be no taxation without Parliament. In light of the implied term of appropriation in chapter 5(1)(b), does this raise an inconsistency? The government cannot change the amount of money it takes, which is created by your labour, without an Act of Parliament. But an employer can take more by making you work harder or longer on the same wages. Is that just?

10. Since the FA 2015, the ITA 2007 s 57A has linked rises in the national minimum wage to the 'personal allowance', under which people do not pay income tax.

This seems laudable: should we make similar changes to NICs (below)? Also, why is the basis for a year's work calculated in s 57A(7) as the hourly wage, eg £7.83 × 30 × 52? How many people work 30 hours a week? Should we nevertheless take up the implication, and move to a three-day weekend? See chapter 7.

11. The Income Tax (Earnings and Pensions) Act 2003 contains the rules for taxing employment, pension and social security income. It covers who counts as resident and subject to tax (ss 14–41L). It says what counts as taxable pay and benefits, such as payments in kind, vouchers, accommodation, cars, loans or shares (ss 63–226E). It creates exemptions from tax for benefits such as certain limited types of transport, education, recreation, moving homes, bridging loans, pensions, redundancy payments, child care, and some health costs (ss 227–326B). Then there are categories of allowable deductions from tax (ie a stated sum in employment earnings is reduced by the item, so reducing the amount of income liable for tax) such as limited types of travel for the purpose of business (ss 327–85). There are special rules for pension, share and social security income (ss 386–681), and finally how the Pay As You Earn system should be administered by HMRC and employers. For detail, see G Loutzenhiser, *Revenue Law* (8th edn 2016) chs 7–18. Why do you think tax law is so voluminous and written with so many exceptions?

12. The Income Tax (Trading and Other Income) Act 2005 concerns trading, property, savings and other income. This, therefore, contains alternative rules for self-employed people. Unlike employees, who get taxed on everything but can get exemptions or deductions, traders get taxed on 'profits' (s 5), which does not include the trader's expenses and allowable deductions. These appear considerably more generous than the tax exemptions for employees, perhaps because it is often thought desirable that entrepreneurs should be encouraged to take on risk, to innovate and develop new businesses. See G Loutzenhiser, *Revenue Law* (8th edn 2016) chs 19–24. Is this fair?

(b) National Insurance Contributions

National Insurance Contributions pay for the state pension, unemployment, incapacity, parental, bereavement and insolvency insurance. The 'National Insurance Fund' is legally separate from the government's 'Consolidated Fund', which comes from tax receipts. But everything is spent by government in each year's budget. There is not a 'fund' of money as such, which is invested, like the 'sovereign wealth funds' of other countries. This legal (if somewhat unreal) separation has existed since the National Insurance Act 1911. But to most people NICs appear simply as another income tax, with a slightly different basis of calculation.

Social Security Contributions and Benefits Act 1992 ss 1, 8–15

1. Outline of contributory system.
  (1) The funds required—
    (a) for paying such benefits under this Act or any other Act as are payable out of the National Insurance Fund and not out of other public money; and

(b) for the making of payments under section 162 of the Administration Act towards the cost of the National Health Service,

shall be provided by means of contributions payable to the Inland Revenue by earners, employers and others, together with the additions under subsection (5) below and amounts payable under section 2 of the Social Security Act 1993.

(2) Contributions under this Part of this Act shall be of the following classes—

(a) Class 1, earnings-related, payable under section 6 below, being—
   (i) primary Class 1 contributions from employed earners; and
   (ii) secondary Class 1 contributions from employers and other persons paying earnings;

(b) Class 1A, payable under section 10 below by persons liable to pay secondary Class 1 contributions and certain other persons;

(bb) Class 1B, payable under section 10A below by persons who are accountable to the Inland Revenue in respect of income tax on general earnings in accordance with a PAYE settlement agreement;

(c) Class 2, flat-rate, payable under section 11 below by self-employed earners;

(d) Class 3, payable under section 13 or 13A below by earners and others voluntarily with a view to providing entitlement to benefit, or making up entitlement;

(da) Class 3A, payable by eligible people voluntarily under section 14A with a view to obtaining units of additional pension; and

(e) Class 4, payable under section 15 below in respect of the profits or gains of a trade, profession or vocation, or under section 18 below in respect of equivalent earnings.

...

8. Calculation of primary Class 1 contributions ...

(2) For the purposes of this Act—

(a) the main primary percentage is 12 per cent; and
(b) the additional primary percentage is 2 per cent;

but the main primary percentage is subject to alteration under sections 143 and 145 of the Administration Act.

...

9. Calculation of secondary Class 1 contributions ...

(2) For the purposes of this Act the secondary percentage is 13.8 per cent; but that percentage is subject to alteration under sections 143 and 145 of the Administration Act.

...

15. Class 4 contributions recoverable under the Income Tax Acts

(3ZA) For the purposes of this Act—

(a) the main Class 4 percentage is 9 per cent; and
(b) the additional Class 4 percentage is 2 per cent;

NOTES AND QUESTIONS

1. An employee (class 1) contributes 12 per cent NICs for earnings of £157 to £866 a week (£8,164 to £45,032 pa in 2017). If you earn over £866 a week, you pay 14 per cent (s 8).

2. An employer contributes 13.8 per cent NICs for earnings over £157 a week (s 9). If the employee is an apprentice or under 21, the employer pays nothing unless the employee earns over £866 per week.

3. If someone is self-employed (class 4), they contribute 9 per cent NICs or 11 per cent for higher earners (s 15). Any contracting party pays nothing.

This means there is a 3 per cent incentive for the labourer to be classified as self-employed. But an employer has a 13.8 per cent incentive to classify their staff as self-employed. If you earn £28,600 a year, that means you pay NICs of £1839.24 instead of £2452.32 (9 per cent instead of 12 per cent of your pay between £8,164 and £28,600), while a contractor (who may in reality be an employer) saves £2820.19 each year.

4.   For example, if drivers for the tech taxi employer Uber earn the median salary, and Uber (if its claims are genuine) has 40,000 drivers in London, it could be evading as much as £112,806,720 per year in NICs alone. What pressures do you think exist against HMRC cracking down on tax evasion? See E McGaughey, 'Uber, the Taylor Review, Mutuality and the Duty to not Misrepresent Rights' (2018) *Industrial Law Journal* (forthcoming).

5.   Should employee and self-employed NICs be the same? If so, do you put self-employed contributions up, or employee contributions down? Do you change the employer contributions at all? What are the implications of each choice?

6.   In *Young and Woods Ltd v West* [1980] EWCA Civ 6, Mr West claimed unfair dismissal as a sheet metal employee, even though he had willingly agreed with Young and Woods Ltd to be classified as self-employed in his contract, to pay less tax. Stephenson LJ held that this could not change Mr West's classification: if needed, the position on tax could be rectified after a judgment on entitlement to statutory rights. As a matter of public policy, neither could be contracted out of. The definition of an 'employee' for tax purposes was to be the same as an 'employee' for the purpose of rights.

7.   D Ariely, 'How Honest People Cheat' [February 2008] *Harvard Business Review* 24, performed a behavioural experiment where he asked people to perform a maths problem, and then report what their own grades were. One group were asked to recall the Ten Commandments before reporting their scores, and a second group were not. The group which recalled the Commandments did not cheat at all. The others did. Does this explain the effectiveness of making people swear to tell the truth before giving evidence in court? Should the law require employers or companies to do this (or something similar) before filing their tax returns?

(4) OCCUPATIONAL PENSIONS

While NICs give people the right to a basic state pension, this is very low. The original model in the Old-Age Pensions Act 1908 was a flat-rate state pension: people might pay in different amounts, but everyone got the same pension. Even after Sir William Beveridge's Report, *Social Insurance and Allied Services* (1942) Cmnd 6404, the state pension system remained a minimum floor through which nobody was meant to fall. The rights to a state pension are in the Social Security Contributions and Benefits Act 1992 ss 43–55C and Sch 3, para 5. In 2017, for someone who meets the minimum qualifications it was £122.30 a week (£6359.60 a year). By contrast, France, Germany, Italy and others created state pensions that would replace, say, two-thirds of pre-retirement income. Some countries, such as Belgium, Denmark, or Sweden, have a mix of a minimum floor system and income replacement up to a low cap.

In the UK, and countries like it (eg Australia, Canada, the Netherlands or the United States), people must have separate pensions, beyond the state pension, to maintain their living standards in retirement. The state, occupational and private pensions are usually called the 'three pillars' of the pension system. Private savings are regulated by ordinary laws on banking and financial products. But occupational pensions, which are linked to the employment relationship, are crucial for labour law. Vast sums of money in occupational pension funds are invested in stock markets. Employees saving for retirement are together the ultimate, beneficial owners of billions of company shares, often including shares in their own companies. This means big potential for the way that corporations are managed, if workers can exercise voice through their capital. This section outlines (a) the right to an occupational pension, and (b) the governance of funds.

(a) Right to an Occupational Pension

Before 2008, there was no right to an occupational pension. Individual contracts or, more often, collective agreements created them. These agreements usually said employees would contribute a percentage of wages to the workplace or industry pension fund, and the employer would 'match' the contribution. Like in National Insurance, a separate entry for 'employee' and 'employer' contributions is accounting hocus-pocus: all contributions are paid for by employees through their work. What matters (except in rare insolvency cases: see chapter 20) is the combined contribution. For example, in 2017 the Universities Superannuation Scheme 'employee' contribution was 8 per cent of salary, and 'employer' contribution was 18 per cent, so 26 per cent of salary in total. Under the Pensions Act (PA) 2008 scheme there will be 5 per cent employee and 3 per cent employer contributions, so 8 per cent of salary from April 2019 (implementation was delayed by the Coalition government).

Another change is that most employers have stopped promising a 'defined benefit' (DB), typically based on an employee's final salary, from retirement to death. For instance, your salary might have been £28,600 at retirement, and your pension promised you 50 per cent of your final salary (£14,300) until death (on top of your state pension). The risk of employees living longer falls on the employer. But in collective pensions, it is easy for an employer's actuaries to calculate the average life expectancy of the workforce: some live longer than expected, some shorter, so it averages out. Yet employers have largely closed DB schemes, and simply offer a fund to save in, which you get back on retirement. For example, imagine (and this is unrealistically simplified) you set aside 10 per cent of your £28,600 salary each year for 40 years of work. Therefore, over the years you saved 40 × £2860, or £114,400. Those were your contributions. Your fund (like in a DB scheme) would have been invested, and usually made money (8 per cent a year should be typical, but is rare). Let us say (again unrealistically simplified) the fund now totals £300,000. You expect to live to 85, 20 years more. You have £15,000 a year. If you live longer, you run out, and you have nothing but the state pension. But if you die quickly, your children or relatives inherit a windfall. The monetary incentive is to die quickly. Company boards and City asset managers have argued that DB pensions mean too much risk and have therefore pushed to shift that risk onto individual workers. However, the same asset managers sell annuity products: if you used your £300,000 on retirement to buy an annuity (for a significant fee) they will insure you have an income for life. In this way, asset managers have a systemic conflict of interest (see further chapter 11(3)). They exercise votes in companies, but also sell companies' products. See E McGaughey, 'Does Corporate Governance Exclude the ultimate Investor?' (2016) 16(1) *Journal of Corporate Law Studies* 221.

But for many people, an even bigger problem is their employers used to offer no occupational pension at all. This would mean retirees only had a minimum state pension (now £6359.60 a year). The PA 2008 began to change this: people are automatically enrolled in a 2 per cent contribution defined contribution scheme.

Pensions Act 2008 ss 1–20

1 Jobholders
(1) For the purposes of this Part a jobholder is a worker—
    (a) who is working or ordinarily works in Great Britain under the worker's contract,
    (b) who is aged at least 16 and under 75, and
    (c) to whom qualifying earnings are payable by the employer in the relevant pay reference period (see sections 13 and 15). ...
    ...

3 Automatic enrolment
(1) This section applies to a jobholder—
    (a) who is aged at least 22,
    (b) who has not reached pensionable age, and
    (c) to whom earnings of more than £10,000 are payable by the employer in the relevant pay reference period (see section 15).
(2) The employer must make prescribed arrangements by which the jobholder becomes an active member of an automatic enrolment scheme with effect from the automatic enrolment date.
(3) Subsection (2) does not apply if the jobholder was an active member of a qualifying scheme on the automatic enrolment date.
    ...

8 Jobholder's right to opt out
(1) This section applies on any occasion when arrangements under section 3(2), 5(2) or 7(3) apply to a jobholder (arrangements for the jobholder to become an active member of an automatic enrolment scheme).
(2) If the jobholder gives notice under this section—
    (a) the jobholder is to be treated for all purposes as not having become an active member of the scheme on that occasion ....
    ...

13 Qualifying earnings
(1) A person's qualifying earnings in a pay reference period of 12 months are the part (if any) of the gross earnings payable to that person in that period that is—
    (a) more than £5,876, and
    (b) not more than £45,000
    ...

20 Quality requirement: UK money purchase schemes
(1) A money purchase scheme that has its main administration in the United Kingdom satisfies the quality requirement in relation to a jobholder if under the scheme—
    (a) the jobholder's employer must pay contributions in respect of the jobholder;

(b)   the employer's contribution, however calculated, must be equal to or more than 3 per cent of the amount of the jobholder's qualifying earnings in the relevant pay reference period;

(c)   the total amount of contributions paid by the jobholder and the employer, however calculated, must be equal to or more than 8 per cent of the amount of the jobholder's qualifying earnings in the relevant pay reference period.

NOTES AND QUESTIONS

1.   PA 2008 requires every 'jobholder' (a 'worker', age 16–75, earning over £5,876) is automatically enrolled in a pension (ss 1–3, 13). But the jobholder may opt-out (s 8). The pension must at least be a defined contribution pension (also termed a 'money purchase scheme') with minimum contributions of 8 per cent of salary (section 20).

2.   Employers administer the scheme, but they have an easy public option pension and asset manager to send employee savings to: the National Employment Savings Trust (NEST), set up under ss 67–69 and Sch 1 (below). Employers can choose another private asset manager, but the intention of NEST was that it would be simple and effectively outcompete the private sector, whose high fees were less a product of effective competition, and more the inherent opacity, and confusing nature, of the market.

3.   The right to opt out of an auto-enrolled pension, and the conditions, are spelled out in the Occupational and Personal Pension Schemes (Automatic Enrolment) Regulations 2010/772. These Regulations were amended after the 2010 election to delay the implementation of the right to a pension, and phase in the contributions by employees and employers (SI 2012/1257). This meant retirement savings did not start building for millions of people for between 2 and 10 years – removing the right to an occupational for as much as a fifth of people's working lives.

4.   OECD, *Pensions at a Glance 2013: OECD and G20 Indicators* (2013) ch 8, 189, showed that the United States had a private pension coverage rate of 47.1 per cent, the UK 43.3 per cent, but Germany had 71.3 per cent (and an income-linked state pension). Auto-enrolment in the UK will significantly change this. Why should it have been delayed at all?

5.   Automatic enrolment in PA 2008 was seen as a major innovation, based on cutting-edge behavioural economics. For example, BC Madrian and DF Shea, 'The Power of Suggestion: Inertia in 401(k) Participation and Savings Behavior' (2001) 116(4) *Quarterly Journal of Economics* 1149, 1151, found in a study of 500 large US companies that when employees could choose to opt in to a pension, only 49 per cent did when they started a new job, but slowly 83 per cent opted in after 20 years worked. But when people were automatically enrolled, with a right to opt out, there was 86 per cent participation from the start. This suggests the power of switching the default rule. That is, 34 per cent of staff lost pension savings before realising the advantages. As human beings we have a behavioural bias for the status quo. In the United States, the Pension Protection Act of 2006 §902 explicitly enabled (but did not require) employers to have auto-enrolment schemes (it would seem this was legal anyway). The PA 2008 made auto-enrolment compulsory, with the opt-out.

6.   If pensions are important, why allow people to opt out at all? According to R Thaler and C Sunstein, *Nudge: Improving Decisions about Health, Wealth and*

Happiness (2008) ch 6, it is because we should value choice. The law should set default, not mandatory rules in all but the rarest cases of market failure: people should always be able to opt out. Scientific understanding of welfare maximisation should inform where default rules are set. The authors argue for opt-outs from all social security (the US equivalent of the state pension) and all labour rights. Thaler and Sunstein call this theory 'libertarian paternalism', and say it has the potential to bridge the political gap between American liberals and conservatives. Is that political aspiration realistic? In any event, would the right to opt out not lead in effect to the abolition of the right, because people are pressured by unequal distribution of wealth, to choose what employers want? On the opt out from the 48-hour week, see chapter 7(2)(b).

7.   Although it is correct, economically, to see 'employee' and 'employer' contributions as economically indistinct (because a rational employer will change the wage rates to reflect mandated benefits), one virtue is that (as with paid holidays) the employer does not typically include their pension contributions in the advertised wage.

8.   Before 1990, it was normal for men and women to have different retirement ages: women usually retired at 60, and men at 65. This was direct sex discrimination, present in the state pension, but also in most occupational pension plans. *Barber v Guardian Royal Exchange Assurance Group* (1990) C-262/88 held that under that different retirement ages for occupational pensions between men and women violated (what is now) the Treaty on the Functioning of the European Union Art 157. An occupational pension was 'pay', and there must be equal pay.

9.   A large portion of money saved in pensions goes into the stock market. When collective bargaining was strong, the share of pension money as the total of investments was rising considerably. That changed by the early 1990s, as shown in Figure 6.4.

Figure 6.4 UK share ownership 1963 to 2008

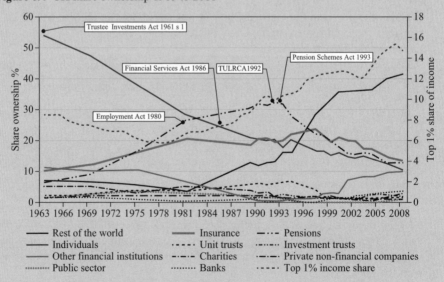

Sources: ONS (2008) and Piketty (2014).

10. Figure 6.4 shows that pensions were steadily rising as a percentage of ownership of all shares up to 1992. Individual ownership of shares was in terminal decline as shareholding became more institutionalised. From 1982, the ownership of UK shares by the rest of the world climbed, and then soared after 1994. Most of this money is pension funds, and other investment funds, from North America and Europe. Life insurance policies have been relatively stable. 'Other financial institutions' include managed or mutual funds, such as open-ended investment companies, bought by wealthier people but also pension funds and asset managers. What do you think explains the relative fall of pension funds' share?

(b) Governance

Who should govern pension funds? When dozens or thousands of employees have contributed their money to a collective occupational pension fund, that money should be invested, and generate a return over time, not dwindle away at the rate of inflation. Pension funds invest in a diversified portfolio (see Trustee Act 2000 s 3) of company shares, corporate bonds, government bonds (called 'gilts' in the UK), mutual funds (listed in the back pages of the *Financial Times*), or in derivative products (futures, options, swaps, etc). Big occupational pension funds (such as the Universities Superannuation Scheme, RPMI Railpen or the BT Pension Scheme) have considerable advantages. They can easily diversify their investments to reduce risk. They can concentrate investments in companies and actively engage in corporate governance. The bigger the pension fund, the more bargaining power they have in negotiating asset manager fees.

Big pension funds could also (if they chose) take all investment decision-making in-house, rather than pay fees to asset managers (eg JP Morgan, Legal & General, BlackRock, Fidelity) to manage investments for them. Asset managers often aim for percentage fees, which can be astronomical over time: a 1.5 per cent yearly fee over 40 years cuts retirement savings by 35 per cent. Imagine a worker on the median UK salary, £28,600, saving 10 per cent of salary or £2860 every year for 40 years. Ignore inflation, changing pay and volatile investment markets. Imagine the worker's fund gets a stable 8 per cent a year return. If there are no fees, the fund will accumulate £800,173 after 40 years. If there is a 1.5 per cent fee on the fund each year, the result will be £518,297. That is, 35.3 per cent vanishes into the City of London (multiply that by every worker who is saving money). For comparison, if the fee is 0.5 per cent, 13.7 per cent of the fund will be eliminated. Should the law require fixed, not percentage-based fees?

Because of these sums, it is often doubted that asset managers generate any meaningful return for their services. This makes pension governance incredibly important. Employing entities may provide or pay for the necessary expertise in setting up pension schemes. But it is questionable whether the vast sums of money spent on financial management are necessary. This is discussed further in chapter 11(3) on 'Votes at work'.

S Webb, 'The Economic Theory of a Legal Minimum Wage' (1912) 20(10)
Journal of Political Economy **973**
Webb argues that a minimum wage, against predictions of disaster and the charge that it
was like wage fixing under the Statute of Labourers, has clear economic benefits. It does
not stop productive competition between employers and among skilled workers. 'All that
it does is to transfer the pressure from one element in the bargain to the other: from the
wage to the work, from price to quality.' Higher wages will also encourage more skilled
people to look for work. Webb concludes by saying, prophetically: 'We may expect to
find all the conditions of employment – wages not excluded – one by one authoritatively
upheld by definite Legal Minima, not in this or that trade only, but in every industry; not
in this or that country alone, but gradually throughout the civilized world.'

D Card and AB Krueger, *Myth and Measurement: The New Economics of the*
Minimum Wage **(1995)**
Card and Krueger argue that, unlike the claims by Friedman and others, the minimum
wage can increase employment. In the United States, where the federal government sets a
nationwide minimum but states and cities can go higher, the authors conducted a study in
1992 on fast food restaurants after New Jersey increased its wage. They found an increase
in employment, controlled by comparison to eastern Pennsylvania: there the same economic conditions held, but there was no minimum wage increase, nor an increase in
levels of employment. Employment growth was higher at restaurants that were forced to
increase their wages, rather than restaurants that already paid the new minimum wage.

G Davidov, 'A Purposive Approach to the National Minimum Wage Act' (2009)
72 *MLR* 581
Davidov argues, consistent with his other work on the purposive approach to labour law,
that minimum wages can be seen as pursuing twin aims of a fair distribution of wealth
or to protect workers' dignity. In the debate about redistribution, Davidov discusses the
literature alleging that minimum wages raises unemployment, and endorses the view that
while the 'debate continues', there is no credible empirical evidence to suggest this is
true. On dignity, Davidov suggests that the goal of preventing unfair competition may be
seen as a sub-goal of enabling people to lead fulfilling lives, and not be treated as commodities. These goals suggest that the broadest possible interpretation for the scope of
minimum wage protection should be applied, making cases such as *Edmonds v Lawson*
QC open to question.

E Albin, 'A Worker-Employer-Customer Triangle: The Case of Tips' (2011)
40 *ILJ* 181
Albin argues that systems where workers rely on tips entail a 'distribution of employing
functions to the customer' which can exacerbate the precarious nature of work. While
wages depend on a customer's discretionary act of generosity, workers are coerced into
adopting 'specific behaviours to please customers and fulfil their wishes' and also hope
a 'good word' will be said to the employer. This can further lead to '"emotional labour"
and 'aesthetic labour', as well as to illegal behaviours of customers, such as sexual

harassment'. After the law changed, so that employers could not subsidise their payment of the minimum wage with tips, Albin suggests that the culture in the worker–employer–customer triangle might change so that waiters feel less forced to please customers in a forced and exploitative way.

L Bebchuk, JM Fried and DI Walker, 'Managerial Power and Rent Extraction in the Design of Executive Compensation' (2002) 69 *University of Chicago Law Review* **751**

The authors argue that because boards of directors pay other members on the board, and that there is no serious arm's-length relationship, corporate executives are able to extract unjustified pay from companies. Their wages become illegitimate 'rents' and the design of executive compensation is corrupt.

7

Working Time
and Child Care

One of labour law's oldest aims is to be free from being subordinated to other people. Partly, this has meant reducing working time: to pursue leisure, have a family, or play an active role in society. The International Labour Organization's first Convention, the Hours of Work (Industry) Convention 1919, Art 2, urged a 48-hour limit on the working week, and 9 hours in any day. An entire era of jurisprudence in the United States was defined when its Supreme Court held that a limit to the working day for bakers was unconstitutional (*Lochner v New York*, 198 US 45 (1905)). A constitutional principle of 'freedom of contract', supposedly derived from the 14th Amendment, remained until 1937. Yet early-twentieth-century collective bargaining brought completely new words and concepts into most people's lives: a 'weekend' consisting of two days (not just the Sabbath), 'retirement' in old age, and 'childhood' for everyone. The late twentieth century brought parental leave, led again by collective bargains that were gradually codified into statute. While chapter 6(4) considered retirement, and while education is outside this book's scope, this chapter focuses on regulation (1) to reduce days, (2) to reduce hours, and (3) to give time off for child care, and (4) the right to request flexible work. That is, more freedom, with a just income.

The essential policy debate that runs through this chapter is between those who oppose working time regulation on the ground that it restricts people's formal freedom, and those who see it as an essential element for human development, which expands freedom itself. These positions, respectively, would encourage a narrow or a broad construction of the law. The great economist, John Maynard Keynes wrote in *The Economic Possibilities of our Grandchildren* (1930) that we could 'make what work there is still to be done to be as widely shared as possible' and with increasing productivity have a 15-hour week by 2030. Although productivity has increased, working hours stopped falling around 1980, and for some people hours have been rising even though the population is more productive. This makes the interpretation of the law's minimum standards all the more important, as well as careful thought about the mechanisms to ensure fair working time within law's limits.

Introductory text: Collins ch 4 (91–94). CEM chs 8, 10. D&M chs 4, 6 (332–48, 737–51).

(1) DAYS

Under the Universal Declaration of Human Rights 1948 Art 24, 'Everyone has the right to rest and leisure, including reasonable limitation of working hours and periodic holidays with pay.' Going further, the European Social Charter 1961 Art 2 required 'the working week to be progressively reduced to the extent that the increase of productivity and other relevant factors permit'. The UK had a series of regulations starting from the Factory Act 1833 to limit working during the nineteenth century. Collective agreements have always gone beyond the minima. The first general regulation was enacted in 1993, now recast in the Working Time Directive (WTD) 2003. This was passed under the Treaty on the Functioning of the European Union Art 153(1)(a), ostensibly as a 'health and safety' measure. Its most debated provisions concern working hours, but by far its most successful – and ubiquitously popular – provisions concern holidays.

(a) What Are Holidays?

The WTD 2003 Art 7 requires that 'every worker' has 'at least four weeks' paid holidays each year. This is confusingly expressed as 5.6 weeks in the Working Time Regulations (WTR) 1998, regs 13 and 13A, because a 'week' was originally interpreted to refer to a 5-day work week. The UK tried to confer only 4 of these 'weeks' (i.e. 20 days paid holiday) on workers (leaving ambiguity over traditional days, New Year, bank holidays, etc). This was not sufficient to comply with the Directive. The Directive means a total of 28 days. The amendment came through SI 2007/2079 regulation 2, but it did not clarify that a 'week' is 7 days: instead it said workers had 5.6 'weeks' (i.e. 5.6 × 5 days = 28) in holidays. The UK government escaped being sued: under *Francovich v Italy* (1991) C-6/90, failure to properly implement a Directive leads to liability of the Member State, unless the words of national law can be interpreted in line with the Directive: *Marleasing SA v La Comercial Internacional de Alimentacion SA* (1990) C-106/89. But if the number of weeks is given, what counts towards holiday pay?

Russell v Transocean International Resources Ltd [2011] UKSC 57

Mr Russell, and his co-workers on an oil and gas rig on the UK continental shelf near Aberdeen, claimed that paid annual leave should reflect the time spent onshore under WTD 2003 Art 7 and WTR 1998 reg 13. Most worked two weeks offshore, and then had two weeks onshore as a 'field break'. During this time they did little work, except for 'training courses, appraisals, grievance and disciplinary hearings, medical assessments and offshore survival courses'. While offshore, they did 12-hour shifts every day. If the time onshore counted as work, their holiday pay would double. The employers argued the field breaks counted as leave, not working, and should not add to the accumulation of paid holidays. The House of Lords held that the time onshore was not work, and did not count toward holiday pay.

Lord Hope:

34. I do not think that is right to describe the contract in this case, as Mr Linden sought to do, as a 26 week contract. The fact is that the appellants were under contract with their employers for the whole of each year. Their working pattern was organised in such a way that working time was limited to the 26 weeks when they were offshore. But their contractual relationship with their employers continued irrespective of where they were at any given time. They had continuity of employment throughout the year. The fact that their pattern of working was a repeating shift pattern was a product of that contractual relationship.

35. The critical question is how that repeating shift pattern falls to be viewed for the purposes of the WTD. How is it to be determined whether the rules that it lays down for what recital 5 of the preamble refers to as daily, weekly and annual periods of rest are satisfied?

36. … the ECJ has not said that a pre-ordained rest period, when the worker is free from all obligations to the employer, can never constitute annual leave within the meaning of that article. I would hold therefore that "rest period" simply means any period which is not working time: see article 2. "Any period" includes every such period irrespective of where the worker is at that time and what he is doing, so long as it is a period when he is not working. I think it is plain that any period when the appellants are on field break onshore will fall into that category.
    …

39. Attention was drawn in the course of the argument to two other problem cases which it was said might give rise to difficulty. The first was the case of teachers, already mentioned by the employment tribunal, who are required to take their annual leave during non-term time. Various other cases fall into this category, such as professional footballers, staff who work in the devolved legislatures such as the Scottish Parliament and in the Parliament at Westminster and people who work full-time during the season in the tourist industry. They are people who are left, for the most part, with no option but to take their paid annual leave during periods when they are not required to work. But the problem in their case disappears if, as I would hold, there is no objection to their being required to take their annual leave during those periods.

40. The other problem was referred to as the Saturday problem, which is illustrated by the case of *Sumsion*. It was said to arise from the ability of employers under regulation 15 of the WTR to designate days within the week when the worker would not otherwise be working as annual leave. Carried to its extreme this could result in workers who worked a five day week, Sundays being treated as the weekly rest period, being required to take their annual leave each Saturday. This would exhaust the possibility of there ever being whole weeks in the year when annual leave could be taken. A literal reading of the employer's rights under regulation 15(2) suggests that this course might be open to him. It would obviously be an abuse of the system as the EAT indicated in *Sumsion v BBC (Scotland)* [2007] IRLR 678, para 26. But the suggestion was that it was an abuse which could not be prevented.

41. This raises a different problem from that which arises in the case of the offshore workers. The question is not whether a worker can be required to take annual leave during a period when he would not otherwise have been working but whether the worker can be forced to take his entitlement to annual leave in periods which are shorter than one week. But it is not

a problem that has to be answered in this case. There seems to me to be much to be said for the view that, when article 7 of the WTD is read together with the purposes identified in the preamble and in the light of what the ECJ said in *Gomez* [2005] ICR 1040, para 30, the entitlement is to periods of annual leave measured in weeks, not days. The worker can opt to take all or part of it in days, if he chooses to do so. But the employer cannot force him to do so. But I do not need to reach a concluded view on this point, and I have not done so.

...

43. I am not persuaded that a reference is necessary in this case on any of the questions that have been listed. We must be mindful of our responsibility as a court against whose decisions there is no judicial remedy under national law. But the ruling in *Srl CILFIT v Ministry of Health* (Case 283/81) [1982] ECR 3415 permits us to decline to make a reference if a decision on the point is not necessary to enable the court to give judgment or the answer to the question is *acte clair*. I do not think that the meaning to be given to article 7, for the purposes of this judgment, is open to any reasonable doubt. The wording and structure of the WTD plainly favours the respondents' argument, and I can find nothing in any of the judgments of the ECJ to which we were referred that casts doubt on the meaning which I think should be given to it. I would refuse the request for a reference.

Lord Brown, **Lord Mance**, **Lord Kerr**, and **Lord Wilson** concurred.

NOTES AND QUESTIONS

1. The Supreme Court held, perhaps not surprisingly, that time spent onshore did not count as working time that had to be counted when calculating the amount of annual leave. It thought this interpretation was 'plain', or *acte clair*, and did not make a preliminary reference to the CJEU to confirm the decision.
2. Historically, there has been no general Act for UK holidays, except legislation such as the Shops Act 1950, which used to limit working on Sundays. The Sunday Trading Act 1994 allowed shop opening on Sundays, but workers could theoretically refuse to work: the Employment Rights Act (ERA) 1996 section 101 makes refusal by shop workers to work Sundays unfair unless they have opted out of the right under section 41.
3. An interesting point of Lord Hope's at [41], though he did not 'reach a concluded view', is that the right to leave is for 'weeks, not days'. This suggests that *Sumison v BBC* [2008] IRLR 678 was wrongly decided. Here, Smith J in the Employment Appeal Tribunal held that the BBC's requirement of a carpenter to take holidays every second Saturday was not unlawful. Mr Sumison was paid £1200 for a six-day week on a 24-week contract. *Russell* suggests that in fact he should have been able to take a week at a time if he chose.
4. In *R (BECTU) v Department of Trade and Industry* (2001) C-173/99, the CJEU held that a 13-week qualifying period for paid annual leave, which the UK's Regulations had contained, was 'manifestly incompatible' with the Directive. This opened the UK government to a damages action under the principle that failure to properly implement a Directive in national law by the expiry date, if it leads to loss, must be compensated by the state: *Francovich v Italy* (1991) C-6/90. In effect, corporations or employers are shielded from liability by the geometric theory that Directives have 'vertical' but not 'horizontal direct effect'. In most cases

this shifts losses from big businesses who find it more convenient not to comply with EU law, onto taxpayers. Does this make sense?

5. In *Dominguez v CICOA* (2012) C-282/10, the CJEU similarly found that a one-month qualifying period in the French Code du travail, L.223-2, for holiday pay in the event that someone was ill for a year was incompatible with the WTD 2003. Fortunately for the French government, the CJEU advised that L.223-4, which defined a work-related absence, could be interpreted to include Ms Dominguez's case because she was injured on her way to work. Thus, under the principle of *Marleasing SA v La Comercial SA* (1990) C-106/89, which requires courts to interpret the words of national laws as far as they can be to achieve compliance with the Directive, the employer could be found liable.

6. The bar on 'horizontal' direct effect was developed by the CJEU in *Marshall v Southampton and South West Hampshire AHA* (1986) C-152/84. This involved Ms Marshall's sex discrimination claim against her NHS employer. In *Marshall (No 2)* (1993) C-271/91, Advocate General van Gerven launched the first of a series of attacks on the rule. In essence the position of the Court of Justice today is that a court must do everything that it can to interpret national law in line with the Directive, and if the state or any emanation of the state is a litigant it must follow the Directive (ie it has 'vertical' effect). However, the court is itself the one state institution that is not bound to apply EU law, and may prefer national law. This exception is arbitrary. *Every* enforcement of a private right is a 'vertical' issue: the very distinction is intellectually indefensible. The consequence, in most labour cases, is to shield businesses from EU rights: an unjustifiable privilege that has no basis in European Treaties. See further P Craig, 'The Legal Effect of Directives: Policy, Rules and Exceptions' [2009] *European Law Review* 349.

7. Can time taken off as sick leave diminish the right to paid holidays?

Stringer v Her Majesty's Revenue and Customs (2009) C-520/06

Ms Stringer and other workers claimed damages from HMRC for holiday pay on the ground that times when they were absent for illness could not subtract from their holidays. The claim was brought under WTR 1998 regs 14–16 and ERA 1996 ss 13 and 23 (to claim for wage deductions, a three-month limitation period). In the Court of Justice, the case was joined to *Schultz-Hoff v Deutsche Rentenversicherung Bund*, where Mr Schultz-Hoff claimed he was entitled to damages for unpaid annual leave for a year in which he was on sick leave from the German Pension Insurance Association due to his long-term disability. On preliminary references, the Court of Justice held that time off taken as sick leave, or for illness, was not holiday.

Grand Chamber:

25. It is common ground that the purpose of the entitlement to paid annual leave is to enable the worker to rest and to enjoy a period of relaxation and leisure. The purpose of the entitlement to sick leave is different. It is given to the worker so that he can recover from being ill.

26. The Court has already held that a period of leave guaranteed by Community law cannot affect the right to take another period of leave guaranteed by that law (see *Merino Gómez,*

paragraphs 32 and 33; Case C-519/03 *Commission v Luxembourg* [2005] ECR I-3067, paragraph 33; and Case C-116/06 *Kiiski* [2007] ECR I-7643, paragraph 56). In the case, in particular, of *Merino Gómez*, the Court held that Article 7(1) of Directive 93/104 must be interpreted as meaning that, where the dates of a worker's maternity leave coincide with those of the general annual leave fixed, by a collective agreement, for the entire workforce, the requirements of that directive relating to paid annual leave cannot be regarded as met.

27. However, by contrast with the rights to maternity leave or parental leave at issue in the case-law cited in the previous paragraph, the right to sick leave and the conditions for exercise of that right are not, as Community law now stands, governed by that law. In addition, the interpretation of Article 7(1) of Directive 93/104 in *Merino Gómez* was necessary, in the light of the other Community directives at issue in that case, in order to guarantee observance of the rights connected with the employment contract of a worker in the event of maternity leave.

28. With regard to the right to paid annual leave, as is clear from the terms of Directive 2003/88 and the case-law of the Court, it is for the Member States to lay down, in their domestic legislation, conditions for the exercise and implementation of that right, by prescribing the specific circumstances in which workers may exercise the right, without making the very existence of that right, which derives directly from Directive 93/104, subject to any preconditions whatsoever (see, to that effect, *BECTU*, paragraph 53).

29. It follows, in those circumstances, on the one hand, that Article 7(1) of Directive 2003/88 does not, as a rule, preclude national legislation or practices according to which a worker on sick leave is not entitled to take paid annual leave during that sick leave, provided however that the worker in question has the opportunity to exercise the right conferred by that directive during another period.

    …

33. … to the extent that it relates to the right to leave and not to the allowance in lieu of paid annual leave not taken, referred in Case C-350/06, the [German] court asks, essentially, whether Article 7(1) of Directive 2003/88 must be interpreted as precluding national legislation or practices according to which the entitlement to paid annual leave is extinguished at the end of the leave year and/or of a carry-over period laid down by national law even where the worker has been on sick leave for the whole or part of the leave year and where his incapacity to work persisted until the end of his employment relationship.

    …

37. As a preliminary point, it should be noted that, according to recital 6 in the preamble, Directive 2003/88 has taken account of the principles of the International Labour Organisation with regard to the organisation of working time.

38. In that regard, under Article 5(4) of Convention No 132 of the International Labour Organisation of 24 June 1970 concerning Annual Holidays with Pay (Revised), '… absence from work for such reasons beyond the control of the employed person concerned as illness, … shall be counted as part of the period of service'.

    …

41. It follows that, with regard to workers on sick leave which has been duly granted, the right to paid annual leave conferred by Directive 2003/88 itself on all workers (BECTU, paragraphs 52 and 53) cannot be made subject by a Member State to a condition concerning the obligation actually to have worked during the leave year laid down by that State.

42. A provision of national law setting out a carry-over period for annual leave not taken by the end of the leave year aims, as a rule, to give a worker who has been prevented from taking his annual leave an additional opportunity to benefit from that leave. The laying down of such a period forms part of the conditions for the exercise and implementation of the right to paid annual leave and therefore falls, as a rule, within the competence of the Member States.

43. It follows that Article 7(1) of Directive 2003/88 does not preclude, as a rule, national legislation which lays down conditions for the exercise of the right to paid annual leave expressly conferred by the directive, including even the loss of that right at the end of a leave year or of a carry-over period, provided, however, that the worker who has lost his right to paid annual leave has actually had the opportunity to exercise the right conferred on him by the directive.

44. It must therefore be held that a worker, who, like the appellant in the main proceedings in Case C-350/06 in relation to the year 2005, is on sick leave for the whole leave year and beyond the carry-over period laid down by national law, is denied any period giving the opportunity to benefit from his paid annual leave.

…

48. It follows that if, under the case-law cited in the previous paragraphs, the right to paid annual leave guaranteed to the worker by Article 7(1) of Directive 2003/88 may not be undermined by provisions of national law which exclude the creation or existence of that right, a different result cannot be allowed in relation to provisions of national law which provide for the loss of that right, in the case of a worker on sick leave for the whole leave year and/or beyond a carry-over period, such as Mr Schultz-Hoff, who has not been able to exercise his right to paid annual leave. As in the circumstances in BECTU, where the Court held that the Member States could not exclude the existence of the right to paid annual leave, in a situation such as that of Mr Schultz-Hoff the Member States may not provide for the loss of that right.

President Skouris, Jann J, Timmermans J, Rosas J, Lenaerts J, Caoimh J, Schiemann J, Makarczyk J, Kūris J, Juhász J, Arestis J, Levits J and **Bay Larsen J.**

NOTES AND QUESTIONS

1. The Court of Justice reasons, on the basis of the ILO Holidays with Pay Convention 1970, that time spent ill cannot be counted as consuming time for holidays because 'sick leave is different' to 'rest and to enjoy a period of relaxation and leisure'. It is possible to prevent the paid leave being used during the time of a long-term illness, but national law cannot allow 'the loss of that right' at the end of the year.
2. *Pereda v Madrid Movilidad* (2009) C-277/08, [19] said national law could allow 'conditions for the exercise of the right to paid annual leave … including even the loss of that right at the end of a leave year or of a carry-over period, provided, however, that the worker who has lost his right to paid annual leave has actually had the opportunity to exercise that right'.
3. However, *KHS AG v Schulte* (2011) C-214/10 found that a limit, from a collective agreement, of 15 months to use paid leave was acceptable. The Grand Chamber of the Court of Justice reasoned at [30] and [33] that 'a worker who is unfit for work several consecutive years … cannot have the right to accumulate,

without any limit, entitlement to paid annual leave'. Beyond 'a certain temporal limit' holiday pay 'ceases to have its positive effect for the worker as a rest period and is merely a period of relaxation and leisure'. This meant that Mr Schulte, a locksmith who could no longer work after a heart attack in 2002, was unable to claim holiday pay for 2006 to 2008, when his employment relationship ended. At [41] the Court of Justice mentioned that the Holidays with Pay Convention 1970 Art 9(1) states holidays must be taken within 18 months. Why, then, was 18 months not the appropriate limit?

4. In *NHS Leeds v Larner* [2012] EWCA Civ 1034 the Court of Appeal upheld a decision by Bean J that it was not necessary that an employee needed to make a request for annual leave for the right to be carried over to the following year. This was because 'she had that right ... [for annual leave] without having to make a formal request for the leave to be carried over'. The employer was not allowed to add conditions.

(b) Level of Pay

How much should workers be paid for annual leave? Two questions have recurred in cases: (i) could employers state that the ordinary wage included, for example, '12.5 per cent holiday pay' on the payslip? (ii) When calculating holiday pay, to what extent would employers have to take into account variable elements of a worker's previous wages?

Robinson-Steele v RD Retail Services Ltd (2006) C-131/04

In three joined appeals, employees claimed that their employers' practice of giving 'rolled up holiday pay' was contrary to the proper interpretation of the WTD 2003 Art 7. Mr Robinson-Steele, who fitted shops and stacked shelves, had a contract stating he was paid 'in addition' holiday pay of 8.33 per cent. Mr Clarke, a brick cutter, was told holiday 'pay is included within the daily rate'. Mr Caulfield was told, under a collective agreement, his pay would 'include 13.36% holiday pay'. Given conflicting decisions in UK courts, the Court of Appeal referred to the European Court of Justice on the proper interpretation.

First Chamber:

47. ... the Court of Appeal is asking, in essence, whether Article 7 of the directive precludes part of the remuneration payable to a worker for work done from being attributed to payment for annual leave without the worker receiving, in that respect, a payment additional to that for work done.

48. In that regard, it must be recalled that the entitlement of every worker to paid annual leave must be regarded as a particularly important principle of Community social law from which there can be no derogations and whose implementation by the competent national authorities must be confined within the limits expressly laid down by the directive itself (see Case C-173/99 *BECTU* [2001] ECR I-4881, paragraph 43).

49. The holiday pay required by Article 7(1) of the directive is intended to enable the worker actually to take the leave to which he is entitled.

50. The term "paid annual leave" in that provision means that, for the duration of annual leave within the meaning of the directive, remuneration must be maintained. In other words, workers must receive their normal remuneration for that period of rest.

51. In those circumstances, it must be held that an agreement under which the amount payable to the worker, as both remuneration for work done and part payment for minimum annual leave, would be identical to the amount payable, prior to the entry into force of that agreement, as remuneration solely for work done, effectively negates, by means of a reduction in the amount of that remuneration, the worker's entitlement to paid annual leave under Article 7 of the directive. Such a result would run counter to what is required by Article 18(3) of the directive.

52. Consequently, the answer to the second question referred in Case C-257/04 must be that Article 7(1) of the directive precludes part of the remuneration payable to a worker for work done from being attributed to payment for annual leave without the worker receiving, in that respect, a payment additional to that for work done. There can be no derogation from that entitlement by contractual arrangement.

    …

59. Accordingly, without prejudice to more favourable provisions under Article 15 of the directive, the point at which the payment for annual leave is made must be fixed in such a way that, during that leave, the worker is, as regards remuneration, put in a position comparable to periods of work.

60. Furthermore, account must be taken of the fact that, under Article 7(2) of the directive, the minimum period of paid annual leave may not be replaced by an allowance in lieu, except where the employment relationship is terminated. That prohibition is intended to ensure that a worker is normally entitled to actual rest, with a view to ensuring effective protection of his health and safety (see, to that effect, *BECTU*, cited above, paragraph 44, and Case C-342/01 *Merino Gómez* [2004] ECR I-2605, paragraph 30).

    …

69. … Article 7 of the directive does not preclude, as a rule, sums paid, transparently and comprehensibly, in respect of minimum annual leave, within the meaning of that provision, in the form of part payments staggered over the corresponding annual period of work and paid together with the remuneration for work done, from being set off against the payment for specific leave which is actually taken by the worker.

Chamber President Jann, Schiemann J, Colneric J, Lenaerts J and Juhász J.

NOTES AND QUESTIONS

1. The Court of Justice holds that the practice of rolled-up holiday pay is unlawful because the aim of paid annual leave is that people actually take leave. However, if a worker's contract has terminated before they have used holidays (because they quit or they are dismissed) then a payment in lieu is owed by the employer. When making a pay in lieu, sums due can be 'set off' against other times that workers 'actually' take 'specific leave'. Presumably this referred to unforeseen instances where workers took time off that was not necessarily designated holiday.

2. *Lyddon v Englefield Brickwork Ltd* [2008] IRLR 198 found that an employee who had been given rolled-up pay, and had then taken two weeks' unpaid leave, was not

entitled to claim back pay when his contract terminated. Elias J seemed to suggest that the rolled-up holiday pay could be 'set off' against the unpaid leave. To what extent does this contradict the Court of Justice and open the UK government to a damages claim? *Köbler v Austria* (2003) C-224/01 requires that a national 'court has manifestly infringed the applicable law', but if so, the state is liable for judicial negligence.

3. In the Court of Appeal, *Caulfield v Marshall Clay Products* [2004] EWCA Civ 422, Laws LJ said the idea of rolled-up holiday pay was a 'far cry from one which would discourage the workers from taking their holidays at all'. He continued, 'it seems to me there is no reason why workers generally should not manage rolled-up holiday pay perfectly sensibly', presumably based on a theory that workers would freely take leave rather than working. Do you agree the more likely situation is that employers who included 'rolled-up holiday pay' simply kept wages the same? This view would suggest employers would be able to do so because a worker would have no bargaining power to get better terms in a standard labour market.

4. Where employers do give paid leave, might some reduce wages to cover the costs of paid holidays actually taken? L Summers, 'Some Simple Economics of Mandated Benefits' (1989) 79(2) *American Economic Review* 177 argues this would be true, on the assumption that all labour markets adjust perfectly to match changes in the marginal cost of production. The argument obviously cannot apply to a minimum-wage worker, because that person must have paid holidays in addition to their minimum wage. (Instead, the contention would be that such a person may lose their job: for the flaws in this logic, see chapters 2(2) and 6(2)(a).) But also, for higher earners, surely employers cannot all reduce wages at once. See JM Keynes, *The General Theory of Employment, Interest and Money* (1936) ch 17, 227. Do you agree that the more realistic view is that most employers, even if their profits are reduced, simply give people paid holidays because everyone else does it?

Williams v British Airways plc (2011) C-155/10

Mr Williams and other British Airways pilots claimed they were entitled to more holiday pay under the Working Time in Civil Aviation Directive 2000/79/EC clause 3 (which is identical in all relevant ways to the WTD 2003 Art 7). The three main components of pilots' pay were (1) a basic fixed salary, (2) supplements for time spent flying, and (3) supplements for expenses while away from their 'base', or ordinary home. The pilots conceded that under the proper construction of their employment contracts, they had contracted to have holiday pay only reflect their basic fixed salary. But they argued that this went below the minimum provided for in the Directive: holiday pay should reflect 'normal remuneration'. BA plc argued that the minimum paid annual leave could reflect the contract, because the UK had failed to enact any specific rules, and had not written the ERA 1996 to include any definition of 'normal working hours'. The UK Supreme Court made a reference to the European Court of Justice on the appropriate rule.

First Chamber:

17. The wording of Article 7 of Directive 2003/88 makes no specific reference to the remuneration to which a worker is entitled during his annual leave. The case-law, however, points out that it follows from the very wording of Article 7(1) – a provision from which that directive allows no derogation – that every worker is entitled to paid annual leave of at least four weeks and that that right to paid annual leave must be regarded as a particularly important principle of Community social law (see Joined Cases C-350/06 and C-520/06 *Schultz-Hoff and Stringer and Others* [2009] ECR I-179, paragraphs 22 and 54 and the case-law cited).

18. The right to such an annual period of paid leave is, moreover, expressly laid down in Article 31(2) of the Charter of Fundamental Rights of the European Union, which Article 6(1) EU recognises as having the same legal value as the Treaties.

19. In that context, the Court has already had occasion to state that the expression 'paid annual leave' in Article 7(1) of Directive 2003/88 means that, for the duration of 'annual leave' within the meaning of that directive, remuneration must be maintained and that, in other words, workers must receive their normal remuneration for that period of rest (see Joined Cases C-131/04 and C-257/04 *Robinson-Steele and Others* [2006] ECR I-2531, paragraph 50, and *Schultz-Hoff and Stringer and Others*, paragraph 58).

  ...

22. However, where the remuneration received by the worker is composed of several components, the determination of that normal remuneration and, consequently, of the amount to which that worker is entitled during his annual leave requires a specific analysis. Such is the case with regard to the remuneration of an airline pilot as a member of the flight crew of an airline, that remuneration being composed of a fixed annual sum and of variable supplementary payments which are linked to the time spent flying and to the time spent away from base.

23. In that regard, although the structure of the ordinary remuneration of a worker is determined, as such, by the provisions and practice governed by the law of the Member States, that structure cannot affect the worker's right, referred to in paragraph 19 of the present judgment, to enjoy, during his period of rest and relaxation, economic conditions which are comparable to those relating to the exercise of his employment.

24. Accordingly, any inconvenient aspect which is linked intrinsically to the performance of the tasks which the worker is required to carry out under his contract of employment and in respect of which a monetary amount is provided which is included in the calculation of the worker's total remuneration, such as, in the case of airline pilots, the time spent flying, must necessarily be taken into account for the purposes of the amount to which the worker is entitled during his annual leave.

25. By contrast, the components of the worker's total remuneration which are intended exclusively to cover occasional or ancillary costs arising at the time of performance of the tasks which the worker is required to carry out under his contract of employment, such as costs connected with the time that pilots have to spend away from base, need not be taken into account in the calculation of the payment to be made during annual leave.

26. In that regard, it is for the national court to assess the intrinsic link between the various components which make up the total remuneration of the worker and the performance of the tasks which he is required to carry out under his contract of employment. That assessment

must be carried out on the basis of an average over a reference period which is judged to be representative and in the light of the principle established by the case-law cited above, according to which Directive 2003/88 treats entitlement to annual leave and to a payment on that account as being two aspects of a single right (see *Robinson-Steele and Others*, paragraph 58, and *Schultz-Hoff and Stringer and Others*, paragraph 60).

Chamber President Tizzano, **Kasel J**, **Borg Barthet J**, **Levits J**, and **Berger J**.

NOTES AND QUESTIONS

1. The Court of Justice reasons that, because the worker should be in the same financial position taking holidays as working, holiday pay had to include all aspects of wages unless 'occasional or ancillary'. UK lawyers will readily understand this, as it mirrors the principle for paying compensatory damages 'as if the contract had been performed', per Parke B in *Robinson v Harman* (1848) 1 Exch 850. The exception, which presumably only refers to benefits that are useful when working (eg cake at lunchtime meeting; ale at an evening reception), must be construed narrowly as a general principle of EU law (see *Pfeiffer*, below at chapter 7(2)(b)).

2. This overrules a prior Court of Appeal case, *British Airways plc v Noble* [2006] EWCA Civ 537, where Mummery LJ approved an employer's practice of reducing holiday pay for shift premiums, on top of their basic rate of pay. Now that it is clear that Mummery LJ was wrong, should the employer be entitled to assert in court that it can retain sums of money that belong to the employees? The perceived difficulty is that Directives are said not to have 'horizontal direct effect', see chapter 7(1)(a) above.

3. In *Lock v British Gas Trading Ltd* (2014) C-539/12 the First Chamber found that Mr Lock, a salesperson who earned around 60 per cent of his average pay through commissions, needed to be given holiday pay that counted his commissions.

4. It was noted above, the European Social Charter 1961 Art 2 requires 'the working week to be progressively reduced to the extent that the increase of productivity and other relevant factors permit'. In fact, pay rises and working-time reduction began to diverge from productivity rises in 1992, but over a longer term, the reduction of working days in the year can be seen moving in a successful direction. If people work a five-day week, and have 28 days of holidays each year, this amounts to 132 from 365 days work. Such people work 66 per cent, less than two-thirds, of the year. To reach working half the year would require a further 51 days off: that is extending to a three-day weekend, or a two-day weekend with 79 paid holidays each year. What measures do you think the UK government could take to comply with its international obligations?

(2) HOURS

(a) Right to Regular Hours

As we saw in chapter 5(2)(b), the Court of Appeal held in *Devonald v Rosser & Sons* [1906] 2 KB 728 that tinplate factory workers had an implied right to pay for the time they would normally work. Particularly after 2010, it became common for standard-form contracts to include a unilateral right for the employer to vary a worker's hours. This had become known as a 'zero-hour contract', because the employer purports to have a power to vary a worker's hours down to 'zero'. In chapter 3(1), *Autoclenz Ltd v Belcher* [2010] UKSC 41, [35] stated: '[T]he relative bargaining power of the parties must be taken into account in deciding whether the terms of any written agreement in truth represent what was agreed.' The same strict approach to total employer discretion was evident through implied-terms cases that emphasise any discretionary power has to be exercised in light of the parties' 'reasonable expectations'. This affects the legality of a 'zero-hours' term.

Borrer v Cardinal Security Ltd [2013] UKEAT 0416_12_1607

Mr Borrer claimed constructive unfair dismissal and unlawful deduction of wages from Cardinal Security Ltd after it purported to unilaterally reduce his hours. He worked as a security guard for Morrison's supermarket in Brighton for around four years until October 2011. For just over two of those years, from 28 September 2009, Cardinal Security Ltd was the relevant intermediary employer. The employer's statement of the contract purported that Mr Borrer could be moved to 'any of the company's assignments', his pay could be 'an increased or decreased hourly rate', and critically it said 'working hours will be specified by your line manager'. In October 2011 a disagreement transpired with a Morrison's manager at Brighton. Borrer was moved to Seaford, but then there was another disagreement with the manager there, and he was told to take 'holiday'. His hours were reduced to zero. Given the absence of notice, or any procedure, Borrer claimed this was a constructive dismissal and unlawful wage deduction. The Havant Employment Tribunal felt that the employers did what they 'were entitled to do and it follows no work no pay'. The Employment Appeal Tribunal reversed this decision.

Supperstone J:

9. 'There is no express term in the contract, as in *Pulse Healthcare Ltd v Carewatch Care Services Ltd* UKEAT/0123/12, that the hours of employment should be zero hours. The question in this case, as in every case, is: what was the true agreement between the parties?' In this regard the Supreme Court in *Autoclenz* approved the approach of this Tribunal in *Consistent Group Ltd v Kalwak* [2007] IRLR 560 and that of the Court of Appeal in *Firthglow Ltd v Szilagyi* [2009] IRLR 365. All of the relevant evidence must be examined, including the written terms of the contract, how the parties conduct themselves in practice and their expectations of each other. The relative bargaining power of the parties must be taken into account in deciding whether the terms of any written agreement (per Lord Clarke, *Autoclenz*, paragraph 35):

> "… in truth represent what was agreed, and the true agreement will often have to be gleaned from all the circumstances of the case of which the written agreement is only part."

10. At paragraph 12 of his witness statement the Claimant stated: "48 per week was agreed by Anya Morbey at my interview, over 2 years ago and there has never been any hint that this might be subject to change or review."

11. Ms Morbey in her witness statement at paragraph 4 says that the Claimant did not have a contractual right to a minimum number of hours per week. The Tribunal does not deal with this evidence in its decision. However, we infer that the Tribunal did not accept that there was

an express agreement that the Claimant would be given 48 hours per week at the interview; if it had, that would have concluded the issue.

...

13. The Tribunal's conclusion that the Claimant had no contractual entitlement to guaranteed hours of work, namely 48 hours, appears to be based on two findings: first, the provision relating to hours of work in the statement of main terms of employment that his working hours would be specified by his line manager; and second, the evidence of the Claimant that he was texted each week, and if not texted would check up with the controller as to where he was working the next week, from which the Tribunal inferred it must follow on which contract and hence for what hours.

...

15. In our view, the two matters that the Tribunal considered to be interrelated – see paragraph 24 of the decision – neither individually nor cumulatively lead to the conclusion that the Claimant had no guaranteed hours of work. We do not accept Mr Morley's submission that the Claimant had no contractual entitlement to be provided with any work. In our judgment, the true agreement between the parties, considering the evidence as a whole and by reference to the specific findings made by the Tribunal that we have referred to, is that the Claimant did have a contractual entitlement to work 48 hours each week. His remuneration for these hours of work would depend on the rate applicable to the assignment to which he is allocated.

...

17. In summary, for the reasons we have given, we are of the view that the Claimant had a contractual entitlement to work 48 hours each week. This case must therefore now be remitted to a Tribunal to determine whether in the light of this conclusion there was a repudiatory breach by the Respondent on the facts, whether there was a constructive dismissal, and if so, whether the constructive dismissal was unfair.

NOTES AND QUESTIONS

1. *Borrer* represents an important application of the *Autoclenz* principle to a so-called 'zero-hours' clause. Read literally, the employer's standard-form statement of Mr Borrer's contract (not the actual contract, but the employer's statement of it) promised no hours, no pay, and maybe that he could be shifted to work anywhere from Tipperary to Timbuktu. 'Flexibility' in this case becomes a euphemism for arbitrary power of a corporate entity. The common law controls it.

2. The phrase 'zero-hours contract' seems first to have appeared around the time of L Dickens, 'Falling through the Net: Employment Change and Worker Protection' (1988) 19(2) *Industrial Relations Journal* 139, 142. However, the essence of the 'zero-hours contract' is simply one aspect of an employer's managerial discretion, applied to unilaterally vary hours down to zero. In outcome, it is no different to what in the United States is known as 'at-will employment'. In one case, the employer may say to the worker 'you have no hours this week', whereas in the other, the employer says 'you are dismissed'. The effect is the same, and the consent of both parties would be necessary for resumption of the relation, unless the law intervened.

3. Are any zero-hours contracts lawful? For an argument that most 'usually lie in a shadowy recess of borderline illegality', see E McGaughey, 'Are Zero Hour

Contracts Lawful?' (2014) ssrn.com/abstract_id=2531913. The essence of the argument is that discretion to vary hours must be exercised according to the parties' 'reasonable expectations' (*Equitable Life Assurance Society v Hyman* [2000] UKHL 39) and this could not decrease expectations of normal hours more than a certain percentage, say 10 or 20 per cent of working time. An express clause in an employment contract will virtually never represent the true agreement of an employee, following *Autoclenz*, who needs work and lacks bargaining power.

4.   Z Adams and S Deakin, *Re-regulating Zero Hours Contracts* (Institute of Employment Rights, 2014) suggest that government welfare policy since 2010 has driven the growth of zero-hours contracts by demanding that job-seekers who claim unemployment insurance take any job, including ones that contain such (potentially unlawful) terms. Accordingly, this suggests that zero-hours contracts are not merely a product of a 'free market' shaped by structurally unequal bargaining power. They also required a regulatory subsidy – however unintended – from government to exist.

5.   While the common law approach of the Employment Appeal Tribunal could protect employees on an ad hoc basis, what models of legislative reform exist? One example is the German Part-time and Fixed-term Work Act 2001 (Teilzeit- und Befristungsgesetz 2001) §12. If a contract is silent on hours, then a period of 10 hours work per week will be deemed to apply. Case law further provides that employers may only vary hours by a maximum of 25 per cent of the norm that the employee works (Federal Labour Court, BAG (7 December 2005) 5 AZR 535/04).

6.   The Small Business, Enterprise and Employment Act 2015 s 153 inserted the ERA 1996 s 27A–B, which makes an exclusivity provision (where the employer purports to prohibit the worker from working for other employers) for a worker on a zero-hours contract unenforceable. This restates the common law on restraint of trade, rather than doing something new (see chapter 4(1)(b)). It was seen as politically important to 'do something' in the run-up to the 2015 general election. See further A Adams, M Freedland and J Prassl, 'The "Zero-Hours Contract": Regulating Casual Work, or Legitimating Precarity?' (2015) Oxford Legal Studies Research Paper No 11/2015.

(b) Maximum Hours

The control of the maximum working day under WTD 2003 Art 6 and WTR 1998 regs 4–5 became the most controversial aspect of working time regulation. During the passage of the original Directive in 1993, the UK government demanded an 'opt-out' from the general rule that 'the average working time for each seven-day period, including overtime, does not exceed 48 hours'. Under WTD 2003 Art 22(1) an employer can require a worker to do longer hours if they 'obtained the worker's agreement'. Under WTR 1998 reg 5, this must be 'in writing'. Thus, there is a default right to maximum hours, but it can be signed away. The employer may not subject the worker to 'any detriment' (WTD 2003 Art 22 and ERA 1996 ss 45A and 101A) for refusing to sign. Other Member States allowed opt outs for more limited groups, by sector or profession.

Pfeiffer v Deutsches Rotes Kreuz (2005) C-397/01

Mr Pfeiffer, and other ambulance workers for the German Red Cross, claimed that a collective agreement that set their hours at 49 hours per week violated the WTD 2003/88 Art 6. The German Working Time Act 1994 (Arbeitszeitgesetz) §3 implemented a maximum 48-hour working week, but §7 created an exception for workers to opt out of that limit in a collective agreement. Pfeiffer argued that §7 was contrary to the Directive, because it required individual agreement. The Red Cross rejected this and further contended that emergency workers were like civil protection service workers or were road transport workers and, under Art 1(3) at the time, fell outside the Directive's scope altogether under. (This exception has since been removed.) The Court of Justice held that the ambulance workers did fall within the Directive's scope, and a collective agreement could not opt out the workers, as they had to give individual consent. Although the workers could not base a claim on the Directive against their employers (as it had no 'horizontal' direct effect) a national court would have to interpret national law as far as possible.

Grand Chamber:

67. Since [the exclusions – now removed – for civil protection service and road transport workers] are exceptions to the Community system for the organisation of working time put in place by Directive 93/104, the exclusions from the scope of the directive provided for in Article 1(3) must be interpreted in such a way that their scope is limited to what is strictly necessary in order to safeguard the interests which the exclusions are intended to protect (see, by analogy, the judgment in *Jaeger*, paragraph 89).

...

69. ... it can hardly be argued that when the Deutsches Rotes Kreuz operates an emergency medical service such as that at issue in the main proceedings its activity pertains to the road transport sector.

...

76. ... it is apparent from Article 118a of the Treaty [now TFEU Art 158(a)], the legal basis for Directive 93/104, from the first, fourth, seventh and eighth recitals in the preamble to the directive and from the actual wording of Article 1(1) of the directive that its objective is to guarantee the better protection of the safety and health of workers by affording them minimum rest periods – especially on a daily and weekly basis – and adequate breaks and by providing for an upper limit on weekly working time.

...

81. In paragraph 74 of *Simap*, the Court concluded that the consent given by trade-union representatives in the context of a collective or other agreement is not equivalent to that given by the worker himself, as provided for in the first indent of Article 18(1)(b)(i) of [the Working Time] Directive 93/104.

82. That interpretation derives from the objective of Directive 93/104, which seeks to guarantee the effective protection of the safety and health of workers by ensuring that they actually have the benefit of, *inter alia*, an upper limit on weekly working time and minimum rest periods. Any derogation from those minimum requirements must therefore be accompanied by all the safeguards necessary to ensure that, if the worker concerned is encouraged to relinquish a social right which has been directly conferred on him by the directive, he must do so freely and with

full knowledge of all the facts. Those requirements are all the more important given that the worker must be regarded as the weaker party to the employment contract and it is therefore necessary to prevent the employer being in a position to disregard the intentions of the other party to the contract or to impose on that party a restriction of his rights without him having expressly given his consent in that regard.

...

84. It follows that, for a derogation from the maximum period of weekly working time laid down in Article 6 of Directive 93/104 (48 hours) to be valid, the worker's consent must be given not only individually but also expressly and freely.

85. Those conditions are not met where the worker's employment contract merely refers to a collective agreement authorising an extension of maximum weekly working time. It is by no means certain that, when he entered into such a contract, the worker concerned knew of the restriction of the rights conferred on him by Directive 93/104.

...

87. By its third question, the national court is essentially asking whether, if Directive 93/104 has been implemented incorrectly, Article 6(2) thereof may be taken to have direct effect.

...

100. ... in view of both the wording of Article 6(2) of Directive 93/104 and the purpose and scheme of the directive, the 48-hour upper limit on average weekly working time, including overtime, constitutes a rule of Community social law of particular importance from which every worker must benefit, since it is a minimum requirement necessary to ensure protection of his safety and health. ...

...

103. In that regard, it is clear from the settled case-law of the Court that, whenever the provisions of a directive appear, so far as their subject-matter is concerned, to be unconditional and sufficiently precise, they may be relied upon before the national courts by individuals against the State where the latter has failed to implement the directive in domestic law by the end of the period prescribed or where it has failed to implement the directive correctly (see, inter alia, Joined Cases C-6/90 and C-9/90 *Francovich and Others* [1991] ECR I-5357, paragraph 11, and Case C-62/00 *Marks & Spencer* [2002] ECR I-6325, paragraph 25).

...

108. ... the Court has consistently held that a directive cannot of itself impose obligations on an individual and cannot therefore be relied upon as such against an individual (see, inter alia, Case 152/84 *Marshall* [1986] ECR 723, paragraph 48; Case C-91/92 *Faccini Dori* [1994] ECR I-3325, paragraph 20; and Case C-201/02 *Wells* [2004] ECR I-0000, paragraph 56).

109. It follows that even a clear, precise and unconditional provision of a directive seeking to confer rights or impose obligations on individuals cannot of itself apply in proceedings exclusively between private parties.

110. However, it is apparent from case-law which has also been settled since the judgment of 10 April 1984 in Case 14/83 *Von Colson and Kamann* [1984] ECR 1891, paragraph 26, that the Member States' obligation arising from a directive to achieve the result envisaged by the directive and their duty under Article 10 EC to take all appropriate measures, whether general or particular, to ensure the fulfilment of that obligation is binding on all the authorities of

Member States including, for matters within their jurisdiction, the courts (see, inter alia, Case C-106/89 *Marleasing* [1990] ECR I-4135, paragraph 8; *Faccini Dori*, paragraph 26 …

…

116. In that context, if the application of interpretative methods recognised by national law enables, in certain circumstances, a provision of domestic law to be construed in such a way as to avoid conflict with another rule of domestic law or the scope of that provision to be restricted to that end by applying it only in so far as it is compatible with the rule concerned, the national court is bound to use those methods in order to achieve the result sought by the directive.

…

118. In this instance, the principle of interpretation in conformity with Community law thus requires the referring court to do whatever lies within its jurisdiction, having regard to the whole body of rules of national law, to ensure that Directive 93/104 is fully effective, in order to prevent the maximum weekly working time laid down in Article 6(2) of the directive from being exceeded (see, to that effect, *Marleasing*, paragraphs 7 and 13).

President Skouris, Jann, Timmermans, Gulmann, Puissochet, Cunha Rodrigues, Schintgen, Macken, Colneric, Bahr and Lenaerts.

NOTES AND QUESTIONS

1. The Court of Justice's reasoning contains three important, general points: (1) exceptions to rules in EU law are to be construed restrictively – in effect *contra proferentem* like for contractual exclusions; (2) the worker is defined in EU law by being the 'weaker party', and rights exist to prevent the employer being able to 'disregard the intentions' of the worker in a contract; and (3) although Mr Pfeiffer could not rely on the Directive against the Red Cross, the German court was bound to use every available interpretative method to reach the result required by the Directive, except contravening express words of a statute, *contra legem*. Otherwise, the German government would be opened to liability in damages.

2. The interpretative method alluded to by the Court of Justice at [116] is to construe some words of a statute as subordinate, so as to give way to an otherwise conflicting rule. The essence of the idea is that sometimes laws conflict, and preference should be given to the one that matches the legal system's overall policy. An example in UK law was the advice of Lord Hoffmann in *AG of Belize v Belize Telecom Ltd* [2009] UKPC 10, a leading statement on implied terms. There, an express term of a company constitution (providing that company directors could not be removed unless shareholders held a special share and a class of ordinary shares) could not 'in the Board's opinion be construed as contradicting the proposed implied term' that the director could be removed by an ordinary resolution of members. The consequence was that an implied term overrode the express term. The express term was nullified by construction. This reflected the parties' 'reasonable expectations' because usually directors are not meant to have jobs for life: they should be accountable. For a contrasting case on commercial contracts (not a director/shareholder relation), see *Marks and Spencer plc v BNP Paribas Securities Services Trust Company (Jersey) Ltd* [2015] UKSC 72.

3. If a worker has *not* opted out, in any given week he or she may still work more than 48 hours, but not more on average over 17 weeks. A collective agreement may extend this to 52 weeks: WTR 1998 reg 4(3)(b).
4. WTD 2003 Art 17, adopted in WTR 1998 reg 20, allows derogation from working hours protection for people with 'autonomous decision making powers', 'family workers', and people working for religious ceremonies or communities. What does 'autonomous' mean? Does it include someone like a manager who only reports to one or a few other people on an organisation's board? No. See *Sayers v Cambridgeshire CC* [2007] IRLR 29. As this exception is to be construed narrowly, it seems necessary to be someone akin to a company director, who only answers to the company general meeting. However, this might not always be the case, for instance, if the person *in effect* is subordinate to orders from another company in the group.
5. WTD 2003 Art 17 and WTR 1998 regs 18–24A contain further miscellaneous derogations, excluding the armed forces, police, road transport workers, etc.
6. A further derogation, allowed when the Directive was first introduced, was for 'doctors in training'. This met the obvious criticism (based on experiences like *Johnstone v Bloomsbury HA*, at chapter 4(1)(c)) that it might not be prudent to allow people to be exhausted and fragile while performing potentially life-and-death medical work. For countries that did not take advantage of the exception, the issue still played out in cases on whether time spent 'on call' counted as working time.

Sindicato de Medicos de Asistencia Publica v Conselleria de Sanidad y Consumo de la Generalidad Valenciana (2000) C-303/98

The Spanish doctors' union, Simap, claimed that the Valencia Ministry of Health was in breach of the WTD 2003. First, the Spanish Royal Decree No 1561/95 was argued to have incorrectly transposed the Directive by excluding doctors, apparently under an exception for core public-sector staff such as armed forces and police, which existed at the time (and has since been removed). Second, the doctors' working time was not being measured to include periods where they were on call. It was alleged that some doctors had to work as long as 31 hours uninterrupted, as the need arose. The Court of Justice held that doctors were included in the Directive's scope, and that on-call time was working time.

The Court:

46. By Questions 2(a) to 2(c), 3(a), 3(b) and 4(c), which it is appropriate to consider together, the national court seeks essentially to determine whether time spent on call by doctors in primary care teams, whether they are required to be present in the health centre or merely contactable, must be regarded as working time or as overtime within the meaning of Directive 93/104.

47. It must be borne in mind that that directive defines working time as any period during which the worker is working, at the employer's disposal and carrying out his activity or duties, in accordance with national laws and/or practice. Moreover, in the scheme of the directive, it is placed in opposition to rest periods, the two being mutually exclusive.

48. In the main proceedings, the characteristic features of working time are present in the case of time spent on call by doctors in primary care teams where their presence at the health centre is required. It is not disputed that during periods of duty on call under those rules, the first two conditions are fulfilled. Moreover, even if the activity actually performed varies according to the circumstances, the fact that such doctors are obliged to be present and available at the workplace with a view to providing their professional services means that they are carrying out their duties in that instance.

...

50. As the Advocate General also states in point 37 of his Opinion, the situation is different where doctors in primary care teams are on call by being contactable at all times without having to be at the health centre. Even if they are at the disposal of their employer, in that it must be possible to contact them, in that situation doctors may manage their time with fewer constraints and pursue their own interests. In those circumstances, only time linked to the actual provision of primary care services must be regarded as working time within the meaning of Directive 93/104.

51. As regards the question whether time spent on call may be regarded as overtime, although Directive 93/104 does not define overtime, which is mentioned only in Article 6, relating to the maximum length of the working week, the fact remains that overtime falls within the concept of working time for the purposes of the directive, which draws no distinction according to whether or not such time is spent within normal hours of work.

52. The answer to Questions 2(a) to 2(c), 3(a), 3(b) and 4(c) is therefore that time spent on call by doctors in primary health care teams must be regarded in its entirety as working time, and where appropriate as overtime, within the meaning of Directive 93/104 if they are required to be present at the health centre. If they must merely be contactable at all times when on call, only time linked to the actual provision of primary care services must be regarded as working time.

President Rodríguez Iglesias, Moitinho de Almeida, Edward, Sevón, Schintgen, Kapteyn, Gulmann, Puissochet, Jann, Ragnemalm and **Wathelet**.

NOTES AND QUESTIONS

1. The essential point of the Court's decision is that doctors whose 'presence is required' at the hospital are working, even if remaining idle for those period 'on call'.
2. The culture of long hours in many countries required the Court to repeat itself.

Landeshauptstadt Kiel v Jaegar (2003) C-151/02

Dr Jaeger, a surgeon at a hospital in Kiel, claimed that all time spent on call should have been included in working time. The collective agreement applicable to him said only time doing work tasks, which was not to exceed 49 per cent of on-call time, counted as working time. Dr Jaeger was given a room and a bed to sleep on at the hospital. This purported to be lawful under the German Working Time Act 1994 §5 III. The State Labour Court for Schleswig-Holstein requested a preliminary ruling, urging that despite the *Simap* decision, the 'majority' German academic opinion (in the court's assessment) was that time on call, where work tasks were not being performed, should not count as working time. The Court of Justice held that all time Dr Jaeger spent on call was working time.

The Court:

47. ... it is clear from the Community Charter of the Fundamental Social Rights of Workers, adopted at the meeting of the European Council held at Strasbourg on 9 December 1989, and in particular points 8 and 19, first subparagraph, thereof, which are referred to in the fourth recital in the preamble to Directive 93/104, that every worker in the European Community must enjoy satisfactory health and safety conditions in his working environment and must have a right, inter alia, to a weekly rest period, the duration of which in the Member States must be progressively harmonised in accordance with national practices.

48. ... in *Simap*, the Court noted that the directive defines that concept as any period during which the worker is working, at the employer's disposal and carrying out his activity or duties, in accordance with national laws and/or practices, and that that concept is placed in opposition to rest periods, the two being mutually exclusive.

...

53. First, it is not disputed that a doctor performing duties such as those at issue in the main proceedings performs his on-call duty under a regime requiring presence in the health centre.

54. Secondly, neither the context nor the nature of the activities of such a doctor are materially different from those in the case which gave rise to the judgment in *Simap* in such a way as to call in question the Court's interpretation of Directive 93/104 in that judgment.

55. In that regard those activities cannot be validly distinguished on the basis that in the case which gave rise to the judgment in *Simap* the doctors assigned to a primary care team were subject to uninterrupted working time which could extend for up to 31 hours without night rest, whereas in the case of on-call duty such as that at issue in the main proceedings, the relevant national legislation ensures that the periods during which the person concerned may be called upon to perform a professional task do not exceed 49% of the totality of the period of on-call duty with the result that he could be inactive during more than half of that period.

...

57. Moreover, even though the figure of 49% appearing in the national legislation at issue in the main proceedings relates to the average time calculated over a certain period linked to the actual performance of services during the period of on-call duty, it is none the less the case that, during that period, a doctor may be required to provide his services as often and as long as proves to be necessary without there being any limitation in that regard under the legislation.

...

59. ... the fact that the definition of the concept of working time refers to national law and/or practice does not mean that the Member States may unilaterally determine the scope of that concept. Thus, those States may not make subject to any condition the right of employees to have working periods and corresponding rest periods duly taken into account since that right stems directly from the provisions of that directive. Any other interpretation would frustrate the objective of Directive 93/104 of harmonising the protection of the safety and health of workers by means of minimum requirements (see Case C-84/94 *United Kingdom v Council* [1996] ECR I-5755, paragraphs 45 and 75).

60. The fact that in the *Simap* judgment the Court did not expressly rule on the fact that doctors performing on-call duty where they are required to be present in the hospital can rest or sleep during the periods when their services are not required is in no way material in that connection.

...

63. According to the Court, the decisive factor in considering that the characteristic features of the concept of working time within the meaning of Directive 93/104 are present in the case of time spent on call by doctors in the hospital itself is that they are required to be present at the place determined by the employer and to be available to the employer in order to be able to provide their services immediately in case of need. In fact, as may be inferred from paragraph 48 of the judgment in *Simap*, those obligations, which make it impossible for the doctors concerned to choose the place where they stay during waiting periods, must be regarded as coming within the ambit of the performance of their duties.

64. That conclusion is not altered by the mere fact that the employer makes available to the doctor a rest room in which he can stay for as long as his professional services are not required.

65. It should be added that, as the Court already held at paragraph 50 of the judgment in *Simap*, in contrast to a doctor on stand-by, where the doctor is required to be permanently accessible but not present in the health centre, a doctor who is required to keep himself available to his employer at the place determined by him for the whole duration of periods of on-call duty is subject to appreciably greater constraints since he has to remain apart from his family and social environment and has less freedom to manage the time during which his professional services are not required. Under those conditions an employee available at the place determined by the employer cannot be regarded as being at rest during the periods of his on-call duty when he is not actually carrying on any professional activity.

66. That interpretation cannot be called in question by the objections based on economic and organisational consequences which, according to the five Member States which submitted observations under Article 20 of the EC Statute of the Court of Justice, would result from the extension to a case such as that in the main proceedings of the solution adopted in the *Simap* judgment.

67. Moreover, it is clear from the fifth recital in the preamble to Directive 93/104 that the improvement of workers' safety, hygiene and health at work is an objective which should not be subordinated to purely economic considerations.'

68. It follows from all the foregoing that the conclusion reached by the Court in the *Simap* judgment, according to which time spent on call by doctors in primary health care teams, where they are required to be physically present in the health centre, must be regarded in its entirety as working time within the meaning of Directive 93/104, irrespective of the work actually performed by the persons concerned, must also apply in regard to on-call duty performed under the same regime by a doctor such as Mr Jaeger in the hospital where he is employed.

69. Under those circumstances Directive 93/104 precludes national legislation such as that at issue in the main proceedings, which treats as periods of rest periods of on-call duty during which the doctor is not actually required to perform any professional task and may rest but must be present and remain available at the place determined by the employer with a view to performance of those services if need be or when he is requested to intervene.

70. In fact that is the only interpretation which accords with the objective of Directive 93/104 which is to secure effective protection of the safety and health of employees by allowing them to enjoy minimum periods of rest. That interpretation is all the more cogent in the case of doctors performing on-call duty in health centres, given that the periods during which their services are not required in order to cope with emergencies may, depending on the case, be of short duration and/or subject to frequent interruptions and where, moreover, it cannot be ruled out that the persons concerned may be prompted to intervene, apart from in emergencies, to monitor the condition of patients placed under their care or to perform tasks of an administrative nature.

President Rodríguez Iglesias, Wathelet, Schintgen, Timmermans, Gulmann, Edward, Jann, Skouris, Macken, Colneric, Bahr, Cunha Rodrigues and Rosas.

NOTES AND QUESTIONS

1. The Court of Justice, in the face of considerable pressure, goes further in emphasising the importance of counting on-call time – even where there is a bed to sleep on – as working time. While emphasising the social nature of the right, that workers are detached from their 'family and social environment', it says people's health should 'not be subordinated to purely economic considerations'. What do 'economic considerations' actually mean? If this means a desire for greater productivity, is there empirical evidence showing that longer hours means more productivity? Is the opposite not true? If it means economic growth in general, unlinked to productivity, does it matter how the gains are shared? In other words, is there actually any evidence that it is good 'economics' to have exhausted workers doing long hours?

2. The consequence of the *Jaeger* judgment in Germany, and 14 other Member States, was those Member States began to allow opt outs from the WTD for doctors and other workers, as the UK had done in general. Furthermore, political pressure led the Commission to propose revision to reverse the effect of the judgment in COM(2004) 607. This was not implemented. The actual application in Member States is reviewed in a Report from the Commission on implementation by Member States of Directive 2003/88/EC ('The Working Time Directive') COM(2010) 802.

3. In *Fuß v Stadt Halle* (2010) C-243/09, a fire officer requested to stop working 54 hours per week on average, and work under 48 hours. The employer transferred him to a job that was less dangerous, and had more social hours, but on less pay. The Administrative Court in Halle, Germany, said that 'objectively' Mr Fuß did not suffer any detriment (in its assessment), but asked whether there was nevertheless a breach of the Directive. The Court of Justice held that this was victimisation. It said 'the effect of a compulsory transfer … deprives of all substance … the right to a maximum working week of 48 hours'. So, it is possible to start a job opting out, but then demand to work less, and be legally protected. What subtle forms of retaliation can you imagine an employer taking? What could you do as a worker to protect yourself?

(c) Breaks and Night Work

WTD 2003 Art 3 and WTR 1998 reg 10 says workers must rest at least 11 consecutive hours in a 24-hour period. Article 5 and reg 11 require a 24-hour period of rest each week. Article 4 says workers must get breaks every 6 hours, and regulation 12(3) sets a 20-minute minimum. Regulation 24 adds that, if a worker does have to work in a designated break, the employer must allow 'an equivalent period of compensatory rest' and if impossible for 'objective reasons … shall afford him such protection … to safeguard the worker's health and safety'. What does this mean?

Hughes v Corps of Commissionaires Management Ltd (No 2)
[2011] EWCA Civ 1061

Mr Hughes, a security guard in Croydon working for the telecoms company Orange, claimed that he did not receive enough rest breaks under WTR 1998 regs 12 and 24. He could break when he chose, but would be on call, as he would be the only security guard on site. If his break was interrupted he could start again. He contended that he should have breaks where he would be guaranteed not to be interrupted, and there were no objective reasons to prevent this.

Elias LJ read the judgment of the court (**Sir Thomas May** and **Thomas LJ**):

35. … the Tribunal made reference to a decision of the ECJ, *Adeneler v Ellinikos Organismos Galkatos* [2006] IRLR 716, where the concept of objective reasons had been discussed. That case was concerned with a different Directive, the Fixed Term Work Directive. The ECJ observed that the concept of objective reasons had to be considered in the light of the objective of the relevant legislation. Having regard to that principle, the Tribunal considered that in determining whether the equivalent period of rest was "not possible" in regulation 24, it should have regard to all the objectives of the Directive. In that context it said this (para 38):

> "… a step which provides compensatory rest for workers that is financially and/or logistically crippling for a small or medium sized employer that is neither immediately terminal to the business nor wholly impossible generally, is unlikely to be envisaged under the Directive as falling outside the exemption of being "not possible objective reasons", particularly having regard to the Recitals to the Directive".

…

54. We would accept that if a period is properly to be described as an equivalent period of compensatory rest, it must have the characteristics of a rest in the sense of a break from work. Furthermore, it must so far as possible ensure that the period which is free from work is at least 20 minutes. If the break does not display those characteristics then we do not think it would meet the criteria of equivalence and compensation. In this case the arrangements plainly did meet those criteria, as the EAT found. Indeed, since the rest break begins again following any interruption, many would say that this was more beneficial than a regulation 12 Gallagher break would be.

55. We would add that we do not think that it is likely to matter in practical terms which paragraph is applicable, at least in circumstances where the employer is unable to offer a Gallagher rest break but adopts arrangements which come as close as possible to replicating that break.

Even if such an arrangement does not fall within paragraph (a), we would have thought that it is bound to fall within paragraph (b).

...

60. ... this was not a case where the only reason for failing to provide the requisite cover was to maximise profits. Any significant additional cost could have undermined the ability of the employers to secure the contract at all and would have threatened the jobs of the security officers or their pay. As the Tribunal pointed out, it will always be possible to provide the requisite rest breaks if money is no object. However, the recitals emphasise that imposing administrative, financial and legal constraints may hold back the creation and development of small and medium-sized undertakings. In our judgment, the Tribunal was fully alive to that consideration, and properly allowed it to enter the equation whether the reasons were objectively justified or not. The appellant's argument ignores it. In addition, the Tribunal found in terms that there were logistical and administrative problems which would arise if additional staff had to be employed. That is a finding of fact, sustainable on the evidence, and there is no basis for going behind it.

We do not accept either that the Tribunal erred in citing, and placing some reliance on, the *Adeneler* decision. This is one of the few ECJ cases where the concept of objective grounds found in various EU Directives has been discussed. The Tribunal recognised in terms that the meaning of objective reasons had to be informed by the objective pursued by the Directive and by the context of Article 17(2), and it specifically had regard to the recitals of the Directive when assessing its objective. It did not make the error attributed to it of simply lifting the language in *Adelener* without any consideration of the very different statutory context.

NOTES AND QUESTIONS

1. The essential point in Elias LJ's reasoning appears to be that Mr Hughes was not denied an uninterrupted break because the employer was not seeking to 'maximise profits'. This was an essential factor that made the reasons (for not giving an uninterrupted break) 'objective'. Do you find the reasoning adequate?

2. Although the case may have appear to raise comparatively small stakes, and one may wonder why it was brought, it is worth recalling how much this may have mattered in practice to Mr Hughes. 'There is no point in dismissive rhetoric whose general purport is that such trivial rules do not rise to the dignity of "law". It matters profoundly to the worker (and his employer) whether his tea break is ten minutes or only five; whether his production quota is 110 per cent or only 90 per cent of what he feels capable of; whether he must silently bear his foreman's abuse or can give as good as he gets without fear of being sacked.' H Arthurs, 'Understanding Labour Law: The Debate over "Industrial Pluralism"' (1985) 38(1) *Current Legal Problems* 83.

3. Under WTD 2003 Art 17 and WTR 1998 reg 21, there can be a derogation from breaks if the job requires 'continuity of service'. In *Gallagher v Alpha Catering* [2004] EWCA Civ 1559, workers catering for airlines claimed they should have paid breaks, although they did have 'downtime' where they would have to be ready for work but not necessarily packing or shipping. Peter Gibson LJ held that there was no need for 'continuity of service', and the 'downtime' if undisturbed would not retrospectively become a 'break'. Ensuring workers had 20-minute breaks would not have 'so apocalyptic a consequence' as counsel for the employer had suggested.

4.   Under WTD 2003 Arts 8–13 and WTR 1998 regs 6–7, a person working at night may only do 8 hours in any 24-hour period on average, or simply 8 hours at most if the work is classified as 'hazardous'. Article 2 defines 'night' as 12am to 5am, but not less than 7 hours around those hours. Exceptions are made for civil protection including armed forces and police.
5.   In *Re Alfred Stoeckel* (1991) C-345/89, the Court of Justice found that the French Code du travail Art L213-1, which said that women should not be employed at night at all, was contrary to the Equal Treatment Directive 76/207/EEC. In this instance, it did not help that it was based on the ILO Night Work (Women) Convention 1948, No 89, which now must itself be seen as incompatible with ILO principles.

(d) Enforcement

As with many individual labour rights, there are significant problems of enforcement. Do people have rights in practice, rather than merely on the books? Trade unions may help put pressure on an employer to comply with the law. A government regulator, such as the Health and Safety Executive, may devote resources to public enforcement. However this is highly dependent on the priorities of the government. Otherwise, the remedies individuals can get will be of great practical importance.

Barber v RJB Mining (UK) Ltd [1999] 2 CMLR 833

Mr Barber, and a group of pit deputies, claimed an injunction to work no more than 48 hours a week on average under WTR 1998 reg 4. This claim came during the course of a trade dispute with the employing entity. They had refused to opt out of the working time limit. RJB Mining Ltd contended that they were merely required to take 'reasonable steps' to ensure the duty was complied with. The High Court issued a declaration that the workers were entitled to refuse working over 48 hours, but declined to give an injunction because this would interfere in the ongoing trade dispute.

Gage J:

38. ... It seems to me clear that Parliament intended that all contracts of employment should be read so as to provide that an employee should work no more than an average of 48 hours in any week during the reference period. In my judgment this is a mandatory requirement which must apply to all contracts of employment. The fact that paragraph (1) does not state that an employer is prohibited from requiring his employee from working longer hours, does not in my view prevent that paragraph from having the effect of placing an obligation on an employer not to require an employee to work more than the permitted number of hours. Such an obligation is in keeping with the stated objective of the Directive of providing for health and safety of employees.

   ...

48. Mr Underhill submits that against the background of the negotiations between NACODS and the defendant and bearing in mind these proceedings were being used as a negotiating tool, it would be grossly disproportionate to grant the relief sought. The court should, accordingly, refuse to exercise its discretion in favour of granting relief.

49. In my judgment the plaintiffs are entitled to the grant of a declaration. In my opinion there is force in Mr Langstaff's submission that they are entitled to have the position under their contracts of employment made clear. The fact that these proceedings must be seen against the background of negotiations and as a tactical manoeuvre in the union's dispute with the defendant, does not in my opinion mean that the plaintiffs are not entitled to the declaration sought. The declaration will have the effect of making it clear that they are entitled, if they so choose, to refuse to continue working until the average working hours come within the specified limit. Subject to discussions with counsel on the precise wording of the declaration I propose to grant that relief.

50. I do not propose to grant either of the injunctions sought. In my judgment in the context of this case it is neither appropriate nor necessary to grant such injunctions. The injunctions sought under paragraph (c) of the prayer to the Statement of Claim are plainly inappropriate. Any detriment which may be caused to the plaintiffs can be the subject of a complaint to an employment tribunal under section 45A of the 1996 Act. So far as the other form of injunction sought, in my opinion, on that matter, the background to this dispute is important. To grant an injunction would be to force the defendant to take action which would be detrimental to its business and to other employees. The benefit to the plaintiffs would be to enable them to stop working for a maximum of five weeks in one case and minimum of two weeks in another case. The effect of injunction would be disproportionate to the benefit to the plaintiffs.

NOTES AND QUESTIONS

1. Gage J reasons that all contracts of employment 'should be read' with the rights created under the Regulations. A declaration of those rights was issued, but no more as the benefits to the claimants of an injunction to enforce working time rights would outweigh the detriment, but purely because of the particular context of the trade dispute. Does this mean that an injunction will be generally available? See further *Edwards v Chesterfield Royal Hospital NHS Foundation Trust* [2011] UKSC 58.

2. *Commission v United Kingdom* (2006) C-484/04 held that the UK government breached its duty under the Directive by allowing Department of Trade and Industry guidance to say: 'Employers must make sure that workers can take their rest, but are not required to make sure that they do take their rest.' The Court of Justice pointed out such guidance could render worker rights 'meaningless and are incompatible with the objective of that directive, in which minimum rest periods are considered to be essential for the protection of workers' health and safety'.

(3) CHILD CARE

Since the Employment Protection Act 1975 gave birth to the first provisions, UK child care rights have grown into an adolescent morass of regulation. In *Halfpenny v IGE Medical Systems Ltd* [1997] ICR 1007, Ward LJ said that for people looking to take child care leave, 'a wet towel around their heads' was 'the single most important aid to the understanding of their rights'. Baffling, repetitious, poorly drafted statutes and statutory instruments conceal conceptually simple issues. Time off for child care is the same as any other working time right: the purpose is to increase people's freedom from work to pursue other valuable activities in life, without unjust financial cost. However, a first major difference is that child care rights are only for 'employees', not workers. Second, gender discrimination is embedded in the very framework of the rights: rights to time off for child care (and therefore, implicitly, the duty for caring for children) are far greater for women. ACL Davies remarks that this has the 'unfortunate side-effect of stereotyping women and perpetuating the view that childcare is their responsibility alone' (*Perspectives on Labour Law* (2004) 111). As entrenched sexism becomes increasingly unacceptable to the next generation, the call for reform is likely.

Table 7.1 summarises the matrix of various UK child care provisions. At present there are four parts, ten different statutes and instruments, and nothing is gained from adding any more words than strictly necessary. Each category summarises the essential rule, and gives the abbreviated source. Further explanations are given below.

Table 7.1

The Matrix of UK child care			
	Maternity	*Paternity*	*Parental*	*Adoption*
Leave	2 compulsory, 24 ordinary, and 26 additional weeks. (14 ordinary and 2 compulsory weeks as EU minimum.)	2 weeks for 56 days past birth. 26 weeks transferable from mother or primary adopter, 20 to 52 weeks past birth.	Up to '18 weeks' until the child is 18 years old. (Phrased as 'four months' in the Directive.)	26 ordinary and 26 additional weeks.
	MPLR regs 7–8. ERA ss 71–3. PWD art 8.	PALR regs 5–6. ERA ss 80A–E. APLR regs 4–5.	MPLR reg 14–15 and Sch 2. ERA ss 76–80. PLD cl 2(2).	PALR regs 18–20. ERA ss 75A–B.
Pay	6 weeks at 90% of pay. 33 weeks at £139.58. (Sick pay equivalent as EU minimum.)	£139.58 or 90% of earnings, whichever is lower.	No pay.	£139.58 or 90% of earnings, whichever is lower.
	SSCBA s 166. SMPR regs 2(2) and 6. PWD art 11(2) and Boyle.	SPPSAPWRR reg 2.		SPPSAPWRR reg 3.
Notice	15 weeks pre-birth for leave.	8 weeks. For transfer, mother's declaration to employer.	21 days before intended leave.	7 days after matching of child and 28 days before placement.
	MPLR reg 4.	APLR regs 5–6. PALR reg 10.	MPLR Sch 2, paras 3–5. PLD cl 3(2).	PALR reg 17.

(continued)

Table 7.1 *(Continued)*

The Matrix of UK child care				
	Maternity	*Paternity*	*Parental*	*Adoption*
Contract	Keep contract, pay and mutual trust and confidence.	Same terms and and conditions, no detriment.	Keep mutual trust and confidence, no detriment.	Same terms and and conditions, no detriment.
	MPLR reg 17. PWD art 11.	PALR regs 12 and 28.	MPLR regs 17 and 19. PLD 5(2).	PALR regs 19 and 28.
Return	Same job during ordinary leave. Same seniority and pay for additional leave.	Suitable and appropriate job.	Similar job, consistent with contract.	Same job unless redundant: right to be redeployed.
	MPLR regs 18–18A. PWD art 11.	PALR reg 13	MPLR regs 18–18A. PLD cl 5–6.	PALR regs 26 and 23.
Dismissal	Unfair.	Unfair.	Unfair.	Unfair.
	ERA s 99. MPLR reg 20. PWD art 10.	PALR reg 29.	MPLR reg 20.	PALR reg 29.
Qualification	None.	26 weeks	1 year.	None.
	(MPLR reg 5 repealed.)	PALR reg 4(2).	MPLR reg 13(1)(a). PLD cl 3(1)(b).	(PALR reg 15(2) (b) repealed.)

NOTES AND QUESTIONS

1. The ERA 1996 ss 55–80E contains general statements of rights across categories of people potentially entitled to child care leave and pay. Specific Regulations follow.

2. In EU law, the Pregnant Workers Directive 92/85/EEC, and the Parental Leave Directive 2010/18/EU set minimum standards. EU law does not provide rights specifically for fathers or adopting parents beyond the unpaid rights for parental leave. As the Directives on maternity leave and pay are confined to women, do you think it is compatible with the general principle of equality in EU law? (See chapter 12(1)(a).)

3. A further question is whether discriminatory child care rights violate the Treaty on the Functioning of the European Union Art 157, 'the principle of equal pay for male and female workers for equal work or work of equal value is applied'. Pay is defined as any consideration 'which the worker receives' from 'his employer'. In *Barber v Guardian Royal Exchange Assurance Group* (1990) C-262/88 the Court of Justice held that discrimination in retirement ages for occupational pensions violated TFEU Art 157. An occupational pension was pay, although it was said, following *Defrenne v Belgium* (1971) Case 80-70, that pay from an employer could not include social security benefits 'directly governed by legislation without any element of agreement within the undertaking'. Does this mean that the

minimum child care rights, paid for by government, are immune from challenge? Is this element of *Barber*, in any event, now incompatible with the general principle of equality? If employers go beyond the statutory minimum, are they bound to give the same rights to men as to women?

4.   The Maternity and Parental Leave, etc Regulations 1999 (SI 1999/3312) contain most rights, other than pay, regarding maternity and parental leave. The Statutory Maternity Pay (General) Regulations 1986 (SI 1986/1960) are routinely updated to upgrade statutory maternity pay in line with inflation, for instance, to £139.58 under the Welfare Benefits Up-rating Order 2015/30. This would amount to £7,242.56 per year (disregarding holidays, the 6 weeks on 90 per cent pay, and that it only lasts a further 33 weeks). (By comparison, the minimum wage, on a 40-hour week, would be around £13,396 per year, before tax and National Insurance.)

5.   The Social Security Contributions and Benefits Act 1992 sections 164–71 duplicate some of the Statutory Maternity Pay (General) Regulations 1986 rules, but also provide that employers are entitled to be reimbursed by the government after paying for statutory maternity leave according to their size and their national insurance contributions. Thus, it is wrong to suppose that businesses suffer any significant financial loss when someone becomes pregnant. Should employers be required to pay more?

6.   In *Boyle v Equal Opportunities Commission* (1998) C-411/96, the Court of Justice held the Pregnant Workers Directive 92/85/EC Art 11(2)(b), on 'maintenance of a payment' during maternity leave, should be at least as high as statutory sick pay. The UK is higher, as this is £88.45 per week in 2015 under the Social Security Contributions and Benefits Act 1992 s 157. For comparison, basic Jobseekers' Allowance is £73.10 per week in 2015.

7.   At all times, employers can (and often will, especially with a good collective agreement) provide better terms and conditions for employees who take child care leave. In particular, many employers who seek to retain talent will wish to maintain full pay.

8.   The Paternity and Adoption Leave Regulations 2002 (SI 2002/2788) concern rules for fathers and parents who adopt. Is there any logic in these regulations being combined, while maternity and parental are combined other than the historical coincidence of their introduction?

9.   The Statutory Paternity Pay and Statutory Adoption Pay (General) Regulations 2002 (SI 2002/2822) and the Statutory Paternity Pay and Statutory Adoption Pay (Weekly Rates) Regulations 2002 (SI 2002/2818) replicate another rule volume to set pay rates.

10.   The Additional Paternity Leave Regulations 2010 (SI 2010/1055) allowed the mother to transfer up to 26 weeks of her maternity leave and pay to the father. The Children and Families Act 2014 s 117 enabled 50 weeks to be transferred. See Mitchell (2015) 44(1) ILJ 125. A primary adopting parent can do the same for the second adopting parent. The difficulty of such transfer regimes (as the Parental Leave Directive 2010 cl 2(2) acknowledges) is that people will often freely choose to perpetuate the entrenched social stereotype. For example, in Sweden by 1999, parents received 15 months of leave and 12 months of this were

compensated at 90 per cent of earnings, but men were only taking 11.9 per cent of benefit days: M Sundström and AE Duvander, 'Gender Division of Childcare and the Sharing of Parental Leave among New Parents in Sweden' (2002) 18(4) *European Sociological Review* 433. Leave is now up to two years, but a split around two to one third between women and men remains. Iceland, by contrast does not allow time-trading, but see HM Sigurdardottir and Ó Garðarsdóttir, 'Backlash in Gender Equality? Fathers' Parental Leave during a Time of Economic Crisis' (2018) *Journal of European Social Policy* 1.

11. The central consequence of women taking more time for child care than men appears to be a continued gender-pay gap. While individuals frequently buck the trend, mothers on average will fall behind in career advancement compared to fathers on average. Couples who find that it is more financially advantageous for the father to keep working because his job is paid more help, unintentionally, to ensure that his job is in fact paid more. Thus, private decisions that appear individually rational become socially irrational, as gender discrimination stubbornly persists.

12. A contrary view might urge that a mother has an inherently more intimate relationship with a child than a father, and this deserves social recognition. That bond is created by the biological fact that the mother carries the child during pregnancy. In a democratic society, it is legitimate for countries to allocate rights and benefits to reflect people's deeply held views about the traditional structure of the family. At the very least, it must be acknowledged that this topic meets genuine religious and cultural sensitivities. But is there any real conflict between having equal child care rights in law and acknowledging biological and cultural differences between men and women?

13. This author suggests, as the foregoing should make clear, that the present legal framework is chaotic, opaque and directly discriminatory on grounds of gender. It would seem desirable to rewrite the law clearly, to ensure children grow up in a world where their parents have equal, decent, transparent rights to care for them.

14. The UK, however, is not alone. There are widespread assumptions internationally that child care is for women. At present, direct sex discrimination is still integral to most systems. See, for example, the Maternity Protection Convention 2000 (c 183).

15. Under ERA 1996 s 57A, following the Parental Leave Directive 2010 cl 7, employees have a further right to 'take reasonable amount of time off' to care for ill or injured dependants, for a death, or an unexpected incident with one's child. The employee must inform the employer 'as soon as reasonably practicable'. In *Qua v John Ford Morrison Solicitors* [2003] ICR 482, Cox J emphasised that there is no additional requirement to deliver updates 'on a daily basis' and that 'the operational needs of the employer cannot be relevant' to decide what is reasonable time off.

(4) RIGHT TO REQUEST FLEXIBLE WORKING TIME

Under the Part-time Work Directive 97/81/EC, clause 5(3) placed a duty on employers to 'give consideration' to employee requests to move from full-time to part-time working.

Initially, the ERA 1996 s 80F–I limited this right to the purpose of caring for children. This was expanded for requests to undergo training, and then simply opened for any reason by the Children and Families Act 2014 s 131. The right to request flexible working (eg Can I work four days a week instead of five? Can I work from home on Thursday? Can I start earlier and finish earlier on a Tuesday?) is therefore not a right to flexible working. But it is seen to function because the employer has a duty to give reasons, in writing, if it feels the request cannot be met. The legitimate reasons to say 'no' are a list of nine grounds in section 80G (see chapter 15(1)(b)) plus any grounds added by Statutory Instrument. These essentially relate to business efficiency.

Commotion Ltd v Rutty [2006] IRLR 171

Mrs Rutty, a warehouse assistant in Tonbridge, Kent, claimed that her employer had breached its duty to provide adequate reasons for denying her request for flexible working under ERA 1996 s 80G. She had worked packing educational toys for Commotion Ltd, but she and her husband had needed to care for Jasmine, their granddaughter. When she asked Mr Wood, the warehouse supervisor, that she needed to move to a three-day week, her request was refused by another manager, Mr Brown. She appealed, and a Mr Coote wrote back saying that she had to remain full time because this would 'help to create a team spirit by having a uniform working day'. She resigned, claiming her application was unreasonably rejected, constructive unfair dismissal and indirect discrimination. The Tribunal found that the refusal was based on incorrect facts and (reflecting the fact that she was close to retirement age, with a difficulty in finding a new job) awarded her £14,038.66. The Employment Appeal Tribunal upheld Mrs Rutty's award, because 'team spirit' was not in the list of legitimate reasons to refuse flexible working.

Judge Burke QC:

37. … There is, we would suggest, a sliding scale of the considerations which a tribunal may be permitted to enter into in looking at such a refusal. The one end is the possibility that all that the employer has to do is to state his ground and there can be no investigation of the correctness or accuracy or truthfulness of that ground. At the other end is perhaps a full inquiry looking to see whether the employer has acted fairly, reasonably, and sensibly in putting forward that ground. Neither extreme is the position, in our judgment, which applies in the relevant statutory situation. We accept Mr Dunn's submission that the tribunal is not entitled to look and see whether it regards the employer as acting fairly or reasonably when he puts forward his reason for rejection of the flexible working request. However, we reject Mr Dunn's submission that the tribunal is not entitled to examine the facts objectively at all; for if it was not so entitled, the jurisdiction set out or the right to make an application set out by section 80H(1)(b) would be of no use. The true position, in our judgment, is that the tribunal is entitled to look at the assertion made by the employer, i e the ground which he asserts is the reason why he has not granted the application, and to see whether it is factually correct. In this case, it does not arise; but, in another case, it may be for instance that the bona fides of the assertion might have to be looked into.

38 In order for the tribunal to establish whether or not the decision by the employer to reject the application was based on incorrect facts, the tribunal must examine the evidence as to the circumstances surrounding the situation to which the application gave rise. In doing so, the tribunal is entitled to inquire into what would have been the effect of granting the application: could it have been coped with without disruption; what did other staff feel about it; could they

make up the time; and matters of that type. We do not propose to go exhaustively through the matters at which a tribunal might wish to look, but if the tribunal were to look at such matters in order to test whether the assertion made by the employer was factually correct, that would not be any misuse of its powers and it would not be committing an error of law.

39 In our judgment, none of the four points made by Mr Dunn under this head is persuasive. We have indicated what the tribunal is entitled to do. In para 11 of its judgment, it did not, in our view, stray outside what was permissible. It pointed out that no evidence had been brought before it to show that working as a part-time warehouse assistant was not feasible. It used its industrial experience to indicate its difficulty in accepting the correctness in fact of the employers' assertion. It pointed out that there was nothing to show that the work could not be done by proper organisation without diminution in the service to customers and that the employers had not carried out any inquiries or investigations to see whether what the claimant wanted could, in fact, be coped with. Those were legitimate points which the tribunal was entitled to consider and on which it was entitled to base its findings. It does refer to justification in the last sentence at para 11; but there it was dealing with the indirect discrimination claim; and, in our judgment, it did not, when considering the flexible working claim, stray from assessing the correctness of the employers' assertion into considering whether it was a justified assertion.

40 As to the second point, the tribunal in its judgment clearly referred to the essential part of the employers' responses to the claimant's application and her appeal and, in para 11, sufficiently addressed the grounds which the employers had put forward.

41 As to the third point, in the case of the warehouse where goods are picked out and packed to the order of customers, as in this case (this being a mail order warehouse) we can see no real difference to any sensible degree between an assertion that somebody working part-time will have a detrimental impact on performance and an assertion that somebody working part-time would have a detrimental effect on the ability to meet customer demand. If there were a detrimental impact on performance, that would constitute a detrimental effect on ability to meet customer demand. The two appear to us to be mirror images of the same. What the tribunal was addressing was, in a practical sense, the true nature of the employers' grounds for rejecting the claimant's request.

42 Lastly, we see no perversity. The tribunal set out the relevant letters; it dealt with the evidence; it reached a conclusion which was a permissible option. We do not propose to say anything more about the well known perversity tests in this section of this judgment, any more than we did in the earlier section of our judgment. We are quite satisfied that the tribunal came to a conclusion which it was open to it to reach and that it had material before it on which to reach that judgment on the facts. The tribunal made findings of facts which were open to it; and we see no ground on which those findings of fact can be successfully attacked.

Mr Evans and **Mrs Gallico** joined.

NOTES AND QUESTIONS

1.   The strict construction of the statute, as applied by Judge Burke QC, accords with the purpose of the Directive and the policy behind s 80F. Arguably, businesses that fail to respond to requests for flexible working adequately, far from merely disappointing their own staff, will damage their own business prospects. Employees who are more content at home will be keener and more productive

in the workplace. Thus, it is important that a genuine legal sanction concentrates the employer's mind on facilitating productivity for its own benefit, as well as employees'.
2. The Flexible Working Regulations 2014/1398 reg 4 adds that an application should be in writing and dated. The ERA 1996 s 80F requires that the employee has worked for at least 26 weeks before making an application.
3. Should there be a right to flexible working time, so that if the employer's reasons are unreasonable, in the view of elected employee representatives or a Tribunal, they will be disregarded?

Problem Question

C Dickens, *A Christmas Carol* (1843)

Bob works as a clerk at a small accounting partnership on Cornhill, in the City. As it is coming up to Christmas, Bob wishes to take some time off. He asks his employer, Scrooge, if he can take off the week between the 25th of December and the 1st of January. Scrooge replies that Bob may only have Christmas Day off. He will have to take his holidays on separate days.

After a cold Christmas, Bob's son Tim is ill. In order to care for Tim, Bob does not come into work. It is three days before he informs Scrooge. Scrooge is very angry when Bob returns to work, shouting about 'that humbug child'. Bob, nevertheless, says he would like to request to become part time from now on. Scrooge says this is impossible because it would damage the 'kindred spirit' in the firm. At the end of the month, when Bob collects his pay cheque, he finds that £15 has been deducted from his wages 'for heating expenses'. This will reduce his average hourly pay to £6 an hour.

Advise Bob on the potential claims he has under UK labour law.

Additional Reading for Chapter 7

L Summers, 'Some Simple Economics of Mandated Benefits' (1989) 79(2) *American Economic Review* 177

Summers puts forward the view that 'mandated benefits' (otherwise known as labour rights) are able to be contracted around by any employer. If, for example, a law requires that people at work have parental leave, 'some simple economics' will in Summers' view lead to the result that the employer can simply lower the wage in order to compensate for the cost of providing the benefit. Although Summers does not consider the existence of bargaining power in how the costs may be shared in practice, the existence of minimum-wage regulation, or the flexibility of businesses in reducing profits in the capital markets that they face, this provides a useful thought exercise, and a starting point for understanding the simplicity of much economic theory.

**C Barnard, S Deakin and R Hobbs, 'Opting Out of the 48 Hour Week' (2003)
32 *ILJ* 223**

The authors argue that the law has had 'little impact on an ingrained culture of long-hours working in the UK'. Their subtitle is 'Employer Necessity or Individual Choice? An Empirical Study of the Operation of Article 18(1)(b) of the WTD in the UK'. It contends that the ability of workers to opt out of the 48-hour limit is a central reason for working time not falling. However, a broader shift toward a reduction of working time would probably require sectoral collective bargaining being restored.

Part Three

Participation

8

Trade Unions

People unionise because they are usually stronger together than alone. By themselves, most employees are offered a contract and told to 'take it or leave it'. But together, employees can collectively bargain. Some do negotiate meaningfully without a union: those with influence over an enterprise's decisions (see chapter 11) or the highly skilled (JS Mill, *Principles of Political Economy* (1848) Book II, ch 14, §14). This may pose risk to fair wages for everyone else: corporate directors, doctors, even law professors, can exploit an arbitrary bargaining position to unjustly enrich themselves. Collective bargaining therefore attempts to create a fair wage scale for everyone. Democratic voice replaces arbitrary power in the distribution of income. Employing entities know that unity matters. They form corporations. Corporations merge into groups. Some groups monopolise markets. Others fix prices in cartels with competitors. Over the twentieth century, law controlled the anticompetitive abuse of capital, and regulated or socialised specific enterprises, while endorsing union organisation to try make a fairer, balanced economy. Unaccountable concentrations of capital have consistently threatened democracy. Unions, from Indian independence, to ending apartheid in South Africa, have been democracy's first and final defenders (chapter 8(1)).

Since 1979, UK unions have been in a state of attrition: from 13 million to 6.5 million members in 2015. This decline began when the Employment Act 1980 prohibited collective agreements to make all employees join the union (a 'closed shop'). Unions have tried to understand how to revive recruitment since (see chapter 9(3)(a)). They remain the largest social networks with active participants of any kind: larger than any political party, voluntary club, public or private enterprise. They are also modernising. Old cumbersome names such as 'National and Local Government Officers Association' are being replaced by brands such as 'Unite'. Unions are organising on social media. They provide services, such as insurance, dismissal protection, advice, and collective bargaining. The three largest are Unite (around 1.4m skilled and technical workers), Unison (1.3m, councils and health), and GMB (613,000, general services). The umbrella body, the Trades Union Congress, covers 5.6 million workers in 50 unions. But size presents its own governance problems. Union executives should represent members' interests. So what accountability strategies will make unions most effective at achieving their goals? Three main mechanisms of accountability are voting rights, other rights in court, and entry or exit rights (cf AO Hirschman, *Exit, Voice, and Loyalty* (1970)). This chapter covers (1) the principle of freedom of association, (2) electing a union's governing body, (3) specific member rights in a union, and (4) rights of members against their employer to join a union without detriment.

Introductory text: Collins ch 6. CEM ch 13, 12 (447–77). D&M chs 7, 8, 10.

(1) FREEDOM OF ASSOCIATION

Freedom of association means organising and acting collectively without undue interference by the state, a corporation or any other powerful group. It is fundamental to democratic society. Not only did the labour movement drive democracy in the UK, workers taking collective action were major, if not the most important, factors contributing to the deposition of the German Kaiser in 1918, Indian independence in 1948, the victory of the US civil rights movement in 1964, the collapse of the Iron Curtain in 1989, and the end of apartheid South Africa in 1994 (to name but a few).[1] All despotic regimes suppress independent centres of power, and must stop them arising. The workplace has historically been the most important location of democratic organisation (whether that was a farm, a factory, an office or a website) because people communicate about their common interest in improving each other's living standards. Freedom of association may have multiple aspects, including the right of people to design their association's own rules (chapter 8(2)–(3)), the right against any detriment or discrimination for joining a union (chapter 8(4)), a duty on the employer to recognise a union and bargain (chapter 9) and the right to take collective action (chapter 10). On this, the European Convention on Human Rights (ECHR) is the most important and binding source of law.

European Convention on Human Rights 1950 Art 11

Article 11 – Freedom of assembly and association

1. Everyone has the right to freedom of peaceful assembly and to freedom of association with others, including the right to form and to join trade unions for the protection of his interests.

2. No restrictions shall be placed on the exercise of these rights other than such as are prescribed by law and are necessary in a democratic society in the interests of national security or public safety, for the prevention of disorder or crime, for the protection of health or morals or for the protection of the rights and freedoms of others. This article shall not prevent the imposition of lawful restrictions on the exercise of these rights by members of the armed forces, of the police or of the administration of the State.

---

[1] See W Deist, 'The Military Collapse of the German Empire: The Reality Behind the Stab-in-the-Back Myth' (1996) 3(2) *War in History* 186, 206–7. B Chandra et al, *India's Struggle for Independence 1857–1947* (2000) ch 36. RA Sense, 'How Poland's Solidarity Won Freedom of Association' (1989) 112 *Monthly Labor Review* 34. On the US civil rights movement, see chapter 1(3)(b). NL Clark and WH Worger, *South Africa: The Rise and Fall of Apartheid* (3rd edn 2016) 111.

NOTES AND QUESTIONS

1. Like other ECHR articles, Art 11 has (1) a general principle and (2) exceptions. Freedom of association, and particularly 'to join trade unions for the protection of his interests', must be guaranteed by the state unless restrictions are (i) 'prescribed by law', (ii) 'necessary in a democratic society' for (iii) national security, public safety, preventing disorder or crime, protecting health or morals, or others' rights and freedoms. The state may (but need not) exclude the military, police and core state administrators from freedom of association, presumably to ensure stability. As always, a core principle of construction is that exceptions to the general rule must be interpreted restrictively.

2. Like most parts of the ECHR, Art 11 was partly inspired by and codified the better side of the common law, equity and traditions of civil law jurisdictions: see eg *Crofter Hand Woven Harris Tweed Co Ltd v Veitch* [1941] UKHL 2.

3. All UK legislation, common law and equity itself, must be interpreted and developed so far as possible to be compatible with ECHR jurisprudence under the Human Rights Act (HRA) 1998 ss 3 and 6(3)(a). It is always possible to develop common law and equity to be compatible. But words in primary legislation may flatly preclude compatible statutory interpretation. If so, a declaration of incompatibility must be made (HRA 1998 s 4). Courts cannot scrap primary legislation that violates human rights. Only Parliament can. But courts can in any case award a remedy (HRA 1998 s 8). In effect, the courts' constitutional position enables them to nullify an Act of Parliament. To what extent do you think courts should be able to limit laws passed by Parliament?

4. Do you think Parliament or the courts are likely to be better defenders of human rights? What might make Parliament fail at this task? What might make courts fail? What should be done if both Parliament and courts fail? What, if anything, can guarantee a positive human rights culture?

5. As chapter 1(2) recounted, unions were originally deemed criminal organisations but slowly won freedom of association, as political democracy was won. In 1834 the Tolpuddle Martyrs were transported to Australia for taking 'unlawful oaths' to press for higher wages, leading to major social protest. In 1868 the Trade Union Congress was established and unions won legal immunity in the Trade Union Act 1871. In 1900 the House of Lords tried to bankrupt the Taff Vale Railway workers for exercising the right to strike. The Trade Disputes Act 1906 re-established statutory freedom for trade unions to strike, but heavy restrictions were reasserted piece by piece from 1980.

6. The ECHR is consistent with, and informed by, the ILO Freedom of Association and Protection of the Right to Organise Convention 1948 (c 87). This says in Art 3: '(1) Workers' and employers' organisations shall have the right to draw up their constitutions and rules, to elect their representatives in full freedom, to organise their administration and activities and to formulate their programmes. (2) The public authorities shall refrain from any interference which would restrict this right or impede the lawful exercise thereof.' Employer organisations aside, given that the right is conferred upon workers, does the right to autonomy of the union presuppose that the union must have democratic structure?

7. Similar principles to ECHR Art 11 are found in the Universal Declaration of Human Rights (UDHR) Art 20 (shorter, and expressly including the right to not associate), the International Covenant on Civil and Political Rights (ICCPR) 1966 Art 22 (identical to the ECHR), and the International Covenant on Economic, Social and Cultural Rights (ICESCR) 1966 Art 8 (identical, but explicitly mentioning the right to strike). The Charter of Fundamental Rights of the European Union 2000 Arts 12 and 28 briefly state the right to association, and then the right to collectively bargain and strike. The UDHR expresses customary international law. It is repeated and expanded upon in the ICCPR and ICESCR, treaties the UK has signed. The Charter of Fundamental Rights of the European Union is not binding on the UK, but codifies what was already inherent in EU law, and is used by the CJEU to interpret all legislation and treaty provisions.

8. Two examples of approaches by dictatorships to unions would have been high in the minds of the ECHR drafters. First, VI Lenin, *The Role and Functions of the Trade Unions Under the New Economic Policy* (12 January 1922) explained: '[I]t is absolutely essential that all authority in the factories should be concentrated in the hands of the management. The factory management, usually built up on the principle of one-man responsibility, must have authority independently to fix and pay out wages, and also distribute rations, working clothes, and all other supplies on the basis and within the limits of collective agreements concluded with the trade unions. ... The trade unions must collaborate closely and constantly with the government, all the political and economic activities of which are guided by the class-conscious vanguard of the working class – the Communist Party.' In this way, unions were simply an extension of and controlled by the state. The early Soviet state itself, despite the hopes of earlier communists, became a ruthless militarised gulag: cf G Orwell, *Animal Farm* (1945).

9. Second, as explained by K Robert, *Hitler's Counterfeit Reich* (1941) 27–28: 'In the Third Reich there exists no longer private associations (*Vereine*) the members of which voluntarily accept leadership for the realization of a common purpose. No democratic methods are admitted, no discussion allowed. The decision of the leader alone is final ... hunting associations, sports clubs, chess clubs, even innocent collectors of stamps [are] all organized according to the Führer principle. Typical of many is the "Labor Front" which has displaced the German Trade Unions.' This 'German Labour Front', created after the free unions were annihilated, was the nationalised Nazi union. Its membership was in effect compulsory. Its leader, an alcoholic called Robert Ley, was directly appointed by Hitler: see the *Deutsche Arbeitsfront Verordnung 1934*. Why do you think the Nazis were concerned about the governance of social groups, if they already controlled the state?

10. Employing entities have also sought to control unions. The United States had particular problems with 'company unions' where representatives were screened, or elections limited, to pre-empt independent union support. See Robert F. Wagner, 'Company Unions: A Vast Industrial Issue' [11 March 1934] *New York Times*, sec 9, 1. The National Labor Relations Act 1935 §8(a)(2) makes it an 'unfair labor practice' for an employer 'to dominate or interfere with the formation or administration of any labor organization, or contribute financial or other support

to it'. The US Republican Party has repeatedly attempted to repeal this provision, for instance, in the 'Teamwork for Employees and Managers Act of 1995'. It argues (falsely) that §8(a)(2) prevented the creation of employee-elected work councils, with binding rights to decide specific workplace issues. Instead, they seek to enable employer-dominated work councils. Given the 2016 election this issue is likely to return. On actual work councils, see chapter 11.

(2) VOTING RIGHTS

Like companies, clubs, trusts or any association lasting over time, trade unions must have standards for how their members and representatives interact. Unions' internal governance can be structured in any way so long as it complies with the law's minimum standards. There is basic 'freedom of contract' or 'freedom of association', subject to minimum members' rights. Very generally, the law's aim is to promote democracy and accountability: that begins with the vote.

Historically, unions wanted to avoid rules administered by potentially hostile courts. They could choose, for example, to incorporate under the Companies Act (CA) 2006 as companies limited by guarantee, but none do. Without any formal registration process, a union is an 'unincorporated association'. Once members agree to act together and contribute 'something of value' (an exchange of promises to cooperate is enough) there is a contract. Any assets are held on trust for members in accordance with the contract's terms. The association will be classed as a 'trade union' under the Trade Union and Labour Relations (Consolidation) Act (TULRCA) 1992 s 1 if its 'principal purposes include the regulation of relations between workers' and employers or other unions. Unions usually apply to the 'Certification Officer' (ss 2–4) to be classed as 'independent' (ss 6–9), ie that they are not interfered with by an employer (s 5). This costs £4,216 (SI 2005/713) and is perceived by some to be useful to get recognition for collective bargaining (chapter 9(1)). Like any other association, or body corporate, unions are subjects of legal rights and duties: they can sue, be sued, make contracts, hold property or commission torts (ss 10–23).

(a) Elections

Probably the most important voting right is for members of the union's governing body.

Trade Union and Labour Relations (Consolidation) Act 1992 ss 46 and 50

46. Duty to hold elections for certain positions.
  (1) A trade union shall secure—
   (a) that every person who holds a position in the union to which this Chapter applies does so by virtue of having been elected to it at an election satisfying the requirements of this Chapter, and
   (b) that no person continues to hold such a position for more than five years without being re-elected at such an election.

(2) The positions to which this Chapter applies (subject as mentioned below) are—
   (a) member of the executive,
   (b) any position by virtue of which a person is a member of the executive,
   (c) president, and
   (d) general secretary.

(3) In this Chapter "member of the executive" includes any person who, under the rules or practice of the union, may attend and speak at some or all of the meetings of the executive, otherwise than for the purpose of providing the committee with factual information or with technical or professional advice with respect to matters taken into account by the executive in carrying out its functions.

[...]

50. Entitlement to vote.

(1) Subject to the provisions of this section, entitlement to vote shall be accorded equally to all members of the trade union.

(2) The rules of the union may exclude entitlement to vote in the case of all members belonging to one of the following classes, or to a class falling within one of the following—
   (a) members who are not in employment;
   (b) members who are in arrears in respect of any subscription or contribution due to the union;
   (c) members who are apprentices, trainees or students or new members of the union. ...

NOTES AND QUESTIONS

1. TULRCA 1992 ss 46 and 50 have the combined effect that all unions must hold direct elections, with equal voting rights for members, for its executive body: that is where the General Secretary will sit. The 'General Secretary' who leads the union's day-to-day policy (like the Chief Executive Officer of a company) will usually be elected separately from other members of the executive, unlike the Prime Minister in Parliament who holds their position only at the will of other Members. The 'President' of a union (like a company Chair) will usually preside over meetings of the executive.

2. TULRCA 1992 s 50(2)(c) does not define what it means by 'new members', but presumably this entitles a union to set a short qualifying period if it wishes before new members have the right to vote. In practice, unions want to give voting rights immediately upon joining, to foster belonging, solidarity and mutual trust.

3. Union governance is not corporate governance, but the similarities are strong. Indeed, union governance is often both informed by, and sets a model for, corporate governance. On corporate governance standards, see D Kershaw, *Company Law in Context: Texts and Materials* (2012) ch 6, 219–29 and ch 7, 252–73. A major difference is that companies only have compulsory rules on the removal of a director, with 28 days notice and a fair hearing (CA 2006 ss 168–69) but not appointment. Unions have compulsory rules on appointment, and not removal. Instead, companies have model rules on appointment that can be changed: Companies (Model Articles) Regulations 2008 Sch 3, para 2 and UK Corporate Governance Code 2016, section B. Is one preferable to the other?

4. Is five years too long (or even too short) as an upper limit for re-election? Five years matches the Fixed-term Parliaments Act 2011, but in practice, the

Fixed-term Parliaments Act 2011 is symbolic: Parliament can scrap it at any time with a simple majority. In any case, in 2017 the Act's requisite two-thirds majority triggered the 'snap election', enabling Theresa May to lose a Conservative majority. The five-year term was opposed by the Labour Party, which advocated four years. Five years is longer than most other countries: Australia, one of the shortest, does federal elections each three years. In companies, the UK Corporate Governance Code 2016 B.7.1 recommends yearly re-appointments for all directors, though this invited criticism for encouraging too much 'short-termism' in business. Is there a principled way to resolve this question? What are the benefits and risks of longer or shorter terms?

5.   The union election rules were first introduced by the notorious Trade Union Act 1984. This was most controversial for its rules on strike ballots (see chapter 10) rather than election rules. Before, the Trade Union Act 1871 merely required disclosure of basic constitutional documents. The Department of Employment, *Democracy in Trade Unions* (1983) Cm 8778, chs 2–3 argued (without much justification) that unions were 'out of touch' with their members and (with more justification) that some were 'militant'. By 'militant' it seems to have meant 'opposed to government policy'.

6.   P Smith, P Fosh, R Martin, H Morris and R Undy, 'Ballots and Union Government in the 1980s' (1993) 31 *British Journal of Industrial Relations* 365, 379–80 argued that direct elections probably increased union executives' opposition to the government, and 'singularly failed to initiate a transformation in the political complexion of union leadership or a reorientation of democracy in a "moderate" direction'. Why do you think that greater democracy would have increased opposition to Conservative Party policy toward labour in the 1980s?

7.   Before the Trades Union Act 1984, most unions had direct elections: 63 out of 101 unions surveyed by R Undy and R Martin, *Ballots and Trade Union Democracy* (1984) 58–59, accounting for 61 per cent of TUC membership at the time.

8.   What rights of voice do union members have aside from elections every five years? Most unions allow members through their branches (rather than individual rights) to attend, speak and submit motions in the annual general meeting: often called a 'national delegate conference: eg Unison (2016) D.1.7 and D.1.10 (cf CA 2006 ss 301 and 314). Most unions require a resolution of the national delegate conference to amend the union's constitution, eg Unison (2016) N.1, without a super-majority (cf CA 2006 s 21).

9.   There is a long-running debate on whether law should bind unions' democratic standards (and what that itself should mean) in all developed societies. Some have argued that unions should be left free, to become 'fighting organisations' in the way they want. Others argue that legally enforceable democratic standards actually improve, rather than hamper, unions' effectiveness. See E McGaughey, 'Democracy or Oligarchy? Models of Union Governance in the UK, Germany and US' (2017) KCL Law School Research Paper No 2017-35. Do you think 'democracy' strengthens or weakens effective and efficient governance? Under what circumstances?

10. If a member is running for election to the executive, TULRCA 1992 s 48 creates a right for candidates to circulate 'election addresses' of at least 100 words to the

union's members by post with voting papers. This allows new candidates, who have perhaps not had established positions in a union already, to get some publicity. What really matters is access to the union's contact and membership list. In practice today, union executive candidates are using Facebook, Twitter, Youtube and email to communicate and publicise themselves.

11. TULRCA 1992 s 51 says the 'method of voting must be by the marking of a voting paper by the person voting'. This must be done by post, and is argued to preclude electronic voting. In 2016, the government asked Sir Ken Knight CBE to review whether this system should remain. Sir Ken was the former Chief Inspector of Fire Services, now retired. While perhaps not the most obvious choice for the government to lead a review on information technology, Sir Ken made headlines in 2013 by advocating job cuts among firefighters to save a predicted £200m in a 'time of austerity'. In pressing for a full review of s 51, the government was resolved to in no way be distracted by criticism that companies, political parties or the *X-Factor* have already used e-voting for some time. The real controversy appears to centre on the fact that change must include strike ballots. E-voting will almost certainly increase turnout and engagement of members with their union (see chapter 10). Do you think anti-union interest groups might have an incentive to tie unions up in 'red tape'?

12. The other provisions of TULRCA 1992 ss 49, 51A–56A are meant to ensure the integrity of the election process. They require the appointment of an independent scrutineer to oversee the ballot process and counting. The scrutineer writes a report. Any member or candidate can complain about misconduct to the Certification Officer, who in turn can require a union to make any changes, or hold a fresh election. The Certification Officer's decisions can be appealed to the Employment Appeal Tribunal on a point of law 'arising in any proceedings before or arising from any decision'.

13. TULRCA 1992 s 47 says: 'No member of the trade union shall be unreasonably excluded from standing as a candidate.' *Breen v AEU* dealt with an analogous exclusion, but after an election (not before) and for a shop steward (not an executive).

Breen v Amalgamated Engineering Union **[1971] 2 QB 175**

Patrick Breen claimed he was unlawfully excluded from being an elected shop steward by the district secretary, Victor Townsend, of the Amalgamated Engineering Union (AEU, now part of Unite) in 1965. Under the AEU's rule 13(21): 'Shop stewards elected by members are subject to approval by the district committee and shall not function until such approval is given.' In 1954, Breen had been elected as a shop steward at the Esso Oil Refinery, Fawley, Hampshire. In 1958, Breen was accused of stealing union funds, but the accusation was found by a union subcommittee to be a false 'trumpery charge'. Townsend had been the subcommittee's secretary at the time. According to the judge, Cusack J, Townsend's evidence had been 'evasive and untrue … he had retained in his own mind since 1958 a belief that the plaintiff was really guilty'. However, he held that rule 13(21) had to be strictly applied, even if the procedure used had breached principles of natural justice. Only bad faith would be enough, and that was not clear on the facts. Breen argued on appeal that there should be good reasons, and a fair hearing. The Court of Appeal held by a majority that, while there is a right to a fair hearing, a union does not need to give good reasons. Lord Denning MR, dissenting, held that natural justice requires good reasons.

Lord Denning MR (dissenting): … the judge was echoing views which were current some years ago, But there have been important developments in the last 22 years which have transformed the situation. It may truly now be said that we have a developed system of administrative law. These developments have been most marked in the review of decisions of statutory bodies: but they apply also to domestic bodies.

Take first statutory bodies. It is now well settled that a statutory body, which is entrusted by statute with a discretion, must act fairly. It does not matter whether its functions are described as judicial or quasi-judicial on the one hand, or as administrative on the other hand, or what you will. Still it must act fairly. It must, in a proper case, give a party a chance to be heard: see *In re H. K. (An Infant)* [1967] 2 QB 617, 630 by Lord Parker CJ in relation to immigration officers; and *R v Gaming Board for Great Britain, Ex parte Benaim and Khaida* [1970] 2 QB 417, 430 by us in relation to the gaming board. The discretion of a statutory body is never unfettered. It is a discretion which is to be exercised according to law. That means at least this: the statutory body must be guided by relevant considerations and not by irrelevant. If its decision is influenced by extraneous considerations which it ought not to have taken into account, then the decision cannot stand. No matter that the statutory body may have acted in good faith; nevertheless the decision will be set aside. That is established by *Padfield v Minister of Agriculture, Fisheries and Food* [1968] AC 997 which is a landmark in modern administrative law.

Does all this apply also to a domestic body? I think it does, at any rate when it is a body set up by one of the powerful associations which we see nowadays. Instances are readily to be found in the books, notably the Stock Exchange, the Jockey Club, the Football Association, and innumerable trade unions. All these delegate power to committees. These committees are domestic bodies which control the destinies of thousands. They have quite as much power as the statutory bodies of which I have been speaking. They can make or mar a man by their decisions. Not only by expelling him from membership, but also by refusing to admit him as a member: or, it may be, by a refusal to grant a licence or to give their approval. Often their rules are framed so as to give them a discretion. They then claim that it is an "unfettered" discretion with which the courts have no right to interfere. They go too far. They claim too much. The Minister made the same claim in the *Padfield* case, and was roundly rebuked by the House of Lords for his impudence. So should we treat this claim by trade unions. They are not above the law, but subject to it. Their rules are said to be a contract between the members and the union. So be it. If they are a contract, then it is an implied term that the discretion should be exercised fairly. But the rules are in reality more than a contract. They are a legislative code laid down by the council of the union to be obeyed by the members. This code should be subject to control by the courts just as much as a code laid down by Parliament itself. If the rules set up a domestic body and give it a discretion, it is to be implied that that body must exercise its discretion fairly. Even though its functions are not judicial or quasi-judicial, but only administrative, still it must act fairly. Should it not do so, the courts can review its decision, just as it can review the decision of a statutory body. The courts cannot grant the prerogative writs such as *certiorari* and *mandamus* against domestic bodies, but they can grant declarations and injunctions which are the modern machinery for enforcing administrative law.

Then comes the problem: ought such a body, statutory or domestic, to give reasons for its decision or to give the person concerned a chance of being heard? Not always, but sometimes. It all depends on what is fair in the circumstances. If a man seeks a privilege to which he has no particular claim – such as an appointment to some post or other – then he can be turned away without a word. He need not be heard. No explanation need be given: see the cases cited in *Schmidt v Secretary of State for Home Affairs* [1969] 2 Ch 149, 170-171. But if he is a man whose property is at stake, or who is being deprived of his livelihood, then reasons should be given why he is being turned down, and he should be given a chance to be heard. I go further. If he is a man who has some right or interest, or some legitimate expectation, of which it would not be fair to deprive him without a hearing, or reasons given, then these should be afforded him, according as the case may demand. The giving of reasons is one of the fundamentals of good administration. Again take *Padfield's case* [1968] AC 997. The dairy farmers had no right to have their complaint referred to a committee of investigation, but they had a legitimate expectation that it would be. The House made it clear that if the Minister rejected their request without reason, the court might infer that he had no good reason: and, that if he gave a bad reason, it might vitiate his decision.

So here we have Mr. Breen. He was elected by his fellow workers to be their shop steward. He was their chosen representative. He was the man whom they wished to have to put forward their views to the management, and to negotiate for them. He was the one whom they wished to tell the union about their needs. ...

...

Seeing that he had been elected to this office by a democratic process, he had, I think, a legitimate expectation that he would be approved by the district committee, unless there were good reasons against him. If they had something against him, they ought to tell him and to give him a chance of answering it before turning him down. It seems to me intolerable that they should be able to veto his appointment in their unfettered discretion. This district committee sit in Southampton some miles away from Fawley. None of them, so far as I know, worked in the oil refinery. Who are they to say nay to him and his fellow workers without good reason and without hearing what he has to say?

To be fair to them, the district committee did not claim that they could act without good reasons. They said that they had good reasons. They were set out by their secretary with their authority in the letter of December 31, 1965. And, when examined, the very first reason they gave was a bad reason. It was that he had misappropriated union funds seven years ago; whereas in truth he had done nothing of the sort and had been acquitted of the charge. So long as that letter stands as the vehicle of their reasons, their disapproval must be utterly invalid: for, on the face of it, they were actuated by a highly prejudicial consideration which was entirely erroneous and which they ought not to have taken into account at all. Call it prejudice, bias, or what you will. It is enough to vitiate the discretion of any body, statutory, domestic, or other. To make it worse, they did not give him a chance of answering it or correcting it. They condemned him unheard.

...

Mr. Townsend certainly was influenced by the bad reason. He wrote it down in the letter. He repeated it later, saying to Mr. Breen "You had the money, brother." I expect the judge thought that Mr. Townsend's state of mind did not matter because he had no vote. But I think it mattered a lot. He was the district secretary, a paid official there permanently. The others were elected annually. They came and went. He stayed on. He knew all about the episode in 1958. It was his job to know it. It is true that he had no vote, but he had a voice and he had a pen.

...

A week later, after the truth was out, they deliberately decided to stand by the reason. They stood by it in their pleading for a long time. They only renounced it years later. It was then too late. On principle it seems to me that, when a committee or body of persons, who are entrusted with a decision, give reasons for it in writing which are clear and unambiguous, then it is not open to the individual members of that body, be they one or many, to give evidence to add to, vary or contradict the reasons which have been given authoritatively on behalf of all. If that were permitted, one of them might say one thing; another another: and no one would know which was correct, especially when the evidence comes years after the meeting, as happened here. More important, the party affected by the decision is entitled to go by the stated reasons. It is on the basis of them that he determines whether to accept the decision or to challenge it. ...

...

5. The Remedy

It said that Mr. Breen has no remedy. His election was only for one year – from December, 1965. That year is long past. So there is no point in making a declaration. As to damages, he has suffered none because he did not lose his job. He still got his wages. All he lost was his standing as a shop steward: and for that no damages should be awarded, any more than a dismissed servant can get such damages: see *Addis v Gramophone Co Ltd* [1909] AC 488. [*On this point, see now chapter 18(1).*]

This argument does not appeal to me in the least. Here was Mr. Breen elected to an office of standing and responsibility amongst his fellows. He was wrongly deprived of it. The effect would not be for that one year only. It would seriously prejudice his chance of being elected another year. Loss of such an office strikes deep, and not the less so because it may not strike at the pocket: see *Lawlor v Union of Post Office Workers* [1965] Ch 712, 734-5. I think that the court should do what it can to vindicate him. It is an appropriate case for the remedies now given by administrative law. The court should grant a declaration that the refusal of approval was invalid: see *Taylor v National Union of Seamen* [1967] 1 WLR 532. This will not make him shop steward for that year. But it will justify him in the eyes of his fellow workmen.

Next, damages. At present these have to be claimed in contract. No action of tort lies against a trade union. The claim must be based on an implied contract that the district committee must not withhold their approval unfairly. But what are the damages? There is no financial loss, because Mr. Breen has remained at work. But he has suffered in reputation and standing. He has been injured in his proper feelings of dignity and pride. He has lost the chance of a career of honour in the union. If the action had been in tort, these would certainly have been the subject of compensation: see *Rookes v Barnard* [1964] AC 1129, 1221, by Lord Devlin. Are they outlawed in contract? I think not. Our law is flexible enough to meet new situations as they arise. It gave damages to a trader when his cheque was wrongly dishonoured, even though he suffered no financial loss. It has given, in this century, damages to actors for loss of publicity. I see no reason why it should not give damages to a shop steward for wrongful deprivation of office.

Edmund Davies LJ: I entertain substantial doubts that the judgment I am about to deliver will serve the ends of justice. That is, to say the least, a most regrettable situation for any judge, but I see no escape from it. Its effect is to turn away empty-handed from this court an appellant who, on any view, has been grossly abused.

...

Directing myself accordingly, while I confess my inability to understand how the trial judge arrived at his vital conclusion of fact, I regard myself as unable to disturb it ... to adopt the words of Viscount Simon in *Watt (or Thomas) v Thomas* [1947] AC 484, 486:

> "This is not to say that the judge of first instance can be treated as infallible in determining which side is telling the truth or is refraining from exaggeration. Like other tribunals, he may go wrong on a question of fact ..."

Cusack J may indeed have gone wrong on the crucial question in this case. But, quite apart from the formidable fact that the plaintiff was given leave to appeal out of time on terms that findings of fact would be left unchallenged, for the reason I have given I cannot say that it has been affirmatively demonstrated that he did.

Megaw LJ delivered a short opinion concurring with **Edmund Davies LJ**.

NOTES AND QUESTIONS

1.   The majority held that Mr Breen had no remedy because the judge's finding of no bad faith could not be disturbed: the union did not have to give good reasons. Natural justice principles did not require this. Lord Denning MR would have held that good reasons needed to be given: Townsend's state of mind was not decisive. But now, TULRCA 1992 s 47 and the oversight of the scrutineer mean that Lord Denning MR's judgment effectively represents the law for elections to a union's executive body.

2.   Does natural justice now require reasonableness in excluding someone from an election? It would seem that, whatever the position in 1971, reasons are now required, and so if Mr Breen's case were run again today, Lord Denning MR's judgment would be the correct one. A test of reasonableness, to overturn a decision of a union executive could choose from at least four standards: (1) the judge thinks the decision was not reasonable, and substitutes their decision; (2) it was not proportionate, ie not appropriate, necessary and reasonable (see chapter 13(1)(b)); (3) it falls outside a reasonable range of responses (see chapter 17); or (4) it was so unreasonable that no reasonable person could decide the same way, as in *Associated Provincial Picture Houses Ltd v Wednesbury Corp* [1948] 1 KB 223. While the *Wednesbury* test was used for public bodies before, it has generally shifted to the reasonable range test, or the proportionality test where human rights are at stake. Given that union governance goes to the heart of freedom of association in ECHR Art 11, and that it is more structured and predictable, it seems the proportionality is the right test in law today.

3.   Lord Denning MR refers to a union's rules as being a 'contract between the members and the union'. He argued that, even if one did not see a union as like a statutory body subject to judicial review in administrative law, the duty to act fairly with good reasons would be 'an implied term that the discretion should be exercised fairly'. Put another way, it does not matter whether an organisation exercising power is public or private, all should be bound by good governance standards. Do you agree?

4.   It has since become clear that the same functional outcomes to control discretionary abuse of power are to be reached through contractual language as much as public or administrative law standards. The two leading cases are *Equitable Life Assurance Society v Hyman* [2000] UKHL 39 (directors of a life insurance company had to exercise discretion to fulfil policyholders' reasonable expectations) and *Attorney General of Belize v Belize Telecom Ltd* [2009] UKPC 10 (company investors' reasonable expectations were that a director could be removed, despite a badly drafted article suggesting the opposite).

5.   In *Ecclestone v National Union of Journalists* [1999] IRLR 166 a former Deputy General Secretary of the NUJ for 40 years claimed he was unfairly excluded from running for election, contrary to TULRCA 1992 s 47. The executive had dismissed Ecclestone after a vote of no confidence and refused his application to run again, stating that to do so, a candidate had to have the NEC's confidence.

This was not in the union's rules, or in a resolution adopted at the NUJ's Annual General Meeting. Smith J held that Ecclestone could not be excluded either at common law or under TULRCA 1992 s 47, applying a 'reasonable range' standard. 'The actions of this NEC', he said, 'fell outside the scope of the discretion provided by the rules because they did not act in accordance with good employment practice.' Thus, Smith J in substance followed Lord Denning MR's reasoning in *Breen*.

6.   In *AB v CD* [2001] IRLR 808 the President of the National Union of Rail, Maritime and Transport Workers (RMT) sought a declaration that Mr Tilley had not 'won' election to the executive for its Regions 2 and 3. Rule 13(1) required a single transferable vote system, but said nothing about a tie situation. In the first round Mr Tilley won 747 votes, Mr Grundy 713 and Mr Puttnam 332. In the second round, the second preference on Mr Puttnam's votes were counted to give Tilley and Grundy 874 each. A union committee recorded Tilley as winning, following the recommended standards of the Electoral Reform Society. Sir Andrew Morritt VC held that it was justified to imply the ERS rules (and obviously so) rather than hold another election.

(b) Political Funds

Trade Union and Labour Relations (Consolidation) Act 1992 ss 71–72 and 82

71. Restriction on use of funds for political objects.
   (1) The funds of a trade union shall not be applied in the furtherance of the political objects to which this Chapter applies unless—
   (a)   there is in force in accordance with this Chapter a resolution (a "political resolution") approving the furtherance of those objects as an object of the union (see sections 73 to 81), and
   (b)   there are in force rules of the union as to – (i) the making of payments in furtherance of those objects out of a separate fund, and (ii) the making of contributions to that fund by members,
which comply with this Chapter (see sections 82, 84 and 85) and have been approved by the Certification Officer.
   ...

72. Political objects to which restriction applies.
   (1) The political objects to which this Chapter applies are the expenditure of money—
   (a)   on any contribution to the funds of, or on the payment of expenses incurred directly or indirectly by, a political party;
   (b)   on the provision of any service or property for use by or on behalf of any political party;
   (c)   in connection with the registration of electors, the candidature of any person, the selection of any candidate or the holding of any ballot by the union in connection with any election to a political office;
   (d)   on the maintenance of any holder of a political office;

(e) on the holding of any conference or meeting by or on behalf of a political party or of any other meeting the main purpose of which is the transaction of business in connection with a political party;

(f) on the production, publication or distribution of any literature, document, film, sound recording or advertisement the main purpose of which is to persuade people to vote for a political party or candidate or to persuade them not to vote for a political party or candidate.

...

82. Rules as to political fund.

(1) The trade union's rules must provide—

(a) that payments in the furtherance of the political objects to which this Chapter applies shall be made out of a separate fund (the "political fund" of the union);

(b) that a member of the union who is not a contributor (see section 84) shall not be under any obligation to contribute to the political fund;

(c) that a member shall not by reason of not being a contributor

(i) be excluded from any benefits of the union, or

(ii) be placed in any respect either directly or indirectly under a disability or at a disadvantage as compared with other members of the union (except in relation to the control or management of the political fund); ...

(ca) that, if the union has a political fund, any form (including an electronic form) that a person has to complete in order to become a member of the union shall include—

(i) a statement to the effect that the person may opt to be a contributor to the fund,

and

(ii) a statement setting out the effect of paragraph (c); and

(d) that contribution to the political fund shall not be made a condition for admission to the union.

(2) A member of a trade union who claims that he is aggrieved by a breach of any rule made in pursuance of this section may complain to the Certification Officer.

NOTES AND QUESTIONS

1. TULRCA 1992 ss 71–72 and 82 require that unions (1) hold a resolution to authorise a political fund, for (2) any financial assistance for or against a political party or candidate, (3) the fund is separated from the union's general funds, and (4) union members must opt-in. Section 72A states the Certification Officer can take complaints about any breach, and s 73 requires resolutions to be renewed at least each 10 years. Section 77 requires voting on 'paper', even though individuals can opt-in electronically under s 82(1)(ca).

2. Under the CA 2006 ss 366–68, company directors cannot make political donations without a resolution by members (or members of a holding company, if a subsidiary) authorising it, at least each four years. However, s 378 exempts donations under £5,000 in each 12-month period from a resolution, or potentially any disclosure. Moreover, members or shareholders have no right to opt-out. Political views of the ultimate investors in companies (as opposed to asset managers) are more likely to be in direct conflict with those of company directors, but union members' views are less likely to conflict with union executives.

Should the £5,000 exemption be removed, or an opt-in rule introduced? Should corporate money be banned in its entirety?

3. Principled concerns could be raised about union executives using funds for causes not all union members share. This concern is more than neutralised by the opt-in. In practice, however, the law was not driven by principles, but rather a desire to defund the Labour Party. In *Amalgamated Society of Railway Servants v Osborne* [1910] AC 87 the House of Lords held any union political spending, when not specifically in a union's objects, was *ultra vires*. Because Members of Parliament were unpaid at that time, Labour Party MPs were threatened with bankruptcy, because unlike Liberal or Conservative MPs they were not individually wealthy. Lloyd-George introduced MP salaries in 1911, and the Trade Union Act 1913 enabled majority union member resolutions to adopt political objects (without a potentially far harder union constitution amendment). Unions that still lacked political objects were also banned by at least one judge from running a newspaper: *Bennett v National Amalgamated Society of Operative House and Ship Painters and Decorators* (1916) 85 LJ Ch 298.

4. After the general strike of 1926, the Conservative government passed the Trade Disputes and Trade Unions Act 1927 to require all union members opt-in the political fund. The first majority Labour government passed Trade Disputes and Trade Unions Act 1946 to say union members could opt-out. The Trade Union Act 1984 again switched the default to require an opt-in. Why do you think the default matters? See chapter 2(2).

5. In *Paul and Fraser v NALGO* [1987] IRLR 413, two members of NALGO (now part of Unison) claimed the union's publications in its 'Make People Matter' campaign before the 1987 local and general elections were unlawful (now TULRCA 1992 s 72(1)(f)). This included leaflets, implying that people should not vote Conservative. It had phrases like 'Decent public services make all the difference' and 'More than 36,000 National Health Service beds – one in 10 of the total – have been cut since 1979.' Sir Nicolas Browne-Wilkinson VC held the literature was unlawful because the union did not have a political objects clause. See now Unison, Rulebook (2016) s J.

6. In 2016, the Certification Officer reported there were 6,948,725 union members, £33,031,003 was contributed to political funds in 25 unions, from 4,859,578 members (69%). 651,140 members in those 25 unions had not opted in: 88% opted in. This suggests opting in had been made extremely easy for most members.

(3) OTHER RIGHTS IN COURT

(a) Right to Enforce the Constitution

While most issues within a union are resolved by voting for representatives, members have more rights under its constitution, and a reasonable expectation that the constitution is followed. Like any contract, the constitution's terms are enforceable as of right by any union member. When union executives exceed their authority, this is called act-ing *ultra vires* (beyond powers), and is unlawful. But all constitutional violations can be restrained. Under TULRCA 1992 s 63, a member's right to access courts cannot be excluded, or nullified by a union's rules (cf CA 2006 ss 171 and 232 for company mem-bers). Therefore, in the unlikely event that executives or officials fail to follow the union's own rules, a court may compel them to do so. There are, of course, good reasons why litigation may not be desirable to resolve every dispute about unions' internal affairs. But a constitution, if not changed, must always be followed.

Edwards v Halliwell [1950] 2 All ER 1064

Edwards claimed that Halliwell, the General Secretary of National Union of Vehicle Builders (NUVB) (now part of Unite), with the executive committee had unconsti-tutionally increased the union's fees. Rule 19 of NUVB's rules required a ballot with a two-thirds vote in favour to increase the union's fees, but this had not happened. Halliwell argued that an old company law principle from *Foss v Harbottle* (1843) 67 ER 189 applied, so that a 'mere irregularity' of internal governance did not entitle individual members to sue: it should be up to the executive, as the union's representative, to rectify any wrongful conduct under the constitution (and here the executive was entitled to do nothing). The Court of Appeal held the union's rules had to be followed. Raising fees without a vote was *ultra vires* and void.

Asquith LJ: Here were men who had a right not to have their contributions increased except after a ballot resulting in a two-thirds majority. This right was clearly violated. An unauthorised increase was sought to be extorted, and when they refused to pay, as they were entitled to do, severe penalties were imposed or threatened. To call this a mere informality or irregularity without any element of oppression or unfairness would be an abuse of language. When in circumstances such as I have described a remedy is sought by an individual, complaining of a particular act in breach of his rights and inflicting particular damage on him, it seems to me the principle of *Foss v Harbottle*, which has been so strongly relied upon by the defendants, does not apply either by way of barring the remedy or supporting the objection that the action is wrongly constituted because the union is not a plaintiff.

Jenkins LJ: The rule in *Foss v Harbottle*, as I understand it, comes to no more than this. First, the proper plaintiff in an action in respect of a wrong alleged to be done to company or asso-ciation of persons is *prima facie* the company or the association of persons itself. Secondly, where the alleged wrong is a transaction which might be made binding on the company or association and on all its members by a simple majority of the members, no individual member of the company is allowed to maintain an action in respect of that matter for the simple reason that, if a mere majority of the members of the company or association is in favour of what has been done, then cadit quaestio. No wrong had been done to the company or association and there is nothing in respect of which anyone can sue. If, on the other hand, a simple majority of members of the company or association is against what has been done, then there is no valid reason why the company or association itself should not sue. In my judgment, it is implicit in the rule that the matter relied on as constituting the cause of action should be a cause of action properly belonging to the general body of corporators or members of the company or associa-tion as opposed to a cause of action which some individual member can assert in his own right.

The cases falling within the general ambit of the rule are subject to certain exceptions. It has been noted in the course of argument that in cases where the act complained of is wholly *ultra vires* the company or association the rule has no application because there is no question of the transaction being confirmed by any majority. It has been further pointed out that where what has been done amounts to what is generally called in these cases a fraud on the minority and the wrongdoers are themselves in control of the company, the rule is relaxed in favour of the aggrieved minority who are allowed to bring what is known as a minority shareholders' action on behalf of themselves and all others. The reason for this is that, if they were denied that right, their grievance could never reach the court because the wrongdoers themselves, being in control, would not allow the company to sue. Those exceptions are not directly in point in this case, but they show, especially the last one, that the rule is not an inflexible rule and it will be relaxed where necessary in the interests of justice.

There is a further exception which seems to me to touch this case directly. That is the exception noted by Romer J in *Cotter v National Union of Seamen*. He pointed out that the rule did not prevent an individual member from suing if the matter in respect of which he was suing was one which could validly be done or sanctioned, not by a simple majority of the members of the company or association, but only by some special majority, as, for instance, in the case of a limited company under the Companies Act, a special resolution duly passed as such. As Romer J pointed out, the reason for that exception is clear, because otherwise, if the rule were applied in its full rigour, a company which, by its directors, had broken its own regulations by doing something without a special resolution which could only be done validly by a special resolution could assert that it alone was the proper plaintiff in any consequent action and the effect would be to allow a company acting in breach of its articles to do de facto by ordinary resolution that which according to its own regulations could only be done by special resolution. That exception exactly fits the present case inasmuch as here the act complained of is something which could only have been validly done, not by a simple majority, but by a two-thirds majority obtained on a ballot vote. In my judgment, therefore, the reliance on the rule in *Foss v Harbottle* in the present case may be regarded as misconceived on that ground alone.

I would go further. In my judgment, this is a case of a kind which is not even within the general ambit of the rule. It is not a case where what is complained of is a wrong done to the union, a matter in respect of which the cause of action would primarily and properly belong to the union. It is a case in which certain members of a trade union complain that the union, acting through the delegate meeting and the executive council in breach of the rules by which the union and every member of the union are bound, has invaded the individual rights of the complainant members, who are entitled to maintain themselves in full membership with all the rights and privileges appertaining to that status so long as they pay contributions in accordance with the tables of contributions as they stood before the purported alterations of 1943, unless and until the scale of contributions is validly altered by the prescribed majority obtained on a ballot vote. Those rights, these members claim, have been invaded. The gist of the case is that the personal and individual rights of membership of each of them have been invaded by a purported, but invalid, alteration of the tables of contributions. In those circumstances, it seems to me the rule in *Foss v Harbottle* has no application at all, for the individual members who are suing sue, not in the right of the union, but in their own right to protect from invasion their own individual rights as members.

Sir Raymond Evershed MR concurred.

NOTES AND QUESTIONS

1.   Jenkins LJ, with whom the whole court agreed, held that (1) the union executive's actions were *ultra vires*, entitling Edwards to sue, (2) the wrongdoers were in control of the union, meaning Edwards and other members had to have the right to sue if the constitutional breach were to be rectified by anyone, (3) special

voting procedures had to be strictly followed, and (4) the right of Edwards that was infringed was a 'personal right' entitling an individual member to claim. Do you agree that arguments (1)–(4) amount to the same thing: union members can enforce their constitution's terms?

2.   *Foss v Harbottle* created a long and confused history of thought in company law. *Foss* was not about enforcing a company's constitution, but the implicit standard of care. A minority shareholder, Foss, claimed that Harbottle and other directors of the Victoria Park Co were negligent in overspending the company's assets in building an estate in Manchester. The standard of care ('do not be negligent') was not expressed in the company constitution: it functions like an implied term. Wigram VC held that there could be no such claim for negligence: it was up to a majority of the company shareholders to claim, not a single minority shareholder. We have higher standards now, and this case might be decided differently, but it reflected the sentiment that members may prefer voting to costly litigation to deal with incompetence. Today, it is generally accepted that members can enforce a company's constitution as of right (CA 2006 s 33), but should only be able to further sue directors for damages for a breach of duty, including negligence, if a court find it in the company's best financial, reputational, social or other interests (CA 2006 ss 171–77 and 260–63). Basically, a union is the same.

3.   In *National Union of Mineworkers (Kent Area) v Gormley* (20 October 1977) The Times, the miners from the Kent area sued Joe Gormley, the NUM's General Secretary, to halt a ballot on whether to endorse the Labour government's national productivity scheme. A positive result on the ballot would avoid a conflict over incomes policy. The NUM's executive had no express constitutional power to hold ballots, rather than a general power of management. Lord Denning MR held that holding a ballot was part of the National Executive Committee's implied powers. He said: '[T]he ballot was a sensible and reasonable proposal by the NEC to take the views by the democratic method of a secret ballot of all the workers affected. It was a far more satisfactory and democratic method than leaving it to the delegates of a conference who might not be truly representative in their individual capacities of the views of the various men they represented.' Do you agree that holding a referendum should be considered part of day-to-day management power? Is there a danger that referenda are used for ulterior purposes, unconnected with the issues, and wreak havoc when an unexpected result transpires?

4.   While there has been no significant litigation, union executives are bound like any agent to exercise care and skill. Also, like anyone in a position of trust and confidence, they are bound to avoid any possibility of a conflict of interest. These standards, familiar from contract, tort, trust and company law, will probably reflect those found in CA 2006 ss 171–77. While there are no codified rules for unions, a court would have to be satisfied that litigation, if any allegation of negligence or conflicts were made, was in the union's interest as a whole.

5.   In *McGahie v Union of Shop, Distributive and Allied Workers* (1965) 1966 SLT 74, Lord Fraser for the Court of Session Outer House held that Euphemia McGahie was entitled to enforce her application for legal aid. A union member

could compel the union to consider his legal aid application, even though if the union agreed to grant it, he could not have enforced the right to it.

6. In *Hodgson v National and Local Government Officials Association* [1972] 1 WLR 130 members of the Leeds branch of NALGO (now part of Unison) sought an injunction against their National Executive Committee to direct conference delegates to support entry into the European Economic Community (now the EU). The union's constitution designated NALGO's conference as being the body that 'directed ... general policy'. Goudling J held the members' claim was well founded, and the rule in *Foss v Harbottle* (of the executive controlling decisions) 'should not be applied if the result may be to deprive the majority of an opportunity of carrying out their will. In other words, if the constitutional machinery of the body cannot operate in time to be of practical effect, the court, in my view, should entertain the suit of a member or members not supported by the association itself.'

(b) Money and Transparent Accounts

Prudent use of a union's money, derived from member contributions or selling services, is important to every member. In corporate governance it is thought that without information and oversight, money may be wasted on excessive managerial pay, vanity projects, needless bureaucracy or political causes that members do not support. Unions committed to democracy and equality differ widely in many ways, but transparency is expected.

Trade Union and Labour Relations (Consolidation) Act 1992 s 28

28. Duty to keep accounting records.
(1) A trade union shall—
   (a) cause to be kept proper accounting records with respect to its transactions and its assets and liabilities, and
   (b) establish and maintain a satisfactory system of control of its accounting records, its cash holdings and all its receipts and remittances.
(2) Proper accounting records shall not be taken to be kept with respect to the matters mentioned in subsection (1)(a) unless there are kept such records as are necessary to give a true and fair view of the state of the affairs of the trade union and to explain its transactions.
...

30. Right of access to accounting records.
(1) A member of a trade union has a right to request access to any accounting records of the union which are available for inspection and relate to periods including a time when he was a member of the union. In the case of records relating to a branch or section of the union, it is immaterial whether he was a member of that branch or section.
...

32. Annual return.
(1) A trade union shall send to the Certification Officer as respects each calendar year a return relating to its affairs. ...

1.   The basic principles are that unions should (1) keep accounts to give a 'true and fair view' of the union's finances (cf CA 2006 ss 495–97), (2) enable members to see the accounts and (3) file returns with the Certification Officer. TULRCA 1992 ss 27–45D elaborate. Accounts must be audited and the essential parts are public. In practice, good financial administration in unions is routine and highly professionalised. Unions hire well-known firms such as Deloitte, Moore Stephens or BDO to audit their books.

2.   The *Annual Report of the Certification Officer 2015–2016* (2016) compiles union member and finance information. Appendix 5 has a table of the salary and benefits of general secretaries. Out of 98 independent unions, the 21 most highly paid are:

Union	£ total pay	£ salary+benefits
Association of School and College Leaders	150,044	127,472+22,572
Royal College of Nursing of the UK	149,169	149,169+0
Trades Union Congress	147,929	108,997+38,932
British Air Line Pilots Association	147,646	120,353+27,293
National Union of Teachers	145,976	103,574+42,402
National Association of Head Teachers	145,492	124,325+21,167
Musicians Union	145,327	112,940+32,387
International Transport Workers Federation	145,000	122,000+23,000
Royal College of Midwives	141,460	117,687+23,773
Association of Teachers and Lecturers	140,494	120,441+20,053
Nationwide Group Staff Union	136,329	119,328+17,001
Accord	136,178	124,844+11,334
Community	135,711	106,842+28,869
Prospect	133,000	109,000+24,000
NASWUT	132,473	101,312+31,161
Chartered Society of Physiotherapy	129,690	110,000+19,690
University and College Union	122,208	102,578+19,630
GMB	121,000	97,000+24,000
Unite the Union	120,886	101,368+19,518
Unison	104,673	97,211+7,462
IBOA The Finance Union (*NB ranking changes*)	€190,928	132,455+58,473 (€)

3.   There is a considerable disparity between these top 21 paying unions and the other 77. Many unions pay wages far closer to their members. For example, the National Union of Journalists pays a £66,221 salary and £7,392 in benefits.

4.   The median UK salary is around £27,195 for full-time employees. The median salary for teachers is around £27,797 and for nurses £23,319. The Prime Minister earns £149,440. Do you think general secretaries should receive five or six times those medians?

5.   Transparency of pay is often thought to have a 'ratcheting effect': executives see their peers earning higher wages than them, and say to themselves either consciously or subconsiously, 'I'm worth that much.' Then they use their influence within an organisation to ratchet up their pay. Members exercising their governance power is probably the main (or only?) method for 'ratcheting down'. Can that work?

6.   Whatever one thinks about general secretaries, the pay of company executives is far more extreme, and has caused far greater social concern. See chapter 6(2), noting that the pay multiple for the average FTSE 100 CEO is 202 times the UK average (ie over £5,400,000, or 36 times the top general secretary). Really extreme wealth is generated by dominating, not just company directorships, but also share ownership and power.

7.   In Unite, Rule 19.5 treats pay for all officials including executives as a management decision, in other words for the executive. In Unison, Rule 3.1 appears to let the executive set the general secretary's pay. The same appears for GMB, Rule 33, Usdaw, Rule 11(13), or UCU, Rule 30.2. By contrast, the UK Corporate Governance Code would insist listed companies have a remuneration committee on the executive that does not include the CEO, and has 'independent directors'. As chapter 6(2) explained, this has been utterly ineffective at preventing exponential pay rises. In unions, it would seem that the closeness of the general meeting, and strong opinion or culture is exercising restraint. It may also be that unions take their cue from public-sector pay scales, which they are involved in writing: top general secretary pay is very similar to that of the prime minister. What do you think?

8.   Is there a principled way to determine top salaries? Should unions have pay ratios? Should general secretary pay rises, or falls, be linked to average member pay? Both these examples raise obvious, immediate problems: linking general secretary pay to member pay would create an incentive to reduce membership to high-paid workers when, presumably, unions urgently need to expand. The hard fact, however, is that in the last 10 or 20 years, and though there are many exceptions, most unions members' pay has stagnated, union membership has fallen dramatically, but general secretary pay has been rising. Most general secretaries are deeply concerned about inequality, and so it would seem all the more urgent to determine a fair method of pay. What do you think?

9.   One notable example to buck the trend was the RMT, the National Union of Rail, Maritime and Transport Workers. The late general secretary Bob Crow attracted *Daily Mail* headlines (10 March 2014) publicising a £145,000 a year 'salary' (somewhat misleading, as this figure included expenses as well as 'salary'). Crow replied to the *Daily Mail* (where editor-in-chief Paul Dacre took £1.85m in 2014) he was 'worth it'. The story was written by Jason Groves, now political editor, whose pay is undisclosed. Crow died from a heart attack the day after the report. Between 2002 and 2014 under Crow, RMT membership rose from around 57,000 to 80,000, while pay for London Underground drivers went from around

> £28,000 to £52,000: probably the most impressive results in modern UK history. The RMT strategy centred heavily upon demanding a voice within the rail governance structure, coupled with proactive protest (not protest for its own sake).

(c) Fairness in Disciplinary or Expulsion

The principles of natural justice, applicable to unions as much as public bodies, are partly codified in TULRCA 1992. Sections 64–67 say union members have a right to not be unjustifiably disciplined: allegations of a breach of union rules must be accurate (s 65(6)). Section 174(2) only permits members to be excluded from unions if they (a) no longer satisfy union rules (b) do not work in the right area (c) or employer (d) or based on conduct. A leading example of this, with a now resolved debate about liability, is found in *Bonsor*.

Bonsor v Musicians' Union [1956] AC 104

Harry Bonsor claimed he was wrongfully expelled by the Musicians' Union after being accused of not paying his dues. He only found out he was expelled after applying to Coventry Orchestra and being rejected because he was no longer a union member: the union ran a 'closed shop' (see chapter 9(3)(a)). Rule 27(7) said: 'Any member not clear on the books at the end of each quarter shall be fined 3d., and any member 26 weeks' subscription in arrears shall be excluded unless a satisfactory reason be assigned.' A branch secretary had deleted Bonsor's name from the member list, and refused to let him repay arrears out of his first orchestra wages. Instead, Bonsor had to work removing rust from Brighton Pier, and at an engineering works earning £6 a week when the trial began. Before he earned over £10 a week. Bonsor died during the appeal and his widow took up the case.

Upjohn J held that the expulsion was wrongful and granted an injunction against Bonsor's expulsion. Lord Evershed MR and Jenkins LJ held that although the secretary had acted *ultra vires*, Bonsor was could not win damages according to *Kelly v NSOPA* (1915) 84 LJKB 2236: the union had no separate legal entity, and apparently an action was barred because the union included Bonsor, and he would be 'suing himself'. Denning LJ dissented, arguing a union could be sued for damages. The House of Lords, while considering by a majority the Court of Appeal was bound by *Kelly*, followed Denning LJ's result.

Denning LJ: I start by observing that as simple matter of fact, not law, a trade union has a personality of its own distinct from its members. Professor Dicey pointed that out long ago. He said: "When a body of twenty, or two thousand, or two hundred thousand men, bind themselves together to act in a particular way for some common purpose, they create a body, which by no fiction of law, but by the very nature of things, differs from the individuals of whom it is constituted" (17 Harvard Law Review, p. 513). and Professor Maitland expressed his wholehearted concurrence with unrivalled clarity and felicity in his *Collected Papers*, Vol. III, p. 305. He quotes the incident in the House of Commons in 1904 when the Prime Minister, Mr. Balfour, spoke of trade unions as corporations. Sir Robert Reid (afterwards Lord Loreburn) interrupted him with "The trade unions are not corporations." "I know that," retorted Mr. Balfour, "I am talking English, not law." I take it to be clear, therefore, that a trade union is an entity in fact. The question is whether it is also an entity in law.

When trade unions were first legalized 83 years ago, their supporters were very anxious that they should not be made corporations, because they wanted to avoid the liabilities which flowed from corporate personality. They desired that a trade union should be able to prosecute an officer or servant who embezzled its funds; but they did not want a trade union to be sued by its members or by outsiders. But when the statutes came to be enacted it was found that this was not a possible state of affairs. The trade unions had, perforce, to be given a legal personality; and one cannot have the benefits of legal personality without the responsibilities attaching to it.

To prove this, take the statutes from 1871 to 1940, and one will find that Parliament has conferred on a registered trade union so many rights and duties, and such ample powers and capacities, as to make it a legal entity virtually indistinguishable from a corporation: (i) a registered trade union has the capacity to own property and to act by agents ... (ii) it can itself make complaints and lodge indictments in the criminal courts ... and it is itself liable to penalties in the criminal courts for non-compliance with statutory provisions ... (iii) it has "its constitution" and "its objects" ... (iv) it is capable of entering into contracts with third persons and with its own members. It is true that Parliament has provided that certain of its contracts are not "directly enforceable" by action ... but that leaves all the rest of its contracts enforceable; (v) it can undertake "engagements" on its own account and become indebted to its own "creditors"; and it can by special resolution transfer "its engagements" to any other trade union without prejudice, however, to the rights of its own creditors. ... In view of this catalogue of enactments from 1871 to 1940, there can, I think, be no doubt at the present day that a trade union is a legal entity.

Turn now to the contract of membership in the present case and see how naturally it fits into the conception of a legal entity. When the plaintiff joined the trade union he signed a printed document addressed to the secretary of the Kilburn branch of the Musicians' Union in these words: "I, the undersigned, do hereby make application to become a member of the Musicians' Union, subject to the constitution and rules which I accept as a condition of my admission to membership. Declaration of new members. I, the undersigned do hereby agree, of my own free will and consent, to conform to and abide by the rules of this union, as also any subsequent rules or alterations thereof that may be made in accordance with the constitution of this union, and I further declare my intention to promote to the best of my ability, the interests of this union and to act in harmony with my fellow members for the maintenance of the objects as expressed in its rules."

The rules of the union read more like a legislative code than anything else, but the significant thing is that throughout the rules the union is treated as a legal person. In the face of these documents I ask myself: suppose the Musicians' Union were only an unincorporated association of individuals with no legal personality of its own, what is the contract evidenced by those documents? Is it a contract by each member with the others jointly, or with them separately? and is a new contract made every time an old member goes out and a new member comes in? and what are the terms of the contract? Every member, of course, promises to pay his subscriptions and obey the rules, but does he do more? Are the officials to be regarded as his agents, so that he is responsible for their wrongdoing or for their breaches of contract? No confident answer can be given to any of these questions.

But once it is held that a trade union is a legal entity, the nature of the contract by every in-coming member becomes clear. It is a contract between him and the union, not a contract between him and his fellow members; and it is a contract whereby he, for his part, agrees to abide by the rules of the union, and the union, for its part, impliedly agrees that he shall not he excluded by the union or its officers except in accordance with the rules. This view is supported by the statement in Mr Citrine's book, *Trade Union Law* (1950), p. 175, when he says that the rules "constitute the contract existing between the members and the union, upon the exact terms of which will depend the objects and powers of the union and the rights and liabilities of both contracting parties."

Once the contract of membership is held to be a contract between the member and the union, then it follows in point of law that if a member is wrongfully excluded by the union or its officers in breach of the contract, he has a remedy in damages against the union.

The position of the trade union is then indistinguishable from the position of a proprietary club which has been held liable in damages for wrongful exclusion. (See *Baird v Wells* (1890) 44 Ch.D. 661; *Young v Ladies' Imperial Club* [1920] 2 KB 523; *Abbott v Sullivan* [1952] 1 KB 189.)

Lord Evershed MR and **Jenkins LJ** gave opinions denying Mr Bonsor damages.

[The case was appealed to the House of Lords.]

Lord Morton: My Lords, the Master of the Rolls and Jenkins L.J. were of opinion, rightly, in my view, that *Kelly v National Society of Operative Printers' Assistants* (1915) 84 LJKB 2236 was binding on the Court of Appeal, but Denning LJ felt himself entitled to disregard that case and delivered a judgment in favour of Mr. Bonsor, which I have found of great assistance. ...

Lord Macdermott: ... I would agree with Denning LJ that a trade union may be regarded as an entity in fact. In common parlance the term is habitually used to connote something that is in some way different from the individuals who form the combination ... the same can be said of many groups which lay no claim to a legal personality, and since [TUA 1871 s 4, equivalent now in TULRCA 1992 s 10] applies to both registered and unregistered unions, the Act's recognition of the factual entity can, in my opinion, offer no sound ground for making the registered union a legal entity as well.

> ...

> ... a registered trade union is recognized by the law as a body distinct from the individuals who from time to time compose it. It is not a corporation; but it is very much like one. The association is not merely the aggregate of the persons who compose it, and the presence of the corporate fiction is not necessary to secure its individuality. In an age of neologism it might be called a 'near-corporation'. As I have already indicated, these expressions of opinion do not seem to me necessarily to involve the decision in *Gillian's case*; but in the present suit Denning LJ accepted them as well founded and they, no less than those I have quoted to the contrary effect, invite the most careful consideration.

> ... the most weighty consideration of all lies in the fact that Parliament has made no effort to incorporate the registered trade union. In the latter half of last century incorporation was the recognized and usual way of conferring upon an association of persons the status of a distinct legal entity, and it is clear that the draftsman of the Act of 1871 had the Companies Act of 1862 before him. Yet there is not a word about the members becoming, on registration, a body corporate, and the only reference to a seal is in relation to the work of the registry. Parliament is not, of course, restricted in its choice of possible methods for producing a given result. But when, as here, it studiously avoids a familiar and appropriate method without purporting to adopt another in its stead, its intention to reach that result may well be open to doubt. For these reasons I am of opinion that a registered trade union is not a juridical person.

Lord Porter and **Lord Keith** concurred. **Lord Somervell** agreed with **Lord Macdermott**.

NOTES AND QUESTIONS

1. *Bonsor* is an easy case of wrongful exclusion. In substance, Bonsor's treatment was disproportionate, and he should not have been expelled. But most of the case is preoccupied with a muddled legal argument about whether there was any remedy. The House of Lords comes to the view that Bonsor had been entitled to damages because of his wrongful exclusion from the Musicians' Union, and it was no

bar that the union was not considered in statute, or up until then, at common law, as having 'legal personality'. Their Lordships seem uncomfortable with Denning LJ's point that a union is a 'legal entity' (carefully avoiding the words 'corporate' or 'person'). But the effect is identical. TULRCA 1992 ss 10 and 174 now make that position clear.

2.   What does it mean to be a 'person' in law? It is being the subject of legal rights and duties: being able to make contracts, hold property, commission torts, sue, be sued, and so on. Although TULRCA 1992 s 10 expressly denies that unions are a body corporate, they have identical attributes. The rest is historical and linguistic nicety.

3.   The old case of *Amalgamated Society of Carpenters and Joiners v Braithwaite* [1922] 2 AC 440 provides an example of an at once literal and creative interpretation of a union's rules to reach a desired result. Braithwaite was expelled from the ASCJ (now part of Unite) for joining an employee share scheme at his employer, Lever Bros (now Unilever), because a rule said members could be expelled if found 'working on a co-partnership system when such system makes provision for the operatives holding only a minority of the shares'. The point of this rule was to ensure employees did not buy into a management-dominated worker participation scheme, to undercut the union, or halt genuine voice at work (see chapter 11). Lord Buckmaster, who seemed to favour employee share schemes, at 442 cleverly reasoned that the rule only allowed expulsion if the scheme enabled employees to hold 'only a minority of the shares' and never acquire a majority. Today, this would likely be seen as wrong, because a reasonable person would construe the rule in its context to mean exactly what the union meant.

4.   Denning LJ had already set out his basic approach to individual rights within associations in *Lee v The Showmen's Guild of Great Britain* [1952] 2 QB 329. Frank Lee claimed wrongful expulsion by the Showmen's Guild after a fairground dispute. The guild decided Lee's *Noah's Ark* roundabout spot should go to another member, Shaw, who had it before the war. Shaw and Lee had a heated argument when they both arrived to take the place. The guild fined Lee. Lee refused to pay and was expelled. Ormerod J granted an injunction, finding that in fact Lee had breached no rule of the guild, the guild had been wrong in law, its action *ultra vires* and void. The Court of Appeal upheld the injunction, Denning LJ stating that any wrongful expulsion would be injuncted if 'necessary to protect a proprietary right of his; or to protect him in his right to earn a livelihood ... but it will not grant an injunction to give a member the right to enter a social club, unless there are proprietary rights attached to it, because it is too personal to be specifically enforced. ... That is, I think, the only relevance of rights of property in this connexion. It goes to the form of remedy, not to the right.' Can the same reasoning be applied to any dismissal of a worker by an employer?

5.   In *Annamunthodo v Oilfield Workers' Trade Union* [1961] AC 945 the Privy Council advised that natural justice required Walter Annamunthodo had to have the chance to answer a charge before he was expelled. Annamunthodo worked in the oil industry in Trinidad, and was accused of four charges, appeared to answer them, but the hearing was delayed. None of those charges could, under the union's rules, have resulted in expulsion. He was then summoned on a day he could not

attend and then told he was expelled under another rule that he had no opportunity to answer. Lord Denning advised: '[I]t should not have been invoked for the purpose of expelling Walter Annamunthodo unless he was given notice of the charge under it and had a fair opportunity of meeting it.'

6. In *Edwards v Society of Graphical and Allied Trades* [1971] Ch 354, Mr Edwards claimed an injunction and damages against SOGAT (now part of Unite) for wrongful exclusion over being in arrears. A union official had made a mistake, but the union's rule 18(4)(k) said there would be no appeal right. The union also threatened his employer with a strike unless Edwards was dismissed. The Court of Appeal held that an unfettered right to withdraw membership was invalid and awarded damages, subject to a duty to mitigate loss.

7. In *Esterman v NALGO* [1974] ICR 625, Miss Esterman claimed she was wrongfully disciplined after she refused to join the strike by NALGO (now part of Unison). Miss Esterman, a senior legal assistant in Islington London Borough Council, did not agree with NALGO's policy of selective strikes to disrupt the May 1974 local elections. Outside her council work, she volunteered to count ballots. Templeman J awarded Esterman an injunction because the union did not have express authority in its rules to interfere with her work outside normal employment. It was appropriate to construe the rules narrowly, in the judge's view, to restrain 'the serious step of interfering' with Miss Esterman's outside activity.

8. In *Stevenson v United Road Transport Union* [1977] ICR 893, Stevenson claimed he was unjustly dismissed from his URTU official position after a report alleged he had not performed his duties. Stevenson, who was described by judge Brian Dillon QC as 'pugnacious' and as having a 'persecution mania', was prevented from seeing the report. The Court of Appeal held that this violated natural justice principles. People have a right to see and meet charges against them. Buckley LJ (Orr LJ and Goff LJ concurring) said: 'Where one party has a discretionary power to terminate the tenure or enjoyment by another of an employment or an office or a post or a privilege, is that power conditional upon the party invested with the power being first satisfied upon a particular point which involves investigating some matter upon which the other party ought in fairness to be heard or to be allowed to give his explanation or put his case? If the answer to the question is "Yes," then unless, before the power purports to have been exercised, the condition has been satisfied after the other party has been given a fair opportunity of being heard or of giving his explanation or putting his case, the power will not have been well exercised.' Do you agree that this principle is expressly applicable to dismissal by an employer?

9. In *Roebuck v National Union of Mineworkers (Yorkshire Area) No 2* [1978] ICR 676, Roebuck successfully claimed he was wrongfully disciplined after giving evidence for the *Sheffield Star* in a libel action by the NUM general secretary, Arthur Scargill. Roebuck's disciplinary hearing was conducted under the union's rules, but Scargill chaired the disciplinary panel (disqualifying Roebuck and others for two years). Templeman J held this breached natural justice principles: it 'undoubtedly gave the impression that the dice were loaded against ... the appearance of bias was inevitable'. The question is 'whether a reasonable man with no inside knowledge might well think that it might be biased'.

10. Taken together, principles of natural justice will at least require the member (1) is told a case against them, *Stevenson*, (2) may answer the charges against them, *Annamunthodo*, (3) has an impartial hearing, *Roebuck*, (4) is only disciplined within the union's rules, *Esterman* and *Annamunthodo*, and (5) is handled proportionately, *Bonsor*.

11. An exception to point (3) is that unions occasionally expel people because of disputes with other unions over who should represent a particular group of workers. In 1924, to ensure that strikes and needless arguments did not result, the TUC adopted an agreement with a basic obligation on unions not to poach each others' members. This was updated in a 1939 meeting in Bridlington, North Yorkshire, giving the name 'Bridlington Principles' that has stuck through revisions up to the current *TUC Disputes Principles and Procedures* (2016). It 'sets out the framework for unions to work together, and to avoid damaging resource-consuming disputes'.

Cheall v APEX [1983] 2 AC 180

Ernest Cheall, a security officer at Vauxhall Motors, claimed he was wrongfully expelled by the Association of Professional, Executive, Clerical and Computer Staff (APEX, now part of the GMB) because he had no hearing. APEX's rule 14 allowed it to expel members on six weeks' notice after a decision by the Trades Union Congress disputes committee. Cheall had resigned from the Association of Clerical, Technical and Supervisory Staff (ACTSS, now part of Unite) after becoming disappointed with it. ACTSS complained to the TUC that APEX had breached the Bridlington Principles, especially principle 2 against trying to recruit other unions' members. It said APEX knew that Cheall was a former ACTSS member. The TUC decided that Cheall should be expelled and rejoin ACTSS. Cheall, who played no part in the TUC's dispute resolution, objected. Bingham J held Cheall had no claim. Lord Denning MR and Slade LJ held that Cheall was wrongfully excluded. Donaldson LJ dissented. The House of Lords held that Cheall had no standing to be heard before the TUC Disputes Committee.

Lord Diplock: The breach of duty which it is suggested disentitled A.P.E.X. in the instant case to rely upon rule 14 as against Cheall was its duty under the Bridlington principles not to poach members from A.C.T.S.S. This duty, though moral only and not legally enforceable, it owed to A.C.T.S.S. and T.G.W.U. and, may be, other trade unions that are members of the T.U.C.; but plainly it cannot have owed such duty to individual members of trade unions, since only trade unions were parties to the agreement embodied in the Bridlington principles.

Since rule 14 can only come into effect when there has been a breach by A.P.E.X. of the duty owed by it to another trade union under the Bridlington principles, it is hopeless to argue that A.P.E.X. is debarred from relying on the rule to terminate the membership of a poached member, merely because it acted in breach of the Bridlington principles in poaching him. So counsel for Cheall felt constrained to introduce the concept of a distinction to be drawn between a "conscious and deliberate" breach of the Bridlington principles and a breach that was merely inadvertent. The former it was argued disentitled A.P.E.X., as a matter of law, ever to rely upon rule 14 to terminate the membership of the person in respect of whom the conscious and deliberate breach was committed, while an inadvertent breach did entitle it to do so.

My Lords, I know of no principle of law which justifies this distinction.

…

Natural justice

It was contended on Cheall's behalf that the termination of his membership was also void because the procedure which resulted in it constituted a denial to him of natural justice. He was entitled, it was suggested, not merely to be present, as he was, at the hearing of the complaint against A.P.E.X. by the disputes committee, but also to make representations, written or oral, to the disputes committee explaining his reasons for wishing to switch his membership from A.C.T.S.S. to A.P.E.X. and the consequences that an award adverse to A.P.E.X. would have upon him personally.

This contention did not find favour with any of the judges in the courts below: the only parties to the dispute that was before the disputes committee were the trade unions concerned. They, and they only, were entitled to make representations written or oral to the committee. Decisions that resolve disputes between the parties to them, whether by litigation or some other adversarial dispute-resolving process, often have consequences which affect persons who are not parties to the dispute; but the legal concept of natural justice has never been extended to give such persons as well as the parties themselves rights to be heard by the decision-making tribunal before the decision is reached. If natural justice required that Cheall should be entitled to be heard, there could be no stopping there; any other member of either union who thought he would be adversely affected by the decision, if it went one way or the other, would have a similar right to be heard. To claim that this is a requirement of "fair play in action" (to borrow Sach LJ's description of natural justice in *Edwards v. Society of Graphical and Allied Trades* [1971] Ch 354, 382) would be little short of ludicrous.

Alternatively, though rather more mutedly, it was submitted that Cheall was entitled to be heard by the executive council of A.P.E.X. before they decided to comply with the award, which was already more than one year old, by giving him notice of termination of his membership under rule 14. In his judgment Bingham J. sets out what had in fact occurred before the executive council reached its decision to act under rule 14 and Cheall's own knowledge of it. That, in the learned judge's view, made it inevitable that the only way in which A.P.E.X. could fulfil its duty to act in the best interest of its members as a whole was by complying with the award of the disputes committee. His conclusion was that, in the circumstances that he recounts, there was no legal obligation on A.P.E.X. to give Cheall prior notice of their decision or grant him an opportunity to be heard. "To have done so," said the learned judge [1982] ICR 231, 250, "where nothing he said could affect the outcome would in my view have been cruel deception." My Lords, I can content myself with saying: "I agree."

Public policy

Finally it was argued that if all the submissions with which I have already dealt failed, as in my opinion they plainly do, the Bridlington principles, which have been in operation since as long ago as 1939, are contrary to public policy, since they restrict the right of the individual to join and to remain a member of a trade union of his choice; and that any attempt to give effect to any such restriction would, upon application by the individual affected by it, be prevented by the courts.

This supposed rule of public policy has, it is claimed, always formed part of the common law of England but it has now been reinforced by the accession of the United Kingdom to the European Convention for the Protection of Human Rights and Fundamental Freedoms (1953) (Cmd. 8969), of which article 11 reads as follows. ... [see above at chapter 8(1)]

My Lords, freedom of association can only be mutual; there can be no right of an individual to associate with other individuals who are not willing to associate with him. The body of the membership of A.P.E.X., represented by its executive council and whose best interests it was the duty of the executive council to promote, were not willing to continue to accept Cheall as a fellow-member. No doubt this was because if they continued to accept him, they ran the risk of attracting the sanction of suspension or expulsion of A.P.E.X. from the T.U.C. and all the attendant disadvantages to themselves as members of A.P.E.X. that such suspension or expulsion would entail. But I know of no existing rule of public policy that would prevent trade unions from entering into arrangements with one another which they consider to be in the interests of their members in promoting order in industrial relations and enhancing their members' bargaining power with their employers; nor do I think it a permissible exercise of your Lordships' judicial power to create a new rule of public policy to that effect. If this is to be done at all it must be done by Parliament.

Different considerations might apply if the effect of Cheall's expulsion from A.P.E.X. were to have put his job in jeopardy, either because of the existence of a closed shop or for some other reason. But this is not the case. All that has happened is that he left a union, A.C.T.S.S., in order to join another union, A.P.E.X., which he preferred. After four years of membership he was compelled, against his will, to leave it and was given the opportunity, which he rejected, of rejoining A.C.T.S.S. if he so wished.

My human sympathies are with Mr. Cheall, but I am not in a position to indulge them. ...

Lord Edmund-Davies, **Lord Fraser**, **Lord Brandon**, and **Lord Templeman** concurred.

NOTES AND QUESTIONS

1. The House of Lords unanimously held that Cheall had no right to speak, and it would in any case have been pointless. Lord Diplock suggests it would have been different if the union had had a closed shop, but here Cheall was effectively just being shifted from one union to the other. The purpose of this arrangement was to ensure the best representation for all workers.
2. The result is that Cheall, though dissatisfied with the ACTSS, was not practically able to 'exit' or 'vote with his feet' as a way to encourage his union to improve. What would you advise are the other practical options for an individual member to improve the quality of the union's service?
3. Cheall's appeal to the ECHR under Art 11 was briskly rejected: *Cheall v United Kingdom* (1986) 8 EHRR CD74.
4. Previously it was not explicit in TULRCA 1992 s 174 that union members could be expelled for acting upon political views that were inconsistent with the implicit political objectives of a union. The Employment Relations Act 2004, s 174(4A)–(4H) elaborates a series of express reasons that cannot be used for ejecting someone, but says in s 174(4B) that present membership of a political party is not one of them. These amendments were thanks to Mr Lee.

ASLEF v United Kingdom [2007] ECHR 184

The Associated Society of Locomotive Engineers and Firemen (ASLEF) claimed the UK breached ECHR Art 11 by not expressly establishing a legal right in TULRCA 1992 s 174 to allow it to exclude Mr Lee. Lee was a member of the British Nationalist Party. He wrote an article in its racist *Spearhead* magazine (now defunct). He distributed anti-Islam leaflets. He harassed a member of the Anti-Nazi League. He took photographs and made throat-cutting gestures. He followed a woman home and wrote her house number down. ASLEF expelled him when they found out, as rule 3 committed it to equal treatment, and rule 4 required no members who sympathised with groups 'diametrically opposed to the objects of the union, such as a fascist organisation'.

Lee claimed this breached TULRCA 1992 s 174, which at the time stated (2)(d) members could be expelled for their conduct, but (3)(a)(iii) this could not include being a member of a political party. The Employment Appeal Tribunal had held s 174 could be compatibly construed with Art 11, so that Lee's conduct led to his expulsion. But on remission the Employment Tribunal held Lee's membership was the main reason for his expulsion. ASLEF argued s 174 violated Art 11.

European Court of Human Rights

1. General principles

37. The essential object of Article 11 is to protect the individual against arbitrary interference by public authorities with the exercise of the rights protected. The right to form and join trade unions is a special aspect of freedom of association which also protects, first and foremost, against State action. The State may not interfere with the forming and joining of trade unions except on the basis of the conditions set forth in Article 11 § 2 (see *Young, James and Webster v. United Kingdom* ...

38. The right to form trade unions involves, for example, the right of trade unions to draw up their own rules and to administer their own affairs. Such trade union rights are explicitly recognised in Articles 3 and 5 of ILO Convention No. 87, the provisions of which have been taken into account by the Convention organs in previous cases (see e.g. *Cheall v United Kingdom ... Wilson & the National Union of Journalists v United Kingdom* ...). Prima facie trade unions enjoy the freedom to set up their own rules concerning conditions of membership, including administrative formalities and payment of fees, as well as other more substantive criteria, such as the profession or trade exercised by the would-be member.

39. As an employee or worker should be free to join, or not join a trade union without being sanctioned or subject to disincentives (e.g. *Young, James and Webster* ..., *Wilson & the National Union of Journalists* ...), so should the trade union be equally free to choose its members. Article 11 cannot be interpreted as imposing an obligation on associations or organisations to admit whosoever wishes to join. Where associations are formed by people, who, espousing particular values or ideals, intend to pursue common goals, it would run counter to the very effectiveness of the freedom at stake if they had no control over their membership. By way of example, it is uncontroversial that religious bodies and political parties can generally regulate their membership to include only those who share their beliefs and ideals. Similarly, the right to join a union "for the protection of his interests" cannot be interpreted as conferring a general right to join the union of one's choice irrespective of the rules of the union: in the exercise of their rights under Article 11 § 1 unions must remain free to decide, in accordance with union rules, questions concerning admission to and expulsion from the union. ...

40. This basic premise holds good where the association or trade union is a private and independent body, and is not, for example, through receipt of public funds or through the fulfilment of public duties imposed upon it, acting in a wider context, such as assisting the State in securing the enjoyment of rights and freedoms, where other considerations may well come into play ...

41. Accordingly, where the State does intervene in internal trade union matters, such intervention must comply with the requirements of Article 11 § 2, namely be "prescribed by law" and "necessary in a democratic society" for one or more of the permitted aims. In this context, the following should be noted.

42. Firstly, "necessary" in this context does not have the flexibility of such expressions as "useful" or "desirable" (*Young, James and Webster* ...).

43. Secondly, pluralism, tolerance and broadmindedness are hallmarks of a "democratic society" (*Handyside v United Kingdom* ...). Although individual interests must on occasion be subordinated to those of a group, democracy does not simply mean that the views of a majority must always prevail: a balance must be achieved which ensures the fair and proper treatment of minorities and avoids any abuse of a dominant position. For the individual right to join a union to be effective, the State must nonetheless protect the individual against any abuse of a dominant position by trade unions (see *Young, James and Webster* ...). Such abuse might occur, for example, where exclusion or expulsion from a trade union was not in accordance with union rules or where the rules were wholly unreasonable or arbitrary or where the consequences of exclusion or expulsion resulted in exceptional hardship (see *Cheall* ...).

44. Thirdly, any restriction imposed on a Convention right must be proportionate to the legitimate aim pursued (amongst many authorities, Handyside, cited above, p. 23, § 49).

45. Fourthly, where there is a conflict between differing Convention rights, the State must find a fair and proper balance (see no. 11366/85, Comm. Dec 16.10.86, DR 50 p. 173; *Gaskin v. the United Kingdom*, judgment of 7 July 1989, Series A no. 160, §§ 42–44).

46. Finally, in striking a fair balance between the competing interests, the State enjoys a certain margin of appreciation in determining the steps to be taken to ensure compliance with the Convention (amongst many authorities, *Hatton and Others v. the United Kingdom* [GC], no. 36022/97, § 98, ECHR 2003 VIII). However, since this is not an area of general policy, on which opinions within a democratic society may reasonably differ widely and in which the role of the domestic policy-maker should be given special weight (see e.g. *James and Others v. the United Kingdom*, judgment of 21 February 1986, Series A no. 98, p. 32, § 46, where the Court found it natural that the margin of appreciation "available to the legislature in implementing social and economic policies should be a wide one"), the margin of appreciation will play only a limited role.

2. Application in the present case

47. The question that arises in the present case concerns the extent to which the State may intervene to protect the trade union member, Mr Lee, against measures taken against him by his union, the applicant.

48. It is accepted by the parties in this case that section 174 had the effect in this case of prohibiting the applicant from expelling Mr Lee as it barred unions from such action where it was motivated, at least in part, by membership of a political party. This constituted an interference with the applicant's freedom of association under the first paragraph of Article 11 which requires to be justified in the terms set out above.

49. In the context of the case, lawfulness is not an issue. Nor is it disputed that the measure had the aim of protecting the rights of individuals, such as Mr Lee, to exercise their various political rights and freedoms without undue hindrance. The crucial question is whether the State has struck the right balance between Mr Lee's rights and those of the applicant trade union.

50. Taking due consideration of the Government's argument as to the importance of safeguarding fundamental individual rights, the Court is not persuaded however that the measure of expulsion impinged in any significant way on Mr Lee's exercise of freedom of expression or his lawful political activities. Nor is it apparent that Mr Lee suffered any particular

detriment, save loss of membership itself in the union. As there was no closed shop agreement for example, there was no apparent prejudice suffered by the applicant in terms of his livelihood or in his conditions of employment. The Court has taken account of the fact that membership of a trade union is often regarded, in particular due to the trade union movement's historical background, as a fundamental safeguard for workers against employers' abuse and it has some sympathy with the notion that any worker should be able to join a trade union (subject to the exceptions set out in Article 11 § 2 in fine). However, as pointed by the applicant, ASLEF represents all workers in the collective bargaining context and there is nothing to suggest in the present case that Mr Lee is at any individual risk of, or is unprotected from, any arbitrary or unlawful action by his employer. Of more weight in the balance is the applicant's right to choose its members. Historically, trade unions in the United Kingdom, and elsewhere in Europe, were, and though perhaps to a lesser extent today are, commonly affiliated to political parties or movements, particularly those on the left. They are not bodies solely devoted to politically-neutral aspects of the well-being of their members, but are often ideological, with strongly held views on social and political issues. There was no hint in the domestic proceedings that the applicant erred in its conclusion that Mr Lee's political values and ideals clashed, fundamentally, with its own. There is no indication that the applicant had any public duty or role conferred on it, or has taken the advantage of state funding, such that it may reasonably be required to take on members to fulfil any other wider purposes.

President J Casadevall, Sir Nicolas Bratza, Mr S Pavlovschi, Mr L Garlicki, Ms L Mijović, Mr J Šikuta, and **Mrs P Hirvelä** unanimously supported the judgment.

NOTES AND QUESTIONS

1. The Court reasoned that no right of Lee's was affected: he could continue to work in his job, as without a closed shop there was no risk that exclusion from the union meant exclusion from work (contrast *Redfearn v United Kingdom* in chapter 12(1)(b)). Instead, the right of ASLEF to carry out its 'strongly held views on social and political issues' carried 'more weight'. By then, of course, the UK's legislation had been amended. But given the HRA 1998 s 3, did the Employment Tribunal fail in the binding duty upon it to construe the law compatibly with Art 11?
2. The Employment Act 2008 s 19 sets out more fair reasons for expulsion.

(4) ANTI-DISCRIMINATION

Beyond the bare principle of freedom of association, this chapter has considered, first, rights of voice (which aim to be self-enforcing, but can be litigated) and, second, other rights exercisable in court. A third mechanism of accountability is the right to join or leave a union freely. If unions and general secretaries are performing well, this might encourage people to 'vote with their feet' by joining. Equally they may leave if the union is not engaging them or improving their standards of living. Entry and exit should send a signal to unions' governing bodies about their performance, both positive and negative. Historically, unions did attempt to prevent people from leaving by putting 'closed shop' clauses in collective agreements: employers would have to dismiss someone who left the union. Closed shop clauses have not been possible since 1980, but functional substitutes, such as automatic enrolment with an opt-out right, are considered further in chapter 9(3).

By contrast, employing entities have continually deterred union membership, even though this is strictly unlawful in international and UK law. Discrimination against union members is prohibited by the Universal Declaration on Human Rights 1948 Art 23(4), the ILO Freedom of Association Convention 1948 (c 87) Art 2, the ILO Collective Bargaining Convention 1949 (c 98) Arts 1 and 2, and the ILO Workers' Representatives Convention 1971 (c 135) Art 1. Nevertheless, shareholding interests (that are not democratic pension funds, etc) often take the view that eliminating union membership will reduce labour costs (ie people's wages). The principle of anti-discrimination requires constant enforcement, not always seen in the UK, and there are exceptions for 'national security'.

Wilson and Palmer v United Kingdom **[2002] ECHR 552**

Wilson and Palmer claimed that the United Kingdom had failed to adhere to the ECHR Art 11 because the House of Lords had held they had no remedy when employers attempted to pay more to people who left their unions.

Mr Wilson worked for the *Daily Mail*, a publication considered by many to be a news source. The owners decided to stop collectively bargaining with the National Union of Journalists in 1990, and offered a 4.5 per cent pay rise for staff who shifted to individual contracts rather than stay on the existing collective agreement. Mr Wilson refused to go onto an individual contract, and so his pay was not increased like that of his colleagues.

Mr Palmer worked for Associated British Ports in Southampton. In 1991, he refused a 10 per cent pay increase and private medical insurance to move to a 'personal contract of employment', and so cease being represented by the National Union of Rail, Maritime and Transport Workers. His pay fell behind that of his colleagues by an average of 8.9 per cent.

At the time, TULRCA 1992 s 146 covered 'employees' but not workers, and s 148(3) only prevented employers taking 'action' which no reasonable employer could take. In 1995, the House of Lords held that employers only had a remedy against employers who took 'action' short of dismissal, not this 'omission' to improve union members' pay. In 2002, the European Court of Human Rights held that financial incentives could not be used to frustrate the right to join a union.

European Court of Human Rights

32. In 1995 the Committee of Independent Experts set up under Article 25 of the Social Charter examined section 13 of the 1993 [inserting TULRCA 1992 s 148(3)] Act with a view to determining whether it was consistent with Article 5 of the Charter and observed as follows (Conclusions XIII-3, Council of Europe, 1996, p. 108):

"... the Committee was of the opinion that the wording of section 148(3)(a) was so general that the effect of this provision was that only in exceptional cases would a tribunal be able to rule that the action taken by the employer was unlawful because it violated freedom of association. It considered that this weakening of the protection of freedom of association was not compatible with the requirements of Article 5. It pointed out that 'the Contracting State is obliged to take adequate legislative or other measures to guarantee the exercise of the right to organise, and in particular to protect workers' organisations from any interference on the part of employers' (see most recently Conclusions XII-2, p. 101). It also referred to its conclusion under Article 6 § 2 and its case-law to the effect that where a fundamental trade union prerogative such as the right to bargain collectively was restricted, this could amount to an infringement of the very nature of trade union freedom (see most recently Conclusions XIII-2, p. 269)."

33. In its next report the Committee again insisted "that the necessary measures be taken to repeal [section 13 of the 1993 Act, inter alia]", commenting (Conclusions XIV-I, 1998, pp. 798 and 800):

"The Committee repeats the criticism raised in its previous conclusion with respect to section 13 of the 1993 Act which is in breach of Article 5 of the Charter as it permits employers to take certain measures such as awarding preferential remuneration to employees in order to persuade them to relinquish trade union activities and collective bargaining ..."

...

1. General principles

41. The Court observes at the outset that although the essential object of Article 11 is to protect the individual against arbitrary interference by public authorities with the exercise of the rights protected, there may in addition be positive obligations to secure the effective enjoyment of these rights. In the present case, the matters about which the applicants complain – principally, the employers' de-recognition of the unions for collective bargaining purposes and offers of more favourable conditions of employment to employees agreeing not to be represented by the unions – did not involve direct intervention by the State. The responsibility of the United Kingdom would, however, be engaged if these matters resulted from a failure on its part to secure to the applicants under domestic law the rights set forth in Article 11 of the Convention (see *Gustafsson v Sweden* (1996) 22 EHRR 409, [45]).

42. The Court reiterates that Article 11(1) presents trade union freedom as one form or a special aspect of freedom of association (see *National Union of Belgian Police v Belgium*, (1979–80) 1 EHRR 578, [38], and *Swedish Engine Drivers' Union v Sweden* (6 February 1976) [39]). The words "for the protection of his interests" in Article 11(1) are not redundant, and the Convention safeguards freedom to protect the occupational interests of trade union members by trade union action, the conduct and development of which the Contracting States must both permit and make possible. A trade union must thus be free to strive for the protection of its members' interests, and the individual members have a right, in order to protect their interests, that the trade union should be heard (see *National Union of Belgian Police*, [39]–[40], and *Swedish Engine Drivers' Union*, [40]–[41]). Article 11 does not, however, secure any particular treatment of trade unions or their members and leaves each State a free choice of the means to be used to secure the right to be heard (see *National Union of Belgian Police*, [38]–[39], and *Swedish Engine Drivers' Union*, [39]–[40]).
...

45. ... the Court does not consider that the absence, under United Kingdom law, of an obligation on employers to enter into collective bargaining gave rise, in itself, to a violation of Article 11 of the Convention.

46. The Court agrees with the Government that the essence of a voluntary system of collective bargaining is that it must be possible for a trade union which is not recognised by an employer to take steps including, if necessary, organising industrial action, with a view to persuading the

employer to enter into collective bargaining with it on those issues which the union believes are important for its members' interests. Furthermore, it is of the essence of the right to join a trade union for the protection of their interests that employees should be free to instruct or permit the union to make representations to their employer or to take action in support of their interests on their behalf. If workers are prevented from so doing, their freedom to belong to a trade union, for the protection of their interests, becomes illusory. It is the role of the State to ensure that trade union members are not prevented or restrained from using their union to represent them in attempts to regulate their relations with their employers.

47. In the present case, it was open to the employers to seek to pre-empt any protest on the part of the unions or their members against the imposition of limits on voluntary collective bargaining, by offering those employees who acquiesced in the termination of collective bargaining substantial pay rises, which were not provided to those who refused to sign contracts accepting the end of union representation. The corollary of this was that United Kingdom law permitted employers to treat less favourably employees who were not prepared to renounce a freedom that was an essential feature of union membership. Such conduct constituted a disincentive or restraint on the use by employees of union membership to protect their interests. However, as the House of Lords' judgment made clear, domestic law did not prohibit the employer from offering an inducement to employees who relinquished the right to union representation, even if the aim and outcome of the exercise was to bring an end to collective bargaining and thus substantially to reduce the authority of the union, as long as the employer did not act with the purpose of preventing or deterring the individual employee simply from being a member of a trade union.

48. Under United Kingdom law at the relevant time it was, therefore, possible for an employer effectively to undermine or frustrate a trade union's ability to strive for the protection of its members' interests. The Court notes that this aspect of domestic law has been the subject of criticism by the Social Charter's Committee of Independent Experts and the ILO's Committee on Freedom of Association (see paragraphs 32–33 and 37 above). It considers that, by permitting employers to use financial incentives to induce employees to surrender important union rights, the respondent State has failed in its positive obligation to secure the enjoyment of the rights under Article 11 of the Convention. This failure amounted to a violation of Article 11, as regards both the applicant trade unions and the individual applicants.

President JP Costa, AB Baka, G Jörundsson, K Jungwiert, M Ugrekhelidze, A Mularoni and **Lord Phillips of Worth Matravers** (ad hoc judge).

NOTES AND QUESTIONS

1. The European Court of Human Rights held that UK law (in TULRCA 1992 ss 146–48 at the time) violated Art 11, because it 'permitted employers to treat less favourably employees who were not prepared to renounce' benefits of union membership, [47]. States have 'positive obligations to secure the effective enjoyment' of human rights, [41]. See further KD Ewing, 'The Implications of Wilson and Palmer' (2003) 32(1) *ILJ* 1.

2. Possibly the most important statement of principle on labour rights in the Court's history, at [46], is that: '[I]t is of the essence of the right to join a trade union for the protection of their interests that employees should be free to instruct or permit the union to make representations to their employer or to take action in support of their interests on their behalf. If workers are prevented from so doing, their

freedom to belong to a trade union, for the protection of their interests, becomes illusory.' In other words, collective bargaining, without the right to strike, is collective begging. See chapter 10.

3. Do you think Mr Wilson and Mr Palmer were adequately served by the justice system? Mr Wilson's case began in 1990, and ended in 2002. Between that time, there were three general elections. TULRCA 1992 was eventually amended by the Employment Relations Act 2004 ss 29–32, to change the word 'employee' to 'worker' and to remove the s 148(3) restrictions for 'legitimate' employer detriment.

4. The reformed TULRCA 1992 s 146 now reads: 'A worker has the right not to be subjected to any detriment as an individual by any act, or any deliberate failure to act, by his employer if the act or failure takes place for the sole or main purpose of (a) ... deterring him from being or seeking to become a member of an independent trade union ... (b) ... taking part in the activities of an independent trade union at an appropriate time ... (ba) ... making use of trade union services ... (c) compelling him to be or become a member of any trade union ...' The section then defines an 'appropriate time' as outside working hours, or within working hours with consent of an employer, and 'working hours' as times when one is required by contract to be at work. Then, since 2013, some extra ss 145A–B add (quite unnecessarily) that there is a right not to have offers 'inducing' someone not to be a union member or party to a collective agreement. Despite the verbiage, the point is clear: any detriment for any worker for associating with a union is unlawful.

5. In chapter 12(4) we saw that 'detriment' under the Equality Act 2010 s 27 ban on victimisation included a council sending letters to dinner ladies that it was 'greatly concerned' about the impact of their equal-pay claim, and detriment was defined as that which is viewed as such when it is 'objectively reasonable in all the circumstances', *St Helen's MBC v Derbyshire* [2007] UKHL 16, [68]. It would seem sensible that the same approach is taken here: any action is unlawful if a reasonable person would consider it as detriment.

6. What if an employer writes threatening emails or letters to staff who are planning collective action? Suppose an employer demands that workers send in their names on whether they are taking part before a strike, or demands names after a strike. Could this count as detriment? The answer is 'yes'. Before a strike has occurred, workers taking part in planning for collective action are undertaking appropriate activities during working time. It follows there is a claim under TULRCA 1992 s 146. But what if an employer threatens to gather names after a strike, in preparation for wage deductions or some other retaliation? The answer, arguably, is this still counts as unlawful detriment. As chapter 11 explores, compelling authority shows that it is an implied term of every contract that stopping work in contemplation or furtherance of a good-faith trade dispute is lawful (from *Mogul Steamship* onwards), and therefore not breaking an employment contract. Actions in good faith, and indeed pursuing fundamental human rights, are not to be considered tortious at common law, whatever the theoretical position put forward over 110 years ago in *Taff Vale*. A strike does not involve an employee breaking a contract of employment (and at the very worst is no breach of a 'condition') because an implied term in every employment contract is that the employer performs in

good faith. It follows under s 146 that employees taking part in a strike are taking part in union activities at an 'appropriate time' because during a good-faith trade dispute there is no contractual obligation to the employer to be working. Any other view would lead to the result that the common law holds the UDHR 1948 in contempt. Workers are protected against detriment whenever they go on strike. This approach encourages employers and unions to negotiate, not retaliate.

7.   Although not in issue in *Wilson*, TULRCA 1992 s 146 was amended in 2004 to protect 'workers' and not just employees from 'detriment'. But s 152, which prohibits 'dismissal' for union association, only covers employees. There are at least three ways to read this. First, Simon Deakin and Gillian Morris, *Labour Law* (2012) 819–20 highlight the 'unusual' possibility that claimants, if dismissed for union activity, might seek to argue 'that they are "workers" other than "employees"'. This would happen if a court accepted a narrower group of people (employees) are protected from dismissal than from detriment (workers). Because dismissal is usually the worst form of detriment, it would be absurd if non-employee workers are protected from detriment but not dismissal: this outcome should therefore be avoided. Second, the word 'employee' in s 152 could be viewed as, in effect, 'zombie-law': it appears to 'alive' in statute, but it is manifestly incompatible with ECHR Art 11 after *Wilson*, and is therefore already 'dead'. In any case where it matters (and one has not yet arisen) a Court's duty under HRA 1993 s 3 is to construe the meaning of the section to be compatible with ECHR Art 11. This means a court has a duty to stretch its meaning, for the purpose of this statute alone, to cover every person at work: everyone is entitled to unionise. Third, as discussed through chapter 3(2), the actual meaning of an 'employee' could rightly be construed so as to eliminate all practical concern. Only if non-employee workers are assumed to exclude vulnerable casual workers, by applying the discredited *O'Kelly* definition of mutuality of obligation, can a concern arise. However, after *Gisda Cyf*, *Autoclenz* and *Bates van Winkelhof*, consistent Supreme Court jurisprudence strongly suggests that the only non-employee workers are people with real autonomy in their terms of work, such as partners in a law firm, and they are unlikely in practice to join unions. This, however, remains unsatisfactory because international human rights standards require that 'everyone' is entitled to unionise (eg UDHR Art 23(4)), not just employees, or workers, but also the fully self-employed.

8.   A fundamental principle of labour rights is that they create minimum standards: party autonomy may improve those standards for the benefit (not detriment) of the employee. What do common law and equity say about union discrimination? A notorious passage in *Allen v Flood* [1898] AC 1, 172 saw Lord Davey remark that: 'An employer may discharge a workman (with whom he has no contract), or may refuse to employ one from the most mistaken, capricious, malicious, or morally reprehensible motives that can be conceived, but the workman has no right of action against him.' However, their Lordships did not consider rival principles of equity. In *Dean v Bennett* (1870) LR 6 Ch 489, 494, Lord Hatherley LC held that a minister was unjustly dismissed, stating: 'No one would expect to find that such a course had been adopted in any assembly of English people, who are accustomed in some degree to the ordinary principles of justice.' Today, the

courts should openly acknowledge that workmen and ministers benefit alike from the conscience of equity: this binds any employing entity or contracting party to treat people providing them services justly. If it is thought desirable, this could be expressed as a requirement of 'good faith': cf in Canada, *Bhasin v Hrynew* 2014 SCC 71. Equity is the gateway for ensuring the common law's essential precepts do not confound international human rights principles.

9.   Why did two general election victories by the Labour Party not swiftly reverse the laws frustrating Wilson and Palmer's rights? Tony Blair, the Prime Minister (1997–2007), wrote in Rupert Murdoch's publication a comment called: 'We won't look back to the 1970s' (31 March 1997) The Times: 'The essential elements of the trade union legislation of the 1980s will remain. There will be no return to secondary action, flying pickets, strikes without ballots, the closed shop and all the rest. The changes that we do propose would leave British law the most restrictive on trade unions in the Western world.'

10. Although people must suffer no detriment for being union members, the European Court of Human Rights has found that employers can implement measures against people in unions for independent reasons. In *Palomo Sanchez v Spain* [2011] ECHR 1319, six union members were dismissed for putting 'allegedly offensive content in the union's newsletter'. This was a comic depicting employees queuing up, and the Human Resources manager, Señor Garcia, 'receiving sexual gratification' under a desk. His speech bubble says: 'I told them they would be released as long as they served me well ... SERVED!' A majority of twelve judges on the European Court of Human Rights found there was no violation in the dismissals. Five judges dissented. Do you agree this (admittedly crass and offensive) comic legitimised a collective dismissal? Do people ridicule their boss often?

11. Although 'everyone' has the right to unionise under UDHR 1948 Art 23(2) and the ILO's conception of 'workers' includes everyone who provides work, including self-employed people, it is generally accepted that limits are legitimate for national security. How far should this go?

Council of Civil Service Unions v Minister for the Civil Service [1984] UKHL 9

The Council of Civil Service Unions (CCSU) claimed that the Minister in 1984 had unlawfully exercised the Royal Prerogative and a power (now in TULRCA 1992 s 275) to prohibit staff at Government Communications Headquarters (GCHQ) from belonging to a trade union. A 1984 Order implemented a public announcement by the Prime Minister, Margaret Thatcher, in 1983. Before 1983, GCHQ staff were encouraged to join and there had been a Whitley Council, where unions and the employer settled a pay scale through periodic negotiation and consultation. Staff who objected had the option of relocation. The House of Lords held that, although the Royal Prerogative was in principle subject to judicial review, actions based on national security could not be reviewed.

Lord Fraser:

My Lords, Government Communications Headquarters ("GCHQ") is a branch of the public service under the Foreign and Commonwealth Office, the main functions of which are to ensure the security of the United Kingdom military and official communications and to provide signals intelligence for the Government. These functions are of great importance and they involve handling secret information which is vital to the national security. The main establishment of GCHQ is at Cheltenham where over 4,000 people are employed. There are also a number of smaller out-stations one of which is at Bude in Cornwall.

...

Starting with Blackstone's *Commentaries*, 15th ed. (1809), p. 251 and Chitty's *Prerogatives of the Crown* (1820), pp. 6–7 [counsel for the Minister submitted] that, within the sphere of its prerogative powers, the Crown has an absolute discretion.

...

It is clear that the employees did not have a legal right to prior consultation. ... The Civil Service handbook (*Handbook for the new civil servant*, 1973 ed. as amended 1983) which explains the normal method of consultation through the departmental Whitley Council, does not suggest that there is any legal right to consultation; indeed it is careful to recognise that, in the operational field, considerations of urgency may make prior consultation impracticable. The Civil Service Pay and Conditions of Service Code expressly states:

> "The following terms and conditions also apply to your appointment in the Civil Service. It should be understood, however, that in consequence of the constitutional position of the Crown, the Crown has the right to change its employees' conditions of service at any time, and that they hold their appointments at the pleasure of the Crown."

But even where a person claiming some benefit or privilege has no legal right to it, as a matter of private law, he may have a legitimate expectation of receiving the benefit or privilege, and, if so, the courts will protect his expectation by judicial review as a matter of public law. This subject has been fully explained by my noble and learned friend, Lord Diplock, in *O'Reilly v Mackman* [1983] 2 AC 237 and I need not repeat what he has so recently said. Legitimate, or reasonable, expectation may arise either from an express promise given on behalf of a public authority or from the existence of a regular practice which the claimant can reasonably expect to continue. ... Accordingly in my opinion if there had been no question of national security involved, the appellants would have had a legitimate expectation that the minister would consult them before issuing the instruction of 22 December 1983. ...

...

I have already explained my reasons for holding that, if no question of national security arose, the decision-making process in this case would have been unfair. The respondent's case is that she deliberately made the decision without prior consultation because prior consultation "would involve a real risk that it would occasion the very kind of disruption [at GCHQ] which was a threat to national security and which it was intended to avoid."

...

The question is one of evidence. The decision on whether the requirements of national security outweigh the duty of fairness in any particular case is for the Government and not for the courts; the Government alone has access to the necessary information, and in any event the judicial process is unsuitable for reaching decisions on national security. But if the decision is successfully challenged, on the ground that it has been reached by a process which is unfair, then the Government is under an obligation to produce evidence that the decision was in fact based on grounds of national security. ...

...

The evidence in support of this part of the respondent's case came from Sir Robert Armstrong in his first affidavit, especially at paragraph 16. Mr. Blom-Cooper rightly pointed out that the affidavit does not in terms directly support paragraph 27(i), ante pp. 401H–402A. But it does set out the respondent's view that to have entered into prior consultation would have served to bring out the vulnerability of areas of operation to those who had shown themselves ready to organise disruption. That must be read along with the earlier parts of the affidavit in which

Sir Robert had dealt in some detail with the attitude of the trade unions which I have referred to earlier in this speech. The affidavit, read as a whole, does in my opinion undoubtedly constitute evidence that the Minister did indeed consider that prior consultation would have involved a risk of precipitating disruption at GCHQ. I am accordingly of opinion that the respondent has shown that her decision was one which not only could reasonably have been based, but was in fact based, on considerations of national security, which outweighed what would otherwise have been the reasonable expectation on the part of the appellants for prior consultation. ...

Lord Scarman:

My Lords, I would dismiss this appeal for one reason only. I am satisfied that the respondent has made out a case on the ground of national security. Notwithstanding the criticisms which can be made of the evidence and despite the fact that the point was not raised, or, if it was, was not clearly made before the case reached the Court of Appeal, I have no doubt that the respondent refused to consult the unions before issuing her instruction of the 22 December 1983 because she feared that, if she did, union-organised disruption of the monitoring services of GCHQ could well result. I am further satisfied that the fear was one which a reasonable minister in the circumstances in which she found herself could reasonably entertain. I am also satisfied that a reasonable minister could reasonably consider such disruption to constitute a threat to national security. I would, therefore, deny relief to the appellants upon their application for judicial review of the instruction, the effect of which was that staff at GCHQ would no longer be permitted to belong to a national trade union. ...

Lord Diplock:

The reason why the Minister for the Civil Service decided on 22 December 1983 to withdraw this benefit was in the interests of national security. National security is the responsibility of the executive government; what action is needed to protect its interests is, as the cases cited by my learned friend, Lord Roskill, establish and common sense itself dictates, a matter upon which those upon whom the responsibility rests, and not the courts of justice, must have the last word. It is par excellence a non-justiciable question. The judicial process is totally inept to deal with the sort of problems which it involves.

The executive government likewise decided, and this would appear to be a collective decision of cabinet ministers involved, that the interests of national security required that no notice should be given of the decision before administrative action had been taken to give effect to it. The reason for this was the risk that advance notice to the national unions of the executive government's intention would attract the very disruptive action prejudicial to the national security the recurrence of which the decision barring membership of national trade unions to civil servants employed at GCHQ was designed to prevent.

There was ample evidence to which reference is made by others of your Lordships that this was indeed a real risk; so the crucial point of law in this case is whether procedural propriety must give way to national security when there is conflict between (1) on the one hand, the prima facie rule of "procedural propriety" in public law, applicable to a case of legitimate expectations that a benefit ought not to be withdrawn until the reason for its proposed withdrawal has been communicated to the person who has theretofore enjoyed that benefit and that person has been given an opportunity to comment on the reason, and (2) on the other hand, action that is needed to be taken in the interests of national security, for which the executive government bears the responsibility and alone has access to sources of information that qualify it to judge what the necessary action is. To that there can, in my opinion, be only one sensible answer. That answer is "Yes."

Lord Roskill and **Lord Brightman** concurred.

NOTES AND QUESTIONS

1. The House of Lords held that the government could derecognise the trade union, without consultation, because there was evidence (perhaps 'ample' (Lord Diplock) or perhaps where 'criticisms could be made' (Lord Scarman)) of 'national security' risks. Otherwise, their Lordships would have held that a union would have a legitimate expectation (and therefore a legal right) to be consulted by an employer, whether private or public. See chapter 9(1).

2. Why and how, exactly, would a union organising a strike in Cheltenham, or Bude in Cornwall, among 4,000 or so GCHQ office staff threaten national security?

3. Historically, trade unions have frequently been vilified as 'threats' to 'national security'. Examples include the Tolpuddle Martyrs who were transported to Australia in 1834 (chapter 1(2)), the German Chancellor Otto von Bismarck using the *Sozialistengesetze* to prohibit almost all union activity until 1890 in Germany's Second Reich, the 'Red scare' in the United States between 1919 and 1921, and the persecutions led by Republican Senator Joseph McCarthy from 1947 to 1956: see A Miller, *The Crucible* (1953). When such people talk about 'national security', are they really thinking of personal privilege?

4. By contrast to civil servants, it is often thought that the military is a legitimate exception to the right to join a trade union. There is no doubt that armies have a revolutionary capacity that can threaten the security of an existing state, as well as its people. For example, in 1918, soldiers' councils in the Germany's Imperial Army went on strike, and so forced an end to World War One. This helped bring about the democratic Constitution of the Weimar Republic. In 1946, Indian naval servicemen went on strike, hastening the British government's agreement to independence. Strikes run directly opposite to normal military governance. The military is thought, unlike other workplaces, to require unquestioning subordination to the leadership. If two or more people organise disobedience, this is regarded as mutiny under the Army Act 1955 s 31, and before HRA 1998 s 21(5) was punishable by death. Despite this, the former death penalty was not applied in 1931 after the largest mutiny in the UK: in the Royal Navy fleet at Invergordon, sailors revolted after 10–25 per cent pay cuts. What reasons do you think there are (if any) to justify soldiers being totally subordinate to their commanders? Should there be limits (if any) to such a principle?

5. In *Fitzpatrick v British Railways Board* [1992] ICR 221, Ms Fitzpatrick claimed she was unlawfully dismissed by the BRB after an *Evening Standard* article publicised she had been in a Trotskyist group called Socialist Action. She had also failed to state that she had worked for Ford Motor Co. The BRB said she was dismissed for 'untruthfulness and lack of trust', rather than her Trotskyist beliefs. Woolf LJ held the dismissal was unlawful and about her 'previous trade union (and possibly her political) activities, which gave her a reputation for being a disruptive force; and that was the prime reason for her dismissal'.

6. Under TULRCA 1992 ss 137–39 it is unlawful to refuse to employ someone, including through an employment agency, because of union membership – protection for union 'activities' seen in other sections is not made explicit. In *Harrison v Kent County Council* [1995] ICR 434 (EAT) Mr Harrison claimed

Kent CC violated this right when it refused to hire him for having 'an uncoopera-tive attitude and anti-management style'. Kent CC tried to argue they were not refusing to hire him because of union membership, but because of his activi-ties. Mummery J held Mr Harrison's right was violated. No distinction, for this purpose, could be drawn between membership and activities: if that reasoning were accepted, the most active union members would be the most discriminated against.

7. The following case illustrates the conflict of managerial authority and union freedom.

Bass Taverns Ltd v Burgess [1995] EWCA Civ 40

Mr Burgess claimed he was constructively dismissed when he was demoted by Bass Taverns Ltd for telling new trainees about the trade union at an induction course. He was a member of the National Association of Licensed House Managers. He had the consent of the company to present about the trade union. He said: '[T]he union who will fight for you, not the company. At the end of the day the company is concerned with profits and this comes before everything else.' The company argued that, implied in their consent, was a duty not to undermine the company in the eyes of the trainees. The Tribunal found there was an unfair dismissal. The Employment Appeal Tribunal overturned this, saying Burgess was not demoted for trade union activities, but rather because of his behaviour. The Court of Appeal unanimously restored the Tribunal's judgment.

Pill LJ:

In the findings of the Industrial Tribunal as to what the Respondent said, I find nothing beyond the rhetoric and hyperbole which might be expected at a recruiting meeting for a trade union or, for that matter, some other organisation or cause. Neither dishonesty nor bad faith are sug-gested. While harmonious relations between a company and a union are highly desirable, a union recruiting meeting cannot realistically be limited to that object. A consent which at the same time prevents the recruiter from saying anything adverse about the employer is no real consent. Given that there was consent to use the meeting as a forum for recruitment, it cannot be regarded as an "abuse of privilege" to make remarks to employees which are critical of the company. An Industrial Tribunal may be surprised at the situation which developed, but it was the employers who, at the start of their induction course, put the Respondent in the position of being both trainer manager and recruiter. Having put him in that position, they cannot reason-ably expect his activities in the latter role to be limited by the fact that he also was performing the role of trainer manager.

Sir Ralph Gibson and **Balcombe LJ** agreed.

NOTES AND QUESTIONS

1. In this short but important case, the Court of Appeal held there was no implied term in the agreement with the union that Mr Burgess would say anything consist-ent with (supposed) management's interests. It recognises there *must* be a conflict of interest, and legitimately, between unions and management, for unions to do their job: 'a union recruiting meeting cannot realistically be limited' to fostering 'harmonious relations' with corporate management.

2. The principle in *Burgess* has profound historic significance: unions must retain absolute intellectual and practical freedom of action from employers. O Kahn-Freund, 'The Social Ideal of the Reich Labour Court – A Critical Examination of the Practice of the Reich Labour Court' (1931) in O Kahn-Freund, R Lewis and J Clark (eds), *Labour Law and Politics in the Weimar Republic* (1981) ch 3, documented how the Reich Labour Court developed legal duties of union organisers to the abstract concept of the 'enterprise' (*Betrieb*), which in fact meant no more than employees owing a duty to their employers. This was emblematic, argued Kahn-Freund, of the descent of the courts into fascist ideology, designed to break organised labour. Two years later, Hitler had usurped power, and Kahn-Freund was dismissed from the judiciary for 'political unreliability', and forced to flee to London. See Otto Kahn-Freund, *Autobiographical Memories of the Weimar Republic: A Conversation with Wolfgang Luthardt* (February 1978) translated by E McGaughey (2016) ssrn.com.

3. Can an employer prohibit workers, including management staff, persuading people through speech to join the union? The answer consistent with ECHR Arts 10 and 11, and basic principles of common law and equity, is 'no'. The ILO Collective Bargaining Convention 1949 (c 98) requires no detriment for union 'activities' outside working hours, or within working hours when an employer's 'consent' is obtained. However, simply talking and promoting a union among colleagues (as opposed to leafleting, holding meetings, picketing or other activities) within the course of employment cannot be prohibited consistently with the right to freedom of expression, unless that freedom positively interferes undermines duties of employment. Simply talking must be regarded as an incident of membership, rather than activities. Under TULRCA 1992 ss 146(2) and 152(2) there is protection from detriment and dismissal for union 'membership', and also 'activities' at an 'appropriate time', which means outside working hours, or inside with employer consent.

4. In *Zucker v Astrid Jewels Ltd* [1978] ICR 1088, Miss Zucker successfully appealed to the Employment Appeal Tribunal that she was unfairly dismissed after she had been talking about her union (1) in the morning and afternoon tea breaks and at lunch (2) while working on her machine. The EAT held that the Tribunal was wrong to assume that while Miss Zucker was being paid this was 'working hours'. The case was remitted to Tribunal to resolve the facts, the EAT pointing out that if employees 'are permitted to converse upon anything' they were impliedly entitled to 'converse upon trade union activities'. What if an employer expressly forbids talking about unions? It is submitted that a proper resolution would have recognised that Miss Zucker, unless she started working more slowly on her machine, was simply acting as a member: there is no requirement for an 'appropriate time' because talking cannot be regarded as an 'activity' within the law's meaning. An employer would have needed to show that her talking – simply talking – was so disruptive that it was conduct justifying dismissal. The fact that it was talking about union membership should have been wholly irrelevant.

5. In *Post Office v Union of Post Office Workers* [1974] 1 WLR 89 a smaller union, the Telecommunications Staff Association (TSA), successfully claimed that it should be entitled to engage in union activities (collecting subscriptions, leafleting, holding meetings) even though the Post Office had decided to exclusively

recognise the Union of Post Office Workers (UPW) for collective bargaining. The House of Lords held the Post Office had to allow the TSA the same facilities as the UPW. Lord Reid specifically held any employee is allowed 'to take part in union activities whilst on employer premises but not actually working'. Adopting the language of equity, and as opposed to being asked 'to incur expense or submit to substantial inconvenience', Lord Reid stated: '[E]mployers must tolerate minor infringements of their strict legal rights which do them no real harm.' Do you agree this is allusion to equitable principle means the fundamental right to organise a union?

6. What if an employer refuses to incur expense, for instance, by sending lists of new employees for union organisers to contact? This would almost certainly violate a specific right of unions to information: TULRCA 1992 s 181, which requires information 'without which' collective bargaining 'would be to a material extent impeded' and fosters 'good industrial relations practice'. Under s 182, an employer is not required to disclose information that 'relates specifically to an individual', but a name and contact details is not information that 'relates' to an individual, and in any case an employer can voluntarily do what they please. See chapter 10(3).

7. Sadly, hardline management practices have developed further to suppress union members, particularly in construction. KD Ewing, *Ruined Lives – Blacklisting in the UK Construction Industry* (IER 2009) recounts how a group called 'The Consulting Association' (TCA) compiled data on 3,213 union members which was shared among construction corporations including Sir Robert McAlpine Ltd, Skanska, Balfour Beatty, Laing O'Rourke and Morgan Ashurst. Blacklisted workers would not be hired after companies performed a name check with TCA for £2.20. Under the Data Protection Act 1998 ss 17–21 it is an offence to 'process' (including holding) any 'personal data' without being registered as a data processor, and without someone's consent. Nevertheless, the Information Commissioner's Office refused to bring criminal prosecutions on behalf of the union members who were persecuted. This caused a Parliamentary investigation, and new Regulations issued under the Employment Relations Act 1999 s 3.

Employment Relations Act 1999 (Blacklists) Regulations 2010 (SI 2010/493)

3. General prohibition

(1) Subject to regulation 4, no person shall compile, use, sell or supply a prohibited list.

(2) A "prohibited list" is a list which—

  (a) contains details of persons who are or have been members of trade unions or persons who are taking part or have taken part in the activities of trade unions, and

  (b) is compiled with a view to being used by employers or employment agencies for the purposes of discrimination in relation to recruitment or in relation to the treatment of workers.

(3) "Discrimination" means treating a person less favourably than another on grounds of trade union membership or trade union activities.

(4) In these Regulations references to membership of a trade union include references to—

  (a) membership of a particular branch or section of a trade union, and

  (b) membership of one of a number of particular branches or sections of a trade union;

and references to taking part in the activities of a trade union have a corresponding meaning.

5. Refusal of employment

(1) A person (P) has a right of complaint to an employment tribunal against another (R) if R refuses to employ P for a reason which relates to a prohibited list, and either—

(a) R contravenes regulation 3 in relation to that list, or

(b) R (i) relies on information supplied by a person who contravenes that regulation in relation to that list, and (ii) knows or ought reasonably to know that the information relied on is supplied in contravention of that regulation.

(2) R shall be taken to refuse to employ P if P seeks employment of any description with R and R—

(a) refuses or deliberately omits to entertain and process P's application or enquiry;

(b) causes P to withdraw or cease to pursue P's application or enquiry;

(c) refuses or deliberately omits to offer P employment of that description;

(d) makes P an offer of such employment the terms of which are such as no reasonable employer who wished to fill the post would offer and which is not accepted; or

(e) makes P an offer of such employment but withdraws it or causes P not to accept it.

(3) If there are facts from which the tribunal could conclude, in the absence of any other explanation, that R contravened regulation 3 or relied on information supplied in contravention of that regulation, the tribunal must find that such a contravention or reliance on information occurred unless R shows that it did not.

6. Refusal of employment agency services

(1) A person (P) has a right of complaint to an employment tribunal against an employment agency (E) if E refuses P any of its services for a reason which relates to a prohibited list, and either—

(a) E contravenes regulation 3 in relation to that list, or

(b) E (i) relies on information supplied by a person who contravenes that regulation in relation to that list, and (ii) knows or ought reasonably to know that information relied on is supplied in contravention of that regulation.

...

9. Detriment

(1) A person (P) has a right of complaint to an employment tribunal against P's employer (D) if D, by any act or any deliberate failure to act, subjects P to a detriment for a reason which relates to a prohibited list, and either—

(a) D contravenes regulation 3 in relation to that list, or

(b) D (i) relies on information supplied by a person who contravenes that regulation in relation to that list, and (ii) knows or ought reasonably to know that information relied on is supplied in contravention of that regulation.

...

11. Remedies in proceedings under regulation 9

(1) Where the employment tribunal finds that a complaint under regulation 9 is well-founded, it shall make a declaration to that effect and may make an award of compensation to be paid by D to P in respect of the act or failure complained of.

(2) Subject to the following paragraphs, the amount of the compensation awarded shall be such as the tribunal considers just and equitable in all the circumstances...

...

(5) Where an award of compensation is made, the amount of compensation before any increase or reduction is made under paragraphs (6), (7) and (8) of this regulation and section 207A of the Trade Union and Labour Relations (Consolidation) Act 1992 shall not be less than £5,000.

1. The essence of the Blacklists Regulations 2010 (which properly construed, should have resulted from existing law) allow full compensation for detriment resulting from being blacklisted, but no less than £5,000.

2. In *Various Claimants v McAlpine* [2016] EWHC 45 (QB) some of the facts of a group claim were outlined by Supperstone J, before the case was brought to an end through settlements, and substantial compensation for the victims. Average settlements were around £80,000 each. The High Court case itself related to a preliminary question of whether the claimants could use expert evidence of a labour economist, Dr Victoria Wass, who would use 'regression analysis' to model the claimants' loss of earnings, hypothesising what they would have had if they had not been blacklisted. Unfortunately for the econometrics profession, Supperstone J was not persuaded that 'there exists a recognised expertise governed by recognised standards and rules of conduct' to perform such a task. Instead, under the Civil Evidence Act 1972 s 3, the analysis would not be proportionate to its expense, compared to traditional methods.

3. The Information Commissioner's Office found that one Mr Ian Kerr had been responsible for managing The Consulting Association, but prosecuted him for a mere £5,000 for not registering as a data processor under the Data Protection Act 1998 s 17, because s 60 states the maximum is a 'fine not exceeding level 5 on the standard scale, found in the Criminal Justice Act 1991 s 17(1)'. Could the claimants have brought a civil claim against Mr Kerr for restitutionary damages – to strip his gains or profits – as a result of his wrongful work?

4. In *Smith v United Kingdom* [2016] ECHR 805 Mr Smith claimed that UK law violated his right to privacy under ECHR Art 8, and his right to associate in a trade union under Art 11, by failing to award him a remedy for being blacklisted. He was an agency worker for the end-user Carillion Ltd, and was blacklisted before the Employment Relations Act 2004 amended TULRCA 1992 s 146 to protect 'workers' and not just employees. As chapters 3(2)(c) and 15(3)(a) note, the Court of Appeal, on wholly inadequate grounds, said that agency staff were not employees of the end-user, and on this flawed presumption the European Court of Human Rights had to decide whether there was adequate protection. However, after parallel criminal proceedings by the Information Commissioner for The Consulting Association not being duly registered as a data processor, Mr Smith had been able to settle for £50,000 in compensation. In the European Court of Human Rights' view, at [40] this meant 'the legal framework provided a combination of domestic remedies which proved to be effective in the applicant's case, resulting in an acknowledgment of the violation of the applicant's rights, and giving appropriate redress'. Similarly, because of the settlement, he had therefore suffered no 'significant disadvantage' under Art 11. This outcome, which focuses on the final result in the individual case, should not be taken as an endorsement of the woefully inadequate reasoning on Mr Smith's civil law remedies: if the criminal proceedings (for whatever reason) had not taken place, and there had been no settlement, logically there would have been a violation of Arts 9 and 11.

S Webb and B Webb, *Industrial Democracy* **(1920) chs 1 and 2**
The Webbs' foundational labour law text is a compelling read on the reasons for labour law. The first two chapters explore the development of democracy in trade unions, from 'primitive' systems which tended to function on the basis of discussion and regular voting by all members, appropriate for smaller and more informal groups, to a more sophisticated and self-regulating system of representative democracy. The Webbs argue that Parliament-like systems of regulation, which enable direct control by the members over the executive through the vote, but also accountability of executives to a union board, is the superior mode of union governance.

KD Ewing and P Elias, *Trade Union Democracy, Members' Rights and the Law* **(1987)**
Ewing and Elias' book on trade union democracy gives a comprehensive account of how members' rights in their unions had developed, to promote internal accountability. This followed the Trade Union Act 1984, where the government had argued that statutory regulation was necessary to control supposed aggressive or militant tendencies in unions. In fact, the authors show that democracy in trade unions had been constantly vibrant, and that detailed regulation was neither necessary nor particularly desirable.

KD Ewing, 'The Function of Trade Unions' (2005) 34 *Industrial Law Journal* **1**
Ewing suggests the main functions of trade unions are fivefold. First, they provide services, eg sickness insurance, death benefits, legal advice and assistance. Second, they provide workplace representation, in employer negotiation, grievance or disciplinary, and collective bargaining. Third, they have a regulatory function, through collective agreements for shaping terms and conditions at work or in lobbying for legislation. Fourth, unions provide political representation, promoting issues in the national or EU arena. Fifth, unions are involved in public administration, and as 'social partners' can frequently be delegated responsibility for administering state policy, such as determining the minimum wage.

E McGaughey, 'Democracy or Oligarchy? Models of Union Governance in the UK, Germany and US' (2017) KCL Law School Research Paper No 2017-35
This paper sets out the empirical evidence that unions succeed more in pursuing their members interests, and are better 'fighting organisations', when executives are directly accountable through the vote to their members. On average, where trade unions require that members vote for delegates, and delegates vote for executives, the successes of the union and the labour relations system in the country as a whole are more limited. The article sets out the historical development of union governance in the UK, Germany and the United States, which suggests that governance structures typically evolved out of habit, and often to match the familiar political structures of a country. Certainly the thesis that there is an iron law of oligarchy has no credible evidence to back it up.

9

Collective Bargaining

Collective bargaining has been the main method to achieve 'just and favourable remuneration' since the early twentieth century (Universal Declaration on Human Rights 1948
Art 23(3)). It is a process, not an outcome, so the results depend on constant activism
by unions. The classic view, advocated by Otto Kahn-Freund, was that if the state established the right legal conditions, trade unions and employers could mostly be left alone.
With 'collective *laissez faire*' there could be a kind of fair market equilibrium. Most
labour lawyers now think this was too optimistic. Trade union strength, like the strength
of capital, depends on active state support (see chapter 1(3)(a)). Moreover organisational
governance, not just markets, is a primary determinant of prices. Nothing is 'left free',
and that became all too obvious in the UK once the state turned hostile after 1979. If fair
wages were so rapidly dismantled before, can the law prevent the same thing happening
again?

   This question presses all developed democracies, though labour law systems do vary.
First, collective bargaining can take place at a sectoral or enterprise level. The UK shifted
from sectoral bargaining to enterprise bargaining after the Donovan Report (1968) Cmnd
3623. This led to a decline in collective agreement coverage: in 2014, just 29 per cent of
UK citizens were covered by a collective agreement. By comparison, France achieves 98
per cent, Sweden 89 per cent. Germany has dropped to 59 per cent since it began allowing enterprise agreements. Second, employing entities might have a duty to bargain in
good faith enforced by some sanction, or not. The UK used to have no such requirement,
but since the Employment Relations Act 1999, it imposes a weak duty to bargain, backed
by a possibility that a collective agreement may become binding (chapter 9(1)). Third,
collective agreement terms are far more ambitious in some systems than others. All try
to raise wages and regulate working time beyond minimum standards. But where unions
are weaker, collective agreements become preoccupied with rudimentary job security.
In strong systems, unions bargain for lasting voting rights in the constitutions of their
enterprise, on boards and through their pension capital. They embed and expand their
membership base with active employer cooperation. This is collective bargaining's frontier: the steady redrafting of the economic constitution, for a more democratic economy
and society. Viewed in this way, collective bargaining should not be an unending fight
against wage cuts, or even as an end in itself: collective bargaining is a right to achieve
rights. This chapter covers (1) recognition of unions to collectively bargain, (2) standard

terms of collective agreements, and (3) rights essential to bargaining, including auto-matic enrolment of workers in unions, and rights to representation and time off.

Introductory text: Collins ch 6. CEM ch 12 (478–88), 14. D&M ch 9 (869–912).

(1) RECOGNITION FOR BARGAINING

Any employing entity may voluntarily recognise and bargain with a trade union at any time. Around 80 of the UK's top 100 companies voluntarily recognise a union, although this does always not equate to meaningful bargaining. Corporations and public bodies may outsource services to (formally) separate corporations. In fragmented enterprises, it takes much more time to secure collective agreements, potentially for thousands of shifting and reorganising corporations across a sector. This means more meetings, nego-tiations, drafting and redrafting of contracts. Without sectoral bargaining, even if collec-tive agreements cover the largest companies, the majority of the workforce may be left without a voice.

Some corporations may also just refuse to collectively bargain with their workforce. This leaves two main options. The first is to organise a strike: workers can start the bar-gaining process by threatening to withdraw their labour, just as employers constantly control their workforce with the threat of dismissal. Two main conditions for this to be possible are that (1) the workforce is organised and willing to withstand reprisals, and (2) the employer has fewer other options, limiting its capacity to hold out. In a competitive private sector, halts in production can swiftly damage an employer's profits. Customers switch to other competitors. The enterprise must concede the union's demands to avoid insolvency. However, in any system of diversified share ownership, shareholders can become indifferent to one company's insolvency, because they equally invest in competi-tors. Profits lost at one corporation may simply increase profits in others. As a whole, this weakens labour's power against capital. In regulated sectors or public services, a strike may halt services to consumers or the public who have nowhere else to go: this causes anger. But managers of a regulated or government entity may be content to hold out, either because they do not need profit, or their ideology defies rational economic choices. Because of these problems, collective action and conflict has been used as a last resort. An alternative since 1999, of doubtful merit, is the long statutory recognition procedure.

Trade Union and Labour Relations (Consolidation) Act 1992 Sch A1, paras 3–7, 11, 12, 18, 22–26 and 35–36

3. (1) This paragraph applies for the purposes of this Part of this Schedule.

(2) The meaning of collective bargaining given by section 178(1) shall not apply.

(3) References to collective bargaining are to negotiations relating to pay, hours and holidays; but this has effect subject to sub-paragraph (4).

(4) If the parties agree matters as the subject of collective bargaining, references to collective bargaining are to negotiations relating to the agreed matters; and this is the case whether the

agreement is made before or after the time when the CAC [Central Arbitration Committee] issues a declaration, or the parties agree, that the union is (or unions are) entitled to conduct collective bargaining on behalf of a bargaining unit.

(5) Sub-paragraph (4) does not apply in construing paragraph 31(3).

(6) Sub-paragraphs (2) to (5) do not apply in construing paragraph 35 or 44.

4. (1) The union or unions seeking recognition must make a request for recognition to the employer. ...

...

6. The request is not valid unless the union (or each of the unions) has a certificate of independence.

7. (1) The request is not valid unless the employer, taken with any associated employer or employers, employs—

(a) at least 21 workers on the day the employer receives the request, or

(b) an average of at least 21 workers in the 13 weeks ending with that day.

(2) To find the average under sub-paragraph (1)(b)—

(a) take the number of workers employed in each of the 13 weeks (including workers not employed for the whole of the week);

(b) aggregate the 13 numbers;

(c) divide the aggregate by 13.

...

11. (1) This paragraph applies if—

(a) before the end of the first period the employer fails to respond to the request, or

(b) before the end of the first period the employer informs the union (or unions) that the employer does not accept the request (without indicating a willingness to negotiate).

(2) The union (or unions) may apply to the CAC to decide both these questions—

(a) whether the proposed bargaining unit is appropriate;

(b) whether the union has (or unions have) the support of a majority of the workers constituting the appropriate bargaining unit.

...

12. (1) Sub-paragraph (2) applies if—

(a) the employer informs the union (or unions) under paragraph 10(2), and

(b) no agreement is made before the end of the second period.

(2) The union (or unions) may apply to the CAC to decide both these questions—

(a) whether the proposed bargaining unit is appropriate;

(b) whether the union has (or unions have) the support of a majority of the workers constituting the appropriate bargaining unit.

(3) Sub-paragraph (4) applies if—

(a) the employer informs the union (or unions) under paragraph 10(2), and

(b) before the end of the second period the parties agree a bargaining unit but not that the union is (or unions are) to be recognised as entitled to conduct collective bargaining on behalf of the unit.

(4) The union (or unions) may apply to the CAC to decide the question whether the union has (or unions have) the support of a majority of the workers constituting the bargaining unit.

...

18. (1) If the CAC accepts an application under paragraph 11(2) or 12(2) it must try to help the parties to reach within the appropriate period an agreement as to what the appropriate bargaining unit is.

(2) The appropriate period is (subject to any notice under sub-paragraph (3), (4) or (5))—

(a) the period of 20 working days starting with the day after that on which the CAC gives notice of acceptance of the application, or

(b) such longer period (so starting) as the CAC may specify to the parties by notice containing reasons for the extension.

...

22. (1) This paragraph applies if—

(a) the CAC proceeds with an application in accordance with paragraph 20 or 21 (and makes no declaration under paragraph 19F(5)),

(b) the CAC is satisfied that a majority of the workers constituting the bargaining unit are members of the union (or unions).

(2) The CAC must issue a declaration that the union is (or unions are) recognised as entitled to conduct collective bargaining on behalf of the workers constituting the bargaining unit.

(3) But if any of the three qualifying conditions is fulfilled, instead of issuing a declaration under sub-paragraph (2) the CAC must give notice to the parties that it intends to arrange for the holding of a secret ballot in which the workers constituting the bargaining unit are asked whether they want the union (or unions) to conduct collective bargaining on their behalf.

(4) These are the three qualifying conditions—

(a) the CAC is satisfied that a ballot should be held in the interests of good industrial relations;

(b) the CAC has evidence, which it considers to be credible, from a signi cant number of the union members within the bargaining unit that they do not want the union (or unions) to conduct collective bargaining on their behalf;

(c) membership evidence is produced which leads the CAC to conclude that there are doubts whether a significant number of the union members within the bargaining unit want the union (or unions) to conduct collective bargaining on their behalf.

(5) For the purposes of sub-paragraph (4)(c) membership evidence is—

(a) evidence about the circumstances in which union members became members;

(b) evidence about the length of time for which union members have been members, in a case where the CAC is satisfied that such evidence should be taken into account.

23. (1) This paragraph applies if—

(a) the CAC proceeds with an application in accordance with paragraph 20 or 21 (and makes no declaration under paragraph 19F(5)), and

(b) the CAC is not satisfied that a majority of the workers constituting the bargaining unit are members of the union (or unions).

(2) The CAC must give notice to the parties that it intends to arrange for the holding of a secret ballot in which the workers constituting the bargaining unit are asked whether they want the union (or unions) to conduct collective bargaining on their behalf.

25. (1) This paragraph applies if the CAC arranges under paragraph 24 for the holding of a ballot.

(2) The ballot must be conducted by a qualified independent person appointed by the CAC.

(3) The ballot must be conducted within—

(a) the period of 20 working days starting with the day after that on which the quali-fied independent person is appointed, or

(b) such longer period (so starting) as the CAC may decide.

(4) The ballot must be conducted—
- (a) at a workplace or workplaces decided by the CAC,
- (b) by post, or
- (c) by a combination of the methods described in sub-paragraphs (a) and (b), depending on the CAC's preference.

(5) In deciding how the ballot is to be conducted the CAC must take into account—
- (a) the likelihood of the ballot being affected by unfairness or malpractice if it were conducted at a workplace or workplaces;
- (b) costs and practicality;
- (c) such other matters as the CAC considers appropriate. …

…

26. (1) An employer who is informed by the CAC under paragraph 25(9) must comply with the following five duties.

(2) The first duty is to co-operate generally, in connection with the ballot, with the union (or unions) and the person appointed to conduct the ballot; and the second and third duties are not to prejudice the generality of this.

(3) The second duty is to give to the union (or unions) such access to the workers constituting the bargaining unit as is reasonable to enable the union (or unions) to inform the workers of the object of the ballot and to seek their support and their opinions on the issues involved.

(4) The third duty is to do the following (so far as it is reasonable to expect the employer to do so)—
- (a) to give to the CAC, within the period of 10 working days starting with the day after that on which the employer is informed under paragraph 25(9), the names and home address of the workers constituting the bargaining unit;
- (b) to give to the CAC, as soon as is reasonably practicable, the name and home address of any worker who joins the unit after the employer has complied with paragraph (a);

(4A) The fourth duty is to refrain from making any offer to any or all of the workers constituting the bargaining unit which–
- (a) has or is likely to have the effect of inducing any or all of them not to attend any relevant meeting between the union (or unions) and the workers constituting the bargaining unit, and
- (b) is not reasonable in the circumstances.

(4B) The fifth duty is to refrain from taking or threatening to take any action against a worker solely or mainly on the grounds that he–
- (a) attended or took part in any relevant meeting between the union (or unions) and the workers constituting the bargaining unit, or
- (b) indicated his intention to attend or take part in such a meeting.

27A. (1) Each of the parties informed by the CAC under paragraph 25(9) must refrain from using any unfair practice.

(2) A party uses an unfair practice if, with a view to in uencing the result of the ballot, the party–
- (a) offers to pay money or give money's worth to a worker entitled to vote in the ballot in return for the worker's agreement to vote in a particular way or to abstain from voting,
- (b) makes an outcome-specific offer to a worker entitled to vote in the ballot,
- (c) coerces or attempts to coerce a worker entitled to vote in the ballot to disclose–
  - (i)   whether he intends to vote or to abstain from voting in the ballot, or
  - (ii) how he intends to vote, or how he has voted, in the ballot,
- (d) dismisses or threatens to dismiss a worker,

> (e) takes or threatens to take disciplinary action against a worker,
> (f) subjects or threatens to subject a worker to any other detriment, or
> (g) uses or attempts to use undue in uence on a worker entitled to vote in the ballot.
> …

30. (1) This paragraph applies if the CAC issues a declaration under this Part of this Schedule that the union is (or unions are) recognised as entitled to conduct collective bargaining on behalf of a bargaining unit.

(2) The parties may in the negotiation period conduct negotiations with a view to agreeing a method by which they will conduct collective bargaining.

(3) If no agreement is made in the negotiation period the employer or the union (or unions) may apply to the CAC for assistance.

(4) The negotiation period is—
> (a) the period of 30 working days starting with the start day, or
> (b) such longer period (so starting) as the parties may from time to time agree.

(5) The start day is the day after that on which the parties are notified of the declaration.

31. (1) This paragraph applies if an application for assistance is made to the CAC under paragraph 30.

(2) The CAC must try to help the parties to reach in the agreement period an agreement on a method by which they will conduct collective bargaining.

(3) If at the end of the agreement period the parties have not made such an agreement the CAC must specify to the parties the method by which they are to conduct collective bargaining.

(4) Any method specified under sub-paragraph (3) is to have effect as if it were contained in a legally enforceable contract made by the parties.

(5) But if the parties agree in writing—
> (a) that sub-paragraph (4) shall not apply, or shall not apply to particular parts of the method specified by the CAC, or
> (b) (b) to vary or replace the method specified by the CAC, the written agreement shall have effect as a legally enforceable contract made by the parties.

(6) Specific performance shall be the only remedy available for breach of anything which is a legally enforceable contract by virtue of this paragraph.

(7) If at any time before a specification is made under sub-paragraph (3) the parties jointly apply to the CAC requesting it to stop taking steps under this paragraph, the CAC must comply with the request.

(8) The agreement period is—
> (a) the period of 20 working days starting with the day after that on which the CAC receives the application under paragraph 30, or
> (b) such longer period (so starting) as the CAC may decide with the consent of the parties.
> …

35. (1) An application under paragraph 11 or 12 is not admissible if the CAC is satisfied that there is already in force a collective agreement under which a union is (or unions are) recognised as entitled to conduct collective bargaining on behalf of any workers falling within the relevant bargaining unit.

(2) But sub-paragraph (1) does not apply to an application under paragraph 11 or 12 if—
> (a) the union (or unions) recognised under the collective agreement and the union (or unions) making the application under paragraph 11 or 12 are the same, and
> (b) the matters in respect of which the union is (or unions are) entitled to conduct collective bargaining do not include all of the following: pay, hours and holidays ("the core topics").

(3) A declaration of recognition which is the subject of a declaration under paragraph 83(2) must for the purposes of sub-paragraph (1) be treated as ceasing to have effect to the extent specified in paragraph 83(2) on the making of the declaration under paragraph 83(2).

(4) In applying sub-paragraph (1) an agreement for recognition (the agreement in question) must be ignored if—

(a) the union does not have (or none of the unions has) a certificate of independence,

(b) at some time there was an agreement (the old agreement) between the employer and the union under which the union (whether alone or with other unions) was recognised as entitled to conduct collective bargaining on behalf of a group of workers which was the same or substantially the same as the group covered by the agreement in question, and

(c) the old agreement ceased to have effect in the period of three years ending with the date of the agreement in question.

(5) It is for the CAC to decide whether one group of workers is the same or substantially the same as another, but in deciding the CAC may take account of the views of any person it believes has an interest in the matter.

(6) The relevant bargaining unit is—

(a) the proposed bargaining unit, where the application is under paragraph 11(2) or 12(2);

(b) the agreed bargaining unit, where the application is under paragraph 12(4).

36. (1) An application under paragraph 11 or 12 is not admissible unless the CAC decides that—

(a) members of the union (or unions) constitute at least 10 per cent of the workers constituting the relevant bargaining unit, and

(b) a majority of the workers constituting the relevant bargaining unit would be likely to favour recognition of the union (or unions) as entitled to conduct collective bargaining on behalf of the bargaining unit.

(2) The relevant bargaining unit is—

(a) the proposed bargaining unit, where the application is under paragraph 11(2) or 12(2); (b) the agreed bargaining unit, where the application is under paragraph 11(4).

NOTES AND QUESTIONS

1. When faced with tomes of procedure or statute, possibly the best thing lawyers can do is identify essential points, count them, and if feasible create an acronym to remember. Schedule A1 can become five points that (optimistically) spell recognition 'IN ABC':

    Independent unions can apply for recognition, paras 4–7
    No collective agreement must already exist for an application to succeed, para 35
    Appropriate bargaining units must be identified for voting on the union, paras 11–18
    Ballots musts be fairly conducted, getting majority union support, para 22–26, 36
    Collective agreements set by the Central Arbitration Committee, if employers resist, bind in law, paras 31–32

2. Neat acronyms aside (can you make your own?) the procedure gives employers many chances to delay recognition as long as possible, and hire lawyers to help. Even if a union completes the procedure, the duty to bargain imposed by the Central Arbitration Committee, which ends in a legally binding agreement, does not require the employer to make any particular terms. Under this law, you can

drag the horse to water, but cannot make it drink. How did the approach of the Ministry of Labour differ under the Trade Boards or Wages Council Acts? See chapter 1(3).

3.   Although statutory recognition purports 'to facilitate transition from a non-union to a unionized governance structure', Bogg points out the 'process assumes a non-union default.' A Bogg, 'The Death of Statutory Union Recognition in the United Kingdom' (2012) 54 *Journal of Industrial Relations* 409, 413. Why should that be? Why should the default be 'no union and no voice', but then a supposed right to follow a complex procedure to get a voice? Why is there not an inherent right to vote in your workplace, just like you can vote for Parliament? See chapter 11.

4.   Why do workers, under paragraph 7, with fewer than 20 colleagues lose the right to statutory recognition? Should small businesses be able to pay unfair wages to their staff, and so engage in unfair competition with medium-size businesses?

5.   The Central Arbitration Committee expected around 150 recognition applications a year, but in 10 years was only getting around half that: 761. Of these, 444 applications were in the first 5 years, but only 116 recognitions were actually completed (ie 23 a year). The peak was 2001/02 with 118 applications. There were 42 applications in 2008/09 and 2009/10, and 28 in 2010/11, with 12 completions. See G Gall, 'The first Ten Years of the Third Statutory Union Recognition Procedure in Britain' (2010) 39 *ILJ* 444. Do you think people are not applying for recognition because they do not want union representation, or because of something else?

6.   Turning to particular issues, a first problem with Sch A1, paras 3–7 and 35, is that while only an independent union may use the statutory recognition procedure, a sham union may be voluntarily recognised by the employer. Quite astonishingly, it has been held an independent union must apply for the employer-dominated, sham union to be derecognised before it can apply for recognition.

Pharmacists' Defence Association Union v Secretary of State for Business, Innovation and Skills [2017] EWCA Civ 66

Workers at Boots Ltd claimed their Pharmacists' Defence Association Union, founded in November 2010, should be recognised for collective bargaining. Boots Ltd argued the application was blocked because it already recognised a listed 'trade union', the 'Boots Pharmacists' Association' (BPA). The BPA is an employer-dominated, sham union, with financial 'support and facilities' from Boots Ltd, and no certificate of independence. Boots Ltd entered into an agreement with the BPA in March 2012, immediately after the Pharmacists' Defence Association Union (PDAU) had withdrawn an application to the Central Arbitration Committee from January 2012, on faith that Boots Ltd would start to bargain. Therefore, the PDAU renewed an application to the Central Arbitration Committee, accepted in December 2012. The Central Arbitration Committee held, although BPA was recognised, under the Human Rights Act (HRA) 1998 s 3, paragraph 35 should be implicitly interpreted to mean that a collective agreement in force had to be at least about 'pay, hours and holidays' (as a normal independent trade union would aim to bargain for). This was necessary to be compatible with ECHR Art 11. Boots Ltd successfully applied for judicial review. Keith J, over two High Court cases, decided the Central Arbitration

Committee could not have reached the interpretation it did, the Committee further was not able to make a declaration of incompatibility under HRA 1998 s 4, and that he was not prepared to make a declaration of incompatibility either, because a union could apply for the sham union's derecognition first. The Court of Appeal reached the same result.

Underhill LJ:

64. I have already noted that under paragraph 137 an application for derecognition under Part VI can only be made by a worker. It cannot be made by a trade union. Mr Hendy argued before the Judge and before us that that meant that the escape-route from paragraph 35 relied on by Boots and the Secretary of State was not reliably available. It was true that if there were a substantial number of Boots employees who wanted to have the PDAU recognised, and thus to have the BPA derecognised as a necessary preliminary, one or more of them of them could be asked by it to make the necessary application; and the PDAU could stand behind and guide the application so far as necessary. But Mr Hendy argued that that was not the same as the union being able to make the application in its own right. It should be entitled to do so as a matter of principle, but in any event there was a further problem that individual workers could not be counted on to go into battle on its behalf. He acknowledged that Part VIII of Schedule A1 enacted various protections for workers who were subjected to a detriment, including dismissal, for exercising their rights under the Schedule, but he submitted that in the real world employees might not have total confidence in that protection. The article 11 rights of the PDAU could only be protected by a mechanism that allowed it to apply in its own right for the derecognition of the BPA.

65. Sir Brian Keith rejected those submissions at paras. 12–13 of his judgment, as follows:

"12. All in all, the PDAU's concern about the impact of these considerations is more theoretical than real. It is very unlikely that the PDAU will be unable to find a single pharmacist within Boots who wants the PDAU to be recognised for the purposes of collective bargaining in place of the BPA, and who is willing to put their head above the parapet. And if the PDAU is not able to find such a pharmacist, that is overwhelmingly likely to have been because there is insufficient support for the PDAU among Boots' pharmacists for any application for statutory recognition to be successful. That is because one of the conditions for the grant of statutory recognition to the PDAU under the Schedule is that it has to have the support of a majority of Boots' pharmacists.

13. Ultimately, the question is whether the machinery in Part VI of the Schedule for securing the de-recognition of an incumbent non-independent trade union, coupled with the machinery in Part VIII of the Schedule for awarding compensation to workers who are subjected to detrimental treatment for seeking to secure that, enables the PDAU to avoid the consequences of para. 35 of the Schedule and to invoke the machinery in Part I of the Schedule for securing its own recognition. Subject, of course, to the issue over the proper construction of the phrase "collective bargaining" in para. 134(1) of the Schedule, I think it does. The mechanism may not be perfect, but the existence of the mechanism means that para. 35 does not render the right of the PDAU to engage in collective bargaining with Boots devoid of substance."

66. Mr Hendy's principal submission in answer to that reasoning was that it was wrong in principle that the PDAU should be dependent for the vindication of its article 11 rights on the action of a third party. I do not accept that. I am prepared to accept for present purposes, although Mr Stilitz did not, that a trade union as well as its members enjoys rights under article 11 in connection with recognition: the ECtHR appears to proceed on that basis in both Demir and Unite, though the issue did not arise for consideration. But it does not follow that a

scheme for compulsory recognition should place all the levers in the hands of a union for which recognition is sought rather than in the hands of those who wish to be represented by it. It is, after all, ultimately for the benefit of the workers that recognition is sought. I appreciate that under Part I the process is initiated by a request, and if necessary an application, by the union rather than a worker or workers; but that does not mean that the same approach needs to be followed in every element of the scheme. In my view the essential question is simply whether there is a reasonably practicable route whereby the recognition of the PDAU can be achieved if the majority of the pharmacists want it.

67. Mr Hendy's secondary submission was that even on that basis the Judge gravely under-estimated the disincentives to a pharmacist taking the necessary first step. He referred not only to the risk (perceived if not actual) that such action would prejudice their relationship with Boots but to other possible considerations, such as a disinclination to be (or appear) dis-loyal to the BPA or colleagues who were active in it. I do not accept that submission. Sir Brian Keith, who has great experience in this area, had to make a realistic assessment of whether the requirement to find a pharmacist who would make the application represented a substantial obstacle to achieving the derecognition of the BPA; and the assessment which he makes at para. 12 of his judgment is unimpeachable.

68. Looking at the point more generally, the observation at the end of para. 13 of Sir Brian Keith's judgment seems to me important. The devising of a statutory scheme of recognition inevitably requires a large number of detailed choices about both substantive and procedural matters, seeking, as Mr Stilitz put it, to "balance and calibrate the interests of multiple stake-holders (e.g. workers, employers and competing trade unions)". There will inevitably be some choices which not only could have been made differently but could have been made better. But I think it is clear from the case-law of the ECtHR referred to above that article 11 cannot be used as a tool to challenge this or that arguably sub-optimal element in a scheme provided that a fair balance has been struck. Both before and after Demir the Court has emphasised the wide margin of appreciation which must be accorded to member states in this area ....

Sales LJ and **Sir James Munby** agreed.

NOTES AND QUESTIONS

1. The Court of Appeal held that because Sch A1 provided a workable way for a sham union to be derecognised, it was compatible with ECHR Art 11. Although 'sub-optimal', the 'large number of detailed choices' was there to 'balance and calibrate the interests of multiple stake-holders'. Do you agree? Do you agree the 'ultimate question' of the case was whether, as Keith J says, 'the machinery in Part VI of the Schedule for securing the de-recognition' existed?
2. Why did the Court of Appeal not interpret Sch A1 para 35 to mean an 'independ-ent' union, when it says 'union'? Regardless of human rights, would that not be a construction that is consistent with any reasonable person's understanding of the Act's purpose? Is this not the plain and binding meaning of the law that Parlia-ment intended, read in its context? Did Boots Ltd have any credible arguments for why the legislation had the purpose of enabling employers to block recognition with sham unions over periods, like here, of 6 years and 3 months and more? On basic principles of construction, see *AG of Belize v Belize Telecom Ltd* [2009] UKPC 10. The essential point is that the statute itself is silent about what a 'union' means in paragraph 35, and so it must be construed in its context.

3.   Why does the Court of Appeal treat ECHR Art 11 as if it is a frustrating external force to be limited as much as possible? The Pharmacists' Union could have continued to submit that under HRA 1998 s 3, Sch A1 has to be interpreted to fulfil the principles (not bare minimum rules) in ECHR Art 11. The point of Boots Ltd's strategy was not merely to refuse to bargain with the PDAU, but to drag out the formal, expensive process as long as possible.

4.   It is almost certain that when a union, like the PDAU, eventually wins recognition in such circumstances, an anti-union management would continue to refuse to bargain. Is this system adequate to improve people's working pay and conditions?

5.   A second problem with Sch A1, para 35, is that it was held that an independent trade union which is already recognised with a collective agreement can block an application by another union, even though the incumbent has virtually no support among the workforce.

R (National Union of Journalists) v CAC [2005] EWCA Civ 1309

The National Union of Journalists (NUJ) claimed it was not blocked under paragraph 35 by the recognition of the British Association of Journalists at the *Racing Post*, owned by the Mirror News Group. The Central Arbitration Committee has rejected the NUJ's application on the grounds that a collective agreement was 'already in force'. The BAJ formed in the early 1990s as a breakaway from the NUJ. While independent, it was not affiliated to the Trades Union Congress. In 2003, it signed an agreement with the Mirror's Sports Division, but only had one member. A majority of people in the bargaining unit were in favour of statutory recognition of the NUJ. The NUJ argued an agreement should be considered 'already in force' for the purpose of para 35, and in any case the Central Arbitration Committee decision breached ECHR Arts 11 and 14.

Buxton LJ:

4. In considering the decision of the CAC and the apparently unusual outcome of it, it is relevant to remind ourselves of what the CAC said in para 42 of its determination:

"We are comforted by two matters in reaching this negative conclusion on the question of support for the voluntarily recognised union. The first is that it coincides with the traditional understanding of voluntary recognition."

They then quote from Deakin & Morris, *Labour Law*, 3rd ed (2001), p 765 in the following terms:

"A further, and less commented on, consequence of the voluntary nature of trade union recognition is that there is no mechanism to control the employer's choice of union. Thus, there is nothing to prevent an employer recognising a union which may have only minimal support among the workforce."

5 The CAC continued:

"Second, and more pertinent, is the emphasis placed in the White Paper which preceded the introduction of the statutory recognition procedure on the desirability of taking inter-union disputes outside the scope of the panel's jurisdiction: see Fairness at Work (1998) (Cm 3968), para 4.19."

6 However, having said that, the CAC indicated that it was very far from satisfied about the outcome that its application of paragraph 35 had produced. It said this in para 43 of its determination, immediately after the passage that I have just read:

"Nevertheless, we should like to put on record our firm belief that the exclusionary rule contained in paragraph 35 has not achieved justice in this case. The employer has been able to defeat what are in all probability the wishes of a majority of the relevant workforce by the simple expedient of concluding a voluntary recognition agreement with a wholly unrepresentative union. It may be said that the principle of avoiding CAC adjudication upon inter-union disputes was regarded by Parliament as more important than the principle of providing collective bargaining where a majority of the appropriate workforce desire it. Even accepting that, we think this case displays a lacuna in the legislation. Were the BAJ a non-independent trade union, which it is not, its recognition by the company could be challenged under Part VI of the Schedule. Were the BAJ affiliated to the Trades Union Congress, which it is not, the NUJ could have recourse to the procedures of the TUC to bring about a resolution of the issues raised by the case. Since the BAJ is independent but not affiliated, the defeated majority union has no avenue of potential redress, once it is excluded from the statutory recognition process. This seems to us highly unsatisfactory."

...

27 Before the CAC and the judge, the NUJ asserted its rights of association under article 11 of the Convention and said that they were being interfered with by the refusal of MGN Ltd to negotiate with them, and the fact that MGN Ltd were able to use paragraph 35 to that end.

28 The only case that was relied on for the proposition that that situation fell under article 11 was *Wilson v United Kingdom* (2002) 35 EHRR 523. Mr Hendy relied on para 42 of that determination, and in particular the words:

"A trade union must thus be free to strive for the protection of its members' interests, and the individual members have a right, in order to protect their interests, that the trade union should be heard."

29 That, it was said, demonstrated that a right to negotiate on the part of the trade union was part of the article 11 rights of its members. That was plainly not what the court thought. It went on in that very paragraph to say: "Article 11 does not, however, secure any particular treatment of trade unions or their members and leaves each state a free choice of the means to be used to secure that right to be heard."

30 It then went on in paras 43 and 44 to expand on that view, and in particular said in para 44: "The court has not yet been prepared to hold that the freedom of a trade union to make its voice heard extends to imposing on an employer an obligation to recognise a trade union."

...

36 The obvious difficulty facing the NUJ in this case is to point to any action by the state that has discriminated against them. They may well say that they have been discriminated against by MGN Ltd, but MGN Ltd is not the state or a state-supported body.

37 Mr Hendy at the end of his submissions therefore reformulated the case in this way:

"By precluding a representative trade union from using the statutory procedure, the legislature is actively impeding the right of the employees to be heard through the negotiating procedure. The state has permitted that state of affairs through the terms of paragraph 35."

38 I have to say that I find that formulation and that description of this case wholly artificial. This case is completely different from the only case that comes even remotely near to it, the closed shop case of *Young, James and Webster v United Kingdom* (1981) 4 EHRR 38. In that case, once the European Court of Human Rights had managed to find a right of non-association lurking within article 11 it had no difficulty in holding that the state was responsible for legislation that allowed, and some would say encouraged, the punishment of workers for their exercise of that right. But in this case paragraph 35 is not limiting or punitive, or aimed at a particular category of workers, but it is even-handed in according primacy to existing voluntary agreements.

39 I would venture respectfully to adopt in that respect paragraph 35 of the skeleton argument of Ms Dinah Rose, on behalf of the CAC, which read:

"Even if there were a difference in treatment, the [NUJ] has failed to identify any ground for that difference in treatment which falls within the ambit of article 14. The reason why the NUJ is denied access to the statutory recognition procedure in paragraph 35 is not because of any particular feature or status of the NUJ to which the legislation is hostile. It is merely because another union has already entered into an agreement with the employer. The result would be identical if it were the NUJ which had entered into an agreement and the BAJ was seeking statutory recognition. This treatment does not disclose any discrimination within the ambit of article 14."

40 In my view, all that can be said, and indeed is said, is that the state should take positive steps to prevent the use of paragraph 35 in the way in which MGN Ltd has used it in this case. But there are at least two objections to that. First, it is inconsistent with the guidance given in the *Wilson* case as to the obligations of the state with regard to collective bargaining. Secondly, a failure to take that general step cannot possibly be characterised as an act of discrimination by the state against the NUJ, and it is that, and not some general issue of the character of the scheme as a whole, that has to be established under article 14.

Latham LJ and **Sir Martin Nourse** agreed.

NOTES AND QUESTIONS

1. The Court of Appeal holds that the Central Arbitration Committee rightly (albeit reluctantly) blocked the NUJ from using the recognition procedure. It adds that ECHR Art 11 provides no assistance, because as interpreted in *Wilson* there is no right of a union to recognition. As the *Pharmacists' Union* case above shows, the position has now become more nuanced, but has not changed. Regardless of human rights, could the Court of Appeal have not simply interpreted 'collective agreement' as one that generally covers a sufficient number in the 'collective'? Would this not be consistent with the purpose of Schedule A1?

2. Unlike the *Pharmacists' Union* case, the union blocking the NUJ was not an employer-dominated sham – but it was still a management-friendly body, with the same functional outcome as a sham union.

3. In *Demir and Baykara v Turkey* [2008] ECHR 1345, the European Court of Human Rights, under the heading 'Evolution of the case law' put its interpretation of *Wilson* differently to what Buxton LJ said was 'plainly' the case. At [145] it said there is, 'the right for a trade union to seek to persuade the employer to hear what it has to say on behalf of its members' based on *Wilson v UK* [2002] ECHR 552, [44]. It went on to hold 'the right to bargain collectively with the employer has, in principle, become one of the essential elements' of Art 11. Should the Court of Appeal now be viewed as wrong? (See *Netjets Management Ltd v CAC* below.)

4. Which duties on the employer should be entailed by this right to bargain collectively? Apparently the UK has positive obligations to ensure there is some minimum level. But what does that mean? Should the UK be seeking only to achieve the minimum?

5. In *Vining v Wandsworth LBC* [2017] EWCA Civ 1092 one thing that 'falls squarely within the "essential elements" protected by article 11' is a right to be consulted, within the meaning of the Trade Union and Labour Relations (Consolidation) Act (TULRCA) 1992 ss 188–92. See chapter 19. What else can you think of?

6. If the Central Arbitration Committee had openly admitted its interpretation defeated the Act's purpose, why did it not choose another interpretation of the Act? It is usually thought that a judge 'must set to work on the constructive task of finding the intention of Parliament, and he must do this not only from the language of the statute, but also from a consideration of the social conditions which gave rise to it, and of the mischief which it was passed to remedy, and then he must supplement the written word so as to give "force and life" to the intention of the legislature'. *Seaford Court Estates Ltd v Asher* [1949] 2 KB 481, 498–99, per Denning LJ. If the Central Arbitration Committee or the Court of Appeal was not doing this, which theory of statutory interpretation was it following?

7. A third problem of Sch A1, reflected in paras 11–18, is that while sectoral collective bargaining tends to produce the best outcomes, the 'appropriate bargaining unit' is often construed narrowly by the Central Arbitration Committee. A bias toward enterprise bargaining hampers sectoral collective agreements. On the other hand, unions rationally aim for smaller bargaining units because there can be a greater likelihood of majority support (it is easier to organise fewer members than more). Whatever the aim, employing entities have another opportunity to litigate, over the proper meaning of the bargaining unit.

R (Kwik-Fit (GB) Ltd) v Central Arbitration Committee [2002] EWCA Civ 512

The Central Arbitration Committee appealed a High Court decision that it had drawn the size of the bargaining unit incorrectly. The Transport and General Workers Union had argued that the bargaining unit should be two separate units in London, under para 11(2), and that the Central Arbitration Committee should determine 'whether the proposed bargaining unit is appropriate or some other bargaining unit is appropriate'. Kwik-Fit argued that the bargaining unit should be company wide. Kwik-Fit complained under Schedule A1 paragraph 19B that the bargaining unit, if confined to the M25, would make management difficult. The Central Arbitration Committee decided that the bargaining unit was workplaces within the M25. Elias J in the High Court quashed the Central Arbitration Committee decision. The Court of Appeal restored the Central Arbitration Committee's finding that the M25 area was an appropriate bargaining unit.

Buxton LJ:

2. ... the CAC was intended by Parliament to be a decision making body in a specialist area, that is not suitable for the intervention of the courts. Judicial review, such as is sought in the present case, is therefore only available if the CAC has either acted irrationally or made an error of law.

3. I am quite clear that the determination of the CAC in this case was entirely in accord with the legal provisions that bind it. Since in so holding I will be venturing to differ from the views of the judge who has great experience in this area of work, I need to set out in some detail my reasons for so thinking, though at the end of the day the point appears to be a short one.
    ...

11. ... the employer may well raise objections to the appropriateness of the union's proposed bargaining unit by urging that only another and different unit could be appropriate. The CAC cannot simply ignore such objections. It has to determine whether the objections, and the availability of alternatives that may form an important part of the argument in support of those objections, render inappropriate for bargaining purposes the unit proposed by the union. What, in my view, however, the CAC does not have to do is to conduct a search for the most appropriate unit from amongst those that are proposed to it.

12. The judge accepted that last point, thereby disagreeing with an important part of the submissions of the employer before him. However, he also disagreed with the contention of the CAC, that the statutory scheme required the union's proposal to receive first consideration. He did so because he appears to have understood the contention to be that the CAC could and must consider the union's proposal, as it were in the air, without reference to possible modifications to it, and without reference to the views of the employers. The latter could only be taken into account if the CAC found that the union's proposal failed the test of appropriateness.

20. ... The employer's position was very simple. The union's unit, limited to London, was not appropriate, because the only appropriate unit in Kwik-Fit's view was a single unit covering the whole country, mirroring the management and management structure of the company. For reasons set out in detail, the CAC did not accept that criticism. Even if the judgment of Elias J were to be upheld, and the issue be remitted to the CAC for the reasons set out therein, I do not see how the CAC could properly come to any other conclusion than that which it has already reached.

21. ... the contest before the CAC was straightforward. It did not partake of the type of case hypothesised by Elias J, where modifications or improvements might be suggested to the union's proposal, or where constructive dialogue was offered by the employer as to proposals different from those of the union. The employer's position in this case was that only his proposal, of a national unit, could meet the statutory criteria. The CAC did not agree. In so determining, they not only upheld the union's proposal but rejected, in a reasoned decision, the employer's criticism of it. Since it is not now contended that the CAC acted irrationally, and plainly could not be so contended, that must necessarily be the end of the case.

Latham LJ and **Sir Denis Henry** concurred.

1. The Court of Appeal held the CAC has broad discretion to determine the appropriate bargaining unit and it must have acted irrationally before it could be overturned by anybody's challenge. This did not, however, stop the union being delayed by an adverse High Court judgment of Elias J, while it was worked out whether this particular concern over legal technicality was pertinent.

2. In *Fullarton Computer Industries Ltd v CAC* [2001] Scot CS 168 the Scottish Court of Session held that the Central Arbitration Committee's discretion could be challenged in judicial review according to ordinary natural justice principles in public law. Fullarton Ltd had claimed that a bargaining unit under Sch A1, para 22, was inappropriate, to avoid recognising the Iron and Steel Trades Confederation. Lord Johnston held that he probably would have personally ordered for a ballot to be retaken, although he would defer to the Central Arbitration Committee on the matter.

3. In another example of employer litigation against Central Arbitration Committee decisions, *Netjets Management Ltd v CAC* [2012] EWHC 2685, Netjets Ltd argued the Central Arbitration Committee had wrongly proposed that all of its 779 pilots were a bargaining unit, on the basis that many were outside the territorial scope of the UK. Netjets Ltd was based in Portugal, and 159 of its pilots began flights in the UK. It argued its employees did not have a close enough connection to the UK (see chapter 4(3)(a)) to be covered by a UK bargaining unit. Supperstone J refused the claim, affirming that Schedule A1 should be construed so as to give effect to the ECHR Art 11 'right to bargain collectively with the employer'. Elias LJ gave permission for an expedited appeal: [2013] EWCA Civ 127. The case then settled.

4. The Court of Appeal was forced to affirm its stance once more that determinations about bargaining units should not be challenged.

Lidl Ltd v Central Arbitration Committee [2017] EWCA Civ 328

Lidl Ltd claimed the Central Arbitration Committee (chaired by Professor Gillian Morris) had wrongly decided Bridgend warehouse workers were an appropriate bargaining unit under para 19B(3)(c). Lidl Ltd supplied staff to Lidl supermarkets, and recognised no union in the UK. The union, GMB, wanted recognition to start with the Bridgend workers, roughly 1.2 per cent of the employer's total workforce. The Central Arbitration Committee found this bargaining unit was appropriate. Lidl Ltd argued this misconstrued Sch A1 para 19B(3)(c) which requires the Central Arbitration Committee have regard to 'the desirability of avoiding small fragmented bargaining units within an undertaking'. The Central Arbitration Committee said that because there was only one bargaining unit, there were no 'small fragmented bargaining units' to avoid. Lewis J rejected Lidl Ltd's appeal. The Court of Appeal rejected Lidl's appeal again.

Underhill LJ:

GROUND 1: CAN A SOLE UNIT BE "FRAGMENTED"?

...

36. ... the CAC was right ... the word "fragmented" naturally connotes a whole which has been broken into parts and thus necessarily implies plurality. But a reading which refers to a plurality of units, or the risk of it, also makes sense in the present context because it would reflect a well-known problem in industrial relations – perhaps more historical than current, but policymakers in this field have long memories. It has long been regarded as undesirable (to use the statutory term) that employers should have to negotiate in more than one forum – and, more particularly, with more than one trade union – in respect of parts of their workforce who were not essentially different. At the very least, conducting two or more sets of negotiations where one would do is wasteful of time and effort. But there is also the risk of inconsistent outcomes, which can breed anomalies and discontent between comparable groups of workers (including, though certainly not only, in an equal pay context). Further, there is a risk of disruption as a result of competition between trade unions: it will be noted that that point is made by the CAC in the decision which was under challenge in the *Cable & Wireless* case. ... The policy expressed by head (c) is evidently that, other things being equal, where a group of employees can appropriately be bargained for by a single trade union in a single bargaining unit it is desirable that they should be. It is thus concerned specifically with fragmentation of collective bargaining.

38. ... that kind of fragmentation is not the mischief referred to by paragraph 19B (3) (c): it does not involve fragmentation between bargaining units or fragmented collective bargaining. That does not mean that Lidl's concerns about having a small island of union recognition in a sea of non-recognition are necessarily irrelevant to the issue of whether the proposed unit is appropriate: it only means that they do not come in under paragraph 19B (3)(c). ...

39. ... For the future I would strongly discourage legal challenges based on the nice parsing of the constituent parts of paragraph 19B: I refer to what I have said at para. 16 above ...

GROUND 2: INADEQUATE REASONS

40. As noted above, Lidl requires permission to raise this ground, which is not part of its claim as originally pleaded. Ms McColgan said that the union had no objection to it having permission, and we allowed the ground to be argued *de bene esse* while making it clear that we would reserve our position on whether it should be allowed to be pursued.

41. Mr Barnett's essential submission was that his arguments to the CAC about "fragmentation", which I have set out at para. 21 above, made a number of distinct points; but that in the single sentence of para. 36 in which the CAC addressed this part of the case it dealt only with one aspect. Specifically:
   (a) he had argued that the recognition of a trade union in respect of one small unit was inconsistent with the "one Lidl concept" – see para. 21 (2) above; and
   (b) he had made points at paras. 31 and 33 of his submissions based on the "tensions" which the recognition of the GMB for the proposed bargaining unit would cause;
but neither point is addressed at all. The only part of his case under this head which the CAC's reasoning responds to, he submitted, was the point made at para. 34 about the risk of proliferation. ...

Longmore LJ agreed.

1. The Court of Appeal held that Lidl's claim failed because the Central Arbitration Committee's determination about the appropriate bargaining unit was sound.

2. Underhill LJ eloquently emphasises he wants to 'strongly discourage legal challenges based on the nice parsing of the constituent parts of paragraph 19B'. But are 'legal challenges based on the nice parsing' of words not precisely what lawyers do for a living? Does the very existence of more words in a statutory recognition procedure increase the likelihood of litigation?

3. The Central Arbitration Committee, *Annual Report 2016/17* (2017) 9, states the average time from receiving an application to deciding recognition was 23 weeks with a ballot, and 14 weeks without a ballot (usually because there is majority union membership). Why does it take 3½ months to decide that a majority union workplace should be able to bargain? Why is this process necessary or desirable?

4. Under para 24, the Central Arbitration Committee must hold a ballot (ie the employer can demand one) if there is not majority membership of a union. If the union fails to secure recognition, under para 39 it must wait 3 years for another ballot. It is submitted that it is impossible to justify that 3 years – an entirely arbitrary date – is proportionate to any legitimate aim, and therefore violates the fundamental right to collectively bargain.

5. Why should majority union support in a workplace be a requirement for collective bargaining? Why should, say, 20 out of 100 workers not have a right to collectively bargain for themselves, even if their colleagues want to maintain individual contracts? They can, in any event, organise a strike and picket. But why should a majority remove the rights of the minority to the statutory recognition procedure?

6. A fourth problem of Schedule A1, paras 22–27, is that an employer can pressure employees during the course of a ballot. Although para 27A prohibits threats, bribes and undue influence, there is a risk that these prohibitions are not interpreted broadly as they should be. Can an employer hire union-busting 'consultants' that require staff to have 'information' meetings about the 'consequences' of having a union? Union-avoidance tactics have been developed and tested over many years in the United States. Since the Taft–Hartley Act of 1947, 29 USC §158(c) 'the expressing of any views, argument or opinion ... shall not constitute or be evidence of an unfair labor practice ... if such expression contains no threat of reprisal or force or promise of benefit'. The US Supreme Court attempted to draw the dividing lines in *NLRB v Gissel Packing Co*, 395 US 575 (1969). This enables employers to actively persuade employees to not vote for a union, even though their interest is diametrically opposed to the workforce, which, when unionised, they will be bargaining with. Why should management say anything?

7. Even if all the problems of the statutory recognition were resolved, including (1) sham unions not delaying real unions, (2) all appropriate bargaining unit requirements being eliminated, (3) any requirement for minimum support before recognition being eliminated, and (4) a duty to bargain in good faith with union

members for the themselves and anyone who wants to join if it is better, would this be enough? If the Central Arbitration Committee carried out meaningful work, there is a risk that an anti-union government might appoint people who simply oppose unions. This happened in the United States: the National Labor Relations Board was shut down by a Republican Senate, which simply refused to approve any appointees. The five Republican appointees on the US Supreme Court, following the desires of corporate donors, held over the four Democrat dissenters that all NLRB rules were invalid without a quorate board: *New Process Steel LP v NLRB*, 560 US 674 (2010). Why should freedom of association depend on any state bureaucracy, which can be captured and throttled by corrupt politicians that serve corporate masters instead of the public interest? On the long-term destruction of democracy in the United States, see E McGaughey, 'Fascism-Lite in America (or the Social Ideal of Donald Trump)' (2018) *British Journal of American Legal Studies*.

(2) COLLECTIVE AGREEMENT TERMS

The terms of a collective agreement, like any individual employment contract, depend on the same rules of enforceability and their standard terms cover similar substance.

(a) Enforceability

The passage of the Trade Union Act 1871 led to the thought that collective agreements would not always be legally enforceable. Section 4 said agreements among trade union members about terms of work were not enforceable between themselves, largely to keep courts away from regulation of internal union affairs. Although the enforcement of a collective agreement with an employer was quite different, the UK labour movement used strikes, not courts, because they perceived judges as anti-working class. This was certainly accurate in the nineteenth and much of the twentieth century. In most other countries, collective agreements are binding. Moreover, they are enforceable in the UK, when 'apt' for incorporation into individual contracts (see chapter 4(2)(b)). Dissatisfaction with employers breaking collective agreements leads to a question about whether collective agreements should normally be enforceable.

Trade Union and Labour Relations (Consolidation) Act 1992 s 179

179 Whether agreement intended to be a legally enforceable contract.
(1) A collective agreement shall be conclusively presumed not to have been intended by the parties to be a legally enforceable contract unless the agreement—
(a) is in writing, and
(b) contains a provision which (however expressed) states that the parties intend that the agreement shall be a legally enforceable contract.

NOTES AND QUESTIONS

1. TULRCA 1992 s 179 goes on to say that (2) written express agreements are legally binding, and (3)–(4) parts of collective agreements may be designated as legally enforceable, or not. This reverses the ordinary contract law presumption that there is an intention to create legal relations, unless otherwise expressed, when people are acting in a commercial sphere of life, as opposed to a social or domestic setting: see *Rose & Frank Co v JR Compton & Bros Ltd* [1925] AC 445 (carbon paper dealers expressly agreeing their transaction would not be subject to legal enforcement).

2. TULRCA 1992 s 179 was only introduced by the Trade Union and Labour Relations Act 1974. The original argument, that collective agreements were not intended to create legal relations, appears in a number of earlier cases, including *Young v Canadian National Railway* [1930] UKPC 94, 5. See B Hepple, 'Intention to Create Legal Relations' (1970) 28(1) *Cambridge Law Journal* 122.

3. In *Ford Motor Co Ltd v Amalgamated Union of Engineering and Foundry Workers* [1969] 2 QB 303, Ford Ltd claimed the AUEFW had breached a collective agreement, which the union was trying to renegotiate. Geoffrey Lane J held that, even if it were true that the union was in breach, it was not legally enforceable. Making the law as he saw it deriving from custom, he said: 'Agreements such as these, composed largely of optimistic aspirations, presenting grave practical problems of enforcement and reached against a background of opinion adverse to enforceability, are, in my judgment, not contracts in the legal sense and are not enforceable at law. Without clear and express provisions making them amenable to legal action, they remain in the realm of undertakings binding in honour. ... In my judgment, the parties, none of them, had the intention to make these agreements binding at law.' Do you think the parties subjectively intended anything at all? Why, if they did not, are we using the euphemism of 'intention', rather than recognising it is a legal presumption to create legal relations driven by (debatable) policy?

4. Should the presumption that collective agreements are not enforceable be scrapped? In some countries, employers seek to include in binding collective agreements no-strike clauses, which plainly limits a union's freedom of action, and probably operates unfairly whenever employers still reserve a right to dismiss workers. Hypothetically, a no-strike clause in a binding contract might be enforced by an injunction. It would be a question of legislative policy whether a union can make a no-strike agreement, or whether that remains in any event a fundamental, not an optional, right. What do you think?

5. In *Gallagher v Post Office* [1970] 3 All ER 712, Mr Gallagher claimed that it should be a binding right, that he be able to remain a member of the National Guild of Telephonists while he worked at the Post Office (which used to be responsible for telecommunications). The Post Office Act 1969 was transforming his employer into a public corporation, and sought to recognise the Union of Postal Workers as the sole bargaining agent. But Mr Gallagher had been told by a trainer when he started work that he was free to join any union or not. Brightman J held this statement was not enough to become a legally actionable term of the contract.

(b) Standard Collective Agreement Terms

What does a collective agreement look like? The answer is that there is no clear standard, and the quality of drafting, transparency and comprehensibility can vary greatly. The following is an example from higher education, which covers the whole sector.

Joint Negotiating Committee for Higher Education Staff

FRAMEWORK AGREEMENT FOR THE MODERNISATION OF PAY STRUCTURES

Preamble
- This agreement has been developed in partnership between employers' and trades unions' representatives under the arrangements detailed in the June 2001 agreement establishing the JNCHES.
- The parties to the agreement are: Amicus, AUT, EIS, GMB, NATFHE [*NB AUT and NATFHE are now UCU*], TGWU, UNISON, and the UCEA [*NB now Universities UK*] on behalf of its subscribing HE institutions.
- The parties are united in their view:
  o of the vital contribution which staff at all levels make to the continuing success of UK higher education, and the need for them to be rewarded properly; and
  o on the need to modernise pay arrangements in the sector to improve the recruitment and retention of staff, to ensure equal pay for work of equal value, to tackle problems of low pay, to recognise and reward the contribution which individuals make, and to underpin opportunities for career and organisational development.
- The agreement recognises that there is much diversity among HE institutions as well as many key features that they hold in common. It provides a common national framework for pay arrangements that fit with institutions' varying missions and circumstances.
  …

Principles
- Every HE institution introducing new pay structures under the terms of this agreement will follow the principles set out in Appendix A.

Pay Spine
- HE institutions applying this agreement will use the single pay spine detailed in Appendix B to determine pay rates for all staff (other than clinical academics) covered by national agreements in force on 31 July 2003.
- The values of the pay points in this spine will be reviewed, through the agreed national negotiating machinery, with effect from 1 August each year.
  …

Staff Development and Review
- Access to training and development is important both for the motivation of staff and to enhance their contribution to the institution. HE institutions will make available suitable training and development opportunities to all staff, irrespective of their present grades or career pathways.
  …

Working Hours
- The application to all staff at the same grade level in an institution of equivalent pay ranges (drawn from the pay spine) assumes comparable working hours, reflecting statutory requirements on equal pay for work of equal value.

- HE institutions will be recommended to harmonise the length of the standard working week for all staff with a defined working week – in particular resulting in a reduction in the nationally agreed hours for manual staff – as early as possible and by no later than 1 August 2005.

   ...

APPENDIX B

NEW SINGLE PAY SPINE

[NB The following numbers have been inserted by the author to be up to date.]

Spine point	2017–18				
1	–	18	22,876	35	37,706
2	15,417	19	23,557	36	38,833
3 (grade 1)	15,721	20 (grade 4)	24,285	37	39,992
4	16,035	21	24,983	38 (grade 7)	41,212
5	16,341	22	25,728	39	42,418
6	16,654	23	26,495	40	43,685
7 (grade 2)	16,983	24	27,285	41	44,992
8	17,326	25 (grade 5)	28,098	42	46,336
9	17,764	26	28,936	43	47,722
10	18,263	27	29,799	44	49,149
11	18,777	28	30,688	45 (grade 8)	50,618
12	19,305	29	31,604	46	52,132
13	19,850	30	32,548	47	53,691
14 (grade 3)	20,411	31 (grade 6)	33,518	48	55,297
15	20,989	32	34,520	49	56,950
16	21,581	33	35,550	50	58,655
17	22,214	34	36,613	51 (grade 9)	60,410

* London Allowance of £2,923 per annum from 1 August 2017 for staff appointed on or after 1 March 2008

NOTES AND QUESTIONS

1. This extract from the collective agreement shows a number of notable features. First, the actual pay in the 'single salary spine' is updated each year through the Joint Negotiating Committee for higher-education staff. The increases have, in the last few years (as many teachers of labour law will be painfully aware), been considerably behind the rates of inflation, and therefore represent a real-terms pay cut. Nevertheless, this collective agreement envisages an ongoing mechanism of voice, based on the historical Whitely Council model. Individual universities may, however, have different policies on where their lecturers, administrative staff or professors are on the salary spine. Senior staff are above it, and negotiate significantly higher pay. Part-time and fixed-term teachers are typically outside of

the spine altogether. Thus, the University and College Union leadership has failed to maintain full coverage by collective agreement.

2. Second, and despite the foregoing, the collective agreement refers to 'staff', rather than technical legal terms of 'employee', 'worker' or 'jobholder', and emphasises its scope is to be universal. However, in practice many universities have outsourced staff. For example, at the time of writing, the University of London is denying that outsourced receptionists, security, post-room and porter staff are joint employees, and therefore refusing to collectively bargain. The employees, represented by the Independent Workers Union of Great Britain, argue that failure to recognise them for collective bargaining violates ECHR Art 11. What do you think?

3. Third, the framework agreement at various points appeals to legal principles such as 'equal pay for work of equal value' and commits to working hours reduction for 'manual staff'. In this way, it is plain that collective agreements that unions negotiate are heavily inspired by the models that the law itself sets, just as the law is itself inspired by the best collective agreements.

4. There is no model collective agreement attached to the TULRCA 1992 or the Employment Rights Act 1996. By contrast, accompanying the Companies Act 2006 there are the Companies (Model Articles) Regulations 2008 which set out model company constitutions. These templates are widely adopted, and function as default rules. Should the law provide model collective agreements, and if so what should be in them?

5. As chapter 11 explains, collective agreements have historically created the critical right of employees to vote at work, both in the governance of enterprise, and in the governance of pension trust funds. Should collective agreements begin to adopt such a policy on a widespread basis? See E McGaughey, 'Votes at work in Britain: Shareholder Monopolisation and the 'Single Channel'' (2018) 47(1) *ILJ* 76.

(3) RIGHTS ESSENTIAL FOR BARGAINING

At least three main rights are essential for collective bargaining. First, a union must have members. It must seek ways to engage, maintain and grow an active base of membership to ensure collective bargaining is real. Second, unions need information from employing entities that is pertinent to collective bargaining, beyond that in the public domain. Third, people need a right to be represented by their trade union. This matters most for dismissal or disciplinary hearings, but forms part of a larger right to have representatives speak in bargaining with management itself. To do this, union representatives need time off from work to perform their duties. This is seen as something management should provide because good workplace relations are in the interest of the enterprise as a whole.

(a) Automatic Enrolment and Closed Shop

Before 1980, unions could rely on 'closed shop' provisions in collective agreements to maintain membership numbers. Either nobody would be hired without first having joined a union (pre-entry closed shop) or they would have to join the union soon after starting work (post-entry closed shop). That is no longer possible. The law presumes a default position that workers have no representation. As chapter 6(4) discussed, a severe, equivalent and connected problem has arisen in pensions. Because collective bargaining declined, more and more people had no occupational pension, and were left to rely on the minimum state pension. The Pensions Act 2008 switched the default by creating a right for most workers ('jobholders') to be automatically enrolled in a workplace pension. For union membership, two questions arise: (1) whether the law should require automatic enrolment of new staff in their union, and (2) how unions in collective agreements to achieve the same result.

This necessarily connects with the provisions ensuring a 'negative' right of association, or to not belong to a union if one so wishes.

Trade Union and Labour Relations (Consolidation) Act 1992 s 146

146. Detriment on grounds related to union membership or activities.
(1) A worker has the right not to be subjected to any detriment as an individual by any act, or any deliberate failure to act, by his employer if the act or failure takes place for the sole or main purpose of—
  (a) preventing or deterring him from being or seeking to become a member of an independent trade union, or penalising him for doing so,
  (b) preventing or deterring him from taking part in the activities of an independent trade union at an appropriate time, or penalising him for doing so,
  (ba) preventing or deterring him from making use of trade union services at an appropriate time, or penalising him for doing so, or
  (c) compelling him to be or become a member of any trade union or of a particular trade union or of one of a number of particular trade unions.
  ...
(3) A worker also has the right not to be subjected to any detriment as an individual by any act, or any deliberate failure to act, by his employer if the act or failure takes place for the sole or main purpose of enforcing a requirement (whether or not imposed by a contract of employment or in writing) that, in the event of his not being a member of any trade union or of a particular trade union or of one of a number of particular trade unions, he must make one or more payments.

NOTES AND QUESTIONS

1. TULRCA 1992 s 146 expresses the idea that there is 'negative' freedom of association (no unjustified compulsion to associate with anyone), as much as 'positive' freedom of association (no unjustified prevention to associate with anyone, *and* positive duties on the state to enable truly free choice to associate). The 'negative' right does not appear in ECHR Art 11, but it does in the Universal Declaration on Human Rights 1948 Art 20(2). This was argued to mean people could not be made to join a union to have a job.
2. Most of the decline in UK union membership dates from the abolition of the closed shop, starting with the Employment Act 1980. The default rule was switched from 'with a job, you'll be in a union, where you'll stay' to 'with a job, you have no union, but you may join'. Between 1983 and 2001 the rate of people who were

never in a union rose from 28 to 48 per cent. Decline in union density 'is almost wholly accounted for by the rise in never-membership': A Bryson and R Gomez, 'Buying into Union Membership' in H Gospel and S Wood (eds), *Representing Workers* (2003) 29, 73. Why not switch the default to 'when you get a job, you'll be enrolled in a union, but you can opt out'?

3. Apart from the rapid acceleration of inequality, without union coverage, pension coverage declined. The Pensions Act 2008 section 1 gives the right to automatic enrolment in a pension, with an opt-out right. Why do people not join unions and pensions themselves, but are likely to stay if enrolled? The answer is a human behavioural bias for the status quo. We stick with what we do already. One study found a rise from 49 per cent enrolment when people had to opt into a pension, to 86 per cent when people were automatically enrolled but could opt out: BC Madrian and DF Shea, 'The Power of Suggestion: Inertia in 401(k) Participation and Savings Behavior' (2001) 116(4) *Quarterly Journal of Economics* 1149, 1151.

4. Do you think most people, if automatically enrolled, would opt out or stay in their union? What factors might affect their decision? Should automatic enrolment in pensions be a model for union membership?

5. One of the major arguments that face automatic enrolment plans is that negative freedom of association provisions, such as in TULRCA 1992 s 146(1)(c), could be inflicting 'detriment' for the 'main purpose' of 'compelling him to be or become a member of any trade union'. It is submitted that all such arguments would fail: if people can opt out of union membership, there is no 'compelling' of anything. Indeed, the requirement of professional qualifications frequently entails compulsion, far more intrusive, for access to jobs. However, this is objectively justified by the need to ensure sound management of enterprise: like union membership.

6. Perhaps the oldest case on the issue was *Tailors of Ipswich Case* (1614) 11 Co Rep 53a, which struck down a rule that one could not work as a tailor in Ipswich unless admitted by masters of the town's Society of Crafts and Mysteries. Lord Coke CJ said it was 'against the liberty and freedom of the subject, and are a means of extortion in drawing money from them, either by delay, or some other subtle device, or of oppression of young tradesmen, by the old and rich of the same trade, not permitting them to work in their trade freely; and all this is against the common law, and the commonwealth: but ordinances for the good order and government of men of trades and mysteries are good, but not to restrain any one in his lawful mystery'. Do you agree that everyone should be able to take up any profession, without any official authorisation or qualification? Lord Coke CJ obviously did not: see *Prohibitions del Roy* (1607) 12 Co Rep 63.

7. The Legal Services Act 2007 sections 12 and 18 prevent anybody undertaking 'reserved legal activity', such as a right of audience, litigation or probate, without authorisation from an 'approved regulator'. In Schedule 10, this is the Legal Services Board, which in turn approves, for example, the Law Society and the Bar Council. Each have a partner 'Independent Regulatory body', the Solicitors Regulation Authority (SRA) and the Bar Standards Board (BSB), which set out membership requirements in order to undertake reserved legal activity. According to the *SRA Practising Regulations 2011* (18th edn 2016), the SRA issues a

'practising certificate' upon various conditions being fulfilled. In *Wouters v Algemene Raad van de Nederlandse Orde van Advocaten* (2002) C-309/99, [97] and [110] the Court of Justice held that solicitor registration rules were outside of competition law because they were necessary for the legal profession's 'integrity and experience' and 'for the proper practice of the legal profession'. Thus, what in substance is a restriction on freedom of association (as well as competition) was justified. Do you think this is positive, or that it should be seen as violating some right of everyone to take up any profession, without any official authorisation? Does the need to join the SRA or BSB violate your ostensible negative right of freedom of association?

8.	Formative in the European approach to compulsory association was the Nazi system from 1933 to 1945. After Hitler murdered or imprisoned all leading trade unionists, from May Day of 1933, everyone was compelled to join the Deutsche Arbeitsfront (DAF, the German Labour Front). Hitler was a product of big business backing. His accession to the Chancellorship was agreed on 4 January 1933 with the conservative leader at the house of a banker (Baron Kurt von Schröder) and was given a million marks on 6 March 1933 for his election campaign by Gustav Krupp and members of the 'Freundeskreis der Wirtschaft' (Circle of Economic Friends). A business-bent state then assumed total control over the labour movement through the DAF. It held to the *Führerprinzip* (leadership principle). Its task was to create understanding among followers for the position of the leaders, and to foster understanding of the leaders for the followers. DAF officials acted, in the words of Ley, as 'the soldier-like kernel of the plant community which obeys the Leader blindly. Its motto is "the Leader is always right".' F Neumann, *Behemoth* (1941) 340.

9.	The Universal Declaration of Human Rights (UDHR) Art 20(2) says: 'No one may be compelled to belong to an association.' This should plainly be interpreted to encompass organisations such as DAF. It would, however, seem absurd if people could not be required to be registered with the Law Society in order to work. A clear distinction is that nobody needs to become a lawyer: they are not compelled to undertake such a profession, but if they do choose to, they must join the club that enforces the rules. Is there any inherent reason why people should not have to join a trade union when they choose to engage in a job in a particular sector?

Young, James and Webster v United Kingdom [1981] ECHR 4

Young, James and Webster claimed that the United Kingdom violated ECHR Art 11, by allowing unions and employers to conclude closed-shop agreements. The claimants, and 54 others out of a total of 250,000 staff, were dismissed by the British Railways Board in 1976, after it had concluded closed-shop agreements with the National Union of Railwaymen (NUR, now the RMT), the Transport Salaried Staffs' Association (TSSA), and the Associated Society of Locomotive Engineers and Firemen (ASLEF). There was an exception for anyone 'who genuinely objects on grounds of religious belief to being a member of any Trade Union whatsoever or on any reasonable grounds to being a member of a particular Trade Union'. Applications for exemption would be heard by a joint employer and union panel. The NUR's objects included to 'work for the suppression of the capitalist system by a Socialistic order of society'. The TSSA contributed to the Labour Party from its political fund. ASLEF was for people doing other tasks. Young, James and Webster claimed they should have freedom to choice, and variously disapproved of the Labour Party, nationalisation, and taking part in strikes for higher pay demands. The Court held that there was a violation of Art 11.

European Court of Human Rights

51. A substantial part of the pleadings before the Court was devoted to the question whether Article 11 (art. 11) guarantees not only freedom of association, including the right to form and to join trade unions, in the positive sense, but also, by implication, a "negative right" not to be compelled to join an association or a union.

Whilst the majority of the Commission stated that it was not necessary to determine this issue, the applicants maintained that a "negative right" was clearly implied in the text. The Government, which saw the Commission's conclusion also as in fact recognising at least a limited negative right, submitted that Article 11 (art. 11) did not confer or guarantee any right not to be compelled to join an association. They contended that this right had been deliberately excluded from the Convention and that this was demonstrated by the following passage in the *travaux préparatoires*:

> "On account of the difficulties raised by the 'closed-shop system' in certain countries, the Conference in this connection considered that it was undesirable to introduce into the Convention a rule under which 'no one may be compelled to belong to an association' which features in [Article 20 par. 2 of] the United Nations Universal Declaration" (Report of 19 June 1950 of the Conference of Senior Officials, Collected Edition of the "Travaux Préparatoires", vol. IV, p. 262).

52. The Court does not consider it necessary to answer this question on this occasion.

The Court recalls, however, that the right to form and to join trade unions is a special aspect of freedom of association (see the National Union of Belgian Police judgment of 27 October 1975, Series A no. 19, p. 17, par. 38); it adds that the notion of a freedom implies some measure of freedom of choice as to its exercise.

Assuming for the sake of argument that, for the reasons given in the above-cited passage from the *travaux préparatoires*, a general rule such as that in Article 20 par. 2 of the Universal Declaration of Human Rights was deliberately omitted from, and so cannot be regarded as itself enshrined in, the Convention, it does not follow that the negative aspect of a person's freedom of association falls completely outside the ambit of Article 11 (art. 11) and that each and every compulsion to join a particular trade union is compatible with the intention of that provision. To construe Article 11 (art. 11) as permitting every kind of compulsion in the field of trade union membership would strike at the very substance of the freedom it is designed to guarantee. …

…

55. The situation facing the applicants clearly runs counter to the concept of freedom of association in its negative sense.

Assuming that Article 11 (art. 11) does not guarantee the negative aspect of that freedom on the same footing as the positive aspect, compulsion to join a particular trade union may not always be contrary to the Convention.

However, a threat of dismissal involving loss of livelihood is a most serious form of compulsion and, in the present instance, it was directed against persons engaged by British Rail before the introduction of any obligation to join a particular trade union.

In the Court's opinion, such a form of compulsion, in the circumstances of the case, strikes at the very substance of the freedom guaranteed by Article 11 (art. 11). For this reason alone, there has been an interference with that freedom as regards each of the three applicants.

56. Another facet of this case concerns the restriction of the applicants' choice as regards the trade unions which they could join of their own volition. An individual does not enjoy the right to freedom of association if in reality the freedom of action or choice which remains available to him is either non-existent or so reduced as to be of no practical value. ...

The Government submitted that the relevant legislation ... not only did not restrict but also expressly protected freedom of action or choice in this area; in particular, it would have been open to the applicants to form or to join a trade union in addition to one of the specified unions. The applicants, on the other hand, claimed that this was not the case in practice, since such a step would have been precluded by British Rail's agreement with the railway unions and by the Bridlington Principles. ... in their view, joining and taking part in the activities of a competing union would, if attempted, have led to expulsion from one of the specified unions. These submissions were, however, contested by the Government.

Be that as it may, such freedom of action or choice as might have been left to the applicants in this respect would not in any way have altered the compulsion to which they were subjected since they would in any event have been dismissed if they had not become members of one of the specified unions.

...

58. The Government expressly stated that, should the Court find an interference with a right guaranteed by paragraph 1 of Articles 9, 10 or 11 ... they would not seek to argue that such interference was justified under paragraph 2.

The Court has nevertheless decided that it should examine this issue of its own motion. ...

59. An interference with the exercise of an Article 11 ... right will not be compatible with paragraph 2 ... unless it was "prescribed by law", had an aim or aims that is or are legitimate under that paragraph and was "necessary in a democratic society" for the aforesaid aim or aims. ...

60. The applicants argued that the restrictions of which they complained met none of these three conditions.

The Court does not find it indispensable to determine whether the first two conditions were satisfied, these being issues which were not fully argued before it. It will assume that the interference was "prescribed by law", within the meaning of the Convention ... and had the aim, amongst other things, of protecting the "rights and freedoms of others", this being the only of the aims listed in paragraph 2 that might be relevant.

61. In connection with the last point, the Court's attention has been drawn to a number of advantages said to flow from the closed shop system in general, such as the fostering of orderly collective bargaining, leading to greater stability in industrial relations; the avoidance of a proliferation of unions and the resultant trade union anarchy; the counteracting of inequality of bargaining power; meeting the need of some employers to negotiate with a body fully representative of the workforce; satisfying the wish of some trade unionists not to work alongside non-union employees; ensuring that trade union activities do not benefit of those who make no financial contribution thereto.

Any comment on these arguments would be out of place in the present case since the closed shop system as such is not under review. ...

62. On the other hand, what has to be determined is the "necessity" for the interference complained of: in order to achieve the aims of the unions party to the 1975 agreement with British

Rail, was it "necessary in a democratic society" to make lawful the dismissal of the applicants, who were engaged at a time when union membership was not a condition of employment?

63. A number of principles relevant to the assessment of the "necessity" of a given measure have been stated by the Court in its *Handyside* judgment of 7 December 1976 (Series A no. 24).

Firstly, "necessary" in this context does not have the flexibility of such expressions as "useful" or "desirable" (p. 22, par. 48). The fact that British Rail's closed shop agreement may in a general way have produced certain advantages is therefore not of itself conclusive as to the necessity of the interference complained of.

Secondly, pluralism, tolerance and broadmindedness are hallmarks of a "democratic society" (p. 23, par. 49). Although individual interests must on occasion be subordinated to those of a group, democracy does not simply mean that the views of a majority must always prevail: a balance must be achieved which ensures the fair and proper treatment of minorities and avoids any abuse of a dominant position. Accordingly, the mere fact that the applicants' standpoint was adopted by very few of their colleagues is again not conclusive of the issue now before the Court.

Thirdly, any restriction imposed on a Convention right must be proportionate to the legitimate aim pursued (p. 23, par. 49).

64. The Court has noted in this connection that a majority of the *Royal Commission on Trade Unions and Employers' Associations*, which reported in 1968, considered that the position of existing employees in a newly-introduced closed shop was one area in which special safeguards were desirable (see paragraph 14 above). Again, recent surveys suggest that, even prior to the entry into force of the Employment Act 1980 (see paragraph 24 above), many closed shop arrangements did not require existing non-union employees to join a specified union (see paragraph 13 above); the Court has not been informed of any special reasons justifying the imposition of such a requirement in the case of British Rail. Besides, according to statistics furnished by the applicants, which were not contested, a substantial majority even of union members themselves disagreed with the proposition that persons refusing to join a union for strong reasons should be dismissed from employment. Finally, in 1975 more than 95 per cent of British Rail employees were already members of NUR, TSSA or ASLEF (see paragraph 31 above).

All these factors suggest that the railway unions would in no way have been prevented from striving for the protection of their members' interests (see the above-mentioned National Union of Belgian Police judgment, p. 18, par. 39) through the operation of the agreement with British Rail even if the legislation in force had not made it permissible to compel non-union employees having objections like the applicants to join a specified union.

65. Having regard to all the circumstances of the case, the detriment suffered by Mr. Young, Mr. James and Mr. Webster went further than was required to achieve a proper balance between the conflicting interests of those involved and cannot be regarded as proportionate to the aims being pursued. Even making due allowance for a State's "margin of appreciation" (see, inter alia, the above-mentioned Sunday Times judgment, p. 36, par. 59), the Court thus finds that the restrictions complained of were not "necessary in a democratic society", as required by paragraph 2 of Article 11 (art. 11-2).

There has accordingly been a violation of Article 11 (art. 11).

President G Wiarda and twenty other judges took part in the decision.

Mr G van der Meersch, Mrs Bindschedler-Robert, Mr Liesch, Mr Gölcüklü, Mr Matscher, Mr Pinheiro Farinha and **Mr Pettiti** gave a concurring opinion. **Mr Evrigenis** also gave a concurring opinion.

Mr Sørensen, Mr Thór Vilhjálmsson and **Mr Lagergren** dissented:

1. The issue under Article 11 (art. 11) is whether or not freedom of association as protected by that Article (art. 11) implies a right for the individual not to be constrained to join or belong to any particular association, or in other words whether or not the so-called negative freedom of association or – in the terminology adopted by the Court – the negative aspect of the freedom of association is covered by Article 11 (art. 11).

2. The answer to this question must take account of the statement made by the Conference of Senior Officials in its report of 19 June 1950 (see paragraph 51 of the judgment). It clearly emerges from this element of the drafting history that the States Parties to the Convention could not agree to assume any international obligation in the matter, but found that it should be subject to national regulation only.

3. The attitude thus adopted was entirely consistent with the attitude previously adopted within the framework of the International Labour Organisation. In dealing with questions of trade union rights and freedom to organise, the competent bodies of that organisation had traditionally held that union security arrangements were matters for regulation in accordance with national law and practice and could not be considered as either authorised or prohibited by the texts adopted in the ILO (see C. Wilfred Jenks, *The International Protection of Trade Union Freedom*, London 1957, pp. 29–30; Nicolas Valticos, *Droit international du travail*, Paris 1970, pp. 268–69; Geraldo von Potobsky, The Freedom of the Worker to Organise according to the Principles and Standards of the International Labour Organisation, in *Die Koalitionsfreiheit des Arbeitnehmers*, Heidelberg 1980, vol. II, at pp. 1132–36). This understanding has been maintained ever since and also been expressed by the States Parties to the European Social Charter of 1961 with respect to the obligations undertaken in virtue of that instrument (See Appendix, Part II, Article 1, paragraph 2).

4. During the proceedings in the present case it was argued on behalf of the respondent Government by the Solicitor-General that "the scale of the closed shop system within Britain and the state of the common law was such that the inclusion within Article 11 (art. 11) of the right not to be compelled to join a union would inevitably have required the United Kingdom to make a reservation in respect of any such right" (verbatim record of the hearing on the morning of 4 March 1981, doc. Cour (81) 19, p. 75).

   ...

6. This conclusion is perfectly compatible with the nature and function of the rights in question. The so-called positive and negative freedom of association are not simply two sides of the same coin or, as the Court puts it, two aspects of the same freedom. There is no logical link between the two.

   The positive freedom of association safeguards the possibility of individuals, if they so wish, to associate with each other for the purpose of protecting common interests and pursuing common goals, whether of an economic, professional, political, cultural, recreational or other character, and the protection consists in preventing public authorities from intervening to frustrate such common action. It concerns the individual as an active participant in social activities, and it is in a sense a collective right in so far as it can only be exercised jointly by a plurality of individuals. The negative freedom of association, by contrast, aims at protecting the individual against being grouped together with other individuals with whom he does not agree or for purposes which he does not approve. It tends to protect him from being identified with convictions, endeavours or attitudes which he does not share and thus to defend the intimate sphere of the personality. In addition, it may serve the purpose of protecting the individual against misuse of power by an association and against being manipulated by its leaders. However strongly such protection of the individual may sometimes be needed, it is neither in logic nor by necessary implication part of the positive freedom of association.

7. It follows that union security arrangements and the practice of the "closed shop" are neither prohibited, nor authorised by Article 11 … of the Convention. Objectionable as the treatment suffered by the applicants may be on grounds of reason and equity, the adequate solution lies, not in any extensive interpretation of that Article … but in safeguards against dismissal because of refusal to join a union, that is in safeguarding the right to security of employment in such circumstances. But this right is not among those recognised by the Convention which – as stated in the Preamble – is only a first step for the collective enforcement of human rights. At present, it is therefore a matter for regulation by the national law of each State.

NOTES AND QUESTIONS

1. The majority of the Court held, first, there was a violation of Art 11, it seems, because the claimants started work before the new closed shop arrangement was introduced, and it led to their dismissal. Do you think there is any meaningful reason to distinguish a closed shop before someone starts a job, and one introduced after?

2. Second, it held that Art 11 encompasses 'freedom of expression' and holding to one's 'convictions' like Arts 9 and 10. There was an interference with those rights, and that could not be justified and dismissal went further than necessary, it seems, because 95 per cent of workers were in a union: allowance could be made for personal convictions. This means, if people can freely opt out of a union, there is no possibility to find any interference with the right to freedom of association in Art 11.

3. A practical (if not meaningful) distinction between a union closed shop and compulsory Law Society membership is the union's interests oppose a firm's management, while the Law Society's interests are synonymous with the managements of law firms.

4. In *Cheall v APEX* [1983] QB 126, Lord Denning MR said: 'Often enough nowadays a man is compelled to join a trade union so as to be able to earn his living. He signs an application form which purports to bind him to the rules. But he hardly ever reads them. Or if he did, he would not understand them. They are dictated to him. He has no choice but to obey. To hold them to be a contract is far more a fiction than in the common standard form of consumer contract – with exemption clauses. … The man is not even told, "Take it or leave it." He is told, "You've got no choice. You must sign." … He is not to be ordered to join this or that trade union without having a say in the matter. He is not to be treated as a pawn on the chessboard. … It might result, when there is a "closed shop," in his being deprived of his livelihood. He would be crushed between the upper and nether millstones. Even though it should result in industrial chaos, nevertheless the freedom of each man should prevail over it. There comes a time in peace as in war – as recent events show – when a stand must be made on principle, whatever the consequences. Such a stand should be made here today.' Leaving aside the hyperbolic echoes of the anti-slavery case, *Somerset v Stewart*, do you agree?

5.   In the United States, the language of a 'right to work' (UDHR Art 23(1)) had been appropriated since the Taft–Hartley Act of 1947 to mean a right to not join a union. US law banned the closed shop, and further lets states ban unions collecting fees (to reflect higher wages from collective bargaining) from employees who do not join a union: Republican governments have called this becoming a 'right to work state'. Democrats call this a 'right to work for less state'.

6.   Under TULRCA 1992 s 146(3) it might appear the UK is one such state. *Samuels v London Bus Services Ltd* (2008) ET Case No 3202466/2008 held a 'fair share agreement', whereby people not in the union would contribute to the cost of collective bargaining, to be unlawful. The Tribunal did not, however, apply the appropriate test of whether a reasonable person would view action as 'detriment'. If you simply pay for the benefits you receive, is 'detriment' a reasonable characterisation?

7.   In *Sigurjonnson v Iceland* (1993) 16 EHRR 462 the European Court of Human Rights decided that Art 11 did encompass a negative right of association after all. Here, an Icelandic taxi driver claimed he should not be made to join a taxi driver rights association. The Court held that (whether or not the taxi association was a trade union) there was a violation, and it was unjustified.

8.   *Gustafsson v Sweden* [1996] ECHR 20 held there was no breach of Art 11 when a restaurant owner refused to sign up to a collective agreement despite being blockaded by the commercial and food unions.

9.   *Sørenson v Denmark* [2006] ECHR 24 held that a pre-entry closed shop violated Article 11. Sørensen got a job as a holiday relief worker in 1996 and was told: 'To obtain the job it is mandatory to be a member of one of the trade unions affiliated to the Danish Confederation of Trade Unions (LO). You will be informed on request of the name of the union.' He was dismissed after not joining. The High Court of Denmark held the dismissal lawful in 1998, because he knew it was a condition of the job. The Supreme Court upheld this. The European Court of Human Rights decided that there should be no distinction between pre- and post-entry closed shop and 'the freedom of choice of the individual inherent in Article 11' must prevail. At [70] the Court said: '[A]ttempts to eliminate entirely the use of closed-shop agreements in Denmark would appear to reflect the trend which has emerged in the Contracting Parties, namely that such agreements are not an essential means for securing the interests of trade unions and their members and that due weight must be given to the right of individuals to join a union of their own choosing without fear of prejudice to their livelihood.' At [75] it said: '[T]here is little support in the Contracting States for the maintenance of closed-shop agreements and that the European instruments referred to above clearly indicate that their use in the labour market is not an indispensable tool for the effective enjoyment of trade-union freedoms.'

10.   Assuming for argument's sake the Court's reasoning is economically or socially justified, what can be done to get higher union membership, without the closed shop?

11.   Figure 9.1 shows the attrition of trade union membership (which appears to directly cause higher inequality) across countries that used to have the closed shop.

Figure 9.1 Union density in Western Europe 1960–2014

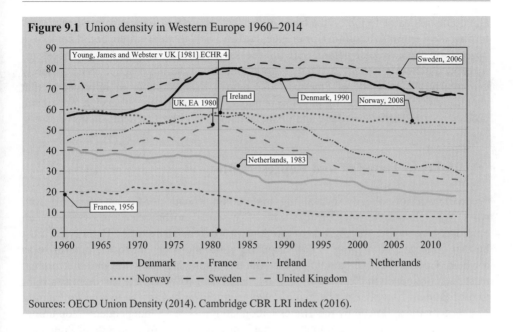

Sources: OECD Union Density (2014). Cambridge CBR LRI index (2016).

(b) Information for Collective Bargaining

Information is essential for collective bargaining, because knowledge of a bargaining adversary's position will improve one's bargaining power (WS Jevons, *Theory of Political Economy* (1888) ch 4, §74). First, a union should inform itself, from the Strategic Report, Directors' Report, and Directors' Remuneration Report, and accounts that are required by the Companies Act 2006 ss 414A, 415, 420, and 423 about a company's financial position, business plans and prospects, and senior pay structure. It should use this information both in its own publicity, its communications with members and in bargaining. Public listed companies must publish accounts on websites (s 430), while private company accounts must be circulated among company members and 'every person who is entitled to receive notice of general meetings'. Therefore, if union members or union pension funds simply own one share in a non-public company, they should be able to receive comprehensive accounting information. This should be the basis to determine whether the workforce is receiving a fair share of a company's product, and to determine whether the distribution of wages is fair.

Second, in TULRCA 1992 s 181 there is a right of (1) a recognised union to (2) information without which collective bargaining would be impeded to a material extent, and which 'good industrial relations practice' would make prudent to disclose. Requests are to be made in writing, and employers need not disclose information concerning national security, anything subject to a statutory prohibition, information given in confidence, relating to any specific individual, anything that would cause substantial injury to the undertaking, anything that might be used in legal proceedings, or that would cost an unreasonable amount to produce. What kind of information is 'for the purpose of collective bargaining? In *R (BTP Tioxide) v Central Arbitration Committee* [1981] ICR 843 a union requested information on 'the break point between grades, job descriptions and points allocated to job on the basis of the factors used'. This was refused, and over-turning the Central Arbitration Committee, Forbes J held that the employer did not have a negotiation, because such details were unnecessary. This old decision does not necessarily carry much weight today, given that 'good industrial relations practice' can constantly evolve. The ACAS Code of Practice No 2 para11 lists examples of information that should be disclosed, including pay and benefits, staff conditions of service, personnel, productivity and efficiency data, and financial data such as profits, debts, loans or assets.

(c) Rights to Time Off and Representation

To do the work of collective bargaining, trade union officials need to have time off from work. Why should the law consider time off essential, to be taken out of time when employers are paying wages, rather than done in workers' spare time? The answer must be that collective bargaining is both a public good and a benefit to the enterprise as a whole. Good collective bargaining benefits the employing entity, by building mutual trust and confidence in the workforce. First, under TULRCA 1992 s 168 there is a right to paid time off for collective bargaining that an employer has agreed to, and for training of a type that is approved by the Trades Union Congress or an independent trade union. What counts as a reasonable amount of time is covered by the ACAS Code of Practice 3 (2010). Types of training could include issues such as legislative changes, organisational change or something related to a union official's special responsibilities. Examples of activity to have time off include attending workplace meetings, voting on action and approach toward employers, regional meetings, and annual conferences for official policy and discussion with other representatives. For example, in *London Ambulance Service v Charlton* [1992] ICR 773, the National Union of Public Employees successfully claimed an entitlement to paid time off to attend a union meeting on their approach to employers in negotiations. The Ambulance Service was only allowing unpaid time off, but this was found to be inadequate. Second, under TULRCA 1992 s 170 there is a right to unpaid time off for activities where an employee acts as a representative. What is reasonable again follows the ACAS Code. In *Luce v Bexley LBC* [1990] ICR 591, Wood J held that attending a protest before Parliament against Conservative Party legislation did not count as a protected activity.

While union officials need time off, union members also need a positive right to be represented, for instance, in grievance or disciplinary hearings. The Employment Relations Act 1999 ss 10–15 create this right, enforceable in Tribunal, and with a further right to suffer no detriment for asserting the right. Who counts as a legitimate representative? *National Union of Gold, Silver, and Allied Trades v Albury Brothers Ltd* [1979] ICR 84 held that officials from a recognised trade union are entitled to be representatives. Recognition means conduct that is 'sufficiently clear and distinct', and would today obviously include completion of the statutory recognition procedure. Do you think ECHR Art 11 could require the representative of a worker's choice, as part of their freedom of association?

Department of Trade and Industry, *Fairness at Work* **(1998) Cm 3968, ch 4**
This set out Tony Blair's policy for collective labour rights. It stated some support for the European Work Council Directive and the Employee Involvement Directive in European Companies, but was 'not persuaded of the need' for national information and consultation. It suggested unions, somewhat ambitiously, 'now focus much more strongly on working with management to develop a flexible, skilled and motivated workforce' (4.7), without recognising that fair pay is probably the primary motivating force at work. Abolition of the closed shop was said to be 'justified', without addressing any alternative for the attrition in union membership or collective agreement coverage. It proposed the statutory recognition procedure 'without the disputes', without recognising either the history of failure in that policy in the United States, weighing up the costs of litigation, or addressing why workers who want to bargain do not automatically have that right. It advocated protection against dismissal and discrimination for union activity, and 'reform' for the ballot and notice procedure.

A Bogg, *The Democratic Aspects of Trade Union Recognition* **(2009) chs 5–7**
In a book on comparative and political theory understanding of recognising unions, Bogg explains in chapters 5–7 why the statutory recognition procedure in TULRCA 1992 Sch A1 was bound to fail. In chapter 5, Bogg charts the American system's failure under the National Labor Relations Act of 1935 to see that the state cannot be 'neutral' to the employer's supposed rights to property and free speech, when employers are typically corporations. A supposedly free cultural marketplace, where an employer and union have 'equal' rights to persuade workers for and against union representation, fails to see the employer can only win. No representation is the default, and representation does not bind the employer, but merely requires a further bargain process, which is evaded. In chapter 7, Bogg reimagines a deliberative collective bargaining procedure. The state could (a) invest more in mediation, (b) expand the scope of lawful bargaining to 'any area of managerial policy', (c) require employers to give more information, (d) lift bans on 'secondary' action, (e) require sectoral bargaining, and (f) a duty to actively bargain.

KD Ewing, J Hendy QC and C Jones (eds), *A Manifesto for Labour Law: Towards a Comprehensive Revision of Workers' Rights* **(IER 2016)**
Authored by a host of the most distinguished labour lawyers in the UK, EU and Commonwealth, the *Manifesto* advocates a new Ministry of Labour, and to restore sectoral collective bargaining. In addition it seeks to advance trade union membership, to lift suppression of collective action, require worker votes in their company meetings and representatives on boards (see chapter 11), a real living wage, child care rights, complete the scope of employment rights, complete health and safety protection, and provide genuine protection from discrimination and dismissal. This was adopted as official policy at the Labour Party Conference of 2016.

Collective Action

Collective action is the foundation of human development. It is the way people build a just society, and to those who abuse their power you can always sit down and just say 'no'. People's ability to strike finished the Kaiser in World War One, ended the British Empire's authority for an independent India, brought down the Iron Curtain, and stopped apartheid South Africa (chapter 8(1)). Every one of those strikes, forging the modern democratic world, was banned by positive law. Even today, democracies are only sustained because they protect people's right to resist illegitimate authority. Despots must suppress independent centres of power because plurality enables democracy. They must suppress unions seeking economic and political freedom, and suppress their most important weapon: strike action. This is because, as American teacher unions said in the 1960s, collective bargaining without the right to strike is 'collective begging' (LJ Siegel (1964) 1 *Industrial & Labor Relations Forum* 1, 46, quoting Jules Kolodney). In the long-term, prohibitions on strikes have consistently proven futile. Some regimes have grown richer while suppressing labour but only by the state redistributing wealth in a way that imitates, but never comes close to improving on, what is possible in an open society. In the short term, suppressing collective action can inflict real damage. Inequality will accelerate, innovation will slow, development will falter, class divisions will entrench, and human freedom will be threatened.

This is why the right to take collective action, and strike, is fundamental to the common law, statute, EU law and international law. As old as work itself, the first recorded strike appears to have been against Rameses III (later murdered in a coup) for not properly paying workers building the Royal Necropolis around 1150 BC: WF Edgerton, 'The Strikes in Ramses III's Twenty-Ninth Year' (1951) 10(3) *Journal of Near Eastern Studies* 137, cf Genesis 11:9 and Exodus 5:7, recording labour disputes. Yet the right itself, and certainly its scope, is fiercely contested, because it disrupts production and causes loss. Of course, the basis of a market economy – competition by the threat of insolvency – is inherently wasteful. Dismissals by employers disrupt work and cause loss as well (chapter 19). So does corporate governance that concentrates power among unaccountable directors and asset managers (chapter 11). The law's dilemma is not how to achieve some 'fair balance' between the power of labour and capital, because unequal property distribution creates systemically unequal bargaining power. The real task is to guarantee that people may act collectively to steadily democratise economic and political life. This chapter considers (1) the right in common law, statute, international and EU law, (2) solidarity strikes in corporate groups, (3) ballot rules, (4) picketing and (5) damages or injunctions against strikes.

Introductory reading: CEM chs 16–17. D&M ch 11.

(1) THE RIGHT TO COLLECTIVE ACTION

The right to take collective action logically begins with who can take collective action, the limits, and the purpose for which collective action may be taken. The general position is (and ought to be) that everyone can take collective action, with only the narrowest exceptions, at (a) common law and equity, (b) under UK statute, (c) under international law and (d) in EU law.

(a) Common Law and Equity

Common law and equity recognise the right to strike as a fundamental right, though this has recently been contested. In two Court of Appeal cases, without any references, it was said the 'common law confers no right to strike in this country' (*RMT v Serco Ltd* [2011] EWCA Civ 226, [2] per Elias LJ) and 'the right to strike has never been much more than a slogan or a legal metaphor' (*Metrobus Ltd v Unite the Union* [2009] EWCA Civ 829, [118] per Maurice Kay LJ). These comments by judges of the Court of Appeal are not lightly to be dismissed. But they must be weighed against other, more influential dicta (that should have been recognised as binding) and the position of Parliament (chapter 10(1)(b)). In *London Underground Ltd v RMT* [1996] ICR 170, Millett LJ said the right to strike is 'a right which was first conferred by Parliament in 1906, which has been enjoyed by trade unions ever since and which is today recognised as encompassing a fundamental human right' (Ward LJ and Butler-Sloss LJ agreeing). In *Morgan v Fry* [1968] 2 QB 710, Lord Denning MR said it 'has been held for over 60 years that workmen have a right to strike' (Davies LJ concurring, Russell LJ dissenting). In *Mogul Steamship Co Ltd v McGregor* [1892] AC 25, 47, Lord Bramwell held the 'a combination of workmen, an agreement among them to cease work except for higher wages, and a strike in consequence, was lawful at common law'. And in *Crofter Hand Woven Harris Tweed Co Ltd v Veitch* [1942] AC 435, 463, Lord Wright held: 'The right of workmen to strike is an essential element in the principle of collective bargaining.'

It follows that even aside from domestic statute, the Human Rights Act (HRA) 1998, EU law or international law (below), common law upholds the right to strike. Even if arguments in *RMT* or *Metrobus* had been referenced, they would need to justify why the common law should reject what is a fundamental human right. The next case, affirming Millett LJ above, further underlines the dominant opinion: there is a positive right to strike at common law.

British Airways Plc v Unite the Union [2010] EWCA Civ 669

British Airways plc (BA) sought an injunction against its own cabin crew, organised by Unite, from taking strike action from 18 May to 3 June over pay cuts, through the withdrawal of perks for flights. Unite held a ballot on 22 February, of which the airline itself was properly informed by the union, which had 9,282 voters, 7,482 for, 1,781 against and 11 spoilt (80 per cent in favour). Unite sent out texts, emails and put the information on the workplace notice board. But BA claimed that Unite had not individually informed its own members of (a) the number of votes cast and (d) the number of spoiled votes, rather than the result. So, said BA, the strike was unlawful under the Trade Union and Labour Relations (Consolidation) Act (TULRCA) 1992 s 231 which requires that information. McCombe J granted an injunction against the strike. Unite appealed.

Lord Judge CJ:

20 ... I cannot, however, refrain from observing that there is a certain irony that it is the employers in this case whose application is based on an asserted non-compliance by the Union with steps created in the interests of the members, when the employers know perfectly well that an overwhelming majority of the members wish to take strike action and that the object of these proceedings is to restrain them from doing so. Nevertheless, in my judgment, the statutory provisions appear to be in wide enough terms to enable BA to take proceedings on this basis, and the contrary has not been argued.

...

29 ... our attention was drawn and Mr Reade QC, on behalf of BA, relied heavily on some observations by Mrs Justice Sharp in *Network Rail Infrastructure Limited v The National Union of Rail, Maritime and Transport Workers* [2010] EWHC 1084 (QB). Mrs Justice Sharp observed:

"It seems to me that section 231, on the face of it, requires active steps to be taken to provide information. I think there is a real distinction between taking active steps by sending information to the members concerned, and identifying for them a place where they can go and get the information if they wish to have it. It may be in this day and age most people would be able to use a computer and have access to it, but that cannot be assumed. It seems to me that for good policy reasons, it is important that members are given the information which they are entitled to by section 231 actively, rather than merely being told where they can go and get it if they wish to have it."

30 Mrs Justice Sharp did not identify the good policy considerations which she had in mind, but for present purposes, perhaps more important, while the distinction she identified between taking active steps to send information to the members, and identifying a place where they could go and find the information, may have been appropriate to the decision in that particular case, universally applied it represents a gloss on the statutory requirements. The important issue is that the members should be informed of the result, that is in the form required by section 231, and in this day and age, when, as here, the members of this union are highly computer literate, and use modern technology on a daily basis, there is no reason why the fact that they have to take a few simple steps themselves at a keyboard could possibly mean that they are not being supplied with information within the ambit of section 231.

31 For all these considerations, I conclude, consistently with the deployment of the concept of reasonableness in section 231, that the Union is not required to prove that literally every eligible member was personally sent his or her own individual report of the full results. A test

of such strictness would be unrealistic and, as it seems to me, McCombe J came very close to applying it when he came to his conclusion in this case.

...

61 In view of this conclusion, it is unnecessary for me to deal with Mr Hendy QC's further submissions that such failures as might have been shown were unimportant, so minimal that in effect they should be ignored. I do not think it possible to brush aside the requirements of section 231. They are embedded in statute. They are, however, less overwhelmingly compelling than perhaps it has previously been thought. But non-compliance with them, if established, matters, and would deprive the Union of the statutory protection in Part V.

62 What I do, however, question is whether as a matter of principle it can be appropriate that even a complete failure to inform the Union members – not the employers – of the fact that an infinitesimal proportion of spoilt ballots were returned which could have had no possible bearing on the outcome of the ballot could leave the Union liable in tort for calling a strike which had the support of the vast preponderance of its members. At the risk of repetition, it does indeed seem curious to me that the employers can rely on a provision designed to protect the interests of members of the Union in order to circumvent their wishes. In the meantime, without making any comment direct or indirect on the merits or otherwise of the proposed industrial action, we must all hope for a speedy and fair resolution of this dispute. It must be resolved by negotiation. Legal processes do not constitute mediation. To the contrary, they often serve to inflame rather than to mollify the feelings of those involved as they are in this case.

Lord Neuberger MR (dissenting):

66 Section 231 requires a trade union "as soon as is reasonably practicable" after the holding of the ballot "to take such steps as are reasonably necessary to ensure that all persons entitled to a vote are informed of the number of (a) votes cast in the ballot, (b) individuals answering "yes" to the question ..., (c) individuals answering "no" to the question ..., and (d) spoilt voting papers ".

67 In my judgment, these provisions are clear, and the court should proceed on the basis that they mean what they say. Unless the court is satisfied that, as soon as reasonably practicable, the trade union has taken steps which are reasonably necessary to ensure that the four pieces of information identified in section 231 (a) to (d) ("the section 231 information") are given to all persons entitled to vote then the ballot would not comply with section 231. It is, in my view, impermissible for the court to dispense with the requirement that the requisite steps are taken to provide one or more of four items of information when the legislature has said in terms that requisite steps must be taken to ensure each such item has to be provided.

68 When a statute stipulates in clear terms that a specific item of information has to be given, or a specific step has to be taken, in order for a person to claim a particular benefit, then in the absence of some statutory warrant to the contrary, it is simply not open to the court to rule that the person is entitled to that benefit where the specific information has not been given, or the specific step has not been taken. ...

Smith LJ:

112 Another major concern at the time of the legislation was that strike ballots often took place in a very informal way, typically in the work's carpark where everyone could see who was voting for and against the strike. There was concern that some workers were not able

to take part. Others who could take part were put under pressure, at times even bullied into supporting the strike. The new provisions now found at sections 226 to 232 of the Act were designed to ensure that ballots for industrial action were secret, free and fair. In short they were designed to ensure that a ballot had democratic legitimacy.

113 These provisions are quite detailed and impose considerable demands on the Union. But it seems to me important to recognise that they are not designed to prevent unions from organising strikes, or even to make it so difficult that it will be impracticable for them to do so. As Lord Justice Millett said in *London Underground Limited v National Union of Railwaymen, Maritime and Transport Staff* [1996] ICR 170, at page 180:

> "Parliament's object in introducing the democratic requirement of a secret ballot is not to make life more difficult for trade unions by putting further obstacles in their way before they can call for industrial action with impunity but to ensure that such action should have the genuine support of the members who are called upon to take part. The requirement has not been imposed for the protection of the employer or the public but for the protection of the Union's own members. It would be astonishing if a right that was first conferred by Parliament in 1906, which has been enjoyed by trade unions ever since and which is today recognised as encompassing a fundamental human right, should have been removed by Parliament by enacting a series of provisions intended to strengthen industrial democracy and governing the relations between a union and its own members."

114 In the present case it is not disputed that most of the requirements of Part V relating to the conduct of the ballot have been complied with. In January 2010 the Union gave notice to BA of its intention to conduct a ballot and the number and types of worker concerned were identified as required by section 226A.

115 No criticism can be made either of the way in which the ballot was conducted. The members entitled to vote received ballot papers, by post, as required. The ballot period covered four weeks so as to give the members a full opportunity to vote. This was thought necessary as cabin crews are often abroad. Electoral Reform Services was appointed as independent scrutineer. The ballot closed on 22 February and the result was declared by the scrutineer later that day. There was a large majority in favour of strike action, 7,482 "yes" votes to 1,789 "no" votes. The scrutineer provided a certificate saying that it was satisfied with the conduct of the ballot. BA was immediately informed of the results. BA has no cause to complain of the conduct of the ballot so far as its own rights and interests are concerned.

...

154 In my view the cabin crew members of Unite have expressed a clear view in a fair and open ballot conducted in February 2010. I consider that it is likely that a judge at trial would hold that the Union had complied with section 231; alternatively, I consider it highly likely that he would hold that the Union had at least substantially complied with that section.

NOTES AND QUESTIONS

1. The Court of Appeal (with three formidable and expert judges) holds by a majority that there was no violation of the balloting rules (chapter 10(3)). Lord Neuberger MR in dissent holds the ballot rules should be applied as they are 'plainly' written. However, Lord Judge CJ and Smith LJ do not accept that the meaning is plain, and do not see the ballot rules' purpose as being to frustrate a union's right to strike. Smith LJ in particular, agreeing with Millett LJ, articulates that the right to

strike is a 'fundamental human right' [113]. This guides construction of the statute. Furthermore, the ballot rules exist for the protection of union members, not employers. Lord Judge CJ echoes the same idea, [20]. On this basis the injunction is refused.

2. While the majority in *BA plc v Unite* supported the right to strike, a minority clearly contests that view. At least three basic positions can be summarised. First, it could be argued that there is no right to strike, except that which is given immunity by statute. At common law, it is argued, strikes are a breach of contract, which requires following directions in virtually all circumstances (see chapter 5(1)(a)). At least three torts are commissioned when a union organises a strike that causes economic loss (chapter 10(1)(b) below). This reductive view of contract and tort law cannot be consistent with *BA plc v Unite*, or *London Underground Ltd v NUR*, *Morgan v Fry* and *Crofter* (as summarised below). Second, it might be said there is a positive right to strike which derives from the infusion of human rights into the common law. Both the UK's accession to the ECHR 1950, and the International Covenant on Economic, Social and Cultural Rights (ICESCR) 1966 brought with it a duty – even before the HRA 1998 – to develop the common law in light of progressive international standards: cf *Hounga v Allen* (chapter 4(1)). The difficulty with this approach is that (by itself) it leaves unaddressed the internal logic of common law – and equity. A third approach is to say that a strike, taken as part of a good-faith trade dispute, is potentially a response to an employer's breach of contract. An implied term in every contract (which cannot be given away but by collective agreement, cf TULRCA 1992 s 180) is that workers can lawfully suspend their performance for any breach of reasonable expectation to fair treatment. The law presumes to be agnostic, without specific reason, about who is at fault in a trade dispute. Without breach of contract there is no tort for procuring breach. 'No secondary liability without primary liability.' Moreover, a court should be 'reluctant to become involved in devising rules of fair competition': *OBG Ltd v Allan* [2007] UKHL 21, [44] and [56] per Lord Hoffmann.

3. *Commonwealth v Hunt* 45 Mass 111 (1842), a landmark for US labour law, is instructive. The Boston Journeymen Bootmakers' Society went on strike for higher wages, and was sued. Shaw CJ held that the law to be applied by the Massachusetts Supreme Judicial Court had evolved from English common law, so 'a conviction in England, in many cases, would not be a precedent for a like conviction here'. People could 'agree together to exercise their own acknowledged rights, in such a manner as best to subserve their own interests'. If a strike were conducted 'by fair or honorable and lawful means' it would itself be lawful. A similar defence was rejected by the House of Lords in *South Wales Miners' Federation v Glamorgan Coal Co* [1905] AC 239. Do you agree that position should be expressly overruled by the UK Supreme Court?

4. In the UK, is it any longer tenable to assert that a strike is a breach of contract? A strike invariably responds to an employer's breach of workers' reasonable expectations, especially for pay cuts, failing to ensure pay is fair, unjust dismissals or ignoring workers' voice. On orthodox contract principles, this may be seen as entitling workers to withhold their performance until settlement is reached. In the context of transfers of undertakings (chapter 19(1)(c)) Potter LJ said in *University*

of Oxford v Humphreys [1999] EWCA Civ 3050: '[T]he threatened breach by the employer of his continuing obligation ... if persisted in despite the objection of the employee, is an anticipatory repudiatory breach of an executory contract.' This analysis resembles P Elias, 'The Strike and Breach of Contract: A Reassessment' in KD Ewing, CA Gearty and BA Hepple, *Human Rights and Labour Law* (1994) ch 11: '[E]mployees may be able to take strike action in response to a repudiatory breach by the employer in one of two ways. Either they may be able to withhold their labour until the employer is willing to perform his part of the contract; or they may be able to give notice to terminate their contracts in response to the repudiatory breach.'

5.   Today it is acknowledged that good faith or mutual trust and confidence is a fundamental and 'continuing obligation' in every employment contract (chapter 5). The foundational case on withholding performance in contract law is *Kingston v Preston* (1773) 2 Doug KB 689. Kingston, a silk-mercer, sued Preston, a business owner, for failing to convey the business to Kingston and his nephew after Kingston served for a year and a quarter. They had agreed Preston would convey the stock in trade over a period of time, in return for Kingston providing security. But Kingston never provided the security. When Kingston sued, Lord Mansfield held that because the security was a condition precedent to Preston's performance, Preston had been entitled to withhold conveyance. Lord Mansfield described the case as involving 'covenants which are conditions and dependant, in which the performance of one depends on the prior performance of another, and, therefore, till this prior condition is performed, the other party is not liable to an action on his covenant'. Applied to employment, it follows that breach of good faith by an employer – eg by announcing a real-terms pay cut – would entitle workers to withhold their performance. Workers have a right to strike.

6.   At the very least, strikes by people who do not accept a contractual obligation to work must have the right to strike. That would mean all zero-hours contract workers: see *Allen v Flood* [1898] AC 1 (where workers hired day by day who went on strike commissioned no breach of contract). But also, since *Allen v Flood* the common law of contract, especially in employment, has moved on. Before one gets anywhere near statute, it would be a very rare thing for an individual to truly agree to give up the right to strike, except perhaps in a collective agreement where the parties are of equal bargaining power (cf TULRCA 1992 s 180). Any such contract term that purports to withdraws the right to strike would at common law be a sham: *Autoclenz Ltd v Belcher* [2011] UKSC 41, [35].

7.   Do you agree the right to withhold performance (including on strike) during a good-faith trade dispute is an implied term in every contract? Do you agree that the conscience of equity bends the common law's strict adherence to contract toward justice?

8.   The first major statement of the common law right to strike derives from Lord Bramwell in *Mogul Steamship Co Ltd v McGregor, Gow & Co* [1892] AC 25. Mogul Steamship Ltd claimed damages for 'conspiracy to injure' against (what we would now recognise as) a cartel of shipping owners, including McGregor, Gow & Co, which gave a 5 per cent discount to organisations that dealt only with their members. Lord Bramwell agreed that there was no liability because

the association pursued lawful objects, and said this: 'There is one thing that is to me decisive. I have always said that a combination of workmen, an agreement among them to cease work except for higher wages, and a strike in consequence, was lawful at common law; perhaps not enforceable inter se, but not indictable. The Legislature has now so declared.' That reference was to the Conspiracy, and Protection of Property Act 1875 s 3. Today small firms could face liability as a cartel under the Competition Act 1998 s 2 and the Treaty on the Functioning of the European Union Art 101, but would simply operate as a corporation, with no risk of liability, not an association of entities.

9.   *Mogul* coincided with the US Sherman Antitrust Act of 1890, codifying a common law prohibition on 'restraint of trade'. It may be read as a rejection of that policy. In retrospect the House of Lords appears to have been too sanguine about business combinations, but Lord Bramwell was certainly on the pulse of the future in relation to labour. Indeed, the Sherman Act was immediately used as a weapon not against business combinations, but trade unions: *United States v Workingmen's Amalgamated Council of New Orleans*, 57 F 85 (5th Cir 1893) after a general strike in New Orleans, and *In re Debs*, 158 US 564 (1895) where the future Presidential candidate for the US Socialist Party, Eugene Debs, was thrown in prison. The Supreme Court directly confirmed its intolerance of labour in *Loewe v Lawlor*, 208 US 274 (1908) until the Clayton Act 1914 §6 forced a change in the law, saying 'the labor of a human being is not a commodity or article of commerce. Nothing contained in the antitrust laws' should 'forbid the existence and operation of labor ... organizations' or 'restrain individual members of such organizations from lawfully carrying out the legitimate objects'. The view that 'labour is not a commodity' became foundational to international law with the ill-fated Versailles Treaty 1919 Part XIII, Art 427, and the Declaration of Philadelphia (10 May 1944).

10.   A decisive shift in UK law came with *Crofter Hand Woven Tweed Co Ltd v Veitch* [1941] UKHL 2. Crofter Ltd sued Veitch for the tort of 'conspiracy' after the Transport and General Workers Union (now part of Unite) ensured that dockworkers refused to handle Crofter Ltd's goods when it came from the island of Lewis to the port at Stornoway, because Crofter Ltd refused to pay adequate wages. The House of Lords unanimously held that the TGWU's solidarity action was lawful, because it aimed to protect legitimate interests. Lord Thankerton said: 'I can see no ground for holding that it was not legitimate for the union to avail itself of the services of its docker members to promote the interests of the union.' Lord Wright said: 'It cannot be merely that the Appellants' right to freedom in conducting their trade has been interfered with. That right is not an absolute or unconditional right ... limitations are inevitable in organised societies where the rights of individuals may clash. In commercial affairs each trader's rights are qualified by the right of others to compete. Where the rights of labour are concerned, the rights of the employer are conditioned by the rights of the men to give or withhold their services. The right of workmen to strike is an essential element in the principle of collective bargaining.'

11.   In *Morgan v Fry* [1968] 2 QB 710 Morgan, a member of a breakaway union, claimed that Fry, the regional secretary of the TGWU (now part of Unite) which

was recognised by the Port of London Authority, was liable for the torts of intimidation and conspiracy. The TGWU told the Port it would strike if Morgan were not dismissed. The Court of Appeal held there was reasonable notice of a strike, so there was no intimidation, and the union was acting honestly and sincerely in their members' interests, so there was no conspiracy. Lord Denning MR in particular, quoted himself in *Stratford (JT) & Son Ltd v Lindley* [1964] 2 WLR 1002, 1016–17, positing that there could be a breach of contract if there was a threat to strike (rather than terminate the contract on notice), but then said: 'It is difficult to see the logical flaw in that argument. But there must be something wrong with it: for if that argument were correct, it would do away with the right to strike in this country. It has been held for over 60 years that workmen have a right to strike (including therein a right to say that they will not work with non-unionists) provided that they give sufficient notice beforehand: and a notice is sufficient if it is at least as long as the notice required to terminate the contract.' Do you agree this is consistent with Lord Mansfield's dictum in *Kingston v Preston*?

12. Why *should* the common law, in contract, tort, and ultimately in its regulation of property rights, recognise a right to strike? One of the best answers was in South Africa.

Certification of the Constitution of the Republic of South Africa [1996] ZACC 26

The Constitutional Court of South Africa, appointed by Nelson Mandela in 1995, was required by an Interim Constitution (21 April 1994) to certify that a 'New Text' complied with a set of general 'Constitutional Principles'. In 1990, the last apartheid President, FW de Klerk, was pushed by massive strikes and growing moral awareness, to agree to release from prison the African National Congress (ANC) leader, legalise the ANC and other political parties, and agree to elections. The ANC leader, Nelson Mandela (who, while in prison, undertook the University of London's external LLB, for his second law degree) was elected by overwhelming majority in elections held on 24–27 April 1994. To guarantee stability during the transition, it was agreed beforehand between the white minority government, the ANC and other parties negotiating an end to apartheid that a new constitution's text with fundamental rights would comply with 'Constitutional Principles' agreed by the negotiating parties, as judged by the new Court. Multiple interest groups made submissions to the Court on compliance. The Court certified some of the New Text, but rejected other parts. The following section concerns labour rights.

The Court:

63 There were two objections to [the New Text of the Constitution (NT)] 23.[1] The first was that the omission of the right of employers to lock out workers is in breach of [Constitutional

---

[1] NT 23 provides as follows:

"(1) Everyone has the right to fair labour practices.
(2) Every worker has the right – (a) to form and join a trade union; (b) to participate in the activities and programmes of a trade union; and (c) to strike.
(3) Every employer has the right – (a) to form and join an employers' organisation; and (b) to participate in the activities and programmes of an employers' organisation.

Principles (CP)] II and XXVIII. The second ground of objection was that NT 23 fails to "recognise and protect" the right of individual employers to engage in collective bargaining as required by CP XXVIII.

Lockout

64 The first and major ground for this objection was based on CP XXVIII which provides that:

> "Notwithstanding the provisions of Principle XII, the right of employers and employees to join and form employer organisations and trade unions and to engage in collective bargaining shall be recognised and protected. Provision shall be made that every person shall have the right to fair labour practices."

The objectors argued that in order to engage effectively in collective bargaining, bargaining parties must have the right to exercise economic power against each other. Accordingly, went the argument, the right to lock out should be expressly recognised in the NT. It is correct that collective bargaining implies a right on the part of those who engage in collective bargaining to exercise economic power against their adversaries. However, CP XXVIII does not require that the NT expressly recognise any particular mechanism for the exercise of economic power on behalf of workers or employers: it suffices that the right to bargain collectively is specifically protected. Once a right to bargain collectively is recognised, implicit within it will be the right to exercise some economic power against partners in collective bargaining. The nature and extent of that right need not be determined now.

65 The objectors also argued that, by including the right to strike but omitting the right to lock out, the employers' right to engage in collective bargaining is accorded less status than the right of workers to engage in collective bargaining. However, the effect of including the right to strike does not diminish the right of employers to engage in bargaining, nor does it weaken their right to exercise economic power against workers. Their right to bargain collectively is expressly recognised by the text.[2]

66 A related argument was that the principle of equality requires that, if the right to strike is included in the NT, so should the right to lock out be included. This argument is based on the proposition that the right of employers to lock out is the necessary equivalent of the right of workers to strike and that therefore, in order to treat workers and employers equally, both should be recognised in the NT. That proposition cannot be accepted. Collective bargaining is based on the recognition of the fact that employers enjoy greater social and economic power than individual workers. Workers therefore need to act in concert to provide them collectively with sufficient power to bargain effectively with employers. Workers exercise collective power primarily through the mechanism of strike action. In theory, employers, on the other hand, may exercise power against workers through a range of weapons, such as dismissal, the employment of alternative or replacement labour, the unilateral implementation of new terms and conditions of employment, and the exclusion of workers from the workplace (the last of these being generally called a lockout).[3] The importance of the right to strike for workers has led to it

(4) Every trade union and every employers' organisation has the right – (a) to determine its own administration, programmes and activities; (b) to organise; (c) to bargain collectively; and (d) to form and join a federation.
(5) The provisions of the Bill of Rights do not prevent legislation recognising union security arrangements contained in collective agreements."

[2] This is subject to the issue we discuss below under the heading *The Right of Individual Employers to Bargain Collectively* in para 69.
[3] In South Africa the lockout has been the subject of elastic statutory definition. Under the Labour Relations Act 28 of 1956, the lockout was given wide definition to include a range of employer conduct aimed at

being far more frequently entrenched in constitutions as a fundamental right than is the right to lock out. The argument that it is necessary in order to maintain equality to entrench the right to lock out once the right to strike has been included, cannot be sustained, because the right to strike and the right to lock out are not always and necessarily equivalent.

67 It was also argued that the inclusion of the right to strike necessarily implies that legislation protecting the right to lock out, such as the LRA, would be unconstitutional. The objectors argued that such a result would be in breach of CP XXVIII. The argument is based on a false premise. The fact that the NT expressly protects the right to strike does not mean that a legislative provision permitting a lockout is necessarily unconstitutional, or indeed that the provisions of the LRA permitting lockouts are unconstitutional. The effect of NT 23 will be that the right of employers to use economic sanctions against workers will be regulated by legislation within a constitutional framework. The primary development of this law will, in all probability, take place in labour courts in the light of labour legislation. That legislation will always be subject to constitutional scrutiny to ensure that the rights of workers and employers as entrenched in NT 23 are honoured.[4]

...

The Right of Individual Employers to Bargain Collectively

69 The second objection levelled at NT 23 is based on the failure to entrench the right of individual employers to engage in collective bargaining. The objection was based on CP XXVIII which provides that "the right of employers ... to engage in collective bargaining shall be recognised and protected." The objectors pointed out that NT 23 specifically entrenches only the rights of employers' associations to engage in collective bargaining, and does not specifically entrench the right of individual employers to engage in collective bargaining. It is true that NT 23 does not protect the right of individual workers to bargain, but individual workers cannot bargain collectively except in concert. As stated above, collective bargaining is based on the need for individual workers to act in combination to provide them collectively with sufficient power to bargain effectively with employers. Individual employers, on the other hand, can engage in collective bargaining with their workers and often do so. The failure by the text to protect such a right represents a failure to comply with the language of CP XXVIII which specifically states that the right of employers to bargain collectively shall be recognised and protected. This objection therefore succeeds.

Chaskalson P, Langa J, Mahomed DP, Madala J, Didcott J, Mokgoro J, Goldstone J, O'Regan J, Kriegler J and **Sachs J** took part in the judgment.

NOTES AND QUESTIONS

1. The Constitutional Court of South Africa rejects the contentions of employer groups that there should be a constitutional right to lock out striking workers, as much as there is a right of workers to strike, because 'employers enjoy greater social and economic power than individual workers. Workers therefore need to act

compelling workers' agreement, including changing the terms and conditions of employment of workers and even the dismissal of workers. The new Labour Relations Act 66 of 1995 gives a much more restricted definition to lockout.

[4] This is not dissimilar to the situation in Germany, although in that country the development of the collective right to strike and lock out is undertaken by the courts with no legislative framework, other than the constitutional one. See, for a discussion, Carl Mischke 'Industrial Action in German Law' (1992) 13 *Industrial Law Journal* 1, 4.

in concert to provide them collectively with sufficient power to bargain effectively with employers' [66]. Thus, the court recognises it is not enough to create some formal parity between abstract concepts of capital and labour. That imbalance of power among people derives from the unequal distribution of resources, coupled with the unequal distribution of contractual, proprietary and corporate rights (chapter 2(1)). This judgment is not binding on the UK courts, yet it exemplifies, free from authority, a principled course of reasoning.

2.   After the *First Certification* judgment, the text was revised, and quickly approved in a *Second Certification* judgment [1996] ZACC 24. The current Constitution of South Africa, ch 2, §23 as amended, shifted §23(4)(c) into a new subsection that now reads fully: 'Every trade union, employers' organisation and employer has the right to engage in collective bargaining. National legislation may be enacted to regulate collective bargaining.' This was essentially to enable the possibility of enterprise bargaining, instead of sectoral collective bargaining. As chapter 9 explained, the undermining of sectoral bargaining was key in weakening labour rights systems in the UK, USA, Canada and elsewhere. Not well understood in 1996, it probably also weakened South African labour rights. Currently just over 25 per cent of South African workers are union members.

3.   A year before the *First Certification* judgment came *London Underground Ltd v RMT* [1996] ICR 170. London Underground Ltd sought an injunction against a strike by the National Union of Railwaymen, Maritime and Transport Staff (RMT) on the basis that the union notified that 692 more employees could take part in a strike than were included in the ballot under TULRCA 1992 s 234A (see chapter 10(3)). Under s 224A, a union has to notify employers of a list of workers entitled to vote in the ballot. There were over 5,000. Over 2,000 voted in favour of a strike, 622 against. Under s 234A a union then has to notify the employer of when a strike will occur, and a list of potential workers who would strike. RMT included 692 people who were hired since the strike. The employer argued this was unlawful. The Court of Appeal held that the whole strike became lawful if a majority voted for it in a ballot, not simply lawful for those included in the ballot. Millett LJ, at 181–82, said: 'It would be astonishing if a right which was first conferred by Parliament in 1906, which has been enjoyed by trade unions ever since and which is today recognised as encompassing a fundamental human right, should have been removed by Parliament by enacting a series of provisions intended to strengthen industrial democracy and governing the relations between a union and its own members. I conclude, therefore, that there is nothing in sections 226 to 235 which curtails a union's long accepted right to induce non-members to support the industrial action called by the union by breaking their own contracts of employment.'

4.   But why did Millett LJ say a worker is breaking his or her contract of employment when he or she goes on strike? If the right to strike is a human right, as Millett LJ rightly says, and it is a breach of contract, it would follow that English contract law (absent statute) violates human rights. Whether or not that conclusion is commonly held, it must be regarded as unacceptable. The very idea of a legal 'system' is that it organises and reconciles different and developing sources – case law,

> human rights, statute – and construes them as a coherent whole: HLA Hart, *The Concept of Law* (1961) ch 5, 95–96 and ch 6. When this does not happen, when the capacity for change is denied, there is a legal regime, not a legal system. It forces its own judiciary into a kind of permanent doublethink, pitching sources of law at war with one another.

(b) Statutory Codified Rights

Since the Trade Union and Labour Relations Act 1974 s 18(4), statute has expressly recognised the positive 'right to take industrial action': TULRCA 1992 s 180. Section 180 says: 'Any terms of a collective agreement which prohibit or restrict *the right of workers to engage in a strike* or other industrial action, or have the effect of prohibiting or restricting that right, shall not form part of any contract' unless contained in an express collective agreement' (emphasis added). Thus, statute codified the common law position (see in *Morgan v Fry* or *Crofter*) that there is a right to strike. While it has been said that there is 'no right to strike in this country', and the right to strike is 'a slogan or a legal metaphor' (chapter 10(1)(a)), those minority views must, with respect, be seen as mistaken, rhetorical and contrary to Parliament's will.

Yet the right to strike, as briskly expressed in statute, is problematic. Historically, the right to strike developed by lifting common law and statutory restrictions on combinations. Concretely, this began with the 'golden formula' in the Conspiracy and Protection of Property Act 1875 s 3 to exempt from criminal liability any action by workers 'in contemplation or furtherance of a trade dispute'. After *Taff Vale* (chapter 1(3)), the Trade Disputes Act 1906 ss 1–4 affirmed protection from civil liability. By contrast there are explicit restrictions on the right to strike for police, prison officers, merchant shipping and in the armed forces. The weight of statute, however, has been concerned with protection from hypothetical torts, to give way to the right to strike, rather than affirmative elaboration of the scope of the right to take collective action.

Is the issue largely semantic? Whether rights are framed negatively or positively, it could be argued, this does not affect the law's functional substance: what workers and unions can do. But on the other hand, the law's frame affects the mind, and lawyers' psychological starting point. It may encourage the illusion that the common law cannot evolve equitably, to align with international human rights, or that statute creates exceptions to a general rule of liability that must be construed restrictively (cf Lord Neuberger MR above). Put at its lowest, it is questionable whether tort liability does and should still apply to collective action. Although statute refers to hypothetical torts, their place in labour disputes is open to severe doubt.

Trade Union and Labour Relations (Consolidation) Act 1992 ss 219 and 244

219. Protection from certain tort liabilities.

(1) An act done by a person in contemplation or furtherance of a trade dispute is not actionable in tort on the ground only—

    (a) that it induces another person to break a contract or interferes or induces another person to interfere with its performance, or

    (b)   that it consists in his threatening that a contract (whether one to which he is a party or not) will be broken or its performance interfered with, or that he will induce another person to break a contract or interfere with its performance.

(2) An agreement or combination by two or more persons to do or procure the doing of an act in contemplation or furtherance of a trade dispute is not actionable in tort if the act is one which if done without any such agreement or combination would not be actionable in tort.

(3) Nothing in subsections (1) and (2) prevents an act done in the course of picketing from being actionable in tort unless—

    (a)   it is done in the course of attendance declared lawful by section 220 (peaceful picketing), and

    (b)   in the case of picketing to which section 220A applies, the requirements in that section (union supervision of picketing) are complied with.

(4) Subsections (1) and (2) have effect subject to sections 222 to 225 (action excluded from protection) and to [sections 226 (requirement of ballot before action by trade union) and 234A (requirement of notice to employer of industrial action); and in those sections "not protected" means excluded from the protection afforded by this section or, where the expression is used with reference to a particular person, excluded from that protection as respects that person.

    ...

244. Meaning of "trade dispute" in Part V.

(1) In this Part a "trade dispute" means a dispute between workers and their employer which relates wholly or mainly to one or more of the following—

    (a)   terms and conditions of employment, or the physical conditions in which any workers are required to work;

    (b)   engagement or non-engagement, or termination or suspension of employment or the duties of employment, of one or more workers;

    (c)   allocation of work or the duties of employment between workers or groups of workers;

    (d)   matters of discipline;

    (e)   a worker's membership or non-membership of a trade union;

    (f)   facilities for officials of trade unions; and

    (g)   machinery for negotiation or consultation, and other procedures, relating to any of the above matters, including the recognition by employers or employers' associations of the right of a trade union to represent workers in such negotiation or consultation or in the carrying out of such procedures.

(2) A dispute between a Minister of the Crown and any workers shall, notwithstanding that he is not the employer of those workers, be treated as a dispute between those workers and their employer if the dispute relates to matters which—

    (a)   have been referred for consideration by a joint body on which, by virtue of provision made by or under any enactment, he is represented, or

    (b)   cannot be settled without him exercising a power conferred on him by or under an enactment.

(3) There is a trade dispute even though it relates to matters occurring outside the United Kingdom, so long as the person or persons whose actions in the United Kingdom are said to be in contemplation or furtherance of a trade dispute relating to matters occurring outside the United Kingdom are likely to be affected in respect of one or more of the matters specified in subsection (1) by the outcome of the dispute.

(4) An act, threat or demand done or made by one person or organisation against another which, if resisted, would have led to a trade dispute with that other, shall be treated as being done or made in contemplation of a trade dispute with that other, notwithstanding that because that other submits to the act or threat or accedes to the demand no dispute arises.

(5) In this section—
"employment" includes any relationship whereby one person personally does work or performs services for another; and
"worker", in relation to a dispute with an employer, means—
  (a) a worker employed by that employer; or
  (b) a person who has ceased to be so employed if his employment was terminated in connection with the dispute or if the termination of his employment was one of the circumstances giving rise to the dispute.

NOTES AND QUESTIONS

1. TULRCA 1992 s 219 says an act is 'not actionable in tort' if done 'in contemplation or furtherance of a trade dispute'. This phrase, repeated since the 1875 and 1906 Acts, was called the 'golden formula' by KW Wedderburn (1965) 28(2) MLR 205, 209, but that formula has plainly lost some of its shine in the last few decades. In its current form it isolates three hypothetical torts from which unions are protected, and then adds that this protection depends on the balloting rules. Section 244 then defines a 'trade dispute' as being at least 'mainly' connected to seven issues relating to workers' contracts and employment relationship. But if strikes are a specific instance of the broader right to collective action, where economic and political interests intersect, focus on a dispute about trade fails to express the scope of the human right: cf *BBC v Hearn* below.
2. What are the torts, that are said to be triggered, and the arguments for their existence, when workers exercise the 'right to take industrial action' (s 180)? Section 219 itself is agnostic about the torts actually arising: it is framed not to endorse them ('not actionable in tort on the ground only …'). However three torts, which certainly apply in fields of commerce or business, are in mind:

   (i) inducing breach of contract: *Lumley v Gye* (below)
   (ii) conspiracy to injure: removed by *Crofter Tweed Ltd v Veitch* (chapter 10(1)(a) above)
   (iii) causing loss by unlawful means: *Rookes Barnard* and *J&T Stratford* (below)

3. These three categories are referred to as 'economic torts', as they enable recovery of damages for loss of expected profits, rather than something that exists now. As applied to strikes, they are disorganised and overlap because they attempt to categorise what is in essence one wrong: against the right to one's 'expectation interest' in contract. For an employer, that means the right to future profits.
4. For the first tort, it is argued that a strike is a breach of contract, and unions organising a strike are procuring their members to breach their contracts. This begins with *Lumley v Gye* (1853) 2 E&B 216. Lumley, who ran Her Majesty's Theatre, sued Gye, who ran Covent Garden Theatre, in tort for persuading a singer, Joanna Wagner, to break her contract with Her Majesty's Theatre and instead sing for Gye at Covent Garden Theatre. Crompton J said: '[A] person who wrongfully and maliciously, or, which is the same thing, with notice, interrupts the relation subsisting between master and servant … commits a wrongful act for which he is responsible at law.' It might be thought that a union, organising a strike, should be analogous to Gye enticing Wagner to his theatre to sell more tickets. However,

Lumley v Gye makes clear that the liability of Gye in tort is secondary or dependent on a breach of contract by Wagner. If it is recognised that an employee who strikes commits no breach of contract (because a strike has a legitimate objective), there can be no liability of a union for this tort. Moreover, a union (eg a singers' union) cannot be likened to a commercial entity making profit. The objective motivation, and policy justifications, for the actions of each differ fundamentally. Finally, it is now recognised that the 'need to segregate intellectually common law principles relating to contract law, even in the field of employment, from statutorily conferred rights is fundamental'. *Gisda Cyf v Barratt* [2010] UKSC 41, [39] (chapter 3(1)). Because statute expressly recognises 'the right to take industrial action' (TULRCA 1992 s 180) common law must be constructed to uphold the right to strike.

5. As chapter 1(2) alluded, a trilogy of cases triggered the Trade Disputes Act 1906, which first embedded the right to strike. First, in *Taff Vale Railway Co v ASRS* [1901] UKHL 1, the Amalgamated Society of Railway Servants was held liable in tort for members who 'illegally watched and beset men to prevent them from working for the company, and illegally ordered men to break their contracts' (per Farwell J). Although *Taff Vale* was quickly decided, in *Quinn v Leathem* [1901] UKHL 2 their Lordships took more time to articulate that the relevant tort was that in *Lumley v Gye*. Lord Lindley added that 'the principle involved in it cannot be confined to inducements to break contracts of service. ... The principle ... reaches all wrongful acts done intentionally to damage a particular individual and actually damaging him.' Then in *South Wales Miners' Federation v Glamorgan Coal Co* [1905] AC 239 the House of Lords added that it was no defence that a union intended to act without malice, in this case by intending to limit the amount workers worked, and so to keep coal prices up which would benefit the employers while enabling higher wages. It is submitted that as well as s 219(1)(a) providing protection in tort, this must longer be regarded as tortious at common law because there is no breach of contract (see chapter 10(1)(a) above).

6. For the second tort, it was seen above that *Crofter Ltd v Veitch* [1941] UKHL 2 removed any liability for conspiracy, even though this is still covered by s 219(2), by establishing the trade union had the right to defend its legitimate interests: Lord Thankerton said: 'I can see no ground for holding that it was not legitimate for the union to avail itself of the services of its docker members to promote the interests of the union.' This was in effect resurrecting a good-faith defence that *South Wales* rejected. It gives a good example of how the common law moves on, even though the Trade Disputes Act 1906 stayed the same.

7. For the third tort, of causing loss by unlawful means, there were three main cases. First, in *Rookes v Barnard* [1964] UKHL 1 the House of Lords reincarnated the tort of intimidation from *Tarleton v M'Gawley* (1790) 1 Peake NPC 270, and applied it to unions because it had not been thought of by the drafters of the Trade Disputes Act 1906, and their Lordships felt like attacking the unions. In *Tarleton*, Lord Kenyon held the master of *The Othello* was liable to a rival shipowner for depriving him of trade by firing a cannon ball across the path of a canoe that was going to the shore of West Africa. Here to enforce its closed shop (chapter 9(3)(a)) the union called a strike against the British Airways Overseas Corp to make

it dismiss Rookes, who had left the union. Lord Devlin said: 'I find therefore nothing to differentiate a threat of a breach of contract from a threat of physical violence or any other illegal threat.' (Whether his Lordship was trying very hard to find something to differentiate is another matter.) Though the tort liability was immediately protected by Parliament in the Trade Disputes Act 1965, the case still stands as good authority for principles to apply punitive damages: see LH Hoffmann (1965) 81 LQR 116. Second, in *JT Stratford & Son v Lindley* [1965] AC 269 the House of Lords held the Watermen, Lightermen, Tugmen and Bargemen's Union could be liable for intentionally procuring breach of a commercial contract: this apparently new tort was made out when union members of different employers at the Port of London refused to handle the barges of JT Stratford & Son, because its parent company did not sign a collective agreement with them. Counsel for Lindley, the general secretary, argued: 'At common law there is an implied right to go on strike after proper notice without terminating one's employment.' But their Lordships, refusing to handle the argument, held there was no trade dispute, and there was 'an actionable interference with contractual relations ... committed by a third party' at 297, citing *DC Thomson & Co Ltd v Deakin* [1952] Ch 646. Third, in *Torquay Hotel Co Ltd v Cousins* [1969] 2 Ch 106 the Court of Appeal held there was liability even for interference with a commercial contract, without procuring its breach. This was so where the Transport and General Workers Union blocked the supply of oil from Esso Co Ltd to Torquay Hotel Co Ltd under a contract which contained a force majeure clause, so there was no breach if oil was not delivered because of a strike. The Court of Appeal held the union official could not rely on the force majeure clause for protection.

8.   Although *Rookes*, *Lindley* and *Cousins* dealt with what were said to be two torts (intimidation and procuring or interfering with commercial contracts) in *OBG Ltd v Allan* [2007] UKHL 21, the House of Lords said that in fact this must be regarded as one tort: of causing loss by unlawful means [7]. Lord Hoffmann at [47] said the tort's elements are '(a) a wrongful interference with the actions of a third party in which the claimant has an economic interest and (b) an intention thereby to cause loss to the claimant'. The interference seems to become 'wrongful' only if one says that one says there is a breach of contract when one goes on strike. But as Lord Hoffmann stressed at [56] the 'common law has traditionally been reluctant to become involved in devising rules of fair competition', citing *Mogul Steamship* where Lord Bramwell clearly approved said 'a combination of workmen, an agreement among them to cease work except for higher wages, and a strike in consequence, was lawful at common law'. It must follow that this third tort, which can still apply in commercial relations like the cases in *OBG* itself, should cease to apply in its entirety to labour.

9.   A fourth tort was once proposed in *Merkur Island Shipping Corporation v Laughton* [1983] 2 AC 570, for procuring a breach of a statutory duty, or indeed any 'interference with a person's legal rights'. However *Merkur Island* was expressly overruled by *OBG Ltd v Allan* at [44] and [185], as their Lordships rejected a unified theory of economic torts, and confined those existing torts to the two categories of (1) procuring breach of contract, or (2) causing loss by unlawful means.

10. It might be argued that statute has codified the tortious liability of trade unions, but such a view cannot be accepted because statute has expressly been drafted to be agnostic. TULRCA 1992 s 20 states that '[w]here proceedings in tort are brought against a trade union' including inducing breach of contract, threatening or interfering in contract, then a union is only liable if the person doing the (hypothetical) wrong had constitutional authority of the union. Under s 21, a union's executive can distance itself from subordinate officials and therefore escape any (hypothetical) liability in tort. Under s 22, unions' liability is limited to £250,000 in damages if there are over 100,000 members, or £10,000 if there are under 5,000 members, £50,000 up to 25,000 members, and £125,000 up to 100,000 members. But this goes for all torts, including personal injury or product liability. Defenders of the notion that there is no right to strike are therefore in a strange position of disavowing that under s 180 the 'right to take industrial action' has any meaning for common law, but assuming the ephemeral reference to tort in s 20 must be immutable.

11. The policy arguments for removing all economic tort liability from workers and unions can be summed up as follows: (1) the right to withhold one's labour in a good-faith trade dispute is necessary to ensure that workers' inequality of bargaining power is not completely hampered, and that the degradation of real wages in the UK does not continue, (2) there is little justification for saying that workers cannot withhold performance of a contract in a good-faith dispute when it is clear that commercial actors can do so in similar circumstances, and (3) the role of a court in a democratic society is to uphold a just system of rules, and a just society is one in which everyone can realise their potential, including by getting a fair day's wage for a fair day's work. Constraining the right to strike is incompatible with the historical view of tort law.

12. Although statute definitely creates a right to strike, the legitimate scope of a strike turns on whether it is a 'trade dispute'. Does that include political issues, and if so, when?

BBC v Hearn [1977] ICR 686

The BBC sought an injunction to restrain Tony Hearn, the general secretary of the Association of Broadcasting Staff (ABS, now part of BECTU), from stopping the broadcast of the FA Cup Final on 21 May 1977 to South Africa. Following a campaign by Peter Hain, of the Action Committee against Racialism, the ABS condemned the discrimination against black South Africans by the proto-fascist apartheid regime. The regime had been condemned by the United Nations General Assembly in Resolution 1598, On Race Conflict in South Africa 1961, after the International Confederation of Free Trade Unions called for economic sanctions. The regime's legislation included the Prohibition of Political Interference Act 1968 (banning mixed-race political parties), the Industrial Conciliation Act 1956 (banning mixed-race trade unions), the Reservation of Separate Amenities Act 1953 (banning different races using the same buses, public buildings, parks, and therefore playing together in sport teams) and the Immorality Act 1927 (banning sex between 'European' and 'non-European' people). The ABS said it would strike. But the BBC's Director-General, Sir Charles Curran, said the BBC did not agree with the demand not to broadcast to South Africa and on 16 May 1977 wrote that it would seek an injunction on the basis that this was not a 'trade dispute'. Pain J held that the proposed action was in contemplation or furtherance of a trade dispute. The Court of Appeal granted the injunction because the action was not formulated as a trade dispute.

Lord Denning MR:

... we turn to the definition of "a trade dispute."

...

It was suggested that those words related only to the contractual terms and conditions. Some of us said as much in *Cory Lighterage Ltd v Transport and General Workers' Union* [1973] 1 WLR 792, 814, 821. But that, I think, would be too limited. Terms and conditions of employment may include not only the contractual terms and conditions but those terms which are understood and applied by the parties in practice, or habitually, or by common consent, without ever being incorporated into the contract.

So I come to the words "in contemplation or furtherance of a trade dispute." There comes the rub. Was a trade dispute in contemplation? This has been discussed in the courts. As long ago as 1908 one of my predecessors, Cozens-Hardy MR in *Conway v Wade* [1908] 2 KB 844, 850, said:

> "The words 'in contemplation' are difficult. but they must embrace an act done by a person with a view to bringing about a trade dispute. If, for example, a minister of religion says to an employer, 'If you do not tomorrow morning discharge all your workmen who are not of my sect, I will call out all my co-religionists,' he may act with impunity."

That view was expressly rejected by the House of Lords [1909] AC 506. Lord Loreburn LC himself said he could not agree (p. 510). And Lord Shaw of Dunfermline, at p. 522, said that he "respectfully but totally" dissented from that view of the Master of the Rolls. Lord Shaw said:

> "... I think the argument was well founded that the contemplation of such a dispute must be the contemplation of something impending or likely to occur, and that they do not cover the case of coercive interference in which the intervener may have in his own mind that if he does not get his own way he will thereupon take ways and means to bring a trade dispute into existence."

Adapting those words to the illustration given by Cozens-Hardy MR it means that if shop stewards – who object to a man's religious belief – say to an employer, "Dismiss this man or we will go out on strike," – that is not a trade dispute. It is coercive interference with the man's freedom of religion and with the employer's business. Take the case which I put in the course of argument: if printers in a newspaper office were to say: "We don't like the article which you are going to publish about the Arabs – or the Jews – or on this or that political issue – you must withdraw it. If you do not do so, we are not going to print your paper." That is not a trade dispute. It is coercive action unconnected with a trade dispute. It is an unlawful interference with the freedom of the press. It is a self-created power of censorship. It does not become a trade dispute simply because the men propose to break their contracts of employment in doing it. Even if the men have a strong moral case, saying, "We have a conscientious objection to this article. We do not want to have anything to do with it," that does not turn it into a trade dispute. The dispute is about the publication of the article, not about the terms and conditions of employment.

Applying those considerations to this case, all that was happening was that the trade union, or its officers, were saying: "Stop this televising by the Indian Ocean satellite, stop it yourself. If you don't, we will ask our own people to stop it for you." That is not a trade dispute. They were hoping, I suppose, that the B.B.C. would give in; but, if they did not give in, they were going to order their members to stop the broadcast. That does not seem to me to be a trade dispute. To become a trade dispute, there would have to be something of the kind which was discussed in the course of argument before us: 'We would like you to consider putting a clause in the contract by which our members are not bound to take part in any broadcast which may be viewed in South Africa because we feel that it is obnoxious to their views and to the views of a great multitude of people. We would like that clause to be put in, or a condition of that kind to be understood.' If the B.B.C. refused to put in such a condition, or refused to negotiate about it, that might be a trade dispute. That, I think, is rather the way in which the judge approached this case. Towards the end of his judgment he said, putting it into the mouths of members through their union:

> "'We wish it established as a condition of employment that we shall not be required to take part in broadcasts to South Africa so long as the South African Government pursues its policy of apartheid.'"

If that request had been made, and not acceded to, there might be a trade dispute as to whether that should be a condition of the employment. But the matter never reached that stage at all. It never reached the stage of there being a trade dispute. There was not a trade dispute "in contemplation." It was coercive interference and nothing more. If that is the right view, it means that the trade union and its officers are not exempt from the ordinary rule of law – which is that men must honour their contracts, and must not unlawfully interfere with the performance of them.

Roskill LJ and **Scarman LJ** gave concurring opinions.

NOTES AND QUESTIONS

1. Lord Denning MR holds that going on strike would be breaking a contract because there was no term in the contract enabling BBC employees to object to broadcasts reaching South Africa. However, Lord Denning MR states it 'might be a trade dispute' if the BBC refused or would not negotiate after the union had said: 'We would like you to consider putting a clause in the contract by which our members are not bound to take part in any broadcast which may be viewed in South Africa because we feel that it is obnoxious to their views and to the views of a great multitude of people.'

2. The result of the 1977 FA Cup was that Manchester beat Liverpool 2 to 1. This close result reflected various factors such as talent, training, teamwork and good fortune.

3. Can a union make every political dispute a trade dispute by bargaining for the substance to be a contract term? *Express Newspapers Ltd Respondents v McShane* [1980] AC 672, 682 and 694 the House of Lords approved *BBC v Hearn*, quoting Lord Denning MR's hypothetical example. *Hadmor Productions Ltd v Hamilton* [1983] 1 AC 191, 227, approved *BBC v Hearn* again. On the other hand, in *Universe Tankships Inc of Monrovia v International Transport Workers Federation* [1983] 1 AC 366, 392 Lord Cross of Chelsea contradicted Lord Denning MR, saying: 'A trade union cannot turn a dispute which in reality has no connection with terms and conditions of employment into a dispute connected with terms and conditions of employment by insisting that the employer inserts appropriate terms

into the contracts of employment into which he enters.' Lord Diplock agreed, but Lords Russell, Scarman and Brandon said nothing on the point.

4.   After quoting Lord Cross in *The Universe Sentinel*, Lord Hoffmann in *P v NASUWT* (chapter 10(3) below) said on the question of making political issues a question of contract: 'The point does not seem to have surfaced in subsequent cases and your Lordships may therefore well leave it there' [34]. It was unnecessary to engage with for the decision. Here the House of Lords held that it was plainly part of a trade dispute for teachers to refuse to teach disruptive pupils: the majority held this was about the contract, while Lord Bingham preferred to say it concerned the employment relationship. Do you agree that every interaction with other people that a worker has, direct or indirectly, through his or her work forms a part of the employment contract?

5.   Whether political objects are a legitimate part of a union's bargaining strategy is a fundamental question for a democratic society. It is arguable that international treaties binding on the UK *already* form part of the implied terms of every contract: it would be a breach of an employee's reasonable expectations for any employer to violate, or support parties who violate, international law as much as statute. This position was approved by a unanimous Court of Appeal in *Saad v SS for the Home Department* [2001] EWCA Civ 2008, [15]–[16] as Lord Phillips MR approved the view that: 'It is a principle of legal policy that the municipal law should conform to public international law. The court, when considering, in relation to the facts of the instant case, which of the opposing constructions of the enactment would give effect to the legislative intention, should presume that the legislator intended to observe this principle.'

6.   Political issues constantly interact with the employment relationship, because people's work, and who they associate with, is so often central to their political identity. When are a union's political and economic objects ever separable? Consider the following cases:

   (i)   a union seeks to guarantee no worker handles supplies from Sweaty Inc, a company that refuses to give an enforceable undertaking that its suppliers use no child labour.

   (ii)   a union bargains for the employer stop exporting products to Yellowstan, a country which has a dire record of human rights abuse against trade unions and women.

   (iii) a union negotiates for all contracts of employment to include a right to restrain the company making any political or lobbying donations in the UK or abroad.

7.   If one accepts that a union should not be allowed to bargain for any contract terms, such as those above, it forces the conclusion that there is a radical constraint on the freedom of contract of employees, but not employers. It would expose a hypocritical position, that 'the freedom was all on the side of the big concern. … No freedom for the little man' or woman who is the worker: cf *George Mitchell (Chesterhall) Ltd v Finney Lock Seeds Ltd* [1982] EWCA Civ 5, per Lord Denning MR. Because that position cannot be justified, it must be rejected.

8.   The notion that some political (or economic) strikes are unlawful has an ironic quality: when the strike is a minor one, unions may tolerate legal defeat but win

the larger dispute in other ways. When the strike is a major one, where law might matter most, attempts to suppress become irrelevant. In the general strike of 1926 nearly the whole of industry shut down, as 1.7 million transport and industry workers stopped work. Coal miner pay had been cut from £6 to £3.90 since the end of World War One with another 13.5 per cent cut advocated by the Samuel Commission (1926). Workers demanded 'Not a penny off the pay, not a minute on the day.' In *National Sailors' and Firemen's Union v Reed* [1926] Ch 536, 539–49, Astbury J said: 'The so-called general strike called by the Trades Union Congress Council is illegal, and persons inciting or taking part in it are not protected by the Trade Disputes Act, 1906.' In his view they were acting unlawfully by taking secondary action. The judgment was irrelevant, as the government prepared for all-out confrontation with workers. Prime Minister Stanley Baldwin, *British Gazette* (5 May 1926) said: 'Constitutional Government is being attacked.' Nine days in, the TUC leadership realised that 'the government could hold out longer than the workers'. But a leading researcher at the TUC, Walter Milne-Bailey wrote that the general strike's defeat proved a 'brilliant failure': 'There has never been a more amazing display of labour solidarity and the effect of such a demonstration must inevitably be deep and enduring. Workers have learnt a new sense of their oneness and their power.' In the May 1929 general election, the Labour Party won more seats than any other party in Parliament, beating Baldwin.

9. Is the identity of your employer, or who owns the company, a legitimate concern for you and your employment contract? If the rules on consultation in chapter 11, or on transfers of undertakings in chapter 19, are anything to go by the answer must be 'yes'. However, in *Mercury Communications Ltd v Scott-Garner* [1984] ICR 74, Mercury Ltd sought an injunction against John Scott-Garner, president of the Post Office Engineering Union (POEU), to make the unions' members at British Telecommunications start connecting the Mercury system to the BT network. The BT Act 1981 enabled the Secretary of State to licence telecomms services to private companies and the POEU opposed this. Mercury Ltd was refused an injunction by Mervyn Davies J. But, represented by Alexander Irvine QC and Patrick Elias, it succeeded before Lord Donaldson MR. He said the union was 'mainly' pursuing a political not a trade dispute, not protecting members' job security. In retrospect, do you think that privatisation and liberalisation raised real employment concerns? On the other hand, today, BT is under a statutory duty to connect its network, or grant access to competitors: see Access Directive 2002/19/EC Arts 3–4 and the Communications Act 2003 s 87. Do you agree that, rather than manipulating the meaning of a contract or an employment relationship to constrain what is a trade dispute, a court should only find a strike is unlawful if it contravenes a statute?

10. While the definition of a 'trade dispute' circumscribes tort protection, four Acts specifically ban strikes in certain sectors. First, under the Police Act 1996 s 91, 'causing disaffection' is considered to include taking strike action. This dates from the Police Act 1919, which set up a system of alternative dispute resolution to settle police pay, after police strikes lasting from before the end of World War One into 1919. Statute did not stop the police force in 2008 from conducting a ballot to hold a, although the dispute was quickly resolved. Further, in 2012, at

least 16,000 police officers (during their days off) joined a protest along White-hall, watched by fellow police officers (who did not have that day off).

11. Second, the Criminal Justice and Public Order Act 1994 s 127 prohibits tak-ing 'any industrial action' that means 'withholding services as a prison officer', although this may be amended by the Secretary of State by order under s 127A. Like for the police, under s 128 the Secretary of State can make regulations estab-lishing a formal negotiation procedure to settle pay from time to time. Like for the police, alternative dispute mechanisms are used, and for prison workers that meant a Joint Industrial Relations Procedural Agreement, which contained a no-strike clause, until the union terminated the agreement in 2008. It argued that the 'Pay Review Body' (PRB) that would settle wages was no longer being listened to by the Secretary of State: the PRB recommended a 2.5 per cent wage rise, but the Secretary of State said this was unaffordable and only gave a 1.9 per cent wage rise. In 2007, the prison workers called and went on strike. In *Ministry of Justice v Prison Officers' Association* [2008] EWHC 239 Wyn Williams J upheld an application for an injunction against strike action to be considered. Apparently the Ministry of Justice should not be deprived of an equitable remedy (the injunc-tion) because it had not acted inequitably by ignoring the PRB recommendation: the union knew this was not binding. Moreover the union had not proven the alter-native dispute mechanism was an insufficient replacement for the right to strike. What do you think?

12. Third, the Merchant Shipping Act 1995 s 59 makes it a criminal offence to 'diso-bey lawful commands which are required to be obeyed at a time while the ship is at sea'. Contrast *Stilk v Myrick* [1809] EWHC KB J58. Given the advances in shipping technology and safety, is such a blanket ban still justified?

13. Fourth, the Army Act 1955 s 31 makes 'mutiny' an offence subject to court-martial, and this means to 'resist lawful authority in Her Majesty's forces', 'diso-bedience subversive of discipline' or 'avoiding any duty … against, the enemy'.

14. Also recall, at Government Communications HQ there is no union at all: see chapter 8(4).

(c) International Law

The right to strike is fundamental to international law. ICESCR 1966 Art 8(1)(d) requires that state parties ensure: 'The right to strike, provided that it is exercised in conformity with the laws of the particular country.' This was ratified by the UK and 166 countries in total, including all 47 countries party to the ECHR except Andorra. This makes the right explicit, though it was already clear in the Universal Declaration of Human Rights (UDHR) 1948 Art 23(4) that: 'Everyone has the right to form and to join trade unions for the protection of his interests.'

The right to strike is also in the ILO Freedom of Association and Protection of the Right to Organise Convention 1948 Convention (c 87), ratified by the UK and 154 coun-tries in total. Article 3(1) says worker organisations 'shall have the right … to organise their administration and activities and to formulate their programmes'. While, like the UDHR 1948, it does not spell out the right to strike, in preparatory discussions the debate was merely whether to codify the right to strike's scope and exceptions. At the ILO Conference Committee on Freedom of Association in 1947, India proposed to exempt police and armed forces from 'the field of application of freedom of association, because they were not authorised to take part in collective negotiations and had not the right to strike'. The worker representative from France objected on the ground that 'public employees should enjoy full freedom of association': ILO, *Background document for the Tripartite Meeting* (Geneva, 23–25 February 2015) para 8. Hence, the amendment was rejected, and the right to strike was not mentioned purely because of lack of agreement on its scope. The ILO Committee of Experts and the Committee on Freedom of Association has consistently interpreted ILO Convention 87 to include the right to strike: B Gernigon, A Odero and H Guido, 'ILO Principles Concerning the Right to Strike' (1998) 137 *International Labour Review* 441.

In the ECHR, the right to strike is in Art 11: 'Everyone has the right to freedom of peaceful assembly and to freedom of association with others, including the right to form and to join trade unions for the protection of his interests.' Protection of one's interests includes the right to strike, but again its scope and exceptions were debated. The European Social Charter 1961 Art 6(4), issued by the Council of Europe and ratified by the UK, explicitly protects 'the right of workers and employers to collective action in cases of conflicts of interest including the right to strike, subject ... to collective agreements'. The European Court of Human Rights finally acknowledged the right, but set the minimum standard low, to afford outlier countries like the UK or Turkey a 'margin of appreciation'.

RMT v United Kingdom [2014] ECHR 366

RMT claimed that UK law failed to adequately protect the right to strike under ECHR Art 11 by suppressing secondary action, and through unduly complex ballot requirements. First, Jarvis plc had two subsidiaries with 1,200 staff and 569 RMT members: Fastline Ltd and Jarvis Rail Ltd. In August 2007, Fastline Ltd transferred 20 employees to Hydrex Equipment (UK) Ltd with terms preserved under the Transfer of Undertakings (Protection of Employment) Regulations 2006, though other Hydrex workers were paid less. In March 2009, Hydrex said it would reduce ex-Fastline workers' salaries by 36–40 per cent, and RMT organised a strike, with pickets at places where the workers performed their jobs, rather than Hydrex Ltd's offices. Because the transferred workers were a small minority in Hydrex Ltd, RMT wanted to bring all Jarvis plc workers out in support of the strike, and claimed it would have been much more effective if so. Instead, it settled (but Hydrex Ltd and Jarvis plc went insolvent anyway by 2011). Second, in June 2009 RMT called a strike against EDF Energy Powerlink Ltd, which operated electricity on the London Underground, after pay negotiations failed. EDF Ltd sought and received an injunction in October 2009 from Blake J on the ground that RMT gave notice of a category of workers as 'Engineer/Technician', while the company said it did not recognise the 'technician' group (only more specific job descriptions), and therefore failed to duly notify details of who was voting in the ballot under TULRCA 1992 s 226A. This dispute was, however, settled. The European Court of Human Rights, Fourth Section, held there was a right to strike, but the UK's legislation on secondary action was lawful by virtue of the margin of appreciation under the Convention. In the EDF case, it refused to consider the merits because the dispute had on the facts already been resolved.

Judgment:

III. RELEVANT INTERNATIONAL LAW

26. In support of its application, the applicant included references to other international legal instruments, and the interpretation given to them by the competent organs. The most relevant and detailed of these materials are referred to below.

A. International Labour Organisation Conventions

27. While there is no provision in the Conventions adopted by the International Labour Organisation expressly conferring a right to strike, both the Committee on Freedom of Association and the Committee of Experts on the Application of Convention and Recommendations (the "Committee of Experts") have progressively developed a number of principles on the right to strike, based on Articles 3 and 10 of the Freedom of Association and Protection of the Right to Organise Convention, 1948 (No. 87) (summarised in Giving globalisation a human face, International Labour Office, 2012, at paragraph 117). This Convention was ratified by the United Kingdom on 27 June 1949.

1. Concerning notice requirements

28. The Committee of Experts has commented several times upon the notice requirements for industrial action in the United Kingdom. The applicant referred to the following statement, adopted in 2008:

> "In its previous comments, the Committee had taken note of comments made by the TUC to the effect that the notice requirements for an industrial action to be protected by immunity were unjustifiably burdensome. The Committee notes that according to the Government, a number of measures have already been taken to simplify sections 226–235 of the TULRA and 104–109 of the 1995 Order; moreover, as part of a plan published in December 2006 to simplify aspects of employment law, the Government explicitly invited trade unions to come forward with their ideas to simplify trade union law further. Since then, the Government has held discussions with the TUC to examine their ideas to simplify aspects of the law on industrial action ballots and notices. These discussions are ongoing. The Committee notes that in its latest comments, the TUC notes that there has been no progress in this reform. **The Committee requests the Government to indicate in its next report progress made in this regard.**"

...

2. Concerning secondary action

30. The Committee of Experts has taken the following view:

> "With regard to so-called 'sympathy' strikes, the Committee considers that a general prohibition of this form of strike action could lead to abuse, particularly in the context of globalization characterized by increasing interdependence and the internationalization of production, and that workers should be able to take such action, provided that the initial strike they are supporting is itself lawful."

(*Giving globalization a human face*, op. cit., at paragraph 125).

31. The Committee on Freedom of Association also considers this form of industrial action to be protected by international labour law:

> "A general prohibition of sympathy strikes could lead to abuse and workers should be able to take such action provided the initial strike they are supporting is itself lawful."
> "A ban on strike action not linked to a collective dispute to which the employee or union is a party is contrary to the principles of freedom of association."

(Freedom of Association, *Digest of the decisions and principles of the Freedom of Association Committee of the Governing Body of the ILO*, Fifth (revised) edition, International Labour Office, 2006, paragraphs 534 and 538).
    …

33. It appears that the Committee of Experts did not take a definitive position on the ban until its 1995 observation concerning the United Kingdom, when it observed as follows:

> "The Committee draws the Government's attention to paragraph 168 of its 1994 General Survey on Freedom of Association and Collective Bargaining where it indicates that a general prohibition on sympathy strikes could lead to abuse and that workers should be able to take such action, provided the initial strike they are supporting is itself lawful. The lifting of immunity opens such industrial action to be actionable in tort and therefore would constitute a serious impediment to the workers' right to carry out sympathy strikes."

It has maintained this view since, stating in its most recent review of the situation (2012 observation):

> "Immunities in respect of civil liability for strikes and other industrial action (sections 223 and 224 of the TULRA): In its previous comments, the Committee had noted that according to the TUC, due to the decentralized nature of the industrial relations system, it was essential for workers to be able to take action against employers who are easily able to undermine union action by complex corporate structures, transferring work, or hiving off companies. The Committee generally raised the need to protect the right of workers to take industrial action in relation to matters which affect them even though, in certain cases, the direct employer may not be party to the dispute, and to participate in sympathy strikes provided the initial strike they are supporting is itself lawful. The Committee takes note of the Government indication that: (1) its position remains as set out in its report for 2006–08, that the rationale has not changed and that it therefore has no plans to change the law in this area; and (2) this issue forms part of a matter brought before the ECHR by the National Union of Rail, Maritime and Transport Workers (RMT) and that the Court has yet to consider the case. The Committee recalls the previous concern it raised that the globalization of the economy and the delocalization of work centres may have a severe impact on the right of workers' organizations to organize their activities in a manner so as to defend effectively their members' interests should lawful industrial action be too restrictively defined. In these circumstances, the Committee once again requests the Government to review sections 223 and 224 of the TULRA, in full consultation with the social partners, and to provide further information in its next report on the outcome of these consultations." [4]

(Report of the Committee of Experts to the International Labour Conference, 102nd Session, 2013, ILC.102/III(1A), pp. 195-196).
    …

(d) The Court's assessment

...

(ii) Lawfulness and legitimacy of the interference

79. There was no dispute between the parties that the interference was prescribed by law. The Court agrees.

80. As to the aim of the interference, the applicant argued that it found no legitimation in Article 11 § 2. It clearly did not concern national security or public safety, the prevention of disorder or crime, or the protection of health or morals. As for the remaining aim recognised as legitimate, namely the "protection of the rights and freedoms of others", the applicant's argument was that it would be illogical to restrict the right to strike on account of the impact of such action on the employer. The very purpose of strike action is to have a strong impact on the employer's position, to induce the employer to meet the demands of labour. It would be erroneous to allow this to serve as a justification for curbing the right to strike. ...

...

82. ... As the Government have argued, by its nature secondary action may well have much broader ramifications than primary action. It has the potential to impinge upon the rights of persons not party to the industrial dispute, to cause broad disruption within the economy and to affect the delivery of services to the public. Accordingly, the Court is satisfied that in banning secondary action, Parliament pursued the legitimate aim of protecting the rights and freedoms of others, not limited to the employer side in an industrial dispute.

(iii) Necessity in a democratic society

83. It remains to be determined whether the statutory ban on secondary industrial action, as it affected the ability of the applicant to protect the interests of its Hydrex members, can be regarded as being "necessary in a democratic society". To be so considered, it must be shown that the interference complained of corresponds to a "pressing social need", that the reasons given by the national authorities to justify it are relevant and sufficient and that it is proportionate to the legitimate aim pursued.

84. The Court will consider first the applicant's argument that the right to take strike action must be regarded as an essential element of trade union freedom under Article 11, so that to restrict it would be to impair the very essence of freedom of association. It recalls that it has already decided a number of cases in which restrictions on industrial action were found to have given rise to violations of Article 11 (see for example *Karaçay v. Turkey*, no. 6615/03, 27 March 2007 ... *Enerji Yapı-Yol Sen v Turkey*, no. 68959/01, 21 April 2009). The applicant placed great emphasis on the last of these judgments, in which the term "indispensable corollary" was used in relation to the right to strike, linking it to the right to organise (*Enerji*, at §24). It should however be noted that the judgment was here adverting to the position adopted by the supervisory bodies of the ILO rather than evolving the interpretation of Article 11 by conferring a privileged status on the right to strike. More generally, what the above-mentioned cases illustrate is that strike action is clearly protected by Article 11. The Court therefore does not discern any need in the present case to determine whether the taking of industrial action should now be accorded the status of an essential element of the Article 11 guarantee.

85. What the circumstances of this case show is that the applicant in fact exercised two of the elements of freedom of association that have been identified as essential, namely the right

for a trade union to seek to persuade the employer to hear what it has to say on behalf of its members, and the right to engage in collective bargaining. The strike by its Hydrex members was part of that exercise, and while it did not achieve its aim, it was not in vain either since it led the company to revise its offer, which the applicant then commended to its members. Although the Government criticised the applicant for supporting the revised offer at the time and then reversing its stance in the present proceedings, the Court recognises that the applicant is bound to respect its members' negative vote. Yet the fact that the process of collective bargaining and industrial action, including strike action against the employer of the union members who were the subject of the dispute, did not lead to the outcome desired by the applicant and its members does not mean that the exercise of their Article 11 rights was illusory. The right to collective bargaining has not been interpreted as including a "right" to a collective agreement (see in this respect §158 of *Demir and Baykara* judgment, where the Court observed that the absence of any obligation on the authorities to actually enter into a collective agreement was not part of the case). Nor does the right to strike imply a right to prevail. As the Court has often stated, what the Convention requires is that under national law trade unions should be enabled, in conditions not at variance with Article 11, to strive for the protection of their members' interests (*Demir and Baykara*, §141; more recently *Sindicatul "Păstorul cel Bun" v. Romania* [GC], no. 2330/09, §34, 9 July 2013). This the applicant and its members involved in the dispute were largely able to do in the present case.

86. In previous trade union cases, the Court has stated that regard must be had to the fair balance to be struck between the competing interests of the individual and of the community as a whole. Since achieving a proper balance between the interests of labour and management involves sensitive social and political issues, the Contracting States must be afforded a margin of appreciation as to how trade-union freedom and protection of the occupational interests of union members may be secured. In its most recent restatement of this point, and referring to the high degree of divergence it observed between the domestic systems in this field, the Grand Chamber, considered that the margin should be a wide one (*Sindicatul "Păstorul cel Bun"*, cited above, §133). The applicant relied heavily on the *Demir and Baykara* judgment, in which the Court considered that the respondent State should be allowed only a limited margin (see §119 of the judgment). The Court would point out, however, that the passage in question appears in the part of the judgment examining a very far-reaching interference with freedom of association, one that intruded into its inner core, namely the dissolution of a trade union. It is not to be understood as narrowing decisively and definitively the domestic authorities' margin of appreciation in relation to regulating, through normal democratic processes, the exercise of trade union freedom within the social and economic framework of the country concerned. ...

87. If a legislative restriction strikes at the core of trade union activity, a lesser margin of appreciation is to be recognised to the national legislature and more is required to justify the proportionality of the resultant interference, in the general interest, with the exercise of trade union freedom. Conversely, if it is not the core but a secondary or accessory aspect of trade union activity that is affected, the margin is wider and the interference is, by its nature, more likely to be proportionate as far as its consequences for the exercise of trade union freedom are concerned.

88. As to the nature and extent of the interference suffered in the present case by the applicant in the exercise of its trade union freedom, the Court considers that it was not as invasive as the applicant would have it. What the facts of the case reveal is that the applicant led a strike, albeit on a limited scale and with limited results. It was its wish to escalate the strike, through the threatened or actual involvement of hundreds of its members at Jarvis, another, separate company not at all involved in the trade dispute in question, that was frustrated. ...

89. As for the object of the interference in issue in the present case, the extracts from the debates in Parliament preceding the passage of the Employment Act 1980 make clear the legislative intention to strike a new balance in industrial relations, in the interests of the broader economy, by curbing what was a very broad right to take secondary action. A decade later, the Government of the day considered that even in its more limited form secondary action posed a risk to the economy and to inward investment in the country's economic activity. As a matter of policy it considered that restricting industrial action to primary strikes would achieve a more acceptable balance within the British economy. The Government have reiterated that position in the present proceedings. That assessment was sharply contested at the time by the opposition in Parliament, and is rejected by the applicant as grounded in animus towards trade unions rather than any clear evidence of direct damage to the economy. Yet the subject-matter in this case is certainly related to the social and economic strategy of the respondent State. In this regard the Court has usually allowed a wide margin of appreciation since, by virtue of their direct knowledge of their society and its needs, the national authorities, and in particular the democratically elected parliaments, are in principle better placed than the international judge to appreciate what is in the public interest on social or economic grounds and what are the legislative measures best suited for the conditions in their country in order to implement the chosen social, economic or industrial policy (see among many authorities *Stummer v. Austria* [GC], no. 37452/02, §89, ECHR 2011).

. . .

98. The foregoing analysis of the interpretative opinions emitted by the competent bodies set up under the most relevant international instruments mirrors the conclusion reached on the comparative material before the Court, to wit that with its outright ban on secondary industrial action, the respondent State finds itself at the most restrictive end of a spectrum of national regulatory approaches on this point and is out of line with a discernible international trend calling for a less restrictive approach. The significance that such a conclusion may have for the Court's assessment in a given case was explained in the *Demir and Baykara* judgment in the following terms (at §85):

> "The consensus emerging from specialised international instruments and from the practice of Contracting States may constitute a relevant consideration for the Court when it interprets the provisions of the Convention in specific cases."

The Grand Chamber's statement reflects the distinct character of the Court's review compared with that of the supervisory procedures of the ILO and the European Social Charter. The specialised international monitoring bodies operating under those procedures have a different standpoint, shown in the more general terms used to analyse the ban on secondary action. In contrast, it is not the Court's task to review the relevant domestic law in the abstract, but to determine whether the manner in which it actually affected the applicant infringed the latter's rights under Article 11 of the Convention (see *Von Hannover v. Germany* (no. 2) [GC], nos. 40660/08 and 60641/08, §116, ECHR 2012; also *Kart v. Turkey* [GC], no. 8917/05, §§ 85–87, ECHR 2009 (extracts)). The applicant as well as the third parties dwelt on the possible effect of the ban in various hypothetical scenarios, which could go as far as to exclude any form of industrial action at all if the workers directly concerned were not in a position to take primary action, thereby, unlike in the present case, striking at the very substance of trade union freedom. They also considered that the ban could make it easy for employers to exploit the law to their advantage through resort to various legal stratagems, such as de-localising work-centres, outsourcing work to other companies and adopting complex corporate structures in order to transfer work to separate legal entities or to hive off companies (see paragraphs 33 and 37 above). In short, trade unions could find themselves severely hampered in the performance of their legitimate, normal activities in protecting their members' interests. These alleged, far-reaching negative effects of the statutory ban do not however arise in the situation at Hydrex. The Court's review is bounded by the facts submitted for examination in the case. ...

Judges Nicolaou, Mahoney, Vehabović and **Araci** joined unreservedly.

Joint concurring opinion of Judges Ziemele, Hirvelä and Bianku:

1. ... the Convention was conceived as a treaty on civil and political rights. However, the division between the so-called three generations of human rights has been rightly abandoned since then (see the 1993 Vienna Declaration and Programme of Action adopted by the World Conference on Human Rights). ...

2. ... At this juncture we should say, however, that we are not impressed with the argument that, merely because Parliament has adopted a particular general measure, the Court may not overrule it, as it were. ... For us, the solution that the Court adopts is not so much about the general measure as such, it is about the character of the right concerned or an aspect thereof. The assessment of the general measure depends on the character of the right in issue. Furthermore, it is about the prejudice sustained by the applicant by virtue of the application of the general measure. The right to strike is not absolute. There are already a number of limitations applicable in view of the general public interest. In the case at hand, we are even further from the core issue in that secondary or sympathy strikes are not necessarily or directly relevant to the rights or interests of those engaged in such strikes.

3. Given the nature of such strikes and the implications for economic policy considerations, the issue is best dealt with as part of the on-going dialogue between the specialised monitoring bodies in the field of social and labour rights. That kind of softer process allows the respondent State to continue examining its economic options. A judgment of the European Court of Human Rights finding a violation would have the effect of putting an abrupt end to such a process. However, it should be pointed out that if the very essence of the applicant's right to strike were affected, there would be no doubt as to what the Court's decision would be.

Concurring opinion of Judge Wojtyczek:

1. ... I disagree with the methodology of the interpretation of the Convention applied by the majority. In my view, it would have been more correct to say that Article 11 is not applicable in this case and that therefore there has been no violation of this provision. ...
    ...

8. The interpretation of treaty provisions pertaining to social rights has to take into account the specific nature of those rights. States have devised specific mechanisms for monitoring the implementation of social rights without having to entrust the adjudication of disputes concerning social rights to international courts. States also make use of optional instruments which leave them some choice as to their undertakings, such as the European Social Charter. Some States have clearly expressed their reluctance to undertake obligations in the field of social rights. An extensive interpretation of existing treaties pertaining to social rights may have a chilling effect on those States when they consider entering into new treaties in this field.
    The right to strike has further peculiarities. The interpretation of the scope of freedom of association under Convention No. 87 is not uncontroversial, as employers' organisations have contested the idea that the freedom to form trade unions encompasses the right to strike. It is important to bear in mind in this context that the right to strike may encroach on the human rights of other persons and have an impact on the national economy. Therefore, the interpretation of international treaty provisions pertaining to the right to strike should take into account

the various conflicting rights and the legitimate private and public interests at stake. Similarly, national legislation implementing the right to strike has to achieve a proper balance between different rights and interests. Broadening the scope of protection of the right to strike may entail the narrowing of the protection of other fundamental human rights.

9. The majority in the present case states that the Court should not adopt an interpretation of the scope of freedom of association of trade unions that is much narrower than that which prevails in international law. I am not persuaded by this argument. Firstly, the scope of trade union freedom may differ from one treaty to another even if the wording of the relevant provisions is similar. Secondly, as pointed out above, the nature and scope of State obligations pertaining to sympathy strikes have not been clearly defined in international law. Thirdly, the different treaty rules protecting the right to strike have not been accepted by all the 47 High Contracting Parties to the Convention for the Protection of Human Rights and Fundamental Freedoms.

   The majority also invokes the fact that many European States have long accepted secondary industrial action as a lawful form of trade union action. For my part, I note that some European States take the opposite view. Not only is there no European consensus on this issue but, moreover, one can observe a strong resistance to recognising sympathy strikes. In any event, the fact that a majority of States adopts a higher standard of protection of a right is not a sufficient argument for imposing this standard on a minority of States which rejects it.

10. To conclude, in my view, the analysis of international law does not support the opinion that Article 11 of the Convention for the Protection of Human Rights Fundamental Freedoms should be interpreted in such a way that it encompasses the right to sympathy strikes. To hold otherwise exposes the Court to the risk of being legitimately criticised for judicial activism.

NOTES AND QUESTIONS

1.   The Fourth Section holds that 'strike action is clearly protected by Article 11' but refuses to say whether it is an 'essential element' [84]. This seems to be because the Court does not want to decide that suppression of secondary action violates Art 11. Given there are exceptions in Art 11(2) anyway, what difference would it make if the right to strike were an 'essential element', rather than 'clearly protected'?

2.   While at times the Court's opinion seems long-winded and poorly structured, it comes to a crucial point at [98] that it could be 'striking at the very substance of trade union freedom' if workers were not in a position to take 'primary action' if companies were structured so as to undermine it. It says, however, it cannot decide that point because Hydrex Ltd was not part of Jarvis plc's corporate group and the Court 'is bounded by the facts submitted'. Do you agree that strikes against legal entities that are part of the same economic entity cannot be considered 'secondary' action? See chapter 10(2) below.

3.   The Court ultimately decides the UK's law is within a 'margin of appreciation' which must be wide, because 'democratically elected parliaments, are in principle better placed than the international judge to appreciate what is in the public interest on social or economic grounds'. Although the UK is at the 'most restrictive end of a spectrum' in repressing the right to strike, the Court would not act. What defines this 'spectrum'?

4.   While the concurring opinion of Judges Ziemele, Hirvelä and Bianku says that it has abandoned the illusory division between civil and political rights from

economic and social rights, the European Court of Human Rights has been very slow to accept the legitimacy of labour rights. In *Schmidt and Dahlstrom v Sweden* [1976] ECHR 1, [36] the Court said that although 'the Convention safeguards freedom to protect the occupational interests of trade union members by trade union action' and 'a right to strike represents without any doubt one of the most important of these means, but there are others. Such a right, which is not expressly enshrined in Article 11 (art. 11), may be subject under national law to regulation of a kind that limits its exercise in certain instances.' With *RMT v UK* it is clear that position has changed, so that limits are not merely dependent on national law, but it would appear that the ECHR is probably not going to be a major engine of change.

5. The express acknowledgement of the right to strike in *RMT v UK* was preceded by two Turkish cases. In *Demir and Baykara v Turkey* [2008] ECHR 1345, Demir and Baykara (member and president of the civil servants' union, Tüm Bel Sen) brought a claim to enforce provisions of a collective agreement from 1993. The Court of Cassation held the union had no authority to enter a collective agreement twice. On application to it, the European Court of Human Rights' Grand Chamber held Art 11 was violated. It emphasised that 'the exceptions set out in Article 11 are to be construed strictly; only convincing and compelling reasons can justify restrictions on such parties' freedom of association' [119]. Turkey had demonstrated no 'pressing social need' for denying capacity to the union. Then, in *Enerji Yapi-Yol Sen v Turkey* [2009] ECHR 2251 the Prime Minister's Public Service Policy Directorate banned a strike by the claimant union. The European Court of Human Rights, albeit with some delay, held this was an unjustified interference in the right to strike, protected by Art 11, saying a 'strike, which allows a trade union to make its voice heard, is an important aspect for trade union members in protecting their interests'. It then said the 'Court recognizes that the right to strike is not absolute' (author's translation). But an absolute ban could not be justified.

6. The limits of the right to strike under the ECHR were considered in *Hrvatski Lijecnicki sindikat v Croatia* [2014] ECHR 1337. Medical practitioners claimed that Croatia had unlawfully banned a strike announced in 2005. This was to pressure the government to adopt an annex to a health care sector collective agreement. The Croatian courts banned this on the pretext that not all unions had made the collective agreement. The European Court of Human Rights held the ban was an unlawful violation of Art 11, because while it might have pursued a legitimate aim of protecting the 'rights of others', the action was disproportionate. Though pursuing a principle of parity in collective bargaining could be a legitimate aim, the action was not 'capable to justify depriving a trade union for three years and eight months of the most powerful instrument to protect occupational interests of its members' [59]. Judge Pinto de Albuquerque gave an emphatic concurring opinion, stressing that the right to strike was fundamental to international law. When, if ever, should it be justified to restrict the right of medical professionals to strike?

7. The Court has now frequently relied on ILO Conventions, and referred to the Committee of Experts. But does the ILO itself go far enough? The ILO was

originally proposed to be a body with only government and employee representation. Superficially it may seem fair to grant equal voice to capital and labour. But from the viewpoint of a democratic society, this seems skewed. Trade unions represent the interests of billions of people. Employer associations represent people who are billionaires. In a democratic society, should international institutions such as the ILO represent people, or continue to be weighted according to groups that had historically significant social power?

(d) European Union

While the right to strike is 'clearly protected' by the ECHR Art 11, it is enshrined in the Charter of Fundamental Rights of the European Union 2000 Art 28. This says workers have the right 'to take collective action to defend their interests, including strike action'. The UK did not sign up to the Charter, although this seems irrelevant because it was a codification of existing human rights principles acknowledged in Court of Justice case law, and it continues to be used to interpret legislation for all member states. The Treaty on European Union does not explicitly state there is a right to strike rather than referring generally in Art 2 to 'freedom, democracy, equality, the rule of law and respect for human rights' and 'pluralism, non-discrimination, tolerance, justice, solidarity'. The Treaty on the Functioning of the European Union Art 153 sets out social or labour policy fields in which the EU may legislate, and Art 153(4) says that 'provisions adopted' under this 'shall not prevent any Member State from maintaining or introducing more stringent protective measures compatible with the Treaties'. However, Art 153(5) says that: 'The provisions of this Article shall not apply to pay, the right of association, the right to strike or the right to impose lock-outs.' This probably refers to the right of the EU to legislate, because pay, collective bargaining and action were seen as sensitive, just as Art 153(4) says that other labour legislation 'must not significantly affect the financial equilibrium' of member states' social security systems.

The first EU cases to deal expressly with the right to strike were, however, seen as a disgrace by European labour lawyers. While acknowledging the right, the Court of Justice attempted to place business rights above. This triggered extensive criticism and legislation.

The Rosella or *ITF v Viking Line ABP* (2007) C-438/05

Viking Line ABP, a Finnish company that operated *The Rosella*, claimed the International Transport Workers Federation (ITF) violated its right of establishment in the Treaty on the Functioning of the European Union Art 49 (then TEC Art 43) by striking. Viking Line ABP renounced a Finnish collective agreement, and put new staff on Estonian contracts, by changing the flag of its ships from Finnish to Estonian. The Finnish Seamen's Union, a member of ITF, headquartered in London, joined with other ITF unions to blockade Viking Line ABP's ships. The company applied to the English High Court for an injunction, which was granted. However, the Court of Appeal quashed the injunction and instead referred the case for a preliminary ruling, as it affected 'the fundamental rights of workers to take industrial action', [2005] EWCA Civ 1299, [22] per Waller LJ. The Court of Justice held that although the right to strike was a fundamental human right, it was a disproportionate infringement of the business's right of establishment.

Grand Chamber:

The first question

32 By its first question, the national court is essentially asking whether Article [49 TFEU] must be interpreted as meaning that collective action initiated by a trade union or a group of trade unions against an undertaking in order to induce that undertaking to enter into a collective agreement, the terms of which are liable to deter it from exercising freedom of establishment, falls outside the scope of that article.

...

39 ... the Danish Government submits that the right of association, the right to strike and the right to impose lock-outs fall outside the scope of the fundamental freedom laid down in Article [49 TFEU] since, in accordance with Article [157(5) TFEU] the Community does not have competence to regulate those rights.

40 In that respect it is sufficient to point out that, even if, in the areas which fall outside the scope of the Community's competence, the Member States are still free, in principle, to lay down the conditions governing the existence and exercise of the rights in question, the fact remains that, when exercising that competence, the Member States must nevertheless comply with Community law (see, by analogy, in relation to social security, Case C-120/95 *Decker* [1998] ECR I-1831, paragraphs 22 and 23, and Case C-158/96 *Kohll* [1998] ECR I-1931, paragraphs 18 and 19; in relation to direct taxation, Case C-334/02 *Commission v France* [2004] ECR I-2229, paragraph 21, and Case C-446/03 *Marks & Spencer* [2005] ECR I-10837, paragraph 29).

41 Consequently, the fact that Article 137 EC does not apply to the right to strike or to the right to impose lock-outs is not such as to exclude collective action such as that at issue in the main proceedings from the application of Article 43 EC.

...

44 Although the right to take collective action, including the right to strike, must therefore be recognised as a fundamental right which forms an integral part of the general principles of Community law the observance of which the Court ensures, the exercise of that right may none the less be subject to certain restrictions. As is reaffirmed by Article 28 of the Charter of Fundamental Rights of the European Union, those rights are to be protected in accordance with Community law and national law and practices. In addition, as is apparent from paragraph 5 of this judgment, under Finnish law the right to strike may not be relied on, in particular, where the strike is *contra bonos mores* or is prohibited under national law or Community law.

45 In that regard, the Court has already held that the protection of fundamental rights is a legitimate interest which, in principle, justifies a restriction of the obligations imposed by Community law, even under a fundamental freedom guaranteed by the Treaty, such as the free movement of goods (see Case C-112/00 *Schmidberger* [2003] ECR I-5659, paragraph 74) or freedom to provide services (see Case C-36/02 *Omega* [2004] ECR I-9609, paragraph 35).

46 However, in *Schmidberger* and *Omega*, the Court held that the exercise of the fundamental rights at issue, that is, freedom of expression and freedom of assembly and respect for human dignity, respectively, does not fall outside the scope of the provisions of the Treaty and considered that such exercise must be reconciled with the requirements relating to rights protected

under the Treaty and in accordance with the principle of proportionality (see, to that effect, *Schmidberger*, paragraph 77, and *Omega*, paragraph 36).

47 It follows from the foregoing that the fundamental nature of the right to take collective action is not such as to render Article 43 EC inapplicable to the collective action at issue in the main proceedings.

48 Finally, FSU and ITF submit that the Court's reasoning in *Albany* must be applied by analogy to the case in the main proceedings, since certain restrictions on freedom of establishment and freedom to provide services are inherent in collective action taken in the context of collective negotiations.

49 In that regard, it should be noted that in paragraph 59 of Albany, having found that certain restrictions of competition are inherent in collective agreements between organisations representing employers and workers, the Court nevertheless held that the social policy objectives pursued by such agreements would be seriously undermined if management and labour were subject to Article 85(1) of the EC Treaty (now, Article 81(1) EC) when seeking jointly to adopt measures to improve conditions of work and employment.

50 The Court inferred from this, in paragraph 60 of Albany, that agreements concluded in the context of collective negotiations between management and labour in pursuit of such objectives must, by virtue of their nature and purpose, be regarded as falling outside the scope of Article [106 TFEU].

51 The Court must point out, however, that that reasoning cannot be applied in the context of the fundamental freedoms set out in Title III of the Treaty.

...

The second question

56 By that question, the referring court is asking in essence whether Article [49 TFEU] is such as to confer rights on a private undertaking which may be relied on against a trade union or an association of trade unions.

...

58 ... the Court has ruled, first, that the fact that certain provisions of the Treaty are formally addressed to the Member States does not prevent rights from being conferred at the same time on any individual who has an interest in compliance with the obligations thus laid down, and, second, that the prohibition on prejudicing a fundamental freedom laid down in a provision of the Treaty that is mandatory in nature, applies in particular to all agreements intended to regulate paid labour collectively (see, to that effect, Case 43/75 *Defrenne* [1976] ECR 455, paragraphs 31 and 39).

59 Such considerations must also apply to Article [49 TFEU] which lays down a fundamental freedom.

...

The third to tenth questions

67 By those questions, which can be examined together, the national court is essentially asking the Court of Justice whether collective action such as that at issue in the main proceedings constitutes a restriction within the meaning of Article [49 TFEU] and, if so, to what extent such a restriction may be justified.

The existence of restrictions

68 The Court must first point out, as it has done on numerous occasions, that freedom of establishment constitutes one of the fundamental principles of the Community and that the provisions of the Treaty guaranteeing that freedom have been directly applicable since the end of the transitional period. Those provisions secure the right of establishment in another Member State not merely for Community nationals but also for the companies or firms referred to in Article [54 TFEU] (Case 81/87 *Daily Mail and General Trust* [1988] ECR 5483, paragraph 15).

...

72 In the present case, first, it cannot be disputed that collective action such as that envisaged by FSU has the effect of making less attractive, or even pointless, as the national court has pointed out, Viking's exercise of its right to freedom of establishment, inasmuch as such action prevents both Viking and its subsidiary, Viking Eesti, from enjoying the same treatment in the host Member State as other economic operators established in that State.

73 Secondly, collective action taken in order to implement ITF's policy of combating the use of flags of convenience, which seeks, primarily, as is apparent from ITF's observations, to prevent shipowners from registering their vessels in a State other than that of which the beneficial owners of those vessels are nationals, must be considered to be at least liable to restrict Viking's exercise of its right of freedom of establishment.

...

Justification of the restrictions

75 It is apparent from the case-law of the Court that a restriction on freedom of establishment can be accepted only if it pursues a legitimate aim compatible with the Treaty and is justified by overriding reasons of public interest. But even if that were the case, it would still have to be suitable for securing the attainment of the objective pursued and must not go beyond what is necessary in order to attain it (see, inter alia, Case C-55/94 *Gebhard* [1995] ECR I-4165, paragraph 37, and *Bosman*, paragraph 104).

76 ITF, supported, in particular, by the German Government, Ireland and the Finnish Government, maintains that the restrictions at issue in the main proceedings are justified since they are necessary to ensure the protection of a fundamental right recognised under Community law and their objective is to protect the rights of workers, which constitutes an overriding reason of public interest.

77 In that regard, it must be observed that the right to take collective action for the protection of workers is a legitimate interest which, in principle, justifies a restriction of one of the fundamental freedoms guaranteed by the Treaty (see, to that effect, *Schmidberger*, paragraph 74) and that the protection of workers is one of the overriding reasons of public interest recognised by the Court (see, inter alia, Joined Cases C-369/96 and C-376/96 *Arblade and Others* [1999] ECR I-8453, paragraph 36 ...).

...

79 Since the Community has thus not only an economic but also a social purpose, the rights under the provisions of the Treaty on the free movement of goods, persons, services and capital must be balanced against the objectives pursued by social policy, which include, as is clear from the first paragraph of Article [156 TFEU], inter alia, improved living and working conditions, so as to make possible their harmonisation while improvement is being maintained, proper social protection and dialogue between management and labour.

80 In the present case, it is for the national court to ascertain whether the objectives pursued by FSU and ITF by means of the collective action which they initiated concerned the protection of workers.

81 First, as regards the collective action taken by FSU, even if that action – aimed at protecting the jobs and conditions of employment of the members of that union liable to be adversely affected by the reflagging of the *Rosella* – could reasonably be considered to fall, at first sight, within the objective of protecting workers, such a view would no longer be tenable if it were established that the jobs or conditions of employment at issue were not jeopardised or under serious threat.

   ...

84 If, following that examination, the national court came to the conclusion that, in the case before it, the jobs or conditions of employment of the FSU's members liable to be adversely affected by the reflagging of the Rosella are in fact jeopardised or under serious threat, it would then have to ascertain whether the collective action initiated by FSU is suitable for ensuring the achievement of the objective pursued and does not go beyond what is necessary to attain that objective.

   ...

86 As regards the appropriateness of the action taken by FSU for attaining the objectives pursued in the case in the main proceedings, it should be borne in mind that it is common ground that collective action, like collective negotiations and collective agreements, may, in the particular circumstances of a case, be one of the main ways in which trade unions protect the interests of their members (European Court of Human Rights, *Syndicat national de la police belge v Belgium*, of 27 October 1975, Series A, No 19, and *Wilson, National Union of Journalists and Others v United Kingdom* of 2 July 2002, 2002-V, § 44).

87 As regards the question of whether or not the collective action at issue in the main proceedings goes beyond what is necessary to achieve the objective pursued, it is for the national court to examine, in particular, on the one hand, whether, under the national rules and collective agreement law applicable to that action, FSU did not have other means at its disposal which were less restrictive of freedom of establishment in order to bring to a successful conclusion the collective negotiations entered into with Viking, and, on the other, whether that trade union had exhausted those means before initiating such action.

88 Secondly, in relation to the collective action seeking to ensure the implementation of the policy in question pursued by ITF, it must be emphasised that, to the extent that that policy results in shipowners being prevented from registering their vessels in a State other than that of which the beneficial owners of those vessels are nationals, the restrictions on freedom of establishment resulting from such action cannot be objectively justified. Nevertheless, as the national court points out, the objective of that policy is also to protect and improve seafarers' terms and conditions of employment.

89 However, as is apparent from the file submitted to the Court, in the context of its policy of combating the use of flags of convenience, ITF is required, when asked by one of its members, to initiate solidarity action against the beneficial owner of a vessel which is registered in a State other than that of which that owner is a national, irrespective of whether or not that owner's exercise of its right of freedom of establishment is liable to have a harmful effect on the work or conditions of employment of its employees. Therefore, as Viking argued during the hearing without being contradicted by ITF in that regard, the policy of reserving the right of collective negotiations to trade unions of the State of which the beneficial owner of a vessel is a national

is also applicable where the vessel is registered in a State which guarantees workers a higher level of social protection than they would enjoy in the first State.

President Skouris, Jann, Rosas, Lenaerts, Lõhmus, Bay Larsen, Rapporteur Schintgen, Silva de Lapuerta, Schiemann, Makarczyk, Kūris, Levits and **Caoimh.**

NOTES AND QUESTIONS

1. The Court of Justice holds (1) the right to strike exists but can be subject to restrictions, (2) freedom of establishment can apply between private parties, by horizontal direct effect, not just vertically between private parties and the state, (3) a union's right to strike can be considered to interfere with a business' freedom of establishment, but (4) it could count as a justifiable, overriding interest if exercised proportionately. The Court then opines that strikes seem unjustified if 'jobs or conditions of employment at issue were not jeopardised or under serious threat' [81]. Where did it get that idea from?
2. The Court assumes business rights to establish are to be placed above human rights (an idea alluded to in the *Schmidberger* and *Omega* cases, but unresolved). This had the effect that (1) strikes must be proportionate to a business right to establish, instead of (2) balancing two conflicting rights, or (3) saying that human rights must be given greater weight than rights of corporations in a democratic society.
3. In *Commission v Germany* (2010) C-271/08 the CJEU suggested at [52] that perhaps instead a 'fair balance' should be achieved between a collective agreement that set up pension benefits and rights of establishment, services and to fair competition. See P Syrpis (2011) 40(2) ILJ 222, who says this gave a 'tantalizing prospect' that social and economic rights could be balanced like conflicting economic rights. If that were true, which right should win, and why?
4. The Court of Justice never had the benefit of submissions on the right of ITF or the Finnish Seamen's Union to establish under TFEU Art 49. On a plain reading of the Treaties, it would appear that unions provide services (under TFEU Art 56) and so they have the right to establish (Art 49). TFEU Art 57 says 'services' mean those 'normally provided for remuneration' and includes 'activities of the professions'. Unions, in return for membership fees, provide their members with collective bargaining, insurance, representation and more. Under Art 49 those with the right to establish 'include' self-employed people and undertakings, but the list is not exhaustive and plainly includes social groups such as trade unions, consumer or environmental groups. Once it is acknowledged that both a union and a business have the right to establish, and a union going on strike is exercising the right to collectively bargain for its members, a business has no more right to complain about economic loss from this than it does when a competitor (exercising its conflicting right to establish) draws customers away.
5. Why was the Court using freedom of establishment to create maximum standards for labour rights when TFEU Art 153(5) makes clear the legislature may not legislate on the issue? Even when legislation is enabled for labour rights, it cannot stop member states passing 'more stringent protective measures compatible with the Treaties'. At [40] the Court simply dismisses this argument, as advanced

by the Danish government. Should the Treaties be amended to make clear that (1) neither the legislature nor the courts may legislate on pay and collective labour rights, and (2) that Member States can always have higher standards? Or should legislation be enabled on pay and collective labour rights, but also explicitly enable Member States to go beyond that minimum floor?

6. In the United States, where the outlook for labour rights and the democratic process has become increasingly desperate, the Fair Labor Standards Act of 1938 explicitly enables states and local governments to pass more protective minimum wage or hour standards. The National Labor Relations Act of 1935, by contrast, is silent. However, A Cox and MJ Seidman, 'Federalism and Labor Relations' (1950) 64 *Harvard Law Review* 211 called for 'an integrated public labor policy' and warned 'enforcement of … state regulation will thwart the development of federal policy'. The US Supreme Court adopted this argument in *Garner v Teamsters Local 776*, 346 US 485 (1953) and *San Diego Building Trades Council v Garmon* 359 US 236 (1959). The result has been unmitigated disaster. See C Estlund, 'The Ossification of American Labor Law' (2002) 102 *Columbia Law Review* 1527 and BI Sachs, 'Despite Preemption: Making Labor Law in Cities and States' (2011) 1224 *Harvard Law Review* 1153.

7. After *Viking*, the Court of Justice deployed a similar (and yet even more wild) line of reasoning for the right to provide services under TFEU Art 56 (ex Art 49 TEC) in *Laval*.

Laval Un Partneri Ltd v Svenska Byggnadsarbetareförbundet (2007) C-319/05

Laval Ltd, a Latvian building company, claimed the Swedish Builders Union violated its right to provide service, now in TFEU Art 56, by striking against it. Laval Ltd refused to sign a collective agreement to pay its Latvian workers the same as their Swedish colleagues. It was blockaded in a strike, and went insolvent. The Posted Workers Directive 1996 Art 3(1) says 'Member States shall ensure that, whatever the law applicable to the employment relationship' undertakings should guarantee workers the terms of 'collective agreements or arbitration awards which have been declared universally applicable'. However, Sweden did not make its collective agreements universally applicable. Similar to TFEU Art 153(4) (ex Art 137(4)), recital 17 says: '[M]andatory rules for minimum protection in force in the host country must not prevent the application of terms and conditions of employment which are more favourable to workers.' Nevertheless, the Court of Justice held that without legislation to raise standards beyond the minima in the Posted Workers Directive 1996, collective action to get a collective agreement, would violate Laval Ltd's right to provide services.

Grand Chamber:

The first question

51 By its first question, the national court is asking whether it is compatible with rules of the EC Treaty on the freedom to provide services and the prohibition of any discrimination on the grounds of nationality and with the provisions of Directive 96/71/EC, for trade unions to attempt, by means of collective action in the form of a blockade, to force a foreign provider of

services to sign a collective agreement in the host country in respect of terms and conditions of employment, such as the collective agreement for the building sector, if the situation in the host country is characterised by the fact that the legislation to implement that directive has no express provision concerning the application of terms and conditions of employment in collective agreements.

52 It is clear from the order of reference that the collective action initiated by Byggnads and Byggettan was motivated by Laval's refusal to guarantee its workers posted in Sweden the hourly wage demanded by those trade unions, even though that Member State does not provide for minimum rates of pay, and Laval's refusal to sign the collective agreement for the building sector, some terms of which lay down, in relation to certain matters referred to in Article 3(1), first subparagraph, (a) to (g) of Directive 96/71, more favourable conditions than those resulting from the relevant legislative provisions, while other terms relate to matters not referred to in that article.

…

The possibilities available to the Member States for determining the terms and conditions of employment applicable to posted workers, including minimum rates of pay

…

69 … the national authorities in Sweden have entrusted management and labour with the task of setting, by way of collective negotiations, the wage rates which national undertakings are to pay their workers and that, as regards undertakings in the construction sector, such a system requires negotiation on a case-by-case basis, at the place of work, having regard to the qualifications and tasks of the employees concerned.

70 As regards the requirements as to pay which can be imposed on foreign service providers, it should be recalled that the first subparagraph of Article 3(1) of Directive 96/71 relates only to minimum rates of pay. Therefore, that provision cannot be relied on to justify an obligation on such service providers to comply with rates of pay such as those which the trade unions seek in this case to impose in the framework of the Swedish system, which do not constitute minimum wages and are not, moreover, laid down in accordance with the means set out in that regard in Article 3(1) and (8) of the directive.

71 It must therefore be concluded at this stage that a Member State in which the minimum rates of pay are not determined in accordance with one of the means provided for in Article 3(1) and (8) of Directive 96/71 is not entitled, pursuant to that directive, to impose on undertakings established in other Member States, in the framework of the transnational provision of services, negotiation at the place of work, on a case-by-case basis, having regard to the qualifications and tasks of the employees, so that the undertakings concerned may ascertain the wages which they are to pay their posted workers.

…

Matters which may be covered by the terms and conditions of work applicable to posted workers

73 In order to ensure that the nucleus of mandatory rules for minimum protection are observed, the first subparagraph of Article 3(1) of Directive 96/71 provides that Member States are to ensure that, whatever the law applicable to the employment relationship, in the framework of the transnational provision of services, undertakings guarantee workers posted to their territory the terms and conditions of employment covering the matters listed in that provision, namely: maximum work periods and minimum rest periods; minimum paid annual holidays; the minimum rates of pay, including overtime rates; the conditions of hiring-out of

workers, in particular the supply of workers by temporary employment undertakings; health, safety and hygiene at work; protective measures with regard to the terms and conditions of employment of pregnant women or women who have recently given birth, of children and of young people; and equality of treatment between men and women and other provisions on non-discrimination.

74 That provision seeks, first, to ensure a climate of fair competition between national undertakings and undertakings which provide services transnationally, in so far as it requires the latter to afford their workers, as regards a limited list of matters, the terms and conditions of employment laid down in the host Member State by law, regulation or administrative provision or by collective agreements or arbitration awards within the meaning of Article 3(8) of Directive 96/71, which constitute mandatory rules for minimum protection.

...

79 It is true that Article 3(7) of Directive 96/71 provides that paragraphs 1 to 6 are not to prevent application of terms and conditions of employment which are more favourable to workers. In addition, according to recital 17, the mandatory rules for minimum protection in force in the host country must not prevent the application of such terms and conditions.

80 Nevertheless, Article 3(7) of Directive 96/71 cannot be interpreted as allowing the host Member State to make the provision of services in its territory conditional on the observance of terms and conditions of employment which go beyond the mandatory rules for minimum protection. As regards the matters referred to in Article 3(1), first subparagraph, (a) to (g), Directive 96/71 expressly lays down the degree of protection for workers of undertakings established in other Member States who are posted to the territory of the host Member State which the latter State is entitled to require those undertakings to observe. Moreover, such an interpretation would amount to depriving the directive of its effectiveness.

...

83 In the main proceedings, certain terms of the collective agreement for the building sector relate to matters which are not specifically referred to in Article 3(1), first subparagraph, (a) to (g) of Directive 96/71. In that regard, it follows from paragraph 20 of this judgment that signing that collective agreement entails undertakings accepting pecuniary obligations such as those requiring them to pay to Byggettan a sum equal to 1.5% of total gross wages for the purposes of the pay review which that section trade union carries out, and to the insurance company, FORA, first, 0.8% of total gross wages for the purposes of a charge called the 'special building supplement', and, second, a further 5.9% for the purposes of a number of insurance premiums.

84 It is common ground, however, that those obligations were imposed without the national authorities' having had recourse to Article 3(10) of Directive 96/71. The terms of the collective agreement for the building sector in question were in fact established through negotiation between management and labour; not being bodies governed by public law, they cannot avail themselves of that provision by citing grounds of public policy in order to maintain that collective action such as that at issue in the main proceedings complies with Community law.

85 It is also necessary to assess from the point of view of Article 49 EC the collective action taken by the trade unions in the case in the main proceedings, both in so far as it seeks to force a service provider established in another Member State to enter into negotiations on the wages to be paid to posted workers and in so far as it seeks to force that service provider to sign a collective agreement the terms of which lay down, as regards some of the matters referred to in Article 3(1), first subparagraph, (a) to (g) of Directive 96/71, more favourable conditions than

those stemming from the relevant legislative provisions, while other terms cover matters not referred to in that provision.

...

Assessment of the collective action at issue in the case in the main proceedings from the point of view of Article 49 EC

...

103 ... the right to take collective action for the protection of the workers of the host State against possible social dumping may constitute an overriding reason of public interest within the meaning of the case-law of the Court which, in principle, justifies a restriction of one of the fundamental freedoms guaranteed by the Treaty (see, to that effect, Joined Cases C-369/96 and C-376/96 *Arblade and Others* [1999] ECR I-8453, paragraph 36 ... and Case C-438/05 *International Transport Workers' Federation and Finnish Seamen's Union* [2007] ECR I-0000, paragraph 77).

...

106 In the case in the main proceedings, Byggnads and Byggettan contend that the objective of the blockade carried out against Laval was the protection of workers.

107 In that regard, it must be observed that, in principle, blockading action by a trade union of the host Member State which is aimed at ensuring that workers posted in the framework of a transnational provision of services have their terms and conditions of employment fixed at a certain level, falls within the objective of protecting workers.

108 However, as regards the specific obligations, linked to signature of the collective agreement for the building sector, which the trade unions seek to impose on undertakings established in other Member States by way of collective action such as that at issue in the case in the main proceedings, the obstacle which that collective action forms cannot be justified with regard to such an objective. In addition to what is set out in paragraphs 81 and 83 of the present judgment, with regard to workers posted in the framework of a transnational provision of services, their employer is required, as a result of the coordination achieved by Directive 96/71, to observe a nucleus of mandatory rules for minimum protection in the host Member State.

109 Finally, as regards the negotiations on pay which the trade unions seek to impose, by way of collective action such as that at issue in the main proceedings, on undertakings, established in another Member State which post workers temporarily to their territory, it must be emphasised that Community law certainly does not prohibit Member States from requiring such undertakings to comply with their rules on minimum pay by appropriate means (see *Seco and Desquenne & Giral*, paragraph 14; *Rush Portuguesa*, paragraph 18, and *Arblade and Others*, paragraph 41).

110 However, collective action such as that at issue in the main proceedings cannot be justified in the light of the public interest objective referred to in paragraph 102 of the present judgment, where the negotiations on pay, which that action seeks to require an undertaking established in another Member State to enter into, form part of a national context characterised by a lack of provisions, of any kind, which are sufficiently precise and accessible that they do not render it impossible or excessively difficult in practice for such an undertaking to determine the obligations with which it is required to comply as regards minimum pay (see, to that effect, *Arblade and Others*, paragraph 43).

President Skouris, Jann, Rosas, Lenaerts, Lõhmus, Bay Larsen, Rapporteur Schintgen, Silva de Lapuerta, Schiemann, Makarczyk, Kūris, Levits and Caoimh.

NOTES AND QUESTIONS

1. The Grand Chamber said (1) the Posted Workers Directive 1996 creates minimum standards, but these cannot be improved upon except by Member State legislation, (2) strikes, though a human right, could infringe a company's right to provide services if exercised disproportionately, and (3) collective bargaining is not 'sufficiently precise' to enable 'an undertaking to determine the obligations' it has to comply with. Where did it get the idea that collective bargaining is imprecise?
2. The case it cites repeatedly, *Criminal Proceedings against Jean-Claude Arblade* (1999) C-369/96, involved (obviously) criminal proceedings where the importance of knowing what one contravenes matters somewhat more than in a collective agreement.
3. As in *Viking*, the court did not have the benefit of submissions on the Swedish Builders' Union right to provide its services to Latvian workers. Here, the Court rejects the notion that the union can strike in order to ensure every worker benefits from the same pay. This has the direct consequence that when posted Latvian workers return to Latvia, they will have less money in their pockets, less to spend on Latvian goods and services, and therefore make Latvia poorer compared to Sweden. This approach entrenches the economic separation and inequalities between EU Member States, dividing, not unifying, the internal market.
4. The consequences of *Viking* and *Laval* were swift and ugly. In 2008, a dispute broke out after Alstom, a power company, contracted Spanish and Polish businesses to build power stations in Nottinghamshire and Kent using labour that was paid 40% less than the collectively agreed wage for UK workers. In 2009, engineers went on strike across the country in sympathy with workers at the Lindsey Oil Refinery in Lincolnshire, who faced similar issues. They carried banners saying 'British Jobs for British Workers'. The Prime Minister Gordon Brown was responsible for this implicitly racist slogan. See further C Kilpatrick, 'British Jobs for British Workers? UK Industrial Action and Free Movement of Services in EU Law' (2009) LSE Law, Society and Economy Working Papers 16/2009. Do you agree that when a government fails to guarantee fair incomes and labour rights, the risk is raised that fascist solutions fill the void?
5. The CJEU's case law was implicitly reversed by Rome I Regulation (EC) No 593/2008 recital 34: 'The rule on individual employment contracts should not prejudice the application of the overriding mandatory provisions of the country to which a worker is posted in accordance with Directive 96/71/EC ... concerning the posting of workers in the framework of the provision of services.' Nevertheless, the CJEU persisted in its reasoning. *Rüffert v Land Niedersachsen* (2008) C-346/06 suggested a state government could not require fair wages in procurement policy. *Commission v Germany* (2010) C-271/08 held Germany violated the Public Procurement Directive by not requiring its councils to put pension contracts out for tender, rather than awarding them according to collective agreement. *Bundesdruckerei GmbH v Stadt Dortmund* (2014) C-549/13 held a city could not require a minimum wage for workers on publicly procured contracts that were not similar to the going rate in regions where the workers worked. *Regiopost GmbH & Co KG v Stadt Landau in der Pfalz* (2015) C-115/14 held that another government tender could not require the bidders to pay the regional minimum

wage. The Public Procurement Directive 2014/25/EU Art 18 changed the law, so that a procuring body can require 'obligations in the fields of environmental, social and labour law established by Union law, national law, collective agreements' or international law. See chapter 16(1)(b). Should a court have to be censured by the legislature twice on the same issue?

6. The idea that EU law could be incompatible with the ECHR has frequently been discussed. See KD Ewing and J Hendy QC, 'The Dramatic Implications of Demir and Baykara' (2010) 39(1) *Industrial Law Journal* 2. However, the CJEU has refused to the EU the right to accede to the ECHR (as it was meant to under the Treaties) in *Opinion 2/13* (2014). By contrast, the European Court of Human Rights has so far refused to engage with questions of the compatibility of EU law with the ECHR, most recently in *Svenska Transport-arbetareförbundet and Seko v Sweden* (2016) App 29999/16. Here a ship owner claimed that the Swedish transport, part of the International Transport Workers' Federation, had violated the Norwegian equivalent of TFEU Art 56 by striking against the owner putting up a Panama flag to pay its crew less. A Swedish labour court held the strike was unlawful under TFEU Art 56 because wage demands were excessive. On application to the European Court of Human Rights, O'Leary J refused any hearing on the pretext that it did not fulfil 'the admissibility criteria set out in Articles 34 and 35'. It would seem however, that those criteria were in fact met. See [2017] 46(3) ILJ 435–43.

7. As well as freedom of establishment and services, the CJEU has raised the spectre of competition law liability if self-employed people organise in *FNV*.

FNV Kunsten Informatie en Media v Staat der Nederlanden (2014) C-413/13

FNV Kunsten Informatie en Media, a union for substitute orchestra workers, sought a declaration that it was able to make a collective agreement without violating competition law. In 2007 the Netherlands Competition Authority wrote a 'reflection document' where the authors asserted that self-employed substitutes, if they bargained for minimum fees, were not excluded from the scope of TFEU Art 101, which prohibits collusion between 'undertakings'. Substitute orchestra workers previously were covered by a collective agreement between orchestra employers and the Netherlands Musicians' Union, which said self-employed substitutes would receive 16 per cent more than substitutes who were regarded as employees. The Hague Court of Appeal referred to the Court of Justice. The First Chamber replied that self-employed people could be regarded as undertakings, but not if the relationship was one of false self-employment.

First Chamber:

21 By its two questions, which must be examined together, the referring court asks essentially whether, on a proper construction of EU law, a provision of a collective labour agreement, which sets minimum fees for self-employed service providers who are members of one of the contracting employees' organisations and perform for an employer, under a works or service contract, the same activity as that employer's employed workers, does not fall within the scope of Article 101(1) TFEU.

22 In that connection, it is to be recalled that, according to settled case-law, although certain restrictions of competition are inherent in collective agreements between organisations representing employers and employees, the social policy objectives pursued by such agreements would be seriously compromised if management and labour were subject to Article 101(1) TFEU when seeking jointly to adopt measures to improve conditions of work and employment (see judgments in *Albany*, EU:C:1999:430, paragraph 59; *International Transport Workers' Federation and Finnish Seamen's Union*, C-438/05, EU:C:2007:772, paragraph 49 and *3F v Commission*, C-319/07 P, EU:C:2009:435, paragraph 50).

...

27 It must be held in that regard that, although they perform the same activities as employees, service providers such as the substitutes at issue in the main proceedings, are, in principle, 'undertakings' within the meaning of Article 101(1) TFEU, for they offer their services for remuneration on a given market (judgment in *Ordem dos Técnicos Oficiais de Contas*, C-1/12, EU:C:2013:127, paragraphs 36 and 37) and perform their activities as independent economic operators in relation to their principal (see judgment in *Confederación Española de Empresarios de Estaciones de Servicio*, C-217/05, EU:C:2006:784, paragraph 45).

28 It is clear, as also observed by the Advocate General in point 32 of his Opinion and the NMa in its reflection document, that, in so far as an organisation representing workers carries out negotiations acting in the name, and on behalf, of those self-employed persons who are its members, it does not act as a trade union association and therefore as a social partner, but, in reality, acts as an association of undertakings.

...

30 In those circumstances, it follows that a provision of a collective labour agreement, such as that at issue in the main proceedings, in so far as it was concluded by an employees' organisation in the name, and on behalf, of the self-employed services providers who are its members, does not constitute the result of a collective negotiation between employers and employees, and cannot be excluded, by reason of its nature, from the scope of Article 101(1) TFEU.

31 That finding cannot, however, prevent such a provision of a collective labour agreement from being regarded also as the result of dialogue between management and labour if the service providers, in the name and on behalf of whom the trade union negotiated, are in fact 'false self-employed', that is to say, service providers in a situation comparable to that of employees.

32 As observed by the Advocate General in point 51 of his Opinion, and by the FNV, the Netherlands Government and the European Commission at the hearing, in today's economy it is not always easy to establish the status of some self-employed contractors as 'undertakings', such as the substitutes at issue in the main proceedings.

...

35. ... the Court has previously held that the classification of a 'self-employed person' under national law does not prevent that person being classified as an employee within the meaning of EU law if his independence is merely notional, thereby disguising an employment relationship (see, to that effect, judgment in *Allonby*, C-256/01, EU:C:2004:18, paragraph 71).

36. It follows that the status of 'worker' within the meaning of EU law is not affected by the fact that a person has been hired as a self-employed person under national law, for tax, administrative or organisational reasons, as long as that persons acts under the direction of his employer as regards, in particular, his freedom to choose the time, place and content of his

work (see judgment in *Allonby*, EU:C:2004:18, paragraph 72), does not share in the employer's commercial risks (judgment in *Agegate*, C-3/87, EU:C:1989:650, paragraph 36), and, for the duration of that relationship, forms an integral part of that employer's undertaking, so forming an economic unit with that undertaking (see judgment in *Becu and Others*, C-22/98, EU:C:1999:419, paragraph 26).

...

41 Accordingly, a provision of a collective labour agreement, in so far as it sets minimum fees for service providers who are 'false self-employed', cannot, by reason of its nature and purpose, be subject to the scope of Article 101(1) TFEU.

President and Rapporteur Tizzano, Borg Barthet, Levits, Berger and **Rodin**.

NOTES AND QUESTIONS

1. The First Chamber holds that 'service providers … are, in principle, "undertakings"' [27] but then says that people who are 'false self-employed' 'cannot … be subject' to TFEU Art 101. The idea of 'false self-employed' is probably the same as a sham, seen in *Autoclenz Ltd v Belcher*.
2. Why should self-employed people not form trade unions, bargain and strike for higher wages? People who personally perform work, who are self-employed, are distant from the problems that competition law is designed to tackle. In February 2016, Hackney carriage taxi drivers in London brought traffic to a standstill, in protest against the app-based taxi corporation, Uber. It is plain that, while those taxi drivers are self-employed, they have the fundamental right to strike or protest. Similarly, in April 2018 self-employed criminal barristers organised a strike against Ministry of Justice budget cuts to legal aid. The position of international law and the International Labour Organisation is that 'everyone' has the right to strike: e.g. UDHR 1948 Art 23 and ICESCR 1966 Art 8. On this basis, the CJEU would be out of line with international law, and UK law.
3. But was the First Chamber saying that *all* service providers are undertakings and therefore subject to competition law? The Court cannot be taken to mean this, because it would be wrong. TFEU Art 49 plainly foresees that many service providers are not undertakings because it reads the right of establishment 'shall include the right to take up and pursue activities as self-employed persons and to set up and manage undertakings'. It follows, plainly, that not all self-employed people are undertakings. On the other hand, by qualifying its statement that 'in principle' service providers are undertakings, it admits a host of exceptions. Those should be that no person, who personally performs work, can ever be classed as an undertaking.
4. The cases cited by the CJEU at [27] have nothing to do with the fundamental policy questions that the First Chamber touches. *Ordem dos Técnicos Oficiais de Contas* (2013) C-1/12 involved a training fee for chartered accountants. *Confederación Española de Empresarios de Estaciones de Servicio* (2006) C-217/05 involved sales commission for petrol stations. Neither case involved people who personally perform work (whether self-employed or employed) or collective agreement to protect terms and conditions, rather than associations of corporations.

5. A sorry history of social democratic repression, using competition law, was experienced by the United States after the Sherman Antitrust Act of 1890. §1 codified the rule that restraint of trade was a federal wrong, but instead of being used against business, the first cases that were brought were against labour. See chapter 10(1)(a) above. The Clayton Act 1914 §6 ended this finally, saying nothing contained in the antitrust laws' should 'forbid the existence and operation of labor ... organizations' or 'restrain individual members of such organizations from lawfully carrying out the legitimate objects'. This does not mean that cases (currently driven by lawyers for Uber) have not threatened to emerge once more in the United States.

(2) SOLIDARITY ACTION AND PICKETING

The act of withholding work, by taking collective action, rarely affects just an employee and employer. When production stops, the employing entity will be unable to continue appropriating the benefits of labour (chapter 5(1)(b)). This may halt profits for shareholders, although shareholders who have diversified investments may gain higher profits from competitors that are not involved in strikes. Strikes may halt goods and services for consumers, unless consumers can easily switch to another supplier. It could well be, however, that some or all of those stakeholders support collective action by workers, and want to join in support, or they blame an employer's management for the dispute. The right of freedom of association suggests that this should be possible, though *RMT v UK* (at chapter 10(1)(c) above) held that limits in UK law were not to be challenged on the facts. Two major issues are (a) the extent to which other workers can join a strike in solidarity, to push an employer to uphold workers' interests, or (b) the extent to which workers can picket, and encourage people to join in collective action.

(a) Solidarity Action and the Corporate Veil

Although chapter 10(1) established that collective action may be taken by every worker, and at the very least for economic purposes, there are restrictions in UK statute on who collective action may be taken against. Under TULRCA Act 1992 s 224, the object of a strike must be someone's 'employer' and strikes against a non-employer means that the action is unlawful 'secondary action'. But who counts as the 'employer'? This is contested.

Trade Union and Labour Relations (Consolidation) Act 1992 s 224

224. Secondary action.
    (1) An act is not protected if one of the facts relied on for the purpose of establishing liability is that there has been secondary action which is not lawful picketing.
    (2) There is secondary action in relation to a trade dispute when, and only when, a person—
        (a) induces another to break a contract of employment or interferes or induces another to interfere with its performance, or

(b) threatens that a contract of employment under which he or another is employed will be broken or its performance interfered with, or that he will induce another to break a contract of employment or to interfere with its performance,

and the employer under the contract of employment is not the employer party to the dispute.

(3) Lawful picketing means acts done in the course of such attendance as is declared lawful by section 220 (peaceful picketing)—

(a) by a worker employed (or, in the case of a worker not in employment, last employed) by the employer party to the dispute, or

(b) by a trade union official whose attendance is lawful by virtue of subsection (1)(b) of that section.

(4) For the purposes of this section an employer shall not be treated as party to a dispute between another employer and workers of that employer; and where more than one employer is in dispute with his workers, the dispute between each employer and his workers shall be treated as a separate dispute.

In this subsection "worker" has the same meaning as in section 244 (meaning of "trade dispute").

(5) An act in contemplation or furtherance of a trade dispute which is primary action in relation to that dispute may not be relied on as secondary action in relation to another trade dispute.

Primary action means such action as is mentioned in paragraph (a) or (b) of subsection (2) where the employer under the contract of employment is the employer party to the dispute.

(6) In this section "contract of employment" includes any contract under which one person personally does work or performs services for another, and related expressions shall be construed accordingly.

NOTES AND QUESTIONS

1. TULRCA 1992 s 224 says that striking is 'secondary' and 'not protected' against hypothetical tort liability when against someone who is not 'the employer under the contract of employment'. Chapter 3 showed it is basic to contract law that (1) the written document almost never expresses the whole of the contract, (2) an employee may have more than one employer, for different purposes, and (3) the 'need to segregate intellectually common law principles relating to contract law, even in the field of employment, from statutorily conferred rights is fundamental': see *Gisda Cyf v Barratt*, [39]. So, if this section means unions are only protected on strike against one's contractual employer, what does that really mean?

2. There used to be no prohibition on secondary action in the UK. This is the case in 25 out of 28 EU countries – only Luxembourg does not permit secondary action. This point was engaged with in *RMT v UK* [2014] ECHR 366, [38]–[40] but relying on an ETUI source that appears to have been wrong to say the Netherlands and Austria do not allow secondary action: the Netherlands has case law on this, while Austria has no statute or case law at all, but did have widespread secondary strikes in 2011: see M Risak, 2012/1 Juridikum 23. Austria's reason seems to be due to its strong system of board codetermination. For the best global source, see Z Adams, L Bishop and S Deakin, *CBR Labour Regulation Index (Dataset of 117 Countries)* (2016). In other words, the vast majority of democratic countries enable secondary action. By contrast, the United States since the Taft–Hartley Act of 1947, 29 USC §158(b)(4) does not.

3. Before statute was changed in 1980, Lord Denning MR tried to limit second-ary action. In *Express Newspapers Ltd v McShane* [1980] AC 672 journalists at Express Ltd in the National Union of Journalists asked Press Association journal-ists to join in a strike. The Court of Appeal upheld an injunction on the ground that sympathy action must provide practical, not just moral support. The House of Lords, disagreeing, held that the strike action was lawful. Lord Wilberforce stated a strike must only pursue a general intention to further a trade dispute, that is reasonably capable of achieving its objective. The concept of what is in 'furtherance of a trade dispute' refers only to the subjective state of mind of the person doing the act. But Lord Denning MR tried again in *Duport Steel Ltd v Sirs* [1980] ICR 161, where the Iron and Steel Trades Confederation (ISTC) was in a dispute with British Steel Corporation, established under the Iron and Steel Act 1975, for failing to raise wages. In March 1980, the government said it would provide no further public funds. The ISTC called on workers of around 100 pri-vate companies to strike, as a way to pressure the government, to reverse a dec-laration that it would not provide funds after March 1980. The Court of Appeal allowed an injunction, reversing the High Court which followed *McShane.* But the House of Lords affirmed again that what is in contemplation or furtherance of a trade dispute is just a subjective test, and one cannot have regard to the remote-ness of the act done from the source of the dispute.

4. In 1982 statute changed. Before, the Department of Employment, *Trade Union Immunities* (1981) Cm 8128, para 149, explained that 'in some cases, secondary action is the only means by which pressure can be brought on an employer in dispute, for example where the employer has sacked all his unionised employees'. It then said total ban 'could tilt the balance of power unacceptably to the benefit of employers'. The Employment Act 1982 s 18 amended the definition of a trade dispute, though at the Second Reading, the Minister, Norman Tebbit MP said: '[W]e do not propose that all sympathetic action should be made unlawful. [Section 18] applies to the position where an employer and his employees have no dispute between them and everyone is working normally. It provides that, in that position, a trade union outside the company cannot declare that it is in dispute with that company because it does not like the way that the company runs its business or because none of the employees is in a trade union. The effect will be that they cannot organise blacking or other secondary action against him. In other words, this change in the definition will affect only one sort of secondary action, although a particularly obnoxious sort of action.' Hansard HC Debs (8 February 1982) vol 17, col 746.

5. A critical issue at common law is whether workers of subsidiary companies can strike together with workers of a parent company, or workers of a firm can strike against a business that substantially controls their direct employer by contract.

Dimbleby and Sons Ltd v NUJ **[1984] 1 WLR 427**

Dimbleby and Sons Ltd (D&S Ltd) claimed an injunction against the National Union of Journalists (NUJ) for telling its members to boycott sending final versions of newspapers ('copy') for printing at TBF (Printers) Ltd. D&S Ltd (the company of the great-grandfather of BBC presenters David and Jonathan Dimbleby) published four newspapers, including the *Richmond and Twickenham Times* (now owned by Newsquest Media Group Ltd). TBF (Printers) Ltd was part of the TBF group. Another company in the group was T Bailey Forman Ltd, which had in 1979 refused to reinstate 28 NUJ journalists who were dismissed in a national strike, even though other newspapers reinstated theirs when the dispute was resolved. The NUJ therefore maintained a boycott against T Bailey Forman Ltd so that no NUJ members should work for it nor supply copy to it. In 1983, another dispute broke out between Dimbleby Printers Ltd (DP Ltd, the printing company of D&S Ltd) and the National Graphical Association (NGA), a printing union. This resulted in all NGA members at DP Ltd going on strike and being dismissed. As DP Ltd ceased to function, D&S Ltd decided to hire TBF (Printers) Ltd, because it was among the only printers that had no union members, and could not be boycotted by the NGA. However, the NUJ instructed its journalists, working at D&S Ltd, not to supply copy to TBF (Printers) Ltd, because it was in the same group. The House of Lords upheld an injunction against the union on the ground that it was unlikely that at trial the NUJ could establish it was really in a trade dispute with D&S Ltd.

Lord Diplock:

Little time needs to be spent upon the argument on behalf of the N.U.J., which is purely one of statutory construction, that T.B.F. [(Printers) Ltd], although a separate corporate entity from T. Bailey Forman Ltd., was nevertheless a party to the trade dispute between the N.U.J. and the latter company.

My Lords, the reason why English statutory law, and that of all other trading countries, has long permitted the creation of corporations as artificial persons distinct from their individual shareholders and from that of any other corporation even though the shareholders of both corporations are identical, is to enable business to be undertaken with limited financial liability in the event of the business proving to be a failure. The "corporate veil" in the case of companies incorporated under the Companies Act is drawn by statute and it can be pierced by some other statute if such other statute so provides; but in view of its *raison d'etre* and its consistent recognition by the courts since *Salomon v Salomon and Co Ltd* [1897] AC 22, one would expect that any parliamentary intention to pierce the corporate veil would be expressed in clear and unequivocal language. I do not wholly exclude the possibility that even in the absence of express words stating that in specified circumstances one company, although separately incorporated, is to be treated as sharing the same legal personality of another, a purposive construction of the statute may nevertheless lead inexorably to the conclusion that such must have been the intention of Parliament. It was argued for the N.U.J. in the instant case that because T.B.F. and T. Bailey Forman Ltd. were operating companies with identical shareholding and were companies of which a single holding company had control, T.B.F. as well as T. Bailey Forman Ltd. was an "employer who is party to the dispute" between the N.U.J. and T. Bailey Forman Ltd. within the meaning of that phrase where it is used in section 17(3) of the Act of 1980.

My Lords, this seems to me to be a quite impossible construction to put upon the phrase "an employer who is a party to the dispute" in the context in which it appears in subsection (3). This subsection is followed immediately by subsection (4) which deals with secondary action against an "associated employer." By subsection (7), the definition of the expression "associated employer" in the Act of 1974 is adopted for the purposes of section 17 of the Act of 1980. That definition in section 30(5) of the Act of 1974 provides that:

"any two employers are to be treated as associated if one is a company of which the other (directly or indirectly) has control, or if both are companies of which a third person (directly or indirectly) has control; and in this Act 'associated employer' shall be construed accordingly."

T.B.F. is thus an associated employer of T. Bailey Forman Ltd. Section 17(4) read in conjunction with section 17(1)(b), legalises a particular kind of secondary action if it is directed against an "associated employer of an employer who is a party to the dispute," although it would be unlawful if it were directed against any other person. If one were to accept the construction of section 17(3) of the Act of 1980 for which the N.U.J. contends, subsection (4) would be entirely otiose; and if an associated employer were ipso facto an employer who is a party to the suit, the phrase in subsection (4), which I have quoted, would make nonsense.

In the passage that I have already cited from *American Cyanamid Co v Ethicon Ltd* [1975] AC 396 it was said that it was no part of the court's function on an application for an interlocutory injunction to decide difficult questions of law which call for detailed argument and mature consideration. The argument that as a matter of statutory construction T.B.F. as an associated company of T. Bailey Forman Ltd. was "an employer who is a party to the dispute" within the meaning of section 17(3) of the Act of 1980, does not raise a question of law which falls within this category. It is, in my view, one which your Lordships are justified in disposing of here and now by saying that it is unsustainable.

Lord Fraser, Lord Scarman, Lord Bridge and **Lord Brandon** agreed.

NOTES AND QUESTIONS

1. The House of Lords held that even though TBF (Printers) Ltd and T Bailey Forman Ltd were controlled by the same shareholder, it could not be said that the NUJ had a trade dispute with T Bailey Forman Ltd. Lord Diplock says that the principle of separate legal personality has existed since *Salomon* to shield a business's 'financial liability in the event of the business proving to be a failure'. He then says clear statutory language should be needed to 'pierce' the corporate veil. But if the rationale for separate personality is to shield shareholders from financial loss in insolvency, why does it follow that a solvent company is able to evade good faith negotiation in a trade dispute?
2. Limited liability is primarily justifiable because creditors may contract around it. It switches the default rule, but contracts for security or guarantees can switch it back. As Lord Macnaghten said in *Salomon*, the creditors who lost money in that case 'may be entitled to sympathy, but they have only themselves to blame for their misfortunes'. When the creditor is 'non-adjusting' or lacks bargaining power, the justification for limited liability is largely gone. This is why *Chandler v Cape plc*, in chapter 3(3) acknowledged that an employee who was injured by asbestos had a claim against a parent company, despite him having no direct contract of employment.
3. Lord Diplock quoted the Trade Union and Labour Relations Act 1974 s 30(5), which is now the Employment Rights Act (ERA) 1996 s 231, stating: '[A]ny two employers shall be treated as associated if (a) one is a company of which the other (directly or indirectly) has control, or (b) both are companies of which a third person (directly or indirectly) has control and "associated employer" shall be construed accordingly.' Lord Diplock took the view that because employers are 'associated', they are separate and a worker is taking secondary action. But why

does this follow? If employers are associated, does it not indicate strongly that a worker may be employed by both – that there is joint employment? Do you agree that the ERA 1996 s 231 definition can and should apply to enable strike action against second employers?

4.   After *Dimbleby* the Employment Act 1990 s 4 changed the law to the present form of words in s 224. At the second reading, Secretary of State Michael Howard MP rationalised this as follows: 'We do not believe that any business should be threatened with disruption unless there is a direct dispute between the employer and his employees. … in March 1988, we saw just how damaging the threat of secondary action could be to British job prospects. In that year, Ford had planned to invest £40 million in a new electronics plant at Dundee, creating 1,000 jobs. It had negotiated a single-union deal with the Amalgamated Engineering Union. Other unions, led by the Transport and General Workers Union, complained that the AEU had thereby broken TUC rules. Mr. Ron Todd announced that all components from the new plant would be blacked. So Ford took its plant, its £40 million and its 1,000 jobs to Spain.' Hansard HC Debs (29 January 1990) vol 166, cols 44–46. Therefore, it would appear that TULRCA 1992 s 224 was neither intended, nor defended, as being a measure to preclude recognition of more than one employer, aside from the one named in the contract, nor was it designed to prevent solidarity action within a corporate group.

5.   In *University College London Hospitals NHS Trust v Unison* [1998] EWCA Civ 1528 the UCL Hospital employers sought an injunction against Unison, after it called a strike to require that employees being transferred to private companies would still be covered by the collective agreement. Unison also generally objected to the policy of privatised outsourcing of services in the National Health Service (Private Finance) Act 1997. The judge granted an injunction, suggesting it was a political strike. The Court of Appeal upheld the injunction, but Lord Woolf MR said that its employment aims were probably not to be held political, but that it still could not be a trade dispute under s 244 because (apparently) the words 'trade dispute' could not be applied 'in a way which covers the terms and conditions of employment of employees of a third party who have never been employed by the employer who is to be the subject of the strike action'. In *Unison v United Kingdom* [2002] IRLR 497, the European Court of Human Rights refused to find any breach of ECHR Art 11. If Unison had simply formulated its complaint as an opposition to transfer of its members, should it have won?

(b) Picketing

When a strike takes place, people picket. Picketers stand outside the entrances to a workplace with signs or megaphones to (1) advertise the dispute, (2) persuade other people to support them, including colleagues who have not yet joined, and (3) exchange ideas among one another, providing mutual support and encouragement as the dispute goes on. They persuade people to not cross the picket line, an act which is widely seen as morally wrong and a breach of solidarity. Psychologically, it can be important for an employer to suppress pickets, or delegitimise them as being unruly, violent or threatening. Under

TULRCA 1992 s 219(3) (above) picketing does not enjoy protection from hypothetical torts merely because the strike itself does. Section 220 requires in addition that the picket is 'peaceful'.

Trade Union and Labour Relations (Consolidation) Act 1992
ss 220–21 and 241

220 Peaceful picketing.
    (1) It is lawful for a person in contemplation or furtherance of a trade dispute to attend—
        (a)   at or near his own place of work, or
        (b)   if he is an official of a trade union, at or near the place of work of a member of the union whom he is accompanying and whom he represents,
for the purpose only of peacefully obtaining or communicating information, or peacefully persuading any person to work or abstain from working.
    (2) If a person works or normally works—
        (a)   otherwise than at any one place, or
        (b)   at a place the location of which is such that attendance there for a purpose mentioned in subsection (1) is impracticable,
his place of work for the purposes of that subsection shall be any premises of his employer from which he works or from which his work is administered.
    (3) In the case of a worker not in employment where—
        (a)   his last employment was terminated in connection with a trade dispute, or
        (b)   the termination of his employment was one of the circumstances giving rise to a trade dispute,
in relation to that dispute his former place of work shall be treated for the purposes of subsection (1) as being his place of work.
    (4) A person who is an official of a trade union by virtue only of having been elected or appointed to be a representative of some of the members of the union shall be regarded for the purposes of subsection (1) as representing only those members; but otherwise an official of a union shall be regarded for those purposes as representing all its members.

220A Union supervision of picketing
    (1) Section 220 does not make lawful any picketing that a trade union organises, or encourages its members to take part in, unless the requirements in subsections (2) to (8) are complied with.
    (2) The union must appoint a person to supervise the picketing.
    (3) That person ("the picket supervisor") must be an official or other member of the union who is familiar with any provisions of a Code of Practice issued under section 203 that deal with picketing.
    (4) The union or picket supervisor must take reasonable steps to tell the police—
        (a)   the picket supervisor's name;
        (b)   where the picketing will be taking place;
        (c)   how to contact the picket supervisor.
    (5) The union must provide the picket supervisor with a letter stating that the picketing is approved by the union.
    (6) If an individual who is, or is acting on behalf of, the employer asks the picket supervisor for sight of the approval letter, the picket supervisor must show it to that individual as soon as reasonably practicable.
    (7) While the picketing is taking place, the picket supervisor must—
        (a)   be present where it is taking place, or
        (b)   be readily contactable by the union and the police, and able to attend at short notice.

(8) While present where the picketing is taking place, the picket supervisor must wear something that readily identifies the picket supervisor as such.

(9) In this section—

"approval letter" means the letter referred to in subsection (5);

"employer" means the employer to which the trade dispute relates;

"picketing" means attendance at or near a place of work, in contemplation or furtherance of a trade dispute, for the purpose of—

(a) obtaining or communicating information, or

(b) persuading any person to work or abstain from working.

(10) In relation to picketing that two or more unions organise or encourage members to take part in—

(a) in subsection (2) "the union" means any one of those unions, and

(b) other references in this section to "the union" are to that union.

NOTES AND QUESTIONS

1. TULRCA 1992 s 220 gives the express right for 'peacefully persuading' or exchanging information at 'any premises of his employer', or a former place of work if dismissed. Under s 220A there must be a 'picket supervisor', who ideally informs the police of the times and places of picket.

2. The DBIS, *Code of Practice on Picketing* (March 2017) is issued under s 203. The picket supervisor is ideally 'familiar with' this. Among some of the interesting ideas in the Code is §56: 'Large numbers on a picket line are also likely to give rise to fear and resentment amongst those seeking to cross that picket line' as they 'exacerbate disputes and sour relations' with management and 'fellow employees'. It therefore suggests 'in general the number of pickets does not exceed six at any entrance to, or exit from, a workplace'. Where is the empirical evidence that pickets exacerbate disputes, rather than the management that refuses to negotiate, and drives people to the picket line?

3. Section 220 is not exhaustive of the whole right to protest either at common law, or under the ECHR Art 11. It follows that non-compliance with s 220A does not make a picket unlawful, as peaceful protests are invariably lawful in any case. Any employer who complained under s 219(3) would presumably have to show loss from a picket, where people peacefully persuading others to support them: it is submitted that this is legally impossible, that it will and never should succeed. See further JS Mill, *On Liberty* (1859).

4. The effect of s 224(1) and (3), which says 'lawful picketing' is not 'secondary action' is that if a picketer persuades someone who is not a worker to join in the picket, there is no unlawful act.

5. Although there is explicit protection for peaceful picketing today, there is a shameful history of suppression. Before he went to the Lords, and gave a similar judgment in *Taff Vale*, Lord Lindley MR decided *J Lyons & Sons v Wilkins* [1896] 1 Ch. 811 and [1899] 1 Ch 255, which held that picketing was unlawful, because to 'watch and beset' was contrary to the Conspiracy and Protection of Property Act 1875 s 7. Here picketers of the Amalgamated Trade Society of Fancy Leather Workers had 'been placing a few men about the plaintiffs' works, and telling them to accost workpeople and to shew them certain cards'. Lord Lindley MR was obviously so shocked by the content of these 'certain cards' that he did not feel

he could say what was on them in his judgment. This was reversed by the Trade Disputes Act 1906 section 2, like *Taff Vale*.

6. TULRCA 1992 s 241 still contains an offence for watching and besetting, as well as persistently following someone, or hiding their tools or clothes, or even following someone through a street 'in a disorderly manner'. However such actions, to be an offence, must be 'with a view to compelling another person'. Thus, there is a bright-line distinction between use of force by 'intimidation or annoyance by violence' and the general rule that peaceful persuasion is always lawful. As an exception to this, and as an offence, section 241 must be construed restrictively. But what does following someone down a street 'in a disorderly manner' look like? For possible inspiration, see *Monty Python's Flying Circus* (1970) season 2, episode 1, on the 'Ministry of Silly Walks'.

7. The Highway Act 1980 s 137 makes it an offence to obstruct a highway. In *Broome v DPP* [1974] AC 587 Broome stood in front of a lorry as part of a picket, in Short Street, Stockport, and refused to move to allow the driver to enter a site. Broome was arrested by a police officer. The House of Lords upheld the conviction, saying that being part of a peaceful protest was not an excuse to block the lorry.

8. In 1989, there were massive protests centred upon Tiananmen Square, Beijing, in China for democratic reform. Estimates of the number of deaths range from official government figures of around 240, to over 10,000 dead according to Sir Alan Donald, British Ambassador to China: A Lusher (23 December 2017) *The Independent*. Among the most famous images of the twentieth century is a sole figure, with a white shirt, black trousers, and two shopping bags, standing in the middle of the road as a column of tanks halt before him. The tanks have been sent to crush democracy. The man steps left and right as the first tank tries to manoeuvre around him, but does not want to run him down. In a few minutes, he is rushed away by other men. We do not know who the 'tank man' was, or what happened to him. In Britain, would he have been convicted of obstructing a highway?

9. It is certain that peaceful assemblies that do not amount to a public or private nuisance are lawful. In *DPP v Jones* [1999] 2 AC 240, the House of Lords held protestors near Stonehenge did not violate the Public Order Act 1986 s 14A by standing near a road, as they committed no private or public nuisance and were using the highway for a reasonable purpose.

10. Obstructing a police officer in the execution of duty is also an offence: Police Act 1996 s 89(2). If an officer (or any citizen) sees that a 'breach of peace' is taking place, or is imminent she or he may act. But the threshold is very high. In *Piddington v Bates* [1961] 1 WLR 162 Lord Parker CJ held it was lawful for Chief Inspector Piddington to arrest a printing worker who 'gently' pushed past to get to a picket at a printing factory in London, when Piddington reached the view that there were already enough people on the pickets. However, in *R (Laporte) v Chief Constable of Gloucestershire* [2006] UKHL 55, [47] where police forcibly escorted three coaches of protestors back to London because they thought there *could* be a 'breach of peace', Lord Bingham said *Piddington* was 'an aberrant decision: the judgment showed no recognition that the police, in this context, enjoyed no powers not enjoyed by the private citizen', and was

inconsistent with previous authority. *Laporte* also casts severe doubt upon *Moss v McLachlan* [1985] IRLR 76, where miners were convicted for pushing past police on the M1 to join a picket at Nottinghamshire collieries. Lord Brown said at [118] that it was 'going to the furthermost limits of any acceptable view of imminence' of breach of peace, and potentially wrong on the facts. Lord Mance at [150] suggested the decision was wrong: '[T]he court's scrutiny of such factual and legal issues should now be closer than is suggested in *Moss v McLachlan*.'

11. 'Whose streets? Our streets!' is a common rally at marches. Why should a peaceful protest not stop the movement of traffic to an employer's business? When the police arrest picketers and protestors, they favour the employer's interests in breaking a strike, and not negotiating. The state is endorsing the use of violence, to favour the interests of capital owners over its citizens. Contrast the approach in *Schmidberger v Austria* (2003) C-112/00, [81] where, endorsing the right of protestors to block trucks on a motorway, the Court of Justice suggested there must be a 'fair balance' between business and human rights.

(3) BALLOTING

The Trade Union Act 1984 first demanded that unions hold a ballot before a strike. Back then, the Department of Employment, *Democracy in Trade Unions* (1983) Cm 8778, 17, argued: 'Strikes damage economic performance, reduce living standards and destroy jobs far beyond the ambit of the parties to the dispute.' It went on to say, at 57: 'The argument of principle for strike ballots is therefore simple and unanswerable. The rules of some trade unions already provide for them and there is evidence that union members increasingly wish and expect to be consulted by voting in secret before they are called out on strike.' In fact, the premise that strikes 'damage economic performance, reduce living standards and destroy jobs' appears wrong: countries with stronger rights to strike historically have higher living standards, greater equality, and as a result superior economic performance. The reason seems to be that, although strikes themselves are obviously bad for production, the possibility of collective action impels management to distribute each enterprise's product more fairly. Countries that suppress strike action have seen rising inequality, stalling productivity, and have witnessed serious gains by far-right political groups.

Legitimate arguments can be made for strike ballots. These might include strengthening accountability of a union's executive, ensuring in the union's own interest that important decisions command majority support, and ensuring real engagement with the membership. Against requiring ballots, it can be argued that strikes should be classed as a decision for the union executive, or that unions' through their own constitutional channels should be free to determine how decisions on important issues are made. The current rules, however, cannot be seen as advancing any coherent goal one way or the other, except to frustrate collective action. They are long-winded, badly drafted, bureaucratic, and probably violate international law.

Trade Union and Labour Relations (Consolidation) Act 1992 ss 226–34A

226. Requirement of ballot before action by trade union.
(1) An act done by a trade union to induce a person to take part, or continue to take part, in industrial action
   (a) is not protected unless the industrial action has the support of a ballot, and
   (b) where section 226A falls to be complied with in relation to the person's employer, is not protected as respects the employer unless the trade union has complied with section 226A in relation to him.
   ...
(2) Industrial action shall be regarded as having the support of a ballot only if—
   (a) the union has held a ballot in respect of the action—
      (i) in relation to which the requirements of section 226B so far as applicable before and during the holding of the ballot were satisfied,
      (ii) in relation to which the requirements of sections 227 to 231 were satisfied,
      (iia) in which at least 50% of those who were entitled to vote in the ballot did so, and
      (iii) in which the required number of persons (see subsections (2A) to (2C)) answered "Yes" to the question applicable in accordance with section 229(2) to industrial action of the kind to which the act of inducement relates;
   (b) such of the requirements of the following sections as have fallen to be satisfied at the relevant time have been satisfied, namely—
      (i) section 226B so far as applicable after the holding of the ballot, and
      (ii) section 231B;
   (bb) section 232A does not prevent the industrial action from being regarded as having the support of the ballot; and
   (c) the requirements of section 233 (calling of industrial action with support of ballot) are satisfied.
   Any reference in this subsection to a requirement of a provision which is disapplied or modified by section 232 has effect subject to that section.
(2A) In all cases, the required number of persons for the purposes of subsection (2)(a)(iii) is the majority voting in the ballot.
(2B) There is an additional requirement where the majority of those who were entitled to vote in the ballot are at the relevant time normally engaged in the provision of important public services, unless at that time the union reasonably believes this not to be the case.
(2C) The additional requirement is that at least 40% of those who were entitled to vote in the ballot answered "Yes" to the question.
(2D) In subsection (2B) "important public services" has the meaning given by regulations made by statutory instrument by the Secretary of State.
(2E) Regulations under subsection (2D) may specify only services that fall within any of the following categories—
   (a) health services;
   (b) education of those aged under 17;
   (c) fire services;
   (d) transport services;
   (e) decommissioning of nuclear installations and management of radioactive waste and spent fuel;
   (f) border security.
(2EA) But regulations under subsection (2D) may not specify services provided by a devolved Welsh authority.

(2F) No regulations shall be made under subsection (2D) unless a draft of them has been laid before Parliament and approved by a resolution of each House of Parliament.

(3) Where separate workplace ballots are held by virtue of section 228(1)—

    (a) industrial action shall be regarded as having the support of a ballot if the conditions specified in subsection (2) are satisfied, and

    (b) the trade union shall be taken to have complied with the requirements relating to a ballot imposed by section 226A if those requirements are complied with,

in relation to the ballot for the place of work of the person induced to take part, or continue to take part, in the industrial action.

(3A) If the requirements of section 231A fall to be satisfied in relation to an employer, as respects that employer industrial action shall not be regarded as having the support of a ballot unless those requirements are satisfied in relation to that employer.

(4) For the purposes of this section an inducement, in relation to a person, includes an inducement which is or would be ineffective, whether because of his unwillingness to be influenced by it or for any other reason.

226A. Notice of ballot and sample voting paper for employers.

(1) The trade union must take such steps as are reasonably necessary to ensure that—

    (a) not later than the seventh day before the opening day of the ballot, the notice specified in subsection (2), and

    (b) not later than the third day before the opening day of the ballot, the sample voting paper specified in subsection (2F),

is received by every person who it is reasonable for the union to believe (at the latest time when steps could be taken to comply with paragraph (a)) will be the employer of persons who will be entitled to vote in the ballot.

(2) The notice referred to in paragraph (a) of subsection (1) is a notice in writing—

    (a) stating that the union intends to hold the ballot,

    (b) specifying the date which the union reasonably believes will be the opening day of the ballot, and

    (c) containing—

        (i) the lists mentioned in subsection (2A) and the figures mentioned in subsection (2B), together with an explanation of how those figures were arrived at, or

        (ii) where some or all of the employees concerned are employees from whose wages the employer makes deductions representing payments to the union, either those lists and figures and that explanation or the information mentioned in subsection (2C).

(2A) The lists are—

    (a) a list of the categories of employee to which the employees concerned belong, and

    (b) a list of the workplaces at which the employees concerned work.

(2B) The figures are—

    (a) the total number of employees concerned,

    (b) the number of the employees concerned in each of the categories in the list mentioned in subsection (2A)(a), and

    (c) the number of the employees concerned who work at each workplace in the list mentioned in subsection (2A)(b).

(2C) The information referred to in subsection (2)(c)(ii) is such information as will enable the employer readily to deduce—

    (a) the total number of employees concerned,

    (b) the categories of employee to which the employees concerned belong and the number of the employees concerned in each of those categories, and

    (c) the workplaces at which the employees concerned work and the number of them who work at each of those workplaces.

(2D) The lists and figures supplied under this section, or the information mentioned in subsection (2C) that is so supplied, must be as accurate as is reasonably practicable in the light of the information in the possession of the union at the time when it complies with subsection (1)(a).

(2E) For the purposes of subsection (2D) information is in the possession of the union if it is held, for union purposes—

(a)   in a document, whether in electronic form or any other form, and

(b)   in the possession or under the control of an officer or employee of the union.

(2F) The sample voting paper referred to in paragraph (b) of subsection (1) is—

(a)   a sample of the form of voting paper which is to be sent to the employees concerned, or

(b)   where the employees concerned are not all to be sent the same form of voting paper, a sample of each form of voting paper which is to be sent to any of them.

(2G) Nothing in this section requires a union to supply an employer with the names of the employees concerned.

(2H) In this section references to the "employees concerned" are references to those employees of the employer in question who the union reasonably believes will be entitled to vote in the ballot.

(2I) For the purposes of this section, the workplace at which an employee works is—

(a)   in relation to an employee who works at or from a single set of premises, those premises, and

(b)   in relation to any other employee, the premises with which his employment has the closest connection.

(4) In this section references to the opening day of the ballot are references to the first day when a voting paper is sent to any person entitled to vote in the ballot.

(5) This section, in its application to a ballot in which merchant seamen to whom section 230(2A) applies are entitled to vote, shall have effect with the substitution in subsection (2F), for references to the voting paper which is to be sent to the employees, of references to the voting paper which is to be sent or otherwise provided to them.

...

227. Entitlement to vote in ballot.

(1) Entitlement to vote in the ballot must be accorded equally to all the members of the trade union who it is reasonable at the time of the ballot for the union to believe will be induced by the union to take part or, as the case may be, to continue to take part in the industrial action in question, and to no others.

...

230. Conduct of ballot.

(1) Every person who is entitled to vote in the ballot must—

(a)   be allowed to vote without interference from, or constraint imposed by, the union or any of its members, officials or employees, and

(b)   so far as is reasonably practicable, be enabled to do so without incurring any direct cost to himself.

(2) Except as regards persons falling within subsection (2A), so far as is reasonably practicable, every person who is entitled to vote in the ballot must—

(a)   have a voting paper sent to him by post at his home address or any other address which he has requested the trade union in writing to treat as his postal address; and

(b)   be given a convenient opportunity to vote by post.

...

232B Small accidental failures to be disregarded.

(1) If—

    (a)   in relation to a ballot there is a failure (or there are failures) to comply with a provision mentioned in subsection (2) or with more than one of those provisions, and

    (b)   the failure is accidental and on a scale which is unlikely to affect the result of the ballot or, as the case may be, the failures are accidental and taken together are on a scale which is unlikely to affect the result of the ballot,

the failure (or failures) shall be disregarded for all purposes (including, in particular, those of section 232A(c)).

(2) The provisions are section 227(1), section 230(2) and section 230(2B).

NOTES AND QUESTIONS

1.   TULRCA 1992 ss 226, 226A, 227(1), 230 and 232B are just a start. The reader will be spared full extracts, which run into 15 or 20 pages. But who wrote this stuff? Did the government find a specialist in medieval enfeoffment with a nasty bump on the head?

2.   The general answer is the Act was drafted by the Major government before 1992, and then amended by the Blair government in 1999 and 2004, partly because of *P* below.

3.   Tony Blair's government was never going to change much. Before the 1997 election, Blair wrote: 'The essential elements of the trade union legislation of the 1980s will remain. There will be no return to secondary action, flying pickets, strikes without ballots, the closed shop and all the rest. The changes that we do propose would leave British law the most restrictive on trade unions in the Western world. The scenes from Wapping, Grunwick or the miners' strike could no more happen under our proposals than under the existing laws.' Tony Blair, 'We Won't Look Back to the 1970s' (31 March 1997) *The Times*. Blair kept his promise to the owner of *The Times*, Rupert Murdoch, and became godfather to Murdoch's daughter in 2011.

4.   Before entering the vortex of the ballot rules in detail, it is worth considering the leading House of Lords case. This found that the Act, in s 232B, contained a 'blatant error', referring to s 230(2A) (on balloting merchant seamen) instead of s 230(2B). The following case did not turn on this point, but is emblematic of the law's problems.

P v NASUWT [2003] UKHL 8

The National Association of School Masters/Union of Women Teachers (NASUWT) went on strike to pressure for the expulsion of an unruly pupil, 'P', from a school in Bromley, London. The student was said to be violent and abusive. He was expelled, but the school's governors allowed the student's appeal. The teachers balloted for a strike and refused to teach P. P (or rather the barrister for P's mother) argued that the strike was not a 'trade dispute' under TULRCA 1992 s 244 because teaching him was ostensibly not something about the terms and conditions of employment, but rather (supposedly) the headmaster's application of rules in the terms of employment. P also argued that NASUWT's ballot to strike was (supposedly) unlawful, because the union failed to notify two school members who were entitled to vote under ss 226(2) and 232A (on members who would be induced to vote). In the Employment Appeal Tribunal, Morison J dismissed the claim. The mother publicly responded by saying: 'Jesus said "Those without sin shall cast the first stone". Faced with adversity, a parent has to do what's right within the law to seek justice for their young.' However, the Court of Appeal, and then the House of Lords, held that the strike was lawful. It was a trade dispute, and everyone was accorded the right to vote 'so far as reasonably practical' in s 230(2).

Lord Bingham:

6 It has been common ground between the parties throughout that the reference to section 230(2A) in section 232B makes no sense. Morison J inferred, reasonably enough, that the reference to section 230(2A) in section 232B was intended to be a reference to section 232A, since when spoken both sound the same (judgment, para 25). The Court of Appeal [2001] ICR 1241 saw the force of this point (judgment of Waller LJ, at p 1258, para 59) but invited further argument, as a result of which it became clear (and was accepted by both sides) that the reference in section 232B(2) should have been, not to section 230(2A), but to section 230(2B). Thus the House has the unenviable task, as did the courts below, of attempting to construe this complicated series of provisions with knowledge that they contain at least one blatant error.

7 In the present case, the number of union members at the school was relatively small and it would not have been unduly onerous for the union both to establish with accuracy who was entitled to vote and also to ensure they received ballot papers. But these statutory provisions would apply equally to industrial action to be undertaken by thousands or tens of thousands. It would be absurd if an immaterial and accidental failure to send a ballot paper to a single member were to invalidate the ballot, so as to deprive the union of immunity, and this contingency is provided for by sections 230(2) and 232B. But it would be equally absurd if an immaterial and accidental failure to establish with accuracy who was entitled to vote were to invalidate the ballot so as to deprive the union of immunity. It is inconceivable that Parliament intended these 1999 amendments to the 1992 Act to have that result. The House must attempt to give the provisions a likely and workable construction. In my opinion, the construction advanced by my noble and learned friend, Lord Hoffmann, achieves that result, and I also would adopt it. I would however hope, an error on the face of the statute having been exposed, that remedial legislative action may be taken.

Lord Hoffmann:

24 In my opinion this was plainly a dispute over terms and conditions of employment, which I regard as a composite phrase chosen to avoid arguments over whether something should properly be described as a "term" or "condition" of employment. It is sufficient that it should be one or the other. Furthermore, the use of such a composite expression shows that it was intended to be given a broad meaning: see Roskill LJ in *British Broadcasting Corpn v Hearn* [1977] 1 WLR 1004, 1015.

25 In the present case, it seems to me that the dispute was about the contractual obligation of the teachers to teach P. It could be characterised as a dispute over whether there was such a contractual obligation: the union, as we have seen, contended that the headmaster's direction was unreasonable. Alternatively it could be characterised as a dispute over whether there should be such a contractual obligation. It does not seem to me profitable to try to analyse it one way or the other. The dispute arose because the headmaster said that the teachers were obliged to teach P and they said that they were not willing to do so. That seems to me a dispute which does not merely "relate to" but is about their terms and conditions of employment.

26 Mr Giffin, who appeared for P, submitted that "terms and conditions of employment" meant the rules which governed the employment relationship ....

27 ... Mr Giffin says ... [a] dispute over whether they should teach P was not a dispute about the rule but about the application of the rule. ...

28 My Lords, I do not think that Parliament could have intended the immunities conferred upon trade unions in industrial disputes to turn upon such fine distinctions. It is in my opinion impossible in this context to formulate a coherent distinction between a rule and the application of the rule to particular cases. A dispute about what the workers are obliged to do or how the employer is obliged to remunerate them, at any level of generality or particularity, is about terms and conditions of employment.

  ...

35 The other point concerns the validity of the ballot. This depends upon an examination of some complicated provisions in the 1992 Act. ...

  ...

38 In my opinion the key provision in section 232A is, for present purposes, condition (c). Is it the case that the two members were not accorded entitlement to vote in the ballot? For this purpose, one must consider what counts as being accorded entitlement to vote.

39 Before the 1999 amendments, the concept of being accorded entitlement to vote was already being used in section 227(1). That provided that entitlement to vote must be accorded equally to all members of the union whom it was reasonable to believe would be induced to take part in the industrial action. Subsection (2), which was repealed by the 1999 Act, provided:

> "The requirement in subsection (1) shall be taken not to have been satisfied if any person who was a member of the trade union at the time when the ballot was held and was denied entitlement to vote in the ballot is induced by the union to take part ... in the industrial action."

40 Here too, there were no exceptions. No one may be denied entitlement to vote. So the previous legislation also raised the question of what counted as being accorded entitlement to vote, or not being denied entitlement to vote. In particular, does the fact that one has not been sent a ballot paper mean that one has not been accorded entitlement to vote? If it did, then failure to send any person a ballot paper would have invalidated the ballot.

41 The answer to this question may be found in section 230(2), which provides that "so far as is reasonably practicable" every person who is entitled to vote must be sent a ballot paper. That provision in my opinion shows that, if it was not reasonably practicable, the omission to send a ballot paper to a person entitled to vote does not amount to a denial of his entitlement. Otherwise there would be no point in the qualifying words "so far as is reasonably practicable". The ballot would have complied with section 230(2) but would nevertheless have been invalidated by section 227(2). ...

Lord Walker:

62 Statutes dealing with employment, trade unions and labour relations are of the highest social importance. Parliament's objective is to frame such statutes in language which is unambiguous and capable of being understood by the members of the general public who may not

Collective Action **469**

have ready access to legal advice. This appeal shows that unfortunately that objective is some-times imperfectly achieved. ...

...

65 Every trade union is required by law to maintain a register of its members (see section 24 of the 1992 Act). But it is a fact of life that no trade union of any size can keep completely full and accurate records of the names and addresses of its ever-changing body of members, still less their current places of work, trade categories and pay grades. ...

66 In theory the union should have been able to produce from its computerised records a printout showing all its members at the B school. In practice it produced a list which was rea-sonably accurate but not wholly accurate: it included the names of five teachers who had by then moved on, and it omitted the names of two teachers who had joined the school staff, in each case without letting the union know about their moves. The inaccurate printout was in practice the source of the error in distributing ballot papers. But there is nothing in the statu-tory provisions, or in the way in which the union's head office seems to have acted, to indicate that the printout was intended to be definitive. Had either of the recently-joined teachers rung up the head office to protest at non-receipt of a ballot paper, the answer might have been, "It is too late to do anything about it" but it would not have been "You are not entitled to vote". The printout was not a definitive document like an electoral roll.

67 This tentative analysis is, I think, given support by the absence of any statutory requirement for a union to send to the employer anything like an electoral roll of those who are to be bal-loted and (if the ballot goes in favour of industrial action) to be called out. On the contrary section 226A(3A) of the 1992 Act, as amended by the 1999 Act, specifically disentitles the employer from a list of names, for reasons which appear from the judgment of Sir Thomas Bingham MR (on section 226A in the original form in which it was inserted by the 1993 Act) in *Blackpool and the Fylde College v National Association of Teachers in Further and Higher Education* [1994] ICR 648.

73 ... the two teachers who had not told their union about their new employment at the B school were not persons who were "not accorded entitlement to vote". The error made in their case fell within section 230(2), to which section 232B does apply. The ballot issue was raised on behalf of the appellant only on the morning of the hearing. Had it been raised at an earlier stage, the judge would probably have had fuller evidence about this aspect of the matter. As it is, the only fair conclusion is that any defect in the ballot can be disregarded under one or both of the exceptions to section 230(2).

Lord Hobhouse agreed with **Lord Hoffmann** and **Lord Walker. Lord Scott** agreed with **Lord Hoffmann.**

NOTES AND QUESTIONS

1.   The House of Lords held that a proper interpretation of the Act made it obvious there was a trade dispute, and that the ballot rules were to be construed to ensure that small mistakes did not affect validity, because TULRCA 1992 s 230(2) says people must be given the vote 'so far as is reasonably practicable'. Lord Bingham says it would be 'absurd' to invalidate a ballot because not everyone did not receive a paper, or if it was not accurately established who was entitled to vote. Lord Walker contrasts the voting process with an electoral roll, where standards

are expected to be higher. Through the black-letter rules, which principles do you think emerge from this decision?

2. In voting law for politics, the clear principles are that (1) if an irregularity would have changed the result a vote must be declared void, and (2) if a vote is conducted 'so badly that it was not substantially in accordance with the law' this can vitiate the result: *Morgan v Simpson* [1975] QB 151. Do you agree that the same principles – and no stricter rule – should apply to ballots in trade unions?

3. What are the other provisions of the ballot rules in TULRCA 1992 ss 226–35? As above, s 226 requires the ballot rules are followed or industrial action is 'not protected'. Section 226A(1) says a union must give notice to employers of intention to hold a ballot seven days in advance, (2A) with categories of employees to be balloted and numbers 'as is reasonably practicable', and (2H) only ballot those entitled. Section 226B requires a scrutineer to prepare a report on the vote. Section 227 requires only those entitled vote. Section 228 requires a separate ballot at each workplace, section 228A or for each employer. Section 229 requires voting on paper with a yes or no question. Section 230 requires the ballot is done by post and is secret. The government refused to allow electronic voting in the Trade Union Act 2016, instead delegating the task of investigating the use of modern technology to a retired fire chief. Section 231A requires the employer is informed of the result. Section 231B requires the scrutineer to be satisfied the law is complied with. Section 233 requires that a specified person in the union call the action. Section 234 constrains the collective action to take place within 4 weeks, or 8 weeks if the employer agrees or a court orders. Section 234A requires the union to tell the employer 7 days in advance about the strike's start date, whether continuous or not, and how many days it will last.

4. Do you agree that the employer has no legitimate interest in irregularities of a ballot, and that failure to be duly informed should lead to, at most, nominal damages because they will have no loss?

5. Of special note is that TULRCA 1992 s 229(4) requires the voting paper must state 'you may be in breach of your contract of employment'. The fact that the law says one 'may' breach a contract by going on strike underlines the fact that at common law there may not – and arguably is not – any breach of contract at all. Even aside from people on zero-hours contracts, it must be an implied term that everyone is allowed to suspend contractual performance in a good-faith trade dispute. It should be plain that if an employer ever tried to include a clause saying 'there is no right to strike', this would not only violate TULRCA 1992 s 180, but also be a sham: *Autoclenz Ltd v Belcher*. See above chapter 10(1)(a) and (b).

6. The financial crisis starting in 2007 led to more strike action, as employers chose to cut wages and make redundancies to cope (see chapters 10(2) and 19). This led to barristers pushing the law to seek injunctions, which for nearly two years met with constant success in the High Court after *Metrobus Ltd v Unite the Union* [2009] EWCA Civ 829. Here the Court of Appeal held the union had not notified the employer of the strike result under s 231A quickly enough, and upheld an injunction even though 90 per cent of workers had voted in favour. Following this, in *British Airways plc v Unite the Union (No 1)* [2009] EWHC 3541 (QB) Cox J granted an injunction because the union accidentally balloted workers who

had taken voluntary redundancy, even though 92.49 per cent of workers voted in favour of strike against BA plc cutting cabin crew pay. In *Network Rail Infrastructure v RMT* [2010] EWHC 1084 (QB) Sharp J awarded an injunction, on 1 April, because the union did not individually notify members of the result's breakdown under s 231, rather than sending a text message with a link to a website with the full result. Sharp J alluded to 'good policy reasons' for this, but did not explain what those were. In *Milford Haven Port Authority v Unite the Union* [2010] EWCA Civ 400, Sweeney J granted an injunction, where the union gave notice of the strike ballot on one piece of paper, but as there would be both continuous and discontinuous action, the employer argued there should have been two pieces of paper. The Court of Appeal, as the employer apparently agreed this was odd, overturned the injunction. In *British Airways plc v Unite the Union (No 2)* [2010] EWCA Civ 669 (above) the Court of Appeal divided, refusing an injunction, and finally in *RMT v Serco Ltd; ASLEF v London & Birmingham Railway* [2011] EWCA Civ 226 the Court of Appeal firmed its stance. While, as it has been urged above, this judgment must be seen as flawed to suggest that the 'common law confers no right to strike', it did hold that trivial mistakes in ballots should never lead to 'the draconian step of invalidating the ballot', that the court's role was not to 'set traps and hurdles for the union which have no legitimate purpose or function' and suggests that regard should be paid to international instruments, at [8].

7.   As *RMT v UK* showed above, it remains to be seen whether the balloting rules as they stand violate the ECHR. It is already possible for the Court of Appeal, or the Supreme Court to evaluate this issue without recourse to Strasbourg. The problem is not one of declaring an Act of Parliament incompatible with ECHR Art 11 under the HRA 1998 s 4. Instead, the problem flows from an illegitimate assumption of tort liability against unions, with an unjustified windfall to employers, for failure to follow ballot rules. It is within the power of the Court of Appeal or Supreme Court to put the common law onto a principled basis.

(4) DISPUTE RESOLUTION, DISMISSAL, DETRIMENT

So far we have seen there are serious arguments to suggest that since the House of Lords and Supreme Court decisions in *OBG v Allan*, *Autoclenz Ltd v Belcher* and *Gisda Cyf v Barratt* there is a common law right to strike, consistent with human rights. On this view, the right to engage in a good-faith strike is an implied term in a worker's contract. Any worker may lawfully withhold performance of a contract when an employer breaches their reasonable expectations. Without a primary breach, there is no tort commissioned by a union, and no unlawful means are used in carrying out collective action. The ballot rules can be relevant for internal claims by union members against their executive, but internal irregularities are of no legitimate concern to an employer. Without amending or contradicting anything in statute, the common law is open to change whenever it may.

All this said, it is clear that a long and tortured history of cases has been footed on the assumption that the common law is hostile to labour rights, which are enshrined in international law and Acts of Parliament for over a century. That assumption can be corrected at any time, but until then we must understand the current system of dispute resolution. This includes the possibility of arbitration, but we must also examine how injunctions and damages have been awarded against unions in the past. The section then deals with unfair dismissal for strikes, and the legality of wage deductions. Sadly, the system looks less like a mechanism for dispute resolution, and more of dispute retaliation.

Trade Union and Labour Relations (Consolidation) Act 1992 ss 20–22 and 212–18

20. Liability of trade union in certain proceedings in tort.
(1) Where proceedings in tort are brought against a trade union—
    (a) on the ground that an act—
        (i) induces another person to break a contract or interferes or induces another person to interfere with its performance, or
        (ii) consists in threatening that a contract (whether one to which the union is a party or not) will be broken or its performance interfered with, or that the union will induce another person to break a contract or interfere with its performance, or
    (b) in respect of an agreement or combination by two or more persons to do or to procure the doing of an act which, if it were done without any such agreement or combination, would be actionable in tort on such a ground,

then, for the purpose of determining in those proceedings whether the union is liable in respect of the act in question, that act shall be taken to have been done by the union if, but only if, it is to be taken to have been authorised or endorsed by the trade union in accordance with the following provisions. …

21. Repudiation by union of certain acts.
(1) An act shall not be taken to have been authorised or endorsed by a trade union by virtue only of paragraph (c) of section 20(2) if it was repudiated by the executive, president or general secretary as soon as reasonably practicable after coming to the knowledge of any of them.
(2) Where an act is repudiated—
    (a) written notice of the repudiation must be given to the committee or official in question, without delay, and
    (b) the union must do its best to give individual written notice of the fact and date of repudiation, without delay—
        (i) to every member of the union who the union has reason to believe is taking part, or might otherwise take part, in industrial action as a result of the act, and
        (ii) to the employer of every such member. …

   …

212. Arbitration.
(1) Where a trade dispute exists or is apprehended ACAS may, at the request of one or more of the parties to the dispute and with the consent of all the parties to the dispute, refer all or any of the matters to which the dispute relates for settlement to the arbitration of—
    (a) one or more persons appointed by ACAS for that purpose (not being officers or employees of ACAS), or
    (b) the Central Arbitration Committee.

   …

215. Inquiry and report by court of inquiry.

(1) Where a trade dispute exists or is apprehended, the Secretary of State may inquire into the causes and circumstances of the dispute, and, if he thinks fit, appoint a court of inquiry and refer to it any matters appearing to him to be connected with or relevant to the dispute.

(2) The court shall inquire into the matters referred to it and report on them to the Secretary of State; and it may make interim reports if it thinks fit.

(3) Any report of the court, and any minority report, shall be laid before both Houses of Parliament as soon as possible.

...

221 Restrictions on grant of injunctions and interdicts.

(1) Where—

(a) an application for an injunction or interdict is made to a court in the absence of the party against whom it is sought or any representative of his, and

(b) he claims, or in the opinion of the court would be likely to claim, that he acted in contemplation or furtherance of a trade dispute,

the court shall not grant the injunction or interdict unless satisfied that all steps which in the circumstances were reasonable have been taken with a view to securing that notice of the application and an opportunity of being heard with respect to the application have been given to him.

(2) Where—

(a) an application for an interlocutory injunction is made to a court pending the trial of an action, and

(b) the party against whom it is sought claims that he acted in contemplation or furtherance of a trade dispute,

the court shall, in exercising its discretion whether or not to grant the injunction, have regard to the likelihood of that party's succeeding at the trial of the action in establishing any matter which would afford a defence to the action under section 219 (protection from certain tort liabilities) or section 220 (peaceful picketing). This subsection does not extend to Scotland.

NOTES AND QUESTIONS

1. TULRCA 1992 s 20 states that a trade union cannot be liable in tort if an action has not been authorised by it, and s 21 says that a general secretary, president or executive may repudiate any action (eg made by exuberant union officials) with written notice and appropriate publicity: cf *Gate Gourmet London Ltd v TGWU* [2005] EWHC 1889. Under s 21(3) a union's repudiatory notice to members must say there is no right to complain of unfair dismissal for repudiated actions, although such a notice cannot presumably be binding on a court. It is submitted dismissal could still be wrongful, in appropriate circumstances, if a worker is dismissed in a good-faith trade dispute. As noted at chapter 10(1)(b), s 22 limits any damages in tort, but none of these sections can credibly be read as a statutory endorsement or codification of the historical common law position.

2. TULRCA 1992 s 221 is commonly thought to deal with cases where employers apply to court for an injunction against a strike. But a union could equally be the applicant for an injunction, eg against a parent company which has taken a decision to dismiss workers at a subsidiary without consultation (this would be procuring a breach of contract or maybe breach of statutory duty). See chapters 11(2) and 19.

3.   TULRCA 1992 s 221 says (1) if an injunction is applied for when a defendant is absent, a court should endeavour to notify that party to ensure it is heard, and (2) not grant an injunction without having regard to 'the likelihood of that party's succeeding at the trial' that there is a defence to any tort under ss 219 and 220. In the case of an employer or a parent company attempting to dismiss workers in breach of statutory duty there is, of course, no protection from tort liability. For workers and unions, for whom tort liability should be at best regarded as contested, what counts as a 'likelihood' falls case law.

4.   The leading case on granting an injunction, pending a full hearing, is *American Cyanamid Co v Ethicon Ltd* [1975] AC 396. This case, not itself concerned with a labour dispute, held that to get an injunction it must be shown there is 'a serious question to be tried', and then a court must 'consider whether the balance of convenience lies in favour of granting or refusing to interlocutory relief that is sought.' But what does the 'balance of convenience' really mean?

The Nawala or *NWL Ltd v Woods* [1979] 1 WLR 1294

NWL Ltd claimed an injunction against the International Transport Workers Federation (ITF) after it went on strike. It had a policy of 'blacking' ships flying a flag of convenience, to encourage owners to join the ITF collective agreement, or transfer the vessel registration to the domicile of the beneficial owners. *The Nawala* had been owned by a Norwegian firm, had a Norwegian crew and flag and was registered in Oslo. But then a Hong Kong company, with Swedish shareholders, bought the ship, and changed the registration to Hong Kong and the flag to British. A new crew from Hong Kong, mostly not unionised, was recruited on wages far lower than European standards. It carried iron ore to England. As *The Nawala* was near Redcar, an ITF representative told the company that on entering the port the stevedores and tug operators would not deal with the ship, unless the collective agreement were complied with. Donaldson J granted an injunction, arguing there was no trade dispute under the Trade Union and Labour Relations Act 1974 s 13. The Court of Appeal discharged the injunction. NWL Ltd then got crew to sign affidavits saying they were 'very happy and content' with their wages and did not want the ITF agreement because it would mean loss of their livelihood. It applied for another injunction. This time Donaldson J refused. The Court of Appeal then also refused an appeal. The House of Lords also rejected an injunction because it was likely that the union would succeed in establishing that there was a trade dispute.

Lord Diplock:

In the normal case of threatened industrial action against an employer, the damage that he will sustain if the action is carried out is likely to be large, difficult to assess in money and may well be irreparable. Further more damage is likely to be caused to customers of the employer's business who are not parties to the action, and to the public at large. On the other hand the defendant is not the trade union but an individual officer of the union who, although he is acting on its behalf, can be sued in his personal capacity only. In that personal capacity he will suffer virtually no damage if the injunction is granted, whereas if it is not granted and the action against him ultimately succeeds it is most improbable that damages on the scale that are likely to be awarded against him will prove to be recoverable from him. Again, to grant the injunction will maintain the status quo until the trial; and this too is a factor which in evenly balanced cases generally operates in favour of granting an interlocutory injunction. So on the face of the proceedings in an action of this kind the balance of convenience as to the grant of an interlocutory injunction would appear to be heavily weighted in favour of the employer.

To take this view, however, would be to blind oneself to the practical realities: (1) that the real dispute is not between the employer and the nominal defendant but between the employer and the trade union that is threatening industrial action; (2) that the threat of blacking or other industrial action is being used as a bargaining counter in negotiations either existing or anticipated to obtain agreement by the employer to do whatever it is the union requires of him; (3) that it is the nature of industrial action that it can be promoted effectively only so long as it is possible to strike while the iron is still hot; once postponed it is unlikely that it can be revived; (4) that, in consequence of these three characteristics, the grant or refusal of an interlocutory injunction generally disposes finally of the action; in practice actions of this type seldom if ever come to actual trial.

...

My Lords, when properly understood, there is in my view nothing in the decision of this House in *American Cyanamid Co v Ethicon Ltd* [1975] AC 396 to suggest that in considering whether or not to grant an interlocutory injunction the judge ought not to give full weight to all the practical realities of the situation to which the injunction will apply. *American Cyanamid Co v Ethicon Ltd*, which enjoins the judge upon an application for an interlocutory injunction to direct his attention to the balance of convenience as soon as he has satisfied himself that there is a serious question to be tried, was not dealing with a case in which the grant or refusal of an injunction at that stage would, in effect, dispose of the action finally in favour of whichever party was successful in the application, because there would be nothing left on which it was in the unsuccessful party's interest to proceed to trial. By the time the trial came on the industrial dispute, if there were one, in furtherance of which the acts sought to be restrained were threatened or done, would be likely to have been settled and it would not be in the employer's interest to exacerbate relations with his workmen by continuing the proceedings against the individual defendants none of whom would be capable financially of meeting a substantial claim for damages. Nor, if an interlocutory injunction had been granted against them, would it be worthwhile for the individual defendants to take steps to obtain a final judgment in their favour, since any damages that they could claim in respect of personal pecuniary loss caused to them by the grant of the injunction and which they could recover under the employer's undertaking on damages, would be very small.

Lord Scarman:

An employer would in most cases have no difficulty in showing that action to disrupt his business contemplated or undertaken by members of the union with which he was in dispute would cause him serious, even catastrophic, loss. Upon a balance of convenience, he would ordinarily have little difficulty in showing that the status quo should be preserved until full investigation at trial. Yet if this argument should prevail, the trade union's bargaining counter would disappear. Its power to bring instant and real pressure upon the employer would be denied. Section 17(2) was introduced by the Act of 1975 after the *Cyanamid* decision. As Lord Denning MR observed in *The Camilla M* [1979] 1 Lloyd's Rep 26, 31, it restores the old law, so far as the defence of acts done in contemplation or furtherance of a trade dispute are concerned. The court must under the subsection have regard to the likelihood of this defence being established before deciding whether or not to grant an interlocutory injunction.

...

The existence of so sweeping a legislative purpose leads me to conclude that, if there is a likelihood as distinct from a mere possibility of a party showing that he acted in contemplation or furtherance of a trade dispute no interlocutory injunction should ordinarily be issued. A balance of probabilities will suffice in most cases for the court to refuse it. I do not rule out the possibility that the consequences to the plaintiff (or others) may be so serious that the court feels it necessary to grant the injunction; for the subsection does leave a residual discretion with the court. But it would, indeed, be a rare case in which a court, having concluded that there was a real likelihood of the defence succeeding, granted the injunction.

Lord Fraser gave a concurring opinion.

NOTES AND QUESTIONS

1. The House of Lords gives a very strong opinion that injunctions should rarely be granted against strikes. Lord Diplock says that courts should give 'full weight to all the practical realities' of a trade dispute, and that this includes the fact that the 'grant or refusal of an interlocutory injunction generally disposes finally of the action'. This is not the role of the court. Lord Scarman says that because there was 'so sweeping a legislative purpose' in giving tort protection for strikes, if there is even a 'distinct' possibility of the union showing it acted lawfully, no injunction should be granted. Considering this emphatic decision, which itself followed Donaldson J's initial injunction being overturned, why do you think High Court judges in the ballot cases at chapter 10(3) got it so consistently wrong?

2. Lord Diplock says that for an employer a strike could cause 'serious, even catastrophic loss' and 'damage is likely to be caused to customers of the employer's business ... and to the public at large'. But to what extent is that actually true? If one conceives the employer as a legal entity, it may well have a loss of profits. But many employing entities may have no such loss: for instance, when university lecturers and professors go on strike, universities appear to have no financial loss whatsoever, as students do not appear to get fees reimbursed, nor does research funding halt. But also in the private sector, diversified shareholders may suffer no loss at all, as one company's loss could be a competitor's gain. For the same reason, customers may suffer no loss whatsoever as they simply switch to a competing supplier. When sectoral collective bargaining is effective, with coordinated strike action across all competitors, shareholders and customers may not be able to diversify or switch to avoid a strike's effects. But even then, why should these losses be characterised as 'serious' if the implication is that losses to workers when a strike is unsuccessful are any less? Unions are typically taking action against the slow-burning degradation of real wages, which result in a thousand daily social and domestic catastrophes: of struggling to pay the rent, missing bills, the stress of overwork, the indignity of unfair pay. Do you agree that the language of relative loss is best avoided, just like judicial intervention in a trade dispute?

3. In *Govia GTR Ltd v Associated Society of Locomotive Engineers and Firemen* [2016] EWCA Civ 1309, Hugh Mercer QC argued Govia Ltd should get an injunction against ASLEF's proposed strike on the ground that it violated its freedom of establishment, because one of Govia Ltd's shareholders is Keolis, a French company which is in turn 70 per cent owned by SNCF, the French state-owned rail company. (It is worth noting that the only government in the world that cannot own UK railways is the UK government: Railways Act 1993 s 25.)

Elias LJ held there was no serious issue to be tried because despite the *Viking* and *Laval* cases, TFEU art 49 'does not protect companies from having to deal with strong or even bloody minded trade unions'. The purpose of TFEU Art 49 'is to allow companies to have access to an open and free market, not to give them a more favourable protection than locally based enterprises' [41]–[42]. For the additional point, that unions also have the freedom to establish and provide services, see chapter 10(1)(d).

4.   For at least the first 12 weeks of a strike, there is explicit protection for employees against dismissal connected to a strike.

Trade Union and Labour Relations (Consolidation) Act 1992 s 238A

238A. Participation in official industrial action.

(1) For the purposes of this section an employee takes protected industrial action if he commits an act which, or a series of acts each of which, he is induced to commit by an act which by virtue of section 219 is not actionable in tort.

(2) An employee who is dismissed shall be regarded for the purposes of Part X of the Employment Rights Act 1996 (unfair dismissal) as unfairly dismissed if—

   (a)   the reason (or, if more than one, the principal reason) for the dismissal is that the employee took protected industrial action, and

   (b)   subsection (3), (4) or (5) applies to the dismissal.

...

(7A) For the purposes of this section "the protected period", in relation to the dismissal of an employee, is the sum of the basic period and any extension period in relation to that employee.

(7B) The basic period is twelve weeks beginning with the first day of protected industrial action.

(7C) An extension period in relation to an employee is a period equal to the number of days falling on or after the first day of protected industrial action (but before the protected period ends) during the whole or any part of which the employee is locked out by his employer.

NOTES AND QUESTIONS

1.   TULRCA 1992 s 238A has the effect that any dismissal connect to a strike will be found to be automatically unfair, and there is no qualifying period: s 239(1). Employers who try to argue that a dismissal after a strike was not mainly to do with the strike should be regarded with intense suspicion by any worker. If a dismissal of someone who was on strike takes place afterwards, the doctrine of *res ipsa loquitur* would seem appropriate. Under s 238A(5) there is a further duty, even after 12 weeks that an employer must have 'taken such procedural steps as would have been reasonable for the purposes of resolving the dispute' before any dismissals can be made. Under s 238B, if the employer enters into conciliation with the union, the period is extended accordingly.

2.   As explained by B Gernigon, A Odero and H Guido, 'ILO Principles Concerning the Right to Strike' (1998) 137 *ILR* 441, 461–65, international law means that 'participating in a lawful strike should be regarded as suspending rather than

terminating the contract of employment, and in the sense also that those who take part in such action should be protected from dismissal with a right to reinstatement at the end of the dispute.'

3. TULRCA 1992 s 237 says there is no right to claim unfair dismissal if industrial action is unofficial. But this does not exclude the right to claim the dismissal violated the right to a fair process, or that a dismissal was unjust at common law: see *Chhabra* and *Wilson*, discussed in chapter 17. There may still be a good faith trade dispute.

4. Apart from the 12-week protection in TULRCA 1992 s 238A, s 238 suggests that if an employer dismisses everyone during a strike or a lockout, then no claim for unfair dismissal can be heard by a Tribunal. The predecessor of this exception, which does not have any principled basis, was used by Rupert Murdoch, and forced the movement of printers for his papers, which many regard as containing news, away from Fleet Street to Wapping. An indication of Murdoch's character was that, in 1983 responding to the Oxford Regius Professor of Modern History, Lord Dacre, declaring 'Hitler diaries' to be fake, Murdoch instructed his editors at the *Sunday Times*: 'Fuck Dacre. Publish.' Afterwards, when challenged, he said 'we're in the entertainment business': A Lusher (5 May 2018) *The Independent*. When the printers went on strike, Murdoch dismissed over 5,500 workers: see *News Group Newspapers Ltd v Society of Graphical and Allied Trades* [1987] ICR 181. Again, the fact that s 238 excludes an unfair dismissal does not prevent a common law dismissal claim. It is submitted that such a mass dismissal is manifestly unfair without a concerted attempt to bargain, and at a minimum for 12 weeks. If an employer does not like the consequences of economic loss of a strike, they should negotiate fair terms and conditions. If a director or shareholder wants to drive through a management plan that the majority of their workers oppose, they should get another job or invest elsewhere. Cases such as *P&O European Ferries (Dover) Ltd v Byrne* [1989] ICR 779, where not everyone was dismissed, but the Court of Appeal allowed the employer to quickly dismiss two more employees, should not be followed.

5. Finally, in chapter 6(1)(d) it was seen how the House of Lords in *Miles v Wakefield MDC* [1987] UKHL 15 enabled employers to deduct wages for workers going on strike. This ruling, however, must now be viewed in light of *Hartley v King Edward VI College* [2017] UKSC 39. Here, teachers claimed that their school has unlawfully deducted their wages pay at a rate of 1/260th of their annual salary for each day of a strike (reflecting each work day). They argued the proper figure was 1/365th for each calendar day. The Supreme Court held that under the Apportionment Act 1870 s 2, the appropriate deduction was 1/365th, given that the employment relationship lasted over all days of the year, not just weekdays. The Supreme Court also stressed, in [1], that the right to deduct pay came from a collective agreement, called the Red Book. Lord Clarke said: 'When sixth form teachers whose contracts of employment incorporate the Red Book go on strike their employer can withhold their pay.' It is strongly arguable, therefore, that there is no inherent right of an employer to withhold pay when workers go on strike.

If workers are withholding their labour in response to a breach of their reasonable expectations, and a breach of contract by the employer, the employer docking pay logically counts as a second breach of contract. On this view, the worker would be able to bring a claim for unlawful wage deductions under ERA 1996 s 13, unless the employer can show that a union has not been on strike in contemplation or furtherance of a trade dispute.

Additional Reading for Chapter 10

HJ Laski, *Liberty in the Modern State* (1937) ch II, IV, 122–41
Laski's theme, from Pericles, is that liberty comes from the 'courage to resist', and in chapter II, part IV, he argues for the proper extent of the right to strike: for political purposes in a general strike, in government employment, or essential public services. Laski agrees with Holmes J in *Coppage v Kansas* 236 US 1 (1915) that 'liberty of contract always begins where equality of bargaining power begins', and that to 'limit the right to strike is a form of industrial servitude. It means, ultimately, that the worker must labour on the employer's terms.' He argues that general strikes cannot be prohibited in practice, nor is it desirable. 'Legal prohibition will merely exacerbate the dispute. It will transfer the discussion of the real problem at issue to a discussion of legality which serves merely to conceal it.' He suggests that, while withdrawing the right to strike in core state functions such as the army are justified to maintain neutrality (including from big business), it is not justified for anything else. 'I do not forget', says Laski, 'the German Republic was saved from the Kapp Putsch by a general strike.' The central principle is this: 'The secret of avoiding general strikes does not lie in their prohibition but in the achievement of the conditions which render them unnecessary.'

O Kahn-Freund & B Hepple, *Laws Against Strikes* (1972) Fabian Research Series 305
Kahn-Freund and Hepple argued that the reason strikes are justified is because of the unequal possession of property and therefore power in society. So, 'the imperative need for a social power countervailing that of property overshadows everything else. If the workers are not free by concerted action to withdraw their labour, their organisations do not wield a credible social force. The power to withdraw their labour is for the workers what for management is its power to shut down production, to switch it to different purposes, to transfer it to different places. A legal system which suppresses that freedom to strike puts the workers at the mercy of their employers.'

P Wallington, 'Policing the Miners' Strike' (1985) 14 *Industrial Law Journal* 145
Wallington gives an account of the miners' strike from the 6 March 1984 to 3 March 1985. He explains how (after the strike was declared unlawful because the union did not hold a ballot) by the end 9,808 people were arrested in England and Wales, and

7,917 charged, and in Scotland 1,483 were arrested, and 1,015 were proceeded against. Three people were killed. While statistics on the number of police deployed by the Thatcher government were unavailable, on a single day at Orgreave there were 3,300. Mansfield Magistrates' Court in Nottinghamshire was particularly active in convicting people, labelled as 'supermarket justice'.

Votes at Work

Democracy, said Pericles, means power 'is in the hands of the many and not of the few' (Thucydides, *History of the Peloponnesian War* (c 404 BC) B Jowett (1881) 117). The big question in the twenty-first century is whether democracy will advance into the economy as it once did into politics. After the Berlin Wall fell, it was argued we had seen an 'end of history'. 'Liberal democracy' and 'free markets' beat all other models: F Fukuyama (1989) 16 *The National Interest* 3. H Hansmann and R Kraakman (2000) 89 *Georgetown Law Journal* 439. Shareholder monopoly on voting rights, or 'shareholder primacy' in large corporations, was supposedly better than state-owned enterprise and labour-oriented models. Every country would converge on the superior US model. But today it is clear there was no 'end'. The right of workers to vote for company boards has spread to a majority of OECD countries, while US politics faces routine 'shutdown'. But also, in the UK and worldwide shareholders are not what they seem. Most shareholder votes are exercised by financial institutions (namely asset managers and banks) who are investing 'other people's money'. Shareholders may have 'primacy', but they are very different from the real investors of capital. These are employees saving for retirement in pension, life insurance and mutual funds. Because of this, the labour movement has pushed for two types of votes at work: (1) for worker representation in enterprise management, and (2) for worker representatives (not financial institutions) to control how shareholder votes are cast on their money.

The UK is behind other countries in some ways, but ahead in others. Historically the labour movement has been uncertain about the right form of 'industrial democracy', and whether collective bargaining by unions should remain a single channel of voice. (cf S Webb and B Webb, *The History of Trade Unionism* (1920) Appendix VIII, 752–60). That uncertainty has dwindled for three reasons. First, the right to vote at work has been one of collective bargaining's greatest achievements worldwide. If you can vote for the people you bargain with, bargaining will be easier. Just as shareholders can get higher dividends, workers can get higher wages. Second, there is growing recognition that guarantees of fair treatment, through voice at work, motivates people to be productive. If people are fairly treated, they want to contribute more (see chapter 2(2)). Why walk out of work on strike against an exploitative boss, when the boss should walk out instead? Third, it has become clear that capital markets foster conflicts of interest, 'negligence and profusion', because asset managers and banks can use votes on 'other people's money' to make companies buy their own products (cf A Smith, *The Wealth of Nations*, at chapter 2(1)). This chapter considers (1) rights over the executives of enterprise, (2) rights in work councils, and (3) votes in capital.

Introductory text: Collins ch 6 (127–30). CEM ch 15. D&M ch 9 (913–84)

(1) RIGHTS OVER ENTERPRISE EXECUTIVES

The rights that workers have over the executive body, in an enterprise they work for, will directly influence wages and conditions. There are four big legal types of enterprise. First, most employers will be companies, registered under the Companies Act (CA) 2006 ss 7–9 and 154. When a company's shares can be traded on the London Stock Exchange its name ends with 'plc' (eg J Sainsbury plc), and when its shares may not be sold to the public, 'Ltd' (eg Specsavers Optical Group Ltd). Second, many employers, especially in the public sector, will be corporate entities, but created by an Act of Parliament, Statutory Instrument or Royal Charter. There are thousands. For instance, if you work for a hospital in the NHS, it is probably a 'foundation trust' created under the National Health Service Act 2006 ss 30–39 and Sch 7. If you work for a university, there is often a special statute under which further rules are made (eg the King's College London Act 1997) or the university will be created by an Order of the Privy Council (see Education Reform Act 1988 ss 124–28 and Schs 7–7A). Third, law, accountancy and investment firms are often partnerships, usually registered under the Limited Liability Partnerships Act 2000 ss 3–4, to limit the partners' liability if the firm goes insolvent (see chapter 20). Some are still formed under the Partnership Act 1890. Fourth, employers can be sole traders, where contract is the governance structure. This section examines (a) rights to vote for corporate board members, and (b) whether workers have rights to enforce directors' duties through derivative claims.

(a) Votes for Corporate Boards

Most types of UK enterprise still have no rights of workers to vote for executive bodies. The one great exception is the university sector. The rules differ for almost every university, but the following is among the most democratic models.

Statutes and Ordinances of the University of Cambridge 2017, Statutes A and C

Statute A The Chancellor and the Government of the University

Chapter I The Chancellor, the Senate, the High Steward, the Depute High Steward and the Commissary

   1. The Chancellor of the University shall be elected by the members of the Senate and shall hold office, in accordance with the laws and customs of the University, until he or she voluntarily resigns or until the Senate otherwise determines.
   ...
   7. The following shall be members of the Senate:
      (a)   the Chancellor and the Vice-Chancellor;

(b) all persons whose names were inscribed on the Roll of the Regent House at the time of the last promulgation;

(c) all persons who hold any of these complete degrees of the University: any Doctor's degree of the University, any Master's degree of the University, or the degree of Bachelor of Divinity of the University; provided always that

  (i) if any member of the Senate wishes to resign her or his membership and so informs the Registrary, and if the Council deems the reasons given sufficient and permits the resignation, that person shall cease forthwith to be a member of the Senate, and shall not be reinstated except by a subsequent decision of the Council which shall not be taken until a period of five years has elapsed from the date of removal;

  (ii) any person who suffers suspension or deprivation of her or his degree shall not be a member of the Senate during the continuance of such suspension or deprivation.

...

Chapter III The Regent House

1. The Regent House shall be the governing body of the University.

2. Any power of making, altering, or repealing Statutes which is assigned to the University by the Universities of Oxford and Cambridge Act 1923, or by any other Act of Parliament, shall be exercised by the Regent House.

3. The powers of enacting, issuing and amending Special Ordinances, Ordinances and Orders, shall be exercised by Grace of the Regent House except so far as such powers are assigned by Statute to any other authority.

...

8. The members of the Regent House at any time shall be those persons whose names were on the Roll of the Regent House at the time of the last promulgation.

...

10. The Registrary shall inscribe on the Roll of the Regent House the names of the following persons:

(a) (i) the Chancellor, the High Steward, the Deputy High Steward, the Commissary, and (ii) the members of the Council in class (e);

(b) other University officers and persons treated as such under Statute J 7;

(c) Heads of Colleges;

(d) Fellows of Colleges, provided that they conform to such conditions of residence as may be determined by Ordinance;

(e) such other persons holding appointments in the University or a College in such categories and subject to such qualifying periods of service as shall be determined from time to time by Ordinance; provided always that any person who is qualified for membership in class (b), class (d), or class (e) shall cease to be so qualified at the next promulgation after he or she attains the age of seventy years

Chapter IV The Council and its Committees

1.(a) The Council shall be the principal executive and policy-making body of the University. The Council shall have general responsibility for the administration of the University, for the planning of its work, and for the management of its resources; it shall have power to take such action as is necessary for it to discharge these responsibilities. It shall also perform such other executive and administrative duties as may be delegated to it by the Regent House or assigned to it by Statute or Ordinance.

...

(d) The Council shall have the power of initiating and submitting Graces to the Regent House and to the Senate. The procedure for the submission of Graces shall be prescribed by Special Ordinance.

...

2. The Council shall consist of the Chancellor, the Vice-Chancellor, and twenty-three members in the following classes:

Members elected by the Regent House
(a) four from among the Heads of Colleges;
(b) four from among the Professors and Readers;
(c) eight from among the other members of the Regent House.
Members in each of classes (a), (b), and (c) shall be elected by the Regent House for a period and in a manner determined by Special Ordinance.

Student members
(d) three student members.
Members in class (d) shall be such persons as shall be prescribed by Special Ordinance and shall serve for a period determined by Special Ordinance.

Appointed members
(e) four persons appointed by Grace of the Regent House who at the time of appointment are not qualified to be members of the Regent House except under Statute A III 10 (a)(ii) nor are employees of the University or a College, one of whom shall be designated by the Council to chair the Audit Committee of the Council.
Members in class (e) shall be appointed by Grace of the Regent House on the nomination of the Council; the arrangements for nomination shall be prescribed by Ordinance.
...

Statute C University Offices and Employment in the University
...

Chapter III The Vice-Chancellor and the Pro-Vice-Chancellors

1. The Vice-Chancellor shall be appointed by the Regent House on the nomination of the Council, who may nominate any person of their choice. ... The procedures for nomination and admission shall be prescribed by Ordinance.
2. The Vice-Chancellor shall be appointed in the first instance for five years or, in exceptional circumstances, for such other period as the University may determine. He or she may be reappointed for a further period or periods, provided that no one shall hold the office of Vice-Chancellor for a total period of more than seven years. The procedure for reappointment shall be prescribed by Ordinance. ...
...
5. Except as provided in Section 6 below,
   (a)   the Vice-Chancellor shall be Chair of the Council and the General Board, and of any other body of which he or she is ex officio a member, provided that the Chancellor shall have the right to take the chair at any meeting of the Council at which he or she is present.
...
6. The Vice-Chancellor shall not be present at any meeting of the Council or of any other body when the body is considering her or his reappointment or the appointment of her or his successor as Vice-Chancellor.
...

Removal of the Vice-Chancellor from office

11. Any three members of the Council may make a complaint to the Chancellor seeking the removal of the Vice-Chancellor from the office of Vice-Chancellor for good cause.
12. If it appears to the Chancellor that the complaint is trivial or invalid or unjustified, he or she may determine that no further action shall be taken upon it.

1. At Cambridge University, real day-to-day management power lies with the 'Council': A.IV.1. This 25-person executive body is elected by (1) staff, with 16 seats, but weighted by seniority, (2) students, with 3 seats but not necessarily by direct election, and (3) existing management, with 6 seats, including the Chancellor and Vice-Chancellor. The all-important 'Regent House' (A.III.10) includes staff members, from 'fellows' upwards in the academic hierarchy. There are around 3,800 members. The Regent House can also pass 'graces' that function as referendums to bind management. These can be important. For example, a recent student-led campaign for a grace forced the Council to adopt a policy of divesting from fossil fuels. The Vice-Chancellor who chairs the Council is appointed by Regent House, but on the Council's nomination. The Chancellor is elected by the Senate, which includes the 'Regent House' and graduates: Statute A.I.7. Do you think that non-management staff and students have enough voice?

2. The Cambridge University 'Council' is analogous to a company's board of directors. Its Regent House is like a company's general meeting of members. The Vice-Chancellor is like a Chief Executive Officer and Chair rolled into one. The Chancellor is a figurehead.

3. Cambridge's Statutes seem to exclude part-time or fixed-term teaching staff from voting rights: they are not 'fellows', even if they do the same work. An objective justification for this discrimination might appeal to a desirability of hierarchy to reward experience or research capacity, but does this still violate the Part-time Workers Regulations 2000 or the Fixed-term Employees Regulations 2002? See chapter 15 and cf Statute A.III.10(e).

4. Other universities in England are either constituted (1) under the Education Reform Act 1988, (2) by Royal Charter and possibly an Act of Parliament, or (3) as a company.

5. In England, there are 46 universities which follow the Education Reform Act 1988 ss 124A, 128, Schs 7 and 7A, para 3. This requires that university governing bodies should have between 12 and 24 members. There should be up to 13 lay members, up to 2 teachers, up to 2 students, and from 1 to 9 members co-opted by the others. Examples include Anglia Ruskin, Birmingham City, Brighton, East London, Kingston, Lincoln, Manchester Metropolitan, Nottingham Trent, Oxford Brookes and Portsmouth.

6. There are 50 English universities incorporated by a Royal Charter, and may also have accompanying Acts of Parliament. For example, as well as a Charter, the King's College London Act 1997 s 15 requires a 38-member Council. There should be 5 ex-officio members, 20 lay appointees, 8 elected by academics, 3 elected by students, and 2 by non-academic staff members. However, this provision was not put into effect on an 'appointed day'. So, currently under KCL's Charter and Statutes, Art 1, 'Membership of the Council', requires a 21-member board, with 12 lay members, 8 staff, 1 student, yet there is no provision for actual elections by staff. Should the University and College Union bring a judicial review claim to require this? Other universities with Charters include Bath, Birmingham, Birkbeck, Bristol, Brunel, City, East Anglia, Essex, Exeter, Kent, Lancaster, Leeds, Leicester, Liverpool, Manchester, Newcastle, Nottingham, the Open

University, SOAS, Queen Mary, Reading, Sheffield, Sussex, UCL, Warwick and York. See D Farrington and D Palfreyman, *The Law of Higher Education* (2nd edn 2012) ch 5, 161–63.

7. The London School of Economics, *Memorandum and Articles of Association* (2006) is a company limited by guarantee, formed under the CA 2006. Its memorandum was signed by Sidney Webb, George Bernard Shaw and others when it was formed by the Fabian socialists in 1896. Under its Articles today, Art 10.5 (as amended) requires a 17-member 'Council' to have 2 students, 3 staff representatives, and the remainder lay representatives. Do you think this reflects the preferences of its founders, or the interests of today's staff and students enough? There are 25 universities that are companies limited by guarantee, also including Chichester, Derby, Greenwich, London Metropolitan, London South Bank, Roehampton and Westminster.

8. The first statutory enactments for votes of staff at universities derive from the Oxford University Act 1854 ss 16 and 21 and the Cambridge University Act 1856 ss 5–6. Oxford's rules are now in Statute IV and VI and Council Regulation 13 of 2002, regs 4–10. See E McGaughey, 'Votes at Work in Britain: Shareholder Monopolisation and the "Single Channel"' (2018) 47(1) *Industrial Law Journal* 76.

9. Universities in Scotland, Wales and Northern Ireland have separate funding and regulator systems to those in England, but have analogous governance rules: charters, company articles, or an Act. The most interesting and democratic arrangements appear in the Universities (Scotland) Act 1966 and the Higher Education Governance (Scotland) Act 2016, which standardise voting rights in university governance.

10. How is the university closest to you regulated? How (if at all) would you improve it?

11. As we can see, universities do not only give staff the right to vote for governing bodies. Many also give students the rights to vote. The NHS gives patients and residents some voice. In which other sectors of enterprise do you think people who receive a service should have a voice? What do you think justifies this?

12. Outside universities, in most UK workplaces default rules of the CA 2006 apply. A company's constitution (or 'articles of association') can be drafted in any way, just like the LSE (a company limited by guarantee) enfranchises staff and students. This has been rare, but may change, because the UK Corporate Governance Code (July 2018) introduced for the first time – a small but momentous step – a legal requirement to have one workforce representative on the board of directors, or explain why not. Before that, the following are the basic rules of corporate governance.

Companies Act 2006 ss 21, 112–13, 154, 168–69 and 282–84

21 Amendment of articles

(1) A company may amend its articles by special resolution.

...

112 The members of a company

(1) The subscribers of a company's memorandum are deemed to have agreed to become members of the company, and on its registration become members and must be entered as such in its register of members.

(2) Every other person who agrees to become a member of a company, and whose name is entered in its register of members, is a member of the company.

113 Register of members

(1) Every company must keep a register of its members.

(2) There must be entered in the register—

   (a)   the names and addresses of the members,

   (b)   the date on which each person was registered as a member, and

   (c)   the date at which any person ceased to be a member.

(3) In the case of a company having a share capital, there must be entered in the register, with the names and addresses of the members, a statement of—

   (a)   the shares held by each member, distinguishing each share – (i) by its number (so long as the share has a number), and (ii) where the company has more than one class of issued shares, by its class, and

   (b)   the amount paid or agreed to be considered as paid on the shares of each member.

…

154 Companies required to have directors

(1) A private company must have at least one director.

(2) A public company must have at least two directors.

…

168 Resolution to remove director

(1) A company may by ordinary resolution at a meeting remove a director before the expiration of his period of office, notwithstanding anything in any agreement between it and him.

(2) Special notice is required of a resolution to remove a director under this section or to appoint somebody instead of a director so removed at the meeting at which he is removed.

…

169 Director's right to protest against removal

(1) On receipt of notice of an intended resolution to remove a director under section 168, the company must forthwith send a copy of the notice to the director concerned.

(2) The director (whether or not a member of the company) is entitled to be heard on the resolution at the meeting.

…

282 Ordinary resolutions

(1) An ordinary resolution of the members (or of a class of members) of a company means a resolution that is passed by a simple majority.

…

283 Special resolutions

(1) A special resolution of the members (or of a class of members) of a company means a resolution passed by a majority of not less than 75%.

…

284 Votes: general rules

(1) On a vote on a written resolution—

    (a) in the case of a company having a share capital, every member has one vote in respect of each share or each £10 of stock held by him, and

    (b) in any other case, every member has one vote.

NOTES AND QUESTIONS

1.   The CA 2006 requires that companies have two basic organs: (1) a general meeting of members, that can (2) remove directors on the board. Sections 112–13 say a company member is whoever is on the register of members. Section 284 presumes each member has a vote. Directors can be removed (s 168) by a majority vote of members (an 'ordinary' resolution, s 282), with 28 days' notice and the opportunity of a director to circulate an argument to stay (s 169). The director removal rights for members are compulsory, and cannot be changed.

2.   Public companies disclose their accounts, and must hold meetings. These extra rules for plc's are meant to ensure small investors (many saving for retirement) are not misinformed and cheated (CA 2006 ss 336, 437, 489, etc, cf *Derry v Peek* (1889) 14 AC 337, exemplifying problems before the Wall Street Crash of 1929).

3.   There are no compulsory rules on how directors are appointed or paid, on their powers over staff, or members' power over directors. There are also no fixed rules on who 'members' of a company are. This is left to 'Model Articles'. These are default rules that can be changed when a company is formed or can usually be altered by a three-quarters vote (a 'special' resolution, s 283) of the general meeting (s 21). The Model Articles for a public company, a 'plc', are as follows.

Companies (Model Articles) Regulations 2008 Sch 3, paras 3–5, 20, 23, 34

Directors' general authority

3. Subject to the articles, the directors are responsible for the management of the company's business, for which purpose they may exercise all the powers of the company.

Members' reserve power

4. (1) The members may, by special resolution, direct the directors to take, or refrain from taking, specified action.

(2) No such special resolution invalidates anything which the directors have done before the passing of the resolution.

Directors may delegate

5. (1) Subject to the articles, the directors may delegate any of the powers which are conferred on them under the articles—

    (a) to such person or committee;

    (b) by such means (including by power of attorney);

    (c) to such an extent;

    (d) in relation to such matters or territories; and

    (e) on such terms and conditions;

as they think fit.

(2) If the directors so specify, any such delegation may authorise further delegation of the directors' powers by any person to whom they are delegated.

(3) The directors may revoke any delegation in whole or part, or alter its terms and conditions.
…

Methods of appointing directors

20. Any person who is willing to act as a director, and is permitted by law to do so, may be appointed to be a director—
    (a) by ordinary resolution, or
    (b) by a decision of the directors ….

…

Directors' remuneration

23. (1) Directors may undertake any services for the company that the directors decide.
(2) Directors are entitled to such remuneration as the directors determine—
    (a) for their services to the company as directors, and
    (b) for any other service which they undertake for the company.

…

Voting: general

34. A resolution put to the vote of a general meeting must be decided on a show of hands unless a poll is duly demanded in accordance with the articles.

NOTES AND QUESTIONS

1.   The Companies (Model Articles) Regulations 2008 Sch 3, para 3 states the board of directors has general management power, subject to members' right to bind the board with a 75 per cent vote (para 4). Directors are themselves employees of the company and can 'delegate any of the powers' conferred upon them (para 5). Every employment contract is a delegation of the company's constitutional authority. Directors can either be appointed by an ordinary resolution of members, or by a decision of directors (para 20). But in practice, as the UK Corporate Governance Code 2018, J.17 presume, directors will set up a nomination committee to appoint themselves and successors. They also pay themselves (para 23). However, members can remove directors (s 168).

2.   Workers or employees *could* be registered as members of a company. There is no need for a member to hold shares (see G Morse (ed), *Palmer's Company Law* (2016) 7.002 and 7.004). Workers can unionise and collectively bargain with management and major shareholders to put support an amendment to any company constitution that they are registered as members with the right to vote in a general meeting. For instance, a new para 34(2) could state: 'The company's employees shall be registered as members and be entitled to 30 per cent of the total votes in the general meeting. Employees shall have one vote each.' What do you think are the likely arguments against such a plan?

3.   Although the Model Articles are only default rules, and can be altered, why do you think they are influential in the way people form companies and distribute power?

4.   Taking effect from January 2019, the new UK Corporate Governance Code now requires employee representation on company boards, or an explanation why not. The Code is addressed to listed companies (e.g. the companies on the London Stock Exchange). This is the first time employee representation has been part of UK law outside universities in a generation.

Financial Reporting Council, *UK Corporate Governance Code* (July 2018)

1. BOARD LEADERSHIP AND COMPANY PURPOSE
Principles
A.   A successful company is led by an effective and entrepreneurial board, whose role is to promote the long-term sustainable success of the company, generating value for shareholders and contributing to wider society.
B.   The board should establish the company's purpose, values and strategy, and satisfy itself that these and its culture are aligned. All directors must act with integrity, lead by example and promote the desired culture.
C.   The board should ensure that the necessary resources are in place for the company to meet its objectives and measure performance against them. The board should also establish a framework of prudent and effective controls, which enable risk to be assessed and managed.
D.   In order for the company to meet its responsibilities to shareholders and stakeholders, the board should ensure effective engagement with, and encourage participation from, these parties.
E.   The board should ensure that workforce policies and practices are consistent with the company's values and support its long-term sustainable success. The workforce should be able to raise any matters of concern.

...

5.   The board should understand the views of the company's other key stakeholders and describe in the annual report how their interests and the matters set out in section 172 of the Companies Act 2006 have been considered in board discussions and decision-making.[1] The board should keep engagement mechanisms under review so that they remain effective.

  For engagement with the workforce,[2] one or a combination of the following methods should be used:
  • a director appointed from the workforce;
  • a formal workforce advisory panel;
  • a designated non-executive director.
If the board has not chosen one or more of these methods, it should explain what alternative arrangements are in place and why it considers that they are effective.
6.   There should be a means for the workforce to raise concerns in confidence and – if they wish – anonymously. The board should routinely review this and the reports arising from its operation. It should ensure that arrangements are in place for the proportionate and independent investigation of such matters and for follow-up action.

NOTES AND QUESTIONS

1.   In a small but momentous step, Provision 5 says that companies should have 'one or a combination' of 'a director appointed from the workforce', a worker advisory panel or a designated non-executive director. If a company chooses to do nothing, it must explain why. In practice, the simplest option will be to have a workforce-wide election for one director on the board. In practice, this will avoid difficult

---

[1] The Companies (Miscellaneous Reporting) Regulations 2018 require directors to explain how they have had regard to various matters in performing their duty to promote the success of the company in section 172 of the Companies Act 2006. The Financial Reporting Council's Guidance on the Strategic Report supports reporting on the legislative requirement.
[2] See the Guidance on Board Effectiveness Section 1 for a description of 'workforce' in this context.

questions from the trade union about why this obvious step is not being taken. Do you agree that companies should seize the initiative, and go beyond the minimum standards by having one-third employee directors? How would you advise a trade union to approach negotiations?

2. FRC, *Guidance on Board Effectiveness* (July 2018) 15, states: 'Whichever method is chosen, the new arrangements are not intended to displace established channels of communication and consultation arrangements where these exist, for example, collective bargaining arrangements and existing worker representative systems established through trade unions.' This seems imperative: board representation, like consultation and work councils, are to be seen as extensions of collective bargaining, to embed employee voice in corporate governance, for the long-term success of enterprise.

3. The FRC (located on Aldwych) is a quasi-governmental body whose power to enforce compliance ultimately comes from Financial Services and Markets Act 2000 s 1B(6)(a). This says the Financial Conduct Authority (in Canary Wharf) has the function of making rules under the Act, which regulate all financial services, including listed companies which sell shares to the public. Under the FCA's Listing Rule 9.8.6 a listed company must put in 'its annual financial report' a statement of compliance with the provisions of the UK Corporate Governance Code, or 'the company's reasons for non-compliance'.

4. A general argument against comply-or-explain rules is that they are not really rules: companies can opt-out, and so make a mockery of the whole process. If the rule is a good idea, then it should apply to everyone, and if it is not a good idea it should not be a rule. An argument for is that companies have diverse practices. The UK Corporate Governance Code's other rules include (1) separating the chair and CEO into two offices (2) requiring independent non-executive directors, who (3) staff the nomination, audit and remuneration committees. It is argued that while the Code's standards may represent 'best practice', there is a legitimate diversity of opinion on these issues: one size may not fit all. In practice, if the market thinks a rule is good, companies will coalesce around the norm because there is shareholder pressure. In fact, this may be more enduring in establishing a lasting culture, than a rule that companies seek to minimise or flout. To what extent do these arguments apply with equal force to minimum representation for employees on boards?

5. What reasons can you think of why companies should embrace worker voice?

6. In *A Manifesto for Labour Law: Towards a Comprehensive Revision of Workers' Rights* (Institute of Employment Rights, 2016) a distinguished body of labour lawyers from the UK, Commonwealth and EU advocated that (1) 'worker directors should be appointed by recognised trade unions', and (2) 'workers through their trade union … should have a minimum percentage of the vote in general meetings of the company'. This was adopted at the Labour Party Conference in 2016 as official Labour Party policy. Should workers get to vote directly for boards, or should trade unions vote for workers, or perhaps a combination of the two?

7. The UK has had many experiments with workers on boards, from the Port of London Act 1908, to the Post Office Act 1977: (2017) 46(4) ILJ 444. Alan

Bullock, *Report of the Committee of Inquiry on Industrial Democracy* (1977) Cmnd 6706 recommended that trade unions should select half of every company's board. The CBI, *In Place of Bullock* (May 1977) promised 'unremitting hostility' to these plans mainly because it objected to union control over voting. The government then watered down its proposals to unions selecting a minority of directors on a new supervisory board: (1978) Cmnd 7231. This also pleased nobody, and Labour soon lost the 1979 election to Margaret Thatcher, who retrenched all existing worker directors, and ended all plans. Do you agree that minimum principles, rather than imposing a detailed and ideal model are the best way to avoid the same thing happening again?

8. Company members are usually shareholders. In private companies, particularly smaller ones, these are usually the people who have contributed capital. They will often have one vote per share. But in big public companies, the registered shareholders are usually asset manager firms, such as JP Morgan, Legal&General, State Street, Fidelity, BlackRock or Schroders. They receive money from pension trust funds, life insurance policyholders and mutual fund policyholders, and do the work of selecting investments. But in standard form contracts, they also take the shares. So, although these asset managers are the registered shareholders, they have invariably made no investment of capital. They exercise voting rights on 'other people's money'. See chapter 11(3) below.

9. Some companies operate 'employee share schemes', where employees are given shares in a company in return for their labour. Usually the theory is that workers will work harder if they have a financial stake in the firm. Apart from being a modern form of truck, share schemes inevitably break the cardinal rule of investment: to diversify one's share portfolio. It is prudent to buy shares in at least 20 companies, so as to spread losses if one company goes insolvent. A notorious example of an employee share scheme operated at the US energy firm Enron before 2001. Staff were encouraged to invest an average of 62.5 per cent of their retirement savings into Enron shares, and lost everything. See PJ Purcell, 'The Enron Bankruptcy and Employer Stock in Retirement Plans' (11 March 2002) CRS Report for Congress. Can you think of arguments in favour of promoting, or indeed prohibiting, share schemes?

10. Nevertheless in 2013, a new ERA 1996 s 205A enabled employees to get at least 'no less than £2000' worth of shares in a company, but give up the right to request training (s 63D), flexible work (s 80F), the right to not be unfairly dismissed (s 94) and redundancy pay (s 135). This law was the brainchild of the Chancellor of the Exchequer, George Osborne, who was dismissed from his job after the 'Brexit' poll (he appears not to have been part of a share scheme himself). A first problem is that because the Part-time Work Directive clause 5(3) requires the right to request going part-time, s 205A(2)(b) violates EU law: the right to request flexible work cannot be sold for shares. Second, s 205A makes no mention about voting rights on shares, and so employees could have no voice. On average, the value of redundancy pay is greater for most people who have worked in a job for over 4 years on the UK average salary (eg £28,600 ÷ 52 = £550). The loss of unfair dismissal protection is also tremendous. This is why few have opted for a rights-for-shares scheme: see J Prassl (2013) 42(4) ILJ 307.

11. Companies can voluntarily create employee share schemes, defined under CA 2006 s 1166 as schemes for 'encouraging or facilitating the holding of shares' by employees, former employees or their relatives. Directors are empowered to allot shares to employees without any shareholder veto (s 549), or right of pre-emption (s 566), and shares can be issued below market value, down to its nominal value (ss 580–86). But even if rights are not lost, share schemes still concentrate employees' financial risks in a single company. Why should employees have to pay twice for voice at work by investing their money, when they have already invested their labour in a company?

12. A majority of EU countries (18 out of 28) plus Norway have worker representation laws (this is also 19 out of 36 OECD countries). See www.worker-participation.eu. One reason for caution about relying on worker representatives on boards alone, rather than also ensuring votes for employees in a general meeting, is that directors representing distinct interest groups (capital and labour) will clash on predictable issues. By contrast, in casting votes in a general meeting, worker votes can (and are likely to) form coalitions of interest with shareholders who represent workers' pensions. This would mean a board is undivided, because conflicts are resolved by votes in the general meeting.

13. In Sweden, the Board Representation (Private sector employees) Act 1987 provides a model that any UK firm could, if it chose, adopt. The Swedish Ministry of Industry, Employment and Communications has an official translation of the law as follows.

Board Representation (Private Sector Employees) Act 1987 (SFS 1987:1245)

Section 1 The purpose of this Act is to afford employees information about and influence over the company's activities through representation on the board of directors.

...

Section 3 An employee of a principal or parent company, who is permanently engaged in an agent or subsidiary, without being employed there, shall also, in the application of this Act, be treated as an employee of the agent or subsidiary.

In the application of this Act, a collective bargaining agreement between a local employees' organisation and a principal or parent company shall also be treated as a collective bargaining agreement in relation to the agent or subsidiary.

The entitlement to board representation

Section 4 The employees of a company that, in the most recent financial year, in Sweden, has employed an average of not less than 25 employees, shall be entitled to two representatives on the board of directors (board representatives) and one alternate for each such member. If the company conducts business in different branches and if it has, in the most recent financial year, in Sweden, employed an average of at least 1,000 employees, the employees shall be entitled to three representatives on the board of directors (board representation) and one alternate for each such member.

The employees' entitlement to board representation pursuant to the first paragraph may not, however, result in the number of employee representatives exceeding the number of other board representatives.

If the company is a parent company, the provisions of the first and second paragraphs relating to companies shall relate to the group in its entirety and the right to board representation shall accrue in favour of all employees in the group.

...

Section 6 The decision to appoint employees' board representatives shall be taken by a local employee organisation that is bound by a collective bargaining agreement with the company.

If the decision relates to a parent company, the decision shall be taken by a local employees' organisation that is bound by a collective bargaining agreement with one of the companies in the group.

...

Duties of the employees' representative, etc

Section 11 Unless this Act provides to the contrary, the provisions of other acts or legislative instruments concerning members of the board of directors and alternate members of a company's board of directors shall apply to employee members and alternates for such members.

NOTES AND QUESTIONS

1. The Swedish Board Representation (Private Sector Employees) Act 1987 says local employee organisations (ie trade unions) appoint board representatives (s 6), and must have at least two representatives in companies with over 25 employees, or three in companies over 1,000 employees. In practice, Swedish board sizes are kept small through consensus about good governance and collective agreement. In effect, most Swedish boards have one third employee representation. How do you think this might change company policy discussion?

2. The German Codetermination Act 1976 is possibly the best known model, but by no means the best. First, dating from the Kingdom of Prussia's desire to control or 'supervise' industry, German companies have two-tier boards. The general meeting elects a supervisory board (*Aufsichtsrat*), and the supervisory board elects the executive (*Vorstand*). On unification of the German Empire in 1871, Hanseatic states won the argument to let the general meeting still directly remove the executive. But then, the Nazi government, which wanted each company to have its own little *Führer*, made sure the *Vorstand* was irremovable by the general meeting (in the *Aktiengesetz 1937*). This was amended but not reversed after World War Two.

3. Second, since 1922, based on a post-World War One collective agreement, German employees have been represented on large enterprise boards (whether a private 'GmbH' or a public 'AG' or any form of partnership). This was abolished by Hitler, but unions again collectively bargained for codetermination after World War Two: E McGaughey, 'The Codetermination Bargains: The History of German Corporate and Labour Law' (2016) 23(1) *Columbia Journal of European Law* 135. Today, in companies with over 500 staff, workers can elect one-third of a company's supervisory board, which in turn elects the executive that has day-to-day power to run the company (One Third Participation Act 2003 §1 ff). With over 2,000 staff, workers get to elect half the supervisory board, but the chairperson with a casting vote is a shareholder (ie bank) representative (Codetermination Act 1976 §§1, 7, 27–29, 33). With over 8,000 staff, workers by default delegate their trade union their votes, but can opt out (CA 1976 §§9 and 18).

4. It is completely unnecessary to have two-tier board in order for workers to have votes. A majority of EU countries now have votes at work laws, with single-tier boards (see Figure 11.1).

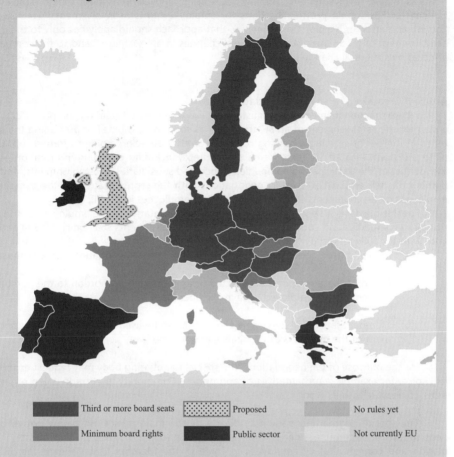

Third or more board seats	Proposed	No rules yet
Minimum board rights	Public sector	Not currently EU

Figure 11.1 Votes at work in the European Union

Source: worker-participation.eu/National-Industrial-Relations/Across-Europe/Board-level-Representation2.

5. Many companies in the EU, especially Germany, have reincorporated as 'European Companies', partly to water down codetermination law. Any company in the EU can reincorporate as a Societas Europaea (SE), although almost no UK companies have done so because there is very little incentive.

6. If a company becomes an 'SE' the basic rules of the Member State the company chooses as its host will apply, subject to minimum standards set out in the European Company Regulation (EC) No 2157/2001. But then, if a Member State has any rules on worker voice (which the UK currently does not), the Employee Involvement Directive 2001/86/EC requires those standards are maintained.

Employee Involvement Directive 2001/86/EC

(18) It is a fundamental principle and stated aim of this Directive to secure employees' acquired rights as regards involvement in company decisions. Employee rights in force before the establishment of SEs should provide the basis for employee rights of involvement in the SE (the "before and after" principle). Consequently, that approach should apply not only to the initial establishment of an SE but also to structural changes in an existing SE and to the companies affected by structural change processes.

...

Article 3 Creation of a special negotiating body

1. Where the management or administrative organs of the participating companies draw up a plan for the establishment of an SE, they shall as soon as possible after publishing the draft terms of merger or creating a holding company or after agreeing a plan to form a subsidiary or to transform into an SE, take the necessary steps, including providing information about the identity of the participating companies, concerned subsidiaries or establishments, and the number of their employees, to start negotiations with the representatives of the companies' employees on arrangements for the involvement of employees in the SE.

2. For this purpose, a special negotiating body representative of the employees of the participating companies and concerned subsidiaries or establishments shall be created in accordance with the following provisions:

    (a) in electing or appointing members of the special negotiating body, it must be ensured:

        (i) that these members are elected or appointed in proportion to the number of employees employed in each Member State ...

...

    (b) Member States shall determine the method to be used for the election or appointment of the members of the special negotiating body ...

...

5. For the purpose of the negotiations, the special negotiating body may request experts of its choice, for example representatives of appropriate Community level trade union organisations, to assist it with its work. ...

...

6. The special negotiating body may decide by the majority set out below not to open negotiations or to terminate negotiations already opened, and to rely on the rules on information and consultation of employees in force in the Member States where the SE has employees. Such a decision shall stop the procedure to conclude the agreement referred to in Article 4. Where such a decision has been taken, none of the provisions of the Annex shall apply.

...

Article 4 Content of the agreement

1. The competent organs of the participating companies and the special negotiating body shall negotiate in a spirit of cooperation with a view to reaching an agreement on arrangements for the involvement of the employees within the SE.

...

Article 7 Standard rules

1. In order to achieve the objective described in Article 1, Member States shall, without prejudice to paragraph 3 below, lay down standard rules on employee involvement which must satisfy the provisions set out in the Annex.

The standard rules as laid down by the legislation of the Member State in which the registered office of the SE is to be situated shall apply from the date of the registration of the SE where either:

(a) the parties so agree; or

(b) by the deadline laid down in Article 5 [*ie six months extendable to one year*], no agreement has been concluded, and:

— the competent organ of each of the participating companies decides to accept the application of the standard rules in relation to the SE and so to continue with its registration of the SE, and

— the special negotiating body has not taken the decision provided in Article 3(6).

...

Annex Standard Rules

...

Part 3: Standard rules for participation

Employee participation in an SE shall be governed by the following provisions

(a) In the case of an SE established by transformation, if the rules of a Member State relating to employee participation in the administrative or supervisory body applied before registration, all aspects of employee participation shall continue to apply to the SE. Point (b) shall apply *mutatis mutandis* to that end.

(b) In other cases of the establishing of an SE, the employees of the SE, its subsidiaries and establishments and/or their representative body shall have the right to elect, appoint, recommend or oppose the appointment of a number of members of the administrative or supervisory body of the SE equal to the highest proportion in force in the participating companies concerned before registration of the SE.

If none of the participating companies was governed by participation rules before registration of the SE, the latter shall not be required to establish provisions for employee participation. ...

NOTES AND QUESTIONS

1. As the 18th recital explains succinctly, the EID's central idea is that when a company transforms into a Societas Europaea, employees in each Member State have a right to at least the same level of representation as existing Member State law gives them (Art 7 and Annex Part 3). Workers should have the same voice before and after, if they want. If one Member State has worse employee participation rules than another, employees can require representation 'equal to the highest proportion in force' (Annex Part 3(b)). However, workers and management in the 'special negotiating body' can negotiate a different arrangement (Arts 3–4), perhaps better or worse. Companies may often want smaller boards, to make management meetings more efficient. Some companies may have two-tier boards (with both an 'administrative' and 'supervisory' body, like in Germany), and they may merge with companies with one-tier boards (with just an 'administrative' or executive body, like in the UK). There is no mathematically exact way to say what is the same, so the Directive left the issue to negotiation.

2. The Directive distinguishes creating new companies by 'transformation' (ie a single company simply changing forms, like a plc changing to an SE) and by other means. The most important is through merger. Companies could merge to

become an SE. But what happens if companies merge across borders and choose a Member State form of company? The Cross Border Merger Directive 2005/56/EC Art 16(2)–(4) requires that when companies situated in different Member States merge, and any company has over 500 staff, the procedure in EID 2000 Arts 3–13 applies. For instance, imagine a German AG merges with a UK plc to become a UK plc. The workers in Germany and the UK will negotiate for representation on the board of directors, which should usually be at least as good as it was in the German AG. (This example is completely hypothetical: it has never happened with UK firms, but could in other Member States.) But what happens if the new UK plc decides to merge again? The CBMD 2005 Art 16(7) says the protection for worker voice lasts for 3 years, but after that, the workers have no *legal* protection to demand they are represented in a new body. The workers would therefore have to threaten a strike. Although the chances of such a cynical series of manoeuvres to avoid votes at work is theoretically possible, it seems to have been unlikely in practice.

3. More problematic could be the EU principle of 'freedom of establishment'. *Centros Ltd v Erhvervs- og Selskabsstyrelsen* (1999) C-212/97 decided that a UK Ltd company could operate in Denmark without being subject to Danish minimum capital rules, which ostensibly protect creditors: if a company goes insolvent there is meant to be *some* money left (at the time about £23,000, which is essentially useless). UK law requires no minimum capital for Ltd companies, and the CJEU held that Denmark's laws were not a proportionate means toward a legitimate aim of protecting creditors. So, the UK company could freely establish. This scared labour lawyers: would votes at work laws be held to violate freedom of establishment? The basic answer was no. In *Überseering BV v Nordic Construction Company Baumanagement GmbH* (2002) C-208/00, [92] the ECJ stressed that: 'It is not inconceivable that overriding requirements relating to the general interest, such as the protection of the interests of creditors, minority shareholders, employees and even the taxation authorities, may, in certain circumstances and subject to certain conditions, justify restrictions on freedom of establishment.' To be justified, as the ECJ repeated, for instance in *Kamer van Koophandel en Fabrieken voor Amsterdam v Inspire Art Ltd* (2003) C-167/01, [133] is that votes at work laws 'must be applied in a non-discriminatory manner; they must be justified by imperative requirements in the public interest; they must be suitable for securing the attainment of the objective which they pursue, and they must not go beyond what is necessary in order to attain it'.

4. Arguably, votes at work are not merely a justifiable and proportionate restriction on freedom of establishment, but fundamental to democracy and social justice, at the heart of the EU treaties. In *Erzberger v TUI AG* (2017) C-566/15 a former law student from the private Bucerius Law School in Hamburg decided he would buy a share in TUI, a German travel company, and argue that the whole scheme of German codetermination violated EU law, by hindering 'free movement of workers'. This argument was based on the idea that TUI workers outside Germany were not being given rights to vote in the German corporate structure (they would be covered by that member state's laws, if any) and this would be a discouragement to move away from Germany (because one might lose voting

rights). Erzberger lost on every count. Crucially, although not yet adopted by the CJEU itself, AG Saugmandsgaard Øe wrote in his Opinion that codetermination is 'an essential element' of 'the German social order' [103]. This would appear to mean that votes at work precede all free movement law and are part of the 'fundamental structures, political and constitutional' of any modern democracy (see TEU Art 4).

5.   The debate is significant in Germany, where a number of high-profile UK companies began operating, without giving workers votes, notably its second biggest airline Air Berlin plc. Unions did not effectively demand workers get votes on the board. But also, Germany's law, the Mitbestimmungsgesetz 1976 (Codetermination Act 1976) §1 was argued by most German corporate lawyers to only cover domestic forms of company, not foreign companies. This is entirely open to dispute, by simply paying regard to the debates in 1976, but some German lawyers have a culture of following the ostensibly authoritative wisdom repeated in leading commentaries – none of which are particularly pro-labour (contrast at chapter 11(3) below the note on Nipperdey and Kahn-Freund). While there has been no authoritative court decision, legislative reform proposals have been made by the Social Democrats to extend codetermination to foreign firms. In any event, Air Berlin plc, after a long series of problems with a demoralised workforce, director incompetence, short-termism and management turnover, went into insolvency in October 2017. Its planes and staff were mostly taken on by Lufthansa AG, which has worker representation on board.

6.   The Draft Fifth Company Law Directive, first proposed in 1972, would have set rules for the whole EC or EU on worker representation on boards. However, disagreements surrounding company structure between Member States meant it did not proceed.

7.   One small general codetermination law, however, is found in the Credit Institutions Directive 2013/36/EU Art 95(2) which requires employee representation on bank board remuneration committees, if national law requires employees in an ordinary company's management body.

8.   The list of private legal enterprise forms (probably unnecessarily long: see J Armour, 'Companies and other Associations' in *English Private Law* (2013) ch 2) is as follows:

1) unlimited companies, private companies limited by shares, public companies, and companies limited by guarantee, including community interest companies: Companies Act 2006 ss 3–6.

2) partnerships, when people act together for a profit, as well as those where liability of sleeping partners is limited: Partnership Act 1890 and Limited Partnerships Act 1908.

3) full limited-liability partnerships, registered at HMRC: Limited Liability Partnerships Act 2000.

4) trusts, by deed or declaration, including those registered under the Charities Act 2011: *Choithram Int SA v Pagarani* [2000] UKPC 46.

5) co-operative or community benefit societies (formerly 'industrial and provident'): Co-operative and Community Benefit Societies Act 2014.

6) friendly societies, overseen by the Financial Conduct Authority: Friendly Societies Act 1992.

7) sole traders, who simply buy and sell things themselves.
8) companies authorised by specific Act of Parliament, eg NHS Act 2006 Sch 7.
9) companies authorised by Royal Charter from the Crown, eg a university.
10) a Societas Europaea, like a plc, which can operate in all Member States.
11) a multitude of entities from other EU Member States that may by virtue of freedom of establishment operate in the UK.

9. Could a UK law that requires worker votes extend to entities from other Member States, incorporated under a foreign law? The answer is probably 'yes'. In the same way as any labour law may apply to foreign companies' workers, the right to vote in a governance structure should not be seen as a violation of freedom of establishment.

(b) Enforcing Directors' Duties?

As well as votes, directors of companies (and the executives of any organisation) can be held accountable through standards enforced in court. The CA 2006 codified directors' duties, which derive from 'common law rules or equitable principles'. These duties, therefore, are found across every organisational form, whether company, contract or partnership. Breaches of duty by a director are wrongs to the company. This means, first, that the board as a whole could sue a director, although that is unlikely because people do not often want to sue their colleagues. Second, a company's administrator after insolvency can sue (see chapter 20). Third, company 'members' can sue through a derivative claim. If employees are members (or shareholders), they can begin derivative claims. Worker-controlled pension funds who own company shares can bring derivative claims against directors. Fourth, if employees are not registered as members, the law may allow claims to be brought, but this remains open to debate.

Companies Act 2006 ss 170–75

170 Scope and nature of general duties
  (1) The general duties specified in sections 171 to 177 are owed by a director of a company to the company.
  (2) A person who ceases to be a director continues to be subject—
    (a) to the duty in section 175 (duty to avoid conflicts of interest) as regards the exploitation of any property, information or opportunity of which he became aware at a time when he was a director, and
    (b) to the duty in section 176 (duty not to accept benefits from third parties) as regards things done or omitted by him before he ceased to be a director.
  To that extent those duties apply to a former director as to a director, subject to any necessary adaptations.
  (3) The general duties are based on certain common law rules and equitable principles as they apply in relation to directors and have effect in place of those rules and principles as regards the duties owed to a company by a director.
  (4) The general duties shall be interpreted and applied in the same way as common law rules or equitable principles, and regard shall be had to the corresponding common law rules and equitable principles in interpreting and applying the general duties.

(5) The general duties apply to a shadow director of a company where and to the extent that they are capable of so applying.

171 Duty to act within powers

A director of a company must—
- (a) act in accordance with the company's constitution, and
- (b) only exercise powers for the purposes for which they are conferred.

172 Duty to promote the success of the company

(1) A director of a company must act in the way he considers, in good faith, would be most likely to promote the success of the company for the benefit of its members as a whole, and in doing so have regard (amongst other matters) to—
- (a) the likely consequences of any decision in the long term,
- (b) the interests of the company's employees,
- (c) the need to foster the company's business relationships with suppliers, customers and others,
- (d) the impact of the company's operations on the community and the environment,
- (e) the desirability of the company maintaining a reputation for high standards of business conduct, and
- (f) the need to act fairly as between members of the company.

(2) Where or to the extent that the purposes of the company consist of or include purposes other than the benefit of its members, subsection (1) has effect as if the reference to promoting the success of the company for the benefit of its members were to achieving those purposes.

(3) The duty imposed by this section has effect subject to any enactment or rule of law requiring directors, in certain circumstances, to consider or act in the interests of creditors of the company.

...

174 Duty to exercise reasonable care, skill and diligence

(1) A director of a company must exercise reasonable care, skill and diligence.

(2) This means the care, skill and diligence that would be exercised by a reasonably diligent person with—
- (a) the general knowledge, skill and experience that may reasonably be expected of a person carrying out the functions carried out by the director in relation to the company, and
- (b) the general knowledge, skill and experience that the director has.

175 Duty to avoid conflicts of interest

(1) A director of a company must avoid a situation in which he has, or can have, a direct or indirect interest that conflicts, or possibly may conflict, with the interests of the company.

(2) This applies in particular to the exploitation of any property, information or opportunity (and it is immaterial whether the company could take advantage of the property, information or opportunity).

(3) This duty does not apply to a conflict of interest arising in relation to a transaction or arrangement with the company.

(4) This duty is not infringed—
- (a) if the situation cannot reasonably be regarded as likely to give rise to a conflict of interest; or
- (b) if the matter has been authorised by the directors.

(5) Authorisation may be given by the directors—
- (a) where the company is a private company and nothing in the company's constitution invalidates such authorisation, by the matter being proposed to and authorised by the directors; or

(b) where the company is a public company and its constitution includes provision enabling the directors to authorise the matter, by the matter being proposed to and authorised by them in accordance with the constitution.

(6) The authorisation is effective only if—

(a) any requirement as to the quorum at the meeting at which the matter is considered is met without counting the director in question or any other interested director, and

(b) the matter was agreed to without their voting or would have been agreed to if their votes had not been counted.

(7) Any reference in this section to a conflict of interest includes a conflict of interest and duty and a conflict of duties.

NOTES AND QUESTIONS

1. CA 2006 s 170 says directors owe duties to a company, that the rules follow those in contract or trust law, and directors are bound by duties even if they have resigned or are 'shadow directors'. Shadow directors are people or entities who are not formally appointed as directors, but still exercise influence on the real directors: CA 2006 s 251. The most important candidates, from whom real directors may have a habit of taking instructions, are major shareholders or banks. Four main duties follow.

2. First, s 171 requires directors follow the rules in the company constitution, ie the model articles. Directors must abide by any constraints on their powers, and exercise powers for a proper purpose. For example, in *Guinness plc v Saunders* [1989] UKHL 2 the House of Lords held that Guinness directors had breached their duty by paying a massive £5.2m bonus to an American lawyer, Ward, who piloted a takeover bid. The company constitution required the whole board to fix remuneration, but this payout was made by a committee of just three directors. This did not follow the constitution, so the directors were liable for the money to be restored.

3. Second, s 174 requires that directors are not negligent: that they exercise 'reasonable care, skill and diligence'. The standard of care requires an objective minimum appropriate for the responsibilities of the director's office. This means a director of a big listed company must exercise more care than a small high-street company. In addition, if a director has any special skills (eg an accountancy degree, or a law degree), they will be held to a higher standard. For example, if something goes wrong with the accounts, the Chief Financial Officer with the accounting degree will be especially culpable. In *Re Barings (No 5)* [2000] 1 BCLC 523, the London directors of the world's oldest merchant bank were found to have been negligent (and disqualified from being directors under the Company Directors Disqualification Act 1986 s 6) after a 'rogue trader' called Nick Leeson made fraudulent trades in the Singapore office and lost £827 million after an earthquake. The Court of Appeal found the directors were negligent because they had ignored an audit report that said the Singapore office was not properly separating its accounting staff from its trading staff. This is what enabled the rogue trader to sign off his own accounts, and perpetuate the massive losses. What kinds of negligent behaviour by directors could affect workers?

4. Third, s 175 requires directors avoid any possibility of a conflict of interest: if they see a business opportunity that the company could be interested in, they should tell the company about it, and only take it themselves if they have express authorisation. For instance in *Cook v Deeks* [1916] 1 AC 554, the Privy Council advised that three directors had breached their duty to the company by taking an opportunity to build a railway line in their own names. Their intention was to exclude the fourth director and shareholder, Cook, from the profits. They were bound to make restitution for all of those profits to the company. Section 177 also follows a similar principle: it prohibits 'self-dealing', as where a director causes her company to enter into a contract with herself, or someone she is connected with. All profits have to be given up. What kinds of conflicts of interest could affect workers?

5. One of the most debated, yet least important sections is 172. This requires directors to 'promote the success of the company for the benefit of its members as a whole' with 'regard to' a list of stakeholders, including employees, supply chains, consumers, the community and so on. That list does not include directors, and it does not mention shareholders, although as we have seen most 'members' will be shareholders. Many have argued this is an 'enlightened shareholder value' norm, requiring directors to maximise dividends over social values if the two conflict. Supposedly, corporate social responsibility is only allowed if it maximises profits. However, this should be regarded as wrong. For example, in *Shepherd v Williamson* [2010] EWHC 2375, a director was found to not have breached a duty to the company after he reported to the Office of Fair Trading that it was engaged in a cartel. After doing so, the company went insolvent – not something one might usually regard as promoting a company's 'success'. Proudman J held that the duty under s 172 was not, however, breached because in essence the director was having regard to the interests of the community in securing fair competition. This means there is no duty to promote shareholder interests at all: directors have the discretion to balance everyone's interests. To the extent it exists, 'shareholder value' is a cultural norm, not a legal norm: see S Deakin, 'The Coming Transformation of Shareholder Value' (2005) 13 *Corporate Governance: An International Review* 11.

6. Section 172 is, however, relevant for the duty of directors under ss 414A–C to prepare a strategic report detailing the company's impact on 'key performance indicators' that include 'environmental matters and employee matters' and 'social, community and human rights issues'. While it is easy to be sceptical about the real impact of corporate social responsibility measures, the aim is to 'mainstream' people's thinking about social factors, to put them into everyday thought, so that profit is not everything. Of course, this is no substitute for hard legal and voting rights.

7. In addition to the CA 2006 s 414C duty, the Modern Slavery Act 2015 s 54 requires any 'commercial organisation' (a company or partnership) with a turnover above £36m (SI 2015/1833 reg 2) to make a statement each financial year on 'steps the organisation has taken … to ensure slavery and human trafficking is not taking place' in any 'supply chains' or 'its own business', or state it has taken no steps. It has to be approved by directors and put on its website 'in a prominent place'. Is this enough?

8. Directors' duties can be enforced by members through a 'derivative claim'.

Companies Act 2006 ss 260–63

260 Derivative claims

(1) This Chapter applies to proceedings in England and Wales or Northern Ireland by a member of a company—

    (a)   in respect of a cause of action vested in the company, and

    (b)   seeking relief on behalf of the company.

This is referred to in this Chapter as a "derivative claim".

(2) A derivative claim may only be brought—

    (a)   under this Chapter, or

    (b)   in pursuance of an order of the court in proceedings under section 994 (proceedings for protection of members against unfair prejudice).

(3) A derivative claim under this Chapter may be brought only in respect of a cause of action arising from an actual or proposed act or omission involving negligence, default, breach of duty or breach of trust by a director of the company. The cause of action may be against the director or another person (or both).

(4) It is immaterial whether the cause of action arose before or after the person seeking to bring or continue the derivative claim became a member of the company.

    …

261 Application for permission to continue derivative claim

(1) A member of a company who brings a derivative claim under this Chapter must apply to the court for permission (in Northern Ireland, leave) to continue it.

(2) If it appears to the court that the application and the evidence filed by the applicant in support of it do not disclose a prima facie case for giving permission (or leave), the court—

    (a)   must dismiss the application, and

    (b)   may make any consequential order it considers appropriate.

    …

263 Whether permission to be given

(1) The following provisions have effect where a member of a company applies for permission (in Northern Ireland, leave) under section 261 or 262.

(2) Permission (or leave) must be refused if the court is satisfied—

    (a)   that a person acting in accordance with section 172 (duty to promote the success of the company) would not seek to continue the claim, or

    (b)   where the cause of action arises from an act or omission that is yet to occur, that the act or omission has been authorised by the company, or

    (c)   where the cause of action arises from an act or omission that has already occurred, that the act or omission—

        (i)   was authorised by the company before it occurred, or

        (ii)   has been ratified by the company since it occurred.

(3) In considering whether to give permission (or leave) the court must take into account, in particular—

    (a)   whether the member is acting in good faith in seeking to continue the claim;

    (b)   the importance that a person acting in accordance with section 172 (duty to promote the success of the company) would attach to continuing it;

    (c)   where the cause of action results from an act or omission that is yet to occur, whether the act or omission could be, and in the circumstances would be likely to be—

        (i)   authorised by the company before it occurs, or

        (ii)   ratified by the company after it occurs;

    (d)   where the cause of action arises from an act or omission that has already occurred, whether the act or omission could be, and in the circumstances would be likely to be, ratified by the company;

    (e)   whether the company has decided not to pursue the claim;

    (f)   whether the act or omission in respect of which the claim is brought gives rise to a cause of action that the member could pursue in his own right rather than on behalf of the company.

  (4) In considering whether to give permission (or leave) the court shall have particular regard to any evidence before it as to the views of members of the company who have no personal interest, direct or indirect, in the matter.

NOTES AND QUESTIONS

1.   CA 2006 s 260 states that derivative claims 'under this Chapter may be brought only' to vindicate breaches of directors duties. Section 261 says members make an application, at which point a court decides whether there is a good prima facie legal case. If so, under s 263, the court has to weigh up an 'enterprise case' for allowing the claim: this centres on whether, hypothetically, a derivative claim will 'promote the success of the company' under the meaning in s 172 (with regard to all stakeholders). The court also weighs up whether the claim could be authorised any way, whether the litigant is acting in good faith, and the views of the members who are unconnected to the claim. Analogous rules for Scotland are in ss 265–69.

2.   Because a derivative claim vindicates wrongs to a company, once a court gives approval, the company must cover the costs of litigation.

3.   In *Re Fort Gilkicker* [2013] EWHC 348, Briggs J (who is now on the UK Supreme Court) held that the codified derivative claim procedure had not excluded a common law right to bring a derivative action. This means that although ss 260–63 codifies the way that 'members' of a company bring claims, it does not exclude a right of non-members to claim. This meant the shareholder of a shareholder in a company could bring a claim, even though it was not a member. This is often called a 'double derivative claim', and is designed to ensure that a person holding the real economic interest in shares can vindicate rights on them. Do you agree that it follows that a pension fund could bring a derivative claim, even though an asset manager is the actual registered shareholder?

4.   What about employees? In *Eley v Positive Government Security Life Assurance Co Ltd* (1876) 1 Ex D 88 the Court of Appeal held that a company's employee was not entitled to claim in court that the constitution was breached, even though the constitution (which he wrote) named him as being the company solicitor. The suggestion, somewhat unarticulated, appeared to be Eley had to plead his claim in his capacity as a company member, not a third-party beneficiary. The position may well have changed now on the rights of third parties at common law. For instance, *Gamlestaden Fastigheter AB v Baltic Partners Ltd* [2007] UKPC 26 appeared to take account of a shareholder's greater interest in pursuing a derivative claim as a loan creditor. In any case, should employees be allowed to vindicate wrongs to the company, given their intrinsic interests in its success?

5.   Other Commonwealth countries have acknowledged the claims of multiple non-shareholder interests in vindicating wrongs to a company. In *BCE Inc v 1976 Debenture Holders* 2008 SCC 69, [44] the Canadian Supreme Court held directors duties are 'not owed solely to the corporation, and thus may be the basis for liability to other stakeholders in accordance with principles governing the law

of tort and extra-contractual liability'. In India, employees have been expressly recognised as having rights to sue under company law: see J Cottrell, 'Indian Judicial Activism, the Company and the Worker' (1990) *39(2) International and Comparative Law Quarterly* 433.

6.   Derivative actions to vindicate breaches of directors' duties are analogous to judicial review in administrative law. There has never been a rigid separation of 'public' and 'private' actions in English law. Indeed, the foundational case on controlling the abuse of government power by Lord Greene MR, *Associated Provincial Picture Houses Ltd v Wednesbury Corporation* [1948] 1 KB 223 was preceded in almost identical terms by a case on controlling the abuse of corporate power: *Re Smith and Fawcett Ltd* [1942] Ch 304. In *Breen v Amalgamated Engineering Union* (chapter 8(2)(a)), Lord Denning MR made this clear: 'we have developed a system of administrative law. These developments have been most marked in the review of decisions of statutory bodies: but they apply also to domestic bodies.' Do you agree that, for the purpose of accountability in law, there is no sensible reason to distinguish government, corporate, or any other organisational power? Do you agree that anybody whose legitimate interests are affected by a corporation is and should be able to bring a claim?

7.   The basic reason why employees should be entitled to bring claims to remedy wrongs to the company is one of proper enforcement. Institutional shareholders may well be apathetic about litigation. As they hold diversified portfolios, they do not see much point in court: they tend to sell, not sue or vote (which leaves the social problems unresolved). On the other hand, it could be argued that less litigation is better for business, and employees or unions might become frivolous litigants. This seems unlikely, because the effort of litigation is deterrence for any party, and a court is capable of guarding against vexatious claims. It is submitted that employees do, and should, have standing.

(2) WORK COUNCILS

A second form of votes at work is through work councils, which may reserve rights (binding or not) to make workplace management decisions. In the UK, work councils have not been common, because trade unions historically achieved their goals by influencing managers in collective bargaining, or 'joint industrial councils' covered whole sectors rather than operating at a macro-level. While successful labour law systems had work councils in each enterprise, but sectoral collective bargaining, the UK opted for enterprise bargaining, and let its sectoral councils break down. But since 2002, work councils have increased in number with the introduction of information and consultation obligations in EU law. In fact, the UK government once wrote an excellent model work council law, just not for its own citizens. This section sets out (a) the principles behind work councils, (b) the requirement for consultation for economic changes in places with over 50 employees, and (c) requirements for consultation with over 1,000 employees, and (d) requirements for information for collective bargaining.

(a) Principles

The following is the official English version of a German work council law, jointly drafted by the UK, US and French governments, and German unions, in post-Word War Two reconstruction.

Control Council Law No 22 (10 April 1946) Works Councils

Article I
The organization and activities of Works Councils (Betriebsräte) to represent the professional, economic and social interests of the workers and employees in each individual enterprise are hereby permitted throughout Germany.

Article II
1. A Works Council for an enterprise shall consist only of persons actually working in that enterprise.
2. No official of the former German Labor Front (Deutsche Arbeitsfront) or former member of the Nazi Party shall be a member of a Works Council.

Article III
1. Members of Works Councils shall be elected by democratic methods. Voting shall be by secret ballot.
2. No person may hold office as a member of a Works Council for more than one year without re-election.

Articles IV
1. Workers and employees of an enterprise may form a Preparatory Committee for the purpose of making recommendations with regard to the composition of the Works Council and the conduct of the election of members thereof. These recommendations shall be subject to the approval by the majority of the workers and the employees of the enterprise.
2. Recognized Trade Unions may participate in the formation of Preparatory Committees and in the organization of elections to Works Councils, and may propose candidates for Works Councils from among workers and employees of the enterprise concerned.

Article V
1. Works Councils may have as their basic functions any of the following matters relating to the protection of the interests of the workers and employees of an enterprise except insofar as these matters are governed by or are subject to any restriction by regulations having the force of law:
   a) Negotiations with employers on the application of collective agreements and of internal regulations to individual enterprises.
   b) Negotiations of agreements with the employers regarding factory regulations for the protection of labor, including such matters as safety pre-cautions, medical facilities, factory hygiene, working conditions, rules for engagements, dismissals, and settlement of grievances.
   c) Submission of proposals to the employer for the improvement of methods of work and organization of production for the purpose of avoiding unemployment.
   d) Investigation of grievances and discussion thereof with the employer; assistance to the workers, employees and Trade Unions in the preparation of cases for

submission to factory inspectors, social insurance and labor protection authorities, labor courts and other agencies for settling labor disputes.

e)   Co-operation with the authorities in the prevention of all war production and in the denazification of public and private enterprises. Participation in the creation of management of social works designed for the welfare of the workers of an enterprise, including nurseries, medical assistance, sports, etc.

2. Each Works Council shall determine its specific functions and procedure within the limits set forth in this law.

Article VI

1. A Works Council or its representatives shall be entitled to meet within the enterprise, and to have access to the employer or his nominated representative for the purpose of discussing matters falling within the competence of the Works Council.

2. The employer shall submit periodically to the Works Council all information necessary to enable the latter to carry out its basic functions.

3. The matters on which [the] employer shall submit reports to the Works Council and the hours and dates of meetings shall be the subject of an agreement between the Works Council and the employer. This agreement may provide, as a method of information, for the attendance of representatives of the Works Council at meetings of the supervisory body of the enterprise.

Article VII

Works Councils shall carry out their functions in cooperation with the recognized Trade Unions.

Article VIII

In addition to their regular meetings, Works Councils shall give a full report of their activities at least once every quarter to a general meeting of the workers and employees concerned.

Article IX

No employer shall hinder the establishment of a Works Council in his enterprise, or interfere with its activities, or discriminate against the members of the Works Council.

NOTES AND QUESTIONS

1.   The central provision of the Work Council Law of 1946 is Art V: work councils have binding rights over (a) enforcing collective agreements in the workplace (b) health and safety (c) measures to avoid unemployment (d) grievance procedures, including relating to social insurance and (e) development of social policy. This law functioned as a template: unions would have to organise and then voluntarily bargain to adopt such a works council structure. It was not imposed on workplaces. Could UK trade unions collectively bargain for an analogous scheme in British workplaces today?

2.   The term 'works council' is usually used by other labour law authors, but this seems to be a mistranslation of the German term *Betriebsrat*. The word *Betrieb* means 'business' or 'workplace' and the word *Rat* means 'council'. At the risk of being pedantic, the 's' in the middle denotes the genitive of *Betrieb*, not a plural, so the literal translation is 'council of work', or 'work council'. This is why this book follows the more natural English sounding 'work council', not the clumsy

and ungrammatical 'works council', though no doubt the effort of swimming against this tide is pointless!

3. Today the German Work Constitution Act 1972 (Betriebsverfassungsgesetz) goes further in the rights work councils have. The most important topic is voice in dismissals. The German government's translation of the key sections follow:

Work Constitution Act 1972 (BGBl I S 2518)

1. Establishment of works councils

(1) Works councils shall be elected in all establishments that normally have five or more permanent employees with voting rights, including three who are eligible. The same shall apply to joint establishments of several companies.

...

87 Right of co-determination

(1) The works council shall have a right of co-determination in the following matters in so far as they are not prescribed by legislation or collective agreement:

1. matters relating to the rules of operation of the establishment and the conduct of employees in the establishment;
2. the commencement and termination of the daily working hours including breaks and the distribution of working hours among the days of the week;
3. any temporary reduction or extension of the hours normally worked in the establishment;
4. the time and place for and the form of payment of remuneration;
5. the establishment of general principles for leave arrangements and the preparation of the leave schedule as well as fixing the time at which the leave is to be taken by individual employees, if no agreement is reached between the employer and the employees concerned;
6. the introduction and use of technical devices designed to monitor the behaviour or performance of the employees;
7. arrangements for the prevention of accidents at work and occupational diseases and for the protection of health on the basis of legislation or safety regulations;
8. the form, structuring and administration of social services [including pensions] whose scope is limited to the establishment, company or combine;
9. the assignment of and notice to vacate accommodation that is rented to employees in view of their employment relationship as well as the general fixing of the conditions for the use of such accommodation;
10. questions related to remuneration arrangements in the establishment, including in particular the establishment of principles of remuneration and the introduction and application of new remuneration methods or modification of existing methods;
11. the fixing of job and bonus rates and comparable performance-related remuneration including cash coefficients;
12. principles for suggestion schemes in the establishment;
13. principles governing the performance of group work; group work within the meaning of this provision is defined as a group of employees performing a complex task within the establishment's workflows, which has been assigned to it and is executed in a largely autonomous way.

(2) If no agreement can be reached on a matter covered by the preceding subsection, the conciliation committee shall make a decision. The award of the conciliation committee shall take the place of an agreement between the employer and the works council.

111 Alterations

In establishments that normally have more than twenty employees with voting rights the employer shall inform the works council in full and in good time of any proposed alterations which may entail substantial prejudice to the staff or a large sector thereof and consult the works council on the proposed alterations. In establishment that have more than 300 employees, the works council may retain a consultant to support it; section 80 (4) shall apply, mutatis mutandis, the foregoing shall be without prejudice to section 80 (3). The following shall be considered as alterations for the purposes of the first sentence above:

1. reduction of operations in or closure of the whole or important departments of the establishment;
2. transfer of the whole or important departments of the establishment;
3. the amalgamation with other establishments or split-up of establishments;
4. important changes in the organization, purpose or plant of the establishment;
5. introduction of entirely new work methods and production processes.

112 Reconciliation of interests in the case of alterations; social compensation plan

(1) If the employer and the works council reach an agreement to reconcile their interests in connection with the proposed alterations, the said agreement shall be recorded in writing and signed by the employer and the works council.

...

(2) If no reconciliation of interests can be achieved in connection with the proposed alterations or if no agreement is reached on the social compensation plan, the employer or the works council may apply to the Executive Board of the Federal Employment Agency for mediation, the Board may entrust other staff members of the Federal Employment Agency with this task.

...

(4) If no agreement is reached on the social compensation plan, the conciliation committee shall make a decision on the drawing up of a social compensation plan ....

...

(5) ... the conciliation committee shall take into account ...

1. When compensating in full or part any financial prejudices sustained, in particular by a reduction in income, the lapse of additional benefits or loss of entitlements to company pensions, removal costs or increased travelling costs, it shall provide for payments which generally make allowances for the circumstances of the individual case.
2. It shall take into account the prospects of the employees concerned on the labour market. It shall exclude from payments employees who may continue to work in reasonable employment in the same establishment or in another establishment of the company or of a company belonging to the combine, but refuse said continued employment; the possibility of continued employment at another location shall not alone be sufficient grounds for claiming unreasonableness.
2a. In particular, it shall duly consider the support schemes aimed at avoiding unemployment provided for in Book Three of the Social Code.
3. When calculating the total amount of the social compensation plan payments, it shall take care that the continuance of the company or the jobs remaining after the implementation of the alterations is not jeopardised.

NOTES AND QUESTIONS

1. The Work Constitution Act (WCA) 1972 says that with over 5 staff, elected work councils get binding rights on 13 issues, including (2, 3) hours and breaks, (4, 10, 11) methods of pay, (7) health and safety, and (8) pensions and social affairs (WCA 1972 §§1 and 87). Which do you think are the most important in the list?
2. With over 20 staff, work councils may defer redundancy dismissals to arbitration on a 'social plan' (WCA 1972 §§111–13). In this way, there is no right for workers

to actually hold onto their jobs. But, in awarding compensation, the conciliation committee must consider the importance of avoiding unemployment. Such a 'social compensation plan' can be very significant.

3. If work councils can defer dismissals, this mitigates employers' inherent conflicts of interest, in driving through dismissals against the interests of the enterprise: see chapter 16.

(b) Economic Changes for 50+ Employees

While the UK has not yet introduced its own legislation, an EU Directive in 2002 made a small start, requiring a minimum framework for 'information and consultation' of employees in the EU. It stops short of binding participation rights, but all countries can go beyond the minimum standards. So can any collective agreement.

Information and Consultation Directive 2002/14/EC Arts 1–7

Article 2 Definitions
For the purposes of this Directive:
  (a) "undertaking" means a public or private undertaking carrying out an economic activity, whether or not operating for gain, which is located within the territory of the Member States;
  (b) "establishment" means a unit of business defined in accordance with national law and practice, and located within the territory of a Member State, where an economic activity is carried out on an ongoing basis with human and material resources;
  ...
  (f) "information" means transmission by the employer to the employees' representatives of data in order to enable them to acquaint themselves with the subject matter and to examine it;
  (g) "consultation" means the exchange of views and establishment of dialogue between the employees' representatives and the employer.

Article 3 Scope
  1. This Directive shall apply, according to the choice made by Member States, to:
  (a) undertakings employing at least 50 employees in any one Member State, or
  (b) establishments employing at least 20 employees in any one Member State.
  Member States shall determine the method for calculating the thresholds of employees employed.

Article 4 Practical arrangements for information and consultation
  1. ... the Member States shall determine the practical arrangements for exercising the right to information and consultation
  2. Information and consultation shall cover:
  (a) information on the recent and probable development of the undertaking's or the establishment's activities and economic situation;
  (b) information and consultation on the situation, structure and probable development of employment within the undertaking or establishment and on any anticipatory measures envisaged, in particular where there is a threat to employment;
  (c) information and consultation on decisions likely to lead to substantial changes in work organisation or in contractual relations, including those covered by the Community provisions referred to in Article 9(1).

3. Information shall be given at such time, in such fashion and with such content as are appropriate to enable, in particular, employees' representatives to conduct an adequate study and, where necessary, prepare for consultation.

4. Consultation shall take place:

(a) while ensuring that the timing, method and content thereof are appropriate;

(b) at the relevant level of management and representation, depending on the subject under discussion;

(c) on the basis of information supplied by the employer in accordance with Article 2(f) and of the opinion which the employees' representatives are entitled to formulate;

(d) in such a way as to enable employees' representatives to meet the employer and obtain a response, and the reasons for that response, to any opinion they might formulate;

(e) with a view to reaching an agreement on decisions within the scope of the employer's powers referred to in paragraph 2(c).

Article 5 Information and consultation deriving from an agreement

Member States may entrust management and labour at the appropriate level, including at undertaking or establishment level, with defining freely and at any time through negotiated agreement the practical arrangements for informing and consulting employees ....

NOTES AND QUESTIONS

1. The core provision is Art 4(2) stating there must at least be consultation with employees on (b) developments or threats to employment, and (c) substantial changes in work organisation or contract changes, and (a) information (only) on probable enterprise developments. When setting up 'practical arrangements', would you advise that a union or group of employees demand consultation, as an opening gambit, in a significant list of workplace issues?

2. There are also (probably superfluous) provisions requiring no disclosure of confidential information (Art 6), protection of employee representatives (Art 7), and 'adequate administrative or judicial procedures are available to enable the obligations deriving from this Directive to be enforced' (Art 8). Article 9 says additional duties regarding collective redundancies and transfer of undertakings take precedence: see chapter 19.

3. The ICED 2002 was implemented in UK law as follows.

Information and Consultation of Employees Regulations 2004 (SI 3426/2004) regs 2–32

3. Application

(1) These Regulations apply to undertakings-

(a) employing in the United Kingdom, in accordance with the calculation in reg 4, at least [50 employees, as under Sch 1]; and

(b) subject to paragraph (2), whose registered office, head office or principal place of business is situated in Great Britain.

(2) Where the registered office is situated in Great Britain and the head office or principal place of business is situated in Northern Ireland or vice versa, these Regulations shall only apply where the majority of employees are employed to work in Great Britain.

4. Calculation of number of employees

(1) Subject to paragraph (4), the number of employees for the purposes of regulation 3(1) shall be determined by ascertaining the average number of employees employed in the previous twelve months. ...

...

7. Employee request to negotiate an agreement in respect of information and consultation

(1) On receipt of a valid employee request, the employer shall, subject to paragraphs (8) and (9), initiate negotiations by taking the steps set out in regulation 14(1).

(2) Subject to paragraph (3), an employee request is not a valid employee request unless it consists of—

(a)   a single request made by at least 10% of the employees in the undertaking; or

(b)   a number of separate requests made on the same or different days by employees which when taken together mean that at least 10% of the employees in that undertaking have made requests, provided that the requests are made within a period of six months.

(3) Where the figure of 10% in paragraph (2) would result in less than 15 or more than 2,500 employees being required in order for a valid employee request to be made, that paragraph shall have effect as if, for the figure of 10%, there were substituted the figure of 15, or as the case may be, 2,500.

(4) An employee request is not a valid employee request unless the single request referred to in paragraph (2)(a) or each separate request referred to in paragraph (2)(b)–

(a)   is in writing;

(b)   is sent to—

(i)   the registered office, head office or principal place of business of the employer; or

(ii)   the CAC; and

(c)   specifies the names of the employees making it and the date on which it is sent.

...

(8) If the employer decides to hold a ballot under regulation 8 or 9, the employer shall not be required to initiate negotiations unless and until the outcome of the ballot is that in regulation 8(5)(b).

(9) If an application is made to the CAC under regulation 13, the employer shall not be required to initiate negotiations unless and until if the CAC declares that there was a valid employee request or that the employer's notification was valid.

8. Pre-existing agreements: ballot for endorsement of employee request

(1) Subject to regulation 9, this regulation applies where a valid employee request has been made under regulation 7 by fewer than 40% of employees employed in the undertaking on the date that request was made and where there exists one or more pre-existing agreements which—

(a)   are in writing;

(b)   cover all the employees of the undertaking;

(c)   have been approved by the employees; and

(d)   set out how the employer is to give information to the employees or their representatives and seek their views on such information.

...

(6) For the purposes of paragraph (5), the employees are to be regarded as having endorsed the employee request if—

(a)   at least 40% of the employees employed in the undertaking; and

(b)   the majority of the employees who vote in the ballot, have voted in favour of endorsing the request.

...

14. Negotiations to reach an agreement

(1) In order to initiate negotiations to reach an agreement under these Regulations the employer must as soon as reasonably practicable—

(a) make arrangements, satisfying the requirements of paragraph (2), for the employees of the undertaking to elect or appoint negotiating representatives; and thereafter

(b) inform the employees in writing of the identity of the negotiating representatives; and

(c) invite the negotiating representatives to enter into negotiations to reach a negotiated agreement.

...

19. Election of information and consultation representatives

(1) ... the employer shall, before the standard information and consultation provisions start to apply, arrange for the holding of a ballot of its employees to elect the relevant number of information and consultation representatives.

...

(3) ... this ... means one representative per fifty employees or part thereof, provided that that number is at least 2 and does not exceed 25. ...

20. Standard information and consultation provisions

(1) Where the standard information and consultation provisions apply pursuant to regulation 18, the employer must provide the information and consultation representatives with information on—

(a) the recent and probable development of the undertaking's activities and economic situation;

(b) the situation, structure and probable development of employment within the undertaking (and such information must include suitable information relating to the use of agency workers (if any) in that undertaking) and on any anticipatory measures envisaged, in particular, where there is a threat to employment within the undertaking; and

(c) subject to paragraph (5), decisions likely to lead to substantial changes in work organisation or in contractual relations, including those referred to in–

(i) sections 188 to 192 of the Trade Union and Labour Relations (Consolidation) Act 1992; and

(ii) regulations 13 to 16 of the Transfer of Undertakings (Protection of Employment) Regulations 2006.

(2) The information referred to in paragraph (1) must be given at such time, in such fashion and with such content as are appropriate to enable, in particular, the information and consultation representatives to conduct an adequate study and, where necessary, to prepare for consultation.

(3) The employer must consult the information and consultation representatives on the matters referred to in paragraph (1)(b) and (c).

(4) The employer must ensure that the consultation referred to in paragraph (3) is conducted—

(a) in such a way as to ensure that the timing, method and content of the consultation are appropriate;

(b) on the basis of the information supplied by the employer to the information and consultation representatives and of any opinion which those representatives express to the employer;

(c) in such a way as to enable the information and consultation representatives to meet the employer at the relevant level of management depending on the subject under discussion and to obtain a reasoned response from the employer to any such opinion; and

(d) in relation to matters falling within paragraph (1)(c), with a view to reaching agreement on decisions within the scope of the employer's powers. ...

1. The central provision of Information and Consultation of Employees Regulations (ICER) 2004 is reg 20, which states the minimum consultation must include (1)(b) the 'probable development of employment' and any 'threat', and (c) substantial changes in work organisation or contracts. This includes collective redundancies and transfers of undertakings, where there are more specific rules (chapter 20). Yet the essence is the same: an 'information and consultation procedure' in effect means a work council, which should serve as a standing institution the employer must go to to consult.

2. While not expressly listed, a takeover or merger must be considered as part of the 'structure' of employment. As chapter 19 discusses, 'transfers of undertakings' mean an asset sale or outsourcing deal, but not where the shareholders of a corporation change (as the corporation, with which an employee has a contract remains legally identical).

3. What, exactly, does 'consultation' mean? ICED 2002 Art 2 and ICER 2004 reg 2 says it means 'exchange of views and establishment of dialogue', but what does that mean? Article 4(4)(e) and reg 20(4)(d) say this means having a 'view to reaching agreement'. In *Junk v Kühnel* (2005) C-188/03, [43] the CJEU, while interpreting the parallel requirements of the Collective Redundancies Directive 1998, said this 'imposes an obligation to negotiate'. In other words, this is what in US labour law might be termed a duty to negotiate in good faith. Is such a duty enforceable in practice against a hostile employer? Would it not be preferable and simpler to give workers binding decision rights, either by board representation or in work councils?

4. ICER 2004 regs 22–23 state that breaches of regulations can be referred to the CAC, and then appealed to an appeal tribunal, but the maximum penalty is £75,000. Is this enough to comply with the ICED 2004 Art 8 requirement of effective enforcement of rights?

5. In *Amicus v Macmillan Publishers Ltd* [2007] IRLR 378 (EAT) Elias J imposed a £55,000 penalty on an employer who failed to set up an election for employee representatives (some distance from actually consulting) as this was 'a very grave breach' and would 'deter others from adopting what can only be described as the wholly cavalier attitude to their obligations that has been demonstrated by the respondent'. What do you think the actual savings to employers might be from not consulting? Outside statutory penalty for simple failure to comply, should punitive damages be imposed for *deliberate* statutory torts that are calculated to make a profit?

6. Under ICER 2004 reg 19, an employer can demand a ballot if there is a pre-existing procedure, or it feels that it is worth fighting and it can argue there is not enough employee support (reg 8). Schedule 2 sets out procedures for a ballot. This says all the 'costs' shall be borne by the employer. But presumably a cut-throat employer seeking to drag out, delay or avoid getting a work council might decide it is worth that cost, and try to manipulate the ballot to that end. Why is a work council not simply a right?

7. In *Moray Council v Stewart* [2006] ICR 1253 (EAT) 500 teachers requested a new procedure. This was over 10 per cent but under 40 per cent of staff. The employer argued a ballot had to be held, because the existing collective agreement

with the union had a protocol on information and consultation. The Employment Appeal Tribunal held the pre-existing procedure was not adequate to force a ballot, because it did not explain how the views of staff would be sought.

8. The Pensions Act (PA) 2004 ss 259–61 enabled the Secretary of State to pass the Occupational and Personal Pension Schemes (Consultation by Employers and Miscellaneous Amendment) Regulations 2006, where regs 11–13 require information and consultation about any 'listed change' (reg 8) including increasing the pension age, closing a scheme to new members, ending employer contributions, and so forth.

9. ICER 2004 reg 4(3) states employees who work under 75 hours a month only count as half-persons for reaching the 50-employee threshold in an undertaking. H Collins, KD Ewing and A McColgan, *Labour Law in Context* (2012) 626, point out 'there is no provision for it in the Directive' and 'it appears to cut across ... the Part-Time Workers Directive'.

10. However, in *Association de médiation sociale v Union locale des syndicats CGT* (2014) C-176/12, [44]–[45] the CJEU's Grand Chamber held French law did not violate EU law by excluding of fixed-term, agency and part-time employees from full rights to count for the information and consultation thresholds (see Code du travail, Art L 1111-3). The Charter of Fundamental Rights of the EU Art 27 says: 'Workers or their representatives must, at the appropriate levels, be guaranteed information and consultation in good time in the cases and under the conditions provided for by Community Union law and national laws and practices.' Because the UK did not sign up, the Charter is not directly binding on the UK, but is an interpretative aid when the CJEU applies any Directive. Yet the CJEU held that Art 27 required further implementation by national law before it is effective. It did not create independent set of rights. This meant there was no ground on which to challenge the French law.

(c) Economic Changes for 1000+ EU Employees

A separate set of rules exist for multinational corporations that operate across the EU.

Transnational Works Council Directive 2009/38/EC arts 6–13

Article 1 Objective

1. The purpose of this Directive is to improve the right to information and to consultation of employees in Community-scale undertakings and Community-scale groups of undertakings.

...

3. Information and consultation of employees must occur at the relevant level of management and representation, according to the subject under discussion. To achieve that, the competence of the European Works Council and the scope of the information and consultation procedure for employees governed by this Directive shall be limited to transnational issues.

Article 2 Definitions

1. For the purposes of this Directive:

(a) 'Community-scale undertaking' means any undertaking with at least 1 000 employees within the Member States and at least 150 employees in each of at least two Member States;

(b) 'group of undertakings' means a controlling undertaking and its controlled undertakings;

(c) 'Community-scale group of undertakings' means a group of undertakings with the following characteristics:
—   at least 1 000 employees within the Member States,
—   at least two group undertakings in different Member States, and
—   at least one group undertaking with at least 150 employees in one Member State and at least one other group undertaking with at least 150 employees in another Member State;

...

Article 3 Definition of 'controlling undertaking'

1. For the purposes of this Directive, 'controlling undertaking' means an undertaking which can exercise a dominant influence over another undertaking (the controlled undertaking) by virtue, for example, of ownership, financial participation or the rules which govern it.

2. The ability to exercise a dominant influence shall be presumed, without prejudice to proof to the contrary, when an undertaking, in relation to another undertaking directly or indirectly:

(a) holds a majority of that undertaking's subscribed capital;

(b) controls a majority of the votes attached to that undertaking's issued share capital; or

(c) can appoint more than half of the members of that undertaking's administrative, management or supervisory body.

...

Article 4 Responsibility for the establishment of a European Works Council or an employee information and consultation procedure

1. The central management shall be responsible for creating the conditions and means necessary for the setting-up of a European Works Council or an information and consultation procedure, as provided for in Article 1(2), in a Community-scale undertaking and a Community-scale group of undertakings.

...

Article 5 Special negotiating body

1. ... the central management shall initiate negotiations for the establishment of a European Works Council or an information and consultation procedure on its own initiative or at the written request of at least 100 employees or their representatives in at least two undertakings or establishments in at least two different Member States.

...

Annex I Subsidiary requirements

1. ... the establishment, composition and competence of a European Works Council shall be governed by the following rules:

(a) The competence of the European Works Council shall be determined in accordance with Article 1(3).

The information of the European Works Council shall relate in particular to the structure, economic and financial situation, probable development and production and sales of the Community-scale undertaking or group of undertakings. The information and consultation of the European Works Council shall relate in particular to the situation and probable trend of employment, investments, and substantial changes concerning organisation, introduction of new working methods or production processes, transfers of production, mergers, cut-backs or closures of undertakings, establishments or important parts thereof, and collective redundancies.

The consultation shall be conducted in such a way that the employees' representatives can meet with the central management and obtain a response, and the reasons for that response, to any opinion they might express. ...

1.   The key provision is the default rule or 'subsidiary requirements' in the Annex, stating that consultation must include employment trends, work method changes, 'mergers, cut-backs or closures of undertakings' and collective redundancies. Although a simple takeover is not expressly included, this must be regarded as part of consultation on 'investments' and 'substantial changes concerning organisation'.

2.   S Laulom, 'The Flawed Revision of the European Works Council Directive' (2010) 39(2) *ILJ* 202, argues the Directive should have (a) expanded upon the issues subject to consultation, not merely transnational issues, (b) should have articulated that consultation must occur before decisions are taken, and (c) should have integrated national and transnational work council structures. Is there any reason why there should not be one work council law for all employees in firms over a minimum size?

3.   The European Works Council Directive (EWCD) 2009 is implemented by Transnational Information and Consultation of Employees Regulations (TICER) 1999, as updated in 2010.

Transnational Information and Consultation of Employees Regulations 1999

3. Controlled and Controlling Undertaking

(1) In these Regulations "controlling undertaking" means an undertaking which can exercise a dominant influence over another undertaking by virtue, for example, of ownership, financial participation or the rules which govern it and "controlled undertaking" means an undertaking over which such a dominant influence can be exercised.

(2) The ability of an undertaking to exercise a dominant influence over another undertaking shall be presumed, unless the contrary is proved, when in relation to another undertaking it directly or indirectly—

(a)   can appoint more than half of the members of that undertaking's administrative, management or supervisory body;

(b)   controls a majority of the votes attached to that undertaking's issued share capital; or

(c)   holds a majority of that undertaking's subscribed capital.

...

5. The central management

(1) The central management shall be responsible for creating the conditions and means necessary for the setting up of a European Works Council or an information and consultation procedure in a Community-scale undertaking or Community-scale group of undertakings where—

(a)   the central management is situated in the United Kingdom;

(b)   the central management is not situated in a Member State and the representative agent of the central management (to be designated if necessary) is situated in the United Kingdom; or

(c)   neither the central management nor the representative agent (whether or not as a result of being designated) is situated in a Member State and—

(i)   in the case of a Community-scale undertaking, there are employed in an establishment, which is situated in the United Kingdom, more employees than are employed in any other establishment which is situated in a Member State, or

(ii) in the case of a Community-scale group of undertakings, there are employed in a group undertaking, which is situated in the United Kingdom, more employees than are employed in any other group undertaking which is situated in a Member State,

and the central management initiates, or by virtue of regulation 9(1) is required to initiate, negotiations for a European Works Council or information and consultation procedure.

...

9. Request to negotiate an agreement for a European Works Council or information and consultation procedure

(1) The central management shall initiate negotiations for the establishment of a European Works Council or an information and consultation procedure where—

(a) a valid request has been made by employees or employees' representatives; and

(b) on the relevant date the undertaking is a Community-scale undertaking or the group of undertakings is a Community-scale group of undertakings.

(2) A valid request may consist of—

(a) a single request made by at least 100 employees, or employees' representatives who represent at least that number, in at least two undertakings or establishments in at least two different Member States; or

(b) a number of separate requests made on the same or different days by employees, or by employees' representatives, which when taken together mean that at least 100 employees, or employees' representatives who represent at least that number, in at least two undertakings or establishments in at least two different Member States have made requests.

...

15. Consultative Committee

(1) Where a consultative committee exists—

(a) no UK member of the special negotiating body shall be elected by a ballot of the UK employees, except in the circumstances specified in paragraphs (2), (3) or (9) below; and

(b) the committee shall be entitled to nominate from its number the UK members of the special negotiating body.

(2) Where the consultative committee fails to nominate any UK members of the special negotiating body, all of the UK members of the special negotiating body shall be elected by a ballot of the UK employees in accordance with regulations 13 and 14.

...

18. Subsidiary requirements

(1) The provisions of the Schedule shall apply if—

(a) the parties so agree;

(b) within the period of six months beginning on the date on which a valid request referred to in regulation 9 was made, the central management refuses to commence negotiations; or

(c) after the expiry of a period of three years beginning on the date on which a valid request referred to in regulation 9 was made, the parties have failed to conclude an agreement under regulation 17 and the special negotiating body has not taken the decision under regulation 16(3).

...

Schedule Subsidiary Requirements

1. Establishment of European Works Council

A European Works Council shall be established in the Community-scale undertaking or Community-scale group of undertakings in accordance with the provisions in this Schedule.

2. Composition of the European Works Council

...

(2) In each Member State in which employees of a Community-scale undertaking or Community-scale group of undertakings are employed to work, those employees shall elect or appoint one member of the European Works Council for each 10% (or fraction of 10%) which those employees represent of the total number of employees of the Community-scale undertaking or Community-scale group of undertakings employed in those Member States.

(3) The European Works Council shall inform the central management and any more appropriate level of management of the composition of the European Works Council.

(4) To ensure that it can co-ordinate its activities, the European Works Council shall elect from among its members a select committee comprising no more than five members who are to act on
behalf of the European Works Council.

...

7. Information and consultation meetings

(1) Subject to paragraph 8, the European Works Council shall have the right to meet with the central management once a year in an information and consultation meeting, to be informed and consulted, on the basis of a report drawn up by the central management, on the progress of the business of the Community-scale undertaking or Community-scale group of undertakings and its prospects.

(2) The central management shall inform the local managements accordingly.

(3) The information provided to the European Works Council shall relate in particular to the structure, economic and financial situation, the probable development of the business and of production and sales of the Community-scale undertaking or Community-scale group of undertakings.

(4) The information and consultation meeting shall relate in particular to the situation and probable trend of employment, investments, and substantial changes concerning organisation, introduction of new working methods or production processes, transfers of production, mergers, cut-backs or closures of undertakings, establishments or important parts of such undertakings or establishments, and collective redundancies ....

NOTES AND QUESTIONS

1. TICER 1999 is materially similar to EWCD 2009, but for some reason the Blair administration, which introduced it, did not want to use the term 'work council' in UK law. This in itself is highly noteworthy, because trade unions are able at any time to bargain for transnational work councils with more rights, and rights of participation, not just consultation in collective agreements.

2. The astonishingly poor, long-winded drafting of TICER 1999 (around 73 pages) could deter trade unions from bothering. This would be a mistake: the simple idea is that a central management must consult with employee representatives, and can be penalised for failing to do so. This gives unions an additional avenue of enforcement to strike action: the right to sue in court.

3. TICER 1999 regs 20–21 state a penalty of up to £100,000 applies for a breach. However, this sum of money is paid to the government, rather than the applicant. Does this allow for adequate enforcement in EU law, given the obvious disincentive to sue when there is no monetary compensation available?

(3) RIGHTS IN WORKERS' CAPITAL

Although the UK is behind in board representation, and work councils, UK unions and employees are advanced in having some voice (by no means adequate) in administering pension funds. Like board representation in Germany, joint pension management in the UK started in collective agreements. Partly this mirrored the UK's history of 'joint industrial councils' or Whitley Councils, where trade unions and employer associations would periodically negotiate sectoral terms and conditions for workers. Retired workers who are beneficiaries of a pension trust also have rights. Because they affect companies, pension rights have massive implications. Codifying previous collective agreements, the PA 2004 set minimum standards for pension trusts to have 'member-nominated trustees'.

Pensions Act 2004 ss 241–43

241 Requirement for member-nominated trustees
  (1) The trustees of an occupational trust scheme must secure—
    (a) that, within a reasonable period of the commencement date, arrangements are in place which provide for at least one-third of the total number of trustees to be member-nominated trustees, and
    (b) that those arrangements are implemented.
  (2) "Member-nominated trustees" are trustees of an occupational trust scheme who—
    (a) are nominated as the result of a process in which at least the following are eligible to participate—
      (i) all the active members of the scheme or an organisation which adequately represents the active members, and
      (ii) all the pensioner members of the scheme or an organisation which adequately represents the pensioner members, and
    (b) are selected as a result of a process which involves some or all of the members of the scheme.
  ...
  (4) The arrangements may provide for a greater number of member-nominated trustees than that required to satisfy the one-third minimum mentioned in subsection (1)(a) only if the employer has approved the greater number.
  ...
  (6) The arrangements must provide that the removal of a member-nominated trustee requires the agreement of all the other trustees.
  ...

242 Requirement for member-nominated directors of corporate trustees
  (1) Where a company is a trustee of an occupational trust scheme and every trustee of the scheme is a company, the company must secure—
    (a) that, within a reasonable period of the commencement date, arrangements are in place which provide for at least one-third of the total number of directors of the company to be member-nominated directors, and
    (b) that those arrangements are implemented.
  ...

243 Member-nominated trustees and directors: supplementary

(1) The Secretary of State may, by order, amend sections 241(1)(a) and (4) and 242(1)(a) and (4) by substituting, in each of those provisions, "one-half" for "one-third".

(2) Regulations may modify sections 241 and 242 (including any of the provisions mentioned in subsection (1)) in their application to prescribed cases.

NOTES AND QUESTIONS

1. PA 2004 s 241 states the basic requirement that one-third of pension trustees must be 'member nominated'. This enables either direct elections by employees and beneficiaries of a pension plan of their trustees, or for the fund to be organised so that a union appoints the pension trustees without an election. Identical rights apply to pension trusts organised as a corporation (s 242). Under s 243, the Secretary of State can raise this minimum standard to one-half. This power has not yet been exercised. What arguments are there for and against raising the standard?

2. Under s 243(2) the Secretary of State may modify the application of ss 241–42 in relation to prescribed cases: a number of collectively bargained pension schemes have 'benefited' from this provision, including the Universities Superannuation Scheme. USS Ltd, where most university professors and lecturers have their retirement savings, is a trust corporation. This trust corporation has three representatives on its board nominated by the union, Universities and College Union, four representatives appointed by the employer association, Universities UK, and five representatives who are 'co-opted', supposedly 'independent' and chosen with agreement of both the union and the employers. At the time of writing, the UUK representatives include Dame Glynis Breakwell (former Vice-Chancellor of Bath, who paid herself £468,000 before resigning under media outcry), a former VC of Birmingham, a former VC of Glasgow, and Deputy VC of Warwick. The UCU members are academics involved with the union. The 'independent' members' backgrounds were from (1) an asset manager, Old Mutual (2) a private equity firm, Warburg Pincus, (3) another asset manager, Schroders, (4) a mining company, Rio Tinto, and (5) another asset manager, JP Morgan. Given the backgrounds, do you think these people represent the views of employees whose money is at stake?

3. PA 2004 derives from the Report by Roy Goode, *Pension Law Reform* (1993) Cm 2342, para 4.5.40. This originally recommended that in defined benefit (DB) schemes active members should have the right to appoint a minimum of one-third of the trustees, but in defined contribution (DC) schemes 'where the employer has no liability beyond the employer's contributions, scheme members should be entitled (but not obliged) to appoint at least two-thirds of the trustees'. Goode's recommendations were only partly put into effect by PA 1995 ss 16–21, but the standard was one-third for DB *and* DC schemes, and employers had a right to opt out. PA 2004 removed the opt out.

4. Before statutory regulation, collective agreements forged the models for pension fund governance. Strong trade unions aimed for 50–50 representation in DB schemes, but there could be much variation. T Schuller and J Hyman, 'Pensions: The Voluntary Growth of Participation' (1983) 14(1) *Industrial Relations Journal* 70,

73–75, found in a study of 57 schemes, there were 3 cases of over 50 per cent employee representation, 16 cases of 50 per cent, 20 cases of 40–49 per cent, 12 between 33 and 40 per cent, and 6 of under 33 per cent. See further E McGaughey, *Participation in Corporate Governance* (2014) ch 6(1).

5. Most pension funds are small. They have less bargaining power. They delegate investment responsibility to asset managers. Asset management is typically classified as either 'passive' or 'active'. In a passive fund, the manager simply invests money across all companies and asset classes in an index (eg an equal share in all FTSE100 companies). This does not require significant intellect or talent. But what is usually marketed as an 'active' fund (where even higher fees are charged) typically means the manager only overweights (buys) or underweights (sells) in, say, 5 or 10 of the FTSE100 companies. This also does not require significant intellect or talent. The financial markets are, however, opaque. Trustees are constantly bamboozled by asset manager marketing on all their 'options' for different 'risk preferences' in funds. This makes what is very simple seem incredibly bewildering. The opacity of the market leads to virtually non-existent competition. According to the Financial Conduct Authority, *Asset Management Market Study* (June 2017) para 1.9, there is 'weak price competition in a number of areas of the asset management industry. Firms do not typically compete on price'. What do you think can be done?

6. Local government pension funds are particularly vulnerable. Although they are organised under an umbrella group, the Local Government Pension Scheme, this is in fact 101 separate pension funds. Each is created by statutory instrument, rather than one big fund, with bargaining power. The Hutton Report, *Independent Public Service Pensions Commission: Final Report* (10 March 2011) suggested mergers would be desirable, but this has not occurred. It also suggested that employees and beneficiaries should have representation: before they had virtually none. However, the Public Service Pensions Act 2013 ss 4–5, elaborated on by the Local Government Pension Scheme Regulations 2013 reg 53(4), only requires that boards with equal employee–employer representation have a role of 'assisting' the scheme manager (ie the employer) 'in relation to securing compliance' with regulations and legislation. Does this sound like enough to secure binding participation rights?

7. NEST, set up by the PA 2008 as the public option pension and asset manager for auto-enrolment savings, has another exemption from PA 2004 s 242.

Pensions Act 2008 ss 67–69 and Sch 1

67 Duty to establish a pension scheme

(1) The Secretary of State must establish a pension scheme and make provision for its administration and management.

(2) A scheme established under this section is to be treated for all purposes as established under an irrevocable trust.

...

(4) It must when registered under Chapter 2 of Part 4 of the Finance Act 2004 be a scheme such that a jobholder's employer, if a participating employer, may comply with an enrolment duty by arranging for the jobholder to become an active member of the scheme.

...

69 Consultation of members and employers

(1) If an order under section 67 establishes a scheme, the Secretary of State must by order under that section require the trustees to make and maintain arrangements for consulting the members of the scheme and participating employers about the operation, development and amendment of the scheme.

(2) The arrangements must include establishment and maintenance of—

    (a) a panel of persons to represent members ("the members' panel"), and

    (b) a panel of persons to represent employers ("the employers' panel").

(3) The composition and functions of the panels are to be determined by order under section 67, or by the trustees under an order.

(4) The functions of the members' panel may include nominating individuals to be members of the trustee corporation.

...

Schedule 1 The trustee corporation

Members

1(1) Appointments of members of the corporation, and of a member as chair of the corporation, are to be made—

    (a) by the Secretary of State, if they take effect on the commencement of section 75(1) or in the initial period;

    (b) by the corporation, if they take effect after the initial period.

(2) Subject to sub-paragraph (3), the Secretary of State must consult the chair of the corporation before appointing an ordinary member (that is, a member who is not, on appointment, also appointed as chair).

(3) A vacancy in the office of chair does not prevent the appointment of an ordinary member.

(4) The Secretary of State and the corporation must aim to ensure that, from the end of the initial period, there are not fewer than 9 and not more than 15 members at any time.

...

(6) An order under section 67 may provide for section 242 of the Pensions Act 2004 (c. 35) (member-nominated directors of corporate trustees) to apply to the members of the corporation as it applies to the directors of a company, subject to any modifications specified in the order.

NOTES AND QUESTIONS

1. PA 2008 Sch 1 requires that the 'trustee corporation' (ie NEST) has 'members' who in effect act as directors of the board. But Sch 1, para 1(6), as spelt out by the National Employment Savings Trust (Consequential Provisions) Order 2010 (SI 2010/9) reg 3, exempts the board from having member-nominated directors.

2. Under Sch 1, para 1, appointments to the NEST board are made by the Secretary of State and the corporation, but under s 69, the NEST board must consult with employer and member panels. Is consultation a substitute for real participation rights?

3. NEST is almost mathematically destined to become one of the world's largest funds, equivalent to what are now often called 'sovereign wealth funds'. Do you think that the board should be selected solely by the Secretary of State or, more

realistically, the existing board and civil servants in Whitehall? Or should the board be selected by the people whose money is really at stake: jobholders saving for retirement?

4. In 2013, this author publicly asked the Secretary of State for Pensions, Steve Webb MP, if he would raise the threshold of member-nominated trustees to one-half under the PA 2004, and ensure that member-nominated directors were elected to NEST. See E McGaughey, 'Member Nominated Trustees and Corporate Governance' (2015) KCLLSRPS No 2015-26. In response, Webb asked the audience for a show of hands whether they thought there should be more member-nominated trustees: a vast majority raised their hands. However, Webb then proceeded to say he thought NEST was sufficiently accountable (see point 2 above). Sadly, Webb lost his seat in Parliament in 2015, although he gained a well-remunerated job as an asset manager with Royal London, and was knighted in 2017. Does a Minister's interest in serving the public conflict with their private interests if they are bought by business after politics?

5. Even given its defects, the UK has a superior system of pension representation than in the German Work Constitution Act 1972 (Betriebsverfassungsgesetz 1972). Pensions are listed among German worker codetermination rights, but there are five legal forms of German pension: a pension by contract with the employer (*Direktzusage*), by an insurance contract *(Versicherungsvertrag)*, a 'pension scheme' (*Pensionskasse*), a 'support scheme' (*Unterstützungskasse*) and a 'pension fund' (*Pensionsfonds*). Even in pension 'schemes' and 'funds', the two-tier constitution means worker representation does not extend to day-to-day management. But also, it was held, following a dubious line of reasoning by a former Federal Labour Court judge, Nipperdey, that contract pensions did not enable work councils to have a voice (BAGE 27, 194 (12 June 1975) 3 ABR 13/74). Those opinions replicated Nipperdey's old coauthored commentary: A Hueck and HC Nipperdey, *Lehrbuch des Arbeitsrechts* (2nd edn 1930) Bd II, §66 Nr 9 (the co-author, Hueck had to be 'de-Nazified' after World War Two). By contract Georg Flatow and Otto Kahn-Freund wrote in their commentary, *Betriebsrätegesetz* (1931) 348 that the law's purpose was to 'constrain the one-sided distribution and administration rights of the employer, and so the potential for arbitrary conduct, by giving employees the ability to participate'. This means today that the German insurance monolith, Allianz, controls a large part of German pensions, and others are simply taken by employers. Is there any good reason to distinguish between the legal form of pensions for codetermination rights?

6. In the UK there are an increasing number of so-called 'contract pensions' where the scheme provider is tacitly trying to argue the scheme is a 'contract' and not a 'trust' and therefore not subject to the PA 2004. In practice this goes unchallenged wherever there is a trade union lacking. In any event, it would seem that just because you call it a 'contract' this does not mean it stops being a trust, especially where rights are at stake: see *Autoclenz* (chapter 3(1)), *Re Spectrum Plus Ltd* (chapter 20) and *Twinsectra Ltd v Yardley* [2002] UKHL 12, [71].

7. After the global financial crisis, a new Association of Member Nominated Trustees (AMNT) formed to organise the voice of employee and union pension trustees. A few years later, the organisation became interested in its potential influence

upon corporate governance. See E McGaughey, 'Member Nominated Trustees and Corporate Governance' (26 June 2013) amnt.org. By 2016, the AMNT had drafted and launched a 'red-line voting' initiative. This seeks to instruct asset managers on how votes on company shares, bought with pension money, must be cast. These are the most notable policies.

Association of Member Nominated Trustees, *The Red Lines: Voting Instructions* (2016)

Introduction

...

The AMNT agrees that trustees should be adopting active responsible investment policies covering environmental, social and corporate governance (ESG) matters and directing how their votes are cast at shareholder meetings of the companies in which they invest. Most pension schemes have found this extremely difficult to achieve in practice, particularly small schemes and those that pool their money with other investors in 'pooled funds' whose fund managers have generally been reluctant to allow investors to direct how the votes associated with their investments are cast.

Red Line Voting, developed by the Association of Member Nominated Trustees, will offer pension scheme trustees (and other asset owners) the opportunity to direct the voting of the UK-listed shares they own on behalf of their members to an extent never before possible for many.

The Red Lines have been designed specifically to enable those investing in pooled funds to direct the votes associated with their investment: the fund managers may receive Red Line Voting instructions from numerous investors in the fund, but they would be the same instructions making them easier to handle. Of about £5.5-trillion of assets under management in the UK in 2014, more than £2.5-trillion was in pooled funds, so this is a major step forward for UK investors. The greater volume of engagement with the process will also benefit those who already participate fully.

...

E1.) If the company does not have an Environmental Sustainability Committee chaired by a board director, or if the company is outside the FTSE 350 and does not have a named board member with responsibility for this area as evidence of appropriate concern, vote against the chair of the board.

...

E4.) Year one: If the company has failed to introduce and disclose emission reduction targets vote against the re-election of the chair of the Environmental Sustainability Committee.

Year two: If the company has failed to commit to introducing and disclose science-based emission reduction targets with a coherent strategy and action plan in line with a 2 degree scenario vote against the re-election of the chair of the Environmental Sustainability Committee.

Year three: if the company has failed to introduce and disclose the above, vote against the re-election of the chair of the Environmental Sustainability Committee.

...

E5.) If the company has a history of major incidents of environmental damage, or a major incident in the year under report, and the directors' report does not include a substantial account of how it is responding to resulting criticism and of the ways in which it proposes to minimise the risks of repetition, vote against the reappointment of the chair. If the remuneration policy proposes any increase in salary or bonus for directors employed at the time of the incident, vote against the remuneration report.

…

S1.) If the company does not have a Corporate Social Responsibility and Health & Safety Committee chaired by a board director, or if the company is outside the FTSE 350 and it does not have a named board member with responsibility for this area as evidence of appropriate concern, vote against the chair of the board.

…

S3.) If there is no diversity strategy in place to address a lack of minority ethnic representation at board or senior management level, and there is no visible minority representation at that level, vote against the chair of the nomination committee

…

S4.) Vote against the re-election of the chair of the nomination committee if there is no strategy in place to address any under-representation of women at board level and fewer than 25% of the company's board members are female.

…

S6.) In furtherance of Principle One of the United Nations Global Compact, vote against the board's remuneration proposals if any members of staff, including subcontracted staff employed in the UK,

- are paid below the Living Wage or where applicable the London Living Wage and the company has no plans to address this;
- do not have employment contracts specifying the number of working hours per week, or (aside from overtime with increased pay) allow more than a 25% increase or decrease on that figure to meet business needs.

…

S7.) Vote against political donations and political expenditure.

…

S8.) Vote against the re-election of the Chair of the main board if there is a failure to abide by the UN Global Compact standards on freedom of association, including the recognition of independent trade unions for the purpose of collective agreement.

…

S9.) Year one: Where a company has breached labour standards or law, vote against the chair of the committee responsible for corporate social responsibility.

Year two: If undertakings made by the company in year one to establish procedures to prevent a repetition are not introduced, and/or there are further breaches, vote against the Chair of the main board.

…

S10.) Where the company has a history of major breakdowns of industrial partnership, or of serious endangerment of health and safety, or of fraud, bribery or other corrupt practices among its staff, or has sustained major damage from any of those causes in the year under report, and the directors' report does not include a substantial account of how it is responding to resulting criticism and of the ways in which it proposes to minimise the risks of repetition, vote against the adoption of that report. If the remuneration policy proposes any increase in salary or bonus for directors employed at the time of the incident, vote against the remuneration report.

…

G19.) Vote against the remuneration report or policy if the total remuneration package of any director is more than 100 times greater than the average pay of the company's UK workforce, other than in exceptional circumstances which must be fully justified.

1. The *Red Lines* are in effect a collective agreement among pension trustees, which may be voluntarily adopted by other pension trustees, and form a common policy in relation to asset managers. They require minimum standards on (1) environmental, (2) social, and (3) governance issues at public companies, where pension fund money is invested. Which 'ESG' issues do you think are most important? Can you think of others?

2. The AMNT's 'red lines' are instructions to asset managers. But do asset managers need to follow them? By the end of 2017, a number of asset managers had agreed to follow instructions, but others had been making various objections. On the fiduciary duty to follow instructions, see *Butt v Kelson* [1952] ch 197. It would be unreasonable to have an exclusion clause excluding such a duty: UCTA 1997 s 3 and Schs 1 and 2. See E McGaughey, 'Does Corporate Governance Exclude the Ultimate Investor?' (2016) 16(1) *Journal of Corporate Law Studies* 221. Should pension funds switch away from their asset managers who fail to comply with instructions? Should they sue?

3. It has been the consistent view of the City that asset managers must act in the interests of the ultimate beneficiary. The Stewardship Code 2012, Principle 1, states that asset managers should have a voting policy: 'The policy should disclose how the institutional investor applies stewardship with the aim of enhancing and protecting the value for the ultimate beneficiary or client.' Similarly, the Hampel Committee, *Committee on Corporate Governance: Final Report* (1998) para 5.7: 'The right to vote is an important part of the asset represented by a share, and in our view an institution has a responsibility to the client to make considered use of it.'

4. Despite the views of the City reports, it is seriously open to question whether asset managers should be voting on 'other people's money' at all. Asset managers are currently exercising votes on shares in companies, and also selling companies' financial products (eg defined contribution pensions). This represents a potential massive conflict of interest, and in principle must be completely prohibited in equity: see *Keech v Sandford* [1726] EWHC Ch J76 and three centuries of jurisprudence since. In Switzerland, a Swiss People's Initiative of 2013, with the second highest majority ever, banned banks voting on shares deposited with them. Pension funds acquired a new duty to vote themselves. Swiss banks are functionally equivalent to UK banks. Do you think asset managers are or should be prohibited from voting on other people's money without specific instructions, or a voting policy democratically approved by the ultimate investors?

5. Asset managers, who are highly paid, have long supported escalating CEO and director pay (eg R Gribben, 'Investors Champion Boardroom Pay Rises' (19 July 1999) *Daily Telegraph*, 27). They side with management, they oppose trade unions, support zero-hours contracts and have been completely complacent about climate damage. Why should this 'financial oligarchy' continue to have any votes in the economy with 'other people's money'? See previously, L Brandeis, *Other People's Money and How the Bankers Use It* (1914) ch I.

Additional Reading for Chapter 11

S Webb and B Webb, *The History of Trade Unionism* (1920) Appendix VIII
In a new Appendix VIII, for the 1920 edition to the book originally from 1894, the Webbs discussed how, in relation to worker involvement in management they should 'put this differently'. While before, in *Industrial Democracy*, they had advocated a split between the three functions of management (determining how to produce), customers (what to produce) and workers (setting conditions of production, in collective bargaining), they now believed there should be no strict 'separation of spheres of authority'. Examples of Swiss workers on railway boards, and time, demonstrated to them that workers could achieve 'real social gain' by being involved in management. They suggested that publicly owned or nationalised companies could be an ideal place to start.

E McGaughey, 'The Codetermination Bargains: the History of German Corporate and Labour Law' (2016) 23(1) *Columbia Journal of European Law* 435
This article argues that codetermination in Germany, with worker representation on company boards and in work councils, came from free collective agreements. It demonstrates that a body of 'law and economics' literature, which argues codetermination is so inefficient that it never arises without a coercive law, is really an ideological myth. Specifically, in Germany both at the end of World Wars One and Two, unions demanded collective agreements to embed democracy in the economy. It was only after this that laws codified the models set up by those collective agreements: the 'codetermination bargains'.

E. McGaughey, 'A Twelve Point Plan for Labour and a Manifesto for Labour Law' (2017) 46(1) *Industrial Law Journal* 169
Reviewing the *Manifesto for Labour Law* (IER 2016), this contribution suggests that the pathbreaking recommendations for a revitalised Ministry of Labour and sectoral collective bargaining can be embedded with a 'twelve point plan'. Regarding votes at work, it suggests that it is necessary to embed democratic voice in the economy through workers having the right to vote in every company general meeting, for elected work councils that have binding rights over dismissals, and critically by democratising pension plans and asset management. Because the vast majority of economic wealth comes from people working and saving for retirement, working people ought to have votes proportionate to their contribution. Instead of directors and asset managers taking the votes in the economy from other people's labour and other people's money, the law should commit to democracy.

E McGaughey, 'Votes at Work in Britain: Shareholder Monopolisation and the 'Single Channel'' (2018) 47(1) *Industrial Law Journal* 76
This article argues that 'votes at work in Britain', far from being alien, has one of the oldest traditions in the world. While it has been said that British workers and unions lacked a 'constitutional conception' of the company, in fact unions were uncertain about seeking voice in management, because they had seen it misused in employee share schemes promoted by those who were ideologically opposed to the labour movement. However, the

UK probably had the oldest law for workers on boards – the Port of London Act 1908 – and saw continual experiments for worker directors, in gas companies, in the post, steel and buses. Laws for votes at work were proposed by every major political party, but largely by misfortune never quite got to statute. With proposals by both the Conservative Party and the Labour Party in 2016 and 2017, there appears to have been a complete change in attitude.

Part Four

Equality

Discrimination

What does 'equality' mean? Usually this indicates a sense that people should be treated the same, irrespective of certain factors. But paradoxically 'equality' in some factors must mean discrimination (or inequality) based on other factors. The really difficult question is what kind of discrimination in life or work is desirable? The language of equality carries an intense rhetorical appeal, but this should not distract from the legal issue. During the US civil rights movement, Martin Luther King Jr called for a world where people 'will not be judged by the color of their skin, but by the content of their character'. Yet the first Civil Rights Act of 1964, whose model the UK follows, did not define factors by which people should positively be judged: when being hired, in their employment terms, or for dismissal. The law could have required that people are judged based on the 'content of their character', skills, performance, and so on. Unfair dismissal law is framed this way (Employment Rights Act (ERA) 1996 s 98; see chapter 17). It could seek to pre-empt the discretionary power of employing entities, which can lawfully be exercised. But instead, today's law lists 'protected characteristics' that must negatively be disregarded by employing entities: it prevents judging people by the 'color of their skin', sex, belief, and so on. If this approach is followed too far, there is a risk that employing entities have unaccountable discretion, except where restricted by the law. This exacerbates the subordination of people at work.

Equality or 'treating like cases alike' may be an important social value, and even 'a general axiom of rational behaviour' (*Matadeen v Pointu* [1998] UKPC 9, Lord Hoffmann). But once it is decided which characteristics are relevant, it must be accompanied by further substantive concepts of justice to have meaning. Everyone being 'equally' subordinate is not a useful goal. Moreover, treating people equally is counterproductive when people are different: treating unequals as equal can be very unequal. Nor is the golden rule always helpful, that we should 'do unto others as you would have them do unto you' (see Leviticus 19:18 or Matthew 7:12), if people's needs and priorities differ. Just as most people value money for what it will buy, most people value equality as a means to get justice. Many standard problems of prejudice that persist today, of racism, sexism, homophobia, ablism or ageism, remain so pressing because there is inequality of income, wealth, education and power. If those prejudices were gone, the world would still be unjust. Identity is frequently exploited to divide people, to dampen their enthusiasm for collective action. If we are taught to fear people who (superficially) seem different, unity and collective action over the issues explored in the rest of this book will diminish.

On this view, prejudice is both a cause and a symptom of the true disease, namely an unjustly hierarchical society. This chapter sets out (1) the principle of equality and protected characteristics in law, (2) the concept of direct discrimination and justifications, (3) harassment and (4) victimisation.

Introductory reading: Collins ch 3. CEM ch 9 (various). D&M ch 6 (601–88).

(1) PRINCIPLES AND PROTECTED CHARACTERISTICS

The Equality Act (EA) 2010 is the main source for discrimination law. This incorporates rules from three EU Directives, and partly codifies general principles developed by common law or equity, and the case law of the Court of Justice of the European Union. Two main questions are (a) the extent to which the law binds or empowers the discretion of property owners or organisation leaders, and (b) how the law formulates who has rights to equality.

(a) General Principle of Equality?

Does the law have a general principle of equality, or should it? The answers to these questions remain essentially unresolved in most countries. This reflects the fact that clear principles of responsibility for property are still settling. The law's classical position was that property rights were strictly enforced, but could not be used to harm others: *sic utere tuo ut alienum non laedas*. Over the twentieth century, the law changed so that organisations which owned property for production (not property for personal consumption) were bound to positive obligations. Just as equity infused the law with duties to use trust property for the benefit of others, duties of equality required property ownership to be consistent with a social inclusion: in employment, housing, access to services (whether privately or publicly owned)[1] and in government. A business owner could no longer refuse to deal with people because of their race or gender by saying 'it is my private property'. While not an employment case, the first example of a general equality principle in English law comes from a landmark administrative law decision.

Kruse v Johnson [1898] 2 QB 91

Kruse claimed that he should be able to sing hymns, as part of a religious service in the Leeds parish of Kent, despite a new council bylaw saying nobody should 'play upon any musical or noisy instrument or sing in any public place or highway within fifty yards of any dwelling-house' if asked to stop by a constable. The bylaw was passed under the

---

[1] NB: this is why the English language, as it is used in England, retains apparently contradictory terms such as 'public schools' for private schools, and 'public houses' (ie pubs) for private drinking and eating establishments.

authority granted by the Local Government Act 1888 s 16. The Divisional Court held that the law was valid, but set out reasons why, in judicial review, a law could be invalidated.

Lord Russell of Killowen CJ:

I have thought it well to deal with these points in some detail, and for this reason that the great majority of the cases in which the question of by-laws has been discussed are not cases of by-laws of bodies of a public representative character entrusted by Parliament with delegated authority, but are for the most part cases of railway companies, dock companies, or other like companies, which carry on their business for their own profit, although incidentally for the advantage of the public. In this class of case it is right that the Courts should jealously watch the exercise of these powers, and guard against their unnecessary or unreasonable exercise to the public disadvantage. But, when the Court is called upon to consider the by-laws of public representative bodies clothed with the ample authority which I have described, and exercising that authority accompanied by the checks and safeguards which have been mentioned, I think the consideration of such by-laws ought to be approached from a different standpoint. They ought to be supported if possible. They ought to be, as has been said, "benevolently" inter-preted, and credit ought to be given to those who have to administer them that they will be reasonably administered. This involves the introduction of no new canon of construction. But, further, looking to the character of the body legislating under the delegated authority of Parlia-ment, to the subject-matter of such legislation, and to the nature and extent of the authority given to deal with matters which concern them, and in the manner which to them shall seem meet, I think courts of justice ought to be slow to condemn as invalid any by-law, so made under such conditions, on the ground of supposed unreasonableness. Notwithstanding what Cockburn C.J. said in *Bailey v. Williamson*,[2] an analogous case, I do not mean to say that there may not be cases in which it would be the duty of the Court to condemn by-laws, made under such authority as these were made, as invalid because unreasonable. But unreasonable in what sense? If, for instance, they were found to be partial and unequal in their operation as between different classes; if they were manifestly unjust; if they disclosed bad faith; if they involved such oppressive or gratuitous interference with the rights of those subject to them as could find no justification in the minds of reasonable men, the Court might well say, "Parliament never intended to give authority to make such rules; they are unreasonable and ultra vires." But it is in this sense, and in this sense only, as I conceive, that the question of unreasonableness can properly be regarded. A by-law is not unreasonable merely because particular judges may think that it goes further than is prudent or necessary or convenient, or because it is not accompa-nied by a qualification or an exception which some judges may think ought to be there.

Matthew J dissented. **Chitty LJ**, **Wright J**, **Darling J**, and **Channell J** concurred.

NOTES AND QUESTIONS

1. Lord Russell CJ holds local governments should be given greater deference than private bodies in their latitude for rulemaking (so the bylaw was valid) but that some principles should still hold. These include (1) a general principle of equal-ity, constraining discrimination that is 'partial and unequal in their operation as between different classes', (2) actions that are 'manifestly unjust', (3) actions that 'disclosed bad faith', or (4) 'oppressive or gratuitous interference with the rights of those subject to them'.

---

[2] (1873) LR 8 QB 118, 124.

2. In administrative law, the case's first principle has been frequently applied, but hardly in a way that made codified equality legislation unnecessary. For example, in South Africa, see *Minister of Posts and Telegraphs v Rasool*, 1934 AD 167. Nevertheless, SH Bailey, *Cases, Materials and Commentary on Administrative Law* (4th edn 2005) 238 refers to *Kruse* 'as illustrating a broader principle of English law requiring equal treatment without unfair discrimination'. The opposite of this principle is the exercise of discretion by an organisation's decision-makers: including a simple employment relation founded on court-enforced contracts, company constitutions or council bylaws.

3. Why did Lord Russell CJ say that profit-making private companies (which are registered through Companies House, a Royal Charter or a special Act of Parliament) should be more constrained than public bodies? For him, the answer seems to be that councils are legitimised by representative accountability (however defective that still was) which derived from the 'delegated authority of Parliament'. This view would suggest that because private enterprise is not (yet) accountable to its stakeholders in a meaningful way, but local government is more so, judicial review should exercise more deference in relation to acts of local government. This would suggest that private enterprise should be held to higher standards, rather than lower, or the same standards. Do you agree?

4. *Kruse v Johnson* is a remarkable endorsement of a prohibition on discrimination 'between different classes'. As we see below, there is not yet a clear codified provision against 'class discrimination' in the UK. Yet it is recognised at common law, and probably in EU and ECHR norms. What would 'class' discrimination mean? In 1898, our class would be heavily reflected in accents and jobs. Divisions were probably more rigid than today. Very generally, the working class (who worked to survive) would comprise most people, while the middle class would be a small group of 'white collar' professionals, and a smaller upper class or aristocracy would derive their income largely through ownership and control of inherited land or capital. These three stylised groups, however, were in practice infinitely more complex. Today, there are infinite gradations of wealth, income and education. The language of 'social mobility' substitutes for an older, more simplistic, class-based analysis, yet it probably serves a similar function. What do you think drives the psychological desire to be in a higher class? Is it possible to simply let go?

5. Class has frequently been seen as the primary factor that either drives or is interwoven with all other discrimination, including gender, religion or race. This is because to stop collective action and break solidarity of working people, the interest groups behind employing entities must divide. Three key examples follow.

6. First, in response to the *Declaration of the Rights of Man and of the Citizen* (1789) in France, Mary Woolstonecroft, *A Vindication of the Rights of Woman* (1792) ch IX, wrote that: 'From the respect paid to property flow, as from a poisoned fountain, most of the evils and vices which render this world such a dreary scene to the contemplative mind. ... One class presses on another, for all are aiming to procure respect on account of their property; and property once gained will procure the respect due only to talents and virtue. ... There must be more equality established in this society, or morality will never gain ground, and this virtuous

equality will not rest firmly even when founded on a rock, if one-half of mankind be chained to its bottom by fate, for they will be continually undermining it through ignorance or pride.' Do you notice any similarity to the Webbs' theory of *Industrial Democracy*? See chapter 2(1).

7. Second, and somewhat notoriously, Karl Marx, *On the Jewish Question* (1844), argued that to liberate Jewish people from religious discrimination and persecution, it was necessary to liberate all people from material dependence and private property. To the extent that being Jewish had become equated with being a 'man of money' and 'haggling and its preconditions', this could only be resolved if the 'subjective basis of Judaism, practical need, had been humanised'. With the French Revolution's liberty, equality and fraternity, said Marx, 'man was not freed from religion, he received religious freedom. He was not freed from property, he received freedom to own property. He was not freed from the egoism of business, he received freedom to engage in business.' The same year Marx published an introduction to *A Contribution to the Critique of Hegel's Philosophy of Right* (1844), in which he argued that: 'Religion is the sigh of a suffering creature, the heart of a heartless world, and the soul of soulless conditions. It is the opium of the people.' Do you agree that racism or religious prejudice would *entirely* dissolve if people were materially equal?

8. Third, Martin Luther King, in his *Speech to the Fourth Constitutional Convention AFL-CIO* (1961) said of the civil rights and labour movement: 'This unity of purpose is not an historical coincidence. Negroes are almost entirely a working people. There are pitifully few Negro millionaires and few Negro employers. Our needs are identical with labor's needs: decent wages, fair working conditions, liveable housing, old age security, health and welfare measures, conditions in which families can grow, have education for their children and respect in the community. That is why Negroes support labor's demands and fight laws which curb labor.' See further chapter 1(3)(b).

9. In *US v Stanley*, known as *The Civil Rights Cases* 109 US 3 (1883), the Supreme Court was faced with a question of whether the Civil Rights Act of 1875, which entitled everyone to access accommodation, public transport and theatres regardless of race or colour, was unconstitutional. During the US Civil War (1860–65) Abraham Lincoln issued the Emancipation Proclamation (1 January 1863) to end US slavery. After the war, the Fourteenth Amendment to the US Constitution (9 July 1868) said: 'No State shall make or enforce any law which shall abridge the privileges or immunities of citizens of the United States; nor shall any State deprive any person of life, liberty, or property, without due process of law; nor deny to any person within its jurisdiction the equal protection of the laws.' Bradley J, for the majority, held this did 'not authorize Congress to create a code of municipal law for the regulation of private rights', as supposedly distinct from 'state' laws. In effect, only state bodies were sufficiently 'public' so as to be regulated: 'private' bodies could not be. Harlan J dissented, and would have held the Civil Rights Act of 1875 valid, because people were left 'practically at the mercy of corporations and individuals wielding power under public authority'. That is, denial of rights against 'private parties' was the denial of the right to go to a public court to sue. A binary distinction between 'public' and 'private' law was, in this

context and in a technical sense, a racist, anti-democratic sham. It took until the Civil Rights Act of 1964 to undo that decision, to reinstate Harlan J's approach. Lord Russell CJ, who visited the United States in 1896, was undoubtedly aware of this when he decided *Kruse* in 1898.

10. In *Constantine v Imperial Hotels Ltd* [1944] KB 693, Birkett J had the opportunity to find a common law right to equal access to accommodation. A star cricketer from the West Indies, Mr Constantine, came to stay at a Russell Square hotel in London, before he played at Lords cricket ground. American troops, many from Southern segregated states, were staying at the hotel and objected to Mr Constantine. Instead of throwing out the troops for racial harassment without a refund (as, it is submitted, is lawfully appropriate today) the hotel owner asked Mr Constantine to relocate to another hotel nearby. Birkett J found that Mr Constantine was entitled to damages, but only nominal, for his 'unjustifiable humiliation and distress'. There was a common law right to reasonable accommodation, and the principle of *Ashby v White* (1703) 92 ER 126 applied, that 'it is a vain thing to imagine a right without a remedy'. A claim for 'exemplary and substantial' damages was declined based on previous authorities. Today they are available. See chapter 12(2)(b).

11. Of course, it was not just Southern state US soldiers who were racist. On just a fragment of the British Empire's vicious institutional racism, see chapter 1(2). In the context of postcolonial migration to the UK in the 1950s, *Scala Ballroom (Wolverhampton) Ltd v Ratcliffe* [1958] 1 WLR 72 was decided. Astonishingly, the company sued a union that took collective action to stop the ballroom's 'colour bar'. If you were black, apparently it was okay to perform on the ballroom's stage, but you could not be a customer. The Musicians' Union organised a boycott, requiring its members not to perform at the ballroom unless the bar was lifted. So, instead of the case being about a black customer suing the ballroom for their racist policy, the union was forced to defend itself for trying to stop the racism. Fortunately the Court of Appeal held union's action was immune from any injunction because they were defending their members' interests. Bob Hepple wrote that this case exemplified how the common law recognised no general tort (outside inn-keeping, as in *Constantine*) for discrimination: (1966) 29(3) MLR 306, 307. Since the point was not argued, it is not clear that this was accurate, but whatever the position more than half a century ago, is that the common law position now?

12. Signs saying things like 'No blacks, no dogs, no Irish' have become legendary in the history of discrimination. There are many witness accounts of such practices, for instance, in a somewhat pious 'Letter to an English Priest' by one Patrick Broughy (1958) 9(4) *The Furrow* 260, 262, saying: 'I have not seen evidence of discrimination against Catholics as such but I have seen it on the grounds of nationality against Irishmen. No doubt the limit was reached by the London landlady whose advertisement ran: Coloured people welcomed. Absolutely no Irish.' (If you are wondering, my parents were from the north of England, and from southern Ireland. My Irish family, who arrived in 1954, got elocution lessons to speak 'properly'.) Also, B Hepple 'The Aims of Equality Law' (2008) 61 *Current Legal Problems* 1, 3, recounts how, when he arrived in Britain from South Africa

in 1964 he was 'appalled to find that many of the racist attitudes and behaviour that I thought I had left behind me were commonplace in the UK. "No Coloureds, No Irish, No dogs" were notices that could be seen in landladies' windows.'

13. Full discussion of common law equality principles largely halted after statutory reform, starting with the landmark Race Relations Act (RRA) 1965. However, it remains important because it affects the psychological starting point of common lawyers: do we accept that 'anything goes' unless banned by Parliament? Or does the legally empowered right to hold property, make contracts and run enterprises carry responsibility? It is submitted that the law does recognise a general principle of equality, along the lines suggested by Harlan J, Lord Russell CJ and Birkett J. It pre-empts all abuses of discretionary power, by requiring that power be exercised for proper purposes. This is analogous to the duty of a company director in the Companies Act 2006 s 171.

14. An example of this principle (albeit in different terminology) being put into effect in employment is *Transco plc v O'Brien* [2002] EWCA Civ 379. The Court of Appeal affirmed it was a breach of mutual trust and confidence to 'single out an employee on capricious grounds'. That was being an agency worker, before there was any legislation on agency workers. Here the principle of equality enters common law through the open-textured standard of good faith. The same is true for open-textured standards such as a duty of care in tort engaged by a refusing to contract (analogous to *Constantine*), or in the power of dismissal (see *Johnson v Unisys Ltd* [2001] UKHL 13, [44] at chapter 17(1)) even in the absence of express statutory regulation.

15. In the CJEU, *Mangold v Helm* (2005) C-144/04 held there was a general principle of equality in EU law with 'horizontal direct effect'. The Court of Justice held that the German Part-time and Fixed-term Work Act 2000 §14(3) was contrary to the general principle of equality in EU law, because it exempted people over the age of 52 from the right to claim permanent, instead of fixed-term, contracts. This was so, even though German law was clear, and the deadline for implementing the Equality Framework Directive 2000 had not yet expired. *Mangold* did not, however, specify its reasoning in great detail, and was generally criticised in academic literature, eg Editorial, 'Horizontal Direct Effect – A Law of Diminishing Coherence?' (2006) 43 *CMLR* 1. The position was then clarified by *Kücükdeveci*.

Kücükdeveci v Swedex GmbH & Co KG (2010) C-555/07

Ms Kücükdeveci claimed that the requirement in the German Civil Code §622 (cf ERA 1996 s 86, chapter 17(1)) to be aged 25 before acquiring rights to notice before dismissal was unlawful age discrimination. In 1996, Kücükdeveci was aged 18 and began to work for Swedex GmbH. She was dismissed on 19 December 2006, with notice until the end of the next calendar month (31 January 2007) because according to §622, introduced in 1926, 'periods prior to the completion of the employee's 25th year of age are not taken into account'. If the time before her 25th birthday had been taken into account, she should have received at least four months' notice. Under the Equality Framework Directive 2000/78, Art 2(2)(a), direct discrimination on the grounds of age would be unlawful unless it was objectively justified under Art 6. The State Labour Court

(*Landesarbeitsgericht*) of Düsseldorf referred to the Court of Justice, asking whether an age qualification (1)(a) could be discriminatory, (1)(b) whether it could be justified, and (2) if it could be relied on by a private party. The Court of Justice held that the national court was bound to disapply the discriminatory part of §622, so that Ms Kücükdeveci would have a directly effective claim against Swedex GmbH for additional notice.

Grand Chamber:

21 ... the Court has acknowledged the existence of a principle of non-discrimination on grounds of age which must be regarded as a general principle of European Union law (see, to that effect, *Mangold*, paragraph 75). Directive 2000/78 gives specific expression to that principle (see, by analogy, Case 43/75 *Defrenne* [1976] ECR 455, paragraph 54).

22 It should also be noted that Article 6(1) TEU provides that the Charter of Fundamental Rights of the European Union is to have the same legal value as the Treaties. Under Article 21(1) of the charter, '[a]ny discrimination based on ... age ... shall be prohibited'.

23 For the principle of non-discrimination on grounds of age to apply in a case such as that at issue in the main proceedings, that case must fall within the scope of European Union law.

24 In contrast to the situation concerned in Case C-427/06 *Bartsch* [2008] ECR I-7245, the allegedly discriminatory conduct adopted in the present case on the basis of the national legislation at issue occurred after the expiry of the period prescribed for the Member State concerned for the transposition of Directive 2000/78, which, for the Federal Republic of Germany, ended on 2 December 2006.

25 On that date, that directive had the effect of bringing within the scope of European Union law the national legislation at issue in the main proceedings, which concerns a matter governed by that directive, in this case the conditions of dismissal.

...

35 The referring court states that the second sentence of Paragraph 622(2) of the BGB reflects the legislature's assessment that young workers generally react more easily and more rapidly to the loss of their jobs and greater flexibility can be demanded of them. A shorter notice period for younger workers also facilitates their recruitment by increasing the flexibility of personnel management.

36 Objectives of the kind mentioned by the German Government and the referring court clearly belong to employment and labour market policy within the meaning of Article 6(1) of Directive 2000/78.

37 It remains to be ascertained, in accordance with the wording of that provision, whether the means of achieving such a legitimate aim are 'appropriate and necessary'.

38 The Member States enjoy a broad discretion in the choice of the measures capable of achieving their objectives in the field of social and employment policy (see *Mangold*, paragraph 63, and *Palacios de la Villa*, paragraph 68).

39 The referring court indicates that the aim of the national legislation at issue in the main proceedings is to afford employers greater flexibility in personnel management by alleviating

the burden on them in respect of the dismissal of young workers, from whom it is reasonable to expect a greater degree of personal or occupational mobility.

40 However, the legislation is not appropriate for achieving that aim, since it applies to all employees who joined the undertaking before the age of 25, whatever their age at the time of dismissal.

41 As regards the aim pursued by the legislature at the time of adoption of the national legislation at issue in the main proceedings, adduced by the German Government, of strengthening the protection of workers according to their length of service in the undertaking, it is clear that, under that legislation, the extension of the notice period for dismissal according to the employee's seniority in service is delayed for all employees who joined the undertaking before the age of 25, even if the person concerned has a long length of service in the undertaking at the time of dismissal. The legislation cannot therefore be regarded as appropriate for achieving that aim.

42 It should be added that, as the referring court points out, the national legislation at issue in the main proceedings affects young employees unequally, in that it affects young people who enter active life early after little or no vocational training, but not those who start work later after a long period of training.

43 It follows from all the above considerations that the answer to Question 1 is that European Union law, more particularly the principle of non-discrimination on grounds of age as given expression by Directive 2000/78, must be interpreted as precluding national legislation, such as that at issue in the main proceedings, which provides that periods of employment completed by an employee before reaching the age of 25 are not taken into account in calculating the notice period for dismissal.
    ...

48 ... in applying national law, the national court called on to interpret it is required to do so, as far as possible, in the light of the wording and the purpose of the directive in question, in order to achieve the result pursued by the directive and thereby comply with the third paragraph of Article 288 TFEU (see, to that effect, *von Colson and Kamann*, paragraph 26; *Marleasing*, paragraph 8; *Faccini Dori*, paragraph 26; and *Pfeiffer and Others*, paragraph 113). The requirement for national law to be interpreted in conformity with European Union law is inherent in the system of the Treaty, since it permits the national court, within the limits of its jurisdiction, to ensure the full effectiveness of European Union law when it determines the dispute before it (see, to that effect, *Pfeiffer and Others*, paragraph 114).

49 According to the national court, however, because of its clarity and precision, the second sentence of Paragraph 622(2) of the BGB is not open to an interpretation in conformity with Directive 2000/78.

50 It must be recalled here that, as stated in paragraph 20 above, Directive 2000/78 merely gives expression to, but does not lay down, the principle of equal treatment in employment and occupation, and that the principle of non-discrimination on grounds of age is a general principle of European Union law in that it constitutes a specific application of the general principle of equal treatment (see, to that effect, *Mangold*, paragraphs 74 to 76).

51 In those circumstances, it is for the national court, hearing a dispute involving the principle of non-discrimination on grounds of age as given expression in Directive 2000/78, to provide, within the limits of its jurisdiction, the legal protection which individuals derive from European

Union law and to ensure the full effectiveness of that law, disapplying if need be any provision of national legislation contrary to that principle (see, to that effect, *Mangold*, paragraph 77).

52 As regards, second, the obligation of the national court, hearing proceedings between individuals, to make a reference to the Court for a preliminary ruling on the interpretation of European Union law before it can disapply a national provision which it considers to be contrary to that law, it is apparent from the order for reference that this aspect of the question has been raised because, under national law, the referring court cannot decline to apply a national provision in force unless that provision has first been declared unconstitutional by the Bundesverfassungsgericht (Federal Constitutional Court).

53 The need to ensure the full effectiveness of the principle of non-discrimination on grounds of age, as given expression in Directive 2000/78, means that the national court, faced with a national provision falling within the scope of European Union law which it considers to be incompatible with that principle, and which cannot be interpreted in conformity with that principle, must decline to apply that provision, without being either compelled to make or prevented from making a reference to the Court for a preliminary ruling before doing so.

54 The possibility thus given to the national court by the second paragraph of Article 267 TFEU of asking the Court for a preliminary ruling before disapplying the national provision that is contrary to European Union law cannot, however, be transformed into an obligation because national law does not allow that court to disapply a provision it considers to be contrary to the constitution unless the provision has first been declared unconstitutional by the Constitutional Court. By reason of the principle of the primacy of European Union law, which extends also to the principle of non-discrimination on grounds of age, contrary national legislation which falls within the scope of European Union law must be disapplied (see, to that effect, *Mangold*, paragraph 77).

55 It follows that the national court, hearing proceedings between individuals, is not obliged but is entitled to make a reference to the Court for a preliminary ruling on the interpretation of the principle of non-discrimination on grounds of age, as given expression by Directive 2000/78, before disapplying a provision of national law which it considers to be contrary to that principle. The optional nature of such a reference is not affected by the conditions of national law under which a court may disapply a national provision which it considers to be contrary to the constitution.

President Skouris, Cunha Rodrigues, Lenaerts, Bonichot, Silva de Lapuerta, Lindh, Toader, Timmermans, Rosas, Kūris, von Danwitz, Arabadjiev and **Kasel**.

NOTES AND QUESTIONS

1. The Court of Justice holds that, because the German Civil Code §622 cut young people out of notice periods, but would carry over to people who are no longer young, it was disproportionate. Because §622 was so clear, the law could not be 'interpreted', however creatively, in conformity with the Directive. Usually, Directives do not enable people to sue anyone except the state for damages when the Directive is not implemented by its deadline. However, because equal treatment is regarded by the Court as a 'general principle' of EU law, there is a significant exception. The Directive, which gives effect to this principle, is elevated

to the rank of a Treaty provision. Even primary legislation that conflicts must be 'disapplied' in a case between non-state parties: the general principle of equality has 'horizontal direct effect'.

2.   In light of the economic 'theory' put forward by the German government, summarised at [35]–[39], do you agree that laws allowing employers to make young people unemployed easily will lead to less youth unemployment? What factors do you think drive these kinds of theories? See further, chapter 20.

3.   *Kücükdeveci* was seen by some as a 'U-turn' on *Mangold*, suggesting that the general principle of equality can only operate between private parties if a Directive gives it 'expression'. The other view is that *Mangold* represented a welcome development in EU law, was principled, justified and remains good law.

4.   There is a plain contrast between the common law principle of equality in *Kruse* and the EU principle. The common law principle would operate to restrict (1) discriminatory contracts or acts of corporations, (2) discriminatory acts of public bodies, but not (3) discriminatory legislation passed by Parliament. Yet, any secondary legislation or government order would be subject to judicial review. EU law can strike down (3) primary legislation of any Member State, (4) acts of EU institutions, and (5) Directives or Regulations passed by the EU. Does the fact that the EU principle is far more powerful, and could be abused in the wrong hands (think of the US Supreme Court in 1883) caution against it?

5.   For Commonwealth jurisdictions, general equality provisions in constitutions were discussed in *Matadeen v Pointu* [1998] UKPC 9. This concerned the interpretation of the Mauritian constitution, and whether it contained a free-standing right to equality so that school exams had to take account of children's native languages. Lord Hoffmann, while accepting that 'treating like cases alike' was 'a general axiom of rational behaviour', asserted that it was also 'banal', because people could legitimately differ on which cases are 'alike'. These comments prefaced advice that a right to equal treatment was limited to specific grounds set out in the constitution. The legislature, rather than the courts would have to add to it by law.

6.   In *Milkova v Izpalnitelen director na Agentsiata za privatizatsia i sledprivatizatsionen control* [2017] IRLR 566 the CJEU indicated that a free standing claim to equal treatment exists under the Charter of Fundamental Rights of the European Union Arts 20–21. The case itself decided that there was no unlawful discrimination in Bulgarian law giving disabled workers the right to not be dismissed without authorisation of the labour inspectorate, but not conferring that positive protection on civil servants because this was 'not inseparably linked to disability'. Regardless of this reasoning, the court then said: 'The principle of equal treatment is a general principle of EU law, now enshrined in Articles 20 and 21 of the Charter, which requires that comparable situations must not be treated differently and that different situations must not be treated in the same way unless such treatment is objectively justified. ... A difference in treatment is justified if it is based on an objective and reasonable criterion, that is, if the difference relates to a legally permitted aim pursued by the legislation in question, and it is proportionate to the aim pursued by the treatment.' How far should this principle develop?

(b) Protected Characteristics

Currently, the EA 2010 ss 5–12 lists eight 'protected characteristics'. Six are under-pinned by the Race Equality Directive 2000 (race), the Equal Treatment Directive 2006 (sex), and the Equality Framework Directive 2000 (religion or belief, disability, age, sexual orientation). To that are added 'gender reassignment' and 'marriage and civil partnership'. In the EU, gender reassignment was already regarded as part of one's sex (*P v S and Cornwall CC* (1996) C-13/94), while marriage or civil partnership is protected under the ECHR Art 9. Elsewhere, the law codifies protection for union member-ship (chapter 9, Trade Union and Labour Relations (Consolidation) Act 1992 ss 137 ff, framed as 'detriment'), and part-time, fixed-term, agency and migrant work (chapter 15) to varying degrees. Do these twelve protected characteristics have anything in common? While the first ones could be seen as things we are born with (eg skin colour, gender, sexual orientation) others are changeable (religion or belief, marriage or civil partner-ship) and others are contractual statuses, rather than inherent attributes (union member-ship, work through an agency). The consistent theme of protected characteristics simply appears to be what democratic society has today, so far, come to regard as irrelevant in access to important social rights (work, housing, etc).

What is not in the (partially codified) list? Additional characteristics in ECHR Art 14 are 'property, birth or other status.' Article 14 only requires equality, however, in the application of other Convention rights: it is not 'free standing'. So inequality of wealth and income – the very things that contribute most to labour's inequality of bargaining power – are not expressly covered by the EA 2010. Discrimination based on accent, class or caste are not yet codified. Other potential protected characteristics, found in some US states, are military background, prior criminal convictions, height and weight. What hap-pens when a characteristic is not expressly protected? Although not about employment, the next case exemplifies the choices of interpretation facing the judiciary.

Mandla v Dowell Lee [1983] QB 1, [1983] 2 AC 548

A Sikh boy and his parents claimed that his refusal of entry to Park Grove School, Birmingham, was unlawful race discrimination. The school headmaster required the boy stop wearing a turban and cut his hair, but his father, supported by the Commission for Racial Equality, insisted that the boy could not do this because of their adherence to the Sikh religion. Mandla brought a claim for 'indirect' discrimination: although the school's rule was formally neutral (nobody was allowed to wear head attire) in substance it had a disproportionate negative impact on certain groups. The school contended that Sikhs were not a 'race'; the former RRA 1976 s 3 defined race to include 'colour, race, nation-ality or ethnic or national origins' (now EA 2010 s 9). Sikhism developed during the 1500s in the Punjab, India, so Sikhs do not have a genetic history different to that of other Indian people from the same region. The Court of Appeal held that Mandla had no claim because Sikhs fell outside the definition of a 'racial group'. The House of Lords allowed an appeal, holding that 'racial group' could be interpreted to cover Sikhs.

Lord Denning MR:

The statute in section 3(1) contains a definition of a "racial group". It means a "group of persons defined by reference to colour, race, nationality or ethnic or national origins." That definition is very carefully framed. Most interesting is that it does not include religion or politics or culture. You can discriminate for or against Roman Catholics as much as you like without being in breach of the law. You can discriminate for or against Communists as much as you please, without being in breach of the law. You can discriminate for or against the "hippies" as much as you like, without being in breach of the law. But you must not discriminate against a man because of his colour or of his race or of his nationality, or of "his ethnic or national origins." You must remember that it is perfectly lawful to discriminate against groups of people to whom you object – so long as they are not a [protected] group. You can discriminate against the Moonies or the Skinheads or any other group which you dislike or to which you take objection. No matter whether your objection to them is reasonable or unreasonable, you can discriminate against them – without being in breach of the law.

[On appeal the House of Lords declined to follow Lord Denning MR's reasoning or outcome.]

Lord Fraser:

It is not suggested that Sikhs are a group defined by reference to colour, race, nationality or national origins. In none of these respects are they distinguishable from many other groups, especially those living, like most Sikhs, in the Punjab. The argument turns entirely upon whether they are a group defined by "ethnic origins". It is therefore necessary to ascertain the sense in which the word "ethnic" is used in the Act of 1976. We were referred to various dictionary definitions. The Oxford English Dictionary (1897 edition) gives two meanings of "ethnic". The first is "pertaining to nations not Christian or Jewish; gentile, heathen, pagan". That clearly cannot be its meaning in the 1976 Act, because it is inconceivable that Parliament would have legislated against racial discrimination intending that the protection should not apply either to Christians or (above all) to Jews. ...

...

For a group to constitute an ethnic group in the sense of the 1976 Act, it must, in my opinion, regard itself, and be regarded by others, as a distinct community by virtue of certain characteristics. Some of these characteristics are essential; others are not essential but one or more of them will commonly be found and will help to distinguish the group from the surrounding community. ...

...

... a group is identifiable in terms of its ethnic origins if it is a segment of the population distinguished from others by a sufficient combination of shared customs, beliefs, traditions and characteristics derived from a common or presumed common past, even if not drawn from what in biological terms is a common racial stock. It is that combination which gives them an historically determined social identity in their own eyes and in the eyes of those outside the group. They have a distinct social identity based not simply on group cohesion and solidarity but also on their belief as to their historical antecedents.

Lord Templeman:

The Court of Appeal thought that the Sikhs were only members of a religion or at best members of a religion and culture. But the evidence of the origins and history of the Sikhs which was adduced by the parties to the present litigation disclosed that the Sikhs are more than a religion and a culture. And in view of the history of this country since the second world war I find it impossible to believe that Parliament intended to exclude the Sikhs from the benefit of the Race Relations Act and to allow discrimination to be practised against the Sikhs in those fields of activity where, as the present case illustrates, discrimination is likely to occur.

Lord Edmund-Davies, Lord Roskill, Lord Brandon of Oakbrook concurred.

1. Lord Fraser reasons that ethnicity can be interpreted to include a group of people with a shared history and culture, and therefore the Sikhs were a protected group. This appears to be motivated by the law's policy behind the law, rather than technical definitions of words. Lord Denning MR does appear, however, motivated by his understanding of the policy behind the law too. Lord Fraser and Lord Templeman appear motivated to ensure the Sikhs were specifically protected. There were no submissions, however, based on the general principle set out in *Kruse v Johnson* [1898] 2 QB 91 above.

2. Would Lord Denning MR be correct (either then or today) that an employer can discriminate for or against the 'hippies', 'Moonies' or 'skinheads'? Or could an employer discriminate against against somebody on a more frivolous basis that they supported, for example, Chelsea Football Club? While it would not attract remedies that are as favourable, it is submitted that detrimental treatment on such irrational grounds would plainly be unlawful. If this led to dismissal, it would justify an unfair dismissal case under ERA 1996 s 94 (chapter 17). If a dismissal was before the two-year qualifying period, there would be a claim for wrongful termination in contract (which could not, however, attract as favourable remedies: see *Johnson v Unisys Ltd*, chapter 17). If it was detriment during the employment relationship, there would be a breach of mutual trust and confidence, justifying a constructive dismissal claim (cf *Wilson v Racher*, chapter 5(1)). If there was a refusal to hire, there would be common law tort (analogous to *Constantine v Imperial Hotels* Ltd [1944] KB 693, above).

3. Regardless of what he was saying by 1982, arguably Lord Denning MR's principled stance in 1951 was infinitely more preferable, that as well as Jews, as 'with all other races, it is a cardinal principle of our law that they shall not suffer any disability or prejudice by reason of their race and shall have equal freedom under the law'. Sir A Denning, *Freedom Under the Law* (1951) 51.

4. While Lord Fraser argues it was 'inconceivable' that Christians and Jews were not protected by the RRA 1976, it originally appeared that Muslims were not protected. Discrimination against Muslims was probably indirect race discrimination, but religious discrimination was not protected in its own right. As we will see in chapter 13, indirect discrimination means that (1) an employing entity applies a rule which is superficially neutral, but (2) has a disproportionate impact on one group, (3) without justification.

5. The ILO Discrimination (Employment and Occupation) Convention 1958 (c 111) which binds the UK as a core Convention, protects 'race, colour, sex, religion, political opinion, national extraction or social origin' and 'such other distinction' that Member States choose to protect. This applies to access and terms and conditions of employment (including dismissal).

6. In 2003, religion or belief was codified as a protected characteristic (now EA 2010 s 10). Beliefs are the only protected characteristics that may (but not necessarily) tell the adherent to treat other people in a certain way. For example, the papacy still maintains that the Catholic Church should not admit women priests or (openly) admit homosexual priests. But there is nothing inherent in being a woman or homosexual that might require treating religious people (or men or heterosexual people) differently. On the other hand, in most cases, a biblical text

(like a law) can be interpreted in multiple ways: thus the Church of England ordains women priests and bishops, while Quakers in the UK formally endorsed same-sex marriage in 2009.

7. In the UK census of 2011, 25.7 per cent of people recorded no religion, 7.2 per cent did not state anything, 59.5 per cent recorded Christianity, 4.4 per cent recorded Islam, 1.3 per cent recorded Hinduism, and 1.9 per cent other religions. The UK census, however, tends to under-record the views of young people or people without stable addresses. The fastest-growing group appears to be people who are not religious: that is, people who describe themselves as agnostics, atheists or humanists.

8. Why would people remain members of a religion, even if it discriminated against them as women or homosexuals, or people they loved? One answer is that there are deep-felt feelings of belonging and commitment, summed up when, after leading the Reformation, and during his trial in 1521, Martin Luther is said to have proclaimed: 'Here I stand, I can do no other.' Many, like Luther, have for generations worked tirelessly, and against the odds, to modernise their religions in light of contemporary social values. Do you agree there are similarities between theology and law?

9. Does someone lose protection if their religion or belief is discriminatory to others?

Redfearn v United Kingdom [2012] ECHR 1878

Arthur Redfearn, a bus driver for Serco Ltd on the West Yorkshire Transport Service in Bradford, claimed he was unlawfully dismissed on grounds of discrimination for his political beliefs. He was disabled and drove a bus for disabled people. He had been rated as a first-class employee by his Asian supervisor. But he was elected as a councillor for the Bradford British National Party (BNP), which was 'wholly opposed to any form of integration between British and non-European peoples'. The bus driver's union, Unison, wrote to Serco Ltd. Serco dismissed Redfearn on 'health and safety' grounds after just under 7 months work, because (apparently) Redfearn's profile would make him a target for violent attacks, making the bus unsafe. Unable to claim unfair dismissal (now ERA 1996 s 108(1)), and without any explicit protection in statute for political belief at the time, Mr Redfearn claimed this was direct and indirect discrimination 'on racial grounds', because white people were disproportionately likely to be members of the BNP. The Court of Appeal held Redfearn was dismissed based on political grounds, not racial grounds so his direct discrimination claim had to fail. The indirect discrimination claim also failed, because in the Court's view there was no neutral rule applied to everyone, to begin with (see chapter 13). On appeal, the European Court of Human Rights held that the UK had failed to protect Redfearn's right to freedom of belief, expression and association with a political party under ECHR Arts 9, 10 and 11. The European Court of Human Rights found by a majority that claims under Arts 10 and 11 would succeed, and held an Art 9 claim was manifestly ill-founded.

President Garlicki, Björgvinsson J, Kalaydjieva J, De Gaetano, and Aracı J:

42. Although the essential object of Article 11 is to protect the individual against arbitrary interference by public authorities with the exercise of the rights protected, the national authorities

may in certain circumstances be obliged to intervene in the relationships between private individuals by taking reasonable and appropriate measures to secure the effective enjoyment of the right to freedom of association. ...

...

44. The Court has recognised that in certain circumstances an employer may lawfully place restrictions on the freedom of association of employees where it is deemed necessary in a democratic society, for example to protect the rights of others or to maintain the political neutrality of civil servants (see, for example, *Ahmed v United Kingdom*, 2 September 1998, § 63, Reports of Judgments and Decisions 1998-VI). In view of the nature of the BNP's policies (see paragraph 9, above), the Court recognises the difficult position that Serco may have found itself in when the applicant's candidature became public knowledge. In particular, it accepts that even in the absence of specific complaints from service users, the applicant's membership of the BNP could have impacted upon Serco's provision of services to Bradford City Council, especially as the majority of service users were vulnerable persons of Asian origin.

45. However, regard must also be had to the fact that the applicant was a "first-class employee" (see paragraph 7, above) and, prior to his political affiliation becoming public knowledge, no complaints had been made against him by service users or by his colleagues. Nevertheless, once he was elected as a local councillor for the BNP and complaints were received from unions and employees, he was summarily dismissed without any apparent consideration being given to the possibility of transferring him to a non-customer facing role. In this regard, the Court considers that the case can readily be distinguished from that of *Stedman v United Kingdom* ... in which the applicant was dismissed because she refused to work the hours required by the post. In particular, the Court is struck by the fact that these complaints ..., were in respect of prospective problems and not in respect of anything that the applicant had done or had failed to do in the actual exercise of his employment.

46. ... at the date of his dismissal he was fifty-six years old and it is therefore likely that he would have experienced considerable difficulty finding alternative employment.

47. Consequently, the Court accepts that the consequences of his dismissal were serious and capable of striking at the very substance of his rights under Article 11 of the Convention (*Sørensen and Rasmussen v Denmark* [GC], nos. 52562/99 and 52620/99, §§ 61 and 62, ECHR 2006-I and *Young, James and Webster v United Kingdom* ... § 55). The Court must therefore determine whether in the circumstances of the applicant's case a fair balance was struck between the competing interests involved, namely the applicant's Article 11 right and the risk, if any, that his continued employment posed for fellow employees and service users. It is also to be borne in mind that what the Court is called upon to do in this case is not to pass judgment on the policies or aims, obnoxious or otherwise, of the BNP at the relevant time (the BNP is, in any case, not a party to these proceedings), but solely to determine whether the applicant's rights under Article 11 were breached in the particular circumstances of the instant case. In this connection it is also worth bearing in mind that, like the Front National-Nationaal Front in *Féret v Belgium* (no. 15615/07, 16 July 2009) the BNP was not an illegal party under domestic law nor were its activities illegal (see, by way of contrast, *Hizb Ut-Tahrir v Germany* (dec.) no. 31098/08, 12 June 2012).

...

52. There is therefore no doubt that the applicant suffered a detriment as a consequence of the one-year qualifying period as it deprived him of the only means by which he could effectively have challenged his dismissal at the domestic level on the ground that it breached his fundamental rights. It therefore falls to the Court to consider whether the respondent State, in

including the one-year qualifying period in the 1996 Act, could be said to have taken reasonable and appropriate measures to protect the applicant's rights under Article 11.

53. The Court observes that the one-year qualifying period was included in the 1996 Act because the Government considered that the risks of unjustified involvement with tribunals in unfair dismissal cases and the cost of such involvement could deter employers from giving more people jobs. Thus, the purpose of the one-year qualifying period was to benefit the domestic economy by increasing labour demand. The Court has received no submissions on the length of the qualifying period but it accepts that one year would normally be a sufficient period for an employer to assess the suitability of an employee before he or she became well-established in a post. Consequently, in view of the margin of appreciation afforded to Contracting States in formulating and implementing social and economic policies, the Court considers that it was in principle both reasonable and appropriate for the respondent State to bolster the domestic labour market by preventing new employees from bringing unfair dismissal claims.

54. However, it observes that in practice the one-year qualifying period did not apply equally to all dismissed employees. Rather, a number of exceptions were created to offer additional protection to employees dismissed on certain prohibited grounds, such as race, sex and religion, but no additional protection was afforded to employees who were dismissed on account of their political opinion or affiliation.

55. The Court has previously held that political parties are a form of association essential to the proper functioning of democracy (*United Communist Party of Turkey v Turkey*, 30 January 1998, § 25, Reports of Judgments and Decisions 1998-I). In view of the importance of democracy in the Convention system, the Court considers that in the absence of judicial safeguards a legal system which allows dismissal from employment solely on account of the employee's membership of a political party carries with it the potential for abuse.

56. Even if the Court were to acknowledge the legitimacy of Serco's interest in dismissing the applicant from its workforce having regard to the nature of his political beliefs, the policies pursued by the BNP and his public identification with those policies through his election as a councillor, the fact remains that Article 11 is applicable not only to persons or associations whose views are favourably received or regarded as inoffensive or as a matter of indifference, but also those whose views offend, shock or disturb (see, mutatis mutandis, *Handyside v United Kingdom*, 7 December 1976, § 49, Series A no. 24, and *Jersild v Denmark*, 23 September 1994, § 37, Series A no. 298). For the Court, what is decisive in such cases is that the domestic courts or tribunals be allowed to pronounce on whether or not, in the circumstances of a particular case, the interests of the employer should prevail over the Article 11 rights asserted by the employee, regardless of the length of the latter's period of employment.

57. Consequently, the Court considers that it was incumbent on the respondent State to take reasonable and appropriate measures to protect employees, including those with less than one year's service, from dismissal on grounds of political opinion or affiliation, either through the creation of a further exception to the one-year qualifying period or through a free-standing claim for unlawful discrimination on grounds of political opinion or affiliation. As the United Kingdom legislation is deficient in this respect, the Court concludes that the facts of the present case give rise to a violation of Article 11 of the Convention.

Bratza J, **Hirvelä J** and **Nicolaou J** dissented:

1. We regret that we are unable to share the view of the majority that there was a violation of Article 11 of the Convention in the present case. In our view, the United Kingdom was not

in breach of its obligations under the Article by reason of any failure to protect the applicant against his dismissal from his employment on grounds of his political opinion.

...

4. We are unable to accept the argument that, having created certain exceptions to the requirement of employment for the qualifying period, the State was obliged to create a further exception in the case of dismissal on grounds of political opinion, still less that the Convention imposes a positive obligation to create a free-standing cause of action, without any temporal limitation. This, in our view, is to press the positive obligation too far. In a complex area of social and economic policy, it is in our view pre-eminently for Parliament to decide what areas require special protection in the field of employment and the consequent scope of any exception created to the general rule. The choice of Parliament of race, sex and religion as grounds requiring special protection can in no sense be seen as random or arbitrary. In this respect we attach importance to the fact that certain grounds of difference of treatment have traditionally been treated by the Court itself as "suspect" and as requiring very weighty reasons by way of justification. These grounds include differences of treatment on grounds of race (*D.H. and others v the Czech Republic* [GC] no. 57325/10, ECHR 2007), sex (*Abdulaziz, Cabales and Balkandali v United Kingdom*, 28 May 1985, Series A No. 94), religion (*Hoffmann v Austria*, 23 June 1993, Series A no. 94) and nationality and ethnicity (*Timishev v Russia*, nos. 55762/00 and 55974/00, ECHR 2005-XII). In addition, the Court has indicated that differences of treatment which are based on immutable characteristics will as a general rule require weightier reasons in justification than differences of treatment based on a characteristic or status which contains an element of choice (*Bah v United Kingdom*, no. 56328/07, 27 September 2011).

5. Doubtless the balance could have been struck by the legislator in a different way and further exceptions to the qualifying period might have been created to cover claims for dismissal of other grounds, including that of political opinion or political affiliation. However, this is a different question from the one which the Court is required to determine, namely whether the United Kingdom exceeded its wide margin of appreciation in not extending the list of exceptions or in not creating a free-standing cause of action covering dismissal on grounds of such opinion or affiliation.

NOTES AND QUESTIONS

1. The majority of the Court seems to reason that Redfearn had a right to associate with the BNP, and the right's bare exercise merited protection, even though the BNP had views that would 'offend, shock or disturb'. It was relevant to the majority that Redfearn had otherwise been a good employee. The minority says it should be for Parliament to decide which characteristics merited special protection. Do you find the reasoning of either the majority or the minority persuasive?

2. In Europe, the Convention had to be sufficiently expansive to accommodate the history of countries where large proportions of some populations had, after the Second World War, been members of Nazi or fascist parties (often compulsorily so), had been involved in the Mediterranean dictatorships up to the 1980s, or after the Cold War had been involved in the apparatus of Soviet police states. To remove protection for people who had such *past* affiliations would obviously have been untenable.

3. The BNP is not prohibited as a terrorist group or otherwise in the United Kingdom, and is politically entitled to run candidates for elections. This is true even though many of its members and leaders are violent criminals who would,

given the chance, launch an assault on democratic institutions and human rights. What do you think might have been the result if the Court had adequately discussed the provisions of Arts 10(2) and 11(2), that there can be restrictions that 'are prescribed by law and are necessary in a democratic society, in the interests of national security, territorial integrity or public safety, for the prevention of disorder or crime'? The argument, which was advanced by the Equality and Human Rights Commission as an intervener, would suggest that there is no legal duty to tolerate the intolerant. On this view, political beliefs and associations that are not compatible with a system of democracy and human rights, on which the Convention is founded, are not be protected. What do you think?

4.   In light of the present global epidemic of far-right parties, from Farage's United Kingdom Independence Party, to Le Pen's National Front, Donald Trump's Republican Party, Austria's 'Freedom' Party, the Swedish 'Democrats', the German Alternative für Deutschland, Putin's 'United Russia', and so on, all of which appear to hold contempt for democracy and human rights, should there be a reassessment of how the law approaches extremism?

5.   The Court simply did not discuss the Art 9 argument, except to regard it as 'manifestly ill-founded' at [58]–[60]. It seems to have taken the view at [36] that *Stedman v United Kingdom* [1997] ECHR 178 was applicable. This held Art 9 did not apply where a Christian employee who refused to work on Sundays was dismissed: apparently this did not pressure the employee to change or stop manifesting their religion, and the UK could not be expected to legislate 'against such dismissals by private employers'. Regardless of whether the public–private distinction is tenable, now that the UK had legislated against such dismissals by private employers, do you think some greater discussion was merited?

6.   The quality of the judiciary in both the European Court of Human Rights in Strasbourg and the Court of Justice in the European Union has attracted increased attention in recent years. The complaints tend to focus on (1) the need to draw judges from each country, regardless of size and traditional quality of legal education, (2) politicised or nepotistic processes for appointment in some countries, (3) the fact that most judgments are prepared, not by the judges themselves, but by the court's clerks or *référendaires* and are merely signed off, after a review by the judge, and (4) that because judgments are issued jointly, there is no possibility to assess the quality of individual judgments, nor an incentive to strive to improve compared to colleagues. Do you think any of these concerns are valid, and if so what could be done to improve the situation?

7.   What are the limits of protection for religious and political beliefs? The belief must be sufficiently deeply held to qualify. In *Grainger plc v Nicholson* [2010] IRLR 4 (EAT) Mr Nicholson was dismissed, he alleged unfairly, from his job at a large corporate landlord. He stated he had 'a strongly held philosophical belief about climate change and the environment. I believe we must urgently cut carbon emissions to avoid catastrophic climate change.' Burton J held that, as a preliminary matter, he was entitled to claim that it had 'a level of cogency, seriousness, cohesion and importance and worthy of respect in a democratic society as well as being not incompatible with human dignity or conflict with others' rights', quoting *Campbell v United Kingdom* (1982) 4 EHRR 293 and *R (Williamson) v SS*

for Education and Employment [2005] UKHL 15. Burton J pointed out that, even though climate damage is scientifically established fact, rather than a theory, it would still merit protection as a 'belief'. He suggested that belief in Darwinian evolution or atheism are also protected. Do you think that this test should have had any relevance to *Redfearn*, to understand Arts 10 and 11?

8.   By contrast in *Harron v Chief Constable of Dorset Police* [2016] IRLR 481 (EAT), a man who expressed a belief 'in the proper and efficient use of public money in the public sector' was found by Langstaff J to not have been protected. This 'belief', which appears to have been associated with support for 'austerity' measures, was not considered to have been sufficiently weighty to warrant protection.

9.   The next case considers 'associative' discrimination. That is whether, in addition to claimants with certain protected characteristics themselves, associated people can claim protection.

Coleman v Attridge Law (2008) C-303/06

Ms Sharon Coleman brought claims for unfair dismissal and disability discrimination against a minor London law firm called Attridge Law (now called EBR Attridge LLP Solicitors), where she had worked as a secretary. She had a disabled son, Oliver, with bronchomalacia and congential laryngomalacia. She was accused her of using her 'fucking child' to manipulate requests for working times and conditions. The Disability Discrimination Act (DDA) 1995 s 4 (contrast now EA 2010 s 13(1)) stated there would be protection for disability discrimination if the treatment is 'against a disabled person'. Because Ms Coleman was not herself disabled, the question was whether the DDA 1995 properly implemented the Equality Framework Directive 2000 Art 2(1). This says there is direct discrimination 'where one person is treated less favourably than another is, has been or would be treated in a comparable situation, on any of the grounds' in Art 1, including disability. This does not explicitly require discriminatory behaviour to be directed at the claimant. Following the Opinion of Advocate General Maduro, the Court of Justice held that Ms Coleman was entitled to bring a claim.

Opinion of AG Maduro:

8 Article 13 EC is an expression of the commitment of the Community legal order to the principle of equal treatment and non-discrimination. Thus, any interpretation of both that article and any directive adopted under this legal basis must be undertaken against the background of the Court's case law on these principles.[3] The Directive itself states in Art.1 that its purpose is:

"[T]o lay down a general framework for combating discrimination ... with a view to putting into effect in the Member States the principle of equal treatment " (my emphasis).

---

[3] It has been pointed out in the literature on discrimination that no conclusive answer as to whether discrimination by association is prohibited flows from Art 13 EC and the directives that were adopted under it. However, it has been suggested that such discrimination will probably be treated as falling within the scope of the anti-discrimination directives. See Schiek, D., Waddington, L. and Bell M. (eds) *Cases, Materials and Text on National, Supranational and International Non-Discrimination Law*, (Hart Publishing, 2007) pp. 169–170.

The Court's case law is clear as regards the role of equal treatment and non-discrimination in the Community legal order. Equality is not merely a political ideal and aspiration but one of the fundamental principles of Community law.[4] As the Court held in Mangold the Directive constitutes a practical aspect of the principle of equality.[5] In order to determine what equality requires in any given case it is useful to recall the values underlying equality. These are human dignity and personal autonomy.

9 At its bare minimum, human dignity entails the recognition of the equal worth of every individual. One's life is valuable by virtue of the mere fact that one is human, and no life is more or less valuable than another. As Ronald Dworkin has recently reminded us, even when we disagree deeply about issues of political morality, the structure of political institutions and the functioning of our democratic states we nevertheless continue to share a commitment to this fundamental principle.[6] Therefore, individuals and political institutions must not act in a way that denies the intrinsic importance of every human life. A relevant, but different, value is that of personal autonomy. It dictates that individuals should be able to design and conduct the course of their lives through a succession of choices among different valuable options.[7] The exercise of autonomy presupposes that people are given a range of valuable options from which to choose. When we act as autonomous agents making decisions about the way we want our life to develop our "personal integrity and sense of dignity and self-respect are made concrete".[8]

10 The aim of Art.13 EC and of the Directive is to protect the dignity and autonomy of persons belonging to those suspect classifications. The most obvious way in which such a person's dignity and autonomy may be affected is when one is directly targeted because one has a suspect characteristic. Treating someone less well on the basis of reasons such as religious belief, age, disability and sexual orientation undermines this special and unique value that people have by virtue of being human. Recognising the equal worth of every human being means that we should be blind to considerations of this type when we impose a burden on someone or deprive someone of a benefit. Put differently, these are characteristics which should not play any role in any assessment as to whether it is right or not to treat someone less favourably.

11 Similarly, a commitment to autonomy means that people must not be deprived of valuable options in areas of fundamental importance for their lives by reference to suspect classifications. Access to employment and professional development are of fundamental significance for every individual, not merely as a means of earning one's living but also as an important way of self-fulfilment and realisation of one's potential. The discriminator who discriminates against an individual belonging to a suspect classification unjustly deprives her of valuable options. As a consequence, that person's ability to lead an autonomous life is seriously compromised since

---

[4] See, inter alia, *R (Omega Air Ltd) v Secretary of State for the Environment, Transport and the Regions* (C-27/00 & C-122/00) [2002] ECR I-2569; [2002] 2 CMLR 9 and the case law cited therein. See also the discussion in Tridimas, T., *The General Principles of EU Law* (2nd edn), (Oxford University Press, 2007); and Dashwood, A., and O'Leary, S., (eds), *The Principle of Equal Treatment in EC Law* (Sweet and Maxwell, 1997).

[5] *Mangold v Helm* (C-144/04) [2005] ECR I-9981; [2006] 1 CMLR 43 at [74].

[6] Dworkin, R., *Is Democracy Possible Here?: Principles for a New Political Debate* (Princeton University Press, 2006) Ch.1.

[7] Raz, J., *The Morality of Freedom* (Oxford University Press, 1986). For the sake of accuracy it should be noted that some authors include the value of personal autonomy within that of dignity. The same happens with the treatment of these two concepts in the case law of some constitutional courts. This, which might be of relevance in the context of the interpretation of legal provisions that refer only to the value of human dignity, is of no relevance for present purposes.

[8] Raz, J., *The Morality of Freedom* (Oxford University Press, 1986) p. 154.

an important aspect of her life is shaped not by her own choices but by the prejudice of someone else. By treating people belonging to these groups less well because of their characteristic, the discriminator prevents them from exercising their autonomy. At this point, it is fair and reasonable for anti-discrimination law to intervene. In essence, by valuing equality and committing ourselves to realising equality through the law, we aim at sustaining for every person the conditions for an autonomous life.

12 Yet, directly targeting a person who has a particular characteristic is not the only way of discriminating against him or her; there are also other, more subtle and less obvious ways of doing so. One way of undermining the dignity and autonomy of people who belong to a certain group is to target not them, but third persons who are closely associated with them and do not themselves belong to the group.

...

17 The fact that the wrongness of discrimination depends on the grounds upon which it is based is reflected in the way relevant legislation is structured. Virtually all anti-discrimination statutes prohibit discrimination on a number of specified grounds. This is the strategy followed by the Community legislature in the Directive which outlaws discrimination based on religion or belief, disability, age and sexual orientation. The main duty imposed by anti-discrimination legislation, such as the Directive, is to treat people in a certain way which is comparable to how others are treated.[9] By adopting the Directive the Council has made it clear that it is wrongful for an employer to rely on any of these grounds in order to treat an employee less well than his or her colleagues. As soon as we have ascertained that the basis for the employer's conduct is one of the prohibited grounds then we enter the realm of unlawful discrimination.

18 In the sense described above, the Directive performs an exclusionary function: it excludes religious belief, age, disability and sexual orientation from the range of permissible reasons an employer may legitimately rely upon in order to treat one employee less favourably than another. In other words, after the coming into force of the Directive it is no longer permissible for these considerations to figure in the employer's reasoning when she decides to treat an employee less favourably.

...

20 Ms Coleman's case raises an issue of direct discrimination. As the order for reference makes clear, she is not complaining of the impact a neutral measure had on her as the mother and carer of a disabled child, but claims that she was singled out and targeted by her employer precisely because of her disabled son. Therefore, the issue for the Court is whether direct discrimination by association is prohibited by the Directive.

21 It is clear that had the claimant been disabled herself the Directive would have been applicable. In the present case, though, the allegation is that it was the disability of the claimant's son which triggered the discriminatory treatment. Thus, the person who is disabled and the person who is the obvious victim or the object of the discriminatory act are not the same. Does this render the Directive inapplicable? Given my analysis up to this point, I think it does not.

---

[9] Gardner, J., "Discrimination as Injustice" (1996) 16 Oxford Journal of Legal Studies 353, 355. As Gardner explains this is a question of justice. Thus, when we say that it is wrong to treat someone less favourably on certain grounds what we mean is that justice requires that we do not rely on those grounds in order negatively to affect that person's position. Put differently, if we do rely on those prohibited grounds we have inflicted on the person concerned an injustice.

22 As stated, the effect of the Directive is that it is impermissible for an employer to rely on religion, age, disability and sexual orientation in order to treat some employees less well than others. To do so would amount to subjecting these individuals to unjust treatment and failing to respect their dignity and autonomy. This fact does not change in cases where the employee who is the object of discrimination is not disabled herself. The ground which serves as the basis of the discrimination she suffers continues to be disability ....

Grand Chamber:

45. The Court defined the concept of 'disability' in its judgment in *Chacón Navas* and, in paragraphs 51 and 52 of that judgment, it found that the prohibition, as regards dismissal, of discrimination on grounds of disability contained in Articles 2(1) and 3(1)(c) of Directive 2000/78 precludes dismissal on grounds of disability which, in the light of the obligation to provide reasonable accommodation for people with disabilities, is not justified by the fact that the person concerned is not competent, capable and available to perform the essential functions of his post. However, it does not follow from this interpretation that the principle of equal treatment defined in Article 2(1) of that directive and the prohibition of direct discrimination laid down by Article 2(2)(a) cannot apply to a situation such as that in the present case, where the less favourable treatment which an employee claims to have suffered is on grounds of the disability of his child, for whom he is the primary provider of the care required by virtue of the child's condition.

46 Although the Court explained at [56] of the judgment in Chacón Navas that, in view of the wording of Art.13 EC, the scope of Directive 2000/78 cannot be extended beyond the discrimination based on the grounds listed exhaustively in Art.1 of the directive, with the result that a person who has been dismissed by his employer solely on account of sickness cannot fall within the scope of the general framework established by Directive 2000/78, it nevertheless did not hold that the principle of equal treatment and the scope ratione personae of that directive must be interpreted strictly with regard to those grounds.

47 So far as the objectives of Directive 2000/78 are concerned, as is apparent from [34] and [38] of the present judgment, the directive seeks to lay down, as regards employment and occupation, a general framework for combating discrimination on one of the grounds referred to in Art.1 – including, in particular, disability – with a view to putting into effect in the Member States the principle of equal treatment. It follows from recital (37) in the preamble to the directive that it also has the objective of creating within the Community a level playing field as regards equality in employment and occupation.

...

51 Where it is established that an employee in a situation such as that in the present case suffers direct discrimination on grounds of disability, an interpretation of Directive 2000/78 limiting its application only to people who are themselves disabled is liable to deprive that directive of an important element of its effectiveness and to reduce the protection which it is intended to guarantee.

...

56 In the light of the foregoing considerations, the answer to the first part of Question 1 and to Questions 2 and 3 must be that Directive 2000/78, and, in particular, Arts 1 and 2(1) and (2)(a) thereof, must be interpreted as meaning that the prohibition of direct discrimination laid down by those provisions is not limited only to people who are themselves disabled. ...

President Skouris, Jann, Timmermans, Rosas, Lenaerts, Tizzano, Ilešič, Klučka, Rapporteur Ó Caoimh, von Danwitz and Arabadjiev.

1. The Court of Justice holds that to limit protection to people who themselves have a protected characteristic would limit the effectiveness of the policy behind the Equal Treatment Directive 2000: that is to create a 'level playing field' in 'employment and occupation'. AG Maduro's Opinion, which probably counts as one of the strongest modern defences of equality, goes significantly further in basing the principles of equality in a defence of human dignity and autonomy.

2. As we will see in chapter 14, there is a duty on employers to make 'reasonable adjustments' for disabled people (EA 2010 ss 20 and 39(5)). Should this duty also extend to make reasonable adjustments for employees who are associated with disabled people? EFD 2000 Art 5 simply states 'reasonable accommodation shall be provided' without saying for who in that sentence. But then the next sentence says this 'means that employers shall take appropriate measures, where needed in a particular case, to enable a person with a disability to have access to, participate in, or advance in employment, or to undergo training, unless such measures would impose a disproportionate burden on the employer'. Does the first sentence include the second, or is the second exclusive?

3. In *Hainsworth v Ministry of Defence* [2014] EWCA Civ 763 Ms Hainsworth claimed disability discrimination, after her request to transfer work from Germany to the UK, where special needs schools were available for her disabled daughter, was rejected. Laws LJ, giving judgment, held that the duty did not extend to Ms Hainsworth, because although the Directive's preamble, and principles set out by AG Maduro, were 'undoubtedly important ideals', in his view, 'care needs to be taken to respect the equally important principle of legal certainty.' Tomlinson LJ and Briggs LJ agreed. Does Laws LJ really mean that legal certainty is 'more' important than equality? If not, do you agree that they are equal? In any case, is there any legal certainty, when enough people appear to have thought the claim was valid? An appeal was, however, refused by the Supreme Court (UKSC 2014/0164) on 1 December 2015 on the ground that *Coleman* at [39] stated the Directive had 'a number of provisions which, as is apparent from their very wording, apply only to disabled people. Thus, Article 5 provides that, in order to guarantee compliance with the principle of equal treatment in relation to persons with disabilities, reasonable accommodation is to be provided.' If the courts will not change this position, should the legislature?

4. The next case concerns 'perceptive' or 'misdirected' discrimination: claims by people who do not in fact share a protected characteristic, but may have been perceived to.

English v Sanderson Blinds Ltd [2008] EWCA Civ 1421

Mr English brought a claim against his former employer for harassment based on sexual orientation. He was the subject of homophobic mockery at his workplace largely, it seems, because he had attended a boarding school, and had lived in Brighton. He was married to a woman and had three children. He claimed harassment under the Employment Equality (Sexual Orientation) Regulations 2003 reg 5 (now EA 2010 ss 12 and 40).

The tribunal rejected his claim, because as he admitted, none of the work colleagues actually thought he was gay. On appeal, Peter Clark J also held that there could be no harassment because nobody had thought he was gay, and he was not gay. The Court of Appeal, reversing the EAT, held by a majority that Mr English was protected.

Laws LJ (dissenting):

21. ... It shows the kind of difficulty that can arise if one seeks to extend the *Showboat* line of reasoning further than the statutory policy strictly requires. I do not think it should be extended so far as to carry the day for Mr Reynold's argument, which proceeds, as I have said, on the basis that harassment on grounds of sexual orientation may occur even though no person's actual, perceived, or assumed sexual orientation has anything whatever to do with the case. In my judgment harassment is perpetrated on grounds of sexual orientation only where some person or persons' actual, perceived, or assumed sexual orientation gives rise to it, that is, is a substantial cause of it. Mr Reynold's case confuses the reason for the conduct complained of with the nature of that conduct. On the facts the reason for the harassment was nothing to do with anyone's actual, perceived, or assumed sexual orientation. It happened to take the form of "homophobic banter" so called, which was thus the vehicle for teasing or tormenting the appellant. In those circumstances sexual orientation was not the grounds of the conduct complained of.

Moreover it seems to me that for the purposes of Mr Reynold's submission the appellant's supposed "stereotypical characteristics associated with homosexuals" are at best the fifth wheel of the coach. On the assumed facts it is nothing to the point what prompted the nature of the perpetrators' thoroughly nasty conduct. They did not actually think he was gay, and the appellant knew as much.

...

27. ... we should recall the premise of [counsel's] argument to which I drew attention in addressing Question (1): that harassment on grounds of sexual orientation may occur even though no person's actual, perceived, or assumed sexual orientation has anything whatever to do with the case. In relation to the Framework Directive, his case must be that the same applies to each of the other forms of discrimination mentioned in Article 1: religion, belief, disability or age. Unwanted conduct relating to any of those matters may amount to harassment even if it does not touch or engage the possession of any of those characteristics by any person.

28. This would amount not to a Pandora's box, but a Pandora's attic of unpredictable prohibitions. I do not believe that the European legislature intended such a state of affairs. And it is to be noted that no such consequence can be said to arise in the case of the amended 1976 Directive [now the Equality Framework Directive 2000]: there, the words in the definition of harassment are "unwanted conduct related to the sex of a person", which must refer only to the sex of a specific person, and manifestly cannot refer to anyone's religion, belief, disability or age. All of the unruly generalities implied by Mr Reynold's argument are excluded ...

Sedley LJ:

37. ... In my judgment it did not matter whether he was gay or not. The calculated insult to his dignity, which depended not at all on his actual sexuality, and the consequently intolerable working environment were sufficient to bring his case both within Regulation 5 and within the 1976 Directive. The incessant mockery ("banter" trivialises it) created a degrading and hostile working environment, and it did so on grounds of sexual orientation. That is the way I would prefer to put it. Alternatively, however, it can be properly said that the fact that the appellant is not gay, and that his tormentors know it, has just as much to do with sexual orientation – his own, as it happens – as if he were gay.

38. If, as is common ground, tormenting a man who is believed to be gay but is not amounts to unlawful harassment, the distance from there to tormenting a man who is being treated as if he were gay when he is not is barely perceptible. In both cases the man's sexual orientation, in both cases imaginary, is the basis – that is to say, the ground – of the harassment. There is no Pandora's box here: simply a consistent application of the principle that, while you cannot legislate against prejudice, you can set out in specified circumstances to stop people's lives being made a misery by it.

Lawrence Collins LJ:

46. If the conduct is "on grounds of sexual orientation" it is plainly irrelevant whether the claimant is actually of a particular sexual orientation. In a case of this kind, even if the claimant is homosexual, it is obviously not for the claimant to show that he is homosexual, any more than a claimant in a racial discrimination case must prove that he is Asian or a Jew.

47. It would follow from the decision of the EAT that if the claimant is actually homosexual, but those who victimise him do not in fact believe him to be so, then Regulation 5(1) would not be engaged. I do not consider that this could have been the intended result of the legislation, and I do not consider that it is its result.

48. In my judgment, where an employee is repeatedly and offensively called a Paki or a Jew-boy even when he is not of Asian or Jewish origin, and even when his tormentors do not believe that he is, that conduct can amount to harassment ...

49. This is not the same as the example of an able-bodied but clumsy person being called "a spastic" which was mentioned in argument. The Disability Discrimination Act 1995, section 3B, provides that a disabled person is subject to harassment where the offensive conduct is engaged in "for a reason which relates to the disabled person's disability." ... Not only does that wording require an actual disability, but also, however unacceptable the word may have become, it does not normally denote actual disability when being used offensively.

50. Does the case-law require the conclusion to which the EAT came? In my judgment it does not.

NOTES AND QUESTIONS

1. Sedley LJ and Lawrence Collins LJ reason that unlawful harassment was made out, regardless of the claimant's actual identity, because this is consistent with the policy of the Act and the Directive, to prevent workplaces being hostile or degrading environments for people with different identities.
2. Do you find the assertion of Laws LJ, that a 'Pandora's attic' would be opened by allowing a claim, a helpful element of his analysis?
3. An important aspect of *English*, which does not appear to be addressed in argument, is how meaningful the principle could be for other people in the workplace. Suppose one of Mr English's colleagues was in fact gay, and had to also suffer watching Mr English's homophobic torment. Do you agree the law is concerned about the social impact of discrimination, as much as its individual impact?
4. People's identities can be considered as much a 'social construct' as inherent features of who we are. Very often, children will never have noticed that they have

lighter or darker skin than the people around them until the day of a first, sad playground incident. The importance of our skin colour may one day seem to people in future as about as relevant as the shape of one's toes. Perhaps a teenager growing up in the future may never think twice about her male friends having male partners, or the lisp when she speaks. While our genetic heritage does not change, social attitudes constantly do. Human beings, with pattern-seeking minds, are prone to classify others, often subconsciously. Racism, sexism and prejudice are often ingrained, but the evidence suggests that there is nothing inherent that requires us to treat other people unequally. As we become more familiar with all the diversity and beauty of people who we share a planet with, this seems to be the likely historical direction.

(2) DIRECT DISCRIMINATION

Direct discrimination (as in *Redfearn* and *Coleman*, in contrast to *Mandla* above) means treating someone less favourably because of a protected characteristic. In order to determine whether this has taken place, the law sets up a series of tests. First, a thought exercise is used in finding a 'comparator', who may be real or hypothetical. This is used to ask if the unwanted treatment was because of the protected characteristic, or in fact something else. Second, because racism, sexism, homophobia and so on are states of mind, discrimination can often be very hard to prove. In order to unearth prejudicial conduct, the claimant has the burden of proof to show facts from which discrimination could be inferred, and the defendant then has to prove the treatment was not the result of discrimination. In addition, remedies should logically be set at a sufficient level to dissuade people from acting upon prejudice. Third, there are exceptions or justifications for direct discrimination which is not socially harmful: an employing entity may argue that hiring someone of a certain protected characteristic, and not others, is a 'genuine occupational requirement' (eg a woman actor to play Desdemona in Shakespeare's *Othello*). For age discrimination, however, there is a more generous rule, which applies to indirect discrimination claims: the employing entity may argue that age discrimination is a 'proportionate means of achieving a legitimate aim'. This usually means the discrimination may be justified for the enterprise's needs as a whole (rather than the job in question).

(a) Comparison

Equality Act 2010 ss 13, 18, 23 and 29

13 Direct discrimination
   (1) A person (A) discriminates against another (B) if, because of a protected characteristic, A treats B less favourably than A treats or would treat others.
   (2) If the protected characteristic is age, A does not discriminate against B if A can show A's treatment of B to be a proportionate means of achieving a legitimate aim.
   (3) If the protected characteristic is disability, and B is not a disabled person, A does not discriminate against B only because A treats or would treat disabled persons more favourably than A treats B.

(4) If the protected characteristic is marriage and civil partnership, this section applies to a contravention of Part 5 (work) only if the treatment is because it is B who is married or a civil partner.

(5) If the protected characteristic is race, less favourable treatment includes segregating B from others.

(6) If the protected characteristic is sex—

   (a) less favourable treatment of a woman includes less favourable treatment of her because she is breast-feeding;

   (b) in a case where B is a man, no account is to be taken of special treatment afforded to a woman in connection with pregnancy or childbirth.

(7) Subsection (6)(a) does not apply for the purposes of Part 5 (work).

(8) This section is subject to section … 18(7).

…

18 Pregnancy and maternity discrimination: work cases

(1) This section has effect for the purposes of the application of Part 5 (work) to the protected characteristic of pregnancy and maternity.

(2) A person (A) discriminates against a woman if, in the protected period in relation to a pregnancy of hers, A treats her unfavourably—

   (a) because of the pregnancy, or

   (b) because of illness suffered by her as a result of it.

(3) A person (A) discriminates against a woman if A treats her unfavourably because she is on compulsory maternity leave.

(4) A person (A) discriminates against a woman if A treats her unfavourably because she is exercising or seeking to exercise, or has exercised or sought to exercise, the right to ordinary or additional maternity leave.

(5) For the purposes of subsection (2), if the treatment of a woman is in implementation of a decision taken in the protected period, the treatment is to be regarded as occurring in that period (even if the implementation is not until after the end of that period).

(6) The protected period, in relation to a woman's pregnancy, begins when the pregnancy begins, and ends—

   (a) if she has the right to ordinary and additional maternity leave, at the end of the additional maternity leave period or (if earlier) when she returns to work after the pregnancy;

   (b) if she does not have that right, at the end of the period of 2 weeks beginning with the end of the pregnancy.

(7) Section 13, so far as relating to sex discrimination, does not apply to treatment of a woman in so far as—

   (a) it is in the protected period in relation to her and is for a reason mentioned in paragraph (a) or (b) of subsection (2), or

   (b) it is for a reason mentioned in subsection (3) or (4).

…

23 Comparison by reference to circumstances

(1) On a comparison of cases for the purposes of section 13, 14, or 19 there must be no material difference between the circumstances relating to each case.

(2) The circumstances relating to a case include a person's abilities if—

   (a) on a comparison for the purposes of section 13, the protected characteristic is disability;

   (b) on a comparison for the purposes of section 14, one of the protected characteristics in the combination is disability.

(3) If the protected characteristic is sexual orientation, the fact that one person (whether or not the person referred to as B) is a civil partner while another is married to a person of the opposite sex is not a material difference between the circumstances relating to each case.

(4) If the protected characteristic is sexual orientation, the fact that one person (whether or not the person referred to as B) is married to a person of the same sex while another is married to a person of the opposite sex is not a material difference between the circumstances relating to each case.

39 Employees and applicants

(1) An employer (A) must not discriminate against a person (B)—
   (a)   in the arrangements A makes for deciding to whom to offer employment;
   (b)   as to the terms on which A offers B employment;
   (c)   by not offering B employment.
(2) An employer (A) must not discriminate against an employee of A's (B)—
   (a)   as to B's terms of employment;
   (b)   in the way A affords B access, or by not affording B access, to opportunities for promotion, transfer or training or for receiving any other benefit, facility or service;
   (c)   by dismissing B;
   (d)   by subjecting B to any other detriment.
(3) An employer (A) must not victimise a person (B)—
   (a)   in the arrangements A makes for deciding to whom to offer employment;
   (b)   as to the terms on which A offers B employment;
   (c)   by not offering B employment.
(4) An employer (A) must not victimise an employee of A's (B)—
   (a)   as to B's terms of employment;
   (b)   in the way A affords B access, or by not affording B access, to opportunities for promotion, transfer or training or for any other benefit, facility or service;
   (c)   by dismissing B;
   (d)   by subjecting B to any other detriment.

NOTES AND QUESTIONS

1.   As one can see, the EA 2010 is not a model of succinct and clear drafting. Nevertheless, the simple idea is that there should be no less favourable treatment based on protected characteristics (s 13), but there are exemptions from this rule so that disabled people and pregnant women may be treated more favourably (ss 13(3) and 18, see further chapter 14), and that when comparing people, they must be the same except for the protected characteristic. The scope is set out in s 39.

2.   EA 2010 s 16 adds special protection to people who are absent from work to undergo gender reassignment, since work absences would usually be a legitimate reason for an employing entity to give the employee a warning, potentially leading to dismissal.

3.   What does it mean in EA 2010 s 23 that comparators must have 'no material difference'?

Shamoon v Chief Constable of the Royal Ulster Constabulary **[2003] UKHL 11**

Ms Shamoon claimed sex discrimination after she was stripped of appraisal duties by the Constabulary, in her job as chief inspector. She had appraised constables in the Urban Traffic Branch. Complaints were made about the way she conducted these appraisals, after which her duties were removed. She made a claim under the Sex Discrimination (Northern Ireland) Order 1976 (for Britain, now EA 2010 s 13). She argued that two appropriate comparators were male chief inspectors who were in the same branch and had the same duties, in which they continued. However, they did not have complaints made against them. The Employment Tribunal held that there was unlawful sex discrimination. The Northern Ireland Court of Appeal rejected her claim because the comparators had no complaints against their appraisal work. The House of Lords agreed that Ms Shamoon's claim failed.

Lord Nicholls:

4. ... the statutory definition calls for a comparison between the way the employer treated the claimant woman ... and the way he treated or would have treated a man. It stands to reason that in making this comparison, with a view to deciding whether a woman who was dismissed received less favourable treatment than a man, it is necessary to compare like with like. The situations being compared must be such that, gender apart, the situation of the man and the woman are in all material respects the same. ...

    ...

10. ... prima facie the comparison with the two male chief inspectors is not apt. So be it. Let it be assumed that, this being so, the most sensible course in practice is to proceed on the footing that the appropriate comparator is a hypothetical comparator: a male chief inspector regarding whose conduct similar complaints and representations had been made. On this footing the less favourable treatment issue is this: was Chief Inspector Shamoon treated less favourably than such a male chief inspector would have been treated? But, here also, the question is incapable of being answered without deciding why Chief Inspector Shamoon was treated as she was. It is impossible to decide whether Chief Inspector Shamoon was treated less favourably than a hypothetical male chief inspector without identifying the ground on which she was treated as she was. Was it grounds of sex? If yes, then she was treated less favourably than a male chief inspector in her position would have been treated. If not, not. Thus, on this footing also, the less favourable treatment issue is incapable of being decided without deciding the reason why issue. And the decision on the reason why issue will also provide the answer to the less favourable treatment issue.

11. This analysis seems to me to point to the conclusion that employment tribunals may sometimes be able to avoid arid and confusing disputes about the identification of the appropriate comparator by concentrating primarily on why the claimant was treated as she was. Was it on the proscribed ground which is the foundation of the application? That will call for an examination of all the facts of the case. Or was it for some other reason? If the latter, the application fails. If the former, there will be usually be no difficulty in deciding whether the treatment, afforded to the claimant on the proscribed ground, was less favourable than was or would have been afforded to others.

Lord Hope:

39. The obvious questions which these provisions raise are: with whom should the comparison be made, and which circumstances are to be considered as relevant: see Daniel Peyton, *Sex and Race Discrimination*, para 3.2.5. But these issues are by no means straightforward. As Sandra Fredman, Discrimination Law, pp 96-99, has explained, the need for a comparator has been one of the most problematic and limiting aspects of direct discrimination as defined in the legislation about discrimination on grounds of sex and race. The requirement is less harsh than in the legislation about equal pay, as the provisions about discrimination on grounds of sex and race permit a "hypothetical" comparison, based – in a sex case, for example – on the question how the woman "would" be treated if it is not possible to find an actual comparator. Nevertheless the choice of comparator requires that a judgment must be made as to

which of the differences between any two individuals are relevant and which are irrelevant. The choice of characteristics may itself be determinative of the outcome: see *Advocate General v MacDonald* 2001 SC 1 and *Pearce v Governing Body of Mayfield School* [2001] EWCA Civ 1347; [2002] ICR 198. This suggests that care must be taken not to approach this issue in a way that will defeat the purpose of the legislation, which is to eliminate discrimination against women on the ground of their sex in all the areas with which it deals.

...

51. For these reasons I am in agreement with the Court of Appeal that, as the facts of their case were different from that of the appellant, the other chief inspectors were not, on their own facts, valid comparators. I also agree that the tribunal, which appears to have proceeded on the basis that they were, misdirected itself on this point. But I think that the Court of Appeal were wrong not to acknowledge that the issue of less favourable treatment can be examined hypothetically, as is indicated by the words "or would treat" in article 3(1)(a). Carswell LCJ said that the court was following the approach which he had described in *Chief Constable of the Royal Ulster Constabulary v A* [2000] NI 261, where he said:

> "To make out a case under section 16(2)(a) of the 1976 Act a complainant has to show that the respondent has treated him 'less favourably than he treats or would treat other persons.' In the absence of evidence of a regular way in which other persons in the same circumstances are treated, he has to prove that at least one other person in comparable circumstances has been treated differently, which may tend to show how others would have been treated if they and not the complainant had been concerned."

In other words, as there was – to apply this formula to the facts of this case – no other chief inspector against whom complaints had been made or about whom representations had been made by the Police Federation, the appellant was bound to fail in her claim that she had been discriminated against. The Court of Appeal held that the appellant's case was bound to fail for the lack of a valid comparator, as she was unable to show that at least one other chief inspector who was in the same position in all respects as she was had been treated differently.

52. The requirement that it must be shown that at least one other person whose circumstances were in fact comparable to those of the complainant was treated differently introduces a step into the exercise which is not found in the legislation. The way the case was argued for the appellant may have invited this approach, as her case depended on accepting the other chief inspectors as valid comparators. But I do not think, with great respect, that this can be regarded as a rule which must be applied in all cases. There could be cases where the position held by the complainant was the only one of its kind and incapable of being compared with that held at the relevant time by anyone else in the employer's organisation. The words "or would treat" in article 3(1) of the Order permit the question whether there was discrimination against a woman on the ground of her sex to be approached on a hypothesis. The crucial question is whether there was discrimination, and it would defeat the purpose of the Order if this question could not be addressed simply because the complainant was unable to point to anyone else who was in fact in the same position as she was. Isolated or unique cases would be left without the protection which the legislation is designed to provide. The flaws which I detect in the Court of Appeal's reasoning lie in its assumption that it was necessary for the appellant to show, as part of the relevant circumstances, that there were in fact other chief inspectors over whom Superintendent Laird had responsibility in whose case too there had been complaints and representations and in its conclusion that, because she had not done this, her case must necessarily fail. ...

Lord Hutton, Lord Scott and **Lord Rodger** gave concurring judgments.

1. The House of Lords emphasises that Ms Shamoon would logically have to find actual comparators or think of a hypothetical comparator who also had complaints made against him. This seems undeniably correct in a technical sense. The question that perhaps received less attention than it should have done, of course, was whether the complaints about Ms Shamoon's appraisal work were themselves tainted by sexist motives. If they were, presumably the complaints should have been disregarded. However, the case proceeds on the footing that the complaints were legitimate, rather than, potentially, the result of a workforce culture where women in positions of authority were unwelcome.

2. In *James v Eastleigh BC* [1990] 2 AC 751 the House of Lords established, by a majority, that motive or intention is irrelevant to whether discrimination has taken place. Lord Goff rejected a test, originally advanced by Sir Nicholas Browne-Wilkinson VC, that an employer should be found to have 'desired' to discriminate. This view was probably advanced, not so much to restrict claims, but to enable 'positive discrimination' to reverse historical disadvantage (see chapter 14). The true test is a wholly objective one, asking on the facts: 'Would the complainant have received the same treatment from the defendant but for his or her sex?' So here, a swimming pool, which gave free entry for women but not men, had engaged in unlawful sex discrimination.

3. In *Smith v Safeway plc* [1996] ICR 868 a man working at Safeway plc's delicatessen was dismissed because he refused to cut his hair. He claimed sex discrimination. He wore his hair in a ponytail. The workplace rules for men said: 'Tidy hair not below shirt collar length. No unconventional hair styles or colouring.' Women were allowed to have long hair. Phillips LJ, remarkably, took the view that different treatment of men, in this case, was not 'less favourable' treatment and the employing entity was entitled to regulate the appearance of its staff. His opening line was that '"Get your hair cut" is an instruction that I suspect most men have heard at some time whether at school, in the armed forces or in the workplace.' Peter Gibson LJ and Leggatt LJ agreed. Have you heard that instruction before at school, in the armed forces, or in the workplace? Was that in real life or a 1950s film? Do you agree with this 'separate but equal' result?

4. Is there any requirement to actually treat someone less favourably for there to be unlawful discrimination? No. In addition to the wording of EA 2010 s 13(1) 'would treat', *Centrum voor Gelijkheid van Kansen en voor Racismebestrijding v Firma Feryn NV* (2008) C-54/07 found that a business owner committed unlawful discrimination when he said in an interview 'people often say: "no immigrants". ... I must comply with my customers' requirements.' The Court of Justice held, in response to a claim by an anti-racism centre, that because there would be a dissuasive effect on applications to work at the firm, there was direct discrimination unless the firm proved that its practices were not in fact discriminatory.

5. Would it be logically preferable to eliminate the requirement for a comparator, and simply make unlawful any detriment because of a protected characteristic? See chapter 10 to compare with trade union discrimination law.

(b) Proof and Remedies

Equality Act 2010 s 136

136 Burden of proof

...

(2) If there are facts from which the court could decide, in the absence of any other explanation, that a person (A) contravened the provision concerned, the court must hold that the contravention occurred.

(3) But subsection (2) does not apply if A shows that A did not contravene the provision.

(4) The reference to a contravention of this Act includes a reference to a breach of an equality clause or rule.

NOTES AND QUESTIONS

1. EA 2010 s 136 reflects EFD 2000 Art 10, and is designed to ensure that, although people may lie that their actions were not motivated by prejudice, when the facts suggest otherwise, they will be liable.

2. In *King v The Great Britain-China Centre* [1992] ICR 516 a Chinese lady, educated in Britain, was not shortlisted for a job interview requiring 'first-hand knowledge of China and fluent spoken Chinese', for deputy director of the centre. All the shortlisted people were white, and the person hired was an English graduate in Chinese. The Tribunal held the employing entity 'had failed to demonstrate that the applicant had not been treated unfavourably, or that such unfavourable treatment was not because of her race'. Neill LJ upheld this finding. Contrast *Igen Ltd v Wong* [2005] EWCA Civ 142.

3. In *Madarassy v Nomura International Plc* [2007] EWCA Civ 33 Mummery LJ emphasised it is necessary to show facts which indicate a defendant did discriminate, not just that it could have done. This meant that Ms Madarassy's claim for sex discrimination failed. Although she had been made redundant from Nomura's equity capital markets team, when two men had not been, this did not in itself mean there was sex discrimination. See also *Bouzir v Country Style Foods Ltd* [2011] EWCA Civ 1519.

4. In *Hewage v Grampian Health Board* [2012] UKSC 37 the Supreme Court approved both *Igen Ltd v Wong* and *Madarassy*, saying there is no substitute for the statutory language, but that 'although the statute involved a two-stage analysis, the tribunal does not in practice hear the evidence and the argument in two stages' per Lord Hope at [30]. At 'stage one', the claimant still has to show there is a 'prima facie' case. The Tribunal makes no assumption. But then at 'stage 2', the court assumes the absence of an adequate explanation. 'The assumption at that stage, in other words, is simply that there is no adequate explanation. There is no assumption as to whether or not a prima facie case has been established.' This meant that Mrs Hewage succeeded in her claim for sex and race discrimination. After a verbal outburst from two colleagues, she made a complaint that was not adequately dealt with. One, Mrs Helen Strachan, had been complained

about before by a Professor Forrester and a Mr Larmour, but they had had their complaints swiftly dealt with. The Supreme Court rejected that, although their situations differed slightly, Forrester and Larmour were not appropriate comparators. The Tribunal was entitled to conclude this, and hold there was no reason for Mrs Hewage's complaints not to be dealt with properly by the Board.

5. EA 2010 s 108 prohibits discrimination and harassment that arises out of and is 'closely connected to a relationship which used to exist between' the parties; ss 109–10 codifies vicarious liability of employers for employees' actions; s 111 prohibits instructions that are in any way discriminatory; and s 112 prohibits 'aiding' unlawful discrimination.

6. For an example at the top end for loss to a claimant, *Chagger v Abbey National plc* [2010] ICR 397 the Court of Appeal upheld a Tribunal award of £1,325,322 for future loss of a financial services industry employee. His career was destroyed after he sued for race discrimination, and the Court took the view that the sum was justified because 'the original employer must remain liable for so-called stigma loss'.

7. EA 2010 s 119 allows remedies that the High Court could grant in a tort or a judicial review case, and state 'damages may include compensation for injured feelings'.

8. *Vento v CC of West Yorkshire Police* [2002] EWCA Civ 1871 stated that for injury to feelings, a 'top band' should be between £15,000 and £25,000 for 'a lengthy campaign of discriminatory harassment on the ground of sex or race'. A middle band of '£5,000 and £15,000 should be used for serious cases, which do not merit an award in the highest band'. In a lower band: 'Awards of between £500 and £5,000 are appropriate for less serious cases, such as where the act of discrimination is an isolated or one off occurrence.' This should be uprated by the Bank of England inflation calculator for the appropriate year.

9. EA 2010 s 123 creates a three-month limit to bring a claim, six months in the armed forces, unless the Tribunal thinks a longer period is just and equitable. By contrast, under s 129 there is a six-month, non-extendable time limit for equal pay claims (chapter 13).

10. The EA 2006 s 1 establishes the Equality and Human Rights Commission (EHRC). Under s 20 it can launch investigations into workplace practices, and under s 30 it can intervene in legal proceedings, apply for judicial review, or suggest to employers that they undertake 'best practice' commitments. One of the reasons that 'Equality Monitoring' forms are so common (where we tick our boxes for being a man, woman, White British, White Irish, Black British, Asian, etc) is that employing entities who use these will be considered to be following best practices. If (particularly indirect) discrimination claims are brought, this may speak in the employing entity's favour. Should the EHRC also have the right, as competition and tax authorities do, to bring representative claims and claims in its own right against private employers? Should trade unions also?

11. Can exemplary or punitive damages be claimed for intentional discrimination calculated to make a profit? The next case sets out the general principle.

Rookes v Barnard [1964] UKHL 1

Douglas Rookes, a draughtsman employed by British Overseas Airways Corporation (BOAC), claimed that his union officials (including the branch chair Mr Barnard) claimed exemplary damages after the union threatened to strike unless Rookes resigned. Rookes had left the Association of Engineering and Shipbuilding Draughtsman (AESD) union, but the AESD had a 'closed shop' agreement (see chapter 9(3)(a)), requiring every BOAC employee to be a union member. When Rookes left the union, BOAC suspended him and after a few months, dismissed him with one week's salary in lieu of proper notice. Rookes argued the union was liable for tortious intimidation, and used unlawful means (apparently the threat to break a contract in a strike) to induce BOAC to terminate his contract. He also sought exemplary damages. The Court of Appeal held that the threat to break a contract was not itself unlawful, and so Barnard was not liable in tort for striking. The House of Lords held that the threat to break a contract was unlawful, but that exemplary damages were not appropriate. Lord Devlin set out principles for claiming exemplary damages.

Lord Devlin:

My Lords, I express no view on whether the Copyright Act, 1956, authorises an award of exemplary, as distinct from aggravated, damages. But there are certainly two other Acts of Parliament which mention exemplary damages by name. The Law Reform (Miscellaneous Provisions) Act, 1934, section 1(2)(a) provides that where a cause of action survives for the benefit of the estate of a deceased person, the damages recoverable shall not include any exemplary damages. The Reserve and Auxiliary Forces (Protection of Civil Interests) Act, 1951, section 13 (2), provides that in any action for damages for conversion in respect of goods falling within the statute the court may take into account the defendant's conduct and award exemplary damages.

These authorities convince me of two things. First, that your Lordships could not, without a complete disregard of precedent, and indeed of statute, now arrive at a determination that refused altogether to recognise the exemplary principle. Secondly, that there are certain categories of cases in which an award of exemplary damages can serve a useful purpose in vindicating the strength of the law and thus affording a practical justification for admitting into the civil law a principle which ought logically to belong to the criminal. I propose to state what these two categories are; and I propose also to state three general considerations which, in my opinion, should always be borne in mind when awards of exemplary damages are being made. I am well aware that what I am about to say will, if accepted, impose limits not hitherto expressed on such awards and that there is powerful, though not compelling, authority for allowing them a wider range. I shall not, therefore, conclude what I have to say on the general principles of law without returning to the authorities and making it clear to what extent I have rejected the guidance they may be said to afford.

The first category is oppressive, arbitrary or unconstitutional action by the servants of the government. I should not extend this category – I say this with particular reference to the facts of this case – to oppressive action by private corporations or individuals. Where one man is more powerful than another, it is inevitable that he will try to use his power to gain his ends; and if his power is much greater than the other's, he might, perhaps, be said to be using it oppressively. If he uses his power illegally, he must of course pay for his illegality in the ordinary way; but he is not to be punished simply because he is the more powerful. In the case of the government it is different, for the servants of the government are also the servants of the people and the use of their power must always be subordinate to their duty of service. It is true that there is something repugnant about a big man bullying a small man and, very likely, the bullying will be a source of humiliation that makes the case one for aggravated damages, but it is not, in my opinion, punishable by damages.

Cases in the second category are those in which the defendant's conduct has been calculated by him to make a profit for himself which may well exceed the compensation payable to the plaintiff. I have quoted the dictum of Erle CJ in *Bell v Midland Railway Co.* 10 C.B.N.S. 287 Maule J in *Williams v Currie* 1 CB 841, 848 suggests the same thing; and so does Martin B. in an obiter dictum in *Crouch v Great Northern Railway Co* (1856) 11 Ex. 742, 759. It is a factor also that is taken into account in damages for libel; one man should not be allowed to sell another man's reputation for profit. Where a defendant with a cynical disregard for a plaintiff's rights has calculated that the money to be made out of his wrongdoing will probably exceed the damages at risk, it is necessary for the law to show that it cannot be broken with impunity. This category is not confined to moneymaking in the strict sense. It extends to cases in which the defendant is seeking to gain at the expense of the plaintiff some object – perhaps some property which he covets – which either he could not obtain at all or not obtain except at a price greater than he wants to put down. Exemplary damages can properly be awarded whenever it is necessary to teach a wrongdoer that tort does not pay.

To these two categories which are established as part of the common law there must of course be added any category in which exemplary damages are expressly authorised by statute.

I wish now to express three considerations which I think should always be borne in mind when awards of exemplary damages are being considered. First, the plaintiff cannot recover exemplary damages unless he is the victim of the punishable behaviour. The anomaly inherent in exemplary damages would become an absurdity if a plaintiff totally unaffected by some oppressive conduct which the jury wished to punish obtained a windfall in consequence.

Secondly, the power to award exemplary damages constitutes a weapon that, while it can be used in defence of liberty, as in the *Wilkes case*, Lofft 1 can also be used against liberty. Some of the awards that juries have made in the past seem to me to amount to a greater punishment than would be likely to be incurred if the conduct were criminal; and, moreover, a punishment imposed without the safeguard which the criminal law gives to an offender. I should not allow the respect which is traditionally paid to an assessment of damages by a jury to prevent me from seeing that the weapon is used with restraint. It may even be that the House may find it necessary to follow the precedent it set for itself in *Benham v Gambling* [1941] AC 157 ... and place some arbitrary limit on awards of damages that are made by way of punishment. Exhortations to be moderate may not be enough.

Thirdly, the means of the parties, irrelevant in the assessment of compensation, are material in the assessment of exemplary damages. Everything which aggravates or mitigates the defendant's conduct is relevant.

Thus a case for exemplary damages must be presented quite differently from one for compensatory damages; and the judge should not allow it to be left to the jury unless he is satisfied that it can be brought within the categories I have specified. But the fact that the two sorts of damage differ essentially does not necessarily mean that there should be two awards. In a case in which exemplary damages are appropriate, a jury should be directed that if, but only if, the sum which they have in mind to award as compensation (which may, of course, be a sum aggravated by the way in which the defendant has behaved to the plaintiff) is inadequate to punish him for his outrageous conduct, to mark their disapproval of such conduct and to deter him from repeating it, then it can award some larger sum. If a verdict given on such direction has to be reviewed upon appeal, the appellate court will first consider whether the award can be justified as compensation and if it can, there is nothing further to be said. If it cannot, the court must consider whether or not the punishment is, in all the circumstances, excessive. There may be cases in which it is difficult for a judge to say whether or not he ought to leave to the jury a claim for exemplary damages. In such circumstances, and in order to save the possible expense of a new trial, I see no objection to his inviting the jury to say what sum they would fix as compensation and what additional sum, if any, they would award if they were entitled to give exemplary damages. That is the course which he would have to take in a claim to which the Law Reform (Miscellaneous Provisions) Act, 1934, applied.

Lord Reid, **Lord Evershed**, **Lord Hodson** and **Lord Pearce** concurred.

NOTES AND QUESTIONS

1. Lord Devlin states that the three categories of case where exemplary damages are to be awarded are (1) 'oppressive, arbitrary or unconstitutional action by the servants of the government', (2) where 'the defendant's conduct has been calculated by him to make a profit for himself which may well exceed the compensation payable to the plaintiff', and (3) where 'exemplary damages are expressly authorised by statute'. He then says a claimant must be the 'victim of punishable behaviour', that an award should not be used to suppress natural liberty, and that the means of the parties, irrelevant in compensation, are relevant in the assessment of exemplary damages.

2. While *Rookes v Barnard* stands as a notorious decision in the history of freedom of association, and was reversed by the Trade Disputes Act 1965, the guidance on exemplary damages has remained authoritative. See LH Hoffmann (1965) 81 LQR 116. Today, the closed shop is unlawful under TULRCA 1992 s 146, as is a strike to enforce one. The principle of exemplary damages has been consistently approved. See *Kuddus v Chief Constable of Leicestershire* [2002] 2 AC 122, and S Deakin, A Johnston and B Markesinis, *Markesinis and Deakin's Tort Law* (7th edn OUP 2012) 800–01.

3. The aim of exemplary damages is not merely to compensate, nor merely to strip an offending party of their gain, but according to Lord Devlin to 'teach a wrongdoer that tort does not pay'. This suggests that exemplary damages acknowledge that tortfeasors may exploit the under-enforcement of the law, and so an award must ensure there is no incentive for wrongdoing.

4. When would exemplary damages be relevant in labour law? Discrimination is a likely candidate, as the very nature of discrimination is that it is 'arbitrary' and 'oppressive' (especially for a public body employer), or may also be connected with a calculation to profit (especially for a private-sector employer). However, despite being clearly available for breaches of the EA 2010 s 124 (see *Harvey on Industrial Relations and Employment Law* (2017) Division Q, Statutes, EA 2010, Part 9 Enforcement, s 124) the number of cases is miniscule, it seems, because counsel are simply not making a plea for them routine. See *Ministry of Defence v Fletcher* [2010] IRLR 25 and *Bradford City Metropolitan Council v Arora* [1991] 2 QB 507, where the Employment Appeal Tribunal in Fletcher suggested that wrongdoing must be 'conscious and contumelious'. Under EU law, exemplary damages are not forbidden, but are also not mandatory: *Arjona Comacho v Securitas Seguridad Espana SA* (2016) C-407/14.

5. If an employee also lives on an employer's premises, and is evicted at the same time as being dismissed, should exemplary damages be awarded by analogy to

> landlord and tenant cases? In *Drane v Evangelou* [1978] 1 WLR 455, the Court
> of Appeal held that an award of £1,000 in exemplary damages was appropriate
> (equivalent to £7,698.07 in 2016) where a landlord had evicted a tenant and his
> wife. The landlord locked the tenants out, put their possessions in the back yard,
> and so forced them both to stay at a friend's house for ten weeks.

(c) Justifications

While rules differ for direct age discrimination, compared to other protected characteristics, the general position is that an employing entity may avoid liability for direct
discrimination by arguing having a protected characteristic was a 'genuine occupational
requirement'.

Equality Act 2010 Sch 9, paras 1–4

Part 1 **Occupational requirements**
General

1(1) A person (A) does not contravene a provision mentioned in sub-paragraph (2) by applying in relation to work a requirement to have a particular protected characteristic, if A shows
that, having regard to the nature or context of the work—

(a) it is an occupational requirement,
(b) the application of the requirement is a proportionate means of achieving a legitimate aim, and
(c) the person to whom A applies the requirement does not meet it (or A has reasonable grounds for not being satisfied that the person meets it).

…

Religious requirements relating to sex, marriage etc., sexual orientation

2(1) A person (A) does not contravene a provision mentioned in sub-paragraph (2) by applying in relation to employment a requirement to which sub-paragraph (4) applies if A shows
that—

(a) the employment is for the purposes of an organised religion,
(b) the application of the requirement engages the compliance or non-conflict principle, and
(c) the person to whom A applies the requirement does not meet it (or A has reasonable grounds for not being satisfied that the person meets it).

…

Other requirements relating to religion or belief

3 A person (A) with an ethos based on religion or belief does not contravene a provision
mentioned in paragraph 1(2) by applying in relation to work a requirement to be of a particular
religion or belief if A shows that, having regard to that ethos and to the nature or context of
the work—

(a) it is an occupational requirement,
(b) the application of the requirement is a proportionate means of achieving a legitimate aim, and
(c) the person to whom A applies the requirement does not meet it (or A has reasonable grounds for not being satisfied that the person meets it).

…

Armed forces

4(1) A person does not contravene section 39(1)(a) or (c) or (2)(b) by applying in relation to service in the armed forces a relevant requirement if the person shows that the application is a proportionate means of ensuring the combat effectiveness of the armed forces.
  (2) A relevant requirement is—
    (a) a requirement to be a man;
    (b) a requirement not to be a transsexual person.

NOTES AND QUESTIONS

1. These provisions implement the EFD 2000 (2000/78/EC) Art 4(1) which contains the genuine occupational requirement formulation, and Art 4(2) which enables exemption for religious organisations.
2. Is the exemption for people 'with an ethos based on religion or belief' a reflection of principle or the reality of interest-group power?
3. How far does the religious exemption extend? In *R (Amicus) v Secretary of State for Trade and Industry* [2004] EWHC 860 (Admin) Richards J applied the standard rule of construction, that such exceptions must be construed narrowly. In the High Court's opinion, a church could not dismiss a gay cleaner who handled religious artefacts, even 'to avoid offending the strongly-held religious convictions of a significant number of adherents', a gay science teacher could not be dismissed by a religious school, nor someone working for a Christian bookshop, nor could a Muslim library refuse to hire someone who appeared gay, even if that would run counter to 'strongly held religious convictions of a significant number of Muslims'. These cases were all distinct from jobs with positions of authority within religious organisations such as a Church itself, which in EA 2010 Schs 22, para 2 appears now to include a 'head teacher' in a school of the 'head' of a university or someone with a canon professorship. See also Sch 23, para 2. Do you agree with either the judgment or the exceptions that were allowed?
4. *Glasgow City Council v McNab* [2007] IRLR 476 confirmed that it was not a genuine occupational requirement to be Catholic to get a job as head teacher at a Catholic school. This is welcome confirmation that education cannot be regarded as anything but a secular task. But aside from employees, why do you think there are still so many schools in the UK which attempt to segregate children by their religion, gender and parents' income? Is this any more acceptable than segregation by race?
5. Article 3(4) enables Member States to not apply the Directive to the armed forces based on disability or age. It is questionable whether Sch 9, para 4(2) complies with this approach, as it suggests a blanket presumption against women in the armed forces is not actually assessing ability. See *Sirdar v The Army Board & SS for Defence* (1999) C-273/97 and *Kreil v Germany* (2000) C-285/98. In addition, EA 2010 s 192 says there will be no contravention of the act by doing anything proportionate 'for the purpose of safeguarding national security'. Is this really necessary, or another lazy stereotype?
6. *Etam plc v Rowan* [1989] IRLR 150 held that a women's clothing store was not entitled to reserve jobs for women on grounds that shop-floor employees would have to staff the women's changing rooms. Mr Rowan 'would have been able to

adequately carry out the bulk of the job of sales assistant, and such parts as he could not carry out could easily have been done by other sales assistants without causing any inconvenience or difficulty for the appellants'.

7.   *Lambeth LBC v Commission for Racial Equality* [1990] ICR 768 rejected a claim by the CRE that, under the old formulation of the law, the council was not entitled to reserve two jobs to black applicants in the housing department. Although Lambeth LBC took the view that this would help because many applicants for housing in the borough were black, the job did not involve personal services. See now chapter 14 on legitimate positive action measures, as opposed to quotas.

8.   Under EA 2010 s 13(2) direct age discrimination can be more easily justified, 'if A can show A's treatment of B to be a proportionate means of achieving a legitimate aim'. This is the same justification test that applies for indirect discrimination (chapter 13). This also makes the approach to age discrimination similar to the approach to part-time, fixed-term and agency work protection. Under EFD 2000 Art 6, Member States had a choice to not give higher protect to age, and the UK took this option. This stance of the UK, enabled by EU law, reflects the much earlier US legislation, the Age Discrimination in Employment Act of 1967 (29 USC §§621–34).

9.   Why should direct age discrimination be more easy to justify? A set of rationales was discussed by Lord Walker in *R (Carson and Reynolds) v SS for Work and Pensions* [2005] UKHL 37. Here Ms Reynolds failed in her claim that jobseekers and income support of £41.35, instead of £52.20 per week, because she was under age 25 was unjustified age discrimination under ECHR Art 14. Lord Walker's view, at [60], was that age 'is different in kind from other personal characteristics. Every human being starts life as a tiny infant and none of us can do anything to stop the passage of the years.' Furthermore, in this case, and following a dictum in *Massachusetts Board of Retirement v Murgia* 427 US 307 (1976), 'lines have to be drawn somewhere', apparently, and this was 'peculiarly a legislative task and an unavoidable one'. Does this persuade you?

10. The next case gives an example of justified direct age discrimination.

Seldon v Clarkson Wright & Jakes [2012] UKSC 16

Mr Seldon, a partner, claimed direct age discrimination after he was compulsorily retired. He joined the partnership in 1971, became an equity partner in 1972, and helped revise the partnership deed in 2005. This restated that partners would retire the December after turning age 65. He asked to stay, but was offered £30,000 to retire instead. He claimed age discrimination under the Employment Equality (Age) Regulations 2006 reg 17 (now EA 2010 ss 5, 13 and 39). The Tribunal held he was less favourably treated, but it was justified (1) to give young associates the opportunity of partnership within a reasonable time, and so to encourage remaining with the firm, (2) by the need for workforce planning, (3) by limiting need to expel underperforming partners. It upheld, however, a victimisation claim. The Supreme Court, endorsing most of the Tribunal, held that Mr Seldon had not suffered unjustifiable direct age discrimination, and rejected the claim that it could not be justified in relation to business need. Employer flexibility was not in itself a legitimate aim. However, it was remitted to Tribunal to decide whether, on the facts, an age of 65 was legitimate.

Lady Hale:

55. ... the United Kingdom has chosen to give employers and partnerships the flexibility to choose which objectives to pursue, provided always that (i) these objectives can count as legitimate objectives of a public interest nature within the meaning of the Directive and (ii) are consistent with the social policy aims of the state and (iii) the means used are proportionate, that is both appropriate to the aim and (reasonably) necessary to achieve it.

56. Two different kinds of legitimate objective have been identified by the Luxembourg court. The first kind may be summed up as inter-generational fairness. This is comparatively uncontroversial. It can mean a variety of things, depending upon the particular circumstances of the employment concerned: for example, it can mean facilitating access to employment by young people; it can mean enabling older people to remain in the workforce; it can mean sharing limited opportunities to work in a particular profession fairly between the generations; it can mean promoting diversity and the interchange of ideas between younger and older workers.

57. The second kind may be summed up as dignity. This has been variously put as avoiding the need to dismiss older workers on the grounds of incapacity or underperformance, thus preserving their dignity and avoiding humiliation, and as avoiding the need for costly and divisive disputes about capacity or underperformance. Either way, it is much more controversial. As Age UK argue, the philosophy underlying all the anti-discrimination laws is the dignity of each individual, the right to be treated equally irrespective of either irrational prejudice or stereotypical assumptions which may be true of some but not of others. The assumptions underlying these objectives look suspiciously like stereotyping. Concerns about capacity, it is argued, are better dealt with, as they were in Wolf and Prigge under article 4(1), which enables them to be related to the particular requirements of the job in question.

58. I confess to some sympathy with the position taken by Age UK. The fact that most women are less physically strong than most men does not justify refusing a job requiring strength to a woman candidate just because she is a woman. The fact that this particular woman is not strong enough for the job would justify refusing it to her. It would be consistent with this principle to hold that the fact that most people over a certain age have slower reactions than most people under that age does not justify sacking everyone who reaches that age irrespective of whether or not they still do have the necessary speed of reaction. But we know that the Luxembourg court has held that the avoidance of unseemly debates about capacity is capable of being a legitimate aim. The focus must therefore turn to whether this is a legitimate aim in the particular circumstances of the case.

...

61. Once an aim has been identified, it has still to be asked whether it is legitimate in the particular circumstances of the employment concerned. For example, improving the recruitment of young people, in order to achieve a balanced and diverse workforce, is in principle a legitimate aim. But if there is in fact no problem in recruiting the young and the problem is in retaining the older and more experienced workers then it may not be a legitimate aim for the business concerned. Avoiding the need for performance management may be a legitimate aim, but if in fact the business already has sophisticated performance management measures in place, it may not be legitimate to avoid them for only one section of the workforce.

62. Finally, of course, the means chosen have to be both appropriate and necessary. It is one thing to say that the aim is to achieve a balanced and diverse workforce. It is another thing to say that a mandatory retirement age of 65 is both appropriate and necessary to achieving this end. It is one thing to say that the aim is to avoid the need for performance management procedures. It is another to say that a mandatory retirement age of 65 is appropriate and necessary to achieving this end. The means have to be carefully scrutinised in the context of the particular

business concerned in order to see whether they do meet the objective and there are not other, less discriminatory, measures which would do so.

Issue 2

63. This leads to the final issue, which is whether the measure has to be justified, not only in general but also in its application to the particular individual. ... Hence, it is argued, the part-nership should have to show, not only that the mandatory retirement rule was a proportionate means of achieving a legitimate aim, but also that applying it to Mr Seldon could be justified at the time.

...

65. I would accept that where it is justified to have a general rule, then the existence of that rule will usually justify the treatment which results from it. In the particular context of inter-generational fairness, it must be relevant that at an earlier stage in his life, a partner or employee may well have benefited from a rule which obliged his seniors to retire at a particular age. Nor can it be entirely irrelevant that the rule in question was re-negotiated comparatively recently between the partners.

Lord Hope, **Lord Brown**, **Lord Mance** and **Lord Kerr** agreed.

NOTES AND QUESTIONS

1. The Supreme Court unanimously accepts a legitimate need for compulsory retire-ment mainly for reasons of intergenerational fairness, and the idea of saving face for elderly employees, but requested assessment of whether age 65 was appropri-ate. The compulsory retirement age for UK Supreme Court judges is currently 70 years old. Would a limited statutory exception, based around the retirement age, be preferable to an open-ended objective justification for age?

2. In *Palacios de la Villa v Cortefiel Servicios SA* (2007) C-411/05 the Court of Justice held that a collective agreement, which set the retirement age at 65, was justified. It pointed to the EFD 2000 Art 6 exception which allows objective jus-tification, 'including legitimate employment policy, labour market and vocational training objectives, and if the means of achieving that aim were appropriate and necessary'. It accepted that a better distribution of work between generations was legitimate. See also *R (Age UK) v Secretary of State for Business, etc* (2009) C-388/07 and [2009] EWHC 2336 (Admin).

3. EA 2010 Sch 9, paras 10–13 also set out a series of age-related exceptions: ben-efits can be based on length of service, young workers and apprentices can be paid a lower minimum wage, and redundancy pay can be longer based on service. Do you find think all of these exceptions are justified?

4. *Wolf v Stadt Frankfurt am Main* (2010) C-229/08 held that an age limit of 30 years for applying to the fire service was a genuine occupational requirement to ensure that fit people were recruited and could have a sufficiently long career ahead. In the Court of Justice's view this was a 'genuine occupational requirement' rather than objectively justified. Did the Grand Chamber confuse requirements for an 'occupation' under Art 4(1) with requirements for the enterprise under Art 6(1),

or as it put them, requirements for 'operational capacity and proper functioning of the professional fire service'?

5. *Rosenbladt v Oellerking Gebäudereinigungsges* (2011) C-45/09 once more upheld a collective agreement ending a woman's job at 65 years old. This was positively enabled by the German Social Code (Sozialgesetzbuch §41). Ms Rosenbladt argued this caused her financial hardship because the statutory old age pension at €228.26 a month was not enough for her to live a decent life. The Court of Justice held that the age was justified as sharing employment between generations. It stated that she was not prevented from seeking alternative work, although this must be severely limited given that collective agreements containing the same retirement age would be common. Given the growing problems of poverty and inequality, including in old age, a full reassessment of social and work policy needs to take place?

6. In *Jivraj v Hashwani* [2011] UKSC 40 a commercial arbitration agreement, requiring the arbitrator to be from the Ismaili community, was held by the Supreme Court to be lawful. An arbitrator was entirely outside the scope of (what is now) the EA 2010 because an arbitrator, held the Supreme Court, does not have the requisite 'subordination' needed to be in 'employment'. The decision may have been motivated in part by a concern for independence of the judiciary, and the notion of 'subordination' appeared antithetical to that. However, it would seem that the appropriate route to this result was to say that people personally performing work were covered (there need be no question of subordination) but that it was a 'genuine occupational requirement' for the arbitrator to be Ismaili, under EA 2010 Sch 9, para 1(1). The legitimate aim would be to have close understanding of the cultural context of the case.

(3) HARASSMENT

Equality Act 2010 ss 26 and 40

26 Harassment

(1) A person (A) harasses another (B) if—
  (a) A engages in unwanted conduct related to a relevant protected characteristic, and
  (b) the conduct has the purpose or effect of—
    (i) violating B's dignity, or
    (ii) creating an intimidating, hostile, degrading, humiliating or offensive environment for B.

(2) A also harasses B if—
  (a) A engages in unwanted conduct of a sexual nature, and
  (b) the conduct has the purpose or effect referred to in subsection (1)(b).

(3) A also harasses B if—
  (a) A or another person engages in unwanted conduct of a sexual nature or that is related to gender reassignment or sex,
  (b) the conduct has the purpose or effect referred to in subsection (1)(b), and
  (c) because of B's rejection of or submission to the conduct, A treats B less favourably than A would treat B if B had not rejected or submitted to the conduct.

(4) In deciding whether conduct has the effect referred to in subsection (1)(b), each of the following must be taken into account—
  (a)   the perception of B;
  (b)   the other circumstances of the case;
  (c)   whether it is reasonable for the conduct to have that effect. ...
  ...

40 Employees and applicants: harassment
  (1) An employer (A) must not, in relation to employment by A, harass a person (B)—
  (a)   who is an employee of A's;
  (b)   who has applied to A for employment.

NOTES AND QUESTIONS

1.   Together, EA 2010 ss 26 and 40 state that employers must not harass their workers. An employing entity will be vicariously liable for acts of employees.
2.   While nasty comments (like in *English*) will obviously be harassment, what else might create an offensive environment? In *Thaine v London School of Economics* [2010] ICR 1422 (EAT) Ms Thaine successfully claimed, after she was dismissed from the LSE's maintenance department, that she had been harassed. Her colleagues had put up (presumably non-gay) pornographic pictures on the wall and had required she sign into a book located in the male changing room. (A separate issue in the case was whether health and family problems had contributed to the dismissal, and whether damages should be reduced.)
3.   A Dignity at Work Bill 2001, which would have outlawed bullying in general (over protected characteristics or not) did not succeed in gaining majority support in Parliament. It is important, however, to recall that hostile, degrading or offensive treatment by an employing entity, or by colleagues which an employer fails to correct having been told, will usually constitute a breach of mutual trust and confidence.
4.   Under the Protection from Harassment Act 1997 s 1(1) a person must not pursue conduct '(a) which amounts to harassment of another, and (b) which he knows or ought to know amounts to harassment of the other'. Otherwise, whether in employment or not, this is a tort.
5.   The next case illustrates vicarious liability for employees' actions.

Majrowski v Guy's and St Thomas's NHS Trust [2006] UKHL 34

William Majrowski claimed Guy's and St Thomas's NHS trust was liable for harassment, carried out by his manager (named Sandra Freeman) under the Protection from Harassment Act (PHA) 1997 s 1. He was a gay man, and worked as a clinical auditor coordinator. The manager bullied and harassed him, and he argued this was because she was homophobic. He said this made the employer vicariously liable. There was an internal investigation, and harassment was found to have occurred, but a year later 'the Trust dismissed Mr Majrowski for reasons unrelated'. Collins J held the PHA 1997 created no statutory tort for which an employer could be vicariously liable. The House of Lords found there was a new statutory tort and the Trust was vicariously liable for the manager's homophobia.

Lord Nicholls:

9. Whatever its historical origin, this common law principle of strict liability for another person's wrongs finds its rationale today in a combination of policy factors. They are summarised in Professor Fleming's *Law of Torts*, 9th ed, (1998) pages 409–410. Stated shortly, these factors are that all forms of economic activity carry a risk of harm to others, and fairness requires that those responsible for such activities should be liable to persons suffering loss from wrongs committed in the conduct of the enterprise. This is 'fair', because it means injured persons can look for recompense to a source better placed financially than individual wrongdoing employees. It means also that the financial loss arising from the wrongs can be spread more widely, by liability insurance and higher prices. In addition, and importantly, imposing strict liability on employers encourages them to maintain standards of 'good practice' by their employees. For these reasons employers are to be held liable for wrongs committed by their employees in the course of their employment.

10. With these policy considerations in mind, it is difficult to see a coherent basis for confining the common law principle of vicarious liability to common law wrongs. The rationale underlying the principle holds good for equitable wrongs. The rationale also holds good for a wrong comprising a breach of a statutory duty or prohibition which gives rise to civil liability, provided always the statute does not expressly or impliedly indicate otherwise. A precondition of vicarious liability is that the wrong must be committed by an employee in the course of his employment. A wrong is committed in the course of employment only if the conduct is so closely connected with acts the employee is authorised to do that, for the purposes of the liability of the employer to third parties, the wrongful conduct may fairly and properly be regarded as done by the employee while acting in the course of his employment: see *Lister v Hesley Hall Ltd* [2002] 1 AC 215, 245, para 69, per Lord Millett, and *Dubai Aluminium Co Ltd v Salaam* [2002] UKHL 48, [2003] 2 AC 366, 377, para 23. If this prerequisite is satisfied the policy reasons underlying the common law principle are as much applicable to equitable wrongs and breaches of statutory obligations as they are to common law torts.

    ...

24. ... Neither the terms nor the practical effect of this legislation indicate that Parliament intended to exclude the ordinary principle of vicarious liability.

25. As to the terms of the legislation, by section 3 Parliament created a new cause of action, a new civil wrong. Damages are one of the remedies for this wrong, although they are not the primary remedy. Parliament has spelled out some particular features of this new wrong: anxiety is a head of damage, the limitation period is six years, and so on. These features do not in themselves indicate an intention to exclude vicarious liability. Vicarious liability arises only if the new wrong is committed by an employee in the course of his employment, as already described. The acts of the employee must meet the 'close connection' test. If an employee's acts of harassment meet this test, I am at a loss to see why these particular features of this newly created wrong should be thought to place this wrong in a special category in which an employer is exempt from vicarious liability. It is true that this new wrong usually comprises conduct of an intensely personal character between two individuals. But this feature may also be present with other wrongs which attract vicarious liability, such as assault.

26. Nor does imposition of criminal liability only on the perpetrator of the wrong, and on a person who aids, abets, counsels or procures the harassing conduct, point to a different conclusion. Conversion, assault and battery may attract criminal liability as well as civil liability, but this does not exclude vicarious liability.

27. I turn to the practical effect of the legislation. Vicarious liability for an employee's harassment of another person, whether a fellow employee or not, will to some extent increase employers' burdens. That is clear. But, here again, this does not suffice to show Parliament intended to exclude the ordinary common law principle of vicarious liability. Parliament added harassment to the list of civil wrongs. Parliament did so because it considered the existing law provided insufficient protection for victims of harassment. The inevitable consequence of Parliament creating this new wrong of universal application is that at times an employee will commit this wrong in the course of his employment. This prompts the question: why should an employer have a special dispensation in respect of the newly-created wrong and not be liable if an employee commits this wrong in the course of his employment? The contemporary rationale of employers' vicarious liability is as applicable to this new wrong as it is to common law torts.

28. Take a case where an employee, in the course of his employment, harasses a non-employee, such as a customer of the employer. In such a case the employer would be liable if his employee had assaulted the customer. Why should this not equally be so in respect of harassment? In principle, harassment arising from a dispute between two employees stands on the same footing. If, acting in the course of his employment, one employee assaults another, the employer is liable. Why should harassment be treated differently?

...

32. ... Harassment means, in short, engaging in unwanted conduct which has the purpose or effect of violating another person's dignity or creating an intimidating, hostile, degrading, humiliating or offensive environment for another person. ... The employer's defence is that in proceedings brought against an employer in respect of an act alleged to have been done by an employee the employer has a defence where he can prove he took such steps as were reasonably practicable steps to prevent the employee from doing that act or acts of that description. ... The Trust contrasted the availability of this defence in proceedings brought under the Race Relations Act 1976 with the position under the 1997 Act if an employer is strictly liable under the 1997 Act for harassment committed by his employees in the course of their employment. The contrast means that if an employer's liability under the 1997 Act is strict, victims of racial harassment can in some circumstances bypass the defence intended to be available to employers under the amendments made to the Race Relations Act 1976. Victims can do so by taking the simple step of bringing their harassment claims under the 1997 Act. By this means victims can also bypass the strict time limits applicable to discrimination claims.

...

38. Given this history, the existence of the employer's defence in the discrimination legislation, embracing harassment as it now does pursuant to the requirements of the directives, and the absence of such a defence from the (earlier) 1997 Act, does not assist materially in the interpretation of the 1997 Act. The discrimination legislation, as it existed in 1997, is too removed from harassment for the inclusion of the employer's defence in that legislation to throw any light on the interpretation of the 1997 Act. The accretion of harassment to the discrimination legislation derives from the directives and came later.

39. Although these later amendments to the discrimination legislation do not assist in the interpretation of the 1997 Act, it must be acknowledged that in the fields they cover they have produced a discordant and unsatisfactory overlap with the 1997 Act.

Lord Hope, Lady Hale, Lord Carswell and **Lord Brown** concurred.

NOTES AND QUESTIONS

1. The House of Lords unanimously holds that the PHA 1997 creates a statutory tort, for which an employing entity will be vicariously liable.
2. The Enterprise and Regulatory Reform Act 2013 chose to remove two subsections from EA 2010 s 40 which stated that (2) employers are liable for third-party harassment if the employer does not take reasonable steps, and (3) it needs to happen twice or more, the employer must be aware, and it does not matter if the third party is the same or a different person. Arguably, this simply codified a common law position on liability for harassment. Now it has been removed it seems fair to suggest there is no need for there to have been two occasions or more of which an employer is aware, if the employer is obviously reckless or negligent, or an instance was reasonably foreseeable and serious.
3. In *Burton and Rheule v De Vere Hotels* [1997] ICR 151, black waitresses were subjected to racist jokes at a 'comedy' performance by a man called Bernard Manning. It was held that the employers had discriminated against the staff. The reasoning was reviewed by the House of Lords in *Pearce v The Governing Body of Mayfield Secondary School* [2003] UKHL 34 and criticised on the basis that an employer might not have actually 'discriminated' against its staff by failing to stop the harassment, because white people might have been subjected to the same abuse. At the time, however, a comparator was necessary for harassment to be made out: now harassment is simply formulated as a tort. So, it would seem that an employer who fails to take steps to prevent customers or third parties is 'creating an intimidating ... [etc] environment' for the employees under s 26(1)(ii). The so called 'bastard defence' (the culprit would have been a bastard to everyone equally) is gone.

(4) VICTIMISATION

Equality Act 2010 s 27

27 Victimisation

(1) A person (A) victimises another person (B) if A subjects B to a detriment because—
    (a)   B does a protected act, or
    (b)   A believes that B has done, or may do, a protected act.

(2) Each of the following is a protected act—
    (a)   bringing proceedings under this Act;
    (b)   giving evidence or information in connection with proceedings under this Act;
    (c)   doing any other thing for the purposes of or in connection with this Act;
    (d)   making an allegation (whether or not express) that A or another person has contravened this Act.

(3) Giving false evidence or information, or making a false allegation, is not a protected act if the evidence or information is given, or the allegation is made, in bad faith.

1.   Together with EA 2010 ss 39(3)–(4) above, s 27 provision is meant to ensure people are not persecuted for exercising their legal rights. In practice, however, a further right to sue is probably not going to be as effective in protecting people as ensuring they have a voice at work, through good union representation, in the first place.

2.   What counts as 'detriment'? In *Chief Constable of West Yorkshire Police v Khan* [2001] UKHL 48 the House of Lords rejected Mr Khan's claim that refusal by the police to give him a reference, after he brought a race discrimination claim, was victimisation. Lord Nicholls stated at 31 that the employing entity 'needs to take steps to preserve his position in the outstanding proceedings'. Lord Hoffmann said, at 59, they were 'adversaries in litigation. The existence of that adversarial relationship may reasonably cause the employer to behave in a way which treats the employee less favourably than someone who had not commenced such proceedings.' In other words, the detriment was justified. But was that not still detriment 'because' of the claim, and ipso facto unlawful under EA 2010 s 27(1)? The House of Lords had the chance to revisit its formulation of the answer.

St Helen's MBC v Derbyshire [2007] UKHL 16

Four hundred and seventy women had brought equal-pay claims against St Helen's MBC, and further claimed they were victimised for doing so. Most had settled, and shared a lump sum of compensation, but Ms Derbyshire with 38 others had pressed their claims. The Council had sent a letter, stating that if they pursued their claims, the budgetary problems could threaten school dinners and lead to redundancies in the workforce. It said 'the continuance of the current claims and a ruling against the council will have a severe impact on all staff'. Another letter was sent to the remaining claimants that the council 'was greatly concerned about the likely outcome of this matter as stated in the letter to all catering staff'. The Tribunal held that this was victimisation because the letter 'amounted to an attempt to induce the acquiescence of individuals despite the view of their union'. It was material that the letters were sent to individuals, rather than their legal representatives. This was intimidatory. The Court of Appeal reversed the finding, saying the letters were 'honest and reasonable' attempts to get a compromise. The House of Lords held a reasonable person would view the letters as a detriment, and therefore victimisation.

Lord Neuberger:

65. My Lords, it is with some diffidence that I suggest that, while the conclusion as expressed in paragraph 31 in *Khan* is correct, both its juridical analysis, founded as it no doubt was, on the arguments addressed to the House, and its subsequent interpretation, are not entirely satisfactory. There are two reasons for my concern, apart from the fact that, as pointed out by Lloyd LJ in paragraph 66 in the Court of Appeal, "the point which has been called the 'honest and reasonable employer' defence is not found in the legislation itself". First, the reasoning in Khan seems to me to place a somewhat uncomfortable and unclear meaning on the words "by reason that".

66. Secondly, under the victimisation provisions, it is primarily from the perspective of the alleged victim that one determines the question whether or not any "detriment" (in this case, in section 6(2)(b) of the 1975 Act) has been suffered. However, the reasoning in *Khan* suggests that the question whether a particular act can be said to amount to victimisation must be judged from the point of view of the alleged discriminator. Of course, the words "by reason that" require one to consider why the employer has taken the particular act (in this case the sending of the two letters) and to that extent one must assess the alleged act of victimisation from the employer's point of view. However, in considering whether the act has caused detriment, one must view the issue from the point of view of the alleged victim.

67. In that connection, Brightman LJ said in *Ministry of Defence v Jeremiah* [1980] ICR 13 at 31 that "a detriment exists if a reasonable worker would or might take the view that the [treatment] was in all the circumstances to his detriment". That observation was cited with apparent approval by Lord Hoffmann in Khan at paragraph 53. More recently it has been cited with approved in your Lordships' House in *Shamoon v Chief Constable of the Royal Ulster Constabulary* [2003] IRLR 285. At paragraph 35, my noble and learned friend, Lord Hope of Craighead, after referring to the observation and describing the test as being one of "materiality", also said that "an unjustified sense of grievance cannot amount to 'detriment'". In the same case, at paragraph 105, Lord Scott of Foscote, after quoting Brightman LJ's observation, added "if the victim's opinion that the treatment was to his or her detriment is a reasonable one to hold, that ought, in my opinion, to suffice".

68. In my judgment, a more satisfactory conclusion, which in practice would almost always involve identical considerations, and produce a result identical, to that in *Khan*, involves focussing on the word "detriment" rather than on the words "by reason that". If, in the course of equal pay proceedings, the employer's solicitor were to write to the employee's solicitor setting out, in appropriately measured and accurate terms, the financial or employment consequences of the claim succeeding, or the risks to the employee if the claim fails, or terms of settlement which are unattractive to the employee, I do not see how any distress thereby induced in the employee could be said to constitute "detriment" for the purposes of sections 4 and 6 of the 1975 Act, as it would not satisfy the test as formulated by Brightman LJ in *Jeremiah*, as considered and approved in your Lordships' House. An alleged victim cannot establish "detriment" merely by showing that she had suffered mental distress: before she could succeed, it would have to be objectively reasonable in all the circumstances. The bringing of an equal pay claim, however strong the claim may be, carries with it, like any other litigation inevitable distress and worry. Distress and worry which may be induced by the employer's honest and reasonable conduct in the course of his defence or in the conduct of any settlement negotiations, cannot (save, possibly, in the most unusual circumstances) constitute "detriment" for the purposes of sections 4 and 6 of the 1975 Act.

Lord Bingham, Lord Hope, Baroness Hale and **Lord Carswell** concurred.

NOTES AND QUESTIONS

1. Lord Neuberger's careful revision of the test suggests that a reasonable person must perceive a 'detriment' as such. This suggests a reasonable person would understand the position of the police in *Khan* in declining to give a reference, because they would recognise the legitimate interest described by Lord Nicholls and Lord Hoffmann.

2. In *Fecitt v NHS Manchester* [2011] EWCA Civ 1190 the Court of Appeal took the view that there is no legal wrong in employees victimising a colleague (as there is for harassment) for whistleblowing under ERA 1996 s 47B. This meant, apparently, the employing entity could not be vicariously liable for the hostile behaviour the employees faced, and was entitled to relocate the whistleblowers, rather than the people doing the victimisation. Do you think that much behaviour amounting to victimisation will inevitably be harassment at the same time?

Problem Question

Philadelphia (1993)

Andrew Beckett works as a corporate lawyer for Wyant-Wheeler. Andrew is gay. Three years ago, Andrew was in the sauna of a tennis club with four law firm colleagues, including a partner Walter Kenton, who tell crude 'jokes' about how a 'faggot' has an orgasm. After this, Andrew keeps his sexual orientation a secret for fear of persecution.

Tragically, in the last few years Andrew has contracted HIV-AIDS, a sexually transmitted disease that without anti-retroviral medicine, slowly attacks the immune system leading to death. Because Andrew was unable to secure treatment in time, his skin develops lesions (known as Kaposi's sarcoma) which are symptomatic of AIDS. The law firm partner, Walter, notices the lesions (which he knows are associated with AIDS) and asks what they are. Because Andrew fears the consequences, he says the lesions are from a sport injury.

The same week, Andrew leaves documents which must be filed for a court case with the partner's assistant a day in advance. The next day, the partner says the case documents could not be located until the last minute. Although the documents reach the court before the deadline, Andrew is summoned to a meeting and dismissed the following morning for submitting work late.

Advise Andrew on his potential claims for harassment, discrimination, the protected characteristics, the process of proof, and available remedies.

Additional Reading for Chapter 12

H Collins, 'Discrimination, Equality and Social Inclusion' (2003) 66 *MLR* 16

Collins suggests that while the rhetoric of discrimination laws is often about 'equality', there are too many deviations from the idea of equal treatment for it to provide a coherent account for equality legislation. The law requires more favourable treatment of specific groups, such as pregnant women, enables justifications for unequal treatment, and also empowers more favourable treatment for groups who are historically disadvantaged. Attempts to refine or adapt the concept of equality (eg to equal opportunity, or equal results) typically fail, and so a preferable view of the law's goals is social inclusion. Ultimately, says Collins, a 'distributive aim or criterion of fairness may be discovered in the aim of social inclusion'. The aims and concept of fairness follow evolving preferences in democratic governance. This may not provide a complete account, but is better than hanging onto equality (ironically) as a reason for (what is now) the EA 2010.

S Fredman, *Discrimination Law* (2nd edn 2011)

Fredman's classic text explores the principles of equality and discrimination law, with a weight of comparative material. Chapter 1 discusses whether general principles of equality or specific protected characteristics ought to be the focus for the law. Chapter 2 discusses the current protected characteristics. Chapter 3 argues for an expansive scope of protection in discrimination law. Chapter 4 examines the 'difficult divide' of direct and indirect discrimination. Chapter 5 discusses reverse discrimination, in different jurisdictions. Chapter 6 examines the limits of today's law, discussing the emergence of positive duties to promote equality.

A McColgan, *Discrimination, Equality and the Law* (2014)

McColgan's masterful treatise draws on a breadth of sources and jurisdictions to reassess the full scope of discrimination/equality law, particularly since the EA 2010. It argues that a regime based upon protected characteristics is 'a necessary corollary of any detailed regime'. By contrast, undefined equality clauses are liable to be subject to implied justifications and therefore cut down and misused. The number of protected grounds are not fixed, and one should focus on whether a protected characteristic remedies an unjust disadvantage. Some grounds differ, but there should be no right to discriminate based on religious or other beliefs: it may often be seen as a proxy for ethnicity.

Disadvantage

Often more insidious than overt or 'direct' discrimination are practices that apply equally to everyone in form, but in substance disadvantage some people more than others. This is known as 'indirect' discrimination in Europe, and 'disparate impact' in the United States. It could also be called 'substantive' (as opposed to formal) discrimination. As we have seen in chapter 12, direct discrimination based on race, sex, belief, disability or sexual orientation can only be justified by showing that this characteristic forms a 'genuine occupational requirement' (plus further exemptions for religious organisations and the military). But, a wider 'objective justification' allowed employing entities to show an age requirement is 'a proportionate means of achieving a legitimate aim' for the employing entity as a whole (not just for that job). This wider justification is open for indirect discrimination on the basis of race, sex, belief, disability and sexual orientation. Even if an employing entity has acted in good faith, and with the best of intentions, if its practices have a discriminatory impact, it must review them to ensure everyone has an equal opportunity. The law's purpose is to remove social disadvantage.

The reality, however, is that most social disadvantage begins some time before people apply for jobs or in the workplace. Education and training of the same quality, with the same investment, is not open to everyone: there is sex segregation and wealth discrimination from pre-school, and since the Teaching and Higher Education Act 1998, up to university. For example, the seven schools listed in the so-called Public Schools Act 1868 were traditionally all for boys, and had fees barring entry to children from low-income families, or children with no families. This is not altered by scholarships for a few students. Rugby and Shrewsbury did permit girls after 1995 and 2014, while Charterhouse and Westminster permit girls in the sixth form. Eton, Harrow and Winchester remain sexually segregated. All segregate children on the basis of wealth. On religion, only Charterhouse is non-Anglican. The UK government has spread this model to many free state schools (on religion and gender) and universities (on wealth), despite overwhelming international evidence that segregated education is inferior. The Equality Act (EA) 2010 does not yet prevent religion, gender or wealth discrimination in education (see ss 4 and 85(1) but then Sch 11), so it may be unsurprising to see problems persist in the workplace. Notably, the gender pay gap in the UK remains at 19.2 per cent across all professions.[1] This makes it a considerable concern that the rules on gender pay discrimination are actually less favourable than the general scheme for pay claims for other protected characteristics.

This chapter sets out (1) general indirect discrimination claims and justifications, and (2) the alternative structure, with reduced protection, in claims for gender pay equality.

Introductory texts: Collins ch 3. CEM ch 9 (331–7, 360–4). D&M ch 6 (629–45, 695–730).

(1) INDIRECT DISCRIMINATION

(a) Particular Disadvantage of Neutral Practices

The test for indirect discrimination follows the Equality Framework Directive 2000 (2000/78/EC) Art 2(2)(b), and identical provisions in the Race Equality Directive 2000 Art 2(2)(b) and the Equal Treatment Directive 2006 Art 2(1)(b) which deals with sex. Indirect discrimination is 'where an apparently neutral provision, criterion or practice' would put people 'at a particular disadvantage compared with' others unless it is 'objectively justified by a legitimate aim and the means of achieving that aim are appropriate and necessary'. This has been translated into UK law as follows.

Equality Act 2010 s 19

19 **Indirect discrimination**

(1) A person (A) discriminates against another (B) if A applies to B a provision, criterion or practice which is discriminatory in relation to a relevant protected characteristic of B's.

(2) For the purposes of subsection (1), a provision, criterion or practice is discriminatory in relation to a relevant protected characteristic of B's if—

  (a) A applies, or would apply, it to persons with whom B does not share the characteristic,

  (b) it puts, or would put, persons with whom B shares the characteristic at a particular disadvantage when compared with persons with whom B does not share it,

  (c) it puts, or would put, B at that disadvantage, and

  (d) A cannot show it to be a proportionate means of achieving a legitimate aim.

NOTES AND QUESTIONS

1.   Both EU and UK law define indirect discrimination in essence as (1) a formally neutral practice that (2) puts people of a protected group at a 'particular disadvantage' compared to others, and (3) is not objectively justified, ie 'a proportionate means of achieving a legitimate aim'.

2.   The phrase 'provision, criterion or practice' (often abbreviated to PCP) seems to be intended to catch anything an employing entity could do that has the *effect* of discriminating against job applicants or employees. Forms of practice are irrelevant.

---

[1] House of Commons Women and Equalities Committee, *Gender Pay Gap* (2016) HC 584, 5.

3.   What, exactly, proves that a group suffers a 'particular disadvantage' compared to others? Suppose an employing entity says that, from Monday, all employees who are not 165 cm (5 feet, 5 inches) tall will be dismissed. This is not a practice that distinguishes between people based on gender, but it turns out that in a workforce of 10 men and 10 women, all the men, but only 5 of the women, were over 165 cm tall. This supposedly neutral practice puts women at a particular disadvantage. Unless the employer can show that it became a proportionate (ie appropriate, necessary and reasonable) means to pursue a legitimate aim on Monday (unlikely!), there is indirect discrimination.

4.   The next case explores the necessary steps of reasoning in an indirect discrimination case. It was brought against the UK government, rather than an employer.

R (Seymour-Smith) v SS for Employment [2000] UKHL 12

Ms Nicole Seymour-Smith and Ms Perez claimed it was indirect sex discrimination for the Secretary of State for Employment, in the Unfair Dismissal (Variation of Qualifying Period) Order 1985, to raise the qualifying period for unfair dismissal from one to two years, contrary to TEEC Art 119 (now TFEU Art 157). Ms Seymour-Smith was dismissed in 1991 from Christo & Co after 15 months, and Ms Perez was dismissed by Matthew Stone Restoration after 15 months and 6 days. Although the gap was beginning to narrow, statistically fewer women had jobs that lasted as long as for men, in data from 1985 to 1991. The High Court held that the differences between men and women were not sufficient. The Court of Appeal held that they were, and there was no objective justification. On a preliminary reference from the House of Lords, the European Court of Justice (1999) C-167/97 held that evidence, including statistics, would be needed and even 'lesser but persistent and relatively constant disparity' would suffice for a finding of indirect discrimination. To objectively justify a disadvantage, responding to the government argument that raising the qualifying period would promote jobs, at [76] it held mere 'generalisations concerning the capacity of a specific measure to encourage recruitment are not enough to show that the aim of the disputed rule is unrelated to any discrimination'. The House of Lords held by a majority that women were placed at a particular disadvantage, but on the evidence available in 1985, there was an objective justification.

Lord Nicholls:

[49] This is not a case of direct discrimination. The 1985 Order drew no distinction between men and women. The contention of Ms. Seymour-Smith and Ms. Perez is that the Order was indirectly discriminatory, because it introduced a qualifying condition which bore more hardly on women than men. Women were treated less favourably than men, because the proportion of women who could comply with the two year qualifying period was smaller than the proportion of men. Before your Lordships two issues arise for decision. The first is whether, at the time of the dismissal of Ms. Seymour-Smith and Ms. Perez in 1991, the 1985 Order did have a disparately adverse impact on women. If it did, the second issue calling for decision is whether the differential impact was objectively justified.

Disparately adverse impact

[50] One of the questions referred by your Lordships' House to the European Court sought guidance on the legal test for establishing whether a measure adopted by a member state

has such a degree of disparate effect as between men and women as to amount to indirect discrimination for the purposes of article 119. ... The European Court, it was submitted, wavered uncertainly between what must be established as a substantive criterion and the evidence needed for that purpose. In paragraph [60] the Court referred to statistical evidence that "a considerably smaller percentage of women than men is able to satisfy the condition", and treated this as evidence of apparent sex discrimination calling for justification. However, in the next paragraph the Court observed that statistical evidence revealing "a lesser but persistent and relatively constant disparity over a long period" could also be evidence of apparent sex discrimination. In paragraph [61], unlike paragraph [60], the Court gave no guidance on the extent of statistical disparity required to establish apparent sex discrimination. ...

[51] ... A considerable disparity can be more readily established if the statistical evidence covers a long period and the figures show a persistent and relatively constant disparity. In such a case a lesser statistical disparity may suffice to show that the disparity is considerable than if the statistics cover only a short period or if they present an uneven picture.

...

[53] Before your Lordships it was common ground that 1991, not 1985, was the relevant date for the purpose of the issue now being considered. The position at this later date was not considered by the European Court. I turn to the available statistics, covering the period from 1985 to 1993, extracted from the annual labour force surveys.

Year	Percentage of men with more than 2 years	Percentage of women with more than 2 years	Disparity
1985	77.4	68.9	8.5
1986	77.2	68.4	8.8
1987	75.3	67.1	8.2
1988	73.4	65.6	7.8
1989	72	63.8	8.2
1990	72.5	64.1	8.4
1991	74.5	67.4	7.1
1992	77.9	72.1	5.8
1993	78.4	74.1	4.3

[54] These figures show that over the period of seven years, from 1985 up to and including 1991, the ratio of men and women who qualified was roughly 10:9. For every 10 men who qualified, only nine women did so. This disparity was remarkably constant for the six years from 1985 to 1990, but it began to diminish in 1991.

[55] These figures are in borderline country. The question under consideration is one of degree. When the borderline is defined by reference to a criterion as imprecise as "considerably smaller" it is inevitable that in some cases different minds may reach different conclusions. The decisions of the two courts below illustrate this. My own impression differs from the majority of your Lordships. I find myself driven to the conclusion that a persistent and constant disparity of the order just mentioned in respect of the entire male and female labour forces of the country over a period of seven years cannot be brushed aside and dismissed as insignificant or inconsiderable. I agree with the Court of Appeal that, given the context of equality of pay or treatment, the latitude afforded by the word "considerably" should not be exaggerated. I think these

figures are adequate to demonstrate that the extension of the qualifying period had a considerably greater adverse impact on women than men.

...

[67] Accordingly, if the Government introduces a measure which proves to have a disparately adverse impact on women, the Government is under a duty to take reasonable steps to monitor the working of the measure. The Government must review the position periodically. The greater the disparity of impact, the greater the diligence which can reasonably be expected of the Government. Depending on the circumstances, the Government may become obliged to repeal or replace the unsuccessful measure.

[68] In the present case the 1985 Order had been in operation for six years when the two claimants were dismissed from their jobs. The Divisional Court and the Court of Appeal noted there was no evidence that the extension of the qualifying period in 1985 led to an increase in employment opportunities. Ought the government to have taken steps to repeal the 1985 Order before 1991? In other words, had the Order, lawful at its inception, become unlawful by 1991?

[69] Here again, the matter is debatable. As time passed, the persistently adverse impact on women became apparent. But, as with the broad margin of discretion afforded to governments when adopting measures of this type, so with the duty of governments to monitor the implementation of such measures: the practicalities of government must be borne in mind. The benefits of the 1985 Order could not be expected to materialise overnight, or even in a matter of months. The government was entitled to allow a reasonable period to elapse before deciding whether the Order had achieved its objective and, if not, whether the Order should be replaced with some other measure or simply repealed. Time would then be needed to implement any decision. I do not think the government could reasonably be expected to complete all these steps in six years, failing which it was in breach of Community law. The contrary view would impose an unrealistic burden on the government in the present case. Accordingly I consider the Secretary of State discharged the burden of showing that the 1985 Order was still objectively justified in 1991.

Lord Goff and **Lord Jauncey** concurred with **Lord Nicholls**.

Lord Slynn dissented on the reasoning, and would have held there was no particular disadvantage to women. **Lord Steyn** concurred in that dissent.

NOTES AND QUESTIONS

1. The majority of the House of Lords held that, while the disparity between women and men who qualified for unfair dismissal rights was 'borderline' (at between 4.3 and 8.8 per cent of all employees), the gap was 'persistent and constant' and could therefore not be 'brushed aside'. Nevertheless, because of the state of evidence about promoting job opportunities, the government discharged the burden of showing it was a proportionate means of achieving a legitimate aim. Do you think the evidence has changed today?

2. How many percentage points is enough to show particular disadvantage? There is no clear answer. Lord Nicholls noted that the Court of Justice did not specify a percentage. Interestingly, the Commission had proposed a 'statistically significant' test. This refers to a well-understood concept in social science, and was

originally discussed by the US Supreme Court in *Castaneda v Partida*, 430 US 482 (1977) per Blackmun J, fn 17, and *Hazelwood School District v US*, 433 US 299 (1977) per Stewart J, fn 14. Usually, a discrepancy over 5 per cent would establish statistical significance. Alternatively two or three 'standard deviations' (eg how far women compared to men are from the qualifying time for average people, using some basic calculus, on a population distribution curve) would suffice. These tests would establish prima facie indirect discrimination. Do you understand how this might work in practice? If so, what do you think would be the advantages or disadvantages of formally adopting statistical methods in law?

3. Presumably, neither Labour nor Conservative governments were particularly concerned about the equality impact of the unfair dismissal qualifying period. They simply wished to be more or less protective to workers or business. Can you think of a more principled way to settle the issue of regulating fair dismissal rights?

4. In *Jones v University of Manchester* [1993] ICR 474 the Court of Appeal agreed that Ms Jones was entitled to claim indirect sex discrimination, when a job was limited to graduate applicants aged 27–35. She was 44 and acquired a degree as a mature student. Balcombe LJ held that, so long as she proved the necessary statistical facts (that significantly more women than men were mature students) this could found indirect discrimination and would need to be justified.

5. In *Rutherford v Secretary of State for Trade and Industry* [2006] UKHL 19, Mr Rutherford claimed that a former rule, which prevented claims for unfair dismissal and redundancy for people reaching retirement, amounted to indirect sex discrimination. Over 65 years of age, 7.6% of men and 3.4% of women were economically active. The House of Lords held there was not a sufficient number of adversely impacted men compared to women to ground a claim.

6. In contrast to discrimination by the government, the next case concerned a discriminatory policy of an employing entity.

Homer v Chief Constable of West Yorkshire Police [2012] UKSC 15

Mr Homer, age 62, claimed indirect age discrimination against the Chief Constable, after a new rule required a law degree to be promoted to the highest pay grade. Mr Homer had worked as a legal adviser since 1995, then age 51, for the Police National Legal Database, when he could either have a law degree or 'exceptional experience in criminal law with a lesser qualification'. After a 2005 review, a law degree would be required. Under (what is now) EA 2010 ss 5, 19 and 39, Mr Homer claimed this put him at a particular disadvantage because the normal retirement age was 65, and a law degree would take at least four years part-time for him to acquire. His internal grievance appeals in 2006 were turned down. The Tribunal allowed his claim in 2008. In 2009 at the Employment Appeal Tribunal Elias J held there was no disadvantage because it was not intrinsically more difficult for older people to get law degrees and, apparently, the consequences related to Mr Homer's retirement age but were not age discrimination. This was upheld by the Court of Appeal in 2009. The Supreme Court held Mr Homer was put at a particular disadvantage and remitted the case to Tribunal to decide whether there was an objective justification.

Lady Hale (with whom **Lord Brown** and **Lord Kerr** agreed):

12. The EAT and Court of Appeal were however persuaded that what put Mr Homer at a disadvantage was not his age but his impending retirement. Had it not been for that, he would have been able to obtain a degree and reach the third threshold. As Mr Lewis argues on behalf of the respondent, the key words in regulation 3(1)(b) are "puts at". What is it that puts him at – or causes – the disadvantage complained of? It is the fact that he is due to leave work within a few years. Regulation 3(2) requires that the relevant circumstances in the complainant's case must be the same, or not materially different, from the circumstances in the case of the persons with whom he is compared. So, argues Mr Lewis, you have to build the relevant circumstance into the comparator group also, in this case the proximity of leaving work. So Mr Homer must be compared with anyone else who is nearing the end of his employment for whatever reason. Anyone who was contemplating leaving within a similar period – whether for family reasons or some other reason – would face the same difficulty. That is what puts him at a disadvantage and not the age group to which he belongs. Indeed, what Mr Homer is arguing for would put people of his age group at an advantage compared with younger people, because they would be able to get the benefits of the third threshold without having a law degree when others would not.

13. This argument involves taking the particular disadvantage which is suffered by a particular age group for a reason which is related to their age and equating it with a similar disadvantage which is suffered by others but for a completely different reason unrelated to their age. If it were translated into other contexts it would have alarming consequences for the law of discrimination generally. Take, for example, a requirement that employees in a particular job must have a beard. This puts women at a particular disadvantage because very few of them are able to grow a beard. But the argument leaves sex out of account and says that it is the inability to grow a beard which puts women at a particular disadvantage and so they must be compared with other people who for whatever reason, whether it be illness or immaturity, are unable to grow a beard.

14. Ironically, it is perhaps easier to make the argument under the current formulation of the concept of indirect discrimination, which is now also to be found in the Equality Act 2010. Previous formulations relied upon disparate impact – so that if there was a significant disparity in the proportion of men affected by a requirement who could comply with it and the proportion of women who could do so, then that constituted indirect discrimination. But, as Mr Allen points out on behalf of Mr Homer, the new formulation was not intended to make it more difficult to establish indirect discrimination: quite the reverse (see the helpful account of Sir Bob Hepple in Equality: the New Legal Framework, Hart 2011, pp 64 to 68). It was intended to do away with the need for statistical comparisons where no statistics might exist. It was intended to do away with the complexities involved in identifying those who could comply and those who could not and how great the disparity had to be. Now all that is needed is a particular disadvantage when compared with other people who do not share the characteristic in question. It was not intended to lead us to ignore the fact that certain protected characteristics are more likely to be associated with particular disadvantages.

15. In any event, it cannot be right to equate leaving work because of impending retirement with other reasons for doing so. They are materially different. A person who leaves work for family reasons or takes early retirement generally has some choice in the matter. Indeed, she may factor into her decision whether it would be advisable to obtain the law degree and with it the higher grading before doing so. A person who is coming up against the mandatory retirement age does not have the same choice. Any extension depends upon the decision of the employer which cannot be depended upon at the relevant time. At the relevant time for this

case, regulation 30 of the Age Regulations provided that the decision to retire an employee at the age of 65 did not need to be justified. Hence, as Mr Allen puts it, this is a case of running up against the buffers of a mandatory retirement age rather than a matter of choice.

16. Nor is this a question of asking for more favourable treatment for people of their age. It obviously has to be possible to cure the discrimination in a non-discriminatory way. In *London Underground Ltd v Edwards (No 2)* [1999] ICR 494, for example, the new rosters for underground train drivers were held to be indirectly discriminatory because all the men could comply with them but not all the women could do so: it was a "striking fact" that not a single man was disadvantaged despite the overwhelming preponderance of men in the pool of train drivers affected. The reason, of course, was that the new rosters had a greater impact upon single parents and single parents are predominantly (though not exclusively) female. But the problem could be solved, not by making an exception for the women, but by making arrangements for single parents of whatever sex. This problem could have been solved by making arrangements for people appointed before the new criterion was introduced.

17. Ingenious though the argument put forward by Mr Lewis is, therefore, to my mind it is too ingenious. The law of indirect discrimination is an attempt to level the playing field by subjecting to scrutiny requirements which look neutral on their face but in reality work to the comparative disadvantage of people with a particular protected characteristic. A requirement which works to the comparative disadvantage of a person approaching compulsory retirement age is indirectly discriminatory on grounds of age. There is, as Lord Justice Maurice Kay acknowledged, "unreality in differentiating between age and retirement" [34]. Put simply, the reason for the disadvantage was that people in this age group did not have time to acquire a law degree. And the reason why they did not have time to acquire a law degree was that they were soon to reach the age of retirement. The resulting scrutiny may ultimately lead to the conclusion that the requirement can be justified. But if it cannot, then it can be modified so as to remove the disadvantage.

    ...

22. The ET (perhaps in reliance on the IDS handbook on age discrimination) regarded the terms "appropriate", "necessary" and "proportionate" as "equally interchangeable" [29, 31]. It is clear from the European and domestic jurisprudence cited above that this is not correct. Although the regulation refers only to a "proportionate means of achieving a legitimate aim", this has to be read in the light of the Directive which it implements. To be proportionate, a measure has to be both an appropriate means of achieving the legitimate aim and (reasonably) necessary in order to do so. Some measures may simply be inappropriate to the aim in question: thus, for example, the aim of rewarding experience is not achieved by age related pay scales which apply irrespective of experience (*Hennigs v Eisenbahn-Bundesamt; Land Berlin v Mai*, Joined Cases C-297/10 and C-298/10 [2012] 1 CMLR 18); the aim of making it easier to recruit young people is not achieved by a measure which applies long after the employees have ceased to be young (*Kücükdeveci v Swedex GmbH & Co KG*, Case C-555/07, [2011] 2 CMLR 33). So it has to be asked whether requiring existing employees to have a law degree before they can achieve the highest grade is appropriate to the aims of recruiting and retaining new staff or retaining existing staff within the organisation. The EAT expressed some scepticism about this [45, 46].

23. A measure may be appropriate to achieving the aim but go further than is (reasonably) necessary in order to do so and thus be disproportionate. The EAT suggested that "what has to be justified is the discriminatory effect of the unacceptable criterion" [44]. Mr Lewis points out that this is incorrect: both the Directive and the Regulations require that the criterion itself be justified rather than that its discriminatory effect be justified (there may well be a difference here between justification under the anti-discrimination law derived from the European

Union and the justification of discrimination in the enjoyment of convention rights under the European Convention of Human Rights).

24. Part of the assessment of whether the criterion can be justified entails a comparison of the impact of that criterion upon the affected group as against the importance of the aim to the employer. That comparison was lacking, both in the ET and in the EAT. Mr Homer (and anyone else in his position, had there been someone) was not being sacked or downgraded for not having a law degree. He was merely being denied the additional benefits associated with being at the highest grade. The most important benefit in practice is likely to have been the impact upon his final salary and thus upon the retirement pension to which he became entitled. So it has to be asked whether it was reasonably necessary in order to achieve the legitimate aims of the scheme to deny those benefits to people in his position? The ET did not ask itself that question.

Lord Hope:

30. It was submitted that to exclude Mr Homer from the requirement to obtain a law degree would be to give him a benefit that was not available to others. It is true that this would have meant that he would not have to go to the trouble of studying and preparing for the examinations. Nor would he have to wait until he had passed the examinations before he got the benefit. But I cannot accept that discrimination on the grounds of age can be regarded as justified simply because eliminating it would put others at a disadvantage that is not related to their age. Any reversal of a discriminatory rule or practice that does not treat everyone equally is likely to have an impact on others which, from their point of view, may seem to be to their disadvantage. This is especially so in the case of age discrimination, where a measure that affects some will inevitably affect others differently. We all grow older as we progress through life. Age is a characteristic which changes with time. A disadvantage to others which is unrelated to their age will not be a ground in itself for holding that the age-related discrimination of the person who complains of it must be regarded as justified.

Lord Mance:

36. ... there was no objective need for an employee as experienced, skilled and knowledgeable as Mr Homer to have had a law degree in order to qualify at the third threshold, then there may have been employees, with more than five years to go to retirement and so with sufficient years ahead in which to complete a law degree, whose experience, skill and knowledge would also have made such a requirement unnecessary. An exception for Mr Homer personally, or a general exception for employees within four or five years of retirement age, could have discriminated unjustifiably against such younger employees on grounds of age.

NOTES AND QUESTIONS

1. The Supreme Court, unanimously disapproving the judgment of Elias J in the EAT and the Court of Appeal, reasons the new requirement for a law degree did affect Mr Homer indirectly because of his age, and unanimously rejected that his retirement date was a somehow unrelated 'true' cause. Given their opinions, it seemed likely they believed the requirement was not objectively justified.

2. It may be worth noting that Mr Homer's case, from the grievance procedure to the Supreme Court, took longer to complete than his part-time law degree would have done.

3. Why do you think the police force required a degree that was probably unnecessary for the job at hand?

4. The EA 2010 s 14, which was not brought into force after the 2010 general election, would explicitly prohibit 'combined discrimination', though it is doubtful this was needed. This relates to what is called 'intersectionality' in a large literature starting in the United States, that social disadvantage may be compounded for people who are in multiple minority groups: see K Crenshaw, 'Mapping the Margins: Intersectionality, Identity Politics, and Violence against Women of Color' (1991) *43(6) Stanford Law Review* 1241. For example, suppose a defendant has nothing against white people in particular, and nothing against men in particular, but just really hates white men. The defendant does not give a white male employee a Christmas bonus, but does give one to everybody else. In *Bahl v Law Society* [2004] EWCA Civ 1070 obiter dicta remarks were made that claims for combined discrimination could not be brought. In effect it was suggested that, to follow the example above, the white male claimant might not succeed because the employer could say they were giving a black male comparator a bonus, and a white woman comparator a bonus, so the fact that the white man did not get one was not due to race or gender. Quite apart from the law's policy, or whether this is logically sound, it seems clear that if nothing else there is indirect discrimination: the practice of not giving a bonus to white men would seem to put both white people and men at a particular disadvantage (and would not seem to be justified). Therefore, EA 2010 s 14 merely restates what is inherent in the law.

5. The idea that combined discrimination is already unlawful was applied in *Ministry of Defence v DeBique* [2010] IRLR 471 (EAT). Cox J held at [164]–[170] that the combined disadvantages of the Ministry's rules to the claimant, as a woman of Vincentian origin who was a single parent, enabled an indirect discrimination claim.

(b) Objective Justification

As *Seymour-Smith* and *Homer* already illustrated, if a practice puts a group at a particular disadvantage, an employing entity may still argue it pursues a legitimate aim, and its actions are proportionate towards that aim. The 'proportionality' test usually has three elements, requiring the practice is (1) appropriate, (2) necessary and (3) reasonable. 'Appropriate' or 'suitable' means the practice must fit the goal. 'Necessary' means that no other method can be found to reach the aim that has a less discriminatory impact: does it go further than needed? If this does not work, a practice could still be judged 'unreasonable' by disproportionately balancing between the interests of the claimant and defendant. This structure of reasoning is widely applied in European law, having systematically originated in Germany (see BVerfGE 3, 383, 399 (1954)). This said, the original case under the US Civil Rights Act of 1964 in Title VII on employment (codified at 42 USC §2000e-2), which developed disparate impact and justification, is still highly instructive.

Griggs v Duke Power Co, 401 US 424 (1971)

Griggs and his colleagues claimed that a requirement to have a high-school diploma or pass an 'intelligence' test was unlawful discrimination. Before the Civil Rights Act of 1964 ended racial segregation, the Duke Power Co in North Carolina had not employed black workers, except in its Labor Department. Afterwards, the Duke Power Co introduced its diploma or test requirements for all departments. Because of chronic school underfunding in southern US states, and particularly in segregated schools for black children, only 34 per cent of white men, but just 12 per cent of black men had high-school diplomas. The company's two 'intelligence' tests, named the 'Wonderlic Personnel Test' and the 'Bennett Mechanical Comprehension Test', were unrelated to the jobs performed in the Duke Power Labor Department. In practice, these requirements confined most black applicants to the Labor Department, where jobs were lower paid than in Coal Handling, Operations, Maintenance, and Laboratory and Test. The US Supreme Court held that the diploma and test requirements, though facially neutral, had a disparate impact on black people and were not justified by business necessity.

Burger CJ:

[10] The Court of Appeals' opinion, and the partial dissent, agreed that, on the record in the present case, 'whites register far better on the Company's alternative requirements' than Negroes.[2] 420 F.2d 1225, 1239 n. 6. This consequence would appear to be directly traceable to race. Basic intelligence must have the means of articulation to manifest itself fairly in a testing process. Because they are Negroes, petitioners have long received inferior education in segregated schools and this Court expressly recognized these differences in *Gaston County v United States*, 395 US 285 ... (1969). There, because of the inferior education received by Negroes in North Carolina, this Court barred the institution of a literacy test for voter registration on the ground that the test would abridge the right to vote indirectly on account of race. Congress did not intend by Title VII, however, to guarantee a job to every person regardless of qualifications. In short, the Act does not command that any person be hired simply because he was formerly the subject of discrimination, or because he is a member of a minority group. Discriminatory preference for any group, minority or majority, is precisely and only what Congress has proscribed. What is required by Congress is the removal of artificial, arbitrary, and unnecessary barriers to employment when the barriers operate invidiously to discriminate on the basis of racial or other impermissible classification.

[11] Congress has now provided that tests or criteria for employment or promotion may not provide equality of opportunity merely in the sense of the fabled offer of milk to the stork and the fox. On the contrary, Congress has now required that the posture and condition of the job-seeker be taken into account. It has – to resort again to the fable – provided that the vessel in which the milk is proffered be one all seekers can use. The Act proscribes not only overt

---

[2] In North Carolina, 1960 census statistics show that, while 34% of white males had completed high school, only 12% of Negro males had done so. U.S. Bureau of the Census, U.S. Census of Population: 1960, Vol. 1, Characteristics of the Population, pt. 35, Table 47.

Similarly, with respect to standardized tests, the EEOC in one case found that use of a battery of tests, including the Wonderlic and Bennett tests used by the Company in the instant case, resulted in 58% of whites passing the tests, as compared with only 6% of the blacks. Decision of EEOC, CCH Empl.Prac. Guide, 17,304.53 (Dec. 2, 1966). See also Decision of EEOC 70 – 552, CCH Empl.Prac. Guide, 6139 (Feb. 19, 1970).

discrimination but also practices that are fair in form, but discriminatory in operation. The touchstone is business necessity. If an employment practice which operates to exclude Negroes cannot be shown to be related to job performance, the practice is prohibited.

[12] On the record before us, neither the high school completion requirement nor the general intelligence test is shown to bear a demonstrable relationship to successful performance of the jobs for which it was used. Both were adopted, as the Court of Appeals noted, without meaningful study of their relationship to job-performance ability. Rather, a vice president of the Company testified, the requirements were instituted on the Company's judgment that they generally would improve the overall quality of the work force.

[13] The evidence, however, shows that employees who have not completed high school or taken the tests have continued to perform satisfactorily and make progress in departments for which the high school and test criteria are now used.[3] The promotion record of present employees who would not be able to meet the new criteria thus suggests the possibility that the requirements may not be needed even for the limited purpose of preserving the avowed policy of advancement within the Company. In the context of this case, it is unnecessary to reach the question whether testing requirements that take into account capability for the next succeeding position or related future promotion might be utilized upon a showing that such long-range requirements fulfill a genuine business need. In the present case the Company has made no such showing.

[14] The Court of Appeals held that the Company had adopted the diploma and test requirements without any 'intention to discriminate against Negro employees.' 420 F.2d, at 1232. We do not suggest that either the District Court or the Court of Appeals erred in examining the employer's intent; but good intent or absence of discriminatory intent does not redeem employment procedures or testing mechanisms that operate as 'built-in headwinds' for minority groups and are unrelated to measuring job capability.

[15] The Company's lack of discriminatory intent is suggested by special efforts to help the undereducated employees through Company financing of two-thirds the cost of tuition for high school training. But Congress directed the thrust of the Act to the consequences of employment practices, not simply the motivation. More than that, Congress has placed on the employer the burden of showing that any given requirement must have a manifest relationship to the employment in question.

[16] The facts of this case demonstrate the inadequacy of broad and general testing devices as well as the infirmity of using diplomas or degrees as fixed measures of capability. History is filled with examples of men and women who rendered highly effective performance without the conventional badges of accomplishment in terms of certificates, diplomas, or degrees. Diplomas and tests are useful servants, but Congress has mandated the commonsense proposition that they are not to become masters of reality.

Black J, Douglas J, Harlan II J, Stewart J, White J, Marshall J and **Blackmun J** joined.

---

[3] For example, between July 2, 1965, and November 14, 1966, the percentage of white employees who were promoted but who were not high school graduates was nearly identical to the percentage of nongraduates in the entire white work force.

1.   A unanimous US Supreme Court in 1971 held that, even though there was not yet a codified provision on indirect discrimination in the law at the time, discrimination in substance was also prohibited. The justification test used by the US Supreme Court was framed as 'business necessity' that is related to 'job performance'.

2.   Between *Griggs* and *Ricci v DeStefano* 557 US 557 (2009) the US Supreme Court had become dominated by Republican appointees who displayed consistent hostility to equality, labour rights and democracy. In *Ricci*, five judges to four held it was unlawful for the City of New Haven, which employed firefighters, to discard test results that the City had concluded may have had a racially discriminatory impact. Going further than the majority, Scalia J said the indirect discrimination concept was (in his opinion) unconstitutional unless it entailed a good-faith defence. His logic was that requiring employing entities to alter their policies, in a way which is sensitive to equal opportunity, was itself 'racial decisionmaking' and that 'is … discriminatory.' Do you agree that equal racial opportunity is less advantageous to white people than a society dominated by white people? Or, is everyone better off by living in an equal society?

3.   Engaging similar issues to *Griggs*, but with a very different turns in argument, was *Essop v Home Office* and *Naeem v Secretary of State for Justice* [2017] UKSC 27. Mr Essop and 49 others claimed that a 'Core Skills Assessment' used for promotion at the UK Border Agency was indirectly discriminatory. Staff over 35 years old were 37.4 per cent less likely to pass, and BME staff were 40.3 per cent less likely to pass, than young or white people. The Home Office had no adequate explanation why. Sir Colin Rimer in the Court of Appeal held the claimants have to prove the reason why there was a lower pass rate, before being able to establish that there was a particular disadvantage. The Supreme Court unanimously rejected this: Lady Hale held it was enough to show a statistical disparity, and no need to prove the reason, at [24]–[25]. The disparity had then to be justified (or the practice removed). Lady Hale remarked at [29]: 'The requirement to justify a PCP should not be seen as placing an unreasonable burden upon respondents. Nor should it be seen as casting some sort of shadow or stigma upon them. There is no shame in it. There may well be very good reasons for the PCP in question – fitness levels in fire-fighters or policemen spring to mind. But … a wise employer will monitor how his policies and practices impact upon various groups and, if he finds that they do have a disparate impact, will try and see what can be modified to remove that impact while achieving the desired result.' In a joined case, Mr Naeem claimed he and other Muslim imams working at the Prison Service were indirectly discriminated against, because their average pay was lower than Christian chaplains. If Muslim imams and Christian chaplains began work at the same time, they would all be paid the same. But because Muslim imams had been only employed on a sessional basis before 2002 (it was thought that there were not enough Muslims in prison to justify full time imams before then), on average imams length of service was lower, leading to lower average pay. After 2002, the Prison Service committed to equalising length of service requirements and pay

> over a number of years. The Tribunal accepted that it did so proportionately, and the Supreme Court held that its finding of justification for the particular disadvantage was justified.
>
> 4.   The UK and EU concepts of 'objective justification' are wider than justifications in the United States: the leading example is found in *Ladele*, joined to *Eweida* below.

Eweida v United Kingdom [2013] ECHR 37

With three others, Ms Eweida claimed that UK law on religious discrimination protection was incompatible with ECHR Arts 9 (freedom of religion) and 14 (equality). Ms Eweida, a Coptic Christian, wore a neckless with a cross in her air hostess job at British Airways plc. After a uniform change, the cross was visible. She was instructed to take it off, and sent home when she refused. In a contrasting workplace, Ms Chaplin claimed that an instruction not to wear a cross at her job with the Royal Devon and Exeter NHS Foundation Trust, after a similar uniform change, was religious discrimination. The NHS Trust had said the necklace could cause injury if a patient pulled on it or it broke. In the Court of Appeal, Ms Eweida, [2010] EWCA Civ 80, and Ms Chaplin both lost on the ground that there was no disadvantage, because there was no evidence that Christians need to wear crosses.

Ms Ladele had claimed that Islington LBC unlawfully discriminated against her as a Christian by requiring she register civil partnerships as well as marriages. Although the Civil Partnership Act 2004 allowed it UK law, she said same-sex unions were 'contrary to God's law'. Initially, Ladele had been allowed to register only marriages, but after two people complained the council had insisted she do all work, and could not be exempt from civil partnership registration, because it followed a 'Dignity for All' equality policy. Her claims failed, Lord Neuberger MR [2009] EWCA Civ 1357 holding the council pursued a legitimate aim.

Mr McFarlane was dismissed from his job as a psychosexual therapist at Relate Avon Ltd after a protracted investigation found he was unwilling to give advice to homosexual couples equally to heterosexual couples. He then claimed this was unlawful discrimination because he said he believed homosexual 'activity' was 'sinful'. After the Employment Appeal Tribunal refused his claim, the Court of Appeal [2010] EWCA Civ 880 also dismissed his case.

The European Court of Human Rights held by a majority that (1) Ms Eweida did suffer unlawful discrimination, but (2) Ms Chaplin, (3) Ms Ladele and (4) Mr McFarlane did not.

Fourth Section:

a. The first applicant

92. In common with a large number of Contracting States ... the United Kingdom does not have legal provisions specifically regulating the wearing of religious clothing and symbols in the workplace. ...

93. When considering the proportionality of the steps taken by British Airways to enforce its uniform code, the national judges at each level agreed that the aim of the code was legitimate, namely to communicate a certain image of the company and to promote recognition of its brand and staff. The Employment Tribunal considered that the requirement to comply with the code was disproportionate, since it failed to distinguish an item worn as a religious symbol from a piece of jewellery worn purely for decorative reasons. This finding was reversed on appeal to the Court of Appeal, which found that British Airways had acted proportionately. In reaching this conclusion, the Court of Appeal referred to the facts of the case as established by the Employment Tribunal and, in particular, that the dress code had been in force for some years and had caused no known problem to the applicant or any other member of staff; that Ms Eweida lodged a formal grievance complaint but then decided to arrive at work displaying her cross, without waiting for the results of the grievance procedure; that the issue was conscientiously addressed by British Airways once the complaint had been lodged, involving a consultation process and resulting in a relaxation of the dress code to permit the wearing of visible religious symbols; and that Ms Eweida was offered an administrative post on identical pay during this process and was in February 2007 reinstated in her old job.

94. It is clear, in the view of the Court, that these factors combined to mitigate the extent of the interference suffered by the applicant and must be taken into account. Moreover, in weighing the proportionality of the measures taken by a private company in respect of its employee, the national authorities, in particular the courts, operate within a margin of appreciation. Nonetheless, the Court has reached the conclusion in the present case that a fair balance was not struck. On one side of the scales was Ms Eweida's desire to manifest her religious belief. As previously noted, this is a fundamental right: because a healthy democratic society needs to tolerate and sustain pluralism and diversity; but also because of the value to an individual who has made religion a central tenet of his or her life to be able to communicate that belief to others. On the other side of the scales was the employer's wish to project a certain corporate image. The Court considers that, while this aim was undoubtedly legitimate, the domestic courts accorded it too much weight. Ms Eweida's cross was discreet and cannot have detracted from her professional appearance. There was no evidence that the wearing of other, previously authorised, items of religious clothing, such as turbans and hijabs, by other employees, had any negative impact on British Airways' brand or image. Moreover, the fact that the company was able to amend the uniform code to allow for the visible wearing of religious symbolic jewellery demonstrates that the earlier prohibition was not of crucial importance.

...

b. The second applicant

99. The Court considers that, as in Ms Eweida's case, the importance for the second applicant of being permitted to manifest her religion by wearing her cross visibly must weigh heavily in the balance. However, the reason for asking her to remove the cross, namely the protection of health and safety on a hospital ward, was inherently of a greater magnitude than that which applied in respect of Ms Eweida. Moreover, this is a field where the domestic authorities must be allowed a wide margin of appreciation. The hospital managers were better placed to make decisions about clinical safety than a court, particularly an international court which has heard no direct evidence.

100. It follows that the Court is unable to conclude that the measures of which Ms Chaplin complains were disproportionate. It follows that the interference with her freedom to manifest her religion was necessary in a democratic society and that there was no violation of Article 9 in respect of the second applicant.

...

c. The third applicant

104. The Court considers that the relevant comparator in this case is a registrar with no religious objection to same-sex unions. It agrees with the applicant's contention that the local authority's requirement that all registrars of births, marriages and deaths be designated also as civil partnership registrars had a particularly detrimental impact on her because of her religious beliefs. In order to determine whether the local authority's decision not to make an exception for the applicant and others in her situation amounted to indirect discrimination in breach of Article 14, the Court must consider whether the policy pursued a legitimate aim and was proportionate.

105. The Court of Appeal held in this case that the aim pursued by the local authority was to provide a service which was not merely effective in terms of practicality and efficiency, but also one which complied with the overarching policy of being "an employer and a public authority wholly committed to the promotion of equal opportunities and to requiring all its employees to act in a way which does not discriminate against others". The Court recalls that in its case-law under Article 14 it has held that differences in treatment based on sexual orientation require particularly serious reasons by way of justification (see, for example, *Karner v. Austria*, no. 40016/98, § 37, ECHR 2003-IX, 38 EHRR 24; *Smith and Grady*, ..., § 90; *Schalk and Kopf v. Austria* ... [2010] ECHR 1996). It has also held that same-sex couples are in a relevantly similar situation to different-sex couples as regards their need for legal recognition and protection of their relationship, although since practice in this regard is still evolving across Europe, the Contracting States enjoy a wide margin of appreciation as to the way in which this is achieved within the domestic legal order (*Schalk and Kopf*, cited above, §§ 99–108). Against this background, it is evident that the aim pursued by the local authority was legitimate.

106. It remains to be determined whether the means used to pursue this aim were proportionate. The Court takes into account that the consequences for the applicant were serious: given the strength of her religious conviction, she considered that she had no choice but to face disciplinary action rather than be designated a civil partnership registrar and, ultimately, she lost her job. Furthermore, it cannot be said that, when she entered into her contract of employment, the applicant specifically waived her right to manifest her religious belief by objecting to participating in the creation of civil partnerships, since this requirement was introduced by her employer at a later date. On the other hand, however, the local authority's policy aimed to secure the rights of others which are also protected under the Convention. The Court generally allows the national authorities a wide margin of appreciation when it comes to striking a balance between competing Convention rights (see, for example, *Evans v. the United Kingdom* [GC], no. 6339/05, § 77, ECHR 2007-I, 46 EHRR 34). In all the circumstances, the Court does not consider that the national authorities, that is the local authority employer which brought the disciplinary proceedings and also the domestic courts which rejected the applicant's discrimination claim, exceeded the margin of appreciation available to them.

...

d. The fourth applicant

108. The Court accepts that Mr McFarlane's objection was directly motivated by his orthodox Christian beliefs about marriage and sexual relationships, and holds that his refusal to undertake to counsel homosexual couples constituted a manifestation of his religion and belief. The State's positive obligation under Article 9 required it to secure his rights under Article 9.

109. ... for the Court the most important factor to be taken into account is that the employer's action was intended to secure the implementation of its policy of providing a service without

discrimination. The State authorities therefore benefitted from a wide margin of appreciation in deciding where to strike the balance between Mr McFarlane's right to manifest his religious belief and the employer's interest in securing the rights of others. In all the circumstances, the Court does not consider that this margin of appreciation was exceeded in the present case.

Garlicki J, **Hirvelä J**, **Kalaydjieva J** were in the majority for all claimants. **Björgvinsson J** and **Bratza J** added a dissenting opinion with respect to Ms Eweida. **Vučinić J** and **De Gaetano J** added a dissenting with respect to Ms Ladele.

NOTES AND QUESTIONS

1. The majority of the European Court of Human Rights reasons that Ms Eweida was entitled wear a cross because there was a more proportionate way for British Airways to achieve a legitimate aim of a common clothing policy: the old uniform. Ms Chaplin's case differed because the NHS Trust's health and safety concerns were found to not be met by changing clothing. Ms Ladele was assumed to suffer a particular disadvantage as a Christian, but Islington LBC's equality policy pursued a legitimate aim, and making people work on all people's registrations was an appropriate, necessary and reasonable way to achieve it. Mr McFarlane's case was the same.

2. The cases of Ms Ladele and Mr McFarlane show how an 'objective' justification in EU law can be wider than a justification of 'business necessity' in US law. An equality policy is not necessary for an enterprise. However, given that context, a finding against religious discrimination is appropriate where a religious claimant herself or himself is attempting to use religious discrimination law to justify their own discriminatory conduct.

3. In *Ladele v London Borough of Islington* [2009] EWCA Civ 1357, [60] Lord Neuberger MR drew on the Constitutional Court of South Africa, in *Christian Education South Africa v Minister of Education* [2000] ZACC 11, [35], where Sachs J said: 'The underlying problem in any open and democratic society based on human dignity, equality and freedom in which conscientious and religious freedom has to be regarded with appropriate seriousness, is how far such democracy can and must go in allowing members of religious communities to define for themselves which laws they will obey and which not. Such a society can cohere only if all its participants accept that certain basic norms and standards are binding. Accordingly, believers cannot claim an automatic right to be exempted by their beliefs from the laws of the land. At the same time, the state should, wherever reasonably possible, seek to avoid putting believers to extremely painful and intensely burdensome choices of either being true to their faith or else respectful of the law.' What do you think?

4. Were the cases distinct, because Ms Eweida's cross affected nobody else, but the desires of Ms Chaplin, Ms Ladele and Mr McFarlane did?

5. In *Azmi v Kirklees Metropolitan Borough Council* [2007] IRLR 434 (EAT) Wilkie J upheld a Tribunal finding that Ms Azmi was not entitled to claim indirect discrimination when she demanded she be able to wear a niqab (which covers the face, except the eyes) as a support worker at a West Yorkshire primary school.

Ms Azmi had attended her interview with a headscarf, where her face was show-ing, but had subsequently decided she wanted to wear a veil covering her face. After a careful investigation, the school found that this obstructed 'her lovely friendly smiling manner with the children and how they responded well to this'. It followed that the council's requirement for Ms Azmi to not cover her face propor-tionately pursued a legitimate educational aim. If Azmi had worked in an office job with adults, would the issue differ?

6. *Achbita v G4S Secure Solutions NV* (2017) C-157/15 the CJEU's Grand Chamber held that although a headscarf ban by an employer could be indirect discrimina-tion, it could be objectively justified by a policy of neutrality toward religious or philosophical belief in a workplace. Does this conflict with *Eweida*?

7. Most theologians in the UK would probably not agree that the Old Testament, New Testament or the Koran, require any particular kind of dress. For instance, the Koran requires 'modest' dress. The practices of the habits worn by Catholic nuns, different forms of headscarf for Muslim women or the Jewish kippah have rather developed as requirements out of different political units: the variety between countries that have a Christian, Muslim or Jewish heritage are infinitely varied, and changing. By contrast, Sikh men generally see a turban as a require-ment. Whatever the position of religious experts, do you agree with the view that head clothing is a symbol of 'oppression', and if so, so what? See further, Aesop, *The North Wind and the Sun* (c 560 BC).

8. What counts as a 'legitimate aim' or not? In *Bilka-Kaufhaus GmbH v Weber von Hartz* (1986) C-170/84, [36] the Court of Justice used the synonym of requir-ing that there is 'a real need on the part of the undertaking'. Here, the company had not given its part-time staff a pension, and argued that this was justified because administrative costs of pensions for part-time workers were propor-tionally higher (ie it costs the same to do pension paper work for full- or part-time workers, but part-time workers work less for the company). Most part-time workers, including Ms Weber von Hartz, were women, and so it was alleged this practice was indirect sex discrimination. The Court of Justice said it would be for the national court to determine an objective justification. In light of *Kutz-Bauer*, below, it is now clear that saving money could not be an excuse for discrimination.

9. In *Rinner-Kühn v FWW Spezial-Gebaudereinigung GmbH & Co KG* (1989) C-171/88 Ms Rinner-Kühn claimed failure to give her and other part-time work-ers sick pay was indirect sex discrimination, as most part-time workers were women. The company's policy mirrored a German law which only required sick pay for people working over 10 hours per week. The Court of Justice rejected the German government's justification that part-time workers were 'not as integrated in, or dependent on' their employers. These were 'only generalizations about cer-tain categories of workers' and did 'not enable criteria which are both objective and unrelated to any discrimination'.

10. The next case said saving money is never a legitimate aim in justifying discrimination.

Kutz-Bauer v Freie und Hansestadt Hamburg (2003) C-187/00

Ms Kutz-Bauer claimed that she ought to be able eligible for the Hamburg government's part-time work scheme, just as men were. The scheme said if newly recruited employees were previously unemployed, between age 55 and retirement, and worked part-time, the government would pay 70 per cent of their wages. However, in the German Social Code (Sozialgesetzbuch VI §§35–39) the retirement age for women was 60, and for men 65. As Ms Kutz-Bauer had turned 60, she was eligible for retirement, and not the part-time work scheme, whereas a comparable man could work part-time (but not yet retire on the state pension). Ms Kutz-Bauer, possibly aware that retirement could mean less money than work, challenged these rules as indirect sex discrimination.

Sixth Chamber:

54 The German Government submits that one of the aims pursued by a scheme such as the one at issue in the main proceedings is to combat unemployment by offering the maximum incentives for workers who are not yet eligible to retire to do so and thus making posts available. To allow a worker who has already acquired entitlement to a retirement pension at the full rate to benefit from the scheme of part-time work for older employees implies, first, that a post which the scheme intends to allocate to an unemployed person would continue to be occupied and, second, that the social security scheme would bear the additional costs, which would divert certain resources from other objectives.

55 As regards the argument which the German Government derives from the encouragement of recruitment, it is for the Member States to choose the measures capable of achieving the aims which they pursue in employment matters. The Court has recognised that the Member States have a broad margin of discretion in exercising that power (see *Seymour-Smith and Perez*, paragraph 74).

56 Furthermore, as the Court stated at paragraph 71 of its judgment in *Seymour-Smith and Perez*, it cannot be disputed that the encouragement of recruitment constitutes a legitimate aim of social policy.

57 However, the fact remains that the broad margin of discretion which the Member States enjoy in matters of social policy cannot have the effect of frustrating the implementation of a fundamental principle of Community law such as that of equal treatment for men and women (see *Seymour-Smith and Perez*, paragraph 75).

58 It follows from the rule referred to at paragraph 51 of this judgment that mere generalisations concerning the capacity of a specific measure to encourage recruitment are not enough to show that the aim of the disputed provisions is unrelated to any discrimination based on sex or to provide evidence on the basis of which it could reasonably be considered that the means chosen are or could be suitable for achieving that aim.

59 As regards the German Government's argument concerning the additional burden associated with allowing female workers to take advantage of the scheme at issue in the main proceedings even where they have acquired entitlement to a retirement pension at the full rate, the Court observes that although budgetary considerations may underlie a Member State's choice of social policy and influence the nature or scope of the social protection measures

which it wishes to adopt, they do not in themselves constitute an aim pursued by that policy and cannot therefore justify discrimination against one of the sexes (Case C-343/92 *De Weerd and Others* [1994] ECR I-571, paragraph 35).

60 Moreover, to concede that budgetary considerations may justify a difference in treatment between men and women which would otherwise constitute indirect discrimination on grounds of sex would mean that the application and scope of a rule of Community law as fundamental as that of equal treatment between men and women might vary in time and place according to the state of the public finances of Member States (*De Weerd and Others*, cited above, paragraph 36, and *Jørgensen*, cited above, paragraph 39).

61 Nor can the City of Hamburg, whether as a public authority or as an employer, justify discrimination arising from a scheme of part-time work for older employees solely because avoidance of such discrimination would involve increased costs (see, to that effect, *Hill and Stapleton*, paragraph 40).

62 It is therefore for the City of Hamburg to prove to the national court that the difference in treatment arising from the scheme of part-time work for older employees at issue in the main proceedings is justified by objective reasons unrelated to any discrimination on grounds of sex. Should it succeed in doing so, the mere fact that the provisions of that scheme which preclude access by workers who have acquired entitlement to a retirement pension at the full rate affect a considerably higher percentage of female workers than of male workers could not be regarded as infringing Articles 2(1) and 5(1) of Directive 76/207.

President Schintgen, Gulmann J, Skouris J, Macken J and **Cunha Rodrigues J.**

NOTES AND QUESTIONS

1. The Court of Justice rejects the German government's contention that 'budgetary considerations' could constitute an 'aim' in themselves. Although budgetary decisions 'underlie' much social policy, the Court implies an allocation of resources is a means to various ends, rather than ends in themselves. Kantian logic aside, the simpler message is that money does not justify discrimination. How many discriminatory policies do you think could be justified if saving money were a legitimate aim?
2. The leading UK case, applying the principle that saving money is not a legitimate aim in itself, is *O'Brien v Ministry of Justice* [2013] UKSC 6 (see chapter 15(1)(a)).
3. If an aim is legitimate, and measures are appropriate and necessary, when might a practice still be found 'unreasonable' (sometimes called disproportionate in the 'narrow' sense)? An example may be *London Underground Ltd v Edwards (No 2)* [1997] IRLR 157. Ms Edwards, a single parent, claimed a new Underground shift system indirectly discriminated against her. She had worked as a train driver for ten years, but could not do her job and childcare under the new shift system. Although the reasoning was not rigidly structured in this way, it appears to have been accepted that the Underground by changing its shift system pursued a legitimate administrative efficiency aim. It was appropriate, but was it either necessary or reasonable? The Tribunal held that they could 'easily, without losing the objectives of their plan and reorganisation, have accommodated the applicant who was

a long-serving employee. ... They did not address themselves to these issues.' In the EAT Morison J held the Underground 'gave in to pressure from its predominantly male workforce' and 'the more clear it is that the employers unreasonably failed to show flexibility in their employment practices, the more willing the tribunal should be to make a finding of unlawful discrimination'. Employing entities 'should carefully consider the impact which a new roster might have on a section of their workforce'. This suggests both that the Underground's changes were not entirely 'necessary'. But also, rethinking was not positive discrimination. Rather, it balanced the legitimate interests of the claimant and the business reasonably.

(2) REDUCED PROTECTION ON GENDER PAY EQUALITY

Unlike any other protected characteristic, there are separate rules for pay solely for sex discrimination. It seems likely that childcare rights (chapter 7) are probably the greatest barrier to gender pay equality, but the persistent gender pay gap of 19.2 per cent makes any difference in regulation very suspect. There are differences on three main points: (1) for pay claims based on sex, a real comparator is required, not a hypothetical comparator; (2) the time limit for claims is a non-extendable 6 months from the time of dismissal or discrimination was discovered (EA 2010 s 129), rather than 3 months that is extendable as just and equitable (s 123); and (3) claims can be brought in the High Court, as well as in an Employment Tribunal, and may be treated like claims for wage deductions under the Employment Rights Act (ERA) 1996 s 13. This carries the normal six-year time limit from when the action accrued under the Limitation Act 1980 s 5. While point (3) is more favourable, points (1) and (2) are far less favourable. Where they are equally favourable, the statutory provisions are convoluted only to reach the same functional outcomes as for other protected characteristics. For these reasons, people argued separate provisions should be scrapped (eg H Mulholland, 'Equal Pay Act 'Should Be Scrapped'' (14 January 2008) *Guardian*). The EA 2010 did not do this.

Is there a principled justification for these rules? No. The reasons are historical, and due to drafting complexity that obscures appropriate attention from Parliament. The United States passed an Equal Pay Act of 1963, which operated to amend its minimum wage law, the Fair Labor Standards Act of 1938. This preceded the general Civil Rights of 1964. The UK followed a similar pattern, with an original Equal Pay Act (EPA) 1970 before it wrote a general Sex Discrimination Act 1975. From the start, the rules were separate (and not equal). The European Union's original treaty provisions (now TFEU Art 157) required equal pay between men and women, but nothing else until the Equality Framework Directive 2000. This apparently 'special' treatment was manifested in a separate Equal Treatment Directive (ETD) 2006. UK law can and does go further than EU rules in many ways, but it has followed a narrow focus on the key question of the appropriate comparator. The effect of EA 2010 s 71 is that direct discrimination claims for gender pay can still be brought under whichever set of rules is most favourable. This means that the reduced protection on gender pay equality is now limited to cases of indirect discrimination.

(a) Comparators

In equal gender pay claims a comparator must be real. This is not required by the Directive, or TFEU Art 157, but has been interpreted by the Court of Justice, and remained in UK law.

Equal Treatment Directive 2006

Article 2 Definitions
...
(b) 'indirect discrimination': where an apparently neutral provision, criterion or practice would put persons of one sex at a particular disadvantage compared with persons of the other sex, unless that provision, criterion or practice is objectively justified by a legitimate aim, and the means of achieving that aim are appropriate and necessary;
...
(e) 'pay': the ordinary basic or minimum wage or salary and any other consideration, whether in cash or in kind, which the worker receives directly or indirectly, in respect of his/her employment from his/her employer;
(f) 'occupational social security schemes': schemes not governed by Council Directive 79/7/EEC of 19 December 1978 on the progressive implementation of the principle of equal treatment for men and women in matters of social security (16) whose purpose is to provide workers, whether employees or self-employed, in an undertaking or group of undertakings, area of economic activity, occupational sector or group of sectors with benefits intended to supplement the benefits provided by statutory social security schemes or to replace them, whether membership of such schemes is compulsory or optional.

Article 4 Prohibition of discrimination
For the same work or for work to which equal value is attributed, direct and indirect discrimination on grounds of sex with regard to all aspects and conditions of remuneration shall be eliminated.
In particular, where a job classification system is used for determining pay, it shall be based on the same criteria for both men and women and so drawn up as to exclude any discrimination on grounds of sex.

Chapter 2 Equal treatment in occupational social security schemes

Article 5 Prohibition of discrimination
Without prejudice to Article 4, there shall be no direct or indirect discrimination on grounds of sex in occupational social security schemes, in particular as regards:
(a) the scope of such schemes and the conditions of access to them;
(b) the obligation to contribute and the calculation of contributions;
(c) the calculation of benefits, including supplementary benefits due in respect of a spouse or dependants, and the conditions governing the duration and retention of entitlement to benefits.

NOTES AND QUESTIONS

1. The ETD 2006 (2006/54/EC) expands upon what would simply be inherent in the Equality Framework Directive 2000, if the word 'sex' had simply been added. This recast the previous Equal Treatment Directive 76/207/EEC, without much rethinking.

2.   Under ETD 2006 Art 7, the 'material scope' of a social security scheme includes five classic pillars of (i) health, (ii) disability, (iii) old age, (iv) workplace accidents and (v) unemployment. The concept of 'pay' has a wide meaning, which in this instance is unfortunate.

3.   In what situations would having a hypothetical comparator make a difference? Suppose that in a fashion company, all designers are men, and all seamsters are women. Their work is not similar. This year, the company announces that, to make savings, Christmas bonuses will need to be reduced by 50 per cent, but this will only apply to seamsters because the market for designers is very 'tight'. Market research has traditionally shown that men are difficult to attract in general to fashion companies without a bonus. This is a neutral practice (reduced bonuses for seamsters) that puts women at a particular disadvantage. Arguably, the real reason for reducing bonuses for women and not men is the state of the market, to attract men to work at fashion companies. Without a hypothetical comparator, the women seamster claimants have no basis to attempt an indirect sex discrimination claim. Why should sex discrimination law be weaker?

4.   An equal pay comparator can include someone who preceded a claimant in a job (eg *Macarthys Ltd v Smith (No 2)* [1981] QB 180) and someone who succeeded a claimant in a job (eg *Diocese of Hallam Trustees v Connaughton* [1996] ICR 860 (EAT)). So there is no need for a hypothetical comparator there. Is that good enough?

5.   Arguably the most important situation where a hypothetical comparator would have helped was seen in *Lawrence v Regent Office Care Ltd* (2002) C-320/00. Dinner ladies, who had previously been directly employed by North Yorkshire County Council, and were then outsourced to Regent Office Care Ltd, claimed they should be able to compare themselves to men who still worked for the council. Their work had been previously rated as equivalent by a collective agreement. The Court of Justice, however, held that there was now no 'single source' that was responsible for a disparity of pay and could rectify it. It took the view that because the council and the subcontracted company were separate legal entities, no comparison could or should be available.

6.   *Allonby* further exemplifies this narrow scope of comparison.

Allonby v Accrington and Rossendale College (2001) C-256/01

Ms Allonby, and other part-time lecturers at Accrington and Rossendale College, claimed indirect sex discrimination (under TFEU Art 157, previously TEC Art 141) and unfair dismissal after they were not allowed access to the Teachers' Superannuation Scheme. Their contracts with the College had not been renewed, and instead they were rehired through an agency, Education Lecturing Services, on a supposedly 'self employed basis' (see chapter 3(1)). More part-time lecturers were women than men. After the Tribunal and EAT had found no sex discrimination claim was available, the Court of Appeal made a preliminary reference to the Court of Justice. It held that a discrimination claim could not succeed because the comparators they attempted to use were at the College and this was a separate legal entity.

Court of Justice:

45 Admittedly, there is nothing in the wording of Article 141(1) EC to suggest that the applicability of that provision is limited to situations in which men and women work for the same employer. The principle established by that article may be invoked before national courts, in particular in cases of discrimination arising directly from legislative provisions or collective labour agreements, as well as in cases in which work is carried out in the same establishment or service, whether private or public (see, inter alia, Case 43/75 *Defrenne II* [1976] ECR 455, paragraph 40, and Case C-320/00 *Lawrence and Others* [2002] ECR I-7325, paragraph 17).

46 However, where the differences identified in the pay conditions of workers performing equal work or work of equal value cannot be attributed to a single source, there is no body which is responsible for the inequality and which could restore equal treatment. Such a situation does not come within the scope of Article 141(1) EC. The work and the pay of those workers cannot therefore be compared on the basis of that provision (*Lawrence*, paragraph 18).

47 It is clear from the order for reference that the male worker referred to by Ms Allonby is paid by the College under conditions determined by the College, whereas ELS agreed with Ms Allonby on the pay which she would receive for each assignment.

48 The fact that the level of pay received by Ms Allonby is influenced by the amount which the College pays ELS is not a sufficient basis for concluding that the College and ELS constitute a single source to which can be attributed the differences identified in Ms Allonby's conditions of pay and those of the male worker paid by the College.

49 Moreover, it is clear from the order for reference that ELS and the College are not associated employers within the meaning of section 1(6)(c) of the Equal Pay Act 1970.

...

75 In order to show that the requirement of being employed under a contract of employment as a precondition for membership of the TSS – a condition deriving from State rules – constitutes a breach of the principle of equal pay for men and women in the form of indirect discrimination against women, a female worker may rely on statistics showing that, among the teachers who are workers within the meaning of Article 141(1) EC and fulfil all the conditions for membership of the pension scheme except that of being employed under a contract of employment as defined by national law, there is a much higher percentage of women than of men.

76 If that is the case, the difference of treatment concerning membership of the pension scheme at issue must be objectively justified. In that regard, no justification can be inferred from the formal classification of a self-employed person under national law.

NOTES AND QUESTIONS

1. The Court of Justice advises that its minimum requirements do not demand that a comparison can be made across legal entities. This does not mean the UK could not have enabled such a claim.
2. Is it unrealistic to suggest that the College could not demand that its outsourced workers be paid equally? The Court of Justice says that just because pay 'is influenced' by the College, this 'is not a sufficient basis' for requiring equal pay. Why does the Court not use the magic word (common in reasoned argument) of 'because'?
3. The UK's provisions to establish appropriate comparators are lengthy.

Equality Act 2010 ss 64–66 and 79

64 Relevant types of work

(1) Sections 66 to 70 apply where—
- (a) a person (A) is employed on work that is equal to the work that a comparator of the opposite sex (B) does;
- (b) a person (A) holding a personal or public office does work that is equal to the work that a comparator of the opposite sex (B) does.

(2) The references in subsection (1) to the work that B does are not restricted to work done contemporaneously with the work done by A.

65 Equal work

(1) For the purposes of this Chapter, A's work is equal to that of B if it is—
- (a) like B's work,
- (b) rated as equivalent to B's work, or
- (c) of equal value to B's work.

(2) A's work is like B's work if—
- (a) A's work and B's work are the same or broadly similar, and
- (b) such differences as there are between their work are not of practical importance in relation to the terms of their work.

(3) So on a comparison of one person's work with another's for the purposes of subsection (2), it is necessary to have regard to—
- (a) the frequency with which differences between their work occur in practice, and
- (b) the nature and extent of the differences.

(4) A's work is rated as equivalent to B's work if a job evaluation study—
- (a) gives an equal value to A's job and B's job in terms of the demands made on a worker, or
- (b) would give an equal value to A's job and B's job in those terms were the evaluation not made on a sex-specific system.

(5) A system is sex-specific if, for the purposes of one or more of the demands made on a worker, it sets values for men different from those it sets for women.

(6) A's work is of equal value to B's work if it is—
- (a) neither like B's work nor rated as equivalent to B's work, but
- (b) nevertheless equal to B's work in terms of the demands made on A by reference to factors such as effort, skill and decision-making.

66 Sex equality clause

(1) If the terms of A's work do not (by whatever means) include a sex equality clause, they are to be treated as including one.

(2) A sex equality clause is a provision that has the following effect—
- (a) if a term of A's is less favourable to A than a corresponding term of B's is to B, A's term is modified so as not to be less favourable;
- (b) if A does not have a term which corresponds to a term of B's that benefits B, A's terms are modified so as to include such a term.

(3) Subsection (2)(a) applies to a term of A's relating to membership of or rights under an occupational pension scheme only in so far as a sex equality rule would have effect in relation to the term.

(4) In the case of work within section 65(1)(b), a reference in subsection (2) above to a term includes a reference to such terms (if any) as have not been determined by the rating of the work (as well as those that have).

...

79 Comparators

(1) This section applies for the purposes of this Chapter.

(2) If A is employed, B is a comparator if subsection (3) or (4) applies.

(3) This subsection applies if—

    (a) B is employed by A's employer or by an associate of A's employer, and

    (b) A and B work at the same establishment.

(4) This subsection applies if—

    (a) B is employed by A's employer or an associate of A's employer,

    (b) B works at an establishment other than the one at which A works, and

    (c) common terms apply at the establishments (either generally or as between A and B).

(5) If A holds a personal or public office, B is a comparator if—

    (a) B holds a personal or public office, and

    (b) the person responsible for paying A is also responsible for paying B.

…

(9) For the purposes of this section, employers are associated if—

    (a) one is a company of which the other (directly or indirectly) has control, or

    (b) both are companies of which a third person (directly or indirectly) has control.

NOTES AND QUESTIONS

1. A legitimate comparator is anybody who does at least broadly similar work, rated as equivalent (usually pursuant to a collective agreement), or work that is equally demanding (s 65). A comparator can be in a different workplace, for instance if he or she is in a different subsidiary of a company group with common terms (s 79(9)). However, this does not yet cover outsourced work (as in *Lawrence* or *Allonby*), or work by other colleagues in a corporate group who do not share similar terms. The number of cases here may be narrow. But do you agree that it is unfair that a race discrimination claim could be brought, and yet a sex discrimination claim could not be?

2. *Could* a race discrimination claim across the corporate veil, and regardless of a single source, be brought? Or would it be argued that a 'hypothetical comparator' cannot cross the veil of an employing entity's separate personhood on policy grounds? It is submitted that the objectives of the equality legislation require that the corporate veil is irrelevant. Artificial limits on comparators risk creating perverse incentives for companies or public bodies to undertake the cost of restructuring merely to evade legal duties: a smaller private gain than the social and economic costs.

3. EA 2010 ss 67–68 concern a 'sex equality rule' which, at some length, sets out an analogous concept to the sex equality clause (s 66) for occupational pension schemes.

4. In *Pickstone v Freemans plc* [1989] AC 66 the House of Lords held that women warehouse operatives were entitled to claim they did work of equal value to men who worked as checker warehouse operatives. It dismissed the argument that, just because there were also some men working as ordinary warehouse operatives, they could not also bring a claim based on a comparison with the checkers.

5. In *British Coal Corporation v Smith* [1996] IRLR 404 the House of Lords held that women canteen and clerical workers could compare themselves to men mineworkers who got extra production bonuses. Lord Slynn emphasised 'the terms

and conditions do not have to be identical', just 'substantially comparable'. Otherwise the rules would be 'far too restrictive'.

6. In *Abdulla v Birmingham CC* [2012] UKSC 47 the Supreme Court held by a majority that under the old EPA 1970 s 2(3) it was not more 'convenient' to hear a pay claim in the Tribunal, when that would have been time barred, as opposed to the High Court where with a six-year limitation period it was not. Lord Sumption and Lord Carnwath dissented.

7. In *North v Dumfries and Galloway Council* [2013] UKSC 45 the Supreme Court held that women classroom and nursery assistants could compare themselves with men who worked as groundskeepers, road and refuse workers, even those who did not work at the schools. It would be too much to require that they worked in the same place. In the old EPA 1970 s 1(6) 'in the same employment' cut across locations. See EA 2010 s 79. Do you agree the problem could be easily solved by the law allowing a claimant to use a hypothetical comparator?

(b) Genuine Material Factor Defence

The 'genuine material factor' defence is identical in substance to objective justification.

Equality Act 2010 s 69

69 Defence of material factor

(1) The sex equality clause in A's terms has no effect in relation to a difference between A's terms and B's terms if the responsible person shows that the difference is because of a material factor reliance on which—

    (a) does not involve treating A less favourably because of A's sex than the responsible person treats B, and

    (b) if the factor is within subsection (2), is a proportionate means of achieving a legitimate aim.

(2) A factor is within this subsection if A shows that, as a result of the factor, A and persons of the same sex doing work equal to A's are put at a particular disadvantage when compared with persons of the opposite sex doing work equal to A's.

(3) For the purposes of subsection (1), the long-term objective of reducing inequality between men's and women's terms of work is always to be regarded as a legitimate aim.

(4) A sex equality rule has no effect in relation to a difference between A and B in the effect of a relevant matter if the trustees or managers of the scheme in question show that the difference is because of a material factor which is not the difference of sex.

(5) "Relevant matter" has the meaning given in section 67.

(6) For the purposes of this section, a factor is not material unless it is a material difference between A's case and B's.

NOTES AND QUESTIONS

1. EA 2010 s 69(1)(b) contains, in substance, the same ideas behind objective justification for indirect discrimination.

2. EA 2010 s 69(3) refers to a practice, adopted in collective agreements, of what is called red-circling. After it was decided that men and women's work in different jobs were of equal value, unions agreed with employing entities to phase in an equalisation of pay, but not do so immediately (usually on grounds of cost).

3.   In *Redcar and Cleveland BC v Bainbridge* [2007] EWCA Civ 929 Mummery LJ
     held that red-circling did not count as a material factor defence because the law
     entitles women and men to equal pay, and not only after a transitionary period.
     This means that, since s 69(3), there is an uneasy tension between primary legisla-
     tion and what the Court of Justice might say if a reference were ever made.
4.   What kind of justifications have not worked in equal-pay cases?

Clay Cross (Quarry Services) Ltd v Fletcher [1978] IRLR 361

Mrs Fletcher claimed that she should be paid equally to a male co-worker. She was paid
£35 per week, along with three other clerks. A colleague left and was replaced by a
Mr Tunnicliffe, aged 24. He was the only suitable candidate and was paid £43 per week,
to match his previous salary. An expert said that clerks' wages should be set at £43.46,
but Mr Tunnicliffe's wage still remained higher, at £49. Ironically, Mrs Fletcher trained
him. When the Equal Pay Act 1970 came into force, in 1975, she complained. The Court
of Appeal held that the disparity was unjustified.

Lord Denning MR:

The issue depends on whether there is a material difference (other than sex) between her
case and his. Take heed to the words "between her case and his." They show that the
tribunal is to have regard to her and to him – to the personal equation of the woman as
compared to that of the man – irrespective of any extrinsic forces which led to the variation
in pay. As I said in *Shields v E Coomes (Holdings) Ltd*, ante, p. 1418E, section 1(3) applies
when "the personal equation of the man is such that he deserves to be paid at a higher rate
than the woman." Thus the personal equation of the man may warrant a wage differential
if he has much longer length of service, or has superior skill or qualifications; or gives bigger output or productivity; or has been placed, owing to downgrading, in a protected pay
category, vividly described as "red-circled"; or to other circumstances personal to him in
doing his job.

   But the tribunal is not to have regard to any extrinsic forces which have led to the man being
paid more. An employer cannot avoid his obligations under the Act by saying: "I paid him more
because he asked for more," or "I paid her less because she was willing to come for less." If any
such excuse were permitted, the Act would be a dead letter. Those are the very reasons why
there was unequal pay before the statute. They are the very circumstances in which the statute
was intended to operate.

   Nor can the employer avoid his obligations by giving the reasons why he submitted to the
extrinsic forces. As for instance by saying: "He asked for that sum because it was what he was
getting in his previous job," or, "He was the only applicant for the job, so I had no option."
In such cases the employer may beat his breast, and say: "I did not pay him more because he
was a man. I paid it because he was the only suitable person who applied for the job. Man or
woman made no difference to me." Those are reasons personal to the employer. If any such
reasons were permitted as an excuse, the door would be wide open. Every employer who
wished to avoid the statute would walk straight through it.

Lawton LJ and **Browne LJ** concurred.

NOTES AND QUESTIONS

1. Lord Denning MR holds, in essence, that market forces cannot justify pay disparities, because then 'the Act would be a dead letter'. There had to be reasons affecting the 'personal equation' between a claimant and the comparator, rather than 'extrinsic' factors.

2. In *Rainey v Greater Glasgow Health Board* [1987] IRLR 26 the House of Lords doubted the test set by Lord Denning MR. A woman prosthetist, recruited directly by the health board, claimed she should not be paid less than new male prosthetists recently hired, who had (apparently) to be paid 40 per cent more to attract them from the private sector. Lord Keith held it was an 'accident' that men in the private sector were paid more. The male comparator was, ostensibly, 'paid more because of the necessity to attract him and other privately employed prosthetists into forming the nucleus of the new service'. Can this judgment stand, given the decisions of *Kutz-Bauer* and *O'Brien v Ministry of Defence* which require that saving money (eg by maintaining lower wages for Ms Rainey) cannot itself be regarded as a legitimate aim?

3. In *Enderby v Frenchay Health Authority* (1993) C-127/92, [26] the Court of Justice said: 'The state of the employment market, which may lead an employer to increase the pay of a particular job in order to attract candidates, may constitute an objectively justified economic ground within the meaning of the case law cited above. How it is to be applied in the circumstances of each case depends on the facts and so falls within the jurisdiction of the national court.' Was this also changed by *Kutz-Bauer* (above)?

4. Is it possible to maintain that the 'employment market' might justify differential treatment, but that saving money cannot? Is the market and money not simply the same thing?

Additional Reading for Chapter 13

RA Epstein, *Forbidden Grounds: The Case against Employment Discrimination Laws* (1992)
Epstein develops a 'case' against all employment discrimination laws, which seem to follow from his commitment to Hobbesian social theory. Epstein advocates total repeal of all discrimination law. Starting with doubly insulting observations such as the 'history of sex discrimination is not as searing as that of race relations', he says the law gets in the way of 'freedom of contract'. He says the moral consensus of academics for equality is 'comfortable, soft' and 'complacent' and apparently people stopped to 'think hard'. Despite this, Epstein does not present any credible evidence that discrimination laws either do not work or cause economic harm. It is, however, a majestic example of hardline ideology.

B Hepple 'The Aims of Equality Law' [2008] 61 *Current Legal Problems* 1

Hepple argues 'we do not need to look far' for the aims of equality law: these are to get a society where 'people's ability to achieve their potential is not limited by prejudice', respect for human rights, dignity of the individual, 'equal opportunity' and 'mutual respect'. Further the law should promote 'equal, real freedom and substantive opportunity to live in the ways people value and would choose, so that everyone can flourish.' Hepple rejects that different parts of the proposed equality law (which became the EA 2010) should have different effects, particularly the reduced protection for equal pay between men and women (see chapter 13). He suggests the largest failure in the law is to place positive duties on both public and private bodies to promote equality. Hepple says his conceptions are similar to Collins's vision of 'social inclusion' but such reconceptualisation runs the 'risk of unravelling clear and consistent legal principles that have been developed with much thought over the past five decades.'

H Collins and T Khaitan (eds), *Foundations of Indirect Discrimination Law* (2018)

The contributors to this edited volume explore the policy and outcomes of indirect discrimination law. The cover depicts a fox and a stork, following Aesop's fable. Here, the fox invites a stork for dinner, serving soup on a shallow plate which the stork with its long beak cannot lap up. When the fox visits the stork for dinner, the stork serves soup in a long-necked jar: each had the theoretical equal opportunity to enjoy dinner but did not. In the context of a US Supreme Court with many judges who appear to oppose the existence of an indirect discrimination claim, they ask whether the law follows the same principles as direct discrimination, its appropriate scope, comparators and justifications.

14

Inclusion

How might the values of 'equality' and 'inclusion' differ? Aristotle once told us that treating unequals equally can be very unequal. Of course, the truth in this quip depends, as chapter 12 recalled, on what we mean by 'equally'. Superficially, an aim of 'equal opportunity' sounds like it is as much about equality as 'equal outcome'. But equal opportunity may lead to unequal outcomes. If equal outcome is desired, opportunities may need to be unequal. The Nobel laureate, Anatole France, captured this difference between process and outcome when he reminded us that 'the law, in its majestic equality, lets rich and poor alike sleep under bridges, beg in the streets, and steal loaves of bread' (*The Red Lily* (1894) ch 7). 'Equality' may turn from a blessing to a curse when focus on 'merit' (understood in a particular way) or traditional qualifications that will systematically exclude some from employment. This is why the law deviates from a presumption that people should be treated equally, towards rules that favour social inclusion. It can even be argued that all equality and discrimination law should be seen as pursuing inclusion as its highest principle (see H Collins, 'Social Inclusion: A Better Approach to Equality Issues' (2004) 14 *Transnational Law and Contemporary Problems* 897).

There are two main challenges for a system of inclusive law. First, there is historical disadvantage. We can all recognise the slow developments in human history: from old empires and colonies, riven with racism and sexism, to a system of 'United Nations', with a quickening global integration, culture and family. The law can allow for groups who have seen historical disadvantage to gain advantage. The 'hard' form, called 'positive discrimination' in Europe and 'affirmative action' in the US, means quotas for jobs. EU and UK law allows this for the 'representative' jobs, but not for workers in general. Instead, 'soft' 'positive action' measures are encouraged. Different approaches might seem more or less legitimate depending on a country's historical starting point. India and South Africa, which bore the brunt of imperialism, caste and apartheid, have very 'hard' rules.

Second, the world of employment may create advantages or disadvantages for people's natural characteristics. One natural characteristic is pregnancy. Plainly, people have to take more care at work, and deserve more care, when they are pregnant. The law partly allows more favourable treatment for expectant mothers because (quite sensibly) it is seen as good to not discourage children. Another natural characteristic is what we call 'disability'. Many people argue that, in truth, *society* has the disability when it fails to include everyone, and adjust to people's natural characteristics. People just are the way they are. Our 'social model' has the problem, not the individual. The law goes so far as to require 'reasonable adjustments' by employing entities for people who merit them. This chapter outlines (1) positive action, (2) rights for pregnant women, and (3) the law on disability.

> **Introductory texts:** Collins ch 3. CEM ch 9 (338–41, 346–9). D&M ch 6 (689–95, 752–65).

(1) POSITIVE ACTION

The UK's central provisions on 'positive action' are found in the Equality Act 2010 (EA 2010) ss 158–59. These allow employing entities, voluntarily, to adopt positive action policies, short of quotas.

Equality Act 2010 ss 158–59

158 Positive action: general
(1) This section applies if a person (P) reasonably thinks that—
  (a) persons who share a protected characteristic suffer a disadvantage connected to the characteristic,
  (b) persons who share a protected characteristic have needs that are different from the needs of persons who do not share it, or
  (c) participation in an activity by persons who share a protected characteristic is disproportionately low.
(2) This Act does not prohibit P from taking any action which is a proportionate means of achieving the aim of—
  (a) enabling or encouraging persons who share the protected characteristic to overcome or minimise that disadvantage,
  (b) meeting those needs, or
  (c) enabling or encouraging persons who share the protected characteristic to participate in that activity.
(3) Regulations may specify action, or descriptions of action, to which subsection (2) does not apply.
(4) This section does not apply to—
  (a) action within section 159(3), or
  (b) anything that is permitted by virtue of section 104.
(5) If section 104(7) is repealed by virtue of section 105, this section will not apply to anything that would have been so permitted but for the repeal.
(6) This section does not enable P to do anything that is prohibited by or under an enactment other than this Act.

159 Positive action: recruitment and promotion
(1) This section applies if a person (P) reasonably thinks that—
  (a) persons who share a protected characteristic suffer a disadvantage connected to the characteristic, or
  (b) participation in an activity by persons who share a protected characteristic is disproportionately low.

(2) Part 5 (work) does not prohibit P from taking action within subsection (3) with the aim of enabling or encouraging persons who share the protected characteristic to—
   (a)   overcome or minimise that disadvantage, or
   (b)   participate in that activity.
(3) That action is treating a person (A) more favourably in connection with recruitment or promotion than another person (B) because A has the protected characteristic but B does not.
(4) But subsection (2) applies only if—
   (a)   A is as qualified as B to be recruited or promoted,
   (b)   P does not have a policy of treating persons who share the protected characteristic more favourably in connection with recruitment or promotion than persons who do not share it, and
   (c)   taking the action in question is a proportionate means of achieving the aim referred to in subsection (2).
(5) "Recruitment" means a process for deciding whether to—
   (a)   offer employment to a person,
   (b)   make contract work available to a contract worker,
   (c)   offer a person a position as a partner in a firm or proposed firm,
   (d)   offer a person a position as a member of an LLP or proposed LLP,
   (e)   offer a person a pupillage or tenancy in barristers' chambers,
   (f)   take a person as an advocate's devil or offer a person membership of an advocate's stable,
   (g)   offer a person an appointment to a personal office,
   (h)   offer a person an appointment to a public office, recommend a person for such an appointment or approve a person's appointment to a public office, or
   (i)   offer a person a service for finding employment.
(6) This section does not enable P to do anything that is prohibited by or under an enactment other than this Act.

NOTES AND QUESTIONS

1.   What exactly does this allow, and what does it not allow? Under EA 2010 s 158(2) employing entities can (voluntarily) undertake measures to correct 'disadvantage' related to a protected characteristic that are proportionate to the legitimate aim of rectifying the disadvantage. Under s 159, it is clear that this does not enable hiring one person over another unless they are equally qualified. This is the 'tie-break' rule originating in EU law.

2.   In policy, the Court of Justice has changed its stance. In *Kalanke v Freie Hansestadt Bremen* (1995) C-450/93, Mr Kalanke and a woman candidate were shortlisted to be a manager at Bremen's city parks. It was accepted that they were equally qualified, and Bremen followed its policy of preferring the woman candidate, since women were underrepresented in the parks service. The Court of Justice held this violated the Equal Treatment Directive 1976 Art 2 because it plainly discriminated against men on grounds of sex. The Court said: '[W]here women and men who are candidates for the same promotion are equally qualified, women are automatically to be given priority in sectors where they are underrepresented, involves discrimination on grounds of sex.'

3.   *Kalanke* caused a political backlash, so after the Amsterdam Treaty, *Marschall v Land Nordrhein Westfalen* (1996) C-409/95 held that a preference for a candidate from an underrepresented group was lawful in a tie-break situation. Mr Marschall complained that a woman candidate got a job over him, even though they were

equally qualified. He contended automatic preference against men (as the overrepresented group, on the facts) should be unlawful. The school's rules said that preference for underrepresented groups would be given 'unless reasons specific to an individual candidate tilt the balance in his favour'. The Court of Justice held that, with this type of 'saving clause' (*Öffnungsklausel*), where an employing entity must truly consider individual merits, an employing entity could lawfully prefer someone from an underrepresented group.

4.   The debate about 'affirmative action' in the United States has been intensive for some time, and many fear a change in the US Supreme Court composition could reverse progress. In *United Steelworkers of America v Weber*, 443 US 193 (1979) the Supreme Court held by a majority that affirmative action was lawful to correct historical disadvantage. In *Johnson v Transportation Agency, Santa Clara County* 480 US 616 (1987) it was again held by a majority that affirmative action was lawful, even in a situation where a woman was less qualified than a male counterpart. It is important to see that – unlike public bodies or companies in India or South Africa – the US rules simply enable employing entities to *voluntarily* adopt such policies. However, they have proved very divisive.

5.   It can be argued that affirmative action is unfair to people who are not hired, despite being more qualified for a job. Even more, people who are given preference may *themselves* not wish to be hired simply because they belong to a 'historically disadvantaged' group. They want to succeed on their own merits. On the other hand, why would the legacy of racism and sexism in the US correct itself? Until there is genuine equality, affirmative action is a part of the solution. What do you think?

6.   Would your answer about the legitimacy of affirmative action (ie positive discrimination, with quotas) change between the contexts of different countries: eg the UK, USA, Sweden, New Zealand or South Africa? Does your answer change for different protected characteristics? If so, why? If not, why not?

7.   In *Abrahamsson and Anderson v Fogelqvist* (2000) C-407/98 the Court of Justice held that, in applying to be a Professor of Hydrospheric Science at the University of Göteborg, the university could not prefer woman candidates where it was shown that a male candidate, Mr Anderson, was better qualified. Only if two candidates were judged to be equally qualified could an employing entity (if it so chose) select someone from an underrepresented group.

8.   If you were advising an employing entity on how to strongly pursue an equality policy under the current law, how would you tell it to arrange its desired job qualifications, to ensure maximum flexibility?

9.   Aside from the question of the tie-break situation, a fuller set of legitimate positive action measures were set out in *Badeck*.

Re Badeck's application (2001) C-158/97

Georg Badeck, the First Minister of the German state of Hesse (capital, Frankfurt am Main) for the Christian Democrat Union party sought judicial review of a Hesse law that set out positive action measures for appointment to public office. He took the view that it potentially violated an ostensible German constitutional duty to get the best people for the job, as well as violating (what is now) the Equal Treatment Directive 2006 (then 76/207/EEC). The Court of Justice summarised its policy in the conclusion to the case.

Court of Justice:

Article 2(1) and (4) of Council Directive 76/207/EEC of 9 February 1976 on the implementation of the principle of equal treatment for men and women as regards access to employment, vocational training and promotion, and working conditions does not preclude a national rule which

—in sectors of the public service where women are under-represented, gives priority, where male and female candidates have equal qualifications, to female candidates where that proves necessary for ensuring compliance with the objectives of the women's advancement plan, if no reasons of greater legal weight are opposed, provided that that rule guarantees that candidatures are the subject of an objective assessment which takes account of the specific personal situations of all candidates,

—prescribes that the binding targets of the women's advancement plan for temporary posts in the academic service and for academic assistants must provide for a minimum percentage of women which is at least equal to the percentage of women among graduates, holders of higher degrees and students in each discipline,

—in so far as its objective is to eliminate under-representation of women, in trained occupations in which women are under-represented and for which the State does not have a monopoly of training, allocates at least half the training places to women, unless despite appropriate measures for drawing the attention of women to the training places available there are not enough applications from women,

—where male and female candidates have equal qualifications, guarantees that qualified women who satisfy all the conditions required or laid down are called to interview, in sectors in which they are under-represented,

—relating to the composition of employees' representative bodies and administrative and supervisory bodies, recommends that the legislative provisions adopted for its implementation take into account the objective that at least half the members of those bodies must be women.

NOTES AND QUESTIONS

1. The Court of Justice holds that the five types of legitimate positive action are (1) preferring underrepresented groups where applicants are equally qualified, (2) targets for hiring to temporary posts, (3) allocating training places equally or proportionately, (4) guaranteeing interview places to equally qualified people, and (5) in any representative body requiring quotas for equal (or proportionate) places.

2. Point (5), which endorsed quotas for 'representative' bodies, is the most significant deviation from the tie-break principle of EU law. This seems to be justified on the basis that the true job of a 'representative' will necessarily be to represent a workforce, a company or a political constituency. Therefore, other qualifications are rightly to be seen as inherently less important than this.

3. Since E Davies, *Women on boards* (February 2011) 4–5 and 22–24, and *6 month Monitoring Report* (October 2011) there has been intensive discussion on how to improve the gender balance in corporate board rooms, particularly for public companies listed on the London Stock Exchange. So far, measures have been

voluntary, with limited progress. Other European countries, beginning with Norway, have adopted quotas. Finland appears to have been most successful, but rather than introducing a fixed legal quota, it has required companies to comply with a parity gender target or publicly explain why they have not been able to do so.

4.   Should directors on boards be treated differently to employees? This is an interesting question, which does not yet seem to have been adequately discussed. This may indicate that the common law has (or will necessarily) shift. First, the starting point is that directors of companies have traditionally been considered 'employees' (eg *Lee v Lee's Air Farming Ltd* [1960] UKPC 33) like anyone else, although Lord Denning MR had advocated (obiter) in *Boulting v ACTAT* [1963] 2 QB 606 that they should not be seen as employees. Under EA 2010 s 83, which covers anyone with 'a contract personally to do work', directors might therefore be subject to the same equal-treatment rules as any other employee, regardless of what *Badeck* had suggested was possible. There is no specific exemption for company directors in EA 2010 ss 158–59. This, however, would lead to the unfortunate result that the Davies Report and action by all of the UK's leading companies to increase woman board members could be challenged as unlawful.

5.   Second, it could be argued that the Supreme Court, since the landmark case of *Clyde & Co LLP v Bates van Winkelhof* [2014] UKSC 32, would acknowledge that, just like Ms Bates van Winkelhof, a law firm partner, was not an employee, neither should company directors be. (It could be argued their dismissal rights are in any case adequately protected by the Companies Act 2006 ss 168–69, and in practice by contract.) However Ms Bates van Winkelhof was still held to be a 'worker', which invites protection from EA 2010 s 83. Moreover, even if directors were not workers, they would still logically 'personally perform work'.

6.   A third alternative could be that the principle elaborated in *Badeck* suggests that when people are hired to representative bodies, as was mentioned above, the most important qualification is legitimately seen as 'representing' people. When companies have potentially thousands of workers and millions of beneficial investors of capital, it is essentially right that representatives do reflect society. Moreover, we know that diversity in groups will usually produce a stronger 'group merit' than when groups are all people of one personality type: eg LR Hoffman, 'Homogeneity of Member Personality and Its Effect on Group Problem-Solving' (1959) 58(1) *Journal of Abnormal and Social Psychology* 27. This suggests that diversity in people of different backgrounds or gender tend to enhance a group's decision-making because a broader range of perspectives interacting will produce more innovative solutions. In this way, in the specific context of representatives who will work together in a group with other representatives, it is not merely that 'being a man' or 'being a woman' does become a decisive qualification in itself. It is also that different qualifications are better, and that intelligent enterprises will see diversity as a genuine occupational requirement for efficient business or public service.

7.   EA 2010 s 78 would have required companies with over 250 employees to publish gender pay gap details. The Coalition government in 2010 decided to delay bringing this into force indefinitely.

(2) PREGNANCY

Pregnancy itself presents no issue of *gender* equality as such (there is no male pregnant comparator), but instead there is a need for positive rights of inclusion for women who are going to have children: the right not to suffer detriment, and the right to reasonable adjustments. These rights are very distinct in effect from rights to pay in maternity and paternity leave (see chapter 7(3)). What at first seems to be 'positive' discrimination for women, while mums are treated better than dads, has a perverse effect. Women take more time out of their careers for childcare. This contributes to the gender pay gap. While it is obvious that women give birth to children, and men do not, there is nothing about caring for children that can reasonably be seen as a 'women's work'. Pay and time-off disparities are unjustified (and liable to be struck down?) under any rational equal-pay principle.

By contrast, the Pregnant Workers Directive 92/85/EEC Art 5(1) requires adjustments for pregnant women to avoid risks such as handling of loads, noise, extreme heat or cold, radiation, chemicals and biological agents (Annex I). Article 5(2) says: '[I]f the adjustment of her working conditions and/or working hours is not technically and/or objectively feasible ... the employer shall take the necessary measures to move the worker concerned to another job.' Further, Art 11 requires that the same employment rights are maintained. What are the standards regarding retention of one's job entitlements?

Parviainen v Finnair Oyj (2010) C-471/08

Sanna Maria Parviainen claimed that her employer, Finnair Oyj, unlawfully reduced her pay. She was transferred from being cabin crew, with average pay of €3,383.04 a month, to office work, which was paid €834.56 a month less because it did not carry variable supplementary allowances (eg overtime pay, pay for night work and extras for long-haul flights). She was moved because, according to the court, cabin crew work exposed her to 'ionising and non-ionising radiation which may cause foetal lesions'. The Helsinki District Court asked the CJEU if this was unlawful under the Pregnant Workers Directive Art 5(2) and 11. The Court of Justice held the pay reduction was unlawful, but there was no entitlement to components of pay which only compensated for disadvantages from performing specific tasks.

Third Chamber:

40 ... women taking maternity leave provided for by Article 8 of that directive [i.e. maternity leave] are in a special position which requires them to be afforded special protection, but which is not comparable either with that of a man or with that of a woman actually at work (see Case C-342/93 *Gillespie and Others* [1996] ECR I-475, paragraph 17, and Case C-147/02 *Alabaster* [2004] ECR I-3101, paragraph 46).

41 In the second place, it is clear from Article 11(3) of Directive 92/85 that the definition of adequate allowance which is mentioned therein applies only to Article 11(2)(b), and thus only to workers on maternity leave (see, to that effect, *Høj Pedersen and Others*, paragraph 39).
    ...

43 The transposition of the case-law of the Court on maternity leave to workers in situations such as those referred to in Article 5(1) and (2) of Directive 92/85 could give rise to an unfair

situation in which a worker, such as the applicant in the main proceedings, who is temporarily transferred, because she is pregnant, to a post other than that which she occupied before the transfer, could have her pay cut during that period to an amount equivalent to the allowance provided for by national social security law, where for health reasons that worker stops working.

44 Such a pay cut for a worker who actually continues working would not only be contrary to the protection of the security and health of pregnant workers pursued by Directive 92/85, but would also undermine the legal provisions of the European Union on equal treatment for male and female workers, contrary to the ninth recital in the preamble thereto.

    …

56 The exercise by the Member States and, where appropriate, management and labour of that discretion when determining the pay to which a pregnant worker, who is temporarily transferred to another job during and on account of her pregnancy, is entitled cannot undermine the objective of protecting the safety and health of pregnant workers pursued by Directive 92/85 nor ignore the fact that such a worker actually continues to work and to perform the tasks entrusted to her by her employer.

57 As is clear from the 16th recital in the preamble to Directive 92/85, measures for the organisation of work concerning the protection of the health of pregnant workers, workers who have recently given birth or workers who are breastfeeding would serve no purpose unless accompanied by the maintenance of rights linked to the employment contract, including maintenance of payment and/or entitlement to an adequate allowance.

58 The pay which must be maintained with respect to a pregnant worker in accordance with Article 11(1) of Directive 92/85, following her temporary transfer to a position other than that which she occupied before her pregnancy, cannot, in any event, be less than that paid to workers occupying the job to which she is temporarily assigned. For the duration of that temporary transfer, the pregnant worker is also entitled to the pay components and supplementary allowances relating to that job provided that she fulfils the conditions of eligibility for them in accordance with Article 11(4) of that directive.

59 Furthermore, as the Advocate General observed, in points 69 and 70 of his Opinion, in defining the pay components of such a worker which must be maintained for the duration of the temporary transfer, in accordance with Article 11(1) of Directive 92/85, the Member States and, where appropriate, management and labour are bound by the nature of the various supplementary allowances paid by the employer and which may, in some cases, such as that at issue in the main proceedings, constitute a substantial part of the overall pay of the pregnant worker concerned.

60 It follows that, in addition to the basic salary relating to her contract or her employment relationship, a pregnant worker temporarily transferred to another job, pursuant to Article 5(2) of Directive 92/85, remains, during that transfer, entitled to the pay components or supplementary allowances which relate to her professional status such as, in particular, her seniority, her length of service and her professional qualifications.

61 However, the Member States and, where appropriate, management and labour are not required pursuant to Article 11(1) of Directive 92/85 to maintain, during the temporary transfer, the pay components or supplementary allowances which, as is clear from paragraph 53 of this judgment, are dependent on the performance by the worker concerned of specific functions in particular circumstances and which are intended essentially to compensate for the disadvantages related to that performance.

62 It is clear from the foregoing that, following her temporary transfer to a job other than that which she occupied before her pregnancy, in accordance with Article 5(2) of Directive 92/85, a pregnant worker is not entitled under Article 11(1) thereof to the pay she received on average before that transfer.

...

69 However, in so far as such a pay scheme, in the calculation of the average monthly pay for pregnant air hostesses who have been temporarily transferred in accordance with Article 5(2) of Directive 92/85, fails to take account of the pay components or supplementary allowances which relate to the professional status of the pregnant worker – which is in no way affected by the temporary transfer – such as supplementary allowances relating to the seniority of the worker concerned, her length of service and her professional qualifications, that scheme cannot be regarded as compatible with the requirements of Article 11(1) of Directive 92/85.

President Cunha Rodrigues, Lindh, Rosas, Caoimh and Arabadjiev.

NOTES AND QUESTIONS

1. The CJEU draws a distinction between pay connected to 'professional status' and pay connected to particular 'disadvantages' in doing a job, but then left it to the Finnish court to decide what among overtime, night work flights or long-haul flight supplements were which. What would you decide?
2. EA 2010 s 4 states that 'maternity and pregnancy' is a protected characteristic, and s 13(6) eliminates the need for a comparator. Under s 18, there is discrimination against a pregnant worker if they are treated 'unfavourably', rather than 'less favourably'.
3. Under ERA 1996 s 99, dismissal is automatically unfair if on grounds of pregnancy.

(3) DISABILITY

The first major statutes on disability came at the conclusion of World Wars One and Two. The first Disabled Men (Facilities for Employment) Act 1919 empowered the Secretary of State to pay employers money for rising expenditures from 'accidents or industrial disease', apparently 'with a view to facilitating the employment' of injured or ill veterans. It appears to have done very little (HC Debs, Written Answers (1 February 1940) vol 356, col 1300). The second Disabled Persons (Employment) Act 1944, with an update in 1958, required that disabled people be employed by entities with over 20 employees, if they had not already filled a quota fixed by the Ministry of Labour. This could be enforced through an injunction, backed by criminal penalties for refusing to take someone into employment. This depended largely on state enforcement, which may have been lacking. It was replaced by the Disability Discrimination Act (DDA) 1995, now integrated in EA 2010. Two main points about disability are (a) its meaning, and (b) the scope of an employing entity's duty to make 'reasonable adjustments'.

(a) Meaning

To some extent, the meaning of disability has to be set by EU law, rather than the provisions about to follow in UK law. Because EU law sets minimum standards, whenever UK law is or seems less favourable, it must be interpreted as far as possible to comply, or it must be disapplied, and the government is open to damages claims. In *Chacón Navas v Eurest Colectividades SA* (2006) C-13/05, [40]–[43] the Court of Justice held that an 'autonomous and uniform' meaning of disability was needed, and this was 'a limitation which results in particular from physical, mental or psychological impairments and which hinders the participation of the person concerned in professional life'. So, the EA 2010 s 6(1) below refers to disability as a 'substantial and long-term' impairment in 'normal day-to-day activities'. But in any situation where this is less favourable than the definition in *Chacón Navas* it is to be disregarded.

Equality Act 2010 s 6 and Sch 1

6 Disability
   (1) A person (P) has a disability if—
      (a)   P has a physical or mental impairment, and
      (b)   the impairment has a substantial and long-term adverse effect on P's ability to carry out normal day-to-day activities.
   (2) A reference to a disabled person is a reference to a person who has a disability.
   (3) In relation to the protected characteristic of disability—
      (a)   a reference to a person who has a particular protected characteristic is a reference to a person who has a particular disability;
      (b)   a reference to persons who share a protected characteristic is a reference to persons who have the same disability.
   (4) This Act (except Part 12 and section 190) applies in relation to a person who has had a disability as it applies in relation to a person who has the disability; accordingly (except in that Part and that section)—
      (a)   a reference (however expressed) to a person who has a disability includes a reference to a person who has had the disability, and
      (b)   a reference (however expressed) to a person who does not have a disability includes a reference to a person who has not had the disability.
      ...

Schedule 1 Disability: supplementary provision
Long-term effects
   2(1) The effect of an impairment is long-term if—
      (a)   it has lasted for at least 12 months,
      (b)   it is likely to last for at least 12 months, or
      (c)   it is likely to last for the rest of the life of the person affected.
   (2) If an impairment ceases to have a substantial adverse effect on a person's ability to carry out normal day-to-day activities, it is to be treated as continuing to have that effect if that effect is likely to recur.

Severe disfigurement
   3(1) An impairment which consists of a severe disfigurement is to be treated as having a substantial adverse effect on the ability of the person concerned to carry out normal day-to-day activities.

Substantial adverse effects

4 Regulations may make provision for an effect of a prescribed description on the ability of a person to carry out normal day-to-day activities to be treated as being, or as not being, a substantial adverse effect.

Effect of medical treatment

5(1) An impairment is to be treated as having a substantial adverse effect on the ability of the person concerned to carry out normal day-to-day activities if—

    (a)   measures are being taken to treat or correct it, and

    (b)   but for that, it would be likely to have that effect.

Certain medical conditions

6(1) Cancer, HIV infection and multiple sclerosis are each a disability.

(2) HIV infection is infection by a virus capable of causing the Acquired Immune Deficiency Syndrome.

NOTES AND QUESTIONS

1.   To continue from above, EA 2010 s 6, with its various elaborations, might be seen as contradicting the binding case law from the Court of Justice, or (preferably) is to be seen as implementing its principles but not doing so very well. There are two clear problems, which require teleological interpretation.

2.   First, there is no EU law requirement that a disability last for 'at least 12 months' (cf Sch 1, para 2(1)). If someone has a shorter-term disability, UK law is best read as meaning that 'long-term' in s 6 means anything long enough to hinder 'participation of the person concerned in professional life', even if that is much shorter than 12 months. Then, Sch 1, para 2(1) is to be read as an example definition, but not exhaustive, ('if' but not 'only if') of the concept of 'long-term' in s 6, defined in reference to *Chacón Navas*.

3.   Second, there is no EU law requirement for a disability to hinder someone in 'normal day-to-day activities' (s 6) *as well as* in 'professional life' (*Chacón Navas*). However, this apparent tension is soluble by recognising that any aspect of work is a central example of a 'normal day-to-day activity', and so it would be irrelevant that a claimant may cope with his or her disability without issue outside work, but finds difficulty at work.

4.   To give examples on the last point, someone *must* now clearly be found disabled who is affected at work because of having paranoid schizophrenia, even if it is under day-to-day control (*Goodwin v Patent Office* [1999] ICR 302), losing hand strength (*Vicary v BT plc* [1999] IRLR 680), or is able to catch a ball but cannot negotiate a pavement due to clinical depression (*Leonard v Southern Derbyshire Chamber of Commerce* [2001] IRLR 19). It is submitted that any detriment from an employing entity due to a medically recognised condition, or judicially recognised impairment, is by definition, hindering a claimant's participation in professional life, and is therefore unlawful disability discrimination.

5.   Under EA 2010 s 6(5) and Sch 1, para 1, the Equality Act 2010 (Disability) Regulations 2010 regs 3–8 were passed, and make certain exemptions. People are deemed not to be disabled simply because they are addicted to alcohol, nicotine or

other non-medically prescribed substances (reg 3). It is not a disability if someone sets fires to things, steals or engages in physical or sexual abuse, exhibitionism, voyeurism, or has seasonal allergic rhinitis ('hay fever') (reg 4). Tattoos and piercings do not count as severe disfigurements (reg 5). But partial sight *does* count as a disability if confirmed by a consultant ophthalmologist (reg 7).

6. Perhaps with *Coleman v Attridge Law* (ch 12(1)(b)) in mind, the Secretary of State chose to add in reg 6 that children under six years of age who cannot carry out normal day-to-day activities do not count as disabled for the purpose of an associative discrimination claim. This would not be an issue under the *Chacón Navas* definition.

7. In *Kaltoft v Municipality of Bilund* (2014) C-354/13, the Court of Justice held that obesity can be a disability if it hinders people in professional life.

(b) Reasonable Adjustments

Together with some clarification of direct discrimination for disability, the duty to make reasonable adjustments is scattered through various sections and Sch 8.

Equality Act 2010 ss 13(3), 15, 20–21, 60 and Sch 8

13 Direct discrimination
...
(3) If the protected characteristic is disability, and B is not a disabled person, A does not discriminate against B only because A treats or would treat disabled persons more favourably than A treats B.
...

15 Discrimination arising from disability
(1) A person (A) discriminates against a disabled person (B) if—
  (a) A treats B unfavourably because of something arising in consequence of B's disability, and
  (b) A cannot show that the treatment is a proportionate means of achieving a legitimate aim.
(2) Subsection (1) does not apply if A shows that A did not know, and could not reasonably have been expected to know, that B had the disability.
...

20 Duty to make adjustments
(1) Where this Act imposes a duty to make reasonable adjustments on a person, this section, sections 21 and 22 and the applicable Schedule apply; and for those purposes, a person on whom the duty is imposed is referred to as A.
(2) The duty comprises the following three requirements.
(3) The first requirement is a requirement, where a provision, criterion or practice of A's puts a disabled person at a substantial disadvantage in relation to a relevant matter in comparison with persons who are not disabled, to take such steps as it is reasonable to have to take to avoid the disadvantage.
(4) The second requirement is a requirement, where a physical feature puts a disabled person at a substantial disadvantage in relation to a relevant matter in comparison with persons

who are not disabled, to take such steps as it is reasonable to have to take to avoid the disadvantage.

(5) The third requirement is a requirement, where a disabled person would, but for the provision of an auxiliary aid, be put at a substantial disadvantage in relation to a relevant matter in comparison with persons who are not disabled, to take such steps as it is reasonable to have to take to provide the auxiliary aid.

(6) Where the first or third requirement relates to the provision of information, the steps which it is reasonable for A to have to take include steps for ensuring that in the circumstances concerned the information is provided in an accessible format.

(7) A person (A) who is subject to a duty to make reasonable adjustments is not (subject to express provision to the contrary) entitled to require a disabled person, in relation to whom A is required to comply with the duty, to pay to any extent A's costs of complying with the duty.

(8) A reference in section 21 or 22 or an applicable Schedule to the first, second or third requirement is to be construed in accordance with this section.

(9) In relation to the second requirement, a reference in this section or an applicable Schedule to avoiding a substantial disadvantage includes a reference to—

    (a)   removing the physical feature in question,

    (b)   altering it, or

    (c)   providing a reasonable means of avoiding it.

(10) A reference in this section, section 21 or 22 or an applicable Schedule (apart from paragraphs 2 to 4 of Schedule 4) to a physical feature is a reference to—

    (a)   a feature arising from the design or construction of a building,

    (b)   a feature of an approach to, exit from or access to a building,

    (c)   a fixture or fitting, or furniture, furnishings, materials, equipment or other chattels, in or on premises, or

    (d)   any other physical element or quality.

…

21 Failure to comply with duty

(1) A failure to comply with the first, second or third requirement is a failure to comply with a duty to make reasonable adjustments.

(2) A discriminates against a disabled person if A fails to comply with that duty in relation to that person.

…

60 Enquiries about disability and health

(1) A person (A) to whom an application for work is made must not ask about the health of the applicant (B)—

    (a)   before offering work to B, or

    (b)   where A is not in a position to offer work to B, before including B in a pool of applicants from whom A intends (when in a position to do so) to select a person to whom to offer work.

…

(3) A does not contravene a relevant disability provision merely by asking about B's health; but A's conduct in reliance on information given in response may be a contravention of a relevant disability provision.

…

(6) This section does not apply to a question that A asks in so far as asking the question is necessary for the purpose of—

    (a)   establishing whether B will be able to comply with a requirement to undergo an assessment or establishing whether a duty to make reasonable adjustments is or will be imposed on A in relation to B in connection with a requirement to undergo an assessment,

(b)   establishing whether B will be able to carry out a function that is intrinsic to the work concerned,

(c)   monitoring diversity in the range of persons applying to A for work,

(d)   taking action to which section 158 would apply if references in that section to persons who share (or do not share) a protected characteristic were references to disabled persons (or persons who are not disabled) and the reference to the characteristic were a reference to disability, or

(e)   if A applies in relation to the work a requirement to have a particular disability, establishing whether B has that disability.

...

Schedule 8 Work: reasonable adjustments

The duty

2(1) A must comply with the first, second and third requirements.

...

Employers (see section 39)

5(1) This paragraph applies where A is an employer.

...

Lack of knowledge of disability, etc.

20(1) A is not subject to a duty to make reasonable adjustments if A does not know, and could not reasonably be expected to know—

(a)   in the case of an applicant or potential applicant, that an interested disabled person is or may be an applicant for the work in question;

NOTES AND QUESTIONS

1.   In total, these sections mean an employing entity has a duty to make reasonable adjustments (literally, reading backwards, Sch 8, paras 5(1), 2(1), and s 21), which includes removing practices that put disabled people at a disadvantage (s 20(3)), changing physical features, and providing auxiliary aids, as is reasonable. Reasonableness means looking at the costs compared to the likely benefits, but recognising that considerable costs could well be inevitable, required by law and just.

2.   The sections and Schedules on disability are not drafted to an adequate standard. This is particularly unfortunate given the stronger than usual need for employing entities to have clear guidance in this field.

3.   EA 2010 s 15 on 'discrimination arising from disability' is meant to clarify that a claim is available, for instance, if someone has a guide dog, and suffers detriment because of the dog, rather than being blind. Although perhaps welcome, this clarification does seem to be unnecessary because the dog owner in that case would plainly have suffered direct discrimination (blindness and the dog are not separate issues). A similar view was posited in *Lewisham LBC v Malcolm and EHRC* [2008] UKHL 43.

4.   In *Stockton on Tees BC v Aylott* [2010] EWCA Civ 910, Mr Aylott successfully claimed direct disability discrimination based on his condition of bipolar affective disorder in the Court of Appeal. This caused Mr Aylott to have to take sick leave, and then it led to an argument with a manager. Such a set of events were mistakenly interpreted as being personal behavioural problems, rather than seeing them as intrinsically connected to or 'arising from' the disability.

5.   Under EA 2010 s 22, the Secretary of State included in the Equality Act 2010 (Disability) Regulations 2010 more details on reasonable adjustments. Under reg 8, reasonable physical adjustments include removal, replacement or provision of chattels, signs and notices, taps and door handles, door bells and entry systems, and changes to the colour of surfaces such as walls or doors.

Archibald v Fife Council [2004] UKHL 32

Mrs Archibald claimed that Fife Council failed to make reasonable adjustments, after she could no longer perform her previous job as a road sweeper. In 1999 she had surgery, with complications and could no longer walk and sweep streets. The Council kept her working in an office, and she was shortlisted for all upcoming vacancies. However, after more than 100 applications for jobs one grade up from a manual worker, she still was turned down for every one. The evidence before Tribunal suggested that her work as a street sweeper had prejudiced the people looking at her credentials. After dismissal for incapacity on 12 March 2001 she brought a claim under the DDA 1995 s 6 (now EA 2010 s 20) for failure to make reasonable adjustments. She contended she should not have had to go through competitive interviews. She lost at Tribunal, in the EAT and the Court of Session, but the House of Lords allowed Mrs Archibald's claim.

Baroness Hale:

47. According to its long title, the purpose of the 1995 Act is 'to make it unlawful to discriminate against disabled persons in connection with employment, the provision of goods, facilities and services or the disposal or management of premises ...' But this legislation is different from the Sex Discrimination Act 1975 and the Race Relations Act 1976. In the latter two, men and women or black and white, as the case may be, are opposite sides of the same coin. Each is to be treated in the same way. Treating men more favourably than women discriminates against women. Treating women more favourably than men discriminates against men. Pregnancy apart, the differences between the genders are generally regarded as irrelevant. The 1995 Act, however, does not regard the differences between disabled people and others as irrelevant. It does not expect each to be treated in the same way. It expects reasonable adjustments to be made to cater for the special needs of disabled people. It necessarily entails an element of more favourable treatment. The question for us is when that obligation arises and how far it goes.

    ...

58. The Disability Rights Commission, which has taken up the case on behalf of Mrs Archibald, argue that in such a case the duty is indeed triggered. The control mechanism lies in the fact that the employer is only required to take such steps as it is reasonable for them to have to take. They are not expected to do the impossible. But among the possible steps is (c) – transfer to fill an existing vacancy, which must include an existing vacancy for a different job. Inability to do the present job cannot mean that there is no duty at all. The Act was clearly intended to apply to existing employees who became disabled as well as to would-be employees who were already disabled. This is reflected in paragraph 4.20 of the Code of Practice, issued by the Secretary of State and laid before Parliament under sections 53 and 54 of the Act, which says this under the heading 'transferring the person to fill an existing vacancy':

    "If an employee becomes disabled, or has a disability which worsens so she cannot work in the same place or under the same arrangements and there is no reasonable adjustment which would enable the employee to continue doing the current job, then she might have to be considered for any suitable alternative posts which are available. (Such a case might also involve reasonable retraining.)"

59. Underlying this debate there may be, as Mr O'Neill on behalf of the council argues, a fundamental philosophical difference about the permissible limits of the positive discrimination which the duty to make reasonable adjustments inevitably entails. The Act predates the Council Directive 2000/78/EC establishing a general framework for equal treatment in employment and occupation (the 'Framework Directive'). That Directive cannot constitute grounds for reducing the level of protection against discrimination already afforded by Member States (article 8.2). Nevertheless both sides seek to rely upon its principles. The council point to the opening words of recital 17 – 'This Directive does not require the recruitment, promotion, maintenance in employment or training of an individual who is not competent, capable and available to perform the essential functions of the post concerned or to undergo the relevant training, … – while the Commission point to its concluding words – '… without prejudice to the obligation to provide reasonable accommodation for people with disabilities.' The council argue that it is a framework for equal, not preferential, treatment. Article 1 provides its purpose:

> "The purpose of this Directive is to lay down a general framework for combating discrimination on the grounds of religion or belief, disability, age or sexual orientation as regards employment and occupation, with a view to putting into effect in the Member States the principle of equal treatment."

> …

65. The duty is to take such steps as it is reasonable in all the circumstances of the case for the employer to have to take. Could this ever include transferring her to fill an existing vacancy at a slightly higher grade without competitive interview? It is noteworthy that the council did do a great deal to help Mrs Archibald. They arranged retraining for her. They kept her on the books for a great deal longer than they normally would have done while she retrained and then looked for alternative posts. They automatically short-listed her for the posts for which she applied. They went rather beyond their normal policies in cases of redundancy or ill-health. They were behaving as if they did have a duty towards her under section 6(1) even if they did not think that they did. They would have been prepared to transfer her without competitive interview to another job at the same or a lower grade, even though there might be others better qualified to do it. But as she was at the bottom of the manual grade and all office jobs were nominally at a higher grade, there was no equal or lower grade job to which she could be transferred.

66. Section 6(3)(c) merely refers to 'an existing vacancy'. It does not qualify this by any words such as 'at the same or a lower grade'. It does refer to 'transferring' rather than 'promoting' her, but as a matter of language a transfer can be upwards as well as sideways or downwards. Furthermore, transferring her 'to fill' an existing vacancy is clearly more than merely allowing her to apply, short-listing or considering her for an existing vacancy. If that were all it meant, it would add nothing to the existing non-discrimination requirements: the employer is already required by section 4(2)(b) not to discriminate against a disabled employee in the opportunities afforded for promotion, transfer, training or any other benefit.

67. On the face of it, therefore, transferring Mrs Archibald to a sedentary position which she was qualified to fill was among the steps which it might have been reasonable in all the circumstances for the council to have to take once she could no longer walk and sweep. Is there any reason to hold to the contrary?

   …

70. This will depend upon all the circumstances of the case, having regard in particular to the factors laid down in section 6(4). An important component in the circumstances must be the council's redeployment policy. This currently distinguishes between transfer to a post at the same or a lower grade and transfer to a post at a higher grade. Generally it must be reasonable for a council to maintain this distinction. But it might be reasonable to expect a small modification either in general or in the particular case to meet the needs of a well-qualified and well-motivated employee who has become disabled. Manual grades are often technically lower than non-manual grades even if the difference in pay is minimal. The possibility of transfer to fill an existing vacancy might become completely illusory for a manual worker who became incapable of manual work but was assessed as very well fitted for low grade sedentary work if that person was always up against the problem presented by her background. We are not talking here of high grade positions where it is not only possible but important to make fine judgments about who will be best for the job. We are talking of positions which a great many people could fill and for which no one candidate may be obviously 'the best'. There is no law against discriminating against people with a background in manual work, but it might be reasonable for an employer to have to take that difficulty into account when considering the transfer of a disabled worker who could no longer do that type of work. I only say 'might' because it depends upon all the circumstances of the case. While the 1995 Act clearly lays great emphasis on the circumstances of the individual case, the general policy of achieving fairness and transparency in local government appointments is also extremely important. The real question may be whether this case should have been seen as a sideways rather than an upwards move.

71. None of this was considered by the Employment Tribunal, which disposed of the case on a ground which was clearly wrong. They did not address the question of reasonableness. They did address the question of justification under section 5(2)(b), but did so without the benefit of the Court of Appeal's decision in Collins v National Theatre [2004] EWCA Civ 144 that the justification must be something other than the circumstances which are taken into account for the purpose of section 6(1). As the council's redeployment policy is an important part of those circumstances, it should not be independently relevant as a justification under section 5(2)(b).

Lord Hope and **Lord Rodger** gave concurring judgments. **Lord Nicholls** and **Lord Brown** concurred.

NOTES AND QUESTIONS

1.   The House of Lords, in probably the most important judgment on disability rights in modern history, held that Mrs Archibald could be entitled to be exempt from competitive interviews: the Tribunal was instructed to consider again. Assuming she won her claim, this would give Mrs Archibald an obvious advantage, and practically amounted to a guarantee for a job. This was probably the very point.

2.   Although not referred to in the judgment, recall that the Disabled Persons (Employment) Act 1944 required employing entities with over 20 employees, in essence, to guarantee quotas of jobs for disabled people. The purpose was to ensure the human potential of people disabled by war were not excluded from society. This was enforceable through injunctions and criminal penalties (summarised in P Davies and M Freedland, *Labour Legislation and Public Policy* (Clarendon Press, 1994) 62–63). It is submitted that neither the DDA 1995 nor the EA 2010 was intended to be a step back from the 1944 Act, but rather a step forward.

3.   It is submitted that a disabled job applicant is legally entitled to succeed in a claim against a large employing entity who refuses to hire them, where (1) the claimant shows a basic capacity to perform a job with all necessary adjustments and assistance, and (2) if that employing entity cannot show, using statistical data, that they employ a percentage of disabled people reflecting the number in the local community. This seems important to combat social exclusion and, it is submitted, is a natural consequence of *Archibald*.

4.   In *Jones v Post Office* [2001] EWCA Civ 558 the Court of Appeal held that the Post Office had not discriminated against Mr Jones on ground of his disability by placing him on limited driving duties following a heart attack, and becoming diabetic and insulin dependent. He was put on bicycle rounds and then limited driving, but not full driving, following the Post Office's own medical appraisal. While the Tribunal decided the medical appraisal was wrong, and Mr Jones could have driven fully, the Court of Appeal held the Tribunal should have deferred to the employer's decision: it should have acknowledged the employer's decision was within a 'reasonable range of responses'. This imports a controversial test from unfair dismissal law, without any apparent basis in the legislation. See further chapter 17.

5.   In *Collins v Royal National Theatre Board Ltd* [2004] EWCA Civ 144 the Court of Appeal, overturning the Emplyment Appeal Tribunal, held that Theatre Board failed to make reasonable adjustments for Mr Collins after he lost part of his finger in a workplace accident. This made his hand clumsy, hindering his work as a carpenter. He turned down surgery that had an improved prospect of fixing his hand on the basis that it was too intrusive. The Theatre Board dismissed him because of this, but according to Sedley LJ they should have accommodated Mr Collins as he was. Brooke LJ and Latham LJ concurred.

6.   In *Eagle Place Services Ltd v Rudd* [2010] IRLR 486, Serota QC held that Mr Rudd, hired through an employment agency, EPS Ltd, to a law firm called Nabarro suffered direct disability discrimination, and that the employing entity failed to make reasonable adjustments. Mr Rudd had detached retinas, which meant office work was strenuous, so he worked at home for some days in the week. He was dismissed because the firm decided this was not an adjustment they should make. But then, they attempted to argue that the real reason for the dismissal was that they simply had a policy of dismissing anyone with whom they had a dispute, as a way to bargain aggressively for a better settlement. Therefore, it was said, Mr Rudd had no comparator to show less favourable treatment, because they would have dismissed a non-disabled person in the same way (the so-called 'bastard defence' – 'we would have been a bastard to anyone'). Serota QC held, at [86]: 'It is simply not open to the respondent to say that it has not discriminated against the claimant because it would have behaved unreasonably in dismissing the comparator. It is unreasonable to suppose that it in fact would have dismissed the comparator for what amounts to an irrational reason.'

7.   *G4S Cash Solutions (UK) Ltd v Powell* [2016] IRLR 820 held that after a claimant suffered a back injury at work, and was redeployed to another job where the pay was lower, the employer could have a duty to protect pay. HH Judge David Richardson held there was no reason why a duty of reasonable adjustment 'should

be read as excluding any requirement upon an employer to protect an employee's pay in conjunction with other measures to counter the employee's disadvantage through disability. The question will always be whether it is reasonable for the employer to have to take that step.'

Additional Reading for Chapter 14

D Bell and A Heitmueller, 'The Disability Discrimination Act in the UK: Helping or Hindering Employment among the Disabled?' (2009) 28 *Journal of Health Economics* **465**

The economist authors find that the DDA 1995 (which was not significantly changed in the EA 2010) coincided with a rate of employment for disabled people that is 5–8 per cent lower. While the authors appear not to appreciate that after World War Two, disabled veterans had to be employed by large companies, they say suggest that more laws decrease employment. They suggest: 'Other countries such as Germany have introduced quota systems which are more transparent and more easily enforced centrally. However, to our knowledge there is little evidence yet that such a system would work any better.' While the conclusion could be the reverse of Bell and Heitmueller's beliefs (that the DDA 1995 represented a de facto reduction in protection), their results do suggest the law could work far better.

15

Atypical Work

What does it mean to be a citizen with a 'standard employment relation'? In the late twentieth century, it came to mean working from 9am to 5pm, Monday to Friday, usually for a corporation or public body, permanently, in one's country of birth. The security of this life was a real achievement of collective bargaining and British social policy. People earned a living wage, with time to raise a family, and had security in retirement. Part-time, fixed-term, agency or migrant work was different. Then, from 1979, government began to say 'flexible' and 'mobile' labour markets were desirable in an increasingly competitive global economy. It was true that some people did not want a standard employment relation. People with children might want to work less than 40 hours a week. A permanent career might not be right just yet. An agency might be convenient for quick jobs. People might look forward to travelling and building their lives abroad. From an employing entity's perspective, a pool of flexible, mobile labour could also enable rapid response to changing technology and demand: business would have stable profits in a dynamic economy. In principle, if enough employees and employers wanted the same flexibility, nothing could be wrong. Some could have security, others could have flexibility, and everyone's needs and wants would be met (see T Wilthagen and F Tros, 'The Concept of "Flexicurity": A New Approach to Regulating Employment and Labour Markets' (2004) 10(2) *Transfer* 166).

But the reality is, while unemployment exists nationally and globally, many are forced to be part-time, fixed-term, agency or migrant workers. Unlike race or gender, each status is created by law: in contract, statute or both. These statuses already purport to restrict rights: less working time (part-time), less job security (fixed-term), intermediated membership in an organisation (agency), partial rights in the nation (migration). People may suffer unequal treatment simply for the status itself. People with limited rights used to be called 'denizens'. 'A denizen', wrote William Blackstone, 'is a kind of middle state, between an alien and a natural-born subject, and partakes of both' (*Commentaries on the Laws of England* (1765) book 1, ch X, 374). Now this term is being applied to precarious workers who do not have real choice of work. Many people in Britain and worldwide are said to have become denizens and together are, writes Guy Standing, *The Precariat: The New Dangerous Class* (2011). Franklin D Roosevelt might have agreed: '"Necessitous men are not free men." People who are hungry and out of a job are the stuff of which dictatorships are made' (*Eleventh State of the Union Address* (1944)). This chapter examines how the law regulates (1) part-time, (2) fixed-term and (3) agency work. For each, there are limited rights to equal treatment and rights to acquire full rights.

Introductory texts: Collins ch 4 (91–4). CEM ch 10 (393–404). D&M ch 3 (199–218).

(1) PART-TIME WORKERS

Part-time jobs tend to be in sectors with lower pay than average. Because of this, it has been calculated that there is an average 'part-time pay penalty' of between 22 and 26 per cent in the UK compared to full-time work (A Manning and B Petrongolo, 'The Part-Time Pay Penalty for Women in Britain' (2008) 118 *Economic Journal* F28). More part-time workers are women. This exacerbates gender inequality. Pay disparities pro rata (ie for each hour) will be rarer within the same employing entity, but certainly exist. Perhaps even more than in fixed-term or agency work, part-time workers face two levels of potential discrimination: first, simply having part-time work may be less favourable for people who want but cannot find full-time work. Second, an employing entity may try to use a worker's contractual status as a reason to justify further less favourable treatment. UK law implements a Directive that was based on an agreement between the European Trade Union Confederation and (what is now) the Confederation of European Business (previously UNICE) and its public sector employer counterpart (CEEP), passed under TFEU Arts 154–55. For this reason, the Directive's essence is found in clauses of the Annex.

(a) Equality or Justification?

Part-time Work Directive 1997 clauses 3–4

Clause 3: Definitions

For the purpose of this agreement:
  1. The term 'part-time worker' refers to an employee whose normal hours of work, calculated on a weekly basis or on average over a period of employment of up to one year, are less than the normal hours of work of a comparable full-time worker.
  2. The term 'comparable full-time worker' means a full-time worker in the same establishment having the same type of employment contract or relationship, who is engaged in the same or a similar work/occupation, due regard being given to other considerations which may include seniority and qualification/skills.
  Where there is no comparable full-time worker in the same establishment, the comparison shall be made by reference to the applicable collective agreement or, where there is no applicable collective agreement, in accordance with national law, collective agreements or practice.

Clause 4: Principle of non-discrimination
  1. In respect of employment conditions, part-time workers shall not be treated in a less favourable manner than comparable full-time workers solely because they work part time unless different treatment is justified on objective grounds.
  2. Where appropriate, the principle of *pro rata temporis* shall apply.
  3. The arrangements for the application of this clause shall be defined by the Member States and/or social partners, having regard to European legislation, national law, collective agreements and practice.

4. Where justified by objective reasons, Member States after consultation of the social partners in accordance with national law, collective agreements or practice and/or social partners may, where appropriate, make access to particular conditions of employment subject to a period of service, time worked or earnings qualification. Qualifications relating to access by part-time workers to particular conditions of employment should be reviewed periodically having regard to the principle of non-discrimination as expressed in Clause 4.1.

NOTES AND QUESTIONS

1. In the Part-time Work Directive (PTWD) 1997 (97/81/EC) clause 3, who can be the comparator (and who cannot)?
2. In clause 4, while 'objective reasons' do not include being a part-time worker itself, what do you think they should include?
3. The PTWD 1997 largely reflects standards in the Part-Time Work Convention 1994 (c 175) except that the Convention does not have any general objective justification clause. Still, it is suggested that for employment rights in general (rather than contractual 'employment conditions') there will never be a justification for treating part-time workers differently, as the Convention suggests.
4. One of the main justifications for the PTWD 1997 was a set of cases in the CJEU which held that discrimination against part-time workers was indirect discrimination against women, because women statistically made up a larger proportion of the part-time workforce. Eventually, it was decided that part-time workers should be protected in their own right.
5. For example, in *R (Equal Opportunities Commission) v SS for Employment* [1994] UKHL 2, [1995] 1 AC 1, the House of Lords held that a requirement to work at least 16 hours a week (or 8 hours after five years' work) to qualify for unfair dismissal protection was unlawful sex discrimination under (what is now) TFEU Art 157. At the time, 90 per cent of part-time employees were women: [1993] 1 CMLR 915, [138]. It followed that direct discrimination against part-time employees was indirect discrimination against women. Lord Keith accepted that 'an increase in the availability of part time work' was 'a beneficial social policy aim' and was a legitimate 'aim'. However, the Department for Employment's affidavit 'did not contain anything capable of being regarded as factual evidence demonstrating the correctness of these views', that removing dismissal protection from part-time workers would 'achieve the stated aim'.
6. What kind of evidence would suffice? In *R (Seymour-Smith and Perez) v SS for Employment* (1999) C-167/97, [76], recall that the Court of Justice stated mere 'generalisations concerning the capacity of a specific measure to encourage recruitment are not enough to show that the aim of the disputed rule is unrelated to any discrimination'. Presumably, this means, even if Member State governments have a wide 'margin of discretion', that falsifiable evidence must at least establish a prima facie case that a policy would achieve its aim. What incentive (if any) can you imagine for an employing entity to hire more people, instead of retaining greater profits, as a result of a reduction in worker rights?
7. The PTWD 1997 was implemented by the Part-time Workers (Prevention of Less Favourable Treatment) Regulations (PTWR) 2000.

Part-time Workers (Prevention of Less Favourable Treatment) Regulations 2000

2. Meaning of full-time worker, part-time worker and comparable full-time worker

...

(4) A full-time worker is a comparable full-time worker in relation to a part-time worker if, at the time when the treatment that is alleged to be less favourable to the part-time worker takes place—

(a) both workers are—
   (i) employed by the same employer under the same type of contract, and
   (ii) engaged in the same or broadly similar work having regard, where relevant, to whether they have a similar level of qualification, skills and experience; and
(b) the full-time worker works or is based at the same establishment as the part-time worker or, where there is no full-time worker working or based at that establishment who satisfies the requirements of sub-paragraph (a), works or is based at a different establishment and satisfies those requirements.

...

5. Less favourable treatment of part-time workers

(1) A part-time worker has the right not to be treated by his employer less favourably than the employer treats a comparable full-time worker—

(a) as regards the terms of his contract; or
(b) by being subjected to any other detriment by any act, or deliberate failure to act, of his employer.

(2) The right conferred by paragraph (1) applies only if—

(a) the treatment is on the ground that the worker is a part-time worker, and
(b) the treatment is not justified on objective grounds.

(3) In determining whether a part-time worker has been treated less favourably than a comparable full-time worker the pro rata principle shall be applied unless it is inappropriate.

(4) A part-time worker paid at a lower rate for overtime worked by him in a period than a comparable full-time worker is or would be paid for overtime worked by him in the same period shall not, for that reason, be regarded as treated less favourably than the comparable full-time worker where, or to the extent that, the total number of hours worked by the part-time worker in the period, including overtime, does not exceed the number of hours the comparable full-time worker is required to work in the period, disregarding absences from work and overtime.

6. Right to receive a written statement of reasons for less favourable treatment

(1) If a worker who considers that his employer may have treated him in a manner which infringes a right conferred on him by regulation 5 requests in writing from his employer a written statement giving particulars of the reasons for the treatment, the worker is entitled to be provided with such a statement within twenty-one days of his request.

(2) A written statement under this regulation is admissible as evidence in any proceedings under these Regulations. ...

NOTES AND QUESTIONS

1. The PTWR 2000 (SI 2000/1551) reg 2(4) follows the PTWD 1997 in the need for a real, not a hypothetical, comparator. Reg 5 creates a general right to equal treatment compared to a full-time worker, unless different treatment is 'justified on objective grounds'. Reg 6 gives the worker the right to written reasons within 21 days. Would you advise a part-time client to request written reasons themselves? Who might be less likely to suffer (overt or covert) retaliation?

(See chapters 8 and 9.) Theoretically, an employer could refuse to give reasons to a third party, and insist a worker makes the request himself or herself, but would you advise an employing entity client to insist on this?

2. PTWR 2000 reg 2(1)–(2) simply defines a full-time worker as someone who 'is identifiable' as such 'having regard to the custom and practice of the employer', and a part-time worker as someone who is not. For the purpose of reg 2(4) on comparable contracts, reg 2(3) specifies that contracts of employment, of apprenticeship and as a worker are to be considered non-comparable, as are 'any other description of worker that it is reasonable for the employer to treat differently'. Reg 3 expressly enables comparison with someone who was full time but whose contract terms were varied, and reg 4 with someone who was full time and returned part time after an absence.

3. A McColgan, 'Missing the Point? The Part-Time Workers (Prevention of Less Favourable Treatment) Regulations 2000' (2000) 29 *ILJ* 260 says that the point about part-time work discrimination is, not so much that part-time workers are paid less pro rata than full-time comparators in the same workplace, but rather 'the difficulties they experience in accessing, as part-time workers, jobs which they would be able to access as full-timers'. In other words, high-paid jobs are not often part time. What do you think can be done to undo the structural segregation of the workforce?

4. Is a full-time employee a valid comparator if they have extra contractual duties?

Matthews v Kent & Medway Towns Fire Authority [2006] UKHL 8

Part-time firefighters of the Kent Fire Brigade claimed that being paid less than full-time firefighters was unlawful discrimination under the PTWR 2000 regulation 5. As well as being contractually obliged to respond to emergencies, full-time firefighters were engaged in educational, preventive and administrative tasks, while the part-time firefighters were not. So, the Kent & Medway Fire Authority contended that the part-time firefighters did not perform 'broadly similar work' to the full-time firefighters under reg 2(4)(a)(ii) because of the difference in duties. The House of Lords by a majority held that the part-time firefighters' work was sufficiently similar to bring a claim.

Baroness Hale:

43. … The sole question for the Tribunal at this stage of the inquiry is whether the work on which the full-time and part-time workers are engaged is "the same or broadly similar". I do not accept the appellants' argument, put at its highest, that this involves looking at the similarities and ignoring any differences. The work which they do must be looked at as a whole, taking into account both similarities and differences. But the question is not whether it is different but whether it is the same or broadly similar. That question has also to be approached in the context of regulations which are inviting a comparison between two types of worker whose work will almost inevitably be different to some extent.

44. In making that assessment, the extent to which the work that they do is exactly the same must be of great importance. If a large component of their work is exactly the same, the question is whether any differences are of such importance as to prevent their work being regarded

overall as "the same or broadly similar". It is easy to imagine workplaces where both full and part-timers do the same work, but the full-timers have extra activities with which to fill their time. This should not prevent their work being regarded as the same or broadly similar overall. Also of great importance in this assessment is the importance of the same work which they do to the work of the enterprise as a whole. It is easy to imagine workplaces where the full-timers do the more important work and the part-timers are brought in to do the more peripheral tasks: the fact that they both do some of the same work would not mean that their work was the same or broadly similar. It is equally easy to imagine workplaces where the full-timers and part-timers spend much of their time on the core activity of the enterprise: judging in the courts or complaints-handling in an ombudsman's office spring to mind. The fact that the full-timers do some extra tasks would not prevent their work being the same or broadly similar. In other words, in answering that question particular weight should be given to the extent to which their work is in fact the same and to the importance of that work to the enterprise as a whole. Otherwise one runs the risk of giving too much weight to differences which are the almost inevitable result of one worker working full-time and another working less than full-time.

45. In my view, looking at the extended reasons of the Tribunal as a whole, it is difficult to escape the conclusion that they saw themselves as conducting essentially the same exercise as that required by the Equal Pay Act. They acknowledged that the fire-fighters' work at the fire ground was the same and said that they gave that factor high importance. But they failed to acknowledge the centrality of that work to the enterprise of the Fire Brigade as a whole. That centrality is demonstrated by the fact that in large areas of the country cover is provided only by retained fire-fighters. Nor did the Tribunal suggest that there was any qualitative difference in the work done by both at the fire ground. Special qualifications, which retained fire-fighters do not have, are needed to operate certain specialist equipment, but not all whole time fire-fighters have those qualifications either. The Tribunal's reliance upon the higher qualification and skills of the whole-time fire-fighters was in connection with the further activities which they were called upon to carry out (para 155).

46. There is a further factor which cannot be ignored, at least in a test case concerning a very large nationwide workforce. This is the extent to which the job description and terms of the part-timer's contract means that he can in fact be required to engage in the same range of tasks as the full-timer, even if in practice he is only rarely called upon to do them. There are likely to be variations in practice across the country, with some places showing greater flexibility in their deployment of their part-timers than others. There are also likely to be variations over time. The recent Audit Commission Report (Comprehensive Performance Assessment. Learning from CPA for the Fire and Rescue Service in England 2005) praises those fire authorities which are making more flexible use of their retained fire-fighting force. It also comments that their lack of involvement in community fire safety work is unlikely to be sustainable in the long term. If more authorities take up the recommendation of the Audit Commission that "the lack of inclusion of retained fire-fighters in community fire safety work is reducing the capacity of fire and rescue authorities to deliver local and national objectives" (p 39) the conclusion that they are not engaged in the same or broadly similar work as the whole-timers is also unlikely to be sustainable in the long term. The Tribunal are, of course, judging the case put before them on the evidence put before them as to the present facts. But the requirements which may and sometimes are placed upon the part-time workers are part of that picture.

47. For these reasons I would remit the case to the Tribunal for reconsideration of whether the retained and whole-time fire-fighters are engaged in the same or broadly similar work.

Lord Nicholls concurred. **Lord Hope** gave a concurring judgment. **Lord Carswell** and **Lord Mance** dissented.

1. Baroness Hale reasons that the part-time firefighters can compare themselves with full-time colleagues under reg 2(4), even though full-time colleagues did extra tasks, because here that was 'the almost inevitable result of one worker working full-time and another working less than full-time'. This suggests that one should look at the dominant role of the workers, and disregard ancillary tasks, to decide whether work is 'broadly similar'.

2. Is it surprising that the first major UK case on part-time work was about men?

3. Differences in contract terms between part-time and full-time workers that are discriminatory also do not affect the ability to use a full-time worker as a comparator. In *Sharma v Manchester City Council* [2008] IRLR 336, Elias J in the Employment Appeal Tribunal held that a reduction of hours for part-time, but not full-time, lecturers in the Manchester Adult Education Service was unlawful under the PTWR 2000 reg 5. A contract term, from a collective agreement, in the part-time contracts said hours had to be a minimum of one-third from the previous years, but the full-time lecturer contracts had no such term. Far from being a reason why the contracts were not comparable, this was the very discrimination complained of, and justified nothing.

4. However, could a part-time worker, whose hours the employer may set at its discretion, compare herself to a full-time worker whose hours did not fluctuate?

Wippel v Peek & Cloppenburg GmbH & Co KG (2005) C-313/02

Ms Wippel claimed that her fluctuating 'on-demand' hours contract meant she was less favourably treated than a full-time worker who received fixed hours in a contract. She worked for a retail clothing business, from age 19 to 21, for initially about three days a week and two Saturdays a month on €6.54 an hour. The Austrian Working Time Act (*Arbeitzeitgesetz*) had a maximum working week for full-time workers. However, Ms Wippel's contract allowed her working hours to be varied to any number. She could also refuse work without having to justify it. Around 90 per cent of part-time workers in Austria were women, while 40 per cent of full-time workers were women. The Court of Justice held that she could be classified as a part-time worker, but she had no full-time comparator with fluctuating hours.

Grand Chamber:

58. ... Clause 3 of the Framework Agreement provides guidelines for determining what is a 'comparable full-time worker'. Such a person is defined as 'a full-time worker in the same establishment having the same type of employment contract or relationship, who is engaged in the same or a similar work/occupation, due regard being given to other considerations which may include seniority and qualification/skills'. Under the same clause, where there is no comparable full-time worker in the same establishment, the comparison is to be made by reference to the applicable collective agreement or, where there is no applicable collective agreement, in accordance with national law, collective agreements or practice.

59. A part-time employee working according to need, such as Ms Wippel, works under a contract which stipulates neither the weekly hours of work nor the manner in which working time

is to be organised, but it leaves her the choice of whether to accept or refuse the work offered by P&C. The work is remunerated by the hour only for hours actually worked.

60. A full-time worker works under a contract which fixes a working week of 38.5 hours, fixing the organisation of the working week and salary, and which requires him to work for P&C for the whole working time thus determined without the possibility of refusing that work even if the worker cannot or does not wish to do it.

61. Under those circumstances, the employment relationship referred to in the preceding paragraph hereof differs, as to subject-matter and basis, from that of a worker such as Ms Wippel. It follows that no full-time worker in the same establishment has the same type of contract or employment relationship as Ms Wippel. It is apparent from the file that in the circumstances of the main proceedings, the same is true of all the full-time workers, in respect of whom the applicable collective agreement provides for a working week of 38.5 hours.

62. In the circumstances of the main proceedings, there is therefore no full-time worker comparable to Ms Wippel within the meaning of the Framework Agreement annexed to Directive 97/81. It follows that a contract of part-time employment according to need which makes provision for neither the length of weekly working time nor the organisation of working time does not result in less favourable treatment within the meaning of Clause 4 of the Framework Agreement.

63. Secondly, in regard to Articles 2(1) and 5(1) of Directive 76/207, it is apparent from the file that, according to Ms Wippel, the situations of the workers to be compared are, first, the situation of part-time employees working according to P&C's needs whose contracts of employment make provision neither for the length of weekly working time nor for the organisation of working time and, secondly, the situation of all P&C's other workers, both full-time and part-time, whose contracts of employment make such provision.

64. Given that the latter category of workers has the obligation to work for P&C for a fixed weekly period, without the possibility of refusing that work should the workers concerned not be able or not wish to work, it is sufficient to note that, for the reasons set out at paragraphs 59 to 61 hereof, the situation of those workers is not analogous to that of part-time employees working according to need.

65. Accordingly, in circumstances such as those of the main proceedings, in which the two categories of workers are not comparable, a contract of part-time employment according to need which makes provision for neither the length of weekly working time nor the organisation of working time does not constitute an indirectly discriminatory measure within the meaning of Articles 2(1) and 5(1) of Directive 76/207.

66. In the light of all the foregoing, the reply to the third question must be that Clause 4 of the Framework Agreement annexed to Directive 97/81 and Articles 2(1) and 5(1) of Directive 76/207 must be interpreted as meaning that, in circumstances where all the contracts of employment of the other employees of an undertaking make provision for the length of weekly working time and for the organisation of working time, they do not preclude a contract of part-time employment of workers of the same undertaking, such as that in the main proceedings, under which the length of weekly working time and the organisation of working time are not fixed but are dependent on quantitative needs in terms of work to be performed determined on a case-by-case basis, such workers being entitled to accept or refuse that work.

President Skouris, Jann, Timmermans, Rosas, Silva de Lapuerta, Lenaerts, Puissochet, Schintgen, Macken, Cunha Rodrigues and **Schiemann.**

1.   The Court of Justice reasons that a full-time employee could have variable hours, and so this type of person (rather than someone who has fixed hours) is the appropriate comparator. The proposed comparator was not similar in all relevant respects to the claimant, and therefore could not be used (see chapter 12(2)(a)). In effect, the Court of Justice refuses to treat the problem of discretionary or zero-hours contracts (chapter 7(2)(a)) as a problem of part-time work. Is this reasoning persuasive? Ms Wippel's contention was that if an employer can vary hours below a given definition of full-time work (in this case 38.5 hours), this person is ipso facto a part-time worker at the employer's discretion. On this view, Ms Wippel should have been able to compare herself to a fixed-hours full-time worker or a variable-hours full-time worker (eg someone who could do overtime). Then, the question would be whether Ms Wippel's hours were being varied in a less favourable manner than a full-time worker's hours.

2.   Advocate General Kokott, unlike the Court of Justice, did consider the position as if Ms Wippel could use a full-time employee as a comparator, but noting the fact of discretionary hours 'does not absolutely conform to traditional ideas of part-time working', Opinion of 18 May 2004, [98]. The clause was unequal treatment compared to a full-time worker [101]. But was it less favourable? In her view, there would need to be specific evidence of discretionary hours resulting in improper social protection (losing holiday pay, sick pay, maternity pay or medical insurance), or abuse (by failing to offer regular work) to show unequal treatment [110]. The very fact of variable hours was not less favourable treatment, especially given the 'positive attitude towards the concept of work on demand displayed by P&C's works council, as its elected staff representative body' [106]. Since the UK is entitled to adopt higher standards than the Directive, UK courts could adopt this reasoning in combating abusive use of zero-hours contracts, in addition to common law reasons (see chapter 7(2)(a)). Do you think they should?

3.   Do you find it odd that a term which makes the worker even more vulnerable than a fixed-hours part-timer is the reason to lose rights? Was the variable-hours term not the very discriminatory treatment complained of?

4.   Did the Court of Justice in *Wippel* tacitly legitimise zero-hours contracts across the EU?

5.   Did the CJEU, maybe distracted by an unspoken policy of labour market flexibility, simply get the law wrong? Once it was established that Wippel, on a part-time contract, had a term in her contract that differed to a full-time comparator, why did that difference not have to be justified? If Wippel was paid €10 an hour, and a full-time comparator was paid €12 an hour, that difference in terms must be justified. So must a variable-hours term. The CJEU's statement that the contract differed 'as to subject-matter and basis' seems to be a very inadequate assertion. How can the very discrimination that is complained of morph into a restriction on the appropriate comparator?

6.   In *McMenemy v Capita Business Ltd* [2007] CSIH 25, at [6] and [14], apparently relying on (its unique understanding of) *Wippel*, the Court of Session's Inner House held that it was lawful not to give a part-time worker an extra bank holiday, as other full-time staff received. Capita's call centre's policy was to allow staff a public holiday 'where these fall on your normal working day'.

Mr McMenemy worked Wednesdays to Fridays, and so he would not ordinarily be scheduled to work Bank Holiday Mondays. The Inner House said an employer needed to have intended to discriminate. Do you agree a requirement for discrimination to be intentional is flatly inconsistent with *Matthews* and most legal history since the civil rights movement? In *Carl v University of Sheffield* [2009] ICR 1286, [43], Peter Clark J politely declined to follow it.

7. What counts as 'objective justification' for treating part-time workers less favourably?

O'Brien v Ministry of Justice [2013] UKSC 6

Mr O'Brien, a part-time recorder (and part-time barrister) claimed that being excluded from pension arrangements was contrary to PTWR 2000 reg 5. He was a recorder from 1978 to 2005 and claimed he should receive a pension pro rata. He was paid a fee for each day sitting, but was not entitled to the same pension scheme as full-time judges. In an initial hearing, [2010] UKSC 34, the Supreme Court referred two questions to the Court of justice, whether (1) national law could determine whether judges were 'workers' under PTWD 1997 cl 2(1); and if so, (2) whether national law could discriminate between full-time and part-time judges on pensions. The Court of Justice, (2012) C-393/10, replied that judges were to be considered workers and not self-employed, and that the PTWD 1997 precluded national law distinguishing full- and part-time judges unless there were objective reasons, that the Supreme Court should determine. The Supreme Court held that no adequate objective justifications were given by the government for excluding pensions.

Lord Hope and **Lady Hale** (delivering a joint judgment):

43. The Part-Time Workers' Directive, like the Fixed-term Work Directive, is unusual in allowing the justification of direct discrimination against part-time workers. Clause 4.1 of the Framework Agreement (quoted at para 14 above) prohibits treating part-time workers less favourably than comparable full-time workers, solely because they work part-time, "unless different treatment is justified on objective grounds". Regulation 5(2) of the domestic 2000 Regulations (quoted at para 17 above) is to the same effect. However, clause 4.2 of the Framework Agreement sets out the general principle that "where appropriate, the principle of *pro rata temporis* shall apply". Regulation 5(3) is to the same effect. ...

44. There is, however, little guidance from the CJEU as to what might constitute such objective grounds, other than that which we have been given in this particular case, at paras 64 to 66 of the judgment of the court:

[... *Paragraphs 64–65 were repeated, without notable guidance* ...]
"66 It must be recalled that budgetary considerations cannot justify discrimination: see, to that effect, *Schönheit v Stadt Frankfurt am Main* ... C-4/02 and C-5/02 ... para 85, and *Zentralbetriebsrat der Landeskrankenhäuser Tirols v Land Tirol* (Case C-486/08) ... para 46."

...

46. The opinion of Advocate General Kokott is slightly more expansive at para 62:

"62 The unequal treatment at issue must therefore be justified by the existence of precise, concrete factors, characterising the employment condition concerned in its specific context and on the basis of objective and transparent criteria for examining the question whether that unequal treatment responds to a genuine need and whether it is appropriate and necessary for achieving the objective pursued: see *Del Cerro Alonso* [2008] ICR 145, para 58, and *Angé Serrano v European Parliament* (Case C-496/08P) [2010] ECR I-1793, para 44."

This court proposes to follow the guidance given by the CJEU and the Advocate General in those passages. ...

...

49. In their pleaded case, the Ministry advance three inter-related aims for the treatment complained of:
  (i)   "fairness" in the distribution of the State's resources that are available to fund judicial pensions;
  (ii) to attract a sufficiently high number of good quality candidates to salaried judicial office; and
  (iii) to keep the cost of judicial pensions within limits which are affordable and sustainable."
  In Mr Cavanagh's written and oral submissions on their behalf, fairness was divided into two elements: (a) the alternative opportunities available to part-timers, but denied to full-timers, to make provision for their retirement; and (b) the greater contribution made by the full-timers to the working of the justice system.

...

51. The Ministry point out that recorders are far removed from the type of part-time worker for whom the protection of the PTWD was designed. These were, it is said, low-paid workers who were driven to take part-time jobs by their personal circumstances, often their childcare or other domestic responsibilities, and were in a very weak bargaining position compared with their full-time and more often unionised colleagues. Many of them were women. Indeed, before the PTWD, there were many cases decided where discrimination against part-time workers was held to be indirect discrimination on grounds of sex because women were so much more likely to be adversely affected by it than men: see, for example, R v Secretary of State for Employment, Ex p Seymour-Smith (No 2) [2000] 1 WLR 435. The aim of the Directive was to promote more flexible working patterns, by eliminating discrimination against part-time workers and assisting the development of opportunities for part-time working in a way which would benefit both employers and workers.

...

55. ... it is irrelevant that the employer is the State. The Ministry should be regarded like any other employer. A private employer would not be able to justify paying part-time workers less or denying them access to its occupational pension scheme and the State should be in no different position. At bottom, this is not an argument about fairness. It is premised on there being a limited pot of money available to fund judicial pensions. That, it is said, is an impermissible premise: budgetary considerations cannot justify discriminatory treatment.

...

62. Promoting a high quality judicial system is of course a legitimate aim but it applies just as much to the part-timers as to the full-timers. Both must be of a high standard, so it is not an aim which divides them. While there is no evidence that the lack of a pension deters good quality candidates from applying to be recorders, the same may not be true of those parts of the justice system which rely upon fee-paid part-timers to do the great majority of the work.

...

71. We agree with the arguments advanced on behalf of Mr O'Brien. The Ministry have struggled to explain what they are seeking to achieve by denying a pension to part-timers while granting one to full-timers. One aim seems to be to give a greater reward to those who are thought to need it most. This might be a legitimate aim, but (as Advocate General Kokott explained) the unequal treatment of different classes of employees must be justified by the existence of precise, concrete factors, characterising the employment condition concerned in its specific context and on the basis of objective and transparent criteria. An employer might devise a scheme which rewarded its workers according to need rather than to their contribution, but the criteria would have to be precise and transparent. That is not so here. Some part-timers will need this provision as much as, if not more than, some of the full-timers. On examination, this objective amounts to nothing more than a blanket discrimination between the different classes of worker, which would undermine the basic principle of the PTWD.

72. Similarly (but inconsistently), an employer might aim to give a greater reward to those who make the greater contribution to the justice system, but the Ministry have failed to demonstrate that fee-paid part-timers, as a class, make a lesser contribution to the justice system than do full-timers, as a class. Once again, the criteria for assessing such contributions are not precise and transparent. They amount to nothing more than a blanket discrimination between the two classes of worker. The proper approach to differential contributions is to make special payments for extra responsibilities. The argument also fails to take into account the benefits to the system in having a cadre of fee-paid part-timers who can be flexibly deployed to meet the changing demands upon it.

73. The aim of recruiting a high quality judiciary is undoubtedly legitimate, but it applies to the part-time judiciary as much as it applies to the full-timers. Nor has it been shown that denying a pension to the part-timers has a significant effect upon the recruitment of full-timers.

74. In effect, the arguments presented to us are the same as the arguments presented by the Kingdom of the Netherlands in *Commission v The Netherlands*: that if recorders get a pension, then the pensions payable to circuit judges will have to be reduced. That is a pure budgetary consideration. It depends upon the assumption that the present sums available for judicial pensions are fixed for all time. Of course there is not a bottomless fund of public money available. Of course we are currently living in very difficult times. But the fundamental principles of equal treatment cannot depend upon how much money happens to be available in the public coffers at any one particular time or upon how the State chooses to allocate the funds available between the various responsibilities it undertakes. That argument would not avail a private employer and it should not avail the State in its capacity as an employer. Even supposing that direct sex discrimination were justifiable, it would not be legitimate to pay women judges less than men judges on the basis that this would cost less, that more money would then be available to attract the best male candidates, or even on the basis that most women need less than most men.

75. It follows that no objective justification has been shown for departing from the basic principle of remunerating part-timers *pro rata temporis*. Although this case is concerned only with the case of a recorder, it seems unlikely that the Ministry's argument could be put any higher than it has been. The court holds that the appellant is entitled to a pension on terms equivalent to those applicable to a circuit judge.

Lord Walker, Lord Clarke and **Lord Dyson** agreed.

1.   The Supreme Court decisively rejects as objective justifications the arguments that part-time workers should be paid less to save money (because that cannot be an independent aim), or that pensions should be higher to recruit quality full-time workers (because good part-time workers are needed too). Given different facts, what can you think of that might, or should, constitute objective justifications?
2.   Suppose that a hypothetical university in central London next to Lincoln's Inn Fields paid its summer school teachers £120 per hour if they were full-time staff members, and £90 per hour if they were part-time staff members, to teach tutorials in a legal subject. What would you advise a part-time staff member to do? What arguments would you anticipate the employing entity to use?
3.   If discrimination based on contractual status is driven by 'budgetary considerations', which is forbidden, and so is 'calculated to make a profit' for the employer (see *Rookes v Barnard* at chapter 12(2)(b)), do claimants have a right to exemplary damages, to prevent the evasion of rights becoming a business strategy?
4.   Does 'prejudice' drive employing entities or the state to treat part-time workers as such less favourably? Assuming (if indeed one can) that there is no obvious prejudice involved (as in race, gender or disability cases) what psychological factors (if any) do you think drive discrimination based on contractual status?
5.   Is it surprising that the second major UK case on part-time work was about a man?

(b) Right to Full-Time Work?

The right to request flexible working time, already seen in chapter 7(4), flows from the PTWD 1997 cl 5(3)(a). Rather than the PTWR 2000, it was placed in the ERA 1996 s 80F–H. As well as the right to request to become a part-time worker, the Directive creates rights for part-time workers to request to move to full-time work. Also, states should review barriers to mobility between different working arrangements.

Part-time Work Directive 1997 clauses 5–6

Clause 5: Opportunities for part-time work
1. In the context of Clause 1 of this Agreement and of the principle of non-discrimination between part-time and full-time workers:
   (a)   Member States, following consultations with the social partners in accordance with national law or practice, should identify and review obstacles of a legal or administrative nature which may limit the opportunities for part-time work and, where appropriate, eliminate them;
   (b)   the social partners, acting within their sphere of competence and through the procedures set out in collective agreements, should identify and review obstacles which may limit opportunities for part-time work and, where appropriate, eliminate them.
2. A worker's refusal to transfer from full-time to part-time work or vice-versa should not in itself constitute a valid reason for termination of employment, without prejudice to termination in accordance with national law, collective agreements and practice, for other reasons such as may arise from the operational requirements of the establishment concerned.

3. As far as possible, employers should give consideration to:
(a) requests by workers to transfer from full-time to part-time work that becomes available in the establishment;
(b) requests by workers to transfer from part-time to full-time work or to increase their working time should the opportunity arise;
(c) the provision of timely information on the availability of part-time and full-time positions in the establishment in order to facilitate transfers from full-time to part-time or vice versa;
(d) measures to facilitate access to part-time work at all levels of the enterprise, including skilled and managerial positions, and where appropriate, to facilitate access by part-time workers to vocational training to enhance career opportunities and occupational mobility;
(e) the provision of appropriate information to existing bodies representing workers about part-time working in the enterprise.

Clause 6: Provisions on implementation

1. Member States and/or social partners may maintain or introduce more favourable provisions than set out in this agreement.

2. Implementation of the provisions of this Agreement shall not constitute valid grounds for reducing the general level of protection afforded to workers in the field of this agreement. This does not prejudice the right of Member States and/or social partners to develop different legislative, regulatory or contractual provisions, in the light of changing circumstances, and does not prejudice the application of Clause 5.1 as long as the principle of non-discrimination as expressed in Clause 4.1 is complied with.

3. This Agreement does not prejudice the right of the social partners to conclude, at the appropriate level, including European level, agreements adapting and/or complementing the provisions of this Agreement in a manner which will take account of the specific needs of the social partners concerned.

4. This Agreement shall be without prejudice to any more specific Community provisions, and in particular Community provisions concerning equal treatment or opportunities for men and women.

5. The prevention and settlement of disputes and grievances arising from the application of this Agreement shall be dealt with in accordance with national law, collective agreements and practice.

6. The signatory parties shall review this Agreement, five years after the date of the Council decision, if requested by one of the parties to this Agreement.

NOTES AND QUESTIONS

1. Clause 5(1) suggests that Member States should review and dismantle barriers to part-time work. An example was seen in *Michaeler v Amt für sozialen Arbeitsschutz and Autonome Provinz Bozen* (2008) C-55/07. The Third Chamber held a requirement to send a copy of every part-time worker's contract to the Italian government was an undue deterrent to part-time work. The aim of 'combating fraud and undeclared work' could be more proportionately pursued with 'surveillance, monitoring and police resources'. Do you agree?

2. In *Zentralbetriebsrat der Landeskrankenhäuser Tirols v Land Tirol* (2010) C-486/08, the First Chamber found that a requirement for full-time employees who wanted to go part-time to have used up holidays, or lose a 'pro rata' part, was unlawful.

3. Clause 5(3)(b) requires employing entities to consider requests to become a full-time worker. How has this been implemented?

Employment Rights Act 1996 s 80F–G

80F Statutory right to request contract variation
(1) A qualifying employee may apply to his employer for a change in his terms and conditions of employment if—
(a) the change relates to—
    (i)   the hours he is required to work,
    (ii)   the times when he is required to work,
    (iii) where, as between his home and a place of business of his employer, he is required to work, or
    (iv)   such other aspect of his terms and conditions of employment as the Secretary of State may specify by regulations.
(2) An application under this section must—
(a) state that it is such an application,
(b) specify the change applied for and the date on which it is proposed the change should become effective, [and] 4
(c) explain what effect, if any, the employee thinks making the change applied for would have on his employer and how, in his opinion, any such effect might be dealt with.
[... *subsection (3) was repealed* ...]
(4) If an employee has made an application under this section, he may not make a further application under this section to the same employer before the end of the period of twelve months beginning with the date on which the previous application was made.

80G Employer's duties in relation to application under section 80F
(1) An employer to whom an application under section 80F is made—
(a) shall deal with the application in a reasonable manner,
(aa) shall notify the employee of the decision on the application within the decision period, and
(b) shall only refuse the application because he considers that one or more of the following grounds applies—
    (i)   the burden of additional costs,
    (ii)   detrimental effect on ability to meet customer demand,
    (iii) inability to re-organise work among existing staff,
    (iv)   inability to recruit additional staff,
    (v)   detrimental impact on quality,
    (vi)   detrimental impact on performance,
    (vii) insufficiency of work during the periods the employee proposes to work,
    (viii) planned structural changes, and
    (ix)   such other grounds as the Secretary of State may specify by regulations ....

NOTES AND QUESTIONS

1. As seen in chapter 7(4) in *Commotion Ltd v Rutty* the right of an employing entity to reject a request on the statutory grounds has been strictly construed. Should there simply be a right to become a full-time worker, unless an employing entity has an objective justification? What benefits or drawbacks can you think of for such a policy?

(2) FIXED-TERM EMPLOYEES

Two years after the PTWD 1997, the Fixed-Term Work Directive (FTWD) 1999 was finalised. Fixed-term work is often also commonly referred to as 'temporary', 'limited-term' or work for a 'specified period'. Like with part-time employees, fixed-term workers are often regarded (consciously or not) as having lesser belonging or status than permanent workers.

(a) Equality or Justification?

Fixed-Term Work Directive 1999 clauses 3–4

Definitions (clause 3)

1. For the purpose of this agreement the term "fixed-term worker" means a person having an employment contract or relationship entered into directly between an employer and a worker where the end of the employment contract or relationship is determined by objective conditions such as reaching a specific date, completing a specific task, or the occurrence of a specific event.

2. For the purpose of this agreement, the term "comparable permanent worker" means a worker with an employment contract or relationship of indefinite duration, in the same establishment, engaged in the same or similar work/occupation, due regard being given to qualifications/skills.
    Where there is no comparable permanent worker in the same establishment, the comparison shall be made by reference to the applicable collective agreement, or where there is no applicable collective agreement, in accordance with national law, collective agreements or practice.

Principle of non-discrimination (clause 4)

1. In respect of employment conditions, fixed-term workers shall not be treated in a less favourable manner than comparable permanent workers solely because they have a fixed-term contract or relation unless different treatment is justified on objective grounds.

2. Where appropriate, the principle of *pro rata temporis* shall apply.

3. The arrangements for the application of this clause shall be defined by the Member States after consultation with the social partners and/or the social partners, having regard to Community law and national law, collective agreements and practice.

4. Period-of service qualifications relating to particular conditions of employment shall be the same for fixed-term workers as for permanent workers except where different length-of-service qualifications are justified on objective grounds.

NOTES AND QUESTIONS

1. FTWD 1999 (99/70/EC) cl 2(1) says the Directive 'applies to fixed-term workers who have an employment contract or employment relationship as defined in law, collective agreements or practice in each Member State'. Fixed-term work is

simply a job with an end date (eg 'this job lasts for 6 months'). Clause 2(2) says Member States can exclude people on apprenticeship or training programmes.

2. In *Della Rocca v Poste Italiane SpA* (2013) C-290/12, the Eighth Chamber held that Mr Della Rocca, who worked for Poste Italiane SpA through an agency named Obiettivo Lavoro, was not entitled to claim he should have a direct contract under cl 5 and 2. The FTWD 2000 cl 2 was only designed to cover claimants as fixed-term workers, and limit abuse as such, and was agnostic to the position of agency workers. Do you see a parallel between this case and *Wippel*, above at chapter 15(1)(a)? What does this suggest about the overall scheme of the three Directives?

3. The FTWD 1999 (99/70/EC) was implemented by Regulations in 2002.

Fixed-Term Employees (Prevention of Less Favourable Treatment) Regulations 2002 regs 2–5

2. Comparable employees

(1) For the purposes of these Regulations, an employee is a comparable permanent employee in relation to a fixed-term employee if, at the time when the treatment that is alleged to be less favourable to the fixed-term employee takes place,

(a) both employees are—
  (i)   employed by the same employer, and
  (ii) engaged in the same or broadly similar work having regard, where relevant, to whether they have a similar level of qualification and skills; and

(b) the permanent employee works or is based at the same establishment as the fixed-term employee or, where there is no comparable permanent employee working or based at that establishment who satisfies the requirements of sub-paragraph (a), works or is based at a different establishment and satisfies those requirements.

(2) For the purposes of paragraph (1), an employee is not a comparable permanent employee if his employment has ceased.

3. Less favourable treatment of fixed-term employees

(1) A fixed-term employee has the right not to be treated by his employer less favourably than the employer treats a comparable permanent employee—

(a) as regards the terms of his contract; or

(b) by being subjected to any other detriment by any act, or deliberate failure to act, of his employer.

(2) Subject to paragraphs (3) and (4), the right conferred by paragraph (1) includes in particular the right of the fixed-term employee in question not to be treated less favourably than the employer treats a comparable permanent employee in relation to—

(a) any period of service qualification relating to any particular condition of service,

(b) the opportunity to receive training, or

(c) the opportunity to secure any permanent position in the establishment.

(3) The right conferred by paragraph (1) applies only if—

(a) the treatment is on the ground that the employee is a fixed-term employee, and

(b) the treatment is not justified on objective grounds.

(4) Paragraph (3)(b) is subject to regulation 4.

(5) In determining whether a fixed-term employee has been treated less favourably than a comparable permanent employee, the *pro rata* principle shall be applied unless it is inappropriate.

...

4. Objective justification

(1) Where a fixed-term employee is treated by his employer less favourably than the employer treats a comparable permanent employee as regards any term of his contract, the treatment in question shall be regarded ... as justified on objective grounds if the terms of the fixed-term employee's contract of employment, taken as a whole, are at least as favourable as the terms of the comparable permanent employee's contract of employment. ...

5. Right to receive a written statement of reasons for less favourable treatment

(1) If an employee who considers that his employer may have treated him in a manner which infringes a right conferred on him by regulation 3 requests in writing from his employer a written statement giving particulars of the reasons for the treatment, the employee is entitled to be provided with such a statement within twenty-one days of his request.

(2) A written statement under this regulation is admissible as evidence in any proceedings under these Regulations.

(3) If it appears to the tribunal in any proceedings under these Regulations—

(a)   that the employer deliberately, and without reasonable excuse, omitted to provide a written statement, or

(b)   that the written statement is evasive or equivocal,

it may draw any inference which it considers it just and equitable to draw, including an inference that the employer has infringed the right in question.

(4) This regulation does not apply where the treatment in question consists of the dismissal of an employee, and the employee is entitled to a written statement of reasons for his dismissal under section 92 of the 1996 Act 1.

NOTES AND QUESTIONS

1.   The Fixed-Term Employees (Prevention of Less Favourable Treatment) Regulations (FTER) 2002 (SI 2002/2034) regs 2–3 state that employees (not 'workers' as for the PTWR 2000) have a right to be treated no less favourably, unless it is 'justified on objective grounds' (reg 3(3)(b)) and that includes, under reg 4, cases where the fixed-term employee is treated equally by looking at the contract 'as a whole'. Under reg 5, employees can request a written statement of reasons for any less favourable treatment. As for part-time workers, would you advise a claimant to write to their employer themselves? What might be a better first step instead?

2.   If, as was suggested in chapter 3, the definition of an 'employee' includes all vulnerable workers (because cases such as *O'Kelly* are properly regarded now as wrong), and the only non-employee workers are comparable to law firm partners such as Ms Bates van Winkelhof who have other sources of protection, there seem to be few problems in the UK using the 'employee' concept. As explained below, this fits the statutory unfair dismissal scheme. On the other hand, if some courts persist in holding vulnerable workers are not employees, could the UK be in breach of its EU obligations in implementing the Directive? While 'national law ... or practice' may define the workers who are covered, would you agree a UK court has a duty to interpret the Regulations in line with EU standards (ie simply following *Autoclenz* and *Bates van Winkelhof*), or it will open the UK to a damages action under *Francovich v Italy* (1991) C-6/90?

3.   FTER 2002 reg 12(2) says: 'Anything done by a person as agent for the employer with the authority of the employer shall be treated for the purposes of these Regulations as also done by the employer.'

4. FTER 2002 reg 18 excludes from the right to a permanent contract in reg 8 'a fixed-term employee who is employed on a scheme, designed to provide him with training or work experience' from the government or an EU institution.

5. In *Hudson v Department for Work and Pensions* [2012] EWCA Civ 1416, Maurice Kay LJ and Elias LJ held that a worker who had worked three and a half years on a 'training' scheme and then six months as a permanent employee was not entitled to claim the right to a permanent job under reg 8: the three and a half years in 'training' did not count under reg 18. Smith LJ dissented, and would have held that on a proper construction of reg 18(1) once a worker is permanent the time spent on a training scheme counts towards the four years. Aside from the point of disagreement, do you agree the Court of Appeal should not have accepted that this so-called training scheme was genuine? Do you think there are many jobs in the Department of Work and Pensions or elsewhere that really require three and a half years training, or like most 'internships', is it just a sham arrangement for cheap labour that exploits people's lack of choice for good work?

6. Unlike for part-time work, there have been few cases on discrimination against fixed-term workers as such, as opposed to cases on the criteria for fixed-term workers having the right to permanent contracts, below at chapter 15(2)(b). *Del Cerro Alonso* is an exception.

Del Cerro Alonso v Osakidetza-Servicio Vasco de Salud (2007) C-307/05

Mrs Yolana Del Cerro Alonso claimed she was entitled to a full length-of-service allowance from her employer, the Basque Health Service, even though she had initially started work as 'temporary regulated staff'. She had become a member of 'permanent regulated staff' and applied for a length-of-service payment, but Basque Decree 231/2000 and Spanish Law 55/2003 of 16 December 2003 stated that these bonuses were only available for permanent staff. This supposedly meant she could not claim for the time that she was a temporary employee. After her queries went unanswered, she brought a claim. The Spanish Court asked the CJEU whether the payments under FTWD 1999 cl 4(1) were 'employment conditions' and if so, whether the fact that the Basque Health Service's rules were in legislation were 'objective grounds' under cl 5 that could justify not giving temporary workers the length-of-service payment. The CJEU upheld her claim.

Second Chamber:

50 The referring court asks ... whether the mere fact that the difference in treatment between the fixed-term workers and permanent workers regarding the length-of-service allowance is provided for by a law or by an agreement between staff union representatives and the administration is capable of constituting such an objective ground.

...

52 ... in that regard, that the Court has already ruled on a similar question concerning the same concept of 'objective reasons' which, according to clause 5(1)(a) of the framework agreement, justify the renewal of contracts or employment relationships for repeated fixed-term contracts.

53 ... 'objective reasons' must be understood as referring to precise and concrete circumstances characterising a given activity, which are therefore capable, in that particular context,

of justifying the use of successive fixed-term employment contracts. Those circumstances may result, in particular, from the specific nature of the tasks for the performance of which such contracts have been concluded and from the inherent characteristics of those tasks or, as the case may be, from pursuit of a legitimate social-policy objective of a Member State (*Adeneler and Others*, paragraphs 69 and 70).

54 On the other hand, a national provision which merely authorises recourse to successive fixed-term contracts, in a general and abstract manner by a rule of statute or secondary legislation, does not accord with the requirements as stated in the previous paragraph (*Adeneler and Others*, paragraph 71).

55 More specifically, recourse to fixed-term employment contracts solely on the basis of a general provision, unlinked to what the activity in question specifically comprises, does not permit objective and transparent criteria to be identified in order to verify whether the renewal of such contracts actually responds to a genuine need, is appropriate for achieving the objective pursued and is necessary for that purpose (*Adeneler and Others*, paragraph 74).

56 The same interpretation is necessary, by analogy, regarding the identical concept of 'objective grounds' within the meaning of clause 4(1) of the framework agreement.

57 In those circumstances, that concept must be understood as not permitting a difference in treatment between fixed-term workers and permanent workers to be justified on the basis that the difference is provided for by a general, abstract national norm, such as a law or collective agreement.

58 On the contrary, that concept requires the unequal treatment at issue to be justified by the existence of precise and concrete factors, characterising the employment condition to which it relates, in the specific context in which it occurs and on the basis of objective and transparent criteria in order to ensure that that unequal treatment in fact responds to a genuine need, is appropriate for achieving the objective pursued and is necessary for that purpose.

59 Accordingly, the reply to the second and third questions is that clause 4(1) of the framework agreement must be interpreted as meaning that it precludes the introduction of a difference in treatment between fixed-term workers and permanent workers which is justified solely on the basis that it is provided for by a provision of statute or secondary legislation of a Member State or by a collective agreement concluded between the staff union representatives and the relevant employer.

President Timmermans, Rapporteur Schintgen, Klučka J, Makarczyk J and Arestis J.

NOTES AND QUESTIONS

1. The Second Chamber reasoned that a national law requiring discrimination against temporary or fixed-term workers was no justification for an employing entity's discrimination: the law itself would be contrary to the FTWD 1999. It further said that the concept of objective justification would be the same under cl 4, as it was interpreted under cl 5 (below) which gives a limited right to be classed as a permanent worker. The CJEU did not say what objective reasons would be. Would it be desirable for legislation to set out a limited list of reasons?
2. Before the CJEU decision, Advocate General Maduro had given an Opinion that the length-of-service payments were not included within the scope of the FTWD

1999, because TFEU Art 153(5) (now TEC Art 137) does not include pay regulation in the scope of the EU's competence; apparently the concept of 'employment conditions' should be interpreted as not including terms relating to pay, for the purpose of equal treatment. AG Maduro said this flowed from the fact that the FTWD 1999 was passed under the authority of Art 153(1), and in Art 153(5) it says the 'provisions of this Article shall not apply to pay'. But equal-pay regulation on the basis of gender or nationality was implicitly embedded in the Treaties for some time both in Art 153(1)(i) and Art 157 (eg *Danfoss* (1989) C-109/88). Yet in *ITWF v Viking Line ABP* (2007) C-438/05, the Advocate General was not deterred by the right to collective bargaining and to strike being outside the EU's competence under Art 153(5), when opining that its use might infringe a business' right of establishment under TFEU Art 49. Why does it make sense to construe a limit to labour rights under a Directive based on Art 153(5), yet refuse to construe a limit to business rights under TFEU Art 49 based on Art 153(5)? See chapter 10.

(b) Right to Permanent Work?

Together, the FTWD 1999 and FTER 2002 reg 8(2) provide the right to claim termination of successive fixed-term contracts is not justified. In form there is a right to be a 'permanent employee', although unless a contract term restricts dismissal, the default position is that any employment contract can be terminated with reasonable notice, for a fair reason, and any due redundancy pay (see chapters 16–19). Nevertheless, combined with ERA 1996 s 1, any employee could claim a written statement of a permanent contract after four years.

Fixed Term Work Directive 1999 clauses 5 and 6

Measures to prevent abuse (clause 5)
  1. To prevent abuse arising from the use of successive fixed-term employment contracts or relationships, Member States, after consultation with social partners in accordance with national law, collective agreements or practice, and/or the social partners, shall, where there are no equivalent legal measures to prevent abuse, introduce in a manner which takes account of the needs of specific sectors and/or categories of workers, one or more of the following measures:
  (a)   objective reasons justifying the renewal of such contracts or relationships;
  (b)   the maximum total duration of successive fixed-term employment contracts or relationships;
  (c)   the number of renewals of such contracts or relationships.
  2. Member States after consultation with the social partners and/or the social partners shall, where appropriate, determine under what conditions fixed-term employment contracts or relationships:
  (a)   shall be regarded as "successive"
  (b)   shall be deemed to be contracts or relationships of indefinite duration.

Information and employment opportunities (clause 6)
  1. Employers shall inform fixed-term workers about vacancies which become available in the undertaking or establishment to ensure that they have the same opportunity to secure

permanent positions as other workers. Such information may be provided by way of a general announcement at a suitable place in the undertaking or establishment.

2. As far as possible, employers should facilitate access by fixed-term workers to appropriate training opportunities to enhance their skills, career development and occupational mobility.

NOTES AND QUESTIONS

1. FTWD 1999 cl 5 requires Member States to introduce some limit on fixed terms: under FTER 2002 reg 8(2) the UK has required a four-year limit unless there are objective reasons for a longer. Clause 6 requires, at least, some information about vacancies be made available. If a job really does require someone only for a fixed term, should the burden of justification not be on the employing entity in the first place?

2. The UK already had in place a right to claim unfair dismissal if a fixed-term contract expired. Under ERA 1996 s 95(1)(b) an employee was regarded as being 'dismissed' if 'he is employed under a contract for a fixed term and that term expires without being renewed under the same contract'. (FTER 2002 'changed' the wording to refer to a 'limited-term contract'.) As we see in chapter 18, this means under s 98 an employing entity must justify the dismissal by saying the employee shows poor capability or qualification, shows poor conduct, is redundant or there is 'some other substantial reason' (eg condition or pay changes are accepted by a workforce majority as a necessary restructure, but individuals object). Assuming 'objective reasons' are (or should be) the same as those listed in s 98, the only thing added by FTER 2002 was a four-year period. But if expiry of a fixed-term contract was a dismissal requiring justification before four years, and after four years fixed-term contracts could still be justified, the position is unchanged.

3. The operation of the fixed-term rule was seen in *Ford v Warwickshire CC* [1983] 2 AC 71, where the House of Lords held that a teacher employed for eight years on fixed-term contracts was entitled to claim unfair dismissal when she was told the contract would end. Under what is now ERA 1996 s 212, their Lordships rejected that breaks in work over the summer holidays were anything more than 'temporary cessations of work', so Ms Ford fulfilled the qualifying period to claim the right to unfair dismissal.

4. Limited protection for fixed-term workers is also found in the Termination of Employment Convention 1982 (c 158) Art 3(3) requiring signatories to stop 'contracts of employment for a specified period of time' that aim to avoid dismissal protection. On this point UK law is more comprehensive, and the UK has not ratified the Convention.

5. In *Adeneler v Ellinikos Organismos Galaktos* (2006) C-212/04, the Grand Chamber held that a Greek law, which stated fixed-term contracts were not successive if they were over 20 days apart, was incompatible with FTWD 1999 cl 5.

6. In *Mascolo v Ministero dell'Istruzione, dell'Università e della Ricerca* (2014) C-22/13, the Third Chamber held that an Italian law limiting conversion from fixed-term to permanent contracts was unlawful.

7. Could a Member State limit the right to permanent contracts to younger employees?

Mangold v Helm **(2005) C-144/04**

Mr Werner Mangold claimed he should have the right to claim a full-time contract, even though the German Employment Promotion Act 1996 (Beschäftigungsförderungsgesetz) reserved that right to people who were under the age of 52. Mangold was 56 years old, and employed on a fixed-term contract. The Act, reflecting the FTWD 1999 cl 5, stated fixed-term contracts should last for a maximum of two years unless continuation could be objectively justified. However, the German government had limited this right to people over age 60, subsequently reduced to age 52, on the theory this limit would 'promote employment'. The Munich Labour Court (Arbeitsgericht München) referred to the CJEU.

Grand Chamber:

18 Paragraph 14 of the TzBfG [Part-time and Fixed Term Work Act 2000], which regulates fixed-term contracts, provides that:

'(1) A fixed-term employment contract may be concluded if there are objective grounds for doing so. Objective grounds exist in particular where:

1. the operational manpower requirements are only temporary,
2. the fixed term follows a period of training or study in order to facilitate the employee's entry into subsequent employment,
3. one employee replaces another,
4. the particular nature of the work justifies the fixed term,
5. the fixed term is a probationary period,
6. reasons relating to the employee personally justify the fixed term,
7. the employee is paid out of budgetary funds provided for fixed-term employment and he is employed on that basis, or
8. the term is fixed by common agreement before a court ….

(3) The conclusion of a fixed-term employment contract shall not require objective justification if the worker has reached the age of 58 by the time the fixed-term employment relationship begins. …'

19 Paragraph 14(3) of the TzBfG has been amended by the First Law for the provision of modern services on the labour market of 23 December 2002 (BGBl. 2002 I, p. 14607, 'the Law of 2002'). The new version of that provision, which took effect on 1 January 2003, is henceforth worded as follows:

'A fixed-term employment contract shall not require objective justification if when starting the fixed-term employment relationship the employee has reached the age of 58. It shall not be permissible to set a fixed term where there is a close connection with a previous employment contract of indefinite duration concluded with the same employer. Such close connection shall be presumed to exist where the interval between two employment contracts is less than six months. Until 31 December 2006 the first sentence shall be read as referring to the age of 52 instead of 58.'

…

40 In Question 1(b), which it is appropriate to consider first, the national court asks whether, on a proper construction of Clause 5 of the Framework Agreement, it is contrary to that

provision for rules of domestic law such as those at issue in the main proceedings to contain none of the restrictions provided for by that clause in respect of the use of fixed-term contracts of employment.

41 Here it is to be noted that Clause 5(1) of the Framework Agreement is supposed to 'prevent abuse arising from the use of successive fixed-term employment contracts or relationships'.

42 Now, as the parties to the main proceedings confirmed at the hearing, the contract is the one and only contract concluded between them.

43 In those circumstances, interpretation of Clause 5(1) of the Framework Agreement is obviously irrelevant to the outcome of the dispute before the national court and, accordingly, there is no need to answer Question 1(b).

...

44 By Question 1(a), the national court seeks to ascertain whether on a proper construction of Clause 8(3) of the Framework Agreement, domestic legislation such as that at issue in the main proceedings which, on transposing Directive 1999/70, lowered from 60 to 58 the age above which fixed-term contracts of employment may be concluded without restrictions, is contrary to that provision.

...

51 The term 'implementation', used without any further precision in Clause 8(3) of the Framework Agreement, does not refer only to the original transposition of Directive 1999/70 and especially of the Annex thereto containing the Framework Agreement, but must also cover all domestic measures intended to ensure that the objective pursued by the directive may be attained, including those which, after transposition in the strict sense, add to or amend domestic rules previously adopted.

52 In contrast, reduction of the protection which workers are guaranteed in the sphere of fixed-term contracts is not prohibited as such by the Framework Agreement where it is in no way connected to the implementation of that agreement.

53 Now, it is clear from both the order for reference and the observations submitted by the German Government at the hearing that, as the Advocate General has noted in paragraphs 75 to 77 of his Opinion, the successive reductions of the age above which the conclusion of a fixed-term contract is permissible without restrictions are justified, not by the need to put the Framework Agreement into effect but by the need to encourage the employment of older persons in Germany.

...

55 By its second and third questions, which may appropriately be considered together, the national court seeks in essence to ascertain whether Article 6(1) of Directive 2000/78 must be interpreted as precluding a provision of domestic law such as that at issue in the main proceedings which authorises, without restriction, unless there is a close connection with an earlier contract of employment of indefinite duration concluded with the same employer, the conclusion of fixed-term contracts of employment once the worker has reached the age of 52. If so, the national court asks what conclusions it must draw from that interpretation.

...

75 The principle of non-discrimination on grounds of age must thus be regarded as a general principle of Community law. Where national rules fall within the scope of Community law, which is the case with Paragraph 14(3) of the TzBfG, as amended by the Law of 2002, as being a measure implementing Directive 1999/70 (see also, in this respect, paragraphs 51 and 64 above), and reference is made to the Court for a preliminary ruling, the Court must provide all the criteria of interpretation needed by the national court to determine whether those rules are compatible with such a principle (Case C-442/00 *Rodríguez Caballero* [2002] ECR I-11915, paragraphs 30 to 32).

76 Consequently, observance of the general principle of equal treatment, in particular in respect of age, cannot as such be conditional upon the expiry of the period allowed the Member States for the transposition of a directive intended to lay down a general framework for combating discrimination on the grounds of age, in particular so far as the organisation of appropriate legal remedies, the burden of proof, protection against victimisation, social dialogue, affirmative action and other specific measures to implement such a directive are concerned.

77 In those circumstances it is the responsibility of the national court, hearing a dispute involving the principle of non-discrimination in respect of age, to provide, in a case within its jurisdiction, the legal protection which individuals derive from the rules of Community law and to ensure that those rules are fully effective, setting aside any provision of national law which may conflict with that law (see, to that effect, Case 106/77 *Simmenthal* [1978] ECR 629, paragraph 21, and Case C-347/96 *Solred* [1998] ECR I-937, paragraph 30).

78 Having regard to all the foregoing, the reply to be given to the second and third questions must be that Community law and, more particularly, Article 6(1) of Directive 2000/78, must be interpreted as precluding a provision of domestic law such as that at issue in the main proceedings which authorises, without restriction, unless there is a close connection with an earlier contract of employment of indefinite duration concluded with the same employer, the conclusion of fixed-term contracts of employment once the worker has reached the age of 52.

It is the responsibility of the national court to guarantee the full effectiveness of the general principle of non-discrimination in respect of age, setting aside any provision of national law which may conflict with Community law, even where the period prescribed for transposition of that directive has not yet expired.

NOTES AND QUESTIONS

1. The Grand Chamber rejects that cl 5 is applicable since Mr Mangold only had one fixed-term contract before bringing the case. Clause 8 did not apply because the German government introduced the age threshold for reasons unrelated to the FTWD 1999. However, there was a 'general principle' of equality that made the age restriction unlawful – even though the expiry period for the Equality Framework Directive 2000 was not yet up, its anticipation effectively solidified age as a ground of unlawful discrimination under the general principle (see chapter 12(1)(a)). Do you agree that, if Mr Mangold had had two contracts, cl 5 would make age limits unlawful themselves?

2. It is interesting to note, at [18], the German legislation's list of objective justifications. Although not set out in EU law, these may influence an interpretation of the FTWD 1999. Do you agree that all should count for the UK context?

Fixed-Term Employees (Prevention of Less Favourable Treatment) Regulations 2002 regs 3(6)–(7) and 8

3. Less favourable treatment of fixed-term employees

...

(6) ... the employee has the right to be informed by his employer of available vacancies in the establishment.

(7) For the purposes of paragraph (6) an employee is "informed by his employer" only if the vacancy is contained in an advertisement which the employee has a reasonable opportunity of reading in the course of his employment or the employee is given reasonable notification of the vacancy in some other way.

...

8. – Successive fixed-term contracts

(1) This regulation applies where—

(a)   an employee is employed under a contract purporting to be a fixed-term contract, and

(b)   the contract mentioned in sub-paragraph (a) has previously been renewed, or the employee has previously been employed on a fixed-term contract before the start of the contract mentioned in sub-paragraph (a).

(2) Where this regulation applies then, with effect from the date specified in paragraph (3), the provision of the contract mentioned in paragraph (1)(a) that restricts the duration of the contract shall be of no effect, and the employee shall be a permanent employee, if—

(a)   the employee has been continuously employed under the contract mentioned in paragraph 1(a), or under that contract taken with a previous fixed-term contract, for a period of four years or more, and

(b)   the employment of the employee under a fixed-term contract was not justified on objective grounds—

(i)   where the contract mentioned in paragraph (1)(a) has been renewed, at the time when it was last renewed;

(ii)   where that contract has not been renewed, at the time when it was entered into.

(3) The date referred to in paragraph (2) is whichever is the later of—

(a)   the date on which the contract mentioned in paragraph (1)(a) was entered into or last renewed, and

(b)   the date on which the employee acquired four years' continuous employment.

(4) For the purposes of this regulation Chapter 1 of Part 14 of the 1996 Act shall apply in determining whether an employee has been continuously employed, and any period of continuous employment falling before the 10th July 2002 shall be disregarded.

(5) A collective agreement or a workforce agreement may modify the application of paragraphs (1) to (3) of this regulation ....

NOTES AND QUESTIONS

1.   FTER 2002 reg 3(6)–(7) requires employers to inform employees of vacancies, at least by adverts the employee has a 'reasonable opportunity of reading'. This might be taken to mean a public advertisement. Is this enough given cl 6(1) requires a 'general announcement *at a suitable place in the undertaking or establishment*'?

2.   FTER 2002 reg 8(2) contains the core rule on the right to a permanent contract after four years.

3.   FTER 2002 reg 8(5) goes on to say collective agreements could specify, for example, a time limit for renewing fixed-term contracts (eg six months, one year), a maximum number (eg one or two), or objective grounds (eg only capability, conduct or redundancy, as under ERA 1996 s 98).

4.   One potential advantage of having a fixed-term contract is that an employing entity is not ordinarily entitled to terminate the contract early. If it does so, damages are payable for the wages up to its end: *Re Joint English Stock Board* (1867) LR Eq 350.

Duncombe v Secretary of State for Children, Schools and Families [2011] UKSC 14

Duncombe and other teachers claimed there was no objective justification for their nine year fixed-term contracts ending under FTER 2002 reg 8, and also claimed unfair dismissal. The UK government employed them to teach in various EU schools, mainly for children of EU officials, under the Statute of the European Schools. One employee, Fletcher, had worked at the European School in Culham, Oxfordshire, while Duncombe had worked at a school in Karlsruhe, Germany. The contracts were limited to nine years, or exceptionally ten years under the Regulations for Members of the Seconded Staff of the European Schools 1996. The Secretary of State claimed it was not for the court of one Member State to question the Regulations. The Court of Appeal held successive fixed-term contracts for work in European schools were not objectively justified. But the Supreme Court held that, in fact, no objective justification was necessary because there was only one fixed-term contract, not a succession of them: this was what FTER 2002 reg 8 stopped. But, after initially reserving judgment, at [2011] UKSC 36, [16] the Supreme Court held the claimants would succeed in a case for unfair dismissal.

Lady Hale (with whom **Lord Rodger** agreed):

12. ... there is no need for objective justification for the current (that is, renewed or successive) contract unless and until the employee has been continuously employed for four years. But once he has, the latest renewal or successive contract has to be justified on objective grounds. Otherwise the contract will automatically be transformed into a contract of indefinite duration. As such it will still, of course, be terminable by whatever is the contractual notice period on either side.

...

18. Before this Court, Mr Crow QC on behalf of the Secretary of State contends that it is not for a court or tribunal in one of the Member States to inquire into the factual merits of the nine year rule. The plain fact of the matter is that the Secretary of State has no choice. The United Kingdom has only one vote on the Board of Governors and has so far failed to persuade them that the rule should be changed. It has to employ teachers for the purpose of seconding them to the European Schools and the Schools will only take them on the basis of the nine year rule. All of this is made perfectly plain to the teachers when they are recruited. This in itself is objective justification for employing the teachers on successive or renewable contracts which mirror the periods in the rule.

...

23. The teachers' complaint is not against the three or four periods comprised in the nine year rule but against the nine year rule itself. In other words, they are complaining about the fixed-term nature of their employment rather than about the use of the successive fixed-term contracts which make it up. But that is not the target against which either the Fixed-term Directive or the Regulations is aimed. Had the Secretary of State chosen to offer them all nine year terms and take the risk that the schools would not have kept them for so long, they would have had no complaint. Employing people on single fixed-term contracts does not offend against either the Directive or the Regulations.

24. This is therefore the answer to Mr Giffin's attractive argument: that fixed-term contracts must be limited to work which is only needed for a limited term; and that where the need for the work is unlimited, it should be done on contracts of indefinite duration. This may well be a desirable policy in social and labour relations terms. It may even be the expectation against which the Directive and Framework Agreement were drafted. But it is not the target against which they were aimed, which was discrimination against workers on fixed-term contracts and abuse of successive fixed-term contracts in what was in reality an indefinite employment. It is not suggested that the terms and conditions on which the teachers were employed during their nine year terms were less favourable than those of comparable teachers on indefinite contracts.

25. It follows that the comprehensive demolition by the Employment Tribunal of the arguments for the nine year rule is nothing to the point. It is not that which requires to be justified, but the use of the latest fixed-term contract bringing the total period up to nine years. And that can readily be justified by the existence of the nine year rule. The teachers were employed to do a particular job which could only last for nine years. The Secretary of State could not foist those teachers on the schools for a longer period, no matter how unjustifiable either he or the employment tribunals of this country thought the rule to be. The teachers were not employed to do any alternative work because there was none available for them to do.

26. The *Adeneler* case is not in point. That concerned a national rule which provided a general 'get-out' from the requirements of the Directive. It is not a question of whether the Staff Regulations 'trump' the Directive. There is no inconsistency between them. The Staff Regulations are dealing with the duration of secondment, not with the duration of employment. In those circumstances it is questionable whether there is any duty of co-operation between the Member States. It appears that the Board of Governors did not see any conflict between the Staff Regulations and the Directive.

27. This is scarcely surprising. The United Kingdom could have chosen to implement the Directive by setting a maximum number of renewals or successive fixed-term contracts, for example by limiting them to three. It could equally have chosen to implement the Directive by setting a maximum duration to the employment, for example by limiting it to nine or ten years in total. It is readily understandable why the alternative route of requiring objective justification after four years was taken: this is more flexible and capable of catering for the wide variety of circumstances in which a succession of fixed term contracts may be used. Unless a very short maximum total had been chosen, it is more favourable to employees than the alternatives. But the fact that the alternatives would have been equally acceptable ways of implementing the Directive is yet another indication that the target is not fixed term employment as such.

Lord Mance, Lord Collins and **Lord Clarke** agreed.

1.   The Supreme Court reasons that, although the FTER 2002 reg 8 does not protect
the employees, unfair dismissal law would. Given the overlap, do you agree that
codifying and recasting these principles in the ERA 1996 would be desirable?
2.   In *Vassallo v Azienda Ospedaliera Ospedale San Martino di Genova* (2006)
C-180/04, the Court of Justice held at [38]–[42] that making an employee permanent is not necessary as a remedy at the end of four years.
3.   *Angelidaki v Organismos Nomarchiakis Autodioikisis Rethymnis* (2009) C-378/07,
held the FTWD 1999 would not have direct effect.
4.   *Kücük v Land Nordrhein-Westfalen* (2012) C-586/10, held that 13 successive
renewals would be justified only if 'actually intended to cover temporary needs'.
It should 'not, in fact, [be] being used to meet fixed and permanent needs'.
5.   *Huet v Université de Bretagne occidentale* (2012) C-251/11 held an employee,
who moved from a fixed-term to a permanent contract, should receive 'overall'
the same working conditions, but some terms can vary. Overall it should not be
unfavourable to the employee.

(3) AGENCY WORK

Because they work through an intermediary, agency staff face special vulnerability. People who are subject to the authority of two entities must please both. Moreover, the
employment agency industry forms a special-interest lobby that influences the progress
of case law, and employment rights in statute. Private agencies profit both from other
people's work and employing entities' demand for labour. There is a real risk that they
use their intermediary position in a way that limits labour supply from matching demand,
regardless of the needs of workers or end-users (see Brandeis J in *Adams v Tanner*, 244
US 590 (1917)). This was why the International Labour Organisation's first ever instruments required abolition of private fee charging agencies, in favour of public employment
services (Unemployment Recommendation 1919 (no 1) and Unemployment Convention
1919 (c 2)). Today the ILO recognises that private employment agencies can provide a
useful service to meet demand, so long as they are properly regulated (Private Employment Agencies Convention 1997 (c 181) and see chapter 16(3)(c)). Yet the existence of
this highly organised economic interest group means agency work rights face unique
pressure.

    In chapter 3(3)(b) it was explained why the better view of the case law means that
agency staff are (1) employees of the agency, confirmed by the TAWD 2008 Art 2 below,
and (2) employees of the end-user where they work, as seen in *Cable & Wireless plc
v Muscat* or *Dacas v Brook Street Bureau Ltd*. The reason the law is right to find joint-
employment in agency situations is that employing functions will be split between
an agency and end-user (see S Deakin, 'The Changing Concept of the 'Employer' in
Labour Law' (2001) 30 *ILJ* 72; J Prassl, *The Concept of the Employer* (2015); and
E McGaughey, 'Social Rights and the Function of Employing Entities' (2017) 37(2)
OJLS 482). While past Court of Appeal cases conflicted, this interpretation follows

sound principle, expressed by the Supreme Court in *Autoclenz* (on bargaining power), *Bates van Winkelhof* (workers must be treated as an intermediate category) and *Catholic Child Welfare Society* (on enterprise responsibility). Where an employment right is breached, the entity whose agents are responsible will be primarily liable, and the other party (whether agency or end-user) will be secondarily liable: this matters in insolvency. However, it is clear that Court of Appeal judgments (described below) have still held agency staff in 'legal limbo'. Those cases are grounded on a flawed understanding of contract law, and ignore binding Supreme Court principles. Ultimately the dispute may have to be resolved, once again, by the Supreme Court in special reference to agency staff (even though *Autoclenz* was a subcontracting case, and cannot be functionally distinguished). These issues aside, the rights focused on in this section are (a) rights of equality or justifications, and (b) rights to direct work.

(a) Equality or Justification?

As we saw in chapter 5(2)(a), *Transco plc v O'Brien* [2002] EWCA Civ 379 held it would be a breach of mutual trust and confidence to single out a person for different treatment simply because they were hired through an agency. This can be seen as an example of a general principle of equality at common law (chapter 12(1)(a)), applied in favour of agency workers. In practice, however, fewer courts have been active in following the lead of *O'Brien*. While the case of *James v Greenwich LBC* [2008] EWCA Civ 35 purported to find an agency worker could bring no claim against anyone for unfair dismissal, Parliament brought a Temporary and Agency Workers (Equal Treatment) Bill to its Second Reading. The government conceded and negotiated through the EU for a new Directive to be finalised, based on plans that the Blair government had blocked up until then.

Temporary Agency Work Directive 2008 Arts 2–3

Article 2 Aim
   The purpose of this Directive is to ensure the protection of temporary agency workers and to improve the quality of temporary agency work by ensuring that the principle of equal treatment, as set out in Article 5, is applied to temporary agency workers, and by recognising temporary-work agencies as employers, while taking into account the need to establish a suitable framework for the use of temporary agency work with a view to contributing effectively to the creation of jobs and to the development of flexible forms of working.

Article 3 Definitions
   1. For the purposes of this Directive: …
   (f) 'basic working and employment conditions' means working and employment conditions laid down by legislation, regulations, administrative provisions, collective agreements and/or other binding general provisions in force in the user undertaking relating to:
        (i)   the duration of working time, overtime, breaks, rest periods, night work, holidays and public holidays;
        (ii) pay.
   …

Article 5 The principle of equal treatment

1. The basic working and employment conditions of temporary agency workers shall be, for the duration of their assignment at a user undertaking, at least those that would apply if they had been recruited directly by that undertaking to occupy the same job.

For the purposes of the application of the first subparagraph, the rules in force in the user undertaking on:

(a) protection of pregnant women and nursing mothers and protection of children and young people; and

(b) equal treatment for men and women and any action to combat any discrimination based on sex, race or ethnic origin, religion, beliefs, disabilities, age or sexual orientation;

must be complied with as established by legislation, regulations, administrative provisions, collective agreements and/or any other general provisions.

2. As regards pay, Member States may, after consulting the social partners, provide that an exemption be made to the principle established in paragraph 1 where temporary agency workers who have a permanent contract of employment with a temporary-work agency continue to be paid in the time between assignments.

3. Member States may, after consulting the social partners, give them, at the appropriate level and subject to the conditions laid down by the Member States, the option of upholding or concluding collective agreements which, while respecting the overall protection of temporary agency workers, may establish arrangements concerning the working and employment conditions of temporary agency workers which may differ from those referred to in paragraph 1.

4. Provided that an adequate level of protection is provided for temporary agency workers, Member States in which there is either no system in law for declaring collective agreements universally applicable or no such system in law or practice for extending their provisions to all similar undertakings in a certain sector or geographical area, may, after consulting the social partners at national level and on the basis of an agreement concluded by them, establish arrangements concerning the basic working and employment conditions which derogate from the principle established in paragraph 1. Such arrangements may include a qualifying period for equal treatment.

NOTES AND QUESTIONS

1. Temporary Agency Work Directive (TAWD) 2008 (2008/104/EC) Art 2 makes clear that the law is now 'recognising temporary-work agencies as employers'. It should be emphasised that it does not say agencies are the exclusive employer, because end-users should invariably be deemed employing entities as well (even if case law still conflicts). Article 5(1) sets out the right to equal treatment for workers, but only in 'basic working conditions' (Art 3(f)). For pay, Art 5(2) allows Member States to set a qualifying period, which the UK took up.

2. TAWD 2008 Art 6 expressly states that rights to 'canteen, child-care facilities and transport services' must be the same unless 'justified by objective reasons'. Article 7 requires agency workers count for all union recognition or workplace representation rights, either in the end-user or agency. Article 8 requires agency workers be informed and consulted like any other worker (see chapter 11).

3. In *Betriebsrat der Ruhrlandklinik gGmbH v Ruhrlandklinik gGmbH* (2016) C-216/15, a company claimed that members of the 'Red Cross Association of Nurses of Essen' were not workers. This would mean, under the German Work Constitution Act 1972 (Betriebsverfassungsgesetz 1972) §99, that the elected work council would not be entitled to object to a nurse being hired to work at the

Ruhrlandklinik. (In Germany, elected work councils have the right to defer both dismissals and hirings of workers, so as to ensure fair pay.) Advocate General Saugmandsgaard Øe gave his opinion that agency workers, thought not classified as such under German law, were workers under EU law in general, and the TAWD 2008 Art 1 in particular. It is notable that before 2003, the nurse association also classified its members as employees. The CJEU agreed.

4. Before the TAWD 2008, the EU had long planned to regulate agency work. On how these proposals initially stalled, see L Zappalà, 'The Temporary Agency Workers' Directive: An Impossible Political Agreement?' (2003) 32(4) *ILJ* 310.

5. As outlined in chapter 3(2)(c) and E McGaughey, 'Should Agency Workers Be Treated Differently?' (2010) LSE Legal Studies Working Paper No 7/2010, one of the reasons why the government had opposed drafts before the TAWD 2008 seems to have been linked to Tony Blair's personal history as a barrister, arguing cases such as *Nethermere*, which favoured reduction of labour rights for vulnerable workers. It is, of course, unfair to suggest that the work people do always affects their moral values about what is right and wrong. Should people have to take cases as lawyers, according to the 'cab rank' rule, which require profiting at other people's expense? Putting criminal law cases aside where considerations of liberty apply, if work appears immoral to most people, is it not correct that the cost should be raised?

6. Regulations were adopted after the TAWD 2008 finally passed.

Agency Workers Regulations 2010 reg 5

3. The meaning of agency worker
(1) In these Regulations "agency worker" means an individual who—
(a)   is supplied by a temporary work agency to work temporarily for and under the supervision and direction of a hirer; and
(b)   has a contract with the temporary work agency which is—
   (i)   a contract of employment with the agency, or
   (ii)   any other contract with the agency to perform work or services personally.
(2) But an individual is not an agency worker if—
(a)   the contract the individual has with the temporary work agency has the effect that the status of the agency is that of a client or customer of a profession or business undertaking carried on by the individual; or
(b)   there is a contract, by virtue of which the individual is available to work for the hirer, having the effect that the status of the hirer is that of a client or customer of a profession or business undertaking carried on by the individual ....
...

5. Rights of agency workers in relation to the basic working and employment conditions
(1) Subject to regulation 7, an agency worker (A) shall be entitled to the same basic working and employment conditions as A would be entitled to for doing the same job had A been recruited by the hirer—
(a)   other than by using the services of a temporary work agency; and
(b)   at the time the qualifying period commenced.
(2) For the purposes of paragraph (1), the basic working and employment conditions are—
(a)   where A would have been recruited as an employee, the relevant terms and conditions that are ordinarily included in the contracts of employees of the hirer;

(b)   where A would have been recruited as a worker, the relevant terms and conditions that are ordinarily included in the contracts of workers of the hirer,

whether by collective agreement or otherwise, including any variations in those relevant terms and conditions made at any time after the qualifying period commenced.

(3) Paragraph (1) shall be deemed to have been complied with where—

(a)   an agency worker is working under the same relevant terms and conditions as an employee who is a comparable employee, and

(b)   the relevant terms and conditions of that comparable employee are terms and conditions ordinarily included in the contracts of employees, who are comparable employees of the hirer, whether by collective agreement or otherwise.

(4) For the purposes of paragraph (3) an employee is a comparable employee in relation to an agency worker if at the time when the breach of paragraph (1) is alleged to take place—

(a)   both that employee and the agency worker are—
(i)   working for and under the supervision and direction of the hirer, and
(ii)   engaged in the same or broadly similar work having regard, where relevant, to whether they have a similar level of qualification and skills; and

(b)   the employee works or is based at the same establishment as the agency worker or, where there is no comparable employee working or based at that establishment who satisfies the requirements of sub-paragraph (a), works or is based at a different establishment and satisfies those requirements.

(5) An employee is not a comparable employee if that employee's employment has ceased.

(6) This regulation is subject to regulation 10.

6. Relevant terms and conditions

(1) In regulation 5(2) and (3) "relevant terms and conditions" means terms and conditions relating to—

(a)   pay;
(b)   the duration of working time;
(c)   night work;
(d)   rest periods;
(e)   rest breaks; and
(f)   annual leave.

…

7. Qualifying period

(1) Regulation 5 does not apply unless an agency worker has …

(2) … work[ed] in the same role with the same hirer for 12 continuous calendar weeks, during one or more assignments.

NOTES AND QUESTIONS

1.   The Agency Workers Regulations (AWR) 2010 (SI 2010/93) suffers from a common virus: long-winded draftsmanship. Nevertheless, the essential ideas are clear: in reg 3 the legal position is confirmed that an agency will be primarily responsible as an employing entity to the employee. Again, this does not exclude that joint employment by the end-user: far from it. There will usually be joint liability. Under reg 5(1)–(2) an employee is entitled to the 'same' conditions as a comparable direct employee. Those conditions are set out in reg 6 as pay and working time. Reg 6(3) elaborates various categories of pay.

2.   Under reg 7, there is a 12-week qualifying period to be able to bring a claim under the AWR 2010. This removes protection for many people. Is a claim in contract available before the qualifying period: a breach of mutual trust and confidence for

irrationally paying someone less simply because they are employed through an agency?

3.   There are few cases regarding unequal treatment so far. One example is *Stevens v Northolt High School, Teach 24 Ltd* (15 July 2014) Unreported, West-law 10246849, where Pettigrew J held a teacher was entitled to compensation for infringement of AWR 2010 reg 5. The agency, Teach 24 got paid £228 a day for Miss Stevens's work, and Miss Stevens got £155 a day. If she had been hired directly, a job of equivalent seniority would have attracted £253 a day. As she was over the qualifying period, she was entitled to equal pay, amounting to £10,878 on the facts. Why did the school not pay the teacher equally in the first place? The transcript does not appear to give any special reason. What does this suggest to you about the reality of employment rights?

4.   AWR 2010 reg 10 provides that, if someone has a permanent employment contract with an agency, the right to equal treatment in reg 5 does not apply. This is known as the 'Swedish derogation', since agencies in Sweden had a habit of working in such a way. Why should agency workers ever not receive equal pay for equal work?

5.   While 'basic working conditions' are covered in the Directive, the most significant problems in the prior case law were in simple access to statutory rights. Which rights had courts denied to agency staff? The major examples have been fair dismissal protection (*James*), discrimination protection (*Muschett*), and protection against blacklisting (*Smith v Carillion Ltd*). It was suggested in chapter 3 that none of these cases were adequately reasoned. The unprincipled stance of these Court of Appeal decisions creates an anticompetitive subsidy for the agency industry. Most importantly, they run contrary to binding Supreme Court authority expressed through the principle of bargaining power in *Autoclenz Ltd v Belcher* (an intermediated employment case) and enterprise responsibility in *CCWS v IBCS*. Nevertheless, they bear outlining again.

6.   In *James v Greenwich LBC* [2008] EWCA Civ 35, Mummery LJ denied an agency worker the right to a fair dismissal.

7.   In *Muschett v HM Prison Service* [2010] EWCA Civ 25, Rimer LJ denied an agency worker the right to bring a claim for race discrimination. Also, it should be recalled that in *Allonby v Accrington and Rossingdale College* [2004] ICR 1328 an agency worker was denied the right to bring a claim for sex discrimination in relation to pay.

8.   In *Smith v JM Carillion Ltd* [2015] EWCA Civ 209, Elias LJ denied an agency worker the right to bring a claim for union membership 'blacklisting'.

9.   Would judges be more likely to decide in favour of employees, if more people had had an employment contract themselves, rather than mostly being self-employed barristers?

(b) Right to Direct Work?

Agency workers do not have clear rights to get direct work, rather than receive information. On the contrary, the Directive seemed more concerned to promote agencies than secure permanent work. This does not, however, mean there is no joint employment.

Temporary Agency Work Directive 2008 Arts 4 and 6

Article 4 Review of restrictions or prohibitions

1. Prohibitions or restrictions on the use of temporary agency work shall be justified only on grounds of general interest relating in particular to the protection of temporary agency workers, the requirements of health and safety at work or the need to ensure that the labour market functions properly and abuses are prevented.
    ...

Article 6 Access to employment, collective facilities and vocational training

1. Temporary agency workers shall be informed of any vacant posts in the user undertaking to give them the same opportunity as other workers in that undertaking to find permanent employment. Such information may be provided by a general announcement in a suitable place in the undertaking for which, and under whose supervision, temporary agency workers are engaged.

2. Member States shall take any action required to ensure that any clauses prohibiting or having the effect of preventing the conclusion of a contract of employment or an employment relationship between the user undertaking and the temporary agency worker after his assignment are null and void or may be declared null and void.

This paragraph is without prejudice to provisions under which temporary agencies receive a reasonable level of recompense for services rendered to user undertakings for the assignment, recruitment and training of temporary agency workers.

3. Temporary-work agencies shall not charge workers any fees in exchange for arranging for them to be recruited by a user undertaking, or for concluding a contract of employment or an employment relationship with a user undertaking after carrying out an assignment in that undertaking.

4. Without prejudice to Article 5(1), temporary agency workers shall be given access to the amenities or collective facilities in the user undertaking, in particular any canteen, child-care facilities and transport services, under the same conditions as workers employed directly by the undertaking, unless the difference in treatment is justified by objective reasons.

5. Member States shall take suitable measures or shall promote dialogue between the social partners, in accordance with their national traditions and practices, in order to:
   (a)   improve temporary agency workers' access to training and to child-care facilities in the temporary-work agencies, even in the periods between their assignments, in order to enhance their career development and employability;
   (b)   improve temporary agency workers' access to training for user undertakings' workers.

NOTES AND QUESTIONS

1.   In *AKT ry v Shell Aviation Finland Oy* (2015) C-533/13 the Grand Chamber, in the first case under the TAWD 2008, held that Art 4 only creating duties on Member States, but did not have horizontal direct affect, so as to be enforceable by national courts. This means that courts did not have some free-ranging licence to review and potentially deregulate the agency industry. See further chapter 20(2)(c).

2.   The AWR 2010 reg 13 implements the main part of TAWD 2008 Art 6.

Agency Workers Regulations 2010 reg 13

13. Rights of agency workers in relation to access to employment

(1) An agency worker has during an assignment the right to be informed by the hirer of any relevant vacant posts with the hirer, to give that agency worker the same opportunity as a comparable worker to find permanent employment with the hirer. ...

NOTES AND QUESTIONS

1.   In *Coles v Ministry of Defence* [2016] ICR 55 Mr Coles claimed that the Ministry of Defence failed to adequately inform him that his job was being advertised. He worked for the Defence Housing Executive through both Building Recruitment Co Ltd and Giant Parkhouse Ltd (ie three employing entities). The job was advertised on the intranet, and 'it would have been visible to the claimant had he chosen to look for it. It found he had ready access to the advertisement.' Langstaff J, upholding the Tribunal, found there was no breach of AWR 2010 reg 13 because there is only a right to the same opportunity as a comparable direct employee. Is this a correct interpretation of the TAWD 2008 Art 6? If so how, if at all, is there any point to the law?

Problem Question

Mary Poppins (1964)

George Banks needs a new nanny for his two troublesome children. His previous nanny, Katie, who was paid £300 a week, has left. He decides to use an employment agency, named Kite Flyers Recruitment. They send him a rosy-cheeked lady named Mary. Because he needs to pay the agency fees, George tells Mary that her wage will be £150 a week. Mary accepts. She is given a room in the Bankses' family house.

Mary finds that her hours were longer than she had expected. Her general duties involve activities with the children in the afternoons. But although the work goes up and down, she is required to remain on call from Monday to Saturday, and she reckons that she is doing more than 5 hours a day, six days a week. When she tells the agency about this, they send one of their 'human resources' consultants to observe her work. They inform her that her work totals no more than 20 hours a week, meaning that she is being paid an average of £7.50 an hour. The consultant requires Mary to sign a form acknowledging this if she is to continue working for the Bankses.

Advise Mary on any claims she has regarding her pay and working time.

T Wilthagen and F Tros, 'The Concept of "Flexicurity": A New Approach to Regulating Employment and Labour Markets' (2004) 10(2) *Transfer* 166
The authors examine the 'new policy concept of "flexicurity" in view of the emerging flexibility-security nexus currently faced by the European Union' and others. Without saying who the 'flexibility' is meant to be for, they say that there is also a 'strong demand for security'. Apparently there was 'a strong need for new theory-inspired policy models and concepts that promise to reconcile these goals'. Acknowledging the analysis of Diamond Ashiagbor, they admit a 'deregulatory agenda is being promoted and pursued' but suggest that 'concepts' such as flexicurity are worth a research agenda. The article exemplifies the cuddly and vapid euphemisms that conceal a hardline managerial drive to cut labour rights, and give agency corporations unrestricted licence. It is full of terms that do not mean anything, such as 'mutual stimulation', 'promoting learning processes' or 'effective trade-off possibilities at decentralised levels'.

A Manning and B Petrongolo, 'The Part-Time Pay Penalty' (2008) 118 *Economic Journal* F28
Manning and Petrongolo measure the average disparity in pay between full-time and part-time workers in the UK. The 'penalty' that an average worker receives for going part time is estimated to be around 24 per cent. Part-time staff are often directly discriminated against for the same work, compared to full-time staff. However, the larger problem is said to be segregation of the workplace, where higher-paid jobs are full time, and part-time jobs are in lower-wage sectors. This also entails indirect sex discrimination.

A McColgan, 'Missing The Point?' (2000) 29 *ILJ* 260
Reviewing the Part-time Workers Regulations 2000, McColgan argues the law misses the point because it does not enable a hypothetical comparator. This 'problem is so overwhelming as to render the PtWRs largely irrelevant to the vast majority of part-time workers'. They 'neglect expressly to prohibit dismissals in connection with a refusal to transfer between part-time and full-time work'. They also unjustifiably 'exclude compensation in respect of injury to feelings'. Given that part-time work discrimination is often about gender, most cases will be brought under sex-discrimination provisions instead.

A McColgan, 'Fiddling while Rome burns?' (2003) 32(3) *ILJ* 194
Reviewing the Fixed-Term Employees Regulations 2002, McColgan argues that 'an increasing culture of casualisation' mean 'financial risks' are passed onto workers 'rather than being borne by the employer'. This has 'really serious implications for the ability of workers to plan their lives, gain access to mortgages, organise childcare, etc'. The Regulations take an unduly strict approach to who can be a comparator. The regulations were probably also inadequate to transpose the Directive because use of the word 'employee' was expressly rejected, and in restricting the scope of the comparator, and potentially because the four-year qualifying period is far too long.

E McGaughey, 'Should Agency Workers Be Treated Differently?' (2010) LSE Legal Studies Working Paper No 7/2010
This article argues that the Temporary Agency Work Directive was inadequate because it failed to address the central issue that faced many agency workers: many were simply not being regarded as 'employees' by anyone, and this had been legitimised by flawed decisions of the Court of Appeal, before *Autoclenz Ltd v Belcher.* Any differential treatment for agency workers enables an unjustified subsidy for the agency industry. While private agencies should probably not be entirely prohibited (as they were under international law in the early twentieth century), they should all be licensed and have to guarantee all labour rights.

M Bell, 'Between Flexicurity and Fundamental Social Rights: The EU Directives on Atypical Work' (2012) *ELR* 31
Bell argues that the Directives, and regulation of atypical workers, has been driven by a desire for efficient labour market regulation, rather than guaranteeing fundamental social rights. He explains the roots of 'flexicurity' rhetoric. Because the debate about economic efficiency of labour rights had been inconclusive, the extent of rights in legislation was limited. By contrast, Bell suggests that judgments of the Court of Justice have in fact been more driven by a rights-based understanding of the law–although the *Wippel* case stands as a notable exception.

E McGaughey, 'A Human Is Not a Resource' (2018) CBR, Cambridge Working Paper 497
This article argues that the language of 'human resource management' treats people as a means to an end. Three core tenets of human resource literature are that it is desirable to have (1) labour 'flexibility' and 'mobility' in a peripheral workforce, (2) individual (not social) responsibility for employment searching, and (3) a manager's right to manage, without accountability. However, where human resource beliefs have pervaded the most, the outcomes are the worst: lower productivity, higher unemployment, more inequality, less growth. To advance prosperity, economic risks must be distributed to the organisations best placed to bear them, people must have security to plan for the future, and people must have real votes at work through collective bargaining and corporate governance. Just as international law once affirmed that 'labour is not a commodity', for social justice in the twenty-first century there must be a conviction that a human is not a resource. 'HR' must change in name and substance, to advance human development and human rights.

Part Five

Job Security

16

Full Employment

Why is there unemployment? When people lose jobs or cannot find work, is this a result of technology, education, welfare, trade unions or job security laws? Are there trade-offs in fiscal and monetary policy, between having the full employment that gives everyone a fair income, and inflation that makes people's incomes worth less? Is unemployment 'natural'? Or is it a policy choice, the result of underinvestment by governments and business? Are the unemployed lazy? Or do the real 'benefits' from unemployment go to employing entities? Debates about work, unemployment and welfare are long running. They go to the heart of labour law. To have labour rights, and especially job security, people need jobs. At least some work is essential for a just society. Most people need to produce or earn income to lead fulfilling lives, and be freed from poverty. But more than this, work gives people esteem among their peers and in themselves. In a just society everyone is able to realise their potential, and they do this in the eyes of others. Often forgotten, the legal policy on full employment, with fair wages, is probably the most important part of all labour law.

There is no doubt that full employment – which means eliminating underemployment as much as unemployment – is an international and fundamental human right. The Universal Declaration of Human Rights 1948, Art 23(1) says: 'Everyone has the right to work, to free choice of employment, to just and favourable conditions of work and to protection against unemployment.' The ILO Employment Policy Convention 1964 (c 122) says 'each Member shall declare and pursue, as a major goal, an active policy designed to promote full, productive and freely chosen employment.' But rights instruments leave the major question unanswered: how should the right be achieved? This chapter covers the four relevant fields of law: (1) fiscal policy or tax and spending by government, (2) monetary policy to affect private investment, (3) unemployment insurance and job agencies, and (4) trade. Some contest the objective. In 1967, Milton Friedman, then American Economic Association President, argued that some unemployment is 'natural'. Full employment simply could not be achieved by government or monetary policy without accelerating to an unacceptable level of inflation in prices. Supposedly the 'natural' rate could be reduced by removing impediments to market forces, which to Friedman meant minimum wages, unions or social security rights. But the role of government was not creating jobs. That would be costly and futile. Friedman's argument attacked the whole of labour law. The evidence shows it is wrong, because the UK, with low inflation, had full employment: 1.2–2.7 per cent unemployment from 1948 to 1970. Since 1974, it has been 4.3–11.9 per cent. This chapter discusses the legal choices that are available, and the choices that have been made.

(1) FISCAL POLICY

Fiscal policy is probably the most controversial method for government to achieve full employment. Experience shows it works, but it has consequences for the distribution of income and power. The Welfare Reform and Work Act 2016 s 1 created a short-lived duty to report to Parliament 'annually on the progress which has been made towards full employment', with its own interpretation of what full employment meant. Because of the Brexit poll and the 2017 election triggered by Theresa May, the section expired and no report was ever laid out. The Act's main function was to cut welfare payments (ss 8–14) and appeared to contain no other measures to achieve full employment.

By contrast, using fiscal policy three options are (a) for investment by government in creating jobs (directly or indirectly) or set rules to spur private and social investment, (b) to use its power in procuring goods and services, and (c) in the long run to ensure training and education create skills that are seen as desirable in future. Why do human rights instruments decline to say how to use fiscal policy? This may reflect a view that there is no 'right' approach to attain full employment (see also European Social Charter 1961 Art 1 and Treaty on European Union Art 3). Nevertheless, in times of sustained full employment, fiscal policy was always ready to be used: see Figure 16.1

Figure 16.1 UK unemployment 1881–2017 and inflation 1948–2016

Sources: Denman and McDonald, Unemploment statistics from 1881 to the present day (Jan 1996) Labour Market Trends, ONS, Unemployment rate MGSX (1995–2017). ONS, RPI All Items: Percentage change over 12 months (2017).

Figure 16.1 depicts long-term patterns of unemployment in the UK. Three main phases are (1) an accelerating period of economic boom and bust up to and through the two world wars, (2) a cross-party commitment to full employment, between 1 and 2.7 per cent from 1948 to 1971, before the Organization of the Petroleum Exporting Countries raised petroleum prices, causing a global recession, and (3) a shift in political consensus from 1979. After that, the unemployment rate never reached below 4.7 per cent until 2017. Since then, unemployment fell, but in its place chronic *under*employment has been soaring. For instance, an extra 0.96 to 1.81 per cent of people were underemployed from 2002 to 2006. But from 2014 to 2018, underemployment reached 3.26 to 3.92 per cent extra (cf ONS, *Labour Market Economic Commentary* (September 2017) Figure 5).

Before examining fiscal policy further, how are unemployment statistics generated? There have been two main methods. First, Jobcentres that distribute unemployment insurance, and supervise people looking for work, can record the number of claimants. This 'claimant count' method obviously fails to record people who are unemployed but choose not to claim. Of those people, some may not want jobs (because, for example, they have money or family to live from) while others do want jobs, but are deterred from claiming unemployment insurance because they feel it is undignified.

Second, the Office for National Statistics, through the Labour Force Survey, uses a survey sample of the population, asking if people are unemployed. This method has become preferred, and is an international standard since the ILO *Resolution Concerning Statistics of the Economically Active Population, Employment, Unemployment and Underemployment* (October 1982). Around 40,000 people in the UK are surveyed each quarter year. The obvious risk is that a sample does not adequately reflect the true position. First, to be surveyed, people need to have a house or a telephone. Second, prisoners are deliberately excluded. In the UK, these factors lead to some inaccuracy but are not *that* significant. But in the United States around 1.5m people become homeless each year, and 2.3m people are in prison (in a 155.5m person workforce). The incarcerated population alone means reported unemployment is around 1.3 per cent lower than reality. Third, people are considered employed if 'economically active'. 'Students and homemakers' are excluded by the ILO definition. In other words, people are working, often very hard without pay, but are invisible because they do not have 'jobs'. Fourth, and most importantly, people can be recorded as 'employed' even if they are working part-time because they cannot find jobs delivering enough hours. To meet this issue, statistical authorities now often record 'underemployment' as well as 'unemployment'. Fifth, the unemployment rate might fall very low, but people might have precarious, low-paid jobs. A government that achieves full employment, but with destitute wages, can be reducing human development. For this reason the Universal Declaration Art 23(3) goes on to say 'Everyone who works has the right to just and favourable remuneration'. These points suggest the ILO *Resolution* (1982) should be updated. At the very least, there are contestable and political choices behind statistical methods. An alternative measure of work is the 'employment rate'. This shows the percentage of the total population actually in work. Over time, an increasing proportion of people have jobs, mainly because over the late twentieth century more women have entered the labour force. The long-term change of the employment rate is therefore independent from the unemployment rate.

(a) Investment

Investment in jobs can be made by anyone with money or capital assets. Governments, private business or social investment funds are the main sources, but not only in the UK. There are global capital markets. Foreign 'direct' investment (buying assets or bonds) and foreign 'portfolio' investment (buying company shares) has increased considerably since 1990. Four major reasons for accelerating globalisation in recent history include the transition of China from Deng Xiaoping in 1978 to a part-market economy (without significant political reform), the Single European Act of 1986 leading to a new emphasis on 'market access' in an expanding EU, the collapse of the Soviet Union in 1989 and its shock privatisation programme (leading to an oligarch 'managed democracy' in Russia), and the World Trade Organization from 1994 which has lowered tariff and customs taxes.

As the scope of global investment markets has increased, wealth and income inequality intensified – in legal terms, an unequal distribution of property or contractual rights. This concentrates the number of parties who have the resources to invest in jobs. If business can make irrational decisions, this logically also increases the volatility of economic cycles. Fewer decision-makers mean a concentrated risk of poor decisions. By contrast, risk is reduced with a diversified capital base, ie when more people have wealth. The following White Paper was the first real attempt to manage volatility in private business and trade. It set out government policy, administered by the Treasury. It is 'soft law'. Policy statements are not legally enforceable alone, but affect statutory interpretation and judicial review. They also have tremendous social implications, because they guide government conduct.

White Paper, *Employment Policy* (May 1944) Cmd 6527

CHAPTER I

THE INTERNATIONAL AND INDUSTRIAL BACKGROUND

1. This Paper is concerned with the course of policy which the Government propose to follow internally in order to maintain the highest possible level of employment. But the level of employment and the standard of living which we can maintain in this country does not depend only upon conditions at home. We must continue to import from abroad a large proportion of our foodstuffs and raw materials, and to a greater extent than ever before we shall have to pay for them by the export of our goods and services. For as the result of two world wars we have had to sacrifice by far the greater part of the foreign investments which we built up over many years when we were the leading creditor country of the world. It will not, therefore, be enough to maintain the volume of our pre-war exports; we shall have to expand them greatly.

2. A country dependent on exports – and relying largely, as we do, on the expert of manufactured goods of high quality – needs prosperity in its oversea markets. This cannot be achieved without effective collaboration among the nations. It is therefore an essential part of the Government's employment policy to co-operate actively with other nations, in the first place for the re-establishment of general economic stability after the shocks of the war, and next for the progressive expansion of trade.

3. The aims of this international co-operation are to promote the beneficial exchange of goods and services between nations, to ensure reasonably stable rates of exchange, and to check the swings in world commodity prices, which alternately inflate and destroy the incomes of the primary producers of food-stuffs and raw materials. It will also be necessary to arrange that countries which are faced with temporary difficulties in their balance of payments shall be able both to take exceptional measures to regulate their imports and to call on other nations, as good neighbours, to come to their help, so that their difficulties may be eased without recourse to measures which would permanently arrest the flow of international trade.

4. ... The Government will also collaborate with other Governments in considering how effect may be given to the principles and recommendations recently put forward by the International Labour Organisation.
...

CHAPTER III

THE BALANCED DISTRIBUTION OF INDUSTRY AND LABOUR

20. Before proceeding (in Chapters IV and V) to describe the long-term policy proposed for maintaining total expenditure, it is necessary to turn aside from the main argument of the paper to describe the measures which the Government will take to check the development of localised unemployment in particular industries and areas ...

21. Apart from temporary unemployment due to the seasonal and other irregularities in particular trades, patches of longer-term unemployment develop in particular industries and areas when the demand for their products is insufficient to provide work for the whole of their labour force. This is due to a temporary or a permanent decline in an industry or group of industries caused by technical change, the trend of fashion, or the growth of foreign competition.

22. Unemployment of this type was a familiar feature in this country's economic life between the wars. The industries affected were mainly export trades – such as cotton and coal – and some of the heavy industries which had been greatly expanded during the last war. Areas which were largely dependent upon depressed industries showed heavy Unemployment percentages, not only in the basic industries, but in subsidiary local trades and occupations as well.

23. The suffering in these areas was enhanced by their lack of a proper industrial balance ....
...

24. The first line of attack on the problem of unemployment in those unbalanced areas must be to promote the prosperity of the basic industries on which they primarily depend, e.g. coal, steel, engineering and shipbuilding. It will be an aim of Government policy to help these industries to reach the highest possible pitch of efficiency, and secure oversea markets.

Secondly, these industries, and the areas which are largely dependent on them, will share in the benefits which will flow from the Government's policy (explained in Chapters IV and V) for maintaining domestic expenditure at a high level. But it will not be enough to rely on the general maintenance of purchasing power to solve all the problems of local unemployment. A solution on these lines alone would be too long drawn out and might involve the partial depopulation of industrial regions which are a national asset that we cannot afford to lose.

25. The Government therefore propose to attack the problems of local unemployment in three ways:—

    (a) By so influencing the location of new enterprises as to diversify the industrial com-position of areas which are particularly vulnerable to unemployment.

    (b) By removing obstacles to the transfer of workers from one area to another, and from one occupation to another.

    (c) By providing framing facilities to fit workers from declining industries for jobs in expanding industries.

    ...

CHAPTER IV

GENERAL CONDITIONS OF A HIGH AND STABLE LEVEL OF EMPLOYMENT

37. In the transition period, as we have seen, employment policy will be primarily concerned with the transfer of men and women to peace-time jobs. But however smoothly this transition can be made, and however rapid may be the return to normal conditions, there will still remain for treatment those long-term problems connected with the maintenance of an adequate and steady volume of employment which eluded solution before the war.

39. If [instability and unemployment] which have afflicted our economic life in the past are to be banished, as it is our resolve to banish them, from the future, three essential conditions must be satisfied:—

    (a) Total expenditure on goods and services must be prevented from falling to a level where general unemployment appears.

    (b) The level off prices and wages must be kept reasonably stable.

    (c) There must be a sufficient mobility of workers between occupations! and localities.

    ...

42. The methods which the Government propose to adopt to maintain total expenditure are described in Chapter V. It will, however, be convenient to analyse here the constituent parts of this total expenditure, for they differ greatly both in their susceptibility to fluctuations and in the ease with which these fluctuations can be controlled.

43. In a country which could ignore the outside world these parts would be four in number:—

    (a) *Private Consumption Expenditure*
        Private expenditure on food, clothing, rent, amusements, etc.

    (b) *Public Expenditure on Current Services*
        Expenditure by public authorities on education, medical services, national defence, etc.

    (c) *Private Investment Expenditure*
        Capital expenditure on buildings, machinery, and other durable equipment and on additions to goods in stock.

    (d) *Public Investment Expenditure*
        Capital expenditure on buildings, machinery, roads and other durable equipment by the central Government, local authorities or public utilities.

    But in a community linked with the outside world some expenditure (i.e. that upon imports) does not directly lead to employment at home, while some, employment at home (i.e. labour engaged in making things for export) arises out of the expenditure of people in other countries.

It is convenient to allow for these facts by adding a fifth item (which may of course be a minus quantity) to the list of the constituents of total expenditure, namely:—

(e) *The Foreign Balance.*
The difference between exports (visible and invisible) and imports (visible and invisible).

44. Expenditure on private consumption is perhaps the element least liable to sudden and spontaneous variation; for so long as people's incomes do not greatly change, their habits of buying are likely to remain much the same. Public expenditure on current services, including national defence, will also be fairly constant as a rule, unless the Government decide as an act of deliberate policy to vary expenditure on some items in order to compensate for swings in other parts of total national expenditure. ...

45. It is, however, in the two remaining components of total expenditure – private expenditure on capital equipment and the foreign balance – that spontaneous variations are likely to be greatest and at the same time most difficult to control. A business man deciding whether it is worth his while to sink more capital into his business will be influenced by a very wide range of considerations: whether his market is likely to grow or decline; what his competitors are doing; whether prices are likely to go up or down; whether the latest type of machinery is much superior to his own, and so on. It is in practice impossible to foresee with any certainty what decisions business managements will reach on these matters: the prevailing atmosphere of optimism or pessimism, particularly in periods of rapid industrial change, probably has as much influence on them as any independent analysis of the facts.

46. In the majority of highly industrialised communities it is expenditure on private invest-ment which is the most usual and most potent cause of instability in total expenditure, and consequently in employment. But this country, because of the relative importance of its export trade ... is also particularly subject to fluctuations in employment arising from fluctuations in international trade ....

47. The most serious obstacles to the maintenance of total expenditure therefore lie in these highly inconvenient facts:—

First, those elements in total expenditure which are likely to. fluctuate most – private invest-ment and the foreign balance – happen also to be the elements which are most difficult to control.

Secondly, an increase in one part of total expenditure can only within limits offset a decrease in another. For if, through a decline in private investment, the construction of new factories is discontinued and building labourers are thrown out of work, it may be useful to stimulate the purchase of clothing but it would be idle to expect the building labourers to turn up the next day, ready to handle sewing machines in the clothing factories. ...

...

48. The guiding principles of the Government's policy in maintaining total expenditure will be as follows:—

(a) To avoid an unfavourable foreign balance, we must export much more than we did before the war.
(b) Everything possible must be done to limit dangerous swings in expenditure on private investment – though success in this field may be particularly difficult to achieve.
(c) Public investment, both in timing and in volume, must be carefully planned to off-set unavoidable fluctuations in private investment.
(d) We must be ready to check and reverse the decline in expenditure on consumers' goods which normally follows as a secondary reaction to a falling off in private investment.

CHAPTER V

METHODS FOR MAINTAINING TOTAL EXPENDITURE

(a) Capital Expenditure

57. If we could stop violent fluctuations in public and private capital expenditure taken together, and could keep the foreign balance reasonably stable, we should have gone far to prevent wide variations in demand and consequently in general employment. ...

58. In ordinary times the volume of capital expenditure is influenced by movement in the rate of interest. If the cost of borrowing money is high, some projects which are not profitable at that rate, will be held back. When it falls again, those projects will be brought forward and others will also be taken in hand.

59. For some time after the end of the war it will be necessary ... to maintain a policy of cheap money. Thereafter, the, possibility of influencing capital expenditure by the variation of interest rates will be kept in view. The experience gained since 1931 of co-operation in this field between the Treasury and the Bank of England and the Joint Stock Banks will make it possible to operate a concerted and effective monetary policy designed to promote stable employment.

60. Monetary policy alone, however, will not be sufficient to defeat the inherent instability of capital expenditure. High interest rates are more effective in preventing excessive investment in periods of prosperity than are low interest fates in encouraging investment in periods of depression.

61. The Government therefore propose to supplement monetary policy by encouraging privately-owned enterprises to plan their own capital expenditure in conformity with a general stabilisation policy. The larger private enterprises may be willing to follow, in their own interests, the example set by the Government in the timing of public investment and to adjust their activities accordingly.
   ...

62. Public, investment can however, be used more directly as an instrument of employment policy.
   Only a small proportion of public capital expenditure is undertaken by the central Government, by far the greater part being within the province of local authorities and public utility undertakings. In the past, capital expenditure by these authorities has generally followed the same trend as private capital expenditure – it has fallen in times of slump and risen in times of boom, and has tended therefore to accentuate the peaks and depressions – of the trade cycle. In the future, Government policy will be directed to correcting this sympathetic movement. It should be possible for the Government to maintain the stability of public investment when private investment is beginning to fall off at the onset of a depression. ...
   ...
   Thus, a large part of the capital expenditure of public authorities – for example on housing, schools and hospitals – is dictated by urgent public needs, the satisfaction of which cannot really be postponed to serve the purpose of employment policy. ... There are, therefore, limits to the policy; but within those limits the Government believe that they can influence public capital expenditure to an extent which will be of material value for the purpose of maintaining employment.

63. The procedure which the Government have in mind is as follows. All local authorities submit annually to appropriate department their programme of capital expenditure for the next five years. For the first of those years, at least, the plans will have been worked out in all details and will be ready for immediate operation; for the later years they will naturally be increasingly tentative and provisional. These programmes will then be assembled by an appropriate co-ordinating body under Ministers and will be adjusted, upward or downward, in the light of the latest information on the prospective employment situation.

...

(c) Central Finance.

74. None of the main proposals contained in this paper involves deliberate planning for a deficit in the National Budget in years of sub-normal trade activity. ...

NOTES AND QUESTIONS

1. The White Paper stated that to maintain full employment central and local government spending should be organised into projected five-year blocks. Spending could be brought forward or backwards to make up for swings in private-sector spending. Monetary policy could also change the interest rate up or down to dampen or stimulate private spending. Private-sector spending, together with the foreign balance of trade (ie how much other countries spend on UK goods that are exported) were the least predictable and the least easy to control. However, the White Paper suggested that within limits a policy of full employment would be successful. However moved, this depends on government spending plans being sufficient to make up for private and international investment volatility. Why might governments not want to provide that money?

2. The White Paper was written under the Minister of Reconstruction, Frederick Marquis, who became chair of the Conservative Party from 1946 to 1955. It coincided with W Beveridge, *Full Employment in a Free Society* (1944), the Liberal Party thinker, who argued government should aim to keep unemployment below 3 per cent. Labour put it into effect. It is a testament to cross-party political consensus, of Labour, Conservatives and Liberals. This consensus explains the complete success of full employment from 1945 to 1973.

3. It seems full employment actually cost almost nothing (even discounting the huge tax receipts from full employment itself). Once government had made the initial investments, and then committed to do 'whatever it takes', this maintained business confidence, economic stability and full employment. According to RCO Matthews, 'Why Has Britain Had Full Employment since the War?' (1968) 78(311) *Economic Journal* 555, far from a 'Keynesian revolution' with persistently or cyclically high government spending, the UK government post-war had a constant current account surplus. This indicated spending restraint.

4. Serious plans to achieve sustained full employment on fair incomes began around the turn of the twentieth century. S Webb, *How the Government Can Prevent Unemployment* (1912) listed four categories of policy: (1) the regularisation of labour through government spending – government as the biggest employer and spender should allocate its resources to counteract changes in foreign trade and private customers; (2) ensuring labour exchanges efficiently match workers to

vacancies at all times; (3) stopping underemployment from people being on call, waiting for shift jobs, by guaranteeing a minimum number of hours per week; and (4) a long-term reduction in the hours of labour for everyone. To what extent is UK labour policy doing any of this today?

5.   Webb also addressed 'How to deal with the "won't works"', arguing people should not be sent to jail but given training and discipline to get them into jobs. For many echoes of the same ideas, see chapter 1(1) and Sir Thomas More.

6.   The UK government did not listen to Webb in the post-World War One economic catastrophe. Demobilisation of soldiers and munitions factory workers, without any credible transition plan, sent the unemployment rate into orbit: 17 per cent by 1921, and 22 per cent by 1932. The latter spike came after the Wall Street Crash in 1929, and the decision by the Republican-controlled US government to lock down international investment with the Smoot–Hawley Tariff Act of 1930. Democrat President Franklin D Roosevelt took office in 1933, and passed the Reciprocal Trade Agreements Act of 1934 to liberalise trade once more. His 'New Deal' also included major programmes to create jobs. The Federal Emergency Relief Act of 1933, followed by the Emergency Relief Appropriation Act of 1935, enabled the President to create the Works Progress Administration, and a host of other agencies, whose funds built infrastructure, such as schools, bridges, hospitals or museums. Substantial sums of money were spent, and unemployment was brought down. However, the sums necessary for full employment could not be secured in Congress. This only happened with the outbreak of World War Two.

7.   JM Keynes, *The General Theory of Employment, Interest and Money* (1936) argued government must create jobs by taxation and spending. Keynes's theory arrived after the US government acted, but is an important restatement of what became a post-World War Two consensus. It developed 'macroeconomics', which roughly maps onto economic aspects of 'public law', while microeconomics roughly maps onto 'private law' (see this book's Preface). Keynes argued classical economics wrongly assumed unemployment was voluntary (ch 2). Involuntary unemployment results when effective 'aggregate demand' for goods and services (and labour) has dropped away (ch 3). In a financial crash, wealth is destroyed, and so people have less money to spend. This reduces aggregate demand. There is nothing inherent in the operation of markets that increases aggregate demand (and therefore stops continuing unemployment) in a depression. Poorer people have a higher 'propensity to consume' their income, because richer people cannot spend all their money, and therefore save or invest capital in the financial sector (ch 9). So, the way to increase aggregate demand, restore growth and a higher 'velocity of money' flowing around the economy (chs 15 and 21), is government spending. Keynes quietly added towards the end of his book that a society might have 'social practices and … a distribution of wealth which result in a propensity to consume which is unduly low' (ch 22). Keynes, a Liberal, was suggesting that stopping unemployment is both a question of active government, and reducing wealth inequality. What do you think?

8.   The most extreme consequences of mass unemployment unfolded in Germany. According to Otto Kahn-Freund: 'The special situation in the Weimar Republic

was the catastrophe of mass unemployment, which followed from the collapse of DANAT Bank, which in turn factually followed from Black Friday in America in the year of 1929. Connected to that, an essential point, was the deflationary economy policy of Brüning [the German Chancellor, 1930–32], whose meaning is not to be underestimated, namely the conscious attempt, by keeping wages low to reinvigorate the performance of Germany's exports. Whatever one wants to think about collective labour law, after the creation of millions of unemployed and the deflationary economic and financial policies of Brüning collective labour law in Germany failed. Because collective labour assumes, among other things, a certain balance of forces. A balance between the representatives of the labour movement and the representatives of employers. This balance was completely destroyed by mass unemployment, and with that the trade unions were robbed of the necessary strength for the maintenance of collective labour law … we found ourselves in complete error about the actual balance of power. We did not know at all what was actually happening. We had no idea of the extent to which what in America is called the "military industrial complex" already dominated the Weimar Republic. Without that Hitler would have been unimaginable. He was its product. And as a consequence the whole building which we had erected, if you like, was a house of cards. We completely overestimated the power of the trade unions in the Weimar Republic and considerably underestimated the power of the Reichswehr (Empire Defence Force).' See O Kahn-Freund, 'Autobiographical Memories of the Weimar Republic. A Conversation with Wolfgang Luthardt' (1981) 14(2) *Kritische Justiz* 183, 195–96, translated by E McGaughey (2016).

9.   Back in the UK, William Beveridge's influential book, *Full Employment in a Free Society* (1944), was as much an attack on fascism as a blueprint for post-war prosperity. It is often said that Mussolini 'got the trains running on time' and that Hitler 'put Germany back to work'. People who survived World War Two felt this was criminally dishonest. This is explained by another labour lawyer who was forced to leave Germany in 1933, Franz Neumann, 'Labor Mobilization in the National Socialist New Order' (1942) 9(3) *Law and Contemporary Problems* 544, 546: 'Slogans such as "plant community," "people's community" and "anti-plutocratic struggle" are designed to capture the working classes. Yet it is precisely on this point that the National Socialist regime offers only propaganda – nothing else. The German worker or salaried employee has received nothing from the regime except promises of a better future. He had, it is true, obtained security before the outbreak of the war. Full employment was the only achievement of the National Socialists. Yet that security is extremely ambiguous. It has paved the way for the utmost physical insecurity, namely for death. Those workers who did not know it before, know it since 1939: that economic security under National Socialism was possible only as a prelude to death. Death in the trenches, death in air raids, death in the factories as a result of physical exhaustion, death in railroad yards, chemical factories, and the like as a result of a terrific increase in industrial accidents. The connection between economic security and death is not incidental, it is essential; it springs from the very nature of National Socialism, which is an aggressive imperialist system seeking to transform markets into colonies.'

10. M Kalecki, 'Political Aspects of Full Employment' (1943) 14(4) *Political Quarterly* 347, 352 argues that under a fascist government, the objections of businessmen and financiers to full employment are removed 'by the fact that the state machinery is under the direct control of a partnership of big business with fascism'. Ordinarily, full employment is unwelcome because 'workers would "get out of hand" and the "captains of industry" would be anxious to "teach them a lesson"'. Kalecki is saying the threat of poverty, when someone can be made unemployed, is a way employers discipline workers. Unemployment reduces worker bargaining power, and instils a sufficient amount of fear to make workers socially subordinate to their employers. Do you agree? Does business have an incentive to maintain higher unemployment at other times?
11. After World War Two, MS Eccles, the chair of the US Federal Reserve (equivalent to the Bank of England) from 1934 to 1948 explained why he thought unemployment soared after 1929.

MS Eccles, *Beckoning Frontiers: Public and Personal Recollections* (1951) 75–77

I began to see that we had reached a stage where further advances in the national income and in our standard of living, even the maintenance of the existing standard, depended on finding an adequate outlet for the nation's savings. For while savings that are invested in new enterprises are beneficial not only to savers but also to the entire economy, savings that find no outlet and accumulate as idle or hoarded funds interrupt the flow of national income and result in a depression.

As mass production has to be accompanied by mass consumption, mass consumption, in turn, implies a distribution of wealth – not of existing wealth, but of wealth as it is currently produced – to provide men with buying power equal to the amount of goods and services offered by the nation's economic machinery. Instead of achieving that kind of distribution, a giant suction pump had by 1929–30 drawn into a few hands an increasing portion of currently produced wealth. This served them as capital accumulations. But by taking purchasing power out of the hands of mass consumers, the savers denied to themselves the kind of effective demand for their products that would justify a reinvestment of their capital accumulations in new plants. In consequence, as in a poker game where the chips were concentrated in fewer and fewer hands, the other fellows could stay in the game only by borrowing. When their credit ran out, the game stopped.

This is what happened to us in the twenties. We sustained high levels of employment in that period with the aid of an exceptional expansion of debt outside of the banking system. This debt was provided by the large growth of business savings as well as savings by individuals, particularly in the upper-income groups where taxes were relatively low. Private debt outside of the banking system increased about fifty per cent. This debt, which was at high interest rates, largely took the form of mortgage debt on housing, office, and hotel structures, consumer installment debt, brokers' loans, and foreign debt. The stimulation to spend by debt-creation of this sort was short-lived and could not be counted on to sustain high levels of employment for long periods of time. Had there been a better distribution of the current income from the national product – in other words, had there been less savings by business and the higher-income groups and more income in the lower groups – we should have had far greater stability in our economy. Had the six billion dollars, for instance, that were loaned by corporations and wealthy individuals for stock-market speculation been distributed to the public as lower prices or higher wages and with less profits to the corporations and the well-to-do, it would have prevented or greatly moderated the economic collapse that began at the end of 1929.

The time came when there were no more poker chips to be loaned on credit. Debtors thereupon were forced to curtail their consumption in an effort to create a margin that could be applied to the reduction of outstanding debts. This naturally reduced the demand for goods of all kinds and brought on what seemed to be overproduction, but was in reality underconsumption when judged in terms of the real world instead of the money world. This, in turn, brought about a fall in prices and employment.

Unemployment further decreased the consumption of goods, which further increased unemployment, thus closing the circle in a continuing decline of prices. Earnings began to disappear, requiring economies of all kinds in the wages, salaries, and time of those employed. And thus again the vicious circle of deflation was closed until one third of the entire working population was unemployed, with our national income reduced by fifty per cent, and with the aggregate debt burden greater than ever before, not in dollars, but measured by current values and income that represented the ability to pay. Fixed charges, such as taxes, railroad and other utility rates, insurance and interest charges, clung close to the 1929 level and required such a portion of the national income to meet them that the amount left for consumption of goods was not sufficient to support the population.

This then, was my reading of what brought on the depression.

NOTES AND QUESTIONS

1. Eccles argues that more inequality means lower 'effective demand'. This makes full employment impossible through private-sector or market action alone. Specifically, Eccles points to the 'idle or hoarded funds' of capital by the private sector, which worsens when inequality increases. As asset owners fail to invest, or actively hoard funds, continued growth may still occur, but only by working people becoming ever more indebted. Debt maintains growth until people can no longer pay, and then 'the game is stopped'. This means a crash.

2. There are multiple reasons why the Wall Street Crash occurred and the Great Depression ensued, on top of the explanation Eccles gives for the depression itself. His reference to 'stock-market speculation' was extensively discussed by AA Berle and GC Means, *The Modern Corporation and Private Property* (1932) part III. This explained how people were sold shares in corporations on the stock market at prices that were far too high. This happened because corporations had few seriously enforced duties, to people buying shares, to present a true and fair view of their accounts, or any other financial detail. Investors were easily misled by share marketing promoters. A stock market 'bubble' grew, and burst on 29 October 1929, when everyone began to sell. The Securities Act of 1933 and Securities and Exchange Act of 1934 wrote Berle and Means's proposals for full disclosure duties into law. The equivalent today in the UK is the Financial Services and Markets Act 2000, backed by a host of EU Directives.

3. Why did the United States (unlike the UK, Germany, etc) have so many ordinary people investing in the stock market? In this author's view, the straightforward explanation is that before the Social Security Act of 1935, there was no public pension system in the USA. Ordinary people had to save for retirement somehow. The result was a tremendous volume of capital flooding into the stock market from small investors. These were the people most vulnerable to misleading

marketing. Why did the United States have no public pension system? Because the
US Supreme Court and state courts, as part of the *Lochner* era, had struck down
all attempts by states to create them for being 'unconstitutional'. See *State Board
of Control v Buckstegge*, 158 Pac 837, 842 (1916), *Busser v Snyder*, 282 Pa 440
(1925) and *Railroad Retirement Board v Alton Railroad Co* 295 US 330 (1935).
In other words, the US Supreme Court was largely responsible for the Wall Street
Crash. This question has been debated many times before. What do you think?

4. Eccles mentions 'hoarded funds'. Later, AA Berle, 'A New Look at Management
    Responsibility' (1962) 2 *Human Resource Management* 3, argued that legal duties
    should develop on private asset owners to assist the government in maintaining
    full employment. 'They ought not to hoard when expenditure is needed; perhaps
    they ought to slow down under some conditions.' Is this desirable? If so, how
    could such a duty be enforced?

5. After World War Two, and Roosevelt's death, the Employment Act of 1946 cre-
    ated a duty on government 'to promote maximum employment, production, and
    purchasing power'. But the original Bill proposed that government would invest
    to assure 'continuing full employment'. It was watered down. Similarly, the
    Humphrey–Hawkins Full Employment Act of 1978 aimed to recreate the
    same duty to achieve full employment, but again failed to pass through Con-
    gress in that form. See KVW Stone, 'A Right to Work in the United States' in
    V Mantouvalou (ed) *The Right to Work* (2015) ch 15. Unlike in the UK, politi-
    cal consensus about stopping unemployment was absent. Figure 16.2 shows that
    every time they left the White House, Democrats had significantly lowered unem-
    ployment, while Republicans raised it.

Figure 16.2 US unemployment with incarcerated population

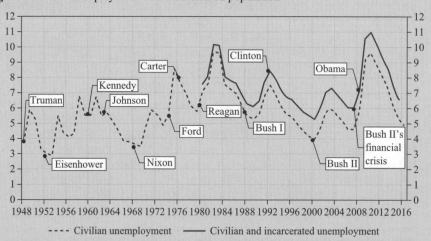

---- Civilian unemployment   ——— Civilian and incarcerated unemployment

Sources: Bureau of Labor Statistics, Labor Force Statistics from the Current Population Survey Bureau
of Justice Statistics, Key Facts at a Glance: Correctional populations.

6. Economic theory, both in the USA and UK, has supported the idea that govern-
    ments cannot and should not aim for full employment. M Friedman, 'The Role of

Monetary Policy' (1968) 58(1) *American Economic Review* 1, argued there is a 'natural' rate of unemployment caused by labour rights and union strength. Friedman based his argument on an analogy to an important paper by AW Phillips, 'The Relation between Unemployment and the Rate of Change of Money Wage Rates in the United Kingdom 1861–1957' (1958) 25 *Economica* 283. This showed that when unemployment in the UK was low, wages tended to rise. This was a perfectly logical conclusion, because low unemployment would tend to raise workers' bargaining power. But Friedman argued that *all prices* would inflate if there were full employment, if that went below the 'natural' unemployment rate. Price inflation, of course, is detrimental because it reduces the real value of the wages people have (eg if I earn £20,000 in 2018 and in 2019, but my rent and bills are rising, my 'real' wage is falling). But why would full employment cause inflation anyway?

7. Logically if there is full employment on fair wages, more people have more money to spend. This will increase demand for goods and services. But if production and supply can expand to meet the demand (because a fully employed people are doing socially useful jobs), prices need not rise. There will be low or no inflation. Therefore, full employment has no necessary connection to inflation whatsoever. What do you think?

8. The claim that full employment accelerates inflation was never backed by evidence. To take just one example, in the UK from 1952 to 1967, there was full employment and inflation averaged 3.12 per cent. The only other 16-year period in modern UK history to do better was 1991 to 2006, at 2.76 per cent inflation. But at that time unemployment, though falling, remained far higher.

9. Friedman's theory was not original. He was restating FA Hayek, 'Full Employment, Planning and Inflation' (1950) 4(6) *Institute of Public Affairs Review* 174. Hayek's theory was equally evidence-free. However, as Friedman became chair of the American Economic Association, his views were influential. His mystical 'natural' rate of unemployment is now termed the 'Non-Accelerating Inflation Rate of Unemployment' (NAIRU) in economic literature. This is the hypothetical rate of unemployment where inflation will not start to spiral. But Friedman said himself, we 'cannot know what the "natural" rate is' (1968) 58(1) *American Economic Review* 1, 10. This makes the theory impossible to falsify.

10. Why would a demonstrably false economic theory be useful? It was adopted by Gerald Ford and Ronald Reagan in the USA, and Margaret Thatcher in the UK. According to Alan Budd, Chief Economic Adviser to HM Treasury under Thatcher, unemployment may have been used as a weapon. 'The nightmare I sometimes have about this whole experience runs as follows. I was involved in making a number of proposals which were partly, at least, adopted by the government and put in play by the government. Now my worry is as follows, that there may have been people making the actual policy decisions or people behind them or people behind them who never believed for a moment that this was the correct way to bring down inflation. They did however see that it would be a very, very good way to raise unemployment, and raising unemployment was an extremely desirable way of, of reducing the strength of the working classes, if you like. That what was engineered there – in Marxist terms – was a crisis of capitalism which

re-created reserve army of labour, and has allowed the capitalist to make high profits ever since. Now again, I'd not say I believe that story, but when I really worry about all this I worry whether indeed that was really what was going on.' *Pandora's Box*, Episode 3: *The League of Gentlemen* (Thursday, 18 June 1992) BBC2. Could Budd's nightmare have been subconscious or conscious reality?

11. The Prices and Incomes Act 1966 Sch 2, para 14, which contained a joint statement of the TUC and employers' organisations contained a different theory of inflationary effects of full employment. It asserted 'experience has shown that in conditions of full employment the normal processes of collective bargaining both at national and local level can result in pay increases which are inflationary in effect. It is accordingly important to ensure that increases in wages and salaries above the norm should be confined to cases in which exceptional treatment can be shown to be required in the national interest.' This suggested there was a trade-off between higher inflation and fuller employment (rather than Friedman or Hayek's theory that inflation would become uncontrollable). But it is simply not clear that experience ever did show that.

12. JL Yellen, 'Monetary Policy: Goals and Strategy' (13 March 1996) NABE Policy Seminar, Washington, DC, appointed chair of the US Federal Reserve by Barack Obama in 2014, remaining until 2017, explained the 'natural rate' or NAIRU as follows: 'That minimum rate – the natural rate or NAIRU – importantly reflects a number of structural aspects of the economy, including the efficiency of the labor market in matching workers to job vacancies, the geographic mobility of workers, the quality of the skills they bring to the labor market, the demographics of the labor force, and the extent of structural mismatch between job vacancies and unemployed workers.' So, in Yellen's summary, factors influencing a 'natural' unemployment rate are (1) private and public employment agencies, (2) mobility, (3), education and (4) a 'structural mismatch'. This makes no explicit mention of labour rights, as Friedman did. But is it implicit? And is the theory of natural unemployment credible even in these terms?

13. The most comprehensive empirical study of labour standards, union rights and job security laws, the 'Labour Regulation Index' of the Centre for Business Research, University of Cambridge, gathers changes in the laws of 117 countries back to 1970. Preliminary results show that between labour rights and employment there is either no correlation, or a positive correlation. See Z Adams, L Bishop, S Deakin, C Fenwick, S Martinsson, G Rusconi, 'Labour Regulation over Time' (2015) RDW Working Paper. That is, if anything, labour rights promote *fuller* employment.

14. Aside from public investment, the 1944 White Paper was concerned to promote private investment. A central method was taxation of idle capital, to compel savings to be invested, not hoarded. Today, private investment promotion has occupied most policy attention, but without any meaningful emphasis on tax. The best example is the 'Europe 2020 Integrated Guidelines'. These are set by the European Council (the heads of EU Member States) and are the successor of the first European Employment Strategy in 1997. They are administered by the EU Commission. The recommendations are constantly updated. Those below expired in 2016, but still reflect Commission thinking. As a full statement of employment policy, it contrasts starkly to the 1944 White Paper.

Economic Policies Recommendation (EU) 2015/1184

Guideline 1: Promoting investment

Increasing the level of productive investment in Europe is key to boosting demand and improving competitiveness and long-term growth potential in Europe. Efforts should focus on mobilising finance for viable investment projects, making finance reach the real economy and improving the investment environment. Macroeconomic and financial stability, as well as regulatory predictability and openness and transparency of its financial sector, are critical for keeping the Union attractive for private sector investment, including foreign investment.

The potential of Union funds, including the European Fund for Strategic Investments and structural funds, and national funds to finance growth enhancing investments in key areas should be fully exploited. ...

Making finance reach the real economy calls for increasing transparency and information provision, in particular through the implementation of a European investment advisory hub under the auspices of the European Investment Bank and the establishment of a transparent pipeline of projects. ...

Guideline 2: Enhancing growth through Member States' implementation of structural reforms

Ambitious implementation of structural reforms by Member States in both product and labour markets, social welfare and pension systems is crucial to strengthen and sustain the economic recovery and ensure sustainable public finances, improve competitiveness, prevent and correct harmful macroeconomic imbalances in line with the macroeconomic imbalance procedure, and increase the growth potential of the Union economies. This would also help achieve higher economic and social cohesion. Competition-enhancing reforms, in particular in the non-tradable sector, a better functioning of the labour markets, and an improved business environment contribute to removing obstacles to growth and investment and increasing the adjustment capacity of the economy. ...

Labour market and social system reforms need to be pursued in order to promote growth and employment, while ensuring access for all to high quality, affordable and sustainable social services and benefits. Action in the area of labour market reforms, for example wage setting mechanisms and an increase in participation rates, should be pursued. ...

Efforts should continue to ... include modernisation of public administration, a reduction in administrative burdens, greater transparency, the fight against corruption, tax evasion and undeclared work, the improvement of the independence, quality and efficiency of judicial systems, alongside with contract enforcement and well-functioning insolvency procedures.

Information and communication technologies and the digital economy are important drivers of productivity, innovation and growth in all sectors of the economy. Promoting private investment in research and innovation should be ... accompanied by in-depth reforms to modernise the research and innovation systems, to enhance cooperation between public institutions and the private sector. ...

Guideline 3: Removing key barriers to sustainable growth and jobs at Union level

...

A well-functioning financial sector is key. ... Measures need to be taken in order to build a sustainable market for securitisation in Europe, which will help improve the effective funding capacity of Union banks. A genuine capital markets Union needs to be established, building on the achievements of the single market for financial services and capital.

... A cost-effective implementation of the 2030 climate and energy framework and transition to a competitive, resource efficient low carbon economy should be pursued. ...

... Union legislation should focus on those issues that are best dealt with at European level, and should be designed taking into account their economic, environmental and social impact. ...

Guideline 4: Improving the sustainability and growth-friendliness of public finances

Sound public finances are key for growth and job creation. Fiscal sustainability is vital to secure investor confidence and the fiscal space necessary to counter unexpected developments and maximise the positive contribution of public finances to the economy. ... Member States should secure long-term control over the deficit and debt levels. Fiscal policies must be conducted within the Union rules-based framework, in particular the Stability and Growth Pact, complemented by sound national budgetary arrangements. ...

In designing and implementing budgetary consolidation, strategies should prioritise growth-enhancing expenditure items within areas such as education, skills and employability, research and development, and innovation and investment in networks with positive impacts on productivity. Expenditure reforms should target efficiency gains in public administration. ...

Expenditure reforms that promote efficient resource allocation to support growth and employment while preserving equity should be complemented by the modernisation of revenue systems, where necessary. A common consolidated corporate tax base should continue to be explored. Shifts towards more growth-friendly taxes, while ensuring compliance with the Stability and Growth Pact, can help correct market inefficiencies. ...

Employment Decision 2015/1848

Guideline 5: Boosting demand for labour

Member States should facilitate the creation of quality jobs, reduce the barriers business faces in hiring people, promote entrepreneurship and, in particular, support the creation and growth of small enterprises. ...

The tax burden should be shifted away from labour to other sources of taxation less detrimental to employment and growth, while protecting revenue for adequate social protection and growth-enhancing expenditure. ...

Member States should, together with social partners and in line with national practices, encourage wage-setting mechanisms allowing for a responsiveness of wages to productivity developments. Differences in skills and divergences in economic performance across regions, sectors and companies should be taken into account. When setting minimum wages, Member States and social partners should consider their impact on in-work poverty, job creation and competitiveness.

Guideline 6: Enhancing labour supply, skills and competences

Member States, in cooperation with social partners, should promote productivity and employability through an appropriate supply of relevant knowledge, skills and competences.

High unemployment and inactivity should be tackled ... reinforcing strategies that include individualised active support for a return to the labour market. Youth unemployment and the high number of young people not in education, employment or training (NEETs), should be comprehensively addressed through a structural improvement in the school-to-work transition, including through the full implementation of the Youth Guarantee.

Barriers to employment should be reduced, especially for disadvantaged groups.
...

Member States should make full use of the European Social Fund and other Union funds to foster employment, social inclusion, lifelong learning and education and to improve public administration.

Guideline 7: Enhancing the functioning of labour markets

Member States should take into account the flexibility and security principles ('flexicurity principles'). They should reduce and prevent segmentation within labour markets and fight undeclared work. Employment protection rules, labour law and institutions should all provide a suitable environment for recruitment. ...

...

Member States should strengthen active labour-market policies ... accompanied by rights and responsibilities for the unemployed to actively seek work. ...

Member States should aim for better, more effective public employment services to reduce and shorten unemployment by providing tailored services to support jobseekers. ...

The mobility of workers should be promoted with the aim of exploiting the full potential of the European labour market. Mobility barriers in occupational pensions and in the recognition of qualifications should be removed. Member States should at the same time prevent abuses of the existing rules and recognise potential 'brain drain' from certain regions.

Guideline 8: Fostering social inclusion, combatting poverty and promoting equal opportunities

Member States should modernise social protection systems. ... Social protection systems should promote social inclusion by encouraging people to actively participate in the labour market and society. Affordable, accessible and quality services such as childcare, out-of-school care, education, training, housing, health services and long-term care are essential. Particular attention should also be given to basic services and actions to prevent early school leaving, reduce in-work poverty and fight poverty and social exclusion. ...

NOTES AND QUESTIONS

1. It is immediately apparent that these 'soft law' instruments (redacted as much as possible) are not written by experts in law, evidence or literature. The language is overlain with jargon, repeats itself, fails to specify what it means should be done, or why any particular outcome should result. Nevertheless, this exemplifies the most prevalent modern political approach to employment policy. It was favoured by the UK and EU since the European Employment Strategy began in 1997. What are the most notable differences between it and the 1944 White Paper? What is not in this 'new' approach?

2. Guideline 1 refers to making finance reach the 'real economy', ie manufacturing and services, rather than the financial sector. It highlights 'regulatory predictability and openness and transparency of its financial sector' but does not say what this entails. The only public investment element in the Guidelines is the European Fund for Strategic Investments, run by the European Investment Bank (EIB). The EIB spent €66.97bn in 2016 (around £58bn) in an EU population of 510m people. In 2017, the EU unemployment rate was recorded as 8% (9.5% in the eurozone): around 20m people without jobs. This means the EU spent about €3,400 (£2,900) per unemployed person, but presumably very little reached those people.

This money is largely spent on the European Investment Advisory Hub giving advice on how to create jobs. For the UK €6.9bn was spent. More money goes to lower-income regions. For perspective, the total UK government budget in 2016–17 was £772bn for 65m people, of which £52.16bn was infrastructure spending. Why not simply increase the sums, to guarantee everyone a job? Do you agree this would achieve the TEU Art 3(3) goal of 'aiming at full employment'? How much money do you think is needed, and spent on what?

3.   In 1993, the European Commission White Paper, *Growth, Competitiveness and Employment* COM (93) 700 final, 1993, proposed a €400 billion plan to invest in jobs. It was rejected by Member States at the Essen Council in 1994.

4.   Guideline 2 talks about 'structural reforms', 'competition-enhancing reforms', 'social security reforms' and 'labour market reforms', and 'reforms to modernise the research and innovation systems' without saying what 'reforms' means. What do you think the Guideline authors mean? Why do you think the authors do not say what they mean? Do they not know what they want, are they are trying to hide what they want, or both? Guideline 3 contains similar but largely benign platitudes: a 'sustainable market for securitisation' and an 'efficient low carbon economy'. But what does this mean?

5.   Guideline 4 says there should be 'control over the deficit and debt levels', refers to the Stability and Growth Pact (annual structural deficits to be limited to 0.5 per cent of GDP), 'efficiency gains in public administration' and runs through various tax policies. In 2016, average EU government debt, as a percentage of annual GDP, was 83.5 per cent. 'Gross Domestic Product' is a country's total income, which could theoretically be taxed. In 2016 UK debt was 89.3 per cent, up from 34 per cent in 2002. Estonia (9.5 per cent debt) and Luxembourg (20 per cent) were closest to being debt free. Government debt is largely owed to banks, asset managers and creditor countries. For the UK, interest on debt has totalled between 2 and 5 per cent of GDP each year. Who benefits by governments maintaining large debts? Is there an easy way to eliminate debt, and achieve a surplus, without cutting government? In any event, is it possible for a government to cut its way to growth?

6.   Guideline 5 says governments should 'reduce the barriers business faces in hiring people'. This appeals to an evidence-free theory that if it is harder to fire people, business will not hire (see chapters 17–19). It says the tax 'burden' should shift away from labour, without distinguishing between people with greater or lesser ability to pay, and again appealing to a theory that income taxes are 'detrimental to employment and growth'. It insinuates that minimum wages 'impact' job creation and competitiveness (see chapter 6). Should economists be allowed to influence law when their grasp on reality is so tenuous?

7.   Guideline 6 talks about 'active support for return to the labour market' and applies a colloquial label, 'NEETs', in the context of youth unemployment. The top entry on UrbanDictionary.com says of NEET: 'like chav, it seems to be particularly applicable to a social under-class lacking drive, motivation or ambition'. The second entry says 'young people have started to use it as a term for bums/layabouts

with no future'. Do you think the European Council should perpetuate name call-
ing and derogatory language, whatever its popularity in economic theory? On
the term's origins, see H Williamson, 'Status Zer0 Youth and the 'Underclass':
Some Considerations' in R Macdonald (ed) *Youth, 'The Underclass' and Social
Exclusion* (1997) 82, referring to the term's use in 'high levels of [the previous
Conservative] central government'.

8.   Guideline 7 talks about 'flexicurity' (see chapter 15) and says 'Employment pro-
     tection rules' should foster 'recruitment', again referring to the theory that if it is
     easier to fire people, more will be hired. It talks about 'tailored services to support
     jobseekers'. What does this mean? It then calls to reduce 'mobility barriers' but
     also prevent 'brain drain'. How, exactly, is that consistent?

9.   Guideline 8 says that social protection should 'modernise'. It refers to making
     services 'affordable', and names 'childcare, out-of-school care, education, train-
     ing, housing, health services and long-term care'. Are these services not often
     provided freely through income tax? What does 'modernise' mean?

10. D Ashiagbor, *The European Employment Strategy: Labour Market Regulation
     and New Governance* (2005) ch 6 suggests that the European Employment Strat-
     egy, although invigorated by the 'New Labour' government of Tony Blair to be
     rolled out across the EU, is not a 'renewal of social democracy', but rather 'accu-
     rately described as no more than "neo-liberalism with a human face"'. Ashiagbor
     doubts whether 'soft law' (even if the policies are not damaging) that 'eschews
     centralized social policy norms can adequately ensure a core of social rights,
     below which no Member State can fall'.

11. It seems a 'hard law' version of the European Employment Strategy was imple-
     mented during the eurozone crisis through the 'Memorandum of Understanding'
     between Greece, the European Central Bank, the Commission and the Interna-
     tional Monetary Fund in 2010. This was a contract under the Vienna Convention
     1969, offered on a take-it-or-leave-it basis to Greece, to get loans to service gov-
     ernment debt (mostly owed to German, French and UK banks).

Greece: *Memorandum of Understanding on Specific Economic Policy Conditionality* (3 May 2010) 60–71

The quarterly disbursements of bilateral financial assistance from euro area Member States
will be subject to quarterly reviews of conditionality for the duration of the arrangement. The
release of the tranches will be based on observance of quantitative performance criteria, and
a positive evaluation of progress made with respect to policy criteria in the MEFP and in this
Memorandum, which specifies the detailed criteria that will be assessed for the successive
reviews, up to the end of 2011. The detailed criteria for the years 2012 and 2013 will be specified at the occasion of the spring 2011 review.

The authorities commit to consult with the European Commission, the ECB and the IMF
on adoption of policies that are not consistent with this memorandum. They will also provide
them with all requested information for monitoring progress during program implementation
and the economic and financial situation (Annex 1). Prior to the release of the instalments, the
authorities shall provide a compliance report on the fulfilment of the conditionality.

1. Actions for the first review (to be completed by end Q2-2010)

...

iv. Structural reforms

...

To strengthen labour market institutions:

Government starts discussions with social partners in order to revise private sector wage bargaining and contractual arrangements.

...

2. Actions for the second review (to be completed by end Q3-2010)

...

ii. Structural fiscal reforms

Parliament adopts legislation to improve the efficiency of the tax administration ...

...

Parliament adopts a reform of the pension system to ensure its medium- and long-term sustainability. It should limit the increase of public sector spending on pensions, over the period 2010–2060, to under 2.5 percent of GDP. The reform will be designed in close consultation with European Commission, IMF and ECB staff, and its estimated impact on long-term sustainability will be validated by the EU Economic Policy Committee. ... The reform should include the following elements:

— ... merging the existing pension funds in three funds and introducing a unified new system for all current and future employees ...;
— ... a unified statutory retirement age of 65 years, including for women in the public sector (phased in immediately after adoption), to be completed by December 2013;
— Gradual increase in the minimum contributory period for retirement on a full benefit from 37 to 40 years by 2015;
— Amendment of the pension award formula ... with accrual rate limited to an average annual rate of 1.2%, and pensions indexed to prices;
— ... an automatic adjustment mechanism that, every three years and starting in 2020, will increase the (minimum and statutory) retirement age in line with the increase in life expectancy at retirement;
— Extend the calculation of the pensionable earnings from the current last five years to the entire lifetime earnings (while retaining acquired rights);
— Reduction of the upper limit on pensions;
— Introduction of a means-tested minimum guaranteed income for elderly people (above the statutory retirement age), to protect the most vulnerable groups, consistent with fiscal sustainability;
— ... restrict access to early retirement. In particular, increase the minimum early retirement age to 60 years by 1st January 2011, including for workers in heavy and arduous professions and those with 40 years of contributions.
— Abolish special rules for those insured before 1993 (while retaining acquired rights). Substantial revision of the list of heavy and arduous professions;
— Reduction of pension benefits (by 6% per year) for people entering retirement between the ages of 60 and 65 with a contributory period of less than 40 years;
— Introduction of stricter conditions and regular re-examination of eligibility for disability pensions.

...

3. Actions for the third review (to be completed by end Q4-2010)
…

iii. Structural reforms
…

To strengthen labour market institutions:

Following dialogue with social partners, the government proposes and parliament adopts legislation to reform wage bargaining system in the private sector, which should provide for a reduction in pay rates for overtime work and enhanced flexibility in the management of working time. Allow local territorial pacts to set wage growth below sectoral agreements and introduce variable pay to link wages to productivity performance at the firm level.

Government amends regulation of the arbitration system, (Law 1876/1990), so that both parties can resort to arbitration if they disagree with the proposal of the mediator.

Following dialogue with social partners, government adopts legislation on minimum wages to introduce sub-minima for groups at risk such as the young and long-term unemployed, and put measures in place to guarantee that current minimum wages remain fixed in nominal terms for three years.

Government amends employment protection legislation to extend the probationary period for new jobs to one year, to reduce the overall level of severance payments and ensure that the same severance payment conditions apply to blue- and white-collar workers, to raise the minimum threshold for activation of rules on collective dismissals especially for larger companies, and to facilitate greater use of temporary contracts and part-time work.
…

6. Actions for the sixth review (to be completed by end Q3-2011)

i. Fiscal consolidation

… Government adopts draft budget for 2012 aiming at a further reduction of the general government deficit …:

— Reduce public employment on top of the rule of 1 recruitment for each 5 retirements in the public sector; the reduction in public employment on top of the 5-to-1 rule should allow savings of at least EUR 600 million; …
— Continue the reorganisation of local government, to generate at least EUR 500 million in savings;
— Nominal freeze in pensions; …
— Reduction of transfers to public enterprises by at least EUR 800 billion following their restructuring;
— Make unemployment benefits means-tested (aiming at savings of EUR 500m) …

NOTES AND QUESTIONS

1. In the extracts, which focus on labour policies, the Memorandum of Understanding with Greece required cuts to (1) pensions, including for the disabled, (2) minimum wages, particularly for young people, (3) dismissal protection and severance pay, including for collective dismissals, (4) for public-sector workers, and (5) in unemployment benefits. It also required (6) changes to 'wage bargaining', without specifying what this would be – but it means a shift from sectoral to enterprise bargaining, and going below sectoral standards if employers can make a union

to agree an 'opening clause' and (7) increasing 'enhanced flexibility'. The full document is found in Commission, DG for Economic and Financial Affairs, *The Economic Adjustment Programme for Greece* (May 2010) Occasional Papers 61. Other parts not extracted deal with many prudent reforms (albeit with varying levels of reasoning and detail) particularly tax enforcement, changes to accounting practice, financial regulation and insolvency law. Others, particularly €3bn of privatisation of public services, are wholly unreasoned. The most consequential changes, however, revolve around labour policy. In what way was the financial or eurozone crisis the result of inflexible labour markets in Greece? How can cuts in labour standards be argued to produce growth?

2. The reason for the eurozone crisis, beginning with Greece, started with the US sub-prime mortgage crisis of 2007. Under George W Bush, the US government had (1) shut down even minimal consumer credit and protection legislation, (2) failed to regulate conflicts of interest of credit-rating agencies, and (3) failed to regulate derivative products. Many Americans had bought homes with teaser rate mortgages, with interest rates variable at will by the lenders (1). The rights to receive income, as struggling Americans paid off their rip-off mortgage debts, were packaged into companies ('special purpose vehicles', SPVs) which issued bonds ('collateralised debt obligations', CDOs) to the securities markets. These CDOs were over-rated by agencies (Moody's, S&P and Fitch) who were paid by the companies selling them (2). Securities traders then sold options or futures or swaps ('derivatives') of the CDOs to pension funds, life insurers and banks around the world, but did not have to disclose much about what 'derivatives of CDOs from SPVs' actually meant (3). In this way, the whole financial system was profiting from families struggling to meet mortgage repayments, as money lenders varied interest at will. By 2006, more and more families were going broke and being evicted from their homes, and money-lenders were writing off losses. By 2007, that meant all the billions of derivatives swirling around the global financial system were suddenly worthless. The UK had to nationalise Northern Rock, and then RBS and Lloyds, which had traded billions in worthless US derivatives. Worldwide governments did the same. See E Warren, 'Product Safety Regulation as a Model for Financial Services Regulation' (2008) 43(2) *Journal of Consumer Affairs* 452 and JC Coffee, 'What Went Wrong? An Initial Inquiry into the Causes of the 2008 Financial Crisis' (2009) 9(1) *Journal of Corporate Law Studies* 1.

3. As the US economy convulsed, international investment locked down. This meant governments everywhere had lower tax receipts, and those with higher public debt faced an even harder task of meeting repayments. Moody's, S&P and Fitch also rate government debt, and began downgrading countries such as Greece to junk. Their own shareholders were betting through credit default swaps that Greece would default on its debt. This sent interest rates (which are variable) for Greek debt into orbit, meaning it was inevitable that Greece could not repay its debts – mainly owed to British, German and French banks. This meant Greece had no choice but to ask the EU for help. Taking the view that this was the fault of an irresponsible Greek people, the European Central Bank, the Commission and the International Monetary Fund only lent money (to pay off British, German and

French banks) with the conditions in the *Memorandum*. See R Janssen, 'Greece and the IMF: Who Exactly Is Being Saved?' (2010) Center for Economic and Policy Research.

4.   Between 2010 and 2014, Greek unemployment rose from 12 to 27 per cent. (See Figure 16.3.) An austerity programme had begun in Spain in January 2010. This did not work, so Spain had to ask the EU for a €100bn loan under a *Memorandum of Understanding* (July 2012) 47, although this merely told Spain: 'Implement the labour market reform adopted in February'. In Portugal, an austerity programme was launched under international pressure in May 2010. That did not work, so it went to the EU for a €78bn loan in May 2011, and received its own *Memorandum of Understanding* (May 2011). Ireland signed a *Memorandum of Understanding* (December 2010) 63, and received a €85bn loan. Although the loan was enough for recovery, it was told to perform measures such as cutting its minimum wage by €1 just to make sure. In no case is there any correlation, let alone credible causative argument, to say destroying labour rights improved prosperity. Recovery took place as global demand was restored, notably after the US government passed the American Recovery and Reinvestment Act of 2009, and it slowly took effect: US unemployment peaked over 9.5% in 2010 but reduced to 5% by 2016. The Obama policy, unlike Cameron, Merkel or Sarkozy in the EU, was growth not austerity.

Figure 16.3 Eurozone unemployment 1998–2016

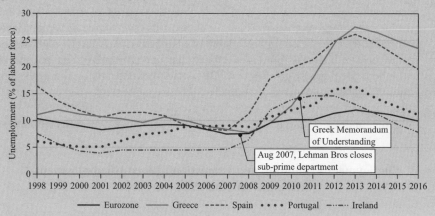

Source: Eurostat, Total unemployment rate.

5.   Its defenders argue that the 'structural reforms' of cutting pensions, minimum wages, collective bargaining, job security and public pay were a necessary period of 'pain' to ensure long-term 'healing'. Does this remind you of a witch doctor? The alternative, logical view, is that alongside the banks' self-induced implosion, destruction of labour rights and public-sector austerity worsened unemployment. Arguably the economy is not like some magic money tree: you cannot prune for prosperity, or cut your way to growth.

6.   There seems little doubt that the *Memorandum* with Greece, at least, violated the right to collective bargaining (ECHR Art 11), just remuneration and social security (UDHR Arts 22–23), consultation, just dismissal and fair working conditions (CFREU Arts 27–28, 30–31, 34). Does the EU have the legal capacity to conclude agreements in international law in a way that is incompatible with human rights norms? Put another way, can the EU do through international agreements with a Member State what it could not achieve through a Directive or Regulation? The answer, so far as an agreement goes, is quite possibly 'no'. Under the Vienna Convention 1969 Arts 6–7: 'Every State possesses the capacity to conclude treaties.' This does not, however, affect the internal liability for acting *ultra vires* (just as a shareholder can sue a director for acting beyond his or her powers, even though a contract remains binding vis-à-vis a third party: Companies Act 2006 ss 31 and 171). Are the Memoranda subject to judicial review, and open to being held void for violation of human rights?

7.   As a whole, the Europe 2020 strategy rests on the theory that private investment will flourish when labour market 'barriers' are removed. This theory is an abject failure. What changes to economic theory and education are needed to protect the economy?

8.   A third source of investment, beyond the private business and the state, are 'social' funds: democratically accountable and not running a profit-making-business. Many (by no means all) pension funds are like this (chapter 6(4)). They take contributions from employees or employers. Pension funds, private or public, whose participants have a degree of social or democratic voice, *may* sidestep both state control and corporate control. If labour controls its own source of capital, which is sufficiently large, it could be capable of maintaining full employment regardless of private business' preference for higher unemployment, and despite any anti-labour ideology of government. Of course, this depends on the fund's constitution. Trade unions have often made collective agreements to exercise greater influence over funds. Interest grew from the 1970s in the possibilities for social investment policy, without the state. An ILO Recommendation reflected this.

Employment Promotion and Protection against Unemployment Recommendation 1988 (no 176)

10. Members should, in accordance, if appropriate, with provisions in multilateral agreements, invest any reserves accumulated by statutory pension schemes and provident funds in such a way as to promote and not to discourage employment within the country, and encourage such investment from private sources, including private pension schemes, while at the same time affording the necessary guarantees of security and yield of the investment.

11. The progressive introduction in rural and urban areas of community services, including health-care services, financed by social security contributions or by other sources, should lead to increased employment and the provision of training of personnel, while at the same time making a practical contribution to the achievement of national objectives regarding employment promotion.

NOTES AND QUESTIONS

1. What does 'invest ... to promote and not to discourage employment' mean? Funds can choose to buy company shares and assets in industries that create desirable jobs, while generating a satisfactory return. An example of a job-discouraging industry could be private equity funds, where the strategy rests on extracting profit for shareholders and lowering wages: see E Appelbaum and R Batt, *Private Equity at Work – When Wall Street Manages Main Street* (2014). The arms industry and tobacco are often avoided out of moral conviction, but arguably these industries diminish employment because their production ends in the inherently wasteful enterprise of killing people.

2. Job-promoting investment logically includes anything that the future economy will soon need more of, or can increase productivity. For example, wind or solar energy and electric transport will inevitably grow in pursuit of a zero-carbon economy. Social care needs will grow. Industries that pay fair wages are more likely to increase jobs, because they contribute to a fairer distribution of wealth. This is why investment decisions are intensely political: they often disfavour people with entrenched economic power.

3. Another example of a social fund is the Norwegian 'Government Pension Fund Global', in which the Norwegian government has saved revenue from North Sea Oil on behalf of every citizen. The UK government chose not to save revenue from its share of North Sea oil, letting BP, Shell, etc, pay all profits to shareholders. Other 'sovereign wealth funds' have been established without natural resources, simply through saving. If the UK developed its own sovereign fund, how would you think it should be governed?

4. Should social funds favour investment to create jobs in the UK or the EU over other countries? In *Cowan v Scargill* [1985] Ch 270, Megarry VC held this would breach a trustee's supposed duty to maximise financial returns. This meant Arthur Scargill, trustee of the mineworkers' pension fund, was not entitled to focus investments in the UK coal industry. This judgment's reasoning was obviously flawed. In *Harries v Church Commissioners of England and Wales* [1992] 1 WLR 1241, Nicholls J (later Lord Nicholls) held that the first duty of a trustee is follow the trust's terms, and trustees should act consistently with the terms. So, this entitled the Church of England pension fund to divest from unethical companies, consistent with Anglican faith.

5. Now, the Trustee Act 2000 s 3(1) states: '[A] trustee may make any kind of investment that he could make if he were absolutely entitled to the assets of the trust.' If *Harries* did not already, this overrides *Cowan*. There is no implied duty on a trustee to maximise financial returns, and therefore not act ethically, or invest money in a way that will help a pension fund's beneficiaries in their capacity as workers. The trouble is that because an appellate court has not firmly resolved these issues, pension trustees and the financial community stick with a rule of maximising financial returns, citing *Cowan* in their defence, for doing nothing.

(b) Procurement

Governments and private enterprise do not only invest themselves: they buy or 'procure' services from others. What conditions should government apply to procurement partners? Once upon a time, in *Roberts v Hopwood* [1925] AC 578, the House of Lords opposed fair labour standards even for a council's own staff. Lord Atkinson said a council's policy of equal pay for men and women expressed 'eccentric principles of socialistic philanthropy ... a feminist ambition to secure the equality of the sexes'. He did not consider the public interest in having well-paid staff to stimulate full employment and social prosperity.

A more modern approach developed in the ILO Labour Clauses (Public Contracts) Convention 1949 (c 94). Article 2 required outsourced workers should have terms equal to those in (a) collective agreements in the sector, (b) arbitration, or (c) national law or regulation. The UK ratified this in 1950, but denounced it in 1982. However, the Public Procurement Directive 2014/24/EU sets out procedural rules that must be followed before awards are made, implemented by the Public Contracts Regulations 2015. Article 18(2) and regulation 56 state operators may decide not to procure from contractors who do not abide by 'applicable obligations in the fields of environmental, social and labour law established by Union law, national law, collective agreements, or by the ... social and labour law provisions listed in Annex X' (ie the eight core ILO Conventions). This is meant to ensure transparency when private companies compete for government contracts. It ensures price competition does not come from wage cutting, which has no inherent economic or social value. This reversed a line of cases, following *Viking* and *Laval*, where the CJEU tried to restrain procurement to advance labour rights.

Rüffert v Land Niedersachsen (2008) C-346/06

Mr Rüffert claimed Lower Saxony's State Procurement Act (the Landesvergabegesetz) violated the Posted Workers Directive 96/71/EC Art 3(8). Rüffert was the liquidator of a bankrupt building company called Objekt and Bauregie GmbH & Co KG. The State Procurement Act §3 said it would only procure building contractors, for jobs over €10,000, where workers were paid according to the minimum terms of collective agreements for public works, and §8 imposed penalties. One of the company's subcontractors paid Polish workers rates 46.57 per cent of the minimum collective agreement rate when building a prison at Rosdorf, near Göttingen. The Higher Regional Court asked the Court of Justice if the penalty under §8 might have been incompatible with the contractor's freedom to provide services (TFEU Art 56).

This question was based on the idea (litigated in *Laval*, now probably reversed: see chaper 10(1)(d)) that the Posted Workers Directive (PWD) 1996/71/EC Arts 1–3 prevents Member States from requiring posted workers to be paid higher than a national minimum wage, according to a collective agreement (cf chapter 15(4)(a)). *Laval* said Art 3(8) means a collective agreement can only set higher rates if it is 'universally applicable', 'generally applicable' or 'concluded by most' representatives of employers and workers. So supposedly, the PWD 1996 does not set a minimum standard but a maximum standard, because any other type of collective agreement violates the employer's freedom to provide services, without regard to the union's equivalent freedom: again, see chapter 10(1)(d). From this deeply flawed reasoning, the Court of Justice said the Polish contractor's freedom was violated.

Second Chamber:

26. In answer to a written question from the Court, Land Niedersachsen confirmed that the 'Buildings and public works' collective agreement is not a collective agreement which has been declared universally applicable within the meaning of the AEntG [the German Posted Worker Act 1996]. In addition, the case file submitted to the Court does not contain any evidence to support the conclusion that that agreement is nevertheless capable of being treated as universally applicable within the meaning of the second indent of the first subparagraph of Article 3(1) of Directive 96/71, read in conjunction with the first subparagraph of Article 3(8) of that directive.

...

28. In addition, a collective agreement such as that at issue in the main proceedings cannot, in any event, be considered to constitute a collective agreement within the meaning of the second subparagraph of Article 3(8) and, more specifically, to be a collective agreement, as mentioned in the first indent to that provision, 'generally applicable to all similar undertakings in the geographical area and in the profession or industry concerned'.

29. In a context such as that in the main proceedings, the binding effect of a collective agreement such as that at issue here covers only a part of the construction sector falling within the geographical area of that agreement, since, first, the law which gives it such an effect applies only to public contracts and not to private contracts and, second, the collective agreement has not been declared universally applicable.

30. It follows that a measure such as that at issue in the main proceedings does not fix a rate of pay according to one of the procedures laid down in the first and second indents of the first subparagraph of Article 3(1) and in the second subparagraph of Article 3(8) of Directive 96/71.

31. Therefore, such a rate of pay cannot be considered to constitute a minimum rate of pay within the meaning of Article 3(1)(c) of Directive 96/71 which Member States are entitled to impose, pursuant to that directive, on undertakings established in other Member States, in the framework of the transnational provision of services (see, to that effect, Case C-341/05 *Laval un Partneri* [2007] ECR I-0000, paragraphs 70 and 71).

32. Likewise, such a rate of pay cannot be considered to be a term and condition of employment which is more favourable to workers within the meaning of Article 3(7) of Directive 96/71.

33. More specifically, that provision cannot be interpreted as allowing the host Member State to make the provision of services in its territory conditional on the observance of terms and conditions of employment which go beyond the mandatory rules for minimum protection. As regards the matters referred to in Article 3(1), first subparagraph, (a) to (g), Directive 96/71 expressly lays down the degree of protection for workers of undertakings established in other Member States who are posted to the territory of the host Member State which the latter State is entitled to require those undertakings to observe. Moreover, such an interpretation would amount to depriving the directive of its effectiveness (see *Laval un Partneri*, paragraph 80).

...

35. It follows that a Member State is not entitled to impose, pursuant to Directive 96/71, on undertakings established in other Member States, by a measure such as that at issue in the

main proceedings, a rate of pay such as that provided for by the 'Buildings and public works' collective agreement.

36. That interpretation of Directive 96/71 is confirmed by reading it in the light of Article 49 EC [now TFEU Art 56], since that directive seeks in particular to bring about the freedom to provide services, which is one of the fundamental freedoms guaranteed by the Treaty.

...

38. In addition, contrary to the contentions of Land Niedersachsen and a number of the Governments which submitted observations to the Court, such a measure cannot be considered to be justified by the objective of ensuring the protection of workers.

39. As stated at paragraph 29 of this judgment, since this case concerns the rate of pay fixed by a collective agreement such as that at issue in the main proceedings, that rate is applicable, as a result of a law such as the Landesvergabegesetz, only to a part of the construction sector falling within the geographical area of that agreement, since, first, that legislation applies solely to public contracts and not to private contracts and, second, that collective agreement has not been declared universally applicable.

40. The case file submitted to the Court contains no evidence to support the conclusion that the protection resulting from such a rate of pay which, moreover, as the national court also notes, exceeds the minimum rate of pay applicable pursuant to the AEntG is necessary for a construction sector worker only when he is employed in the context of a public works contract but not when he is employed in the context of a private contract.

41. For the same reasons as those set out at paragraphs 39 and 40 of this judgment, the restriction also cannot be considered to be justified by the objective of ensuring protection for independence in the organisation of working life by trade unions, as the German Government contends.

Rapporteur Timmermans, President Makarczyk, Klūris, Bonichot and Toader.

NOTES AND QUESTIONS

1. *Rüffert* held the State Procurement Act violated the Polish contractor's freedom to provide services (saying nothing of the employees' right to receive a union's services) because it required compliance with collective agreements, which went beyond the procedure set out in PWD 1996 Art 3(8). The fact that collective agreements, which were not universally applicable, only applied to workers providing services to the public sector meant that the Act could not be justified.

2. Arguably the mistakes made in this judgment are failing to understand that (1) that the PWD 1996 lays down minimum standards: it does not harmonise or create maximum standards, as *Laval* wrongly decided, (2) an employer's freedom to provide services cannot be used to attack a collective agreement, or any law supporting collective agreements, which involve a union's freedom to provide its services, (3) even if points (1) and (2) are not accepted, it is irrelevant that collective agreements only apply to contractors from the public sector, because the employer's right to provide services cannot logically affect the right of its contracting party to set the contract terms it chooses. This flows from the basic

right of freedom of association, and indeed freedom of contract, in the CFREU, Arts 12 and 16.

3. A shift in approach was seen in *Commission v Germany* (2010) C-271/08. The CJEU held that Germany had breached the Public Procurement Directives 92/50/EEC and 2004/18/EC by failing to require that local councils put out contracts to public tender. Councils had signed a collective agreement with two unions, ver.di and dbb tarrifunion, that said pension services would be provided by the Sparkasse (a mutual bank network) or local authority insurance companies. The Grand Chamber held that the Procurement Directives expressed, specifically, principles of the right to provide services and establish (in TFEU Arts 49 and 56), [43]–[46]). Where a collective agreement set terms for contract awards was not inherently outside the scope of the Directives, [50]. The CJEU gave passing mention to *Viking* and *Laval* but was concerned to argue that requiring a tender, before pension contracts were awarded to a bank, 'does not prove irreconcilable with attainment of the social objective' of the collective agreement, [66]. It is submitted that this is a convincing and soundly reasoned case, because *Viking*, *Laval* and employers' supposedly unquestionable freedoms play virtually no role in the *ratio decidendi*. See Sypris (2011) 42(2) ILJ 222. It was a straightforward application of the Directives. Would employees have been better off if the collective agreement set up its own pension fund, where workers could manage their own money? See chapter 6(4).

4. However, *Bundesdruckerei GmbH v Stadt Dortmund* (2014) C-549/13 suggested a minimum wage of €8.62 might not be payable to Polish workers. The Dortmund City Council required minimum wage rates be complied with by all workers of all subcontractors in a tender to digitalise its data and records, whichever Member State those workers were in. The corporation, Bundesdruckerei GmbH (which is German), was refused an exemption so it could get Polish workers to do the job at less cost. The corporation took the view that it could not afford to use a Polish subcontractor and pay Polish workers €8.62. The Ninth Chamber held, without any Advocate General opinion, that TFEU Art 56 could preclude this. It said at [34] a minimum wage could not be imposed 'which bears no relation to the cost of living in the Member State in which the services relating to the public contract at issue are performed and for that reason prevents subcontractors established in that Member State from deriving a competitive advantage from the differences between the respective rates of pay, that national legislation goes beyond what is necessary to ensure that the objective of employee protection is attained'. Was the CJEU saying it is okay for a German corporation to get a 'competitive advantage' by exporting jobs to Poland? Have the self-annointed economists at the CJEU missed the fact that if all employers (Polish or German) pay the *same* wages there can *never* be any competitive disadvantage for any company, and they compete on quality and profit margins? Do you think Polish workers benefit from the CJEU reducing the right to Germany's minimum wage, or does it only benefit the (German) corporate employers? Why did the CJEU not think it necessary to explain its formula for reducing the minimum wage to reflect the 'cost of living' elsewhere? Given that the CJEU had no formula, why did it think itself competent to engage in highly political questions of social and economic policy?

5.   Although *Bundesdruckerei* was decided after the Public Procurement Directive 2014 Art 18, it applied to facts before the Directive. Under the new law, it is submitted that it would be wrong and obviously so. The PPD 2014 recital 37 states that Member States should ensure compliance with labour laws or collective agreements 'at the place where the works are executed or the services provided'. Therefore, where workers 'executed' work in Poland, and their corporate employer up the supply chain has 'provided' the workers' 'services' in Germany, the most favourable norm for the worker applies: in this case German law. This is crystal clear from the wording, although it is open to ambiguity and not resolved in Art 18 of the Directive. For a contrasting view, see Barnard (2017) 46(2) ILJ 208, 238, fn 144 (who does not claim that an opposite interpretation is defensible from a policy perspective: it clearly is not). If the ambiguity is accepted, it is submitted the issue must be left to the procuring party's discretion.

6.   *Regiopost GmbH & Co KG v Stadt Landau in der Pfalz* (2015) C-115/14 held that the City of Landau could lawfully exclude any business which refused to pay the regional minimum wage, set in state law of €8.50. It stated that under Directive 2004/18, which was to be read in conjunction with the Posted Workers Directive 1996, it was lawful to require a minimum wage: here it was in a law. It was (ostensibly) a restriction on freedom to provide services, [69]. But it was justified to protect workers who were 'in the *Land* of Rhineland-Palatinate', [75].

7.   In the United States, there are three main procurement Acts. First, the Davis–Bacon Act of 1931 (41 USC §3141-8) applies to contracts with federal funding over $2,000, and requires the prevailing wage rate be paid for construction of any building works procured by the Federal Government. Second, the Walsh–Healey Public Contracts Act of 1936 (41 USC §6501-11) applies to contracts over $10,000, and requires government contractors to pay overtime, and the prevailing wage rate. Third, the McNamara–O'Hara Service Contract Act of 1965 (41 USC §6701-7) applies to contracts over $2,500 and requires wages be paid at 'prevailing rates in the locality'. Milton Friedman smeared these Acts as contributing to higher 'natural' unemployment: (1968) 58(1) AER 1, 9. It appears that in *Bundesdruckerei*, the CJEU may have been trying to interpret EU law to match the minimum standard set by US law, on the 'prevailing rates in the locality'. Regardless of this, why should a federal minimum be what previously 'prevails', rather than what the democratically elected government in office says is fair?

8.   In the UK, the Local Government Act 1988 s 17(1) banned councils and some public bodies considering 'non-commercial matters' when procuring services. This is defined in s 17(5) to include 'terms and conditions of employment by contractors of their workers', whether provision is by 'self-employed persons', the 'conduct of contractors or workers in industrial disputes', the 'territory of origin of supplies', and 'political, industrial or sectarian affiliations'. Section 17 is therefore an exception to the general rule that public bodies have discretion to procure services from the best provider. It must be construed restrictively. Councils may not consider the 'terms and conditions' of workers. But this does not bar a council, for example, requiring the contractor recognises an independent trade union for collective bargaining, an elected work council with binding rights, or employee representation on a company board. This relates to the process of getting terms

of employment, not the substance. Councils are only barred from requiring terms and conditions of a particular content. Do you agree? In any event, should s 17 be scrapped?

9. The Local Government Act 1999 s 3 made a slight reform that councils and some public bodies (eg police or Transport for London) should seek the 'best value' in procurement, and that meant 'having regard to a combination of economy, efficiency and effectiveness'. In this way it is thought that social (or environmental) factors can be considered where it may be argued that social standards create better value for money. For instance, a council may state that, in its view, requiring contractors to pay at least the local average wage in principle will ensure productivity. Facing judicial review, the council would submit that its policy does not have regard to 'terms and conditions of employment': this is only incidental because its direct concern is productivity and quality. Do you think this would work?

10. The Scottish, Northern Irish, Welsh and London governments can set any procurement policies as they choose, within the scope of EU law.

(c) Education and Retraining

Full employment can be achieved without it being very productive. John Maynard Keynes remarked in *The General Theory* (1936) ch 10, VI, if the Treasury were to: 'fill old bottles with banknotes, bury them at suitable depths in disused coalmines' and then put out tenders for private enterprise to dig them up 'there need be no more unemployment' and the community's growth in income would increase. Keynes was obviously joking (in part), but also pre-empting Friedrich von Hayek's view (chapter 16(1)(a)) that some people's skills were so useless that full employment would accelerate inflation. Full employment cannot depend on current states of education or training, but a highly skilled workforce, aligned to society's present and future needs, is preferable to one performing work of limited value. Many people recoil, rightly, from the notion that school and university education should must merely teach 'skills'. Education ensures not merely that people get skills to fulfil a future employer's orders, but the people learn how to think, create and enlighten the human condition. But if pursuit of skills is subordinated to human enlightenment, work should be 'as productive as possible': Employment Policy Convention 1964 (c 122) Art 1(2).

Does enlightenment, creativity and innovation raise its own problems? In *The Economic Possibilities of our Grandchildren* (1931) Keynes pointed to 'technological unemployment', or 'unemployment due to our discovery of means of economising the use of labour outrunning the pace at which we can find new uses for labour'. Recently, a theory of automation and artificial intelligence replacing billions of jobs has gone 'viral'. Keynes himself said technology would only create a 'temporary phase of maladjustment', and this seems accurate then as now. All studies known by this author that predict mass technological unemployment have as scientific a method as guessing future stock prices or racehorse winners: they gaze at job statistics, hypothesise about gadgets and robots which Google or Apple say they may invent, and pronounce '47 per cent' of jobs are at risk 'over some unspecified number of years'. See E McGaughey, 'Will

Robots Automate Your Job Away? Full Employment, Basic Income and Economic Democracy' (2018) CBR, Cambridge Working Paper 496. But it is clear that when new technology can be introduced, employees can be redundant. If people cannot be redeployed, they must be compensated (chapter 19). People may also need retraining for new skills.

The Promotion and Protection against Unemployment Convention 1988 (c 168) Art 7 requires 'vocational training and vocational guidance' to promote full employment but does not specify any particular measures. These questions necessarily refer us to education policy more broadly. How do you think education should be governed to promote full employment? Should we establish a 'National Education Service' to deliver universal, lifelong learning, where all education is free at the point of use? This would require a larger proportion of the government budget to be invested in education, although it would seem that the dividends (particularly in future tax receipts) would be greater than the investment.

(2) MONETARY POLICY

Monetary policy is not a substitute, but can influence employment almost as much as fiscal policy. More people will have jobs if private enterprise is expanding, and hiring people. To expand, private enterprise may save and finance themselves. Large corporations usually do finance themselves. But small and medium-size enterprises need to sell shares to investors (like on TV's *Dragon's Den*) or go to a bank for loans. Loans carry interest rates. Interest might be high or low. If interest rates are low, so credit is cheap, more businesses will borrow, and usually hire more employees, and vice versa. Using its financial size, and legal power, the Bank of England can influence other banks' interest rates, and therefore employment.

Conversely, if credit is cheap and productivity or supply of goods and services is not expanding, prices will usually rise. Rising prices may be very good for asset owners. It may be bad for consumers, who in effect face a wage cut because their wages now buy less. But some asset prices may be rising (eg housing or company shares), while in other markets prices are stable. This means monetary policy has considerable distributional implications.

Bank of England Act 1998 ss 1–2, 10–13 and 19

1 Court of directors.
(1) There shall continue to be a court of directors of the Bank.
(2) The court shall consist of the following directors appointed by Her Majesty—
    (a) a Governor,
    (b) a Deputy Governor for financial stability,
    (ba) a Deputy Governor for markets and banking,
    (c) a Deputy Governor for monetary policy,
    (d) a Deputy Governor for prudential regulation, and
    (e) not more than 9 non-executive directors. ...
    ...

2 **Functions of court of directors**.

(1) The court of directors of the Bank shall manage the Bank's affairs, other than the formulation of monetary policy.

...

10 **Operational responsibility**.

In section 4(1) of the Bank of England Act 1946 (power of the Treasury to give directions to the Bank), at the end there is inserted ", except in relation to monetary policy".

11 **Objectives**.

In relation to monetary policy, the objectives of the Bank of England shall be—
   (a)   to maintain price stability, and
   (b)   subject to that, to support the economic policy of Her Majesty's Government, including its objectives for growth and employment.

...

13 **Monetary Policy Committee**.

(1) There shall be a committee of the Bank, to be known as the Monetary Policy Committee of the Bank of England, which shall have responsibility within the Bank for formulating monetary policy.

(2) The Committee shall consist of—
   (a)   the Governor of the Bank,
   (aa)   the Deputy Governor for financial stability,
   (aaa)   the Deputy Governor for markets and banking,
   (ab)   the Deputy Governor for monetary policy,
   (b)   one member (to be known as the Chief Economist of the Bank) appointed by the Governor of the Bank after consultation with the Chancellor of the Exchequer, and
   (c)   4 members appointed by the Chancellor of the Exchequer.

(3) The member appointed under subsection (2)(b) shall be a person who carries out monetary policy analysis within the Bank. ...

...

19 **Reserve powers**.

(1) The Treasury, after consultation with the Governor of the Bank, may by order give the Bank directions with respect to monetary policy if they are satisfied that the directions are required in the public interest and by extreme economic circumstances.

(2) An order under this section may include such consequential modifications of the provisions of this Part relating to the Monetary Policy Committee as the Treasury think fit.

(3) A statutory instrument containing an order under this section shall be laid before Parliament after being made.

(4) Unless an order under this section is approved by resolution of each House of Parliament before the end of the period of 28 days beginning with the day on which it is made, it shall cease to have effect at the end of that period.

NOTES AND QUESTIONS

1.   The Bank of England Act (BEA) 1998 ss 1, 2 and 13 state the Bank of England ('the Bank') is controlled by its court of directors, and a subset of those – the Governor, three Deputy Governors, a Chief Economist, plus four appointees of

the Chancellor – conduct 'monetary policy'. Under s19, the Treasury has can override the Bank's policy but only in 'extreme economic circumstances'. By this framework, the BEA 1998 was meant to guarantee the Bank's operational 'independence' from political pressure, and especially the temptations to manufacture a short-term boom before an election that could not be sustained afterwards. Many agree with this, but can monetary policy be regarded as an objective science that should be left to 'independent' experts?

2.   Do any factors of psychology or background make 'independence' a bit suspect?

3.   Section 11 states the 'objectives' are 'price stability' and 'subject to that' HM Government's economic policy objectives 'including its objectives for growth and employment'. Price stability means stopping excessive inflation, and preventing any deflation: the Bank target is normally 2 per cent inflation. What do you think is more important: price stability or full employment? Why?

4.   Inflation is measured in two ways. Before 2003, a 'Retail Price Index' was used by the Bank of England to track around 650 prices, including house prices. After 2003, it shifted to a 'Consumer Price Index' as traditionally used by the US government. It excludes house price rises. For your wages, would you prefer the RPI or CPI?

5.   Other things being equal, if there is 2 per cent inflation means without wage rises, this means a 2 per cent reduction of people's wages every year (compounded, a 25 per cent wage cut over 15 years), and a 2 per cent annual increase in asset owner profits. That means employment contracts or collective agreements must ensure a 2 per cent pay rise every year just to stand still. Why would 2 per cent inflation be a legitimate target in a democratic society? Why, in any event, is price 'stability' interpreted to mean a constant 2 per cent change?

6.   The Bank exercises three main powers to attain monetary policy objectives: (1) setting the Bank interest rate, (2) increasing reserve requirements, and (3) open market transactions. First, the Bank of England interest rate is paid by private banks (Barclays, Lloyds, Royal Bank of Scotland, HSBC, etc) who have accounts with, and can borrow from the Bank. The Bank interest (or 'base') rate ranged between 3.5 and 7.5 per cent from May 1997 to the 2007–08 financial crisis, was 0.5 per cent from March 2009, and 0.25 per cent from August 2016. In 2017, mortgage rates were around 3.75 per cent, and business loans charged around 5 per cent interest. Why should private banks be able to borrow money from the Bank at 0.25 per cent interest, when you have to pay 3.75 or 5 per cent interest? Who owns the Bank of England anyway?

7.   It is thought that when the Bank cuts or raises interest rates, savings or costs will be passed onto the borrowing public. If that happens, a *higher* Bank interest rate reduces business or consumer borrowing, and so reduces total economic activity. This may *reduce* inflation. A *lower* Bank interest rate increases business or consumer borrowing, and so increases total economic activity. This may *increase* inflation (as more people have more credit to spend: if they compete for finite resources, prices go up). The problem is, private banks will pass on borrowing costs, but may not pass on savings. This is why 'it is not feasible for the authorities to exercise an exact control over bank lending through interest rates in the short run', *Monetary Control* (1980) Cmnd 7858, para 1.7.

8.   Second, the Bank may increase its 'reserve requirements': it can order private banks to hold cash and liquid assets in a deposit account with the Bank that the private bank is not allowed to trade with (BEA 1946 s 4(3)). If reserve requirements go up, this raises the cost of lending for private banks (because the percentage of private banks' capital that it may profit from is reduced), this makes private banks raise their interest rates, and so dampens inflation, or vice versa. No order has ever been issued, but the Bank's suggested reserve ratios are complied with out of habit (knowing an Order may be issued if there is non-compliance).

9.   Third, the Bank can conduct 'open market transactions'. Today this has become the dominant method of monetary policy. The Bank does three main things. (1) Buy ('discount') or sell corporate bonds and other commercial bills. If I buy your bond, I give you money now, you pay me interest on the bond (or bill), and may buy it back over time. It is simply like any loan. (2) Sell or buy back government bonds (or 'gilt-edged securities') from banks or other lenders. This is called a 'repo'. (3) Advance credit to banks. The Bank aims to affect the quantity of money in circulation through its market power: it is using its financial size, ultimately underwritten by the UK government's ability to tax, to influence the total volume of credit. 'Quantitative easing' was the jargon from the financial and eurozone crisis for buying masses of government and corporate bonds. This has a distributional impact. It makes credit cheap for people in the financial sector, while people without access to the same credit are outcompeted when they try to purchase assets that those with cheap credit want.

10. The Treasury, under BEA 1946 s 4(3), has another option. Fourth, it can directly control bank lending policy, directing how much banks take and receive. This is not done at the moment. It is thought to be too interfering. Do you agree?

11. Fifth, with new legislation, the government could establish public retail and investment banks that compete with the private sector. Exchange rates could be offered that are the same or as close as possible to the Bank of England interest rate, which is given to other banks. This would eliminate banks' excess profits. Why not do this?

12. The Bank of England was originally a private bank. The Bank of England Act 1694, a statute, established it, like for most other large corporations at the time, but it had private shareholders. Its original purpose was to raise money to fund war against Louis XIV of France. The Bank's backers were Whigs, and their political rivals, the Tories (a word deriving from the Irish for 'thief', *Toriadh*), wanted a financial institution they controlled to fund the government. The opportunity came with the South Sea Company Act 1711, which was meant to exploit the slave trade in the seas around South America, after the Spanish purported to allow British trade in the Treaty of Utrecht. Shares in the South Sea Company were sold, and sold, and the share price rose. In 1717, as the speculative boom continued, it was agreed the Company should take over the UK government's national debt. Then, in 1719, people realised the South Sea Company had in fact done no 'business' (slave trading) because the Spanish had reneged on their promise to allow trading ships into their waters. The share price crashed, the government fell, and the Chancellor of the Exchequer was imprisoned for his involvement with selling shares. This left the Bank of England as the dominant source of finance for the

UK government. The Royal Exchange and London Assurance Corporation Act 1719, passed before the crash to protect the South Sea Company's monopoly, banned corporations being created without a statute. This remained until the Bubble Companies, etc Act 1825.

13. Over the eighteenth and nineteenth centuries, the Bank of England became established as the government's primary financier. See generally J Clapham, *The Bank of England – A History* (1944) and W Bagehot, *Lombard Street: A Description of the Money Market* (1873). It was fully nationalised by the BEA 1946, although in practice it had operated as an arm of the state with monopolistic legal power for some time: the 1946 Act merely confirmed the bank was meant to act in the public interest. Is it clear that it does that now?

14. Within the EU, the European Central Bank took over the functions of Member State central banks upon the creation of the euro. This is used by 19 countries, with Denmark in the Exchange Rate Mechanism (fixing an exchange of €1 to 7.46038 Danish krone), but not adopting the currency. The UK joined the ERM but was forced to leave after speculators crashed the pound in October 1990. With a common currency comes common monetary policy: the ECB sets interest rates for all euro countries and conducts open market operations for the whole bloc at once.

Treaty on European Union, Art 3

Article 3

1. The Union's aim is to promote peace, its values and the well-being of its peoples.

...

3. The Union shall establish an internal market. It shall work for the sustainable development of Europe based on balanced economic growth and price stability, a highly competitive social market economy, aiming at full employment and social progress, and a high level of protection and improvement of the quality of the environment. It shall promote scientific and technological advance.

It shall combat social exclusion and discrimination, and shall promote social justice and protection, equality between women and men, solidarity between generations and protection of the rights of the child.

...

4. The Union shall establish an economic and monetary union whose currency is the euro.

Treaty on the Functioning of the European Union, Arts 9, 127 and 282

Article 9

In defining and implementing its policies and activities, the Union shall take into account requirements linked to the promotion of a high level of employment, the guarantee of adequate social protection, the fight against social exclusion, and a high level of education, training and protection of human health.

...

Article 127

1. The primary objective of the European System of Central Banks (hereinafter referred to as "the ESCB") shall be to maintain price stability. Without prejudice to the objective of price

stability, the ESCB shall support the general economic policies in the Union with a view to contributing to the achievement of the objectives of the Union as laid down in Article 3 of the Treaty on European Union. The ESCB shall act in accordance with the principle of an open market economy with free competition, favouring an efficient allocation of resources, and in compliance with the principles set out in Article 119.

2. The basic tasks to be carried out through the ESCB shall be:
— to define and implement the monetary policy of the Union,
— to conduct foreign-exchange operations consistent with the provisions of Article 219,
— to hold and manage the official foreign reserves of the Member States,
— to promote the smooth operation of payment systems.

3. The third indent of paragraph 2 shall be without prejudice to the holding and management by the governments of Member States of foreign-exchange working balances.

4. The European Central Bank shall be consulted:
— on any proposed Union act in its fields of competence,
— by national authorities regarding any draft legislative provision in its fields of competence, but within the limits and under the conditions set out by the Council in accordance with the procedure laid down in Article 129(4).

The European Central Bank may submit opinions to the appropriate Union institutions, bodies, offices or agencies or to national authorities on matters in its fields of competence.

5. The ESCB shall contribute to the smooth conduct of policies pursued by the competent authorities relating to the prudential supervision of credit institutions and the stability of the financial system.

6. The Council, acting by means of regulations in accordance with a special legislative procedure, may unanimously, and after consulting the European Parliament and the European Central Bank, confer specific tasks upon the European Central Bank concerning policies relating to the prudential supervision of credit institutions and other financial institutions with the exception of insurance undertakings.

...

Article 282

1. The European Central Bank, together with the national central banks, shall constitute the European System of Central Banks (ESCB). The European Central Bank, together with the national central banks of the Member States whose currency is the euro, which constitute the Eurosystem, shall conduct the monetary policy of the Union.

2. The ESCB shall be governed by the decision-making bodies of the European Central Bank. The primary objective of the ESCB shall be to maintain price stability. Without prejudice to that objective, it shall support the general economic policies in the Union in order to contribute to the achievement of the latter's objectives. ...

NOTES AND QUESTIONS

1. The ECB's main objective, in conducting monetary policy for the 19 eurozone countries, is price stability. Why should price stability be the overriding goal instead of being equal in rank to 'full employment' or 'social justice' as the TEU Art 3 mandates? As with the Bank of England, the ECB targets 2 per cent inflation. Why should 2 per cent per year in inflation be considered price stability?

2. M Roth, 'Employment as a Goal of Monetary Policy of the European Central Bank' (2015) ssrn.com makes a convincing argument that a proper interpretation of the treaties does not require the ECB to place reduction of inflation above full employment under TEU Art 3.

3. In the United States the Federal Reserve Act of 1913, 12 USC §225a, says: '[The] Board of Governors of the Federal Reserve System and the Federal Open Market Committee shall maintain long run growth of the monetary and credit aggregates commensurate with the economy's long run potential to increase production, so as to promote effectively the goals of maximum employment, stable prices, and moderate long-term interest rates.' This sees maximum employment as equal to other goals, although 'maximum' is not exactly 'full' employment. This language was introduced in the Employment Act of 1946, 15 USC §1021. KVW Stone, 'A Right to Work in the United States' in V Mantouvalou (ed) *The Right to Work* (2015) ch 15 explains how a statutory commitment to 'continuing full employment' was scrapped after the opposition of people such as Senator Robert Taft (of the disastrous Taft–Hartley Act of 1947).

4. Unlike the Bank of England, the ECB's governance is highly protected from representative accountability. TFEU Art 283(2), states the Executive Board of the ECB (a president, vice-president and four members) are appointed by the European Council by qualified majority, after consulting the European Parliament and the ECB's own Governing Council (which is the ECB Executive, plus governors of eurozone central banks). Board members have an eight-year, non-renewable term, and they can only be removed for gross misconduct after review by the CJEU: ECB Statute Arts 10–11. Is monetary policy a matter of technical expertise, or does it have massive distributional implications that must be subject to democratic accountability?

5. In the eurozone, like in any large country, growth and recession may be occurring at the same time in different regions. Cities may be (and often are) booming, while the local economies of remoter countryside are shrinking. North or west may be growing, while south or east are in recession. One interest rate, and one monetary policy, is unavoidable for one currency: the price of credit that the dominant financial institution gives in the jurisdiction with that currency. There is currently no system to distinguish different recipients of ECB credit by region (is one possible or desirable?). This means, if the ECB sets a low interest rate, credit is cheap in booming, overheating countries as much as struggling, busting countries, and if the ECB sets a high interest rate, credit is scarce in struggling, busting countries and booming, overheating countries. You cannot please everyone with monetary policy.

6. Although countries do have a single currency and monetary policy, governments can use fiscal policy to spend money and promote growth in depressed areas. But, the Treaties prevent an EU fiscal policy. The European Investment Bank has a budget of €62bn, but this is inflexible and at least 20 times too small to maintain stable, full employment. If Member States are in heavy debt, TFEU Art 123 prohibits the EU lending money directly to them. This was originally thought to ensure sound financial policy, and avoid a (supposedly) politically difficult result of one country 'bailing out' another. But the main consequence is that when countries using the euro get into trouble, especially under uniform EU interest rates, the law says that fiscally, they should be on their own. What the EU found out in 2007–10 is that if one country goes bankrupt it would crash everyone's currency, and so something has to be done.

7. In the financial crisis of 2007–08, international investment withdrew. In the EU, Greece, Ireland, Portugal, Spain were most vulnerable. Their tax income shrank, and so they struggled to repay their sovereign debt. In particular, as Greece looked under pressure, banks and fund managers began 'betting' (by making credit default swap contracts) that Greece would be forced to default on its debt repayments. (This was often called going 'bankrupt' or 'insolvent', as debts are not paid as they fall due, though a state controls property rights in its jurisdiction, and is therefore cannot be compared to personal or corporate insolvency.) Interest rates on sovereign debt generally fluctuate according to market conditions (countries do not demand fixed interest rates). So, as the international bond market took the view that Greece would go 'bankrupty', interest rates rose, making it more difficult for Greece to repay: a speculation-driven, self-fulfilling prophecy. In May 2010, the European Commission, ECB and International Monetary Fund was forced to offer a €110bn loan agreement.

8. Although TFEU Art 123 prohibited the EU lending money to Member States, in *Gauweiler v Deutsche Bundestag* (2015) C-62/14 the CJEU held it was lawful for the EU to buy Member State government bonds on secondary markets. This is like saying you are prohibited from buying a car from Volkswagen directly, but you can buy a second-hand (or new) one from a Volkswagen dealer. This followed the announcement of ECB president Mario Draghi that he would do 'whatever it takes' to save the eurozone, including buying bonds. In fact, once that announcement was made, the ECB did not need to buy any Member State bonds, because the guarantee stopped market volatility.

9. After World War Two, the US Foreign Assistance Act of 1948 gave $12.7bn in grants and loans to Western Europe. According to this 'Marshall Plan', the assistance was to 'provide a cure rather than a mere palliative' for 'restoring the confidence of the people of Europe in the economic future'. The results were tremendous: it was a new era of European and American prosperity, and especially benefited the UK and Germany. Have we stopped using fiscal policy because it does not work, or because it does?

10. What does price stability mean? Most economic literature assumes this refers to the evil of inflation: if prices for bread, water, clothing, energy, housing, transport, etc all escalate, this is equivalent to everyone's wages being cut. However, if someone's main source of income is not wages, but the sale of bread, water, clothing, etc, inflation is a benefit. Asset owners gain from inflation, relative to wage earners. In the last century, the highest periods of general inflation in the UK were after World War One, the OPEC oil crisis in 1973, in 1980 and in the housing bubble and collapse of 1989 to 1992. However, prices of different things may inflate at different times. 'Wage inflation' (ie real wage growth) relative to other prices is good for most people. House price inflation is good for house owners, and very bad for renters or first-time buyers. Wage inflation may occur for top earners, and there may be deflation for low or middle earners. This could have a knock-on consequence for different assets: if high earners invest in housing, for example, house prices might inflate much faster than prices of goods and services. In this way, inequality is a serious price stability issue. However, the Bank of England's normal target for inflation is 2 per cent a year. Do you think this figure has any intrinsic merit?

(3) INCOME INSURANCE AND EMPLOYMENT AGENCIES

If you do not have a job, what do you do? If you have no savings, assets or family support, you will probably need a new job, and income insurance until you find one. In the UK, the local Jobcentre administers (a) unemployment insurance, and (b) acts as an employment agency, though people usually find jobs through friends, adverts or register with private employment agencies. Each is covered in turn.

(a) Unemployment Insurance

Unemployment insurance is probably the most important part of a modern social democracy. It is often called 'benefits'. This is language is politically loaded and should be avoided, even though it has entered statute. 'Benefits' suggests people get something for free that they do not work for, or somehow do not deserve. But the National Insurance fund, created first by the National Insurance Act 1911, is paid into by people while they work, so they may withdraw money if they lose their jobs in future. In addition, so called 'benefits' are funded by tax – even by people who cannot work – for instance through Value Added Tax. The social nature of the insurance system protects people when there are not enough jobs. Some people may never have had a job when they first claim insurance, and some people may need longer-term insurance because society fails to maintain full employment. The fact that people make different contributions and claims must not distract from the social security that *all* workers get from the unemployed having income insurance. Unemployment insurance a right people pay for, not a benefit for which we should beg.

How does unemployment insurance affect the labour rights of people who never claim? First, it sustains aggregate demand, limiting collapse in recessions. If people lose jobs, they spend less money: less income for business, fewer people hired. Income insurance means unemployed people spend something: it maintains fuller employment than otherwise. It insures society as a whole, not just individuals. Second, if government must maintain funds to pay unemployment insurance, it has an incentive to reach full employment, to keep the bills down (unless government is controlled by interest groups that are willing to accept such a cost in order to benefit employers). Insurance 'internalises' unemployment's social costs, putting the bill on the body best placed to prevent it: the state, which may alter property rights or tax. Third, if unemployed people have insurance, both they *and* employed workers have more bargaining power. 'Many workmen', wrote Adam Smith in 1776, 'could not subsist a week, few could subsist a month, and scarce any a year without employment' (*The Wealth of Nations* (1776) book I, ch 8, §12). After the enclosure movement removed common land (see chapter 1(1)–(2)), and before unemployment insurance in 1911, people without jobs or resources were put into workhouses, had to beg, steal or starve. If unemployment insurance is a right, employees need not accept any terms an employer fixes. This makes work less exploitative, and raises standards for everyone.

These arguments constantly meet the time-honoured accusation that people without work are lazy, or maybe morally deficient. But the view that poverty is a social (not an individual) problem, and that justice requires it is addressed, is probably even older (eg Deuteronomy 15: 7–11). Plainly, some people are lazy, but they are just as likely to be rich as poor. There is simply no empirical evidence to show that unemployed people are less industrious than people in jobs. There is, however, a wealth of evidence that people become demoralised and downtrodden from having job applications constantly rejected. The belief that laziness accounts for high unemployment since 1973 runs against the fact that governments abandoned full employment. Income insurance is therefore a question of both sound economic policy, and justice. Now there are two names and tiers of unemployment insurance: (i) 'contributory benefit' under the Jobseekers Act 1995 paid for up to half a year to any who has made National Insurance contributions, and (ii) a 'universal credit' for people who have not paid in for long enough, or who have been unemployed for too long, under the Welfare Reform Act 2012.

Jobseekers Act 1995 ss 1–6J

1. The jobseeker's allowance
(1) An allowance, to be known as a jobseeker's allowance, shall be payable in accordance with the provisions of this Act.
(2) Subject to the provisions of this Act, a claimant is entitled to a jobseeker's allowance if he
    (b)   has accepted a claimant commitment;
    (d)   satisfies the conditions set out in section 2;
    (e)   is not engaged in remunerative work;
    (f)   does not have limited capability for work;
    (g)   is not receiving relevant education;
    (h)   is under pensionable age; and
    (i)   is in Great Britain.
(3) A jobseeker's allowance is payable in respect of a week.

2. The contribution based conditions
(1) The conditions referred to in section 1(2)(d) are that the claimant—
    (a)   has actually paid Class 1 contributions in respect of one ("the base year") of the last two complete years before the beginning of the relevant benefit year and satisfies the additional conditions set out in subsection (2);
    (b)   has, in respect of the last two complete years before the beginning of the relevant benefit year, either paid Class 1 contributions or been credited with earnings and satisfies the additional condition set out in subsection (3);
    (c)   does not have earnings in excess of the prescribed amount; and
    (d)   is not entitled to income support.
(2) The additional conditions mentioned in subsection (1)(a) are that—
    (a)   the contributions have been paid before the week for which the jobseeker's allowance is claimed;
    (b)   the claimant's relevant earnings for the base year upon which primary Class 1 contributions have been paid or treated as paid are not less than the base year's lower earnings limit multiplied by 26.
    ...

4. Amount payable by way of a jobseeker's allowance
(1) In the case of a jobseeker's allowance, the amount payable in respect of a claimant ("his personal rate") shall be calculated by—
    (a)   determining the age-related amount applicable to him; and

(b) making prescribed deductions in respect of earnings, pension payments, PPF payments and FAS payments.

(2) The age-related amount applicable to a claimant, for the purposes of subsection (1)(a), shall be determined in accordance with regulations.

. . .

5. Duration of a jobseeker's allowance

(1) The period for which a person is entitled to a jobseeker's allowance shall not exceed, in the aggregate, 182 days in any period for which his entitlement is established by reference under section 2(1)(b) to the same two years.

(2) The fact that a person's entitlement to a jobseeker's allowance ("his previous entitlement") has ceased as a result of subsection (1), does not prevent his being entitled to a further jobseeker's allowance if—

(a) he satisfies the contribution-based conditions; and

(b) the two years by reference to which he satisfies those conditions includes at least one year which is later than the second of the two years by reference to which his previous entitlement was established.

. . .

6. Work-related requirements

(1) The following provisions of this Act provide for the Secretary of State to impose work-related requirements with which claimants must comply for the purposes of this Act.

(2) In this Act "work-related requirement" means—

(a) a work-focused interview requirement (see section 6B);

(b) a work preparation requirement (see section 6C);

(c) a work search requirement (see section 6D);

(d) a work availability requirement (see section 6E).

. . .

6C Work preparation requirement

(1) In this Act a "work preparation requirement" is a requirement that a claimant take particular action specified by the Secretary of State for the purpose of making it more likely in the opinion of the Secretary of State that the claimant will obtain paid work (or more paid work or better-paid work).

. . .

(3) Action which may be specified under subsection (1) includes in particular—

(a) attending a skills assessment;

(b) improving personal presentation;

(c) participating in training;

(d) participating in an employment programme;

(e) undertaking work experience or a work placement;

(f) developing a business plan;

(g) any action prescribed for the purpose in subsection (1).

. . .

6J Higher-level sanctions

(1) The amount of an award of jobseeker's allowance is to be reduced in accordance with this section in the event of a failure by a claimant which is sanctionable under this section.

(2) It is a failure sanctionable under this section if a claimant—

(a) fails for no good reason to comply with a requirement imposed by the Secretary of State under a work preparation requirement to undertake a work placement of a prescribed description;

(b)   fails for no good reason to comply with a requirement imposed by the Secretary of State under a work search requirement to apply for a particular vacancy for paid work;

(c)   fails for no good reason to comply with a work availability requirement by not taking up an offer of paid work;

(d)   by reason of misconduct, or voluntarily and for no good reason, ceases paid work or loses pay.

(3) It is a failure sanctionable under this section if, at any time before making the claim by reference to which the award is made, the claimant—

(a)   for no good reason failed to take up an offer of paid work, or

(b)   by reason of misconduct, or voluntarily and for no good reason, ceased paid work or lost pay.

...

14 Trade disputes

(1) Where—

(a)   there is a stoppage of work which causes a person not to be employed on any day, and

(b)   the stoppage is due to a trade dispute at his place of work,

that person is not entitled to a jobseeker's allowance for the week which includes that day unless he proves that he is not directly interested in the dispute.

(2) A person who withdraws his labour on any day in furtherance of a trade dispute, but to whom subsection (1) does not apply, is not entitled to a jobseeker's allowance for the week which includes that day.

NOTES AND QUESTIONS

1.   The Jobseekers Act (JSA) 1995 creates Jobseeker's Allowance. This comes from the National Insurance Fund, and you can get it for up to 182 days if you have paid in for two years.

2.   In 2018, people over 25 could claim up to £73.10 a week, for under 25 year olds £57.90 a week, while couples could get just £114.85 (i.e. £57.43 each). Given that couples get less, is it government policy to punish families, especially of the poor?

3.   The real value of Jobseeker's Allowance, or other unemployment insurance has been continually cut in real terms since 1993 when (at 2012 prices) it stood at £77.01 a week. Insurance was steadily increased from 1948 (£39.81 per week in 2012 prices, or £1.30) to 1974 (£75 a week in 2012 prices) but thereafter remained roughly similar. In 2012, Jobseeker's Allowance stood at £71 a week, after being cut by the new government from £73.72 in 2009: T Rutherford, *Historical Rates of Social Security Benefits* (22 November 2013) HC Library, SN/SG 6762. Today's rate of £73.10 is just over £63 in 2012 prices: a real-terms pay cut of 11 per cent since 2012, and a cut of 18 per cent since 1993. There is, however, also a housing benefit available to pay for rent, with different categories for private landlords, and lower rates for people living in council homes. In total terms, this has been rising quite dramatically. Given that there is currently no rent regulation in the UK, is housing benefit subsidising private landlords, who are using their superior bargaining position to impose escalating rents on everyone? Should welfare be designed to benefit landlords or the unemployed?

4.   It seems noteworthy that 'Jobseeker's Allowance' in the legislation is framed, by the innocent placement of an apostrophe, as an individual allowance for the job-seeker. It is not called 'Jobseekers' Allowance'. This subconsciously frames the issue as one of individual, not social responsibility. The fact that an unemployed person is called a 'Jobseeker' also suggests, quite falsely, that there are always jobs to be found.

5.   Before the National Insurance Act 1911, and the National Insurance Act 1946, and still after, trade unions set up mutual assistance funds to ensure that their members did not suffer unduly from poverty if they became unemployed. Like healthcare, pensions, adult education or codetermination, to a great extent, the unemployment insurance part of modern welfare state is a codification of vol-untary social practices. See S Webb and B Webb, *Industrial Democracy* (1920) part II, ch 1, 164, on the 'method of mutual insurance'. Crucially, unions required people to take work if they found it but not 'below the "Standard Rate" of remu-neration' to ensure collective bargaining was not undermined. As you read below, ask yourself: how does the law compare today?

6.   JSA 1995 ss 6–6J involve the notorious 'workfare' requirements. The Secretary of State is empowered to write rules to make people work to get income insurance. People can be made to work even when they have paid for their National Insur-ance contributions.

7.   This idea of 'workfare' came in the midst of the global financial crisis, and mas-sive growth in unemployment. Prime Minister Gordon Brown decided to pass the Welfare Reform Act (WRA) 2009, which inserted a new JSA 1995 s 17A under the heading of '"Work for your benefit" schemes' for 'assisting persons to obtain employment'. Just ten months earlier, the Secretary of State, James Purnell, had told Parliament 'workfare' would not be enacted because 'Workfare is a system whereby people are punished and distanced from the labour market by removing their entitlement to work search and by stigmatising them'. Hansard HC Debs (27 January 2009) col 192. But then, that Secretary left, Yvette Cooper took his place, and the government changed its minds, perhaps thinking workfare was a strategy to try and win the May 2010 election, which Brown did not. Why in a crisis, created by reckless practices of bankrupt banks, were the unemployed pun-ished for their unemployment?

8.   JSA 1995 s 17A empowered the Secretary of State to write more rules for making people work for their insurance income. While the *Reilly* case (below) was being litigated, s 17A was replaced in the WRA 2012. This also covers the second type of unemployment insurance, available for people who have not yet made enough National Insurance Contributions, or who have been out of work too long: the 'universal' credit.

Welfare Reform Act 2012 ss 1–17

1. Universal credit
(1) A benefit known as universal credit is payable in accordance with this Part.
(2) Universal credit may, subject as follows, be awarded to—
   (a)   an individual who is not a member of a couple (a "single person"), or

(b)   members of a couple jointly.
(3) An award of universal credit is, subject as follows, calculated by reference to—
   (a)   a standard allowance,
   (b)   an amount for responsibility for children or young persons,
   (c)   an amount for housing, and
   (d)   amounts for other particular needs or circumstances.
…

4. Basic conditions

(1) For the purposes of section 3, a person meets the basic conditions who—
   (a)   is at least 18 years old,
   (b)   has not reached the qualifying age for state pension credit,
   (c)   is in Great Britain,
   (d)   is not receiving education, and
   (e)   has accepted a claimant commitment.
(2) Regulations may provide for exceptions to the requirement to meet any of the basic conditions (and, for joint claimants, may provide for an exception for one or both).

5. Financial conditions

(1) For the purposes of section 3, the financial conditions for a single claimant are that—
   (a)   the claimant's capital, or a prescribed part of it, is not greater than a prescribed amount, and
   (b)   the claimant's income is such that, if the claimant were entitled to universal credit, the amount payable would not be less than any prescribed minimum.
(2) For those purposes, the financial conditions for joint claimants are that—
   (a)   their combined capital, or a prescribed part of it, is not greater than a prescribed amount, and
   (b)   their combined income is such that, if they were entitled to universal credit, the amount payable would not be less than any prescribed minimum.
…

13 Work-related requirements: introductory

(1) This Chapter provides for the Secretary of State to impose work-related requirements with which claimants must comply for the purposes of this Part.
(2) In this Part "work-related requirement" means—
   (a)   a work-focused interview requirement (see section 15);
   (b)   a work preparation requirement (see section 16);
   (c)   a work search requirement (see section 17);
   (d)   a work availability requirement (see section 18).
(3) The work-related requirements which may be imposed on a claimant depend on which of the following groups the claimant falls into—
   (a)   no work-related requirements (see section 19);
   (b)   work-focused interview requirement only (see section 20);
   (c)   work-focused interview and work preparation requirements only (see section 21);
   (d)   all work-related requirements (see section 22).
…

14 Claimant commitment

(1) A claimant commitment is a record of a claimant's responsibilities in relation to an award of universal credit.
(2) A claimant commitment is to be prepared by the Secretary of State and may be reviewed and updated as the Secretary of State thinks fit. …
…

16 Work preparation requirement

(1) In this Part a "work preparation requirement" is a requirement that a claimant take particular action specified by the Secretary of State for the purpose of making it more likely in the opinion of the Secretary of State that the claimant will obtain paid work (or more paid work or better-paid work).

(2) The Secretary of State may under subsection (1) specify the time to be devoted to any particular action.

(3) Action which may be specified under subsection (1) includes in particular—

    (a) attending a skills assessment;

    (b) improving personal presentation;

    (c) participating in training;

    (d) participating in an employment programme;

    (e) undertaking work experience or a work placement;

    (f) developing a business plan;

    (g) any action prescribed for the purpose in subsection (1).

...

19 Claimants subject to no work-related requirements

(1) The Secretary of State may not impose any work-related requirement on a claimant falling within this section.

(2) A claimant falls within this section if—

    (a) the claimant has limited capability for work and work-related activity,

    (b) the claimant has regular and substantial caring responsibilities for a severely disabled person,

    (c) the claimant is the responsible carer for a child under the age of 1, or

    (d) the claimant is of a prescribed description.

NOTES AND QUESTIONS

1. 'Universal' credit is available to people who are between education and retirement (s 4), who prove they do not have enough capital or income (s 5). While most claimants will claim because they are unemployed, people may also claim if they are already in work, but working few hours on low wages. If people are in jobs on low pay, but surviving because they receive income from the government, do you agree that the government is effectively subsidising low-paying employers? Should welfare be about subsidising low-paying employers or the unemployed?

2. In 2018, universal credit's basic payment was £317.82 per month (£73.14 a week, £3813.84 a year) for people over 25 years (£251.77 for people under 25), and £498.89 for joint claimants (or £395.20 under 25): that is £249.45 per month (or £197.60 under 25). So, if you're in a relationship, claiming together, and aged under 25, the UK government thinks you are fine with £6.50 a day: less than an hour's work on the minimum wage (£7.83). Why is it assumed that younger people need to eat less, or should have less financial autonomy? Why is it government policy to penalise people who have relationships?

3. Additional payments can be received for childcare costs, disability costs and housing. It replaces, under one label, what were individual benefits (WRA 2012 s 33). Although such administrative combination could in principle be good, it coincided with cuts, which have become increasingly politically toxic.

WRA 2012 s 96 created a 'benefit cap', which in 2018 stood at £1,116.67 per month for a single person (£1,284.17 in London), or £1,666.67 for a lone parent or couple (£1,916.67 in London). Further, the Welfare Reform and Work Act 2016 s 11 requires a 'benefit freeze' in those amounts up to 5 April 2020. In principle this appears wrong because the decision was not taken with reference to the empirically defensible needs of people, but rather to look tough on the poor, while cutting the size of the state, and reducing corporate tax.

4.   Sections 13–19 set out the 'work-related' requirements (formerly JSA 1995 s 17A). Section 16(3) enables the Secretary of State to write rules that make people do 'training' or a 'work placement' if a Jobcentre takes 'the opinion' that it makes a person 'more likely' to 'obtain work'. The reality of this 'workfare' was seen in *Reilly*.

R (Reilly) v Secretary of State for Work and Pensions [2013] UKSC 68

Ms Reilly and Mr Wilson claimed that the Secretary of State had acted *ultra vires* by requiring them to attend training and work to get Jobseeker's Allowance. Under the Jobseekers Act 1995 s 17A (now Welfare Reform Act 2012 s 16(3)(e)) the Secretary of State was empowered to write rules requiring claimants to take part in schemes of a 'prescribed description', which under s 35 should be 'determined in accordance with regulations'. However, the Jobseeker's Allowance (Employment, Skills and Enterprise Scheme) Regulations 2011 regulation 2 only contained a repeat of s 17A. Still, Jobcentres made people take part in the 'Employment, Skills and Enterprise Scheme'.

Reilly, a geology graduate from Birmingham (who had not yet made sufficient National Insurance contributions), was told in October 2011 that it was mandatory for her to take part in 'training', and then a work 'scheme' at Poundland. She had put down retail as one of her work areas in a Jobseeker's Agreement. She was not paid for her work at Poundland, but she worked like any employee. She merely received Jobseeker's Allowance.

Wilson had been a Heavy Goods Vehicle driver from 1994 to 2008, when (in the financial crisis) he became unemployed. He started receiving Jobseeker's Allowance in 2009, but by August 2011 when he was still unable to find a job (because unemployment remained at crisis levels) he was told he would have to do 'up to six months of near full-time work experience with additional weekly job search support requirements'. He was told he could lose income if he refused to participate. He refused and was denied income.

The JASR 2011 regulation 4(2)(c) required written notice of what claimants were 'required to do', but they were never given notice. Both claimed (1) the Regulations were *ultra vires* for failing to describe the work schemes, (2) the Secretary was further in breach of the notice requirement, (3) there should have been a published policy on the nature of work schemes, and (4) the Act's requirement to take unpaid work violated the prohibition on forced labour in ECHR Art 4. The Supreme Court found the Regulations were *ultra vires*, and that notice should have been given, but not that the government needed to publish a policy, nor that there was forced labour.

Lord Neuberger and **Lord Toulson:**

15. In March 2012, jobseeker's allowance was being received by just over 1.6 million people aged over 18, of whom around 357,000 had been in receipt of the allowance for more than a year. About 480,000 were aged under 24, of whom 55,000 had been in receipt of the allowance for more than a year. Forecast expenditure on the allowance in the year 2011/12 was just under £5bn.

16. In a nutshell, the amendments to the 1995 Act effected in 2009, including section 17A, envisaged that regulations would (i) require participants to undertake unpaid work, or work-related activity, during a prescribed period, to improve their prospects of employment and (ii) impose sanctions (in particular, loss of the allowance) on those who without good cause failed to participate in such schemes. Those regulations materialised as the 2011 Regulations ...

    ...

45. Whether one takes the Employment, Skills and Enterprise Scheme (which is really a group of schemes including the [sector-based work academy, sbwa] scheme and the CAP) as a single scheme, or whether, as seems more natural, one takes the sbwa scheme and the CAP as separate schemes, they were undoubtedly schemes which fell within the ambit of regulation 2.

47. ... it appears clear to us that regulation 2 does not satisfy the requirements of section 17A(1). The courts have no more important function than to ensure that the executive complies with the requirements of Parliament as expressed in a statute. Further, particularly where the statute concerned envisages regulations which will have a significant impact on the lives and livelihoods of many people, the importance of legal certainty and the impermissibility of sub-delegation are of crucial importance. The observations of Scott LJ in *Blackpool Corporation v Locker* [1948] 1 KB 349, 362 are in point: "John Citizen" should not be "in complete ignorance of what rights over him and his property have been secretly conferred by the minister", as otherwise "[f]or practical purposes, the rule of law ... breaks down because the aggrieved subject's legal remedy is gravely impaired".

    ...

50. Given the conclusion that the 2011 Regulations are ultra vires because they fail to provide a "prescribed description" of any scheme, it is strictly unnecessary to consider the further grounds raised by Miss Reilly and Mr Wilson for contending that the 2011 Regulations were invalid, but we will do so briefly.

    ...

53. As described in para 21 above, no written notice was given to Miss Reilly, contrary to regulation 4(1) and 4(2) set out in para 12 above.

54. In relation to Mr Wilson, there is a dispute which falls to be determined, namely whether the letter of 16 November 2011, quoted in para 24 above, complied with regulation 4(2)(c) and regulation 4(2)(e). In agreement with Foskett J, the Court of Appeal held that it did not satisfy the latter provision, but they also found that it did not satisfy regulation 4(2)(c).

55. In our opinion, there was a failure to comply with regulation 4(2)(c). The letter of 16 November 2011 merely informed Mr Wilson that he had to perform "any activities" requested of him by Ingeus, without giving him any idea of the likely nature of the tasks, the hours of work, or the place or places of work. It seems to us, therefore, that the letter failed to give Mr Wilson "details of what [he was] required to do by way of participation".

    ...

65. Fairness therefore requires that a claimant should have access to such information about the scheme as he or she may need in order to make informed and meaningful representations to the decision-maker before a decision is made. Such claimants are likely to vary considerably in their levels of education and ability to express themselves in an interview at a Jobcentre at a time when they may be under considerable stress. The principle does not depend on the categorisation of the Secretary of State's decision to introduce a particular scheme under statutory powers as a policy: it arises as a matter of fairness from the Secretary of State's proposal to invoke a statutory power in a way which will or may involve a requirement to perform work and which may have serious consequences on a claimant's ability to meet his or her living needs.

...

80. Ms Lieven's argument involves two steps. First, Ms Reilly's work at Poundland was "exacted ... under menace of [a] penalty", ie disallowance of jobseeker's allowance, and was therefore prima facie forced labour, and for that she relies on the decision of the Strasbourg court in *Van Der Mussele v Belgium* (1983) 6 EHRR 163, para 34. Secondly, the Secretary of State could not rely on article 4.3(d) because the illegality of the regulations and the notice prevented the Secretary of State being able to argue that the work was part of Ms Reilly's "normal civic obligations."

81. In our judgment the argument fails at the first step. As the court noted in *Van Der Mussele* at para 32, article 4 was largely based on Convention 29 of the International Labour Organisation, the main aim of which was to stop exploitation of labour in the colonies. Forced labour is not fully defined and may take various forms, but exploitation is at its heart. Article 4.3 contains particular instances of obligatory labour which are common features of life in democratic societies and do not represent the mischief at which the article is aimed.

...

83. In the present case we are concerned with a condition imposed for the payment of a claim for a state benefit. Jobseeker's allowance, as its name suggests, is a benefit designed for a person seeking work, and the purpose of the condition is directly linked to the purpose of the benefit. The provision of a conditional benefit of that kind comes nowhere close to the type of exploitative conduct at which article 4 is aimed. Nor is it to the point that according to Ms Reilly the work which she did for Poundland was unlikely in fact to advance her employment prospects. Whether the imposition of a work requirement as a condition of a benefit amounts to exacting forced labour within the meaning of article 4 cannot depend on the degree of likelihood of the condition achieving its purpose.

...

86. In *Talmon v Netherlands* [1997] ECHR 207 the applicant was a scientist. He claimed unemployment benefit and was required as a condition to accept work which he considered unsuitable. Because of his refusal to do it, his benefit payments were reduced. He complained that by having his benefits reduced he was being forced to do work to which he had a conscientious objection, contrary to article 4. The application was declared manifestly ill-founded and inadmissible.

87. In *Schuitemaker v Netherlands* (Application No 15906/08) (unreported) 4 May 2010 the applicant was a philosopher by profession. She claimed unemployment benefit and was told that her benefits would be reduced unless she was willing to take up a wider range of employment than she considered suitable. She complained under article 4 that she was being forced to take up labour irrespective of whether it would be suitable for her. The court held that her application was inadmissible. It noted that the obligation of which she complained was in

effect a condition for the granting of benefits, and it stated as a general principle that a state which has introduced a system of social security is fully entitled to lay down conditions which have to be met for a person to be eligible for benefits under that system.

88. *Van Der Mussele*, on which Ms Lieven relies, was a different type of case. The applicant was a trainee advocate. He was required to represent at his own expense some criminal defendants who were entitled to legal aid. The sanction if he refused to do so was that he would not be registered as an advocate. He complained of a violation of article 4. The obvious difference between that case and the present is that it was not a simple case of a conditional benefit, where the purpose of the benefit was intended to be enhanced by the condition. Rather, it was a case of the state fulfilling its legal obligations to third parties at the expense of the applicant. The court accepted, at para 32, that the menace of the penalty and the lack of voluntariness on the part of the applicant met the starting point for considering whether he had been subjected to forced labour in violation of article 4.

89. However, that was only the beginning of the inquiry. To amount to a violation of article 4, the work had to be not only compulsory and involuntary, but the obligation to work, or its performance, must be "unjust", "oppressive", "an avoidable hardship", "needlessly distressing" or "somewhat harassing". As we read the judgment, the court was not there setting out five different categories but was using a variety of expressions to elucidate a single underlying concept, which we have referred to as exploitation. In *Van Der Mussele*, at para 40, the court concluded for a combination of reasons that there had been no forced labour within the meaning of article 4.2, having regard to the social standards generally obtaining in Belgium and in other democratic societies. The court therefore considered it unnecessary to decide whether the work in question was in any event justified under article 4.3 (d).

90. We do not consider that the imposition of the work condition in this case, intended as it was to support the purpose for which the conditional benefit was provided, met the starting point for a possible contravention of article 4. If it did, we do not consider that it fell within article 4.2, having regard to the Strasbourg guidance and the underlying objective of the article.

91. Does it make a difference to this analysis that what Ms Reilly was told about her obligation to take part in the sbwa scheme, as a condition of receiving jobseeker's allowance, was unauthorised and wrong as a matter of domestic law? The answer is no. The fact that the requirement was invalid does not of itself mean that it also fulfilled the characteristics of forced labour within the meaning of article 4.2. The logic of the contrary argument would produce strange results. If, for example, a public sector employee were wrongly directed to do something which was in fact beyond the terms of his contract of employment, and the employee did as he was told from fear of disciplinary action, we do not accept that the invalidity of the order would of itself trigger a violation of article 4. Equally, if the 2011 Regulations had unjustifiably discriminated between jobseekers on the ground of gender, and hence had been unlawful, it cannot be right that anyone required to work pursuant to such regulations would therefore have had their article 4 rights infringed. Whether the requirement was invalid under domestic law and whether it involved a violation of article 4 are different issues, and proof of the former does not of itself determine the latter.

Lord Clarke, **Lord Mance** and **Lord Sumption** agreed.

1. The Supreme Court held unanimously that there was no violation of ECHR Art 4 by making someone work for benefits, but that the Regulations were *ultra vires*. See A Paz-Fuchs and A Eleveld, 'Workfare Revisited' (2016) 45(1) *ILJ* 29.

2. Reilly had never had a stable job since leaving education when she claimed. Mr Wilson lost his job because of the financial crisis. Their unemployment was in no way their fault. Why was government forcing them to work for income insurance, instead of investing enough money to ensure that full employment returned?

3. The Supreme Court, like the European Court of Human Rights, confidently rejected that a requirement to work for unemployment insurance does not violate ECHR Art 4, 'to perform forced or compulsory labour'. Ignoring the fact that unemployment insurance *was paid for* by Reilly and Wilson's taxes, both future and past, the argument that work is not coerced must be scrutinised. Supposedly the 'starting point' for an Art 4 violation will be that 'the state [is] fulfilling its legal obligations to third parties at the expense of the applicant' [88]. But if you are hungry and out of a job, you have no alternative but to work on the terms set by the owners of property, who offer employment – if any. If there is no work, you now have no alternative but a government work scheme. Moreover, the state *was* providing work to a third party (Poundland) at the expense of the worker (Reilly). The European Court of Human Rights has said that work needs to be 'unjust', etc [89]. But this is a gloss not found in the Convention: the very fact of being compelled to work or starve is degrading. This is why Wilson had such strong objections: a previously fully employed trucker, whose industry offered no jobs, found it degrading to be made to work without a living wage. The Courts should have turned their attention to ECHR Art 4(3)(d) which says that forced labour should not include 'any work or service which forms part of normal civic obligations'. It is submitted that in a free society, workfare lies beyond the outer limits 'of normal civic obligations'. The Convention is not an ossified document bound to the standards of the immediate aftermath of the World War Two. Workfare is a humiliating policy, and forced labour, that operates to decrease everyone's wages. Again, as the Secretary of State put it in 2009, it means 'people are punished and distanced from the labour market by removing their entitlement to work search and by stigmatising them'.

4. This issue goes to the heart of the modern economic system, as it developed since the abolition of slavery and the Master and Servant Acts. While we are formally free to take or not take a job, the inequality of wealth, resources and property rights – which has grown dramatically since 1979 – compels people to work for the owners of property. Property owners do not own people any more, but people have to rent themselves out. Violence is not the instrument of force to make people work, but the threat of poverty is comparably effective. So long as property, held by corporations and asset managers, is not democratically owned and controlled, freedom is rhetoric, and for the people in the precarious margins of society – perhaps not something the typical judge has ever felt – forced labour is reality.

5.   Work at Poundland, like any retail store, could be rewarding and fulfilling if workers had fair wages, real voice and autonomy over their working lives. However, Poundland continued to take labour from the government without paying for it: see S Butler and J Halliday, 'Poundland "Gets Jobless to Work for Free under Government Scheme"' (30 August 2017) *Guardian*. When the current Poundland CEO, Andy Bond, was the chair of Asda, he wrote that the government's state and welfare 'cuts will strengthen Britain's economy by allowing the private sector to generate more jobs' (18 October 2010) *Daily Telegraph*, saying the 'private sector should be more than capable of generating additional jobs to replace those lost in the public sector'. But outside the pages of the *Telegraph*, his actions were not to create jobs but to make people work for him for free. Do you agree that such directors should be held accountable by shareholders and workers? See ch 11.

6.   After the Supreme Court held that the government's scheme was *ultra vires* and void, would Reilly and others be entitled to claim restitution from Poundland for the value that their labour had conferred on Poundland? See chapter 4(1)(b).

7.   While *Reilly* was litigated, the government changed the law by passing the Jobseekers (Back to Work Schemes) Act 2013, where s 1 purported to retroactively validate the 2011 Regulations, which the Supreme Court duly declared were void. The day the Supreme Court gave judgment, the Secretary of State issued Jobseeker's Allowance (Schemes for Assisting Persons to Obtain Employment) Regulations 2013 (SI 2013/276), adding the notice requirements said to be lacking. This led to the next case, *Reilly v Secretary of State for Work and Pensions* [2016] EWCA Civ 413, where Reilly argued that the 2013 Act violated ECHR Art 6, on the right to a fair trial, because the government's action was pre-empting the outcome of litigation, and being passed to affect the result of pending proceedings: see *Zielinski v France* (2001) 31 EHRR 19. The Court of Appeal agreed, and issued a declaration of incompatibility under the Human Rights Act 1998 s 4. However, Underhill LJ, in giving the judgment of the court appeared to undermine his own decision by saying: '[I]t is up to the Government, subject to any further appeal, to decide what action to take in response.'

8.   With respect, Underhill LJ is mistaken. It is not 'up to the Government', because the government has a duty under international law to comply with the obligations it has undertaken. The rule of law is a fundamental constitutional principle of the United Kingdom. This is why in *R (Unison) v Lord Chancellor* [2017] UKSC 51, [68] Lord Reed said: 'Courts exist in order to ensure that the laws made by Parliament, and the common law created by the courts themselves, are applied and enforced. That role includes ensuring that the executive branch of government carries out its functions in accordance with the law.' Do you think that a senior judge should encourage respect for the institutions of justice, and therefore not invite a government to do nothing to comply with the Human Rights Act 1998?

9.   What sanctions do unemployment insurance claimants face? JSA 1995 s 18, inserted in the Social Security Administration Act 1992 s 71A, enables recovery of overpayments if an adjudication officer decides someone made a misrepresentation before they received income insurance. Under WRA 2012 ss 26–29

a system of sanctions exists for non-compliance with duties to work: benefits, like for Mr Wilson, can be cancelled. Jobcentre staff are often professional and compassionate, but are bound to apply a legal regime that is designed to stigmatise claimants.

10. Seen historically, the return to 'workfare' must be regarded as a sign of de-development, a return to cruel and unusual social ethic that scarred English and British history for centuries. In the Statute of Cambridge 1388 county hundreds (sub-counties) were made responsible for people who could not work, and people were prevented from moving without permission. The Act for the Relief of the Poor 1601 required 'Houses of Industry' to be created for each parish where the 'able-bodied poor' were set to work, while the Poor Relief Act 1662 (or Settlement and Removal Act) continued to bind people to their parishes as one had to get a certificate of settlement to leave and work elsewhere. In a meeting at Speenhamland in 1795, people who worked and were still poor also started receiving benefits, and wages began to plummet as employers viewed the poor relief payments as an excuse to cut wages. The Poor Law Amendment Act 1834, which followed a *Poor Law Commissioners' Report of 1834*, abolished this, requiring that poor 'relief' would only be given to people in workhouses, and workhouses were deliberately made so ghastly that people would not apply. This is where Charles Dickens' character *Oliver Twist* (1838) asks the master: 'Please, sir, I want some more.' See S Deakin and F Wilkinson, *The Law of the Labour Market: Industrialization, Employment, and Legal Evolution* (2005) ch 3, 'The Duty to Work'. Today while people are being forced to work for income insurance, there of course is no restriction on moving between parishes. Indeed, free movement of people is fundamental to UK law because it is a member of the European Union: people can move and work anywhere in the EU. At the time of writing, however, the UK government in pursuit of its interpretation of the 'Brexit' poll appears to be intent on removing that right of free movement for its own citizens.

11. Workfare violates international law. Under the Universal Declaration of Human Rights of 1948, Art 23(1): 'Everyone has the right to work, to free choice of employment, to just and favourable conditions of work and to protection against unemployment.' Under the International Covenant on Economic and Social Rights 1966 Art 9 'the right of everyone to social security, including social insurance' is not conditional. The Employment Promotion and Protection against Unemployment Convention 1988 (c 168) Art 2 states members shall 'ensure that its system of protection against unemployment, and in particular the methods of providing unemployment benefit, contribute to the promotion of full, productive and freely chosen employment, and are not such as to discourage employers from offering and workers from seeking productive employment'. Poundland was not a 'free choice of employment' for Reilly, and the practice undercuts the paying of good wages to everyone.

(b) Employment Agencies

As well as administering Jobseeker's Allowance and Universal Credit, Jobcentres act as a public sector employment agency: its predecessors were first created under the Labour

Exchange Act 1909. Employers who would like to hire people who are registered at Jobcentres may choose to advertise there. The problem is, employers may not want to advertise with Jobcentres because may have preconceptions about recruiting from a pool of applicants that includes the longer-term unemployed. Many employers will choose private channels of advertising, including UK and local government employers.

Should private employment *agencies* exist? Such agencies register people looking for work, and spend most of their time calling employers to advertise and attempt to place candidates for a fee: typically a percentage of the worker's future wages. Private agencies have rolls of people who make money for them, maybe indefinitely. The first ever ILO Recommendation and the second Convention, the Unemployment Convention 1919 (c 2), required abolition of private agencies, and the establishment of public job exchanges. This took the view that private employment agencies existed solely to exploit people's labour, and often restricted access of information and opportunities for workers in finding work to boost their fees. This was articulated by Brandeis J dissenting in *Adams v Tanner* 244 US 590 (1917) where a hostile US Supreme Court majority struck down a Washington state law that prohibited private agencies. The ILO did shift with the Private Employment Agencies Convention 1997 (c 181), as it was believed that private agencies could in fact provide a useful service. However, this is accompanied by important requirements for regulation: particularly an absolute prohibition on charging fees to workers (Art 7(1)).

The next case shows demonstrates how many countries were pushed into enabling private employment agencies, under EU competition law.

Höfner and Elser v Macrotron GmbH (1991) C-41/90

Mr Höfner and Mr Elser, two executive recruitment consultants, claimed the German Work Promotion Act (Arbeitsförderungsgesetz) §13 violated EU competition law by retaining a monopoly on labour recruitment for the Federal Office for Employment (Bundesanstalt). Because of §13, contracts made by anyone for employee placement, without the Federal Office's permission, were void under the Civil Code (Bürgerliches Gesetzbuch) §134. In practice the Federal Office turned a blind eye to private businesses doing executive recruitment. However, after Höfner and Elser placed a sales director at Macrotron GmbH, Macrotron GmbH had decided they did not like the person, refused to pay and argued its contract was void. So, to get their fee, Höfner and Elser decided to argue the whole law was void: they argued that the statutory monopoly was an abuse of a dominant position under TFEU Art 102 (ex TEC Art 82) and 106 (ex Art 90). The Court of Justice first decided that the Federal Office was subject to competition law, despite being a state agency, because apparently any entity engaged in 'economic activity' is an 'undertaking'. It then agreed that the law violated article 102 if the Federal Office was not satisfying demand.

Sixth Chamber:

21 It must be observed, in the context of competition law, first that the concept of an undertaking encompasses every entity engaged in an economic activity, regardless of the legal status of the entity and the way in which it is financed and, secondly, that employment procurement is an economic activity.

22 The fact that employment procurement activities are normally entrusted to public agencies cannot affect the economic nature of such activities. Employment procurement has not always been, and is not necessarily, carried out by public entities. That finding applies in particular to executive recruitment.

...

24 It must be pointed out that a public employment agency which is entrusted, under the legislation of a Member State, with the operation of services of general economic interest, such as those envisaged in Article 3 of the AFG, remains subject to the competition rules pursuant to Article 90(2) of the Treaty unless and to the extent to which it is shown that their application is incompatible with the discharge of its duties (see judgment in Case 155/73 *Sacchi* [1974] ECR 409).

25 As regards the manner in which a public employment agency enjoying an exclusive right of employment procurement conducts itself in relation to executive recruitment undertaken by private recruitment consultancy companies, it must be stated that the application of Article 86 of the Treaty cannot obstruct the performance of the particular task assigned to that agency in so far as the latter is manifestly not in a position to satisfy demand in that area of the market and in fact allows its exclusive rights to be encroached on by those companies.

26 Whilst it is true that Article 86 concerns undertakings and may be applied within the limits laid down by Article 90(2) to public undertakings or undertakings vested with exclusive rights or specific rights, the fact nevertheless remains that the Treaty requires the Member States not to take or maintain in force measures which could destroy the effectiveness of that provision (see judgment in Case 13/77 *Inno* [1977] ECR 2115, paragraphs 31 and 32). Article 90(1) in fact provides that the Member States are not to enact or maintain in force, in the case of public undertakings and the undertakings to which they grant special or exclusive rights, any measure contrary to the rules contained in the Treaty, in particular those provided for in Articles 85 to 94.

27 Consequently, any measure adopted by a Member State which maintains in force a statutory provision that creates a situation in which a public employment agency cannot avoid infringing Article 86 is incompatible with the rules of the Treaty. ...

President Mancini, O'Higgins J, Kakouris J, Schockweiler J and **Kapteyn J.**

NOTES AND QUESTIONS

1. *Höfner* held that Germany was infringing EU competition law by maintaining a law that kept a monopoly on job placements for the Federal Office, when it was 'manifestly not in a position to satisfy demand'. It follows that there is no prohibition in competition law on maintaining a statutory monopoly on job placement if a Member State does in fact ensure that demand is fully satisfied.
2. At least two arguments can be advanced in favour of private employment agencies. (1) The existence of a private market does not sap significant expertise from the public service. It could be argued there is no 'natural monopoly' or high barriers to entering and competing to provide work placement services. (2) Because the market for jobs is dynamic and changing, agencies motivated by profit may actively seize upon new demands for services quicker than an expert public service, which may be more suited to industries where people's basic needs change

less. In this way a private market can perform innovative functions better. Where it cannot, it will lose the competition to a public service. See E McGaughey, 'Should Agency Workers Be Treated Differently?' (2010) LSE Legal Studies Working Paper No 7/2010, 7–10.

3. On the other hand, given developments of massive online networks, could it be argued that there is greater efficiency in there simply being one big network as the source for all jobs? Just as most people want to be on one social network like Facebook (contrast WhatsApp or Instagram), or one interconnected telephone system, or one short-term rental network like AirBnB, does it make sense for every employer and employee to know where to go to find what they need? What do you think?

4. The government has an online job search facility: jobsearch.direct.gov.uk. Apart from the clumsy domain name, the page is very basic and unattractive. Should the UK invest more in creating a site that everyone knows about and wants to use?

5. The UK allowed private agencies to operate under strict licensing requirements, in the Employment Agencies Act 1973. The licensing requirements originally in ss 1–3 were, however, scrapped by the Deregulation and Contracting Out Act 1994, and replaced with a possibility to prohibit agencies. This led to a massive growth in agencies, many importing a business model pioneered in the United States. The central regulatory measure still in place is the prohibition on agencies charging fees to workers to find work.

Employment Agencies Act 1973

3A. Power to make orders

(1) On application by the Secretary of State, an employment tribunal may by order prohibit a person from carrying on, or being concerned with the carrying on of—

    (a) any employment agency or employment business; or

    (b) any specified description of employment agency or employment business.

    ...

(4) Subject to subsections (5) and (6) of this section, an [employment tribunal] 2 shall not make a prohibition order in relation to any person unless it is satisfied that he is, on account of his misconduct or for any other sufficient reason, unsuitable to do what the order prohibits.

6. Restriction on charging persons seeking employment, etc

(1) Except in such cases or classes of case as the Secretary of State may prescribe—

    (a) a person carrying on an employment agency shall not request or directly or indirectly receive any fee from any person for providing services (whether by the provision of information or otherwise) for the purpose of finding him employment or seeking to find him employment;

    (b) a person carrying on an employment business shall not request or directly or indirectly receive any fee from an employee for providing services (whether by the provision of information or otherwise) for the purpose of finding or seeking to find another person, with a view to the employee acting for and under the control of that other person;

    (c) a person carrying on an employment business shall not request or directly or indirectly receive any fee from a second person for providing services (whether by the provision of information or otherwise) for the purpose of finding or seeking to find a third person, with a view to the second person becoming employed by the first person and acting for and under the control of the third person.

(2) Any person who contravenes this section shall be guilty of an offence and liable—

(a)   on conviction on indictment, to a fine;

(b)   on summary conviction, to a fine not exceeding the statutory maximum.

...

9. Inspection

(A1) This section does not apply to an officer acting for the purposes of this Act in relation to England and Wales if the officer is a labour abuse prevention officer within the meaning of section 114B of the Police and Criminal Evidence Act 1984 (PACE powers for labour abuse prevention officers).

(1) Any officer acting for the purposes of this Act may at all reasonable times on producing, if so required, written evidence of his authority—

(a)   enter any relevant business premises;

(b)   inspect those premises and

(i)   any records or other documents kept in pursuance of this Act or of any regulations made thereunder;

(ii)   any financial records or other financial documents not falling within paragraph (i) which he may reasonably require to inspect for the purpose of ascertaining whether the provisions of this Act and of any regulations made thereunder are being complied with or of enabling the Secretary of State to exercise his functions under this Act;

(c)   subject to subsection (2) of this section, require any person on those premises to furnish him with such information as he may reasonably require for the purpose of ascertaining whether the provisions of this Act and of any regulations made thereunder are being complied with or of enabling the Secretary of State to exercise his functions under this Act.

13. Interpretation

(2) For the purposes of this Act "employment agency" means the business (whether or not carried on with a view to profit and whether or not carried on in conjunction with any other business) of providing services (whether by the provision of information or otherwise) for the purpose of finding [persons] 9 employment with employers or of supplying employers with [persons] 9 for employment by them.

(3) For the purposes of this Act "employment business" means the business (whether or not carried on with a view to profit and whether or not carried on in conjunction with any other business) of supplying persons in the employment of the person carrying on the business, to act for, and under the control of, other persons in any capacity.

NOTES AND QUESTIONS

1.   The EAA 1973 has some potentially strong provisions, enabling the Secretary of State to inspect agencies, take financial information (s 9), and apply for a ban of the company at a Tribunal if misconduct is uncovered (s 3A). The problem is, this requires an active government and funding to uncover abuse. That does not exist. The Employment Agency Standards Inspectorate (which few have heard of) had a £500,000 budget in 2016–17, and achieved one prosecution and one prohibition, despite 828 complaints: DBIS, *EASI Annual Report 2016–017* (November 2017).

2.   Section 13 distinguishes, unhelpfully, 'agencies' and 'businesses'. Nothing significant turns on this.

3.   As well as the prohibition on charging fees (s 6) with some exemptions, the Conduct of Employment Agencies and Employment Businesses Regulations 2003 (SI 2003/3319, amended several times) contain a host of other important rules, which are routinely broken, as is evident by a casual inspection of an agency's shop window or by working through agencies. Under reg 6, an agency may not subject workers to detriment for taking other jobs. But this practice is common: internal 'blacklisting' of 'problematic' workers is routine. Reg 27 prohibits adverts for jobs that do not exist: but such vaguely worded ads, designed to get people in the door but not get a job, are all over most high streets. Reg 7 bans agencies from supplying workers to employers who face strikes. But this did not the Royal Mail trying this in 2009, and then arguing the law only applied to agencies, not end-users: 'Postal Union to Take Legal Action against Royal Mail over Agency Staff' (3 November 2009) *New Statesman*.

4.   The decision to remove the licensing requirement for agencies had fatal consequences when, on 5 February 2004, a group of 23 Chinese migrant undocumented workers drowned. They were shellfishing (or 'cockle picking') in Morecambe Bay, near the Lake District in Cumbria, and could not get back to shore as the tide came in. They were recruited by a rogue agency that had no concern for their safety, wages, or conditions. Parliament, without the government, reacted swiftly by requiring licensing for employment agencies in specific sectors with vulnerable workers.

Gangmasters Licensing Act 2004 ss 4–13

1 The Gangmasters and Labour Abuse Authority.

(1) The body known as the Gangmasters Licensing Authority is to continue to exist and is to be known as the Gangmasters and Labour Abuse Authority (in this Act referred to as "the Authority").

…

3 Work to which this Act applies

(1) The work to which this Act applies is—

(a)   agricultural work,

(b)   gathering shellfish, and

(c)   processing or packaging—

(i)   any produce derived from agricultural work, or

(ii)   shellfish, fish or products derived from shellfish or fish.

…

4 Acting as a gangmaster

(2) A person ("A") acts as a gangmaster if he supplies a worker to do work to which this Act applies for another person ("B").

…

7 Grant of licence

(1) The Authority may grant a licence if it thinks fit.

(2) A licence shall describe the activities authorised by it and shall be granted for such period as the Authority thinks fit.

…

8 General power of Authority to make rules

(1)The Authority may with the approval of the Secretary of State make such rules as it thinks fit in connection with the licensing of persons acting as gangmasters.

(2) The rules may, in particular—

(a) prescribe the form and contents of applications for licences and other documents to be filed in connection with applications;

(b) regulate the procedure to be followed in connection with applications and authorise the rectification of procedural irregularities;

(c) prescribe time limits for doing anything required to be done in connection with an application and provide for the extension of any period so prescribed;

(d) prescribe the requirements which must be met before a licence is granted;

(e) provide for the manner in which the meeting of those requirements is to be verified;

(f) allow for the grant of licences on a provisional basis before it is determined whether the requirements for the grant of a licence are met and for the withdrawal of such licences (if appropriate) if it appears that those requirements are not met;

(g) prescribe the form of licences and the information to be contained in them;

(h) require the payment of such fees as may be prescribed or determined in accordance with the rules;

(i) provide that licences are to be granted subject to conditions requiring the licence holder—

(i) to produce, in prescribed circumstances, evidence in a prescribed form of his being licensed, and

(ii) to comply with any prescribed requirements relating to the recruitment, use and supply of workers.

NOTES AND QUESTIONS

1. The Gangmasters Licensing Act (GLA) 2004 ss 4–13 is a model example regulation for operating without a licence. The Gangmasters' Licensing Authority is able to require compliance with all labour rights through the simple threat of withdrawal of the licence. The problem remains, that like any government body, its funding depends on the commitment by government to ensuring it functions.

2. Under GLA 2004 ss 12 and 13, people who act as gangmasters without a licence face up to 10 years in prison, and employers who enter into arrangements with gangmasters face up to 51 weeks in prison unless they prove they took reasonable steps to ensure the gangmaster was legal.

3. Should all agencies be licensed?

4. The Temporary and Agency Work Directive 2008/104/EC Art 4, somewhat unhelpfully, required Member States to review restrictions on the use of temporary agency work. Fortunately in *Auto-ja Kuljetusalan Työntekijäliitto AKT ry v Öljytuote ry* (2015) C-533/13, the CJEU Grand Chamber held this did not require adoption of any specific legislation.

(4) TRADE POLICY

Trade policy is critical for fair wages, but it is treated in this section on job security because people often use the metaphor of jobs being 'exported', or 'losing' their jobs to people abroad. The White Paper, *Employment Policy* (1944) said that trade (or the 'balance of payments') was often volatile and therefore, with the private sector's volatility, the biggest challenge for full employment. Other governments can be unpredictable, but usually private enterprise (without adequate regulation) abroad is unstable. The UK government in 1944 said it would cooperate with other countries for 'progressive expansion of trade' and see how 'effect may be given to the principles and recommendations recently put forward by the International Labour Organisation' (paras 2–4). In other words, trade was good when it was accompanied by improvement of labour rights.

Why do labour standards matter in international trade? First, and theoretically, when the UK trades with other countries with lower labour standards it means corporations can relocate their production (or be outcompeted) to pay their workforce less. Corporations may also move to the UK from jurisdictions with better labour standards. Without legally enforceable labour standards, if unions are not active in both jurisdictions, and are not making collective agreements to cover all workers, free movement of capital may weaken labour's bargaining power. Second, if labour standards are reduced, other countries are more prone to prolonged depressions, affecting their ability to buy UK exports. Third, higher labour standards, particularly to enhance collective bargaining and votes at work, promotes equality. If inequality grows abroad, this reduces aggregate demand and dampens full employment. All this said, in practice open trade has not led to a decrease in labour standards, rather than cuts to standards by governments themselves. Although capital moves faster than workers in a global economy, ideas move faster still. Countries can maintain full employment and strong labour rights if they choose to.

After World War Two, the world economic system became composed of the World Bank, the International Monetary Fund and, since 1994, the World Trade Organization (formerly the General Agreement on Tariffs and Trade). These global institutions are flanked by thousands of bilateral investment treaties (BITs). Like standard form contracts, BITs copy each other. Recently they have moved from reducing tariffs, custom barriers or discriminatory taxes, to change regulations of certain sectors. 'Free trade' treaties today have become, in many cases, 'deregulation treaties'. This potentially damages full employment.

This is why there has been a growing movement to put labour standards into trade agreements. The problem is that what is currently there does very little other than restate International Labour Organisation core conventions, and there may be no real enforcement. The following is a good example.

EU–South Korea Free Trade Agreement (14 May 2011) [2011] OJ L127, Art 13

Article 13.1 Context and objectives
1. Recalling Agenda 21 on Environment and Development of 1992, the Johannesburg Plan of Implementation on Sustainable Development of 2002 and the 2006 Ministerial Declaration of the UN Economic and Social Council on Full Employment and Decent Work, the Parties reaffirm their commitments to promoting the development of international trade in such a way as to contribute to the objective of sustainable development and will strive to ensure that this objective is integrated and reflected at every level of their trade relationship.
...

Article 13.2 Scope
...
2. The Parties stress that environmental and labour standards should not be used for protectionist trade purposes. The Parties note that their comparative advantage should in no way be called into question.

Article 13.3 Right to regulate and levels of protection

Recognising the right of each Party to establish its own levels of environmental and labour protection, and to adopt or modify accordingly its relevant laws and policies, each Party shall seek to ensure that those laws and policies provide for and encourage high levels of environmental and labour protection, consistent with the internationally recognised standards or agreements referred to in Articles 13.4 and 13.5, and shall strive to continue to improve those laws and policies.

Article 13.4 Multilateral labour standards and agreements

1. The Parties recognise the value of international cooperation and agreements on employment and labour affairs as a response of the international community to economic, employment and social challenges and opportunities resulting from globalisation. They commit to consulting and cooperating as appropriate on trade-related labour and employment issues of mutual interest.

2. The Parties reaffirm the commitment, under the 2006 Ministerial Declaration of the UN Economic and Social Council on Full Employment and Decent Work, to recognising full and productive employment and decent work for all as a key element of sustainable development for all countries and as a priority objective of international cooperation and to promoting the development of international trade in a way that is conducive to full and productive employment and decent work for all, including men, women and young people.

3. The Parties, in accordance with the obligations deriving from membership of the ILO and the ILO Declaration on Fundamental Principles and Rights at Work and its Follow-up, adopted by the International Labour Conference at its 86th Session in 1998, commit to respecting, promoting and realising, in their laws and practices, the principles concerning the fundamental rights, namely:

    (a) freedom of association and the effective recognition of the right to collective bargaining;
    (b) the elimination of all forms of forced or compulsory labour;
    (c) the effective abolition of child labour; and
    (d) the elimination of discrimination in respect of employment and occupation.

The Parties reaffirm the commitment to effectively implementing the ILO Conventions that Korea and the Member States of the European Union have ratified respectively. The Parties will make continued and sustained efforts towards ratifying the fundamental ILO Conventions as well as the other Conventions that are classified as 'up-to-date' by the ILO.

...

Article 13.7 Upholding levels of protection in the application and enforcement of laws, regulations or standards

1. A Party shall not fail to effectively enforce its environmental and labour laws, through a sustained or recurring course of action or inaction, in a manner affecting trade or investment between the Parties.

2. A Party shall not weaken or reduce the environmental or labour protections afforded in its laws to encourage trade or investment, by waiving or otherwise derogating from, or offering to waive or otherwise derogate from, its laws, regulations or standards, in a manner affecting trade or investment between the Parties.

...

Article 13.16 Dispute settlement

For any matter arising under this Chapter, the Parties shall only have recourse to the procedures provided for in Articles 13.14 and 13.15 [ie Government Consultation and setting up a Panel of Experts].

1. While the EU–South Korea agreement was supposed to be a significant advance, it becomes obvious on a simple reading how weak the ambition is for labour and environmental standards. And even if, for example, the duty to ensure freedom of association were to be enforced, the 'only' recourse to complain of breaches is through soft-talk enforcement, not sanctions or – most importantly – a private right of action against corporations that violate labour rights.

2. In a new generation of deregulation treaties, such as the Comprehensive Economic and Trade Agreement between Canada and the EU, or the proposed and now stalled (ironically, because of Donald Trump) Transatlantic Trade and Investment Partnership (between the USA and EU), or the Trans-Pacific Partnership (between the USA, Canada, Mexico and nine Pacific countries) it has become common to refer to international labour standards. However, the key fact is that under Investor State Dispute Settlement (ISDS) provisions, a corporation may sue a government for breach of a treaty provision, but real people may not. This is altering the reality of international law, which was supposedly about the relationships among sovereign states, not individuals. ISDS provisions create enforceable rights in international law for corporations. But how often is a corporation going to sue to enforce labour (or environmental) rights? Do you agree that individual citizens and trade unions should have the same rights as corporations?

3. Also lacking is a requirement to progressively improve labour standards. A good example is the European Social Charter 1961 Art 2(1) which requires members to take action for 'the working week to be progressively reduced to the extent that the increase of productivity and other relevant factors permit'. Do you agree that trade treaties should require signatories to (i) raise the minimum wage, (ii) progressively grow union membership and collective bargaining coverage, and (iii) decrease the gender pay gap? What do you think should become standard trade treaty terms?

4. The mention in Art 13.2 of using labour standards for 'protectionist' purposes recalls a debate that came to a head in the Singapore Ministerial Declaration (13 December 1996). People had campaigned for the WTO to implement global labour standards. The WTO said it renewed 'its commitment to the observance of internationally recognized core labour standards'. However, it declined to amend the treaties to put them into trade agreements. Labour was the ILO's job. The governments of a number of Asian countries (of varying commitment to democracy at the time) objected to labour standards on the ground that cheap labour was, for them, a supposed comparative advantage in trade and growth. The alternative view, which should be preferred, is that labour rights promote innovation, growth and development. The main result of the WTO failing to include labour rights was the inclusion of labour standards in bilateral treaties. See BA Hepple, *Labour Laws and Global Trade* (2005).

W Beveridge, *Full Employment in a Free Society* (1944)
In his classic book, Beveridge developed a script for the next thirty years of prosperity in the Western world. Arguing that 'full employment' means people have all the hours of work they need 'at fair wages', Beveridge explains why government policy can guarantee everyone jobs. Full employment during peacetime, in a free society (not like the fascist dictatorships that caused the war) required (1) adequate total outlay, or full investment made up by government and corporations, (2) controlled location of industry, to ensure that jobs were spread around the regions of the country, and not just concentrated in cities, and (3) organising the mobility of labour, to ensure people have the freedom to move where jobs are available, and that jobs come to people. Ultimately, full employment is a question of conscience, and the moral decision to ensure that people's lives are fulfilling.

D Ashiagbor, *The European Employment Strategy: Labour Market Regulation and New Governance* (2005)
Ashiagbor's book surveys the modern policies for employment pursued in the EU with outstanding clarity. Covering contemporary economic theory, which accepts there is a 'natural' rate of unemployment, Ashiagbor explains how it leads to a policy of 'downward flexibility in wage levels, the decentralization of collective bargaining to enterprise level and the relaxing of restrictions on employment contracts and on working time'. The book suggests why these theories are flawed, and how they were unlikely to achieve full employment. Although the European Employment Strategy has been conducted through soft law, it has in fact been very effective, and damaging.

M Freedland et al, *Public Employment Services and European Law* (2007)
With P Craig, C Jacqueson and N Kountouris, the authors summarise and theorise the laws and practice of public employment agencies in EU law, and under national law. They explain the historical background and rationales for public employment service, set in the context of EU policies, that drifted away from full employment to 'active labour market policy', 'activation' and 'workfare'. There is a particular focus on the experience of the UK, France, Germany, Italy and Denmark.

A Paz-Fuchs, *Welfare to Work: Conditional Rights in Social Policy* (2008) ch 3
Paz-Fuchs provides a stunning and devastating account of workfare policies, both historically, and their development in modern times from the United States in 1968, affirmed by the Supreme Court in *New York State Department of Social Services v Dublino* 413 US 405, 413 (1973). Paz-Fuchs explains how the language of a 'social contract' has been appropriated and is used to justify responsibility on individuals for the income insurance they receive: 'commissioning the mechanism of the contract to the task of disentitling poor individuals and limiting their options instead of emancipating, empowering and allowing one to realize his or her wishes.'

V Mantouvalou (ed), *The Right to Work: Legal and Philosophical Perspectives* **(2015)**
This edited volume holds a superb range of essays on the idea of the 'right to work', as it is found in the Universal Declaration of Human Rights 1948. Essays deal with topics such as the idea as a human rights concept, on the limited jurisprudence which establishes that there should not be unjustified barriers to work, and critically on the policies for full employment. KVW Stone's chapter, in particular, gives an excellent summary of the attempts to get the federal government to enact legislation guaranteeing full employment in 1945 and 1978. This debate has now returned, with proposals for a Federal Job Guarantee.

E McGaughey, 'Will Robots Automate Your Job Away? Full Employment, Basic Income and Economic Democracy' (2018) CBR, Cambridge Working Paper 496
This article engages with the currently popular idea that automation from robots and artificial intelligence will lead to mass unemployment, and the appropriate policy response is to create a universal basic income. Although this has support from tech billionaires and some academics, the article instead argues for full employment and universal fair incomes. It explains the central theories of unemployment, and shows why the only credible theory with evidential support is that unemployment exists where the law enables asset owners to restrict the supply of capital to the job market. It explains how full employment was created through the post-World War Two era, even though 42 per cent of jobs were immediately redundant on armistice. The social problems from demobilisation and wounded veterans were infinitely more complex than any credible prediction about automation. Based on history and evidence, it suggests the best way to ensure lasting prosperity is to ensure work and capital is democratically accountable, to extend democracy from politics to the economy.

17

Dismissal Concept and Process

Full employment might mean people find new jobs easily, but dismissal can traumatise for life. It often harms people's sense of self-worth, relationships with co-workers and family, and may mean significant financial loss. Virtually every country has rights to prevent unjustified dismissals. People expect a fair process (chapter 17), fair reasons (chapter 18), and for redundancies to be justified (chapter 19). People also want to know their contributions are socially valuable, and that neither their jobs, nor the jobs of co-workers are wasting time. There is little merit in a social policy that lets people hold jobs despite inadequate professional conduct, or when better technology or administrative efficiency makes the jobs unnecessary. But who should decide when dismissals are justified? Individual employees may often want to hold their jobs. Their co-workers might be more objective. But employers, who currently make dismissals, have at least three powerful conflicts of interest. First, managers can dismiss staff because of irrational *personal* conflicts. Enterprises have an interest in a fair process and reasons, to stop bad managers ousting good staff. Second, enterprises may dismiss staff because of *stakeholder* conflicts. Directors may make redundancies to inflate shareholders' profits or directors' pay in the short-term, despite the cost to long-term sustainable enterprise. Third, there are *social* conflicts of interest, particularly in economic crises. If markets crash, individual firms may rationally cut staff bills, in response to falling business. But if every firm does the same, aggregate incomes fall, spending declines, and business is forced to dismiss more people: a socially irrational spiral to depression and mass unemployment. The social costs outweigh any private gains.

How can employers' conflicts of interest be eliminated? So far, UK law relies on courts to enforce minimum job security standards. First, after one month's work, employees receive at least one week's notice before dismissal (unless there is gross misconduct), two weeks after two years, and so on, up to twelve weeks after twelve years (chapter 17(2)). Second, after two years' work, an employee may claim a dismissal is unfair in a Tribunal (chapters 17(3) and 18(2)). Third, after two years, if dismissed for an economic reason, employees have the right to a redundancy payment (chapter 19(1)). Because workers cannot diversify their investment of labour, they have the greatest interest in long-term enterprise sustainability. But there is not yet an express role in statute for worker voice. Furthermore there are no clear statutory dismissal rights for non-employee workers (chapter 3(2)(d)) although on both counts, law and equity has recognised (and may advance) some minimum rights for everyone. This chapter starts with (1) the concept of dismissal, (2) minimum notice before dismissal, (3) the right to a fair hearing, and (4) injunctions to follow procedure.

> ***Introductory texts:*** Collins ch 8 (160–175). CEM chs 18–19 (various). D&M ch 5 (various).

(1) CONCEPT OF DISMISSAL

When do people have rights to complain of an unjust dismissal? First, an employee may voluntarily resign from a job. The employee may want a holiday, have found a better job or just be fed up. Unless an employee is forced to leave, there is no dismissal, and no significant legal problem. Second, an employee may have been forced to resign because the employer has made work objectively intolerable. If an employer conducts its business in a way that fundamentally breaches the parties' reasonable expectations, the employee will be able to claim there was a 'constructive dismissal'. The employer does not say it expressly, and the employee terminates the contract, but the employer's conduct is a dismissal in effect. The employee is objectively justified in quitting to claim damages. A crucial point (which may not have been clearly acknowledged before) is that there is no qualifying period for claiming constructive dismissal in an Employment Tribunal (see *Wilson v Racher* [1974] ICR 428, at chapter 5(1)(a) approved by *West London Mental Health NHS Trust v Chhabra* [2013] UKSC 80, at chapter 5(2)(d)). Everyone has this common law right against a grossly unjust dismissal (see further, chapter 18(1)).

Third, an employer may actively dismiss an employee, saying 'we regret that we no longer require your service, but we wish you the very best in future', or some equivalent. Here there are two possibilities. First, in the normal case of dismissals for questionable conduct, poor performance, lacking skills or redundancy, the employer must give the employee reasonable notice of dismissal (chapter 17(2)), after a fair hearing (chapter 17(3)). The employer must also give a substantively fair reason, reviewable by an Employment Tribunal, if the employee has worked for two years or more (chapter 18(2)). Second, an employer may be objectively justified in dismissing an employee summarily (ie without proper notice) for gross misconduct. Here there is no requirement for giving notice of a week or more. But summary dismissal is only justified in exceptional cases. Pointing a tiny finger and barking 'You're fired!' might attract TV viewers, in the same way that it is hard to peel one's eyes away from a road accident. But this model of workplace relations will violate UK law. An appropriate action is to suspend an employee, before an investigation and a fair hearing (see the ACAS Code and Trade Union and Labour Relations (Consolidation) Act (TULRCA) 1992 s 207A below). The majority view is that constructive dismissals by definition are *always* unfair, but not all unfair dismissals are constructive or grossly unjust (chapter 18(1)).

The next case held that an employee resigned, and was not constructively dismissed.

Western Excavating (ECC) Ltd v Sharp [1977] EWCA Civ 2

Mr Colin Sharp claimed he was constructively dismissed from Western Excavating (ECC) Ltd in Cornwall, by being suspended without pay for five days. He had worked for the company for twenty months. He asked his foreman for three hours off to play cards, but the foreman said no. Mr Sharp left and played cards anyway, and the foreman dismissed him. Mr Sharp complained to the company disciplinary panel, which decided that Mr Sharp should be suspended for five days, but not dismissed, because 'there was room for confusion the way the situation was left'. Nevertheless, losing five days' pay put Mr Sharp in financial difficulty, because he had a partner and two children. The company welfare officer refused to advance a £40 loan. He quit so he could immediately collect £117.17 in holiday pay. He then claimed he was constructively and unfairly dismissed. Under the Employment Rights Act (ERA) 1996 s 95(1)(c) (then, Trade Union and Labour Relations Act 1974 Sch 1, para 5), a dismissal includes cases where an employee 'is entitled to terminate' a contract 'without notice by reason of the employer's conduct'. The Tribunal held that the company 'ought to have leant over backwards' to help Mr Sharp. One Tribunal member dissented, arguing that Mr Sharp should have visited the welfare officer again. The Employment Appeal Tribunal upheld the decision, but only on the basis that the Tribunal had made findings of fact that it could not disturb. The Court of Appeal unanimously held that Mr Sharp was not constructively dismissed.

Lord Denning MR:

Until recently, an ordinary servant had no security of tenure. He could be dismissed on a month's notice or a month's salary in lieu of notice, although he might have served his master faithfully for years. That was altered by the provisions of the Industrial Relations Act 1971, which have now been re-enacted in Schedule 1 to the Trade Union and Labour Relations Act 1974. Paragraph 4 [now ERA 1996 s 94] says: "... every employee shall have the right not to be unfairly dismissed by his employer ..." If he is unfairly dismissed, he can complain to an industrial tribunal. The tribunal may recommend that he be reinstated in his job, if that is practicable. Alternatively, it may award him compensation in such amount as is fair and equitable. ... So, whereas at common law an employer could dismiss a man on a month's notice or a month's wages in lieu, nowadays an employer cannot dismiss a man even on good notice, except at the risk of having to pay him a large sum should the industrial tribunal find that the dismissal was unfair.

These provisions are not confined to cases where the employer himself dismisses the man. They also apply to cases where the man leaves of his own choice, if he can show that it was due to the way the employer treated him. In other words, compensation is payable, not only for actual dismissal, but also for "constructive dismissal." We have here to consider the doctrine of "constructive dismissal."

...

If the employer is guilty of conduct which is a significant breach going to the root of the contract of employment, or which shows that the employer no longer intends to be bound by one or more of the essential terms of the contract, then the employee is entitled to treat himself as discharged from any further performance. If he does so, then he terminates the contract by reason of the employer's conduct. He is constructively dismissed. The employee is entitled in those circumstances to leave at the instant without giving any notice at all or, alternatively, he may give notice and say he is leaving at the end of the notice. But the conduct must in either case be sufficiently serious to entitle him to leave at once. Moreover, he must make up his mind soon after the conduct of which he complains: for, if he continues for any length of time without leaving, he will lose his right to treat himself as discharged. He will be regarded as having elected to affirm the contract.

...

In my opinion, the contract test is the right test. My reasons are as follows. (i) The statute itself draws a distinction between "dismissal" in [ERA 1996 s 95(1)(c)] and "unfairness" in [ERA 1996 s 98].

...

[ERA 1996 s 95(1)(a) ...] deals with cases where the employer himself terminates the contract by dismissing the man with or without notice. That is, when the employer says to the man: "You must go." [ERA 1996 s 95(1)(c) ...] deals with the cases where the employee himself terminates the contract by saying: "I can't stand it any longer. I want my cards."

Conclusion

The present case is a good illustration of a "whimsical decision." Applying the test of "unreasonable conduct," the industrial tribunal decided by a majority of two to one in favour of the employee. All three members of the Employment Appeal Tribunal would have decided in favour of the employers, but felt that it was a matter of fact on which they could not reverse the industrial tribunal. So counting heads, it was four to two in favour of the employers, but yet the case was decided against them – because of the test of "unreasonable conduct."

If the contract test had been applied, the result would have been plain. There was no dismissal, constructive or otherwise, by the employers. The employers were not in breach at all. Nor had they repudiated the contract at all. The employee left of his own accord without anything wrong done by the employers. His claim should have been rejected. The decision against the employers was most unjust to them. I would allow the appeal, accordingly.

Lawton LJ and **Eveleigh LJ** concurred.

NOTES AND QUESTIONS

1. The Court of Appeal held that the employer's conduct toward Mr Sharp was not 'sufficiently serious to entitle him to leave at once'. He could not claim constructive dismissal. Tacitly, the Court suggested it was reasonable for the company to suspend (without dismissing) Mr Sharp on no pay as punishment for missing work. Do you think that the same result should always hold? What if the employee is on a zero-hours contract, where the employer has stated there is no obligation to accept work, but then is frustrated when employees actually take that seriously?

2. The test for constructive dismissal is a matter of degree. What is '*sufficiently serious*' to be a repudiatory breach of contract? It cannot rationally be articulated any further, except by learning examples of how Tribunals may think. Inevitably, there will be some diversity in Tribunal members' opinions. Can you think of any standards that a Tribunal might apply when making a decision?

3. In *Woods v WM Car Services (Peterborough) Ltd* [1982] ICR 693, Ms Woods, the company's chief secretary and accounts clerk, claimed she was constructively dismissed when she was told she would have to accept less pay, or work more, and change job titles. Her solicitor advised her to resign and claim constructive dismissal. The Tribunal held there was no constructive dismissal. Lord Denning MR held that the Tribunal's finding was not to be overturned unless there was a misdirection in law, or its finding was perverse. This is meant to 'lead to the shortening

of the hearings ... and the length of their reasons. At any rate it should reduce the number of appeals ...'. By contrast, Watkins LJ plainly agreed with the Tribunal: 'The obdurate refusal of the employee to accept conditions very properly and sensibly being sought to be imposed upon her was unreasonable.' The employer could not unilaterally change its employee's contract terms: see *Rigby v Ferodo Ltd*, at chapter 5(3)(a). It could, however, dismiss the employee (with reasonable notice, and a fair procedure) and then offer to rehire her on a different contract. However, this opens the potential for a claim that the dismissal was unfair. Such an employer would probably argue that it had dismissed the employee for 'some other substantial reason': see chapter 19. Before you read that, when (if at all) do you think it might be fair for an employer to make staff accept a pay cut?

4. In *Sandle v Adecco UK Ltd* [2016] IRLR 941 a commercial lawyer working through an agency claimed unfair dismissal after the end of a two-year assignment, as the agency did not check if she was interested in further assignments. The agency denied there was any dismissal. The Tribunal held Sandle had never been dismissed, and was still employed by the agency. In the Employment Appeal Tribunal, Judge Eady QC held an agency worker can be dismissed by inaction, but to prove this there must be an express communication of the employer's 'unequivocal intention' to termination a contract. Ostensibly, a 'dismissal does have to be communicated. Communication might be by conduct ... but it has to be something of which the employee was aware.' Unlike a standard employment relationship where failure to provide work might amount to communication of a dismissal, 'agency workers may well experience gaps between assignments that will not fit the standard direct employment model'. Apparently, the claimant might have treated the agency's conduct as a constructive dismissal, but there was no finding that the agency itself considered that the claimant's contract had come to an end. Do you agree that any different standard between employers and agencies lacks any credible basis in statute? Why was the law firm, where Sandle worked for two years, not jointly liable with the agency for both redundancy and unfair dismissal? Why was the agency not under a duty to plan and find work, when it knew a fixed-term contract would expire?

5. The next case, *Buckland*, exemplifies a constructive dismissal.

Buckland v Bournemouth University [2010] EWCA Civ 121

Professor Buckland resigned and claimed he was constructively dismissed by Bournemouth University after its examiner board chair unilaterally elevated student exam marks, in order to inflate the number of students who passed Prof Buckland's course. Prof Buckland had failed a higher than normal proportion of students, but his grades were endorsed by a second marker, and the examiner board as a whole. The chair, however, appeared to be motivated by a university policy of not failing students, so as to attract international fee-paying students (ie making the University money, by cheapening the integrity of a degree). Prof Buckland objected to his grades being altered. This led to the 'Vinney Report' which criticised the board chair, and vindicated Prof Buckland, but the marks were not revoked. So, Prof Buckland resigned and claimed constructive dismissal. The Tribunal held the University committed a fundamental breach of good faith, and this was not rectified by doing a Report. The University attempted to argue that its decision to alter the marks was within a reasonable range of responses, a test that applies to assessing substantive fairness of a dismissal. The Employment Appeal Tribunal and Court of Appeal disagreed, and unanimously upheld the Tribunal in Prof Buckland's favour.

Sedley LJ:

18. In their logical order, the issues now raised, or contingently raised, are these:

(a) Is the occurrence of a fundamental breach of a contract of employment, at least on the employer's part, to be gauged by a conventional contract test or by a 'range of reasonable responses' test? The University raises this issue by way of cross-appeal. If it succeeds in principle, the court is invited to find that the University's conduct, notwithstanding the tribunal's criticisms of it, lay within the range of reasonable responses to the problem which confronted it.
(b) Does the law permit a party which has committed a repudiatory breach of a contract of employment to preclude acceptance by curing the breach? This represents the claimant's principal ground of appeal.
(c) If it does, was the tribunal's decision that the University had failed cure its breach of the claimant's contract of employment (i) legally sound and (ii) factually tenable. This represents the claimant's fallback ground of appeal.
(d) Did the University advance a triable case that, if there had been a constructive dismissal, it had been fair? If it did, the tribunal overlooked it and if necessary the respondent seeks a remission.

(a) What is the correct test of repudiatory conduct by an employer?

19. Modern employment law is a hybrid of contract and status. The way Parliament has done this is to graft statutory protections on to the stem of the common law contract. Thus by s.94 of the Employment Rights Act 1996, every employee is given the right not to be unfairly dismissed. By s.95 dismissal is exhaustively defined for the purposes of the statutory right as – in short – termination by the employer with or without notice, termination by effluxion of time, or termination by the employee "in circumstances in which he is entitled to terminate it without notice by reason of the employer's conduct". The last of these, in legal terms, is constructive dismissal – that is to say an act which is not an explicit dismissal but which in law has the same effect.

20. What circumstances can bring about a constructive dismissal is determined not by the Act, which is silent on the subject, but by the common law. The common law holds that they must be circumstances amounting to a fundamental or repudiatory breach of contract by the employer. The first question, raised by the cross-appeal, is whether to have that character the employer's conduct must fall outside the range of reasonable responses to whatever situation has arisen. Jason Galbraith-Marten for the University submits to us, as he submitted to EAT, that it must do so if it is to constitute a repudiatory breach. Antony White QC for Dr Buckland contends that there is no such test: the question is an objective and unitary one.

21. The fundamental term of Professor Buckland's contract of employment which the tribunal held to have been breached was the requirement of mutual trust and confidence. The University does not contend that this finding was not open to the tribunal, but by its cross-appeal it contends that it was a response to the wrong question: the tribunal should have asked whether what the University had done was within the range of reasonable responses open to it in the situation confronting it in and after July 2006.

...

24. ... Mr Galbraith-Marten contends that the "range of reasonable responses" test forms part of the *Mahmud* exercise at stage (1), as well as of the fairness issue at stage (4), if that is reached.

25. I would unhesitatingly reject this submission. It ignores what the EAT clearly, and correctly, meant when it spoke of "the unvarnished *Mahmud* test". In *Mahmud v BCCI* [1998] AC 20, 35, Lord Nicholls reiterated that the test of breach of a fundamental term of a contract of employment was objective: "A breach occurs when the proscribed conduct takes place". Lord Steyn (at 47) said much the same.

26. Mr Galbraith-Marten accepts this without demur. But – he says – the conduct of an employer which is said to have objectively broken the contract of employment is often (as here) conduct which the claimant alleges was in fundamental breach because it was unreasonable. This must entitle the employer to show that it was not – in other words to argue that it lay within the band of reasonable responses. He accepts that this has the effect of replicating the same issue at stages (1) and (4), but that simply means that by the time stage (4) is reached, if it is reached at all, the job is done.

27. This approach finds support in the EAT's decision in *Abbey National plc v Fairbrother* [2007] IRLR 320, and with qualification in *Claridge v Daler Rowney Ltd* [2008] ICR 1267, §30. But, without retracing the complex path which the EAT was compelled to take, it is an approach which cannot stand with the authority of *Western Excavating v Sharp* [1978] ICR 221, in which this court counterposed the objective test and the unreasonableness test of constructive dismissal and held in clear terms that the former was the correct one.

...

32. The tribunal, having found a repudiatory breach on the University's part, asked and answered a question which neither party had put to it: by the time Professor Buckland purported to accept the breach by giving notice of termination, had it been cured?

33. The case for saying that the Vinney report had cured it was not inconsiderable. It had, as the tribunal found, vindicated Professor Buckland, whose own petulance had kept the wound festering. But, in a balanced and fair-minded judgment, the tribunal concluded that the breach had, even so, not been cured because the slur on his integrity remained.

...

44. Albeit with some reluctance, I accept that if we were to introduce into employment law the doctrine that a fundamental breach, if curable and if cured, takes away the innocent party's option of acceptance, it could only be on grounds that were capable of extension to other contracts, and for reasons I have given I do not consider that we would be justified in doing this. That does not mean, however, that tribunals of fact cannot take a reasonably robust approach to affirmation: a wronged party, particularly if it fails to make its position entirely clear at the outset, cannot ordinarily expect to continue with the contract for very long without losing the option of termination, at least where the other party has offered to make suitable amends. The present case, for reasons explained by Jacob LJ, may be seen as the kind of exception which proves the rule.

Carnwath LJ agreed.

Jacob LJ:

52. ... I do not share Sedley LJ's regret in holding that a repudiatory breach of contract, once it has happened, cannot be "cured" by the contract breaker. Once he has committed a breach of contract which is so serious that it entitles the innocent party to walk away from it, I see no

reason for the law to take away the innocent party's right to go. He should have a clear choice: affirm or go. Of course the wrongdoer can try to make amends – to persuade the wronged party to affirm the contract. But the option ought to be entirely at the wronged party's choice.

53. That has been the common law rule for all kinds of contract for centuries. It works. It spells out clearly to parties to contracts that if they actually commit a repudiatory breach, then whether the contract continues is completely out of their hands. The rule itself discourages repudiatory breach. In the context of employment law it means that employers know that if they treat an employee so badly as to commit a repudiatory breach, then they cannot hang on to the employee unless they can persuade him or her to decide to stay.

54. Next, a word about affirmation in the context of employment contracts. When an employer commits a repudiatory breach there is naturally enormous pressure put on the employee. If he or she just ups and goes they have no job and the uncomfortable prospect of having to claim damages and unfair dismissal. If he or she stays there is a risk that they will be taken to have affirmed. Ideally a wronged employee who stays on for a bit whilst he or she considered their position would say so expressly. But even that would be difficult and it is not realistic to suppose it will happen very often. For that reason the law looks carefully at the facts before deciding whether there has really been an affirmation.

NOTES AND QUESTIONS

1. The Court of Appeal held Professor Buckland was entitled to claim constructive dismissal because the University, by overruling the Professor's academic judgement, committed a repudiatory breach of contract. The test for repudiatory breach does not ask whether an employer's conduct was within a 'reasonable range of responses'. That test, which shows deference to an employer's business judgement, is used for statutory unfair dismissal (chapter 18(2)) but both its meaning and its place in the statutory framework is disputed. At common law, *Buckland* makes clear it is irrelevant: the question is whether an employer breaches an important term of the contract that amounts to repudiation.

2. While Prof Buckland had worked for Bournemouth University for some time, a second critical example of a successful constructive dismissal claim – which exists at common law without any qualification period – is *Wilson v Racher* [1974] ICR 428, at chapter 5(1)(a). Recall that Mr Wilson, the gardener, was shouted at by Mr Racher, the landed aristocrat, so Wilson said 'Get stuffed, go and shit yourself', walked off, claimed constructive dismissal, and won. Mr Wilson had worked for forty-three days. He did not qualify for the new statutory right to unfair dismissal. But the Court of Appeal held that his claim succeeded because: 'We have by now come to realise that a contract of service imposes upon the parties a duty of mutual respect.'

3. The common law right against an unjust dismissal may not have yet been fully acknowledged, but it is nonetheless binding upon every Tribunal, based on incontestable precedent and principle. The right to claim constructive dismissal does not depend on fulfilling any qualifying period, and exists by virtue of common law. *Wilson* was approved by *West London Mental Health NHS Trust v Chhabra* [2013] UKSC 80, at chapter 5(2)(d). The right, without any qualifying period

against a non-constructive, but grossly unjust dismissal by the employer is discussed in chapter 18(1).

4.   A third example of constructive dismissal is *Kwik-Fit (GB) Ltd v Lineham* [1992] ICR 183. Mr Lineham used the toilet after hours at the depot where he worked on returning from the pub. The employer publicly rebuked him, and gave a final written warning. Outraged, Mr Lineham threw down his keys and drove off. He phoned the company the day after, asked for his wages and told Mr Kattner he was going to Tribunal. At Tribunal, the company argued that Mr Lineham's phone call was a voluntary resignation. Wood J held that Mr Lineham was constructively dismissed. The public rebuke was a repudiatory breach of contract. Implicitly the court was holding this violates the 'duty of mutual respect', and a 'quiet word' would invariably be more appropriate.

5.   Can an employee affirm the contract, despite a breach? Employers argued that when *Cheung* kept working after an event, this stopped a constructive dismissal claim.

Adamas Ltd v Cheung [2011] UKPC 32

Mrs Cheung claimed she was constructively dismissed as a senior jewellery salesperson in Adamas Ltd's duty-free shop, Floreal, Mauritius, after she was moved to a coastal shop at Belle Mare. Cheung was paid on commission, but in September 2001 this was removed, and she wrote a letter of objection to the management. Then, in October 2001 she was moved to Belle Mare. She wrote that she saw this 'very much to be a punitive transfer in view of my recent dispute with management concerned fixed commission'. She continued to work at Belle Mare, and fulfilled a request twice to deliver jewellery by car to Floreal. A third time she refused. Her manager stated her 'attitude towards management has now become very alarming and rude'. Cheung complained to the Mauritian Ministry of Labour in February 2002, and then relations deteriorated. She received a written warning over leaving jewellery in the shop window overnight and was dismissed in June for 'gross misconduct'. Cheung argued that she was already constructively dismissed in October 2001, when her job's terms had been, according to her, wrongfully altered. The employer argued, whether a breach or not, she accepted the changes by continuing to work. The Privy Council advised that Mrs Cheung's continued work was not acceptance of the wrongful changes. It referred to *Western Excavating*, and three Mauritian cases, and continued.

Lord Mance:

23. In none of these cases was the situation considered of a change of the nature or terms of employment, which although improper was not sufficiently serious to be repudiatory or therefore capable of constituting a constructive dismissal. In none of them was the situation considered of an announced change of terms which, although repudiatory, did not call for any immediate response or action by the employee, who could and did continue to perform his or her original job as if no change had been requested.

24. In the present case, the Board considers that two questions arise which are not, therefore, covered by these previous decisions. First, were the appellants in Mr Samba's letters of 13 and 27 December 2001 insisting on a change which was repudiatory, in the sense that Mrs Cheung could, if she had wished, have brought her employment to an end on the ground

that she had been constructively dismissed? Secondly, assuming that the change was repudia-tory, was Mrs Cheung obliged to treat it as such, bearing in mind that she could perform her contractual duties (as she correctly saw them) perfectly adequately? Could she not simply await and then refuse any instructions to deliver jewellery that might be given, leaving it to the appel-lants, if they wanted, actually to dismiss her and thereby expose themselves to her present claim for unjustified dismissal?

25. On one view, the words "stay in his employment under changed terms" ... might be read as suggesting that any employee, who continues in employment after any breach by his or her employer consisting of a requirement to do work outside the scope of the original employment contract, thereby accepts the new conditions. But this would not represent a rational legal position. If the change demanded was, although outside the scope of the original contract, so minor as not to be repudiatory, the employee would have no right to treat him or herself as constructively dismissed. It could not be right in such circumstances to treat an employee as having waived any claim for damages for the breach. The Board understood Mr Ahnee to accept that whether conduct is sufficiently serious to justify termination of a contract always depends on an analysis of the particular circumstances. It may be open to question whether the change proposed in this case was repudiatory, when Mrs Cheung could simply refuse to undertake deliveries if and when asked. But, even if one assumes that most if not all unilateral changes of job or terms by an employer including the present would be repudiatory if outside the scope of the original contract, the Board sees no reason why an employee, faced with an employer's demand for what the employee regards as unjustified changes, should then be obliged to treat the contract of employment as terminated on pain of being held, otherwise, to have accepted such changes. Where, as here, the original contractual job continues to exist and to be capable of performance by the employee, the employee can continue to perform; it is the employer who in such circumstances has to decide what stance to take.

...

34. In the Board's view, the fact that Mrs Cheung did not reply to the letter dated 27 December is unsurprising. It is true that one paragraph (B) of the letter dated 27 December addressed the question of performance of duties but it did so only in the most general fashion. It did no more than call Mrs Cheung's attention to her admitted contractual duty to manage the shop and perform any other duty suitable to her post, and ask her to inform Mr Samba immediately should she feel unable to carry out these duties or like to return to the post of sales representa-tive. No specific reference was made to jewellery deliveries and no answers were attempted to any of the detailed contents of Mrs Cheung's letter dated 20 December, by which she had made very clear that she did not regard such deliveries as within the scope of her contract and why she objected to their being treated as such.

35. Nothing can in these circumstances be inferred, by way of consent on her side to undertake such deliveries, from the fact that Mrs Cheung did not reply, repeating what she had already made clear on 20 December. If there is any inference, it seems to be that Mr Samba could not on 27 December think of a convincing response to her detailed objections, rather than vice versa. The Supreme Court was therefore right to regard the issue as remaining open or unre-solved after December 2001.

...

37. In these circumstances, the Board is unable to see any basis on which it could properly be concluded that Mrs Cheung agreed, either expressly or impliedly, to vary the scope of her contract of employment to bring within her duties an obligation to make jewellery deliveries from Belle Mare to Floreal when and if requested. The request made of her on 25 May 2002 was thus one which she was entitled to refuse, as she did, and her dismissal on account of such refusal was unjustified.

Lady Hale and **Lord Clarke** agreed.

NOTES AND QUESTIONS

1. The Privy Council advised that Mrs Cheung did not lose the right to claim a contract was unjustifiably altered by continuing to work. She was not 'obliged to treat the contract of employment as terminated on pain of being held, otherwise, to have accepted such changes'.

2. What happens if a worker falls so ill, or has such a bad accident, that he or she will be unable to work again? Can an employer argue that the contract has been 'frustrated', as in the common law on commercial contracts, to avoid any statutory or other right of a fair dismissal? The doctrine of frustration states, in essence, that if a contract proves to be impossible to perform, it becomes void (eg *Taylor v Caldwell* (1863) 122 ER 309, where a contract to rent a music hall was void after the hall burnt down). It is a default rule that can be contracted around with *force majeure* clauses: something that an employee is inherently unlikely to know about or have the bargaining power to insert into any individual contract. In *Hart v AR Marshall & Sons (Bulwell) Ltd* [1978] 2 All ER 413, Phillips J remarked that 'there is no doubt that the concept is alien to both employers and employees'. And in *Harman v Flexible Lamps Ltd* [1980] IRLR 418, Bristow J stated the doctrine, if allowed, 'would be a very convenient way in which to avoid the provisions of' what is now the ERA 1996.

3. Nevertheless in *Notcutt v Universal Equipment Co (London) Ltd* [1986] EWCA Civ 3 the Court of Appeal held that Mr Notcutt's employment contract was frustrated after he had a heart attack, meaning he did not get wages during his twelve-week notice period (see below). Dillon LJ said 'I feel much sympathy with the employee in that his working life has been cut short by illness or incapacity' but dismissed Mr Notcutt's case. Can you find any statutory exceptions to the minimum right to a fair dismissal or reasonable notice?

4. In favour of *Notcutt*, and other cases like it, it might be argued that a precondition to an employment right is the existence of a contract. If an employment contract is frustrated, there is no contract to which a statutory right may attach. But this argument fails to distinguish contract law's role in the consensual creation of an employment relation (an enforceable agreement), and the subsequent relationship from that point when rights become mandatory. These rights set minimum rules to favour the employee. Common law rules should be more favourable to the employee, but not less. Common law cannot destroy a contract, once created, if this undermines a right. Do you agree? If so, would different considerations exist for 'common mistake', where the event that makes a contract impossible to perform occurs (unknown to the parties) before the agreement is made?

5. It is submitted that, whatever the position in 1986, the decision in *Notcutt* must now be regarded as wrong. In *Gisda Cyf v Barratt* [2010] UKSC 41, [39] the Supreme Court said: 'The need to segregate intellectually common law principles relating to contract law, even in the field of employment, from statutorily conferred rights is fundamental.' Do you agree *Notcutt* is incapable of standing against this 'fundamental' principle?

(2) NOTICE

The right to reasonable notice before dismissal exists at common law, but minimum standards were also introduced in statute. A first, often forgotten, example of this was the Companies Act 1947, which stated company directors could be removed with a simple majority vote of the company general meeting (rather than the prior practice of a 75 per cent vote), but were entitled to 28 days notice and a hearing (now CA 2006 ss 168–69, see chapter 11(1)(a)). For other employees, the Contracts of Employment Act (CEA) 1963 introduced a statutory right of reasonable notice. The common law, and contracts of employment, can be more protective for the employee (but not a director in removal from office). As the Conservative Minister for Labour, John Hare MP said in the Bill's Second Reading: '[The] object of the Bill is not only to bring everybody up to the minimum but also to encourage employers to improve on the minimum on a voluntary basis', Hansard HC Debs (14 February 1963) vol 671, col 1505. The right to notice does not apply when an employee or worker commits gross misconduct. The rights are now in the ERA 1996 ss 86–89.

Employment Rights Act 1996 ss 86 and 89

86 Rights of employer and employee to minimum notice.
(1) The notice required to be given by an employer to terminate the contract of employment of a person who has been continuously employed for one month or more—
    (a) is not less than one week's notice if his period of continuous employment is less than two years,
    (b) is not less than one week's notice for each year of continuous employment if his period of continuous employment is two years or more but less than twelve years, and
    (c) is not less than twelve weeks' notice if his period of continuous employment is twelve years or more.
(2) The notice required to be given by an employee who has been continuously employed for one month or more to terminate his contract of employment is not less than one week.
(3) Any provision for shorter notice in any contract of employment with a person who has been continuously employed for one month or more has effect subject to subsections (1) and (2); but this section does not prevent either party from waiving his right to notice on any occasion or from accepting a payment in lieu of notice.
    ...
(6) This section does not affect any right of either party to a contract of employment to treat the contract as terminable without notice by reason of the conduct of the other party.
    ...

89 Employments without normal working hours.
(1) If an employee does not have normal working hours under the contract of employment in force in the period of notice, the employer is liable to pay the employee for each week of the period of notice a sum not less than a week's pay.
(2) The employer's liability under this section is conditional on the employee being ready and willing to do work of a reasonable nature and amount to earn a week's pay.
(3) Subsection (2) does not apply—
    (a) in respect of any period during which the employee is incapable of work because of sickness or injury,

(b) in respect of any period during which the employee is absent from work wholly or partly because of pregnancy or childbirth or on adoption leave, shared parental leave, parental leave or paternity leave, or

(c) in respect of any period during which the employee is absent from work in accordance with the terms of his employment relating to holidays.

NOTES AND QUESTIONS

1. ERA 1996 s 86(1) states that every employee gets one week's notice before dismissal after one month's work, two weeks after two years, three weeks after three years, and so on up to twelve years. An employee (2) only need give one week's notice. Instead of working during the notice period (3) an employee can take their contractual pay. But (6) an employee can be dismissed for bad conduct without notice. Under s 89, an employee who has no working hours is entitled to a normal week's pay. Under ERA 1996 s 224, a 'week's pay' is defined as the average over the last twelve weeks.

2. W Blackstone, *Commentaries on the Lawes of England* (1765) book I, ch 14, 413, suggested that people who were hired without any period being stated were to be presumed to be hired for a year. Their jobs could only be terminated upon at least one quarter's notice before the end of such a period, unless 'reasonable cause' was found by a justice of the peace. Why, in a pre-industrial society, do you think this presumption of one year's work existed?

3. An employer can always dismiss a worker without giving notice (summarily) if gross misconduct is found. An old example is *Atkin v Acton* (1830) 172 ER 67. Mr Acton hired Jonathan Atkin as his clerk and traveller for a year. Atkin arrived in the morning at Acton's house, where only a maid servant was home. He 'assaulted his employer's maid servant, with intent to ravish her' until interrupted by a postman and a porter. Lord Tenterden CJ held that 'the defendant had a right to discharge him' and 'was not liable to pay him any more than for the time during which he actually served'.

4. Is the refusal to obey an instruction enough to automatically justify dismissal? No. In *Laws v London Chronicle (Indicator Newspapers) Ltd* [1959] 1 WLR 698 a managing director, Mr Brittain, and a supervisor, Mr Delderfield, were in a fierce argument, while Ms Laws was in the room. Mr Brittain accused Mr Delderfield of being drunk, and needing a black coffee to calm down. He left, saying he was taking his employees with him. Mr Brittain said to both: 'Stay where you are.' Ms Laws left the room after being told to do so by her supervisor, so ignoring the managing director. But what was she meant to do? Disobey her direct supervisor or disobey the director? She was then given a letter that said: 'It is impossible for the company to overlook your behaviour and actions in leaving the conference last Friday in defiance of the managing director's request that you remain.' The Court of Appeal held that while Ms Laws was in breach of contract, the breach was not fundamental, and so summary dismissal was not justified.

5. Before the CEA 1963, the common law simply required reasonable notice before an ordinary (non-summary) dismissal, but had no clear rules on what that was

meant to be. In *Creen v Wright* (1875–76) LR 1 CPD 591, Mr Creen successfully claimed that he was entitled to reasonable notice before dismissal from his job as master mariner on Mr Wright's ship. Creen's contract said he would be paid £180 per annum. Wright purported to dismiss Creen without any notice or cause. Lord Coleridge CJ rejected that no notice was due, remarking on another case that 'a month's notice was held reasonable to determine an indefinite hiring of a clerk'. What sort of principles (if any) do you think could or should determine the common law length of notice?

6. The ILO Termination of Employment Convention 1982 (c 158) Art 11 merely states a worker 'shall be entitled to a reasonable period of notice or compensation in lieu thereof, unless he is guilty of serious misconduct' without articulating times.

7. The UK's statutory notice periods fall far below standards of most other developed countries. For example, Germany's Civil Code §622 requires four weeks for all workers, and then two months for workers over five years, three months for eight years, four months for ten years, five months for twelve years, six months for fifteen years, and seven months for twenty years. Who do you think can find a replacement more easily: an employee looking for a job, or an employer looking for a worker?

8. In *Richardson v Koefod* [1969] 1 WLR 1812, 1816, Lord Denning MR held the presumption of a year's hiring, from 'olden times, when England was an agricultural community', no longer applied to the manager of the Wimpy bar, cafe and snack bar in Shirley, Hampshire: 'In the absence of express stipulation, the rule is that every contract of service is determinable by reasonable notice. The length of notice depends on the circumstances of the case. There are many cases in the books showing what has been held reasonable for various employments. They are conveniently set out in Halsbury's Laws of England, 3rd ed., vol. 25, p. 490.'

9. The CEA 1963 and the ERA 1996 s 86 were not intended to displace the common law requirement of reasonable notice before dismissal, but rather set minimum standards. Any contract can improve upon the minimum, and it would seem that in any case an employee may argue they were entitled to more notice than in statute, even if their contract is silent on the matter. In what circumstances do you think that more notice might be due to an employee or worker than the current statutory minimum?

10. ERA 1996 s 86(3) says that employees can agree to let employers make a payment in lieu of notice, so that they leave their jobs with money, instead of continuing to work. But if an employer does make such a payment, does that automatically, and unilaterally bring the contract to an end? *Geys* held 'no', unless this was agreed to.

Société Générale, London Branch v Geys [2012] UKSC 63

Raphael Geys claimed he should receive a €12.5m termination payment upon dismissal from Société Générale (a major French bank) rather than €7m, because his contract of employment only terminated on 6 January 2008, not on 18 December 2007. Geys was a managing director of the European Fixed Income Sales, Financial Institutions Division.

As the global financial crisis unfolded (chapter 16(1)(a)), on 29 November 2007 he was called into a meeting and given a letter that his employment was terminated 'with immediate effect'. Under Geys's contract, para 5.15, if his job was terminated before 2008 he would receive a termination payment that was 65 per cent of half his pay in 2006, but if his job was terminated after 1 January 2008 he would get 65 per cent of half his pay in 2007. 2007 was a much better year than 2006 (€12.5m for 2007, rather than a mere €7m for 2006). The company handbook, cl 8.3 said: 'SG reserves the right to terminate your employment at any time with immediate effect by making a payment to you in lieu of notice' of basic salary and benefits. Geys argued Société Générale could not unilaterally terminate the contract: he had to accept an employer's repudiation. Société Générale paid a sum of money into Geys's bank account on 18 December reflecting his basic salary and benefits, but did not say what this was for until a letter on 4 January 2008, that Geys read on 6 January 2008. Geys argued he never accepted the bank's termination, nor a payment in lieu of notice until that point (when he happily elected to). The High Court held Geys's contract was only validly terminated on 6 January. The Court of Appeal held Geys's contract was unilaterally terminated on 18 December when the payment in lieu of notice was made. The Supreme Court reversed the Court of Appeal and held Société Générale had not unilaterally terminated a contract with a payment in lieu of notice. The contract ended on 6 January 2008.

Lord Hope:

15. For the reasons given by Lord Wilson, I too would hold that the elective theory is to be preferred – that a party's repudiation terminates a contract of employment only if and when the other party elects to accept the repudiation. I am persuaded by his careful analysis of the authorities that provide support for the view that repudiation of a contract of employment terminates the contract without the necessity of acceptance by the other party was not as authoritative or as consistent as Lord Sumption indicates in para 128 below. I also think that there are cases, of which this case is a good example, where it really does matter which of the two theories is adopted. The automatic theory can operate to the disadvantage of the injured party in a way that enables the wrongdoer to benefit from his own wrong. The law should seek to avoid such an obvious injustice. Where there is a real choice as to the direction of travel, the common law should favour the direction that is least likely to do harm to the injured party. I agree that we should be very cautious before reaching a conclusion whose result is that a breach is rewarded rather than its adverse consequences for the innocent party negatived: see para 66.

16. Was Sir John Donaldson clearly right when he declared in *Sanders v Ernest A Neale Ltd* [1974] ICR 565 at p 571 that an unaccepted repudiation brought a contract of employment to an end? Lord Sumption says that this was an accurate summary of the position as it then stood: paras 128 and 139, below. But I find it hard to disagree with Buckley LJ's observation in *Gunton v Richmond-upon-Thames London Borough Council* [1981] Ch 448, 466 that *Sanders v Ernest A Neale Ltd* was the first case in which the automatic theory was part of the basis for the decision in an employment case. In *Thomas Marshall (Exports) Ltd v Guinle* [1979] Ch 227 Sir Robert Megarry V-C in his review of the authorities also took that case as his starting point. He described it as the high-water-mark of the doctrine of automatic determination, but said that the authorities on the point were in a state that was far from satisfactory. Shaw LJ, in his dissenting judgment in Gunton, referred to the field that Buckley LJ had covered in his review of the authorities as dubious. He said that, as a result of the ebb and flow of the tide of judicial opinion, the court was left in the slack water of first principles. Only a few months later, in

London Transport Executive v Clarke [1981] ICR 355, the majority view in the Court of Appeal was in favour of the position that Sir Robert Megarry V-C adopted in Marshall.

17. The fact has to be faced that there is still a degree of oscillation between the two theories: David Cabrelli and Rebecca Zahn, The Elective and Automatic Theories of Termination at Common Law: Resolving the Conundrum? (2012) 41 Industrial Law Journal 346, 349. In any case, the question which of the two theories should be adopted is an open question at our level. Which result is, in principle, the most desirable? One must be careful not to assume that, just because in practice the employee may have little choice but to accept the repudiation, he has in law no alternative but to do so. I would endorse Ralph Gibson LJ's criticism in *Boyo v Lambeth London Borough Council* [1994] ICR 727, 743 of Buckley LJ's observation in the Gunton case that in a case of wrongful dismissal the court should easily infer that the innocent party has accepted the guilty party's repudiation of the contract. If the law requires acceptance of the repudiation, the requirement is for a real acceptance – a conscious intention to bring the contract to an end, or the doing of something that is inconsistent with its continuation. So the question is whether there are sound reasons of principle for holding that the general rule of law that requires acceptance of a repudiation does not apply.

18. The fact that an application of the automatic theory may produce an injustice is, for me, the crucial point. The question that Sir John Donaldson asked himself in *Sanders v Ernest A Neale Ltd* [1974] ICR 565, 571 is at the heart of the issue: why should the employee not sue for wages if it is the act of the employer which has prevented his performing the condition precedent of rendering his services? There may be grounds for thinking that the court is less reluctant than it once was to give injunctive relief in such cases, but I would not rest my decision on that point. It is the objection that the party who is in the wrong should not be permitted to benefit from his own wrong that is determinative. The timing of the repudiation may be crucial, and if the automatic theory were to prevail an employer may well be tempted to play this to his advantage – by getting in first before a rise in pay or pension entitlement takes place or, as in this case, a rise in the entitlement to bonuses. I note too that, as Professor Douglas Brodie has pointed out, it is not always true that work is the counterpart of the entitlement to wages. In some contracts wages are given to employees for holding themselves available for work: *The Contract of Employment* (2008), para 18-09.

19. The essential difference between the two theories may be said to be that under the automatic theory the decision as to whether the contract is at an end is made beyond the control of the innocent party in all circumstances, whereas under the elective theory it is for the innocent party to judge whether it is in his interests to keep the contract alive. Manifest justice favours preferring the interests of the innocent party to those of the wrongdoer. If there exists a good reason and an opportunity for the innocent party to affirm the contract, he should be allowed to do so: *London Transport Executive v Clarke* [1981] ICR 355, 367, per Templeman LJ.

Lady Hale:

45. Amid the welter of case law and academic commentary upon the subjects of both wrongful and unfair dismissal, there appears to be remarkably little discussion of the requirements for a lawful dismissal under the terms of the employment contract. Ever since indefinite terms of employment became the norm, the courts have implied a term that either party may bring it to an end by giving notice (see S Deakin and GS Morris, *Labour Law*, 6th ed, 2012, paras 5.13, 5.14). In 1963, statute intervened to lay down minimum periods of notice to which the employee is entitled and a lesser period to which the employer is entitled (see now, Employment Rights Act 1996, sections 86 et seq). But the parties are, of course, free to provide expressly in their contracts for longer periods of notice. Statute also permits either party to waive his right to notice on any occasion or to accept a payment in lieu of notice (1996 Act, section 86(3)).

46. Statute is, however, silent as to the manner in which such notice is to be given. "Notice" is, of course, an ambiguous term. It can refer to the period between the time when an employer or employee is notified that the contract is to be terminated and the expiry of the specified period. Or it can refer to the notification itself. Or both. The statutory provisions focus upon the period of notice required. This is clear from section 86(6), which provides that the section does not affect the right of either party "to treat the contract as terminable without notice by reason of the conduct of the other party".

...

54. In my view, it is quite clear that paragraph 8.3 is not dispensing with whatever requirement there is that the employee be notified of the termination of his employment. The words in brackets ("or, if notice has already been given, the balance of your notice period") draw a clear distinction between the notice period and notification of the termination of employment and thus strongly suggest that the word "notice" which precedes them also refers to the notice period. The question therefore becomes, to what notification was the employee entitled under the express or implied terms of his contract of employment?

55. In this connection, it is important to distinguish between two different kinds of implied terms. First, there are those terms which are implied into a particular contract because, on its proper construction, the parties must have intended to include them: see *Attorney General of Belize v Belize Telecom Ltd* [2009] UKPC 10, [2009] 1 WLR 1988. Such terms are only implied where it is necessary to give business efficacy to the particular contract in question. Second, there are those terms which are implied into a class of contractual relationship, such as that between landlord and tenant or between employer and employee, where the parties may have left a good deal unsaid, but the courts have implied the term as a necessary incident of the relationship concerned, unless the parties have expressly excluded it: see *Lister v Romford Ice & Cold Storage Co Ltd* [1957] AC 555, *Liverpool City Council v Irwin* [1977] AC 239.

56. A great deal of the contractual relationship between employer and employee is governed by implied terms of the latter kind. Some are of long-standing, such as the employer's duty to provide a safe system of work. Some are of more recent discovery, such as the mutual obligations of trust and confidence. This was referred to by Dyson LJ in *Crossley v Faithful and Gould Holdings Ltd* [2004] IRLR 377 as an "evolutionary process". He also described the "necessity" involved in implying such terms as "somewhat protean", pointing out that some well-established terms could scarcely be said to be essential to the functioning of the relationship. At para 36, he said this:

> "It seems to me that, rather than focus upon the elusive concept of necessity, it is better to recognise that, to some extent at least, the existence and scope of standardised implied terms raise questions of reasonableness, fairness and the balancing of competing policy considerations."

There is much to be said for that approach, given the way in which those terms have developed over the years.

57. Whatever the test to be applied, it seems to me to be an obviously necessary incident of the employment relationship that the other party is notified in clear and unambiguous terms that the right to bring the contract to an end is being exercised, and how and when it is intended to operate. These are the general requirements applicable to notices of all kinds, and there is every reason why they should also be applicable to employment contracts. Both employer and employee need to know where they stand. They both need to know the exact date upon which the employee ceases to be an employee. In a lucrative contract such as this one, a good deal of money may depend upon it. But even without that, there may be rights such as life and

permanent health insurance, which depend upon continuing to be in employment. In some contracts there may also be private health insurance. A person such as Mr Geys, going on holiday over Christmas and the New Year, needs to know whether he should be arranging these for himself. At the other end of the scale, an employee who has been sacked needs to know when he will become eligible for state benefits.

58. It is necessary, therefore, that the employee not only receive his payment in lieu of notice, but that he receive notification from the employer, in clear and unambiguous terms, that such a payment has been made and that it is made in the exercise of the contractual right to terminate the employment with immediate effect. He should not be required to check his bank account regularly in order to discover whether he is still employed. If he does learn of a payment, he should not be left to guess what it is for and what it is meant to do.

59. This is not an unreasonable requirement to place upon an employer (or indeed upon an employee giving notice). When an employer sacks an employee it ought to know what it is doing: is it with immediate effect or on notice? If it is with immediate effect, is it because of some misconduct on the part of the employee or in the exercise of a PILON clause? It is not good enough to purport summarily to dismiss the employee without stating a cause and without making a payment, then to realise that there is no right to do that, but that there is the right to terminate under a PILON clause, and so decide to exercise that right without telling the employee that the right is being exercised and the payment has been made.

60. Given that such a notice is a necessary incident of the relationship, a wise employer would take care to give it in writing. But if the contract does not require writing, it would be possible for an employer to hand over the correct money and clearly state at the same time that this brings the employment to an immediate end, in place of the notice period to which the employee would otherwise be entitled. In the days when wages were normally paid in cash, this would have been a common practice. But if, as is now common, payment is made direct to the employee's bank account, the employee's bank is his agent for the receipt of payment, but it is not without more his agent for the receipt of notification of what the payment is for. That notification has to be given to the employee.

61. On any view, such clear and unambiguous notification was not given in this case. The Bank could easily have done things properly. But for whatever reason they did not do so. Subject, therefore, to the repudiation issue, it was not until 6 January 2008, when Mr Geys must be deemed to have received the Bank's letter of 4 January 2008, that the contractual right to terminate under the PILON method provided for by paragraph 8.3 of the Handbook was validly exercised and his employment with the Bank came to an end.

Lord Wilson:

63. In the absence of any direct authority of real weight at this level, the court is required to make a difficult and important choice between a conclusion that a party's repudiation (albeit perhaps only an immediate and express repudiation) of a contract of employment automatically terminates the contract ("the automatic theory") and a conclusion that his repudiation terminates the contract of employment only if and when the other party elects to accept the repudiation ("the elective theory"). It is common ground that, whichever theory be chosen, it should apply equally to wrongful repudiations by employers (i.e. wrongful dismissals) and wrongful repudiations by employees (i.e. wrongful resignations); and it is only for convenience, and because it is reflective of the facts of the present case, that I will, at times, refer to the wrongful repudiator as the employer and to the innocent party as the employee.

64. In light of the fact that a central incident of the automatic theory is that, upon the automatic termination of the contract, the innocent party has a right to damages, the first question must be whether it matters that the contract is terminated forthwith upon repudiation or, instead, survives until some further, terminating, event? The answer is that sometimes it does matter. It depends on the terms of the contract. The date of termination fixes the end of some contractual obligations and, sometimes, the beginning of others. An increase in salary may depend on the survival of the contract until a particular date. The amount of a pension may be calculated by reference to the final salary paid throughout a completed year of service or to an aggregate of salaries including the final completed year. An entitlement to holiday pay may similarly depend on the contract's survival to a particular date. In some cases an award of damages will compensate the employee for any such loss. But often it will fail to do so. Such failure flows from application of the "least burdensome" principle, namely that damages should reflect only the losses sustained by the employer's decision to repudiate the contract unlawfully rather than by his having hypothetically proceeded, in the manner "least profitable to the plaintiff, and the least burthensome to the defendant", to terminate the contract lawfully: see *Cockburn v Alexander* (1848) 6 CB 791, 136 ER 1459, at pp 814 and 1468, (Maule J), and *McGregor on Damages*, 18th ed (2009) para 8-093. So, where under the terms of the contract it had been open to the wrongfully repudiating employer to have taken a course which would have terminated the contract quickly as well as lawfully, the damages will be small.

65. These propositions are well demonstrated by the facts of the present case. Lord Hope explains in para 6 above why the appellant's termination payment would be substantially increased if his contract of employment were to have terminated after 31 December 2007. Had the effect of the Bank's wrongful repudiation been to terminate it on or prior to that date, his damages would not cover his loss of the increase in payment. For, as Lady Hale observes in para 61 above, it would have been easy for the Bank lawfully to have operated the PILON clause in para 8.3 of the Handbook. Indeed it could, by proper operation of that clause, lawfully have dismissed the appellant on 29 November 2007 itself. So his damages for the Bank's unlawful repudiation of the contract on that date would, by application of the least onerous principle, be no more than nominal. Superficially, however, it may be said to be paradoxical that the principle should demand a hypothesis that the Bank would have operated the PILON clause immediately and validly in circumstances in which in fact it delayed its attempted operation of the clause until 18 December 2007 and thereafter, until 6 January 2008, it operated it invalidly.
...

91. In the course of the affirmation of the elective theory by the Saskatchewan Court of Appeal in *Smart v Board of Governors of South Saskatchewan Hospital Centre* (1989) 60 DLR (4th) 8, Bayda CJS commented on the observations of Buckley LJ, at p 17:

> This position of 'being better off to accept the repudiation' in which the innocent employee so often finds himself in practice and the courts' commensurate readiness to find acceptance have, in my respectful view, tended to seduce some legal analysts into concluding that the innocent employee is obliged in law to accept the repudiation, or, alternatively, does not have the option in law to treat the contract as continuing. But, as ... Buckley [LJ] explicitly pointed out, that conclusion is erroneous. It is important to remember that there are times when it is in the innocent employee's practical interest to continue the contract in law."

92. But Buckley LJ's suggestion that acceptance of a wrongful repudiation should easily be inferred – and his consequent dilution of the effect of the theory which he himself was commending – has attracted powerful criticism, not least by Professor Brodie in *The Contract of Employment* (2008), para 18.10, and by Ralph Gibson LJ in the *Boyo* case [1994] ICR 727, 743. There is certainly no point in conferring upon a party an election to which some other principle of law is applied so as to deprive it of real value; and in my view Buckley LJ's suggestion should

be treated cautiously. Ralph Gibson LJ proceeded to accept that, following a wrongful repudiation, contractual obligations which did not depend on the existence of the relationship of master and servant, such as terms as to disciplinary procedures and competition, continued to exist. But, "subject", so he said, "to that qualification", he would, in the absence of the binding authority of the *Gunton* case, have preferred the automatic theory. I do not understand how a theory can be preferred "subject to" a qualification which is entirely inconsistent with it.

93. Apart from the decision in 1994 in the *Boyo* case, cited above, in which the employee represented himself and the court felt reluctantly obliged to apply the elective theory in accordance with the decision in the *Gunton* case, the most recent domestic decision of significance is *London Transport Executive v Clarke* [1981] ICR 355. Its date demonstrates that, for an entire generation, the issue between the two theories has been substantially quiescent. The employee went to Jamaica for seven weeks contrary to the terms of the contract and to the employer's express instructions. So it was a repudiatory breach falling short of purported resignation. On the contrary, the employee wished to resume his employment upon his return. While he was away, however, the employer told him, by letter, that his employment was at an end. The first question posed by his complaint of unfair dismissal to the industrial tribunal related to the identity of the party who had terminated the contract. Lord Denning MR, evidently prepared to apply the automatic theory even to a repudiatory breach falling short of purported resignation, held, at p 366, that, upon his departure, the employee had himself terminated the contract. But Templeman and Dunn LJJ held that the termination had occurred only when, by its letter, the employer had accepted his repudiatory breach. So he had indeed been dismissed, albeit (so they proceeded to hold) not unfairly. Templeman LJ, with whose reasoning Dunn LJ agreed, said at pp 366–367:

> "The general rule is that a repudiated contract is not terminated unless and until the repudiation is accepted by the innocent party …
>
> [C]ontracts of employment cannot provide a general exemption to that rule because it would be manifestly unjust to allow a wrongdoer to determine a contract by repudiatory breach if the innocent party wished to affirm the contract for good reason. Thus in *Thomas Marshall (Exports) Ltd v Guinle* [1978] ICR 905, which contains a full discussion of principles and of the conflicting authorities, a contract of employment was repudiated by the employee. The court could not enforce specific performance of the contract for personal services, but Sir Robert Megarry VC enforced against the wrongdoing employee at the behest of the innocent employer who had not accepted the repudiation a confidentiality and non-competition obligation which was only effective during the continuance of the contract. Repudiation cannot determine a contract of service or any other contract while there exists a reason and an opportunity for the innocent party to affirm the contract."

Templeman LJ added, at p 368, that the suggested exception was "contrary to principle, unsupported by authority binding on this court and undesirable in practice".

94. Such might have been good quotations with which to conclude my judgment. For I entirely agree with them and cannot improve on them; and they seem particularly apt to the present case, in which the appellant had an obvious reason – and in my view a good reason – for not accepting the Bank's wrongful attempt to terminate his contract until after 2007.

Lord Carnwath:

99. The most significant issue, which has divided the court, is the repudiation issue. Lord Sumption's historical analysis of the development of the law in this area is powerful and of

great interest. However, I am not in the end persuaded that it should provide the answer to this case. That review, like Lord Wilson's equally powerful response, shows how both courts and academics have grappled with, and sought to reconcile, the apparently conflicting rules and remedies which judicial pragmatism has devised to meet the special features of employment contracts.

100. In choosing between them, I attach particular weight to the fact that, in spite of the force of the criticisms directed at the election theory, and at some of the reasoning of the majority in *Gunton* [1981], the law as there stated has stood for 30 years, apparently without evidence of practical difficulty or injustice. ...

101. That approach seems apt also to the particular context of paragraph 5.15, under which the termination payment arises. I am not persuaded that a general distinction can be drawn, as Lord Sumption suggests, between the existential ("obligations which go to the continued existence of the employment relationship"); and the collateral. Nor do I find it helpful (as in some of the submissions before us) to talk of the continuation of a mere "shell" or "husk" contract. As in any other case, the nature and extent of the contractual remedies at any time must depend on the context, the terms of the contract, and the circumstances of the breach.

102. In the present case, the contract provided a detailed code for what was to happen during and after the period of service. The elaborate provisions for termination were an important part of the contractual rights provided to the employee. Paragraph 5.15 fixed the amount of the termination payment by reference to when "your employment terminates". I see no reason why, for the purposes of that clause, the employer should not be held to the date of termination in accordance with the contract, rather than permitted to advance that date by repudiatory breach.

103. On the termination issue, after some hesitation, I have come to the conclusion, for the reasons given by Lady Hale, that the payment on 18 December 2007 did not effect a lawful termination. ...

Lord Sumption (dissenting):

108. Mr Geys is a lucky man. He had a responsible and highly paid job with an entitlement to participate in a profit-sharing bonus scheme dependent on the performance of his division, in addition to discretionary bonuses. The other side of the coin was that he had no contractual job security. Under his contract of employment, his employers, Société Générale ("SG"), were entitled to dismiss him at any time without cause either upon three months' notice or "with immediate effect by making a payment to you in lieu of notice." This is what happened to Mr Geys. He was called to a meeting on 29 November 2007 and given a letter informing him that SG had decided to terminate his employment with immediate effect and that the "appropriate termination documentation" would follow. In accordance with the time-honoured ritual, he was then taken to clear his desk and escorted from the building by security staff. There could not have been the slightest doubt that his employment relationship with SG was at an end. He cannot have supposed that he had been dismissed for cause, for no cause was stated. The only reasonable inference was that SG was purporting to dismiss him summarily without cause, as they were entitled in principle to do.

109. Fortunately for Mr Geys, SG did not understand their own contract. It is common ground that if they had handed him a cheque for his payment in lieu of notice at the meeting on 29 November, his dismissal would have taken effect according to his contract at once. Because the right to terminate with immediate effect is exercisable "by making a payment in

lieu of notice", it is common ground that the purported dismissal with immediate effect on 29 November was a repudiatory breach of contract by SG. They were not entitled to dismiss him with immediate effect from 29 November, but only with effect from the payment in lieu. It was, however, a repudiation of the most technical kind. There was no doubt about SG's right to dismiss him with immediate effect if they set about it in the right way. ...

NOTES AND QUESTIONS

1. The Supreme Court majority holds that Société Générale did not terminate the contract when, in the November meeting, it purported to terminate without making a payment (and therefore wrongfully repudiated the contract). Nor did it terminate until January 6.

2. However, the reasons given by the majority appear not to have completely settled *why* the letter that Mr Geys read on January 6 terminated the contract. Lord Hope and Lord Wilson clearly state that Geys must have accepted the offer to terminate (the 'elective' theory) while it appears that Lady Hale [45] and Lord Carnwath [103] say the contract did not terminate before, because clear and proper notice was not given (it seems avoiding answering whether it would automatically terminate). Lord Sumption suggests that 'it is common ground' that if a payment in lieu of notice were made dismissal would have taken effect immediately [109]. But it is completely unclear this is accurate (Lord Hope and Lord Wilson reject it) and if so why. Should Mr Geys have had to accept early termination on payment in lieu of notice, or would he have a right to continue employment until that notice was complete (whether by continuing to work or not)?

3. The Supreme Court did not settle whether an employer should be allowed give any employee standard terms, purporting to enable immediate termination with a payment in lieu of notice. Section 86(3) says the right to notice 'does not prevent either party from waiving his right to notice on any occasion or from accepting a payment in lieu of notice'. If one follows the elective theory in full, this logically implies that the point of 'acceptance' of a payment in lieu of notice must take place after the employer's offer to terminate. Do you agree it would be unfair to bind an employee to unilateral termination at any point without knowing (in the future) exactly which rights (such as pay increases, pensions or holiday pay as outlined by Lord Wilson at [64]) will be jeopardised?

4. Could different rules apply depending on the bargaining power of the employee? Mr Geys had a multimillion-pound income. Perhaps he was in a position to negotiate his salary and terms. Someone else with less bargaining power would not be able to negotiate PILON clauses: why should they lose the protection of s 86(3)?

5. At [55]–[57] Lady Hale states that the right to notice is a standard incident (at common law) of the contract of employment. It does seem that the tests for implied terms recited at [55] come from an older formulation in commercial cases, of implied terms being based on 'business efficacy', rather than the modern test of implying terms as essential to reflect the parties' reasonable expectations in *Belize* [23], and see chapter 5 generally. Whatever the test, it is welcome recognition that notice before dismissal is a common law right. Can it go beyond statute?

6. Among the previous cases discussed in *Geys* was *Gunton v Richmond upon Thames LBC* [1980] ICR 755. This held that Mr Gunton, a council worker, was able to insist upon a contractual disciplinary procedure being followed, and his contract not terminating once he was given pay in lieu of notice. Buckley LJ held that on a purported instant termination, an employee has a choice of whether to claim damages, whether to affirm the repudiation or insist on the contract continuing. This was upheld.

7. However in *Boyo v London Borough of Lambeth* [1994] EWCA Civ 28 the Court of Appeal followed *Gunton* only reluctantly after Boyo, an accountant for Lambeth Council, was charged by the police with fraud. Boyo was dismissed upon the charges being made, but claimed this was wrongful and Lambeth Council should have followed the contractual disciplinary procedure. Reluctantly the Court of Appeal held that the employer could only terminate a contract lawfully after notice and disciplinary time, unless the employee otherwise accepted termination (in this case when Boyo's trial began). Do you agree that that reluctance should now be abandoned? If in *Boyo* an employer could be justified in summarily dismissing the employee, then there is no need for notice. Otherwise, there is, and this is a right whatever the contract says.

(3) FAIR HEARING

The right to a fair hearing when people are in trouble is fundamental the common law. As chapter 5(2)(d) explained, *West London Mental Health NHS Trust v Chhabra* [2013] UKSC 80, [37] held there is 'an implied contractual right to a fair process' in any dismissal. This meant a hostile 'human resources' director being involved 'undermined the fairness of the disciplinary process'. This chapter's introduction further suggested the right to a fair hearing (both at common law or in statute) before dismissal is complicated by three fundamental conflicts of interest by employers: personal conflicts among managerial and other staff (as in *Chhabra*), stakeholder conflicts over an enterprise's share of the product (chapter 18), and social conflicts when enterprises make redundancies in a crisis while social policy requires jobs to be maintained (chapter 16(1)).

Once upon a time, the Magna Carta 1215 chapter 29 held up the standard for procedural fairness: a hearing by one's 'peers, or by the Law of the Land'. Dismissal procedure must follow the law, but there is not yet a statutory requirement for review by one's peers, even though workforce participation can neutralise managerial conflicts. There are, however, models: the UK government helped draft Control Council Law No 22 (10 April 1946) in occupied Germany, where Art V(b) enabled elected work councils to have binding rights on dismissals (chapter 11(2)(a)). Today, as unions have been squeezed out of many British workplaces, and until they revive, a majority of employers can freely act upon conflicted interests, exacerbating unfairness and fuelling excessive litigation. The current Code by the Advisory, Conciliation and Arbitration Service recognises employer conflicts to some extent as it sets a dismissal procedure.

ACAS Code of Practice 1: Disciplinary and Grievance Procedures (2015)

4. ... whenever a disciplinary or grievance process is being followed it is important to deal with issues fairly. There are a number of elements to this:

- Employers and employees should raise and deal with issues **promptly** and should not unreasonably delay meetings, decisions or confirmation of those decisions.
- Employers and employees should act **consistently**
- Employers should carry out any necessary **investigations**, to establish the facts of the case
- Employers should inform employees of the basis of the problem and give them an opportunity to **put their case** in response before any decisions are made
- Employers should allow employees to be **accompanied** at any formal disciplinary or grievance meeting
- Employers should allow an employee to **appeal** against any formal decision made.

Discipline

Keys to handling disciplinary issues in the workplace

Establish the facts of each case

5. It is important to carry out necessary investigations of potential disciplinary matters without unreasonable delay to establish the facts of the case. In some cases this will require the holding of an investigatory meeting with the employee before proceeding to any disciplinary hearing. In others, the investigatory stage will be the collation of evidence by the employer for use at any disciplinary hearing.

6. In misconduct cases, where practicable, different people should carry out the investigation and disciplinary hearing.

7. If there is an investigatory meeting this should not by itself result in any disciplinary action. Although there is no statutory right for an employee to be accompanied at a formal investigatory meeting, such a right may be allowed under an employer's own procedure.

8. In cases where a period of suspension with pay is considered necessary, this period should be as brief as possible, should be kept under review and it should be made clear that this suspension is not considered a disciplinary action.

Inform the employee of the problem

9. If it is decided that there is a disciplinary case to answer, the employee should be notified of this in writing. This notification should contain sufficient information about the alleged misconduct or poor performance and its possible consequences to enable the employee to prepare to answer the case at a disciplinary meeting. It would normally be appropriate to provide copies of any written evidence, which may include any witness statements, with the notification.

10. The notification should also give details of the time and venue for the disciplinary meeting and advise the employee of their right to be accompanied at the meeting.

Hold a meeting with the employee to discuss the problem

11. The meeting should be held without unreasonable delay whilst allowing the employee reasonable time to prepare their case.

12. ... At the meeting the employer should explain the complaint against the employee and go through the evidence that has been gathered. The employee should be allowed to set out their case and answer any allegations that have been made. The employee should also be given a reasonable opportunity to ask questions, present evidence and call relevant witnesses. They should also be given an opportunity to raise points about any information provided by witnesses. Where an employer or employee intends to call relevant witnesses they should give advance notice that they intend to do this.

Allow the employee to be accompanied at the meeting

...

14. The statutory right is to be accompanied by a fellow worker, a trade union representative, or an official employed by a trade union. A trade union representative who is not an employed official must have been certified by their union as being competent to accompany a worker. ...

...

16. If a worker's chosen companion will not be available at the time proposed for the hearing by the employer, the employer must postpone the hearing to a time proposed by the worker provided that the alternative time is both reasonable and not more than five working days after the date originally proposed.

17. The companion should be allowed to address the hearing to put and sum up the worker's case, respond on behalf of the worker to any views expressed at the meeting and confer with the worker during the hearing. The companion does not, however, have the right to answer questions on the worker's behalf, address the hearing if the worker does not wish it or prevent the employer from explaining their case.

Decide on appropriate action

18. After the meeting decide whether or not disciplinary or any other action is justified and inform the employee accordingly in writing.

19. Where misconduct is confirmed or the employee is found to be performing unsatisfactorily it is usual to give the employee a written warning. A further act of misconduct or failure to improve performance within a set period would normally result in a final written warning.

20. If an employee's first misconduct or unsatisfactory performance is sufficiently serious, it may be appropriate to move directly to a final written warning. This might occur where the employee's actions have had, or are liable to have, a serious or harmful impact on the organisation.

...

Provide employees with an opportunity to appeal

26. Where an employee feels that disciplinary action taken against them is wrong or unjust they should appeal against the decision. Appeals should be heard without unreasonable delay and ideally at an agreed time and place. Employees should let employers know the grounds for their appeal in writing.

27. The appeal should be dealt with impartially and wherever possible, by a manager who has not previously been involved in the case.

28. Workers have a statutory right to be accompanied at appeal hearings. ...

NOTES AND QUESTIONS

1. These standards set out what a responsible body of employers, using following good workplace relations practice, ought to do for a disciplinary or grievances. It is issued by ACAS under TULRCA 1992 s 199. If it is not followed, employees get more in damages under TULRCA 1992 s 207A below.

2. To some extent the ACAS Code acknowledges the systematic conflicts of interest that employing entities have in making dismissals. For instance, at para 6, it requires that investigations and disciplinary hearings are handled by different people. At para 27, it says an appeal should be dealt with 'impartially' and 'by a manager who has not previously been involved'. But do you think managers will be more sympathetic to the side of the story from other managers, or the person in trouble?

3. In more and more countries, employees have the right to take part in the actual dismissal decision. The German Work Constitution Act 1972 (Betriebsverfassungsgesetz 1972) §102 requires a work council to be consulted before every dismissal: any dismissal is void without consultation. A court may then confirm that a dismissal is justified or not. Different rules apply to redundancy dismissals. Under §111, in workplaces with over twenty staff the work council can oppose a dismissal, but cannot prevent it: the employer can insist on redundancies subject to a 'social plan' that is determined by court.

4. Could courts take account of inherent conflicts in procedures for dismissal, by altering their standards of fairness review (chapter 17(2))? For instance, if an elected work council under the consultation procedures in chapter 11(2) is empowered to review and affirm or object to dismissals, those which are affirmed by a work council could be subject to a *Wednesbury* unreasonableness or a proportionality test. If an employer makes a dismissal decision, completely unconfined by union or work council voice, the omnipresent spectre of conflicted interests suggests that courts should engage in a full replacement reasonableness review of the employer decision.

5. The ACAS Code also contains grievance procedure standards. Employees should formally raise grievances if they cannot be informally resolved. Employers should hold a meeting, let the employee be accompanied, decide action, and allow the employee to appeal in writing to someone not previously involved in the case.

6. In *West Midlands Cooperative Society v Tipton* [1986] AC 536 the House of Lords held that an employer's failure to follow its own dismissal procedure would be relevant to a finding of unfair dismissal. Mr Tipton's contract incorporated a collective agreement requiring that the Cooperative's disciplinary procedure allowed for an appeal after any dismissal decision. Mr Tipton had worked for the Coop as a milk worker for thirty-seven years, but he had a record of absenteeism, and in 1980 was absent for 108 out of 250 days. A manager wrote to him requiring 'immediate, dramatic and lasting improvement' or his 'employment will be terminated. No further warnings will be issued.' After another eleven out of seventy-five working days' absence by February 1982, the manager wrote saying he had 'no alternative' but to terminate his job immediately. An appeal was refused by the CEO. The Tribunal found the dismissal was unfair, because the appeal was denied. The House of Lords found that the employer's failure to follow its own contractual disciplinary code made the dismissal unfair.

7. In an obiter remark in *Tipton* Lord Bridge added there could be 'cases where, on the undisputed facts, the dismissal was inevitable, as for example where a trusted employee, before dismissal, was charged with, and pleaded guilty to, a serious offence of dishonesty committed in the course of his employment. In such a case the employer could reasonably refuse to entertain a domestic appeal on the ground that it could not affect the outcome.' But even if there is a confession, why should that eliminate the right to a fair procedure? If the employee resigns, there is obviously no problem.

8.   On quite different facts to that hypothetical, in *Polkey v AE Dayton Services Ltd*
     [1987] UKHL 8 the House of Lords held that damages for unfair dismissal might
     be reduced to zero if a redundancy dismissal were 'inevitable', but that reinstate-
     ment could be ordered. Mr Polkey had driven vans for Dayton Services Ltd for
     four years, before being summoned to a manager's office, told he was redundant
     on the spot, and then driven home by a co-worker. The Tribunal held this was a
     'heartless disregard of the provisions of the code of practice', but then held that
     redundancies would have occurred even if there had been consultation and proper
     procedure, so the dismissal was not unfair. The Employment Appeal Tribunal and
     Court of Appeal rejected appeals. But the House of Lords found that the right to
     a fair dismissal could not be abrogated: a Tribunal was bound to assess whether
     the dismissal was fair at the time. Only in a remedy could the (ostensible) inevi-
     tability of redundancy be taken into account. At that point, said Lord Bridge, a
     'tribunal may conclude, as in the instant case that the appropriate procedural steps
     would not have avoided the employee's dismissal as redundant. But if, as your
     Lordships now hold, that conclusion does not defeat his claim of unfair dismissal,
     the industrial tribunal, apart from any question of compensation, will also ...
     if it thinks fit, make an order for re-engagement ... and in so doing exercise a very
     wide discretion as to the terms of the order.' So if 'redundancy would have been
     inevitable at the time when it took place even if the appropriate procedural steps
     had been taken' this would not 'preclude a discretionary order for re-engagement
     on suitable terms'. Do you agree?
9.   Parliament did not. If the Code is not followed, employees get more compensation.

Trade Union and Labour Relations (Consolidation) Act 1992 s 207A

207A Effect of failure to comply with Code: adjustment of awards
   (1) This section applies to proceedings before an employment tribunal relating to a claim by
an employee under any of the jurisdictions listed in Schedule A2.
   (2) If, in the case of proceedings to which this section applies, it appears to the employment
tribunal that—
     (a)   the claim to which the proceedings relate concerns a matter to which a relevant
           Code of Practice applies,
     (b)   the employer has failed to comply with that Code in relation to that matter, and
     (c)   that failure was unreasonable,
the employment tribunal may, if it considers it just and equitable in all the circumstances to do
so, increase any award it makes to the employee by no more than 25%.
   (3) If, in the case of proceedings to which this section applies, it appears to the employment
tribunal that—
     (a)   the claim to which the proceedings relate concerns a matter to which a relevant
           Code of Practice applies,
     (b)   the employee has failed to comply with that Code in relation to that matter, and
     (c)   that failure was unreasonable, the employment tribunal may, if it considers it just
           and equitable in all the circumstances to do so, reduce any award it makes to the
           employee by no more than 25%.
   (4) In subsections (2) and (3), "relevant Code of Practice" means a Code of Practice issued
under this Chapter which relates exclusively or primarily to procedure for the resolution of
disputes.

(5) Where an award falls to be adjusted under this section and under section 38 of the Employment Act 2002, the adjustment under this section shall be made before the adjustment under that section. ...

NOTES AND QUESTIONS

1. TULRCA 1992 s 207A, introduced by the Employment Act 2008 s 3, and creates what is known as an 'ACAS uplift' to the types of claim listed in Sch A2. This is 25 per cent more than the compensation for unfair dismissal, redundancy, etc.
2. Schedule A2 lists essentially all the claims that can be brought in an Employment Tribunal. For reference, these are:

    – union discrimination and detriment (TULRCA 1992 ss 145A–46)
    – detriment for union recognition rights (Sch A1, para 146)
    – wage deductions (ERA 1996 s 23)
    – detriment in employment (s 48)
    – unfair dismissal (s 111)
    – redundancy (s 163)
    – minimum wage detriment (NMWA 1998 s 24)
    – anti-discrimination rights (EA 2010 ss 120 and 127)
    – breach of employment contract (Employment Tribunal Extension of Jurisdiction (England and Wales) Order 1994)
    – working time claims (WTR 1998 reg 30 and Cross-border Railway Services (Working Time) Regulations 2008 reg 17)
    – information and consultation (TICER 1999 reg 32, EPLLCR 2004 reg 45 and ICER 2004 reg 33)
    – pension scheme consultation (Occupational and Personal Pension Schemes (Consultation by Employers and Misc Amendment) Regs 2006 Sch, para 8)
    – European Cooperative Society (Involvement of Employees) Regulations 2006 reg 34
    – the Employment Relations Act 1999 (Blacklists) Regulations 2010 reg 9.

3. The statutory reform was welcome in principle because, even if limited, it recognises that procedures do change minds, even if people think they never will. Two simple examples suffice. First, nobody credibly argues that the right to a fair trial is not valuable in itself because 'we all know he did it'. Who knows what a fair trial may reveal? Second, directors, trustees and other fiduciaries must avoid any possibility of a conflict of interest. Unlike in Delaware and other US states, English courts for almost three centuries have affirmed that a court may not (once the possibility of conflict is found) assess whether there was an actual conflict that really made a difference to the fiduciary's decisions. This in itself would enable fiduciaries to threaten litigation over their honesty, rather than avoid conflicts to begin with: *Keech v Sandford* [1726] EWHC Ch J76 and *Whelpdale v Cookson* (1747) 27 ER 856. This makes fiduciaries honest.
4. Before TULRCA 1992 s 207A, the government had passed the Employment Act 2002 s 29–33, which required that every employer follow a statutory dismissal

procedure, found in a new ERA 1996 s 98A and EA 2002 Sch 2. This new procedure did not please many people. Employers found it to be a bureaucratic hurdle. Trade unions opposed it because it encouraged a tick-box culture for dismissal proceedings, over ensuring a procedure was truly fair. This is why the EA 2008 created the ACAS uplift, which sets out guidelines and standards, rather than rigid rules.

5.   A few cases were decided under the EA 2002 rules. In *Cartwright v King's College, London* [2010] EWCA Civ 1146, a non-clinical teaching fellow successful claimed his dismissal from KCL's Department of Medical Engineering was unfair for failure to follow a correct procedure. He was sent an email on 9 July 2007 saying there was not enough work, and redeployment and voluntary severance was contemplated, but not that redundancy would be. In October 2007, he was emailed saying that his post was at risk of redundancy, but Cartwright was not invited to a meeting to discuss the possibility. The Court of Appeal held EA 2002 Sch 2 was violated, because step 1 required notification once redundancy was contemplated, and then a meeting to discuss it. So, Cartwright was awarded damages for unfair dismissal.

6.   If an employee is summarily dismissed, for instance because they have asked for unpaid wages, does the ACAS uplift apply? Must a grievance procedure be initiated first?

7.   Some dismissals will be more damaging to an employee than others, if the reason for a dismissal or its consequences are grave. *Roldan* held this affects procedural rights.

Salford Royal NHS Foundation Trust v Roldan **[2010] EWCA Civ 522**

Roldan, a nurse who worked at the NHS for four years, claimed she was unfairly dismissed after she was alleged to have thrown cleaning wipes at a patient, tapped a patient's foot with a saturation probe, slapped a patient's hand, and stuck two fingers up before checking to see if anyone noticed. Those allegations came from a healthcare assistant who had worked at the NHS for four months. As Roldan was from the Philippines, the dismissal resulted in losing her work permit and right to remain in the UK. Roldan admitted to throwing the wipes, but said her two fingers were meant to signify peace, and denied the other accusations. In a disciplinary hearing the evidence of the care assistant was preferred, without any other witnesses being found. The Tribunal held proper investigations were not carried out, and the dismissal was unfair. Judge McMullen QC in the Employment Appeal Tribunal found the Tribunal's decision was perverse. The Court of Appeal held Roldan was unfairly dismissed because the accuser's evidence was not tested.

Elias LJ:

13. ... it is particularly important that employers take seriously their responsibilities to conduct a fair investigation where, as on the facts of that case, the employee's reputation or ability to work in his or her chosen field of employment is potentially apposite. ...

...

51. Before considering these grounds of appeal, I would make this preliminary observation. It is not disputed that the Tribunal properly directed themselves in accordance with the principles established in *Burchell v British Home Stores*, as further explained in a case of this kind by *A v B*. In these circumstances, save at least where there is a proper basis for saying that the Tribunal simply failed to follow their own self direction, the EAT should not interfere with that decision unless there is no proper evidential basis for it, or unless the conclusion is perverse. That is a very high hurdle. In *Yeboah v Crofton* [2002] IRLR 634 Mummery LJ said that this would require an "overwhelming case" that the decision was one which no reasonable tribunal, properly appreciating the law and the evidence, could have made.

...

53. I agree with Mr Cohen that the EAT misunderstood the basis of the Employment Tribunal's criticisms of the disciplinary process. ...

...

56. ... the Employment Tribunal was also entitled to conclude that given in particular the fact that the case turned on the conflict of evidence, the employers ought at least to have tested the evidence of Ms Denton where it was possible to do so. The one objective area where the evidence might have been tested concerned the question whether it was likely that the appellant would have been able to see out of the window or whether the blinds would have been drawn. If there is indeed a strong practice that the window blinds are drawn, as the appellant and Mrs Pemberton both asserted, then this would have cast doubt on this aspect of the complainant's account.

57. It is common experience that if part of a story begins to unravel, other aspects may do so also. Doubts begin to emerge, and the interpretation of actions changes. Mr Powell properly makes the point that it was only at the Employment Tribunal that Mrs Pemberton gave evidence that the blinds would have been closed – this providing an explanation why it would have been futile to see if other members of staff might have seen anything – but the potential significance of this matter was firmly drawn to the appeal body's attention. Mrs Pemberton's evidence merely confirmed that there was potentially considerable force in the appellant's contention on this point.

...

60. In my judgment, therefore, the Employment Tribunal were entitled to find, subject to the section 98A(2) issue, that that the dismissal was unfair for the reasons they gave. This is particularly so given that here was a woman who had given service to the employers over 4 years, apparently without complaint, and there was a real risk that her career would be blighted by this dismissal. It would certainly lead to her deportation and destroy her opportunity for building a career in this country. In my judgment, the case of *A v B*, not specifically referred to in the EAT's judgment, reinforces the justification for the Tribunal's conclusion.

...

73. The second point raised by this appeal concerns the approach of employers to allegations of misconduct where, as in this case, the evidence consists of diametrically conflicting accounts of an alleged incident with no, or very little, other evidence to provide corroboration one way or the other. Employers should remember that they must form a genuine belief on reasonable grounds that the misconduct has occurred. But they are not obliged to believe one employee and to disbelieve another. Sometimes the apparent conflict may not be as fundamental as it seems; it may be that each party is genuinely seeking to tell the truth but is perceiving events from his or her own vantage point. Even where that does not appear to be so, there will be

cases where it is perfectly proper for the employers to say that they are not satisfied that they can resolve the conflict of evidence and accordingly do not find the case proved. That is not the same as saying that they disbelieve the complainant. For example, they may tend to believe that a complainant is giving an accurate account of an incident but at the same time it may be wholly out of character for an employee who has given years of good service to have acted in the way alleged. In my view, it would be perfectly proper in such a case for the employer to give the alleged wrongdoer the benefit of the doubt without feeling compelled to have to come down in favour of on one side or the other.

Etherton LJ and the **Chancellor of the High Court** agreed.

NOTES AND QUESTIONS

1. The Court of Appeal held that the more grave the consequences for an employee, the greater must be the procedural integrity of the employer. The Tribunal's factual findings that the employer's procedure was flawed should not have easily been overturned by the Employment Appeal Tribunal.
2. The Enterprise and Regulatory Reform Act 2013 ss 7–24 introduced a new set of requirements in the Employment Tribunals Act 1996 to start a complaint with ACAS before bringing a claim in an Employment Tribunal. It is hoped that if claims are resolved by ACAS first, then fewer lead to the expense of court. In practice, an employer who has unfairly dismissed an employee often refuses to cooperate at all, or can simply use the opportunity to drag out a hearing. Should this be seen, like Tribunal fees, as another attempt to frustrate access to justice?
3. Could some dismissals raise, not just an important right, but a human right, and if so what procedural requirements should be followed?

R (G) v Governors of X School **[2011] UKSC 30**

G, a 22-year-old sessional music assistant, claimed a right to legal representation under ECHR Art 6 for a disciplinary hearing on sexual misconduct at the X School. In October 2007, he was suspended after allegations of kissing and texting M, a 15-year-old boy. The claimant's solicitor advised him not to participate in the school's investigations until the police did their investigation. In February 2008, the Crown Prosecution Service decided they would take no further action. But the School found there was strong evidence that the allegations were proven, and scheduled a hearing. G was told he could have a trade union or a colleague representing him, but not solicitors. He attended the hearing with his father and refused to answer questions because he said the proceedings were unfair. If he was dismissed for sexual misconduct he would be reported to the Independent Safeguarding Authority (ISA) and put on a 'children's barred list' under the Safeguarding Vulnerable Groups Act 2006 Sch 3, paras 3–4, which would prevent him working with children again. The ISA itself had to decide facts afresh, and could hold hearings though it had not done so before. A barred person could appeal to the Upper Tribunal. After the school hearing, G was summarily dismissed for gross misconduct. He applied for judicial review in May 2008, arguing denial of legal representation breached ECHR Art 6. His appeal was allowed by the High Court and Court of Appeal.

But the Supreme Court allowed the School's appeal, finding that ECHR Art 6 did not apply to the school's proceedings.

Lord Dyson:

32. The issue is whether the governors' decision not to allow the claimant to have legal representation at the disciplinary hearing violated his rights under article 6 of the ECHR which, so far as material, provides:

> 1. In the determination of his civil rights and obligations or of any criminal charge against him, everyone is entitled to a fair and public hearing within a reasonable time by an independent and impartial tribunal established by law. …"

33. It is common ground that the civil right with which we are concerned is the claimant's right to practise his profession as a teaching assistant and to work with children generally. There is no doubt that this right would be directly determined by a decision of the ISA to include him in the children's barred list. He does not, however, contend that the proceedings before the ISA would violate his article 6(1) rights. His case is that (i) the disciplinary proceedings would have such a powerful influence on the ISA proceedings as to engage article 6(1) in both of them and (ii) the consequences of being placed on the children's barred list by the ISA would be so grave for him that the right to a fair hearing vouchsafed by article 6(1) meant that he was entitled to legal representation in both proceedings.

…

68. Thus, in deciding whether article 6(1) applies, the ECtHR takes into account a number of factors including (i) whether the decision in proceedings A is capable of being dispositive of the determination of civil rights in proceedings B or at least causing irreversible prejudice, in effect, by partially determining the outcome of proceedings B; (ii) how close the link is between the two sets of proceedings; (iii) whether the object of the two proceedings is the same; and (iv) whether there are any policy reasons for holding that article 6(1) should not apply in proceedings A. This last factor was taken into account by the ECtHR in Fayed 18 EHRR 393 (see para 43 above).

…

81. I accept, however, that there may occasionally be a case where the critical factor which leads an employer to find that there has been gross misconduct by an employee is the demeanour shown by the employee when giving his or her account to the disciplinary panel. But Mr Drabble does not submit that article 6(1) is engaged at the disciplinary proceedings stage only in order to accommodate such cases. His submission is that the Court of Appeal was correct to hold that findings of fact made by an employer's disciplinary panel are generally and in most cases likely to exercise a profound influence on the decision-making process before the ISA. I do not agree. The guidance notes and case worker guidance have been drafted in meticulous detail. They repeatedly make the point that it is for the ISA to make its own findings of fact on the basis of all the available material. Any case worker who follows the guidance notes and the case worker guidance knows that he or she should not defer to the findings of the referring body. The case worker guidance contains worked examples of evidence evaluation, including examples of both good and bad practice. I see no reason to doubt that case workers do as they are instructed.

82. The lack of an oral hearing does not prevent the ISA from making its own findings of fact. In the present case, it would have to look at all the evidence, including the investigation report and appendices, the notes of the disciplinary hearing, the notes of any appeal hearing before

the governors and the representations of the claimant himself. It would also consider any other information which was made available to it. There is no reason to believe that, contrary to its statutory duty and guidance, the ISA would be unable to form its own view of the facts independently of the view formed by the school authorities and governors.

83. The second feature identified by Laws LJ is that the ISA would be influenced "especially [by the governors'] judgment as to how [the primary] facts should be viewed": [2010] 1 WLR 2218, para 47. In other words, the panel's decision that it is appropriate that the employee should be placed on the barred list would profoundly influence the view taken by the ISA as to the appropriateness of that course. But as Miss Lieven points out, it is difficult to see why this should be so. Save where there is a conviction for a specified offence, a person can be included in a barred list only if the ISA is satisfied that he has engaged in the "relevant conduct" and it appears to the ISA that it is "appropriate" to include the person in the list (paragraph 3(3) of Schedule 3 to the 2006 Act). Stage 3 of the barring process (the case assessment) requires case workers to apply the ISA "structured judgment procedure" which contains a list of detailed questions that they must ask. To assist them in the process, they can obtain specialist advice: see para 6.11 of the guidance notes. The school's disciplinary panel reaches its conclusions as part of an inquiry into a question which is different from that which is addressed by the ISA. More fundamentally, the case workers know that they are required to form their own opinion on the gravity and significance of the facts and on whether it is appropriate to include the referred person in the barred list. There is no reason to suppose that the ISA will be influenced profoundly (or at all) by the school's opinion of how the primary facts should be viewed.

Lord Walker agreed. **Lord Hope** and **Lord Brown** gave concurring opinions.

Lord Kerr:

103. For the reasons given by Lord Dyson, I agree that the Court of Appeal correctly identified the test to be applied on the nature of the connection that is required between various stages of a process in order to determine whether article 6 of the Convention for the Protection of Human Rights and Fundamental Freedoms ("ECHR") is engaged at a point in the process other than that at which the final decision is taken. The premise of the appellants' argument was that the decisive influence that the disciplinary hearing in this case had to have on the decision of the Independent Safeguarding Authority ("ISA") must be determinative if article 6 was to apply to that disciplinary hearing. In other words, for article 6 of ECHR to be in play, the decision on whether G's name was placed on the barred list must, the appellants suggested, be dictated by the outcome of the disciplinary proceedings. Lord Dyson's authoritative survey of the Strasbourg jurisprudence has effectively demonstrated the fallacy of that argument.

104. The centrepiece of the case made on behalf of both the appellant and the Secretary of State has therefore failed. What the majority of this court has decided, however, is that although the Court of Appeal correctly identified the test, it failed to apply it properly. ...
    ...

109. I have said that the hearing before the disciplinary panel is the only remotely adversarial stage of the entire process. Whether ISA has power to hold an oral hearing remains imponderable. ... What is clear is that it has not in the past held one and it may safely be assumed that it will not convene such a hearing in the present case. One must proceed on the basis, therefore, that the only occasion on which oral evidence was or will be given about the extremely serious allegations which form the case against the respondent both on the disciplinary proceedings and the barring proceedings is during the hearing before the panel. In fact, of course, this was not an adversarial proceeding in any real sense for the respondent did not put any questions to

the witnesses who gave evidence against him and refused to answer any questions put to him (because he considered that the proceedings were unfair).

...

113. It is precisely because the disciplinary proceedings provide the only occasion when the competing cases can be presented in direct opposition to each other that legal advice at that point is so crucial. That is the critical time for the testing of the evidence – not merely by observing the demeanour of the witnesses (although that may play its part in the assessment of the reliability of the respective accounts) but by the probing of the allegations against the respondent and the evaluation of the plausibility of his defence to them. It is to be remembered that this young man faced extremely grave accusations. If those were found proved, quite apart from what I consider to be the virtually certain impact that they will have on the barring proceedings, they will place an irretrievable stain on his character and reputation. To recognise his right to be legally represented at that stage, although it may give rise to administrative difficulties for the conduct of disciplinary proceedings, seems to me to be entirely consonant with the proper safeguarding of his article 6 rights. ...

NOTES AND QUESTIONS

1. The Supreme Court's majority held that the school's disciplinary procedure did not 'determine' G's 'civil rights' because the real determination was in the hands of the ISA, which had to decide all facts afresh. Lord Kerr dissented on the ground that the school's disciplinary and fact findings would be influential, and the ISA had no record of actually holding hearings where legal representatives would be heard.
2. The 'civil right' at stake for G was to be able to practice his profession at all. But a question underlying this and all other dismissal cases under the ECHR is why the very fact of a dismissal is not removing a civil right, and therefore requiring (if not a judicial procedure with legal representation) minimum rights to a fair hearing. Article 6 says that in the 'determination of his civil rights and obligations … everyone is entitled to a fair and public hearing within a reasonable time by an independent and impartial tribunal established by law'. Why is the loss of a job not a 'civil right', since loss of a right to pursue a profession anywhere is? Could the Convention evolve?
3. The Charter of Fundamental Rights of the European Union Art 30 says: 'Every worker has the right to protection against unjustified dismissal, in accordance with Community Union law and national laws and practices.' This has yet to have had any significant impact. However its existence makes statements like that in *Harvey on Industrial Relations* (2017) Division DI, authored by Ian Smith, that 'there is no human right to have or remain in employment' flatly incorrect.
4. The Universal Declaration of Human Rights 1948 Art 22 states: 'Everyone, as a member of society, has the right to social security and is entitled to realization, through national effort and international co-operation and in accordance with the organization and resources of each State, of the economic, social and cultural rights indispensable for his dignity and the free development of his personality.' The International Covenant on Economic, Social and Cultural Rights 1966 Art 9 states: 'The States Parties to the present Covenant recognize the right of everyone to social security, including social insurance.' These sources do not explicitly state

that job security is part of social security, but job security is implicit in every scheme of social protection. For example, the understandings behind the UDHR 1948 derive in large measure from the US experience of the New Deal. As part of this, while no federal job security statute was enacted, the Social Security Act of 1935, now partly codified in 29 USC §469, attempted to encourage employers through the social security system to retain workers. This part of social security plays a functionally equivalent role to direct job security measures. It follows that job security is part of the human right to social security.

5. *Vining v London Borough of Wandsworth* [2017] EWCA Civ 1092 held an unfair dismissal claim, not involving privacy, does not engage ECHR Arts 8 or 14.

(4) INJUNCTIONS TO FOLLOW PROCEDURE

As Lord Holt CJ wrote in *Ashby v White* (1703) 92 ER 126, 'it is a vain thing to imagine a right without a remedy; for want of right and want of remedy are reciprocal'. While a full range of remedies are available following a dismissal, a dismissed employee is clearly in a far more vulnerable position after having been removed (and left to protest) than before. In *Edwards* the Supreme Court gave pathbreaking approval to the basic right to an injunction, to compel an employer to follow a contractual disciplinary procedure before dismissal.

Edwards v Chesterfield Royal Hospital NHS Foundation Trust
[2011] UKSC 58

Mr Edwards claimed he was unfairly dismissed as a surgeon without having his contractual disciplinary procedure followed. He was alleged to have performed 'an inappropriate internal examination of a female patient and had then denied that the examination had taken place'. The NHS summarily dismissed him after a disciplinary hearing. One aspect of the case was that he claimed £3.8m in lost earnings and damage to his reputation. The Supreme Court held by a majority that he was not entitled to claim more than the statutory damages cap (see chapter 17(3)(a)). In this respect, Mr Edwards lost badly. However, a second aspect of the claim (less help to Mr Edwards, but of great relevance as a precedent) was that the disciplinary panel was improperly constituted. Mr Edwards's contract required it should have had a legally qualified chair and a medical clinician in his disciplinary hearing (neither of which were present). Mr Edwards argued that if the procedure were done properly, the panel would not have made the findings of fact against him. The Supreme Court held that an injunction could compel the employer to follow a contractual disciplinary procedure.

Lord Dyson (with whom **Lord Walker** agreed):

29. … Parliament has gone further than merely providing that if an employer has applicable disciplinary rules and procedures, they will normally have contractual effect. It has recognised that a breach of disciplinary rules and procedures in the course of a dismissal process is relevant to the question whether the dismissal is unfair. It has from time to time adopted different

statutory mechanisms to encourage or enforce compliance with appropriate disciplinary procedures in order to protect employees from dismissals which are procedurally unfair.

...

37. ... under section 207 of the 1992 Act, any non-compliance with the ACAS Code of Practice relevant to a question arising in unfair dismissal proceedings was to be taken into account in determining that question. Under the [Employment Act 2002], Parliament adopted the direct approach of introducing mandatory dispute resolution procedures and, if a statutory procedure had not been completed for reasons attributable to the employer, providing for the employee to be regarded as unfairly dismissed and for an adjustment of awards in unfair dismissal proceedings. Under the 2008 Act, Parliament reverted to the earlier model (but with modifications) of providing that an unreasonable failure to comply with a relevant Code of Practice may be reflected in the amount of an award of compensation for unfair dismissal. The important point is that in each case, Parliament linked a failure to comply with disciplinary or dismissal procedures with the outcome of unfair dismissal proceedings. To adopt the language of Lord Hoffmann at para 63 of Johnson, the provisions about disciplinary procedure were intended to operate within the scope of the law of unfair dismissal.

38. It follows that, if provisions about disciplinary procedure are incorporated as express terms into an employment contract, they are not ordinary contractual terms agreed by parties to a contract in the usual way. ...

...

44. That is not to say that an employer who starts a disciplinary process in breach of the express terms of the contract of employment is not acting in breach of contract. He plainly is. If that happens, it is open to the employee to seek an injunction to stop the process and/or to seek an appropriate declaration. Miss O'Rourke QC submitted that, if in such a situation there is a breach of contract sufficient to support the grant of an injunction but (for whatever reason) the employee does not obtain an injunction, it is anomalous if the normal common law remedy of damages is in principle not available to him. The short answer to this submission is that an injunction to prevent a threatened unfair dismissal does not cut across the statutory scheme for compensation for unfair dismissal. None of the objections based on the co-existence of inconsistent parallel common law and statutory rights applies. The grant of injunctive or declaratory relief for an actual or threatened breach of contract would not jeopardise the coherence of our employment laws and would not be a recipe for chaos in the way that, as presaged by Lord Millett in Johnson, the recognition of parallel and inconsistent rights to seek compensation for unfair dismissal in the tribunal and damages in the courts would be.

Lord Phillips and **Lord Mance** gave concurring opinions.

Lady Hale:

122. I am uncertain as to how the majority would regard the case of an employee with the contractual right only to be dismissed for cause. Like Lord Kerr, I am puzzled as to how it can be possible for an employee with a contractual right to a particular disciplinary process to enforce that right in advance by injunction but not possible for him to claim damages for its breach after the event. And I am also puzzled why it should make a difference if the right to claim damages is expressly spelled out in the contract.

Lord Kerr (with whom **Lord Wilson** agreed):

137. The Trust accepts that, if the facts as he asserts them are established, Mr Edwards could have applied for an injunction to prevent the tribunal from considering his case. That (rightly

made) concession must proceed on the premise that, on those facts, he already had a cause of action at that stage. On Lord Nicholls' analysis in Eastwood, therefore, if Mr Edwards can establish his case on the pleaded factual assertions, he had a cause of action at law before his dismissal which should remain unimpaired by his subsequent dismissal.

NOTES AND QUESTIONS

1. The Supreme Court held, by a majority of four to three, that Mr Edwards was not in principle entitled to more damages than the statutory cap. However, they were unanimous that he would have been able to apply for an injunction to prevent the NHS constituting a disciplinary panel in breach of contract, and a declaration that it should be properly constituted. The minority would have held that there should be no damages cap to a breach of contract.
2. It would seem this right to an injunction extends to an implied right to a fair hearing from *Chhabra* before any dismissal. It would further seem that in principle that right cannot be contracted out of unless two parties have equal bargaining power, for instance, pursuant to a collective agreement, following the principle of *Autoclenz*.
3. In *Hill v CA Parsons & Co Ltd* [1972] Ch 305 an engineer was dismissed after he joined a trade union against a closed shop rule, at age sixty-three. Sachs LJ granted an injunction for Hill to remain in the job, because he retained mutual trust and confidence with the employer, if not the union.
4. In *Irani v Southampton AHA* [1985] ICR 590 a part-time ophthalmologist successfully applied for an interlocutory injunction, pending a trial, to follow the disciplinary procedure in his health authority's Blue Book, s 33. Mr Irani had only to not attend the hospitals where a senior colleague, Mr Walker, worked, because the dismissal had started with a quarrel with him. For a capability dismissal, see also *Mezey v South West London & St George's Mental Health NHS Trust* [2010] IRLR 512. Do you agree that in large organisations, any dismissal involving personal conflicts present no problems for the award of an injunction?
5. In *Jones v Gwent CC* [1992] IRLR 521 a college lecturer who had complained of sex discrimination, succeeded in an injunction against dismissal for 'gross misconduct', and for a disciplinary procedure to be properly followed. The High Court said, as in the contract, a dismissal for gross misconduct could only happen after such an allegation was upheld by a disciplinary committee.

Problem Question

The Apprentice (2004)

A businessman, who has been bankrupted a number of times, is sitting in a boardroom with a group of apprentice employees. The businessman points an unusually small finger, and tells an employee, who has worked for 12 weeks, 'You're fired'. He then says 'Go'.

Advise the parties under UK law of the possible legal problems in this procedure.

KD Ewing, 'Remedies for Breach of the Contract of Employment' [1993] 52(3) *CLJ* 405
Ewing argues that the remedies for breach of employment contracts was developing too slowly to enable injunctions against wrongful dismissals, and that such developments were desirable. He criticises the 'automatic' theory of contract termination favoured by a dissenting judge in *Gunton*, which 'would make it difficult to develop equitable relief to restrain the employer form acting in breach of a contract which no longer exists'. It appears that, among other things, both of these criticisms were eventually adopted as the Supreme Court in *Edwards* and *Geys* changed the law.

A Döse-Digenopoulos and A Höland, 'Dismissal of Employees in the Federal Republic of Germany' (1985) 48(5) *Modern Law Review* 539
The authors explain German dismissal law in 1985 (although it has not basically changed), as it was experiencing mounting unemployment from the early 1980s recessions (and as government abandoned full employment: see chapter 16). It describes the remedies for unjustified dismissal (enabling reinstatement in just under one in four cases), and the all-important role of employee-elected work councils (*Betriebsräte*) in the dismissal process. While employees can only be dismissed, similar to the UK, for a 'just cause', the work council participates in deciding whether such a cause exists before the employer's decision takes effect. An employer's failure to consult the work council makes a dismissal invalid, and on specific grounds the work council can oppose the dismissal. The court then may decide whether a dismissal was 'socially justifiable', based on personal reasons, conduct, or 'urgent operational requirements'. To give some idea of the scale, in 1984 there were 35,343 elected work councils in the private sector with 190,000 members in West Germany. Although elections do not go through German trade unions, in practice 77 per cent of work council members, and 90 per cent of the work council chairs, are trade union members.

18

Fair Reasons for Dismissal

Even if a procedure before dismissal is fair, the reasons for dismissal might not be. Many oppose the idea that an employer's discretion should be challenged, even if employers who say 'You're fired' are obviously conflicted and irrational. For instance Richard Epstein, 'In Defense of the Contract at Will' (1984) 57 *University of Chicago Law Review* 947 argued an employer should be able to hire, manage and fire, for reasons good or bad, or for no reason at all. He argued that an employer should have the freedom to deal with its business property, or to associate with whoever it wants, as if it is some fundamental right. He also argued that unrestricted freedom to fire at will is good for the economy, and employer power does not increase inequality. Both types of argument have failed to persuade people in almost all democratic countries. First, in principle, an employer's right to property is paid for by taxpayer-funded courts. It is legitimate that property carries responsibility that society sees to be just. Most employers are corporations, where no issue of personal freedom of association arises, and in any case damages rather than an injunction can be awarded if personal liberty is truly at stake (chapter 17(4)). Second, the empirical data strongly suggests that fairness in dismissal promotes prosperity. It is arbitrary exercise of power that damages the economy (chapter 2(3)), while labour's share of income and inequality has in fact been rising. In this way, fair treatment turns out to be good economics after all.

But if all this is true, what standard of review should apply to dismissals? Ideally, the law should try to encourage fair decisions from the outset, to avoid litigation. As Lord Eldon LC once said in a partnership case, a 'Court is not to be required on every Occasion to take the Management of every Playhouse and Brewhouse in the Kingdom' (*Carlen v Drury* (1812) 35 ER 61). The choices in judicial review of dismissals are common to administrative, company, trust and contract law, and the debates repeat themselves. Should a dismissal be 'reasonable', or 'proportionate', in a 'band of reasonable responses' or 'not so unreasonable that no reasonable person could make it'? In the Employment Rights Act (ERA) 1996 s 98(4), it appears Parliament chose the first option: a court should decide if 'the employer acted reasonably or unreasonably' according to 'equity' and the 'substantial merits' of the case. The judiciary, however, has interpreted their role with more latitude. This chapter discusses (1) the right against unjust dismissal at common law and equity, (2) the right to a fair dismissal under statute, (3) remedies after a dismissal.

Introductory texts: Collins ch 8 (172–82). CEM chs 18–19 (various). D&M ch 5 (various).

(1) RIGHT AGAINST UNJUST DISMISSAL

The right against an unjust dismissal in common law and equity has been heavily contested, across the Commonwealth and in the United States, as well as the UK. Historically, there was no consensus on whether the right should exist. Many employees did succeed in claims against unjust dismissal (*Dean v Bennett* extracted below), but others failed (*Addis v Gramophone* noted below). That lack of consensus remained as the ILO Termination of Employment Recommendation 1963 (no 119) urged that dismissals required a 'valid reason' adjudicated by a 'body established under a collective agreement' or a 'neutral body'. Yet in *Ridge v Baldwin* [1964] AC 40, Lord Reid advanced obiter dicta that 'the master can terminate the contract with his servant at any time and for any reason or for none'. He said this even as the House of Lords decided that, in administrative law, the lack of a fair hearing invalidated a police officer's dismissal. In practice, fairness in dismissal was already achieved through collective agreements. After the Donovan Report (1968) Cmnd 3623, ch IX, it took place by the statutory enactment of unfair dismissal rights.

Whether Lord Reid's opinion was right or wrong (or to be more honest, affirming or creating law) a consistent line of cases changed the position. *Wilson v Racher* [1974] ICR 428 (chapter 5(1)(a)) held an employee could claim his (constructive) dismissal was unjust (quite separately from statute) because 'a contract of service imposes upon the parties a duty of mutual respect'. This principle has been consistently affirmed in *Malik v BCCI SA*, in *Johnson v Unisys Ltd*, and in *West London Mental Health NHS Trust v Chhabra* (chapter 5). There is no conflict with statute. The norm precedes statute. It recognises basic equitable principles that apply to every work engagement. The following case articulates them best.

Dean v Bennett (1870) LR 6 Ch 489

Thomas Bennett, a minister of a Baptist chapel in Barnoldswick, Lancashire, claimed he was unjustly dismissed. After being declared bankrupt in 1867, a group of 48 people in his congregation alleged he had 'uttered deliberate falsehoods' and had 'on several occasions been seen drunk'. They held a meeting at which they were outvoted. Then they held another meeting which Bennett argued was illegal, and neither he nor his supporters attended. At that meeting Bennett was purportedly removed as minister. Bennett attempted to take possession of the chapel, and Dean filed an action to restrain him because, argued Dean, Bennett had been validly dismissed. Bennett argued that no valid meeting and no dismissal had taken place. The Court of Chancery held the dismissal was invalid because the meeting had not soundly exercised its discretion.

Lord Hatherley LC:

If this had been a case in which the power of dismissal was not simply and entirely arbitrary, no question could have arisen, because the course taken here was utterly inconsistent with any notion of justice or propriety. They first invite people to bring charges without saying what they are, and they then state in this vague fashion that the charges are established when the person supposed to be criminated has not heard what any one of the charges is. No one would expect to find that such a course had been adopted in any assembly of English people, who are accustomed in some degree to the ordinary principles of justice, though they may not have any accurate idea of its form; and the only point I have to consider is, how far the *Darlington School Case* 12 LJ (QB) 124; 14 LJ (QB) 67 goes, and whether by it the Court is compelled to hold that a resolution come to in this manner was legitimate and operative.

That case undoubtedly does create great difficulty. ... The Court there laid great weight on the finding that the minister was unfit, and said that there was no traverse of the sound discretion; and if the meeting had a sound discretion, and if they found that he was unfit, in addition to the other things that they had found, there was no fault in the decision they had come to, and the decision must be upheld.

I cannot say that I am altogether satisfied with that reasoning, and I do not know how far that case was determined upon the point which arose upon the pleadings. If a number of reasons are assigned by those who are called upon to vote on a given subject, and those reasons are not merely expressed as arguments in the course of a debate, but are averred as those upon which the decision is founded, although the facts have never been investigated, then it seems clear that the proceedings have been altogether erroneous, and it cannot be said that we have got the true mind and judgment of the body.

Upon the whole, I do not feel myself so bound by that case as to hold here that a discretion has been exercised by a meeting which, on charges mentioned for the first time, the person charged not being present, comes to a vague general finding that he has been guilty of falsehood and drunkenness. Although they undoubtedly add unfitness, I cannot find that they have arrived at a sound judgment on this subject, or have exercised any discretion at all in such a strange and wholly irregular meeting. I think that they acted very oppressively, and in a manner which ought not to be in any way sanctioned or assisted by this Court interfering by injunction.

Now, I do not think it enough, on the occasion of the dismissal of a minister, to bring at the first meeting such vague charges, and then to say merely that the resolutions passed at the first meeting were to be confirmed at the second. It is not like the case of a board of directors, who have proper books provided and ordered by law to be kept so that every one can go and ascertain what has been done. It does not appear that there were proper books or any proper officer to keep them. In that state of circumstances they are called upon to confirm a resolution passed on a certain day without being told what that resolution was; and when I look at the deed and at the careful provisions as to the dismissal of the minister, I do not think this a sufficient compliance with the deed. The whole matter was to have been reconsidered at the second meeting, and the persons entitled to be present ought to have been told what they were asked to do.

Feeling, then, as I do, some doubt as to the soundness of the *Darlington School Case*, and that the conduct towards the Defendant has been oppressive, I do not consider myself fettered by that case; and, agreeing, as I do, with the Vice-Chancellor on the second point in this case, I can only dismiss this appeal with costs.

NOTES AND QUESTIONS

1. The Lord Chancellor holds that Bennett was unjustly dismissed, because the meeting had neither 'arrived at a sound judgment' nor 'exercised any discretion at all in such a strange and wholly irregular meeting'. Equity therefore recognised both a requirement for substantive and procedural fairness in dismissal. 'English people' (and presumably we can now say all people) 'are accustomed in some degree to the ordinary principles of justice'.

2.   The law gives employers 'discretion', but this does not mean 'arbitrary power' as the term is sometimes used colloquially. Discretion in law means reasoned and justified use of one's power of decision.-making faculties. According to *Rooke's Case* (1598) 77 ER 209, 201: '[D]iscretion is a science or understanding to discern between falsity and truth, between wrong and right, between shadows and substance, between equity and colourable glosses and pretences, and not to do according to their wills and private affections.'

3.   Admittedly, *Dean v Bennett*, as it concerns the dismissal of a minister, could be argued to be confined to decisions about associations, rather than an ordinary employment contract. However this would seem erroneous, given that the Lord Chancellor's comments were general in nature. By contrast, in *President of the Methodist Conference v Preston* [2013] UKSC 29 the majority of the Supreme Court held a minister was not an employee, able to pursue unfair dismissal rights under ERA 1996 s 230 because he had no contract, and apparently the status of his office was solely determined by the church's constitution. Baroness Hale, dissenting, said: 'Everything about this arrangement looks contractual.' Whichever position one prefers, Preston could have claimed that at common law and equity she had a right not to be unjustly dismissed.

4.   The principle of just dismissal should be seen as fundamental to the common law's regulation of corporate discretion, whether there is a contract, trust or other association. In *R v Richardson* (1758) 97 ER 426, bailiffs of the Corporation of Ipswich purported to remove the elected portmen from office, and then hold an election where another bailiff, Richardson, was appointed in their place. Lord Mansfield held there was no power to remove the portmen, because the 'amotion' was not effected by the corporation, and there was no good cause. Lord Mansfield said that if a director was to be removed, 'where the offence is merely against his duty as a corporator, he can only be tried for it by the corporation'. See also *Lord Bruce's Case* (1728) 93 ER 870 and *Baggs Case* (1615) 81 ER 448. Directors of corporations could only be removed for reasonable cause, but a corporation's meeting (as a neutral body) would have the competence to define what is reasonable: *Inderwick v Snell* (1850) 42 ER 83, 85–87, per Lord Commissioner Langdale. See further E McGaughey, *Participation in Corporate Governance* (2014) ch 4.

5.   While *Dean v Bennett* was a case in equity, and took place before the Supreme Court of Judicature Act 1873 s 25(11) merged equity with common law courts, there is no doubt that the principle of fair dismissal exists also at common law. In *Pearce v Forster* (1886) 17 QBD 536, Pearce unsuccessfully claimed that he was wrongfully dismissed from his job as a clerk for Foster's stockbroking firm, when it was found he engaged in large-scale securities dealings for clients. His contract was silent about when he could be dismissed. Lord Esher MR said: '[T]he question is, whether the breach of duty is a good ground for dismissal.' He said the 'rule of law' is that if an employee 'does anything incompatible with the due or faithful discharge of his duty' there is 'a right to dismiss'. Put the other way, there is no right to dismiss when there is no 'good ground'.

6.   In *Clouston & Co Ltd v Corry* [1906] AC 122, the Privy Council advised that it was a question for the jury whether an agent, who bought barley for a

New Zealand firm, and who was dismissed after a year and two months, was dismissed wrongfully. Mr Corry was said to have made purchases against the company directors' wishes, and was arrested for being drunk outside work. Lord James stated: 'There is no fixed rule of law defining the degree of misconduct which will justify dismissal. … misconduct inconsistent with the fulfilment of the express or implied conditions of service will justify dismissal.' There may be, he said, 'an isolated act committed under circumstances of festivity and in no way connected with or affecting the employer's business. In such a case the question whether the misconduct proved establishes the right to dismiss the servant must depend upon facts – and is a question of fact. If this be so, the questions raised in the present case had to be tried by the jury.' Although today's Tribunals substitute for a jury, his Lordship clearly proceeds on the assumption that agents (not just employees) are entitled to a fair process, including an impartial hearing.

7. However in *Addis v Gramophone Co Ltd* [1909] AC 488 the House of Lords held that Mr Addis, a manager in Calcutta for Gramophone Co Ltd, was unable to claim £600 to reflect the stigma or, as Lord Collins (dissenting) put it, 'the discredit thus thrown upon him' by the dismissal. Lord James (it seems adjusting his position from *Corry*) said there should be no damages 'in consequence of the manner of dismissal'. *Addis* is ambiguous about whether this referred to merely upset or stigma, or also to economic loss. In any event, *Malik v BCCI SA* (chapter 5) reversed *Addis* insofar as there was an bar to stigma damages.
8. *R v Richardson, Dean v Bennett, Corry* and other major authorities were no discussed in *Addis v Gramophone Ltd*. It appears that because they were not raised, the principles of equity in those cases override opinions on the facts of *Addis* about the law.
9. The common law right against unjust dismissal was revisited in *Johnson* (facts in chapter 3).

Johnson v Unisys Ltd [2001] UKHL 13

Lord Hoffmann:

42. My Lords, in the face of this express provision that Unisys was entitled to terminate Mr Johnson's employment on four weeks notice without any reason, I think it is very difficult to imply a term that the company should not do so except for some good cause and after giving him a reasonable opportunity to demonstrate that no such cause existed.

43. On the other hand, I do not say that there is nothing which, consistently with such an express term, judicial creativity could do to provide a remedy in a case like this. In *Wallace v United Grain Growers Ltd* (1997) 152 DLR (4th) 1, 44–48, McLachlin J (in a minority judgment) said that the courts could imply an obligation to exercise the power of dismissal in good faith. That did not mean that the employer could not dismiss without cause. The contract entitled him to do so. But in so doing, he should be honest with the employee and refrain from untruthful, unfair or insensitive conduct. He should recognise that an employee losing his or her job was exceptionally vulnerable and behave accordingly. For breach of this implied obligation, McLachlin J would have awarded the employee, who had been dismissed in brutal circumstances, damages for mental distress and loss of reputation and prestige.

44. My Lords, such an approach would in this country have to circumvent or overcome the obstacle of *Addis v Gramophone Co Ltd* [1909] AC 488, in which it was decided that an employee cannot recover damages for injured feelings, mental distress or damage to his reputation, arising out of the manner of his dismissal. Speaking for myself, I think that, if this task was one which I felt called upon to perform, I would be able to do so. In *Mahmud v Bank of Credit and Commerce International SA* [1998] AC 20, 51 Lord Steyn said that the true ratio of *Addis's case* was the damages were recoverable only for loss caused by a breach of contract, not for loss caused by the manner of its breach. As McLachlin J said in the passage I have quoted, the only loss caused by a wrongful dismissal flows from a failure to give proper notice or make payment in lieu. Therefore, if wrongful dismissal is the only cause of action, nothing can be recovered for mental distress or damage to reputation. On the other hand, if such damage is loss flowing from a breach of another implied term of the contract, Addis's case does not stand in the way. That is why in *Mahmud's case* itself, damages were recoverable for financial loss flowing from damage to reputation caused by a breach of the implied term of trust and confidence.

...

46. It may be a matter of words, but I rather doubt whether the term of trust and confidence should be pressed so far. In the way it has always been formulated, it is concerned with preserving the continuing relationship which should subsist between employer and employee. So it does not seem altogether appropriate for use in connection with the way that relationship is terminated. If one is looking for an implied term, I think a more elegant solution is McLachlin J's implication of a separate term that the power of dismissal will be exercised fairly and in good faith. But the result would be the same as that for which Mr Johnson contends by invoking the implied term of trust and confidence. As I have said, I think it would be possible to reach such a conclusion without contradicting the express term that the employer is entitled to dismiss without cause.

Lord Millett:

71. In *Addis's case* the House of Lords treated a contract of employment as an ordinary commercial contract terminable at will by either party provided only that sufficient notice was given in accordance with the terms of the contract. This was the classical approach to such contracts which the House of Lords was content to confirm more than half a century later. In *Ridge v Baldwin* [1964] AC 40, 65 Lord Reid observed that an employer can terminate the contract of employment at any time and for any reason or for none. It follows that the question whether damages are recoverable does not depend on whether the employer had a good reason for dismissing the employee, or had heard him in his own defence, or had acted fairly towards him: it depends on whether the dismissal was in breach of contract. In *Malloch v Aberdeen Corporation* [1971] 1 WLR 1578, 1581 Lord Reid restated the position:

"At common law a master is not bound to hear his servant before he dismisses him. He can act unreasonably or capriciously if he so chooses but the dismissal is valid. The servant has no remedy unless the dismissal is in breach of contract and then the servant's only remedy is damages for breach of contract."

72. The common law, which is premised on party autonomy, treated the employer and the employee as free and equal parties to the contract of employment. Each had the right, granted by the contract itself, to bring the contract to an end in accordance with its terms. But by 1971 there was a widespread feeling, shared by both sides of industry, that the legal position was unsatisfactory. In reality there was no comparison between the consequences for an employer if the employee terminated his employment and the consequences for an employee if he was dismissed. Many people build their lives round their jobs and plan their future in the

expectation that they will continue. For many workers dismissal is a disaster. In 1964 the Government announced that it would discuss with representatives of employers and trade unions the provision of procedures to give employees effective safeguards against arbitrary dismissal. In 1968 the Royal Commission on Trade Unions and Employers' Associations under the Chairmanship of Lord Donovan reported that it was urgently necessary for employees to be given better protection against unfair dismissal and recommended the establishment of statutory machinery to achieve this. ...

...

77. But the common law does not stand still. It is in a state of continuous judicial development in order to reflect the changing perceptions of the community. Contracts of employment are no longer regarded as purely commercial contracts entered into between free and equal agents. It is generally recognised today that "work is one of the defining features of people's lives"; that "loss of one's job is always a traumatic event"; and that it can be "especially devastating" when dismissal is accompanied by bad faith: see *Wallace v United Grain Growers Ltd* (1997) 152 DLR (4th) 1, 33 per Iacobucci J. This change of perception is, of course, partly due to the creation by Parliament of the statutory right not to be unfairly dismissed. If this right had not existed, however, it is possible that the courts would have fashioned a similar remedy at common law, though they would have proceeded by implying appropriate terms into the contract of employment. It would have been a major step to subject the employer's right to terminate the relationship on proper notice to an obligation not to exercise the right in bad faith, and a still greater step to subject it to an obligation not to exercise it without reasonable cause: (a difficult distinction, but one drawn by McLachlin J in *Wallace's* case, at p 44). Even so, these are steps which, in the absence of the statutory right, the courts might have been prepared to take, though there would have been a powerful argument for leaving the reform to Parliament. If the courts had taken the step themselves, they could have awarded common law damages for unfair dismissal consistently with *Addis's* case [1909] AC 488, because such damages would be awarded for the breach of an implied but independently actionable term (as in *Mahmud's* case [1998] AC 20) and not for wrongful dismissal. But the courts would have been faced with the difficult task of distinguishing between the mental distress and other non-pecuniary injury consequent upon the unfairness of the dismissal (for which the employer would be liable) and the similar injury consequent upon the dismissal itself (for which he would not). In practice, they would probably have been reduced to awarding conventional sums by way of general damages much as the industrial tribunals do.

78. I agree with Lord Hoffmann that it would not have been appropriate to found the right on the implied term of trust and confidence which is now generally imported into the contract of employment. This is usually expressed as an obligation binding on both parties not to do anything which would damage or destroy the relationship of trust and confidence which should exist between them. But this is an inherent feature of the relationship of employer and employee which does not survive the ending of the relationship. The implied obligation cannot sensibly be used to extend the relationship beyond its agreed duration. Moreover, manipulating it for such a purpose would be unrealistic. An employer who summarily dismisses an employee usually does so because, rightly or wrongly, he no longer has any trust or confidence in him, and the real issue is: whose fault is that? That is why reinstatement or re-engagement is effected in only a tiny proportion of the cases that come before the industrial tribunals.

79. But the courts might well have developed the law in a different way by imposing a more general obligation upon an employer to treat his employee fairly even in the manner of his dismissal. They could not, of course, have overridden any express terms of the contract or have held the dismissal itself to be invalid. As in the case of the statutory right, employers would probably have responded by introducing their own procedures of complaint and warning before eventual dismissal. But there would have been this difference; they would surely

have taken care to incorporate such procedures into the contract of employment so that an employee who was dismissed in accordance with the procedure laid down in his contract could not claim damages for breach of an implied term.

Lord Bingham agreed with **Lord Hoffmann** and **Lord Millett**. **Lord Nicholls** and **Lord Steyn** gave shorter judgments concurring with the result.

NOTES AND QUESTIONS

1. Both Lord Hoffmann and Lord Millett doubt that UK employment would be 'at-will' if it were not for statutory reform. Lord Hoffmann explicitly says that he 'would be able to' overcome any barrier represented by *Addis* to award damages for dismissal at common law. They accept that the common law has probably not 'stood still' since statute required fair reasons for dismissal. Lord Millett suggests that mutual trust and confidence might not be the best foundation for such a rule, but whatever one calls it, both acknowledge the right against unjust dismissal would be there. On the facts of *Johnson* there was no need to do so.
2. In making these remarks, their Lordships had not had the benefit of submissions on the effect of *Wilson v Racher*. This matters (1) for people who are dismissed before period to qualify for a Tribunal claim, (2) for the event (unlikely, but not unthinkable) that unfair dismissal rules are repealed.
3. Lord Millett soon restated a major exception (therefore suggesting the rule) for directors of companies. Company directors are classified in law as employees, but the default standards of a fair dismissal are specifically, and precisely, defined in the Companies Act 2006 ss 168–69. Company directors in UK law can be dismissed by the company's general meeting of members on a simple majority vote, with 28 days' notice, and a right for the director to circulate arguments that she or he should stay. In a Bermuda case, *Reda v Flag Ltd* [2002] UKPC 38, Lord Millett advised that an implied term based on mutual trust and confidence could not circumscribe an express contractual power to dismiss the director. This should be seen as an appropriate decision for directors, who might legitimately bargain for different contractual rights, in stark contrast to ordinary employees.
4. *R (Shoesmith) v Ofsted* [2011] EWCA Civ 642 held that it was contrary to 'natural justice' principles of administrative law for the former Secretary of State for Children, Schools and Families, Ed Balls, to have dismissed Sharon Shoesmith, the Director of Children's Services at Haringey Council, after a campaign by *The Sun*, a publication which many people consider to be 'news'. While Shoesmith was director, a baby referred to as 'P' was repeatedly beaten, but Haringey's social services did not take the child away from its mother and abusive boyfriend (who was later found guilty of raping another child). Nevertheless, the Court of Appeal held that summary dismissal was unfair. It is quite absurd to think that employees of public bodies are entitled to different standards of justice at work to those of private bodies. See the *Civil Rights Cases*, 109 US 3 (1883) per Harlan J.
5. As well as a general right against unjustified dismissal in CFREU art 30, there is guidance for international standards in the ILO Termination of Employment Convention 1982 (c 158). This has not yet been adopted by the UK, but gives a structured indication of norms that can be expected.

6. It is submitted that the right against unjustified dismissal at common law and equity is not the same as the statutory norm which is about to follow. An unjust dismissal exhibits bad faith or amounts to a repudiatory breach of contract. The burden of proof lies on the claimant to establish evidence of bad faith. This is different to successful statutory cases where there has been a procedure followed, and yet the decision is still found to be unreasonable. Facts akin to *Wilson v Racher* would suffice. The essential point to recognise that employers that abuse their power cannot escape the consequences of their actions. The claim can be made in an Employment Tribunal for breach of contract, and also in the High Court.

(2) FAIRNESS OF DISMISSAL

A statutory right against an unfair dismissal was introduced by the Industrial Relations Act 1971, and goes beyond common law rights. The common law right prohibits dismissals only for conduct that amounts to a repudiatory breach of the contract. In length of service, there are no qualifications. In scope, every worker or employee is protected. But the employer's conduct must have been 'sufficiently serious' to be a repudiatory breach.

By contrast, the statutory right to a fair dismissal enables full judicial review of the reasonableness of employer's decision (chapter 18(2)(b)–(c)) but damages are limited by a somewhat arbitrary cap (chapter 18(3)(a)). The basic norm ERA 1996 s 94: 'An employee has the right not to be unfairly dismissed by his employer.' This right, subject to ss 95–110, opens a more searching enquiry. However (a) there are qualifications or limitations for the statutory right, (b) there is considerable debate over the appropriate standard of review, (c) there is flexibility deciding the conduct or capability which justifies dismissal. Dismissal for redundancy is considered in chapter 19.

(a) Qualifications for the Statutory Right

To qualify for the statutory right to a fair dismissal, there are four main hurdles. First, one must be an employee, not just a worker (see chapter 3(2)(d)). Second, the employee by their 'effective date of termination' (s 97) must have worked for 'two years' to qualify for the statutory right (s 108). But, there is no qualifying period if the employee has attempted to assert another statutory right, and has been victimised for it: the dismissal will be 'automatically' unfair (s 108(2)–(5)). Third, an employee usually has 'three months' to bring a claim in a Tribunal (s 111). Fourth, an employee must have worked continuously, or without more than temporary cessations of work (s 212).

Employment Rights Act 1996 ss 97, 108, 111 and 212

97 Effective date of termination.
(1) Subject to the following provisions of this section, in this Part "the effective date of termination"—
  (a) in relation to an employee whose contract of employment is terminated by notice, whether given by his employer or by the employee, means the date on which the notice expires,

(b) in relation to an employee whose contract of employment is terminated without notice, means the date on which the termination takes effect, and

(c) in relation to an employee who is employed under a limited-term contract which terminates by virtue of the limiting event without being renewed under the same contract, means the date on which the termination takes effect.

(2) Where—

(a) the contract of employment is terminated by the employer, and

(b) the notice required by section 86 to be given by an employer would, if duly given on the material date, expire on a date later than the effective date of termination (as defined by subsection (1)),

for the purposes of sections 108(1), 119(1) and 227(3) the later date is the effective date of termination.

...

108 Qualifying period of employment.

(1) Section 94 does not apply to the dismissal of an employee unless he has been continuously employed for a period of not less than two years ending with the effective date of termination.

...

111 Complaints to employment tribunal.

(1) A complaint may be presented to an employment tribunal against an employer by any person that he was unfairly dismissed by the employer.

(2) Subject to the following provisions of this section, an employment tribunal shall not consider a complaint under this section unless it is presented to the tribunal—

(a) before the end of the period of three months beginning with the effective date of termination, or

(b) within such further period as the tribunal considers reasonable in a case where it is satisfied that it was not reasonably practicable for the complaint to be presented before the end of that period of three months.

...

212 Weeks counting in computing period.

(1) Any week during the whole or part of which an employee's relations with his employer are governed by a contract of employment counts in computing the employee's period of employment.

(3) Subject to subsection (4), any week (not within subsection (1)) during the whole or part of which an employee is—

(a) incapable of work in consequence of sickness or injury,

(b) absent from work on account of a temporary cessation of work, or

(c) absent from work in circumstances such that, by arrangement or custom, he is regarded as continuing in the employment of his employer for any purpose,

counts in computing the employee's period of employment.

(4) Not more than twenty-six weeks count under subsection (3)(a) between any periods falling under subsection (1).

NOTES AND QUESTIONS

1. Section 97 establishes the 'effective date of termination' as the point where one's notice period legitimately expires, not simply when an employer purports to terminate the contract. Subsections 97(3)–(5) are analogous provisions for notice

by employees. Practically this matters to qualify for dismissal rights (s 108), and for the three-month time limit to bring a claim in tribunal (s 111). Suppose you have worked for one year, eleven months and twenty-five days, and your employer says 'You're fired' on 1 April, thinking that it has escaped the two-year qualifying period. Unless a summary dismissal is justified (chapter 17(2)), you are entitled to one week's notice. By the end of your one week's notice, you will have worked for two years and two days. You have the right to claim unfair dismissal in a tribunal. You have three months from the 8 April to do so.

2. The Donovan Report (1968) Cmnd 3623, ss 555–56 recommended no qualifying period to claim unfair dismissal, but to take into account a contract's own probation terms. However, as it was introduced by a new Conservative government, the Industrial Relations Act 1971 ss 22–33 set a qualifying period for fair dismissal rights at **two years**. When Labour regained power the Trade Union and Labour Relations Act 1974 Sch 1, para 10 reduced the period to **twenty-six weeks**. When the Conservatives came back, it was raised by the Unfair Dismissal (Variation of Qualifying Period) Order 1979 to **one year**, and then **two years** for businesses with under twenty employees by the Employment Act 1980, and all businesses in 1985. While litigation leading to *R (Seymour-Smith) v Secretary of State for Employment* [2000] UKHL 12 (at chapter 13(1)(a) on the discrimination impact of changing the qualifying period) was fought, the new Labour government's Unfair Dismissal and Statement of Reasons for Dismissal (Variation of Qualifying Period) Order 1999, Art 3 put the period back to **one year**. The next Conservative government raised the period again, with the Unfair Dismissal and Statement of Reasons for Dismissal (Variation of Qualifying Period) Order 2012, to **two years**. This happened without primary legislation because the qualifying period can be changed by the Secretary of State under ERA 1996 s 209. It was like 'a game of political ping-pong. Few laws have bounced back and forth over such a long time without any kind of principled conclusion having emerged', E McGaughey, 'Unfair Dismissal Reform: Political Ping-Pong with Equality?' [2012] *Equal Opportunities Review*, issue 226. Since there is no qualifying period for the common law right, why should there be any for statutory fair dismissal at all?

3. Like the common law right, some dismissals have no qualifying period. These are listed in s 108(2)–(5). Dismissal will be unfair if it is for activities relating to:
   - undertaking jury service, s 98B
   - childcare rights and emergency time off, s 99 (chapter 6(3))
   - health and safety activities, s 100
   - refusing as a shop or betting worker to work or do more hours on Sundays, ss 101–ZA
   - refusing to break rights under the Working Time Regulations 1998, s 101A (chapter 6(1))
   - acting as an occupational pension trustee, s 102 (chapter 5(4))
   - being any employee representative or candidate, s 103 (chapter 10)
   - making any protected disclosure, s 103A
   - asserting statutory rights under the ERA 1996, TULRCA 1992, etc, s 104
   - for anything connected to minimum wage rights or prosecutions, s 104A

- rights related to the Tax Credits Act 2002 (though this is mostly repealed), s 104B
- rights relating to flexible working, s 104C
- rights relating to automatic pension enrolment, s 104D
- study and training, s 104E
- blacklisting, 104F
- employee shareholder status, s 104G
- claims relating to redundancy, s 105
- the Transnational Information and Consultation of Employees Regulations 1999
- part-time, fixed-term work, or agency work, see chapter 15
- European Public Limited-Liability Company Regulations 2004 reg 42
- Information and Consultation of Employees Regulations 2004 reg 30
- occupational pension scheme consultation, OPPS(CEMA)R 2006 Sch, para 5
- European Cooperative Society (Involvement of Employees) Regulations 2006 reg 31
- Companies (Cross-Border Mergers) Regulations 2007 regs 46–47
- European Public Ltd-Liability Company (Employee Involvement) (GB) Regs 2009
- Agency Worker Regulations 2010 reg 17
- for political opinions or affiliation
- for membership of a reserve force under the Armed Forces Act 2006 s 374
- *and* the qualifying period is *one month* if dismissal is for taking sick leave, s 64(2)

4. As chapter 4(1)(a) explained, in *Ford v Warwickshire CC* [1983] ICR 273 the House of Lords held that under what is now s 212, a lecturer stopping work over the summer holidays counted as a 'temporary cessation of work', even though it lasted months. If there was no qualifying period for the statutory right, this would be unnecessary.

5. In *Welton v Deluxe Retail Ltd (t/a Madhouse)* [2013] ICR 428, Mr Welton success-fully claimed unfair dismissal from Deluxe Retail Ltd, after he had been shifted between their 'Madhouse' stores. He worked for around a year at their Sheffield store until it closed on 23 February 2010, but was offered a new position at their Blackpool store and started on 8 March 2010. He quit and claimed constructive unfair dismissal around nine months later. The Tribunal held he had no sufficient continuity and could not claim, because they were two different jobs. Langstaff J in the Employment Appeal Tribunal reversed this and affirmed that he both had sufficient continuity, and that there was only a temporary cessation of work in the contract with his employer.

6. As chapter 3(1) explained, in *Gisda Cyf v Barratt* [2010] UKSC 41 the Supreme Court held the three-month time limit in ERA 1996 s 111 to bring a claim only starts running once an employer actually informs an employee of a dismissal, not merely when an employee might be able to open a letter. This differs to the posi-tion for notices in commercial contracts, a context which Lord Kerr said must be 'segregated intellectually' from statutory rights.

(b) Reasonableness

Once it is established that an employee qualifies for the right to bring a statutory claim, a Tribunal must review whether a dismissal was reasonable.

Employment Rights Act 1996 s 98

98 General.
(1) In determining for the purposes of this Part whether the dismissal of an employee is fair or unfair, it is for the employer to show—
    (a) the reason (or, if more than one, the principal reason) for the dismissal, and
    (b) that it is either a reason falling within subsection (2) or some other substantial reason of a kind such as to justify the dismissal of an employee holding the position which the employee held.
(2) A reason falls within this subsection if it—
    (a) relates to the capability or qualifications of the employee for performing work of the kind which he was employed by the employer to do,
    (b) relates to the conduct of the employee,
    (c) is that the employee was redundant, or
    (d) is that the employee could not continue to work in the position which he held without contravention (either on his part or on that of his employer) of a duty or restriction imposed by or under an enactment.
(3) In subsection (2)(a)—
    (a) "capability", in relation to an employee, means his capability assessed by reference to skill, aptitude, health or any other physical or mental quality, and
    (b) "qualifications", in relation to an employee, means any degree, diploma or other academic, technical or professional qualification relevant to the position which he held.
(4) Where the employer has fulfilled the requirements of subsection (1), the determination of the question whether the dismissal is fair or unfair (having regard to the reason shown by the employer)—
    (a) depends on whether in the circumstances (including the size and administrative resources of the employer's undertaking) the employer acted reasonably or unreasonably in treating it as a sufficient reason for dismissing the employee, and
    (b) shall be determined in accordance with equity and the substantial merits of the case.

NOTES AND QUESTIONS

1. Upon a claim for unfair dismissal, s 98(1) requires an employer to state the reason for dismissal. This must be for conduct, capability, redundancy or some other substantial reason (s 98(1)(b)–(3)).
2. In *Abernethy v Mott, Hay and Anderson* [1974] ICR 323 the Court of Appeal held that an employer who told a civil engineer he was dismissed for 'redundancy' could subsequently argue that its real reason was capability. Mott, Hay and Anderson had tried to make Mr Abernethy accept a secondment at the Greater London Council, but when he refused, gave him redundancy pay of £850, plus £750 out of favour. Abernethy claimed the dismissal was unfair, but the employer succeeded in showing the dismissal was for incapability. It appeared they used the word

'redundancy' by mistake when they really meant incapability. Lord Denning MR said: 'The principal reason was his inflexibility, his lack of adaptability and his limited potential.'

3. In contrast, if someone is really told they are redundant, and the employer means it but is simply trying to be 'nice', and does not ever say that there is any problem with their conduct or their capability to do the job, the employer is presumably acting unfairly. The employee never has warning or a chance to improve, as the ACAS Code on disciplinaries requires: see chapter 17(3).

4. In *Smith v Glasgow City DC* [1987] ICR 796 Mr Smith successfully claimed he was unfairly dismissed from the council's buildings and works department. The employer said he was dismissed because (a) he unduly expanded the workforce, (b) he failed to respond to numerous legitimate requests for information, and (c) he engaged in expenditure and improvement without written authority. The employers did not say which of these was the principal reason, or distinguish between them. The Tribunal held (b) was not established, but he was dismissed fairly anyway. The House of Lords held that the Tribunal was wrong, and should have established the principal reason. Moreover, it must be proven that this reason is true. Lord Mackay said unless it was clear that reason (b) 'was not treated by the council as the reason which the council treated as sufficient for dismissing Mr Smith or that it formed no important part of the reason which the council treated as sufficient for dismissing Mr Smith, I am of opinion that the tribunal erred in law'. Could the employer state, and prove, that three, or six reasons were individually and simultaneously grounds for dismissing an employee?

5. Section 98(4) says a Tribunal must decide whether 'the employer acted reasonably or unreasonably'. This appears to mandate, straightforwardly, that a court should substitute its decision on what is reasonable (following social standards not private opinions) for the employer's decision.

6. However, in *British Leyland UK Ltd v Swift* [1981] IRLR 91, Mr Swift claimed that after eighteen years' work he was unfairly dismissed, after he was convicted of theft. A policeman stopped Mr Swift, while driving a Land Rover, and checked his 'tax disc', or the Road Fund Licence. It transpired it was taken from his company, British Leyland, and he pleaded guilty to fraudulent use. The Tribunal held that his dismissal was too severe a penalty for the misconduct, given long years of service. The Court of Appeal held the dismissal was fair. Lord Denning MR said as follows: 'The correct test is: Was it reasonable for the employers to dismiss him? If no reasonable employer would have dismissed him, then the dismissal was unfair. But if a reasonable employer might reasonably have dismissed him, then the dismissal was fair. It must be remembered that in all these cases there is a band of reasonableness, within which one employer might reasonably take one view: another quite reasonably take a different view.' Do you agree that this appears to say three contradictory things at once? Is the test (1) whether an employer was 'reasonable', (2) if 'no reasonable employer would have dismissed' or (3) in a 'band of reasonableness'?

7. In *Iceland Frozen Foods Ltd v Jones* [1983] ICR 17 (EAT) an employee claimed he was unfairly dismissed as a warehouse distribution manager in Deeside, Wales, after being accused of failing to lock a door, and taking part in a 'go-slow' strategy to earn more overtime pay. The Tribunal held the test was whether the dismissal

was 'so unreasonable that [no] reasonable employer would have decided to dismiss'. Browne-Wilkinson J remitted the case to another Tribunal, holding that the correct test was whether an employer's decision fell within 'a band of reasonable responses to the employee's conduct'.

8. The 'band' approach could sensibly be seen as a counterpart to that in *Bolam v Friern Hospital Management Committee* [1957] 1 WLR 582, that no negligence liability exists where a 'responsible body of medical opinion' would have acted similarly. See S Deakin and G Morris, *Labour Law* (5th edn 2009) 446. However, in tort law itself, *Bolam* was discarded by *Montgomery v Lanarkshire Health Board* [2015] UKSC 11 as the Supreme Court held that, in the context of patients' right to give fully informed consent, the *Bolam* test unjustifiably enabled 'divergent attitudes among doctors as to the degree of respect owed to their patients'.

9. In *Haddon v Van Den Bergh Foods Ltd* [1999] ICR 1150 (EAT) the outgoing President of the Employment Appeal Tribunal, Morrison J said Tribunals should decide if dismissals are reasonable or not 'without embellishment'. This led to an 'expedited' hearing in *Madden*.

HSBC Bank plc v Madden [2000] EWCA Civ 3030

In two joined cases, first, Mr Madden claimed he was unfairly dismissed from HSBC after three debit cards went missing from the Enfield Town and then Palmers Green branches where he worked. A 'Nixdorf' computer system was used to look up the status of the cards at times when, said HSBC, only Madden was there. The cards were used to obtain goods by deception. Madden was arrested but not charged, but the bank summarily dismissed him. The Tribunal and the Employment Appeal Tribunal found the dismissal was unfair. HSBC appealed.

Second, Mr Foley was dismissed from the Post Office for 'unauthorised absence from duty for part of a duty on 16 May 1997'. That evening, Mr Foley asked to go home at 7.30pm instead of 11pm because his wife had a 'bad state of nerves'. But a co-worker reported seeing him at the pub at 8.47pm. He argued, supported by his wife, that he had gone to the pub to phone for a taxi, but was not believed and was dismissed, even though he had a 'clean conduct record'. The Tribunal and the Employment Appeal Tribunal found his dismissal was fair.

The Court of Appeal held test was whether these decisions by the employers were in a band of reasonable responses. So, both Madden and Foley were fairly dismissed.

Mummery LJ:

A reminder of the fundamental constitutional difference between the interpretation of legislation, which is a judicial function, and the enactment and amendment of legislation, which is a parliamentary function, is required in view of the number of occasions on which reference was made in the submissions to a "judicial gloss" on the legislation. As Lord Nicholls said in *Inco Europe Ltd v First Choice Distribution* [2000] 1 WLR 586 at 592E–F:

"The courts are ever mindful that their constitutional role in this field is interpretative. They must abstain from any course which might have the appearance of judicial legislation. A statute is expressed in language approved and enacted by the legislature."

In this case the interpretation placed by the tribunals and courts, including this court, on [the ERA 1996 s 98] in the cases of *Iceland Foods* and *Burchell* has not led Parliament to amend the relevant provisions, even though Parliament has from time to time made other amendments to the law of unfair dismissal, since those authoritative rulings on interpretation were first made. So those rulings, which have been followed almost every day in almost every Employment Tribunal and on appeals for nearly 20 years, remain binding.

...

In accordance with section 98(4) the tribunal considered all the relevant circumstances and determined the question whether the dismissal was fair or unfair in accordance with the equity and substantial merits of the case. ...

Appeal Rehearing Point

Although the tribunal found that the disciplinary hearing by Ms Johnson was not conducted as fairly as it might have been, because she had not followed up lines of inquiry with the minicab company and the licensee of the pub, this deficiency was remedied on the appeal.

There is no error of law in that approach. The appeal was a rehearing and not merely a review of the unsatisfactory initial disciplinary hearing by Ms Johnson. The appeal was properly regarded as part of the overall process of terminating Mr Foley's employment. ... The rehearing was conducted thoroughly by Miss Little. She investigated the documentation with the minicab company and the licensee of the Innisfree Public House and weighed that against the evidence of Mr Kowalski, whom she had no reason to disbelieve.

Range of Reasonable Responses Approach

The Employment Tribunal then followed, as it was bound by authority to do, the *Iceland Foods* approach and held that, although it was of the view that the decision to dismiss was "harsh", it was not entitled to substitute itself for the employer and impose its "decision upon that of a reasoned on the spot management decision (para 23)". Instead it asked, as required by authority, whether the dismissal was "within the range of reasonable responses for this employer to have dismissed this employee". It found that it was.

That finding is not erroneous in law, unless it can be characterised by an appellate body as one which no reasonable tribunal could have reached. That is not, however, the basis on which Mr Reade, on behalf of Mr Foley, attacked the decision of the tribunal. His submission, based on Haddon, was that the tribunal ought to have started from the position of considering what it would do in the circumstances and then consider on the objective test in section 98(4) whether the decision to dismiss was reasonable or unreasonable. It should not simply have applied what was described in Haddon as the "mantra" (i.e. the band of reasonable responses and the warning against substituting its own judgment for that of the employer) which drove Employment Tribunals to subvert the provisions of section 98 and in effect apply a more extreme perversity test.

If the tribunal had taken the approach in *Haddon* it would have given effect to its express view that the decision to dismiss was "harsh" and it would have concluded that the dismissal of Mr Foley, who had a clean record, for an offence which was not gross misconduct, was manifestly unreasonable.

I would reject these submissions on the perversity point and on the substitution point as contrary to authority binding on this court.

Perversity Point

It was made clear in Iceland Foods at p.25B-D that the provisions of section 57(3) of the 1978 Act (which were re-enacted in section 98(4) of the 1996 Act) did not require "such a high degree of unreasonableness to be shown that nothing short of a perverse decision to dismiss can be held to be unfair within the section". The tribunals were advised to follow the formulation of the band of reasonable responses approach instead.

If an Employment Tribunal in any particular case misinterprets or misapplies that approach, so as to amount to a requirement of a perverse decision to dismiss, that would be an error of law with which an appellate body could interfere.

The range of reasonable responses approach does not, however, become one of perversity nor is it rendered "unhelpful" by the fact that there may be extremes and that (as observed in Haddon at p.1160D) "dismissal is the ultimate sanction". Further, that approach is not in practice required in every case. There will be cases in which there is no band or range to consider. If, for example, an employee, without good cause, deliberately sets fire to his employer's factory and it is burnt to the ground, dismissal is the only reasonable response. If an employee is dismissed for politely saying "Good morning" to his line manager, that would be an unreasonable response. But in between those extreme cases there will be cases where there is room for reasonable disagreement among reasonable employers as to whether dismissal for the particular misconduct is a reasonable or an unreasonable response. In those cases it is helpful for the tribunal to consider "the range of reasonable responses".

Substitution Point

It was also made clear in Iceland Foods at pp.24G–25B that the members of the tribunal must not simply consider whether they personally think that the dismissal is fair and they must not substitute their decision as to what was the right course to adopt for that of the employer. Their proper function is to determine whether the decision to dismiss the employee fell within the band of reasonable responses "which a reasonable employer might have adopted".

In one sense it is true that, if the application of that approach leads the members of the tribunal to conclude that the dismissal was unfair, they are in effect substituting their judgment for that of the employer. But that process must always be conducted by reference to the objective standards of the hypothetical reasonable employer which are imported by the statutory references to "reasonably or unreasonably" and not by reference to their own subjective views of what they would in fact have done as an employer in the same circumstances. In other words, although the members of the tribunal can substitute their decision for that of the employer, that decision must not be reached by a process of substituting themselves for the employer and forming an opinion of what they would have done had they been the employer, which they were not.

Rix LJ and **Nourse LJ** agreed.

NOTES AND QUESTIONS

1. The Court of Appeal held that the correct test was whether an employer's decision to dismiss was within a 'band of reasonable responses', bolstering its view that this must be correct because Parliament had not changed the law for twenty years. Do you agree that (1) it is Parliament's role to correct judicial mistakes, or (2) the courts cannot reinterpret the rules they have set out themselves?

2. In *University of Technology, Jamaica v Industrial Disputes Tribunal* [2017] UKPC 22, [21] Lady Hale said the *Burchell* or *Madden* 'approach has not proved uncontroversial'. It would seem the main point of controversy is that a 'band of reasonable responses' test is inherently unprincipled. How long is the 'band', and whose standards inform what is reasonable? Of course, the fact that it is unprincipled does not mean it is unworkable.

3. An example of the 'band of reasonable responses' test is *Parr v Whitbread and Co plc* [1990] ICR 427. Here a Threshers Wine Merchants manager was summarily dismissed, along with three other employees, after £4,600 was stolen.

The employer investigated, found nothing and dismissed all four. The Tribunal held the reason for dismissal was 'a genuine belief in the employees' guilt', without any proof. Although it seems unlikely the real thief would have brought a Tribunal claim, Wood J said at 432: '[A]s between members of the group the employer could not reasonably identify the individual perpetrator; then, provided that the beliefs were held on solid and sensible grounds at the date of dismissal, an employer is entitled to dismiss each member of the group.' Is that compatible with any notion of justice? Does an employer have a legitimate interest in protecting its property? Yes. But there are alternatives available, which do not trample on employees' job security, and which will achieve the aim of ensuring that thefts will not recur, such not leaving cash piles on-site. Moreover, it could be a breach of director's duty of care to fail to have systems that prevent theft. Do you think Tribunals should empower negligent employers to shift the blame onto innocent staff?

4.   The original Donovan Report (1968) Cmnd 3623, ch IX, which led to the introduction of fair dismissal rights, justified court-based review as follows. §526: 'In practice there is usually no comparison between the consequences for an employer if an employee terminates the contract of employment and those which will ensue for an employee if he is dismissed. In reality people build much of their lives around their jobs. Their incomes and prospects for the future are inevitably founded in the expectation that their jobs will continue. For workers in many situations dismissal is a disaster. For some workers it may make inevitable the breaking up of a community and the uprooting of homes and families. Others, and particularly older workers, may be faced with the greatest difficulty in getting work at all.' §528 added that unfair dismissal law was necessary to stop strikes about dismissal disputes. It did not exactly clarify what standard of review should be followed, but said there should be a 'valid reason' for dismissal 'connected' to capacity, conduct or redundancy (§545). It said that a Tribunal should also be able to consider 'the reasonableness of the rule' that an employer relied on (§565).

5.   At the Second Reading of the Industrial Relations Act 1971, Hansard, HC Deb (14 December 1970) vol 808, col 967 the Secretary of State for Employment, Robert Carr, said: 'Even if the employer does show that he dismissed the man on one of those grounds he still has to show that he did not act unreasonably in doing so. In the light of this, I do not accept that we have tilted the burden of proof to the disadvantage of the employee. We accept that it must be for the employer, since he carried out the dismissal, to show the tribunal what the reasons for his action were.'

6.   The Donovan Report was significantly influenced by Otto Kahn-Freund's participation and expertise. Kahn-Freund co-authored a commentary, before he was dismissed as a Berlin Labour Court judge and forced to flee Nazi Germany, on the German Work Councils Act: G Flatow and O Kahn-Freund, *Betriebsrätegesetz* (13th edn 1931). This enabled elected work council to participate in dismissal decisions, and prohibited dismissals that caused unreasonable hardship: Work Councils Act 1920 §§84–87. The critical fact is that the decision on which dismissals were fair would be informed through worker voice in the elected work council.

7.   Is it philosophically possible to identify an objective standard of fairness outside the society whose values are at stake?

8.   A clear alternative to the 'band of reasonable responses' test is proportionality. This requires courts to (1) identify a legitimate aim, (2) show action is appropriate, (3) necessary, and (4) strikes a reasonable balance between individual and social interests. This would mean, for instance, that *Swift* and *Madden* were rightly decided, but *Foley* and *Parr* were wrong. See further H Collins, *Nine Proposals for the Reform of the Law on Unfair Dismissal* (Institute of Employment Rights 2004).

9.   Despite criticisms of the 'band of reasonable responses' test, *Turner* affirmed it again.

Turner v East Midlands Trains Ltd [2012] EWCA Civ 1470

Heather Turner, a senior train conductor, claimed she was unfairly dismissed for alleged ticket fraud. Records from her 'Avantix' machine showed that Ms Turner had issued 132 'automatic non-issued tickets' (which are faulty, but still usable, and not issued to a customer) whereas the next highest senior conductor had issued just twenty. The employer suspected that she was selling these tickets to the public, and pocketing the money herself (rather than engaging in a habit of printing off extra tickets by mistake). The employer investigated, found nothing, except a set of statistics and inferences. She was dismissed for dishonesty. The Tribunal held that she could legitimately be found to have engaged in 'spasmodic pilfering', upheld by the Employment Appeal Tribunal. Ms Turner claimed that, as her honesty was in issue, the long-term reputational damage engaged her right to a private life under ECHR art 8 was not adequately protected by the 'band of reasonable responses' test. The Court of Appeal rejected Ms Turner's appeal.

Elias LJ:

17. … the band of reasonable responses test does not simply apply to the question whether the sanction of dismissal was permissible; it bears upon all aspects of the dismissal process. This includes whether the procedures adopted by the employer were adequate: see *Whitbread plc v Hall* [2001] IRLR 275 CA; and whether the pre-dismissal investigation was fair and appropriate: see *Sainsbury's Supermarkets v Hitt* [2003] IRLR 23 CA.

18. There are two important points to note about this test. The first, as the judgment of Aikens LJ makes clear, is that it must not be confused with the classic Wednesbury test adopted in administrative law cases whereby a court can interfere with the substantive decision of an administrator only if it is perverse. This point has been made on a number of occasions. [His Lordship continued, citing *Madden* and *Roldan*.]
   …

19. The band of reasonable responses test is not a subjective test and it is erroneous so to describe it. It provides an objective assessment of the employer's behaviour whilst reminding the employment tribunal that the fact that it would have assessed the case before it differently from the employer does not necessarily mean that the employer has acted unfairly.

20. The second observation is that when determining whether an employer has acted as the hypothetical reasonable employer would do, it will be relevant to have regard to the nature

and consequences of the allegations. These are part of all the circumstances of the case. So if the impact of a dismissal for misconduct will damage the employee's opportunity to take up further employment in the same field, or if the dismissal involves an allegation of immoral or criminal conduct which will harm the reputation of the employee, then a reasonable employer should have regard to the gravity of those consequences when determining the nature and scope of the appropriate investigation.

  …

22. The test applied in *A v B* and *Roldan* is still whether a reasonable employer could have acted as the employer did. However, more will be expected of a reasonable employer where the allegations of misconduct, and the consequences to the employee if they are proven, are particularly serious.

  …

28. The appellant relies upon three consequences of the dismissal which, she submits, whether taken individually or cumulatively, engage Article 8. These are the damage to her reputation caused by a finding of dishonesty; the potential restriction on her ability to obtain other employment as a consequence of that finding and the stigma flowing from it; and the damage wrought by the dismissal on the social relationships which she had developed with her work colleagues.

29. There is no doubt that in an appropriate case each of these interests is in principle capable of engaging Article 8. As to reputation, the European Court of Human Rights observed in *Pfeifer v Austria* (2009) 48 EHRR 8 (para 35) that:

> "a person's reputation, even if that person is criticised in the context of a public debate, forms part of his or her personal identity and psychological integrity and therefore also falls within the scope of his or her private life".

In that case a person had committed suicide as a result of a highly critical article. In *Petrenco v Moldova* [2011] EMLR 5, another case involving an alleged defamatory newspaper article, the Strasbourg court held that a state's positive obligation to protect Article 8 rights might require it to take steps to protect the right to reputation from interference by private bodies.

30. Typically the damage to reputation will result from some publication, but Article 8 is not limited to such cases. The House of Lords has accepted in an employment context that the stigma of removal from a post for allegedly immoral or criminal conduct may, in an appropriate case, engage Article 8: *R (Wright) v Secretary of State for Health* [2009] 1 AC 739. Baroness Hale, with whose judgment Lords Phillips, Hope, Hoffmann and Brown agreed, held that where care workers were entered on a list for alleged misconduct without any right to make representations, the effect of which was to bar them from working in their chosen profession because they were considered unsafe to work with vulnerable adults, their Article 8 rights were infringed. This was partly because of the practical effect on their ability to earn a living, but also because of the inevitable stigma attached to being on the list. This was so even though the list was supposed to be kept private.

  …

53. … in the employment sphere, the Strasbourg court has recognised that some leeway should be given to the employer in the discharge of his powers of dismissal. In *Sanchez v Spain* (2012) 54 EHRR 24 four applicants before the Court had published two articles, worded in vulgar language, which criticised two fellow employees for giving evidence in favour of the employer in proceedings brought against the employer by the trade union. The articles were published in the workplace. In addition they published a cartoon showing the two employees giving sexual

favours to the director of human resources. The applicants were dismissed for serious misconduct. They alleged a breach of their Article 10 rights and also claimed that the real reason for their dismissal was their trade union activities. Their dismissals were found to be justified under Spanish law and their appeal to the Strasbourg Court was unsuccessful. The majority of the Grand Chamber (presided over by Judge Bratza) recognised that disproportionate penalties could conceal anti-union hostility but concluded that the courts had carefully examined the facts and reached a legitimate conclusion taking account of the competing interests at stake.

...

56. Strasbourg therefore adopts a light touch when reviewing human rights in the context of the employment relationship. It may even be that the domestic band of reasonable responses test protects human rights more effectively. Whether that is so or not, Sanchez shows that the interests of the employer are given significant weight when carrying out the balancing exercise which Article 8(2) requires. *Sanchez* strongly reinforces my conclusion that the band of reasonable responses test provides a sufficiently robust, flexible and objective analysis of all aspects of the decision to dismiss to ensure compliance with Article 8.

57. More specifically, I am satisfied that so far as procedures are concerned, the domestic test of fairness does not fall short of the procedural safeguards required by Article 8. In that context, I reject the appellant's submission that the concept of proportionality is either a helpful or relevant one when considering the fairness of the procedures. The Strasbourg court does not use that language when referring to Article 8 procedural safeguards; it uses the language of fairness, a concept universally adopted when speaking of procedures. Recourse to a concept of proportionality – a word not found in Article 8(2) itself – in my judgment simply obfuscates and potentially complicates the essentially simple concept of a fair procedure.

58. Since in this case the employee has conceded that the procedures satisfied domestic standards, and given my conclusion that these reflect Article 8 requirements, it follows that the appeal must fail. However, in case I am wrong about that, I will consider the strength of the case on its merits and address the question whether, even if there is a difference between domestic and Strasbourg procedural standards, the adoption of a stricter test might have led to a different conclusion.

...

60. More specifically, the particular allegations were as follows:

> (1) The appellant claimed that sometimes when her machine issued an ANI this was because the machine was temporarily broken. She would return to the back cab and fix the machine. It may be that one of the ticket inspectors (those who inspect tickets and randomly check that passengers have bought tickets) may have sold passengers the appropriate ticket before the appellant had fixed her machine and been able to do so. The appellant submitted that the employers would have been able to show from their records which inspectors were on the appellant's train during various journeys and for what stages of those journeys, and that might have indicated that there were occasions when this had in fact happened.
> (2) The appellant contended that she had particular problems with the Avantix machine and was regularly returning to the back cab to fix it.
> (3) She contended that it was extremely difficult to manipulate an Avantix machine so as to produce a sufficiently authentic ANI.
> (4) She also claimed that the ANIs had not necessarily been retained satisfactorily by the employers and some of her missing ANIs could be ascribed to the fact that they may have been lost after having been returned by her.

61. The Tribunal did address each of these matters, all of which were advanced before them. As to the question whether the employers should have investigated the possibility that tickets were provided by inspectors, the Tribunal said this (para 33):

> "The explanation for not pursuing this line of enquiry is perfectly satisfactory. It does not constitute a failure on the part of any investigating officer to look for exculpating matters. This is not, of course, any more than a possible means of establishing that at some point an identical ticket to one of the missing ANIs may have been issued by another person, it would not establish that this was in fact a replacement ticket in any particular case nor would it answer the question of why the ANI was missing or go directly to the issue of why the claimant had a disproportionate number of suspicious ANIs."

62. With regard to the breaking down of the Avantix machine, these machines were handed out at random and there was no basis to suppose that the appellant would, over a significant period at least, have any more problems with her machine than any other conductor.

63. The submission that the ANIs were difficult to reproduce was categorically denied by the employers who carried out tests of their own and concluded that it was easy to do. Again, the Tribunal expressly referred to that fact in its judgment.

64. Finally, although there was apparently some evidence to the effect that management processing of the non-issue tickets was unsatisfactory, the tribunal noted that management did not accept that there was the substantial level of non-compliance with procedures alleged by the appellant. Again, even if they had been stored haphazardly, one would have expected the same lackadaisical care to have applied equally to other conductors.

65. The striking feature here was that the appellant had 132 ANIs and the next figure was 20. Her total was reduced to 50 by a series of further reductions all of which made assumptions in her favour. But as the Tribunal noted, that did not leave a contrast of 50 to 20 because had similar principles been applied to the other conductors, there is every reason to assume that the figure of 20 would itself have been reduced.

    …

69. The Tribunal was persuaded by the cogent explanations of the employers for why that step had not been taken, and I can see no basis on which their analysis on that point can be properly criticised. So I would in any event have dismissed the appeal on the ground that even if the Tribunal had applied the wrong test, it would inevitably have reached the same conclusion had it applied the right one.

Sir Stephen Sedley:

73. … the employer's band of reasonable responses is itself catholic enough to accommodate whatever standard of due process article 8 calls for in a particular case. Since that test is exegetic of the statutory provision, this approach in my judgment fulfils the mandate of s.3 of the Human Rights Act. It requires the tribunal to be satisfied that the employer's standard of inquiry and decision-making was apt. …

Maurice Kay LJ agreed.

NOTES AND QUESTIONS

1. The Court of Appeal held that Ms Turner was fairly dismissed, based on the employer's 'cogent explanations', and further held that the band of reasonable responses itself would be enough to account for any human rights claim (here the effect on Ms Turner's life with a dishonesty dismissal hanging over her) under ECHR Art 8. This is mainly because of the principle Elias LJ sets out at [22] that the more serious the allegation, the greater an investigation must be done.

2. If what the Court of Appeal has said is true, and the 'band of reasonable responses' test is 'catholic enough' or can amount to the same thing as the proportionality test, it logically follows that it is open to every Tribunal to apply a proportionality test in its reasoning. The difference will be that its process of reasoning is sharper, more coherent and transparent. What do you think?

3. If the proportionality and 'band' tests, however, are not the same, then *Turner* should be regarded as wrong. The outcome on the facts is, with respect, completely inadequate in principle, as the employer has plainly acted unreasonably. *Turner* fails to engage with the very simple question: what if Ms Turner were innocent? Once East Midlands turned up the statistics of 132 extra ticket issues, its 'investigation' entailed gazing at those same statistics, questioning the employee, and being unsatisfied. It gave no warning to Ms Turner when too many tickets were issued to begin with (say at thirty issues). The judgment itself finds that most ticket issues were 'usually low value', meaning that any theft was probably irrelevant. There is no indication (rather than an assumption) that East Midlands suffered any loss. A suspicion of dishonesty, without any loss, is in principle an unsatisfactory ground for a dismissal. If Ms Turner said she was having difficulty with the machine, why not believe her, and help her?

4. The 'hypothetical reasonable employer' test advanced at [20], which itself derives from *Orr v Milton Keynes Council* [2011] EWCA Civ 62, seems very unhelpful. In *Attorney General of Belize v Belize Telecom Ltd* [2009] UKPC 10, [25] Lord Hoffmann said the similar and 'imaginary' inquiry into what hypothetical people might do only leads to 'barren argument'.

5. If the Court of Appeal had applied a proportionality test (regardless of whether this was required by privacy rights, or simply justice in dismissal) the result should have been as follows. First, did the employer pursue a legitimate aim? Yes, its dismissal, even though it had not proof of dishonesty, was motivated by wanting honest staff. Second, was its action appropriate to achieve that aim? No. Although it can be appropriate to dismiss dishonest people, it is inappropriate to dismiss honest staff. Third, was its action necessary (and no more) to achieve the aim? No. It could have warned its employee on the need to improve or given guidance about how to use the machine. Fourth, did its actions strike a reasonable balance between the interests of the individual and society? No. In principle it is worse to occasionally dismiss an innocent person than occasionally let a guilty person get away.

(c) Reasons: Conduct and Capability

As we have seen, ERA 1996 s 98 states four main reasons can justify dismissal: (1) conduct, (2) capability or qualifications for a job, (3) redundancy, (4) some other substantial reason. It also says dismissal is fair if a statute requires it. Redundancy and 'some other substantial reason' are handled in chapter 19, so this part focuses on conduct and capability. In essence there is no right answer as to what conduct is bad enough, or what kind of incapability is severe enough, to justify dismissal. Tribunals are given deference to decide what is right in the circumstances, applying their experience and judgement with two lay members (representing unions and employers). Obviously, social norms can shift.

Bowater v Northwest London Hospitals NHS Trust [2011] EWCA Civ 63

Laura Bowater claimed she was unfairly dismissed as a senior staff nurse by the NHS after an 'incident'. About to go home, Bowater had to help physically restrain a patient who was naked and having an epileptic fit. While doing this she said, 'It's been a few months since I have been in this position with a man underneath me.' Because of apparent concerns that a member of the public might have heard this, Bowater was dismissed for failing 'to behave in a way that upholds the reputation of the profession'. The Tribunal found the dismissal was unfair. The Employment Appeal Tribunal allowed the NHS appeal, but the Court of Appeal upheld the Tribunal.

Stanley Burton LJ:

7. On behalf of the Respondent, Mr Cooper … criticised the decision of the ET under four heads. He submitted:

(1)   The ET had wrongly substituted its own opinion for that of the respondent.
(2)   The ET had had regard to an irrelevant factor, namely the fact that the remark would be regarded by a large proportion of the population as merely humorous.
(3)   There was no proper evidential basis for the ET's decision.
(4)   The decision of the ET was perverse. …

…

9. As to (1), the decision for the ET was whether the employer's decision to dismiss the appellant was within the range of reasonable responses open to a reasonable employer. The ET correctly directed itself in the first sentence of paragraph 8.3 of its decision and later again in the same paragraph. Furthermore in paragraph 12 of its decision, when summarising the view of the dissenting member of the Tribunal, the ET stated:

"Although the decision to dismiss the Claimant could be considered harsh, it could not be considered to be outside the range of reasonable responses available to a reasonable employer in the circumstances."

It is evident that the majority of the ET applied the correct legal test.

10. As to (2), it is common ground that the remark in question was intended to be humorous. That it was so was clearly relevant, just as it would have been relevant if the remark had been

seen as insulting to a patient. In my view, the EAT was overcritical and wrong in its criticism of paragraph 8.3(v) of the ET's decision. Moreover, the EAT was wrong to hold that this subparagraph demonstrated that the ET had substituted its opinion of what would have been reasonable for that of the respondent: this was a non sequitur.

11. As to (3), the ET carefully set out the primary facts and the respondent's view of them. Mr Cooper criticised the ET for not having set out and specifically addressed the views of Miss Mackie and Mrs Robb to the effect that the appellant's remark justified her summary dismissal. But those views were expressions of judgment, based on primary facts. As I have already stated, the ET carefully addressed the primary facts; it was clearly aware of the context in which the events in question took place; and the majority made it clear why they disagreed with Miss Mackie's and Mrs Robb's judgment as to their seriousness.

12. Contention (4) involves a judgment on the seriousness of the appellant's conduct. It was not and is not suggested that she was not at fault in making the remark she did. However, I have no doubt that the majority of the ET were entitled to find that summary dismissal was outside the range of reasonable responses to the appellant's conduct. The appellant made a misguided and wholly inappropriate remark, intended as humorous. No member of the public was present. There was no evidence that the patient was conscious of its having been made. It is significant that neither Dr Tong nor Charge Nurse Lee admonished the appellant at the time, or reported her conduct. The matter was not reported as a disciplinary matter for some 6 weeks.

13. The appellant's conduct was rightly made the subject of disciplinary action. It is right that the ET, the EAT and this Court should respect the opinions of the experienced professionals who decided that summary dismissal was appropriate. However, having done so, it was for the ET to decide whether their views represented a reasonable response to the appellant's conduct. It did so. In agreement with the majority of the ET, I consider that summary dismissal was wholly unreasonable in the circumstances of this case. ...

Longmore LJ:

18. I agree with Stanley Burnton LJ that dismissal of the appellant for her lewd comment was outside the range of reasonable responses open to a reasonable employer in the circumstances of the case. The EAT decided that the ET had substituted its own judgment for that of the judgment to which the employer had come. But the employer cannot be the final arbiter of its own conduct in dismissing an employee. It is for the ET to make its judgment always bearing in mind that the test is whether dismissal is within the range of reasonable options open to a reasonable employer.

Laws LJ agreed.

NOTES AND QUESTIONS

1. The Court of Appeal holds that the dismissal 'was wholly unreasonable' and 'outside the range of reasonable responses'. It seems their Lordships go beyond saying that they defer to the Tribunal. Although Stanley Burton LJ says the conduct was 'rightly the subject of disciplinary action', do you agree? Without going into why, is it not clear that Bowater's comment was entirely self-deprecating? It was, surely, in no way making fun of the patient, but of herself, making light of what

could be an embarrassing situation. The Court of Appeal is to be commended for
not being too serious.

2.   Do you think the same decision would have been reached by a Tribunal or a Court
of Appeal when the statutory right to a fair dismissal was introduced in 1971?

3.   What about conduct outside of work? In *Mathewson v RB Wilson Dental
Laboratory Ltd* [1988] IRLR 512, Mr Mathewson, a dental technician, was
arrested for possessing cannabis in his lunch break, and returned one hour late.
He explained what happened, and was dismissed. The Employment Appeal
Tribunal held the dismissal was fair because of 'involvement in the use of
prohibited drugs; the intervention of the police; the admission by the appellant ...
the possible influence on other members of staff; and the suitability of continuing
to employ the appellant in the job for which he was employed'. The Misuse of
Drugs Act 1971 prohibited marijuana in the same year as unfair dismissal rights
were introduced. Given that 35 per cent of the UK population has smoked
marijuana or used drugs currently deemed illegal, it would seem the policy of
criminalisation is an abject failure. In any case, do you think an out-of-work drug
charge should be relevant to an employer? Why should the employer be able to
punish someone a second time for a minor crime?

4.   By contrast, some activities outside of work are lawful but still felt to be unacceptable. In *Pay v United Kingdom* [2008] ECHR 1007 the claimant was
dismissed as a probation officer for sex offenders when it was revealed he had
a website for bondage and sadomasochism. The Employment Appeal Tribunal
held the dismissal was justified (although it applied a proportionality test, not a
band of reasonable responses test) and compatible with Pay's right to a private life
under ECHR Art 8. The European Court of Human Rights agreed, saying 'given
in particular the nature of the applicant's work with sex offenders and the fact that
the dismissal resulted from his failure to curb even those aspects of his private life
most likely to enter into the public domain, the Court does not consider that the
measure was disproportionate'.

5.   In *Barbulescu v Romania* [2016] ECHR 61, an employee who worked as a sales
engineer was dismissed after he told his employers it was criminal for them to
read his personal correspondence on work computers over Yahoo Messenger.
The employer had a policy against using work computers for personal purposes.
The European Court of Human Rights held that there was an infringement of
Barbulescu's private life under ECHR Art 8, but this was justified because 'it
is not unreasonable for an employer to want to verify that the employees are
completing their professional tasks during working hours' [59]. In response to
this largely unreasoned assertion, Pinto de Albuquerque J said in dissent: 'Internet
surveillance in the workplace runs the risk of being abused by employers acting as
a distrustful Big Brother lurking over the shoulders of their employees, as though
the latter had sold not only their labor, but also their personal lives to employers.'
What do you think?

6.   An employer can dismiss an employee for capability (recall *Smith v Glasgow
DC*) or qualifications. What if the employer is part responsible for an employee's
incapability?

McAdie v Royal Bank of Scotland plc [2007] EWCA Civ 806

Mrs McAdie claimed she was unfairly dismissed as an assistant manager of the Bromley branch of RBS. She was asked to move to the Swanley branch by a new manager, Mr O'Shaughnessy. She had previously brought a successful grievance against him, after he downgraded her role when she returned from maternity leave. The move would have made her childcare arrangements much harder. But the manager insisted on the move. As McAdie complained to a more senior manager about the proposal on 3 July 2003, she became increasingly stressed. The bank knew that McAdie suffered from stress, which was thought to exacerbate the possibility of her contracting breast cancer. Eventually, on 10 September 2003, she was signed off as sick. She remained off until December 2004, when the bank wrote to dismiss her on grounds of lack of capability. The Tribunal awarded her £53,083.75 in compensation, although the compensatory sum was reduced by 50 per cent under the *Polkey* principle of the possibility of being dismissed in any case.

Wall LJ:

37. In relation to those authorities, the EAT commented in the following terms:

> In *Betty* Morison P appeared to say that the fact that the employer had been responsible for the incapacity which was the reason for a dismissal should as a matter of principle be ignored in deciding whether it was reasonable to dismiss for that reason. But Bell J in Edwards and Judge Reid QC in Frewin expressed the view that, if that was what Morison P meant, it over-stated the position. We agree. It seems to us that there must be cases where the fact that the employer is in one sense or another responsible for an employee's incapacity is, as a matter of common sense and common fairness, relevant to whether, and if so when, it is reasonable to dismiss him for that incapacity. It may, for example, be necessary in such a case to "go the extra mile" in finding alternative employment for such an employee, or to put up with a longer period of sickness absence than would otherwise be reasonable. (We need not consider the further example, suggested by Bell J in Edwards, of a case where the employer, or someone for whose acts he is responsible, has maliciously injured the claimant, since there is no suggestion that those are the facts here. But we should say that we find some difficulty with the implication that in such a case there could never be a fair dismissal.) However, we accept, as did Bell J and Judge Reid, that much of what Morison P said in Betty was important and plainly correct. Thus it must be right that the fact that an employer has caused the incapacity in question, however culpably, cannot preclude him for ever from effecting a fair dismissal. ...

> ...

38. The EAT thus proceeded on the basis that the Tribunal had not erred in principle in being prepared to take into account the fact (as it found) that the Bank was responsible, and culpably so, for the appellant's ill-health. The EAT went on, however, to add the following observations:

> it is important to focus not, as such, on the question of that responsibility but on the statutory question of whether it was reasonable for the Bank, "in the circumstances" (which of course include the Bank's responsibility for her illness), to dismiss her for that reason. On ordinary principles, that question falls to be answered by reference to the situation as it was at the date that the decision was taken. Thus the question which the Tribunal should have

asked itself was "was it reasonable for the Bank to dismiss Mrs. McAdie on 22 December 2004, in the circumstances as they then were, including the fact that their mishandling of the situation had led to her illness?"

That was not the approach which the Tribunal avowedly took. The elegantly-expressed reasoning at para. 87 of the Judgment – "no reasonable employer would have dismissed in these circumstances because no reasonable employer would have found themselves in these circumstances" – focuses explicitly not on what it was reasonable for the Bank to do in the circumstances in which it found itself (however culpably) but on whether it should have got into those circumstances in the first place. If that is really the approach taken by the Tribunal it was plainly a misdirection. It would apply in any case where the employer has negligently injured an employee and would have the result, which as we have said above is not the law, that the employer in such circumstances could never fairly dismiss. ...

...

40. I have cited at length from the EAT's judgment because I find myself both in complete agreement with it and, at the same time, reluctant to add to it.

Rix LJ and **Burton LJ** concurred.

NOTES AND QUESTIONS

1. The Court of Appeal upholds the Employment Appeal Tribunal judgment on the basis that an employer that creates a situation, where an employee is rendered incapable (here through illness) of doing a job will be able to dismiss an employee, but must pay compensation for the unfairness they create.

(3) REMEDIES AFTER DISMISSAL

The remedies for statutory unfair dismissal limit the effectiveness of the right. One positive fact is that *Unison v Lord Chancellor* [2017] UKSC 51 abolished any requirement to pay fees to bring a case to an Employment Tribunal: chapter 3(4). From 2013, these were ordinarily £1,200. After *Unison*, by December 2017, the Ministry of Justice had refunded £1.8m. However (a) damages are subject to a cap that operates against people with long-term losses, or who have high incomes, and (b) the right to reinstatement is used rarely. In the shadow of these rules, (c) an employee and employer can make a compromise agreement.

(a) Damages, Statutory Cap and Exceptions

Damages for unfair dismissal are usually small. In 2013, the median unfair dismissal award was just £4,560: DBIS, *Unfair Dismissal Compensatory Awards: Final Impact Assessment* (2013). Nevertheless, the government proceeded to introduce £1,200 fees (now abolished) and imposed a limit of one year's pay (SI 2013/1949). Before these fees, there were the following number of claims, which will be suggestive of the level now fees are gone again:

Table 18.1 Outcomes of tribunal claims disposed of in 2011/2012

Outcome	Number	Percentage
Total	46,100	100
Withdrawn	11,300	24
ACAS-conciliated settlements	19,500	42
Struck out not at a hearing	4,000	9
Successful at tribunal	3,900	8
Dismissed at a preliminary hearing	1,300	3
Unsuccessful at hearing	4,800	10
Default judgement	1,200	3

Damages consist of a 'basic' plus a 'compensatory' award (s 118), calculated as follows:

Employment Rights Act 1996 ss 119, 123–24 and 227

119 Basic award.
  (1) Subject to the provisions of this section, sections 120 to 122 and section 126, the amount of the basic award shall be calculated by—
    (a) determining the period, ending with the effective date of termination, during which the employee has been continuously employed,
    (b) reckoning backwards from the end of that period the number of years of employment falling within that period, and
    (c) allowing the appropriate amount for each of those years of employment.
  (2) In subsection (1)(c) "the appropriate amount" means—
    (a) one and a half weeks' pay for a year of employment in which the employee was not below the age of forty-one,
    (b) one week's pay for a year of employment (not within paragraph (a)) in which he was not below the age of twenty-two, and
    (c) half a week's pay for a year of employment not within paragraph (a) or (b).
  (3) Where twenty years of employment have been reckoned under subsection (1), no account shall be taken under that subsection of any year of employment earlier than those twenty years.
    …

123 Compensatory award.
  (1) Subject to the provisions of this section and sections 124, 124A and 126, the amount of the compensatory award shall be such amount as the tribunal considers just and equitable in all the circumstances having regard to the loss sustained by the complainant in consequence of the dismissal in so far as that loss is attributable to action taken by the employer.
    …
  (6) Where the tribunal finds that the dismissal was to any extent caused or contributed to by any action of the complainant, it shall reduce the amount of the compensatory award by such proportion as it considers just and equitable having regard to that finding.

124 Limit of compensatory award etc.
(1) The amount of—
    (a) any compensation awarded to a person under section 117(1) and (2), or
    (b) a compensatory award to a person calculated in accordance with section 123,
shall not exceed the amount specified in subsection (1ZA).
(1ZA) The amount specified in this subsection is the lower of—
    (a) £83,682, and
    (b) 52 multiplied by a week's pay of the person concerned.

NOTES AND QUESTIONS

1. Section 119 states that the basic award for unfair dismissal is one week's pay for each year one is employed when aged 22–40, half a week's pay for people 21 and under, and one and a half week's pay for people 41 and over. On what basis is this justifiable? Is the dignity of younger people worth less? Is youth unemployment not significantly worse than unemployment for people in their forties or fifties? And why should you get no basic award if you have not worked for a year?

2. Section 120 says the minimum award for unfair redundancy selections, and for auto-unfair dismissals in ss 100–03 is £6,203, and £5,000 for blacklisting. Section 121 says the basic award for redundancies is two weeks' pay. Section 122 requires a reduction of an award if an employee refused a reasonable offer of reinstatement. Section 126 says there should be no double-recovery for joint unfair dismissal and discrimination claims.

3. ERA 1996 s 227 adds that for basic, compensatory or redundancy awards, the maximum amount of a 'week's pay' is £508. Assuming 6 weeks' holidays in a year, this affects anyone earning over £22,494, a figure significantly below the UK median income. Because the most anyone can receive for a basic award is a week for each of 20 years, and one and a half week's pay, the maximum basic award is $30 \times £508 = £15,240$.

4. Section 123 states that the compensatory award (practically far more important) should be 'such amount as the tribunal considers just and equitable' regarding 'the loss sustained' that is 'attributable to action taken by the employer'. (But this is subject to an overall cap, see below.) Do you agree this means that the employee should be put in the same position as if the tort had not occurred?

5. When the system was first set up, Sir John Donaldson pronounced in *Norton Tool Co Ltd v Tewson* [1972] EW Misc 1 there were four categories of damages for (a) immediate loss of wages, (b) manner of dismissal, which meant 'making [an employee] less acceptable to potential employers or exceptionally liable to selection for dismissal', (c) future loss of wages, and (d) loss of protection in respect of unfair dismissal or dismissal by reason of redundancy. He also said at [14]: '"Loss," in the context of the section, does not include injury to pride or feelings.' That was probably wrong at the time (see *Jarvis v Swans Tours Ltd* [1972] EWCA Civ 8) but must certainly be regarded as wrong in principle now. The House of Lords in *Farley v Skinner* [2001] UKHL 49 held that whenever an 'important part' of a contract, when breached, would lead to non-pecuniary losses, such damages are available. Employment contracts founded on mutual trust and confidence, so in principle injury to feelings, for an employer's bad faith conduct, should be

available. Employment contracts should be more favourable to the employee than ordinary contract law, not less.

6. One might have thought that Lord Hoffmann in *Johnson* at [55] agreed with the foregoing note. But in *Dunnachie v Kingston-upon-Hull CC* [2004] UKHL 36, the House of Lords held that Mr Dunnachie could not claim injury for feelings as part of a compensatory award under section 123. Mr Dunnachie, who worked for the council since 1986, claimed constructive dismissal in 2001 following a campaign of authoritarian harassment by a line manager. The Tribunal awarded compensation, including £10,000 for distress for the manner of dismissal. Lord Steyn, with whom Lord Nicholls, Lord Hoffmann, Lord Rodger and Lord Brown agreed, said at [27]: 'Professor Collins argued that *Norton Tool* reversed the grammar of the statute. He said that *Norton Tool* "elevated the sub-principle of causation of loss to the main principle, and then relegated the general standard of just and equitable compensation to the status of a minor limitation on the application of the principles of causation of economic loss": at 202. For substantially the same reasons as I have already given I find this argument unpersuasive.' Before this at [15] Lord Steyn remarks: 'With the solitary exception of a critical note in 1991 on *Norton Tool* by Professor Hugh Collins ... I am not aware of any academic criticism of this decision.' However, today it appears that Professor Collins's view has become the majority view, and that *Norton Tool* is to be regarded as wrong.

7. What about punitive damages? In *Clarkson International Tools Ltd v Short* [1973] ICR 191, 196, Sir John Donaldson said: 'The purpose of assessing compensation is not to express disapproval of industrial relations policy. It is to compensate for financial loss.' Whether or this was true at the time, in principle punitive damages are available at common law for every statutory tort that is 'calculated to make a profit': *Rookes v Barnard*.

8. The Donovan Report (1968) Cmnd 3623, s 553, stated: '"Punitive" considerations should not normally enter into its assessment except where discrimination is clearly proved.' In other words, punitive damages should be awarded 'where discrimination is clearly proved' but otherwise not 'normally'. It follows that the view of the Donovan Report was that in exceptional cases punitive damages for unfair dismissal should be available. This could follow by analogy to landlord and tenant cases, where landlords have acted with contempt toward tenants. For example, in *Drane v Evangelou* [1978] 1 WLR 455 the Court of Appeal held that an award of £1,000 in exemplary damages was appropriate (nearly £8,000 in 2018), where a landlord locked out a tenant and his wife, put their possessions in the back yard, and so forced them both to stay at a friend's house for ten weeks. For further examples, see S Deakin, A Johnston and B Markesinis, *Markesinis and Deakin's Tort Law* (7th edn OUP 2012) 800–01.

9. In *GAB Robins (UK) Ltd v Triggs* [2008] EWCA Civ 17, Rimer LJ held that a woman who was overworked and bullied, became ill, who submitted a grievance, and then resigned could not claim damages for reduced income that later would flow from her illness. It was found that she was constructively dismissed. But Rimer LJ said this at [34]: 'It is correct that the dismissal was a constructive one, that is that it was the result of, and followed upon, her acceptance of the employer's antecedent breaches of the implied term of trust and confidence

that had caused her illness and, in turn, her reduced earning capacity. But it is fallacious to regard those antecedent breaches as constituting the dismissal. The dismissal was effected purely and simply by her decision in February 2005 that she wished to discontinue her employment. On a claim for unfair dismissal, that entitled her to compensation for whatever loss flowed from that dismissal. But that loss did not include loss (including future loss) flowing from wrongs already inflicted upon her by the employer's prior conduct: those losses (including any future lost income) were not caused by the dismissal.' Is this coherent? If Ms Triggs had been treated properly at work, she would not have been ill. She would not have resigned and successfully claimed constructive dismissal. The Court of Appeal failed to stick to the basic question of what was necessary to put her in the position as if the wrong had not occurred.

10. Section 124(6) allows reduction of compensation for unfair dismissal. This appears to be a statutory analogue to the idea that one must come to equity with 'clean hands'. In *Nelson v British Broadcasting Corporation (No 2)* [1980] ICR 110 Brandon LJ held that Mr Nelson, in refusing the BBC to let him transfer him, should have damages reduced to zero for his behaviour, which was 'perverse or foolish ... or ... bloody minded'. This could go too far: two wrongs (by a claimant and defendant) does not make a defendant right.

11. The most significant and unprincipled limit is the cap on compensatory damages at one year's earnings in s 124(1ZA)(b). If someone is dismissed and remains unemployed for five years, they will have nothing for the remaining four years. This change was made by statutory order, not Parliament. Given that *Unison v Lord Chancellor* struck down tribunal fees for violating the rule of law, should the 2013 Order be subject to similar review? At stake here is an equally fundamental constitutional principle: the effectiveness of a remedy. This is recognised in CFREU Art 47, on the 'right to an effective remedy before a tribunal' (which applies to the right against unjustified dismissal in Art 30), in ECHR Art 13 (albeit that this only applies to other Convention rights), and most critically in common law, *Ashby v White* (1703) 92 ER 126, per Lord Holt CJ: '[I]t is a vain thing to imagine a right without a remedy; for want of right and want of remedy are reciprocal.'

12. The other major cap in s 124(1ZA)(a) is £83,682 (SI 2018/194) in 2018, though this is only likely to affect higher earners. Should the statutory damages cap be ignored if common law would award more?

Johnson v Unisys Ltd [2001] UKHL 13

For the facts, see chapter 3(1) and preceding parts of the judgment, chapter 18(1).

Lord Steyn dissenting on reasoning:

23. The unfair dismissal legislation must be put in context. At the time of the Donovan Report collective bargaining was seen as the main form of protection of individuals. It apparently covered about 83% of the workforce in 1980. It has, however, been contracting steadily. It fell to 35% in 1998. In the result individual legal rights have now become the main source of protection of employees: see Brown, Deakin, Nash and Oxenbridge, "The Employment Contract:

From Collective Procedures to Individual Rights" (2000) 38, British Journal of Industrial Relations, 611, 613–616. At the time of the Donovan Report reinstatement was envisaged as a major remedy: paras 551–552. In practice, however, only about 3% of applicants are reinstated: see Davies and Freedland, *Labour Legislation and Public Policy*, (1993), p 210, citing statistics dating from 1987/8. My understanding is that about 3% still represents the reinstatement figure. Not surprisingly, the award of compensation by a tribunal has to be the primary remedy. The 1971 Act in section 116 adopted the formula, which appears with minor changes in the current law, that the compensation should be "such amount as the ... tribunal considers just and equitable in all the circumstances, having regard to the loss sustained by the aggrieved party in consequence of the matters to which the complaint relates, in so far as the loss was attributable to action taken by or on behalf of the party in default". Hugh Collins, *Justice in Dismissal*, (1992), pp 218–223 has shown how the award of compensation, by reason of artificial limits, has markedly failed to meet the aim of corrective justice in accordance with the employee's contractual rights. One of those limits was the requirement of the unfair dismissal system that such cases had to be resolved in accordance with a very expeditious timetable. Initially, the claim had generally to be lodged within four weeks, that being a period within which the seriousness of damage to employment prospects would often not have become clear: see sections 22, 106(4) and (5) read with schedule 6, para 5 of the Industrial Relations Act 1971. Even now section 111(2) of the Employment Rights Act 1996 provides that such claims must generally be lodged within 3 months, that still being a period within which the seriousness of damage to employment prospects may not have become clear. More importantly, the low statutory limit on the award of compensation made the attainment of corrective justice impossible. At the inception of the statutory regime section 118(1) of the Industrial Relations Act 1971 placed a limit on the maximum amount of compensation of two years pay or £4,160 (whichever was the lesser). In 1975 the alternative way of expressing the limit was abolished. The monetary limit was from time to time increased. In April 1998 it reached £12,000. In October 1999 the maximum was increased to £50,000. It is now index-linked. It has been pointed out that allowing for inflation, £4,160 in 1971 is now worth about £50,000: HC Research Paper 98/99. The statutory system was therefore always only capable of meeting the requirements of cases at the lower end of seriousness. Manifestly, it was always incapable, for example, of affording any significant financial compensation to employees with substantial salaries and pension entitlements in cases where they suffered a serious loss of employment prospects due to the manner of their dismissal. In such cases, inter alia, the artificial statutory limits from the inception inhibited significant compensation. If Parliament is deemed to have been aware of the Addis decision, one must also deem Parliament to have been aware that the system it was creating was only capable of dealing effectively and justly with less serious cases where the threshold of a breach of contract was not necessarily established. Moreover, the changing nature of the relationship between employer and employee, and numerous judicial inroads in case law on Addis's case were already well documented before 1971. The third edition of Treitel, *The Law of Contract*, was published in 1970. Treitel observed, at p 813, that "the rule may be that general damages cannot be recovered for injury to reputation by a non-trader, but that special damages can be recovered for actual loss resulting from such injury" (author's emphasis). In my view the headnote in *Addis's case* (and its recitation in the Donovan Report) in respect of special damages is based on a misconception. But at the very least the relevant part of the rule in *Addis's case* was controversial. In all these circumstances it is unrealistic to say that Parliament would have assumed the common law as reflected in the headnote in *Addis's case* to be set in stone and incapable of principled development. I would therefore reject this argument. ...

Lord Hoffmann:

47. I must however make it clear that, although in my opinion it would be jurisprudentially possible to imply a term which gave a remedy in this case, I do not think that even if the

courts were free of legislative constraint (a point to which I shall return in a moment) it would necessarily be wise to do so. It is not simply an incremental step from the duty of trust and confidence implied in *Mahmud v Bank of Credit and Commerce International SA* [1998] AC 20. The close association between the acts alleged to be in breach of the implied term and the irremovable and lawful fact of dismissal give rise to special problems. So, in *Wallace v United Grain Growers Ltd* (1997) 152 DLR (4th) 1, the majority rejected an implied duty to exercise the power of dismissal in good faith. Iacobucci J said, at p 28, that such a step was better left to the legislature. It would be "overly intrusive and inconsistent with established principles of employment law".

48. Some of the potential problems can be illustrated by the facts of this case, in which Mr Johnson claims some £400,000 damages for the financial consequences of psychiatric damage. This form of damage notoriously gives rise at the best of times to extremely difficult questions of causation. But the difficulties are made greater when the expert witnesses are required to perform the task of distinguishing between the psychiatric consequences of the fact of dismissal (for which no damages are recoverable) and the unfair circumstances in which the dismissal took place, which constituted a breach of the implied term. The agreed statement of facts records that for the purposes of this appeal against a strike-out it is accepted that Mr Johnson's psychiatric illness was caused by "the circumstances and the fact" of his dismissal. At a trial, however, it would be necessary to decide what was caused by what.

49. Another difficulty is the open-ended nature of liability. Mr Johnson's case is that Unisys had knowledge of his psychological fragility by reason of facts lodged in the corporate memory in 1985–87 and therefore should have foreseen when he was engaged that a failure to comply with proper disciplinary procedures on dismissal might result in injury which deprived him of the ability ever to work again. On general common law principles it seems to me that if the necessary term is implied and these facts are made out, the claim should succeed. It may be that such liability would be grossly disproportionate to the employer's degree of fault. It may be likely to inhibit the future engagement of psychologically fragile personnel. But the common law decides cases according to principle and cannot impose arbitrary limitations on liability because of the circumstances of the particular case. Only statute can lay down limiting rules based upon policy rather than principle. In this connection it is interesting to notice that although the majority in *Wallace v United Grain Growers Ltd* were unwilling to accept an implied term as to the manner of dismissal, they treated it as relevant to the period of notice which should reasonably have been given. McLachlin J said that this was illogical and so perhaps it is. But one can understand a desire to place some limit upon the employer's potential liability under this head.

50. It follows, my Lords, that if there was no relevant legislation in this area, I would regard the question of whether judges should develop the law by implying a suitable term into the contract of employment as finely balanced. But now I must consider the statutory background against which your Lordships are invited to create such a cause of action.

51. In 1968 the Royal Commission on Trade Unions and Employers' Associations under Lord Donovan recommended a statutory system of remedies for unfair dismissal. The recommendation was accepted by the government and given effect in the Industrial Relations Act 1971. Unfair dismissal was a wholly new statutory concept with new statutory remedies. Exclusive jurisdiction to hear complaints and give remedies was conferred upon the newly created National Industrial Relations Court. Although the 1971 Act was repealed by the Trade Union and Labour Relations Act 1974, the unfair dismissal provisions were re-enacted and, as subsequently amended, are consolidated in Part X of the Employment Rights Act 1996. The jurisdiction is now exercised by employment tribunals and forms part of the fabric of English employment law.

...

54. My Lords, this statutory system for dealing with unfair dismissals was set up by Parliament to deal with the recognised deficiencies of the law as it stood at the time of *Malloch v Aberdeen Corporation* [1971] 1 WLR 1581. The remedy adopted by Parliament was not to build upon the common law by creating a statutory implied term that the power of dismissal should be exercised fairly or in good faith, leaving the courts to give a remedy on general principles of contractual damages. Instead, it set up an entirely new system outside the ordinary courts, with tribunals staffed by a majority of lay members, applying new statutory concepts and offering statutory remedies. Many of the new rules, such as the exclusion of certain classes of employees and the limit on the amount of the compensatory award, were not based upon any principle which it would have been open to the courts to apply. They were based upon policy and represented an attempt to balance fairness to employees against the general economic interests of the community. And I should imagine that Parliament also had in mind the practical difficulties I have mentioned about causation and proportionality which would arise if the remedy was unlimited. So Parliament adopted the practical solution of giving the tribunals a very broad jurisdiction to award what they considered just and equitable but subject to a limit on the amount.

55. In my opinion, all the matters of which Mr Johnson complains in these proceedings were within the jurisdiction of the industrial tribunal. His most substantial complaint is of financial loss flowing from his psychiatric injury which he says was a consequence of the unfair manner of his dismissal. Such loss is a consequence of the dismissal which may form the subject-matter of a compensatory award. The only doubtful question is whether it would have been open to the tribunal to include a sum by way of compensation for his distress, damage to family life and similar matters. As the award, even reduced by 25%, exceeded the statutory maximum and had to be reduced to £11,000, the point would have been academic. But perhaps I may be allowed a comment all the same. I know that in the early days of the National Industrial Relations Court it was laid down that only financial loss could be compensated: see *Norton Tool Co Ltd v Tewson* [1973] ICR 45; *Wellman Alloys Ltd v Russell* [1973] ICR 616. It was said that the word "loss" can only mean financial loss. But I think that is too narrow a construction. The emphasis is upon the tribunal awarding such compensation as it thinks just and equitable. So I see no reason why in an appropriate case it should not include compensation for distress, humiliation, damage to reputation in the community or to family life.

56. Part X of the Employment Rights Act 1996 therefore gives a remedy for exactly the conduct of which Mr Johnson complains. But Parliament had restricted that remedy to a maximum of £11,000 [£83,682 in 2018], whereas Mr Johnson wants to claim a good deal more. The question is whether the courts should develop the common law to give a parallel remedy which is not subject to any such limit.

57. My Lords, I do not think that it is a proper exercise of the judicial function of the House to take such a step. Judge Ansell, to whose unreserved judgment I would pay respectful tribute, went in my opinion to the heart of the matter when he said:

"there is not one hint in the authorities that the ... tens of thousands of people that appear before the tribunals can have, as it were, a possible second bite in common law and I ask myself, if this is the situation, why on earth do we have this special statutory framework? What is the point of it if it can be circumvented in this way? ... it would mean that effectively the statutory limit on compensation for unfair dismissal would disappear."

58. I can see no answer to these questions. For the judiciary to construct a general common law remedy for unfair circumstances attending dismissal would be to go contrary to the evident intention of Parliament that there should be such a remedy but that it should be limited in application and extent.

59. The same reason is in my opinion fatal to the claim based upon a duty of care. It is of course true that a duty of care can exist independently of the contractual relationship. But the grounds upon which I think it would be wrong to impose an implied contractual duty would make it equally wrong to achieve the same result by the imposition of a duty of care.

...

66. My Lords, given this background to the disciplinary procedures, I find it impossible to believe that Parliament, when it provided in section 3(1) of the 1996 Act that the statement of particulars of employment was to contain a note of any applicable disciplinary rules, or the parties themselves, intended that the inclusion of those rules should give rise to a common law action in damages which would create the means of circumventing the restrictions and limits which Parliament had imposed on compensation for unfair dismissal. The whole of the reasoning which led me to the conclusion that the courts should not imply a term which has this result also in my opinion supports the view that the disciplinary procedures do not do so either. It is I suppose possible that they may have contractual effect in determining whether the employer can dismiss summarily in the sense of not having to give four weeks' notice or payment in lieu. But I do not think that they can have been intended to qualify the employer's common law power to dismiss without cause on giving such notice, or to create contractual duties which are independently actionable.

Lord Bingham, **Lord Nicholls** and **Lord Millett** agreed with **Lord Hoffmann**.

NOTES AND QUESTIONS

1. The House of Lords held that common law damages for breach of mutual trust and confidence during a dismissal could not be applied to circumvent the statutory damages cap. As chapter 18(1) showed, the issue was not that a duty to dismiss in good faith was impossible to create, nor that it would necessarily be undesirable at common law, but the much narrower point that damages should be capped according to the balance that Parliament (or more accurately, the Secretary of State) has struck. Lord Steyn dissents on the reasoning, but agreed that Johnson's appeal should be dismissed because he did not think it right to overturn the Court of Appeal's view that Johnson's loss was too remote from the fact of dismissal.

2. On the one hand, *Johnson* excludes claims by very high earners for economic loss. This benefits large firms, and essentially makes it relatively less costly to fire senior staff who, one could argue, might be more likely to litigate. One might say this precludes a 'damages lottery' for high earners in unfair dismissal cases. During their submissions, counsel for Unisys Ltd was apparently very persuasive by merely repeating the figure of '£400,000' over and again. On the other hand, *Johnson* could be argued to illegitimately limit the development of common law, as Lord Steyn urges. There was no indication, this argument would go, that the Industrial Relations Act 1971 was intended to freeze the common law in its tracks: on the contrary it was designed to remedy the defects of the common law.

3. The same issue has been repeatedly addressed and challenged. In *Eastwood v Magnox Electric plc* [2004] UKHL 35 the House of Lords held that if there was a breach of mutual trust and confidence before a dismissal, then the so-called *Johnson* exclusion zone does not apply. Mr Eastwood was victimised by managers who had apparently organised bogus sexual harassment disciplinary hearings. He settled a claim for unfair dismissal, and then claimed wrongful dismissal, for

breach of mutual trust and confidence during the performance of the contract (rather than at the point of dismissal). In a joined appeal, Mr McCabe succeeded in an unfair dismissal claim, as an allegation of indecency toward school pupils was never proven, he was not informed of the allegation for five months, there was no investigation and he contracted a psychiatric illness. The House of Lords held both cases succeeded and stated that they could proceed to claim damages beyond the statutory cap (in McCabe's case, for £200,000). Lord Nicholls, referring to this inconsistency, said: 'This situation merits urgent attention by the government and legislature.' Do you agree that it is the legislature's problem, rather than one of the courts?

4. *Barber v Somerset CC* [2004] UKHL 13 similarly held that a maths teacher's claim for damages for psychiatric injury could be awarded for breach of duty during the employment relationship: these significantly exceeded the statutory cap.

5. In *Edwards v Chesterfield Royal Hospital NHS Foundation Trust* [2011] UKSC 58 Lady Hale said in her dissenting opinion at [121]: 'We have seen how the "Johnson exclusion area" has been productive of anomalies and difficulties. There is no reason at all to extend it any further than the ratio of that case. As the Court of Appeal held in this case, it should be limited to the consequences of dismissal in breach of the implied term of trust and confidence. The House of Lords was persuaded that the common law implied term, developed for a different purpose, should not be extended to cover the territory which Parliament had occupied. In fact, the territory which Parliament had occupied was the lack of a remedy for loss of a job to which the employee had no contractual right beyond the contractual notice period. Parliament occupied that territory by requiring employers to act fairly when they dismissed their employees. But there was and is nothing in the legislation to take away the existing contractual rights of employees. There was and is nothing to suggest that Parliament intended to limit the entitlement of those few employees who did and do have a contractual right to the job, the right not to be dismissed without cause. It is for that reason that I am afraid that I cannot agree that the key distinction is between the consequences of dismissal and the consequences of other breaches. The key distinction must be between cases which must rely on the implied term to complain about the dismissal and cases which can rely on an express term.' What do you think?

6. In *Horkulak v Cantor Fitzgerald International* [2004] EWCA Civ 1287, the Court of Appeal held that it could calculate the quantum of a bonus that a derivatives trader should receive under his contract after he was constructively and wrongfully dismissed following bullying and abuse. It held that the bonus calculation of £450,000 should be reduced by £116,667. Do you think the law, as developed by the courts, is in a consistent and defensible state?

(b) Injunctions After Dismissal

Once litigation is underway, many people do not want their jobs back. However, particularly in large institutions, many people do want to keep their jobs if it does not mean working with potentially unpleasant people they had previously encountered. The majority of people in the UK are employed in workplaces with over 250 staff. There are 8,825 such large enterprises, employing 16.47m of a total 30.44m workforce: ONS, *Small and Medium-Size Enterprises (SME) Count, Employment and Turnover 2010 to 2017* (2017). The larger the workplace, the easier a workable reinstatement remedy is. But plainly the best solution is that someone is not unfairly dismissed to start with, and makes use of the right to an injunction to follow proper, fair procedure, before any dismissal takes effect (chapter 17(4)). If the dismissal or suspension has already happened, courts can order reinstatement or re-engagement.

Employment Rights Act 1996 ss 114–15

114 Order for reinstatement.
(1) An order for reinstatement is an order that the employer shall treat the complainant in all respects as if he had not been dismissed.
(2) On making an order for reinstatement the tribunal shall specify—
  (a) any amount payable by the employer in respect of any benefit which the complainant might reasonably be expected to have had but for the dismissal (including arrears of pay) for the period between the date of termination of employment and the date of reinstatement,
  (b) any rights and privileges (including seniority and pension rights) which must be restored to the employee, and
  (c) the date by which the order must be complied with.
(3) If the complainant would have benefited from an improvement in his terms and conditions of employment had he not been dismissed, an order for reinstatement shall require him to be treated as if he had benefited from that improvement from the date on which he would have done so but for being dismissed. …
  …

115 Order for re-engagement.
(1) An order for re-engagement is an order, on such terms as the tribunal may decide, that the complainant be engaged by the employer, or by a successor of the employer or by an associated employer, in employment comparable to that from which he was dismissed or other suitable employment.
(2) On making an order for re-engagement the tribunal shall specify the terms on which re-engagement is to take place, including—
  (a) the identity of the employer,
  (b) the nature of the employment,
  (c) the remuneration for the employment,
  (d) any amount payable by the employer in respect of any benefit which the complainant might reasonably be expected to have had but for the dismissal (including arrears of pay) for the period between the date of termination of employment and the date of re-engagement,
  (e) any rights and privileges (including seniority and pension rights) which must be restored to the employee, and
  (f) the date by which the order must be complied with. …
  …

116 Choice of order and its terms.
(1) In exercising its discretion under section 113 the tribunal shall first consider whether to make an order for reinstatement and in so doing shall take into account—
  (a) whether the complainant wishes to be reinstated,
  (b) whether it is practicable for the employer to comply with an order for reinstatement, and

(c) where the complainant caused or contributed to some extent to the dismissal, whether it would be just to order his reinstatement.

...

117 Enforcement of order and compensation.

(1) An employment tribunal shall make an award of compensation, to be paid by the employer to the employee, if—

    (a) an order under section 113 is made and the complainant is reinstated or re-engaged, but

    (b) the terms of the order are not fully complied with.

(3) ... if an order under section 113 is made but the complainant is not reinstated or re-engaged in accordance with the order, the tribunal shall make—

    (a) an award of compensation for unfair dismissal (calculated in accordance with sections 118 to 126, and

    (b) except where this paragraph does not apply, an additional award of compensation of an amount not less than twenty-six nor more than fifty-two weeks' pay, to be paid by the employer to the employee.

(4) Subsection (3)(b) does not apply where—

    (a) the employer satisfies the tribunal that it was not practicable to comply with the order ...

NOTES AND QUESTIONS   •

1.   ERA ss 113–17 say in effect that Tribunals can require employees get their jobs back and enforce such orders for re-engagement or reinstatement with a damages claim. However, employers can argue that reinstatement is impracticable.

2.   ERA 1996 s 128 enables employees to apply for interim relief, which can include under s 130 an order for the continuation of a contract of employment.

3.   In *O'Laire v Jackal Ltd* [1990] IRLR 70, 73, Lord Donaldson MR gave an opinion that reinstatement is 'wholly unenforceable'. This appears to be an unfortunate contradiction of Parliament's will, but it has not altogether been ignored.

Port of London Authority v Payne [1993] EWCA Civ 26

Payne and others claimed that they should be re-engaged in their jobs with the Port of London Authority at Tilbury. In July 1989, dockworkers were dismissed including seventeen shop stewards. They successfully claimed in the Tribunal their dismissals were motivated by their union official status. The Tribunal ordered re-engagement for twelve applicants, and awarded compensation to others. It held it was practicable to comply with the order. The Employment Appeal Tribunal allowed the Port of London Authority's Appeal, as did the Court of Appeal, against re-engagement, taking the view that it would be disruptive for the employer to make more redundancies to make way for the reinstatement.

Neill LJ:

On the one hand it is necessary to bear in mind that the issue of practicability was a question of fact for the industrial tribunal to decide. An appellate court must therefore be very careful before it interferes with such a finding. But the test is practicability not possibility. The industrial tribunal, though it should carefully scrutinise the reasons advanced by an employer, should give due weight to the commercial judgment of the management unless of course the witnesses are disbelieved. The standard must not be set too high. The employer cannot be expected to explore every possible avenue which ingenuity might suggest. The employer does not have to show that reinstatement or re-engagement was impossible. It is a matter of what is practicable in the circumstances of the employer's business at the relevant time.

In the end I have come to the conclusion that the industrial tribunal misdirected itself as to the standard to be applied. It may be that in other circumstances the right course would have been to send the case back to the industrial tribunal to consider whether one or more individuals might have been re-engaged. That would not be a sensible course in this case. One has to look at the matter as a whole. I am satisfied that if the industrial tribunal had directed itself correctly it would have been bound to find in the light of the evidence given by Mr. Burton and Mr. Hills that it would have not been practicable to re-engage these 12 applicants. I can well understand why the orders for re-engagement were made in the first place but it seems to me that, once the matter was looked at again and in greater detail at the practicability hearing, the case for the P.L.A. was made out.

Staughton LJ and **Nolan LJ** agreed.

NOTES AND QUESTIONS

1. Why is the 'commercial judgement' of employers who victimise people who join unions given any weight?

2. If you cannot get your job back, do you really have a right to not be unfairly dismissed?

3. *McBride v Scottish Police Authority* [2016] UKSC 27 saw a rare claim for reinstatement succeed, at least partially. A Tribunal has no power under ERA 1996 s 114 to order reinstatement on different contractual terms, but can recognise practical limitations. In this case, Ms McBride's fingerprint expert team was caught in a media scandal after suggesting one DC McKie was present at a murder scene, when she said she was not. DC McKie narrowly avoided a perjury conviction only after it transpired at trial that the fingerprints could have been wrong. McBride was suspended, until a report said the fingerprint experts were guilty of no malicious wrongdoing and there should be no disciplinary action: all playing out through the papers. She was put back in her job but not giving court evidence, because evidence by her could be used to 'weaken the significance of the fingerprint evidence in the eyes of the jury' in a trial, [7]. In 2007 a new manager, Mr David Mulhern, carrying through a reorganisation (perhaps playing to the papers) stated that McBride and the fingerprint experts involved in the scandal would not be reinstated under him and she was dismissed. The Tribunal held that she was unfairly dismissed, and ordered reinstatement, recognising that she was not go to court, as had been the status quo. Rejecting the view that this amounted to a contractual variation against s 114, Lord Hodge in the Supreme Court held that the reinstatement order was sound.

4. Do you think 9 years of litigation makes it easy to go back to the same job? Do you agree it would be preferable if the manager, Mr Mulhern, had not been capable of pushing through an unfair dismissal in the first place?

(c) Compromise Agreements

Employees can agree to settle their claims under a 'compromise agreement'.

Employment Rights Act 1996 s 203

203 Restrictions on contracting out.
(1) Any provision in an agreement (whether a contract of employment or not) is void in so far as it purports—
    (a) to exclude or limit the operation of any provision of this Act, or
    (b) to preclude a person from bringing any proceedings under this Act before an employment tribunal.
(2) Subsection (1)—
    (a) does not apply to any provision in a collective agreement excluding rights under section 28 if an order under section 35 is for the time being in force in respect of it,
    (b) does not apply to any provision in a dismissal procedures agreement excluding the right under section 94 if that provision is not to have effect unless an order under section 110 is for the time being in force in respect of it,
    (c) does not apply to any provision in an agreement if an order under section 157 is for the time being in force in respect of it,
    (e) does not apply to any agreement to refrain from instituting or continuing proceedings where a conciliation officer has taken action under any of sections 18A to 18C of the Employment Tribunals Act 1996], and
    (f) does not apply to any agreement to refrain from instituting or continuing any proceedings within the following provisions of section 18(1) of the Employment Tribunals Act 1996 (cases where conciliation available)—
        (i) paragraph (b) (proceedings under this Act),
        (ii) paragraph (l)] (proceedings arising out of the Part-time Workers (Prevention of Less Favourable Treatment) Regulations 2000),] if the conditions regulating [F8settlement] agreements under this Act are satisfied in relation to the agreement
        (iii) paragraph (m)] (proceedings arising out of the Fixed-term Employees (Prevention of Less Favourable Treatment) Regulations 2002),
(3) For the purposes of subsection (2)(f) the conditions regulating [F8settlement] agreements under this Act are that—
    (a) the agreement must be in writing,
    (b) the agreement must relate to the particular [F12proceedings],
    (c) the employee or worker must have received [F13advice from a relevant independent adviser] as to the terms and effect of the proposed agreement and, in particular, its effect on his ability to pursue his rights before an [F1employment tribunal],
    (d) there must be in force, when the adviser gives the advice, a [F14contract of insurance, or an indemnity provided for members of a profession or professional body,] covering the risk of a claim by the employee or worker in respect of loss arising in consequence of the advice,
    (e) the agreement must identify the adviser, and
    (f) the agreement must state that the conditions regulating [F8settlement] agreements under this Act are satisfied.

1. ERA 1996 s 203 states that statutory rights, unsurprisingly, cannot be contracted away. This provisions underlines the idea that rights are not for sale. It follows the point, emphasised in chapter 3, that there must be no element of consent built into the concept of an employee or worker. Section 203 goes on to enable employers and employees to make compromise agreements, effectively to settle their claims, so long as an employee is properly advised.

2. In *Igbo v Johnson, Matthey Chemicals Ltd* [1986] ICR 505, Ms Igbo was granted three extra days holiday for signing an agreement that if she failed to return on a set date 'your contract of employment will automatically terminate'. She was ill, and sent in a medical note, but her job was still terminated. Parker LJ held that agreed terminations are very often still dismissals, as under s 95(1)(b) where fixed-term contracts expire, or where there is notice under s 95(1)(a). Here the provision for automatic termination had the effect, if valid, of limiting the operation of the sections. It was therefore void by virtue of s 203.

3. In *Logan Salton v Durham CC* [1989] IRLR 99 a union official negotiated a settlement before any disciplinary hearing where a bad outcome was expected on the employee's behalf. Salton had been pressing to return to an old post and other grievances. With the settlement, employment was terminated and Salton claimed unfair dismissal. Tribunal held there was no dismissal. The Emploment Appeal Tribunal held the agreement was not the product of duress and because it was agreed there was no dismissal. Wood J said this was different from Igbo because it was entered willingly, on good advice, without duress, it was not varying an existing contract and did not depend on a possible future event which if known could change the employee's mind (like getting sick or being hit by a car). Moreover, 'the resolution of industrial disputes it is in the best interests of all concerned'.

4. *Norman v Yellow Pages Sales Ltd* [2010] EWCA Civ 1395, Ms Norman had reached an ACAS settlement with Yellow Pages for her sex, race, victimisation and wrongful dismissal allegations for £53,000. Yellow Pages paid £47,650, the deduction necessary to reflect tax and national insurance, and Norman sued for the shortfall. Pill LJ, Longmore LJ and Jacob LJ held that Yellow Pages were not in breach of contract.

R Epstein, 'In Defense of the Contract at Will' (1984) 57 *University of Chicago Law Review* **947**

Epstein argues employers should be empowered by law to be able to fire anyone at will. (Parts are extracted in chapter 2(2).) He doubts inequality of bargaining power exists, and argues that if it did, labour's total share of income in the economy would logically be declining. But then Epstein argues that, even if the empirical evidence went against him (and clearly today it does), he would deny the public concern in private ordering because intervention is usually damaging.

H Collins, *Nine Proposals for the Reform of the Law on Unfair Dismissal* (Institute of Employment Rights 2004)

Collins proposes nine reforms to improve justice in dismissal. He argues that protection should extend, not just to employees but all workers, that age discrimination should go (this was achieved), that the doctrine of frustration should have no application (this is possible by reversing *Notcutt* in chapter 17(1)), that the qualifying period should be eliminated (this is already the case, it seems, at common law, chapter 18(1) above), that the test for fairness should be changed to a proportionality test (chapter 18(2) explains this may be possible since *Turner*), that disciplinary procedures should be required to be fair (contrast chapter 17(3)), that workers should have an alternative to tribunals, specifically 'consultation with collective representatives of the workforce as to the composition and procedures for internal appeals' (which should mean elected work councils: see chapter 11(2)), that compensation should be truly just (contrast chapter 17(4)), and that dismissals violating other social rights should be effectively sanctioned.

19

Redundancy and Transfers

If enterprises are to be sustainable and productive in the long term, they must adopt the best technology and organisational practices. But who should decide how? Redundancy and transfers of enterprise bring the conflicting interests among stakeholders into sharp focus. Directors or managers, shareholders and workers should be entitled to a reasonable return for their inputs of labour or capital. Public or regulated enterprises, where competition fails, should ensure the interests of service-users and society are protected. But if any stakeholder unduly influences the enterprise governance structure, they may redistribute wealth to themselves at others' expense. To inflate executive bonuses or shareholder profit in the short term, employees might be sacked or their pay might be cut. Thousands of people are regularly made redundant, even while there are healthy profits, and the redundancies are publicised in business news to signal shareholders' interests have primacy (see www.theguardian.com/business/job-losses). Long term, this damages workforce trust and productivity. It probably harms innovation, as empirical evidence suggests job security fosters creative production: V Acharya et al, 'Labor Laws and Innovation' (2013) 56(4) *Journal of Law and Economics* 997; chapter 2(3). Security, not insecurity, promotes success.

Relatively fewer people are made redundant each year in the UK than in the United States, but UK redundancies are higher than in Germany or France. Between November 2016 and October 2017 around 1.4 per cent of UK employees, 417,000 people, become redundant out of a 30m employee workforce (with self-employed people, the workforce is 35m). ONS, *UK Labour Market: March 2018*, tables 5 and 22. Turnover in jobs might be argued to reflect an economy's dynamism and flexibility: turnover could be said to reflect improving technology and organisation. But it is more credible to think the opposite is true: redundancies are like a wasteful byproduct of defective legal rights. Short-term decisions by shareholders or managers externalise the social costs of economic change, and those costs outweigh the private gains. If workers have a proportionate voice in redundancy decisions, one would expect redundancies to occur when actually necessary. Workers will require that ex-colleagues are compensated in full for time unemployed, or for retraining, and because they pay tax, for enterprises to minimise the social costs of unemployment insurance or education for new skills. In practice the law falls short of these standards. This chapter discusses (1) the concept of redundancy that triggers rights under individual, collective and transfer rules, or dismissals for 'some other substantial reason', (2) the duty of employers to consult with individuals and in collective redundancy cases, (3) the right to receive redundancy pay or to be redeployed to another job.

Introductory texts: Collins ch 9. CEM chs 20. D&M ch 5 (561–92).

(1) CONCEPTIONS OF REDUNDANCY

Three fields of labour law use a conception of a redundancy, or more generally 'economic dismissals'. First, UK statute has two definitions of redundancy, for the purpose consultation and for severance pay. Second, in the statutory unfair dismissal provisions (chapter 18(2)(b)), an employer is able to dismiss employees for 'some other substantial reason'. Although it is wholly unclear this was intended, it has been interpreted by the courts to justify dismissals when an employer wants to cut pay or working time and employees do not accept it after a consultation. Third, when there is a transfer of an undertaking (mainly a sale of one business' assets, and potentially also employment contracts, to another) employers cannot dismiss employees unless there is a justified 'economic, technical or organisational' reason. In each case there are duties of consultation (chapter 19(2)). Someone who meets the definition of redundancy will receive severance pay and has a weak right to be redeployed (chapter 19(3)). Despite different words, these statutory concepts fulfil largely the same function. Different constructions would not serve any legitimate aim.

(a) Redundancies

The concept of redundancy at the moment is meant to ensure that people who are dismissed, because their positions are unnecessary for the firm, are fully consulted and compensated. There are, however, two definitions: one for collective consultation (Trade Union and Labour Relations (Consolidation) Act (TULRCA) 1992 s 195), and another for compensation (Employment Rights Act (ERA) 1996 s 139).

Trade Union and Labour Relations (Consolidation) Act 1992 s 195

195 Construction of references to dismissal as redundant etc.
(1) In this Chapter references to dismissal as redundant are references to dismissal for a reason not related to the individual concerned or for a number of reasons all of which are not so related.
(2) For the purposes of any proceedings under this Chapter, where an employee is or is proposed to be dismissed it shall be presumed, unless the contrary is proved, that he is or is proposed to be dismissed as redundant.

1. TULRCA 1992 s 195 defines redundancy for collective consultation, and is broad: anything 'not related to the individual'. The statutory duty to consult in s 188 is triggered if 20 people over 90 days are made collectively redundant (chapter 19(2)).
2. As we saw in chapter 18(2) the statutory list in ERA 1996 s 98(2) says fair reasons for dismissal are for (a) capability, (b) conduct, (c) redundancy, (d) statute, or in s 98(1)(b) for 'some other substantial reason'. Presumably under s 195, reasons that would be 'related to the individual concerned' are capability and conduct.
3. A longer definition is found in the ERA 1996 s 139, for the right to severance pay.

Employment Rights Act 1996 s 139

139 Redundancy.
   (1) For the purposes of this Act an employee who is dismissed shall be taken to be dismissed by reason of redundancy if the dismissal is wholly or mainly attributable to—
   (a)   the fact that his employer has ceased or intends to cease—
      (i)   to carry on the business for the purposes of which the employee was employed by him, or
      (ii) to carry on that business in the place where the employee was so employed, or
   (b)   the fact that the requirements of that business—
      (i)   for employees to carry out work of a particular kind, or
      (ii) for employees to carry out work of a particular kind in the place where the employee was employed by the employer,
   have ceased or diminished or are expected to cease or diminish.
   (2) For the purposes of subsection (1) the business of the employer together with the business or businesses of his associated employers shall be treated as one (unless either of the conditions specified in paragraphs (a) and (b) of that subsection would be satisfied without so treating them).

1. ERA 1996 s 139(1) contains two main ideas, that someone is redundant (a) if a business does or will close, or (b) if the need for work diminishes. Put another way, if an enterprise closes or cuts, there is a redundancy. At its lowest, even if 'the requirements' for 'employees to carry out work' have 'diminished', there is a redundancy. On a plain reading, there is no need for a whole job to be lost: a cut to part of a job is enough.
2. Between the two definitions, there does not seem to be any substantive difference. However, in *Commission v United Kingdom* (1994) C-382/92, the Commission argued that the UK had not properly implemented the definition in the Collective Redundancies Directive (now recast as 98/59/EC) because the UK definition, which reflects what is now in ERA 1996 s 139, did not cover 'cases where workers have been dismissed as a result of new working arrangements within an undertaking unconnected with its volume of business'. The UK government at the time

> conceded that this was right, and amended the wording of TULRCA 1992 s 195 to its present form. However, it would seem that ERA 1996 s 139 is adequate, so long as one does not construe the 'requirements' of a business to mean the same thing as 'volume'. For example, if the consumer demand of a business is the same, but jobs are cut because of new technological or administrative efficiency, then there is still a redundancy under ERA 1996 s 139.
>
> 3. There is a formal difference of procedure between TULRCA 1992 s 195 and ERA 1996 s 139. For consultation in s 195(2) it is presumed that dismissals are for redundancy. For compensation in s 98 the employer has the burden of proof to demonstrate a reason. Either way, the employer is going to have to prove (if it wants to) that an employee is not redundant to avoid consultation, or to avoid redundancy pay. This means showing that dismissals are for conduct or capability – something that will usually be impossible for collective redundancies.
>
> 4. The next case concerns when s 195 is triggered.

University and College Union v University of Stirling [2015] UKSC 26

The University and College Union (UCU) claimed that the University of Stirling had a duty to consult on redundancies with fixed-term staff, as well as permanent members of staff, before any dismissals. In 2009–10 the University projected a future (not present) deficit of £4.4m. So it proposed to make 140 redundancies among permanent employees. After it began consultation, it received 134 applications for voluntary redundancy (where people choose to take severance pay, and may retire, or simply have found other jobs) and so decided to make no compulsory redundancies among permanent staff. However, it did not consult fixed-term staff, and it subsequently resolved not to renew a large number of people's contracts. UCU organised four test cases, claiming that non-renewal of a fixed-term contract was a dismissal, and under TULRCA 1992 s 195, that this counted as redundancy. The Supreme Court, overturning all courts below, held all the fixed-term staff were dismissed and redundant, and the University must consult.

Lady Hale:

4. Dr Harris was employed as a post-doctoral research assistant. Her contract was due to expire on 16 August 2009 and the University resolved not to renew it. Dr Doyle was employed to co-ordinate and deliver three undergraduate modules in English Studies in the spring semester of 2009. Her contract was not renewed when the semester ended on 29 May 2009. Ms Fife was employed to provide maternity cover, initially until 2 May 2009, extended until 4 September 2009, and again until 9 October 2009. Between 10 October 2009 and 10 September 2010 she was employed on a casual basis. Ms Kelly was originally employed to provide sick leave cover for one month in July 2007, and then from 1 October 2007 to 31 March 2008. Her employment was then extended until 30 September 2008 and then to 30 September 2009, partly because she was a named researcher on a number of projects and partly to cover for a colleague who was working reduced hours after returning from maternity leave.

    ...

13. As we are dealing with a definition which is for the particular purpose of the duty to consult about proposed collective redundancies, the statutory purpose and content of that duty are of some relevance. Under section 188(2), the consultation has to include consultation about ways

of avoiding the dismissals, reducing the numbers of employees to be dismissed, and mitigating the consequences of the dismissals. Under section 188(4), the employer has to disclose the reasons for his proposals, the numbers and description of employees whom it is proposed to dismiss as redundant, the total number of employees of any such description employed by the employer at the establishment in question, the proposed method of selecting the employees who may be dismissed, the proposed method of carrying out the dismissals, and the proposed method of calculating any redundancy payments to be made.

14. For completeness, if an employer fails to comply with section 188(1), the trade union may present a complaint to an Employment Tribunal (section 189(1)). If the tribunal finds the complaint well founded it must make a declaration to that effect and also has power to make a protective award (section 189(2)). This is an award of remuneration for the protected period to those employees who have been dismissed as redundant, in respect of whose dismissal or proposed dismissal the employer failed to comply with section 188 (section 189(3)). The protected period is also within the discretion of the tribunal but cannot be for more than 90 days (section 189(4)). The employer also has a duty to give advance notice of proposed collective redundancies to the Secretary of State (section 193) and failure to do so is a criminal offence (section 194).

15. Finally, by virtue of section 298 of the 1992 Act, "dismiss" and "dismissal" are to be construed in accordance with Part X of the Employment Rights Act 1996. Section 95(1)(b) of that Act provides that an employee is dismissed if "he is employed under a limited term contract and that contract terminates by virtue of the limiting event without being renewed under the same contract". It is common ground, therefore, that these employees were dismissed. The only question is whether they were "dismissed as redundant" within the meaning of section 195(1) of the 1992 Act. This in turn depends upon whether the reasons for the dismissal were "not related to the individual concerned".

...

20. It is, however, important to bear in mind that Parliament will certainly not have intended to narrow the scope of the consultation duty from the classic redundancy situations covered under the earlier law: the cessation or reduction in business. Furthermore, it intended to add to those situations the reorganisation of the business: classically, where employees are dismissed and offered new contracts so that their terms and conditions of employment can be changed. This lends powerful support to Mr Glyn's contention that the terms and conditions of the employees' contracts of employment cannot be a "reason related to the individual", because if they were, such business rearrangements, although the very reason why the definition was changed, would not be covered.

21. The context and content of the duty to consult all suggest that it is concerned with the needs of the business or undertaking as a whole. The employer has to explain why he wishes to make a substantial number of employees redundant, which descriptions of employee he proposes to make redundant, and how he proposes to choose among the employees within those descriptions. Employees on LTCs [Limited Term Contracts] might be a description of employees for this purpose, and being on an LTC might be a criterion for selecting for dismissal, but it is a collective description rather than a reason relating to the individual concerned.

22. Where an LTC comes to an end, the "dismissal" in question is the non-renewal of the LTC – or rather the failure to offer a new contract, the LTC having come to an end. The fact that it was an LTC, or even that the employee agreed to it, cannot by itself be a reason for the non-renewal. Many LTCs are in fact renewed or new contracts offered. The question is whether the reasons for the failure to offer a new contract relate to the individual or to the needs of the

business. Sometimes, no doubt, it will relate to the individual. The employer may still need to have the work done, but for one reason or another considers that this employee is not suitable to do it. That would not be a dismissal for redundancy. But the ending of a research project or the ending of a particular undergraduate course would not be a reason related to the individual employee but a reason related to the employer's business. The business no longer has a need for someone to do the research or someone to teach the course. The same would usually be true of the ending of maternity or sickness cover. The need for the job would not have ended but the need for the job to be done by someone other than the person who usually does it would have ended. That too is not a reason related to the individual employee but a reason related to the employer's business.

23. In short, the Employment Appeal Tribunal stated an admirable test: "A reason relates to the individual if it is something to do with him such as something he is or something he has done. It is to be distinguished from a reason relating to the employer, such as his (or in the case of insolvency, his creditors') need to effect business change in some respect". The error was to place the coming to an end of an LTC into the first rather than the second category.

Lord Wilson, **Lord Sumption**, **Lord Reed** and **Lord Hughes** agreed.

NOTES AND QUESTIONS

1. Lady Hale holds for a unanimous Supreme Court that a limited or fixed-term contract ending is a dismissal. Plainly a fixed-term contract, as the Supreme Court holds, is not a reason related to the employee. Do you agree that this is because the employer usually dictates the terms, and decides (against the employee's will) to not renew a fixed-term contract? The employee is told to take-it-or-leave-it and usually has no choice.

2. Lady Hale at [22] also makes clear that when someone is employed to cover for maternity (and presumably paternity: see chapter 7(3)) or sickness of another employee, the ending of their contract is a redundancy. Usually such a person would not be employed for two years, and then would not qualify for redundancy pay, but they must be consulted and redeployed.

3. Lady Hale says at [13] that because the case deals with a definition for the purpose of consultation duties 'the statutory purpose and content of that duty are of some relevance'. It seems possible that this was a humorous understatement, and might tentatively be read as a jibe at lower courts who did not think about that.

4. The first UK legislation on redundancies was the Redundancy Payments Act 1965. *North Riding Garages v Butterwick* [1967] 2 QB 56 was one of the first appellate decisions. Mr Alexander Butterwick claimed he was being made redundant as a car repairs shop manager of 30 years in Whitby, Yorkshire, after new owners introduced new working methods: more paperwork and providing customers cost estimates in advance. Mr Butterwick could not adjust to these new methods, and was found to be redundant by the Industrial Tribunal. But on appeal, Lord Parker CJ, Glyn-Jones J and Widgery J held there was no redundancy because a manager was still needed, just with new skills. Widgery J said Butterwick 'could not do his job in accordance with the new methods and new standards required by the appellants'. While the unfair dismissal rules were not in force at the time, this finding would logically be classified today as a dismissal on the ground of 'capability'. Do you agree that such a finding must place an implied duty on the

employer having done everything to retrain their staff? Surely an employer cannot introduce a new method and sack someone without skills to adapt.

5. Lady Hale says at [20] that Parliament 'intended to add to those situations the reorganisation of the business: classically, where employees are dismissed and offered new contracts so that their terms and conditions of employment can be changed'. This suggests that new contracts which cut rights will always trigger redundancy claims. But what if an employer's written statement of the contract (as opposed to the contract in law) contains a flexibility clause, or an employer's discretion to vary an employee's rights? Do you agree that if a written clause is relied upon by an employer in a way that undermines the employees' reasonable expectations that this will break the contract, and potentially trigger redundancy? Do you agree that any other result would enable an employer to effectively contract out of statutory redundancy rights?

6. After *UCU v University of Stirling* some older decisions appear questionable. For example, in *Lesney Products & Co v Nolan* [1976] EWCA Civ 8 (which was not referred to in *UCU v Stirling*) Nolan claimed that he was redundant after Lesney Products & Co removed its night shift, divided its day shift into two, and stopped giving overtime to workers at its Hackney factory. Demand for its children's toys had fallen. Many employees' wages dropped by a third. Some refused to work on the new day shift and were dismissed. They claimed they were redundant. Overturning the Tribunal, Lord Denning MR said that while this was 'a very difficult case' it was 'important that nothing should be done to impair the ability of employers to reorganise their work force and their times and conditions of work so as to improve efficiency. They may reorganise it so as to reduce overtime and thus to save themselves money, but that does not give the man a right to redundancy payment.' Do you agree that if an employer cuts everyone's working time by 30 per cent, this has the same economic result for the employer (minus fixed costs) as sacking three out of ten workers? Do you agree that the duty to consult and compensate workers itself does 'nothing … to impair the ability of employers to reorganise', and ensures that their decision making is credible? Surely Lord Denning MR was correct when he said in *Re Vandervell's Trusts (No 2)* [1974] Ch 269, 322, that 'when people say hard cases [or 'very difficult' cases] make bad law, they often mean unjust cases make good law, and this is wrong'.

7. Some managers are fond of branding job and pay cuts with happy-sounding, yet sinister words. For example in *Safeway Stores plc v Burrell* [1997] ICR 523 Safeway Stores plc had a 'Safeway 2000' plan for its staff, which envisaged 'delayering' its departments. For Mr Burrell, a petrol station 'manager' in Penzance, what 'Safeway 2000' actually meant was that his job was being 'replaced' by a petrol station 'controller' on less pay for essentially the same work. The facts and proceedings in the case itself were that Mr Burrell did not apply for the 'new' post, and received redundancy pay, but also claimed his dismissal was unfair because he said he was not actually redundant. The Tribunal held that the employers failed to demonstrate that Mr Burrell was redundant, as the job was similar to that before, but Peter Clark J in the Employment Appeal Tribunal held the Tribunal should hear the case again because it failed to ask whether the dismissal was caused by diminished need for employees.

8. The test of 'diminished demand' was explored in *Murray*.

Murray v Foyle Meats Ltd [1999] UKHL 30

Mr Murray and Mr Doherty claimed that they were not redundant, and so were unfairly dismissed, from the slaughter hall of Foyle Meats Ltd in Londonderry. As its business was declining, Foyle Meats Ltd eliminated a production line, and 35 employees were told they were redundant. However, their contracts contained flexibility clauses, requiring that they could be rotated to the boning or loading hall. Murray and Doherty argued they were unfairly selected for redundancy, because employees in any department (not just the slaughter hall) could have been selected. On this basis they argued they were not redundant under the Industrial Relations (Northern Ireland) Order 1976 Art 2(7), which is materially identical to ERA 1996 s 139(1). The House of Lords held the employees were redundant.

Lord Irvine LC:

My Lords, the language of paragraph (b) [of ERA 1996 s 139(1)] is in my view simplicity itself. It asks two questions of fact. The first is whether one or other of various states of economic affairs exists. In this case, the relevant one is whether the requirements of the business for employees to carry out work of a particular kind have diminished. The second question is whether the dismissal is attributable, wholly or mainly, to that state of affairs. This is a question of causation. In the present case, the Tribunal found as a fact that the requirements of the business for employees to work in the slaughter hall had diminished. Secondly, they found that that state of affairs had led to the appellants being dismissed. That, in my opinion, is the end of the matter.

This conclusion is in accordance with the analysis of the statutory provisions by Judge Peter Clark in *Safeway Stores Plc v Burrell* [1997] IRLR 200 and I need to say no more than that I entirely agree with his admirably clear reasoning and conclusions. But I should, out of respect for the submissions of Mr Declan Morgan QC for the appellants, say something about the earlier cases which may have encouraged a belief that the statute had a different meaning.

In *Nelson v British Broadcasting Corporation* [1977] IRLR 148 Mr Nelson was employed by the BBC under a contract which required him to perform any duties to which he might be assigned. In fact he worked for the General Overseas Service broadcasting to the Caribbean. In 1974 the BBC reduced its services to the Caribbean, as a result of which Mr. Nelson's services in that capacity were no longer required. When he refused alternative employment, he was dismissed on grounds of redundancy. The Industrial Tribunal concluded that he had been dismissed for redundancy, apparently on the grounds that a term could be implied into Mr Nelson's contract of employment that he should carry out work on Caribbean programmes. The Court of Appeal rightly rejected the implication of such a term. But they went on to hold that Mr Nelson was therefore not redundant. This was wrong. Whatever the terms of Mr Nelson's contract, it was open to the Tribunal to find that he had been dismissed because the BBC's requirements for work on Caribbean programmes had diminished. This was a question of fact.

The basis for the fallacy is to be found in the judgment of Brandon LJ in *Nelson v British Broadcasting Corporation (No 2)* [1979] IRLR 346, when Mr Nelson's case came again before the Court of Appeal. He said (at p. 353) that Mr. Nelson had been right in law in maintaining that "because the work which he was employed to do continued to exist, he was not redundant." In saying this Brandon LJ appears to have meant that because Mr. Nelson was employed to do any work to which he might be assigned with the BBC and because the BBC was still carrying on business, he could not be redundant. In my opinion this cannot be right. The fact was that the BBC's requirements for employees in the General Overseas Service in general and for Caribbean broadcasts in particular had diminished. It must therefore have been open to the Tribunal to decide that Mr. Nelson's dismissal was attributable to that state of affairs.

Of course, the BBC did not necessarily have to respond in that way. They could, for example, have transferred Mr. Nelson to broadcasts which were still being maintained at full strength (say, to West Africa) in the place of a less experienced employee and made the latter redundant instead. In that case, it would have been open to the Tribunal to find that the other employee had been dismissed on account of redundancy. (Compare *Safeway Stores Plc v Burrell* [1997] IRLR 200 at p. 207.) In each case, the factual question of whether the dismissal was "attributable" to the statutory state of affairs is one for the Tribunal.

The judgments in the two Nelson cases have caused understandable difficulty for Industrial Tribunals. They have been treated as authority for what has been called the "contract test", which requires consideration of whether there was a diminution in the kind of work for which, according to the terms of his contract, the employee had been engaged. I give one example. In *Pink v White* [1985] IRLR 489, Mr Pink was engaged to work in a shoe factory as a "making and finishing room operative." In practice, he did more specialised work as sole layer/pre-sole fitter. Because of a reduction in demand, the employer's requirements for making and finishing room operatives in general diminished, but their need for sole layers and pre-sole fitters remained the same. Nevertheless, they selected Mr. Pink for redundancy, apparently because he had been absent for lengthy periods and the employer had had to train someone else to do his work while he was away. The argument before the Employment Appeal Tribunal turned on whether the "contract test" ought to be applied (i.e. did the company need less [*sic*] employees of the kind specified in Mr. Pink's contract), in which case he was redundant, or the "function test" (did it need less employees to do the kind of work he was actually doing), in which case he was not. It held that it was bound by *Nelson v British Broadcasting Corporation* [1977] IRLR 148 to apply the contract test and held that Mr. Pink was redundant. I have no doubt that on its facts the case was rightly decided, but both the contract test and the function test miss the point. The key word in the statute is "attributable" and there is no reason in law why the dismissal of an employee should not be attributable to a diminution in the employer's need for employees irrespective of the terms of his contract or the function which he performed. Of course the dismissal of an employee who could perfectly well have been redeployed or who was doing work unaffected by the fall in demand may require some explanation to establish the necessary causal connection. But this is a question of fact, not law.

Lord Clyde:

The present case concerns the construction and application of section 11(2)(b) of the Contracts of Employment and Redundancy Payments Act (Northern Ireland) 1965. In relation to that subsection, and to the equivalent provision which applies in the United Kingdom, the so-called "contract test" has come in practice to be identified and indeed recognised as proper and even obligatory. I find its paternity and origin somewhat obscure. The terms of the contract in *Nelson v. The British Broadcasting Corporation (No. 1)* were invoked in order to show that the reason for Mr. Nelson's dismissal was not redundancy but his refusal to be directed to other work which was within the scope of his contract of employment. The reference to the terms of the contract however provided the seed which was then fertilised in *Nelson v. The British Broadcasting Corporation (No. 2)* [1979] I.R.L.R. 346 and blossomed into the proposition regarded as established law in *Cowen v. Haden Carrier Ltd* [1982] IRLR 225 at para. 17 of the decision of the EAT (to which the Court of Appeal gave some support [1983] ICR 1), that employers required to show not only that the work of the kind on which the employee was actually engaged had ceased or diminished, but that the same was true of any work which he could have asked under his contract to do. I am not persuaded that this development of the law was necessarily justified by the basis on which it purported to proceed, but in any event I do not consider that the so-called test is appropriate.

Counsel for the appellants sought to justify the proposition that reference must be made to the terms of the employee's contract by pointing to the word "employees" in section 11(2)(b). But that is a perfectly natural and proper word to use in the particular context and cannot bear the significance which he sought to put upon it. It is properly used to distinguish work being done by employees of the particular employer as distinct from work done by others than persons employed by that employer. I cannot spell out of the use of the word "employees" a necessity to treat the terms of the contract of employment as the conclusive measure of the "work of a particular kind" to which the subsection refers. On the contrary the appellants' approach seems to require a rewriting of the section so that it would refer to "employees of a particular kind" or to "work specified in their contracts of employment." But that is not what the paragraph says. It is not to the actual contractual arrangements which the employees have made that the paragraph directs attention but to the requirements of the business. The requirements of the business may call for a particular number of employees and for employees of particular skills and abilities. But the contractual provisions which the employer may make with the employees are not necessarily a requirement of the business: they are rather a means whereby the requirements of the business in respect of the workforce may be met. That is not to say that the provisions of the contracts of employment are necessarily irrelevant; in some circumstances they may be useful, for example in throwing light on the kinds of work carried out or the place of employment. But the contractual terms are not determinative of the application of the subsection.

Lord Jauncey and **Lord Hoffmann** agreed with both opinions. **Lord Slynn** agreed with **Lord Irvine LC**.

NOTES AND QUESTIONS

1. The House of Lords held that Murray and Doherty were redundant because, says Lord Irvine LC, the statutory test is 'simplicity itself' and diminished demand led to the need to make cuts. But does this address the point of the claim? Some employees could logically have been redundant, but these employees could also have been unfairly selected. Cuts were needed, but was the process fair? If the process was unfair, should the employees not have been both redundant and unfairly dismissed? Today this issue would probably be resolved by TULRCA 1992 s 207A, which would allow compensation for redundancy to be lifted up by 25 per cent to reflect an unfair procedure.

2. Lord Irvine LC, as we saw in chapter 3, was not exactly the same as other judges: rather he was a political appointee of Prime Minister Tony Blair, and the last to decide cases before the Constitutional Reform Act 2005 abolished the ability of the Lord Chancellor to impose himself upon judicial work. While a respected QC, Lord Irvine LC never held judicial office before his elevation to the Lords. This may account, like in *Carmichael*, for some of the unusual rhetoric in the opinion ('simplicity itself', 'I need to say no more than', 'caused understandable difficulty') as well as common grammatical errors. For instance, 'did the company need less employees' should be 'fewer employees', because employees are individual human beings, not a volume that can be liquidated.

3. *Murray* was not referred to by *UCU v University of Stirling*, although it covers very similar ground. This is similar to the way that *Carmichael* was not referred to by *Autoclenz Ltd v Belcher*, although it covered very similar ground.

4. Like in *Murray*, employees may want to claim they were not redundant so that they can argue their dismissal was unfair, and a higher compensation award (eg median of £4,560, see chapter 18(3)(a)) than for redundancy (eg one week's

pay for each year worked, see chapter 19(3)). *High Table Ltd v Horst* [1997] EWCA Civ 2000 was another such case. Mrs Christine Horst and two others claimed they were unfairly dismissed, not redundant as they were told, as silver service wait staff through High Table Ltd. They usually worked for a bank in the City of London, Hill Samuel, but the staff handbook said their workplace could be transferred 'within reasonable daily travelling distance'. So, they argued they were not redundant because there were other jobs available. Peter Gibson LJ held they were redundant from their workplace, Hill Samuel, and a place of work should be established by a 'factual enquiry' rather than contract terms on the ability to transfer. He said: '[I]t defies common sense to widen the extent of the place' where an employee is employed 'merely because of the existence of a mobility clause … it cannot be right to let the contract be the sole determinant, regardless of where the employee actually worked for the employer.' Is it problematic that a mobility clause binds the employee when the employer wants it (subject only to use in good faith: chapter 4), but it does not bind the employer when the employee wants it?

(b) Some Other Substantial Reason

What does, and should, this phrase in ERA s 98(1)(b) actually mean?

Employment Rights Act 1996 s 98(1)(b)

98 General.
  (1) In determining for the purposes of this Part whether the dismissal of an employee is fair or unfair, it is for the employer to show—
  (a) the reason (or, if more than one, the principal reason) for the dismissal, and
  (b) that it is either a reason falling within subsection (2) or some other substantial reason of a kind such as to justify the dismissal of an employee holding the position which the employee held.

NOTES AND QUESTIONS

1. At the second reading of the Industrial Relations Act 1971, the government minister introducing the law, the Attorney General, Sir Geoffrey Howe, said the wording of 'some other substantial reason' was meant to refer to 'some other substantial reason relevant to the work which the dismissed employee was doing'. Hansard HC Debs (2 August 1971) vol 822, col 1236.
2. Based on the second reading (which should be highly influential in interpretation: *Pepper v Hart* [1992] UKHL 3) it would appear that 'some other substantial reason' should logically relate to work of an employee: what 'the dismissed employee was doing'. In this way, a dismissal for some other substantial reason should logically be a residual category for reasons related to 'capability or qualifications' or 'conduct' in s 98(2). An example could be a dismissal of an employee who intends to defect to a competitor: *Davidson v Comparisons* [1980] IRLR 360.

It may be debated whether any 'conduct' has occurred yet that is in breach of contract, but any ambiguity over the scope of that word can be covered by 'some other substantial reason'. See Lady Hale in *Reilly* [32] below. The clause should not be construed as analogous to redundancy, nor the refusal of an employee to accept unilateral cuts to pay or deteriorating rights.

3. This construction (which as we are about to see has not been followed) is all the more important when taking into account the purpose of the legislation. If an employer makes a contract, an employee is entitled to expect statutory rights as a minimum for the duration of the relationship. First, shareholders ought to bear the heaviest brunt in any situation of insolvency or business difficulty, because they can easily diversify their investments (it is often a duty to do so: Trustee Act 2000 s 4(3)(b)). Employees certainly cannot. Second, where elimination of dividends for the foreseeable future is not enough, directors or managers of an enterprise are logically next best placed to absorb the costs of business failure, not only because they may be responsible for it, but because they will invariably be more highly paid. Employees, third, usually cannot accept pay cuts without a deterioration in their standards of living: affecting families, the ability to pay the rent, or maintain a dignified livelihood. The social costs of employees' diminishing living standards will often fall back on the state, and therefore taxpayers. In effect, if the law is interpreted so that employers can impose unilateral pay cuts, the state is being asked to subsidise shareholder profit and managerial pay. This is unjust.

4. In 1979, *Hollister* said the interpretation of 'some other substantial reason' enables employers to impose unilateral pay cuts, though there must usually have 'been a properly consulted-upon reorganisation'. The question is whether this is still right.

Hollister v National Farmers' Union [1979] ICR 542

Mr Hollister claimed he was unfairly dismissed by the National Farmers' Union (NFU) after he refused to accept new contract terms. The NFU employed Mr Hollister as a group secretary in Cornwall; he initially received a small salary, but was mainly paid by fluctuating commissions from sales at the Cornish Mutual Assurance Co Ltd. As this was unlike NFU employees in the rest of the country, the head office in London negotiated with the secretaries after their complaints to change the pay arrangements to a minimum salary. But also, it proposed to cut pension provision as compensation. Mr Hollister refused to accept a new contract with higher pay, but also pension cuts, that his colleagues accepted. He was dismissed. The Court of Appeal held the dismissal was fair, and for 'some other substantial reason'.

Lord Denning MR:

There was a great deal of correspondence between London and Cornwall about the new terms and arrangements which were being offered to the group secretaries. Mr. Hollister was not at all satisfied. He did not like the new proposals which were being made to him. For instance, the pension rights under the new arrangements would not be so good. There were meetings at Bristol and elsewhere. But Mr. Hollister could not be persuaded to accept the new arrangements. So the National Farmers' Union felt they could do nothing else in the matter but dismiss him. On October 25, 1976, this letter was written by the Director General in London to Mr. Hollister:

> "Dear Mr. Hollister, Further to correspondence and discussion which has already taken place over the new contract of employment which has been offered to you. On behalf of the Council of the Union I hereby give you notice terminating your present contract with effect from January 25, 1977. I enclose herewith the new contract which the Council of the Union will be pleased to enter into with you. If you wish to accept this, please sign it and return it to me before November 8, 1976. As already mentioned to you the Council of the Union is agreeable to your making application to the National Farmers' Union Mutual Insurance Society Ltd. for their insurance agency for your area and if you accept the new contract I trust you will approach the local branch manager as soon as you have indicated your acceptance in order that the agency may become effective as soon as possible."

There it is. Mr. Hollister did not accept this new contract. So his employment was terminated. He was paid up to the end of it. Then, almost immediately, he took out an application to go before the industrial tribunal, claiming that he had been unfairly dismissed and claiming compensation under the Trade Union and Labour Relations Act 1974. The National Farmers' Union gave as their answer that they had to reorganise their arrangements for Cornwall. They felt they had no option. They had offered him a new contract on good and reasonable terms: and, as he would not take it, they felt they had to dismiss him.

...

The question which is being discussed in this case is whether the reorganisation of the business which the National Farmers' Union left they had to undertake in 1976, coupled with Mr. Hollister's refusal to accept the new agreement, was a substantial reason of such a kind as to justify the dismissal of the employee. Upon that there have only been one or two cases. One we were particularly referred to was *Ellis v Brighton Co-operative Society Ltd* [1976] IRLR 419, where it was recognised by the court that reorganisation of business may on occasion be a sufficient reason justifying the dismissal of an employee. They went on to say, at p. 420:

> "Where there has been a properly consulted-upon reorganisation which, if it is not done, is going to bring the whole business to a standstill, a failure to go along with the new arrangements may well – it is not bound to, but it may well – constitute 'some other substantial reason.'"

Certainly, I think, everyone would agree with that. But in the present case Arnold J. expanded it a little so as not to limit it to where it came absolutely to a standstill but to where there was some sound, good business reason for the reorganisation. I must say I see no reason to differ from Arnold J.'s view on that. It must depend on all the circumstances whether the reorganisation was such that the only sensible thing to do was to terminate the employee's contract unless he would agree to a new arrangement. It seems to me that that paragraph may well be satisfied, and indeed was satisfied in this case, having regard to the commercial necessity of rearrangements being made and the termination of the relationship with the Cornish Mutual, and the setting up of a new relationship via the National Farmers' Union Mutual Insurance Society Ltd. On that rearrangement being made, it was absolutely essential for new contracts to be made with the existing group secretaries: and the only way to deal with it was to terminate the agreements and offer them reasonable new ones. It seems to me that that would be, and was, a substantial reason of a kind sufficient to justify this kind of dismissal. I stress the word "kind."

Apart from that being a reason, there is a further paragraph in the Schedule. It is paragraph 6 (8) [now ERA 1996 s 98(4)] which provides as follows:

> "... the determination of the question whether the dismissal was fair or unfair, having regard to the reason shown by the employer, shall depend on whether the employer can satisfy the

tribunal that in the circumstances (having regard to equity and the substantial merits of the case) he acted reasonably in treating it as a sufficient reason for dismissing the employee."

Here we come to a point which was discussed in the appeal tribunal. It seems to have been said on several occasions that in order for a dismissal to be justified there nearly always ought to be consultation before a person is dismissed. A man should not be dismissed without proper consultation. That is said to be based on some phrases in the *Industrial Relations Code of Practice* (HMSO 1972), which of course has some statutory effect. Paragraph 65 says:

"Consultation means jointly examining and discussing problems of concern to both management and employees. It involves seeking mutually acceptable solutions through a genuine exchange of views and information."

In the present case it was stressed several times in the course of the judgment of the appeal tribunal that there had been no negotiations. We were referred to several passages, one of which is at [1978] ICR 712, 720G: "In particular, nothing was said about any future course of negotiation. The matter was left as it was." In the absence of a finding that there had been any negotiation – and, in that sense, consultation – the appeal tribunal felt there had been a failure in this case by the employers to do all they ought to have done, and therefore the dismissal was unfair.

I must say that I think that is going too far and is putting a gloss on the statute. It does not say anything about "consultation" or "negotiation" in the statute. It seems to me that consultation is only one of the factors. Negotiation is only one of the factors which has to be taken into account when considering whether a dismissal is fair or unfair. ...

Eveleigh LJ and **Sir Stanley Rees** agreed.

NOTES AND QUESTIONS

1.   The Court of Appeal holds that Mr Hollister was fairly dismissed because after there has 'been a properly consulted-upon reorganisation', refusal to accept the outcome is not unfair. But then Lord Denning MR adds that in not all circumstances is consultation necessary, and consultation does not mean the same thing as negotiation.

2.   In the final analysis, the employer is making pay cuts: this logically means both diminished demand for employees, for reasons unrelated to the employee. But under statute 'some other substantial reason' cannot logically be a subcategory of either, without triggering full rights to consultation and severance pay. *Hollister* must be regarded as an impermissible interpretation of the statute.

3.   Today, consultation has been interpreted as the same thing as 'an obligation to negotiate' under the Collective Redundancies Directive 1998, reflected in TULRCA 1992 s 188 (ch 19(2)): *Junk v Kühnel* (2005) C-188/03, [43]. On any reasonable view, consultation cannot mean an employer may merely do the following: send someone an email or a letter, proposing their pay is cut, waiting to receive a response, and writing again to say 'Thanks for your consultation, and after considering everything you said, we will be proceeding with our proposals'. To the extent that this practice is widespread, it is a farce that cannot have reflected any sensible intention of Parliament.

4.   Lord Denning MR says that it is 'putting a gloss on the statute' to say consultation is required. It seems reasonable to say that when there is collective negotiation

(ie consultation) with elected representatives, then individual consultation should not be required. This would be unmanageable, and tedious. However, it is plainly a gloss on the statute to say 'some other substantial reason' should be in any way interpreted as enabling the employer to cut pay (or pensions) without agreement. This interpretation effectively uses statute as a method to diminish workers' rights at common law: cf *Rigby v Ferodo Ltd* [1988] ICR 29 in chapter 4. That cannot be correct.

5. Why should consultation – without negotiation and an agreement – ever be enough to cut someone's pay? This extra-statutory interpretation finds no basis in the text of the statute, nor in Hansard, nor in a rational interpretation of the law's purpose. To change a contract, an employer should gain the consent of the workforce's elected representatives, and ideally a trade union. No consent, no change. If an employer does not like sticking to its contracts, should it be in business?

6. *Hollister* has been followed. In *Richmond Precision Engineering Ltd v Pearce* [1985] IRLR 179 Mr Pearce claimed he was unfairly dismissed after he rejected a new contract, from an owner that had recently taken over the business, on lower pay, more hours, reduced holidays, and pension and benefits eliminated. The Tribunal upheld the unfair dismissal claim, but Beldam J in the Employment Appeal Tribunal held that the dismissal was not unfair: 'Merely because there are disadvantages to the employee, it does not, by any means, follow that the employer has acted unreasonably in treating his failure to accept the terms which they have offered as a reason for dismissal.' Do you agree this is unreasoned assertion that has no basis in statute or principle?

7. By contrast, in *Catamaran Cruisers Ltd v Williams* [1994] IRLR 384, Williams and six other claimants argued they were unfairly dismissed after the business, nearing insolvency, was purchased by a new French owner. The Transport and General Workers' Union negotiated a new contract, offered to all employees, but the seven did not accept and were dismissed. Tudor Evans J held that the dismissal was fair. Do you think such circumstances – assuming full union representative involvement – should justify dismissal? But if so, is the proper reason not simply that the employees were redundant?

8. Despite these cases, it was suggested by Lady Hale in *Reilly v Sandwell MBC* that the meaning of 'some other substantial reason' could be construed as (and confined to) 'not contractual conduct'.

Reilly v Sandwell Metropolitan Borough Council [2018] UKSC 16

Ms Reilly claimed she was unfairly dismissed as head teacher of a primary school, after it transpired that her friend, Mr Selwood, had been convicted of making child pornography. They had been close friends since 1998 and had bought a house together in 2003, but were not in a relationship. In 2009, a month after starting work at the school, Mr Selwood's house was searched and he was arrested. She did not tell the school, and went on holiday with him in 2010, although her contract said she was to 'advise, assist and inform the Governing Body in the fulfilment of its responsibilities'. Those responsibilities, under the Education Act 2002 s 175(2) include 'safeguarding and promoting the welfare of children'. The governing body, on learning of the relationship, summoned

Reilly to a disciplinary hearing, and was concerned that she should have informed the governing body, so that any risk could be minimised. She refused to accept that she had such a duty. The Supreme Court held the dismissal was fair, and in doing so Lady Hale discussed the grounds.

Lord Wilson:

28. … Had she disclosed her relationship to them, it is highly unlikely that she would have been dismissed, still less that the tribunal would have upheld any dismissal as fair. Far more likely would have been the extraction by the governors of promises by Ms Reilly that she would not allow Mr Selwood to enter the school premises and perhaps, for example, that outside the school she would not leave information about pupils, for example stored electronically, in places where he might be able to gain access to it. …

Lady Hale:

31 I agree entirely, for the reasons given by Lord Wilson, that Ms Reilly was in breach of her contract of employment by not informing her employers of her connection with Mr Selwood. Ms Reilly had a duty to "advise, assist and inform" the Governing Body in the fulfilment of its safeguarding responsibilities towards the school's pupils. Those who are guilty of sexual offences against children pose a risk to the safety of other children both directly and indirectly. There are many ways in which Mr Selwood, should he choose to do so, might have used his friendship with Ms Reilly to gain access to the school's pupils: not only through being allowed to visit the school but also through finding out information about the pupils. Reporting the connection would have enabled a serious discussion to take place about how those risks might be avoided. There is no reason to think that it would have been a resigning matter. Issues could have been identified and solutions found. It is the absence of that full and frank disclosure and discussion which was the cause for serious concern. And it is the absence of any acknowledgement of what she should have done which makes the decision to dismiss her reasonable, indeed some might think it inevitable.

32 The case might have presented an opportunity for this court to consider two points of law of general public importance which have not been raised at this level before. The first is whether a dismissal based on an employee's "conduct" can ever be fair if that conduct is not in breach of the employee's contract of employment. Can there be "conduct" within the meaning of section 98(2)(b) which is not contractual misconduct? Can conduct which is not contractual misconduct be "some other substantial reason of a kind such as to justify the dismissal" within the meaning of section 98(1)(b) ? It is not difficult to think of arguments on either side of this question but we have not heard them – we were only asked to decide whether there was a duty to disclose and there clearly was.

33 Nor have we heard any argument on whether the approach to be taken by a tribunal to an employer's decisions, both as to the facts under section 98(1) to (3) of the Employment Rights Act 1996 and as to whether the decision to dismiss was reasonable or unreasonable under section 98(4), first laid down by the Employment Appeal Tribunal in *British Homes Stores Ltd v Burchell (Note)* [1978] ICR 303 and definitively endorsed by the Court of Appeal in *Foley v Post Office* [2000] ICR 1283, is correct. As Lord Wilson points out, in para 20 above, the three requirements set out in *Burchell* are directed to the first part of the inquiry, under section 98(1) to (3), and do not fit well into the inquiry mandated by section 98(4). The meaning of section 98(4) was rightly described by Sedley LJ, in *Orr v Milton Keynes Council* [2011] ICR 704, at para 11, as "both problematical and contentious". He referred to the "cogently reasoned" decision of the Employment Appeal Tribunal (Morison J presiding) in

Haddon v Van den Burgh Foods [1999] ICR 1150, which was overruled by the Court of Appeal in *Foley*. Even in relation to the first part of the inquiry, as to the reason for the dismissal, the *Burchell* approach can lead to dismissals which were in fact fair being treated as unfair and dismissals which were in fact unfair being treated as fair. Once again, it is not difficult to think of arguments on either side of this question but we have not heard them.

34 There may be very good reasons why no-one has challenged the *Burchell* test before us. First, it has been applied by Employment Tribunals, in the thousands of cases which come before them, for 40 years now. It remains binding upon them and on the Employment Appeal Tribunal and Court of Appeal. Destabilising the position without a very good reason would be irresponsible. Second, Parliament has had the opportunity to clarify the approach which is intended, should it consider that *Burchell* is wrong, and it has not done so. Third, those who are experienced in the field, whether acting for employees or employers, may consider that the approach is correct and does not lead to injustice in practice.

35 It follows that the law remains as it has been for the last 40 years and I express no view about whether that is correct.

NOTES AND QUESTIONS

1. *Reilly* as a decision itself is fairly straightforward: the dismissal was within a reasonable band of responses. But, first, Lady Hale both questions whether that test is in fact correct given the 'cogently reasoned' decision of Morison J in *Haddon* (chapter 18(2)(b)). Lady Hale does seem to stress the missed opportunity in arguing this point before the Supreme Court. Second, the notion of 'some other substantial reason' is identified as potentially embracing 'not contractual misconduct'. In other words, it should arguably be construed as relating to 'misconduct'.
2. Do you agree that, apart from changes reached by collective agreement, no employee is guilty of misconduct when they insist upon their existing contractual rights?

(c) Transfer of Undertakings

A third conception of redundancy appears for transfer of undertakings. Often business owners switch, and normally *without* a transfer of undertakings by an asset sale. There is a transfer of company shares: a share sale. For example, the chocolate company, Cadbury plc, was owned by various shareholders until 2009 when the American cheese brand, Kraft Foods Inc, made a hostile takeover bid to buy all the shares. A bid is 'hostile' if an offer does not have endorsement from the board of a 'target' company. After negotiation, Kraft settled on an offer with the board for £8.40 a share, valuing Cadbury at £11.5bn. The identity of the company that employees worked for, Cadbury plc, always stayed the same (though it was later delisted from the stock market and became Cadbury Ltd). It subsequently embarked on a programme of redundancies, contrary to its public assurances before the takeover. Those redundancies fell within the definitions already discussed, and trigger the rights of consultation, severance pay or redeployment.

By contrast, a transfer of undertaking means the sale to another of an enterprise's assets: buildings, vehicles, supply contracts, employment contracts, anything of economic value. Usually this means one company selling a business 'as a going concern' to another. Imagine that Cadbury Ltd decided to sell one division, at a building in Bourneville with thirty employees, to Nestlé. It can also mean a public body 'outsourcing' employees. Imagine that the National Gallery in London decides to subcontract G4S to run its security, instead of hiring security guards directly. Or suppose the National Gallery, two years later, decides to stop the G4S contract and use Serco for its security. In these cases, the Transfer of Undertakings Directive (TUD) 2001 and the Transfer of Undertakings (Protection of Employment) Regulations (TUPER) 2006 (SI 2006/246) may apply. The basic rule is, contracts of employees where an undertaking is transferred bind the new employer (Art 3(1)). Before and after the transfer, dismissals connected to a transfer will be unfair, when these are not independently justified by an 'economic, technical or organisational' reason (Art 4(1)). A dismissed justified by independent economic, technical or organisational reasons requires consultation and a redundancy payment. There is a further duty to consult about a transfer itself (chapter 19(2)).

The two main issues are (i) when there is a transfer, and (ii) which rights transfer.

Transfer of Undertakings Directive 2001/23/EC Arts 1, 3–4 and 6

Article 1

1. (a) This Directive shall apply to any transfer of an undertaking, business, or part of an undertaking or business to another employer as a result of a legal transfer or merger.

(b) Subject to subparagraph (a) and the following provisions of this Article, there is a transfer within the meaning of this Directive where there is a transfer of an economic entity which retains its identity, meaning an organised grouping of resources which has the objective of pursuing an economic activity, whether or not that activity is central or ancillary.

(c) This Directive shall apply to public and private undertakings engaged in economic activities whether or not they are operating for gain. An administrative reorganisation of public administrative authorities, or the transfer of administrative functions between public administrative authorities, is not a transfer within the meaning of this Directive.

2. This Directive shall apply where and in so far as the undertaking, business or part of the undertaking or business to be transferred is situated within the territorial scope of the Treaty.

3. This Directive shall not apply to seagoing vessels.

...

Article 3

1. The transferor's rights and obligations arising from a contract of employment or from an employment relationship existing on the date of a transfer shall, by reason of such transfer, be transferred to the transferee.

Member States may provide that, after the date of transfer, the transferor and the transferee shall be jointly and severally liable in respect of obligations which arose before the date of transfer from a contract of employment or an employment relationship existing on the date of the transfer.

...

3. Following the transfer, the transferee shall continue to observe the terms and conditions agreed in any collective agreement on the same terms applicable to the transferor under that agreement, until the date of termination or expiry of the collective agreement or the entry into force or application of another collective agreement.

Member States may limit the period for observing such terms and conditions with the proviso that it shall not be less than one year.

4. (a) Unless Member States provide otherwise, paragraphs 1 and 3 shall not apply in relation to employees' rights to old-age, invalidity or survivors' benefits under supplementary company or intercompany pension schemes outside the statutory social security schemes in Member States.

(b) Even where they do not provide in accordance with subparagraph (a) that paragraphs 1 and 3 apply in relation to such rights, Member States shall adopt the measures necessary to protect the interests of employees and of persons no longer employed in the transferor's business at the time of the transfer in respect of rights conferring on them immediate or prospective entitlement to old age benefits, including survivors' benefits, under supplementary schemes referred to in subparagraph (a).

Article 4

1. The transfer of the undertaking, business or part of the undertaking or business shall not in itself constitute grounds for dismissal by the transferor or the transferee. This provision shall not stand in the way of dismissals that may take place for economic, technical or organisational reasons entailing changes in the workforce.

Member States may provide that the first subparagraph shall not apply to certain specific categories of employees who are not covered by the laws or practice of the Member States in respect of protection against dismissal.

2. If the contract of employment or the employment relationship is terminated because the transfer involves a substantial change in working conditions to the detriment of the employee, the employer shall be regarded as having been responsible for termination of the contract of employment or of the employment relationship.

...

Article 6

1. If the undertaking, business or part of an undertaking or business preserves its autonomy, the status and function of the representatives or of the representation of the employees affected by the transfer shall be preserved on the same terms and subject to the same conditions as existed before the date of the transfer by virtue of law, regulation, administrative provision or agreement, provided that the conditions necessary for the constitution of the employee's representation are fulfilled. ...

NOTES AND QUESTIONS

1. TUD 2001 Art 1 states: '[T]here is a transfer of an economic entity which retains its identity, meaning an organised grouping of resources which has the objective of pursuing an economic activity, whether or not that activity is central or ancillary.' This is mirrored in TUPER 2006 reg 3. Article 3(1) states that 'rights and obligations' from a 'contract of employment' will 'transfer to the transferee'. This (3) includes collective agreements, but (4) need not include pension and survivor benefits: TUPER 2006 regs 4–5. Article 4 states that transfers cannot be grounds for a dismissal, but there can be independent 'economic, technical or organisational reasons' for dismissals: TUPER 2006 reg 7. Article 6 says worker representatives' 'status and function ... shall be preserved on the same terms': TUPER 2006 reg 6.

2. An 'undertaking' appears to have a common meaning in EU law, first laid out in *Höfner and Elser v Macrotron GmbH* (1991) C-41/90, [21] albeit for the 'context of competition law' but very similar to how it has been defined in the TUD

2001 Art 1(1)(c): 'This Directive shall apply to public and private undertakings engaged in economic activities whether or not they are operating for gain.' It then clarifies that 'administrative reorganisation' of 'public administrative authorities' is not a transfer.

3.   A risk in many takeovers, mergers and transfers of undertakings is that companies buy other companies (by a share or asset sale) to exploit the fact that a previous management had not sufficiently pressed its employee wage bill down, or customer prices high enough, to extract more 'shareholder value'. A large literature says there are 'implicit contracts' between business managers and stakeholders that reflect the maintenance of trust and confidence: employees stay because they feel they are getting a fair deal, customers are loyal to a brand because they feel they are getting a good product. While these relationships may or may not be recognised as having legal value (in the United States, where most literature comes from; reasonable expectations are the basis for implied terms in English law) those implicit contracts certainly have economic value. A sufficiently aggressive management, for instance run by a private equity group, could redistribute this value from workers, customers or the public to shareholders. Defenders of private equity would contend private equity generates 'efficiencies' by improving management practice, without unfairly redistributing wealth among stakeholders. See E Appelbaum and R Batt, *Private Equity at Work – When Wall Street Manages Main Street* (2014) and J Prassl, *The Concept of the Employer* (2015) ch 2(2).

4.   The TUD 2001 may be seen as an incomplete attempt to pre-empt opportunistic transfers of undertakings. Its purpose is to halt corporations whose business plan is to buy the assets of a company or public body, not in order to run it better, but to redistribute wealth to shareholders and managers, by sacking and cutting the pay of workers who have little bargaining power. The law stops this sort of practice to the extent that there must be an 'economic, technical or organisational reason' that is not connected to the transfer itself.

5.   However, because the TUD 2001 only applies to the form of transfers of legal entities (ie asset sales) it cannot tackle functionally identical opportunistic behaviour during takeover bids or mergers (ie share sales). A proposal to expressly cover private equity takeovers by share sale was made in the Private Equity (Transfer of Undertakings and Protection of Employment) Bill 2008. This would have codified the principle that takeovers through share transactions, rather than an asset sale, are covered by the Transfer of Undertakings (Protection of Employment) Regulations 2006. It would have expressly required employee agreement, and conferred injunctive relief, and would have reformed the 'arbitrary impact of the Directive': P Davies, 'Transfers – The UK Will Have to Make Up its Own Mind' (2001) 30 *ILJ* 231, 234. The government, under Prime Minister Gordon Brown, declined to support it.

6.   The ordinary law could be even more effective at pre-empting opportunistic takeovers than adding more form-specific regulation. Even without an asset or share, there is nothing special to stop an existing management simply changing its mind and sacking workers or cutting pay, except the general law on governance and redundancies. The incidence of takeover bids is highest in the USA, high in the UK and low in continental Europe where employees have strong rights to a voice

in enterprise governance. First, if workers have votes for the board of directors, they will oppose takeovers designed to damage their welfare. Second, if workers have the right to be consulted and fully compensated for any redundancies (whether connected to an asset or share sale or not), this will raise the cost, and nullify the advantages of business strategies that seek purely to exploit workers' vulnerability. See chapter 11.

7.   A more formalistic justification for the transfer of undertakings provisions is that, at common law, an old case called *Nokes v Doncaster Amalgamated Collieries Ltd* [1940] AC 1014 held that an employee's contract could not transfer to a new employer without that employee's consent. This case was subsequently distorted into the proposition that employment contracts became void upon a purported transfer. Reform was needed.

8.   An analogy to transfer of undertakings elsewhere in the law is that the Land Registration Act 2002 Sch 3, para 2 entitles tenants to remain in their homes when the landlord sells to another landlord: the tenants' interests override those of the new property buyer. Many jurisdictions in Europe do not characterise leases as a proprietary interest, but nevertheless legislate so that a rental contract overrides a property right (eg in Germany, BGB §566, cf §613). Similarly, the employee's contract of employment overrides a new business owners' freedom to do what they like with the business.

9.   In the United States, a notorious case on the same issue is *Howard Johnson Co v Detroit Local Joint Executive Board* 417 US 249 (1974) where Marshall J held for an 8:1 majority that a company had no duty to bargain in good faith with employees of a transferred motor lodge business. The union (Detroit Local) claimed Howard Johnson Co should bargain with it over terms of its members (under the Taft–Hartley Act of 1947, 29 US §185, placing that duty on an 'employer') after Howard Johnson Co bought a motor lodge business from Grissom & Son, but only kept nine workers and sacked forty-four. Marshall J held there was no 'substantial continuity of identity in the workforce hired'. Douglas J dissented, saying: 'Howard Johnson had substantial control over the Grissoms' operation of the business; it was no stranger to the enterprise it took over. The business continued without interruption at the same location, offering the same products and services to the same public, under the same name and in the same manner, with almost the same number of employees. The only change was Howard Johnson's replacement of the Union members with new personnel.' Do you agree that UK and EU law (as first introduced by Acquired Rights Directive 77/187/EC) would follow Douglas J's dissent?

10. On the political and ideological breakdown of the US judicial system, beginning around the time of *Howard*, and Powell J's appointment to the Supreme Court, see E McGaughey, 'Fascism-Lite in America (or the Social Ideal of Donald Trump)' (2018) *British Journal of American Legal Studies*, forthcoming.

11. *Howard* involved a simple sale of a business's assets from one firm (A) to a second firm (B). Another form of transfer could be when an enterprise, often public, (X) has contracted with a supplier (A) and then switches the supplier (B) often after a new procurement tender has been won. In this case, there is no contractual or business connection between the old supplier (A) and the new supplier (B) but

often the new supplier may hire some of the same workers: little changes but the management. Do you agree the safeguards against irrational redundancies should hold regardless of the corporate form, or management, that executes them?
12.   There is a transfer under TUD 2001 Art 1(1)(b) when an 'entity retains its identity'. But what does that actually mean?

Oy Liikenne Ab v Liskjärvi and Juntunen (2001) C-172/99

Mr Liskjärvi and Mr Juntunen, bus drivers in Helsinki, claimed they should have the same contractual terms from their new employer, Oy Liikenne Ab (Transport Ltd), as they had before with the previous bus company, Hakunlian Liikenne Oy (Hakunlian Transport Ltd). The Greater Helsinki Joint Board (YTV) had decided to change the contracting firm for seven bus routes. The tender procedure followed the Public Procurement Directive 92/50/EC. Forty-five drivers were dismissed by Hakunlian Liikenne Oy when it lost a contract, 33 of those drivers were rehired by Oy Liikenne Ab, and 18 new drivers were hired. Oy Liikenne Ab bought 22 new buses, but leased two buses from Hakunlian Liikenne as it waited for the new vehicles. The Court of Justice held that the Finnish court should determine the matter based on the balance between labour and capital intensiveness of the sector.

Sixth Chamber:

32 It is for the national court to establish if necessary, in the light of the guiding factors set out above, whether the operation of the bus routes at issue in the main proceedings was organised as an economic entity within Hakunilan Liikenne before being entrusted to Liikenne.

33 However, to determine whether the conditions for the transfer of an economic entity are satisfied, it is also necessary to consider all the factual circumstances characterising the transaction in question, including in particular the type of undertaking or business involved, whether or not its tangible assets such as buildings and movable property are transferred, the value of its intangible assets at the time of the transfer, whether or not the core of its employees are taken over by the new employer, whether or not its customers are transferred, the degree of similarity between the activities carried on before and after the transfer, and the period, if any, for which those activities were suspended. These are, however, merely single factors in the overall assessment which must be made, and cannot therefore be considered in isolation (see, in particular, *Spijkers*, paragraphs 13, and *Süzen*, paragraph 14).

34 So the mere fact that the service provided by the old and the new contractors is similar does not justify the conclusion that there has been a transfer of an economic entity between the two undertakings. Such an entity cannot be reduced to the activity entrusted to it. Its identity also emerges from other factors, such as its workforce, its management staff, the way in which its work is organised, its operating methods or indeed, where appropriate, the operational resources available to it (*Süzen*, paragraph 15 ...).

35 As pointed out in paragraph 32 above, the national court, in assessing the facts characterising the transaction in question, must take into account among other things the type of undertaking or business concerned. It follows that the degree of importance to be attached to the various criteria for determining whether or not there has been a transfer within the

meaning of the directive will necessarily vary according to the activity carried on, and indeed the production or operating methods employed in the relevant undertaking, business or part of a business (*Süzen*, paragraph 18 …).

36 On this point, the Commission submits, referring to *Süzen*, that the absence of a transfer of assets between the old and new holders of the contract for bus transport is of no importance, whereas the fact that the new contractor took on an essential part of the employees of the old contractor is decisive.

37 The Court has indeed held that an economic entity may, in certain sectors, be able to function without any significant tangible or intangible assets, so that the maintenance of the identity of such an entity following the transaction affecting it cannot, logically, depend on the transfer of such assets (*Süzen*, paragraph 18 …).

38 The Court thus held that, since in certain sectors in which activities are based essentially on manpower a group of workers engaged in a joint activity on a permanent basis may constitute an economic entity, it must be recognised that such an entity is capable of maintaining its identity after it has been transferred where the new employer does not merely pursue the activity in question but also takes over a major part, in terms of their numbers and skills, of the employees specially assigned by his predecessor to that task. In those circumstances, the new employer takes over an organised body of assets enabling him to carry on the activities or certain activities of the transferor undertaking on a regular basis (*Süzen*, paragraph 21 …).

39 However, bus transport cannot be regarded as an activity based essentially on manpower, as it requires substantial plant and equipment (see, reaching the same conclusion with respect to driveage work in mines, *Allen*, paragraph 30). The fact that the tangible assets used for operating the bus routes were not transferred from the old to the new contractor therefore constitutes a circumstance to be taken into account.

40 At the hearing, the representative of the defendants in the main proceedings emphasised the economic value of the contract between the contracting authority YTV and Liikenne, and submitted that this was a significant intangible asset. That value cannot be denied; but in the context of an award which is to be renewed, the value of such an intangible asset in principle falls to nil on the expiry of the old contract, since the award is necessarily thrown open again.

41 If an award procedure such as that at issue in the main proceedings provides for the new contractor to take over the existing contracts with customers, or if the majority of the customers may be regarded as captive, then it should nevertheless be considered that there is a transfer of customers.

42 However, in a sector such as scheduled public transport by bus, where the tangible assets contribute significantly to the performance of the activity, the absence of a transfer to a significant extent from the old to the new contractor of such assets, which are necessary for the proper functioning of the entity, must lead to the conclusion that the entity does not retain its identity.

43 Consequently, in a situation such as that in the main proceedings, Directive 77/187 does not apply in the absence of a transfer of significant tangible assets from the old to the new contractor.

President Gulmann, Skouris, Puissochet (Rapporteur)**, Schintgen** and **Colneric**.

1. The Court of Justice suggests that, while the Finnish court must ultimately make the decision, if there is no 'transfer to a significant extent' of 'tangible assets' [42] where the sector that is heavily reliant on capital (like buses), then an entity cannot be said to retain its identity: there would be no transfer. It says bus 'transport cannot be regarded as an activity based essentially on manpower' [39]. On the other hand, the court stresses that there is a 'transfer of customers' who in the case of bus services 'may be regarded as captive'. Although buses are capital intensive, do you think that (1) the lease of two buses to the new company, (2) the re-engagement of most of the workers, and (3) a captive customer market, means that a transfer should take effect?

2. Companies that are procured to perform a public service frequently fail to invest adequately in updated capital and infrastructure. Often, when services are outsourced, investment takes place only because public subsidies are made available, either (1) by direct transfer of funds, (2) in the licence fee set by the public service for the private company, and primarily (3) by raising the cost of the service to customers (eg bus fares). In this context, why should a new company ever have the benefit of an extra subsidy – an immunity from the duty to consult and make severance payments – if the capital intensiveness of its industry is significantly, or wholly, subsidised by taxpayers?

3. The test of an 'entity retaining its identity' is plainly not a test that can be mechanically applied: precisely because it consists of multiple factors, there is always room for a court to assess those with the purpose of the law in mind: to prevent firms profiting excessively, without regard to the social cost. In *Spijkers v Gebroeders Benedik Abattoir CV* (1986) Case 24/85, Mr Spijkers claimed he was unjustly dismissed after his work at a slaughterhouse (in Ubach over Worms, the Netherlands) was transferred from Gebroeders Colaris Abattoir BV to another firm, Benedik Abattoir CV. Benedik CV retained all employees except Mr Spijkers and one other, although because of the poor business, it retained no customers. At [13] the Court highlighted the enterprises' (1) assets, such as buildings and movable property, (2) intangible assets, (3) whether a majority of employees move, (4) customers, and (5) similarity between activities. How would you have decided this case if you were the Dutch court?

4. In *Süzen v Zehnacker Gebaeudereingung GmbH Krankenhausservice* (1997) C-13/95 Ms Süzen claimed she was still employed as a cleaner at a secondary school, the Aloisiuskolleg in Bonn-Bad-Godesberg, Germany. Her initial employer was Zehnacker GmbH, and it lost the school cleaning contract to Lefarth GmbH. The Court remarked there was no evidence of an offer by Lefarth GmbH to the previous Zehnacker GmbH workers, [4]. It affirmed that it 'is certainly not conclusive' that there was no contractual link between the two cleaning firms. It then set out a similar multifactor test to *Spijkers*, [14]. This suggests Ms Süzen would count as transferred.

5. Do you think that if a cleaner works at a school, or a security guard works at a university, even though they outsourced, that in law he or she is still employed by the end-user? Do you agree there is joint employment? See chapter 3(3).

6. In *CLECE SA v Valor* (2011) C-463/09, Mrs Valor claimed she was unjustly dismissed as a cleaner at a school, working through a company called CLECE SA.

The Court of Justice's Third Chamber held 'in certain labour-intensive sectors' an entity usually retains its identity 'where the new employer ... takes over a major part, in terms of their numbers and skills, of the employees' [39]. But then it said an entity's identity 'cannot be retained if the majority of its employees are not taken on by the alleged transferee' [41]. Do you agree that the Third Chamber's opinion creates a perverse incentive? By fixing an arbitrary figure of employees (a majority), a new employer may be encouraged to dismiss a few more workers, and therefore purport to have liability for none of them. Do you agree that this is incompatible with the multifactor test in TUD 2001 Art 1? To some extent it does not matter what the Court of Justice says, as it is merely interpreting the minimum standard of protection: Member States can in their own law require higher (just not lower) standards.

7. In the UK, *RCO Support Services Ltd v Unison* [2002] EWCA Civ 464, Unison claimed that cleaners and catering staff at the Aintree Hospitals NHS Trust were transferred from Initial Hospital Services Ltd to RCO Support Services Ltd. This occurred as patient services shifted buildings, from Walton to Fazakerley (near Liverpool). RCO Ltd had won the contract partly by assuring the NHS that the transfer rules would not apply, yet it agreed to guarantee six cleaners continuity of employment, and to hire them if they applied. The 'new' jobs were on lower pay and the staff did not reapply, instead choosing to unionise and argue that they were transferred. The Court of Appeal affirmed the Tribunal's decision that had been a transfer. Mummery LJ said: 'I am, however, unable to accept RCO's submissions that ... there can never be a transfer of an undertaking in a contracting out case if neither assets nor workforce are transferred. ... That interpretation of the Directive would run counter to... the "multifactorial approach" to the retention of identity test in *Spijkers*' [25]–[26]. Hale LJ and Pill LJ agreed.

8. TUD 2001 Arts 3–4 (and TUPER 2006 regs 4–7) suggest that contract terms and rights must remain the same unless there are economic, technical or organisational reasons. But how far does this go? Once there is a transfer, which rights transfer?

9. In *Werhof v Freeway Traffic Systems GmbH & Co KG* (2006) C-499/04 Mr Werhof claimed he should have a 2.6 per cent pay increase under a collective agreement between IG Metall and AGV (an employer federation) after his job was transferred by Siemens DUEWAG GmbH to Freeway KG in October 1999. Freeway KG was not an AGV member, and made Mr Werhof sign an agreement waiving individual rights to wage increases in 2001 in return for a one-off lump sum. Nevertheless he argued that, because his individual contract referred to a collective agreement, future collective agreements after a transfer should be incorporated into his. It was held by the Düsseldorf State Labour Court that no claim was available under settled German case law on BGB §631 (the equivalent of TUD 2001 Art 3) but it asked the Court of Justice whether EU law might require that updated collective agreements compulsorily transfer. The Third Chamber answered that EU law did not preclude German law refusing to make the transferee bound, because the transferee was not a party to the collective agreement. It placed weight on the right not to join a collective agreement, as part of the right to not associate [34].

10. But then, when it came to English law, the Third Chamber appeared not to adapt its reasoning, though as we shall see in 2017 it backtracked once more.

Parkwood Leisure Ltd v Alemo-Herron (2013) C-426/11

Mark Alemo-Herron and 23 other staff who worked in leisure services for Lewisham LBC claimed that their rights to receive pay increases under a collective agreement transferred, when their employer shifted from CCL Ltd to Parkwood Leisure Ltd in 2004. Their contracts had initially given them a right to receive pay increases in line the rates agreed on the National Joint Council for Local Government Services (NJC). The NJC is composed of Unison and public-sector employers, and at the time did not allow private-sector employers to be members. Parkwood Leisure Ltd initially agreed to raise pay in line with NJC scales, but soon stopped doing so. The Tribunal held that Parkwood Leisure could not be bound to a collective agreement where it was not a party. McMullen J on appeal held that it could be bound. Rimer LJ, for the Court of Appeal held that the UK regulations did not more than implement the bare-minimum standards of the TUD 2001, and that only 'static' but not 'dynamic' rights that can later change will transfer. The Supreme Court [2011] UKSC 26, Lord Hope giving judgment, decided to refer the case to the Court of Justice. The Third Chamber suggested that a 'static' interpretation of the Directive was a maximum standard.

Lord Hope:

9. The view that was taken in those decisions about the effect of conditions of the kind that the appellants rely on in this case was, in my opinion, entirely consistent with the common law principle of freedom of contract. There can be no objection in principle to parties including a term in their contract that the employee's pay is to be determined from time to time by a third party such as the NJC of which the employer is not a member or on which it is not represented. It all depends on what the parties have agreed to, as revealed by the words they have used in their contract. The fact that the employer has no part to play in the negotiations by which the rates of pay are determined makes no difference. Unless the contract itself provides otherwise, the employee is entitled to be paid according to the rates of pay as determined by the third party. This is simply what the parties have agreed to in their contract. The same is true of the transferee in the event of the transfer of an undertaking regulated by TUPE. Domestic law tells us that the term in the contract is enforceable against the transferee in just the same way as it was against the original employer.

    ...

Is a dynamic interpretation precluded by article 3(1)?

43. The Advocate General's summary of the facts indicates that the system under national law which applied in *Werhof* was different from that which formed the context for the appellants' contracts of employment with the council. Among other things, the German employment law with reference to which Mr Werhof's employment contract was framed assumes that the employer is a member of the employer's federation which is a party to the collective agreement and, in consequence, is bound by statute to comply with it: Advocate General, para 12; see also *Employment Law In Europe* 2nd ed (2009), paras 11.197–11.200. There is no such statutory obligation in our domestic law, nor is membership of the negotiating body a prerequisite for the enforceability of any agreement that has been reached collectively. It all depends upon what the parties have provided for in their individual contracts. There is therefore something to be said for Mr Linden's submission that the decision in *Werhof* is distinguishable on its facts, especially as to the point that the Court of Justice made in paras 31–35 of its judgment about the transferee's fundamental right not to be required to join an employer's federation.

44. The more important point of distinction for present purposes, however, is the second point on which Mr Linden relies: see para 34, above. The question which the Court of Justice addressed by its ruling in *Werhof* is not the same as that which requires to be answered in this case. It was sufficient to resolve the issue that had been raised by the referring court for it to say that the ruling of the Federal Labour Court summarised by the Advocate General in para 35 of his opinion was not precluded by article 3(1) of the Directive. In our case the question has to be looked at the other way round. This is because, as the Court of Justice recognised in *Criminal Proceedings against Lindqvist* [2004] QB 1014, para 98, there is nothing to prevent a member state from extending the scope of the national legislation implementing the provisions of the Directive to areas not included within it, so long as no other provisions of Community law preclude this. It would, of course, not be open to the national court to adopt that approach if the effect of the Directive was that it was precluded by it. That is why the way in which the Court of Justice framed its ruling in Werhof does not answer directly the question that needs to be resolved in this case.

45. The absence of a direct answer to it would not have given rise to difficulty if it had been possible to infer from the judgment how the question would have been answered. Mr Lynch invited us to draw that inference, as his case is that the principle enunciated in the judgment is that the transfer of dynamic contractual rights is inconsistent with the Directive so regulation 5 of TUPE must be confined to static contractual rights. But it is not obvious, if it is open to the national courts to interpret legislation that was intended to give effect to the Directive more generously in favour of employees than the Directive itself envisaged, why this should be so.

46. The first of the two reasons for the court's decision, that the object of the Directive was merely to safeguard the rights and obligations of employees in force on the date of the transfer, would not seem to preclude a more generous interpretation if the national court thought that this was appropriate to give effect to the ordinary meaning of TUPE. There are various reasons for thinking that, when TUPE was originally being framed, it was thought that employment contracts such as those which the appellants entered into which provided for a dynamic approach to be taken to collective agreements were permitted by the Directive. The aim of the Directive was to promote approximation of laws among the member states, not their harmonisation. None of the recitals in the preamble refer to a need to balance protection for employers against the protection given to employees in the event of a change of employer. And it was stated in article 7 of the Directive that it was not to affect the right of member states to introduce laws which are more favourable to employees. It hardly needs to be said that the question whether *Werhof* precludes the dynamic approach, if this is indeed what the employment contract interpreted according to the principles of domestic law provides for, is of fundamental importance to the many employees who work in sectors where their terms and conditions of employment are commonly determined through collective bargaining.

47. The second reason for the court's decision was its finding that, when interpreting the Directive, account had to be taken of the principle of the coherence of the Community legal order which required secondary Community legislation to be interpreted in accordance with the general principles of Community law among which was that the right not to join an association or a union was protected in the Community legal order: paras 32–33. As I have already mentioned, this point was directly relevant in Mr Werhof's case because of the way German employment law deals with collective agreements. Our domestic law is entirely different. There is no equivalent statutory framework. The matter depends entirely on the domestic law of contract, under which parties are at liberty to agree to abide by agreements arrived at by a process in which they do not, and are not required to, participate. Parkwood has not sought to argue that regulation 5 of TUPE is objectionable because it breached its article 11 Convention right of freedom not to join an association. There is no question of its being forced to become

a member of one of the participants in the NJC. The appellants' contracts do not require this, and in any event it would not be eligible to do so.

[*The Court of Justice gave the following reply to the UK Supreme Court.*]

Third Chamber:

20 By its three questions, which should be examined together, the referring court asks, in essence, whether Article 3 of Directive 2001/23 must be interpreted as precluding a Member State from providing, in the event of a transfer of an undertaking such as that at issue in the main proceedings, that dynamic clauses referring to collective agreements negotiated and agreed after the date of transfer are enforceable against the transferee.

...

22 First, in paragraph 37 of *Werhof*, the Court held that Article 3(1) of Directive 77/187 must be interpreted as not precluding, in a situation where the contract of employment refers to a collective agreement binding the transferor, that the transferee, who is not party to such an agreement, is not bound by collective agreements subsequent to the one which was in force at the time of the transfer of the business.

23 Next, it is apparent from Article 8 of Directive 2001/23 that that directive does not affect the right of Member States to apply or introduce laws, regulations or administrative provisions which are more favourable to employees or to promote or permit collective agreements or agreements between social partners more favourable to employees.

...

25 However, Directive 77/187 does not aim solely to safeguard the interests of employees in the event of transfer of an undertaking, but seeks to ensure a fair balance between the interests of those employees, on the one hand, and those of the transferee, on the other ....

...

28 ... a dynamic clause referring to collective agreements negotiated and agreed after the date of transfer of the undertaking concerned that are intended to regulate changes in working conditions in the public sector is liable to limit considerably the room for manoeuvre necessary for a private transferee to make such adjustments and changes.

29 In such a situation, such a clause is liable to undermine the fair balance between the interests of the transferee in its capacity as employer, on the one hand, and those of the employees, on the other.

30 Secondly, it is settled case-law that the provisions of Directive 2001/23 must be interpreted in a manner consistent with the fundamental rights as set out by the Charter of Fundamental Rights of the European Union ('the Charter') (see, to that effect, Case C-179/11 *Cimade and GISTI* [2012] ECR, paragraph 42).

31 In that regard, the referring court does indeed indicate that the right not to join an association is not at issue in the main proceedings. However, the interpretation of Article 3 of Directive 2001/23 must in any event comply with Article 16 of the Charter, laying down the freedom to conduct a business.

32 That fundamental right covers, inter alia, freedom of contract, as is apparent from the explanations provided as guidance to the interpretation of the Charter (OJ 2007 C 303, p. 17)

and which, in accordance with the third subparagraph of Article 6(1) TEU and Article 52(7) of the Charter, have to be taken into account for the interpretation of the Charter (Case C-283/11 *Sky Österreich* [2013] ECR, paragraph 42).

33 In the light of Article 3 of Directive 2001/23, it is apparent that, by reason of the freedom to conduct a business, the transferee must be able to assert its interests effectively in a contractual process to which it is party and to negotiate the aspects determining changes in the working conditions of its employees with a view to its future economic activity.

34 However, the transferee in the main proceedings is unable to participate in the collective bargaining body at issue. In those circumstances, the transferee can neither assert its interests effectively in a contractual process nor negotiate the aspects determining changes in working conditions for its employees with a view to its future economic activity.

35 In those circumstances, the transferee's contractual freedom is seriously reduced to the point that such a limitation is liable to adversely affect the very essence of its freedom to conduct a business.

36 Article 3 of Directive 2001/23, read in conjunction with Article 8 of that directive, cannot be interpreted as entitling the Member States to take measures which, while being more favourable to employees, are liable to adversely affect the very essence of the transferee's freedom to conduct a business (see, by analogy, Case C-544/10 *Deutsches Weintor* [2012] ECR, paragraphs 54 and 58).

37 Having regard to all the foregoing, the answer to the three questions referred is that Article 3 of Directive 2001/23 must be interpreted as precluding a Member State from providing, in the event of a transfer of an undertaking, that dynamic clauses referring to collective agreements negotiated and adopted after the date of transfer are enforceable against the transferee, where that transferee does not have the possibility of participating in the negotiation process of such collective agreements concluded after the date of the transfer.

President Silva de Lapuerta, Lenaerts, Arestis, Rapporteur Malenovský and Šváby.

NOTES AND QUESTIONS

1. The Third Chamber held that the Directive, read in conjunction with a previously undiscovered right of 'freedom of contract' in CFREU 2000 Art 16, creates a maximum standard that prevents a 'dynamic' provision transferring. Does the Court adequately respond to Lord Hope's carefully reasoned argument that in English law one may simply be bound to whatever one has signed? Are the responsibilities of contract not as or more important than freedom of contract?
2. Mr Alemo-Herron did not get a lump sum payment to go off the collective agreement, so why was his situation in any way analogous to Mr Werhof's?
3. If Parkwood Leisure Ltd felt disadvantaged by not being represented on the National Joint Committee for Local Government Services, why did it not seek a collective agreement to get such representation? Would this not be a more appropriate use of its right to 'freedom of contract'?
4. Parkwood Leisure's contract with Lewisham London Borough Council was cancelled in 2011, after the Labour Party regained a majority on the Council.

It changed the supplier to 'Fusion Lifestyle Ltd'. Parkwood Leisure still operates in 25 councils.

5. *Alemo-Herron* may be seen as an extension of the ideological turn initiated with *Viking* and *Laval*. The idea of a fundamental right to 'freedom of contract' under CFREU 2000 does not immediately spring to mind when one reads Art 16: 'The freedom to conduct a business in accordance with Community Union law and national laws and practices is recognised.' A sensible construction would suggest that a business has the freedom to operate without unjustified restrictions, such as for the right of freedom of establishment, and that no labour law and no collective agreement could reasonably be seen as an unjustified restriction. The doctrine of 'freedom of contract' harks back to the nasty history of *Lochner v New York*, 198 US 45 (1905). At the very best, the Third Chamber's opinion lacked historical awareness of the meaning of its words.

6. In *Asklepios Kliniken Langen-Seligenstadt GmbH v Felja* (2017) C-680/15 the Third Chamber decided to have another go at the issue of *Werhof* and *Alemo-Herron*. After *Werhof* Germany amended its law so that BGB §613a now says that upon a transfer a collective agreement or work council agreement will transfer, and cannot be amended for one year. It was intended to ensure that 'dynamic' terms also transfer. Asklepios GmbH claimed this violated CFREU 2000 Art 16. The CJEU wisely rejected this argument, holding the Directive 'should not be read as intended to prevent a 'dynamic' clause from producing its effects under all circumstances' [20]. Should the Third Chamber simply have said *Alemo-Herron* got it wrong?

7. Under TUD 2001 Art 3 and TUPER 2006 reg 4, employees employed 'immediately before' a transfer will be transferred. Of course, the law would make little sense if an transferor could sack workers just before a transfer (with tacit or actual collusion of the transferee) and then argue they had no rights. In *Litster v Forth Dry Dock & Engineering Co Ltd* [1988] UKHL 10 the receiver of Forth Dry Dock Ltd sacked twelve employees an hour before a transfer to Forth Estuary Engineering Ltd. The House of Lords held the employees transferred anyway, and the dismissals are 'required to be treated as ineffective' and employment is 'statutorily continued'. Having rights to unfair dismissal solely against an 'insolvent transferor, said Lord Oliver, would be 'largely illusory unless they can be exerted against the transferee.'

8. However, in *Wilson v St Helens BC* [1998] UKHL 37 Mr Wilson and eight other staff claimed their pay had been unlawfully deducted after the Red Bank Community Controlled Home, a school, was transferred from Lancashire County Council to St Helens Borough. The St Helens BC contracts paid less to some staff. This was joined to *British Fuels Ltd v Baxendale*, where Mr Baxendale claimed to still be employed after his job was shifted from National Fuels Distributors Ltd (a British Coal Corp subsidiary) to British Fuels Ltd. Lord Slynn held that the employees could claim damages, but there was no right of specific performance for Mr Baxendale to retain his job. According to Lord Slynn, 'neither the Regulations nor the Directive nor the jurisprudence of the Court create a community law right to continue in employment which does not exist under national law'. Should this decision be regarded as outdated by *Edwards v Chesterfield NHS* [2011]

UKSC 58 (chapter 17(4)) where the Supreme Court affirmed that an injunction is available to continue a contractual disciplinary procedure? Do you agree that especially in large organisations the policy objections to specific enforcement of contracts or right can be bypassed?

9. The inclusion of new terms that are disadvantageous, rather than just the cutting of pay or benefits, can also breach TUPER 2006. In *Credit Suisse First Boston (Europe) Ltd v Lister* [1999] ICR 794 Mr Lister, previously head of European Equities, claimed an injunction against a gardening clause inserted into his and 208 other employees' new contracts when they were transferred from Barclays de Zoete Wedd to Credit Suisse Ltd. Clarke LJ approved the injunction. Is an injunction to hold to a contract's terms any different in kind to specific performance to keep one's job as it is?

10. A claimant can enforce their rights either against a new or an old employer. In *University of Oxford v Humphreys* [1999] EWCA Civ 3050, Mr Humphreys claimed he was wrongfully and constructively dismissed from his job as an A level examination moderator at Oxford University, when it transferred those functions to the Associated Examining Board on worse pay. Mr Humphreys objected before the transfer, and the University argued this prevented him from claiming against it, and the only claim could go against the AEB. Potter LJ upheld the Tribunal's refusal to strike out the claim against the University, holding that 'prior to transfer, the threatened breach by the employer of his continuing obligation to employ the employee for the period of his contract, if persisted in despite the objection of the employee, is an anticipatory repudiatory breach of an executory contract, open to acceptance by the employee at any time prior to its withdrawal'.

11. Taken together, it can be seen that the law on transfers is overcomplicated by (1) a lack of generosity in interpreting when a transfer takes place, and (2) failing to acknowledge that all rights, which should be fully enforceable, transfer. But the bigger picture is that transfers that redistribute wealth from workers and customers to shareholders will continue to the limits of judicial tolerance as long as shareholders monopolise governance.

(2) CONSULTATION, SELECTION, NOTIFICATION

To ensure employers do not make irrational redundancy decisions, they must be properly informed. The requirement to consult serves two key functions. First, there is a business information function. Management may simply be divorced from the reality of its own enterprise, confined to offices where they cannot easily be reached, nor reaching out to staff except in episodes of crisis. Consultation can improve management's awareness of how staff can be deployed to make an enterprise run efficiently. Second, there is a social information function. The act of consultation can humanise management decisions: by talking to people as human beings, managers may see their decisions' real consequences, before they dig in their heels. The law also partially serves a vital psychological function: consultation should begin before decisions are made, not after. This is important because once people have made a decision, few of us have the presence of mind to change: eg EB Andrade and D Ariely, 'The Enduring Impact of Transient Emotions on Decision Making' (2009) 109(1) *Organizational Behavior and Human Decision Processes* 1. But as it stands, it is doubtful that the law can fulfil this psychological function when worker participation does not shape the governance of enterprises already when decisions are initially formed.

This section deals with (a) the general duty to consult (b) consultation for twenty or more redundancies, in an 'establishment' and 'good time', and (c) the limits of EU competence.

(a) General Duty to Consult

Williams v Compair Maxam Ltd [1982] ICR 156 (EAT)

Mr Williams and four other employees of Compair Maxam Ltd claimed there was no adequate consultation, and their dismissals on grounds of redundancy were procedurally unfair. During the economic crisis beginning in 1980 (inflation reached 22 per cent and unemployment 12.5 per cent by 1982) the company had lost business. From its 200 employees, it accepted 35 voluntary redundancies, called short-time working and, with the consent of the union APEX called for 21 further voluntary redundancies. After only seven people volunteered, department managers drew up lists of who they wanted to keep, based on personal preference, without further consultation. The Employment Appeal Tribunal, overturning the Tribunal, held this was unfair.

Browne-Wilkinson J:

At some stage, and it is not clear to us whether this was before or after 16th January, the departmental managers did draw up lists of those to be retained and those to be made redundant. The basis of those lists was apparently that each manager picked the employees he wanted to make his department viable. All four appellants were in the department to be managed by Mr. Hennessy. Mr. Hennessy in evidence said that he really started again in restaffing his department: he drew up a list of vacancies and from the existing staff filled those vacancies with those employees whom he considered would be best to retain in the interests of the Company in the long run. Although the industrial tribunal in its reasons did not refer to this, in his evidence Mr. Hennessy said that his choice was quite subjective and that he had known all the people since he joined the Company. Length of service was not a factor taken into account.
...
The union asked for a list of the names of those to be made redundant but this was refused. The management agreed to postpone the dismissals until the following morning. ...
...
... the question is whether the dismissal lay within the range of conduct which a reasonable employer could have adopted. The second point of law. particularly relevant in the field of dismissal for redundancy, is that the tribunal must be satisfied that it was reasonable to dismiss each of the applicants on the grounds of redundancy. It is not enough to show simply that it was reasonable to dismiss an employee; it must be shown that the employer acted reasonably in treating redundancy "as a sufficient reason for dismissing the employee," i.e. the employee complaining of dismissal. Therefore, if the circumstances of the employer make it inevitable that some employee must be dismissed, it is still necessary to consider the means whereby the applicant was selected to be the employee to be dismissed and the reasonableness of the steps taken by the employer to choose the applicant, rather than some other employee, for dismissal.

In law therefore the question we have to decide is whether a reasonable tribunal could have reached the conclusion that the dismissal of the applicants in this case lay within the range of conduct which a reasonable employer could have adopted. It is accordingly necessary to try to set down in very general terms what a properly instructed industrial tribunal would know to be the principles which, in current industrial practice, a reasonable employer would be expected to adopt. This is not a matter on which the chairman of this appeal tribunal feels that he can contribute much, since it depends on what industrial practices are currently accepted as being normal and proper. The two lay members of this appeal tribunal hold the view that it would be impossible to lay down detailed procedures which all reasonable employers would follow in all circumstances: the fair conduct of dismissals for redundancy must depend on the circumstances of each case. But in their experience, there is a generally accepted view in industrial relations that, in cases where the employees are represented by an independent union recognised by the employer, reasonable employers will seek to act in accordance with the following principles:

1. The employer will seek to give as much warning as possible of impending redundancies so as to enable the union and employees who may be affected to take early steps to inform themselves of the relevant facts, consider possible alternative solutions and, if necessary, find alternative employment in the undertaking or elsewhere.

2. The employer will consult the union as to the best means by which the desired management result can be achieved fairly and with as little hardship to the employees as possible. In particular, the employer will seek to agree with the union the criteria to be applied in selecting the employees to be made redundant. When a selection has been made, the employer will consider with the union whether the selection has been made in accordance with those criteria.

3. Whether or not an agreement as to the criteria to be adopted has been agreed with the union, the employer will seek to establish criteria for selection which so far as possible do not depend solely upon the opinion of the person making the selection but can be objectively checked against such things as attendance record, efficiency at the job, experience, or length of service.

4. The employer will seek to ensure that the selection is made fairly in accordance with these criteria and will consider any representations the union may make as to such selection.

5. The employer will seek to see whether instead of dismissing an employee he could offer him alternative employment.

The lay members stress that not all these factors are present in every case since circumstances may prevent one or more of them being given effect to. But the lay members would expect these principles to be departed from only where some good reason is shown to justify such departure. The basic approach is that, in the unfortunate circumstances that necessarily attend redundancies, as much as is reasonably possible should be done to mitigate the impact on the work force and to satisfy them that the selection has been made fairly and not on the basis of personal whim.

That these are the broad principles currently adopted by reasonable employers is supported both by the practice of the industrial tribunals and to an extent by statute. A very large number of appeals on cases of alleged unfair selection for redundancy come before this Appeal Tribunal. In the experience of all of us, without exception hitherto the approach of the industrial tribunals has reflected the canons of good industrial relations set out above.

...

We must add a word of warning. For the purpose of giving our reasons for reaching our exceptional conclusion that the decision of the industrial tribunal in this case was perverse, we have had to state what in our view are the steps which a reasonable and fair employer at the present time would seek to take in dismissing unionised employees on the ground of redundancy. We stress two points. First, these are not immutable principles which will stay unaltered for ever. Practices and attitudes in industry change with time and new norms of acceptable industrial relations behaviour will emerge. Secondly the factors we have stated are not principles of law, but standards of behaviour. ...

For the reasons that we have stated, we allow the appeal and substitute a finding that the four appellants were unfairly dismissed. We will remit the case to a differently constituted tribunal to assess the compensation.

Mr RV Cooper and **Mrs D Lancaster** joined in the proceedings.

NOTES AND QUESTIONS

1. Browne-Wilkinson J holds that when redundancies are being made, employers must prove they follow five principles, or show 'some good reason ... to justify such departure'. That is, employers must (1) give 'as much warning as possible', (2) 'consult the union ... to agree', particularly on any selection criteria, which should be followed (3) even if there is no agreement, establish objective criteria, (4) follow the criteria, (5) redeploy employees 'instead of dismissing'. These are not 'immutable principles' and represent not law but 'standards of behaviour'. Do you agree that those principles will have 'mutated' further towards higher standards now than in 1980?

2. *Williams* is less specific in its requirements than CRD 1998 Art 2 and TULRCA 1992 s 188(2)–(4) below, but not necessarily less consequential. First, do you agree that giving 'as much warning as possible ... to consider possible alternative solutions' should mean at least 30 days' notice, and wherever 'possible' more? Do you agree that the requirement of finding 'alternative solutions' must logically mean that no decision may have been taken before consultation begins?

3. Second, it would appear the requirement to 'consult the union' carries the same meaning, as Browne-Wilkinson J expressed it, as in *Junk v Kühnel* (2005) C-188/03, [43], ie an 'obligation to negotiate' on management over fair results without hardship. Agreement on selection criteria, should it come to that, is merely one particular aspect of this general duty of consultation. This mirrors the hierarchy of objectives below in s 188(2) of avoiding, reducing or mitigating redundancies.

4. Third, selection criteria must be objectively justifiable, and verifiable. The requirement for verifiability was discussed in *British Aerospace plc v Green* [1995] EWCA Civ 26, where 235 employees claimed that individual assessment scores should be disclosed, after 530 redundancies from British Aerospace's 7,000-person plant were planned. The claimants had scored the lowest on the test, and demanded that the forms be disclosed, so that the method could be challenged. However the Court of Appeal held that, while forms could be disclosed if a specific allegation of unfairness was made, there was no general duty of disclosure. Waite LJ said to force 'disclosure ... designed to provide individual applicants with grounds for specific allegations of anomaly or mistake in particular instances would have done nothing to ease the task in hand – which was limited to the selection of sample cases – and would have run a serious risk of subjecting these multiple applications to procedural chaos'. What do you think?

5. A common method of selection, which is objective, is 'last in first out', or some other form of giving points for experience. However, in *Rolls Royce plc v Unite the Union* [2009] EWCA Civ 387 the company, evidently dissatisfied with both its older workers and the collective agreement it had signed, tried to argue that giving employees extra credit for each year of service constituted unlawful age discrimination (under what is now the Equality Act 2010 ss 5, 19 and 39). The Court of Appeal rejected the claim because though it indirectly discriminated against younger people, it pursued a legitimate aim and was proportionate, particularly where it came from a collective agreement.

(b) Over 20 Redundancies

The CRD 1998 specifies requirements for over 20 redundancies, as the UK implements it.

Collective Redundancies Directive 98/59/EC

Definitions and scope

Article 1
1. For the purposes of this Directive:
    (a) 'collective redundancies' means dismissals effected by an employer for one or more reasons not related to the individual workers concerned where, according to the choice of the Member States, the number of redundancies is:
        (i) either, over a period of 30 days:
            — at least 10 in establishments normally employing more than 20 and less than 100 workers,
            — at least 10 % of the number of workers in establishments normally employing at least 100 but less than 300 workers,
            — at least 30 in establishments normally employing 300 workers or more,
        (ii) or, over a period of 90 days, at least 20, whatever the number of workers normally employed in the establishments in question …
    …

Information and consultation

Article 2
1. Where an employer is contemplating collective redundancies, he shall begin consultations with the workers' representatives in good time with a view to reaching an agreement.
2. These consultations shall, at least, cover ways and means of avoiding collective redundancies or reducing the number of workers affected, and of mitigating the consequences by recourse to accompanying social measures aimed, inter alia, at aid for redeploying or retraining workers made redundant.
    Member States may provide that the workers' representatives may call on the services of experts in accordance with national legislation and/or practice.
3. To enable workers' representatives to make constructive proposals, the employers shall in good time during the course of the consultations:
    (a) supply them with all relevant information and

(b)   in any event notify them in writing of:
   (i)   the reasons for the projected redundancies;
   (ii)   the number of categories of workers to be made redundant;
   (iii)   the number and categories of workers normally employed;
   (iv)   the period over which the projected redundancies are to be effected;
   (v)   the criteria proposed for the selection of the workers to be made redundant in so far as national legislation and/or practice confers the power therefor upon the employer;
   (vi)   the method for calculating any redundancy payments other than those arising out of national legislation and/or practice.

The employer shall forward to the competent public authority a copy of, at least, the elements of the written communication which are provided for in the first subparagraph, point (b), subpoints (i) to (v).

4. The obligations laid down in paragraphs 1, 2 and 3 shall apply irrespective of whether the decision regarding collective redundancies is being taken by the employer or by an undertaking controlling the employer.

Final provisions

Article 5
This Directive shall not affect the right of Member States to apply or to introduce laws, regulations or administrative provisions which are more favourable to workers or to promote or to allow the application of collective agreements more favourable to workers.

NOTES AND QUESTIONS

1.   CRD 1998 Art 1 defines redundancies as dismissals 'not related to the individual workers' and gives Member States a choice about when the information and consultation duties in Art 2 are triggered: the UK opted for the twenty dismissals within ninety days in the 'establishments'. This is implemented by TULRCA 1992 s 188.

Trade Union and Labour Relations (Consolidation) Act 1992 s 188

188. Duty of employer to consult representatives.
(1) Where an employer is proposing to dismiss as redundant 20 or more employees at one establishment within a period of 90 days or less, the employer shall consult about the dismissals all the persons who are appropriate representatives of any of the employees who may be affected by the proposed dismissals or may be affected by measures taken in connection with those dismissals.

(1A) The consultation shall begin in good time and in any event—
   (a)   where the employer is proposing to dismiss 100 or more employees as mentioned in subsection (1), at least 45 days, and
   (b)   otherwise, at least 30 days,
before the first of the dismissals takes effect.

(1B) For the purposes of this section the appropriate representatives of any affected employees are–
   (a)   if the employees are of a description in respect of which an independent trade union is recognised by their employer, representatives of the trade union, or

    (b) in any other case, whichever of the following employee representatives the employer chooses:—

        (i)   employee representatives appointed or elected by the affected employees otherwise than for the purposes of this section, who (having regard to the purposes for and the method by which they were appointed or elected) have authority from those employees to receive information and to be consulted about the proposed dismissals on their behalf;

        (ii) employee representatives elected by the affected employees, for the purposes of this section, in an election satisfying the requirements of section 188A(1).

(2) The consultation shall include consultation about ways of—

    (a) avoiding the dismissals,

    (b) reducing the numbers of employees to be dismissed, and

    (c) mitigating the consequences of the dismissals,

and shall be undertaken by the employer with a view to reaching agreement with the appropriate representatives.

(3) In determining how many employees an employer is proposing to dismiss as redundant no account shall be taken of employees in respect of whose proposed dismissals consultation has already begun.

(4) For the purposes of the consultation the employer shall disclose in writing to the appropriate representatives—

    (a) the reasons for his proposals,

    (b) the numbers and description of employees whom it is proposed to dismiss as redundant,

    (c) the total number of employees of any such description employed by the employer at the establishment in question,

    (d) the proposed method of selecting the employees who may be dismissed,

    (e) the proposed method of carrying out the dismissals, with due regard to any agreed procedure, including the period over which the dismissals are to take effect,

    (f) the proposed method of calculating the amount of any redundancy payments to be made (otherwise than in compliance with an obligation imposed by or by virtue of any enactment) to employees who may be dismissed,

    (g) the number of agency workers working temporarily for and under the supervision and direction of the employer,

    (h) the parts of the employer's undertaking in which those agency workers are working, and

    (i) the type of work those agency workers are carrying out.

(5) That information shall be given to each of the appropriate representatives by being delivered to them, or sent by post to an address notified by them to the employer, or (in the case of representatives of a trade union) sent by post to the union at the address of its head or main office.

(5A) The employer shall allow the appropriate representatives access to the affected employees and shall afford to those representatives such accommodation and other facilities as may be appropriate.

(7) If in any case there are special circumstances which render it not reasonably practicable for the employer to comply with a requirement of subsection (1A), (2) or (4), the employer shall take all such steps towards compliance with that requirement as are reasonably practicable in those circumstances. Where the decision leading to the proposed dismissals is that of a person controlling the employer (directly or indirectly), a failure on the part of that person to provide information to the employer shall not constitute special circumstances rendering it not reasonably practicable for the employer to comply with such a requirement.

(7A) Where—

    (a) the employer has invited any of the affected employees to elect employee representatives, and

(b)   the invitation was issued long enough before the time when the consultation is required by subsection (1A)(a) or (b) to begin to allow them to elect representatives by that time,

the employer shall be treated as complying with the requirements of this section in relation to those employees if he complies with those requirements as soon as is reasonably practicable after the election of the representatives.

(7B) If, after the employer has invited affected employees to elect representatives, the affected employees fail to do so within a reasonable time, he shall give to each affected employee the information set out in subsection (4). ...

NOTES AND QUESTIONS

1.   TULRCA 1992 s 188 says (1) consultation must occur when over 20 workers 'may be affected by proposed dismissals' over 90 days. Under (1A) the consultation period must be 30 days, or 45 days if over 100 workers' jobs are at risk. The employer must (1B) consult the recognised trade union or ensure employee representatives are elected to consult. The employer cannot hide behind the fact that a controlling company is really making the decision: the controlling company must also consult.

2.   The Trade Union and Labour Relations (Consolidation) Act 1992 (Amendment) Order 2013/763 Art 3 reduced the consultation time for over 100 redundancies to 45 days, down from 90 days. Do you think a month and a half is enough time for 100 or more sacked workers to reorganise their working lives? Should Parliament require more?

3.   Employers must follow a collective consultation for 30 days, to avoid, reduce or mitigate dismissals (s 188(2)) and provide written disclosure of reasons, numbers of staff, selection methods, calculating redundancy payments, and affected agency workers (s 188(4)) if there are over 20 workers affected in 90 days (or 45 days for 100 employees) in 'one establishment'.

4.   The remedies for failure to consult are in TULRCA 1992 ss 189–90. If employers fail to consult, or fail to organise elections for representatives to consult with, they will face claims for a 'protective award' (s 189(1)) which is up to 90 days' pay from the date when the first (unlawful) dismissals were made, as the court this is just and equitable (ss 189(4) and 190(1)). The complaint must be made in 3 months, extendable if reasonable, from the last dismissal (s 189(5)) to a Tribunal (s 192). Every employee is entitled to one week's pay for each week (s 190(2)). The period halts, however, if the employee is fairly dismissed or resigns (s 191).

5.   Who can bring a claim for a protective award? In *Northgate HR Ltd v Mercy* [2007] EWCA Civ 1304, an employee applied for a protective award individually. There was an Employee Consultation Council in place with elected and appointed members. Wilkie J held that Mr Mercy was barred by s 189(1)(b) from claiming himself. Maurice-Kay LJ agreed, so that individual claims could only be brought when there were no employee representatives. The Lord Justice dismissed the notion that CRD 1998 Art 6 required enforcement by both, even though it says: 'Member States shall ensure that judicial and/or administrative procedures for the enforcement of obligations under this Directive are available to the workers' representatives and/or workers.' Was Maurice Kay LJ wrong? (See also chapter 10(1)

and *Metrobus*.) What if there is a difference of view between a majority of representatives and an employee?

6. How much should the Tribunal exercise its discretion in fixing the number of days for a protective award under s 189(4)? In *Susie Radin Ltd v GMB* [2004] EWCA Civ 180, [45] Peter Gibson LJ held that the purpose 'was to provide a sanction for breach by the employer ... it was not to compensate the employees for loss', so 'a proper approach ... is to start with the maximum period and reduce it only if there are mitigating circumstances justifying a reduction to an extent which the [tribunal] consider appropriate'.

7. Looking back to s 188(4), why do you think agency 'workers' seem to be treated as disposable? If agency staff are in law to be treated as employees, they must be consulted. Do you agree that staff hired through an agency are entitled to dignity and security at work as well?

8. What is 'one establishment'? Is it intended to be a legal, physical or economic concept? In *E Green & Son (Castings) Ltd v Association of Scientific, Technical and Managerial Staffs* [1984] ICR 352 (EAT) the union of 157 employees (now covered by Unite) working at one premises claimed there should have been longer consultation. They worked for three subsidiaries of Green Economisers Group plc: 97 for EG&S (Castings) Ltd, 36 for EG&S Ltd, 24 for EG&S (Site Services) Ltd. The employer(s) argued that because those subsidiaries were separate legal entities, and in none were over 100 employees were dismissed, there was no need for longer consultation. Nolan J, overturning the Tribunal, held the 'establishment' concept did not pierce the corporate veil. Do you agree this must be regarded as wrong, and would encourage the artificial creation of legal entities to evade statutory rights? On consistent jurisprudence, there is no need to 'pierce the veil', rather than construe the meaning of the statute or common law right to uphold its purpose: see *Daimler Co Ltd v Continental Tyre and Rubber Co (Great Britain) Ltd* [1916] 2 AC 307, holding that the Trading with the Enemy Act 1914 applied to a UK incorporated firm, because it had German shareholders, and *Chandler v Cape plc* [2012] EWCA Civ 525, ch 3(3), holding that an employee of a subsidiary could claim in tort against a parent company for breach of health and safety duties because it interfered in the subsidiary's affairs.

9. *Rockfon A/S v Specialarbejderforbundet i Danmark* (1995) C-449/93 cast heavy doubt on *E Green & Son*. Rockfon A/S dismissed 24 or 25 employees out of its 162 workforce without consulting. It was part of the Danish multinational Rockwool Group with 5,300 workers worldwide and 1,435 workers in Denmark. The Danish law had opted for the threshold of a duty to consult if over 10 per cent of the workforce is dismissed (= 16.2 workers at Rockfon, but 143.5 workers in the Rockwool Group), or over 30 employees, now in the CRD 1998 Art 1(a)(i). The Rockwool Group it argued there was no duty to consult, and that Rockfon A/S, though a separate firm, was not a separate 'establishment' because such large-scale redundancies could only be effected at group level. The Court of Justice noted at [25] that 'establishment' must be defined by EU law. It then said at [30] that: 'an interpretation of the term "establishment" like that proposed by Rockfon would allow companies belonging to the same group to try to make it more difficult for the Directive to apply to them by conferring on a separate decision-making

body the power to take decisions concerning redundancies. By this means, they would be able to escape the obligation to follow certain procedures for the protection of workers and large groups of workers could be denied the right to be informed and consulted which they have as a matter of course under the directive. Such an interpretation therefore appears to be incompatible with the aim of the Directive.' This suggests that both legal and managerial structures should not be relevant, and never capable of manipulation, to 'escape the obligation' to consult. That principle suggests *E Green & Son* was wrong.

10. *Lyttle* suggests 'establishment' is a geographical concept. This creates its own issues.

Lyttle v Bluebird UK Bidco 2 Ltd (2015) C-182/13

Ms Lyttle and three others (organised in the union USDAW) claimed their dismissals from Bonmarché stores in Northern Ireland were unlawful, because there was no consultation. Bonmarché had become insolvent and was sold to Bluebird Ltd in January 2012. There had been 20 stores in Northern Ireland, employing 180 people, but 12 stores closed, and 105 employees were dismissed. However, the claimants each worked at stores with under 20 staff. They claimed that because Northern Ireland was treated as one 'region', there should have been consultation. The company argued that each store, usually in different towns, was an 'individual cost centre' and therefore not an establishment, and no duty to consult under CRD 1998 Art(1)(a)(ii), as implemented by the Employment Rights (Northern Ireland) Order 1996, which is identical to TULRCA 1992 s 188. The Northern Ireland Industrial Tribunal asked the Court of Justice whether an 'establishment' can include 'more than one local employment unit' and whether the number 20 could cover more than one. The Fifth Chamber replied that one unit was enough to be an establishment.

Fifth Chamber:

28 In paragraph 31 of the judgment in *Rockfon* (C-449/93, EU:C:1995:420), the Court observed … an employment relationship is essentially characterised by the link existing between the worker and the part of the undertaking or business to which he is assigned to carry out his duties. The Court therefore decided, in paragraph 32 of the judgment in *Rockfon* (C-449/93, EU:C:1995:420), that the term 'establishment' in Article 1(1)(a) of Directive 98/59 must be interpreted as designating, depending on the circumstances, the unit to which the workers made redundant are assigned to carry out their duties. It is not essential in order for there to be an 'establishment' that the unit in question is endowed with a management that can independently effect collective redundancies.

   …

30 In the judgment in *Athinaïki Chartopoiïa* (C-270/05, EU:C:2007:101), the Court further clarified the term 'establishment', inter alia by holding, in paragraph 27 of that judgment, that, for the purposes of the application of Directive 98/59, an 'establishment', in the context of an undertaking, may consist of a distinct entity, having a certain degree of permanence and stability, which is assigned to perform one or more given tasks and which has a workforce, technical means and a certain organisational structure allowing for the accomplishment of those tasks.

31 By the use of the words 'distinct entity' and 'in the context of an undertaking', the Court clarified that the terms 'undertaking' and 'establishment' are different and that an establishment normally constitutes a part of an undertaking. That does not, however, preclude the establishment being the same as the undertaking where the undertaking does not have several distinct units.

32 In paragraph 28 of the judgment in *Athinaïki Chartopoiïa* (C-270/05, EU:C:2007:101), the Court held that since Directive 98/59 concerns the socio-economic effects that collective redundancies may have in a given local context and social environment, the entity in question need not have any legal autonomy, nor need it have economic, financial, administrative or technological autonomy, in order to be regarded as an 'establishment'.

...

42 As regards the question raised by the referring tribunal as to whether Article 1(1)(a)(ii) of Directive 98/59 requires that account be taken of the dismissals effected in each establishment considered separately, interpreting that provision so as to require account to be taken of the total number of redundancies across all the establishments of an undertaking would, admittedly, significantly increase the number of workers eligible for protection under Directive 98/59, which would correspond to one of the objectives of that directive.

43 However, it should be recalled that the objective of that directive is not only to afford greater protection to workers in the event of collective redundancies, but also to ensure comparable protection for workers' rights in the different Member States and to harmonise the costs which such protective rules entail for EU undertakings (see, to that effect, judgments in *Commission v United Kingdom*, C-383/92, EU:C:1994:234, paragraph 16 ...).

44 Interpreting the term 'establishment' in the manner envisaged in paragraph 42 above would, first, be contrary to the objective of ensuring comparable protection for workers' rights in all Member States and, secondly, entail very different costs for the undertakings that have to satisfy the information and consultation obligations under Articles 2 to 4 of that directive in accordance with the choice of the Member State concerned, which would also go against the EU legislature's objective of rendering comparable the burden of those costs in all Member States.

...

46 It should be recalled, however, that Directive 98/59 establishes minimum protection with regard to informing and consulting workers in the event of collective redundancies (see judgment in Confédération générale du travail and Others, C-385/05, EU:C:2007:37, paragraph 44). Article 5 of that directive gives Member States the right to apply or to introduce laws, regulations or administrative provisions which are more favourable to workers or to promote or to allow the application of collective agreements more favourable to workers.

...

48 Although the Member States are therefore entitled to lay down more favourable rules for workers on the basis of Article 5 of Directive 98/59, they are nevertheless bound by the autonomous and uniform interpretation given to the EU law term 'establishment' in Article 1(1)(a)(i) and (ii) of that directive, as set out in paragraph 33 above.

...

51. ... it appears that each of the stores at issue in the main proceedings is a distinct entity that is ordinarily permanent, entrusted with performing specified tasks, namely primarily the sale of goods, and which has, to that end, several workers, technical means and an organisational structure in that the store is an individual cost centre managed by a manager.

52. Accordingly, such a store is capable of satisfying the criteria set out in the case law cited at [28], [30] and [32] above relating to the term "establishment" in Art.1(1)(a) of Directive 98/59; this is, however, a matter for the referring tribunal to establish in the light of the specific circumstances of the dispute in the main proceedings.

President von Danwitz, Vajda, Rosas, Rapporteur Juhász and Šváby.

NOTES AND QUESTIONS

1. The Fifth Chamber holds that the meaning of 'establishment' which must be uniform does not extend to multiple locations, even if it is within one undertaking (or company). While this probably follows the natural meaning of the word 'establishment', its rationalisation at [42]–[44] that otherwise this could lead to 'very different costs' for undertakings in different countries is incoherent. If the CJEU had held that the minimum, and fixed, meaning of establishment could include all the stores in a geographical region, this would be the case in every EU Member State: there would be no variation, because whenever there are more than twenty people, there would be a duty to consult. This rationalisation (which lacks any basis in the Directive itself or the recitals, despite the dictum in *Commission v UK*, [16] that the CJEU cites) also makes no sense because Art 5 explicitly encourages Member States to provide greater protection. What is being harmonised is minimum standards: no maximum standard was ever intended.

2. The CRD 1998 Art 2(1) says that consultation should begin where 'an employer is contemplating collective redundancies' and 'in good time'. Article 2(4) also says this applies 'irrespective of whether the decision ... is being taken ... by an undertaking controlling the employer'. What does that mean?

AEK ry v Fujitsu Siemens Computers Oy (2009) C-44/08

Workers from a factory of Fujitsu Siemens Computers Oy, in Kilo, Finland, represented by Akavan Erityisalojen Keskusliitto AEK ry (a branch of Akava, one of Finland's largest unions) claimed they were made redundant without genuine consultation, because the decision was made before consultation began. 450 out of 490 employees at FSC Oy were made redundant. The IT businesses of Fujitsu Ltd and Siemens AG had merged on 1 October 1999. FSC Oy became a subsidiary of the new merged company, incorporated in the Netherlands, Fujitsu Siemens Computers BV. On 7 December 1999, a group of executives proposed to the whole (parent company) board to sell the Kilo factory. On 14 December, the board decided to support the proposal, and FSC Oy 'proposed consultations, which took place' (as the CJEU put it, [22]) on 20 December 1999 and 31 January 2000. On 1 February the board decided to terminate FSC Oy's operations in Finland, except for computer sales. AEK argued the decision to close the Kilo factory was taken on 14 December before consultations began. FSC Oy argued that no specific decision on the Kilo plant was taken by the parent board, because alternatives still existed its operations could have been sold. The decision to terminate was only taken on 1 February. The Fourth Chamber held (without specifying dates) that consultation should begin once a 'commercial decision compelling him to contemplate or to plan for collective redundancies has been taken', although the subsidiary, as the direct employer, does the actual consulting.

Fourth Chamber:

37 First, it is to be noted that the present case relates to economic and commercial decisions which might have repercussions on the employment of a number of workers within an undertaking, and not to decisions which are directly concerned with terminating specific employment relationships.

38 In that regard, it must be recalled that, as is clear from the wording of arts 2(1) and 3(1) of Directive 98/59, the obligations of consultation and notification imposed on the employer come into being prior to the employer's decision to terminate employment contracts (see, to that effect, *Junk v Kuhnel* (C-188/03) [2005] ECR I-885; [2005] 1 CMLR 42 at [36] and [37]). In such a case, there is still a possibility of avoiding or at least reducing collective redundancies, or of mitigating the consequences.

...

44 Against an economic background marked by the increasing presence of groups of undertakings, [art 2(4)] serves to ensure, where one undertaking is controlled by another, that the purpose of Directive 98/59, which, as is stated in recital 2 of its preamble, seeks to promote greater protection for workers in the event of collective redundancies, is actually achieved (*Athinaiki Chartopoiia AE v Panagiotidis* (C-270/05) [2007] ECR I-1499 at [25]).

45 Moreover, as the United Kingdom Government rightly observes, a premature triggering of the obligation to hold consultations could lead to results contrary to the purpose of Directive 98/59, such as restricting the flexibility available to undertakings when restructuring, creating heavier administrative burdens and causing unnecessary uncertainty for workers about the safety of their jobs.

46 Lastly, the raison d'être and effectiveness of consultations with the workers' representatives presuppose that the factors to be taken into account in the course of those consultations have been determined, given that it is impossible to undertake consultations in a manner which is appropriate and consistent with their objectives when there has been no definition of the factors which are of relevance with regard to the collective redundancies contemplated. Those objectives are, under art.2(2) of Directive 98/59, to avoid termination of employment contracts or to reduce the number of workers affected, and to mitigate the consequences (see *Junk* [2005] 1 CMLR 42 at [38]). However, where a decision deemed likely to lead to collective redundancies is merely contemplated and where, accordingly, such collective redundancies are only a probability and the relevant factors for the consultations are not known, those objectives cannot be achieved.

47 On the other hand, it is clear that to draw a link between the requirement to hold consultations arising under art 2 of Directive 98/59 and the adoption of a strategic or commercial decision which makes the collective redundancies of workers necessary may deprive that requirement, in part, of its effectiveness. As is clear from the first subparagraph of that art 2(2), the consultations must cover, inter alia, the possibility of avoiding or reducing the collective redundancies contemplated. A consultation which began when a decision making such collective redundancies necessary had already been taken could not usefully involve any examination of conceivable alternatives with the aim of avoiding them.

48 It must therefore be held that, in circumstances such as those of the case in the main proceedings, the consultation procedure must be started by the employer once a strategic or commercial decision compelling him to contemplate or to plan for collective redundancies has been taken ....

...

52 It follows from [art 2(3)(b)] that that information can be provided during the consultations, and not necessarily at the time when they start.

...

54 It follows that the time at which consultations are to start cannot be dependent on whether the employer is already able to supply to the workers' representatives all the necessary information referred to in art.2(3)(b) of Directive 98/59.

...

57 ... it is clear that, under art.2(1) and (3) and art.3(1) and (2) of Directive 98/59, the only party on whom the obligations to inform, consult and notify are imposed is the employer, in other words a natural or legal person who stands in an employment relationship with the workers who may be made redundant.

58 An undertaking which controls the employer, even if it can take decisions which are binding on the latter, does not have the status of employer.

59 As stated by the Commission of the European Communities, first, how the management of a group of undertakings is organised is an internal matter and, secondly, it is not the purpose of Directive 98/59, any more than it was of Directive 75/129, to restrict the freedom of such a group to organise their activities in the way which they think best suits their needs (see, to that effect, as regards Directive 75/129, *Rockfon A/S v Specialarbejderforbundet i Danmark* (C-449/93) [1995] ECR I-4291 at [21]).

...

62 Consequently, art.2(1) and the first subparagraph of art.2(4) of Directive 98/59 are to be interpreted to the effect that, under those provisions, irrespective of whether collective redundancies are contemplated or projected as a result of a decision of the undertaking which employs the workers concerned or a decision of its parent company, it is always the former which is obliged, as the employer, to start consultations with the representatives of its workers.

63 As regards the time at which that obligation arises, it is evident, as observed by the Finnish Government, that consultations with the workers' representatives can be started only if it is known in which undertaking collective redundancies may be made. Where the parent company of a group of undertakings adopts decisions likely to have repercussions on the jobs of workers within that group, it is for the subsidiary whose employees may be affected by redundancies, in its capacity as their employer, to start consultations with the workers' representatives. It is therefore not possible to start such consultations until such time as that subsidiary has been identified.

64 In addition, with regard to the intended objectives of the consultations, under art.2(2) of Directive 98/59, those consultations are, at least, to cover ways and means of avoiding collective redundancies or reducing the number of workers affected, and of mitigating the consequences by recourse to accompanying social measures aimed, inter alia, at aid for redeploying or retraining workers made redundant. If a consultation on those matters is to have

any meaning, the subsidiary whose employees will be affected by the contemplated collective redundancies must be known.

...

67 ... the obligation to hold consultations laid down in art.2(1) of Directive 98/59 is binding solely on the employer.

68 There is no provision in that directive which can be interpreted to the effect that it may impose such an obligation on the parent company.

69 It follows that it is always for the subsidiary, as the employer, to undertake consultations with the representatives of the workers who may be affected by the collective redundancies contemplated and, if necessary, itself to bear the consequences of failure to fulfil the obligation to hold consultations if it has not been immediately and properly informed of a decision by its parent company making such redundancies necessary. ...

President Lenaerts, Silva de Lapuerta, Rapporteur Juhász, Arestis and Malenovský.

NOTES AND QUESTIONS

1. The Fourth Chamber tries to distinguish a 'strategic or commercial decision' that could lead one to 'contemplate' redundancies from a decision that makes redundancies 'necessary' at [47], but does not say where on the facts that should have actually been. Presumably, the 'strategic or commercial decision' was taken by the parent company on 14 December 1999, and therefore Fujitsu Siemens Computers Oy breached its consultation duties.
2. Decision-making by any collective entity, including a group company, is usually multifaceted, and it is very rare that there are no alternatives. An analogy for the appropriate time to consult can be found in the judiciary. Judges will consult with one another, with an open mind, on points of law throughout a hearing and after before they right a judgment. They may have preliminary views on the papers, but the very purpose of a hearing is to ensure that those views can change. By contrast, when a judgment is issued it is too late for any consultation. For instance, when the CJEU issues an opinion to a Member State, the decision about the relevant principles to determine liability have already been made. Do you agree that the CRD 1998 aims to ensure management and workers consult with one another as equal peers under Art 2(1) 'with a view to reaching an agreement', and are not to be treated as in a relationship of subordination?
3. Is it adequate that when a board decision was made in December 1999, the issue of failure to consult should be decided by the CJEU in September 2009? In April 2009, Fujitsu had already bought out Siemens's interest in the company, so that had the employees won their claim, this would have been enforced against Fujitsu Technology Solutions (Holding) BV, which is owned by Fujitsu Ltd, incorporated in Japan.
4. The parent company, according to the Fourth Chamber at [67], is under no obligation to consult, because that duty is 'binding solely on the employer', and at [68] there is no basis in the Directive for regarding the parent as an employer. In most cases this may not matter, because with effective enforcement a parent company

will effectively have to consult through its subsidiary, and will as a shareholder bear the economic costs of breaching the law. On the other hand, if a subsidiary goes insolvent, while the subsidiary may have the duty to consult, do you agree the parent company does owe an obligation to pay damages for the subsidiary's failure to consult? This would appear even more important given that the 'right to an effective remedy' is a fundamental human right in CFREU 2000 Art 47. In any event, Member State law can plainly go further than the minimum EU standards. See chapter 3(3).

5. Employees also have rights to be consulted under the Information and Consultation of Employees Directive 2002 and the European Works Council Directive 2009, see chapter 11.

6. In *United States v Nolan* [2015] UKSC 63 some of the ambiguities in *Fujitsu* were brought out. Mrs Nolan with around 200 employees were unjustly dismissed from a watercraft repair centre, RSA Hythe, Hampshire run by the US Army. The US Army decided it would close RSA Hythe on 13 March 2006. The BBC reported this on 21 April. On 24 April the employees were told the base would close. On 9 May, the US Army told the UK government. Notices of dismissal were issued and 'consultation' began on 30 June, while the contracts terminated on 29 September. One issue was whether the USA could be bound by the CRD 1998 at all because Art 1(2)(b) grants an exception for 'public administrative bodies'. The CJEU (2012) C-583/10 held it had no jurisdiction, and added that the USA could have also relied upon 'their immunity as a sovereign state'. However, UK law has no such exemption for public administrative bodies, as a result of an amendment in TULRCA 1992 s 188 by amending Regulations in 1995 (SI 1995/2587). On return to the Supreme Court, it was held by a majority that the 1995 Regulations had not been ultra vires the Minister's powers under the European Communities Act 1972, and that there was no possibility on the facts for the USA to claim sovereign immunity. It had (plainly) breached its duty to consult in good time.

7. *Claes v Landsbanki Luxembourg SA* (2011) C-235/10 held that the duty to consult exists even where an order for an insolvent company to be liquidated was made by a court. This judgment, which is obviously correct, ensures that multiple alternatives to redundancies can still be realised, in particular a transfer of the business with a commitment to avoid, minimise, or mitigate all job losses.

8. Unfortunately, TULRCA 1992 s 188(7) purports to contain an exception to the duty to consult, where there are 'exceptional circumstances'. This is not compatible with EU law, and in any case as a restriction must be construed restrictively (eg there is no duty to consult if a disaster leaves all employers and employees dead). Such an exception must plainly be (1) interpreted into non-existence, (2) disapplied by a UK court, or (3) open the UK state to a *Francovich* damages claim. *Clark's of Hove v Bakers Union* [1978] ICR 1076 already set the path for option (1). Here 380 workers were made redundant, and they claimed there was a failure to consult. Clark's of Hove claimed the 'exceptional circumstance' was that it ceased trading on 24 October 1976 after being in financial difficulty since

the summer. The Court of Appeal held that 'insolvency is, on its own, neither here nor there' and particularly where, as here, there was 'a gradual run-down of the company'. Do you agree that after *Claes*, even an immediate disaster, which necessitates immediate liquidation, there must still be consultation?

9. Realistically, do you think the decision to close Kilo would have been taken before the merger between Siemens and Fujitsu? Usually increase profit global operations would be assessed before a merger, takeover or transfer of business occurred: this would form the basis of the new management's expectation to achieve a profit. For Kilo, which began as a Nokia factory, it would appear neither the German Siemens executives, nor Japanese Fujitsu executives, saw any advantage in maintaining Finnish production.

10. Although (as we saw at chapter 19(1)(c)) it does not cover mergers or takeovers, there is an extra duty to consult on transfers, whether or not redundancies are proposed.

Transfer of Undertakings Directive 2001/23/EC Art 7

Article 7
1. The transferor and transferee shall be required to inform the representatives of their respective employees affected by the transfer of the following:
   — the date or proposed date of the transfer,
   — the reasons for the transfer,
   — the legal, economic and social implications of the transfer for the employees,
   — any measures envisaged in relation to the employees.
The transferor must give such information to the representatives of his employees in good time, before the transfer is carried out.

The transferee must give such information to the representatives of his employees in good time, and in any event before his employees are directly affected by the transfer as regards their conditions of work and employment.

2. Where the transferor or the transferee envisages measures in relation to his employees, he shall consult the representatives of this employees in good time on such measures with a view to reaching an agreement.

...

4. The obligations laid down in this Article shall apply irrespective of whether the decision resulting in the transfer is taken by the employer or an undertaking controlling the employer.

In considering alleged breaches of the information and consultation requirements laid down by this Directive, the argument that such a breach occurred because the information was not provided by an undertaking controlling the employer shall not be accepted as an excuse.

...

6. Member States shall provide that, where there are no representatives of the employees in an undertaking or business through no fault of their own, the employees concerned must be informed in advance of:
   — the date or proposed date of the transfer,
   — the reason for the transfer,
   — the legal, economic and social implications of the transfer for the employees,
   — any measures envisaged in relation to the employees.

1. TUD 2001 Art 7(1), implemented by TUPER 2006 regs 13–15, requires consultation 'in good time' on the transfer's date, reasons, implications, and 'measures envisaged in relation to the employees'.
2. This duty to consult is triggered regardless of whether there are over twenty staff in an establishment.
3. Does TUD 2001 Art 7(1) presuppose that a decision to transfer has already been taken? If a transferee has 'envisaged' redundancies before it buys an undertaking, is it (or the transferor) logically under a duty from the CRD 1998 to begin consultation already, and to therefore halt the transfer if the central strategy of shareholders is to profit from redundancies? It seems this must be the case for Art 7(2) to have substance, to enable 'a view to reaching an agreement' for any measures relating to redundancies.
4. The requirements of TUD 2001 Art 2(2) to consult are mandatory and must be regarded as more than simply providing information: as in *Junk v Kühnel* (2005) C-188/03, [43] this means an 'obligation to negotiate'. In *Royal Mail Group Ltd v CWU* [2009] EWCA Civ 1045, as Royal Mail was rolling out a privatisation strategy, selling branches to private companies such as WH Smith, it failed to inform staff that the transfers were in fact a transfer of an undertaking. There was discussion with the union, but it took the view the regulations (as the union had before this case) that the regulations did not apply because no job terminations were planned. Waller LJ held that the duty to inform and consult does not mean that the employer had to warrant the accuracy of the 'legal … implications' of a transfer, and so getting it wrong was not a breach of duty. What do you think?

(c) Limits of EU Competence

Under TULRCA 1992 ss 193–94, an employer making over 20 or 100 redundancies in an establishment in under 90 days must notify the Secretary of State either 30 or 45 days in advance, unless it was not reasonably practicable. This implements CRD 1998 Arts 3–4. However some countries go further and require authorisation of collective redundancies by the government. Rules like this in Greece were challenged in *AGET Iraklis*.

AGET Iraklis v Ypourgos Ergasias, Koinonikis Asfalisis kai Koinonikis Allilengyis (2016) C-201/15

AGET Iraklis, a subsidiary of French multinational Lafarge (now LafargeHolcim Ltd a construction company that bid to build a Mexico–US border wall), claimed that the refusal of the Greek Minister for Labour (Yprougos Ergasias) to authorise it to make collective redundancies violated the CRD 1998 and its right to freedom of establishment. Under the CRD 1998 Arts 3–4 employers may be required to notify Member State authorities of projected redundancies, and Member States can require longer consultation periods. But Greek law also said that if the parties reached no agreement on a collective redundancy plan, the Minister could refuse to authorise redundancies based on (1) labour market conditions, (2) the undertaking's situation and (3) national economic interests. The Minister argued that Greek law was consistent with the Directive, but even if not, it could be justified by the fact that Greece suffered from an acutely high unemployment rate. The Grand Chamber held that, while the CRD 1998 creates minimum standards, the ability to make collective redundancies could not be completely 'ruled out' by Greek law. Greece had, on this reasoning, therefore violated TFEU Art 49.

Grand Chamber:

Articles 49 and 63 TFEU

...

45 Freedom of establishment ... entails, in accordance with Article 54 TFEU, for companies or firms formed in accordance with the law of a Member State and having their registered office, central administration or principal place of business within the European Union, the right to exercise their activity in the Member State concerned through a subsidiary, a branch or an agency (see, in particular, judgment of 13 December 2005, *Marks & Spencer*, C-446/03, EU:C:2005:763, paragraph 30 ...).

...

48 It is settled case-law that the concept of a 'restriction' within the meaning of Article 49 TFEU covers, in particular, measures which, even though they are applicable without discrimination on grounds of nationality, are liable to impede the exercise of freedom of establishment or render it less attractive. ...

49 That concept thus covers, in particular, measures taken by a Member State which, although applicable without distinction, affect access to the market for undertakings from other Member States and thereby hinder intra-Community trade (see, in particular, judgment of 28 April 2009, *Commission v Italy*, C-518/06, EU:C:2009:270, paragraph 64 ...)

...

52 Actual exercise of freedom of establishment thus entails, in particular, as a necessary adjunct to that freedom, that the subsidiary, agency or branch set up by a legal person established in another Member State must be able, where relevant, and if the activity which it proposes to carry out in the host Member State so requires, to take on workers in that Member State (see, to that effect, judgment of 10 July 1986, *Segers*, 79/85, EU:C:1986:308, paragraph 15).

53 Such exercise also entails, in principle, the freedom to determine the nature and extent of the economic activity that will be carried out in the host Member State, in particular the size of the fixed establishments and the number of workers required for that purpose, and also, as the Advocate General has observed in point 65 of his Opinion, the freedom subsequently to scale down that activity or even the freedom to give up, should it so decide, its activity and establishment.

54 It must be noted, in connection with those various observations, that under the legislation at issue in the main proceedings it is the very ability of such an establishment to effect collective redundancies that is subject, in this instance, to a requirement that there be no opposition on the part of the competent public authority. The decision to effect collective redundancies is, however, a fundamental decision in the life of an undertaking (see, by analogy, in respect of decisions relating to voluntary winding-up, demerger or merger, judgment of 13 May 2003, *Commission v Spain*, C-463/00, EU:C:2003:272, paragraph 79).

55 Such national legislation constitutes a significant interference in certain freedoms which economic operators generally enjoy (see, by analogy, judgment of 28 April 2009, *Commission v Italy*, C-518/06, EU:C:2009:270, paragraph 66). That is true of the freedom of economic operators to enter into contracts with workers in order to be able to carry out their activities or the freedom, for their own reasons, to bring the activity of their establishment to an end, and their freedom to decide whether and when they should formulate plans for collective redundancies on the basis, in particular, of factors such as a cessation or reduction of the activity of the undertaking or a decline in demand for the product which they manufacture, or as a result of new working arrangements within an undertaking unconnected with its level of activity (see, to that effect, judgments of 12 February 1985, *Dansk Metalarbejderforbund and Specialarbejderforbundet i Danmark*, 284/83, EU:C:1985:61, paragraph 15, and of 8 June 1994, *Commission v United Kingdom*, C-383/92, EU:C:1994:234, paragraphs 29 and 32).

56 National legislation such as that at issue in the main proceedings is thus such as to render access to the Greek market less attractive and, following access to that market, to reduce considerably, or even eliminate, the ability of economic operators from other Member States who have chosen to set up in a new market to adjust subsequently their activity in that market or to give it up, by parting, to that end, with the workers previously taken on.

57 Accordingly, it must be held that such national legislation is liable to constitute a serious obstacle to the exercise of freedom of establishment in Greece.

...

59 ... even if the legislation at issue in the main proceedings were to have restrictive effects on the free movement of capital, those effects would, in such a case, be the unavoidable consequence of any restriction on freedom of establishment and would not warrant independent examination in the light of Article 63 TFEU (see, to that effect, judgments of 26 March 2009, *Commission v Italy*, C-326/07, EU:C:2009:193, paragraph 39 ...

...

Possible justification

61 According to settled case-law, a restriction on freedom of establishment is permissible only if it is justified by overriding reasons in the public interest. ...

...

66 In the present instance, as the referring court has pointed out, national legislation such as that at issue in the main proceedings entails a limitation on exercise of the freedom to conduct a business enshrined in Article 16 of the Charter.

67 The Court has indeed already held that the protection afforded by that provision covers the freedom to exercise an economic or commercial activity, freedom of contract and free competition (judgment of 22 January 2013, *Sky Österreich*, C-283/11, EU:C:2013:28, paragraph 42).

68 As regards freedom of contract, the Court has thus held, in relation to the negotiation of collective labour agreements, that Article 16 of the Charter means, in particular, that an undertaking must be able to assert its interests effectively in a contractual process to which it is party and to negotiate the aspects determining changes in the working conditions of its employees with a view to its future economic activity (judgment of 18 July 2013, *Alemo-Herron and Others*, C-426/11, EU:C:2013:521, paragraph 33).

...

72 As regards safeguarding the interests of the national economy, it is settled case-law that purely economic grounds, such as, in particular, promotion of the national economy or its proper functioning, cannot serve as justification for obstacles prohibited by the Treaty (see to that effect, in particular, judgments of 5 June 1997, *SETTG*, C-398/95, EU:C:1997:282, paragraphs 22 and 23 ...

...

73 On the other hand, the overriding reasons in the public interest that are recognised by the Court include the protection of workers ... [the CJEU refers to *Viking*, [77] see ch 10(1)(d)]

74 The same is true of the encouragement of employment and recruitment which, being designed in particular to reduce unemployment, constitutes a legitimate aim of social policy ...

...

80 ... those restrictions must be appropriate for ensuring attainment of the objective in the public interest which they pursue and must not go beyond what is necessary to attain it.

...

89 ... it should be recalled that Article 52(1) of the Charter accepts that limitations may be imposed on the exercise of rights enshrined by the Charter as long as, in particular, in accordance with the principle of proportionality, they are necessary and genuinely meet recognised objectives of general interest or the need to protect the rights and freedoms of others. As regards such rights and freedoms, it is to be noted that Article 30 of the Charter states that every worker has the right to protection against unjustified dismissal, in accordance with EU law and national laws and practices.

...

100 ... the employers concerned do not know in what specific objective circumstances that power may be applied, as the situations allowing its exercise are potentially numerous, undetermined and indeterminable and leave the authority concerned a broad discretion that is difficult to review. Such criteria which are not precise and are not therefore founded on objective, verifiable conditions go beyond what is necessary in order to attain the objectives stated and cannot therefore satisfy the requirements of the principle of proportionality (see, to that effect, judgments of 4 June 2002, *Commission v France*, C-483/99, EU:C:2002:327, paragraphs 51 and 53; of 26 March 2009, *Commission v Italy*, C-326/07, EU:C:2009:193, paragraphs 66 and 72; and of 8 November 2012, *Commission v Greece*, C-244/11, EU:C:2012:694, paragraphs 74 to 77 and 86).

...

103 On identical grounds, such legislation also fails to comply with the principle of proportionality laid down in Article 52(1) of the Charter and, therefore, with Article 16 thereof.

...

106 ... the fact that the national context is one of acute economic crisis and a particularly high unemployment rate most certainly likewise does not authorise a Member State to deprive the provisions of the directive of practical effect, as the directive does not contain a safeguard clause for the purpose of authorising by way of exception a derogation, in the event of such a national context, from the harmonising provisions which it lays down.

President Lenaerts, Vice-President Tizzano, Silva de Lapuerta, von Danwitz, da Cruz Vilaça, Juhász, Berger, Rapporteur Prechal, Vilaras, Rosas, Borg Barthet, Šváby and Jarašiūnas.

1. The Grand Chamber held that Greece violated the French–Swiss multinational corporation's right of establishment. Whether or not you approve of Greece's law, it is not preferable to let the Greek Parliament rather than a court make the decision?

2. Before the CJEU gave judgment, Advocate General Wahl started his Opinion with the statement that: 'The European Union is based on a free market economy, which implies that undertakings must have the freedom to conduct their business as they see fit. What are the limits, then, to Member State intervention in order to ensure the job security of workers?' AG Wahl seems to lack familiarity with the Treaty on European Union. This says in Art 3(3) that the EU aims for 'a highly competitive social market economy, aiming at full employment and social progress'. Do you think AG Wahl did not notice this, or that he has misunderstood the difference between a 'free market' and a 'social market', or that he did not care?

3. The CJEU's line of reasoning is both that Greece's requirement for authorisation violates freedom of establishment (it says considering freedom of capital is superfluous, but one may guess its answer) and it violates a business' supposed right to 'freedom of contract', invented by *Alemo-Herron* in Art 16. At [89] it pays lip service to the express right in the Charter (not a right invented by the Court) not to be unjustifiably dismissed. But presumably because both rights should be exercised 'in accordance with Union and national law and practices', and the Court feels it may invent the law according to its own preferences, Art 30 becomes quite irrelevant. Its basic justification for saying this is that Greece's law means (apparently) 'employers concerned do not know' what criteria are applied, because it enables 'broad discretion that is difficult to review'. Why is the certainty for a multinational corporation so much more important than the uncertainty of workers who face years of uncertainty and poverty through unemployment? Did Lafarge not invest in Greece with its eyes open to the laws that applied, and could it not hire lawyers to calculate those risks? Why is a multinational corporation being empowered by the CJEU to attack laws passed by the elected representatives of Greece?

4. Did the CJEU elevate the right to make redundancies into an aspect of freedom of establishment? Is this a court putting the '"Donald Trump" model of workplace relations' – where authority figures feel they have an inalienable right to bark 'You're fired!'–into EU law? cf E McGaughey, 'Fascism-Lite in America (or the Social Ideal of Donald Trump)' (2018) *British Journal of American Legal Studies*, forthcoming.

5. In *Guisado v Bankia SA* (2018) C-103/16, the CJEU was asked whether the Pregnant Workers Directive 92/85/EC should apply so as to protect pregnant workers from selection in a collective dismissal. Article 10(2) says an 'employer must cite duly substantiated grounds' to dismiss a pregnant worker, unconnected with pregnancy. The CJEU said that by itself, pregnant workers were not protected from collective redundancies without some additional reason. Unlike *AGET Iraklis*, the CJEU did not mention CFREU 2000, where Art 33 says 'everyone shall have the right to protection from dismissal for a reason connected with maternity and

the right to paid maternity leave and to parental leave following the birth or adoption of a child.' The difficulty a dismissed pregnant woman faces is one of proof, and the quite unthinkable stress of litigation when one has better things to concentrate on. Should the CJEU not have developed a presumption that such a dismissal is unfair unless the employer shows otherwise? Or should legislation give positive, additional protection for parents who are having children?

(3) RIGHT TO PAY OR REDEPLOYMENT

While meaningful consultation should avoid any redundancies at all, if some redundancies are agreed to be unavoidable the employer must 'pay a redundancy payment' (s 135). This can be seen to have three functions. First redundancy pay may internalise the social costs of redundancy, pressing an employer to think before making irrational choices to dismiss. Second, a payment reduces the social cost to taxpayers, by giving dismissed workers funds until finding another job. This may reduce the burden on unemployment insurance, simply because many people will not actually make claims. Third, redundancy pay recognises that while one's job is a contract, it is also represents loss of something valuable, like any other property right. To this it is commonly argued that increased costs for employers in dismissal will raise the unemployment rate, by reducing employers' freedom of choice, and therefore willingness to hire. There are three answers to this. First, following its own logic this seems doubtful because if employers can profit, they will hire. Second, employers are not all rational calculating machines: like other people, they have a behavioural tendency to discount future risks, and so hiring decisions are unlikely to be affected in practice by firing costs. Third, there is no empirical evidence to support the claim. The evidence shows that on the whole countries with stronger job security rights have higher employment: S Deakin et al, 'The Economic Effects of Laws Relating to Employment Protection and Different Forms of Employment: Analysis of a Panel of 117 Countries, 1990–2013' (2018) CBR Working Paper, forthcoming.

The employer's consultation duties from *Williams v Compair Maxam Ltd* and TULRCA 1992 s 188 imply a duty to attempt to redeploy staff. It is not spelt out in statute. Instead, s 141 removes the right to a redundancy payment when an employee is offered a contract renewal or re-engagement and this is at least 'an offer of suitable employment in relation to the employee' (s 141(3)(b)). Otherwise the amount of redundancy pay is one week's wages for each year worked for people aged 22–40, but only half a week for people 21 or under, and one and a half week's pay for people 41 and over.

Employment Rights Act 1996 ss 135, 141, 162

135 The right.
   (1) An employer shall pay a redundancy payment to any employee of his if the employee—
      (a)   is dismissed by the employer by reason of redundancy, or

(b) is eligible for a redundancy payment by reason of being laid off or kept on short-time.

...

141. Renewal of contract or re-engagement.

(1) This section applies where an offer (whether in writing or not) is made to an employee before the end of his employment—

(a) to renew his contract of employment, or

(b) to re-engage him under a new contract of employment,

with renewal or re-engagement to take effect either immediately on, or after an interval of not more than four weeks after, the end of his employment.

(2) Where subsection (3) is satisfied, the employee is not entitled to a redundancy payment if he unreasonably refuses the offer.

(3) This subsection is satisfied where—

(a) the provisions of the contract as renewed, or of the new contract, as to—

(i) the capacity and place in which the employee would be employed, and

(ii) the other terms and conditions of his employment,

would not differ from the corresponding provisions of the previous contract, or

(b) those provisions of the contract as renewed, or of the new contract, would differ from the corresponding provisions of the previous contract but the offer constitutes an offer of suitable employment in relation to the employee.

(4) The employee is not entitled to a redundancy payment if—

(a) his contract of employment is renewed, or he is re-engaged under a new contract of employment, in pursuance of the offer,

(b) the provisions of the contract as renewed or new contract as to the capacity or place in which he is employed or the other terms and conditions of his employment differ (wholly or in part) from the corresponding provisions of the previous contract,

(c) the employment is suitable in relation to him, and

(d) during the trial period he unreasonably terminates the contract, or unreasonably gives notice to terminate it and it is in consequence terminated.

...

162 Amount of a redundancy payment.

(1) The amount of a redundancy payment shall be calculated by—

(a) determining the period, ending with the relevant date, during which the employee has been continuously employed,

(b) reckoning backwards from the end of that period the number of years of employment falling within that period, and

(c) allowing the appropriate amount for each of those years of employment.

(2) In subsection (1)(c) "the appropriate amount" means—

(a) one and a half weeks' pay for a year of employment in which the employee was not below the age of forty-one,

(b) one week's pay for a year of employment (not within paragraph (a)) in which he was not below the age of twenty-two, and

(c) half a week's pay for each year of employment not within paragraph (a) or (b).

(3) Where twenty years of employment have been reckoned under subsection (1), no account shall be taken under that subsection of any year of employment earlier than those twenty years. ...

1. Together, ERA 1996 ss 135 and 162 create rights to a redundancy payment, favouring older workers. Is it justified to value someone's job who is young at one half a week for each year worked, but value someone 41 years or older at one and a half weeks? Youth unemployment is consistently higher in the UK and EU than adult unemployment, which suggests it is even harder for young people to find jobs. Could the high incidence of youth unemployment be the result of inadequate and unequal job security rights?
2. Aside from direct age discrimination, is the redundancy pay adequate to internalise the social costs of unemployment, and deter the employer from making irrational redundancies?
3. Under s 141, if an employer has offered an alternative job, an employee can refuse and take a redundancy payment if it is not 'suitable'. *Taylor v Kent CC* [1969] 2 QB 560 said this meant substantially equivalent in terms of status, wages and types of duties. This suggests any pay cut could be refused.
4. In *Thomas Wragg & Sons Ltd v Wood* [1976] ICR 313, Mr Wood claimed he was entitled to redundancy pay after a new job offer the day before his planned termination. Lord McDonald in the Employment Appeal Tribunal held refusing the job was not unreasonable, as he had already committed to a future job, and was legitimately concerned about future layoffs. Therefore the employer had to pay a redundancy payment.
5. Under ERA 1996 s 138, if the employee takes up a new job offer she or he still has a four-week trial period in which he can terminate the contract and still claim for redundancy dismissal, but this new termination must be reasonable under ERA 1996 s 141(4)(d). In *Optical Express Ltd v Williams* [2007] IRLR 936, Ms Williams claimed redundancy after trying a redeployed job for six weeks. She had been working at a dental clinic but was moved to an optical store, expressing reservations, and asking if she could still claim redundancy if the job did not work out. The employer remained silent. The Tribunal held that a 'common law' trial period could be longer than four weeks, and her rejection was within a reasonable time. Burton J in the Employment Appeal Tribunal overturned the Tribunal, holding the four-week limit could not be ignored. If the employer's delay in proper consultation stops it from relying on the statutory period, why not ignore it?
6. The alternative job offer under ERA 1996 s 146 could also be an associated employer, within the meaning of ERA 1996 s 231 (where one company controls another, typically in a group) or TULRCA 1992 s 297. See further *Secretary of State for Employment v Chapman* [1989] ICR 771, holding that a sole trader who converted into a limited company in 1980, and then back to being a sole trader in 1982, had continuously employed an employee since 1980. The owner, in whatever multiple form, was an 'associated employers'.

The Office (2001–02)

David Brent is the sub-manager at the office of Wernham Hogg, a paper-making company, in Slough. In early July, as a practical joke, Brent tells an employee, Dawn Tinsley, that she is fired for stealing post-it notes. When Dawn begins to cry, David tells her it was just a joke, and to forget it.

On 20 July the manager of Wernham Hogg, Jennifer, is contemplating twenty-five staff redundancies in either the Slough or Swindon offices, although a firm proposal has not been finalised. On the 1st of September, Jennifer finalises the proposals and tells the thirty employees in Swindon that their office will be closed, that twenty-five will be given the statutory minimum redundancy pay, and that the remaining five will be transferred to Slough. She says there will be a 'consultation' that runs until the 1st of October, and that the transfers will take place on 1st of November.

Meanwhile, back at the Slough Office, David Brent is called into a meeting with Jennifer. Brent is told that he must accept a redundancy package, because his position will no longer be necessary. Brent asks for one last chance, and says he is sure that he can make his position appear valuable, or be redeployed, but his pleas are ignored.

Advise the parties.

EP Lazear, 'Job Security Provisions and Employment' (1990) 105(3) *Quarterly Journal of Economics* 699

Lazear's article exemplifies a prominent strand of economic theory: dismissal laws create unemployment. He says that job security, in 'anything less than a perfectly functioning market [has] effects of the provisions on employment. Incumbents are more likely to retain their jobs, but new workers are less likely to be hired. An examination of the European data suggests that severance pay requirements reduce employment.' The author claimed to have found this result by looking at data in twenty-two countries from 1956 to 1984 on the number of months in severance pay, and months in notice, after ten years' employment. Apart from the primitive sample and method, this result is misleading for many reasons. For instance, it fails to take account of the strong dismissal protections that US trade unions had in collective agreements before the Reagan administration of 1980, or the operation of the Social Security Act of 1935, giving tax incentives against redundancies.

VV Acharya, RP Baghai and KV Subramanian, 'Labor Laws and Innovation' (2013) 56(4) *Journal of Law and Economics* 997

Based on data at the Centre for Business Research in Cambridge, the authors argue that 'strong dismissal laws appear to have a positive effect on the innovative pursuits of firms and their employees'. They assess the USA, UK, France, Germany and India, and the changes in labour law since 1970, and the result of labour rights strength for the number of patents that are filed.

Z Adams, L Bishop, S Deakin, C Fenwick, S Martinsson and G Rusconi, 'The Economic Significance of Laws Relating to Employment Protection and Different Forms of Employment' (2018) CBR Working Paper, WP 500.
Based on the Centre for Business Research, Labour Regulation Index (2016), this paper's subtitle is 'Analysis of a Panel of 117 Countries, 1990–2013'. The result, in this comprehensive study, is that increased protections for atypical workers (chapter 15) 'are correlated with rising employment and falling unemployment over the long run. … Similar results are found for employment protection laws in general.'

Index

abuse of power, 334–5
ACAS Codes of Practice:
  failure to comply with (legislation), 767–7
  Practice 1, 764
  Practices 2, and 3, 404
access to justice, right of and fees order, 152–4
action, propriety of (A Smith), 46
affirmative action (US), 618
age, non-discrimination on, 659
agency work, 136–45, 663–70
  case law, 140–1
  discussion of, 136
  temporary, 2008 Directive for, 664–6, 669
    (case law)
agency workers, 144–5 (case law), 668 (case law)
  access to employment, 670 (case law)
  definition, 666
  right to direct work, 668–70
  2010 Regulations, 666–8, 670
  unequal treatment of, 668
  workers classified as (EU law), 665–6 (case law)
agents' entitlement to fair process, 782–3
  (case law)
alienation (Karl Marx), 59
annuities, 277–8
anti-discrimination, 354–68
apprentice defined, 106
apprenticeship and employment, 128–30
arbitration clauses in employment
  contracts, 167 (case law)
Article 11 (ECHR), 352–4 (case law)
  breach of and expulsion, 351–4 (case law)
  closed shop agreements and, 396–401 (case law)
  collective bargaining, on, 356–7 (case law)
  freedom of expression and, 401 (case law)
asset managers:
  conflict of interest, 528
  instructions from pensions trustees, 528
  ultimate beneficiary's interests, 528
associated employees:
  conditions for, 457
  secondary action against, 455–7 (case law)
associations, dismissal from, 782 (case law)
at-will employment, 79–80

Balfour Committee on Industry and Trade (1924),
  25–6
balloting and ballots, 462–71
  ballot rules, 470
  employees' participation in, 418 (case law)
  employers' pressure on employees through, 388
  injunctions after irregularities in, 470–1
  irregularities in ballots, 466–9, 469–71
  legislation for, 463–6

  results, communication of, 409–12
  strike action, for, 409–12 (case law)
'bank nurses', minimum wage payment for, 253–5
Bank of England, 708–9, 710–11
  history and development of, 711–12
  monetary policy objectives, attainment of, 710
bargaining:
  Central Arbitration Committee and, 386 (case law)
  unit, fragmented, 386 (case law)
bargaining power (S and B Webb), 64–5
  contract at will and inequality of, 70–1
  'free to choose' and, 111 (case law)
  inequality of, 71–2, 74
barristers as employees, 129–30
'basic working and employment conditions'
  defined, 664
*Beckoning Frontiers: Public and Personal
  Recollections* (MS Eccles, 1951), 686–7
behavioural psychology and labour law, 75–82
benefits and pay, 248 (case law)
blacklists, 366–8
  case law, 368
  remedies not awarded for, (Carillon), 368
    (case law)
  2010 Regulations, 366–7
Blair, Tony, 360
  collective labour rights, on, 405
  trade union legislation, on, 466
board directors *see* company directors
Bolam test, 793 (case law)
bonus scheme, company directors' 'absolute
  discretion' to change, 227–8 (case law)
bonuses, 79
  discretionary, non-award of breach of contract,
    180–1 (case law)
breach of contract:
  discretionary bonus not awarded, 180–1
    (case law)
  interest-free bridging loan refused, 182–4
    (case law)
  non-award of and discretionary bonus, 180–1
    (case law)
  restitution and, 219
  strikes as, 412–13 (case law)
  wages cuts are, 236–9 (case law)
breach of duty due to fair dismissal, 782
  (case law)
breach of good faith, withholding performance,
  413 (case law)
breach of peace, picketing as, 461–2
breaks and night work (working time), 308–10
  derogation from breaks, 309
  interrupted breaks, 308–10 (case law)
  regulations for, 308

bridging loan, refusal of is breach of contract,
182–4 (case law)
Bridlington principles, 350
British Airways crew reduced under collective
agreement, 186–7 (case law)
Bullock Committee (1975), 29, 30–1
by-laws, 534–5 (case law)

capability (unfair dismissal), 802–6 (case law)
capital:
    'capital market friendly policies', 85
    equipment, private expenditure on, 681
    expenditure, 682–3
    workers, rights in, 521–8
Capital: A Critique of Political Economy
    (Karl Marx, 1867), 53–8
capitalist:
    accumulation and appropriation (Karl Marx),
        56–7
    production, 54
Catholic Child Welfare Society sexual abuse case,
    133–6
Cave Committee (1921), 25
Central Arbitration Committee, 377–8
    bargaining and, 386 (case law)
    inter-union disputes, 382
Charter of the Forest 1217, 4, 6
child care, 311–15
    regulations for, 313–15
    UK, in, 312–13 (table)
    women by and gender-pay gap, 315
    working time and, 285–319
children:
    child labour, nineteenth-century reports, 17
    employment conditions in coal
        mines, 15–16
    legislation for working conditions in coal
        and iron mines, 16
China, democratic reform protests, 461
choice and conflicts of law, 191–203
choice of law, separated from
    jurisdiction, 194
circuit judges, pensions of, 646 (case law)
civil rights and fair hearing, 774
class discrimination, 536
closed shop, 401 (case law)
    trade unions, in, 393–403
closed shop agreements:
    ECHR Article 11, violation of, 396–401
    eliminating, 402 (case law)
coal mining:
    children's employment conditions, 15–16
    miners' living conditions, 15
    working conditions in (1844), 15–18
codetermination, 31, 73, 87, 88, 157, 498–9
    Germany, in, 494, 495, 499, 525, 529
coercive interference, 424, 426
'collateralised debt obligations' (CDOs), 698
collective action, 407–80
    pay deduction after, 259–63
    right to, 407–53
    trade union members' rights and, 358–9

collective agreements, 185–7 (case law), 371
    breach of by unions, 390 (case law)
    cabin crew, reduction of under, 186–7 (case law)
    compliance with, 704
    compulsory redundancy and, 185–6 (case law)
    enforceability of, 389–90
    example, 391–3
    49 hours per week violates WTD, 300–3
        (case law)
    legislation for, 184–5
    part-time workers' employment contracts, in, 641
        (case law)
    pay increase under, 847 (case law), 848–53
        (case law)
    pension trustees governed by, 522–3
    Posted Workers Directive 1996, Article 3(1) and,
        445–9 (case law)
    terms, 389–93
    transfer of, 852 (case law)
    wage level (UK), 449
collective bargaining, 29, 371–405
    cessation of, 355–60 (case law)
    ECHR Article 11 on, 356–7 (case law)
    essential rights, 393–404
    'fair share agreement', 402 (case law)
    information for, 403–4
    legislation for, 372–7
    Posted Workers Directive Article 3(1), 449
    recognition of unions, 372–89
    sham union, derecognition of, 378–81
        (case law)
    South Africa, in, 417, 418
collective redundancies:
    Directive, 857–8
    pregnant workers and, 874–5
colonisation (Karl Marx and F Engels), 57–8, 60
commerce and public works, 49–50
commissions to be included in holiday pay, 296
    (case law)
common law:
    English, applied in US, 14
    equity and, 408–19
    trial period, 877
'common' ownership (S Webb), 66
Communist Manifesto **(Karl Marx),** 59–60
companies:
    allocation or disposition of resources, 28
    board composition, 490–1
    incorporation of, 273
    'interest of the company', 29–30
    legislation of, 486–8
    management, 488
    quoted, 269
    standard of care of, implicit, 340 (case law)
    'three-tier' structure, 28
    'two-tier' structure, 28, 32
    undermining of, unfair dismissal due to, 364–6
        (case law)
    see also corporate entries
companies' model articles, legislation for, 488–9
Companies (Model Articles) Regulations 2008,
    266–9

company boards:
consumer interest and, 30
employee representation on, 28–9
shareholder representation on, 28–9
'2 X plus Y' formula, 29
company directors:
bonus payments, discretion to chanjge, 227–8
(case law)
derivative claims against, 500, 504–5
employees, treated differently from, 620
remuneration policy, approval of, 269–70
(case law)
representation of, (Germany and Sweden), 493–4
salaries of, 268–9
share options and, 226–8
workers as, 490–3
company directors' duties, 500–6
conflict of interest and, 503
legislation for, 500–2
promoting company success, 503
rules observed, 502
slavery statement, 503
social responsibilities of, 503
standard of care, 502
company information, trade union's right to, 403–4
comparative advantage (D Ricardo), 50
comparators, 610
case law, 610–11, 632
compensation:
loss of earnings, for, 221–4
psychiatric injury, for, 810–14 (case law)
unfair dismissal, for, 810 (case law)
competition law (US), 453
compromise agreements, 819–20
legislation for, 819
compulsory association, Nazi system of, 396
**compulsory redundancy reliance on collective
agreements,** 185–6 (case law)
conduct, contract formation by, 166–7 (case law)
conduct (unfair dismissal), 802–6 (case law)
outside work, 804 (case law)
confidence and mutual trust, 96–8 (case law)
conflict of interest, asset managers', 528
conflicts of law and choice, 191–203
Constitution of South Africa, certification of,
415–19
construction:
case law and principles, 96–105
**constructive damages, and injury for feelings
and,** 809
constructive dismissal, 742, 743–5 (case law)
change of hours and pay reduction, 744 (case law)
duty of mutual respect and, 748–9
transfer of undertakings, under, 853 (case law)
university exam marks raised, 745–51
wrongful changes of employment contract,
749–51 (case law)
consultation, 853–75
Collective Redundancies Directive, violation of,
870–1 (case law)
duty to consult, 868–9
establishment size and, 861–2 (case law)

fixed-term staff and redundancy, 826–9
freedom of establishment and, 874
general duty to consult, 854–7
inadequate consultation on redundancy, 854–7
(case law)
limits of EU competence, 870–5
over 20 redundancies *see* over 20 redundancies
period for, 860
protection award, 860–1
consumer interest and company boards, 30
'continuing financial losses', 221–2
contract at will (RA Epstein), 70–2
equality of bargaining power and, 70–1
contract formation by conduct, 166–7 (case law)
contract of employment:
business owners' freedom and, 843
transfer of, 843 (case law)
contract of service:
book written by former employee, 214–16
conditions of, 139 (case law)
consideration of, 108–11 (case law)
continuing existence of, 143 (case law)
control of, 109 (case law)
implied, 141–5 (case law), 144 (case law),
independent suppliers of, 141–5 (case law)
mutual respect, duty of and, 780
triangular, 136–40
contract terms:
new, unfair dismissal claimed due to, 834–7
renegotiated, refusal to accept, 241–2
(case law)
same terms in new contract, 844–7
contracts:
common theory of, 75
contractual consideration, 210
European Union, in, 192–201
European Union Regulation for, 192–4
implicit, 842
incorporation of terms, 181–91
international treaties as part of, 427
medical and personal injury damages, 178–9
mutuality and, 122 (case law)
public tender, put to, 705 (case law)
right to statement of, 189
service of *see* contract of service
statutory rights and, 200
test, 744
umbrella, 121–4 (case law)
contracts of employment, 163–205
formation of, 164–81
illegal, 170–7 (case law)
unjust or vitiating factors, 169–77
**contractual disciplinary procedures, requirement
to follow,** 763 (case law)
control:
contract of service and, 109 (case law)
test for, 107
co-operation (Karl Marx), 53–6
capitalistic, 55–6
copyright, book written by former employee,
214–16
corporate boards, votes for, 482–500

corporate discretion and just dismissal, 782 (case law)
corporate governance (OE Williamson), 73–4
corporate groups, 145–8 (case law)
corporate tax rates, 273
'corporate veil':
　piercing, 456
　solidarity action and, 453–8
corporations as separate legal personalities, 457
'corrective justice', vi, 811
courts, constitutional right of access to, 149–51 (case law)
creditor protection and freedom of association, 498

damages:
　asbestosis, for, 145–8 (case law)
　compensatory, 810
　fair hearings and, 333
　holiday pay, for, 289–91
　mental distress, for, 783–7 (case law)
　punitive, 809
　reduced income, for, 809–10 (case law)
　restitutionary, 217–18
　stigma after dismissal, for, 783 (case law)
　wages cut, claimed for, 236–9 (case law)
damages (unfair dismissal), 805–15
　categories of, 808–9
　redundancy dismissal and, 767 (case law)
days (working time), 286–96
Declaration on Fundamental Principles and Rights at Work (ILO, 1998), 39
defence of illegality:
　integrity of law and, 172–3 (case law)
　public policy and, 172–3
　racial discrimination and, 170–2
deficit and debt levels, 692, 694
defined benefit (DB) pension, 277, 522
democratic reform protests (China), 461
democracy, 21–32
　democratic society and individual interests, 399
　trade unionism and (S and B Webb), 64
deregulation treaties, 738
derivative claims:
　company's directors, against, 500
　double, 505
　judicial review analogous to, 506
　legislation for, 504–5
derogation, breaks from, 309 (case law)
detriment, 471–9, 580 (case law), 581 (case law)
direct discrimination, 559–75
　legislation for, 559–61
direct participation, 31
direct work, agency workers' right to, 668–70
disability, 623–33
　EU law requirements, 625
　health and, 627–8 (legislation)
　legislation for, 623, 624–5
　meaning of, 624–6
　reasonable adjustment for, 626–33
disability discrimination:
　bi-polar disorder and, 626–8, 688 (case law)
　unlawful, examples of, 625

disability rights, 631–3 (case law)
　job adjustments after surgery, 629–31
　road sweeper's changed circumstances, 629–31
disadvantage, 585–614
disciplinary hearings:
　Germany, in, 766
　stages of, 764–5
disciplinary procedure:
　employer's failure to follow, 775–7
　injunctions for, 775–7
discipline or expulsion affairs, 344 (legislation)
　fairness in, 344–54 (case law)
discretion defined, 782
discretionary bonus, non-award of is breach of contract, 180–1 (case law)
discrimination, 533–83
　associative, 552–5 (case law)
　case law, 565–6
　class, 536
　combined, 594
　compensation for unjust feelings, 566 (case law)
　detrimental treatment, 546
　direct *see* direct discrimination
　direct age, of, 572–5 (case law)
　disability *see* disability discrimination
　exemplary damages and, 569 (case law)
　indirect and niqab wearing, 601–2
　justifications, 570–5
　labour movement (US) and, 33
　political grounds, on, 547–50 (case law)
　racial (UK) *see* racial discrimination
　recruitment and, 637 (case law)
　religious, Karl Marx on, 537
　sex *see* sex discrimination
　test for, 564 (case law)
　trade union, 359–60
　unlawful *see* unlawful discrimination
　women, against, 571–2 (case law)
'discrimination arising from a disability', 628 (case law)
dismissal, 471–78
　associations, from, 782 (case law)
　capability grounds, on is not redundancy, 828–9 (case law)
　concept of, 742–51
　employers' conflict of interest and, 741–2
　fair process for, 233–5
　fixed term contract's termination is, 820 (case law)
　gross misconduct, for, injunction against, 777 (case law)
　injunctions after, 815–19
　notice for, 233–5
　procedure, failure to follow, 776 (case law)
　reasons for, 741
　summary, 742
　unjust, 780–7
　variation, after, 241–2
　'without cause', 235 (case law)
dispossession, 8
　Thomas More on, 6–7
dispute solution, 471–9
domestic bodies and fair hearings, 331

Donovan Report (1968), 796
duty of care, damages for asbestosis, 145–8
**duty of good faith, intelligence services book's
    publication breaches,** 216–21
duty of mutual respect, 214, 223 (case law)
duty to bargain with employees, 843 (case law)
duty to inform, breach of, 190–1 (case law)

'economic activity' defined, 82
economic changes (1000 + employees), 516–20
economic efficiency, 67–82
economic entity, transfer of, 841, 844–7
economic harm, 20 (case law)
Economic Institutions of Capitalism **1985,** 72–5
economic loss, trade union's liability for, 20
    (case law)
economic organisation (S and B Webb), 66
Economic Policies Recommendation 2015 (EU),
    691–2
**economic theory, traditional and information
    economics,** 84
economics:
    neoclassical and labour, 67
    normative, 67
education and training, 707–8
effectiveness principle, 153 (case law)
efficiency and power, 73
Employee Involvement Directive, 496–7
    mergers and, 497–8
employee rights:
    implied, 221–35
    transfer of undertakings and, 852, (case law)
employee share scheme, 492–3
    membership of, expulsion due to, 347 (case law)
employees:
    ballots, participation in, 418
    barristers as, 129–30
    CEGB tour guides are not, 119–21
    company board, representation on, 28–9
    company directors treated differently
        from, 620
    definition, 105, 106
    duty to bargain with, 843 (case law)
    fixed term *see* fixed-term employees
    home workers as, 116–19 (case law)
    loyalty, rights to and limits, 216–21
    managerial staff are not, 127 (case law)
    mutuality of obligation and, 112–24
    permanent status of, 224–6 (case law)
    representation, regulation of, 30
    safety of and safe system of work, 231
        (case work)
    share schemes, 492–3
    status, multiple factors, 106–21
    statutory tests for, 105–6
    sub-contracted employee, 127–8
    subsidiary, of, health and safety for, 145–8
        (case law)
    tips are property of, 263–5 (case law)
    transfer of undertakings, rights under, 852–3
    Transnational Information and Consultation of
        Employees Regulations 1999, 518–20

    vulnerable workers are, 652
    work, some other substantial reason for
        dismissals, refers to, 833–4
**employer and employee relationship
    (O Kahn-Freund),** 65
employers, 133–48
    associated, secondary action against, 455–7
    conflict of interest and dismissal, 741–2
    definition, 133
    employee's labour, appropriates benefits from,
        214–16
    employees, pressure on via ballots, 388
    harm to, and wages improvement, 20 (case law)
    misconduct, allegations of, approach to, 769–71
    premises of, trade union activities on, 365–6
    types of, 482
    unfair dismissal and, 769–71, 775–7
    workmen, relations between (Whitley
        Committee), 22–3
employment, 82
    agency worker's access to, 670 (case law)
    apprenticeship and, 128–30 (case law)
    'employment business' defined, 733
    full and fair incomes, 683–4
    high level of, maintained, 680–1
    market and pay increases, 613 (case law)
    minimum wage, legislation's effect on, 84
    notice for normal working hours, without, 752
        (legislation)
    permanent, claim to right of, 653 (case law)
    policy, international and industrial background
        for, 678–9
    political issues and, 427
    employment rate, 677
    rearrangement of workforce is not redundancy,
        829 (case law)
    refusal of due to trade union membership, 363–4
        (case law)
    relationship, national policy for, 160–1
    removal of, 680
    restructuring under redundancy, 829 (case law)
    settlement and termination, 820 (case law)
    short breaks in, 115 (case law)
    statement of employment, 188–9
    three-party employment relationship, 104–5
        (case law)
    withholding performance and breach of good
        faith, 413 (case law)
Employment Act 2002 rules, 769 (case law)
employment agencies, 729–35, 732–3 (legislation)
    definition, 733
    fees charged by, 732–3, 734
    private, 730
    unfair dismissal by, 745
Employment Appeal Tribunal, fees for, 149–54
    (case law)
employment contracts:
    arbitration clauses in, 167 (case law)
    frustration of, 751
    individual, EU Regulation for, 193
    repudiatory breach of, 746–8, (case law)
    same contract terms in new contract, 844–7

staff sickness practice, unilateral variation of,
   239–41 (case law)
standard terms re notice for, 762
termination of *see* termination of contract
transfer of, 846–7 (case law)
variation of, 649 (legislation)
wrongful change of is constructive dismissal,
   749–51 (case law)
Employment Decision 2015/1848, 692–3
employment income, 271–2 (legislation)
taxation of, 270–4
Employment Policy **(1944, cmd 6527),** 678–86
**Employment Promotion and Protection against
   Unemployment Recommendation 1988
   (no 176),** 700–1
**Employment Protection Index (EPI)
   (OECD),** 87
**'Employment, social justice and societal
   well-being' (J Stiglitz, 2002),** 82–6
Employment Tribunals:
claims, 155, 768
fees for, 149–54 (case law)
legislation for, 389–90
enforceability of rights and sex discrimination, 176
   (case law)
enforceable agreements, 164–9
basic rule of, 164
enforcement, 310–11, 148
bodies, 148–58
individual claims and, 148–9
scope of, 95–161
enterprise:
executives, rights over, 482–506
subcontracting, through, 133–6
'entity retaining its identity', 846
environmental damage, EU Regulation for,
   202, 203
Epstein, RA, 70–2
equal pay, 36 (legislation)
Act 1970, cause of, 37
definitions, 35
disparity in clerk's wages, 612–13 (case law)
employment market and pay increases, 613
   (case law)
market forces and, 36
private sector, in, 613 (case law)
situations of, 35–6
**Equal Pay Bill, second reading (Hansard Debate,
   1970),** 35–7
equal pay comparators, 606–11
case law, 607
equal pay scheme claims and victimisation,
   580–1 (case law)
equal treatment, 665
2006 Directive on, 606–7
**Equal Treatment Directive 2000 and
   protection,** 556
equality, 32–7
access to accommodation, in, 538
administrative law, in, 536
age discrimination and, 539–42 (case law)
case law, 32

civil rights and, 537
classes, between, 536
common law principle and EU law principle, 543
Commonwealth constitutions, in, 543
equal treatment as general principle of EU law,
   542–3
ethnicity, of, 544–5, 546
freedom and, 46–66
general principle in law, 534–43 (case law)
indirect discrimination, 544–5 (case law)
legislation for, 609–10
Mary Woolstonecroft on, 536
monitoring, 566
principles of, 534–59
private companies and public bodies lack, 536
proof of, 565–70 (legislation)
protected characteristics of, 534–59
racial (US), 537–8
religion as protected characteristic, 546–7
establishment defined, 863, 684
estoppels, proprietary rights for, 167 (case law)
EU-South Korea Free Trade Agreement (2011),
   736–7
European Central Bank, 712, 713
European Convention on Human Rights (ECHR):
Article 6, breach of, 771–5
Article 8 and unfair dismissal, 798–9
   (case law}
Article 11 *see* Article 11
incompatibility with EU law, 450 (case law)
labour rights legitimacy, 437–8
right to strike not absolute, 438
UK legislation's compatibility with, 325
European Employment Strategy, 695
European System of Central Banks (ESCB),
   712–13
functions and governance, of, 713
European Union (EU), 72
contract in, 192–201
entry to, local government support for, 341
   (case law)
fiscal policy and full employment, 714
right to strike and, 439–53
European Union law:
incompatibility with ECHR, 450 (case law)
norms and labour policies, 38–9
European Union legislation and labour law, 38–9
European Union Regulations on tort, 201–3
eurozone crisis:
reason for, 698
unemployment rates (1998–2016) and, 699 (fig)
evidence:
accuser's in unfair dismissals, 769–71
libel trial, given in, 348
exemplary damages, 567–70 (case law)
award of, 569
discrimination and, 569 (case law)
expulsion:
ECHR Article 11, breach of, 351–4 (case law)
employee share scheme membership, due to, 347
   (case law)
wrongful *see* wrongful expulsion

fair dismissal, 787–806
  basis of, 786 (case law)
  breach of duty, due to, 782 (case law)
  court-based review of, 796
  legislation for, 787
fair hearings, 763–75
  ACAS Code of Practice for, 764–5
  civil rights and, 774
  damages and, 333
  domestic bodies and, 331
  explanation of decision, 331–2
  statutory bodies and, 331
fair incomes, full employment on, 683–4
fair market equilibrium, 371
fair process:
  agent's entitlement to, 782–3
  dismissal for, 233–5
fairness, 645
  discipline or expulsion affairs, in, 344–54
    (case law)
  dismissal, in, 779–821
  productivity and, 76–8
  work schemes and, 725 (case law)
fascism and post-war prosperity, 685–6
fees:
  EAT, for, 149–54 (case law)
  employment tribunals, for, 149–54
  order and right of access to justice, 152–4
    (case law)
  remedies (unfair dismissal), for, 806 (case law)
fiscal consolidation and policy, 697, 676
    (legislation)
  full employment and, 676–7
fixed-term contracts, 663 (case law)
  nine-year, unfair dismissal claim for, 661–3
  successive, 660
  termination of is dismissal, 820 (case law)
fixed-term employees, 650–63
  less favourable treatment, prevention of, 651–3
    (legislation)
  1999 Directive for, 650
  non-discrimination of, 650
  prevention of less favourable treatment, 660–1
    (Regulation)
fixed-term employment, grounds for, 657
fixed-term staff, redundancy not consultation,
    826–9 (case law)
fixed-term work, 656 (case law)
  1999 Directive, 655–6
  unfair dismissal claim for, 656
**fixed term worker's application for length of
    service payment,** 653–5 (case law)
'flexibility clauses' *see* **unilateral variation**
flexible working, 315–16 (legislation), 318
    (legislation)
  refusal of requests for and productivity,
    317–18
  request for refused due to 'team spirit', 316–17
    (case law)
  right to request, 315–18
flexicurity, 79–80
floating charge, identification of, 104 (case law)

fragmentation of bargaining units, 386–7 (case law)
'free to choose 'and bargaining power, 111
    (case law)
freedom and equality, 46–66
freedom of association, 324–7, 395–6 (case law)
  conventions and charters on, 326
  creditor protection and, 498
  definition, 324
  ECHR Article 11 on, 324–5
  trade unions', 325, 388–9
**Freedom of Association and Protection of the Right
    to Organise Convention 1948,** 325
freedom of choice, EU Regulation for, 192–3
freedom of contract, 11–20, 70, 97–8 (case law), 852
    (case law)
freedom of establishment:
  consultation and, 874
  creditor protection and, 498
  right to strike and, 444
  votes at work and, 488–9
freedom of expression and Article 11, 401
    (case law)
**freedom to provide services, State Procurement
    Act (Germany) violates,** 702–4 (case law)
Friedman, M, 67–9
frustration of contracts, 751
full employment, 675–740
  EU fiscal policies and, 714
  fair incomes, on, 683–4
  fiscal policy and, 677
  inflation and, 689, 690
  US, in, 714
Full Employment in a Free Society **(William
    Beveridge, 1944),** 683
full-time contract, claim to, 657–9 (case law)
full-time work:
  'on demand' hours contract is compared to, 643
  part-time worker's right to, 647–63
full-time workers:
  'comparable full-time worker' defined, 641
  definition, 638

gangmasters, licensing of, 735
Gangmasters Licensing Authority, legislation for,
    734–5
**GCHQ staff prohibited from trade union
    membership,** 360–4 (case law)
gender equality, 34
gender pay:
  equality, origin of and, 605–13
  gap and childcare by women, 315
general secretaries, salaries of, 342–4
general strike (1926) effects, 428
General Theory of Employment, Interest and Money
    (JM Keynes, 1936), 684
Germany:
  codetermination, 494, 495, 499, 525, 529
  company directors, representation of, 493–4
  disciplinary hearings, 766
  labour recruitment and Federal Office of
    Employment, 730–2 (case law)
  pension trustees in, 525

Polish workers, minimum wage, right to, 705 (case law)
State Procurement Act violates freedom to provide services, 702–4 (case law)
work councils legislation, 507–8 (post-WWII), 509–10
'genuine material factor' defence, 611–13
legislation for, 611
red-circling (equal pay) is not, 612 (case law)
good faith, 221–8
definition, 224
government agencies for labour rights enforcement, 155
government bonds on secondary markets (EU), purchase of, 715
government departments and labour rights enforcement, 156
Grand National Consolidated Trades Union, 13–14
influence of, 13–14
petitions raised by, 13–14
Graphic Representation of the Laws of Supply and Demand and other Essays on Political Economy (1887), 61
great depression, causes of, 686–7
Greece:
Memorandum of Understanding on Specific Economic Policy Conditionality (2010), 695–7
unemployment, rise of (2010–14), 699
gross misconduct:
disciplinary procedure for, 233–5 (case law)
dismissal for, injunction against, 777 (case law)

harassment, 575–6 (legislation), 575–9
conditions for, 579
manager's homophobia, due to, 576–9 (case law)
sexual orientation, due to, 556–8 (case law)
Hawthorne experiments and effects of, 80
health and safety, subsidiary's employees for, 145–8 (case law)
holiday pay:
absence for illness and damages claim, 289–91
commissions to be counted in, 296 (case law)
entitlement to, 101–5 (case law)
'normal 'remuneration, should reflect, 294–6 (case law)
onshore time does not count, 296–89 (case law)
pay levels, 292–6 (case law)
pilot's, 294–6 (case law)
qualifying periods, 288–9 (case law)
rolled-up holiday pay is contrary to WTD, 292–4 (case law)
'Saturday problem', 287 (case law), 288 (case law)
holidays, 286–92
case law, 286–91
paid holidays, 286
homeworkers as employees, 116–19 (case law)
homosexuality and unlawful discrimination, 598 (case law)
'horizontal' direct effect, 289 (case law)
hours (working time), 296–311
change of and pay reduction, 744 (case law)
maximum, 299–207

How the Government Can Prevent Unemployment (S Webb, 1912), 683–4
human behaviour's effect on labour markets, 46–7
human development, 82–90
human rights:
right of establishment and, 444
violations and Tolpuddle Martyrs, 14
work schemes and, 728
human trafficking, 173–5 (case law)

illegality:
defence of see defence of illegality
principle's inconsistence with rule of law, 247
public policy, 172–3
illness, absence for, holiday pay damages claim, 289–91 (case law)
imperfect information:
imperfect competition and, 83
unemployment and, 83–4
implementation defined, 658
implied employee rights, 221–35
implied rights of employing entities, 208–21
implied terms, 98 (case law)
types of, 757
unreasonableness in, 227 (case law)
variation and, 207–43
works accidents, for, 208–11
'inappropriate behaviour', 98–100 (case law)
incapacity (unfair dismissal), 805–6 (case law)
inclusion, 615–33
inclusive law:
challenges of, 615–16
employment and, 615–16
historical disadvantages of, 615
income:
distribution alternative and power, 73
high earners', 273
inequality, 267
reduced, damages for, 809–10
taxation of, 274 (legislation)
income tax, 272, 273
incorporation of terms, 181–91
indemnity for works accidents, 208–11 (case law)
indirect discrimination, 586–604
age for, degree required for promotion, 590–3
legislation for, 586–7
neutral practices for, 586–94
niqab wearing and, 601–2 (case law)
indirect sex discrimination:
degree required for promotion, 590–3
failure to pay sick leave is, 602 (case law)
graduate applicants aged 27–35 for, 590 (case law)
London Underground shift is, 604–5 (case law)
part-time work scheme, woman's eligibility for, 603–5
pensions for part-time staff, 602 (case law)
teachers' superannuation scheme, no access to, 607–8
unfair dismissal claims for retirement-aged people, 590 (case law)

individual interests and democratic society, 399
individuals:
    best interests of, 51–2
    judgments, legal interference for, 52
industrial action:
    EU Regulation for, 202
    torts and, 421–2
industrial democracy, 27, 481–2
    Otto Kahn-Freund on, 28–31
    proposals for, 28–9
Industrial Democracy (S and B Webb) (1897),
    62–4
industrial relations, Ministry of Labour's
    intervention in (1918–21), 24
inflation:
    full employment and, 689, 690
    measurement of, 710
information and consultation:
    Directive on, 511–12
    employees, of, 2004 Regulations and, 512–16
information economics and traditional economic
    theory, 84
injunctions:
    ballot irregularities, after, 470–1
    broadcast, restraint of is not a trade dispute,
        424–6
    disciplinary procedures, following, 775–7
    dismissal, after, 815–19
    dismissal for gross misconduct, against, 777
        (case law)
    48 hours per week under WTR, for, 310–11
        (case law)
    legislation for, 473, 474
    restitution, used instead of, 220
    restrictions on, 473 (legislation), 474 (legislation)
    strikes, against, 474–6 (case law)
*Inquiry into the Nature and Causes of the Wealth of
    Nations* (1776), 48–51
insurance and works accidents, 208–11
intellectual property, copyright on book written by
    employee, 214–16
intelligence tests and assessments unrelated to
    jobs, 595–8
inter-union disputes and Central Arbitration
    Committee, 382
interest rates (EU), 710, 714, 715
international investment and US sub-prime
    mortgage crisis, 698–99
International Labour Conference, 39–40
International Labour Organisation
    conventions, 40
    right to strike and, 438–9
international law, right to strike in, 429–39
international trade and labour standards, 736
international treaties as part of contract, 427
internationalism, 38–41
investment:
    jobs, in, 678–201
    promotion of, 691
    social funds as source of, 700
iron mining, children's employment conditions,
    15–16

job security, 37
    social security and, 774–5
    trade policy and, 735–8
jobs:
    creation by taxation and spending, 684
    cuts due to redundancy, 830–3
    investment in, 678–701
    jobcentres, 729–30
    job-discouraging industry, 701
    'job holder' defined, 106
    job-promoting investment, 701
jobseeker's allowance:
    duration of, 718
    legislation for, 717–19
    trade disputes, during, 719
    training and work requirements under, 723–6
    work types as condition of, 725–6
Joint Representation Committee, 29
Joint Standing Industrial Councils (JICs), 22–3, 26
    1923–48, in, 24–5
joint stock company, 49–50
jurisdiction separate from choice of law, 194
just dismissal and corporate discretion, 782
    (case law)
just enrichment and *quantum meruit*, 246–9
    (case law)
justice, access to and fees order, 152–4

Kahn-Freund, Otto:
    collective laissez-faire, on, 21–2
    industrial democracy, on, 28–31
King, Martin Luther, 1961 speech, 32–4

Labour and neoclassical economics, 83–6
labour:
    demand and supply, boosting of, 692–3
    forced, consideration of, 727
labour history, 3–41
    slavery and serfdom and, 3–11
labour law (US), 445
    behavioural psychology and, 75–82
    EU legislation and, 38–9
    1979 onward, 21–41
    policy and WTO, 41
    slavery and, 9
    time trends in, 84
labour laws in OECD countries (1970–2010),
    88–9 (fig)
labour markets:
    flexibility of, 84–5
    functioning of, 693
    helping others and, 47
    human behaviour's effect on, 46–7
labour movement (US):
    discrimination and, 33
    Martin Luther King's speech on (1961), 32–4
    racial discrimination and, 33
labour policies and EU law norms, 38–9
labour recruitment (Germany) and Federal Office
    for Employment, 730–2 (case law)
labour regulation, four-tier system, 184
Labour Regulation Index (LRI), 87–8, 690

labour rights:
'binary divide', 107–8
categories of, 96
collective, Tony Blair on, 405
scope and enforcement, 95–161
unemployment benefit and, 716–17
labour rights enforcement:
government agencies for, 155
government departments and, 156
trade unions and, 156
works councils and, 156
labour standards, 738
international trade and, 736
labour theory, 45–92, 208
laissez-faire:
collective laissez-faire, 21–2, 26
exceptions to, 51–2
Mill on, 53
theory, 11
law:
individual's judgments, interference for, 52
integrity of and defence of illegality, 172–3
(case law)
worker combinations and, 50
**law firm partners treated differently from
employees,** 620
legal aid, application for trade union member,
340–1 (case law)
legal representation, 154–5
sexual misconduct, for, 771–5 (case law)
length of service payment, 654–5
fixed-term worker applied for, 653–5
(case law)
**Liberal government 1905, legislation
under,** 20
limits of right to direct, 208–14 (case law)
local government union support for entry to EU,
341 (case law)
lock out, right to (South Africa), 416–17
loss of earnings, compensation for, 221–4
losses, strikes caused by, 476

'macroeconomics' (J M Keynes), 66
Madurai game studies, 78–80
management:
companies, of, 488
universities, of, 485–6
market imperfections, 85
marriage, dismissal due to, 100 (case law)
'Marshallian cross' (economics), 61
Marx, K, 53–61
religious discrimination, on, 537
maximum hours (working time), 299–307
**meeting, illegal, and unfair
dismissal,** 780–3
*Memorandum of Understanding on Specific
Economic Policy Conditionality*
(Greece 2010), 695–8
men, sex discrimination against, 617–18
mental distress, damages for, 783–7
mergers and Employee Involvement Directive,
497–8

**military services, trade union membership is
exception to,** 363
Mill, JS, 51–3
Millennium Development Goals (UN), 40
minimum living wage, 249–53
legislation for, 249
minimum wage, 67–9
bank nurses, payment to, 253–5
care worker's claim for, 255–6
employment system, 256
entitlement to, 101–5 (case law)
legislation effect on employment, 84
refusal to pay, 706 (case law)
right to, 705–6 (case law)
shortfall for claims, 249–50
tips put towards, 263–5 (case law)
**Ministry of Labour and industrial relations
(1918–21),** 24
misconduct, employer's approach to allegations of,
769–71
monetary policy, 708–15
legislation for, 708–9
money and transparent accounts, 341–4
legislation for, 341
Musicians' Union, wrongful expulsion from, 344–9
(case law)
mutual respect, duty of:
constructive dismissal and, 748–9
contract of service and, 780 (case law)
mutual trust, 96–8 (case law)
confidence and, 221–8
mutuality and contract, 122
mutuality of obligation, 116–19 (case law)
CEGB tour guides do not have, 119–21

National Insurance, creation of, 716
National Insurance Contributions, 270, 274–6
calculation of, 275–6
case law, 276
definition, 274
legislation for, 274–5
payment of, 108–12 (case law)
national productivity scheme, ballot for, 340
(case law)
**national security and right to trade union
membership,** 360–4
natural justice:
withholding report violates, 348 (case law)
panel chair breaches, 348 case law)
reasonableness and, 334
wrongful expulsion without warning, 350
(case law)
'necessary' defined, 594
**non-commercial matters banned under
procurement (UK),** 706–7
non-contractual obligations, EU Regulation for,
202
non-discrimination principles, 636–7
age grounds, on, 659
fixed term employees, of, 650
non-interference principle *see* **laissez-faire**
'no-strike' clause, 20 (case law)

notice, 752–63
  dismissal, for, 233–5
  employment without normal working hours,
    752–3 (legislation)
  legislation for, 752–3
  minimum, 752 (legislation)
  payment in lieu of, 754–62 (case law)
  statutory notice periods (UK), 754

oaths and obligation, 12 (case law)
objective justification, 594–604
obligation, mutuality of employee's defined, 112–13
occupational pensions, 276–81
  combined contribution, 277
  extra contributions to scheme, 190–1
  legislation for, 278–9
  retirement ages for, 280
  right to, 277–9
on-call time is working time, 303–7 (case law)
**'on-demand' hours contract, full-time work
  compared to,** 641–3
'open market transactions' (Bank of England), 711
opt-outs (doctors) allowed under WTD, 307
  (case law)
'ordinary contractual principles', 183–4
  (case law)
organisation of labour, 72–3
'output work' defined, 254
over 20 redundancies, 857
  Directive for, 857–8
  legislation for, 858–60
overwork, personal injury due to, 230–3

paid annual leave:
  right to, 291 (case law)
  temporal limits for, 291–2 (case law)
  wage reduction and, 294
participation and productivity, 80–1
part-time work:
  holiday leave allocation, 648 (case law)
  'on-demand' hours contract is classed as, 641–4
    (case law)
  opportunities for, 647–8 (legislation)
  provisions for implementation, 648 (legislation)
**part-time work scheme, women's eligibility for is
  indirect sex discrimination,** 603–5 (case law)
part-time workers, 636–49
  collective agreements in employment contracts,
    641 (case law)
  'comparable full-time worker' definition, 636
  definition, 636
  full-time work, right to, 647–63
  1997 Directive for, 636–7
  prevention of less favourable treatment
    regulations, 638
  public holiday, extra, 643–4 (case law)
patient confidentiality, disciplinary procedure for,
  233–5
pay:
  benefits and, 248 (case law)
  contractual 28-day notice period, in, 228–30
    (case law)

  part-time firefighters' pay is unlawful
    discrimination, 639–41 (case law)
  right to for normal working hours, 296–7
  unjustified, 265–70 (legislation)
pay deductions, 256–65
  collective action, after, 259–63
  legislation, 257–9 (case law)
  limits to, 265
pay increases:
  collective agreement, under, 847 (case law),
    848–56 (case law)
pay period, 253–6
pay ratios (US), 267
pay reduction due to pregnancy, 621–3 (case law)
pension funds:
  asset management, 523
  vulnerability, 523
pensions:
  automatic enrolment in, 395
  circuit judges, of, 646 (case law)
  governance, 281
  'no detriment guarantee', 239 (case law)
  opting out of, 279–80
  part-time recorders, for, 644–7 (case law)
  part-time staff, for is indirect sex discrimination,
    602 (case law)
  schemes, 279
  share ownership and, 280–1 (fig)
pensions trustees:
  association of member-nominated, 525–6
  collective agreements govern, 522–3
  Germany, in, 525
  instructions to asset managers, 528
  legislation, 521–2, 523–4
  member-nominated proportions, 525
  University Superannuation Scheme, backgrounds
    of, 522
  voting instructions (collective agreement),
    526–7, 528
performance-related pay, 79
permanent work, right to, 655–63
personal injury:
  damages, breach of medical contract, 178–9
    (case law)
  asbestosis, damages for, 145–8 (case law)
  overwork, from, 230–3 (case law)
  parent company's liability for, 148
picketing, 453–62
  breach of peace, as, 461–2
  code of practice, 460
  legislation for, 20, 459–60
  peaceful, 460
  watching and besetting, 460–1
Polish workers, minimum wage, right to, 705
  (German case law)
political democracy, 27
political funds, 335–7
  legislation for, 335–6
**political issues and employment
  relationship,** 427
**political power and property
  qualification,** 14–15

positive action, 616–20
  legislation for, 616–17
  public office appointments, for, 618–20 (case law)
  types of, 619
positive economics:
  definition, 67–9
  methodology of (Friedman), 67–9
Posted Workers Directive 1996 Art 3 (1):
  collective agreements, 445–9 (case law)
  collective bargaining, 449
**Posted Workers Directive 1996, State Procurement
  Act violated,** 702–4 (case law)
power:
  alternative distribution of income and, 73
  definition, 65
  efficiency and, 73
pregnancy, 621–3
  pay reduction, due to, 621–3
  positive rights of inclusion, 621
Principles of Political Economy (JS Mill,1848), 51–2
private consumption, expenditure on, 681
private copartnery, 49
**private employment agencies, advantages
  of,** 731–2
private enterprise, types of, 499–500
private equity takeovers, 842
private investment, 690
private property, economic systems for, 57–8
private rights regulation (US), 537–8
procurement, 702–7
  non-commercial maters banned under (UK),
  706–7
procurement acts (US), 706
productivity:
  fairness and, 76–8
  flexible working, refusal of requests for and,
  317–18
  participation and, 80–1
  security and, 78–80
**profits, restitution of, from book on security and
  intelligence services,** 216–21
property, unequal division of, 50
property qualification and political power, 14–15
proportionality, 797
proportionality test, 801
  definition, 594
proprietary rights, estoppel for, 167 (case law)
protected industrial action, legislation for, 477
protection:
  Equal Treatment Directive and, 556
  political and religious beliefs, for, 550–1
public finances:
  deficit and debt levels, 692, 694
  sustainability of improved, 692
public holidays, part-time workers' leave on, 643–4
  (case law)
**public office appointments, positive action
  measures for,** 618–20 (case law)
public policy:
  defence of illegality and, 172–3
  wrongful expulsion without hearing, 350–1
  (case law)

**Public Procurement Directive, public tendering of
  contracts breaches,** 705 (case law)
**public tender, contracts to, Public Procurement
  Directive breaches,** 705 (case law)
public works and commerce, 49–50

quantum meruit:
  claims, 248–9
  just enrichment and, 246–9
quoted companies, 269

race discrimination, no claim under, 132 (case law)
racial discrimination (UK):
  defence of illegality and, 170–2 (case law)
  labour movement (US) and, 33
  unfair dismissal and, 170–7 (case law)
reasonable responses test, 799–801 (case law)
reasonableness, 791–801
  case law, 791–3
  legislation for, 791
  natural justice and, 334
recorder, part-time, pensions for, 644–7 (case law)
recruitment and discrimination, 637 (case law)
redeployment, 875–7
redundancies, 824–33
  collective, *see* collective redundancies
  fixed-term staff not consulted, 826–9 (case law)
  legislation for, 824–6
  over 20, 857–70
redundancy:
  damages for unfair dismissal and, 767 (case law)
  decision taken before consultation, 864–7
  (case law)
  definition, 824
  dismissal on capability grounds is not, 828–9
  employment restructuring under, 829 (case law)
  inadequate consultation on, 854–7 (case law)
  job cuts, due to, 830–3 (case law)
  principles of, 856
  reorganisation of workforce is not, 829
  (case law)
  selection criteria, 856 (case law)
  'some other substantial reason' *see* 'some other
  substantial reason' (redundancy)
  transfers and, 823–79
  unfair dismissal, due to, 198–201 (case law)
redundancy pay, 875–7 (legislation)
  enhanced contractual, failure to pay, 224–6
  (case law)
**redundancy payment, claim for after trial
  period,** 877
Reform Act 1867, opposition to, 17–18
regular hours, right to, 296–9
reinstatement, 816–18
  case law, 817–18
  legislation for, 816–17
relative bargaining power, 103 (case law)
religious discrimination, 571 (case law), 598–602
  (case law)
  consideration, 601, 602
remedies (unfair dismissal), 806–21
  fees for, 806 (case law)

remuneration, 263–4 (case law)
   'normal' holiday pay should reflect, 294–6
     (case law)
   tips as, 263–4 (case law)
reserve requirements (Bank of England), 711
restitution:
   breach of contract and, 219
   case law, 219–20
   injunctions used instead of, 220
   profits from book on, 216–21
   restitutionary damages, 217–18
restraint of trade, 176–7 (case law)
Retail Price Index, wage increases in line with,
   164–8 (case law)
retirement ages for occupational pensions, 280
right of access to courts, 149–52 (case law)
right of association, 'negative', 397
right of establishment, 439–44 (case law)
   human rights, and, 444
   trade unions have, 444
right to appropriate and limits, 214–16
right to collective action, 407–53
right to direct, and limits of, 208–14 (case law)
right to notice of terms, 188–91 (legislation)
right to pay, 875–7
right to strike, 408 (case law), 413–15 (case law),
   422 (case law)
   EU and, 439–53
   European Treaties, in, 439
   freedom of establishment and, 444
   International Labour Organisation Convention
     and, 431–2, 438–9
   international law, in, 429–39
   statutory recognition of, 419
   UK law fails to protect, 430–7 (case law)
'right to work' (US) and trade unions, 402
rights:
   capital workers', 521–8
   enterprise executives, over, 482–506
   implied *see* implied rights
Royal Commissioners' Final Report Into Trade
   Union Organisation (1868–69), 18–20
   dissent from, 19
rule of law's inconsistency with illegality principle,
   242 (case law)

safe system of work, 230–3 (case law)
   employee safety and, 231 (case law)
salaried work, definition, 254
'Saturday problem', (holiday pay), 287 (case law),
   288 (case law)
scope and enforcement (labour rights), 95–161
secondary action, 430
   associated employer, against, 453–4 (legislation),
     455–7 (case law)
   countries allowing, 454
   suppression of, 437
security and productivity, 78–80
self-employed workers:
   TFEU Art 101 excludes, 450–2 (case law)
   undertakings, as, 452
   workers, can be, 124–8

separate legal personalities, corporations as, 457
serfdom and slavery *see* **slavery and serfdom**
servants' duties, 209
'service charge', 265
service providers, undertakings, as, 452
sex discrimination:
   appraisal duties, complaints about, 561–4
     (case law)
   case law, 565–6
   enforceability of rights and, 176 (case law)
   indirect *see* indirect sex discrimination
   men, against, 617–18 (case law)
   unlawful, unfair dismissal is, 637 (case law)
'sex equality rule', 610
sexual abuse cases, Catholic Child Welfare
   Society's (CCWS) liability for, 133–6
sexual misconduct, legal representation, for, 771–5
   (case law)
sexual orientation, harassment due to, 556–8
   (case law)
share options and company directors, 226–8
   (case law)
share ownership and pensions, 280–1 (fig)
shareholder representation on company board,
   28–9
shares:
   employee share schemes, 492–3
   shareholders in companies, 492
shop steward's election, fair hearing for, 330–1
   (case law)
Showmen's Guild, wrongful expulsion by, 347
   (case law)
sick pay, failure to pay is indirect sex
   discrimination, 602 (case law)
simple economics of mandated benefits, 69
slave trade:
   abolition of, 10–11
   legislation for, 10–11
slavery and serfdom, 6
   case law, 9–11
   labour history and, 3–11
   labour law and, 9
   unlawfulness of, 9–11 (case law)
Smith, A, 46–51
social benefits, receipt of full superannuation
   benefits, 190–1 (case law)
social compensation plan and work councils,
   510–11
social funds, 701
   investment source, as, 700
social protection systems (EU), 693
social security and job security, 774–5
Societas Europaea, outline, 495
   worker representation directive, 496–7
society, stationary state of, 51
solidarity action, 453–62
   corporate veil and, 453–8
'some other substantial reason'
   (dismissal), 833–9
   employee's work, reference to, 833–4
   legislation for, 833
standard collective agreement terms, 391–3

standard of care (companies), implicit, 340
  (case law)
state intervention, 22–7
  definition, 22
  voluntarism and, 25–6
State Procurement Act 2004 (Germany):
  freedom to provide services, violates, 702–4
    (case law)
  Posted Workers Directive violated, 702–4
    (case law)
statement, right to, and contract, 189
Statute of Labourers 1351 and, 6
statutory bodies and fair hearings, 331
statutory codified rights, 419–29
statutory control of unfair terms, 177–81 (case law)
statutory rights and contract, 200
statutory right (fair dismissal), 789–90
  'effective date of termination', 788–9
  legislation for, 787–8
Stiglitz, J, 82–7
stigma, damages for, 783 (case law)
strike action:
  ballot for, 409–12 (case law)
  tort law and, 412 (case law)
strikes, 372
  breach of contract, as, 412–13 (case law)
  closed shop enforcement by, 567 (case law)
  injunctions against, 474–6 (case law)
  legislation for, 20
  losses caused by, 476
  sympathy, 431–2
  unfair dismissal and, 477–8
  wage deductions during, 478–9
structural fiscal reforms, 696
structural reforms:
  labour market institutions, for, 696, 697
  Member States, by, 641
subcontracting, 133–6 (case law)
  'enterprise' through, 133–6
summary dismissal, 742, 753 (case law)
supply and demand graphs, 61
surplus value (Karl Marx), 58–9
sustainable growth, removal of barriers to,
  691–2

taxation, job creation by, 684
**Teachers' Superannuation Scheme, no access
  to is indirect sex discrimination,** 607–8
  (case law)
Temporary Agency Work Directive 2008, 664–6,
  669 (case law)
**'temporary cessation of work', unfair dismissal
  due to,** 168–9 (case law), 790 (case law)
termination and employment settlement, 820
  (case law)
termination of contract:
  elective and automatic theories, 756, 759–60
    (case law)
  payment in lieu of notice, 754–62 (case law)
Theory of Moral Sentiments **(1759),** 46–7
time off, trade union officials' right to, 404
'time work' defined, 254

tips:
  employees' property, are, 263–5 (case law)
  remuneration, as, 263–4 (case law)
Tolpuddle Martyrs, 12–13, 325
torts, 201–3
  case law, 422–4
  EU regulation on, 201–3
  industrial action and, 421–2
  strike action and, 412 (case law)
total expenditure, maintenance of, 680–1, 682–3
Trade Boards, 23–4
  Cave Committee on, 25
trade dispute, 419–21 (legislation)
  action in furtherance of, 455
  definition amended by Employment
    Act 1982 s18, 455
  injunction to restrain broadcast, 424–6
  jobseekers' allowance during, 719
trade policy and job security, 735–8
trade union activities, 394 (legislation)
  discussion of during working hours, 365
    (case law)
  employers' premises, on, 365–6 (case law)
trade union constitution and right to enforce,
  337–41
trade union discrimination, 359–60
trade union elections, 327–35, 335 (case law)
  election addresses, 329–30
  election process, 330
  legislation for, 327–9
  rules, 329
trade union members:
  legal aid, application for, 340–1 (case law)
  right of representation in hearings, 404
  rights and collective action, 358–9
trade union membership, 394 (legislation)
  contract of, 345
  decline of, 394–5
  GCHQ staff prohibited from, 360–4 (case law)
  majority, 388
  military services and, 363
  Post Office, at, 390 (case law)
  refusal of employment due to, 363–4 (case law)
  right to and national security, 360–4 (case law)
  withdrawal of, expulsion due to, 348 (case law)
trade union organisation, 104 (case law), 113–16
  (case law)
  eighteenth century, in, 11–12 (case law)
  inquiry into (1868–69), 18–20
trade union strikes:
  refusal to join, 348 (case law)
  reliance on, 27
trade unionism:
  democracy and (S and B Webb), 64
  history of, 12–14
trade unions, 323–69
  accounts, 342
  automatic enrolment, 393–403
  closed shop, 393–403
  collective agreements, breach of by, 390
    (case law)
  economic loss, liability for, 20 (case law)

employers' pressure on employees against, via
    ballots, 388
fees, increase of without vote, 388–9 (case law)
financial incentives for non-members, 355–60
    (case law)
freedom and managerial authority, 364–6
    (case law)
freedom of association of, 325, 388–9
goals of, 18–19
illegality and, 18 (case law)
labour rights enforcement and, 156
legal entities, are, 345
legislation for, 19–20, 466, 472, 473
literature on, 326
non-members' pay increases, 355–60 (case law)
organisation of *see* trade union organisation
political spending, 337 (case law)
publications, unlawful, 337 (case law)
recognition for bargaining, 372–89
recognition of blocked, 381–4 (case law)
resolutions, *ultra vires*, 339
right of establishment and, 444
right of representation and time off, 404
right to company information, 403–4
rules and agreements, 19–20 (legislation)
United States, in, 326–7
voting rights, 327
transactions, 72–3
labour market, 72
product market, 73
transfer of undertakings, 839–53
constructive dismissal under, 853 (case law)
directive, 869
employee rights under, 852–3 (case law)
pay increases under, collective agreement, 848–53
    (case law)
2001 Directive, 840–1
transfers and redundancy, 823–79
**transnational information and consultation of
    employees, 1999 Regulations,** 518–20
transnational works council, 2009 Directive,
    516–18
**Treaty on the Functioning of the European Union
    (1957):**
Art 101, self-employed workers excluded, 450–2
Art 153, 38
tribunal claims, 2011/12, 806–7
trust and confidence:
obligation breached, 211–14
term, 222

UK Corporate Governance Code:
compliance requirements, 491
extract, 490
UK law:
peripatetic workers not subject to, 194–7
right to strike fails to protect, 430–7
workers subject to, 198 (case law)
UK legislation compatibility with ECHR, 325
undertakings:
self-employed workers as, 452
service providers as, 452

unemployment:
control of, 679–80
imperfect information and, 83–4
mass unemployment in Weimar Republic,
    684–5
natural rate of, 689, 690
rise of in Greece (2010–14), 699
statistics, 677
United States, in, 688
unemployment insurance:
benefits, 716–29
labour rights and, 716–17
types of, 717
unfair contract terms, 177–8 (legislation)
unfair dismissal, 742
accuser's evidence not tested, 769–71
allegations of misconduct, employer's approach
    to, 769–71
awards, 807–8 (legislation)
case law, 96–100, 113–16
compensation for, 810 (case law)
constructive, wage reduction, due to, 297–9
    (case law)
contract test and, 744
damages for and redundancy dismissal, 767
    (case law)
ECHR Art 8 and, 798–9
employer's failure to follow disciplinary
    procedure, 775–7
employment agency, by, 745 (case law)
failure to perform duties violates natural justice,
    348 (case law)
fixed-term work and, 656 (case law)
illegal meeting, due to, 780–3
lap dancer, of, 121–4 (case law)
men and women, disparity between, 587–9
    (case law)
mental-health hostel, from, 136–41
new contract terms not accepted, 834–7
    (case law)
nine-year fixed-term contracts, for, 661–3
no consultation for, 862–7 (case law)
non-disclosure of relationship, 837–9 (case law)
people reaching retirement, for, 590 (case law)
peripatetic workers, for, 194–7
perversity of, 794–5 (case law)
qualifying period for, 587–9 (case law),
    789–90
racial discrimination and, 120–7 (case law)
'reasonable responses' test applied, 797–801
    (case law)
reasonable responses to, 793–7 (case law)
redundancy, due to, 198–201
rehearing appeals, 794 (case law)
remedies after *see* remedies (unfair dismissal)
renegotiated contract terms, refusal to accept,
    241–2 (case law)
reputation of nurse and, 802–4 (case law)
strikes, after, 477–8
substitution, 795 (case law)
'temporary cessation of work', due to, 168–9
    (case law), 790 (case law)

trust and confidence obligation breached, 211–14
(case law)
undermining the company, due to, 364–6
(case law)
unlawful sex discrimination, qualifies for, 637
(case law)
unreasonable conduct test and, 744
volunteers, of, 130–2
unfair terms, statutory control for *see* **statutory**
control of unfair terms
unilateral variation, 239–41
staff sickness practices, of, 239–41 (case law)
UNISON, 149–54 (case law)
United Nations Inequality-adjusted Human
Development Index, 82
United States (US):
English common law applied in, 14
full employment in, 714
pay ratios, 267
procurement acts, 706
sub-prime mortgage crisis and international
investment, 689–99
Universal Credit, 720–2 (legislation)
payments, 722–3
universities, management of, 485–6
university grades, elevation of (constructive
dismissal), 745–51, 746 (case law)
unlawful discrimination:
homosexuality and, 498 (case law)
intelligence tests required for jobs, 595–8
part-time firefighters, rate of pay is, 639–41
(case law)
sinfulness of homosexuality, 598 (case law)
untruthfulness and lack of trust, for, 363
(case law)
unmeasured work:
careworker's pay is, 255–6 (case law)
definition, 254
unreasonable conduct test, 744
unreasonableness, implied terms, in, 227
Utilitarianism **(JS Mill) (1863),** 52
utility:
effect of, 46–7
Karl Marx on, 60
pursuance of (Mill), 52–3
Utopia **(1516) (Thomas More),** 6–7, 8

variation, 236–43
dismissal after, 241–2
implied terms and *see* implied terms
and variation
without consent, 236–9 (case law)
VAT, 272
victimisation, 579–82
equal pay scheme claims, due to, 580 (case law)
legislation for, 579–80
whistleblowing, due to, 582 (case law)
volunteers, unfair dismissal of, 130–2
voluntarism and state intervention, 25–6
votes:
corporate boards, for, 482–500
university councils, 485–6

votes at work, 481–529
freedom of establishment and, 498–9
voting rights, 327–37
vulnerable workers are employees, 652

wage reduction:
constructive unfair dismissal, due to, 297–9
(case law)
paid annual leave, 294
'wage theft', 265
wages, 250–2
clerks', disparity in and equal pay, 612–3
contracts (S and B Webb), 62–4
deductions, 478–9
improvement, 20 (case law)
improvement of in eighteenth century, 11–12
(case law)
increases in line with RPI, 164–8
labour, of, 48–9
labourers, co-operation of, 54–5
living, work for, 246–9
minimum, Polish workers' right to, 705 (case law)
reduction of and paid leave, 294
regulation of, 8
unfair, effect of, 77–8
unlawful deduction of, 297–9 (case law)
unpaid, claim for, 246–7 (case law)
wage level (UK), collective agreement, 449
wages cuts:
breach of contract, are, 236–9 (case law)
damages claimed for, 236–7 (case law)
watching and besetting, picketing as, 460–1
Webb, Sidney and Beatrice, 12–14, 62–4
Weimar Republic, mass unemployment
in, 684–5
welfare reform, 720–2 (legislation)
whistleblowing, 124–8 (case law)
victimisation and, 582 (case law)
Whitley Committee (1916), 22–3
Williamson, OE, 72–5
women:
child care responsibilities and gender
pay-gap, 315
discrimination against, 571–2 (case law)
work councils, 506–20
labour rights enforcement and, 156
legislation (Germany), 507–8, 509–10
multinational *see* consultation requirements for
economic changes (1000+ employees)
principles, 507–11
rights in, 521–8
social compensation plan, 510–11
template for, 508
work patterns, 635–72
workplace rule-book, 182–4 (case law)
work schemes, 723–6 (case law)
fairness and, 725 (case law)
human rights and, 728
workers:
agency workers are classified as (EU law), 665–6
(case law)
combinations of and law, 50

company directors, as, 490–3
definition, 105, 106
expatriate, 197
non-union, 20 (case law)
peripatetic workers and, 194–7
representation, Societas
    Europaea, 496–7
self-employed workers *see* self-employed
    workers
status of, 124–8 (case law)
statutory tests for, 105–6
test for status, 127
UK law, subject to, 194–7, 198 (case law)
'**workfare**', 720, 729
**working conditions, children's in mines, legislation
    for,** 16
**workmen and employers, relationship between
    (Whitley Committee),** 22–3
working hours:
long, discussion of, 232–3
normal, right to pay for, 296–7 (case law)
protection, derogation from Working Time
    Directive, 303
working time, 285
child care and, 285–319
48 hours per work under WTR, injunction for,
    310–11 (case law)
on-call time is, 303–7 (case law)

Working Time Directive (WTD):
derogation from working hours protection, 303
doctors' opt-outs allowed, 307 (case law)
49 hours per work collective agreement violates,
    300–3 (case law)
rolled-up holiday pay is contrary to, 292–4
    (case law)
**Working Time Regulations 1998 (WTR), 48 hours
    per work under injunction for,** 310–11
    (case law)
works accidents and insurance, 208–11 (case law)
world economic system, development of, 736
World Trade Organisation and labour law policy,
    41
written statement, interpretation of, 189
wrongful disciplining:
evidence given in libel trial, 348 (case law)
refusal to join a strike, 348 (case law)
wrongful expulsion:
answering charges, opportunity for, 347–8
    (case law)
Musicians' Union, from, 344–9
no hearing before, 349–51 (case law)
Showmen's Guild, by, 347 (case law)
withdrawal of union membership, due to, 348
    (case law)

zero-hours contracts, 298–9 (case law)